Useful Accounting Links

AICPA
www.rutgers.edu/accounting/raw/aicpa/home

American Accounting Association
www.rutgers.edu/accounting/raw/aaa/aaa.htm

FASB
www.rutgers.edu/accounting/raw/fasb

Rutgers Accounting Web
www.rutgers.edu/accounting

EDGAR
www.edgar_online.com

Public Accounting Firms

Arthur Andersen
www.arthurandersen.com

Coopers and Lybrand
www.colybrand.com

**Deloitte Touche Tohmatsu
    International**
www.dttus.com

Ernst & Young
www.ey.com

KPMG
www.us.kpmg.com

Price Waterhouse
www.pw.com/us

FINANCIAL ACCOUNTING

SECOND EDITION

*F*INANCIAL ACCOUNTING

►**JERRY J. WEYGANDT** *Ph.D., C.P.A.*

Arthur Andersen Alumni Professor of Accounting
University of Wisconsin
Madison, Wisconsin

►**DONALD E. KIESO** *Ph.D., C.P.A.*

KPMG Peat Marwick Emeritus Professor of Accountancy
Northern Illinois University
DeKalb, Illinois

►**PAUL D. KIMMEL** *Ph.D., C.P.A.*

Associate Professor of Accounting
University of Wisconsin—Milwaukee
Milwaukee, Wisconsin

 JOHN WILEY & SONS, INC.
New York • Chichester • Weinheim • Brisbane • Singapore • Toronto

ACQUISITIONS EDITOR   Susan Elbe
SUPPLEMENT EDITOR   David B. Kear
MARKETING MANAGER   Wendy Goldner
PRODUCTION COORDINATOR   Suzanne Ingrao
DESIGNER   Kevin Murphy
SENIOR PRODUCTION EDITOR   Tony VenGraitis
PHOTO EDITOR   Mary Ann Price, Hilary Newman
PHOTO RESEARCHER   Jennifer Atkins, Elaine Paoloni
ILLUSTRATION COORDINATOR   Anna Melhorn
COVER PHOTO   Powerstock Photos/Index Stock Photography, Inc.
Coke can   Courtesy Coca-Cola Company
Pepsi can   Reprinted with permission of Pepsi-Cola Company

This book was set in 10.5/12 Palatino by CRWaldman Graphic Communications, Inc. and printed and bound by Von Hoffmann Press. The cover was printed by Phoenix Color Corp.

Recognizing the importance of preserving what has been written, it is a policy of John Wiley & Sons, Inc. to have books of enduring value published in the United States printed on acid-free paper, and we exert our best efforts to that end.

The paper in this book was manufactured by a mill whose forest management programs include sustained yield harvesting of its timberlands. Sustained yield harvesting principles ensure that the number of trees cut each year does not exceed the amount of new growth. The specimen financial statements, Appendix A, are printed with permission of PepsiCo, Inc.

ABOUT THE AUTHORS

••

Jerry J. Weygandt, Ph.D., CPA, is Arthur Andersen Alumni Professor of Accounting at the University of Wisconsin-Madison. He holds a Ph.D. in accounting from the University of Illinois. Articles by Professor Weygandt have appeared in the *Accounting Review, Journal of Accounting Research,* the *Journal of Accountancy,* and other professional journals. These articles have examined such financial reporting issues as accounting for price-level adjustments, pensions, convertible securities, stock option contracts, and interim reports. He is a member of the American Accounting Association, the American Institute of Certified Public Accountants, and the Wisconsin Society of Certified Public Accountants. He has served on numerous committees of the American Accounting Association and as a member of the editorial board of the *Accounting Review.* In addition, he is actively involved with the American Institute of Certified Public Accountants and has been a member of the Accounting Standards Executive Committee (AcSEC) of that organization. He has served on the FASB task force that examined the reporting issues related to "accounting for income taxes" and is presently a trustee of the Financial Accounting Foundation. Professor Weygandt has received the Chancellor's Award for Excellence in Teaching; he also has served as President and Secretary-Treasurer of the American Accounting Association. Recently he received the Wisconsin Institute of CPA's Outstanding Educator's Award and the Lifetime Achievement Award.

Donald E. Kieso, Ph.D., CPA, received his bachelors degree from Aurora University and his doctorate in accounting from the University of Illinois. He has served as chairman of the Department of Accountancy and is currently the KPMG Peat Marwick Emeritus Professor of Accountancy at Northern Illinois University. He has public accounting experience with Price Waterhouse & Co. (San Francisco and Chicago) and Arthur Andersen & Co. (Chicago) and research experience with the Research Division of the American Institute of Certified Public Accountants (New York). He is a recipient of NIU's Teaching Excellence Award and four Golden Apple Teaching Awards. He has served as a member of the Board of Directors of the Illinois CPA Society, the Board of Governors of the American Accounting Association's Administrators of Accounting Programs Group, and AACSB's Accounting Accreditation and Visitation Committees, the State of Illinois Comptroller's Commission, as Secretary-Treasurer of the Federation of Schools of Accountancy, and as Secretary-Treasurer of the American Accounting Association. Professor Kieso is currently serving as Vice-Chairman and member of the Board of Trustees and Executive Committee of Aurora University, the Boards of Directors of Castle BancGroup and the Sandwich State Bank, and the Board of Directors and as Treasurer of The Sandwich Community Hospital. From 1989 to 1993 he served as a charter member of the national Accounting Education Change Commission. In 1988 he received the Outstanding Accounting Educator Award from the Illinois CPA Society; in 1992 he received the FSA's Joseph A. Silvoso Award of Merit and the NIU Foundation's Humanitarian Award for Service to Higher Education; and in 1995 he received a Distinguished Service Award from the Illinois CPA Society.

Paul D. Kimmel, Ph.D., CPA, received his bachelors degree from The University of Minnesota and his doctorate in accounting from University of Wisconsin. He is an Associate Professor at the University of Wisconsin-Milwaukee. He has public accounting experience with Deloitte & Touche (Minneapolis). He is the recipient of the UWM School of Business Advisory Council Teaching Award, the Reggie Taite Excellence in Teaching Award, a three-time winner of the Outstanding Teaching Assistant Award at the University of Wisconsin, and a recipient of the Elijah Watts Sells Award for Honorary Distinction for his results on the CPA exam. He is a member of the American Accounting Association and has published articles in the *Accounting Review, Accounting Horizons, Issues in Accounting Education,* and the *Journal of Accounting Education* as well as other journals. His research interests include accounting for financial instruments and innovation in accounting education. He has published papers and given numerous talks on incorporating critical thinking into accounting education, and helped prepare a catalog of critical thinking resources for the Federated Schools of Accountancy.

Dedicated to
Enid, **Donna**, and **Merlynn**
for their
Love, Support, and Understanding

and to
Clarence P. and Marilyn Hankes
for their humor, patience, and friendship

TO THE INSTRUCTOR

In the previous edition of *Financial Accounting*, we sought to create a book about business that made the subject clear and fascinating to beginning students. And that is still our passion: to provide a link between accounting principles, student learning, and the real world.

Motivation: The Catalyst for Learning

In our effort to create an even more effective text, we listened to reviewers, talked to instructors, and held focus groups. Everyone agreed that one of the biggest challenges instructors face is motivating their students, regardless of how the course is taught.

In this edition, we believe we have created a text that truly motivates students. We took the basic elements of a text—relevancy, content, pedagogy, and study aids—and added the crucial component that sets this edition apart from other introductory texts—*motivation*.

Goals and Features of the Second Edition

The Second Edition of *Financial Accounting* provides an opportunity to improve a textbook that has set high standards for quality. Users and reviewers continue to comment positively on the writing style, the use of real-world examples, pedagogical features, and the fact that the textbook is not only about accounting but about business as well.

The primary purpose of this revision was to maintain these successful features and improve on them. We gathered three consistent messages from all our developmental research:

- Some complex topics that were beyond the scope of the introductory accounting course needed to be eliminated. We've carefully evaluated all topics regarding their suitability for beginning accounting students. Those topics more suitable for an advanced course in accounting were deleted from this edition.
- The pedagogical effectiveness of the text should be as high as possible. Although we believe our First Edition was a market leader in pedagogical effectiveness, we've added many pedagogical elements that are truly unique; they are described below.
- The book should continue to involve the student in the learning process and ensure that the student understands the *why* as well as the *how*. The message is consistent with the recent Accounting Education Change Commission recommendations, which encourage an emphasis on communication skills, interpersonal skills, critical thinking and decision-making skills, ethics, international accounting, and real-world issues.

Content Changes in the Second Edition

In the Second Edition, we tried to simplify and condense the textual material. To achieve this goal, the text was carefully reviewed and carefully edited to ensure its clarity and exposition. We have streamlined the presentation where appropriate to emphasize accounting concepts. Many constructive suggestions came from adopters and users of our First Edition.

Chapter 1, Characteristics and Basic Concepts of Accounting, has deleted the sections describing the accounting profession and careers in accounting (but now includes an ethics presentation). This made room to include a complete set of The Coca Cola Company's financial statements which allow for Comparative Analysis assignments in every chapter in contrast with PepsiCo, Inc.'s financial data.

Chapter 2, The Accounting Information System, has been updated to reflect the latest changes in technology.

Chapters 3 and 4 end-of-chapter assignment material has been expanded.

Chapter 5, Accounting for Merchandising Operations, has been entirely rewritten and based on the perpetual inventory system instead of the periodic inventory system, resulting in a much simpler presentation (coverage of the periodic system is now entirely in *Chapter 9*).

Chapter 6, Financial Statement Concepts and Analysis, is simplified due to deletion of coverage of constant dollar, current cost, percentage of completion, and installment method. The new ratio integration includes coverage of current ratio, working capital, profit margin percentage, return on assets, return on equity, and debt to total assets ratios.

Chapter 8, Accounting for Receivables, has added ratio analysis and now integrates accounts receivable turnover ratio and average days' receivables uncollected.

Chapter 9, Inventories, has been revised to cover periodic inventory system and enhance the comparison of the periodic inventory system to the perpetual system. New ratio integration includes inventory turnover ratio and average days to sell inventory.

Chapter 10, Assets, has been rewritten, revised, and simplified. Topics deleted include: lump-sum purchase, additions, improvments, no increase in useful life, and increase in useful life, and MACRS tax depreciation. A new section on ratio analysis has been added with average life of assets, average age of assets, and asset turnover ratio integrated.

Chapter 11, Liabilities, has deleted coverage of zero interest bearing notes and using a bond sinking fund. Ratio analysis sections have been added with working capital, current ratio, debt to total assets ratio, and times interest earned have been integrated.

Chapter 12, Corporation: Organization, Stock, and Dividends, now covers stockholder's equity entirely in one chapter, including retained earnings. Book value coverage has been moved to an appendix. These topics have been deleted: participating dividends, convertible perferred stock, and callable preferred stock. A new section on analysis and integration of return on common stockholder's equity has been added.

Chapter 13, Investments (formerly Corporations: Retained Earnings and Investments) is now devoted entirely to investments and has been simplified with clearer coverage. Consolidated financial statements has been added to this chapter as an appendix.

Chapter 14, Statement of Cash Flows, has been reorganized to eliminate duplicate coverage under indirect and direct methods. The usefulness of statements of cash flows has been moved to the front of the chapter and ratio topics (current cash debt coverage, cash return on sales, and cash debt coverage) have been integrated into the chapter.

Chapter 15, Financial Statement Analysis, includes the three ratios covering statement of cash flows and summarizes all ratios.

Appendixes at the end of the book include: *A.* PepsiCo Financial Statements, *B.* Time Value of Money (expanded to include future values as well as present values), *C.* Payroll Accounting, *D.* Special Journals & Subsidiary Ledgers, and *E.* Other Significant Liabilities.

Unique Pedagogical Framework

Financial Accounting has provided tools to help students learn accounting concepts and procedures and apply them to the real world. The Second Edition places increased emphasis on the *processes* students undergo as they learn.

- **How to Use the Study Aids** begins the text to help students understand the value of the text's pedagogy and how to use it. They then get tips on in-class and at-home learning strategies, as well as help in identifying the text pedagogy that would be most useful to them when they study. Finally, Chapter 1 contains notes that explain each pedagogical element the first time it appears.

- **Concepts for Review**, listed at the beginning of each chapter from Chapter 2 on, identify concepts that will apply in the chapter to come. In this way, students see the relevance to the current chapter of concepts covered earlier.

- **Study Objectives** form a learning framework throughout the text, with each objective being repeated in the margin at the appropriate place in the main body of the chapter and in the **Summary**. Further, end-of-chapter assignment material is linked to the **Study Objectives**.

- A **Chapter-Opening Vignette** presents a scenario, based on an actual college or business situation, which relates the topic of the chapter to students' lives. The vignette also serves as a running example in the chapter and is the topic of a review question at the end of the chapter.

- A chapter **Preview** links the **Chapter-Opening Vignette** with the major topics of the chapter. First, an introductory paragraph explains how the vignette applies to the topics to be discussed, and then a graphic outline of the chapter provides a visual road map, useful for seeing the big picture as well as the connections between subtopics.

- **Accounting in Action** boxes give students insight into how real companies practice accounting. The boxes, highlighted with effective photographs, cover business, ethics, and international issues.

- **Technology in Action** boxes, also illustrated with photographs, explain how computers are continuing to revolutionize accounting, how they are used in accounting practice today, and what the future holds.

- **Color illustrations** continue to support and reinforce the concepts of the text. **Infographics** are a special type of illustration that helps students visualize and apply accounting concepts to the real world.

- **Before You Go On** sections occur at the end of each key topic and consist of two parts: *Review It* serves as a learning check within the chapter by asking students to stop and answer questions about the material just covered. A mini-demonstration problem, in a section called *Do It*, gives immediate practice of the material just covered. Solutions are provided to help students understand the reasoning involved in reaching an answer. The last *Do It* exercise in each chapter asks students to take a critical look back at the **Chapter-Opening Vignette**.

- **Helpful Hints** in the margin offer students succinct examples to clarify the concept under discussion. This feature actually makes this book an Annotated *Student* Edition.

- Marginal **International Notes** and **Ethics Notes** provide a helpful and convenient way for instructors to expose students to international issues in accounting and to sensitize students to the real-world ethical dilemmas of accounting.

- A **Demonstration Problem** gives students the opportunity to refer to a detailed solution to a representative problem as they do homework assignments. **Problem-Solving Strategies** assist students in understanding the solution and establishing a logic for approaching similar types of problems.

- **Brief Exercises** help build students' confidence and test their basic skills. Each exercise focuses on one of the **Study Objectives**.

- Each of the **Exercises** focuses on one or more **Study Objectives**. These tend to take a little longer to complete, and they present more of a challenge to students than **Brief Exercises**. These **Exercises** help instructors and students make a manageable transition to more challenging problems.

- **Problems** stress the applications of the concepts presented in the chapter and are paired with **Alternate Problems** to give instructors greater flexibility in assigning homework. Certain problems, marked with a pencil icon, help build business writing skills.

- Each **Brief Exercise, Exercise, Problem**, and **Alternate Problem** has a description of the concept covered and is keyed to **Study Objectives**. Key figures from the solutions to the exercises and problems are available for the instructor to use as preferred.
- Each chapter contains selected exercises and problems, identified with an icon, that can be solved utilizing **Solving Financial Accounting Problems Using Lotus 1-2-3**.
- Selected problems, identified with an icon, can be solved utilizing the new **General Ledger Software**, available with this edition of the text.
- **Broadening Your Perspective** is a unique section at the end of each chapter that lets students put it all together and serves as a resource for those instructors who want to teach a more conceptual course. It includes a *Financial Reporting Problem, Comparative Analysis Problem, Interpretation of Financial Statements, Decision Case, Communication Activity, Group Activity, Ethics Case, Research Assignment* and *Critical Thinking: A Real-World Focus* case.
- **Specimen Financial Statements:** Excerpts from the PepsiCo, Inc. 1995 Annual Report are included as Appendix A at the end of the text and are referred to in the end-of-chapter material. The Coca-Cola Company's 1995 financial statements appear in Chapter 1, for comparison and contrast.

Pedagogical Improvements in Second Edition

We have also refined the pedagogical elements to help teachers to teach and students to learn basic accounting concepts.

- **Comparative Analysis Problems** have been added in every chapter. The book now contains two well-known companies' financial statements. The financial statements of PepsiCo, Inc. and The Coca Cola Company give students the chance to review statements from competing companies in the same industry. Every chapter includes assignment material which asks students to analyze, compare and contrast these companies' financial information.
- **Chapter Opening Previews** visually represent the chapter, showing the skeleton and hierarchy of chapter coverage. These visual previews immediately illuminate important concepts and show the relationship of topics.
- **Infographics** are a special type of illustration that appear throughout the text that help to pictorially link concepts to the real world.
- **Before You Go On,** which occur at the end of major sections, include "Review It" questions to serve as a learning check, brief "Do It" exercises to help students apply what they are learning, and "Solutions" to show how the "Do It" exercises should be solved.
- **Marginal Notes** serve several purposes. "Helpful Hints" give tips for students to avoid common pitfalls. "International Notes" provide an effective way to introduce international issues and problems in account-

ing. "Ethics Notes" sensitize students to the real world ethical dilemmas encountered by accountants.
- **Broadening Your Perspective** assignment section has been expanded to include comparative analysis questions, interpretation of financial statements cases, and research assignments.

Accounting Education Change Commission Recommendations Applied

As indicated earlier, we must involve the student in the learning process and ensure that the student understands the why as well as the how. We therefore have provided material that should help students in the following areas as recommended by the Accounting Education Change Commission.

Communication Skills. Each chapter requires answers to certain exercises and problems, identified by a pencil icon, to be in the form of written business communications such as memos or reports. In addition, we have provided an entire section called Broadening Your Perspective, which includes a Financial Reporting Problem, Decision Case, Communication Activity, Group Activity, Ethics Case, and Critical Thinking: A Real-World Focus case. Each of these items provides the student with an opportunity to use both oral and written communication skills.

Interpersonal Skills. Each chapter has a Group Activity assignment intended to develop team-building, collaborative effort skills. Working as part of a group, students exercise leadership skills and learn the art of compromise and concession.

Critical Thinking and Decision-Making Skills. Every chapter has a Critical Thinking case based on a real-world company. In addition, before the end of the chapter proper, students are asked to recall the opening vignette of each chapter in a critical thinking exercise. There is also at least one Decision Case per chapter. These cases require an evaluation of a manager's decision or lead to a decision concerning alternative courses of action. In addition, many exercises and problems require analysis and interpretation of financial statements. In the management chapters, students are asked to evaluate the performance of managers and to make managerial decisions.

Ethics. A discussion of ethics appears in Chapter 1 of the text. Each chapter has an Ethics Case that is relevant to the chapter. In addition, selected real-world Accounting in Action: Ethics Insights are provided in the text and Ethics Notes are provided in the margins.

International Accounting. This topic is covered in Chapter 6. First, the importance of international trade is explained, and the magnitude of foreign sales for major U.S. companies is illustrated. The section concludes with an explanation of financial statements and the setting of uniform international accounting standards. In addition, Accounting in Action: International Insights are provided in the text and International Notes are provided in the margins to illustrate interesting international accounting issues.

Real-World Emphasis. *Financial Accounting* has been the leader in the use of real-world vignettes. The vignettes, called Accounting in Action, are classified as (1) Business Insight, (2) International Insight, and (3) Ethics Insight. In the Second Edition, we continue to use real-world vignettes extensively in every chapter. We have also added a Comparative Analysis Problem (Coca-Cola vs. Pepsi), an Interpretation of Financial Statements (real companies), and a new Critical Thinking: A Real-World Focus case to each chapter. We also changed a number of the chapter-opening vignettes to orient them more towards the business world. As in earlier editions, an appendix at the end of the text includes the annual report of a major U.S. corporation, PepsiCo, Inc. Most of the Financial Reporting Problems require the student to use these data and to analyze and interpret the PepsiCo financial statements and accompanying notes. In addition, specimen financial statements for Coca Cola appear in Chapter 1 so students may compare and contrast statements from two companies in the same industry.

Computer Vignettes. *Accounting Principles* was the pioneer text in using computer vignettes. These real-world vignettes, called Technology in Action, give the student an opportunity throughout the text to see how computers are used in the accounting and business worlds.

A Comprehensive Package of Supplements

Financial Accounting, Second Edition, features a full line of teaching and learning resources developed and revised to help you create a more dynamic and innovative learning environment.

The relevance of accounting in the student's daily life is a major theme of the entire supplements package. Vital current topics such as communication skills, critical thinking and decision making, ethics, and real-world emphasis are integrated throughout. These resources also take an *active learning approach* to help build students' skills and analytical abilities.

The Second Edition supplements package has been revised with Benjamin Bloom's *Taxonomy of Educational Objectives* as a foundation. Throughout the instructor's materials, problems and exercises are classified by their placement within Bloom's taxonomy, allowing instructors to tailor assignments to their students' needs and to develop their students' cognitive ability. The exercise material has been written both to offer instructors a range of options and to guide students step by step from the simpler levels of cognitive ability (Knowledge and Comprehension) to the more complex (such as Evaluation, which includes critical thinking and creative problem solving). The Instructor's Resource Guide and the Solutions Manual contain tables indicating the relationship between each end-of-chapter exercise, its placement within Bloom's taxonomy, and the Study Objectives the exercise reinforces. Additionally, each item in the Test Bank and Exam Book is classified according to Bloom's taxonomy, allowing instructors to tailor their tests even more closely to their objectives.

More than just classifying according to Bloom's, all of the exercises and problem material in each of the supplements—for student and instructor—have been designed and written to achieve very specific behavioral objectives, to help instructors accurately test their students' performance, and to help students learn accounting principles and develop their cognitive ability.

Instructor's Resources

For the instructor, we have designed an extensive support package to help you maximize your teaching effectiveness. We offer useful supplements for instructors with various levels of experience and different instructional circumstances.

Solutions Manual

The Solutions Manual contains detailed solutions to all exercises and problems in the textbook and suggested answers to the questions and cases. Print is large and bold for easy readability in lecture settings. Each chapter includes an *assignment classification table* (identified end-of-chapter items by study objectives), an *assignment characteristics table* (describes each problem and alternate problem), a *Bloom's taxonomy table* (classifies end-of-chapter items by Bloom's taxonomy of learning skills and objectives), and identifies difficulty level and estimated completion time.

Examination Book and Test Bank

The Second Edition now features a comprehensive testing package designed to allow instructors to tailor examinations according to study objectives, learning skills and objectives, and selected content. This package consists of a Test Bank of over 2,000 examination questions and exercises accompanied by answers and solutions. Each chapter includes a *Summary of Questions by Objectives* and a *Summary of Objectives by Questions* (linking test items to Study Objectives), and an indication of placement among Bloom's taxonomy. Exercises are also identified by estimated completion time. In addition to the examination material provided for each chapter, comprehensive examinations covering three to five chapters are also included.

The Examination Book also includes a series of pre-printed Achievement Tests for easy testing of major concepts. Each test covers two chapters from the textbook. The tests, easy to photocopy and distribute directly to students, consist of multiple-choice, matching, true/false, and problems and exercises (computation and journal entries). Solutions are included at the end of each Achievement Test.

Test Preparation Service

Simply call Wiley's special number (1-800-541-5602) with the questions you want on an examination. Wiley will provide a customized master exam within 24 hours. If you prefer, random selection from a number of chapters is possible.

Solutions Transparencies

Packaged in an organizer box with chapter file folders, these transparencies feature detailed solutions to all exercises and problems in the textbook, and suggested answers to the cases. They feature large, bold type for better projection and easy readability in large classroom settings. Accuracy is assured—all solutions were extensively checked by the authors and reviewers.

Teaching Transparencies

One hundred and fifty illustrations are available in four-color format. The authors have selected these illustrations from the text and from original exhibits outside the text as well. Designed to support and clarify concepts in the text, the Teaching Transparencies will enhance lectures. Suggestions on how to integrate the Teaching Transparencies are included in the Instructor's Manuals.

Instructor's Manual

The Instructor's Manual is a comprehensive resource guide designed to assist professors in preparing lectures and assignments. Each manual is set in a print size large enough for easy reading or use as transparency masters. Each volume includes sample syllabi for two-semester and three-quarter use of the textbook. A correlation chart for all end-of-chapter exercises and problems and a correlation chart of chapter contents helps instructors adapt their lecture materials for a smooth transition to the Second Edition.

Included for each chapter are an *assignment classification table*, an *assignment characteristics table*, a *list of study objectives* in extra large, bold-face print for transparencies; a *chapter review* of the significant topics and points contained in the chapter; *enhanced lecture outlines* with teaching tips and references to text material; *suggestions for integrating supplements* into the classroom; a *20-minute quiz* in the form of 10 true/false and 5 multiple-choice questions (with solutions); and illustrations, including diagrams, graphs, questions and exercises, for use as classroom hand-outs, overhead transparencies, in-class quizzes, or demonstrations (solutions are provided).

Additional Solutions Manuals

Solutions Manuals are also available for the following:

- University Bookstore, Inc.: A Corporate Practice Set
- Solving Financial Accounting Problems Using Excel and Lotus 1-2-3

Technology Supplements for Instructors

Technology's increasing application to education has created an environment that is both dynamic and stimulating. Wiley has carefully developed technology supplements to meet the needs of instructors changing the course of accounting and business education today. These supplements provide instructors with state-of-the-art, flexible educational tools.

Computerized Test Bank

The collection of objective questions and exercises with answers for each chapter in the textbook is available for use with IBM and IBM-true compatibles. The Computerized Test Bank offers a number of valuable options. You can:

- Quickly generate a large number of test questions randomly or manually.
- Modify and customize test questions by either changing existing problems or by adding your own problems.
- Create multiple versions of the same test by scrambling questions by type, chapter, or number.
- Customize exams with headers, page and margin size, and question numbering.
- Preview tests prior to printing (the answer key prints with the test).
- Store tests on a separate disk or hard drive and retrieve them later for playback.
- Save tests as ASCII files for export into other word-processing applications.

PowerPoint Presentation Material

This powerful PowerPoint lecture aid contains a combination of key concepts, images, and problems from the textbook for use in the classroom. Designed according to the organization of the material in the textbook, this series of electronic transparencies can be used to reinforce accounting principles visually and graphically. PowerPoint viewer is included, so users are not required to have PowerPoint already installed. However, users with PowerPoint will be able to add their own material to the presentation, or modify existing material to meet their needs.

General Ledger Software Evaluator Disk

This program is a simple way to evaluate students' answers prepared using the General Ledger Software. It evaluates both the transactions that were posted and the ending balances for each of the accounts. The program also includes many reporting options, allowing instructors to print detailed or summary reports for a student or a class using a variety of sort sequences.

Videos

Videos are valuable resources for today's students. Wiley has produced a series of videos to enliven accounting principles and concepts through graphics and visual aids. Presented by three dynamic instructors, all known for their excellence in teaching, they also bring additional insight to the material covered in each chapter of *Financial Accounting*, Second Edition.

The videos are designed for student self-study and review, and they cover each major accounting topic. The whole set is approximately 30 hours in length. Each module covers a chapter and averages 40 to 60 minutes.

Within each chapter, topics are covered in 15-minute segments. The format is designed to aid in maximum student retention.

Wiley Nightly Business Report *Video*

This video contains segments from the highly respected *Nightly Business Report*, which have been selected for their applicability to accounting principles and for their reinforcement of key concepts in the text. Each of the segments is approximately 3 to 5 minutes long and can be used to introduce topics to the students, enhance lecture material, and provide real-world context for related concepts. Suggestions for integrating the material into the classroom are included in the Instructor's Manual.

Technical Support

If you need assistance for any Wiley technology product, please contact Wiley at either of these addresses:

Tech support e-mail: techhelp@jwiley.com
Tech support hotline: 1-212-850-6753

Student Active Learning Aids

In addition to the innovative pedagogy included in the text, we offer a number of valuable learning aids for the student. These are intended to enhance true understanding so that students will be able to apply accounting concepts. A full description of these learning aids is found in the Student Text Preface.

Working Papers

Working Papers are partially completed accounting forms for all end-of-chapter exercises, problems, and cases. A convenient resource for organizing and completing homework assignments, they demonstrate how to correctly set up solution formats and are directly tied to textbook assignments. Each page of the Working Papers has the problem number and company name, and space for students to write their name and course information, providing instructors with consistent forms to grade.

Student Study Guide

The Student Study Guide is a comprehensive review of accounting and a powerful tool for students to use in the classroom. It guides students through chapters by tying content to study objectives and provides resources for use during lectures. This is an excellent resource when preparing for exams. Each chapter of the Student Study Guide includes:

- Study Objectives and a chapter review consisting of 20 to 30 key points to reinforce the material in the textbook.
- A demonstration problem linked to study objectives in the textbook.
- Additional opportunities for students to practice their knowledge and skills through true/false, multiple-choice, and matching questions related to key terms, and exercises linked to study objectives.
- Solutions to the exercises explaining the hows and whys so students get immediate feedback.
- A chapter outline with space provided for students to take lecture notes.

- Blank working papers for students to record any problems and examples presented in class.

Self-Study Problems/Solutions Book

This Self-Study tutorial is designed to improve students' success rates in solving accounting principles homework assignments and exam questions. The Self-Study also provides additional insight and tips on how to study accounting. Each chapter includes:

- An overview of key chapter topics and a review of chapter Study Objectives.
- Purpose statements for each question, case, or exercise, and a direct link to Study Objectives.
- Tips to alert students to common pitfalls and misconceptions, as well as reminders of concepts and principles to help solve problems.
- A selection of multiple-choice questions, exercises, and cases representative of common exam questions or homework assignments to enhance student proficiency.
- Detailed solutions and explanations to assist students in the approach, setup, and completion of problems.

Practice Set

University Bookstore, Inc. is a corporate practice set that exposes students to a real-world simulation of maintaining a complete set of accounting records for a business, integrating business events, accounting concepts, and records. Performed either independently or in a group, the set includes few transactions and thus reinforces students' analytical and creative problem-solving skills.

Technology Supplements for Students

General Ledger Software

The General Ledger Software (GLS) is one of the most exciting technology supplements that accompanies the Second Edition. Available in a DOS, Windows, or Network version, the General Ledger Software program allows students to solve selected end-of-chapter text problems, which are identified by a diskette icon in the margin in the text.

- GLS is ideal for instructors who want their students to gain a hands-on feel for a computerized accounting system. The program demonstrates the immediate effects of each transaction, helping students understand the use of computers in a real-world accounting environment.
- GLS has the ability to modify the existing chart of accounts and beginning balances when creating new problems. This increases the instructor's flexibility in assigning alternate problems within the textbook. This feature also provides students with more opportunity to practice with computerized accounting systems.
- GLS is user-friendly and easy to use, with little start-up time. The DOS version is on only one disk, and the Windows version is on only two, plus a data disk.

Computerized Practice Sets

The General Ledger Software is used to computerize University Bookstore, Inc.: A Corporate Practice Set.

Students receive the same materials as for the manual versions, but use GLS to input the transaction data. Screens for inputting data closely resemble those of general ledger packages that students will encounter in real-world business settings. The program will automatically post, close, and generate all financial statements.

Solving Financial Accounting Problems Using Lotus 1-2-3

These electronic spreadsheet templates allow students to complete selected end-of-chapter exercises and problems identified by a spreadsheet icon in the margin of the text. The manual, which includes the disks, guides students step-by-step from an introduction to computers and Lotus, to completing preprogrammed spreadsheets, to designing their own spreadsheets. Prepared for students with a range of experience in spreadsheet applications, these templates and tutorials help students develop and hone their computer skills and expose them to software packages often used in real-world business environments.

Computerized Study Guide

MicroStudy is a computerized version of the Student Study Guide, designed to provide more flexible movement through the content to meet the particular needs of each student. It offers students both extensive review information and hundreds of self-testing questions from every chapter in the text. The student can select from a number of self-study options including: chapter summaries, chapter study objectives, and self-test questions. Multiple-choice questions offer students explanations of why the wrong choices are not correct. All questions can be automatically scrambled to avoid duplication of identical tests.

Web Site at www.wiley.com/college

Recognizing that the World Wide Web is a valuable resource for students and instructors, we have developed a web site as www.wiley.com/college to provide a variety of additional resources. Internet cases, company websites and useful accounting links will be included. Students will also be provided with an e-mail feedback form that, when sent, goes to the authors.

Instructor's Resource System on CD-ROM

Responding to the changing needs of instructors, the Supplement CD-ROM provides the instructor support material in an easy to use and navigate electronic format. This CD-ROM contains all the print supplements, as well as the electronic ones, for use in the classroom, for printing out material, or for downloading and modifying.

Jerry J. Weygandt
Madison, Wisconsin

Donald E. Kieso
DeKalb, Illinois

Paul D. Kimmel
Milwaukee, Wisconsin

ACKNOWLEDGMENTS

· ·

During the course of development of *Financial Accounting* the authors benefited greatly from manuscript reviewers and ancillary authors and proofers. The constructive suggestions and innovative ideas of the reviewers and the creativity and accuracy of the ancillary authors and checkers is greatly appreciated.

Reviewers and Focus Group Participants

Angela H. Bell, Jacksonville State University;
Sarah Ruth Brown, University of North Alabama;
George M. Dow, Valencia Community College-West;
Craig R. Ehlen, University of Southern Indiana;
Edwin R. Etter, Syracuse University;
Larry R. Falcetto, Emporia State University;
Sheila D. Foster, The Citadel;
Jessica J. Frazier, Eastern Kentucky University;
David Gotlob, Indiana University-Purdue University Fort Wayne;
Ellsworth C. Granger, Jr., Mankato State University;
Tracey J. Hawkins, University of Cincinnati-Clermont;
Elliot Kamlet, SUNY at Binghamton;

Alvin Koslofsky, San Jose City College;
Jerry G. Kreuze, Western Michigan University;
Robert W. McGee, Seton Hall University;
Noel McKeon, Florida Community College-Downtown;
Gale E. Newell, Western Michigan University;
Marc A. Rubin, Miami University;
Victoria S. Rymer, University of Maryland;
LaVerne Thompson, St. Louis Community College-Meramec;
Donna Ulmer, St. Louis Community College-Meramec;
Linda G. Wade, Tarleton State University;
Joni J. Young, University of New Mexico

Ancillary Authors, Contributors, and Proofers

Anne-Lee Bain (University of Wisconsin)—Administrative Assistant;
John C. Borke (University of Wisconsin-Platteville)—Solutions Manual Proofer and Technical Advisor;
Larry Falcetto (Emporia State University)—Supplements Coordinator and Instructor's Manual Author;
David Gotlob (Indiana University-Purdue University Fort Wayne)—Technical and Pedagogical Advisor;
Wayne Higley (Buena Vista College)—Content Proofer and Technical Advisor;
Douglas W. Kieso (University of California at Irvine)—Study Guide Author;
David R. Koeppen (Boise State University)—Lotus Problems Author;
Gary Lubin—General Ledger Software Programmer

We appreciate the exemplary support and professional commitment given us by our solutions manual compositor Elm Street Publications (Ingred Mocant and Barb Lange) our word processor Mary Ann Benson, our executive editor Susan Elbe, the vice president of college production and manufacturing Ann Berlin, our supplements editor David Kear, our marketing manager Wendy Goldner, and our production coordinator Suzanne Ingrao.

We thank PepsiCo, Inc. for permitting us the use of its 1995 Annual Report for our specimen financial statements and accompanying notes.

Suggestions and comments from users are encouraged and appreciated. Please feel free to contact any one of us.

Jerry J. Weygandt
Donald E. Kieso
Paul D. Kimmel

HOW TO USE THE STUDY AIDS
IN THIS BOOK

● ●

Concepts for Review, listed at the beginning of each chapter from Chapter 2 on, are the accounting concepts you learned in previous chapters that you will need to know in order to understand the topics you are about to cover. Page references are provided if you need to review before reading the chapter.

● ● ● ● ● ● ▶ **Concepts for Review**

Before studying this chapter, you should know or, if necessary, review:

a. *How cash transactions are journalized in special journals.*
(Ch. 6, pp. 244–47, 250–52)
b. *How postings are made to the cash account from special journals.*
(Ch. 6, pp. 244–47, 250–52)
c. *The phases in developing an accounting system. (Ch. 6, pp. 237–38)*

No Free Lunch

NEW YORK, NY — At Columbia University, thousands of dollars in cash changes hands between students and dining facility cashiers. Making sure that all of the money received by cashiers gets to where it's supposed to go requires various control measures. In accounting, these measures are called internal control.

One control measure used in the cafeteria at Columbia is that the register tape that records the sale and the amount of cash received must reconcile with the amount of cash in the cash drawer at the end of the day. "We see if there are significant overages or shortages at the end of each day for each register," says Susan McLaughlin, director of Columbia's dining facilities. Do cash differences happen very often? "No, because the cashier knows that if there are repeated or significant shortages, disciplinary action will be

taken," she says. "Ther be a variance of more either over or under, time—or else it indica handling."

If a student buying register sees that a sal

CHAPTER · 7
● ● ● ● ● ● ● ● ● ● ● ● ● ● ●

*I*NTERNAL CONTROL
AND CASH

▶ **STUDY OBJECTIVES** ◀
● ●

After studying this chapter, you should be able to:

1. *Define internal control.*
2. *Identify the principles of internal control.*
3. *Explain the applications of internal control principles to cash receipts.*
4. *Describe the applications of internal control principles to cash disbursements.*
5. *Explain the operation of a petty cash fund.*
6. *Indicate the control features of a bank account.*
7. *Prepare a bank reconciliation.*
8. *Explain the reporting of cash.*

The **Chapter-Opening Vignette** is a brief story that helps you picture how the topics of the chapter relate to the real worlds of accounting and business. Throughout the chapter, references to the opening vignette will help you put new ideas in context, organize them, and remember them.

Study Objectives appear at the beginning of each chapter to provide you with a learning framework. Each study objective then reappears at the point within the chapter where the concept is discussed and each is also summarized at the end of the chapter.

The **Preview** starts with an introductory paragraph linking the vignette with the major topics of the chapter. It is followed by a graphic outline of major topics and subtopics that will be discussed. This narrative and visual preview gives you a mental framework upon which to arrange the new information you are learning.

Technology in Action sections, identified by a CD icon, show how computers are one of the most important tools to the accountant and users of accounting information.

PREVIEW OF CHAPTER 7

As the story about the dining facilities at Columbia University indicates, control of cash is important. Similarly, controls are needed to safeguard other types of assets. For example, Columbia University undoubtedly has controls to prevent the theft of food served in the cafeteria and controls to prevent the theft of computer equipment and supplies from its computer laboratories.

In this chapter, we explain the essential features of an internal control system and then describe how those controls apply to cash. The applications include some controls with which you may be already familiar. Toward the end of the chapter, we describe the use of a bank and explain how cash is reported on the balance sheet. The organization and content of Chapter 7 are as follows:

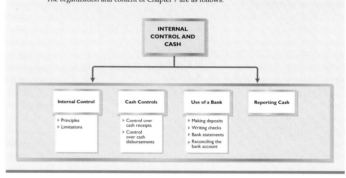

Use of a Bank • 303

Technology in Action

A malfunctioning computer software program doubled all withdrawals and transfers made at Chemical Bank automatic teller machines (ATMs) in New York state for about 12 hours. The printed record of transactions spit out by the ATM was accurate, but the computerized posting of the transactions was automatically doubled. The bank corrected all errors, which in the aggregate may have been $15 million.

Source: Denver Post, February 19, 1994.

The incidence of errors depends on the effectiveness of the inte maintained by the depositor and the bank. Bank errors are infreque either party could inadvertently record a $450 check as $45 or $540 the bank might mistakenly charge a check drawn by C. D. Berg to of C. D. Burg.

Reconciliation Procedure

To obtain maximum benefit from a bank reconciliation, the reconciliation should be prepared by an employee who has no other responsibilities pertaining to cash. When the internal control principle of independent internal verification is not followed in preparing the reconciliation, cash embezzlements may escape unnoticed. For example, a cashier who prepares the reconciliation can embezzle cash and conceal the embezzlement by misstating the reconciliation. Thus, the bank accounts would reconcile and the embezzlement would not be detected.

In reconciling the bank account, it is customary to reconcile the balance per books and balance per bank to their adjusted (correct or true) cash balances. The reconciliation schedule is divided into two sections, as shown in Illustration 7-12. The starting point in preparing the reconciliation is to enter the balance per bank statement and balance per books on the schedule. The following steps should reveal all the reconciling items that cause the difference between the two balances.

1. Compare the individual deposits on the bank statement with deposits in transit from the preceding bank reconciliation and with the deposits per company records or copies of duplicate deposit slips. Deposits recorded by the depositor that have not been recorded by the bank represent deposits in transit and are added to the balance per bank.

2. Compare the paid checks shown on the bank statement or the paid checks returned with the bank statement with (a) checks outstanding from the preceding bank reconciliation and (b) checks issued by the company as recorded in the cash payments journal. Issued checks recorded by the company that have not been paid by the bank represent outstanding checks that are deducted from the balance per bank.

3. Note any errors discovered in the foregoing steps and list them in the appropriate section of the reconciliation schedule. For example, if a paid check correctly written by the company for $195 was mistakenly recorded by the company for $159, the error of $36 is deducted from the balance per books. All errors made by the depositor are reconciling items in determining the adjusted cash balance per books. In contrast, all errors made by the bank are reconciling items in determining the adjusted cash balance per bank.

Helpful hint Deposits in transit and outstanding checks are reconciling items because of time lags.

t employees in the business that you own or manage? ver sometimes is Yes. For example, the financial press lowing:

small company diverted $750,000 of bill payments to a nt over a 3-year period.

th 28 years of service shipped $125,000 of merchandise

r embezzled $21 million from Wells Fargo Bank over a

borrowed'' $150,000 of church funds to finance a friend's

ize the need for a good system of internal control.

Helpful Hints in the margins help clarify concepts being discussed.

Key Terms and concepts are printed in blue where they are first explained in the text and are defined again in the end-of-chapter glossary.

Accounting in Action boxes give you more glimpses into the real world of accounting by discussing actual challenges faced by accountants. Each type of issue—business, ethics, and international—is identified by its own icon. Don't skip over the photos, figures, and tables.

302 CHAPTER 7 ▸ Internal Control and Cash

Accounting in Action ▸ Business Insight

As copying machines have become ever more sophisticated, check counterfeiting has flourished. For example, in the second quarter of a recent fiscal year, the Woolworth Corporation had a $5 million loss from bad checks. Most of the total occurred in the Foot Locker division of the company, a spokesperson said. In the U.S. business community as a whole, some $10 billion worth of bad checks are written every year.

Checkmate Electronic Inc. thinks it has at least a partial answer to this problem. It makes electronic devices that read the magnetic ink used to print account and routing numbers on checks. By identifying the magnetic frequencies as well as the precise shape and size of the numbers, the machine can determine if a check is a fake. Checkmate has a machine small enough to be installed beside cash registers, and it is now in use by such retailers as J.C. Penney, Neiman-Marcus, and Pier 1 Imports.

Source: *Wall Street Journal,* March 31, 1994, p. C2; and *Business Week,* May 23, 1994, p. 9.

Credit Memorandum

A depositor may ask the bank to collect its notes receivable. In such a case, the bank will credit the depositor's account for the cash proceeds of the note, as illustrated on the bank statement by the symbol CM. It will issue a credit memorandum which is sent with the statement to explain the entry. Many banks also offer interest on checking accounts. The interest earned may be indicated on the

---

with the depositor's name and address. Each check and with both a bank and a depositor identification number computer processing of the transaction.

Many companies have more than one bank accou ations and better control, national retailers like Wal-Ma have regional bank accounts. Similarly, a company such as Exxon with more than 150,000 employees may have a payroll bank account, as well as one or more general bank accounts. In addition, a company may maintain several bank accounts in order to have more than one source for obtaining short-term loans when needed.

Making Bank Deposits

Bank deposits should be made by an authorized employee, such as the head cashier. Each deposit must be documented by a deposit slip (ticket), as shown in Illustration 7-9.

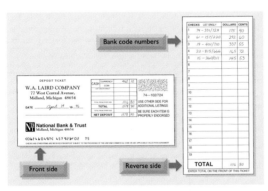

Illustration 7-9

Deposit slip

Color Illustrations visually reinforce important concepts and therefore often contain material that may appear on exams.

Deposit slips are prepared in duplicate. The original is retained by the bank; the duplicate, machine stamped by the bank to establish its authenticity, is retained by the depositor.

Internal Control ◂ 289

Independent internal verification is especially useful in comparing recorded accountability with existing assets. The reconciliation of the cash register tape with the cash in the register in the Columbia University dining facility is an example of this internal control principle. Another common example is the reconciliation by an independent person of the cash balance per books with the cash balance per bank. The relationship between this principle and the segregation of duties principle is shown graphically in Illustration 7-3.

Infographics, a special type of illustration, pictorially link concepts to the real world.

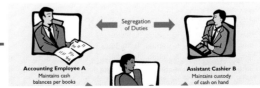

Illustration 7-3

Comparison of segregation of duties principle with independent internal verification principle

Before You Go On *Review It* questions serve as a learning check. If you cannot answer these questions, you should go back and read the section again. Brief *Do It* exercises help you apply what you are learning; their solutions help you see how the problem should be solved. (Keyed to homework exercises.)

A petty cash fund should be replenished at the end of the accounting period regardless of the cash in the fund. Replenishment at this time is necessary in order to recognize the effects of the petty cash payments on the financial statements.

Internal control over a petty cash fund is strengthened by (1) having a supervisor make surprise counts of the fund to ascertain whether the paid vouchers and fund cash equal the imprest amount and (2) canceling or mutilating the paid vouchers so they cannot be resubmitted for reimbursement.

Before You Go On . . .

► **Review It**

1. How do the principles of internal control apply to cash receipts?
2. How do the principles of internal control apply to cash disbursements?
3. When are entries required in a petty cash system?

► **Do It**

L. R. Cortez is concerned about the control over cash receipts in his fast-food restaurant, Big Cheese. The restaurant has two cash registers. At no time do more than two employees take customer orders and ring up sales. Work shifts for employees range from 4 to 8 hours. Cortez asks your help in installing a good system of internal control over cash receipts.

Reasoning: Cortez needs to understand the principles of internal control, especially the principles of establishing responsibility, the use of electronic controls, and independent internal verification. Using this knowledge, an effective system of control over cash receipts can be designed and implemented.

Solution: Cortez should assign a cash register to each employee at the start of each work shift, with register totals set at zero. Each employee should be instructed to use only the assigned register and to ring up all sales. At the end of each work shift, Cortez or a supervisor/manager should total the register and make a cash count to see whether all cash is accounted for.

Related exercise material: BE7–3 and E7–2.

▼ Use of a Bank

The use of a bank contributes significantly to good internal control over cash. A company can safeguard its cash by using a bank as a depository and clearing house for checks received and checks written. Use of a bank minimizes the amount of currency that must be kept on hand. In addition, the use of a bank facilitates the control of cash because a double record is maintained of all bank transactions—one by the business and the other by the bank. The asset account, Cash, maintained by the depositor is the reciprocal of the bank's liability account for each depositor. It should be possible to **reconcile these accounts** (make them agree) at any time.

Opening a bank checking account is a relatively simple procedure. Typically, the bank makes a credit check on the new customer and the depositor is required to sign a **signature card**. The card should contain the signatures of each person authorized to sign checks on the account. The signature card is used by bank employees to validate signatures on the checks.

As soon as possible after an account is opened, the bank will provide the depositor with a book of serially numbered checks and deposit slips imprinted

STUDY OBJECTIVE

6

Indicate the control features of a bank account.

Teaching help Stress that the counterpart to a cash register for cash receipts is the use of a bank account for cash disbursements.

EASTMAN KODAK COMPANY

Current assets (in millions)
Cash and cash equivalents

Cash equivalents are highly liquid investments, with m[...] less when purchased, that can be converted into a specifi[...] include money market funds, money market savings certi[...] of deposit, and U.S. Treasury bills and notes.

A company may have cash that is restricted for a spe[...] include a payroll bank account for paying salaries and w[...] sion fund cash for financing new construction. If the res[...] to be used within the next year, the amount should be rep[...] However, when this is not the case, the restricted funds [...] noncurrent asset. Since a payroll bank account will be u[...] payday for employees, it is reported as a current asset. [...] new construction will begin within the next year, plant [...] classified as a noncurrent asset.

In making loans to depositors, it is common for banks to require the borrowers to maintain minimum cash balances. These minimum balances, called *compensating balances*, provide the bank with support for the loans. Compensating balances are a restriction on the use of cash that may affect a company's liquidity. Accordingly, compensating balances should be disclosed in the financial statements.

Before You Go On . . .

► **Review It**

1. What is generally reported as cash on a company's balance sheet?
2. What is meant by cash equivalents and compensating balances?

► *A Look Back at Columbia University*

Refer to the opening story about Columbia University, and answer the following questions:

1. Does Susan McLaughlin have a valid basis for establishing responsibility for overages or shortages? Why or why not?
2. What internal control principles are applicable to reconciling cash register tapes and the amount of cash in the cash drawer at the end of the day?
3. What internal control principle is involved in seeing that a student gets a receipt when buying a meal at a register? How does this requirement contribute to good internal control?
4. Do you think the cashiers are, or should be, bonded?

Solution

1. Establishing responsibility for overages or shortages is made only at the end of the day. This will provide a valid basis for evaluation only if one person worked the register for the entire day. If more than one person works the register during the day, the single count will not provide a valid basis for establishing who is responsible for the overage or shortage.
2. Applicable internal control principles are: (a) Segregation of duties—the cashier(s) should not be involved in performing the reconciliation. (b) Documentation proce-

---

The last **Before You Go On** exercise takes you back for a critical look at the chapter-opening vignette.

Under the Foreign Corrupt Practices Act of 1977, all major U.S. corporations are required to maintain an adequate system of internal control. Companies that fail to comply are subject to fines, and company officers may be imprisoned. Also, the National Commission on Fraudulent Financial Reporting concluded that all companies whose stock is publicly traded should maintain internal controls that can provide reasonable assurance that fraudulent financial reporting will be prevented or subject to early detection.[1]

Principles of Internal Control

To safeguard its assets and enhance the accuracy and reliability of its accounting records, a company follows specific control principles. Of course, internal control measures vary with the size and nature of the business and with management's control philosophy. However, the six principles listed in Illustration 7-1 apply to most enterprises:

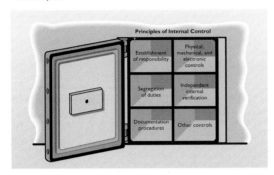

▶ *International note*

U.S. companies also adopt model business codes that guide their international operations to provide for a safe and healthy workplace, avoid child and forced labor, abstain from bribes, and follow sound environmental practices.

International Notes provide a helpful way of introducing international issues and problems in accounting.

STUDY OBJECTIVE
▼ 2
Identify the principles of internal control.

Illustration 7-1
Principles of internal control

Study Objectives reappear in the margins at each point that the topic is discussed. End-of-chapter exercises and problems are keyed to study objectives.

▶ *Ethics note*

Fundamental to internal control systems is the assumption that employees are honest and ethical and will not commit wrongdoing. As a result, most control measures are more effective in preventing and detecting errors than irregularities.

Ethics Notes help sensitize you to the real-world ethical dilemmas of accounting.

[1]Report of the National Commission on Fraudulent Financial Reporting, October 1987, p. 11.

---

dures—the cash register tape provides the documentation for total receipts for the day. (c) Independent internal verification—a supervisor should perform the reconciliation.
3. The internal control principle of documentation procedures is involved. The control does not reside in the receipt itself. For example, there will not be any subsequent reconciliation of cash register receipts with cash at the end of the day. The control is forcing the cashier to ring up each sale so that a receipt is produced. Each receipt is recorded on the cash register tape. At the end of the day, the tape is used in determining overages or shortages.
4. If the dining facility has nonstudent employees who work as cashiers, they may be bonded. However, if students work part-time as cashiers, it is doubtful that they are bonded. From the employer's standpoint, bonding is protection against major embezzlements. The risk of this occurring with student help is relatively low.

The **Summary of Study Objectives** relates the chapter summary to the study objectives located throughout the chapter. It gives you another opportunity to review as well as to see how all the key topics within the chapter are related.

Summary of Study Objectives

1. *Define internal control.* Internal control is the plan of organization and related methods and procedures adopted within a business to safeguard its assets and to enhance the accuracy and reliability of its accounting records.

2. *Identify the principles of internal control.* The principles of internal control are: establishment of responsibility; segregation of duties; documentation procedures; physical, mechanical, and electronic controls; independent internal verification; and other controls.

3. *Explain the applications of internal control principles to cash receipts.* Internal controls over cash receipts include: (a) designating only personnel such as cashiers to handle cash; (b) assigning the duties of receiving cash, recording cash, and custody of cash to different individuals; (c) obtaining remittance advices for mail receipts, cash register tapes for over-the-counter receipts, and deposit slips for bank deposits; (d) using company safes and bank vaults to store cash with access limited to authorized personnel, and using cash registers in executing over-the-counter receipts; (e) making independent daily counts of register receipts and daily comparisons of total receipts with total deposits; and (f) bonding personnel that handle cash and requiring them to take vacations.

4. *Describe the applications of internal control principles to cash disbursements.* Internal controls over cash disbursements include: (a) having only specified individuals such as the treasurer authorized to sign checks; (b) assigning the duties of approving items for payment, paying the items, and recording the payment to different individuals; (c) using

prenumbered checks and accounting for all checks, with each check supported by an approved invoice; (d) storing blank checks in a safe or vault with access restricted to authorized personnel, and using a checkwriter to imprint amounts on checks; (e) comparing each check with the approved invoice before issuing the check, and making monthly reconciliations of bank and book balances; and (f) after payment, stamping each approved invoice "paid."

5. *Explain the operation of a petty cash fund.* In operating a petty cash fund, it is necessary to establish the fund, make payments from the fund, and replenish the fund.

6. *Indicate the control features of a bank account.* A bank account contributes to good internal control by providing physical controls for the storage of cash, minimizing the amount of currency that must be kept on hand, and creating a double record of a depositor's bank transactions.

7. *Prepare a bank reconciliation.* In reconciling the bank account, it is customary to reconcile the balance per books and balance per bank to their adjusted balances. The steps in determining the reconciling items are to ascertain deposits in transit, outstanding checks, errors by the depositor or the bank, and unrecorded bank memoranda.

8. *Explain the reporting of cash.* Cash is listed first in the current assets section of the balance sheet. In some cases, cash is reported together with cash equivalents. Cash restricted for a special purpose is reported separately as a current asset or as a noncurrent asset depending on when the cash is expected to be used.

The **Glossary** defines all the terms and concepts introduced in the chapter.

GLOSSARY

Bank service charge A fee charged by a bank for the use of its services. (p. 301).

Bank statement A statement received monthly from the bank that shows the depositor's bank transactions and balances. (p. 300).

Cash Resources that consist of coins, currency, checks, money orders, and money on hand or on deposit in a bank or similar depository. (p. 291).

Cash equivalents Highly liquid investments, with matur-

End-of-Chapter Appendices address topics considered optional by some instructors.

APPENDIX ▶ Alternative Treatment of Prepaid Expenses and Unearned Revenues

In our discussion of adjusting entries for prepaid expenses and unearned revenues, we illustrated transactions for which the initial entries were made to balance sheet accounts. That is, in the case of prepaid expenses, the prepayment was debited to an asset account, and in the case of unearned revenue, the cash received was credited to a liability account. Some businesses use an alternative treatment: (1) At the time an expense is prepaid, it is debited to an expense account; (2) at the time of a receipt for future services, it is credited to a revenue account. The circumstances that justify such entries and the different adjusting entries that may be required are described below. The alternative treatment of prepaid expenses and unearned revenues has the same effect on the financial statements as the procedures described in the chapter.

STUDY OBJECTIVE

After studying this appendix, you should be able to:

9. Prepare adjusting entries for the alternative treatment of prepayments.

DEMONSTRATION PROBLEM

Trillo Company's bank statement for May 1996 shows the following data:

Balance 5/1	$12,650	Balance 5/31	$14,280
Debit memorandum:		Credit memorandum:	
NSF check	$ 175	Collection of note receivable	$ 505

The cash balance per books at May 31 is $13,319. Your review of the data reveals the following:

1. The NSF check was from Hup Co., a customer.
2. The note collected by the bank was a $500, three-month, 12% note. The bank charged a $10 collection fee. No interest has been accrued.
3. Outstanding checks at May 31 total $2,410.
4. Deposits in transit at May 31 total $1,752.
5. A Trillo Company check for $352 dated May 10 cleared the bank on May 25. This check, which was a payment on account, was journalized for $325.

Instructions

(a) Prepare a bank reconciliation at May 31.
(b) Journalize the entries required by the reconciliation.

Solution to Demonstration Problem

(a)

TRILLO COMPANY
Bank Reconciliation
May 31, 1996

Cash balance per bank statement		$14,280
Add: Deposits in transit		1,752
		16,032
Less: Outstanding checks		2,410
Adjusted cash balance per bank		$13,622
Cash balance per books		$13,319
Add: Collection of note receivable $500, plus $15 interest less collection fee $10		505
		13,824

Demonstration Problems are the final step before you begin homework. These sample problems provide you with **Problem-Solving Strategies** and **Solutions**.

Problem-Solving Strategies
1. Follow the four steps used in reconciling items (pp. 303–4).
2. Work carefully to minimize mathematical errors in the reconciliation.
3. All entries are based on reconciling items per books.
4. Make sure the cash ledger balance after posting the reconciling entries agrees with the adjusted cash balance per books.

	$175	
...check	27	202
...r books		$13,622
...Expense	505	
...able	10	
...nue		500
(...collection of note by bank)		15
...vable—Hup Co.	175	
(...NSF check from Hup Co.)		175
...le	27	
(...error in recording check)		27

SELF-STUDY QUESTIONS

Answers are at the end of the chapter.

Self-Study Questions are a practice test, keyed to Study Objectives, that gives you an opportunity to check your knowledge of important topics. Answers appear on the last page of the chapter.

(SO 1) 1. Internal control is used in a business to enhance the accuracy and reliability of its accounting records and to:
   a. safeguard its assets.
   b. prevent fraud.
   c. produce correct financial statements.
   d. deter employee dishonesty.

(SO 2) 2. The principles of internal control do not include:
   a. establishment of responsibility.
   b. documentation procedures.
   c. management responsibility.
   d. independent internal verification.

(SO 2) 3. Physical controls do not include:
   a. safes and vaults to store cash.
   b. independent bank reconciliations.
   c. locked warehouses for inventories.
   d. bank safety deposit boxes for important papers.

(SO 3) 4. Which of the following items in a cash drawer at November 30 is not cash?
   a. Money orders.
   b. Coins and currency.
   c. A customer check dated December 1.
   d. A customer check dated November 28.

(SO 3) 5. Permitting only designated personnel such as cashiers to handle cash receipts is an application of the principle of:
   a. segregation of duties.
   b. establishment of responsibility.
   c. independent check.
   d. other controls.

(SO 4) 6. The use of prenumbered checks in disbursing cash is an application of the principle of:
   a. establishment of responsibility.
   b. segregation of duties.
   c. physical, mechanical, and electronic controls.
   d. documentation procedures.

(SO 5) 7. A check is written to replenish a $100 petty cash fund when the fund contains receipts of $94 and $3 in cash. In recording the check,
   a. Cash Over and Short should be debited for $3.
   b. Petty Cash should be debited for $94.
   c. Cash should be credited for $94.
   d. Petty Cash should be credited for $3.

(SO 6) 8. The control features of a bank account do not include:
   a. having bank auditors verify the correctness of the bank balance per books.
   b. minimizing the amount of cash that must be kept on hand.
   c. providing a double record of all bank transactions.
   d. safeguarding cash by using a bank as a depository.

(SO 7) 9. In a bank reconciliation, deposits in transit are:
   a. deducted from the book balance.
   b. added to the book balance.
   c. added to the bank balance.
   d. deducted from the bank balance.

(SO 7) 10. The reconciling item in a bank reconciliation that will result in an adjusting entry by the depositor is:
   a. outstanding checks.
   b. deposit in transit.
   c. a bank error.
   d. bank service charges.

(SO 8) 11. The statement that correctly describes the reporting of cash is:
   a. Cash cannot be combined with cash equivalents.
   b. Restricted cash funds may be combined with Cash.
   c. Cash is listed first in the current asset section.
   d. Restricted cash funds cannot be reported as a current asset.

Questions allow you to explain your understanding of concepts and relationships covered in the chapter.

QUESTIONS

1. "Internal control is concerned only with enhancing the accuracy of the accounting records." Do you agree? Explain.

2. What principles of internal control apply to most business enterprises?

3. In the corner grocery store, all sales clerks make change out of one cash register drawer. Is this a violation of internal control? Why?

4. J. Duma is reviewing the principle of segregation of duties. What are the two common applications of this principle?

5. How do documentation procedures contribute to good internal control?

6. What internal control objectives are met by physical, mechanical, and electronic controls?

7. (a) Explain the control principle of independent internal verification. (b) What practices are important in applying this principle?

8. The management of Cobo Company asks you, as the company accountant, to explain (a) the concept of reasonable assurance in internal control and (b) the importance of the human factor in internal control.

9. Midwest Inc. owns the following assets at the balance sheet date:

Cash in bank-savings account	$ 5,000
Cash on hand	850
Cash refund due from the IRS	1,000
Checking account balance	12,000
Postdated checks	500

What amount should be reported as cash in the balance sheet?

10. What principle(s) of internal control is (are) involved in making daily cash counts of over-the-counter receipts?

11. Dent Department Stores has just installed new electronic cash registers in its stores. How do cash registers improve internal control over cash receipts?

12. In Allen Wholesale Company, two mail clerks open all mail receipts. How does this strengthen internal control?

13. "To have maximum effective internal control over cash disbursements, all payments should be made by check." Is this true? Explain.

14. Handy Company's internal controls over cash disbursements provide for the treasurer to sign checks imprinted by a checkwriter after comparing the check with the approved invoice. Identify the internal control principles that are present in these controls.

15. How do the principles of (a) physical, mechanical, and electronic controls and (b) other controls apply to cash disbursements?

16. (a) What is a voucher system? (b) What principles of internal control apply to a voucher system?

17. What is the essential feature of an electronic funds transfer (EFT) procedure?

18. (a) Identify the three activities that pertain to a petty cash fund, and indicate an internal control principle that is applicable to each activity. (b) When are journal entries required in the operation of a petty cash fund?

19. "The use of a bank contributes significantly to good internal control over cash." Is this true? Why?

20. Paul Pascal is confused about the lack of agreement between the cash balance per books and the balance per the bank. Explain the causes for the lack of agreement to Paul, and give an example of each cause.

21. What are the four steps involved in finding differences between the balance per books and balance per banks?

22. Mary Mora asks your help concerning an NSF check. Explain to Mary (a) what an NSF check is, (b) how it is treated in a bank reconciliation, and (c) whether it will require an adjusting entry per bank.

23. (a) "Cash equivalents are the same as cash." Do you agree? Explain. (b) How should restricted cash funds be reported on the balance sheet?

Brief Exercises help you focus on one Study Objective at a time and thus help you build confidence in your basic skills and knowledge. (Keyed to Study Objectives.)

BRIEF EXERCISES

BE7–1 Gina Milan is the new owner of Liberty Parking. She has heard about internal control but is not clear about its importance for her business. Explain to Gina the two purposes of internal control and give her one application of each purpose for Liberty Parking.

Explain the importance of internal control.
(SO 1)

BE7–2 The internal control procedures in Marion Company provide that:

(a) Employees who have physical custody of assets do not have access to the accounting records.

Identify internal control principles.
(SO 2)

EXERCISES

Identify the principles of internal control.
(SO 2)

E7–1 Joe Marino is the owner of Marino's Pizza. Marino's is operated strictly on a carryout basis. Customers pick up their orders at a counter where a clerk exchanges the pizza for cash. While at the counter, the customer can see other employees making the pizzas and the large ovens in which the pizzas are baked.

Instructions
Identify the six principles of internal control and give an example of each principle that you might observe when picking up your pizza. (Note: It may not be possible to observe all the principles.)

Exercises, which gradually increase in skills, understanding, and time necessary to complete them, help you continue to build your confidence. (Keyed to Study Objectives.)

Certain exercises or problems marked with an icon ▊▊▊▶ help you practice business **writing skills**.

Instructions
(a) List the weaknesses in internal control over cash disbursements.
(b) ▊▊▊▶ Write a memo to your boss indicating your recommendations for improvement.

E7–5 Ramona Company uses an imprest petty cash system. The fund was established on March 1 with a balance of $100. During March the following petty cash receipts were found in the petty cash box:

Prepare journal entries for a petty cash fund.
(SO 5)

Date	Receipt No.	For	Amount
3/5	1	Stamp Inventory	$38
7	2	Freight-in	19
9	3	Miscellaneous Expense	12
11	4	Travel Expense	24
14	5	Miscellaneous Expense	5

There was no cash over or short. The fund was replenished on March 15. On March 20, the amount in the fund was increased to $150.

Instructions

(a) Prepare the bank reconciliation at September 30.
(b) Prepare the adjusting entries at September 30, assuming (1) the NSF check was from a customer on account, and (2) no interest had been accrued on the note.

E7–10 The cash records of Kuwait Company show the following:

1. The June 30 bank reconciliation indicated that deposits in transit total $850. During July the general ledger account Cash shows deposits of $15,750, but the bank statement indicates that only $15,600 in deposits were received during the month.
2. The June 30 bank reconciliation also reported outstanding checks of $920. During the month of July, Kuwait Company books show that $17,200 of checks were issued, yet the bank statement showed that $16,400 of checks cleared the bank in July.
3. In September, deposits per the bank statement totaled $26,700, deposits per books were $25,400, and deposits in transit at September 30 were $2,400.
4. In September, cash disbursements per books were $23,700, checks clearing the bank were $25,000, and outstanding checks at September 30 were $2,100.

There were no bank debit or credit memoranda, and no errors were made by either the bank or Kuwait Company.

Instructions

Answer the following questions:

(a) In situation (1), what were the deposits in transit at July 31?
(b) In situation (2), what were the outstanding checks at July 31?
(c) In situation (3), what were the deposits in transit at August 31?
(d) In situation (4), what were the outstanding checks at August 31?

Compute deposits in transit and outstanding checks for two bank reconciliations.
(SO 7)

PROBLEMS

P7–1 Red River Theater is located in the Red River Mall. A cashier's booth is located near the entrance to the theater. Two cashiers are employed. One works from 1–5 P.M., the other from 5–9 P.M. Each cashier is bonded. The cashiers receive cash from customers and operate a machine that ejects serially numbered tickets. The rolls of tickets are inserted and locked into the machine by the theater manager at the beginning of each cashier's shift.

After purchasing a ticket, the customer takes the ticket to a doorperson stationed at the entrance of the theater lobby some 60 feet from the cashier's booth. The doorperson tears the ticket in half, admits the customer, and returns the ticket stub to the customer. The other half of the ticket is dropped into a locked box by the doorperson.

At the end of each cashier's shift, the theater manager removes the ticket rolls from the machine and makes a cash count. The cash count sheet is initialed by the cashier. At the end of the day, the manager deposits the receipts in total in a bank night deposit vault located in the mall. In addition, the manager sends copies of the deposit slip and the initialed cash count sheets to the theater company treasurer for verification and to the company's accounting department. Receipts from the first shift are stored in a safe located in the manager's office.

Identify internal control weaknesses over cash receipts.
(SO 2, 3)

Instructions

(a) Identify the internal control principles and their application to the cash receipts transactions of the Red River Theater.
(b) If the doorperson and cashier decide to collaborate to misappropriate cash, what actions might they take?

P7–2 MTR Company maintains a petty cash fund for small expenditures. The following transactions occurred over a 2-month period:

July 1 Established petty cash fund by writing a check on Metro Bank for $200.
15 Replenished the petty cash fund by writing a check for $194.30. On this date the fund consisted of $5.70 in cash and the following petty cash receipts: Freight-in $94.00, postage expense $42.40, entertainment expense $46.60, and miscellaneous expense $10.70.
31 Replenished the petty cash fund by writing a check for $192.00. At this date, the fund consisted of $8.00 in cash and the following petty cash receipts: Freight-in

Journalize and post petty cash fund transactions.
(SO 5)

Each **Problem** helps you pull together and apply several concepts of the chapter. Included in these are problems that help you develop the writing skills that are so important in business. (Keyed to multiple Study Objectives.)

General Ledger Problems, identified by an icon are selected problems that can be solved using the General Ledger Software package.

Paired with the Problems, **Alternate Problems** provide additional opportunities to apply concepts learned in the chapter. (Each Alternate Problem is keyed to the same Study Objectives as its counterpart in the Problems set.)

Spreadsheet Problems identified by an icon are selected exercises and problems that can be solved using *Solving Principles of Accounting Problems Using Lotus 1-2-3 or Excel.* •

---

230   CHAPTER 5 ► *Accounting for Merchandising Operations*

Prepare correct multiple-step and single-step income statements.
(SO 5, 7)

P5–5A A part-time bookkeeper prepared the following income statement for the Tao Company for the year ending December 31, 1996.

TAO COMPANY
Income Statement
December 31, 1996

Revenues		
Sales		$702,000
Less: Freight-in	$ 17,200	
Discounts	4,100	21,300
Net sales		680,700
Other revenues (net)		1,300
Total revenues		682,000
Expenses		
Purchases	470,000	
Selling expenses	100,000	
Administrative expenses	50,000	
L. Tao, Drawings	12,000	
Total expenses		632,000
Net income		$ 50,000

As an experienced, knowledgeable accountant you review the statement and determine the following facts:

1. Sales includes $10,000 of deposits from customers for future sales orders.
2. Discounts consist of purchase discounts earned $7,200 and sales discounts granted $11,300.
3. Other revenues contains two items: interest expense $4,000 and interest revenue $5,300.
4. Purchases includes freight-out $14,000 less purchase returns and allowances $9,000.
5. Ending merchandise inventory increased $20,000 from a beginning inventory of $35,000.
6. Selling expenses consist of sales salaries $76,000, advertising $10,000, depreciation on store equipment $7,500, and sales commissions expense $6,500.
7. Administrative expenses consist of office salaries $19,000, utilities expense $8,000, rent expense $16,000, and insurance expense $7,000. Insurance expense includes $1,200 of insurance applicable to 1994.

▶*B*roadening Your Perspective

The **Broadening Your Perspective** section helps you pull together various concepts covered in the chapter and apply them to real-life business decisions.

*F*INANCIAL REPORTING PROBLEM

The financial statements of PepsiCo, Inc. are presented in Appendix A of this textbook together with two reports: (1) a management report, Management's Responsibility for Financial Statements, and (2) an auditor's report, Report of Independent Auditors.

Instructions
Using the financial statements and reports, answer the following questions about PepsiCo's internal controls and cash.

1. What comments, if any, concerning the company's system of internal control are included in each report?
2. What reference, if any, is made to internal auditors in each report?
3. What comments, if any, are made about cash in the report of the independent auditors?

A **Financial Reporting Problem** familiarizes you with the format, content, and uses of financial statements prepared by major U.S. companies.

*C*OMPARATIVE ANALYSIS PROBLEM— THE COCA-COLA COMPANY VS. PEPSICO, INC.

The financial statements of The Coca-Cola Company are presented at the end of Chapter 1, and PepsiCo's financial statements are presented in Appendix A.

Instructions:
(a) Based on the information contained in these financial statements, determine each of the following for each company:
   1. Cash and cash equivalents balance at December 31, 1995.
   2. Increase (decrease) in cash and cash equivalents from 1994 to 1995.
   3. Cash provided by operating activities during 1995 (from Statement of Cash Flows).
(b) What conclusions concerning the management of cash can be drawn from these data?

A **Comparative Analysis Problem** requires you to compare and analyze both quantitatively and qualitatively the financial information contained in the Coca-Cola Company's and PepsiCo's financial statements.

*I*NTERPRETATION OF FINANCIAL STATEMENTS

Case—Microsoft, Inc.
Microsoft is the leading developer of software in the world. To continue to be successful Microsoft must generate new products. Generating new products requires significant amounts of cash. Shown below is the current assets section of Microsoft's June 30, 1995, balance sheet and excerpts from a footnote describing the first item listed in the balance sheet, "cash and short-term investments." Below Microsoft is the current asset section of Oracle, another major software developer.

(all dollar amounts in millions)

Microsoft		
Current assets:	1994	1995
Cash and short-term investments (1)	$3,614	$4,750
Accounts receivable—net of allowances of $92 and $139	475	581
Inventories	102	88
Other	121	201
Total current assets	4,312	5,620
Total current liabilities	913	1,347

An **Interpretation of Financial Statements Case** requires you to interpret financial information presented either in a real world's financial statements or the accompanying notes.

*D*ECISION CASE

The board of trustees of a local church is concerned about the internal accounting controls pertaining to the offering collections made at weekly services. They ask you to serve on a three-person audit team with the internal auditor of the university and a CPA who has just joined the church.

At a meeting of the audit team and the board of trustees you learn the following:

1. The church's board of trustees has delegated responsibility for the financial management and audit of the financial records to the finance committee. This group prepares the annual budget and approves major disbursements but is not involved in collections or record keeping. No audit has been made in recent years because the same trusted employee has kept church records and served as financial secretary for 15 years. The church does not carry any fidelity insurance.

Instructions
(a) Indicate the weaknesses in internal accounting control over the handling of collections.
(b) List the improvements in internal control procedures that you plan to make at the next meeting of the audit team for (1) the ushers, (2) the head usher, (3) the financial secretary, and (4) the finance committee.
(c) What church policies should be changed to improve internal control?

A **Decision Case** helps you build your decision-making skills by analyzing accounting information in a less structured situation. At the same time it provides practice in your writing skills.

*C*OMMUNICATION ACTIVITY

As a new auditor for the CPA firm of Rawls, Keoto, and Landry you have been assigned to review the internal controls over mail cash receipts of Adirondack Company. Your review reveals the following: Checks are promptly endorsed "For Deposit Only," but no list of the checks is prepared by the person opening the mail. The mail is opened either by the cashier or by the employee who maintains the accounts receivable records. Mail receipts are deposited in the bank weekly by the cashier.

Instructions
Write a letter to L. S. Osman, owner of the Adirondack Company, explaining the weaknesses in internal control and your recommendations for improving the system.

Communication Activities ask you to engage in real-life business situations using your writing, speaking, or presentation skills.

Group Activities prepare you for the business world, where you will be working with many people, by giving you practice in solving problems with colleagues.

Through the **Ethics Cases** you will reflect on ethical situations an accountant typically confronts.

Instructions
Write a letter to L. S. Osman, owner of the Adirondack Company, explaining the weaknesses in internal control and your recommendations for improving the system.

GROUP ACTIVITY

From your employment or personal experiences, identify situations in which cash was received or disbursed.

Instructions
In groups of five or six students:
   (a) Identify the internal control principles used for cash receipts.
   (b) Identify the internal control principles used for cash disbursements.
   (c) Identify any weaknesses in internal control related to cash receipts and disbursements.

ETHICS CASE

You are the assistant controller in charge of general ledger accounting at Lemon Twist Bottling Company. Your company has a large loan from an insurance company. The loan agreement requires that the company's cash account balance be maintained at $200,000 or more as reported monthly. At June 30 the cash balance is $80,000, which you report to Sam Williams, the financial vice-president. Sam excitedly instructs you to keep the cash receipts book open for one additional day for purposes of the June 30 report to the insurance company.

Instructions
   (a) Who will suffer negative effects if you do not comply with Sam Williams' instructions? Who will suffer if you do comply?
   (b) What are the ethical considerations in this case?
   (c) What alternatives do you have?

Sam says, "If we don't get that cash balance over $200,000, we'll default on our loan agreement. They could close us down, put us all out of our jobs!" Sam continues, "I talked to Grochum Distributors (one of Lemon Twist's largest customers) this morning and they said they sent us a check for $150,000 yesterday. We should receive it tomorrow. If we include just that one check in our cash balance, we'll be in the clear. It's in the mail!"

Instructions
   (a) Who will suffer negative effects if you do not comply with Sam Williams' instructions? Who will suffer if you do comply?
   (b) What are the ethical considerations in this case?
   (c) What alternatives do you have?

RESEARCH ASSIGNMENT

The "Fortune 500" issue of *Fortune* magazine can serve as a useful reference. This annual issue of *Fortune*, generally appearing in late April or early May, contains a great deal of information regarding the largest U.S. industrial and service companies. Examine the most recent edition and answer the following questions.

   (a) Identify the three largest U.S. corporations in terms of revenues, profits, assets, market value, and employees.
   (b) Identify the largest corporation headquartered (or operating, if needed) in your state (by total revenue). How does this corporation rank in terms of revenues, profits, assets, market value, and number of employees?

CRITICAL THINKING CASE
► *A Real-World Focus: Alternative Distributor Corp.*

Alternative Distributor Corp., a distributor of groceries and related products, is headquartered in Medford, Massachusetts. It was founded in 1980 and today has seven employees, with a total sales of $7 million.

During its audit, the Alternative Distributor Corp. was advised that previously existing internal controls necessary for the company to develop reliable financial statements were inadequate. The audit report stated that the current system of accounting for sales, receivables, and cash receipts constituted a material weakness.

Among other items, the report focused on non-timely deposit of cash receipts, exposing Alternative Distributor to potential loss or misappropriation; excessive past due accounts receivable due to lack of collection efforts; disregard of advantages offered by vendors for prompt payment of invoices; absence of appropriate segregation of duties by personnel consistent with appropriate control objectives; inadequate procedures for applying accounting principles; lack of qualified management personnel; lack of supervision by an outside board of directors; and overall poor recordkeeping.

Instructions
Identify the principles of internal control violated by Alternative Distributor Corporation.

Answers to Self-Study Questions
1. a   2. c   3. b   4. c   5. b   6. d   7. a   8. a   9. c   10. d   11. c

---

A **Research Assignment** requires you to find the source of the data (in a publication, in your library, in an Annual Report, on the World Wide Web or the Internet) and then interpret or analyze the data and evaluate it

Critical Thinking: A Real-World Focus asks you to decide how to apply the concepts you have learned to specific situations faced by actual companies.

Answers to Self-Study Questions provide feedback on your understanding of concepts.

HOW DO YOU LEARN BEST?

Now that you have looked at your Owner's Manual, take time to find out how you learn best. This quiz was designed to help you find out something about your preferred learning method. Research on left brain/right brain differences and also on learning and personality differences suggests that each person has preferred ways to receive and communicate information. After taking the quiz, we will help you pinpoint the study aids in this text that will help you learn the material based on your learning style.

Circle the letter of the answer that best explains your preference. If a single answer does not match your perception, please circle two or more choices. Leave blank any question that does not apply.

1. You are about to give directions to a person. She is staying in a hotel in town and wants to visit your house. She has a rental car. Would you
   - V) draw a map on paper?
   - R) write down the directions (without a map)?
   - A) tell her the directions?
   - K) pick her up at the hotel in your car?

2. You are staying in a hotel and have a rental car. You would like to visit friends whose address/location you do not know. Would you like them to
   - V) draw you a map on paper?
   - R) write down the directions (without a map)?
   - A) tell you the directions by phone?
   - K) pick you up at the hotel in their car?

3. You have just received a copy of your itinerary for a world trip. This is of interest to a friend. Would you
   - A) call her immediately and tell her about it?
   - R) send her a copy of the printed itinerary?
   - V) show her on a map of the world?

4. You are going to cook a dessert as a special treat for your family. Do you
   - K) cook something familiar without need for instructions?
   - V) thumb through the cookbook looking for ideas from the pictures?
   - R) refer to a specific cookbook where there is a good recipe?
   - A) ask for advice from others?

5. A group of tourists has been assigned to you to find out about national parks. Would you
   - K) drive them to a national park?
   - R) give them a book on national parks?
   - V) show them slides and photographs?
   - A) give them a talk on national parks?

6. You are about to purchase a new stereo. Other than price, what would most influence your decision?
   - A) A friend talking about it.
   - K) Listening to it.
   - R) Reading the details about it.
   - V) Its distinctive, upscale appearance.

7. Recall a time in your life when you learned how to do something like playing a new board game. (Try to avoid choosing a very physical skill, e.g., riding a bike.) How did you learn best? By

   - V) visual clues—pictures, diagrams, charts?
   - A) listening to somebody explaining it?
   - R) written instructions?
   - K) doing it?

8. Which of these games do you prefer?
   - V) *Pictionary*
   - R) *Scrabble*
   - K) Charades

9. You are about to learn to use a new program on a computer. Would you
   - K) ask a friend to show you?
   - R) read the manual that comes with the program?
   - A) telephone a friend and ask questions about it?

10. You are not sure whether a word should be spelled "dependent" or "dependant." Do you
    - R) look it up in the dictionary?
    - V) see the word in your mind and choose the best way it looks?
    - A) sound it out in your mind?
    - K) write both versions down?

11. Apart from price, what would most influence your decision to buy a particular textbook?
    - K) Using a friend's copy.
    - R) Skimming parts of it.
    - A) A friend talking about it.
    - V) It looks OK.

12. A new movie has arrived in town. What would most influence your decision to go or not to go?
    - A) Friends talked about it.
    - R) You read a review of it.
    - V) You saw a preview of it.

13. Do you prefer a lecturer/teacher who likes to use
    - R) handouts and/or a textbook?
    - V) flow diagrams, charts, slides?
    - K) field trips, labs, practical sessions?
    - A) discussion, guest speakers?

Results: To determine your learning preference, add up the number of individual Vs, As, Rs, and Ks you have circled. Take the letter you have the greatest number of and match it to the same letter in the Learning Styles Chart. Next to each letter in the Chart are suggestions that will refer you to different learning aids throughout this text.

LEARNING STYLES CHART

TYPE	WHAT TO DO IN CLASS	WHAT TO DO WHEN STUDYING	TEXT FEATURES THAT MAY HELP YOU THE MOST	WHAT TO DO PRIOR TO AND DURING EXAMS
V VISUAL	Underline. Use different colors. Use symbols, charts, arrangements on the page.	Use the "In Class" strategies. Reconstruct images in different ways. Redraw pages from memory. Replace words with symbols and initials.	**Preview** **Infographics/ Illustrations** **Photos** **Accounting in Action** **Technology in Action** **Key Terms in blue** **Words in bold** **Questions/Exercises/ Problems** **Financial Reporting Problem**	Recall the "pictures of the pages." Draw, use diagrams where appropriate. Practice turning visuals back into words.

TYPE	WHAT TO DO IN CLASS	WHAT TO DO WHEN STUDYING	TEXT FEATURES THAT MAY HELP YOU THE MOST	WHAT TO DO PRIOR TO AND DURING EXAMS
A AURAL	Attend lectures and tutorials. Discuss topics with students. Explain new ideas to other people. Use a tape recorder. Describe overheads, pictures, and visuals to somebody not there. Leave space in your notes for later recall.	You may take poor notes because you prefer to listen. Therefore: Expand your notes. Put summarized notes on tape and listen. Read summarized notes out loud. Explain notes to another "aural" person.	**Infographics/Illustrations** **Accounting in Action** **Technology in Action** **Review It/Do It** **Summary of Study Objectives** **Glossary** **Demonstration Problem** **Self-Study Questions** **Questions/Exercises/ Problems** **Financial Reporting Problem** **Decision Case** **Communication Activity** **Group Activity** **Ethics Case** **Critical Thinking** **Videos**	Listen to your "voices" and write them down. Speak your answers. Practice writing answers to old exam questions.

Source: Adapted from Neil D. Fleming and Colleen Mills, "Not Another Inventory, Rather a Catalyst for Reflections," *To Improve the Academy*, Volume II (1992), pp. 137-155. Used by permission.

TYPE	WHAT TO DO IN CLASS	WHAT TO DO WHEN STUDYING	TEXT FEATURES THAT MAY HELP YOU THE MOST	WHAT TO DO PRIOR TO AND DURING EXAMS
R R E A D I N G / W R I T I N G 	Use lists, headings. Use dictionaries and definitions. Use handouts and textbooks. Read. Use lecture notes.	Write out words again and again. Reread notes silently. Rewrite ideas into other words. Organize diagrams into statements.	**Study Objectives** **Preview** **Review It/Do It** **Summary of Study Objectives** **Glossary** **Self-Study Questions** **Questions/Exercises/ Problems** **Writing Problems** **Financial Reporting Problem** **Decision Case** **Communication Activity** **Group Activity** **Ethics Case** **Critical Thinking**	Practice with multiple-choice questions. Write out lists. Write paragraphs, beginnings and endings.

TYPE	WHAT TO DO IN CLASS	WHAT TO DO WHEN STUDYING	TEXT FEATURES THAT MAY HELP YOU THE MOST	WHAT TO DO PRIOR TO AND DURING EXAMS

K
 	
K I N E S T H E T I C

	Use all your senses.
	Go to labs, take field trips.
	Use trial-and-error methods.
	Listen to real-life examples.
	Use hands-on approach.
		You may take notes poorly because topics do not seem relevant. Therefore:
		   Put examples in note summaries.
		   Use pictures and photos to illustrate.
		   Talk about notes with another "kinesthetic" person.
			Concepts for Review
			Vignettes
			Preview
			Infographics/Illustrations
			Review It/Do It
			A Look Back at . . .
			Summary of Study Objectives
			Demonstration Problem
			Self-Study Questions
			Questions/Exercises/ Problems
			Financial Reporting Problem
			Decision Case
			Communication Activity
			Group Activity
				Write practice answers.
				Role-play the exam situation.

BRIEF TABLE OF CONTENTS

CONTENTS

Strike Three?

MILWAUKEE, Wis. — "It might be ... it could be ... it IS ... a home run!" That phrase was not heard in major league baseball stadiums from August 11, 1994, until April 25, 1995. During that time major league baseball was benched by a players' strike. Who was at fault? Some argue that the reason for the strike was the greed of *both* the players and the owners. Each side—players and owners—thinks the other makes too much money, and each believes its side should be receiving more.

It would seem easy to prove how much the owners make—or lose—each year. Interim baseball commissioner Bud Selig stated that "losses for many teams are not only real, they are staggering." Selig points out that teams like the Kansas City Royals and the Detroit Tigers would have lost over $20 million if play had continued in 1994. Thus, owners argue they need to limit salaries and other expenses in order to bring financial stability to the nation's pastime. Players' association union chief Donald Fehr, on the other hand, has said repeatedly that you can do anything with numbers. He contends that better management and more honest bookkeeping would show that most baseball teams are making money. And, he notes, the value of a baseball franchise is increasing yearly.

Which argument makes more sense to you—that of the owners or the players? ◀

CHAPTER · **1**

*U*SERS AND USES OF FINANCIAL STATEMENTS

► STUDY OBJECTIVES ◄

After studying this chapter, you should be able to:

1. *Explain the meaning of accounting.*
2. *Identify the users and uses of accounting.*
3. *Understand why ethics is a fundamental business concept.*
4. *Explain the meaning of generally accepted accounting principles and the cost principle.*
5. *Explain the meaning of the monetary unit assumption and the economic entity assumption.*
6. *State the basic accounting equation and explain the meaning of assets, liabilities, and stockholders' equity.*
7. *Analyze the effect of business transactions on the basic accounting equation.*
8. *Prepare an income statement, retained earnings statement, balance sheet, and statement of cash flows.*

The opening story about the major league baseball strike highlights the need for accurate and sound reporting of financial information. It follows that regardless of one's pursuits or occupation, the need for financial information is inescapable. You cannot earn a living, spend money, buy on credit, make an investment, or pay taxes without receiving, using, or dispensing financial information. Good decision making depends on good information.

The purpose of this chapter is to show you that accounting is the system used to provide useful financial information. The content and organization of the chapter are as follows:

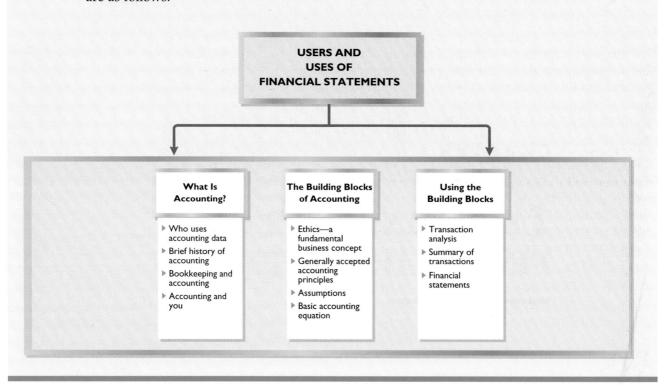

The Preview describes and outlines the major topics and subtopics you will see in the chapter. It will also help you when it is time to review the chapter before exams.

*W*hat Is Accounting?

STUDY OBJECTIVE

1

Explain the meaning of accounting.

As a financial information system, accounting is a process of three activities: **identifying**, **recording**, and **communicating** the economic events of an organization (business or nonbusiness) to interested users of the information. Let's take a closer look at these three activities:

1. The first part of the process—**identifying**—involves selecting those events that are considered **evidence of economic activity relevant to a particular organization**. The sale of goods by J.C. Penney Company, the rendering of services by American Telephone & Telegraph, the payment of wages by Ford Motor Company, and the collection of ticket and broadcast money and the payment of expenses by major league baseball teams are examples of economic events.

2. Once identified and measured in dollars and cents, economic events are **recorded** to provide a permanent history of the financial activities of the or-

ganization. Recording consists of keeping a **chronological diary of measured events in an orderly and systematic manner**. In recording, economic events are also classified and summarized.

3. This identifying and recording activity is of little use unless the information is **communicated** to interested users. The information is communicated through the **preparation and distribution of accounting reports**, the most common of which are called **financial statements**. To make the reported financial information meaningful, accountants describe and report the recorded data in a standardized way. Information resulting from similar transactions is accumulated and totaled. Such data are said to be reported **in the aggregate**. For example, all sales transactions of Apple Computer are accumulated over a certain period of time and reported as one amount in the financial statements of Apple Computer. By presenting the recorded data in the aggregate, the accounting process simplifies a multitude of transactions and renders a series of activities understandable and meaningful.

A vital element in communicating economic events is the accountant's ability and responsibility to **analyze** and **interpret** the reported information. Analysis involves the use of ratios, percentages, graphs, and charts to highlight significant financial trends and relationships. Interpretation involves **explaining the uses, meaning, and limitations of reported data**. Included in Appendix A of this textbook are specimen financial statements and accompanying notes and graphs from PepsiCo, Inc. We will refer to them at various places throughout the text. At this point, they probably strike you as complex and confusing. By the end of this course, you'll be surprised at how much about them you understand.

In summary, the accounting process may be diagrammed as follows:

Illustrations such as the one below convey information in pictorial form to help you visualize and apply the information as you study.

Illustration 1-1

Accounting process

Identification — Select economic events (transactions)

Recording — Record, classify, and summarize

Communication — Prepare accounting reports / Analyze and interpret for users

Accounting should consider the needs of the users of financial information. As a consequence, you should know who these users are and something about their needs for information.

Who Uses Accounting Data?

Because it communicates financial information about a business enterprise, accounting is often called "the language of business." The information that a specific user of financial information needs depends upon the kinds of decisions that user makes. The differences in the decisions divide the users of financial information into two broad groups: internal users and external users. **Internal users** are those who manage the business (officers and other decision makers). **External users** are those outside the business who have either a **present or potential direct financial interest** (investors and creditors) or an **indirect financial interest** (taxing authorities, regulatory agencies, labor unions, customers, and economic planners). The relationship of these users to the accounting process and to one another is diagrammed in Illustration 1-2.

Helpful hint Accounting is the language of business because it communicates vital information about a business to interested parties.

Illustration 1-2

Users of accounting information

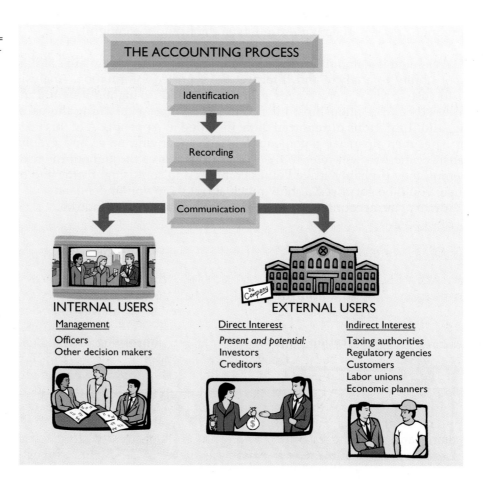

Internal Users

Management at all levels uses accounting information in planning, controlling, and evaluating business operations. To perform these functions, managers need detailed information on a timely basis. For example, the managers of a company might ask:

> Is cash sufficient to pay our debts?
> Are customers paying their bills promptly?

What is the cost of manufacturing each unit of product?

What costs exceed budget?

Can we afford to give employee pay raises this year?

Which product line is the most profitable?

How much money must be borrowed to expand the factory?

To assist management in answering these questions, accounting provides **internal reports**. Examples include financial comparisons of operating alternatives, projections of income from new sales campaigns, and forecasts of cash needs for the next year. In addition, statements on the financial position and results of operations of the entire business are prepared.

External Users—Direct Interest

External users with a direct interest are the company's investors and creditors. **Investors** (owners) make their decisions to buy, hold, or sell their financial interests on the basis of accounting information. **Creditors** (suppliers and bankers) evaluate the risks of granting credit or lending money on the basis of available accounting information. Some of the questions asked by investors and creditors about a company might be:

Is the company earning satisfactory income?

How does the company compare in size and profitability with competitors?

Will the company be able to pay its debts as they come due?

Are interest payments and dividends protected by an adequate inflow of cash from operations?

External Users—Indirect Interest

The information needs and questions of those with indirect financial interests vary considerably. **Taxing authorities** (such as the Internal Revenue Service) want to know if the company complies with the tax laws. **Regulatory agencies** (such as the Securities and Exchange Commission or the Federal Trade Commission) want to know if the company is operating within prescribed rules. **Customers** are interested in whether a company will continue to honor product warranties and otherwise support its product lines. **Labor unions** (such as the major league players' association in the opening story) want to know if the owners have the ability to pay increased wages and benefits. **Economic planners** use accounting information to analyze and forecast economic activity.

The many and varied uses of accounting information clearly attest to its importance. **Without accounting, our existing systems of production, investment, credit, and taxation would be seriously impaired.**

Helpful hint The IRS has long required businesses to prepare and retain a set of records that can be audited. Also, the Foreign Corrupt Practices Act requires public companies to keep books and records.

Brief History of Accounting

The **origins of accounting** are generally attributed to the work of Luca Pacioli, a famous Italian Renaissance mathematician. Pacioli was a close friend and tutor to Leonardo da Vinci and a contemporary of Christopher Columbus. In his text *Summa de Arithmetica, Geometria, Proportione et Proportionalite*, Pacioli described a system to ensure that financial information was recorded efficiently and accurately.

With the advent of the **industrial age** in the nineteenth century and, later, the emergence of large corporations, a separation of the owners from the man-

▶Accounting in Action ▸ *International Insight*

When the chief engineer of Irkutsk Energo, a public utility in Moscow, addressed a gathering of international investors recently, he provided them with all kinds of financial information about the company. The reason: Russians are learning that corporate openness lures much-needed foreign investment. Foreign investors, however, have been reluctant to invest because Russian firms have been secretive (and sometimes deceptive) about their financial affairs. Now, however, things will probably change because firms such as Irkutsk Energo have enjoyed stock price surges after providing candid accounting information. In short, good accounting information may help Russia solve some of its economic problems.

Source: Wall Street Journal, June 9, 1995, p. A-6.

Throughout this textbook, you will find Accounting in Action examples highlighted like this. These examples illustrate important and interesting information as it relates to actual accounting situations in business. Different icons highlight each type of issue—a globe, as here, for international insights, scales for ethics insights, and a city skyline for business insights.

agers of businesses took place. As a result, the need to report the status of the business enterprise took on increasing importance, to ensure that managers acted in accord with owners' wishes. In addition, transactions between businesses became more complex, making necessary improved approaches for reporting financial information.

Our economy has now evolved into a post-industrial age—**the information age**—in which the "products" are information services. The computer, as the information processor, has been the driver of the information age.

The pace of business change has also increased, partly in response to international competition. Companies must remake themselves rapidly, and they are doing it by a whole assortment of actions: downsizing, worker empowerment, process reengineering, mergers, alliances, and novel financial instruments. Accounting is constantly adapting to this changing environment, by examining carefully the types of financial information needed in this fast-paced environment.

Distinguishing between Bookkeeping and Accounting

Many individuals mistakenly consider bookkeeping and accounting to be one and the same. This confusion is understandable because the accounting process **includes the bookkeeping function**. However, accounting also includes much more. Bookkeeping usually involves only the **recording of economic events** and is therefore just one part of the accounting process. In total, accounting involves the **entire process** of identification, recording, and communication.

The bookkeeping function is often performed by individuals with limited skills in accounting. As a result, it is not surprising that the increased use of computers by business enterprises has resulted in much of the detailed work that is part of the bookkeeping process being performed by machines.

▶Technology in Action

With the phenomenal growth in computers, more and more record keeping is being performed electronically. Businesses, small as well as large, are finding that through the use of the computer the entire recording process has become more efficient. However it is important to know the procedures used in a manual system to understand the operations a computer performs.

Throughout this textbook you will find computer notes highlighted like this. These notes are designed to show how computer technology is used in accounting and business.

Accounting and You

One question frequently asked by students of accounting is, "How will the study of accounting help me?" It should help you a great deal, because a working knowledge of accounting is desirable for virtually every field of endeavor. Some illustrations of how accounting is used in other careers include:

General management: Imagine running General Motors, a major hospital, a school, a McDonald's franchise, a bike shop; all general managers need to understand and have access to accounting data in order to make wise business decisions.

Marketing/Advertising: A marketing specialist is someone who develops strategies to help the sales force be successful. But making a sale is meaningless unless it is a profitable sale. Marketing people must be sensitive to costs and benefits, which accounting helps them quantify and understand.

Marketing people are also involved in advertising. What would a flashy field such as advertising have to do with accounting? Just ask anybody who works in the media department of a company or an ad agency: If you buy a commercial on a radio station, you'll want to know the cost per thousand listeners. You'll deal in ratings numbers and budgets all day. And ad agencies are always under pressure to cut costs, because their clients can be very fickle—particularly if the ad campaign doesn't work.

Finance: Do you want to be a banker, an investment analyst, a stock broker? These fields rely heavily on accounting. Suppose you decide to go into banking. You could become a lending officer, a money manager, a deal-maker, a foreign currency trader, or a retail branch supervisor. You could work with huge companies or with a mom-and-pop business down the street. You might specialize in one industry, such as health care, or be a generalist. Whatever the situation, you will regularly examine financial statements to understand the financial standing of your customer. In fact, it is difficult to get a good job in a finance function without two or three courses in accounting.

Real estate: Perhaps the most prevalent career in real estate is that of a broker, a person who sells residential or commercial real estate. Because a third party—the bank—is almost always involved in financing a real estate transaction, brokers must understand the numbers involved: Can the buyer of the house afford to make the payments to the bank on a given salary? Does the cash flow from the industrial property justify the purchase price in this market? What are the tax benefits of making the purchase?

►*A*ccounting in *A*ction ► *Business Insight*

Help Wanted: Forensic CPAs

Tom Taylor's job at the FBI has changed. He used to pack a .357 magnum; now he wields a No. 2 pencil. Taylor, age 37, for two years an FBI agent, is a forensic accountant, somebody who sniffs through company books to ferret out white-collar crime.

Demand for this service has surged in the past few years. In one recent year, a recruiter for San Diego's Robert Half International, a headhunting firm, had requests for more than 1,000 such snoops.

Qualification: a CPA with FBI, IRS, or similar government experience. Interestingly, despite its macho image, the FBI has long hired mostly accountants and lawyers as agents.

Accounting is useful even for occupations you might think completely unrelated. If you become a doctor, a lawyer, a social worker, a teacher, an engineer, an architect, or an entrepreneur—you name it—a working knowledge of accounting is relevant.

Review It questions at the end of major text sections offer an opportunity to stop and check the key points you have studied. Sometimes *Review It* questions stand alone, as here; other times, they are accompanied by practice exercises, as on page 14.

Before You Go On . . .

▸ *Review It*

1. What is accounting?
2. Who uses accounting information?
3. What is the difference between bookkeeping and accounting?
4. How can you use your accounting knowledge?

The Building Blocks of Accounting

Every profession develops a body of theory consisting of principles, assumptions, and standards. Accounting is no exception. Just as a doctor follows certain standards in treating a patient's illness, an accountant follows certain standards in reporting financial information. For these standards to work, however, a fundamental business concept is followed—ethical behavior.

Ethics—A Fundamental Business Concept

STUDY OBJECTIVE
3

Understand why ethics is a fundamental business concept.

Wherever you make your career—whether in accounting, marketing, management, finance, government, or elsewhere—your behavior and actions will affect other people and organizations. The standards of conduct by which one's actions are judged as right or wrong, honest or dishonest, fair or not fair, are ethics. Imagine trying to carry on a business, perform an audit, or invest money if you could not depend on the individuals you deal with to be honest. If managers, customers, investors, co-workers, and creditors all consistently lied, effective communication and economic activity would be impossible. Information would have no credibility.

Fortunately most individuals in business are ethical. Their actions are both legal and responsible, and they consider the organization's interests in their decision making. However, in some situations public officials, business executives, and respected leaders act unethically. For example, a former chief of the finance committee of the House of Representatives was indicted for possible illegal behavior; Sears was accused of widespread customer overcharging on car repairs; Woolworth Corp. executives were dismissed because they reported false income numbers. As one business leader noted: "We are all embarrassed by the events that make *The Wall Street Journal* read like the *Police Gazette*."

To sensitize you to ethical situations and to give you practice at solving ethical dilemmas, we have included in the book three types of ethics materials: (1) marginal notes that provide helpful hints for developing ethical sensitivity, (2) ethics in accounting boxes that highlight ethics situations and issues, and (3) an ethics case simulating a business situation at the end of the chapter. In the process of analyzing these ethics cases, you should apply the steps outlined in Illustration 1-3.

Generally Accepted Accounting Principles

STUDY OBJECTIVE
4

Explain the meaning of generally accepted accounting principles and the cost principle.

The accounting profession has attempted to develop a set of standards that is generally accepted and universally practiced. Its efforts have resulted in a common set of standards called generally accepted accounting principles (GAAP). These standards indicate how to report economic events.

Two organizations are primarily responsible for establishing generally accepted accounting principles. The first is the Financial Accounting Standards

Illustration 1-3

Steps in analyzing ethics cases

Solving an Ethical Dilemma

1. Recognize an ethical situation and the ethical issues involved.

Use your personal ethics to identify ethical situations and issues. Some businesses and professional organizations provide written codes of ethics for guidance in some business situations.

2. Identify and analyze the principal elements in the situation.

Identify the *stakeholders*— persons or groups who may be harmed or benefited. Ask the question: What are the responsibilities and obligations of the parties involved?

3. Identify the alternatives, and weigh the impact of each alternative on various stakeholders.

Select the most ethical alternative, considering all the consequences. Sometimes there will be one right answer. Other situations involve more than one right solution; these situations require an evaluation of each and a selection of the best alternative.

Board (FASB), a private organization that establishes broad reporting standards of general applicability as well as specific accounting rules. The second, the Securities and Exchange Commission (SEC), is a governmental agency that requires companies filing financial reports with it to follow generally accepted accounting principles. In situations where no principles exist, the SEC often mandates that certain guidelines be used. In general, the FASB and the SEC work hand in hand to assure that timely and useful accounting principles are developed.

One important principle is the cost principle, which states that assets should be recorded at their cost. **Cost is the value exchanged at the time something is acquired.** If you buy a house today, the cost is the amount you pay for it, say $100,000. If you sell the house in two years for $120,000, the sales price is its market value—the value determined by the market for homes at that time. At the time of acquisition, cost and fair market value are the same. In subsequent periods, cost and fair market value may vary, **but the cost amount continues to be used**.

For example, at one time, Greyhound Corporation had 128 bus stations nationwide that cost approximately $200 million. The current market value of the stations is approximately $1 billion. Under the cost principle, the bus stations are recorded and reported at $200 million, not $1 billion. Until the bus stations are actually sold, estimates of market values are considered too subjective.

As the Greyhound example indicates, cost has an important advantage over other valuations: it is reliable. Cost is definite and verifiable. The values exchanged at the time something is acquired generally can be objectively measured. To rely on the information supplied, users must know that the information is based on fact. However, critics argue that cost is often not relevant and that market values provide more useful information. Despite its shortcomings, cost continues to be used in the financial statements because of its reliability.

Assumptions

In developing generally accepted accounting principles, certain basic assumptions are made. These assumptions provide a foundation for the accounting process. Two main assumptions are the **monetary unit assumption** and the **economic entity assumption**.

Helpful hint The FASB has issued over 120 standards, and the SEC has issued over 200 financial reporting releases.

► *International note*

The standard-setting processes in Canada, Mexico, and the United States are quite similar in most respects. All three have relatively open deliberations on new rules, and they support efforts to follow international standards. The use of similar accounting principles within North America has implications for the success of the North American Free Trade Agreement (NAFTA).

Helpful hint The cost principle is often referred to as the *historical cost principle*.

Helpful hint Assumptions for accounting are like the foundation for the Empire State Building—indispensable and unchanging (we hope!).

Monetary Unit Assumption

The monetary unit assumption requires that only transaction data that can be expressed in terms of money be included in the accounting records of the economic entity. Because money is the commonly used medium of exchange, this assumption enables accounting to quantify (measure) the economic event. The monetary unit assumption is vital to applying the cost principle discussed earlier. This assumption prevents such relevant information as the health of the owner, the quality of service, and the morale of employees from being included in the accounting records because they cannot be quantified in terms of money.

An important corollary to the monetary unit assumption is the added assumption that the unit of measure remains sufficiently constant over time. However, the assumption of a stable monetary unit has been challenged because of the significant decline in the purchasing power of the dollar. For example, what used to cost $1.00 in 1960, costs over $4.00 in 1996, an increase of fourfold. In such situations, adding, subtracting, or comparing 1960 dollars with 1996 dollars is highly questionable. The profession has recognized this problem and encourages companies to disclose the effects of changing prices.

Economic Entity Assumption

▸ *Ethics note*

An IRS investigation uncovered the following violation of the economic entity assumption: Gucci Shops, the international retail chain, issued checks payable to "Gucci," supposedly to pay for expenses of acquiring merchandise through a buying office in Italy. However, the checks actually went into founder Aldo Gucci's personal bank accounts, and the cash diverted from the business was divided among Gucci family members. (*Source: Wall Street Journal*, 1/20/86.)

An economic entity can be any organization or unit in society. It may be a business enterprise (such as General Electric Company), a governmental unit (such as the state of Ohio), a municipality (such as Seattle), a school district (such as St. Louis District 48), or a social organization such as a church (Southern Baptist), a fraternity (Theta Chi), or a sorority (Chi Omega). The economic entity assumption states that economic events can be identified with a particular unit of accountability. This assumption requires that the activities of the entity be kept separate and distinct from (1) the activities of its owner and (2) all other economic entities. To illustrate, if Sally Rider, owner of Sally's Boutique, charges any of her personal living costs as expenses of the Boutique, the economic entity assumption is violated. Similarly, the economic entity assumption assumes that the activities of McDonald's, Wendy's, and Burger King can each be segregated into separate economic entities for accounting purposes.

Although the economic entity assumption can be applied to any unit of accountability, we will generally discuss it in relation to a business enterprise, which may be organized as a proprietorship, partnership, or corporation.

▸Accounting in Action ▸ *Ethics Insight*

A violation of the entity assumption contributed to the recent resignation by the chief executive of W.R. Grace and Company. Investors were angered to learn that company funds were used for personal medical care, a Manhattan apartment, and a personal chef for the company's chief. Funds were also used to support a hotel interest owned by the chief executive's son.

Source: New York Times, March 10, 1995.

Proprietorship. A business owned by one person is generally a proprietorship. The owner is often the manager/operator of the business. Small service-type businesses (barber shops, law offices, plumbing companies, and auto repair shops), farms, and small retail stores (antique shops, clothing stores, and book stores) are often sole proprietorships. **Usually only a limited amount of money (capital) is necessary to start in business as a proprietorship, and the owner receives any profits, suffers any losses, and is personally liable for all debts**

of the business. Although there is no legal distinction between the business as an economic unit and the owner, the records of the business activities are kept separate from the personal records and activities of the owner. Although sole proprietorships represent the largest number of businesses in the United States, they are typically the smallest in size and volume of business.

Partnership. A business owned by two or more persons associated as partners is a partnership. In most respects a partnership is similar to a sole proprietorship except that more than one owner is involved. When a partnership is created, an agreement (written or oral) should set forth such terms as initial investment of each partner, duties of each partner, division of net income (or net loss), and settlement to be made upon death or withdrawal of a partner. Each partner generally has unlimited personal liability for the debts of the partnership. **Like a proprietorship, for accounting purposes the partnership affairs must be kept separate from the personal activities of the partners.** Partnerships are often used to organize retail and service-type businesses, including professional practices (lawyers, doctors, architects, and certified public accountants).

Corporation. A business organized as a separate legal entity under state corporation law and having ownership divided into transferable shares of stock is called a corporation. The holders of the shares (stockholders) **enjoy limited liability**; they are not personally liable for the debts of the corporate entity. Stockholders **may transfer all or part of their shares to other investors at any time** (i.e., sell their shares in the securities market). The ease with which ownership can change adds to the attractiveness of investing in a corporation. Because ownership can be transferred without dissolving the corporation, the corporation **enjoys an unlimited life**.

Although the combined number of proprietorships and partnerships in the United States is more than five times the number of corporations, the revenue produced by corporations is eight times greater. Most of the largest enterprises in the United States—for example, Exxon, General Motors, Sears Roebuck, Citicorp, and Pacific Gas and Electric—are corporations.

Basic Accounting Equation

Other essential building blocks of accounting are the categories into which economic events are classified. The two basic elements of a business are what it owns and what it owes. **Assets** are the resources owned by a business. For example, Eastman Kodak has total assets of approximately $15 billion. **Equities** are the rights or claims against these resources. Thus, a company such as Eastman Kodak that has $15 billion of assets also has $15 billion of claims against those assets. This relationship can be shown in equation form as follows:

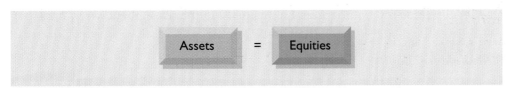

Equities may be further subdivided into two categories: claims of creditors and claims of owners. Claims of creditors are called **liabilities**. Claims of owners are called **stockholders'** or **owners' equity**. For example, Eastman Kodak has liabilities of $11 billion and stockholders' equity of $4 billion. The equation above can, then, be expanded as follows:

Helpful hint A recent survey noted that approximately 70% of the companies in the United States are proprietorships; however, they account for only 6.5% of gross revenues. Corporations, on the other hand, are approximately 19% of all companies, but account for 90% of the revenues.

STUDY OBJECTIVE
••••••••• 6 •••••••••
State the basic accounting equation and explain the meaning of assets, liabilities, and stockholders' equity.

Illustration 1-4

Relationship between assets and equities

Illustration 1-5

The basic accounting equation

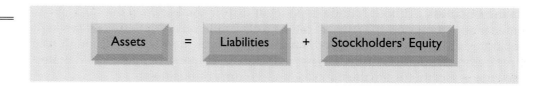

This equation is referred to as the basic accounting equation. Assets must equal the sum of liabilities and stockholders' (owners') equity. Because creditors' claims are paid before ownership claims if a business is liquidated, liabilities are shown before stockholders' (owners') equity in the basic accounting equation.

The accounting equation applies to all **economic entities** regardless of size, nature of business, or form of business organization. Thus, it applies to a small proprietorship such as a corner grocery store as well as to a giant corporation such as AT&T. The equation provides the underlying framework for recording and summarizing the economic events of a business enterprise.

Let's look in more detail at the categories in the basic accounting equation.

Assets

As indicated above, assets are resources owned by a business. Thus, they are the things of value used in carrying out such activities as production, consumption, and exchange. The common characteristic possessed by all assets is the capacity to provide future services or benefits to the entities that use them. In a business enterprise, that service potential or future economic benefit eventually results in cash inflows (receipts) to the enterprise.

For example, the enterprise Campus Pizza owns a delivery truck that provides economic benefits because it is used in delivering pizzas. Other assets of Campus Pizza are tables, chairs, jukebox, cash register, oven, mugs and silverware, and, of course, cash.

Liabilities

Helpful hint Identify a future payment or service that does not qualify as a liability of Campus Pizza. Answer: Next week's wages of employees, because Campus Pizza does not owe the employees until they have worked.

Liabilities are claims against assets. Put more simply, **liabilities are existing debts and obligations.** For example, businesses of all sizes and degrees of success usually find it necessary to borrow money and to purchase merchandise on credit. Campus Pizza, for instance, purchases cheese, sausage, flour, and beverages on credit from suppliers; these obligations are called **accounts payable.** Additionally, Campus Pizza has a **note payable** to First National Bank for the money borrowed to purchase its delivery truck. Campus Pizza may also have **wages payable** to employees, and **sales and real estate taxes payable** to the local government. Persons or entities to whom Campus Pizza owes money are called **creditors.**

Most claims of creditors attach to **total** enterprise assets rather than to the specific assets provided by the creditor. In the event of nonpayment, creditors may legally force the liquidation of a business. In that case, the law requires that creditor claims be paid before ownership claims.

Stockholders' Equity

The ownership claim on total assets is known as stockholders' equity. It is equal to total assets minus total liabilities. Here is why: The assets of a business are supplied or claimed by either creditors or stockholders. To determine what belongs to stockholders, we therefore subtract creditors' claims—the liabilities—from assets. The remainder—stockholders' equity—is the stockholders' claim on the assets of the business. It is often referred to as residual equity. The stockholders' equity section of a corporation's balance sheet consists of (1) paid-in (contributed) capital and (2) retained earnings (earned capital).

Paid-in Capital. **Paid-in capital** is the term used to describe the total amount paid in by stockholders. The principal source of paid-in capital is the investment of cash and other assets in the corporation by stockholders in exchange for capital stock. Corporations may issue several classes of stock, but the stock representing ownership interest is common stock.

Retained Earnings. The **retained earnings** section of the balance sheet is determined by three items: revenues, expenses, and dividends.

Revenues. Revenues are the gross increase in stockholders' equity resulting from business activities entered into for the purpose of earning income. Generally, revenues result from the sale of merchandise, the performance of services, the rental of property, and the lending of money.

> **Helpful hint** The effect of revenues is positive—an increase in stockholders' equity coupled with an increase in assets or a decrease in liabilities.

Revenues usually result in an increase in an asset. They may arise from different sources and are identified by various names depending on the nature of the business. Campus Pizza, for instance, has two categories of sales revenues—pizza sales and beverage sales. Other titles for and sources of revenue common to many businesses are: sales, fees, services, commissions, interest, dividends, royalties, and rent.

Expenses. Expenses are **the decreases in stockholders' equity that result from operating the business.** They are the cost of assets consumed or services used in the process of earning revenue. Expenses represent actual or expected cash outflows (payments). Like revenues, expenses take many forms and are identified by various names depending on the type of asset consumed or service used. For example, Campus Pizza recognizes the following types of expenses: cost of ingredients (meat, flour, cheese, tomato paste, mushrooms, etc.); cost of beverages; wages expense; utility expense (electric, gas, and water expense); telephone expense; delivery expense (gasoline, repairs, licenses, etc.); supplies expense (napkins, detergents, aprons, etc.); rent expense; interest expense; and property tax expense. When revenues exceed expenses, net income results. When expenses exceed revenues, a net loss results.

> **Helpful hint** The effect of expenses is negative—a decrease in stockholders' equity coupled with a decrease in assets, or an increase in liabilities.

Dividends. When a company is successful, it generates net income. **Net income** represents an increase in net assets which are then available to distribute to stockholders. When cash or other assets are distributed to stockholders, it is called a dividend. Dividends reduce retained earnings. However, dividends are not an expense of a corporation. A corporation first determines its revenues and expenses and then computes net income or net loss. At this point, a corporation may decide to distribute a dividend.

In summary, the principal sources (increases) of stockholders' (owners') equity are (1) investments by stockholders and (2) revenues from business' operations. In contrast, reductions (decreases) in stockholders' equity are a result of (1) expenses and (2) dividends. These relationships are shown in Illustration 1-6.

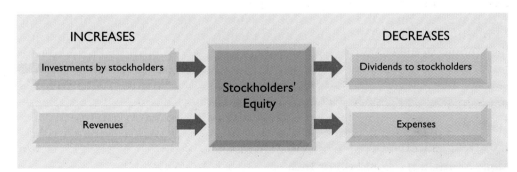

Illustration 1-6

Relationships among subdivisions of stockholders' equity

Before You Go On . . .

► Review It

1. Why is ethics considered a fundamental business concept?
2. What are generally accepted accounting principles? Give an example of an accounting principle.
3. Explain the monetary unit and the economic entity assumptions.
4. What is the basic accounting equation?
5. What are assets, liabilities, and stockholders' equity?

Do It exercises give you immediate practice of the material just covered. These exercises outline the reasoning necessary to complete the exercise and a solution.

► Do It

Classify the following items as issuance of stock (I), dividends (D), revenues (R), or expenses (E), and indicate whether these items increase or decrease stockholders' equity: (1) Rent Expense, (2) Service Revenue, (3) Dividends, and (4) Salaries Expense.

Reasoning: Both investments and service revenue increase stockholders' equity; however, service revenue arises from the sale of merchandise, the performance of services, the rental of property, or the lending of money. Investments are resources contributed to the business by the stockholders. Similarly, expenses and dividends decrease stockholders' equity; however, expenses arise from consuming assets or services. Dividends are distributions of cash or other assets to stockholders.

Solution:
(1) Rent Expense is classified as an expense (E); it decreases stockholders' equity.
(2) Service Revenue is classified as revenue (R); it increases stockholders' equity.
(3) Dividends is classified as stockholders' equity (D); it decreases stockholders' equity.
(4) Salaries Expense is classified as an expense (E); it decreases stockholders' equity.

Related exercise material: BE1–1, BE1–2, BE1–3, BE1–4, BE1–5, BE1–6, BE1–7, BE1–9, E1–1, E1–2, E1–3, E1–4, E1–6, and E1–7.

Using the Building Blocks

STUDY OBJECTIVE 7

Analyze the effect of business transactions on the basic accounting equation.

Helpful hint Transactions are events that cause a change in individual assets, liabilities, or one of the subdivisions of stockholders' equity.

Transactions (often referred to as business transactions) are the economic events of the enterprise that are recorded. Transactions may be identified as external or internal. **External transactions involve economic events between the company and some outside enterprise or party.** For example, for Campus Pizza the purchase of cooking equipment from a supplier, the payment of monthly rent to the landlord, and the sale of pizzas to customers are external transactions. **Internal transactions are economic events that occur entirely within one company.** The use of office supplies illustrates this type of transaction for Campus Pizza.

A company may carry on many activities that do not in themselves represent business transactions. Hiring employees, answering the telephone, talking with customers, and placing an order for merchandise with a supplier are examples. Some of these activities, however, may lead to a business transaction: employees will earn wages, and merchandise will be delivered by the supplier. Each transaction must be analyzed in terms of its effect on the components of the basic accounting equation. This analysis must identify the specific items affected and the amount of the change in each item.

The equality of the basic equation must be preserved. Therefore, each transaction must have a dual effect on the equation. For example, if an individual asset is increased, there must be a corresponding:

1. Decrease in another asset, or
2. Increase in a specific liability, or
3. Increase in stockholders' equity.

It follows that two or more items could be affected when an asset is increased. For example, as one asset is increased $10,000, another asset could decrease $6,000, and a specific liability could increase $4,000. Note also that any change in an individual liability or ownership claim is subject to similar analysis.

Transaction Analysis

The following examples are business transactions for a new computer programming business during its first month of operations. You will want to study these transactions until you are sure you understand them. They are not difficult but they are important to your success in this course. The ability to analyze transactions in terms of the basic accounting equation is essential for an understanding of accounting.

Transaction (1). Investment by Stockholders. Ray and Barbara Neal decide to open a computer programming company that they incorporate as Softbyte, Inc. They invest $15,000 cash in the business in exchange for $15,000 of common stock. The common stock indicates the ownership interest that the Neals have in Softbyte, Inc. The transaction results in an equal increase in both assets and stockholders' equity. In this case, there is an increase in the asset Cash of $15,000, and an increase in Common Stock of $15,000. To the right of Common Stock is the reason why stockholders' equity changed, i.e., investment.

The effect of this transaction on the basic equation is:

	Assets	=	Liabilities	+	Stockholders' Equity	
					Common	
	Cash	=			Stock	
(1)	+$15,000	=			+$15,000	Investment

Observe that the equality of the basic equation has been maintained. Note also that the source of the increase in stockholders' equity is indicated, to make clear that the increase is an investment rather than revenue from operations. Why does this matter? Because investments by stockholders do not represent revenues, they are excluded in determining net income. Additional investments (i.e., investments made by stockholders after the corporation has been initially formed) have the same effect on stockholders' equity as the initial investment.

Transaction (2). Purchase of Equipment for Cash. Softbyte purchases computer equipment for $7,000 cash. This transaction results in an equal increase and decrease in total assets, though the composition of assets is changed: Cash is decreased $7,000, and the asset Equipment is increased $7,000. Both the specific effect of this transaction and the cumulative effect of the first two transactions are:

		Assets			=	Liabilities	+	Stockholders' Equity	
								Common	
		Cash	+	Equipment	=			Stock	
	Old Bal.	$15,000						$15,000	
(2)		−7,000		+$7,000					
	New Bal.	$ 8,000	+	$7,000	=			$15,000	
			$15,000						

Observe that total assets are still $15,000 and stockholders' equity also remains at $15,000, the amount of the original investment.

Transaction (3). Purchase of Supplies on Credit.   Softbyte, Inc. purchases computer paper and other supplies expected to last several months from Acme Supply Company for $1,600. Acme agrees to allow Softbyte to pay this bill in October, a month later. This transaction is often referred to as a purchase on account or a credit purchase. Assets are increased by this transaction because of the expected future benefits of using the paper and supplies, and liabilities are increased by the amount due Acme Company. The asset Supplies is increased $1,600, and the liability Accounts Payable is increased by the same amount. The effect on the equation is:

		Assets						=	Liabilities	+	Stockholders' Equity
		Cash	+	Supplies	+	Equipment	=	Accounts Payable	+	Common Stock
	Old Bal.	$8,000				$7,000						$15,000
(3)				+$1,600						+$1,600		
	New Bal.	$8,000	+	$1,600	+	$7,000	=	$1,600	+	$15,000
				$16,600						$16,600

Total assets are now $16,600. This total is matched by a $1,600 creditor's claim and a $15,000 stockholders' claim.

Transaction (4). Services Rendered for Cash.   Softbyte, Inc. receives $1,200 cash from customers for programming services. This transaction represents the principal revenue-producing activity of Softbyte. Recall that **revenue increases stockholders' equity**. Both assets and stockholders' equity are then increased. In this case, Cash is increased $1,200, and Retained Earnings is increased $1,200. The new balances in the equation are:

		Assets					=	Liabilities	+		Stockholders' Equity		
		Cash	+	Supplies	+	Equipment	=	Accounts Payable	+	Common Stock	+	Retained Earnings	
	Old Bal.	$8,000		$1,600		$7,000		$1,600		$15,000			
(4)		+1,200										+$1,200	Service Revenue
	New Bal.	$9,200	+	$1,600	+	$7,000	=	$1,600	+	$15,000	+	$1,200	
				$17,800						$17,800			

The two sides of the equation balance at $17,800. Note that stockholders' equity is increased when revenues are earned. The source of the increase in stockholders' equity is indicated as service revenue. Service revenue is included in determining Softbyte, Inc's. net income.

Transaction (5). Purchase of Advertising on Credit.   Softbyte, Inc. receives a bill for $250 from the *Daily News* for advertising the opening of its business but postpones payment of the bill until a later date. This transaction results in an increase in liabilities and a decrease in stockholders' equity. The specific items involved are Accounts Payable and Retained Earnings. The effect on the equation is:

		Assets				=	Liabilities +		Stockholders' Equity		
							Accounts	Common	Retained	
		Cash	+ Supplies	+ Equipment	=		Payable	+ Stock	+ Earnings	
(5)	Old Bal.	$9,200	$1,600	$7,000			$1,600	$15,000	$1,200	
							+250		−250	Advertising Expense
	New Bal.	$9,200 +	$1,600 +	$7,000	=		$1,850 +	$15,000 +	$950	
			$17,800					$17,800		

The two sides of the equation still balance at $17,800. Observe that Retained Earnings is decreased when the expense is incurred, and the specific cause of the decrease is noted. Expenses do not have to be paid in cash at the time they are incurred. When payment is made at a later date, the liability Accounts Payable will be decreased and the asset Cash will be decreased [see Transaction (8)]. The cost of advertising is considered an expense as opposed to an asset because the benefits have been used. This expense is included in determining net income.

Transaction (6). Services Rendered for Cash and Credit. Softbyte provides programming services of $3,500 for customers. Cash amounting to $1,500 is received from customers, and the balance of $2,000 is billed to customers on account. This transaction results in an equal increase in assets and stockholders' equity. Three specific items are affected: Cash is increased $1,500; Accounts Receivable is increased $2,000; and Retained Earnings is increased $3,500. The new balances are as follows:

			Assets				=	Liabilities +		Stockholders' Equity		
			Accounts					Accounts	Common	Retained	
		Cash	+ Receivable	+ Supplies	+ Equipment	=		Payable	+ Stock	+ Earnings	
(6)	Old Bal.	$9,200		$1,600	$7,000			$1,850	$15,000	$950	
		+1,500	+$2,000							+3,500	Service Revenue
	New Bal.	$10,700 +	$2,000 +	$1,600 +	$7,000	=		$1,850 +	$15,000 +	$4,450	
				$21,300					$21,300		

Why increase Retained Earnings by $3,500 when only $1,500 has been collected? Because the inflow of assets resulting from the earning of revenues does not have to be in the form of cash. Remember that stockholders' equity is increased when revenues are earned, and in Softbyte's case that is when the service is provided. When collections on account are received at a later date, Cash will be increased and Accounts Receivable will be decreased [see Transaction (9)].

Transaction (7). Payment of Expenses. Expenses paid in cash for September are store rent, $600, salaries of employees, $900, and utilities, $200. These payments result in an equal decrease in assets and stockholders' equity. Cash is decreased $1,700 and Retained Earnings is decreased by the same amount. The effect of these payments on the equation is:

Helpful hint The terms *Fees Receivable* instead of Accounts Receivable and *Fees Earned* instead of Service Revenue are often used when services are provided.

		Assets			= Liabilities +		Stockholders' Equity	
	Cash	+ Accounts Receivable	+ Supplies	+ Equipment =	Accounts Payable	+ Common Stock	+ Retained Earnings	
Old Bal.	$10,700	$2,000	$1,600	$7,000	$1,850	$15,000	$4,450	
(7)	−1,700						−600	Rent Expense
							−900	Salaries Expense
							−200	Utilities Expense
New Bal.	$ 9,000 +	$2,000 +	$1,600 +	$7,000 =	$1,850 +	$15,000 +	$2,750	
		$19,600				$19,600		

The two sides of the equation now balance at $19,600. Three lines are required in the analysis to indicate the different types of expenses that have been incurred.

Transaction (8). Payment of Accounts Payable. Softbyte, Inc. pays its *Daily News* advertising bill of $250 in cash. In analyzing the effect of this transaction, we must recall that the bill has previously been recorded in Transaction (5) as an increase in Accounts Payable and a decrease in Retained Earnings. Thus, this payment "on account" decreases both assets and liabilities. In this case, the asset Cash and the liability Accounts Payable are decreased by $250. The effect of this transaction on the equation is:

		Assets			= Liabilities +	Stockholders' Equity	
	Cash	+ Accounts Receivable	+ Supplies	+ Equipment =	Accounts Payable	+ Common Stock	+ Retained Earnings
Old Bal.	$9,000	$2,000	$1,600	$7,000	$1,850	$15,000	$2,750
(8)	−250				−250		
New Bal.	$8,750 +	$2,000 +	$1,600 +	$7,000 =	$1,600 +	$15,000 +	$2,750
		$19,350				$19,350	

Observe that the payment of a liability related to an expense that has previously been incurred does not affect stockholders' equity. Both the Common Stock and Retained Earnings do not change as a result of this transaction.

Transaction (9). Receipt of Cash on Account. The sum of $600 in cash is received from customers who have previously been billed for services in Transaction (6). This transaction does not change total assets, but it changes the composition of Softbyte's assets. Cash is increased $600 and Accounts Receivable is decreased $600. The new balances are:

		Assets			= Liabilities +	Stockholders' Equity	
	Cash	+ Accounts Receivable	+ Supplies	+ Equipment =	Accounts Payable	+ Common Stock	+ Retained Earnings
Old Bal.	$8,750	$2,000	$1,600	$7,000	$1,600	$15,000	$2,750
(9)	+600	−600					
New Bal.	$9,350 +	$1,400 +	$1,600 +	$7,000 =	$1,600 +	$15,000 +	$2,750
		$19,350				$19,350	

Note that a collection on account for services previously billed and recorded does not affect stockholders' equity. Revenue was already recorded in Transaction (6) and should not be recorded again.

Transaction (10). Dividends. The corporation pays a dividend of $1,300 in cash to Ray and Barbara Neal, the stockholders of Softbyte, Inc. The transaction results in an equal decrease in assets and stockholders' equity. Thus, both Cash and Retained Earnings are decreased $1,300 as shown below.

		Assets				= Liabilities +	Stockholders' Equity	
	Cash	+ Accounts Receivable	+ Supplies	+ Equipment =		Accounts Payable +	Common Stock +	Retained Earnings
Old Bal.	$9,350	$1,400	$1,600	$7,000		$1,600	$15,000	$2,750
(10)	−1,300							−1,300 Dividends
New Bal.	$8,050 +	$1,400	+ $1,600	+ $7,000	=	$1,600	+ $15,000 +	$1,450
			$18,050				$18,050	

Note that the dividend reduces retained earnings which is part of stockholders' equity. Dividends do not represent expenses. Like stockholders' investments, dividends are not included in determining net income.

Summary of Transactions

The transactions of Softbyte, Inc. are summarized in Illustration 1-7 to show their cumulative effect on the basic accounting equation. The transaction number, the

Illustration 1-7

Tabular summary of Soft-byte, Inc. transactions

		Assets				= Liabilities +	Stockholders' Equity		
Transaction	Cash	+ Accounts Receivable	+ Supplies	+ Equipment =		Accounts Payable +	Common Stock +	Retained Earnings	
(1)	+$15,000						+$15,000		Investment
(2)	−7,000			+$7,000					
	8,000	+		7,000	=		15,000		
(3)			+$1,600			+$1,600			
	8,000	+	1,600 +	7,000	=	1,600 +	15,000		
(4)	+1,200							+1,200	Service Revenue
	9,200	+	1,600 +	7,000	=	1,600 +	15,000	1,200	
(5)						+250		−250	Advert. Expense
	9,200	+	1,600 +	7,000	=	1,850 +	15,000	950	
(6)	+1,500	+$2,000						+3,500	Service Revenue
	10,700 +	2,000 +	1,600 +	7,000	=	1,850 +	15,000	4,450	
(7)	−1,700							−600	Rent Expense
								−900	Salaries Expense
								−200	Utilities Expense
	9,000 +	2,000 +	1,600 +	7,000	=	1,850 +	15,000	2,750	
(8)	−250					−250			
	8,750 +	2,000 +	1,600 +	7,000	=	1,600 +	15,000	2,750	
(9)	+600	−600							
	9,350 +	1,400 +	1,600 +	7,000	=	1,600 +	15,000	2,750	
(10)	−1,300							−1,300	Dividends
	$ 8,050 +	$1,400 +	$1,600 +	$7,000	=	$1,600 +	$15,000 +	$1,450	
			$18,050				$18,050		

specific effects of the transaction, and the balances after each transaction are indicated. The illustration demonstrates a number of significant facts:

1. Each transaction must be analyzed in terms of its effect on:
   a. the three components of the basic accounting equation.
   b. specific types (kinds) of items within each component.
2. The two sides of the equation must always be equal.
3. The causes of each change in the stockholders' claim on assets must be indicated in the Common Stock and Retained Earnings columns.

There! You made it through transaction analysis. If you feel a bit shaky on any of the transactions, it would probably be a good idea at this point to get up, take a short break, and come back again for a 10- to 15-minute review of the transactions, to make sure you understand them before you go on to the next section.

Financial Statements

After transactions are identified, recorded, and summarized, four financial statements are prepared from the summarized accounting data:

1. An income statement presents the revenues and expenses and resulting net income or net loss of a company for a specific period of time.
2. A retained earnings statement summarizes the changes in retained earnings for a specific period of time.
3. A balance sheet reports the assets, liabilities, and stockholders' equity of a business enterprise at a specific date.
4. A statement of cash flows summarizes information concerning the cash inflows (receipts) and outflows (payments) for a specific period of time.

STUDY OBJECTIVE
8
Prepare an income statement, retained earnings statement, balance sheet, and statement of cash flows.

Helpful hint   The income statement, retained earnings statement, and statement of cash flows are all for a *period* of time, whereas the balance sheet is for a *point* in time.

Helpful hint   There is only one group of notes for each set of financial statements and not separate sets of notes for each financial statement.

Each statement provides management, stockholders, and other interested parties with relevant financial data. The financial statements of Softbyte, Inc. and their interrelationships are shown in Illustration 1-8. The statements are interrelated: **(1) Net income of $2,750 shown on the income statement is added to the beginning balance of retained earnings in the retained earnings statement. (2) Retained earnings of $1,450 at the end of the reporting period shown in the retained earnings statement is reported on the balance sheet. (3) Cash of $8,050 on the balance sheet is reported on the statement of cash flows.**

Additionally, every set of financial statements is accompanied by explanatory notes and supporting schedules that are an integral part of the statements. Examples of these notes and schedules are illustrated in later chapters of this textbook.

Be sure to carefully examine the format and content of each statement. The essential features of each are briefly described in the following sections.

Income Statement

Helpful hint   The income statement is sometimes referred to as the statement of operations, earnings statement, or profit and loss statement.

The income statement for Softbyte, Inc. is prepared from the data appearing in the retained earnings column of Illustration 1-7. The heading of the statement identifies the company, the type of statement, and the time period covered by the statement. Note that the primary focus of the income statement is on reporting the success or profitability of the company's operations over a specified period of time. To indicate that it applies for a period of time, the income statement is dated "For the Month Ended September 30, 1996."

Illustration 1-8

Financial statements and their interrelationships

SOFTBYTE, INC.
Income Statement
For the Month Ended September 30, 1996

Revenues		
Service revenue		$4,700
Expenses		
Salaries expense	$900	
Rent expense	600	
Advertising expense	250	
Utilities expense	200	
Total expenses		1,950
Net income		$2,750

SOFTBYTE, INC.
Retained Earnings Statement
For the Month Ended September 30, 1996

Retained earnings, September 1	$0
Add: Net income	2,750
	2,750
Less: Dividends	1,300
Retained earnings, September 30	$1,450

①

SOFTBYTE, INC.
Balance Sheet
September 30, 1996

Report format ②

Assets

Cash	$ 8,050
Accounts receivable	1,400
Supplies	1,600
Equipment	7,000
Total assets	$18,050

Liabilities and Stockholders' Equity

Liabilities		
Accounts payable		$ 1,600
Stockholders' equity		
Common stock	$15,000	
Retained earnings	1,450	16,450
Total liabilities and stockholders' equity		$18,050

③

SOFTBYTE, INC.
Statement of Cash Flows
For the Month Ended September 30, 1996

Cash flows from operating activities		
Cash receipts from revenues *(Source)*		$ 3,300
Cash payments for expenses		(1,950)
Net cash provided by operating activities		1,350
Cash flows from investing activities		
Purchase of equipment *(Uses)*		(7,000)
Cash flows from financing activities		
Sale of common stock	$15,000	
Payment of cash dividends	(1,300)	13,700
Net increase in cash		8,050
Cash at the beginning of the period		0
Cash at the end of the period		$ 8,050

Helpful hint The four financial statements are prepared in the sequence shown for the following reasons: Net income is computed first and is needed to determine the ending balance in retained earnings. The ending balance in retained earnings is needed in preparing the balance sheet. The cash shown on the balance sheet is needed in preparing the statement of cash flows.

Revenues are listed first, followed by expenses. Finally net income (or net loss) is determined. Although practice varies considerably on this matter, we have chosen in our illustrations and solutions to homework to list expenses in order of magnitude. Alternative formats for the income statement will be considered in later chapters.

Note that investment and dividend transactions between the stockholders and the business are not included in the measurement of net income. For example, the cash dividend from Softbyte, Inc. was not regarded as a business expense, as explained earlier. This type of transaction is considered a reduction of retained earnings which causes a decrease in stockholders' equity.

Retained Earnings Statement

Data for the preparation of the retained earnings statement are obtained from the retained earnings column of the tabular summary (Illustration 1-7) and from the income statement in Illustration 1-8. The heading of this statement identifies the company, the type of statement, and the time period covered by the statement. The time period is the same as that covered by the income statement and therefore is dated "For the Month Ended September 30, 1996." The beginning retained earnings amount is shown on the first line of the statement. Then, net income and dividends are identified in the statement. The retained earnings ending balance is the final amount on the statement. The information provided by this statement indicates the reasons why retained earnings increased or decreased during the period. If there is a net loss, it is deducted with dividends in the retained earnings statement.

Balance Sheet

The balance sheet for Softbyte, Inc. is prepared from the column headings and the month-end data shown in the last line of the tabular summary (Illustration 1-7). The heading of a balance sheet must identify the company, the statement, and the date. To indicate that the balance sheet is at a specific date, it is dated "September 30, 1996." Observe that the assets are listed at the top, followed by liabilities and stockholders' equity. Total assets must equal total liabilities and stockholders' equity. In the Softbyte illustration, only one liability, accounts payable, is reported on the balance sheet. In most cases, there will be more than one liability. When two or more liabilities are involved, a customary way of listing is as follows:

Illustration 1-9

Presentation of liabilities

Liabilities	
Notes payable	$10,000
Accounts payable	63,000
Salaries payable	18,000
Total liabilities	$91,000

The balance sheet is like a snapshot of the company's financial condition at a specific moment in time (usually the month-end or year-end).

Statement of Cash Flows

Helpful hint Investing activities pertain to investments made by the company, not investments made by the stockholders.

The primary purpose of a statement of cash flows is to provide financial information about the cash receipts and cash payments of an enterprise for a specific period of time. To achieve this purpose and to aid investors, creditors, and others in their analysis of cash, **the statement of cash flows reports (1) the cash effects** of a company's operations during a period, (2) its investing transactions, (3) its financing transactions, (4) the net increase or decrease in cash during the period, and (5) the cash amount at the end of the period.

Reporting the sources, uses, and net increase or decrease in cash is useful because investors, creditors, and others want to know what is happening to a company's most liquid resource. The statement of cash flows, therefore, provides answers to the following simple but important questions:

1. Where did the cash come from during the period?
2. What was the cash used for during the period?
3. What was the change in the cash balance during the period?

Helpful hint The cash at the end of the period reported in the statement of cash flows equals the cash reported in the balance sheet.

A statement of cash flows for Softbyte, Inc., is provided in Illustration 1-8.

As shown in the statement, cash increased $8,050 during the year. This increase resulted because net cash flow provided from operating activities increased cash $1,350, cash flow from investing transactions decreased cash $7,000 and cash flow from financing transactions increased cash $13,700. At this time, you need not be concerned with how these amounts are determined. Chapter 14 will examine in detail how the statement is prepared.

Before You Go On . . .

▶ Review It

1. If an asset increases, what are the three possible effects on the basic accounting equation?
2. What are the income statement, retained earnings statement, balance sheet, and statement of cash flows?
3. Indicate how the financial statements are interrelated.

▶ A Look Back at the Baseball Strike

Refer to the opening story about the baseball strike, and answer the following questions:

1. If you represented the baseball players' union, what two financial statements would you request from the owners?
2. What would these financial statements tell you?
3. Would you request audited financial statements? Explain.
4. Will the financial statements show the market value of the baseball team? Explain.

This set of exercises refers back to the chapter opening story. These exercises help you analyze that real-world situation in terms of the accounting topic of the chapter.

Solution:

1. The two statements that you would probably want to request are the balance sheet and the income statement.
2. The balance sheet reports the assets, liabilities, and stockholders' equity of the team. The income statement presents the revenues and expenses and resulting net income (or net loss) for a specific period of time. The balance sheet is like a snapshot of the team's financial condition at a point in time. The income statement should give you a good indication of the profitability of the team. Also, the sources of the team's revenues and a picture of its expenses are provided in the income statement.
3. The players should request **audited** financial statements—statements that a CPA has examined and expressed an opinion as to the fairness of presentation. Players should not make decisions without having audited financial statements.
4. The financial statements will not show the market value of the team. As indicated, one important principle of accounting is the cost principle, which states that assets should be recorded at cost. Cost has an important advantage over other valuations: it is reliable.

Financial Statements of Coca-Cola Company and PepsiCo, Inc.

In the previous pages you studied the business transactions and financial statements of Softbyte, Inc., a small computer programming *service company*. Softbyte's transactions and financial statements were simple. In order for you to see the financial statements of a recognizable, large, real-world company, we present on the following pages the financial statements of **The Coca-Cola Company**. The Coca-Cola Company is a multinational beverage *merchandising business*, unlike Softbyte, which is a small, local, service business. As a result, Coca-Cola's financial statements contain some items (such as "inventories" in the balance sheet and "cost of goods sold" in the income statement) that are not contained in Softbyte's financials.

At this time you are not expected to understand all of the contents of Coca-Cola Company's financial statements. But by the end of this financial accounting course, you will have a much greater appreciation for the items reported in Coca-Cola's financial statements—because that is what this book is all about.

Another complete set of financial statements (accompanied by a complete set of notes and management's discussions relating to the statements as well as the auditor's and management's reports) are presented for PepsiCo, Inc. in Appendix A at the end of this book. The contents of Coca-Cola's and PepsiCo's financial statements, as two competitors in the same industry, may be compared and analyzed as you proceed through the chapters of this book.

The Coca-Cola Company

Financial Highlights

Year Ended December 31,	1995	1994	Percent Change
(In millions except per share data and ratios as reported)			
Total return (share price appreciation plus reinvested dividends)	45.9%	17.1%	—
Closing market price per share	$ 74.25	$ 51.50	44%
Total market value of common stock	$92,983	$65,711	42%
Net operating revenues	$18,018	$16,181	11%
Operating income	$ 4,092	$ 3,716	10%
Net income	$ 2,986	$ 2,554	17%
Net income per share	$ 2.37	$ 1.98	20%
Cash dividends per share	$ .88	$ .78	13%
Average shares outstanding	1,262	1,290	(2)%
Share-owners' equity at year-end	$ 5,392	$ 5,235	3%
Return on equity	56.2%	52.0%	—

The Coca-Cola Company and Subsidiaries

Selected Financial Data

(In millions except per share data, ratios and growth rates)	Compound Growth Rates		Year Ended December 31,	
	5 Years	10 Years	**1995**	1994
Summary of Operations				
Net operating revenues	12.0%	11.9%	**$18,018**	$16,181
Cost of goods sold	10.5%	9.1%	**6,940**	6,168
Gross profit	12.9%	14.1%	**11,078**	10,013
Selling, administrative and general expenses	11.4%	12.4%	**6,986**	6,297
Operating income	16.0%	17.6%	**4,092**	3,716
Interest income			**245**	181
Interest expense			**272**	199
Equity income			**169**	134
Other income (deductions)-net			**20**	(104)
Gain on issuance of stock by equity investees			**74**	–
Income from continuing operations before income taxes and changes in accounting principles	16.5%	17.2%	**4,328**	3,728
Income taxes	16.3%	15.6%	**1,342**	1,174
Income from continuing operations before changes in accounting principles	16.7%	18.0%	**$ 2,986**	$ 2,554
Net income	16.7%	15.3%	**$ 2,986**	$ 2,554
Preferred stock dividends			**–**	–
Net income available to common share owners	17.0%	15.3%	**$ 2,986**	$ 2,554
Average common shares outstanding			**1,262**	1,290
Per Common Share Data				
Income from continuing operations before changes in accounting principles	18.4%	20.7%	**$ 2.37**	$ 1.98
Net income	18.4%	17.8%	**2.37**	1.98
Cash dividends	17.1%	13.4%	**.88**	.78
Market price on December 31	26.1%	26.6%	**74.25**	51.50
Total Market Value of Common Stock	24.5%	23.9%	**$92,983**	$65,711
Balance Sheet Data				
Cash, cash equivalents and current marketable securities			**$ 1,315**	$ 1,531
Property, plant and equipment–net			**4,336**	4,080
Depreciation			**421**	382
Capital expenditures			**937**	878
Total assets			**15,041**	13,873
Long-term debt			**1,141**	1,426
Total debt			**4,064**	3,509
Share-owners' equity			**5,392**	5,235
Total capital			**9,456**	8,744
Other Key Financial Measures				
Total debt-to-total capital			**43.0%**	40.1%
Net debt-to-net capital			**28.8%**	22.6%
Return on common equity			**56.2%**	52.0%
Return on capital			**34.9%**	32.7%
Dividend payout ratio			**37.2%**	39.4%
Economic profit			**$ 2,172**	$ 1,881

The Coca-Cola Company and Subsidiaries

Consolidated Statements of Income

Year Ended December 31,	1995	1994	1993
(In millions except per share data)			
Net Operating Revenues	$18,018	$16,181	$13,963
Cost of goods sold	6,940	6,168	5,160
Gross Profit	11,078	10,013	8,803
Selling, administrative and general expenses	6,986	6,297	5,695
Operating Income	4,092	3,716	3,108
Interest income	245	181	144
Interest expense	272	199	168
Equity income	169	134	91
Other income (deductions)-net	20	(104)	(2)
Gain on issuance of stock by Coca-Cola Amatil	74	–	12
Income before Income Taxes and Change in Accounting Principle	4,328	3,728	3,185
Income taxes	1,342	1,174	997
Income before Change in Accounting Principle	2,986	2,554	2,188
Transition effect of change in accounting for postemployment benefits	–	–	(12)
Net Income	$ 2,986	$ 2,554	$ 2,176
Income per Share			
Before change in accounting principle	$ 2.37	$ 1.98	$ 1.68
Transition effect of change in accounting for postemployment benefits	–	–	(.01)
Net Income per Share	$ 2.37	$ 1.98	$ 1.67
Average Shares Outstanding	1,262	1,290	1,302

See Notes to Consolidated Financial Statements.

The Coca-Cola Company and Subsidiaries

Consolidated Balance Sheets

December 31,	1995	1994
(In millions except share data)		
Assets		
Current		
Cash and cash equivalents	$ 1,167	$ 1,386
Marketable securities	148	145
	1,315	1,531
Trade accounts receivable, less allowances of $34 in 1995 and $33 in 1994	1,695	1,470
Finance subsidiary receivables	55	55
Inventories	1,117	1,047
Prepaid expenses and other assets	1,268	1,102
Total Current Assets	5,450	5,205
Investments and Other Assets		
Equity method investments		
Coca-Cola Enterprises Inc.	556	524
Coca-Cola Amatil Limited	682	694
Other, principally bottling companies	1,157	1,114
Cost method investments, principally bottling companies	319	178
Finance subsidiary receivables and investments	351	255
Marketable securities and other assets	1,246	1,163
	4,311	3,928
Property, Plant and Equipment		
Land	233	221
Buildings and improvements	1,944	1,814
Machinery and equipment	4,135	3,776
Containers	345	346
	6,657	6,157
Less allowances for depreciation	2,321	2,077
	4,336	4,080
Goodwill and Other Intangible Assets	944	660
	$15,041	$13,873
Liabilities and Share-Owners' Equity		
Current		
Accounts payable and accrued expenses	$ 2,894	$ 2,564
Loans and notes payable	2,371	2,048
Current maturities of long-term debt	552	35
Accrued taxes	1,531	1,530
Total Current Liabilities	7,348	6,177
Long-Term Debt	1,141	1,426
Other Liabilities	966	855
Deferred Income Taxes	194	180
Share-Owners' Equity		
Common stock, $.25 par value		
Authorized: 2,800,000,000 shares		
Issued: 1,711,839,497 shares in 1995; 1,707,627,955 shares in 1994	428	427
Capital surplus	1,291	1,173
Reinvested earnings	12,882	11,006
Unearned compensation related to outstanding restricted stock	(68)	(74)
Foreign currency translation adjustment	(424)	(272)
Unrealized gain on securities available for sale	82	48
	14,191	12,308
Less treasury stock, at cost (459,540,663 shares in 1995; 431,694,661 shares in 1994)	8,799	7,073
	5,392	5,235
	$15,041	$13,873

See Notes to Consolidated Financial Statements.

The Coca-Cola Company and Subsidiaries

Consolidated Statements of Share-Owners' Equity

Three Years Ended December 31, 1995	Number of Common Shares Outstanding	Common Stock	Capital Surplus	Reinvested Earnings	Outstanding Restricted Stock	Foreign Currency Translation	Unrealized Gain on Securities	Treasury Stock
(In millions except per share data)								
Balance December 31, 1992	1,307	$424	$871	$ 8,165	$(100)	$(271)	$ –	$(5,201)
Stock issued to employees exercising stock options	7	2	143	–	–	–	–	–
Tax benefit from employees' stock option and restricted stock plans	–	–	66	–	–	–	–	–
Stock issued under restricted stock plans, less amortization of $19	–	–	6	–	15	–	–	–
Translation adjustments	–	–	–	–	–	(149)	–	–
Purchases of stock for treasury	(17)[1]	–	–	–	–	–	–	(680)
Net income	–	–	–	2,176	–	–	–	–
Dividends (per share–$.68)	–	–	–	(883)	–	–	–	–
Balance December 31, 1993	1,297	426	1,086	9,458	(85)	(420)	–	(5,881)
Transition effect of change in accounting for certain debt and marketable equity securities, net of deferred taxes	–	–	–	–	–	–	60	–
Stock issued to employees exercising stock options	4	1	68	–	–	–	–	–
Tax benefit from employees' stock option and restricted stock plans	–	–	17	–	–	–	–	–
Stock issued under restricted stock plans, less amortization of $13	–	–	2	–	11	–	–	–
Translation adjustments	–	–	–	–	–	148	–	–
Net change in unrealized gain on securities, net of deferred taxes	–	–	–	–	–	–	(12)	–
Purchases of stock for treasury	(25)[1]	–	–	–	–	–	–	(1,192)
Net income	–	–	–	2,554	–	–	–	–
Dividends (per share–$.78)	–	–	–	(1,006)	–	–	–	–
Balance December 31, 1994	1,276	427	1,173	11,006	(74)	(272)	48	(7,073)
Stock issued to employees exercising stock options	**4**	**1**	**85**	–	–	–	–	–
Tax benefit from employees' stock option and restricted stock plans	–	–	**26**	–	–	–	–	–
Stock issued under restricted stock plans, less amortization of $12	–	–	**7**	–	**6**	–	–	–
Translation adjustments	–	–	–	–	–	**(152)**	–	–
Net change in unrealized gain on securities, net of deferred taxes	–	–	–	–	–	–	**34**	–
Purchases of stock for treasury	**(29)[1]**	–	–	–	–	–	–	**(1,796)**
Treasury stock issued in connection with an acquisition	**1**	–	–	–	–	–	–	**70**
Net income	–	–	–	**2,986**	–	–	–	–
Dividends (per share–$.88)	–	–	–	**(1,110)**	–	–	–	–
Balance December 31, 1995	**1,252**	**$428**	**$1,291**	**$12,882**	**$ (68)**	**$(424)**	**$82**	**$(8,799)**

[1]*Common stock purchased from employees exercising stock options amounted to 280 thousand, 208 thousand and 2.7 million shares for the years ending December 31, 1995, 1994, 1993, respectively.*

See Notes to Consolidated Financial Statements.

The Coca-Cola Company and Subsidiaries

Consolidated Statements of Cash Flows

Year Ended December 31,	1995	1994	1993
(In millions)			
Operating Activities			
Net income	$ 2,986	$ 2,554	$ 2,176
Transition effect of change in accounting principle	–	–	12
Depreciation and amortization	454	411	360
Deferred income taxes	157	58	(62)
Equity income, net of dividends	(25)	(4)	(35)
Foreign currency adjustments	(23)	(6)	9
Gains on sales of assets	–	–	(84)
Other noncash items	(29)	41	78
Net change in operating assets and liabilities	(405)	129	54
Net cash provided by operating activities	3,115	3,183	2,508
Investing Activities			
Additions to finance subsidiary receivables	(144)	(94)	(177)
Collections of finance subsidiary receivables	46	50	44
Acquisitions and investments, principally bottling companies	(338)	(311)	(611)
Purchases of securities	(190)	(201)	(245)
Proceeds from disposals of investments and other assets	580	299	690
Purchases of property, plant and equipment	(937)	(878)	(800)
Proceeds from disposals of property, plant and equipment	44	109	312
Other investing activities	(74)	(11)	(98)
Net cash used in investing activities	(1,013)	(1,037)	(885)
Net cash provided by operations after reinvestment	2,102	2,146	1,623
Financing Activities			
Issuances of debt	754	491	445
Payments of debt	(212)	(154)	(567)
Issuances of stock	86	69	145
Purchases of stock for treasury	(1,796)	(1,192)	(680)
Dividends	(1,110)	(1,006)	(883)
Net cash used in financing activities	(2,278)	(1,792)	(1,540)
Effect of Exchange Rate Changes on Cash and Cash Equivalents	(43)	34	(41)
Cash and Cash Equivalents			
Net increase (decrease) during the year	(219)	388	42
Balance at beginning of year	1,386	998	956
Balance at end of year	$ 1,167	$ 1,386	$ 998

See Notes to Consolidated Financial Statements.

As previously demonstrated in Illustration 1-8 on page 21, the four primary financial statements are interrelated. It is important that you understand this interrelatedness. To understand how these financial statements interrelate, **trace each of the following relationships to Coca-Cola's statements**.

(a) The 1995 income statement reports net income of $2,986 million. Net income is reported on the 1995 statement of share-owners' equity as an increase to retained earnings (see the "Reinvested Earnings" column).

(b) The ending balance of $12,882 million in reinvested earnings (the term used by Coca-Cola instead of retained earnings), as reported in the 1995 statement of share-owners' equity, is carried over to the balance sheet at the end of 1995 (see the share-owners' equity section).

(c) Net income as reported at $2,986 million in the 1995 income statement appears as the first item in the operating activities section of the 1995 statement of cash flows. Net income of $2,986 million is adjusted to "net cash provided by operating activities" of $3,115 million.

(d) The cash balance of $1,386 million that is reported on the balance sheet at the end of 1994 is reported at the bottom of the statement of cash flows where it is added to the net decrease of $219 million in cash during the year 1995. The result is the ending balance in cash of $1,167 as reported in the 1995 balance sheet and the statement of cash flows.

▸ *Summary of Study Objectives*

1. *Explain the meaning of accounting.* Accounting is the process of identifying, recording, and communicating the economic events of an organization (business or nonbusiness) to interested users of the information.

2. *Identify the users and uses of accounting.* The major users and uses of accounting are: (a) Management uses accounting information in planning, controlling, and evaluating business operations. (b) Investors (owners) judge the wisdom of buying, holding, or selling their financial interests on the basis of accounting data. (c) Creditors (suppliers and bankers) evaluate the risks of granting credit or lending money to particular businesses on the basis of the accounting information obtained about those businesses. Other groups with an indirect interest are taxing authorities, regulatory agencies, customers, labor unions, and economic planners.

3. *Understand why ethics is a fundamental business concept.* Ethics are the standards of conduct by which one's actions—both personal and business—are judged as right or wrong. If you cannot depend on the honesty of the individuals you deal with, effective communication and economic activity would be impossible and information would have no credibility.

4. *Explain the meaning of generally accepted accounting principles and the cost principle.* Generally accepted accounting principles are a common set of standards used by accountants. One important principle is the cost principle, which states that assets should be recorded at their cost.

5. *Explain the meaning of the monetary unit assumption and the economic entity assumption.* The monetary unit as-

sumption requires that only transaction data capable of being expressed in terms of money be included in the accounting records of the economic entity. The economic entity assumption states that economic events can be identified with a particular unit of accountability.

6. *State the basic accounting equation and explain the meaning of assets, liabilities, and stockholders' equity.* The basic accounting equation is:

$$\text{Assets} = \text{Liabilities} + \text{Stockholders' Equity}$$

Assets are resources owned by a business. Liabilities are creditorship claims on total assets. Stockholders' equity is the ownership claim on total assets. It is often referred to as residual equity.

7. *Analyze the effect of business transactions on the basic accounting equation.* Each business transaction must have a dual effect on the accounting equation. For example, if an individual asset is increased, there must be a corresponding: (1) decrease in another asset, or (2) increase in a specific liability, or (3) increase in stockholders' equity.

8. *Prepare an income statement, retained earnings statement, balance sheet, and statement of cash flows.* An income statement presents the revenues and expenses of a company for a specified period of time. A retained earnings statement summarizes the changes in retained earnings that have occurred for a specific period of time. A balance sheet reports the assets, liabilities, and stockholders' equity of a business at a specific date. A statement of cash flows summarizes information concerning the cash inflows (receipts) and outflows (payments) for a specific period of time.

GLOSSARY

Accounting The process of identifying, recording, and communicating the economic events of an organization to interested users of the information. (p. 2).

Assets Resources owned by a business. (p. 12).

Balance sheet A financial statement that reports the assets, liabilities, and stockholders' equity at a specific date. (p. 20).

Basic accounting equation Assets = Liabilities + Stockholders' Equity. (p. 12).

Bookkeeping A part of accounting that involves only the recording of economic events. (p. 6).

Corporation A business organized as a separate legal entity under state corporation law having ownership divided into transferable shares of stock. (p. 11).

Cost principle An accounting principle that states that assets should be recorded at their cost. (p. 9).

Dividend A distribution by a corporation to its stockholders on a pro rata (equal) basis. (p. 13).

Economic entity assumption An assumption that economic events can be identified with a particular unit of accountability. (p. 10).

Ethics The standards of conduct by which one's actions are judged as right or wrong, honest or dishonest, fair or not fair. (p. 8).

Expenses The cost of assets consumed or services used in the process of earning revenue. (p. 13).

Financial Accounting Standards Board (FASB) A private organization that establishes generally accepted accounting principles. (p. 8).

Generally accepted accounting principles (GAAP) A common set of standards that indicate how to report economic events. (p. 8).

Income statement A financial statement that presents the revenues and expenses and resulting net income or net loss of a company for a specific period of time. (p. 20).

Liabilities Creditorship claims on total assets. (p. 12).

Monetary unit assumption An assumption stating that only transaction data that can be expressed in terms of money be included in the accounting records of the economic entity. (p. 10).

Net income The amount by which revenues exceed expenses. (p. 13).

Net loss The amount by which expenses exceed revenues. (p. 13).

Partnership An association of two or more persons to carry on as co-owners of a business for profit. (p. 11).

Proprietorship A business owned by one person. (p. 10).

Retained earnings statement A financial statement that summarizes the changes in retained earnings for a specific period of time. (p. 20).

Revenues The gross increase in stockholders' equity resulting from business activities entered into for the purpose of earning income. (p. 13).

Securities and Exchange Commission (SEC) A governmental agency that requires companies to file financial reports in accordance with generally accepted accounting principles. (p. 9).

Statement of cash flows A financial statement that provides information about the cash inflows (receipts) and cash outflows (payments) of an entity for a specific period of time. (p. 20).

Stockholders' equity The ownership claim on total assets of a corporation. (p. 12).

Transactions The economic events of the enterprise recorded by accountants. (p. 14).

DEMONSTRATION PROBLEM

Legal Services, Inc. was incorporated on July 1, 1996. During the first month of operations, the following transactions occurred:

1. Stockholders invested $10,000 in cash in exchange for shares of stock.
2. Paid $800 for July rent on office space.
3. Purchased office equipment on account, $3,000.
4. Rendered legal services to clients for cash, $1,500. (use Fees Earned)
5. Borrowed $700 cash from a bank on a note payable.
6. Rendered legal services to client on account, $2,000.
7. Paid monthly expenses: salaries, $500; utilities, $300; and telephone, $100.

The Demonstration Problems are a final review before you begin homework. The problem-solving strategies in the margins give you tips about how to approach the problem, and the solutions provided demonstrate both the form and content of complete answers.

Instructions

(a) Prepare a tabular summary of the transactions.

(b) Prepare the income statement, retained earnings statement, and balance sheet at July 31 for Legal Services, Inc.

Solution to Demonstration Problem

Problem-Solving Strategies

1. Remember that assets must equal liabilities and stock-holders' equity after each transaction.

2. Investments and revenues increase stockholders' equity.

3. Dividends and expenses decrease stockholders' equity.

4. The income statement shows revenues and expenses for a period of time.

5. The retained earnings statement shows the changes in retained earnings for a period of time.

6. The balance sheet reports assets, liabilities, and stockholders' equity at a specific date.

(a)

Trans-action	Cash	+	Accounts Receivable	+	Equipment	=	Notes Payable	+	Accounts Payable	+	Common Stock	+	Retained Earnings	
							Assets = Liabilities + Stockholders' Equity							
(1)	+$10,000										+$10,000			
(2)	−800												−$800	Rent Expense
	9,200					=					10,000 +		−800	
(3)					+$3,000				+$3,000					
	9,200	+			3,000	=			3,000 +		10,000		−800	
(4)	+1,500												+1,500	Fees Earned
	10,700	+			3,000	=			3,000 +		10,000 +		700	
(5)	+700						+$700							
	11,400	+			3,000	=	700 +		3,000 +		10,000 +		700	
(6)			+$2,000										+2,000	Fees Earned
	11,400 +		2,000	+	3,000	=	700 +		3,000 +		10,000 +		2,700	
(7)	−900												−500	Salaries Expense
													−300	Utilities Expense
													−100	Telephone Expense
	$10,500 +		$2,000	+	$3,000	=	$700 +		$3,000 +		$10,000 +		$1,800	

(b)

LEGAL SERVICES, INC.
Income Statement
For the Month Ended July 31, 1996

Revenues			
Fees earned			$3,500
Expenses			
Rent expense		$800	
Salaries expense		500	
Utilities expense		300	
Telephone expense		100	
Total expenses			1,700
Net income			$1,800

LEGAL SERVICES, INC.
Retained Earnings Statement
For the Month Ended July 31, 1996

Retained earnings, July 1	$ –0–
Add: Net income	1,800
Retained earnings	$1,800

LEGAL SERVICES, INC.
Balance Sheet
July 31, 1996

Assets

Cash	$10,500
Accounts receivable	2,000
Equipment	3,000
Total assets	$15,500

Liabilities and Stockholders' Equity		
Liabilities		
Notes payable		$ 700
Accounts payable		3,000
Total liabilities		3,700
Stockholders' Equity		
Common stock	$10,000	
Retained earnings	1,800	11,800
Total liabilities and stockholders' equity		$15,500

SELF-STUDY QUESTIONS

Answers are at the end of the chapter.

(SO 1)
1. The accounting process does *not* include:
   a. identification
   b. verification
   c. recording
   d. communication

(SO 2)
2. One of the following statements about users of accounting information is *incorrect*. The incorrect statement is:
   a. Management is considered an internal user.
   b. Taxing authorities are considered external users.
   c. Present creditors are considered external users.
   d. Regulatory authorities are considered internal users.

(SO 3)
3. Generally accepted accounting principles are:
   a. the guidelines used to resolve ethical dilemmas.
   b. established by the Internal Revenue Service.
   c. are primarily established by the Financial Accounting Standards Board and the Securities Exchange Commission.
   d. immutable truths derived from the laws of nature.

(SO 4)
4. The cost principle states that:
   a. assets should be recorded at cost and adjusted when the market value changes.
   b. activities of an entity be kept separate and distinct from its owner.
   c. assets should be recorded at their cost.
   d. only transaction data capable of being expressed in terms of money be included in the accounting records.

(SO 5)
5. Which of the following statements about basic assumptions is *incorrect*?
   a. Basic assumptions are the same as accounting principles.
   b. The economic entity assumption states that there should be a particular unit of accountability.
   c. The monetary unit assumption enables accounting to measure economic events.

   d. An important corollary to the monetary unit assumption is the stable monetary unit assumption.

(SO 6)
6. Net income will result during a time period when:
   a. assets exceed liabilities.
   b. assets exceed revenues.
   c. expenses exceed revenues.
   d. revenues exceed expenses.

(SO 7)
7. The effects on the basic accounting equation of performing services on account are:
   a. increase assets and decrease stockholders' equity.
   b. increase assets and increase stockholders' equity.
   c. increase assets and increase liabilities.
   d. increase liabilities and increase stockholders' equity.

(SO 7)
8. As of December 31, 1996, Graceland Company has assets of $3,500 and stockholders' equity of $2,000. What are the liabilities for Graceland Company as of December 31, 1996?
   a. $1,500.
   b. $1,000.
   c. $2,500.
   d. $2,000.

(SO 8)
9. Exodus Company buys a $900 machine on credit. This transaction will affect the:
   a. income statement only.
   b. balance sheet only.
   c. income statement and retained earnings statement only.
   d. income statement, retained earnings statement, and balance sheet.

(SO 8)
10. The financial statement that reports assets, liabilities, and stockholders' equity is the:
    a. income statement.
    b. retained earnings statement.
    c. balance sheet.
    d. statement of cash flow.

QUESTIONS

1. "Accounting is ingrained in our society and it is vital to our economic system." Do you agree? Explain.

2. Identify and describe the steps in the accounting process.

3. (a) Who are internal users of accounting data?
   (b) How does accounting provide relevant data to these users?

4. Distinguish between the two types of external users of accounting data and give examples of each.

5. "Bookkeeping and accounting are the same." Do you agree? Explain.

6. Travelynn Agency Inc. purchased land for $75,000 cash on December 10, 1996. At December 31, 1996, the land's value has increased to $93,000. What amount should be reported for land on Travelynn's balance sheet at December 31, 1996? Explain.

7. What is the monetary unit assumption? What impact does inflation have on the monetary unit assumption?

8. What is the economic entity assumption?

9. What are the three basic forms of business organizations for profit-oriented enterprises?

10. Betsy Ross is the owner of a successful printing shop. Recently her business has been increasing, and Betsy has been thinking about changing the organization of her business from a proprietorship to a corporation. Discuss some of the advantages Betsy would enjoy if she were to incorporate her business.

11. What is the basic accounting equation?

12. (a) Define the terms assets, liabilities, and stockholders' equity. (b) What items affect stockholders' equity?

13. Which of the following items are liabilities of Hot Jewelry Stores?
   (a) Cash.   (f) Equipment.
   (b) Accounts payable.   (g) Salaries payable.
   (c) Inventory   (h) Service revenue.
   (d) Accounts receivable.   (i) Rent expense.
   (e) Supplies.

14. Can a business enter into a transaction in which only the left side of the basic accounting equation is affected? If so, give an example.

15. Are the following events recorded in the accounting records? Explain your answer in each case.
   (a) The president of the company dies.
   (b) Supplies are purchased on account.
   (c) An employee is fired.

16. Indicate how the following business transactions affect the basic accounting equation.
   (a) Paid cash for janitorial services.
   (b) Purchased equipment for cash.
   (c) Invested cash in the business for stock.
   (d) Paid an accounts payable in full.

17. Listed below are some items found in the financial statements of Ruth Weber, Inc. Indicate in which financial statement(s) the following items would appear.
   (a) Advertising expense.   (d) Cash.
   (b) Equipment.   (e) Common stock.
   (c) Service revenue.   (f) Wages payable.

18. In February of 1995, Paul Jones invested $5,000 in Environs, Inc. Environ's accountant, Donna Wortham, recorded this receipt as an increase in cash and revenues. Is this treatment appropriate? Why or why not?

19. A company's net income appears directly on the income statement and the retained earnings statement, and it is included indirectly in the company's balance sheet. Do you agree? Explain.

20. Hernandez Enterprises, Inc. had a stockholders' equity balance of $138,000 at the beginning of the period. At the end of the accounting period, the stockholders' equity balance was $198,000.
   (a) Assuming no additional investment or distributions during the period, what is the net income for the period?
   (b) Assuming an additional investment of $13,000 but no distributions during the period, what is the net income for the period?

21. Summarized operations for the Cora L. King Co. for the month of July are as follows:

   Revenues earned: for cash $45,000; on account $80,000.

   Expenses incurred: for cash $26,000; on account $40,000.

   Indicate for Cora L. King Co. (a) the total revenues, (b) the total expenses, and (c) net income for the month of July.

BRIEF EXERCISES

BE1–1 Presented below is the basic accounting equation. Determine the missing amounts:

Basic accounting equation.
(SO 6)

	Assets	=	Liabilities	+	Stockholders' Equity
(a)	$90,000		$50,000		? 40,000
(b)	118,000		$48,000		$70,000
(c)	$94,000		? 22,000		$72,000

BE1–2 Given the accounting equation, answer each of the following questions:

Basic accounting equation.
(SO 6)

1. The liabilities of Hogan Company are $90,000 and the stockholders' equity is $240,000. What is the amount of Hogan Company's total assets?
2. The total assets of Potter Company are $170,000 and its stockholders' equity is $90,000. What is the amount of its total liabilities?
3. The total assets of Barren Co. are $700,000 and its liabilities are equal to one half of its total assets. What is the amount of Barren Co.'s stockholders' equity?

BE1–3 At the beginning of the year, Lamson Company had total assets of $700,000 and total liabilities of $500,000. Answer the following questions:

Basic accounting equation.
(SO 6)

1. If total assets increased $150,000 during the year and total liabilities decreased $80,000, what is the amount of stockholders' equity at the end of the year?
2. During the year, total liabilities increased $100,000 and stockholders' equity decreased $70,000. What is the amount of total assets at the end of the year?
3. If total assets decreased $90,000 and stockholders' equity increased $110,000 during the year, what is the amount of total liabilities at the end of the year?

BE1–4 Presented below are three business transactions. On a sheet of paper, list the letters a, b, c with columns for assets, liabilities, and stockholders' equity. For each column, indicate whether the transactions increased (+), decreased (−) or had no effect (NE) on assets, liabilities, and stockholders' equity:

Determine effect of transactions on basic accounting equation.
(SO 7)

(a) Purchased supplies on account.
(b) Received cash for providing a service.
(c) Expenses paid in cash.

BE1–5 Follow the same format as BE1-4 above. Determine the effect on assets, liabilities, and stockholders' equity of the following three transactions:

Determine effect of transactions on basic accounting equation.
(SO 7)

(a) Invested cash in the business.
(b) Paid cash dividend.
(c) Received cash from a customer who had previously been billed for services provided.

BE1–6 Classify each of the following items as asset (A), liability (L), revenue (R), or expense (E).

Classify various items.
(SO 6, 7)

E	Advertising expense	A	Cash
R	Commission revenue	R	Rent revenue
E	Insurance expense	E	Utilities expense
E	Salaries expense	A	Accounts payable

BE1–7 Presented below are three transactions. Mark each transaction as affecting common stock (C), dividends (D), revenue (R), expense (E), or not affecting stockholders' equity (NSE):

Determine effect of transactions on stockholders' equity.
(SO 7)

_____ Received cash for services performed
_____ Paid cash to purchase equipment
_____ Paid employee salaries

BE1–8 In alphabetical order below are balance sheet items for Gidget Company at December 31, 1996. Prepare a balance sheet, following the format of Illustration 1-8.

Prepare a balance sheet.
(SO 8)

Accounts payable	$90,000
Accounts receivable	$81,000
Cash	$40,500
Common stock	$31,500

Identify assets, liabilities, and stockholders' equity.
(SO 6)

BE1–9 Indicate whether each of the following items is an asset (A), liability (L), or part of stockholders' equity (SE):

A Accounts receivable   A Office supplies
L Salaries payable   SE Common stock
A Equipment   L Notes payable

Determine where items appear on financial statements.
(SO 8)

BE1–10 Indicate whether the following items would appear on the income statement (IS), balance sheet (BS), or retained earnings statement (RE):

____ Notes payable   ____ Cash
____ Advertising expense   ____ Fees earned
____ Common stock

EXERCISES

Classify accounts as assets, liabilities, and stockholders' equity.
(SO 6)

E1–1 The Ace Cleaners has the following balance sheet items:

Accounts payable	Accounts receivable
Cash	Notes payable
Cleaning equipment	Salaries payable
Cleaning supplies	Common stock

Instructions
Classify each item as an asset, liability, or stockholders' equity.

Analyze the effect of transactions.
(SO 6, 7)

E1–2 Selected transactions for Green Lawn Care Company are listed below:

1. Made cash investment to start business.
2. Paid monthly rent.
3. Purchased equipment on account.
4. Billed customers for services performed.
5. Paid dividends.
6. Received cash from customers billed in (4).
7. Incurred advertising expense on account.
8. Purchased additional equipment for cash.
9. Received cash from customers when service was rendered.

Instructions
List the numbers of the above transactions and describe the effect of each transaction on assets, liabilities, and stockholders' equity. For example, the first answer is: (1) Increase in assets and increase in stockholders' equity.

Analyze the effect of transactions on assets, liabilities, and stockholders' equity.
(SO 6, 7)

E1–3 Li Wang Computer Timeshare Company entered into the following transactions during May 1996.

1. Purchased computer terminals for $19,000 from Digital Equipment on account.
2. Paid $4,000 cash for May rent on storage space.
3. Received $15,000 cash from customers for contracts billed in April.
4. Provided computer services to Brieske Construction Company for $3,000 cash.
5. Paid Southern States Power Co. $11,000 cash for energy usage in May.
6. Stockholders' invested an additional $32,000 in the business.
7. Paid Digital Equipment for the terminals purchased in (1) above.
8. Incurred advertising expense for May of $1,000 on account.

Instructions
Indicate with the appropriate letter whether each of the transactions above results in:

(a) an increase in assets and a decrease in assets.
(b) an increase in assets and an increase in stockholders' equity.
(c) an increase in assets and an increase in liabilities.
(d) a decrease in assets and a decrease in stockholders' equity.
(e) a decrease in assets and a decrease in liabilities.

(f) an increase in liabilities and a decrease in stockholders' equity.

(g) an increase in stockholders' equity and a decrease in liabilities.

E1–4 A tabular analysis of the transactions made by Roberta Mendez & Co., a certified public accounting firm, for the month of August is shown below. Each increase and decrease in owner's equity is explained.

Analyze transactions and compute net income. (SO 7)

	Cash	+ Accounts Receivable	+ Supplies	+ Office Equipment	= Accounts Payable	+ Stockholders' Equity
1.	+$15,000					+$15,000 Investment
2.	−2,000			+$5,000	+$3,000	
3.	− 750		+$750			
4.	+4,600	+3,400				+8,000 Fees Earned
5.	−1,500				−1,500	
6.	−2,000					−2,000 Dividends
7.	− 650					− 650 Rent Expense
8.	+ 450	−450				
9.	−2,900					−2,900 Salaries Expense
10.					+ 500	− 500 Utilities Expense

Instructions

(a) [pencil icon] Describe each transaction that occurred for the month.

(b) Determine how much stockholders' equity increased for the month.

(c) Compute the amount of net income for the month.

E1–5 The tabular analysis of transactions for Roberta Mendez & Co. is presented in E1–4.

Prepare an income statement, retained earnings statement, and a balance sheet. (SO 8)

Instructions

Prepare an income statement and a retained earnings statement for August and a balance sheet at August 31, 1996.

E1–6 The Debra Company had the following assets and liabilities on the dates indicated:

Determine net income (or loss). (SO 7)

December 31	Total Assets	Total Liabilities
1996	$380,000	$250,000
1997	$460,000	$310,000
1998	$590,000	$400,000

Debra began business on January 1, 1996, with an investment of $100,000.

Instructions

From an analysis of the change in stockholders' equity during the year, compute the net income (or loss) for:

(a) 1996, assuming Debra paid $15,000 in dividends for the year.

(b) 1997, assuming stockholders made an additional investment of $50,000 and Debra paid no dividends in 1997.

(c) 1998, assuming stockholders made an additional investment of $10,000 and Debra paid dividends of $20,000 in 1998.

E1–7 Two items are omitted from each of the following summaries of balance sheet and income statement data for two corporations for the year 1996, Kate Cordova, Inc., and Maxim Enterprises.

Analyze financial statements items. (SO 6, 7)

	Kate Cordova, Inc.	Maxim Enterprises
Beginning of year:		
Total assets	$ 90,000	$130,000
Total liabilities	80,000	(c)
Total stockholders' equity	(a)	95,000
End of year:		
Total assets	160,000	180,000
Total liabilities	120,000	50,000
Total stockholders' equity	40,000	130,000

Changes during year in stockholders' equity:		
Additional investment	(b)	25,000
Dividends	24,000	(d)
Total revenues	215,000	100,000
Total expenses	165,000	80,000

Instructions
Determine the missing amounts.

Prepare income statement and retained earnings statement.
(SO 8)

E1–8 The following information relates to Tone Kon Co. for the year 1996.

Common stock, January 1, 1996	$45,000	Advertising expense	1,800
Dividends, during 1996	5,000	Rent expense	10,400
Fees earned	50,000	Utilities expense	3,100
Salaries expense	28,000		

Instructions
After analyzing the data, prepare an income statement and a retained earnings statement for the year ending December 31, 1996. Beginning retained earnings was $5,000.

Correct an incorrectly prepared balance sheet.
(SO 8)

E1–9 Kit Lucas is the bookkeeper for Aurora Company. Kit has been trying to get the balance sheet of Aurora Company to balance. Aurora's balance sheet is as follows:

AURORA COMPANY
Balance Sheet
December 31, 1996

Assets		Liabilities	
Cash	$16,500	Accounts payable	$20,000
Supplies	8,000	Accounts receivable	(10,000)
Equipment	46,000	Common stock	50,000
Dividends	7,000	Retained earnings	17,500
Total assets	$77,500	Total liabilities and stockholders' equity	$77,500

Instructions
Prepare a correct balance sheet.

Compute net income and prepare a balance sheet.
(SO 8)

E1–10 Deer Park, Inc. a public camping ground near the Lake Mead National Recreation Area, has compiled the following financial information as of December 31, 1996.

Revenues during 1996—camping fees	$147,000	Notes payable	60,000
Revenues during 1996—general store	40,000	Expenses during 1996	150,000
Accounts payable	11,000	Supplies on hand	2,500
Cash on hand	7,000	Common stock	50,000
Original cost of equipment	115,500	Retained earnings	?
Market value of equipment	140,000		

Instructions
  (a) Determine Deer Park's net income for 1996.
  (b) Prepare a balance sheet for Deer Park as of December 31, 1996.

Prepare an income statement.
(SO 8)

E1–11 Presented below is financial information related to the 1996 operations of the Sanibel Cruise Company, Inc.

Boat rental expense	$ 90,000
Property tax expense (on dock facilities)	10,000
Salaries expense	142,000
Advertising expense	3,500
Ticket revenue	325,000

Instructions
Prepare the 1996 income statement for the Sanibel Cruise Company.

E1–12 Presented below is information related to Wet Sprocket, Inc.

Retained earnings, January 1, 1996	$150,000
Legal fees earned—1996	380,000
Total expenses—1996	205,000
Dividends—1996	76,000

Prepare a retained earnings statement.
(SO 8)

Instructions
Prepare the 1996 retained earnings statement for Wet Sprocket, Inc.

PROBLEMS
••

P1–1 On April 1, Alschuler Travel Agency, Inc. was established. The following transactions were completed during the month:

1. Stockholders invested $20,000 cash, receiving common stock in exchange.
2. Paid $400 cash for April office rent.
3. Purchased office equipment for $2,500 cash.
4. Incurred $300 of advertising costs in the Chicago Tribune, on account.
5. Paid $600 cash for office supplies.
6. Earned $9,000 for services rendered: Cash of $1,000 is received from customers, and the balance of $8,000 is billed to customers on account.
7. Paid $200 cash dividend.
8. Paid Chicago Tribune amount due in transaction (4).
9. Paid employees' salaries, $1,200.
10. Cash of $8,000 is received from customers who have previously been billed in transaction (6).

Analyze transactions and compute net income.
(SO 6, 7)

Instructions
(a) Prepare a tabular analysis of the transactions using the following column headings: . Cash, Accounts Receivable, Supplies, Office Equipment, Accounts Payable, Common Stock and Retained Earnings.
(b) From an analysis of the column, Retained Earnings, compute the net income or net loss for April.

P1–2 Hillary Brennan Corporation was formed on July 1, 1996. On July 31, the balance sheet showed Cash $4,000, Accounts Receivable $1,500, Supplies $500, Office Equipment $5,000, Accounts Payable $4,200, Common Stock $6,500, and Retained Earnings $300. During August the following transactions occurred:

1. Collected $1,400 of accounts receivable.
2. Paid $2,700 cash on accounts payable.
3. Earned fees of $6,400, of which $3,000 is collected in cash and the balance is due in September.
4. Purchased additional office equipment for $1,000, paying $400 in cash and the balance on account.
5. Paid salaries $1,500, rent for August $900, and advertising expenses $350.
6. Dividends of $550 were paid.
7. Received $1,000 from Standard Federal Bank—money borrowed on a note payable.
8. Incurred utility expenses for month on account, $250.

Analyze transactions and prepare income statement and retained earnings statement.
(SO 6, 7, 8)

Instructions
(a) Prepare a tabular analysis of the August transactions beginning with July 31 balances. The column heading should be as follows: Cash + Accounts Receivable + Supplies + Office Equipment = Notes Payable + Accounts Payable + Common Stock + Retained Earnings.

(b) Prepare an income statement for August, a retained earnings statement for August, and a balance sheet at August 31.

Prepare income statement, retained earnings statement, and balance sheet.
(SO 8)

P1–3 On June 1, Cindy Crawford Cosmetics was started with an investment in the company of $26,200 in cash. Following are the assets and liabilities of the company at June 30 and the revenues and expenses for the month of June.

Cash	$12,000	Notes Payable	$13,000
Accounts Receivable	3,000	Accounts Payable	1,200
Fees Earned	6,500	Supplies Expense	1,200
Cosmetic Supplies on Hand	2,400	Gas and Oil Expense	800
Advertising Expense	500	Utilities Expense	300
Equipment	25,000		

No additional investments were made in June, but dividends of $1,700 were paid during the month.

Instructions
Prepare an income statement and retained earnings statement for the month of June and a balance sheet at June 30, 1996.

Prepare income statement and retained earnings statement.
(SO 8)

P1–4 Charlie Doss Consulting Co. was organized on March 1, 1996. The retained earnings column of the tabular summary for the month of March contained the following recorded data:

Transaction	Amount	Description
(4)	750	Rent expense
(6)	3,250	Fees earned
(8)	400	Advertising expense
(11)	1,000	Salaries expense
(12)	2,100	Fees earned
(15)	250	Utilities expense
(18)	500	Dividends
(20)	3,200	Fees earned
(22)	200	Repair expense
(24)	1,000	Advertising expense
(27)	250	Dividends
(29)	1,100	Fees earned
(32)	900	Salaries expense
(34)	200	Supplies expense
(36)	150	Utilities expense

All data were properly recorded except the following:

In transaction (36), $80 was applicable to repairs on business property.

Instructions
(a) Prepare an income statement for the month of March.
(b) Prepare a retained earnings statement for March.

Determine financial statement amounts and prepare retained earnings statements.
(SO 7, 8)

P1–5 Financial statement information about four different companies is as follows:

	Zarle Company	Wasicsko Company	McKane Company	Russe Company
January 1, 1996:				
Assets	$ 80,000	$100,000	(g)	$150,000
Liabilities	50,000	(d)	75,000	(j)
Stockholders' equity	(a)	60,000	45,000	90,000
December 31, 1996:				
Assets	(b)	130,000	180,000	(k)
Liabilities	55,000	62,000	(h)	80,000
Stockholders' equity	45,000	(e)	110,000	145,000

Stockholders' equity changes in year:

Additional investment	(c)	8,000	10,000	15,000
Dividends	15,000	(f)	12,000	10,000
Total revenues	350,000	400,000	(i)	500,000
Total expenses	330,000	385,000	360,000	(l)

Instructions

(a) Determine the missing amounts.

(b) Prepare the retained earnings statement for Zarle Company. Assume that the beginning balance in retained earnings is zero.

(c) ▭▭▭▭▭▶ Write a memorandum explaining the sequence for preparing financial statements and the interrelationship of the retained earnings statement to the income statement and balance sheet.

ALTERNATE PROBLEMS
···

P1–1A On May 1, Better Bob, Inc. was started. A summary of May transactions is presented below.

Analyze transactions and compute net income.
(SO 6, 7)

1. Stockholders invested $15,000 cash in the Fox Valley Bank in the name of the business.
2. Purchased equipment for $5,000 cash.
3. Paid $400 cash for May rent.
4. Paid $500 cash for parts and supplies.
5. Incurred $250 of advertising costs in the Beacon News on account.
6. Received $4,100 in cash from customers for repair service.
7. Dividends of $500 were paid.
8. Paid part-time employee salaries $1,000.
9. Paid utility bills $140.
10. Provided repair service on account to customers, $200.
11. Collected cash of $150 for services billed in transaction (11).

Instructions

(a) Prepare a tabular analysis of the transactions, using the following column headings: Cash, Accounts Receivable, Supplies, Equipment, Accounts Payable, Common Stock and Retained Earnings. Revenue is called service revenue.

(b) From an analysis of the column, Retained Earnings, compute the net income or net loss for May.

P1–2A On August 31, the balance sheet of Cook Corporation showed Cash $9,000, Accounts Receivable $1,700, Supplies $600, Office Equipment $6,000, Accounts Payable $3,600, Common Stock $13,000, and Retained Earnings $700. During September the following transactions occurred:

Analyze transactions and prepare income statement and retained earnings statement.
(SO 6, 7, 8)

1. Paid $3,100 cash on accounts payable.
2. Collected $1,300 of accounts receivable.
3. Purchased additional office equipment for $2,100, paying $800 in cash and the balance on account.
4. Earned fees of $5,900, of which $2,500 is paid in cash and the balance is due in October.
5. Dividends of $600 were paid.
6. Paid salaries $700, rent for September $900, and advertising expense $100.
7. Incurred utility expenses for month on account, $170.
8. Received $8,000 from Hilldale Bank—money borrowed on a note payable.

Instructions

(a) Prepare a tabular analysis of the September transactions beginning with August 31 balances. The column headings should be as follows: Cash + Accounts Receivable +

Supplies + Office Equipment = Notes Payable + Accounts Payable + Common Stock + Retained Earnings.

(b) Prepare an income statement for September, a retained earnings statement for September, and a balance sheet at September 30.

Prepare income statement, retained earnings statement, and balance sheet.
(SO 8)

P1–3A Skyline Flying School, Inc. was started on May 1 with an investment of $45,000 cash. Following are the assets and liabilities of the company on May 31, 1996, and the revenues and expenses for the month of May.

Cash	$ 8,000	Notes Payable	$30,000
Accounts Receivable	7,000	Rent Expense	1,200
Equipment	64,000	Repair Expense	400
Fees Earned	9,600	Fuel Expense	2,200
Advertising Expense	500	Insurance Expense	400
		Accounts Payable	800

No additional investments were made by stockholders in May, but a dividend of $1,700 in cash was paid.

Instructions

(a) Prepare an income statement and retained earnings statement for the month of May and a balance sheet at May 31.

(b) Prepare an income statement and retained earnings statement for May assuming the following data are not included above: (1) $800 of fees were earned and billed but not collected at May 31, and (2) $5,300 of fuel expense was incurred but not paid.

Prepare income statement and retained earnings statement.
(SO 8)

P1–4A Presented below are the November 1996 transactions that affected the retained earnings account of the Michael Bolton Corp.

Transaction	Amount	Description
(7)	$ 700	Property tax expense
(9)	6,000	Service revenue
(10)	350	Supplies expense
(13)	4,000	Wage expense
(16)	300	Utilities expense
(18)	1,250	Rent expense
(19)	450	Advertising expense
(22)	2,000	Service revenue
(23)	800	Dividends
(25)	600	Repair expense
(27)	400	Auto expense
(31)	9,000	Service revenue
(32)	1,800	Dividends
(33)	4,000	Wage expense
(34)	500	Utilities expense

In reviewing the account, Mr. Bolton realized that his new bookkeeper had made the following error:

Transaction (27) was actually a payment for wage expense.

Instructions

(a) Prepare an income statement for the month of November.

(b) Prepare a retained earnings statement for November, assuming that the beginning retained earnings balance was $9,500 on November 1.

Determine financial statement amounts and prepare retained earnings statements.
(SO 7, 8)

P1–5A Financial statement information about four different companies is as follows:

	Yanni Company	Selena Company	Candlebox Company	Winans Company
January 1, 1996:				
Assets	$ 90,000	$110,000	(g)	$160,000
Liabilities	50,000	(d)	75,000	(j)
Stockholders' equity	(a)	60,000	55,000	90,000

December 31, 1996:

Assets	(b)	150,000	200,000	(k)
Liabilities	55,000	65,000	(h)	80,000
Stockholders' equity	58,000	(e)	130,000	170,000
Stockholders' equity changes in year:				
Additional investment	(c)	15,000	10,000	15,000
Dividends	25,000	(f)	14,000	20,000
Total revenues	350,000	420,000	(i)	520,000
Total expenses	320,000	385,000	350,000	(l)

Instructions

(a) Determine the missing amounts.

(b) Prepare the retained earnings statement for Selena Company. Assume that the beginning balance of retained earnings was zero.

(c) ▭▭▭▭▭► Write a memorandum explaining the sequence for preparing financial statements and the interrelationship of the retained earnings statement to the income statement and balance sheet.

►*Broadening Your Perspective*

*F*INANCIAL REPORTING PROBLEM—PEPSICO, INC.
• •

The actual financial statements of PepsiCo, Inc., as presented in the company's 1995 Annual Report, are contained in Appendix A (at the back of the textbook). Refer to PepsiCo's financial statements and answer the following questions:

1. What were PepsiCo's total assets at December 30, 1995? At December 31, 1994?
2. How much cash (and cash equivalents) did PepsiCo have on December 30, 1995?
3. What amount of accounts payable did PepsiCo report on December 30, 1995? On December 31, 1994?
4. What were PepsiCo's net sales in 1993? In 1994? In 1995?
5. What is the amount of the change in PepsiCo's net income from 1994 to 1995?
6. The accounting equation is: Assets = Liabilities + Stockholders' Equity. Replacing the words in that equation with dollar amounts, what is PepsiCo's accounting equation at December 30, 1995? (Hint: Stockholders' equity is equivalent to shareholders' equity.)

*C*OMPARATIVE ANALYSIS PROBLEM—
COCA-COLA COMPANY VS. PEPSICO, INC.
• •

The financial statements of Coca-Cola Company are presented at the end of this chapter and PepsiCo's financial statements are presented in Appendix A.

Instructions

(a) Based on the information contained in these financial statements, determine the following for each company:
   (1) Total assets at December 31, 1995.
   (2) Accounts (notes) receivable, less allowances at December 31, 1995.
   (3) Net sales for 1995.
   (4) Net income for 1995.

(b) What conclusions concerning the two companies can be drawn from these data?

INTERPRETATION OF FINANCIAL STATEMENTS

Mini-Case One—Med/Waste, Inc.

Med/Waste, Inc. provides commercial cleaning and medical waste disposal services to hospitals and other large healthcare providers, primarily in the state of Florida. In its 1995 statement of cash flows, Med/Waste showed increases in cash from investing and financing activities and a net decrease in cash from operations. The largest sources of cash were the sale of investments and the repayment of a loan to a director.

Instructions

1. What concerns might a creditor of Med/Waste have about this information reported in the statement of cash flows? What additional information might a creditor seek to confirm or soften these concerns?
2. Would an investor view this information from the statement of cash flows as negative or positive if the overall cash position improved? Explain.

Mini-Case Two—Lincoln Village Properties, Inc.

Lincoln Village Properties, Inc. is a property management firm in Springfield, Missouri that provides residential rental property management, such as grounds maintenance, minor repair service, and trash collection for an annual fee. A portion of Lincoln Village's 1995 balance sheet follows:

Assets	
Cash	$10,000
Accounts Receivable	2,000
Supplies Inventory	8,000
Machinery and Equipment, net	80,000
Other noncurrent assets	5,000
Total Assets	$105,000

During 1996, the following events occurred:

1. $25,000 of machinery, net, was sold for cash
2. $5,000 in supplies were used
3. $100,000 was received from cash sales
4. $115,000 was paid for cash expenses
5. Customers contracted for $150,000 in services on credit.
6. Lincoln Village Properties collected $148,000 from accounts receivable.

Instructions

Prepare the 1996 Assets portion of the balance sheet for Lincoln Village Properties.

DECISION CASE

Betsy and Bill King, local golf stars, formed Parbuster Corporation on March 1, 1996. They invested $10,000 of their cash savings in the business and received $10,000 of common stock. A caddy shack was constructed for cash at a cost of $4,000 and $800 was spent on golf balls and golf clubs. The corporation leased five acres of land at a cost of $1,000 per month and paid the first month's rent. During the first month, advertising costs totaled $750 of which $150 was unpaid at March 31, and $400 was paid to members of the high school golf team for retrieving golf balls. All fees from customers were deposited in the company's bank account. On March 15, a dividend of $700 in cash was paid. A $100 utility bill was received on March 31 but it was not paid. On March 31, the balance in the company's bank account was $8,650.

Betsy and Bill thought Parbuster had a pretty good first month of operations. However, their estimates of profitability ranged from a loss of $1,350 to net income of $3,200.

Instructions

(a) How could the Kites have concluded that the business operated at a loss of $1,350? Was this a valid basis on which to determine net income?

(b) How could the Kites have concluded that the business operated at a net income of $3,200? (Hint: Prepare a balance sheet at March 31.) Was this a valid basis on which to determine net income?

(c) Without preparing an income statement, determine the actual net income for March.

(d) What were the fees earned in March?

COMMUNICATION ACTIVITY

Debra Joan is the bookkeeper for Vermont Company. Debra has been trying to get the balance sheet of Vermont Company to balance. Vermont's balance sheet is as follows:

VERMONT COMPANY
Balance Sheet
For the Month Ended December 31, 1996

Assets		Liabilities	
Equipment	$20,500	Common stock	$15,000
Cash	9,000	Retained Earnings	6,000
Supplies	2,000	Accounts receivable	(3,000)
Accounts payable	(5,000)	Dividends	(2,000)
	$26,500	Notes payable	10,500
			$26,500

Instructions
Explain to Debra Joan in a memo why the original balance sheet is incorrect and what should be done to correct it.

GROUP ACTIVITY

Hattie Company had the following account balances:

Rent expense	$ 800	Utilities expense	$ 300
Notes payable	700	Accounts receivable	2,000
Cash	10,500	Telephone expense	100
Common stock	10,000	Accounts payable	3,000
Salaries expense	500	Equipment	3,000
Revenue	3,500	Retained earnings, July 1	–0–

Instructions
Your instructor will divide the class into groups of five or six students. When you are told to begin, prepare Hattie Company's income statement, retained earnings statement, and balance sheet for July 31. The first group to finish with the correct answer wins!

ETHICS CASE

After numerous campus interviews, Joe Catmus, a senior at Great Eastern College, received two office interview invitations from the Baltimore offices of two large firms. Both firms offered to cover his out-of-pocket expenses (travel, hotel, and meal). He scheduled the interviews for both firms on the same day, one in the morning and one in the afternoon. At the conclusion of each interview, he submitted to both firms his total out-of-pocket expenses for the trip to Baltimore, $244: mileage $70 (280 miles at $.25), hotel $120, meals $36, parking and tolls $18, for a total of $244. He believes this approach is appropriate. If he had made two trips, his cost would have been two times $244. He is also certain that neither firm knew he had visited the other on that same trip. Within ten days Joe received two checks in the mail, each in the amount of $244.

Instructions
   (a) Who are the stakeholders (affected parties) in this situation?
   (b) What are the ethical issues in this case?
   (c) What would you do in this situation?

RESEARCH ASSIGNMENT

1. *The Wall Street Journal* (WSJ), published weekdays by Dow Jones & Company, Inc., is a premier source of business information. Examine a recent copy of the WSJ and answer the following questions.

   (a) How many separate sections are included in the WSJ? What are the contents of each section?
   (b) An index of the companies referenced in each edition is included on page 2 of section B. Select a company from the index and read the associated article. What is the article about? Identify any accounting-related issues discussed in the article?

2. Most libraries have company annual reports on file or available on microfiche. Obtain copies of the financial statements of two companies and answer the following questions.

   (a) What were the total assets, total liabilities, and total stockholders' equity at the most recent balance sheet date?
   (b) Mathematically demonstrate that the basic accounting equation holds for each company.
   (c) What were the total current assets and total current liabilities at the most recent balance sheet date?
   (d) What were the net sales (or revenue) and net income in the most recent income statement?

CRITICAL THINKING
▸ *A Real-World Focus: Air Transportation Holding Company Inc.*

Founded in 1980, **Air Transportation Holding Company** *operates contract cargo shipping, specializing in small, overnight deliveries throughout the eastern United States. The company flies approximately 80 routes, as specified in its contracts with Federal Express. It has hangars and maintenance facilities in North Carolina, Michigan, and South Carolina.*

The specific assets, liabilities, and subdivisions of stockholders' equity of any business depend on the type of business being operated. Management of Air Transportation Holding Company explained the year's results of operations as follows:

Operating expenses increased $5,498,000 (29.9%) to $23,904,000 for 1993 compared to 1992. The increase in operating expenses consisted of the following changes: cost of flight operations increased $2,313,000 (25.7%) as a result of increases in pilot and flight personnel and costs associated with travel and landing fees which were partially offset by decreased aircraft lease and fuel costs; maintenance expense increased $2,850,000 (42.9%) primarily as a result of increases in aircraft parts purchases and mechanic and maintenance personnel costs (due to start-up of satellite maintenance facility and the operation of additional aircraft); the general and administrative expense increase of $470,000 (17.3%) resulted from increases in operational and clerical staffing related to expansion of the aircraft fleet operated.

Instructions
   (a) Recall the definition of an asset. Can you identify three specific types of assets owned by Air Transportation Holding Company?
   (b) The discussion above is largely about the operating expenses of the company. Identify five expenses of operations that Air Transportation incurs.
   (c) When this company renders service by providing air transportation, what account affecting stockholders' equity is increased?

Answers to Self-Study Questions
1. b   2. d   3. c   4. c   5. a   6. d   7. b   8. a   9. b   10. c

Before studying this chapter, you should know or, if necessary, review:

a. *What are assets, liabilities, common stock, retained earnings, dividends, revenues, and expenses. (Ch. 1, pp. 11–14)*
b. *Why assets equal liabilities plus stockholders' equity. (Ch. 1, pp. 11–13)*
c. *What transactions are and how they affect the basic accounting equation. (Ch. 1, pp. 15–19)*

Concepts for Review highlight accounting concepts that you need to understand from earlier chapters before starting the new chapter.

Her Classroom Is the Real World

SAN DIEGO, Calif. — Gabriella Torres of San Diego learned how to record transactions on a computer before she took her first accounting course. The reason: by day, she manages the office of Diabetes & Endocrine Associates, a medical practice with an office located near San Diego State University. The doctors' office uses a computer package that makes recording transactions quite easy for Gabriella. She attends night school and hopes to graduate within six years. "The doctors have really been accommodating to my school schedule."

Working during the day allows Gabriella to bring a real-world perspective to the classroom. In turn, studying business subjects at night makes her job easier. She is in charge of paying the bills for the medical practice, making sure the bank statement reconciles with the checkbook, hiring office staff, pre-paring patient bills, and maintaining accounts receivable. "I really love my job," she says, which is one reason she prefers to work days and go to school at night.

Taking her first accounting course helped Gabriella understand how the journal entries, the accounts, and financial statements fit together. Unlike doing homework assignments, though, the computer package at work catches some of her errors. "It won't let you proceed from one accounting entry to the next unless the entry balances," she says. In fact, there are no "books" at all, just diskettes and printouts. ◀

CHAPTER · **2**

*T*HE RECORDING PROCESS

▶ **STUDY OBJECTIVES** ◀

After studying this chapter, you should be able to:

1. *Explain what an account is and how it helps in the recording process.*
2. *Define debits and credits and explain how they are used to record business transactions.*
3. *Identify the basic steps in the recording process.*
4. *Explain what a journal is and how it helps in the recording process.*
5. *Explain what a ledger is and how it helps in the recording process.*
6. *Explain what posting is and how it helps in the recording process.*
7. *Prepare a trial balance and explain its purposes.*
8. *Identify the key points in comparing manual and computerized accounting systems.*

In Chapter 1, we analyzed business transactions in terms of the accounting equation and presented the cumulative effects of these transactions in tabular form. Imagine a medical practice such as Diabetes & Endocrine Associates using the same tabular format as Softbyte Inc. to keep track of every one of its transactions. In a single day, this medical practice engages in hundreds of business transactions. To record each transaction this way would be impractical, expensive, and unnecessary.

As a result, a set of procedures and records are used to make it possible to keep track of and accumulate transaction data more easily. In this chapter we will introduce and illustrate the basic procedures and records that are used. The organization and content of the chapter are as follows:

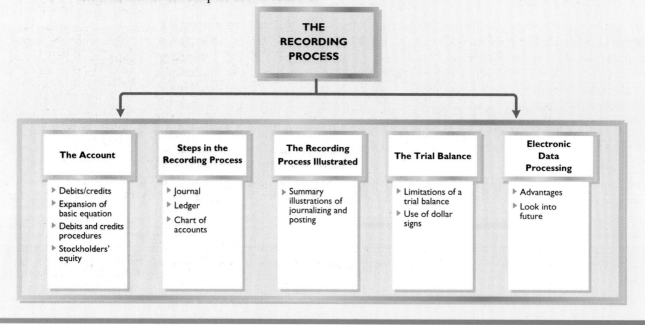

THE RECORDING PROCESS				
The Account	**Steps in the Recording Process**	**The Recording Process Illustrated**	**The Trial Balance**	**Electronic Data Processing**
▸ Debits/credits ▸ Expansion of basic equation ▸ Debits and credits procedures ▸ Stockholders' equity	▸ Journal ▸ Ledger ▸ Chart of accounts	▸ Summary illustrations of journalizing and posting	▸ Limitations of a trial balance ▸ Use of dollar signs	▸ Advantages ▸ Look into future

◤he Account

An account is an individual accounting record of increases and decreases in a specific asset, liability, or stockholders' equity item. For example, Softbyte Inc. (discussed in Chapter 1) would have separate accounts for Cash, Accounts Receivable, Accounts Payable, Service Revenue, Salaries Expense, and so on. In its simplest form, an account consists of three parts: (1) the title of the account, (2) a left or debit side, and (3) a right or credit side. Because the alignment of these parts of an account resembles the letter T, it is referred to as a T account. The basic form of an account is shown in Illustration 2-1.

Illustration 2-1

Basic form of account

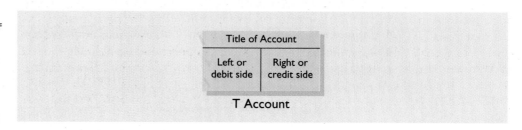

Title of Account	
Left or debit side	Right or credit side

T Account

Helpful hint The T account is a standard shorthand in accounting that helps make clear the effects of transactions on individual accounts.

This form of account will be used often throughout this book to explain basic accounting relationships.

►*T*echnology in *A*ction

Computerized and manual accounting systems basically parallel one another. Most of the procedures are handled by electronic circuitry in computerized systems. They seem to occur invisibly. Therefore, to fully comprehend how computerized systems operate, it is necessary to illustrate and understand manual approaches for processing accounting data.

Debits and Credits

The terms **debit** and **credit** mean left and right, respectively. They are commonly abbreviated as Dr. for debit and Cr. for credit.[1] These terms do not mean increase or decrease. The terms debit and credit are used repeatedly in the recording process. For example, the act of entering an amount on the left side of an account is called **debiting** the account, and making an entry on the right side is **crediting** the account. When the totals of the two sides are compared, an account will have a **debit balance** if the total of the debit amounts exceeds the credits. Conversely, an account will have a **credit balance** if the credit amounts exceed the debits.

The procedure of having debits on the left and credits on the right is an accounting custom, or rule. We could function just as well if debits and credits were reversed. However, the custom of having debits on the left side of an account and credits on the right side (like the custom of driving on the right-hand side of the road) has been adopted in the United States. **This rule applies to all accounts.**

The procedure of recording debits and credits in an account is shown in Illustration 2-2 for the cash transactions of Softbyte Inc. The data are taken from the cash column of the tabular summary in Illustration 1-7.

STUDY OBJECTIVE

2

Define debits and credits and explain how they are used to record business transactions.

Helpful hint The word credit has a different meaning in accounting than it has in everyday life. For accounting purposes, think of the terms debit and credit solely as directional signals. Debit—use the left side of the account; credit—use the right side.

Illustration 2-2

Tabular summary compared to account form

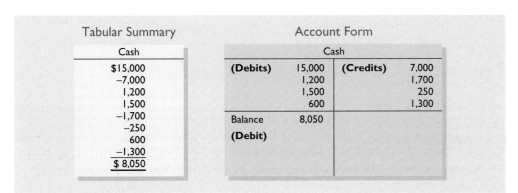

Every positive item in the tabular summary represents a receipt of cash; every negative amount constitutes a payment of cash. Notice that in the account form the increases in cash are recorded as debits, and the decreases in cash are recorded as credits. Having increases on one side and decreases on the other helps in determining the totals of each side of the account as well as the balance in the account. The account balance, a debit of $8,050, indicates that Softbyte Inc. has had $8,050 more increases than decreases in cash. That is, it has $8,050 in its Cash account.

[1]These abbreviations come from the Latin words *debere* (Dr.) and *credere* (Cr.).

Helpful hint   Debits must equal credits for each transaction.

Debit and Credit Procedure

In Chapter 1 you learned the effect of a transaction on the basic accounting equation. Remember that each transaction must affect two or more accounts to keep the basic accounting equation in balance. In other words, for each transaction debits must equal credits in the accounts. The equality of debits and credits provides the basis for the double-entry system of recording transactions (sometimes referred to as double-entry bookkeeping).

Under the universally used double-entry system, the dual (two-sided) effect of each transaction is recorded in appropriate accounts. This system provides a logical method for recording transactions. It also offers a means of proving the accuracy of the recorded amounts. If every transaction is recorded with equal debits and credits, then the sum of all the debits to the accounts must equal the sum of all the credits.

The double-entry system for determining the equality of the accounting equation is much more efficient than the plus/minus procedure used in Chapter 1. There, it was necessary after each transaction to compare total assets with total liabilities and stockholders' equity to determine the equality of the two sides of the accounting equation.

▸ *International note*

As indicated in Chapter 1, an Italian named Luca Pacioli published the first accounting textbook in 1494. His book is famous for showing how to use the double-entry system.

Assets and Liabilities

In the Softbyte Inc. illustration above, increases in cash—an asset—were entered on the left side, and decreases in cash were entered on the right side. We know that both sides of the basic equation (assets = liabilities + stockholders' equity) must be equal; it then follows that increases and decreases in liabilities will have to be recorded opposite from increases and decreases in assets. Thus, increases in liabilities must be entered on the right or credit side, and decreases in liabilities must be entered on the left or debit side. The effects that debits and credits have on assets and liabilities are summarized as follows:

Illustration 2-3

Debit and credit effects—assets and liabilities

Debits	Credits
Increase assets	Decrease assets
Decrease liabilities	Increase liabilities

Debits to a specific asset account should exceed the credits to that account, and credits to a liability account should exceed debits to that account. Thus, asset accounts normally show debit balances, and liability accounts normally show credit balances. The normal balances may be diagrammed as follows:

Illustration 2-4

Normal balances—assets and liabilities

Helpful hint   The normal balance for an account is always the same as the increase side.

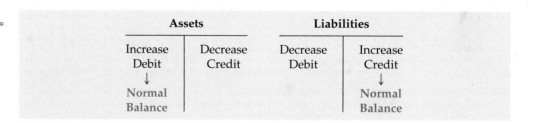

An awareness of the normal balance in an account may help you when you are trying to trace errors. For example, a credit balance in an asset account such as Land or a debit balance in a liability account such as Wages Payable would indicate errors in recording. Occasionally, however, an abnormal balance may

►Technology in Action

In automated systems, the computer is programmed to flag these normal balance exceptions and to print out error or exception reports. In manual systems, careful visual inspection of the accounts is required to detect normal balance problems.

be correct. The Cash account, for example, will have a credit balance when a company has overdrawn its bank balance (i.e., written a "bad" check).

Stockholders' Equity

As indicated in Chapter 1, there are five subdivisions of stockholders' equity: Common stock, retained earnings, dividends, revenues, and expenses. In a double-entry system, accounts are kept for each of these subdivisions as explained below.

Common Stock. Common stock is issued in exchange for the owners' investment paid in to the corporation. The Common Stock account is increased by credits and decreased by debits. When cash is invested in the business in exchange for shares of the corporation's stock, Cash is debited and Common Stock is credited.

The rules of debit and credit for the Common Stock account are stated as follows:

Debits	Credits
Decrease Common Stock	Increase Common Stock

Illustration 2-5

Debit and credit effect—common stock

The normal balance in this account may be diagrammed as follows:

Common Stock

Decrease Debit	Increase Credit ↓ Normal Balance

Illustration 2-6

Normal balance—common stock

Helpful hint The rules for debit and credit and the normal balance of common stock are the same as for liabilities.

Retained Earnings. Retained earnings is net income that is retained in the business. It represents the portion of stockholders' equity which has been accumulated through the profitable operation of the business. Retained earnings is increased by credits (net income) and decreased by debits (dividends or net losses) as shown below.

Retained Earnings

Decrease Debit	Increase Credit ↓ Normal Balance

Illustration 2-7

Debit and credit effect and normal balance—retained earnings

Dividends.   A dividend is a distribution by a corporation to its stockholders on a pro rata (equal) basis. The most common form of a distribution is a cash dividend. Dividends can be declared (authorized) only by the board of directors and are a reduction of the stockholders' claims on retained earnings. The Dividends account is increased by debits and decreased by credits with a normal debit balance as shown below.

Illustration 2-8

Debit and credit effect and normal balance—dividends

	Dividends	
Increase Debit ↓ Normal Balance		Decrease Credit

Revenues and Expenses

Helpful hint Because revenues increase stockholders' equity, a revenue account has the same debit and credit rules as does the common stock account. Conversely, expenses have the opposite effect.

When revenues are earned, stockholders' equity is increased. Revenues are a subdivision of stockholders' equity that provides information as to why stockholders' equity increased. Revenue accounts are increased by credits and decreased by debits. Accordingly, **the effect of debits and credits on revenue accounts is identical to their effect on stockholders' equity**.

On the other hand, expenses decrease stockholders' equity. As a result, expenses are recorded by debits. Since expenses are the negative factor in the computation of net income, and revenues are the positive factor, it is logical that the increase and decrease sides of expense accounts should be the reverse of revenue accounts. Thus, expense accounts are increased by debits and decreased by credits. The effect of debits and credits on revenues and expenses may be stated as follows:

Illustration 2-9

Debit and credit effects— revenues and expenses

Debits	Credits
Decrease revenues Increase expenses	Increase revenues Decrease expenses

Credits to revenue accounts should exceed the debits, and debits to expense accounts should exceed credits. Thus, revenue accounts normally show credit balances and expense accounts normally show debit balances. The normal balances may be diagrammed as follows:

Illustration 2-10

Normal balances—revenues and expenses

	Revenues			Expenses	
Decrease Debit		Increase Credit ↓ Normal Balance	Increase Debit ↓ Normal Balance		Decrease Credit

Accounting in Action ► *Business Insight*

The Chicago Cubs baseball team has the following major revenue and expense accounts:

Revenues	**Expenses**
Admissions (ticket sales)	Players' salaries
Concessions	Administrative salaries
Television and radio	Travel
Advertising	Ballpark maintenance

Stockholders' Equity Relationships

As indicated in Chapter 1, common stock and retained earnings are reported in the stockholders' equity section of the balance sheet. Dividends are reported on the retained earnings statement. Revenues and expenses are reported on the income statement. Dividends, revenues, and expenses are eventually transferred to retained earnings at the end of the period. As a result, changes in any one of these three items affects stockholders' equity. The relationships related to stockholders' equity are shown in Illustration 2-11.

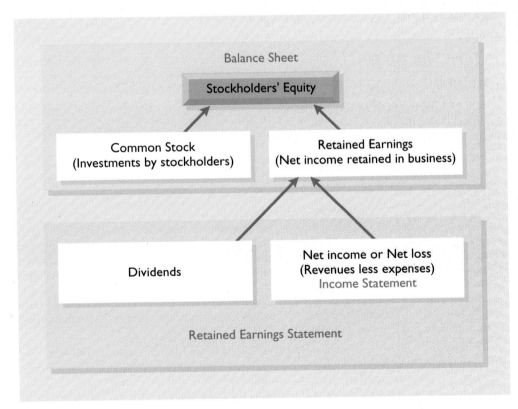

Illustration 2-11

Stockholders' equity relationships

Expansion of Basic Equation

You have already learned the basic accounting equation. Illustration 2-12 expands this equation to show the accounts that comprise stockholders' equity. In addition, the debit/credit rules and effects on each type of account are illustrated.

Study this diagram carefully. It will help you understand the fundamentals of the double-entry system. Like the basic equation, the expanded basic equation must be in balance (total debits equal total credits).

Illustration 2-12

Expanded basic equation and debit/credit rules and effects

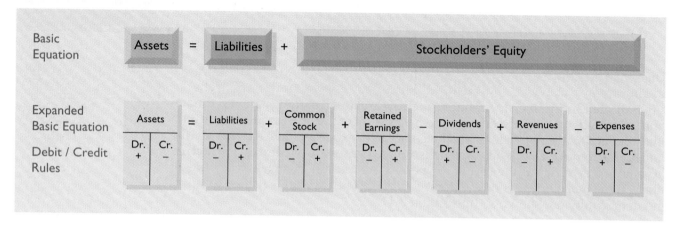

Before You Go On . . .

▶ Review It

1. What do the terms debit and credit mean?
2. What are the debit and credit effects on assets, liabilities, and stockholders' equity?
3. What are the debit and credit effects on revenues, expenses, and dividends?
4. What are the normal balances for individual asset, liability, and stockholders' equity accounts?

▶ Do It

Kate Browne, president of Hair It Is, Inc., has just rented space in a shopping mall for the purpose of opening and operating a beauty salon. Long before opening day and before purchasing equipment, hiring assistants, and remodeling the space, Kate is strongly advised to set up a double-entry set of accounting records in which to record all of her business transactions.

Identify the balance sheet accounts that Hair It Is, Inc. will likely need to record the transactions necessary to establish and open for business. Also, indicate whether the normal balance of each account is a debit or a credit.

Reasoning: To start the business, Hair It Is, Inc. will need to have asset accounts for each different type of asset invested in the business. In addition, the corporation will need liability accounts for debts incurred by the business. Hair It Is, Inc. will only need one stockholders' equity account for common stock when it begins the business. The other stockholders' equity accounts will be needed only after business has commenced.

Solution: Hair It Is, Inc. would likely need the following accounts in which to record the transactions necessary to establish and ready the beauty salon for opening day: Cash (debit balance); Equipment (debit balance); Supplies (debit balance); Accounts Payable (credit balance); Notes Payable (credit balance), if the business borrows money; and Common Stock (credit balance).

Related exercise material: BE2–1, BE2–2, E2–1, and E2–3.

Steps in the Recording Process

Although it is possible to enter transaction information directly into the accounts, few businesses do so. In practically every business, the basic steps in the recording process are:

1. Analyze each transaction in terms of its effect on the accounts.
2. Enter the transaction information in a journal (book of original entry).
3. Transfer the journal information to the appropriate accounts in the ledger (book of accounts).

The actual sequence of events begins with the transaction. Evidence of the transaction comes in the form of a **business document**, such as a sales slip, a check, a bill, or a cash register tape. This evidence is analyzed to determine the effect of the transaction on specific accounts. The transaction is then entered in the journal. Finally, the journal entry is transferred to the designated accounts in the ledger. The sequence of events in the recording process can be diagrammed as follows:

> **STUDY OBJECTIVE**
> ····· **3** ·····
> *Identify the basic steps in the recording process.*

> **Helpful hint** Proper analysis of documentary evidence is as critical to correct accounting records as turning the ignition is to starting an automobile. You can't have one without the other.

> **Illustration 2-13**
>
> *The recording process*

The Recording Process

Analyze each transaction

Enter transaction in a journal

Transfer journal information to ledger accounts

The basic steps in the recording process occur repeatedly in every business enterprise. The analysis of transactions has already been illustrated, and further examples of this step will be given in this and later chapters. The other steps in the recording process are explained in the next sections.

The Journal

Transactions are initially recorded in chronological order in a journal before being transferred to the accounts. Thus, the journal is referred to as the book of original entry. For each transaction the journal shows the debit and credit effects on specific accounts. Companies may use various kinds of journals, but every company has the most basic form of journal, a general journal. Typically, a general journal has spaces for dates, account titles and explanations, references, and two money columns. Whenever the term journal is used in this textbook without a modifying adjective, it will mean the general journal.

> **STUDY OBJECTIVE**
> ····· **4** ·····
> *Explain what a journal is and how it helps in the recording process.*

The journal makes several significant contributions to the recording process:

1. It discloses in one place the complete effect of a transaction.
2. It provides a chronological record of transactions.
3. It helps to prevent or locate errors because the debit and credit amounts for each entry can be readily compared.

Journalizing

Entering transaction data in the journal is known as journalizing. Separate journal entries are made for each transaction. A complete entry consists of: (1) the date of the transaction, (2) the accounts and amounts to be debited and credited, and (3) a brief explanation of the transaction.

To illustrate the technique of journalizing, the first two transactions of Softbyte Inc. are journalized in Illustration 2-14 using the first page (J1) of the general journal. These transactions were: September 1, stockholders invested $15,000 cash in the corporation in exchange for shares of stock, and computer equipment was purchased for $7,000 cash.

Illustration 2-14

Technique of journalizing

GENERAL JOURNAL					J1
Date	Account Titles and Explanation	Ref.	Debit	Credit
1996 Sept. 1	Cash		15,000	
	Common Stock			15,000
	(Issued shares of stock for cash)			
1	Computer Equipment		7,000	
	Cash			7,000
	(Purchased equipment for cash)			

Helpful hint Practice makes perfect in journalizing. Use the correct form and content every time.

The standard form and content of journal entries are as follows:

1. The date of the transaction is entered in the Date column. The date recorded should include the year, month, and day of the transaction.
2. The debit account title (that is, the account to be debited) is entered first at the extreme left margin of the column headed Account Titles and Explanation. The credit account title (that is, the account to be credited) is then entered on the next line, indented under the line above. The indentation decreases the possibility of switching the debit and credit amounts.
3. The amounts for the debits are recorded in the Debit (left) column and the amounts for the credits are recorded in the Credit (right) column.
4. A brief explanation of the transaction is given.
5. A space is left between journal entries. The blank space separates individual journal entries and makes the entire journal easier to read.
6. The column entitled Ref. (which stands for reference) is left blank at the time the journal entry is made. The Reference column is used later when the journal entries are transferred to the ledger accounts. At that time, the ledger account number is placed in the Reference column to indicate where the amount in the journal entry was transferred.

It is important to use correct and specific account titles in journalizing. Since most accounts appear later in the financial statements, erroneous account titles lead to incorrect financial statements. Some flexibility exists initially in selecting account titles. The main criterion is that each title must appropriately describe the content of the account. For example, the account title used for the cost of delivery trucks may be Delivery Equipment, Delivery Trucks, or Trucks. Once a company chooses the specific title to use, all subsequent transactions involving the account should be recorded under that account title.[2]

If an entry involves only two accounts, one debit and one credit, it is considered a **simple entry**. For some transactions, however, it may be necessary to use more than two accounts in journalizing. Imagine, for example, the numerous accounts needed by General Electric to record the acquisition of all the assets and liabilities of RCA in what was one of the largest mergers ever completed. When three or more accounts are required in one journal entry, the entry is referred to as a **compound entry**. To illustrate, assume that on July 1, Butler Company purchases a delivery truck costing $14,000 by paying $8,000 cash and the balance on account (to be paid at a later date). The entry is as follows:

Illustration 2-15

Compound journal entry

GENERAL JOURNAL				J1
Date	Account Titles and Explanation	Ref.	Debit	Credit
1996 July 1	Delivery Equipment		14,000	
	Cash			8,000
	Accounts Payable			6,000
	(Purchased truck for cash with balance on account)			

In a compound entry, it is important to determine that the total debit and credit amounts are equal. Also, the standard format requires that all debits be listed before the credits are listed.

Before You Go On . . .

► *Review It*

1. What is the correct sequence of the steps in the recording process?
2. What contribution does the journal make to the recording process?
3. What is the standard form and content of a journal entry made in the general journal?

► *Do It*

In establishing her beauty salon, Hair It Is, Inc., Kate Browne as president and sole stockholder engaged in the following activities:

1. Opened a bank account in the name of Hair It Is, Inc. and deposited $20,000 of her own money in this account in exchange for shares of common stock.
2. Purchased on account (to be paid in 30 days) equipment, for a total cost of $4,800.
3. Interviewed three persons for the position of beautician.

In what form (type of record) should Hair It Is, Inc. record these three activities? Prepare the entries to record the transactions.

---

[2]In homework problems, when specific account titles are given, they should be used. When account titles are not given, you may select account titles that identify the nature and content of each account. The account titles used in journalizing should not contain explanations such as Cash Paid or Cash Received.

Reasoning: Hair It Is, Inc. should record the transactions in a journal, which is a chronological record of the transactions. The record should be a complete and accurate representation of the transactions' effects on the business's assets, liabilities, and stockholders' equity.

Solution: Each transaction that is recorded is entered in the general journal. The three activities would be recorded as follows:

1. Cash   20,000
        Common Stock   20,000
            (Issued shares of stock for cash)
2. Equipment   4,800
        Accounts Payable   4,800
            (Purchased equipment on account)
3. No entry because no transaction has occurred.

Related exercise material: BE2–3, BE2–5, BE2–6, E2–2, E2–4, E2–6, E2–7, and E2–8.

The Ledger

STUDY OBJECTIVE
5
Explain what a ledger is and how it helps in the recording process.

The entire group of accounts maintained by a company is referred to collectively as the ledger. The ledger keeps in one place all the information about changes in specific account balances.

Companies may use various kinds of ledgers, but every company has a general ledger. A general ledger contains all the assets, liabilities, and stockholders' equity accounts, as shown in Illustration 2-16. A business can use a looseleaf binder or card file for the ledger with each account kept on a separate sheet or card. Whenever the term ledger is used in this textbook without a modifying adjective, it will mean the general ledger.

Illustration 2-16

The general ledger

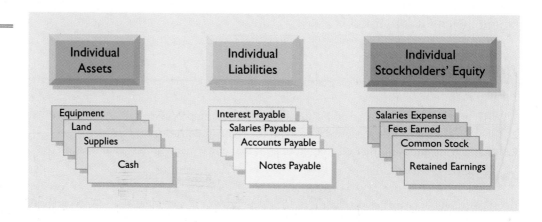

The ledger should be arranged in statement order beginning with the balance sheet accounts. First in order are the asset accounts, followed by liability accounts, stockholders' equity accounts, revenues, and expenses. Each account is numbered for easier identification.

The information in the ledger provides management with the balances in various accounts. For example, the Cash account enables management to determine the amount of cash that is available to meet current obligations. Amounts due from customers and the amounts owed to creditors can be determined by examining the Accounts Receivable and Accounts Payable accounts, respectively.

►Accounting in Action ► *Business Insight*

In his autobiography Sam Walton described the double-entry accounting system he began the Wal-Mart empire with: "We kept a little pigeonhole on the wall for the cash receipts and paperwork of each [Wal-Mart] store. I had a blue binder ledger book for each store. When we added a store, we added a pigeonhole. We did this at least up to twenty stores. Then once a month, the bookkeeper and I would enter the merchandise, enter the sales, enter the cash, and balance it."

Source: Sam Walton, Made in America *(New York: Doubleday, 1992), p. 53.*

Standard Form of Account

The simple T-account form of an account used in an accounting textbook is often very useful for illustration and analysis purposes. However, in practice, the account forms used in ledgers are much more structured. A form widely used in a manual system is shown in Illustration 2-17, using assumed data from a cash account.

| CASH | | | | | No. 10 |
Date	Explanation	Ref.	Debit	Credit	Balance
1996					
June 1			25,000		25,000
2				8,000	17,000
3			4,200		21,200
9			7,500		28,700
17				11,700	17,000
20				250	16,750
30				7,300	9,450

Illustration 2-17
Three-column form of account

Helpful hint When there is only one balance column, the amount shown is assumed to be the normal balance unless the balance is specifically identified as abnormal by putting it in parentheses or in red. Alternatively, there are forms that contain two balance columns.

This form has three money columns—debit, credit, and balance. The balance in the account is determined after each transaction. Thus, this form is often called the three-column form of account. Note that the explanation space and reference columns are used to provide special information about the transaction.

Posting

The procedure of transferring journal entries to the ledger accounts is called posting. **This phase of the recording process accumulates the effects of journalized transactions in the individual accounts.**

STUDY OBJECTIVE 6

Explain what posting is and how it helps in the recording process.

►Technology in Action

Determining what to record is the most critical (and for most businesses the most expensive) point in the accounting process. In computerized systems, after this phase is completed, your input and all further processing just boil down to file merging and report generation. Programmers and management information system types with good accounting backgrounds (such as they should gain from a good principles textbook) are better able to develop effective computerized systems.

Helpful hint Posting is essentially a copying procedure that should be done carefully if correct account balances are to be obtained.

Posting involves the following steps:

1. In the ledger, enter in the appropriate columns of the account(s) debited the date, journal page, and debit amount shown in the journal.
2. In the reference column of the journal, write the account number to which the debit amount was posted.
3. In the ledger, enter in the appropriate columns of the account(s) credited the date, journal page, and credit amount shown in the journal.
4. In the reference column of the journal, write the account number to which the credit amount was posted.

These four steps are diagrammed in Illustration 2-18 using the first journal entry of Softbyte, Inc. The boxed numbers indicate the sequence of the steps.

Illustration 2-18

Posting a journal entry

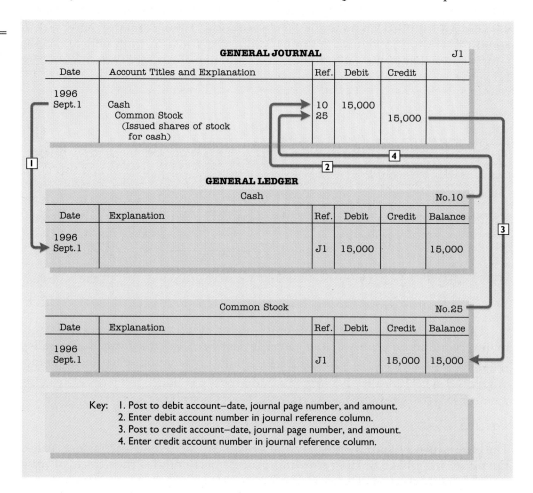

Posting should be performed in chronological order. That is, all the debits and credits of one journal entry should be posted before proceeding to the next journal entry. Under the journalizing procedures described in this chapter, postings should be made on a timely basis to ensure that the ledger is up to date.[3]

---

[3]In homework problems, it will be permissible to journalize all transactions before posting any of the journal entries.

The reference column **in the journal** serves several purposes. The numbers in this column indicate the entries that have been posted. After the last entry has been posted, the journal reference column should be scanned to see that all postings have been made.

The reference column **of a ledger** account indicates the journal page from which the transaction has been posted. The explanation space of the ledger account is used infrequently because an explanation already appears in the journal. It generally is used only when detailed analysis of account activity is required.

Chart of Accounts

The number and type of accounts used differ depending on the size, complexity, and type of business involved. For example, the number of accounts depends on the amount of detail desired by management. The management of one company may want one account for all types of utility expense. Another may keep separate expense accounts for each type of utility expenditure, such as gas, electricity, and water. Similarly, a small corporation like Softbyte Inc. will not have many accounts compared with a corporate giant like Ford Motor Company. Softbyte Inc. may be able to manage and report its activities in 20 to 30 accounts, while Ford requires thousands of accounts to keep track of its worldwide activities.

Accounting in Action ▸ *Business Insight*

 The numbering system used to identify accounts can be quite sophisticated or relatively simple. For example, at Goodyear Tire & Rubber Company an 18-digit system is used. The first three digits identify the division or plant. The second set of three-digit numbers contains the following account classifications:

100–199 Assets	300–399 Revenues
200–299 Liabilities and Stockholders' Equity	400–599 Expenses

Other digits describe the location of a specific plant, product line, region of the country, and so on.

Most companies have a chart of accounts that lists the accounts and the account numbers which identify their location in the ledger. The numbering system used to identify the accounts usually starts with the balance sheet accounts and follows with the income statement accounts.

▶Technology in Action

The first step in designing a computerized accounting system is to create a chart of accounts. The chart of accounts establishes the framework for the entire data base of accounting information.

From the chart of accounts, the general ledger can be created. Journal entries are simultaneously posted to the ledger accounts when the journal entry is made in most computerized systems. The balances are available at any point in time in such systems.

Obvious errors in the recording process (e.g., unbalanced entries or use of nonexistent accounts) are "flagged" by the system and are not processed until corrected. This correction usually takes place immediately after the error is discovered by the system. Because the initial entry is so important, many systems search for more subtle errors, such as unreasonable dollar amounts for specific accounts.

In this and the next two chapters, we will be explaining the accounting for a small corporation, Pioneer Advertising Agency Inc. (a service enterprise). Accounts 1–19 indicate asset accounts; 20–39 indicate liabilities; 40–49 indicate stockholders' equity accounts; 50–59, revenues; and 60–69, expenses. The chart of accounts for Pioneer Advertising Agency Inc. is shown in Illustration 2-19. It contains the following accounts, some of which are explained in later chapters:

Illustration 2-19

Chart of accounts

Pioneer Advertising Agency Inc.

Assets	Stockholders' Equity
1. **Cash**	40. **Common Stock**
6. Accounts Receivable	41. **Retained Earnings**
8. **Advertising Supplies**	42. Dividends
10. **Prepaid Insurance**	49. Income Summary
15. **Office Equipment**	**Revenues**
16. Accumulated Depreciation—Office Equipment	50. **Fees Earned**
Liabilities	**Expenses**
25. **Notes Payable**	60. **Salaries Expense**
26. **Accounts Payable**	61. **Advertising Supplies Expense**
27. Interest Payable	62. **Rent Expense**
28. **Unearned Fees**	63. Insurance Expense
29. Salaries Payable	64. Interest Expense
	65. Depreciation Expense

You will notice that there are gaps in the numbering system of the chart of accounts for Pioneer Advertising Inc. Gaps are left to permit the insertion of new accounts as needed during the life of the business.

The Recording Process Illustrated

Illustration 2-20 through Illustration 2-29 show the basic steps in the recording process, using the October transactions of the Pioneer Advertising Agency Inc. Its accounting period is a month. A basic analysis and a debit-credit analysis precede the journalizing and posting of each transaction. Study these transaction analyses carefully. **The purpose of transaction analysis is first to identify the type of account involved, and then to determine whether a debit or a credit to the account is required.** You should always perform this type of analysis before preparing a journal entry. Doing so will help you understand the journal entries discussed in this chapter as well as more complex journal entries to be described in later chapters.

Keep in mind that every journal entry affects one or more of the following items: assets, liabilities, stockholders' equity, revenues, or expenses. By becoming skilled at transaction analysis, you will be able to recognize quickly the impact of any transaction on these five items. For simplicity, the T-account form is used in the illustrations instead of the standard account form.

Illustration 2-20

Investment of cash by stockholders

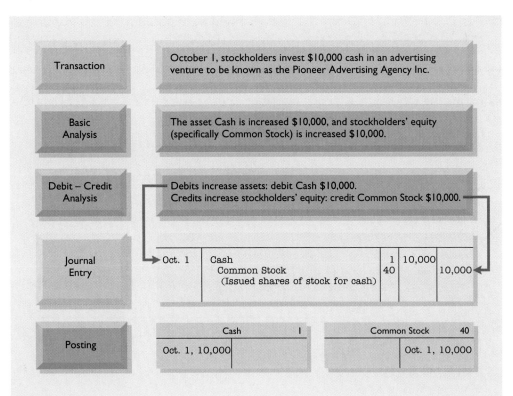

| Transaction | October 1, stockholders invest $10,000 cash in an advertising venture to be known as the Pioneer Advertising Agency Inc. |

| Basic Analysis | The asset Cash is increased $10,000, and stockholders' equity (specifically Common Stock) is increased $10,000. |

| Debit – Credit Analysis | Debits increase assets: debit Cash $10,000. Credits increase stockholders' equity: credit Common Stock $10,000. |

Journal Entry

Oct. 1	Cash	1	10,000	
	Common Stock	40		10,000
	(Issued shares of stock for cash)			

Posting

| Cash | 1 | | Common Stock | 40 |
| Oct. 1, 10,000 | | | | Oct. 1, 10,000 |

Illustration 2-21

Purchase of office equipment

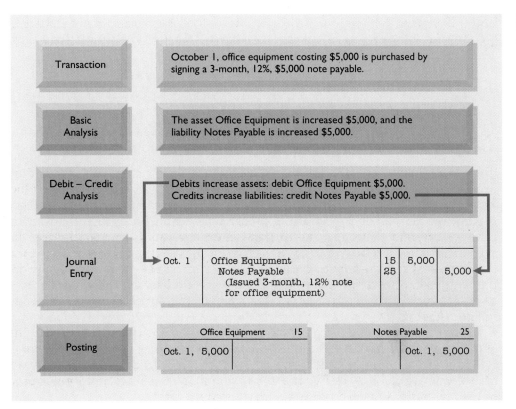

| Transaction | October 1, office equipment costing $5,000 is purchased by signing a 3-month, 12%, $5,000 note payable. |

| Basic Analysis | The asset Office Equipment is increased $5,000, and the liability Notes Payable is increased $5,000. |

| Debit – Credit Analysis | Debits increase assets: debit Office Equipment $5,000. Credits increase liabilities: credit Notes Payable $5,000. |

Journal Entry

Oct. 1	Office Equipment	15	5,000	
	Notes Payable	25		5,000
	(Issued 3-month, 12% note for office equipment)			

Posting

| Office Equipment | 15 | | Notes Payable | 25 |
| Oct. 1, 5,000 | | | | Oct. 1, 5,000 |

Illustration 2-22

Receipt of cash for future service

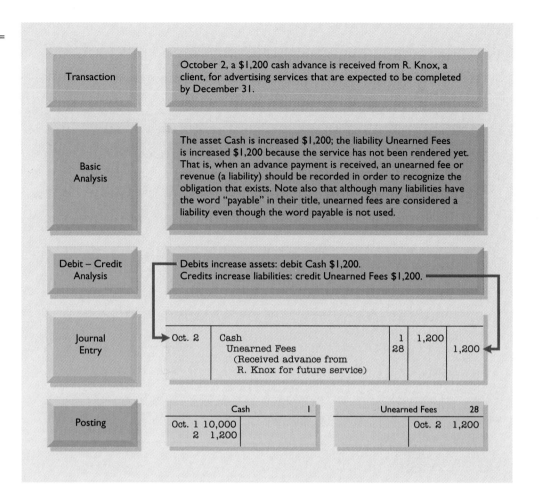

Transaction	October 2, a $1,200 cash advance is received from R. Knox, a client, for advertising services that are expected to be completed by December 31.
Basic Analysis	The asset Cash is increased $1,200; the liability Unearned Fees is increased $1,200 because the service has not been rendered yet. That is, when an advance payment is received, an unearned fee or revenue (a liability) should be recorded in order to recognize the obligation that exists. Note also that although many liabilities have the word "payable" in their title, unearned fees are considered a liability even though the word payable is not used.
Debit – Credit Analysis	Debits increase assets: debit Cash $1,200. Credits increase liabilities: credit Unearned Fees $1,200.

Journal Entry

Oct. 2	Cash	1	1,200	
	Unearned Fees	28		1,200
	(Received advance from			
	R. Knox for future service)			

Posting

Cash	1
Oct. 1 10,000	
2 1,200	

Unearned Fees	28
	Oct. 2 1,200

Illustration 2-23

Payment of monthly rent

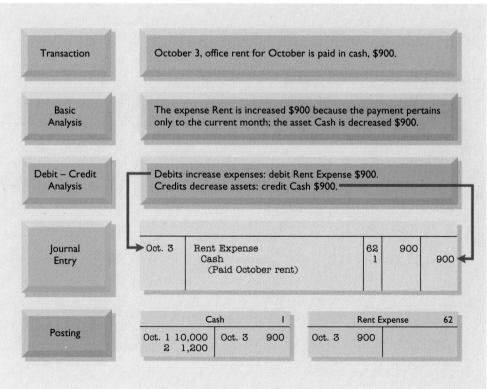

Transaction	October 3, office rent for October is paid in cash, $900.
Basic Analysis	The expense Rent is increased $900 because the payment pertains only to the current month; the asset Cash is decreased $900.
Debit – Credit Analysis	Debits increase expenses: debit Rent Expense $900. Credits decrease assets: credit Cash $900.

Journal Entry

Oct. 3	Rent Expense	62	900	
	Cash	1		900
	(Paid October rent)			

Posting

Cash	1
Oct. 1 10,000	Oct. 3 900
2 1,200	

Rent Expense	62
Oct. 3 900	

Illustration 2-24

Payment for insurance

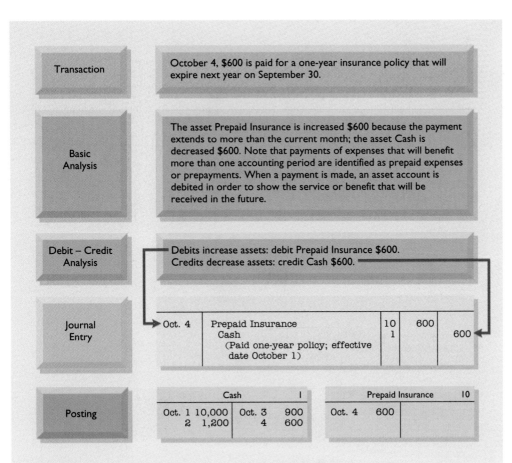

Transaction	October 4, $600 is paid for a one-year insurance policy that will expire next year on September 30.		
Basic Analysis	The asset Prepaid Insurance is increased $600 because the payment extends to more than the current month; the asset Cash is decreased $600. Note that payments of expenses that will benefit more than one accounting period are identified as prepaid expenses or prepayments. When a payment is made, an asset account is debited in order to show the service or benefit that will be received in the future.		
Debit – Credit Analysis	Debits increase assets: debit Prepaid Insurance $600. Credits decrease assets: credit Cash $600.		

Journal Entry	Oct. 4	Prepaid Insurance
		  Cash
		    (Paid one-year policy; effective
		    date October 1)
			10
			1
				600
				
					600

Posting

Cash			1
Oct. 1	10,000	Oct. 3	900
2	1,200	4	600

Prepaid Insurance		10
Oct. 4	600	

Illustration 2-25

Purchase of supplies on credit

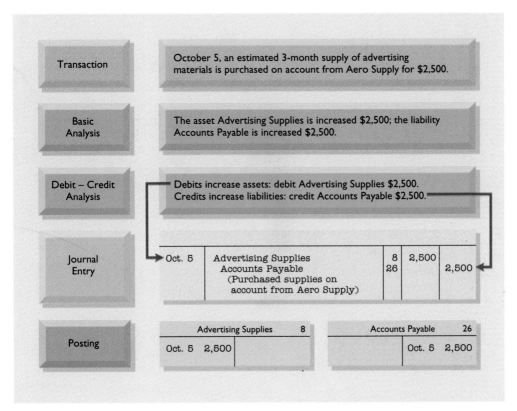

Transaction	October 5, an estimated 3-month supply of advertising materials is purchased on account from Aero Supply for $2,500.		
Basic Analysis	The asset Advertising Supplies is increased $2,500; the liability Accounts Payable is increased $2,500.		
Debit – Credit Analysis	Debits increase assets: debit Advertising Supplies $2,500. Credits increase liabilities: credit Accounts Payable $2,500.		

Journal Entry	Oct. 5	Advertising Supplies
		  Accounts Payable
		    (Purchased supplies on
		    account from Aero Supply)
			8
			26
				2,500
				
					2,500

Posting

Advertising Supplies		8
Oct. 5	2,500	

Accounts Payable		26
	Oct. 5	2,500

Illustration 2-26

Hiring of employees

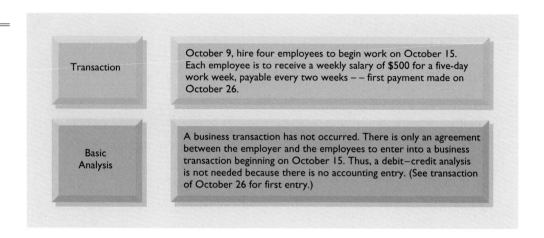

Illustration 2-27

Declaration and payment of dividend by corporation

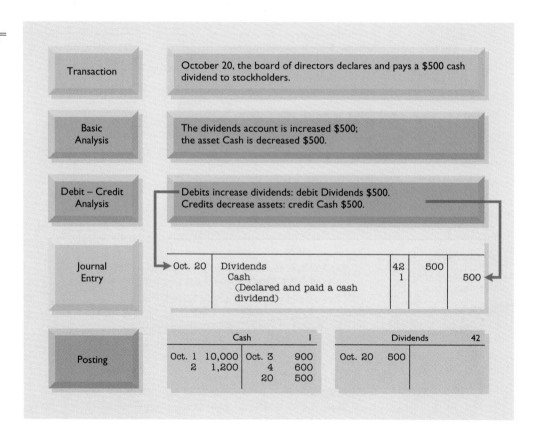

Illustration 2-28

Payment of salaries

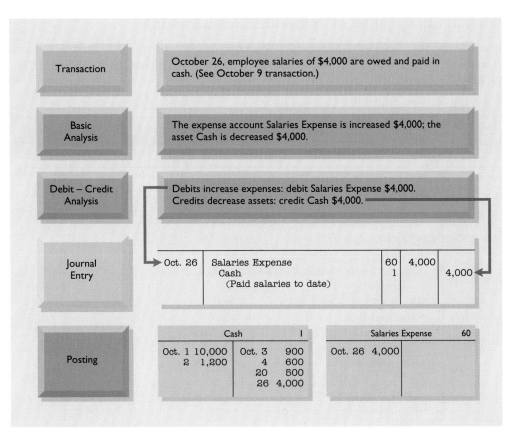

Transaction	October 26, employee salaries of $4,000 are owed and paid in cash. (See October 9 transaction.)
Basic Analysis	The expense account Salaries Expense is increased $4,000; the asset Cash is decreased $4,000.
Debit – Credit Analysis	Debits increase expenses: debit Salaries Expense $4,000. Credits decrease assets: credit Cash $4,000.

Journal Entry

Oct. 26	Salaries Expense	60	4,000	
	Cash	1		4,000
	(Paid salaries to date)			

Posting

Cash				1
Oct. 1	10,000	Oct. 3	900	
2	1,200	4	600	
		20	500	
		26	4,000	

Salaries Expense		60
Oct. 26	4,000	

Illustration 2-29

Receipt of cash for fees earned

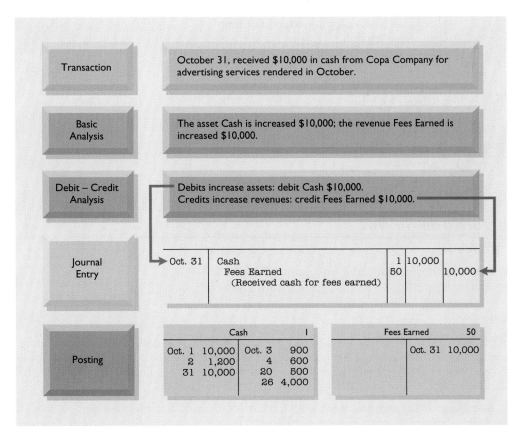

Transaction	October 31, received $10,000 in cash from Copa Company for advertising services rendered in October.
Basic Analysis	The asset Cash is increased $10,000; the revenue Fees Earned is increased $10,000.
Debit – Credit Analysis	Debits increase assets: debit Cash $10,000. Credits increase revenues: credit Fees Earned $10,000.

Journal Entry

Oct. 31	Cash	1	10,000	
	Fees Earned	50		10,000
	(Received cash for fees earned)			

Posting

Cash				1
Oct. 1	10,000	Oct. 3	900	
2	1,200	4	600	
31	10,000	20	500	
		26	4,000	

Fees Earned		50
	Oct. 31	10,000

Summary Illustration of Journalizing and Posting

The journal for Pioneer Advertising Agency for the month of October is summarized in Illustration 2-30. The ledger is shown in Illustration 2-31 with all balances in color.

Illustration 2-30

General journal entries

GENERAL JOURNAL				Page J1
Date	Account Titles and Explanation	Ref.	Debit	Credit
1996 Oct. 1	Cash	1	10,000	
	Common Stock	40		10,000
	(Issued shares of stock for cash)			
1	Office Equipment	15	5,000	
	Notes Payable	25		5,000
	(Issued three-month, 12% note for office equipment)			
2	Cash	1	1,200	
	Unearned Fees	28		1,200
	(Received advance from R. Knox for future service)			
3	Rent Expense	62	900	
	Cash	1		900
	(Paid October rent)			
4	Prepaid Insurance	10	600	
	Cash	1		600
	(Paid one-year policy; effective date, October 1)			
5	Advertising Supplies	8	2,500	
	Accounts Payable	26		2,500
	(Purchased supplies on account from Aero Supply)			
20	Dividends	42	500	
	Cash	1		500
	(Declared and paid a cash dividend)			
26	Salaries Expense	60	4,000	
	Cash	1		4,000
	(Paid salaries to date)			
31	Cash	1	10,000	
	Fees Earned	50		10,000
	(Received cash for fees earned)			

Before You Go On . . .

▶ *Review It*

1. How does journalizing differ from posting?
2. What is the purpose of (a) the ledger and (b) a chart of accounts?

▶ *Do It*

In the week following its successful grand opening, Hair It Is, Inc. collected $2,280 in cash for hair styling services, and paid $400 in wages and $92 for utilities. The company recorded these transactions in a general journal and posted the entries to the general ledger. Explain the purpose and process of journalizing and posting these transactions.

Reasoning: Every business must keep track of its financial activities (receipts, payments, receivables, payables, etc.); journalizing does this. However, just recording every transaction

Illustration 2-31

General ledger

GENERAL LEDGER

Cash   No. 1

Date	Explanation	Ref.	Debit	Credit	Balance
1996					
Oct. 1		J1	10,000		10,000
2		J1	1,200		11,200
3		J1		900	10,300
4		J1		600	9,700
20		J1		500	9,200
26		J1		4,000	5,200
31		J1	10,000		**15,200**

Advertising Supplies   No. 8

Date	Explanation	Ref.	Debit	Credit	Balance
1996					
Oct. 5		J1	2,500		**2,500**

Prepaid Insurance   No. 10

Date	Explanation	Ref.	Debit	Credit	Balance
1996					
Oct. 4		J1	600		**600**

Office Equipment   No. 15

Date	Explanation	Ref.	Debit	Credit	Balance
1996					
Oct. 1		J1	5,000		**5,000**

Notes Payable   No. 25

Date	Explanation	Ref.	Debit	Credit	Balance
1996					
Oct. 1		J1		5,000	**5,000**

Accounts Payable   No. 26

Date	Explanation	Ref.	Debit	Credit	Balance
1996					
Oct. 5		J1		2,500	**2,500**

Unearned Fees   No. 28

Date	Explanation	Ref.	Debit	Credit	Balance
1996					
Oct. 2		J1		1,200	**1,200**

Common Stock   No. 40

Date	Explanation	Ref.	Debit	Credit	Balance
1996					
Oct. 1		J1		10,000	**10,000**

Dividends   No. 42

Date	Explanation	Ref.	Debit	Credit	Balance
1996					
Oct. 20		J1	500		**500**

Fees Earned   No. 50

Date	Explanation	Ref.	Debit	Credit	Balance
1996					
Oct. 31		J1		10,000	**10,000**

Salaries Expense   No. 60

Date	Explanation	Ref.	Debit	Credit	Balance
1996					
Oct. 26		J1	4,000		**4,000**

Rent Expense   No. 62

Date	Explanation	Ref.	Debit	Credit	Balance
1996					
Oct. 3		J1	900		**900**

in chronological order does not make the entries useful. To be useful, the entries need to be classified and summarized; posting the entries to specific ledger accounts does this.

Solution: The purpose of journalizing is to record in chronological order every transaction. Journalizing involves dating every transaction, measuring the dollar amount of each transaction, identifying or labeling each amount with account titles, and recording in a standard format equal debits and credits. Posting involves transferring the journalized debits and credits to specific accounts in the ledger.

Related exercise material: BE2–7, BE2–8, E2–5, E2–6, and E2–8.

*T*he Trial Balance

Helpful hint A trial balance is so named because it is a test to determine if the sum of the debit balances equals the sum of the credit balances.

A trial balance is a list of accounts and their balances at a given time. Customarily, a trial balance is prepared at the end of an accounting period. The accounts are listed in the order in which they appear in the ledger, with debit balances listed in the left column and credit balances in the right column. The totals of the two columns must be in agreement.

The primary purpose of a trial balance is to prove the mathematical equality of debits and credits after posting. Under the double-entry system this equality will occur when the sum of the debit account balances equals the sum of the credit account balances. **A trial balance also uncovers errors in journalizing and posting. In addition, it is useful in the preparation of financial statements**, as will be explained in the next two chapters. The procedures for preparing a trial balance consist of:

1. Listing the account titles and their balances.
2. Totaling the debit and credit columns.
3. Proving the equality of the two columns.

The trial balance prepared from the ledger of Pioneer Advertising Agency Inc. is presented below:

Illustration 2-32

A trial balance

Helpful hint To sum a column of figures is sometimes referred to as to foot the column. The column is then said to be footed.

Helpful hint If only the debit portion of a journal entry is posted, what procedure should bring this error to light? Answer: Taking a trial balance.

PIONEER ADVERTISING AGENCY INC.
Trial Balance
October 31, 1996

	Debit	Credit
Cash	$15,200	
Advertising Supplies	2,500	
Prepaid Insurance	600	
Office Equipment	5,000	
Notes Payable		$ 5,000
Accounts Payable		2,500
Unearned Fees		1,200
Common Stock		10,000
Dividends	500	
Fees Earned		10,000
Salaries Expense	4,000	
Rent Expense	900	
	$28,700	$28,700

Note that the total debits $28,700 equal the total credits $28,700. Account numbers are sometimes shown to the left of the account titles in the trial balance.

Limitations of a Trial Balance

Helpful hint A trial balance is a necessary check point before proceeding to other steps in the accounting process.

A trial balance does not prove that all transactions have been recorded or that the ledger is correct. Numerous errors may exist even though the trial balance columns agree. For example, the trial balance may balance even when (1) a transaction is not journalized, (2) a correct journal entry is not posted, (3) a journal entry is posted twice, (4) incorrect accounts are used in journalizing or posting, or (5) offsetting errors are made in recording the amount of a transaction. In

►*T*echnology in *A*ction

In a computerized system, the trial balance is often only one column (no debit or credit columns), and the accounts have plus and minus signs associated with them. The final balance therefore is zero. Any errors that develop in a computerized system will undoubtedly involve the initial recording rather than some error in the posting or preparation of a trial balance.

other words, as long as equal debits and credits are posted, even to the wrong account or in the wrong amount, the total debits will equal the total credits.

Use of Dollar Signs

Note that dollar signs do not appear in the journals or ledgers. Dollar signs are usually used only in the trial balance and the financial statements. Generally, a dollar sign is shown only for the first item in the column and for the total of that column. A single line is placed under the column of figures to be added or subtracted; the total amount is double underlined to indicate the final sum.

Helpful hint We have avoided the use of cents in the text to save you time and effort.

▼*E*lectronic Data Processing

Electronic data processing (also called computerized or automated systems) encompasses all processing steps from the initial entry of data into the system to the preparation of financial reports for management.

Many students ask, "Why then study manual systems if the real world uses computerized systems?" The accounting concepts and principles do not change whether the system is manual or computerized. However, the concepts are more easily illustrated in a manual system than in a computerized system. In addition, the exact procedures in a computerized system depend on the computer hardware and software being used. Thus, manual systems have been used up to now in this textbook and will continue to be used in the remainder of the chapters.

Comparative Advantages of Manual versus Computerized Systems

There are similarities and differences between manual and computerized systems. One should not conclude that computerized systems are always better. As with any selection, the costs and benefits of each alternative should be weighed before the choice is made. The following key points should be considered when evaluating and comparing manual and computerized systems.

STUDY OBJECTIVE
•••••••••• 8 ••••••••••
Identify the key points in comparing manual and computerized accounting systems.

Dollar Costs

The costs of bookkeepers' salaries and manual accounting records must be compared to the costs of computer hardware and software. Computer systems have some hidden costs that must be considered. Such costs include computer training of personnel and salary differences between bookkeepers and competent computer operators to run the system. Another consideration is the possibility that fewer individuals are needed to run a computer system. And, in general, with microcomputers widely available, as well as an abundance of user-friendly software packages, the manual system is losing its comparative advantage in even the smallest businesses.

Processing Speed

When the number of transactions is large, computerized systems offer real advantages. Thousands of transactions can be processed quickly by a computer, and high-speed printers can generate reports. However, delays in computer processing can occur. For example, if transactions are **batched** (grouped together into like categories and processed at a later time), records and balances may not contain the most up-to-date information. This delay can be avoided by processing transactions using **real-time** (on-line) processing systems in which data are processed as soon as received. In addition, if back-up hardware and software are not kept, malfunctions and breakdowns may bring the system to a standstill.

Processing Errors

Unless a hardware failure occurs, the computer will not make a processing error. Both hardware and software controls generally ensure accurate processing. Because humans perform the processing in a manual system, the potential for processing errors is greater in the manual system. However, humans may be involved with data entry in a computerized system, so some errors may creep into the system.

Responsiveness

Have you ever tried to call the computer to get your bill corrected? Errors and other problems are generally handled more swiftly and readily in a manual system than in a computerized system. For example, a bookkeeper may be more responsive to customer complaints. Also, an important psychological factor differentiates manual systems from computer systems. In a computerized system, customers become numbers, and customers generally prefer not to be treated as numbers; they like personalized relationships. The computer becomes a mechanical intermediary that neither recognizes individuality nor appreciates the customer's business; it never says "Thank you!"

Report Generation

A definite advantage of computerized systems is the ease with which reports can be prepared. Once the system contains the information, useful manipulations of the information can be performed and printed in a matter of minutes. These "demand" reports are also a result of the computer system's ability to bring together information from different parts of the system, such as sales transactions and the accounts receivable subsidiary ledger.

Although some trade-offs exist between the efficiencies of computers and the personal responsiveness of manual systems, computer systems are gaining so significantly in popularity that manual accounting systems are becoming an endangered species.

A Look into the Future

Helpful hint An electronic cash register is a good example of computer use in accounting. At the time of each cash receipt, cash, inventory, and sales are updated and posted. In other words, the posting process occurs at the time the transaction takes place.

Initially, computer technology in business was used to automate the accounting system. Much of the clerical work involved in recording and summarizing accounting transaction data was eliminated. However, there was still a problem—a sales transaction was first processed by accountants. Then, this same sales information was reprocessed by production, marketing, and so on for use in their decision making.

Accountants are now beginning to use computer systems to capture all the organizational information and then provide this information to executives in the forms they desire. As one writer noted: Accountants are becoming organization historians by (a) recording complete histories of organizational events and (b) interpreting these histories for decision makers. Thus, an organizational data base of events is developed. This data base is then used to provide information for decision making for both internal and external purposes. These new developments will make accounting even more enjoyable and useful in the future.[4]

Before You Go On . . .

▶ *Review It*

1. What is a trial balance and how is it prepared?
2. What is the primary purpose of a trial balance?
3. What are the limitations of a trial balance?
4. Why study a manual system?
5. What are the advantages of using a computerized system to record business transactions?

▶ *A Look Back at Gabriella Torres, Diabetes & Endocrine Associates*
• •

Now that you have learned the details of the recording process, think back to the beginning of the chapter to Gabriella Torres and her position as office manager at Diabetes & Endocrine Associates, and answer the following questions:

1. What accounting entries would Gabriella be likely to make to record (a) the rent payment, (b) billing a patient for services rendered, and (c) collecting cash from a patient on account.
2. In what way might Gabriella's day-time job as office manager help in her studies as a night student in accounting and business?
3. Prepare a likely list of asset accounts Gabriella has in her general ledger at Diabetes & Endocrine Associates.

Solution:

1. Gabriella would likely make the following entries:
    (a) Rent Expense
         Cash
            (Paid rent)
    (b) Accounts Receivable
         Fees Earned
            (Billed a patient for services performed)
    (c) Cash
         Accounts Receivable
            (Collected cash for amount due)
2. As a result of her office manager's position, Gabriella is able to relate the subject matter as well as much of the assignment material in her business courses to a real-world context. From her job she knows how bills are paid; how to reconcile a bank statement; how employees are hired, managed, evaluated, and paid; how the individual accounts receivable accounts are maintained; how accounting functions are performed on a computer; and much more.
3. A likely list of asset accounts is: Cash, Accounts Receivable, Medical Supplies, Land and Building (if owned), Medical Equipment, Office Furniture and Fixtures, and Prepaid Insurance.

---

[4]Adapted from an article by Eric L. Denna, "Real Time Accounting," *New Accounting*.

Summary of Study Objectives

1. *Explain what an account is and how it helps in the recording process.* An account is an individual accounting record of increases and decreases in specific asset, liability, and stockholders' equity items.

2. *Define debits and credits and explain how they are used to record business transactions.* The terms debit and credit are synonymous with left and right. Assets, dividends, and expenses are increased by debits and decreased by credits. Liabilities, common stock, retained earnings, and revenues are increased by credits and decreased by debits.

3. *Identify the basic steps in the recording process.* The basic steps in the recording process are: (a) analyze each transaction in terms of its effect on the accounts, (b) enter the transaction information in a journal, (c) transfer the journal information to the appropriate accounts in the ledger.

4. *Explain what a journal is and how it helps in the recording process.* The initial accounting record of a transaction is entered in a journal before the data are entered in the accounts. A journal (a) discloses in one place the complete effect of a transaction, (b) provides a chronological record of transactions, and (c) prevents or locates errors because the debit and credit amounts for each entry can be readily compared.

5. *Explain what a ledger is and how it helps in the recording process.* The entire group of accounts maintained by a company is referred to collectively as a ledger. The ledger keeps in one place all the information about changes in specific account balances.

6. *Explain what posting is and how it helps in the recording process.* Posting is the procedure of transferring journal entries to the ledger accounts. This phase of the recording process accumulates the effects of journalized transactions in the individual accounts.

7. *Prepare a trial balance and explain its purposes.* A trial balance is a list of accounts and their balances at a given time. The primary purpose of the trial balance is to prove the mathematical equality of debits and credits after posting. A trial balance also uncovers errors in journalizing and posting and is useful in preparing financial statements.

8. *Identify the key points in comparing manual and computerized accounting systems.* The key points in comparing manual and computerized accounting systems are (a) cost considerations, (b) processing speed, (c) processing errors, (d) responsiveness, and (e) generation of reports on demand.

Glossary

Account An individual accounting record of increases and decreases in specific asset, liability, and stockholders' equity items. (p. 50).

Chart of accounts A list of accounts and the account numbers which identify their location in the ledger. (p. 63).

Common stock Issued in exchange for the owners' investment paid in to the corporation. (p. 53).

Compound entry An entry that involves three or more accounts. (p. 59).

Credit The right side of an account. (p. 51).

Debit The left side of an account. (p. 51).

Dividend A distribution by a corporation to its stockholders on a pro rata (equal) basis. (p. 54).

Double-entry system A system that records the dual effect of each transaction in appropriate accounts. (p. 52).

General journal The most basic form of journal. (p. 57).

General ledger A ledger that contains all asset, liability, and stockholders' equity accounts. (p. 60).

Journal An accounting record in which transactions are initially recorded in chronological order. (p. 57).

Journalizing The procedure of entering transaction data in the journal. (p. 58).

Ledger The entire group of accounts maintained by a company. (p. 60).

Posting The procedure of transferring journal entries to the ledger accounts. (p. 61).

Retained earnings Net income that is retained in the business. (p. 53).

Simple entry An entry that involves only two accounts. (p. 59).

T account The basic form of an account. (p. 50).

Three-column form of account A form containing money columns for debit, credit, and balance amounts in an account. (p. 61).

Trial balance A list of accounts and their balances at a given time. (p. 72).

DEMONSTRATION PROBLEM

Bob Sample and other student investors opened the Campus Laundromat Inc. on September 1, 1997. During the first month of operations the following transactions occurred:

Sept. 1 Stockholders invested $20,000 cash in the business.
  2 Paid $1,000 cash for store rent for the month of September.
  3 Purchased washers and dryers for $25,000 paying $10,000 in cash and signing a $15,000 six-month 12% note payable.
  4 Paid $1,200 for one-year accident insurance policy.
  10 Received bill from the Daily News for advertising the opening of the laundromat, $200.
  20 Declared and paid a cash dividend to stockholders, $700.
  30 Determined that cash receipts for laundry fees for the month were $6,200.

The chart of accounts for the company is the same as in Pioneer Advertising Agency Inc. except for the following: No. 15 Laundry Equipment and No. 61 Advertising Expense.

Instructions
(a) Journalize the September transactions. (Use J1 for the journal page number.)
(b) Open ledger accounts and post the September transactions.
(c) Prepare a trial balance at September 30, 1997.

Solution to Demonstration Problem

(a) **GENERAL JOURNAL** J1

Date	Account Titles and Explanation	Ref.	Debit	Credit
1997				
Sept. 1	Cash	1	20,000	
	Common Stock	40		20,000
	(Stockholders invested cash in business)			
2	Rent Expense	62	1,000	
	Cash	1		1,000
	(Paid September rent)			
3	Laundry Equipment	15	25,000	
	Cash	1		10,000
	Notes Payable	25		15,000
	(Purchased laundry equipment for cash and six-month 12% note payable)			
4	Prepaid Insurance	10	1,200	
	Cash	1		1,200
	(Paid one-year insurance policy)			
10	Advertising Expense	61	200	
	Accounts Payable	26		200
	(Received bill from Daily News for advertising)			
20	Dividends	42	700	
	Cash	1		700
	(Declared and paid a cash dividend)			
30	Cash	1	6,200	
	Fees Earned	50		6,200
	(Received cash for laundry fees earned)			

Problem-Solving Strategies

1. Separate journal entries are made for each transaction.
2. In journalizing, make sure debits equal credits.
3. In journalizing, use specific account titles taken from the chart of accounts.
4. Provide appropriate description of journal entry.
5. Arrange ledger in statement order, beginning with the balance sheet accounts.
6. Post in chronological order.
7. Numbers in the reference column indicate the amount has been posted.
8. The trial balance lists accounts in the order in which they appear in the ledger.
9. Debit balances are listed in the left column, and credit balances in the right column.

(b)   **GENERAL LEDGER**

Cash   No. 1

Date	Explanation	Ref.	Debit	Credit	Balance
1997					
Sept. 1		J1	20,000		20,000
2		J1		1,000	19,000
3		J1		10,000	9,000
4		J1		1,200	7,800
20		J1		700	7,100
30		J1	6,200		13,300

Prepaid Insurance   No. 10

Date	Explanation	Ref.	Debit	Credit	Balance
1997					
Sept. 4		J1	1,200		1,200

Laundry Equipment   No. 15

Date	Explanation	Ref.	Debit	Credit	Balance
1997					
Sept. 3		J1	25,000		25,000

Notes Payable   No. 25

Date	Explanation	Ref.	Debit	Credit	Balance
1997					
Sept. 3		J1		15,000	15,000

Accounts Payable   No. 26

Date	Explanation	Ref.	Debit	Credit	Balance
1997					
Sept. 10		J1		200	200

Common Stock   No. 40

Date	Explanation	Ref.	Debit	Credit	Balance
1997					
Sept. 1		J1		20,000	20,000

Dividends   No. 42

Date	Explanation	Ref.	Debit	Credit	Balance
1997					
Sept. 20		J1	700		700

Fees Earned   No. 50

Date	Explanation	Ref.	Debit	Credit	Balance
1997					
Sept. 30		J1		6,200	6,200

Advertising Expense   No. 61

Date	Explanation	Ref.	Debit	Credit	Balance
1997					
Sept. 10		J1	200		200

Rent Expense   No. 62

Date	Explanation	Ref.	Debit	Credit	Balance
1997					
Sept. 2		J1	1,000		1,000

(c)

CAMPUS LAUNDROMAT INC.
Trial Balance
September 30, 1997

	Debit	Credit
Cash	$13,300	
Prepaid Insurance	1,200	
Laundry Equipment	25,000	
Notes Payable		$15,000
Accounts Payable		200
Common Stock		20,000
Dividends	700	
Fees Earned		6,200
Advertising Expense	200	
Rent Expense	1,000	
	$41,400	$41,400

SELF-STUDY QUESTIONS

Answers are at the end of the chapter.

(SO 1) 1. Which of the following statements about an account is true?
   a. In its simplest form, an account consists of two parts.
   b. An account is an individual accounting record of increases and decreases in specific asset, liability, and stockholders' equity items.
   c. There are separate accounts for specific assets and liabilities but only one account for stockholders' equity items.
   d. The left side of an account is the credit or decrease side.

(SO 2) 2. Debits:
   a. increase both assets and liabilities.
   b. decrease both assets and liabilities.
   c. increase assets and decrease liabilities.
   d. decrease assets and increase liabilities.

(SO 2) 3. A revenue account:
   a. is increased by debits.
   b. is decreased by credits.
   c. has a normal balance of a debit.
   d. is increased by credits.

(SO 2) 4. Accounts that normally have debit balances are:
   a. assets, expenses, and revenues.
   b. assets, expenses, and common stock.
   c. assets, liabilities, and dividends.
   d. assets, dividends, and expenses.

(SO 3) 5. Which of the following is not part of the recording process?
   a. Analyzing transactions.
   b. Preparing a trial balance.
   c. Entering transactions in a journal.
   d. Posting transactions.

(SO 4) 6. Which of the following statements about a journal is false?
   a. It is not a book of original entry.

   b. It provides a chronological record of transactions.
   c. It helps to locate errors because the debit and credit amounts for each entry can be readily compared.
   d. It discloses in one place the complete effect of a transaction.

(SO 5) 7. A ledger:
   a. contains only asset and liability accounts.
   b. should show accounts in alphabetical order.
   c. is a collection of the entire group of accounts maintained by a company.
   d. is a book of original entry.

(SO 6) 8. Posting:
   a. normally occurs before journalizing.
   b. transfers ledger transaction data to the journal.
   c. is an optional step in the recording process.
   d. transfers journal entries to ledger accounts.

(SO 7) 9. A trial balance:
   a. is a list of accounts with their balances at a given time.
   b. proves the mathematical accuracy of journalized transactions.
   c. will not balance if a correct journal entry is posted twice.
   d. proves that all transactions have been recorded.

(SO 7) 10. A trial balance will not balance if:
   a. a correct journal entry is posted twice.
   b. the purchase of supplies on account is debited to Supplies and credited to Cash.
   c. a $100 cash dividend by the corporation is debited to Dividends for $1,000 and credited to Cash for $100.
   d. a $450 payment on account is debited to Accounts Payable for $45 and credited to Cash for $45.

QUESTIONS

1. Why is an account referred to as a T account?

2. The terms *debit* and *credit* mean increase and decrease, respectively. Do you agree? Explain.

3. José Amaro, a fellow student, contends that the double-entry system means each transaction must be recorded twice. Is José correct? Explain.

4. Teresa Alvarez, a beginning accounting student, believes debit balances are favorable and credit balances are unfavorable. Is Teresa correct? Discuss.

5. State the rules of debit and credit as applied to (a) asset accounts, (b) liability accounts, and (c) stockholders' equity account.

6. What is the normal balance for each of the following accounts? (a) Accounts Receivable. (b) Cash. (c) Dividends. (d) Accounts Payable. (e) Fees Earned. (f) Salaries Expense. (g) Common Stock.

7. Indicate whether each of the following accounts is an asset, a liability, or a stockholders' equity account and whether it would have a debit or credit balance: (a) Accounts Receivable, (b) Accounts Payable, (c) Equipment, (d) Dividends, (e) Supplies.

8. For the following transactions, indicate the account debited and the account credited:
   (a) Supplies are purchased on account.

(b) Cash is received on signing a note payable.

(c) Employees are paid salaries in cash.

9. Presented below is a series of accounts. Indicate whether these accounts generally will have (a) debit entries only, (b) credit entries only, (c) both debit and credit entries.
   (1) Cash.
   (2) Accounts Receivable.
   (3) Dividends.
   (4) Accounts Payable.
   (5) Salaries Expense.
   (6) Fees Earned.

10. What are the basic steps in the recording process?

11. What are the advantages of using the journal in the recording process?

12. (a) When entering a transaction in the journal, should the debit or credit be written first?
    (b) Which should be indented, the debit or credit?

13. Give an example of a compound entry.

14. (a) Can business transaction debits and credits be recorded directly in the ledger accounts?
    (b) What are the advantages of first recording transactions in the journal and then posting to the ledger?

15. The account number is entered as the last step in posting the amounts from the journal to the ledger. What is the advantage of this step?

16. Journalize the following business transactions.
    (a) Doris Wang invests $9,000 in the business in exchange for shares of common stock.
    (b) Insurance of $800 is paid for the year.
    (c) Supplies of $1,500 are purchased on account.

(d) Cash of $7,500 is received for services rendered.

17. (a) What is a ledger? (b) Why is a chart of accounts important?

18. What is a trial balance and what are its purposes?

19. Kap Shin is confused about how accounting information flows through the accounting system. He believes the flow of information is as follows:
    (a) Debits and credits posted to the ledger.
    (b) Business transaction occurs.
    (c) Information entered in the journal.
    (d) Financial statements are prepared.
    (e) Trial balance is prepared.
    Indicate to Kap the proper flow of the information.

20. Two students are discussing the use of a trial balance. They wonder whether the following errors, each considered separately, would prevent the trial balance from balancing.
    (a) The bookkeeper debited Cash for $600 and credited Wages Expense for $600 for payment of wages.
    (b) Cash collected on account was debited to Cash for $900 and Fees Earned was credited for $90. What would you tell them?

21. What are the key points to be considered in evaluating and comparing manual and computerized systems?

22. What are the trade-offs between the efficiencies of computers and the personal responsiveness of manual systems?

*B*RIEF EXERCISES

Indicate debit and credit effects and normal balance.
(SO 2)

BE2–1 For each of the following accounts indicate (a) the effect of a debit or a credit on the account and (b) the normal balance.
1. Accounts Payable.
2. Advertising Expense.
3. Fees Earned.
4. Accounts Receivable.
5. Common Stock.
6. Dividends.

Identify accounts to be debited and credited.
(SO 2)

BE2–2 Transactions for the H. J. Oslo Company for the month of June are presented below. Identify the accounts to be debited and credited for each transaction.

June 1 H. J. Oslo invests $2,500 cash in exchange for shares of common stock in a small welding corporation.
      2 Buys equipment on account for $900.
      3 Pays $500 to landlord for June rent.
      12 Bills J. Kronsnoble $300 for welding work done.

Journalize transactions.
(SO 4)

BE2–3 Using the data in BE2–2, journalize the transactions. (You may omit explanations.)

Identify and explain steps in recording process.
(SO 3)

BE2–4 ◼◼◼▷ Tage Shumway, a fellow student, is unclear about the basic steps in the recording process. Identify and briefly explain the steps in the order in which they occur.

Indicate basic and debit-credit analysis.
(SO 4)

BE2–5 J. A. Norris Corporation has the following transactions during August of the current year. Indicate (a) the basic analysis and (b) the debit-credit analysis illustrated on pages 51–54 of the text.

Aug. 1 Opens an office as a financial advisor, investing $5,000 in cash in exchange for common stock.

4 Pays insurance in advance for 6 months, $1,800.

16 Receives $900 from clients for services rendered.

27 Pays secretary $500 salary.

BE2–6 Using the data in BE2–5, journalize the transactions. (You may omit explanations.)

Journalize transactions.
(SO 4)

BE2–7 Selected transactions for the Gonzales Company are presented in journal form below. Post the transactions to T accounts.

Post journal entries to T accounts.
(SO 6)

J1

Date	Account Titles and Explanation	Ref.	Debit	Credit
May 5	Accounts Receivable		3,200	
	Fees Earned			3,200
12	Cash		2,400	
	Accounts Receivable			2,400
15	Cash		2,000	
	Fees Earned			2,000

BE2–8 Selected journal entries for the Gonzales Company are presented in BE2–7. Post the transactions using the standard form of account.

Post journal entries to standard form of account.
(SO 6)

BE2–9 From the ledger balances given below, prepare a trial balance for the P. J. Carland Company at June 30, 1996. List the accounts in the order shown on page 65 of the text. All account balances are normal.

Prepare a trial balance.
(SO 7)

Accounts Payable $4,000, Cash $3,800, Common Stock $20,000, Dividends $1,200, Equipment $17,000, Fees Earned $6,000, Accounts Receivable $3,000, Salaries Expense $4,000, and Rent Expense $1,000.

BE2–10 An inexperienced bookkeeper prepared the following trial balance that does not balance. Prepare a correct trial balance, assuming all account balances are normal.

Prepare a correct trial balance.
(SO 7)

GOMEZ COMPANY
Trial Balance
December 31, 1996

	Debit	Credit
Cash	$18,800	
Prepaid Insurance		$ 3,500
Accounts Payable		3,000
Unearned Fees	2,200	
Common Stock		17,000
Dividends		4,500
Fees Earned		25,600
Salaries Expense	18,600	
Rent Expense		2,400
	$39,600	$56,000

EXERCISES

E2–1 Selected transactions for A. Mane Inc., an interior decorator, in her first month of business, are as follows:

Identify debits, credits, and normal balances.
(SO 2)

1. Invested $10,000 cash in business in exchange for common stock.
2. Purchased used car for $4,000 cash for use in business.
3. Purchased supplies on account for $500.
4. Billed customers $1,800 for services performed.
5. Paid $200 cash for advertising start of business.
6. Received $700 cash from customers billed in (4) above.

7. Paid creditor $300 cash on account.
8. Declared and paid a $500 cash dividend.

Instructions
For each transaction indicate (a) the basic type of account debited and credited (asset, liability, stockholders' equity); (b) the specific account debited and credited (cash, rent expense, fees earned, etc.); (c) whether the specific account is increased or decreased; and (d) the normal balance of the specific account. Use the following format, in which transaction (1) is given as an example:

	Account Debited				Account Credited			
Trans-action	(a) Basic Type	(b) Specific Account	(c) Effect	(d) Normal Balance	(a) Basic Type	(b) Specific Account	(c) Effect	(d) Normal Balance
(1)	Asset	Cash	Increase	Debit	Stockholders' Equity	Common Stock	Increase	Credit

Journalize transactions
(SO 4)

E2–2 Data for A. Mane Inc., interior decorating, are presented in E2–1.

Instructions
Journalize the transactions using journal page J1.

Analyze transactions and determine their effect on accounts.
(SO 2)

E2–3 Presented below is information related to Marx Real Estate Agency Inc.:

Oct. 1 Lynn Marx begins business as a real estate agent with a cash investment of $13,000 in exchange for common stock.
    2 Hires an administrative assistant.
    3 Buys office furniture for $1,900, on account.
    6 Sells a house and lot for B. Rollins; fees due from Rollins, $3,200 (not paid by Rollins at this time).
   10 Receives cash of $140 as fees for renting an apartment for the owner.
   27 Pays $700 on the balance indicated in the transaction of October 3.
   30 Pays the administrative assistant $960 in salary for October.

Instructions
Prepare the debit-credit analysis for each transaction as illustrated on pages 51–54.

Journalize transactions.
(SO 4)

E2–4 Transaction data for Marx Real Estate Agency Inc. are presented in E2–3.

Instructions
Journalize the transactions.

Post journal entries and prepare a trial balance.
(SO 6, 7)

E2–5 Selected transactions from the journal of J. L. Kang Inc., investment brokerage firm, are presented below.

Date	Account Titles and Explanation	Ref.	Debit	Credit
Aug. 1	Cash		1,600	
	Common Stock			1,600
10	Cash		2,400	
	Fees Earned			2,400
12	Office Equipment		4,000	
	Cash			1,000
	Notes Payable			3,000
25	Accounts Receivable		1,400	
	Fees Earned			1,400
31	Cash		900	
	Accounts Receivable			900

(b) Trial balance totals $8,400

Instructions
(a) Post the transactions to T accounts.
(b) Prepare a trial balance at August 31, 1996.

E2–6 The T accounts below summarize the ledger of Lush Landscaping Corporation at the end of the first month of operations:

Journalize transactions from account data and prepare a trial balance.
(SO 4, 7)

Cash			No. 101
4/1	8,000	4/15	600
4/12	900	4/25	1,500
4/29	400		
4/30	800		

Unearned Fees		No. 205
	4/30	800

Accounts Receivable		No. 112
4/7	3,200	4/29	400

Common Stock		No. 311
	4/1	8,000

Supplies		No. 126
4/4	1,800	

Fees Earned		No. 400
	4/7	3,200
	4/12	900

Accounts Payable		No. 201
4/25	1,500	4/4	1,800

Salaries Expense		No. 726
4/15	600	

Instructions
(a) Prepare the complete general journal (including explanations) from which the postings to Cash were made.
(b) Prepare a trial balance at April 30, 1996.

E2–7 Presented below is the ledger for Holly Corp.

Journalize transactions from account data and prepare a trial balance.
(SO 4, 7)

Cash			No. 101
10/1	4,000	10/4	400
10/10	650	10/12	1,500
10/10	5,000	10/15	250
10/20	500	10/30	300
10/25	2,000	10/31	500

Common Stock		No. 311
	10/1	4,000
	10/25	2,000

Dividends		No. 332
10/30	300	

Accounts Receivable		No. 112
10/6	800	10/20	500
10/20	940		

Service Revenue		No. 407
	10/6	800
	10/10	650
	10/20	940

Supplies		No. 126
10/4	400	

Store Wages Expense		No. 628
10/31	500	

Furniture		No. 149
10/3	2,000	

Rent Expense		No. 729
10/15	250	

Notes Payable		No. 200
	10/10	5,000

Accounts Payable		No. 201
10/12	1,500	10/3	2,000

Instructions
(a) Reproduce the journal entries for the transactions that occurred on October 1, 10, and 20 and provide explanations for each.
(b) Prepare a trial balance at October 31, 1996.

Prepare journal entries and post using standard account form.
(SO 4, 6)

E2–8   Selected transactions for Craig Stevenson Corporation during its first month in business are presented below.

Sept. 1 Invested $15,000 cash in the business in exchange for common stock.
     5 Purchased equipment for $10,000 paying $5,000 in cash and the balance on account.
   25 Paid $3,000 cash on balance owed for equipment.
   30 Declared and paid a $500 cash dividend.

Stevenson's chart of accounts shows: Cash, No. 101; Equipment, No. 157; and Accounts Payable, No. 201; Common Stock, No. 311; and Dividends, No. 332.

Instructions
(a) Journalize the transactions on page J1 of the journal.
(b) Post the transactions using the standard account form.

Analyze errors and their effects on trial balance.
(SO 7)

E2–9   The bookkeeper for John Castle's Equipment Repair made a number of errors in journalizing and posting, as described below:

1. A credit posting of $400 to Accounts Receivable was omitted.
2. A debit posting of $750 for Prepaid Insurance was debited to Insurance Expense.
3. A collection on account of $100 was journalized and posted as a debit to Cash $100 and a credit to Fees Earned $100.
4. A credit posting of $300 to Property Taxes Payable was made twice.
5. A cash purchase of supplies for $250 was journalized and posted as a debit to Supplies $25 and a credit to Cash $25.
6. A debit of $465 to Advertising Expense was posted as $456.

Instructions
For each error, indicate (a) whether the trial balance will balance; if the trial balance will not balance, indicate (b) the amount of the difference, and (c) the trial balance column that will have the larger total. Consider each error separately. Use the following form, in which error (1) is given as an example.

Error	(a) In Balance	(b) Difference	(c) Larger Column
(1)	No	$400	debit

Prepare a trial balance.
(SO 2, 7)

E2–10   The accounts in the ledger of Speedy Delivery Service contain the following balances on July 31, 1997:

Accounts Receivable	$ 7,642	Prepaid Insurance	$ 1,968
Accounts Payable	7,396	Repair Expense	961
Cash	?	Service Revenue	8,610
Delivery Equipment	49,360	Dividends	700
Gas and Oil Expense	758	Common Stock	40,000
Insurance Expense	523	Wages Expense	4,428
Notes Payable	18,450	Wages Payable	815
		Retained Earnings	4,636

Trial balance totals $79,907

Instructions
Prepare a trial balance with the accounts arranged as illustrated in the chapter and fill in the missing amount for Cash.

PROBLEMS

Journalize a series of transactions.
(SO 2, 4)

P2–1   The Surepar Miniature Golf and Driving Range Inc. was opened on March 1 by Jim McInnes. The following selected events and transactions occurred during March:

Mar. 1 Invested $50,000 cash in the business in exchange for common stock.
    3 Purchased Lee's Golf Land for $38,000 cash. The price consists of land, $23,000, building, $9,000, and equipment, $6,000. (Make one compound entry.)
    5 Advertised the opening of the driving range and miniature golf course, paying advertising expenses of $1,600.

6 Paid cash $1,480 for a one-year insurance policy.

10 Purchased golf clubs and other equipment for $1,600 from Palmer Company payable in 30 days.

18 Received golf fees of $800 in cash.

19 Sold 100 coupon books for $15.00 each. Each book contains 10 coupons that enable the holder to one round of miniature golf or to hit one bucket of golf balls.

25 Declared and paid a $500 cash dividend.

30 Paid salaries of $600.

30 Paid Palmer Company in full.

31 Received $500 of fees in cash.

McInnes uses the following accounts: Cash; Prepaid Insurance; Land; Buildings; Equipment; Accounts Payable; Unearned Golf Fees; Common Stock; Dividends; Golf Fees Earned; Advertising Expense; and Salaries Expense.

Instructions

Journalize the March transactions.

P2–2 Patricia Perez incorporated as a licensed architect. During the first month of the operation of her business, the following events and transactions occurred.

Journalize transactions, post, and prepare trial balance.
(SO 2, 4, 6, 7)

April 1 Invested $13,000 cash in exchange for common stock.

1 Hired a secretary-receptionist at a salary of $300 per week payable monthly.

2 Paid office rent for the month, $800.

3 Purchased architectural supplies on account from Halo Company, $1,500.

10 Completed blueprints on a carport and billed client $900 for services.

11 Received $500 cash advance from R. Welk for the design of a new home.

20 Received $1,500 cash for services completed and delivered to P. Donahue.

30 Paid secretary-receptionist for the month, $1,200.

30 Paid $600 to Halo Company on account.

Patricia uses the following chart of accounts: No. 101 Cash, No. 112 Accounts Receivable, No. 126 Supplies, No. 201 Accounts Payable, No. 205 Unearned Fees, No. 311 Common Stock, No. 400 Fees Earned, No. 726 Salaries Expense, and No. 729 Rent Expense.

Instructions

(a) Journalize the transactions.

(b) Post to the ledger accounts.

(c) Prepare a trial balance on April 30, 1996.

P2–3 The trial balance of Jane's Laundry Corp. on September 30 is shown below:

Journalize transactions, post, and prepare a trial balance.
(SO 2, 4, 6, 7)

JANE'S LAUNDRY CORP.
Trial Balance
September 30, 1996

Account No.		Debit	Credit
101	Cash	$ 8,500	
112	Accounts Receivable	2,200	
126	Supplies	1,700	
157	Equipment	8,000	
201	Accounts Payable		$ 5,000
206	Unearned Revenue		700
311	Common Stock		14,700
		$20,400	$20,400

The October transactions were as follows:

Oct. 5 Received $900 cash from customers on account.

10 Billed customers for services performed $5,500.

15 Paid employee salaries $1,200.

17 Performed $400 of services for customers who paid in advance in August.

20   Paid $1,600 to creditors on account.
29   Declared and paid $500 in cash dividends.
31   Paid utilities $600.

Instructions

(a) Enter the opening balances in the ledger accounts as of October 1. Write "Balance" in the explanation space and insert a check mark (√) in the reference column. Provision should be made for the following additional accounts: No. 332 Dividends; No. 426 Laundry Revenue; No. 726 Salaries Expense; and No. 732 Utilities Expense.
(b) Journalize the transactions.
(c) Post to the ledger accounts.
(d) Prepare a trial balance on October 31, 1996.

Prepare a correct trial balance.
(SO 7)

P2–4   The trial balance of Thom Wargo Corp. shown below does not balance.

THOM WARGO CORP.
Trial Balance
June 30, 1996

	Debit	Credit
Cash		$ 2,840
Accounts Receivable	$ 3,231	
Supplies	800	
Equipment	3,000	
Accounts Payable		2,666
Unearned Fees	1,200	
Common Stock		9,000
Dividends	800	
Fees Earned		2,380
Salaries Expense	3,400	
Office Expense	910	
	$13,341	$16,886

Each of the listed accounts has a normal balance per the general ledger. An examination of the ledger and journal reveals the following errors.

1. Cash received from a customer on account was debited for $570 and Accounts Receivable was credited for the same amount. The actual collection was for $750.
2. The purchase of a typewriter on account for $340 was recorded as a debit to Supplies for $340 and a credit to Accounts Payable for $340.
3. Services were performed on account for a client for $890. Accounts Receivable was debited for $890 and Fees Earned was credited for $89.
4. A debit posting to Salaries Expense of $600 was omitted.
5. A payment on account for $206 was credited to Cash for $206 and credited to Accounts Payable for $260.
6. The dividend of $400 cash to stockholders' was debited to Salaries Expense for $400 and credited to Cash for $400.

Instructions

Prepare a correct trial balance.

Journalize transactions, post, and prepare a trial balance.
(SO 2, 4, 6, 7)

P2–5   The Star Theater Corp. owned by Leo Baerga, will begin operations in March. The Star will be unique in that it will show only triple features of sequential theme movies. As of February 28, the ledger of Star showed: No. 101 Cash $16,000; No. 140 Land $42,000; No. 145 Buildings (concession stand, projection room, ticket booth, and screen) $18,000; No. 157 Equipment $16,000; No. 201 Accounts Payable $12,000; and No. 311 Common Stock $80,000. During the month of March the following events and transactions occurred:

Mar. 2   Acquired the three *Star Wars* movies (*Star Wars, The Empire Strikes Back*, and *The Return of the Jedi*) to be shown for the first 3 weeks of March. The film rental was $12,000; $4,000 was paid in cash and $8,000 will be paid on March 10.

3   Ordered the first three *Star Trek* movies to be shown the last 10 days of March. It will cost $400 per night.

9 Received $6,500 cash from admissions.

10 Paid balance due on *Star Wars* movies rental and $3,000 on February 28 accounts payable.

11 Hired M. Brewer to operate concession stand. Brewer to pay Star Theater 15% of gross receipts payable monthly.

12 Paid advertising expenses $800.

20 Received $7,200 cash from admissions.

20 Received the *Star Trek* movies and paid the rental fee of $4,000.

31 Paid salaries of $3,800.

31 Received statement from M. Brewer showing gross receipts from concessions of $8,000 and the balance due to Star Theater of $1,200 for March. Brewer paid one-half the balance due and will remit the remainder on April 5.

31 Received $12,500 cash from admissions.

In addition to the accounts identified above, the chart of accounts includes: No. 112 Accounts Receivable, No. 405 Admission Revenue, No. 406 Concession Revenue, No. 610 Advertising Expense, No. 632 Film Rental Expense, and No. 726 Salaries Expense.

Instructions
(a) Enter the beginning balances to the ledger. Insert a check mark (√) in the reference column of the ledger for the beginning balance.
(b) Journalize the March transactions.
(c) Post the March journal entries to the ledger. Assume that all entries are posted from page 1 of the journal.
(d) Prepare a trial balance on March 31, 1996.

ALTERNATE PROBLEMS
••

P2–1A The Frontier Park Corp. was started on April 1 by Ed Quinn. The following selected events and transactions occurred during April.

Journalize a series of transactions.
(SO 2, 4)

Apr. 1 Invested $60,000 cash in the business in exchange for common stock.

4 Purchased land costing $30,000 for cash.

8 Incurred advertising expense of $1,800 on account.

11 Paid salaries to employees $1,500.

12 Hired park manager at a salary of $4,000 per month, effective May 1.

13 Paid $1,500 for a one-year insurance policy.

17 Declared and paid a $600 cash dividend.

20 Received $5,700 in cash for admission fees.

25 Sold 100 coupon books for $25 each. Each book contains 10 coupons that entitle the holder to one admission to the park.

30 Received $5,900 in cash admission fees.

30 Paid $700 on account for advertising incurred on April 8.

Frontier uses the following accounts: Cash; Prepaid Insurance; Land; Accounts Payable; Unearned Admissions; Common Stock; Dividends; Admission Revenue; Advertising Expense; and Salaries Expense.

Instructions
Journalize the April transactions.

P2–2A Iva Holz is a licensed incorporated CPA. During the first month of operations of her business, the following events and transactions occurred:

Journalize transactions, post, and prepare a trial balance.
(SO 2, 4, 6, 7)

May 1 Invested $42,000 cash in exchange for common stock.

2 Hired a secretary-receptionist at a salary of $1,000 per month.

3 Purchased $1,200 of supplies on account from Read Supply Company.

7 Paid office rent of $900 for the month.

11 Completed a tax assignment and billed client $1,100 for services rendered.

12 Received $3,500 advance on a management consulting engagement.

17 Received cash of $1,200 for services completed for H. Arnold Co.

31   Paid secretary-receptionist $1,000 salary for the month.

31   Paid 40% of balance due Read Supply Company.

Iva uses the following chart of accounts: No. 101 Cash, No. 112 Accounts Receivable, No. 126 Supplies, No. 201 Accounts Payable, No. 205 Unearned Fees, No. 311 Common Stock, No. 400 Fees Earned, No. 726 Salaries Expense, and No. 729 Rent Expense.

Instructions
(a) Journalize the transactions.
(b) Post to the ledger accounts.
(c) Prepare a trial balance on May 31, 1996.

Journalize transactions, post, and prepare a trial balance.
(SO 2, 4, 6, 7)

P2–3A   The trial balance of Sterling Dry Cleaners Inc. on June 30 is shown below.

STERLING DRY CLEANERS INC.
Trial Balance
June 30, 1996

Account No.		Debit	Credit
101	Cash	$12,532	
112	Accounts Receivable	10,536	
126	Supplies	4,844	
157	Equipment	25,950	
201	Accounts Payable		$15,878
206	Unearned Revenue		1,730
311	Common Stock		30,000
320	Retained Earnings		6,254
		$53,862	$53,862

The July transactions were as follows:

July 8   Collected $4,936 in cash on June 30 accounts receivable.

9   Paid employee salaries $2,100.

11   Received $4,325 in cash for services rendered.

14   Paid June 30 creditors $10,750 on account.

17   Purchased supplies on account $554.

22   Billed customers for services rendered, $4,700.

30   Paid employee salaries $3,114, utilities $1,384, and repairs $692.

31   Declared and paid a $700 cash dividend.

Instructions
(a) Enter the opening balances in the ledger accounts as of July 1. Write "Balance" in the explanation space and insert a check mark (√) in the reference column. Provision should be made for the following additional accounts: No. 332 Dividends; No. 428 Dry Cleaning Revenue; No. 622 Repair Expense; No. 726 Salaries Expense; and No. 732 Utilities Expense.
(b) Journalize the transactions.
(c) Post to the ledger accounts.
(d) Prepare a trial balance on July 31, 1996.

Prepare a correct trial balance.
(SO 7)

P2–4A   The trial balance of the Saginaw Corporation shown below does not balance.

SAGINAW CORPORATION
Trial Balance
May 31, 1996

	Debit	Credit
Cash	$ 5,850	
Accounts Receivable		$ 2,750
Prepaid Insurance	700	
Equipment	8,000	
Accounts Payable		4,500
Property Taxes Payable	560	

	Debit	Credit
Common Stock		11,700
Fees Earned	6,690	
Salaries Expense	4,200	
Advertising Expense		1,100
Property Tax Expense	800	
	$26,800	$20,050

Your review of the ledger reveals that each account has a normal balance. You also discover the following errors.

1. The totals of the debit sides of Prepaid Insurance, Accounts Payable, and Property Tax Expense were each understated $100.
2. Transposition errors were made in Accounts Receivable and Fees Earned. Based on postings made, the correct balances were $2,570 and $6,960, respectively.
3. A debit posting to Salaries Expense of $200 was omitted.
4. A $700 cash dividend by the corporation was debited to Common Stock for $700 and credited to Cash for $700.
5. A $420 purchase of supplies on account was debited to Equipment for $420 and credited to Cash for $420.
6. A cash payment of $250 for advertising was debited to Advertising Expense for $25 and credited to Cash for $25.
7. A collection from a customer for $210 was debited to Cash for $210 and credited to Accounts Payable for $210.

Instructions
Prepare a correct trial balance. (Note: The chart of accounts includes the following: Dividends; Supplies; and Supplies Expense.

P2–5A Lake Theater Inc. opens on April 1. All facilities were completed on March 31. At this time, the ledger showed: No. 101 Cash $6,000; No. 140 Land $10,000; No. 145 Buildings (concession stand, projection room, ticket booth, and screen) $8,000; No. 157 Equipment $6,000; No. 201 Accounts Payable $2,000; No. 275 Mortgage Payable $8,000; and No. 311 Common Stock $20,000. During April, the following events and transactions occurred.

Journalize transactions, post, and prepare a trial balance.
(SO 2, 4, 6, 7)

Apr. 2 Paid film rental of $800 on first movie.
     3 Ordered two additional films at $500 each.
     9 Received $1,800 cash from admissions.
    10 Made $2,000 payment on mortgage and $1,000 on accounts payable.
    11 Hired R. Thoms to operate concession stand. Thoms to pay The Lake Theater 17% of gross receipts payable monthly.
    12 Paid advertising expenses $300.
    20 Received one of the films ordered on April 3 and was billed $500. The film will be shown in April.
    25 Received $4,200 cash from admissions.
    29 Paid salaries $1,600.
    30 Received statement from R. Thoms showing gross receipts of $1,000 and the balance due to The Lake Theater of $170 for April. Thoms paid one-half of the balance due and will remit the remainder on May 5.
    30 Prepaid $700 rental on special film to be run in May.

In addition to the accounts identified above, the chart of accounts shows: No. 112 Accounts Receivable, No. 136 Prepaid Rentals, No. 405 Admission Revenue, No. 406 Concession Revenue, No. 610 Advertising Expense, No. 632 Film Rental Expense, and No. 726 Salaries Expense.

Instructions
(a) Enter the beginning balances in the ledger as of April 1. Insert a check mark (✓) in the reference column of the ledger for the beginning balance.
(b) Journalize the April transactions.
(c) Post the April journal entries to the ledger. Assume that all entries are posted from page 1 of the journal.
(d) Prepare a trial balance on April 30, 1996.

▼*B*roadening Your Perspective

*F*INANCIAL REPORTING PROBLEM—PEPSICO, INC.
•••

The financial statements of PepsiCo in Appendix A at the back of this textbook and the notes accompanying the statements contain the following selected accounts, and stated in millions of dollars:

Accounts Payable	$1,556	Income Taxes Payable	387
Accounts Receivable	2,407	Interest Income	127
Interest Expense	682	Prepaid Expenses	590
Land	1,327		

Instructions
(a) Answer the following questions:
1. What is the increase and decrease side for each account?
2. What is the normal balance for each account?
(b) Identify the probable other account in the transaction and the effect on that account when
1. Accounts Receivable is decreased.
2. Income Taxes Payable is decreased.
3. Prepaid Expenses are increased.
(c) Identify the other account(s) that ordinarily would be involved when
1. Interest Expense is increased.
2. Land is increased.

*C*OMPARATIVE ANALYSIS PROBLEM— COCA-COLA COMPANY VS. PEPSICO, INC.
•••

The financial statements of Coca-Cola Company are presented at the end of Chapter 1, and PepsiCo's financial statements are presented in Appendix A.

Instructions
(a) Based on the information contained in these financial statements, determine the following for each company:

The normal balance for:

Coca-Cola's	PepsiCo's
1. Accounts receivable	1. Inventories
2. Land	2. Machinery and equipment
3. Loans and notes payable	3. Short-term borrowing
4. Common stock	4. Retained earnings
5. Interest expense	5. Interest income

(b) Identify the other account ordinarily involved when:
1. Accounts receivable is increased.
2. Notes payable is decreased.
3. Machinery is increased.
4. Interest income is increased.

*I*NTERPRETATION OF FINANCIAL STATEMENTS
•••

Mini-Case One—Bob Evans Farms, Inc.
Bob Evans Farms, Inc. operates 354 restaurants and several food processing plants. The food processing plants primarily process pork into sausage, some of which are used in the res-

taurants, and some of which are sold to grocery stores. The food processing plants also produce "fast-food"-type frozen sandwiches, which are marketed to grocery stores.

The 1995 balance sheet of Bob Evans Farms showed a cash balance of $10 million and trade accounts receivable of $16 million.

The notes to the financial statements revealed that there was a line of credit available of $63 million, of which $26 million was then outstanding.

Instructions
  (a) Explain why most of the trade accounts receivable would probably not pertain to the restaurant business.
  (b) What kind of individuals or companies would you expect to find in the individual accounts receivable accounts?
  (c) Why might Bob Evans Farms be keeping the $10 million in cash, instead of using most of it, for example $8 million, to help pay off the line of credit debt?

Mini-Case Two—Chieftain International, Inc.
Chieftain International, Inc. is an oil and natural gas exploration and production company. The company's 1994 balance sheet reported $208 million in assets with only $4.6 million in liabilities, all of which were short-term accounts payable.

During the year, Chieftain expanded its holdings of oil and gas rights, drilled 37 new wells, and invested in expensive 3-D seismic technology.

The company generated $19 million cash from operating activities in 1994 and paid no dividends. It had a cash balance of $102 million at the end of the year.

Instructions
  (a) What are some of the advantages to Chieftain from having no long-term debt? Name at least two. Can you think of any disadvantages?
  (b) What are some of the advantages to Chieftain from having this large a cash balance? What is a disadvantage?
  (c) Why do you suppose that Chieftain has the $4.6 million balance in accounts payable, since it appears that it could have made all its purchases for cash?

DECISION CASE
••

Lucy Lars operates the Lucy Riding Academy Inc. The academy's primary sources of revenue are riding fees and lesson fees, which are provided on a cash basis. Lucy also boards horses for owners, who are billed monthly for boarding fees. In a few cases, boarders pay in advance of expected use. For its revenue transactions, the academy maintains the following accounts: No. 1 Cash, No. 5 Boarding Accounts Receivable, No. 27 Unearned Boarding Fees, No. 51 Riding Fees Earned, No. 52 Lesson Fees Earned, and No. 53 Boarding Fees Earned.

The academy owns 10 horses, a stable, a riding corral, riding equipment, and office equipment. These assets are accounted for in accounts No. 11 Horses, No. 12 Building, No. 13 Riding Corral, No. 14 Riding Equipment, and No. 15 Office Equipment.

The academy employs stable helpers and an office employee, who receive weekly salaries. At the end of each month, the mail usually brings bills for advertising, utilities, and veterinary service. Other expenses include feed for the horses and insurance. For its expenses, the academy maintains the following accounts: No. 6 Hay and Feed Supplies, No. 7 Prepaid Insurance, No. 21 Accounts Payable, No. 60 Salaries Expense, No. 61 Advertising Expense, No. 62 Utilities Expense, No. 63 Veterinary Expense, No. 64 Hay and Feed Expense, and No. 65 Insurance Expense.

Lucy Lars' sole source of income is dividends from the academy. Thus, the corporation declares and pays periodic dividends. To record stockholders' equity in the business and dividends, two accounts are maintained: No. 50 Common Stock, and No. 51 Dividends.

During the first month of operations an inexperienced bookkeeper was employed. Lucy Lars asks you to review the following nine entries of the 50 entries made during the month.

In each case, the explanation for the entry is correct.

May	1	Cash	15,000	
		Common Stock		15,000
		(Invested $15,000 cash in business in exchange for common stock)		
	5	Cash	250	
		Riding Fees Earned		250
		(Received $250 cash for lesson fees)		
	7	Cash	500	
		Boarding Fees Earned		500
		(Received $500 for boarding of horses beginning June 1)		
	9	Hay and Feed Expense	1,700	
		Cash		1,700
		(Purchased estimated two months' supply of feed and hay for $1,700 on account)		
	14	Riding Equipment	80	
		Cash		800
		(Purchased desk and other office equipment for $800 cash)		
	15	Salaries Expense	400	
		Cash		400
		(Declared and paid dividend to Lucy Lars)		
	20	Cash	145	
		Riding Fees Earned		154
		(Received $154 cash for riding fees)		
	31	Veterinary Expense	75	
		Accounts Payable		75
		(Received bill of $75 from veterinarian for services rendered)		

Instructions

(a) For each journal entry that is correct, so state. For each journal entry that is incorrect, prepare the entry that should have been made by the bookkeeper.

(b) Which of the incorrect entries would prevent the trial balance from balancing?

(c) What was the correct net income for May, assuming the bookkeeper reported net income of $4,500 after posting all 50 entries?

(d) What was the correct cash balance at May 31, assuming the bookkeeper reported a balance of $12,475 after posting all 50 entries?

COMMUNICATION ACTIVITY

Milly Maid Company offers home cleaning service. Two recurring transactions for the company are billing customers for services rendered and paying employee salaries. For example, on March 15 bills totaling $6,000 were sent to customers and $2,000 was paid in salaries to employees.

Instructions

Write a memorandum to your instructor that explains and illustrates the steps in the recording process for each of the March 15 transactions. Use the format illustrated in the text under the heading, "The Recording Process Illustrated" (p. 58).

GROUP ACTIVITY

The expanded basic accounting equation contains six account categories: assets, liabilities, common stock, dividends, revenues, and expenses.

Instructions

With the class divided into six groups, each group should choose one of the six account categories and should:

   (a) Explain for its category: (1) the increase/decrease side of the account, and (2) the normal balance of the account.
   (b) Give an example of a transaction that will result in an increase in the assigned category.

ETHICS CASE

Julietta Gilbert is the assistant chief accountant at Zarle Company, a manufacturer of computer chips and cellular phones. The company presently has total sales of $20 million. It is the end of the first quarter and Julietta is hurriedly trying to prepare a general ledger trial balance so that quarterly financial statements can be prepared and released to management and the regulatory agencies. The total credits on the trial balance exceed the debits by $1,000. In order to meet the 4 p.m. deadline, Julietta decides to force the debits and credits into balance by adding the amount of the difference to the Equipment account. She chose Equipment because it is one of the larger account balances: percentage-wise it will be the least misstated. Julietta plugs the difference! She believes that the difference is quite small and will not affect anyone's decisions. She wishes that she had another few days to find the error but realizes that the financial statements are already late.

Instructions

   (a) Who are the stakeholders in this situation?
   (b) What are the ethical issues involved in this case?
   (c) What are Julietta's alternatives?

RESEARCH ASSIGNMENT

There are several commonly available indexes which enable individuals to locate articles previously included in numerous business publications and periodicals. Articles can generally be searched for by company or by subject matter. Four common indexes are *The Wall Street Journal Index*, *Business Abstracts* (formerly the *Business Periodical Index*), *Predicasts F&S Index*, and *ABI/Inform*. Use one of these resources to find an article about a New York Stock Exchange company of your choosing. Read the article and answer the following questions. (**Note:** Your library may have hard copy or CD-ROM versions of these indexes.)

   (a) What is the article about?
   (b) What company-specific information is included in the article?
   (c) Is the article somehow related to anything you read in Chapter 2 of your accounting textbook?
   (d) Identify any accounting-related issues discussed in the article.

CRITICAL THINKING
► A Real-World Focus: Automated Security Holdings

Automated Security Holdings operates multinationally, with principal markets in the United States and the United Kingdom. The company designs, produces, installs, and maintains security systems to safeguard life and property from a wide range of hazards. The markets for these security products include commercial, industrial, and residential customers.

The following notes to the financial statements identify a few of the accounts found in the general ledger of Automated Security Holdings.

FINANCIAL NOTES:

	November 30, 1993	1994
	(thousands of dollars)	
Income Tax Payable	3,929	3,919
Accounts Payable	6,499	9,620
Salaries Expense	16,353	9,213
Cash	4,749	2,869
Unearned Fees	1,211	1,434
Notes Payable	52,000	40,000
Prepaid Insurance	1,333	2,000

Instructions

(a) Identify the accounts of Automated Security Holdings that have debit balances in the trial balance.

(b) What date has Automated Security Holdings adopted for its accounting year-end?

(c) Are the accounts listed above in the order in which they would appear in Automated Security Holdings' general ledger? Explain.

Answers to Self-Study Questions

1. b   2. c   3. d   4. d   5. b   6. a   7. c   8. d   9. a   10. c

Before studying this chapter, you should know, or, if necessary, review:

a. *What a double-entry system is. (Ch. 2, p. 52)*

b. *How to increase or decrease assets, liabilities, and stockholders' equity using debit and credit procedures. (Ch. 2, pp. 52–54)*

c. *How to journalize a transaction. (Ch. 2, pp. 58–59)*

d. *How to post a transaction. (Ch. 2, pp. 61–63)*

e. *How to prepare a trial balance. (Ch. 2, p. 72)*

When Students Leave Campus, This College Adjusts Its Books

TEMPE, Ariz. — Like many colleges, Arizona State University (ASU) uses a June 30 date as the end of its annual accounting period. Rather than using December 31, most colleges use the school year as their primary period of activity. Having an ending date like that seems neat and tidy—and it is in many respects. (If it were not, schools would choose an end-date that made more sense.) But colleges, just like any business organization, have some loose ends that need tying up at the end of the accounting period. For example, at ASU, the second summer session begins around July 5, but registration for the session takes place the prior February. The school collects tuition for the session in one accounting period but will provide the services in the next accounting period. "We have lots of students who are paying tuition in February for a session that begins in July," says Carol Balk, ASU's manager of student tuition payments. In the new accounting year, following completion of the summer session, "we have to account for the revenue collection of five months earlier."

Similarly, ASU has to account for supplies purchased in one accounting year but used the next. Supplies purchased on April 1 for use in the summer session will need to be reported as an expense in the new accounting year. ◀

CHAPTER · 3

ADJUSTING THE ACCOUNTS

In Chapter 2 we examined the basic steps in the recording process through the preparation of the trial balance. Before we will be ready to prepare financial statements from the trial balance, additional steps need to be taken. The timing mismatch between revenues and expenses of Arizona State University illustrates the types of situations that make these additional steps necessary. For example, computer equipment purchased in the prior accounting year is being used to keep student records and accounts in the current year. What portion of the computer cost, if any, should be recognized as an expense of the current period? Before financial statements can be prepared, these and other questions relating to the recognition of revenues and expenses must be answered. With the answers in hand, the relevant account balances can then be adjusted.

The organization and content of the chapter are as follows:

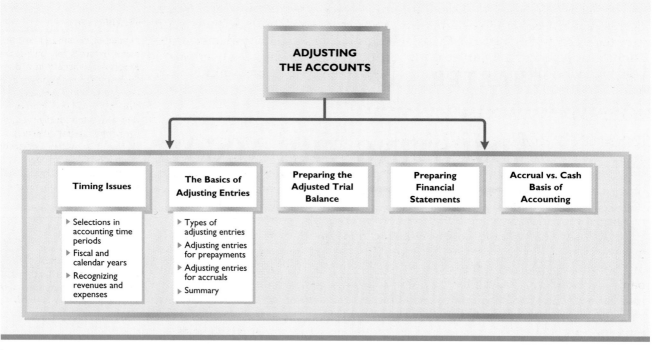

Timing Issues

STUDY OBJECTIVE

••••••••••▼••••••••••

Explain the time period assumption.

No adjustments would be necessary if we waited to prepare financial statements until a company ended its operations. At that point, we could readily determine its final balance sheet and the amount of lifetime income it earned. The following anecdote illustrates one way to compute lifetime income:

> A grocery store owner from the old country kept his accounts payable on a spindle, accounts receivable on a note pad, and cash in a cigar box. His daughter, having just passed the CPA exam, chided the father: "I don't understand how you can run your business this way. How do you know what your profits are?"
>
> "Well," the father replied, "when I got off the boat 40 years ago, I had nothing but the pants I was wearing. Today your brother is a doctor, your sister is a college professor, and you are a CPA. Your mother and I have a nice car, a well-furnished house, and a lake home. We have a good business and everything is paid for. So, you add all that together, subtract the pants, and there's your profit."

Selecting an Accounting Time Period

Although the old grocer may be correct in his evaluation, it is impractical to wait so long for the results of operations. All entities, from the corner grocery, to a global company like PepsiCo, to your college or university, find it desirable and necessary to report the results of their activities more frequently. For example, management usually wants monthly financial statements, and the Internal Revenue Service requires all businesses to file annual tax returns. As a consequence, **accountants make the assumption that the economic life of a business can be divided into artificial time periods.** This assumption is referred to as the time period assumption.

Many business transactions affect more than one of these arbitrary time periods. For example, the milking machine bought by Farmer Brown in 1995 and the airplanes purchased by Delta Airlines 5 years ago are still in use today. Therefore it is necessary to determine the relevance of each business transaction to specific accounting periods. Doing so may involve subjective judgments and estimates. Generally, the shorter the time period (e.g., a month or a quarter of a year), the more difficult it becomes to determine the proper adjustments to be made.

Helpful hint The time period assumption is also called the periodicity assumption.

Fiscal and Calendar Years

Both small and large companies prepare financial statements on a periodic basis in order to assess their financial condition and results of operations. **Accounting time periods are generally a month, a quarter, or a year.** Monthly and quarterly time periods are often referred to as interim periods. Most large companies are required to prepare both interim (quarterly) and annual financial statements.

An accounting time period that is one year in length is referred to as a fiscal year. A fiscal year usually begins with the first day of a month and ends 12 months later on the last day of a month. The accounting period used by most businesses coincides with the calendar year (January 1 to December 31). Companies whose fiscal year differs from the calendar year include Delta Air Lines, June 30; Walt Disney Productions, September 30; Kmart Corp., January 31; and Dunkin' Donuts, Inc., October 31. Arizona State University's fiscal year is July 1 through June 30, which is typical of universities and governmental agencies.

►Ethics note

In addition to annual numbers, many investors rely on interim reports. The Securities and Exchange Commission recently charged two former executives of the Union Corporation with intentionally reporting in one quarter revenues that were earned in a different quarter, in order to meet quarterly income targets. The misstatement had no effect on year-end totals.

Helpful hint A business normally selects a fiscal year that ends when business activity is at a relatively low ebb.

Recognizing Revenues and Expenses

Determining the amount of revenues and expenses to be reported in a given accounting period can be difficult. Therefore, accountants have developed two principles as part of generally accepted accounting principles (GAAP) that help in this determination: the revenue recognition principle and the matching principle.

The revenue recognition principle dictates that revenue be recognized in the accounting period in which it is earned. In a service enterprise, revenue is considered to be earned at the time the service is performed. To illustrate, assume that a dry cleaning business cleans clothing on June 30 but customers do not claim and pay for their clothes until the first week of July. Under the revenue recognition principle, revenue is earned in June when the service is performed and not in July when the cash is received. At June 30, the dry cleaner would report a receivable on its balance sheet and revenue in its income statement for the service performed.

In recognizing expenses, accountants follow the approach of "let the expenses follow the revenues." Thus, expense recognition is tied to revenue recognition. In the preceding example, this principle means that the salary expense incurred in performing the cleaning service on June 30 should be reported in the income statement for the same period in which the service revenue is recognized.

STUDY OBJECTIVE
••••••••••2••••••••••
Distinguish between the revenue recognition principle and the matching principle.

Helpful hint Another example is ASU's need to account for supplies purchased in one year but used in the next.

▸Accounting in Action ▸ *Business Insight*

Suppose you are a filmmaker and spend $15 million to produce a film. Over what period should the $15 million be expensed? Yes, it should be expensed over the economic life of the film. But what is its economic life? The filmmaker must estimate how much revenue will be earned from box office sales, video sales, and television—a period that easily can stretch five years or more. If a filmmaker allocates the cost over five years, and the film produces revenue in the sixth year, proper matching has not occurred. Furthermore, in some cases, films flop, and yet the costs are spread out over five years in the hopes that the films will eventually succeed. For example, in the mid-1980s Orion Pictures (now bankrupt) earned $7.3 million in one year, but lost $32 million the next year because it expensed 40 films that were not producing revenue. It was alleged that the company had overstated its income in earlier years because it did not expense these costs earlier. This case demonstrates the difficulty of properly matching expenses to revenues.

The critical issue in expense recognition is when the expense makes its contribution to revenue. This may or may not be the same period in which the expense is paid. If the salary incurred on June 30 is not paid until July, the dry cleaner would report salaries payable on its June 30 balance sheet. The practice of expense recognition is referred to as the matching principle because it dictates that efforts (expenses) be matched with accomplishments (revenues).

Once the assumption is made that the economic life of a business can be divided into artificial time periods, it follows that the revenue recognition and matching principles can be applied. This one assumption and two principles thus provide guidelines as to when revenues and expenses should be reported. These relationships are shown in Illustration 3-1.

Illustration 3-1

GAAP relationships in revenue and expense recognition

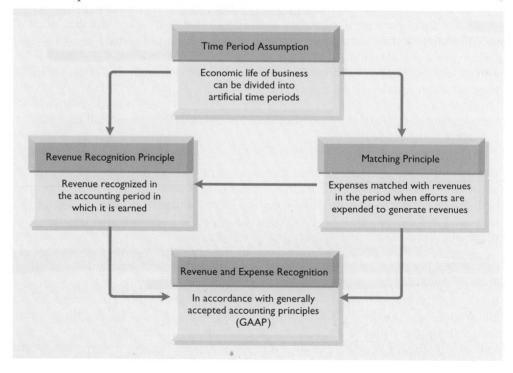

Before You Go On . . .

▸ *Review It*

1. What is the relevance of the time period assumption to accounting?
2. What are the revenue recognition and matching principles?

The Basics of Adjusting Entries

In order for revenues to be recorded in the period in which they are earned, and for expenses to be recognized in the period in which they are incurred, adjusting entries are made at the end of the accounting period. In short, adjusting entries are needed to ensure that the revenue recognition and matching principles are followed.

STUDY OBJECTIVE
3
Explain why adjusting entries are needed.

The use of adjusting entries makes it possible to report on the balance sheet the appropriate assets, liabilities, and stockholders' equity at the statement date and to report on the income statement the proper net income (or loss) for the period. However, the trial balance—the first pulling together of the transaction data—may not contain up-to-date and complete data. This is true for the following reasons:

1. Some events are not journalized daily because it is inexpedient to do so. Examples are the consumption of supplies and the earning of wages by employees.
2. Some costs are not journalized during the accounting period because these costs expire with the passage of time rather than as a result of recurring daily transactions. Examples of such costs are building and equipment deterioration and rent and insurance.
3. Some items may be unrecorded. An example is a utility service bill that will not be received until the next accounting period.

Helpful hint Adjusting entries are needed to enable financial statements to be in conformity with GAAP.

Adjusting entries are required every time financial statements are prepared. An essential starting point is an analysis of each account in the trial balance to determine whether it is complete and up-to-date for financial statement purposes. The analysis requires a thorough understanding of the company's operations and the interrelationship of accounts. The preparation of adjusting entries is often an involved process. In accumulating the adjustment data, the company may need to make inventory counts of supplies and repair parts. Also it may be desirable to prepare supporting schedules of insurance policies, rental agreements, and other contractual commitments. Adjustments are often prepared after the balance sheet date. However, the adjusting entries are dated as of the balance sheet date.

Types of Adjusting Entries

Adjusting entries can be classified as either prepayments or accruals. Each of these classes has two subcategories as shown below:

STUDY OBJECTIVE
4
Identify the major types of adjusting entries.

Prepayments

1. **Prepaid Expenses.** Expenses paid in cash and recorded as assets before they are used or consumed.
2. **Unearned Revenues.** Revenues received in cash and recorded as liabilities before they are earned.

Accruals

3. **Accrued Revenues.** Revenues earned but not yet received in cash or recorded.
4. **Accrued Expenses.** Expenses incurred but not yet paid in cash or recorded.

Specific examples and explanations of each type of adjustment are given in subsequent sections. Each example is based on the October 31 trial balance of Pioneer Advertising Agency Inc., reproduced in Illustration 3-2 from Chapter 2.

Illustration 3-2

Trial balance

PIONEER ADVERTISING AGENCY INC.
Trial Balance
October 31, 1996

	Debit	Credit
Cash	$15,200	
Advertising Supplies	2,500	
Prepaid Insurance	600	
Office Equipment	5,000	
Notes Payable		$ 5,000
Accounts Payable		2,500
Unearned Fees		1,200
Common Stock		10,000
Retained Earnings		–0–
Dividends	500	
Fees Earned		10,000
Salaries Expense	4,000	
Rent Expense	900	
	$28,700	$28,700

Helpful hint   Analyzing each account in the trial balance is the starting point for adjusting entries.

We assume that Pioneer Advertising Agency Inc. uses an accounting period of one month. Thus, monthly adjusting entries will be made. The entries will be dated October 31.

Adjusting Entries for Prepayments

STUDY OBJECTIVE
··········· 5 ···········
Prepare adjusting entries for prepayments.

As indicated earlier, prepayments are either prepaid expenses or unearned revenues. Adjusting entries for prepayments are required at the statement date to record the portion of the prepayment that represents the **expense incurred or the revenue earned** in the current accounting period. Assuming an adjustment is needed for both types of prepayments, the asset and liability are overstated and the related expense and revenue are understated. For example, in the trial balance, the balance in the asset, Supplies, shows only supplies purchased. This balance is overstated; the related expense account, Supplies Expense, is understated because the cost of supplies used has not been recognized. Thus the adjusting entry for prepayments will decrease a balance sheet account and increase an income statement account. The effects of adjusting entries for prepayments are graphically depicted in Illustration 3-3.

Helpful hint   Remember that credits decrease assets and increase revenues. Debits increase expenses and decrease liabilities.

Prepaid Expenses

Helpful hint   Prepaid expenses are also called deferred expenses.

As stated on page 101, expenses paid in cash and recorded as assets before they are used or consumed are identified as prepaid expenses. When a cost is incurred, an asset account is debited to show the service or benefit that will be received in the future. Prepayments often occur in regard to insurance, supplies, advertising, and rent. In addition, prepayments are made when buildings and equipment are purchased.

Prepaid expenses expire either with the passage of time (e.g., rent and insurance) or through use and consumption (e.g., supplies). The expiration of these costs does not require daily recurring entries, which would be unnecessary and impractical. Accordingly, it is customary to postpone the recognition of such cost expirations until financial statements are prepared. At each statement date, adjusting entries are made to record the expenses that apply to the current accounting period and to show the unexpired costs in the asset accounts.

An asset-expense relationship exists with prepaid expenses. Prior to adjustment, assets are overstated and expenses are understated. **Thus, the prepaid**

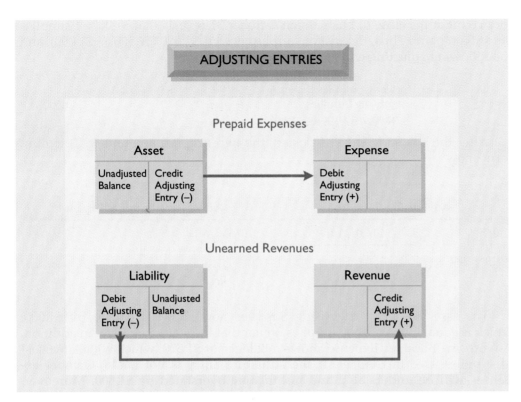

Illustration 3-3

Adjusting entries for prepayments

expense adjusting entry results in a debit to an expense account and a credit to an asset account.

Supplies. Several different types of supplies are used in a business enterprise. For example, a CPA firm will have **office supplies** such as stationery, envelopes, and accounting paper. In contrast, an advertising firm will have **advertising supplies** such as graph paper, video film, and poster paper. Supplies are generally debited to an asset account when they are acquired. During the course of operations, supplies are depleted or entirely consumed. However, recognition of supplies used is deferred until the adjustment process when a physical inventory (count) of supplies is taken. The difference between the balance in the Supplies (asset) account and the cost of supplies on hand represents the supplies used (expense) for the period.

Pioneer Advertising Agency Inc. purchased advertising supplies costing $2,500 on October 5. The debit was made to the asset Advertising Supplies, and this account shows a balance of $2,500 in the October 31 trial balance. An inven-

Supplies

Oct. 5

Supplies purchased; record asset

Oct. 31

Supplies used; record supplies expense

►Accounting in Action ► *Business Insight*

The costs of advertising on radio, television, and magazines for such products as burgers, bleaches, athletic shoes, and so on are sometimes considered prepayments. As a manager for Procter & Gamble noted, "If we run a long ad campaign for soap and bleach, we sometimes report the costs as prepayments if we think we'll receive sales benefits from the campaign down the road." Presently it is a judgment call whether these costs should be prepayments or expenses in the current period. Developing guidelines consistent with the matching principle is difficult because situations vary widely from company to company. The issue is important since the outlays for advertising can be substantial. Recent big spenders: Procter & Gamble, the biggest U.S. advertiser, spent $2.3 billion, Sears Roebuck spent $1.5 billion, and McDonald's $760 million.

tory count at the close of business on October 31 reveals that $1,000 of supplies are still on hand. Thus, the cost of supplies used is $1,500 ($2,500 − $1,000), and the following adjusting entry is made:

Oct. 31	Advertising Supplies Expense	1,500	
	Advertising Supplies		1,500
	(To record supplies used)		

After the adjusting entry is posted, the two supplies accounts in T-account form show:

Illustration 3-4

Supplies accounts after adjustment

Advertising Supplies				Advertising Supplies Expense		
10/5	2,500	10/31 **Adj.**	1,500	10/31 **Adj.**	1,500	
10/31 **Bal.**	1,000					

The asset account Advertising Supplies now shows a balance of $1,000, which is equal to the cost of supplies on hand at the statement date. In addition, Advertising Supplies Expense shows a balance of $1,500, which equals the cost of supplies used in October. **If the adjusting entry is not made, October expenses will be understated and net income overstated by $1,500. Moreover, both assets and stockholders' equity will be overstated by $1,500 on the October 31 balance sheet.**

Insurance.   Most companies have fire and theft insurance on merchandise and equipment, personal liability insurance for accidents suffered by customers, and automobile insurance on company cars and trucks. The cost of insurance protection is determined by the payment of insurance premiums. The term and coverage are specified in the insurance policy. The minimum term is usually one year, but three- to five-year terms are available and offer lower annual premiums. Insurance premiums normally are charged to the asset account Prepaid Insurance when paid. At the financial statement date it is necessary to debit Insurance Expense and credit Prepaid Insurance for the cost that has expired during the period.

On October 4, Pioneer Advertising Agency Inc. paid $600 for a one-year fire insurance policy. The effective date of coverage was October 1. The premium was charged to Prepaid Insurance when it was paid, and this account shows a balance of $600 in the October 31 trial balance. An analysis of the policy reveals that $50 ($600 ÷ 12) of insurance expires each month. Thus, the following adjusting entry is made:

Insurance

Oct.4

Insurance purchased; record asset

Insurance Policy			
Oct $50	Nov $50	Dec $50	Jan $50
Feb $50	March $50	April $50	May $50
June $50	July $50	Aug $50	Sept $50
1 YEAR $600			

Oct.31

Insurance expired; record insurance expense

Oct. 31	Insurance Expense	50	
	Prepaid Insurance		50
	(To record insurance expired)		

After the adjusting entry is posted, the accounts show:

Illustration 3-5

Insurance accounts after adjustment

Prepaid Insurance				Insurance Expense		
10/4	600	10/31 **Adj.**	50	10/31 **Adj.**	50	
10/31 **Bal.**	550					

The asset Prepaid Insurance shows a balance of $550, which represents the unexpired cost applicable to the remaining 11 months of coverage. At the same time, the balance in Insurance Expense is equal to the insurance cost that has expired in October. **If this adjustment is not made, October expenses will be understated by $50 and net income overstated by $50. Moreover, both assets and stockholders' equity also will be overstated by $50 on the October 31 balance sheet.**

Helpful hint If financial statements were prepared quarterly, what would be the amount of the adjusting entry at December 31? Answer: $150 ($50 × 3).

Depreciation. A business enterprise typically owns a variety of productive facilities such as buildings, equipment, and motor vehicles. These assets provide a service for a number of years. The term of service is commonly referred to as the useful life of the asset. Because an asset such as a building is expected to provide service for many years, it is recorded as an asset, rather than an expense, in the year it is acquired. As explained in Chapter 1, such assets are recorded at cost, as required by the cost principle.

According to the matching principle, a portion of the cost of a long-lived asset should be reported as expense during each period of the asset's useful life. Depreciation is the process of allocating the cost of an asset to expense over its useful life in a rational and systematic manner.

Helpful hint Depreciation is an estimate—one of many estimates inherent in accounting.

Need for Depreciation Adjustment.   From an accounting standpoint, the acquisition of productive facilities is viewed essentially as a long-term prepayment for services. The need for making periodic adjusting entries for depreciation is, therefore, the same as described before for other prepaid expenses; that is, to recognize the cost that has expired (expense) during the period and to report the unexpired cost (asset) at the end of the period.

In determining the useful life of a productive facility, the primary causes of depreciation are actual use, deterioration due to the elements, and obsolescence. At the time an asset is acquired, the effects of these factors cannot be known with certainty, so they must be estimated. Thus, you should recognize that depreciation is an estimate rather than a factual measurement of the cost that has expired. A common procedure in computing depreciation expense is to divide the cost of the asset by its useful life. For example, if cost is $10,000 and useful life is expected to be 10 years, annual depreciation is $1,000.[1]

For Pioneer Advertising, depreciation on the office equipment is estimated to be $480 a year, or $40 per month. Accordingly, depreciation for October is recognized by the following adjusting entry:

Depreciation

Oct. 1

Office equipment purchased; record asset

Office Equipment			
Oct	Nov	Dec	Jan
$40	$40	$40	$40
Feb	March	April	May
$40	$40	$40	$40
June	July	Aug	Sept
$40	$40	$40	$40
Depreciation = $480/year			

Oct. 31

Depreciation recognized; record depreciation expense

Oct. 31	Depreciation Expense	40	
	Accumulated Depreciation—Office Equipment		40
	(To record monthly depreciation)		

After the adjusting entry is posted, the accounts show:

Office Equipment

10/1	5,000	

Accumulated Depreciation— Office Equipment

	10/31 Adj. 40

Depreciation Expense

10/31 Adj. 40	

Illustration 3-6

Accounts after adjustment for depreciation

Helpful hint Note that the account containing the prepayment is not used in the adjusting entry.

---
[1]Additional consideration is given to computing depreciation expense in Chapter 10.

The balance in the accumulated depreciation account will increase $40 each month. Therefore, after journalizing and posting the adjusting entry at November 30, the balance will be $80.

Statement Presentation.   Accumulated Depreciation—Office Equipment is a contra asset account. A contra asset account is an account that is offset against an asset account on the balance sheet. This means that the accumulated depreciation account is offset against Office Equipment on the balance sheet and that its normal balance is a credit. This account is used instead of crediting Office Equipment in order to permit disclosure of **both the original cost** of the equipment **and the total cost that has expired to date**. In the balance sheet, Accumulated Depreciation—Office Equipment is deducted from the related asset account as follows:

Office equipment	$5,000	
Less: Accumulated depreciation—office equipment	40	$4,960

The difference between the cost of any depreciable asset and its related accumulated depreciation is referred to as the book value of that asset. In Illustration 3-7, the book value of the equipment at the balance sheet date is $4,960. It is important to realize that the book value and the market value of the asset are generally two different values. The reason the two are different is that depreciation is not a matter of valuation but rather, a means of cost allocation.

Note also that depreciation expense identifies that portion of the asset's cost that has expired in October. As in the case of other prepaid adjustments, the omission of this adjusting entry would cause total assets, total stockholders' equity, and net income to be overstated and depreciation expense to be understated.

If additional equipment is involved, such as delivery or store equipment, or if the company has buildings, depreciation expense is recorded on each of these items. Related accumulated depreciation accounts also are established. These accumulated depreciation accounts would be described in the ledger as follows: Accumulated Depreciation—Delivery Equipment; Accumulated Depreciation—Store Equipment; and Accumulated Depreciation—Buildings.

Unearned Revenues

As stated on page 101, revenues received in cash and recorded as liabilities before they are earned are called unearned revenues. Such items as rent, magazine subscriptions, and customer deposits for future service may result in unearned revenues. Airlines such as United, American, and Delta treat receipts from the sale of tickets as unearned revenue until the flight service is provided. Similarly, tuition received prior to the start of a semester, as in the opening story about Arizona State University, is considered to be unearned revenue. Unearned revenues are the opposite of prepaid expenses. Indeed, unearned revenue on the books of one company is likely to be a prepayment on the books of the company that has made the advance payment. For example, if identical accounting periods are assumed, a landlord will have unearned rent revenue when a tenant has prepaid rent.

When the payment is received for services to be provided in a future accounting period, an unearned revenue (a liability) account should be credited to recognize the obligation that exists. Unearned revenues are subsequently earned through rendering service to a customer. During the accounting period it may not be practical to make daily recurring entries as the revenue is earned. In such cases, the recognition of earned revenue is delayed until the adjustment process. Then an adjusting entry is made to record the revenue that has been earned and to show the liability that remains. **A liability–revenue account relationship therefore exists with unearned revenues.** In the typical case, liabilities are overstated and revenues are understated prior to adjustment. Thus, **the adjusting entry for unearned revenues results in a debit (decrease) to a liability account and a credit (increase) to a revenue account**.

Pioneer Advertising Agency Inc. received $1,200 on October 2 from R. Knox for advertising services expected to be completed by December 31. The payment was credited to Unearned Fees, and this account shows a balance of $1,200 in the October 31 trial balance. When analysis reveals that $400 of those fees has been earned in October, the following adjusting entry is made:

Oct. 31	Unearned Fees	400	
	Fees Earned		400
	(To record fees earned)		

After the adjusting entry is posted, the accounts show:

Unearned Fees					Fees Earned			
10/31 Adj.	400	10/2	1,200				10/31 Bal.	10,000
							31 Adj.	400
		10/31 Bal.	800					

Unearned Revenues

Oct.2

Thank you in advance for your work

I will finish by Dec. 31

~$1,200

Cash is received in advance; liability is recorded

Oct.31

Service is provided; revenue is recorded

Illustration 3-8

Fees accounts after adjustment

The liability Unearned Fees now shows a balance of $800, which represents the remaining advertising services expected to be performed in the future. At the same time, Fees Earned shows total revenue earned in October of $10,400. **If this adjustment is not made, revenues and net income will be understated by $400 in the income statement. Moreover, liabilities will be overstated and stockholders' equity will be understated by $400 on the October 31 balance sheet.**

Before You Go On . . .

► Review It

1. What are the four types of adjusting entries?
2. What is the effect on assets, stockholders' equity, expenses, and net income if a prepaid expense adjusting entry is not made?
3. What is the effect on liabilities, stockholders' equity, revenues, and net income if an unearned revenue adjusting entry is not made?

► Do It

The ledger of Hammond, Inc., on March 31, 1996, includes the following selected accounts before adjusting entries are prepared:

	Debit	Credit
Prepaid Insurance	3,600	
Office Supplies	2,800	
Office Equipment	25,000	
Accumulated Depreciation—Office Equipment		5,000
Unearned Fees		9,200

An analysis of the accounts shows the following:

1. Insurance expires at the rate of $100 per month.
2. Supplies on hand total $800.
3. The office equipment depreciates $200 a month.
4. One-half of the unearned fees were earned in March.

Prepare the adjusting entries for the month of March.

Reasoning: In order for revenues to be recorded in the period in which they are earned, and for expenses to be recognized in the period in which they are incurred, adjusting entries are made at the end of the accounting period. Adjusting entries for prepayments are required at the statement date to record the portion of the prepayment that represents the expense incurred or the revenue earned in the current accounting period. The failure to adjust for the prepayment leads to overstatement of the asset or liability and a related understatement of the expense or revenue.

Solution:

1. Insurance Expense	100	
Prepaid Insurance		100
(To record insurance expired)		
2. Office Supplies Expense	2,000	
Office Supplies		2,000
(To record supplies used)		
3. Depreciation Expense	200	
Accumulated Depreciation—Office Equipment		200
(To record monthly depreciation)		
4. Unearned Fees	4,600	
Fees Earned		4,600
(To record fees earned)		

Related exercise material: BE3–3, BE3–4, BE3–5, BE3–6, E3–1, E3–2, E3–3, E3–4, E3–5, E3–6, E3–7, E3–8 and E3–9.

Adjusting Entries for Accruals

The second category of adjusting entries is **accruals**. Adjusting entries for accruals are required to record revenues earned and expenses incurred in the current accounting period that have not been recognized through daily entries. If an accrual adjustment is needed, the revenue account (and the related asset account) and/or the expense account (and the related liability account) is understated. Thus, the adjusting entry for accruals will **increase both a balance sheet and an income statement account**. Adjusting entries for accruals are graphically depicted in Illustration 3-9.

Accrued Revenues

Helpful hint Accrued revenues are also called accrued receivables.

As explained on page 101, revenues earned but not yet received in cash or recorded at the statement date are accrued revenues. Accrued revenues may accumulate (accrue) with the passing of time, as in the case of interest revenue and rent revenue. Or they may result from services that have been performed but neither billed nor collected, as in the case of commissions and fees. The former are unrecorded because the earning of interest and rent does not involve daily transactions; the latter may be unrecorded because only a portion of the total service has been provided.

An adjusting entry is required to show the receivable that exists at the balance sheet date and to record the revenue that has been earned during the period. **An asset-revenue account relationship exists with accrued revenues.** Prior to adjustment both assets and revenues are understated. Accordingly, **an adjusting**

Illustration 3-9

Adjusting entries for accruals

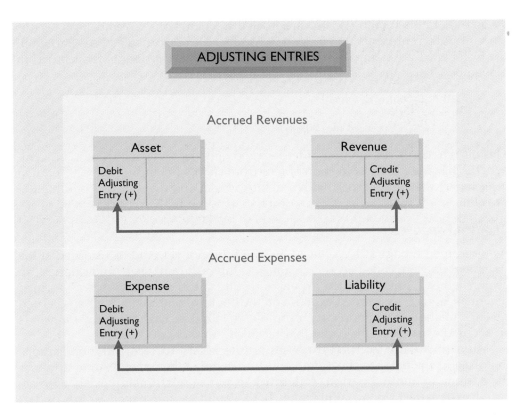

Accrued Revenues

Oct. 31

My fee is $200

Revenue and receivable are recorded for unbilled services

Nov.
Cash is received; receivable is reduced

entry for accrued revenues results in a debit (increase) to an asset account and a credit (increase) to a revenue account.

In October Pioneer Advertising Agency Inc. earned $200 in fees for advertising services that were not billed to clients before October 31. Because these services have not been billed, they have not been recorded. Thus, the following adjusting entry is made:

Oct. 31	Accounts Receivable	200	
	Fees Earned		200
	(To accrue fees earned but not billed or collected)		

After the adjusting entry is posted, the accounts show:

Illustration 3-10

Receivable and revenue accounts after accrual adjustment

Accounts Receivable		Fees Earned	
10/31 Adj. 200		10/31 10,000	
		31 400	
		31 Adj. 200	
		10/31 Bal. 10,600	

The asset Accounts Receivable shows that $200 is owed by clients at the balance sheet date. The balance of $10,600 in Fees Earned represents the total fees earned during the month ($10,000 + $400 + $200). **If the adjusting entry is not made, assets and stockholders' equity on the balance sheet, and revenues and net income on the income statement, will all be understated.**

In the next accounting period, the clients will be billed. When this occurs, the entry to record the billing should recognize that $200 of fees earned in October have already been recorded in the October 31 adjusting entry. To illustrate, assume that bills totaling $3,000 are mailed to clients on November 10. Of this amount, $200 represents fees earned in October and recorded as Fees Earned in the October 31 adjusting entry. The remaining $2,800 represents fees earned in November. Thus, the following entry is made:

Nov. 10	Accounts Receivable	2,800	
	Fees Earned		2,800
	(To record fees billed)		

This entry records the amount of fees earned between November 1 and November 10. The subsequent collection of fees from clients (including the $200 earned in October) will be recorded with a debit to Cash and a credit to Accounts Receivable.

Accrued Expenses

As indicated on page 101, expenses incurred but not yet paid or recorded at the statement date are called accrued expenses. Interest, rent, taxes, and salaries can be accrued expenses. Accrued expenses result from the same causes as accrued revenues. In fact, an accrued expense on the books of one company is an accrued revenue to another company. For example, the $200 accrual of fees by Pioneer is an accrued expense to the client that received the service.

Helpful hint Accrued expenses are also called accrued liabilities.

Adjustments for accrued expenses are necessary to record the obligations that exist at the balance sheet date and to recognize the expenses that apply to the current accounting period. **A liability–expense relationship exists with accrued expenses.** Prior to adjustment both liabilities and expenses are understated. Therefore, **the adjusting entry for accrued expenses results in a debit (increase) to an expense account and a credit (increase) to a liability account.**

Accrued Interest.   Pioneer Advertising Agency Inc. signed a 3-month note payable in the amount of $5,000 on October 1. The note requires interest at an annual rate of 12%. The amount of the interest accumulation is determined by three factors: (1) the face value of the note, (2) the interest rate, which is always expressed as an annual rate, and (3) the length of time the note is outstanding. In this instance, the total interest due on the $5,000 note at its due date 3 months hence is $150 ($5,000 × 12% × 3/12), or $50 for one month. The formula for computing interest and its application to Pioneer Advertising Agency Inc. for the month of October[2] are shown in Illustration 3-11.

Helpful hint Interest is a cost of borrowing money that accumulates with the passage of time.

Illustration 3-11

Formula for computing interest

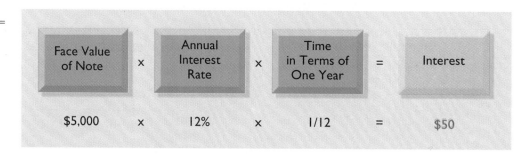

Note that the time period is expressed as a fraction of a year. The accrued expense adjusting entry at October 31 is as follows:

Oct. 31	Interest Expense	50	
	Interest Payable		50
	(To accrue interest on notes payable)		

---

[2]The computation of interest will be considered in more depth in later chapters.

After this adjusting entry is posted, the accounts show:

Illustration 3-12

Interest accounts after adjustment

Interest Expense		Interest Payable	
10/31 50			10/31 50

Interest Expense shows the interest charges applicable to the month of October. The amount of interest owed at the statement date is shown in Interest Payable. It will not be paid until the note comes due at the end of three months. The Interest Payable account is used instead of crediting Notes Payable to disclose the two types of obligations (interest and principal) in the accounts and statements. **If this adjusting entry is not made, liabilities and interest expense will be understated, and net income and stockholders' equity will be overstated.**

Accrued Salaries. Some types of expenses, such as employee salaries and commissions, are paid for after the services have been performed. At Pioneer Advertising, salaries were last paid on October 26; the next payment of salaries will not occur until November 9. As shown in the calendar below, three working days remain in October (October 29–31).

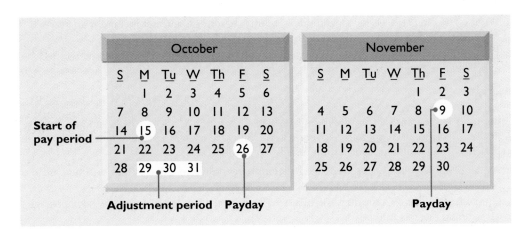

At October 31, the salaries for these days represent an accrued expense and a related liability to Pioneer Advertising. As explained on page 68, the employees receive total salaries of $2,000 for a five-day work week, or $400 per day. Thus, accrued salaries at October 31 are $1,200 ($400 × 3), and the adjusting entry is:

Helpful hint Although we call these entries accruals we do not put accrued in the account title.

Oct. 31	Salaries Expense	1,200	
	Salaries Payable		1,200
	(To record accrued salaries)		

After this adjusting entry is posted, the accounts show:

Illustration 3-13

Salary accounts after adjustment

Salaries Expense		Salaries Payable	
10/26 4,000			10/31 Adj. 1,200
31 Adj. 1,200			
10/31 Bal. 5,200			

After this adjustment, the balance in Salaries Expense of $5,200 (13 days $\times$ $400) is the actual salary expense for October. The balance in Salaries Payable of $1,200 is the amount of the liability for salaries owed as of October 31. **If the $1,200 adjustment for salaries is not recorded, Pioneer's expenses will be understated $1,200, and its liabilities will be understated $1,200.**

At Pioneer Advertising, salaries are payable every two weeks. Consequently, the next payday is November 9, when total salaries of $4,000 will again be paid. The payment consists of $1,200 of salaries payable at October 31 plus $2,800 of salaries expense for November (7 working days as shown in the November calendar $\times$ $400). Therefore, the following entry is made on November 9:

Nov. 9	Salaries Payable	1,200	
	Salaries Expense	2,800	
	Cash		4,000
	(To record November 9 payroll)		

This entry eliminates the liability for Salaries Payable that was recorded in the October 31 adjusting entry and records the proper amount of Salaries Expense for the period between November 1 and November 9.

Before You Go On . . .

▶ *Review It*

1. What is the effect on assets, stockholders' equity, revenues, and net income if an accrued revenue adjusting entry is not made?
2. What is the effect on liabilities, stockholders' equity, and interest expense if an accrued expense adjusting entry is not made?

▶ *Do It*

Calvin and Hobbs are the new owners of Micro Computer Services. At the end of August 1996, their first month of operations, Calvin and Hobbs are trying to prepare monthly financial statements. The following information relates to August:

1. At August 31, Micro Computer owed its employees $800 in salaries that will be paid on September 1.
2. On August 1, Micro Computer borrowed $30,000 from a local bank on a 15-year mortgage. The annual interest rate is 10%.
3. Fees earned but unrecorded for August totaled $1,100.

   Prepare the adjusting entries needed at August 31, 1996.

   Reasoning: Adjusting entries for accruals are required to record revenues earned and expenses incurred in the current accounting period that have not been recognized through daily entries. An adjusting entry for accruals will increase both a balance sheet and an income statement account.

   Solution:

1.	Salaries Expense	800	
	Salaries Payable		800
	(To record accrued salaries)		
2.	Interest Expense	250	
	Interest Payable		250
	(To record accrued interest)		
	($30,000 $\times$ 10% $\times$ 1/12 = $250)		
3.	Accounts Receivable	1,100	
	Fees Earned		1,100
	(To accrue fees earned but not billed or collected)		

Related exercise material: BE3–7, E3–1, E3–2, E3–3, E3–4, E3–5, E3–6, E3–7, E3–8, and E3–9.

Summary of Basic Relationships

Pertinent data on each of the four basic types of adjusting entries are summarized in Illustration 3-14. Take some time to study and analyze the adjusting entries shown in the summary. Be sure to note that **each adjusting entry affects one balance sheet account and one income statement account**.

Illustration 3-14

Summary of adjusting entries

Type of Adjustment	Accounts before Adjustment	Adjusting Entry	Examples
1. Prepaid expenses	Assets overstated Expenses understated	Dr. Expenses Cr. Assets	Insurance, rent, supplies
2. Unearned revenues	Liabilities overstated Revenues understated	Dr. Liabilities Cr. Revenues	Subscriptions, deposits, rent
3. Accrued revenues	Assets understated Revenues understated	Dr. Assets Cr. Revenues	Interest, rent
4. Accrued expenses	Expenses understated Liabilities understated	Dr. Expenses Cr. Liabilities	Salaries, wages interest, taxes

Helpful hint (1) Remember that adjusting entries should not involve debits and credits to cash. (2) Evaluate whether the adjustment makes sense. For example, an adjustment to recognize supplies used should increase supplies expense. (3) Double-check all computations.

The journalizing and posting of adjusting entries for Pioneer Advertising Agency Inc. on October 31 are shown in Illustrations 3-15 and 3-16. All adjustments are identified in the ledger by the reference J2 because they are journalized on page 2 of the general journal. A center caption entitled Adjusting Entries may be inserted between the last transaction entry and the first adjusting entry to identify these entries. When reviewing the general ledger in Illustration 3-16, note that the adjustments are highlighted in color.

Illustration 3-15

General journal showing adjusting entries

	GENERAL JOURNAL			J2
Date	Account Titles and Explanation	Ref.	Debit	Credit
1996	Adjusting Entries			
Oct. 31	Advertising Supplies Expense	61	1,500	
	Advertising Supplies	8		1,500
	(To record supplies used)			
31	Insurance Expense	63	50	
	Prepaid Insurance	10		50
	(To record insurance expired)			
31	Depreciation Expense	65	40	
	Accumulated Depreciation—Office Equipment	16		40
	(To record monthly depreciation)			
31	Unearned Fees	28	400	
	Fees Earned	50		400
	(To record fees earned)			
31	Accounts Receivable	6	200	
	Fees Earned	50		200
	(To accrue fees earned but not billed or collected)			
31	Interest Expense	64	50	
	Interest Payable	27		50
	(To accrue interest on notes payable)			
31	Salaries Expense	60	1,200	
	Salaries Payable	29		1,200
	(To record accrued salaries)			

Helpful hint The standard form and content of journal entries stated in Chapter 2 also applies to adjusting entries.

Illustration 3-16

General ledger after adjustment

GENERAL LEDGER

Cash — No. 1

Date	Explanation	Ref.	Debit	Credit	Balance
1996					
Oct. 1		J1	10,000		10,000
2		J1	1,200		11,200
3		J1		900	10,300
4		J1		600	9,700
20		J1		500	9,200
26		J1		4,000	5,200
31		J1	10,000		15,200

Accounts Receivable — No. 6

Date	Explanation	Ref.	Debit	Credit	Balance
1996					
Oct. 31	Adj. entry	J2	200		200

Advertising Supplies — No. 8

Date	Explanation	Ref.	Debit	Credit	Balance
1996					
Oct. 5		J1	2,500		2,500
31	Adj. entry	J2		1,500	1,000

Prepaid Insurance — No. 10

Date	Explanation	Ref.	Debit	Credit	Balance
1996					
Oct. 4		J1	600		600
31	Adj. entry	J2		50	550

Office Equipment — No. 15

Date	Explanation	Ref.	Debit	Credit	Balance
1996					
Oct. 1		J1	5,000		5,000

Accumulated Depreciation—Office Equipment — No. 16

Date	Explanation	Ref.	Debit	Credit	Balance
1996					
Oct. 31	Adj. entry	J2		40	40

Notes Payable — No. 25

Date	Explanation	Ref.	Debit	Credit	Balance
1996					
Oct. 1		J1		5,000	5,000

Accounts Payable — No. 26

Date	Explanation	Ref.	Debit	Credit	Balance
1996					
Oct. 5		J1		2,500	2,500

Interest Payable — No. 27

Date	Explanation	Ref.	Debit	Credit	Balance
1996					
Oct. 31	Adj. entry	J2		50	50

Unearned Fees — No. 28

Date	Explanation	Ref.	Debit	Credit	Balance
1996					
Oct. 2		J1		1,200	
31	Adj. entry	J2	400		800

Salaries Payable — No. 29

Date	Explanation	Ref.	Debit	Credit	Balance
1996					
Oct. 31	Adj. entry	J2		1,200	1,200

Common Stock — No. 40

Date	Explanation	Ref.	Debit	Credit	Balance
1996					
Oct. 1		J1		10,000	10,000

Retained Earnings — No. 41

Date	Explanation	Ref.	Debit	Credit	Balance
1996					

Dividends — No. 42

Date	Explanation	Ref.	Debit	Credit	Balance
1996					
Oct. 20		J1	500		500

Fees Earned — No. 50

Date	Explanation	Ref.	Debit	Credit	Balance
1996					
Oct. 31		J1		10,000	10,000
31	Adj. entry	J2		400	10,400
31	Adj. entry	J2		200	10,600

Salaries Expense — No. 60

Date	Explanation	Ref.	Debit	Credit	Balance
1996					
Oct. 26		J1	4,000		4,000
31	Adj. entry	J2	1,200		5,200

Advertising Supplies Expense — No. 61

Date	Explanation	Ref.	Debit	Credit	Balance
1996					
Oct. 31	Adj. entry	J2	1,500		1,500

Rent Expense — No. 62

Date	Explanation	Ref.	Debit	Credit	Balance
1996					
Oct. 3		J1	900		900

Insurance Expense — No. 63

Date	Explanation	Ref.	Debit	Credit	Balance
1996					
Oct. 31	Adj. entry	J2	50		50

Interest Expense — No. 64

Date	Explanation	Ref.	Debit	Credit	Balance
1996					
Oct. 31	Adj. entry	J2	50		50

Depreciation Expense — No. 65

Date	Explanation	Ref.	Debit	Credit	Balance
1996					
Oct. 31	Adj. entry	J2	40		40

Preparing the Adjusted Trial Balance

After all adjusting entries have been journalized and posted, another trial balance is prepared from the ledger accounts. This trial balance is called an adjusted trial balance. It shows the balances of all accounts, including those that have been adjusted, at the end of the accounting period. The purpose of an adjusted trial balance is to **show the effects of all financial events that have occurred during the accounting period.** The procedures for preparing an adjusted trial balance are identical to those described in Chapter 2 for preparing a trial balance.

An adjusted trial balance proves the equality of the total debit balances and the total credit balances in the ledger after all adjustments have been made. The proof provided by an adjusted trial balance, like the proof contained in a trial balance, extends only to the mathematical accuracy of the ledger. Because the accounts contain all data that are needed for financial statements, the adjusted trial balance provides the primary basis for the preparation of financial statements.

The adjusted trial balance for Pioneer Advertising Agency Inc. presented in Illustration 3-17 has been prepared from the ledger accounts shown in Illustration 3-16. To facilitate the comparison of account balances before and after adjustment, the adjusted data are presented with the trial balance data shown in Illustration 3-2, on page 102. In addition, the amounts affected by the adjusting entries are highlighted in color in the After Adjustment columns.

STUDY OBJECTIVE

7

Describe the nature and purpose of an adjusted trial balance.

PIONEER ADVERTISING AGENCY INC.
Trial Balances
October 31, 1996

	Before Adjustment Dr.	Before Adjustment Cr.	After Adjustment Dr.	After Adjustment Cr.
Cash	$15,200		$15,200	
Accounts Receivable			200	
Advertising Supplies	2,500		1,000	
Prepaid Insurance	600		550	
Office Equipment	5,000		5,000	
Accumulated Depreciation—				
Office Equipment				$ 40
Notes Payable		$ 5,000		5,000
Accounts Payable		2,500		2,500
Interest Payable				50
Unearned Fees		1,200		800
Salaries Payable				1,200
Common Stock		10,000		10,000
Retained Earnings		–0–		–0–
Dividends	500		500	
Fees Earned		10,000		10,600
Salaries Expense	4,000		5,200	
Advertising Supplies				
Expense			1,500	
Rent Expense			900	
	900			
Insurance Expense			50	
Interest Expense			50	
Depreciation Expense			40	
	$28,700	$28,700	$30,190	$30,190

Illustration 3-17

Trial balance and adjusted trial balance compared

▶*T*echnology in *A*ction

In many computer systems, the adjusting process is handled like any other transaction, with the accountant inputting the adjustment at the time required. The main difference between adjusting entries and regular transactions is that with adjusting entries, one part of the computer system may perform the required calculation for such items as depreciation or interest and then "feed" these figures to the journalizing process.

Such systems are also able to display information before and after changes were made. Management may be interested in such information to highlight the impact that adjustments have on the various accounts and financial statements.

*P*reparing Financial Statements

Illustration 3-18

Preparation of the income statement and retained earnings statement from the adjusted trial balance

Financial statements can be prepared directly from an adjusted trial balance. The preparation of financial statements from the adjusted trial balance of Pioneer Advertising Agency Inc. and the interrelationship of data are presented in Illustrations 3-18 and 3-19. As shown in Illustration 3-18 the income statement is prepared from the revenue and expense accounts; the retained earnings statement is derived from the retained earnings and dividends accounts and the net income (or net loss) shown in the income statement. As shown in Illustration 3-19 the balance sheet is then prepared from the asset and liability accounts, the common stock account, and the ending retained earnings balance as reported in the retained earnings statement.

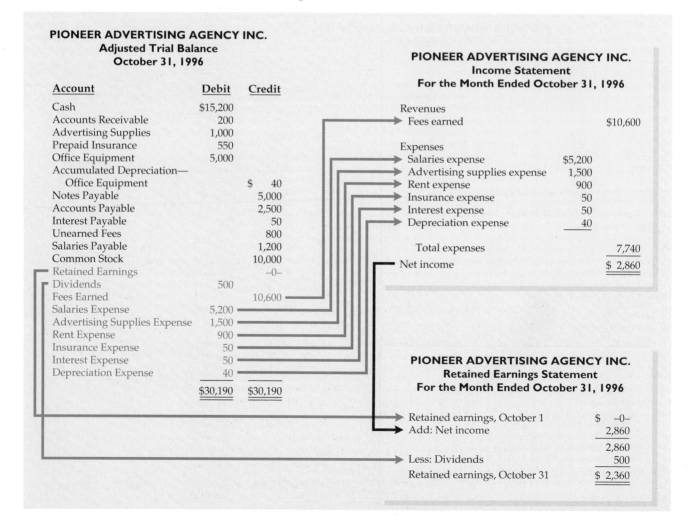

PIONEER ADVERTISING AGENCY INC.
Adjusted Trial Balance
October 31, 1996

Account	Debit	Credit
Cash	$15,200	
Accounts Receivable	200	
Advertising Supplies	1,000	
Prepaid Insurance	550	
Office Equipment	5,000	
Accumulated Depreciation—		
Office Equipment		$ 40
Notes Payable		5,000
Accounts Payable		2,500
Interest Payable		50
Unearned Fees		800
Salaries Payable		1,200
Common Stock		10,000
Retained Earnings		–0–
Dividends	500	
Fees Earned		10,600
Salaries Expense	5,200	
Advertising Supplies Expense	1,500	
Rent Expense	900	
Insurance Expense	50	
Interest Expense	50	
Depreciation Expense	40	
	$30,190	$30,190

PIONEER ADVERTISING AGENCY INC.
Income Statement
For the Month Ended October 31, 1996

Revenues		
Fees earned		$10,600
Expenses		
Salaries expense	$5,200	
Advertising supplies expense	1,500	
Rent expense	900	
Insurance expense	50	
Interest expense	50	
Depreciation expense	40	
Total expenses		7,740
Net income		$ 2,860

PIONEER ADVERTISING AGENCY INC.
Retained Earnings Statement
For the Month Ended October 31, 1996

Retained earnings, October 1		$ –0–
Add: Net income		2,860
		2,860
Less: Dividends		500
Retained earnings, October 31		$ 2,360

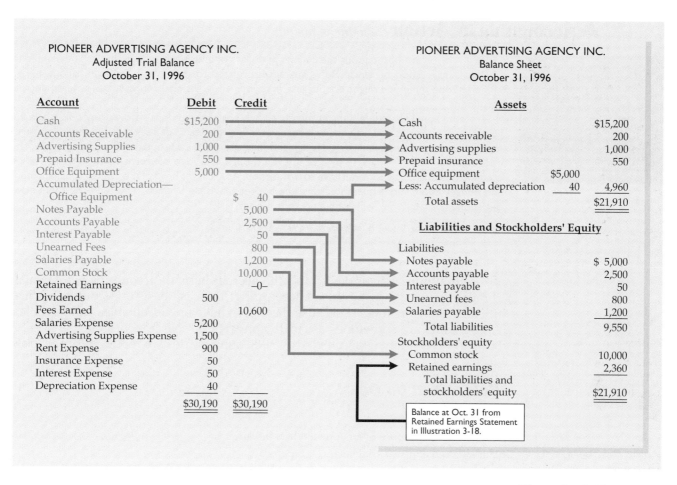

PIONEER ADVERTISING AGENCY INC.
Adjusted Trial Balance
October 31, 1996

Account	Debit	Credit
Cash	$15,200	
Accounts Receivable	200	
Advertising Supplies	1,000	
Prepaid Insurance	550	
Office Equipment	5,000	
Accumulated Depreciation—Office Equipment		$ 40
Notes Payable		5,000
Accounts Payable		2,500
Interest Payable		50
Unearned Fees		800
Salaries Payable		1,200
Common Stock		10,000
Retained Earnings		–0–
Dividends	500	
Fees Earned		10,600
Salaries Expense	5,200	
Advertising Supplies Expense	1,500	
Rent Expense	900	
Insurance Expense	50	
Interest Expense	50	
Depreciation Expense	40	
	$30,190	$30,190

PIONEER ADVERTISING AGENCY INC.
Balance Sheet
October 31, 1996

Assets

Cash		$15,200
Accounts receivable		200
Advertising supplies		1,000
Prepaid insurance		550
Office equipment	$5,000	
Less: Accumulated depreciation	40	4,960
Total assets		$21,910

Liabilities and Stockholders' Equity

Liabilities		
Notes payable		$ 5,000
Accounts payable		2,500
Interest payable		50
Unearned fees		800
Salaries payable		1,200
Total liabilities		9,550
Stockholders' equity		
Common stock		10,000
Retained earnings		2,360
Total liabilities and stockholders' equity		$21,910

> Balance at Oct. 31 from Retained Earnings Statement in Illustration 3-18.

Illustration 3-19

Preparation of the balance sheet from the adjusted trial balance

Accrual vs. Cash Basis of Accounting

What you have learned in this chapter is the accrual basis of accounting. Accrual basis accounting means that transactions that change a company's financial statements are recorded **in the periods in which the events occur**, rather than in the periods in which the company receives or pays cash. For example, using the accrual basis to determine net income means recognizing revenues when earned rather than when the cash is received, and recognizing expenses when incurred rather than when paid. Information presented on an accrual basis reveals relationships that are likely to be important in predicting future results. To illustrate, under accrual accounting, revenues are generally recognized when services are performed so they can be related to the economic environment in which they occur. Trends in revenues are thus more meaningful for decision-making purposes.

Under cash basis accounting, revenue is recorded only when the cash is received, and an expense is recorded only when cash is paid. As a result, the cash basis of accounting often leads to misleading financial statements. For example, it fails to record revenue which has been earned but for which the cash has not been received, violating the revenue recognition principle. In addition, expenses are also not matched with earned revenues and therefore the matching principle is not followed. Therefore, **the cash basis of accounting is not in accordance with generally accepted accounting principles.**

STUDY OBJECTIVE

8

Explain the accrual basis of accounting.

▶ *International note*

Although different accounting standards are often used in other major industrialized countries, the accrual basis of accounting is followed by all these countries.

Helpful hint The cash basis is used in filing personal federal income tax returns with the Internal Revenue Service.

▸Accounting in Action ▸ *Business Insight*

If you are upset about the billions of dollars of taxpayers' money that will be needed to make good on Uncle Sam's guarantees related to the savings and loan bailout, here's one thing you might do: Suggest that your congressional representatives learn accrual accounting.

Presently, the U.S. federal budget measures only cash transactions—how many dollar bills the government pays out and how many it receives in a given year. Let's say that the federal government guarantees loans made by a savings and loan. Since no cash outlay takes place initially, the budget deficit doesn't increase by a cent, even though everyone concerned knows there will be credit losses that Uncle Sam will have to make good. As a former head of the Office of Management and Budget noted, "loan guarantees are the budget's invisible Pacmen. You can't see them now, but sooner or later they will gobble up your money."

Source: Adapted from "Phony Bookkeeping," *Forbes*, May 1990.

Although most companies use the accrual basis of accounting, some small companies use the cash basis of accounting. The cash basis of accounting is justified by these businesses because they often have few receivables and payables. Accountants are sometimes asked to convert cash basis records to the accrual basis. As you might expect, extensive adjusting entries are required for this task.

Before You Go On . . .

▸ *Review It*

1. What is the purpose of an adjusted trial balance?
2. How is an adjusted trial balance prepared?
3. What are the differences between the cash and accrual bases of accounting?

▸ *A Look Back at Arizona State University*

Refer to the opening story about Arizona State University, and answer the following questions.

1. What are the purposes of adjusting entries?
2. Why should Arizona State be concerned about the period in which revenue is recognized?
3. What adjusting entries should be made for tuition revenue and supplies expense at the end of the summer session?
4. What other types of adjusting entries do you believe Arizona State University might make?

Solution:

1. Adjusting entries are necessary to make the financial statements complete and accurate. Adjusting entries are made to record revenues in the period in which they are earned and to recognize expenses in the period in which they are incurred. Therefore, adjustments ensure that the revenue recognition and matching principles are followed.
2. As a not-for-profit institution Arizona State University must operate within its state appropriations and its own budget. It must know what revenues are attributable to each operating/accounting period. Assignment of revenues to the proper operating periods (namely, in the period earned) is necessary in order to make operating/accounting periods (years) comparable.
3. ASU probably used Unearned Tuition Revenue because tuition is generally received before the semester begins. The adjusting entry is debit Unearned Tuition Revenue

and credit Tuition Revenue. When supplies were purchased, ASU probably debited Supplies. The adjusting entry is a credit to Supplies and a debit to Supplies Expense.
4. (a) Accrued expenses: rent, salaries, utilities, interest.
   (b) Accrued revenues: unpaid tuition, lab fees, interest earned.
   (c) Prepaid expenses: insurance, depreciation.
   (d) Unearned revenues: tuition, lab fees, theatre tickets, athletic tickets.

Summary of Study Objectives

1. *Explain the time period assumption.* The time period assumption assumes that the economic life of a business can be divided into artificial time periods.

2. *Distinguish between the revenue recognition principle and the matching principle.* The revenue recognition principle dictates that revenue be recognized in the accounting period in which it is earned. The matching principle dictates that expenses be recognized when they make their contribution to revenues.

3. *Explain why adjusting entries are needed.* Adjusting entries are made at the end of an accounting period. They ensure that revenues are recorded in the period in which they are earned and that expenses are recognized in the period in which they are incurred.

4. *Identify the major types of adjusting entries.* The major types of adjusting entries are prepaid expenses, unearned revenues, accrued revenues, and accrued expenses.

5. *Prepare adjusting entries for prepayments.* Prepayments are either prepaid expenses or unearned revenues. Adjusting entries for prepayments are required at the statement date to record the portion of the prepayment that represents the expense incurred or the revenue earned in the current accounting period.

6. *Prepare adjusting entries for accruals.* Accruals are either accrued revenues or accrued expenses. Adjusting entries for accruals are required to record revenues earned and expenses incurred in the current accounting period that have not been recognized through daily entries.

7. *Describe the nature and purpose of an adjusted trial balance.* An adjusted trial balance is a trial balance that shows the balances of all accounts, including those that have been adjusted, at the end of an accounting period. The purpose of an adjusted trial balance is to show the effects of all financial events that have occurred during the accounting period.

8. *Explain the accrual basis of accounting.* Accrual basis accounting means that events that change a company's financial statements are recorded in the periods in which the events occur, rather than in the periods in which the company receives or pays cash.

APPENDIX ► *Alternative Treatment of Prepaid Expenses and Unearned Revenues*

In our discussion of adjusting entries for prepaid expenses and unearned revenues, we illustrated transactions for which the initial entries were made to balance sheet accounts. That is, in the case of prepaid expenses, the prepayment was debited to an asset account, and in the case of unearned revenue, the cash received was credited to a liability account. Some businesses use an alternative treatment: (1) At the time an expense is prepaid, it is debited to an expense account; (2) at the time of a receipt for future services, it is credited to a revenue account. The circumstances that justify such entries and the different adjusting entries that may be required are described below. The alternative treatment of prepaid expenses and unearned revenues has the same effect on the financial statements as the procedures described in the chapter.

STUDY OBJECTIVE

After studying this appendix, you should be able to:

9. Prepare adjusting entries for the alternative treatment of prepayments.

Prepaid Expenses

Prepaid expenses become expired costs either through the passage of time, as in the case of insurance, or through consumption, as in the case of advertising supplies. If, at the time of purchase, the company expects to consume the supplies before the next financial statement date, **it may be more convenient initially to debit (increase) an expense account rather than an asset account**. Assume, for example, that Pioneer Advertising expects that all of the supplies purchased on October 5 will be used before October 31. A debit of $2,500 to Advertising Supplies Expense rather than to the asset account, Advertising Supplies, on October 5 will eliminate the need for an adjusting entry on October 31, if all the supplies are used. At October 31, the Advertising Supplies Expense account will show a balance of $2,500, which is equal to the cost of supplies used between October 5 and October 31.

Assume, however, that the company does not use all the supplies, and an inventory of $1,000 of advertising supplies remains on October 31. What then? Obviously, in such a case an adjusting entry is needed. Prior to adjustment, the expense account, Advertising Supplies Expense, is overstated $1,000, and the asset account, Advertising Supplies, is understated $1,000. Thus the following adjusting entry is made:

Oct. 31	Advertising Supplies	1,000	
	Advertising Supplies Expense		1,000
	(To record supplies inventory)		

After posting the adjusting entry, the accounts show:

Advertising Supplies				Advertising Supplies Expense			
10/31 Adj.	1,000			10/5	2,500	10/31 Adj.	1,000
				10/31 Bal.	1,500		

After adjustment, the asset account, Advertising Supplies, shows a balance of $1,000, which is equal to the cost of supplies on hand at October 31. In addition, Advertising Supplies Expense shows a balance of $1,500, which is equal to the cost of supplies used between October 5 and October 31. If the adjusting entry is not made, expenses will be overstated and net income will be understated by $1,000 in the October income statement. Moreover, both assets and stockholders' equity will be understated by $1,000 on the October 31 balance sheet.

A comparative summary of the entries and accounts for advertising supplies is shown in Illustration 3A-2.

	Prepayment Initially Debited to Asset Account (per chapter)				Prepayment Initially Debited to Expense Account (per appendix)		
Oct. 5	Advertising Supplies	2,500		Oct. 5	Advertising Supplies		
	Accounts Payable		2,500		Expense	2,500	
					Accounts Payable		2,500
Oct. 31	Advertising Supplies			Oct. 31	Advertising Supplies	1,000	
	Expense	1,500			Advertising Supplies		
	Advertising Supplies		1,500		Expense		1,000

After posting the entries, the accounts appear as follows:

(per chapter) Advertising Supplies			(per appendix) Advertising Supplies		
10/5	2,500	10/31 Adj. 1,500	10/31 Adj. 1,000		
10/31 Bal.	1,000				

Advertising Supplies Expense			Advertising Supplies Expense		
10/31 Adj.	1,500		10/5	2,500	10/31 Adj. 1,000
			10/31 Bal.	1,500	

Note that the account balances under each alternative are the same at October 31; that is, Advertising Supplies $1,000, and Advertising Supplies Expense $1,500.

Unearned Revenues

Unearned revenues become earned either through the passage of time, as in the case of unearned rent, or through rendering the service, as in the case of unearned fees. Like prepaid expenses, a revenue account may be credited when cash is received for future services and a different adjusting entry may be necessary.

To illustrate, assume that when Pioneer Advertising received $1,200 in fees for future services on October 2 the services were expected to be performed before October 31.[3] In such a case, Fees Earned would be credited. If these fees are in fact earned before October 31, no adjustment is needed. However, if, at the statement date, $800 of the services have not been provided, an adjusting entry is required. Prior to adjustment, the revenue account, Fees Earned, is overstated $800, and the liability account, Unearned Fees, is understated $800. Thus, the following adjusting entry is made:

Oct. 31	Fees Earned		800	
	Unearned Fees			800
	(To record unearned fees)			

After posting the adjusting entry, the accounts show:

Unearned Fees			Fees Earned		
	10/31 Adj. 800	10/31 Adj.	800	10/2	1,200
				10/31 Bal.	400

---

[3]This example focuses only on the alternative treatment of unearned revenues. In the interest of simplicity, the entries to Fees Earned pertaining to the immediate earning of fees ($10,000) and the adjusting entry for accrued fees ($200) have been ignored.

The liability account, Unearned Fees, shows a balance of $800, which is equal to the services that will be rendered in the future. In addition, the balance in Fees Earned equals the services rendered in October. If the adjusting entry is not made, both revenues and net income will be overstated by $800 in the October income statement. Moreover, liabilities will be understated by $800, and stockholders' equity will be overstated by $800 on the October 31 balance sheet.

A comparative summary of the entries and accounts for fees earned and unearned is presented in Illustration 3A-5:

Illustration 3A-5

Adjustment approaches— a comparison

	Unearned Revenue Initially Credited to Liability Account (per chapter)			Unearned Revenue Initially Credited to Revenue Account (per appendix)	
Oct. 2	Cash	1,200	Oct. 2	Cash	1,200
	Unearned Fees	1,200		Fees Earned	1,200
Oct. 31	Unearned Fees	400	Oct. 31	Fees Earned	800
	Fees Earned	400		Unearned Fees	800

After posting the entries, the accounts will show:

Illustration 3A-6

Comparison of accounts

	(per chapter) Unearned Fees				(per appendix) Unearned Fees		
10/31 Adj.	400	10/2	1,200			10/31 Adj.	800
		10/31 Bal.	800				

	(per chapter) Fees Earned				(per appendix) Fees Earned		
		10/31 Adj.	400	10/31 Adj.	800	10/2	1,200
						10/31 Bal.	400

Note that the balances in the accounts are the same under the two alternatives: Unearned Fees $800, and Fees Earned $400.

Summary of Additional Adjustment Relationships

The use of alternative adjusting entries requires additions to the summary of basic relationships presented earlier in Illustration 3-14. The additions are shown in color in Illustration 3A-7.

Alternative adjusting entries do not apply to accrued revenues and accrued expenses because **no entries occur before these types of adjusting entries are made**. Hence, the summary data shown in Illustration 3-14 for these two types of adjustments remains unchanged.

Type of Adjustment	Account Relationship	Reason for Adjustment	Account Balances before Adjustment	Adjusting Entry
1. Prepaid Expenses	Assets and Expenses	(a) Prepaid expenses initially recorded in asset accounts have been used.	Assets overstated Expenses understated	Dr. Expenses Cr. Assets
		(b) Prepaid expenses initially recorded in expense accounts have not been used.	Assets understated Expenses overstated	Dr. Assets Cr. Expenses
2. Unearned Revenues	Liabilities and Revenues	(a) Unearned revenues initially recorded in liability accounts have been earned.	Liabilities overstated Revenues understated	Dr. Liabilities Cr. Revenues
		(b) Unearned revenues initially recorded in revenue accounts have not been earned.	Liabilities understated Revenues overstated	Dr. Revenues Cr. Liabilities

Summary of Study Objectives for Chapter 3 Appendix

9. Prepare adjusting entries for the alternative treatment of prepayments. When prepayments are initially recorded in expense and revenue accounts, these accounts are overstated prior to adjustment. The adjusting entries for prepaid expenses are a debit to an asset account and a credit to an expense account. Adjusting entries for unearned revenues are a debit to a revenue account and a credit to a liability account.

GLOSSARY

Accrual basis of accounting Accounting basis in which transactions that change a company's financial statements are recorded in the periods in which the events occur, rather than in the periods in which the company receives or pays cash. (p. 117).

Accrued expenses Expenses incurred but not yet paid in cash or recorded. (p. 110).

Accrued revenues Revenues earned but not yet received in cash or recorded. (p. 108).

Adjusted trial balance A list of accounts and their balances after all adjustments have been made. (p. 115).

Adjusting entries Entries made at the end of an accounting period to ensure that the revenue recognition and matching principles are followed. (p. 101).

Book value The difference between the cost of a depreciable asset and its related accumulated depreciation. (p. 106).

Calendar year An accounting period that extends from January 1 to December 31. (p. 99).

Cash basis accounting Revenue is recorded only when cash is received and an expense is recorded only when cash is paid. (p. 117).

Contra asset account An account that is offset against an asset account on the balance sheet. (p. 106).

Depreciation The process of allocating the cost of an asset to expense over its useful life in a rational and systematic manner. (p. 105).

Fiscal year An accounting period that is one year in length. (p. 99).

Interim periods Monthly or quarterly accounting time periods. (p. 99).

Matching principle The principle that efforts (expenses) be matched with accomplishments (revenues). (p. 100).

Prepaid expenses Expenses paid in cash and recorded as assets before they are used or consumed. (p. 102).

Revenue recognition principle The principle that revenue be recognized in the accounting period in which it is earned. (p. 99).

Time period assumption   An assumption that the economic life of a business can be divided into artificial time periods. (p. 99).

Unearned revenues   Revenues received in cash and recorded as liabilities before they are earned. (p. 106).

Useful life   The length of service of a productive facility. (p. 105).

•••

DEMONSTRATION PROBLEM

Terry Thomas and a group of investors incorporates the Green Thumb Lawn Care Corporation on April 1. At April 30, the trial balance shows the following balances for selected accounts:

Prepaid Insurance	$ 3,600
Equipment	28,000
Notes Payable	20,000
Unearned Fees	4,200
Fees Earned	1,800

Analysis reveals the following additional data pertaining to these accounts:

1. Prepaid insurance is the cost of a two-year insurance policy, effective April 1.
2. Depreciation on the equipment is $500 per month.
3. The note payable is dated April 1. It is a six-month, 12% note.
4. Seven customers paid for the company's six months' lawn service package of $600 beginning in April. These customers were serviced in April.
5. Lawn services rendered other customers but not billed at April 30 totaled $1,500.

Instructions
Prepare the adjusting entries for the month of April. Show computations.

Solution to Demonstration Problem

Problem-Solving Strategies

1. Note that adjustments are being made for one month.
2. Make computations carefully.
3. Select account titles carefully.
4. Make sure debits are made first and credits are indented.
5. Check that debits equal credits for each entry.

GENERAL JOURNAL   J2

Date	Account Titles and Explanation	Ref.	Debit	Credit
	Adjusting Entries			
Apr. 30	Insurance Expense		150	
	Prepaid Insurance			150
	(To record insurance expired:			
	$3,600 ÷ 24 = $150 per month)			
30	Depreciation Expense		500	
	Accumulated Depreciation—Equipment			500
	(To record monthly depreciation)			
30	Interest Expense		200	
	Interest Payable			200
	(To accrue interest on notes payable:			
	$20,000 × 12% × 1/12 = $200)			
30	Unearned Fees		700	
	Fees Earned			700
	(To record fees earned: $600 ÷ 6 = $100;			
	$100 per month × 7 = $700)			
30	Accounts Receivable		1,500	
	Fees Earned			1,500
	(To accrue fees earned but not billed or			
	collected)			

*Note: All **asterisked** Questions, Exercises, and Problems relate to material contained in the Appendix to the chapter.

SELF-STUDY QUESTIONS

Answers are at the end of the chapter.

(SO 1)   1. The time period assumption states that:
     a. revenue should be recognized in the accounting period in which it is earned.
     b. expenses should be matched with revenues.
     c. the economic life of a business can be divided into artificial time periods.
     d. the fiscal year should correspond with the calendar year.

(SO 2)   2. The principle which dictates that efforts (expenses) be matched with accomplishments (revenues) is the:
     a. matching principle.
     b. cost principle.
     c. periodicity principle.
     d. revenue recognition principle.

(SO 3)   3. Adjusting entries are made to ensure that:
     a. expenses are recognized in the period in which they are incurred.
     b. revenues are recorded in the period in which they are earned.
     c. balance sheet and income statement accounts have correct balances at the end of an accounting period.
     d. All of the above.

(SO 4)   4. Each of the following is a major type (or category) of adjusting entries *except*:
     a. prepaid expenses.
     b. accrued revenues.
     c. accrued expenses.
     d. earned revenues.

(SO 5)   5. The trial balance shows Supplies $1,350 and Supplies Expense $0. If $600 of supplies are on hand at the end of the period, the adjusting entry is:

     a. Supplies   600
          Supplies Expense   600
     b. Supplies   750
          Supplies Expense   750
     c. Supplies Expense   750
          Supplies   750
     d. Supplies Expense   600
          Supplies   600

(SO 5)   6. Adjustments for unearned revenues:
     a. decrease liabilities and increase revenues.
     b. have an assets and revenues account relationship.
     c. increase assets and increase revenues.
     d. decrease revenues and decrease assets.

(SO 6)   7. Adjustments for accrued revenues:
     a. have a liabilities and revenues account relationship.
     b. have an assets and revenues account relationship.
     c. decrease assets and revenues.
     d. decrease liabilities and increase revenues.

(SO 6)   8. Kathy Siska earned a salary of $400 for the last week of September. She will be paid on October 1. The adjusting entry for Kathy's employer at September 30 is:
     a. No entry is required
     b. Salaries Expense   400
          Salaries Payable   400
     c. Salaries Expense   400
          Cash   400
     d. Salaries Payable   400
          Cash   400

(SO 7)   9. Which of the following statements is *incorrect* concerning the adjusted trial balance?
     a. An adjusted trial balance proves the equality of the total debit balances and the total credit balances in the ledger after all adjustments are made.
     b. The adjusted trial balance provides the primary basis for the preparation of financial statements.
     c. The adjusted trial balance lists the account balances segregated by assets and liabilities.
     d. The adjusted trial balance is prepared after the adjusting entries have been journalized and posted.

(SO 8)   10. One of the following statements about the accrual basis of accounting is *false*. That statement is:
     a. Events that change a company's financial statements are recorded in the periods in which the events occur.
     b. Revenue is recognized in the period in which it is earned.
     c. This basis is in accord with generally accepted accounting principles.
     d. Revenue is recorded only when cash is received, and expense is recorded only when cash is paid.

(SO 9)   *11. The trial balance shows Supplies $0 and Supplies Expense $1,500. If $800 of supplies are on hand at the end of the period, the adjusting entry is:
     a. debit Supplies $800 and credit Supplies Expense $800.
     b. debit Supplies Expense $800 and credit Supplies $800.
     c. debit Supplies $700 and credit Supplies Expense $700.
     d. debit Supplies Expense $700 and credit Supplies $700.

QUESTIONS

1. (a) How does the time period assumption affect an accountant's analysis of business transactions?
   (b) Explain the terms *fiscal year, calendar year,* and *interim periods.*

2. Identify and state two generally accepted accounting principles that relate to adjusting the accounts.

3. Tony Galego, a lawyer, accepts a legal engagement in March, performs the work in April, and is paid in May. If Connel's law firm prepares monthly financial statements, when should it recognize revenue from this engagement? Why?

4. In completing the engagement in (3) above, Galego incurs $2,000 of expenses in March, $2,500 in April, and none in May. How much expense should be deducted from revenues in the month the revenue is recognized? Why?

5. "Adjusting entries are required by the cost principle of accounting." Do you agree? Explain.

6. Why may a trial balance not contain up-to-date and complete financial information?

7. Distinguish between the two categories of adjusting entries and identify the types of adjustments applicable to each category.

8. What account relationship exists with prepaid expenses? What is the debit/credit effect of a prepaid expense adjusting entry?

9. "Depreciation is a process of valuation that results in the reporting of the fair market value of the asset." Do you agree? Explain.

10. Explain the differences between depreciation expense and accumulated depreciation.

11. Cher Company purchased equipment for $12,000. By the current balance sheet date, $7,000 had been depreciated. Indicate the balance sheet presentation of the data.

12. What account relationships exist with unearned revenues? What is the debit/credit effect of an unearned revenue adjusting entry?

13. A company fails to recognize revenue earned but not yet received. Which of the following accounts are involved in the adjusting entry: (a) asset, (b) liability, (c) revenue, or (d) expense? For the accounts selected, indicate whether they would be debited or credited in the entry.

14. A company fails to recognize an expense incurred but not paid. Indicate which of the following accounts is debited and which is credited in the adjusting entry: (a) asset, (b) liability, (c) revenue, or (d) expense.

15. A company makes an accrued revenue adjusting entry for $900 and an accrued expense adjusting entry for $600. How much was net income understated prior to these entries? Explain.

16. On January 9, a company pays $5,000 for salaries of which $1,700 was reported as Salaries Payable on December 31. Give the entry to record the payment.

17. For each of the following items before adjustment, indicate the type of adjusting entry (prepaid expense, unearned revenue, accrued revenue, and accrued expense) that is needed to correct the misstatement. If an item could result in more than one type of adjusting entry, indicate each of the types.
    (a) Assets are understated.
    (b) Liabilities are overstated.
    (c) Liabilities are understated.
    (d) Expenses are understated.
    (e) Assets are overstated.
    (f) Revenue is understated.

18. One half of the adjusting entry is given below. Indicate the account title for the other half of the entry.
    (a) Salaries Expense is debited.
    (b) Depreciation Expense is debited.
    (c) Interest Payable is credited.
    (d) Supplies is credited.
    (e) Accounts Receivable is debited.
    (f) Unearned Fees is debited.

19. "An adjusting entry may affect more than one balance sheet or income statement account." Do you agree? Why or why not?

20. Why is it possible to prepare financial statements directly from an adjusted trial balance?

21. Why do accrual basis financial statements provide more useful information than cash basis statements?

*22. The Alpha Company debits Supplies Expense for all purchases of supplies and credits Rent Revenue for all advanced rentals. For each type of adjustment, give the adjusting entry.

BRIEF EXERCISES

Indicate why adjusting entries are needed.
(SO 3)

BE3–1 The ledger of the Lena Company includes the following accounts. Explain why each account may require adjustment.
a. Prepaid Insurance   c. Unearned Fees
b. Depreciation Expense   d. Interest Payable

BE3–2 The Riko Company accumulates the following adjustment data at December 31. Indicate (a) the type of adjustment (prepaid expense, accrued revenues and so on), (b) the account relationships (asset/revenue, liability/expense, and so on), and (c) the accounts before adjustment (overstated or understated).

Identify the major types of adjusting entries.
(SO 4)

1. Supplies of $600 are on hand.
2. Fees earned but unbilled total $900.
3. Interest of $200 has accumulated on a note payable.
4. Rent collected in advance totaling $800 has been earned.

BE3–3 The Sain Advertising Company's trial balance at December 31 shows Advertising Supplies $9,700 and Advertising Supplies Expense $0. On December 31, there are $1,500 of supplies on hand. Prepare the adjusting entry at December 31 and, using T accounts, enter the balances in the accounts, post the adjusting entry, and indicate the adjusted balance in each account.

Prepare adjusting entry for supplies.
(SO 5)

BE3–4 At the end of its first year, the trial balance of the Shah Company shows Equipment $25,000 and zero balances in Accumulated Depreciation—Equipment and Depreciation Expense. Depreciation for the year is estimated to be $3,000. Prepare the the adjusting entry for depreciation at December 31, post the adjustments to T accounts, and indicate the balance sheet presentation of the equipment at December 31.

Prepare adjusting entries for depreciation.
(SO 5)

BE3–5 On July 1, 1996, Bere Co. pays $15,000 to Marla Insurance Co. for a three-year insurance contract. Both companies have fiscal years ending December 31. For Bere Co. journalize and post the entry on July 1 and the adjusting entry on December 31.

Prepare adjusting entries for prepaid expense.
(SO 5)

BE3–6 Using the data in BE3–5, journalize and post the entry on July 1 and the adjusting entry on December 31 for Marla Insurance Co. Marla uses the accounts Unearned Insurance Revenue and Insurance Revenue.

Prepare adjusting entry for unearned revenue.
(SO 5)

BE3–7 The bookkeeper for the DeVoe Company asks you to prepare the following accrued adjusting entries at December 31.

Prepare adjusting entries for accruals.
(SO 6)

1. Interest on notes payable of $400 is accrued.
2. Fees earned but unbilled total $1,400.
3. Salaries earned by employees of $700 have not been recorded.

Use the following account titles: Fees Earned, Accounts Receivable, Interest Expense, Interest Payable, Salaries Expense, and Salaries Payable.

BE3–8 The trial balance of the Hoi Company includes the following balance sheet accounts. Identify the accounts that require adjustment. For each account that requires adjustment, indicate (a) the type of adjusting entry (prepaid expenses, unearned revenues, accrued revenues, and accrued expenses) and (b) the related account in the adjusting entry.

Analyze accounts in an adjusted trial balance.
(SO 7)

Accounts Receivable	Notes Payable
Prepaid Insurance	Interest Payable
Equipment	Unearned Fees
Accumulated Depreciation—Equipment	

BE3–9 The adjusted trial balance of the Lumas Company at December 31, 1996, includes the following accounts: Retained Earnings $15,600; Dividends $6,000; Fees Earned $35,400; Salaries Expense $13,000; Insurance Expense $2,000; Rent Expense $4,000; Supplies Expense $1,500; and Depreciation Expense $1,000. Prepare an income statement for the year.

Prepare an income statement from an adjusted trial balance.
(SO 7)

BE3–10 Partial adjusted trial balance data for the Lumas Company is presented in BE3–9. The balance in Retained Earnings is the balance as of January 1. Prepare a retained earnings statement for the year assuming net income is $14,000 for the year.

Prepare a retained earnings statement from an adjusted trial balance.
(SO 7)

*BE3–11 The Tower Company records all prepayments in income statement accounts. At April 30, the trial balance shows Supplies Expense $2,800, Fees Earned $9,200, and zero balances in related balance sheet accounts. Prepare the adjusting entries at April 30 assuming (a) $1,300 of supplies on hand and (b) $900 of the fees are unearned.

Prepare adjusting entries under alternative treatment of prepayments.
(SO 9)

EXERCISES

•••

Identify types of adjustments and account relationships.
(SO 4, 5, 6, 7)

E3–1   The Rafael Company accumulates the following adjustment data at December 31.

1. Fees earned but unbilled total $600.
2. Store supplies of $300 have been used.
3. Utility expenses of $225 are unpaid.
4. Fees of $260 collected in advance have been earned.
5. Salaries of $800 are unpaid.
6. Prepaid insurance totaling $350 has expired.

Instructions

For each of the above items indicate:

(a) The type of adjustment (prepaid expense, unearned revenue, accrued revenue, or accrued expense).
(b) The account relationship (asset/revenue, liability/revenue, and so on).
(c) The accounts before adjustment (overstatement or understatement).

Prepare adjusting entries from selected account data.
(SO 5, 6, 7)

E3–2   The ledger of Easy Rental Agency on March 31 of the current year includes the following selected accounts before adjusting entries have been prepared.

	Debit	Credit
Prepaid Insurance	$ 3,600	
Supplies	2,800	
Equipment	25,000	
Accumulated Depreciation— Equipment		$ 8,400
Notes Payable		20,000
Unearned Rent Revenue		9,300
Rent Revenue		60,000
Interest Expense	–0–	
Wage Expense	14,000	

An analysis of the accounts shows the following:

1. The equipment depreciates $500 per month.
2. One-third of the unearned rent was earned during the quarter.
3. Interest of $600 is accrued on the notes payable.
4. Supplies on hand total $850.
5. Insurance expires at the rate of $200 per month.

Instructions

Prepare the adjusting entries at March 31, assuming that adjusting entries are made quarterly. Additional accounts are: Depreciation Expense, Insurance Expense, Interest Payable, and Supplies Expense.

Prepare adjusting entries.
(SO 5, 6, 7)

E3–3   Mike Maroscia, D.D.S., opened a dental practice on January 1, 1996. During the first month of operations the following transactions occurred.

1. Performed services for patients who had dental plan insurance. At January 31, $750 of such services was earned but not yet billed to the insurance companies.
2. Utility expenses incurred but not paid prior to January 31 totaled $650.
3. Purchased dental equipment on January 1 for $80,000, paying $20,000 in cash and signing a $60,000, three-year-note payable. The equipment depreciates $400 per month. Interest is $600 per month.
4. Purchased a one-year malpractice insurance policy on January 1 for $12,000.
5. Purchased $1,800 of dental supplies. On January 31, determined that $500 of supplies were on hand.

Instructions

Prepare the adjusting entries on January 31. Account titles are: Accumulated Depreciation—Dental Equipment, Depreciation Expense, Fees Earned, Accounts Receivable, Insurance Expense, Interest Expense, Interest Payable, Prepaid Insurance, Supplies, Supplies Expense, Utilities Expense, and Utilities Payable.

E3–4 The trial balance for the Pioneer Advertising Agency Inc. is shown in Illustration 3-2, p. 92. In lieu of the adjusting entries shown in the text at October 31, assume the following adjustment data:

Prepare adjusting entries.
(SO 5, 6, 7)

1. Advertising supplies on hand at October 31 total $1,300.
2. Expired insurance for the month is $100.
3. Depreciation for the month is $50.
4. Unearned fees earned in October total $500.
5. Fees earned but unbilled at October 31 are $300.
6. Interest accrued at October 31 is $70.
7. Accrued salaries at October 31 are $1,600.

Instructions
Prepare the adjusting entries for the items above.

E3–5 The income statement of Weller Co. for the month of July shows net income of $1,400 based on Fees Earned $5,500, Wages Expense $2,300, Supplies Expense $1,200, and Utilities Expense $600. In reviewing the statement, you discover the following:

Prepare correct income statement.
(SO 2, 5, 6, 7)

1. Insurance expired during July of $300 was omitted.
2. Supplies expense includes $400 of supplies that are still on hand at July 31.
3. Depreciation on equipment of $150 was omitted.
4. Accrued but unpaid wages at July 31 of $300 were not included.
5. Fees earned but unrecorded totaled $750.

Instructions
Prepare a correct income statement for July.

E3–6 A partial adjusted trial balance of the Cordero Company at January 31, 1996, shows the following:

Analyze adjusted data
(SO 2, 4, 5, 6, 7)

Adjusted Trial Balance

	Debit	Credit
Supplies	$ 800	
Prepaid Insurance	2,400	
Salaries Payable		700
Unearned Fees		750
Supplies Expense	950	
Insurance Expense	400	
Salaries Expense	1,800	
Fees Earned		2,500

Instructions
Answer the following questions, assuming the year begins January 1:

(a) If the amount in Supplies Expense is the January 31 adjusting entry, and $850 of supplies was purchased in January, what was the balance in Supplies on January 1?
(b) If the amount in Insurance Expense is the January 31 adjusting entry, and the original insurance premium was for one year, what was the total premium and when was the policy purchased?
(c) If $2,500 of salaries was paid in January, what was the balance in Salaries Payable at December 31, 1995?
(d) If $1,600 of fees was received in January for services performed in January, what was the balance in Unearned Fees at December 31, 1995?

E3–7 Selected accounts of the Alamo Company are shown below:

Journalize basic transactions and adjusting entries.
(SO 5, 6, 7)

Supplies Expense

7/31	400	

Supplies

7/1	Bal.	1,100	7/31	400
7/10		300		

Salaries Payable

	7/31	1,200

Accounts Receivable			Unearned Fees			
7/31	500		7/31	800	7/1 Bal.	1,500
					7/20	700

Salaries Expense			Fees Earned		
7/15	1,200			7/14	3,000
7/31	1,200			7/31	800
				7/31	500

Instructions

After analyzing the accounts, journalize (a) the July transactions and (b) the adjusting entries that were made on July 31. (Hint: July transactions were for cash.)

Prepare adjusting entries from analysis of trial balances.
(SO 5, 6, 7)

E3–8 The trial balances before and after adjustment for the Apachi Company at the end of its fiscal year are presented below.

APACHI COMPANY
Trial Balance
August 31, 1996

	Before Adjustment		After Adjustment	
	Dr.	Cr.	Dr.	Cr.
Cash	$10,400		$10,400	
Accounts Receivable	8,800		9,500	
Office Supplies	2,300		700	
Prepaid Insurance	4,000		2,500	
Office Equipment	14,000		14,000	
Accumulated Depreciation—Office Equipment		$ 3,600		$ 4,800
Accounts Payable		5,800		5,800
Salaries Payable		–0–		1,000
Unearned Rent Revenue		1,500		700
Common Stock		10,000		10,000
Retained Earnings		5,600		5,600
Fees Earned		34,000		34,700
Rent Revenue		11,000		11,800
Salaries Expense	17,000		18,000	
Office Supplies Expense	–0–		1,600	
Rent Expense	15,000		15,000	
Insurance Expense	–0–		1,500	
Depreciation Expense	–0–		1,200	
	$71,500	$71,500	$74,400	$74,400

Instructions

Prepare the adjusting entries that were made.

Prepare financial statements from adjusted trial balance.
(SO 5, 6, 7)

E3–9 The adjusted trial balance for the Apachi Company is given in E3–8.

Instructions

Prepare the income statement and a retained earnings statement for the year and the balance sheet at August 31.

Distinguish between cash and accrual basis of accounting.
(SO 8)

E3–10 On numerous occasions proposals have surfaced to put the federal government on the accrual basis of accounting. This is no small issue because if this basis were used, it would mean that billions in unrecorded liabilities would have to be booked and the federal deficit would increase substantially.

Instructions

(a) What is the difference between accrual basis accounting and cash basis accounting?
(b) Comment on why politicians prefer a cash basis accounting system over an accrual basis system.

(c) Write a letter to your senator explaining why you think the federal government should adopt the accrual basis of accounting.

Journalize transactions and adjusting entries using appendix.
(SO 9)

*E3–11 At the Devereaux Company, prepayments are debited to expense when paid and unearned revenues are credited to revenue when received. During January of the current year, the following transactions occurred:

Jan. 2 Paid $3,600 for fire insurance protection for the year.
  10 Paid $1,700 for supplies.
  15 Received $5,100 in fees for services to be performed in the future.

On January 31, it is determined that $1,200 of the services fees have been earned and that there are $800 of supplies on hand.

Instructions
(a) Journalize and post the January transactions. (Use T accounts.)
(b) Journalize and post the adjusting entries at January 31.
(c) Determine the ending balance in each of the accounts.

PROBLEMS

P3–1 The trial balance before adjustment of Scenic Tours Inc. at the end of its first month of operations is presented below:

Prepare adjusting entries, post, and prepare an adjusted trial balance.
(SO 5, 6, 7)

SCENIC TOURS INC.
Trial Balance
June 30, 1996

	Debit	Credit
Cash	$ 3,000	
Prepaid Insurance	7,200	
Office Equipment	1,800	
Buses	140,000	
Notes Payable		$ 62,000
Unearned Fees		15,000
Common Stock		70,000
Fees Earned		15,900
Salaries Expense	9,000	
Advertising Expense	800	
Gas and Oil Expense	1,100	
	$162,900	$162,900

Other data:

1. The insurance policy has a one-year term beginning June 1, 1996.
2. The monthly depreciation is $50 on office equipment and $2,000 on buses.
3. Interest of $700 accrues on the notes payable each month.
4. Deposits of $1,500 each were received for advanced tour reservations from 10 school groups. At June 30, three of these deposits have been earned.
5. Bus drivers are paid a combined total of $400 per day. At June 30, 3 days' salaries are unpaid.
6. A senior citizen's organization that had not made an advance deposit took a Canyon tour on June 30 for $1,200. This group was not billed for the services rendered until July 3.

Instructions
(a) Journalize the adjusting entries at June 30, 1996.
(b) Prepare a ledger using the three-column form of account. Enter the trial balance amounts and post the adjusting entries. (Use J2 as the posting reference.)
(c) Prepare an adjusted trial balance at June 30, 1996.

Prepare adjusting entries,
adjusted trial balance, and
financial statements.
(SO 5, 6, 7)

P3–2   The River Run Hotel Corp. opened for business on May 1, 1996. Its trial balance before adjustment on May 31 is as follows:

RIVER RUN HOTEL CORP.
Trial Balance
May 31, 1996

	Debit	Credit
Cash	$ 2,500	
Prepaid Insurance	1,800	
Supplies	1,900	
Land	15,000	
Lodge	70,000	
Furniture	16,800	
Accounts Payable		$ 4,700
Unearned Rent Revenue		3,600
Mortgage Payable		35,000
Common Stock		60,000
Rent Revenue		9,200
Salaries Expense	3,000	
Utilities Expense	1,000	
Advertising Expense	500	
	$112,500	$112,500

Other data:
1. Insurance expires at the rate of $200 per month.
2. An inventory of supplies shows $1,350 of unused supplies on May 31.
3. Annual depreciation is $3,600 on the lodge and $3,000 on furniture.
4. The mortgage interest rate is 12%. (The mortgage was taken out on May 1.)
5. Unearned rent of $1,500 has been earned.
6. Salaries of $300 are accrued and unpaid at May 31.

Instructions
(a) Journalize the adjusting entries on May 31.
(b) Prepare a ledger using the three-column form of account. Enter the trial balance amounts and post the adjusting entries. (Use J1 as the posting reference.)
(c) Prepare an adjusted trial balance on May 31.
(d) Prepare an income statement and a retained earnings statement for the month of May and a balance sheet at May 31.

Prepare adjusting entries and
financial statements.
(SO 5, 6, 7)

P3–3   The Ozaki Co. was organized on July 1, 1996. Quarterly financial statements are prepared. The trial balance and adjusted trial balance on September 30 are shown below.

	Trial Balance		Adjusted Trial Balance	
	Dr.	Cr.	Dr.	Cr.
Cash	$ 6,700		$ 6,700	
Accounts Receivable	400		800	
Prepaid Rent	1,500		900	
Supplies	1,200		1,000	
Equipment	15,000		15,000	
Accumulated Depreciation—Equipment				$ 350
Notes Payable		$ 5,000		5,000
Accounts Payable		1,510		1,510
Salaries Payable				600
Interest Payable				50
Unearned Rent Revenue		900		600
Common Stock		14,000		14,000
Retained Earnings		–0–		–0–
Dividends	600		600	
Commission Revenue		14,000		14,400

Rent Revenue		400		700
Salaries Expense	9,000		9,600	
Rent Expense	900		1,500	
Depreciation Expense			350	
Supplies Expense			200	
Utilities Expense	510		510	
Interest Expense			50	
	$35,810	$35,810	$37,210	$37,210

Instructions
(a) Journalize the adjusting entries that were made.
(b) Prepare an income statement and a retained earnings statement for the 3 months ending September 30 and a balance sheet at September 30.
(c) If the note bears interest at 12%, how many months has it been outstanding?

P3–4   A review of the ledger of the Montana Company at December 31, 1996, produces the following data pertaining to the preparation of annual adjusting entries:

Prepare adjusting entries.
(SO 5, 6)

1. Prepaid Insurance $12,800. The company has separate insurance policies on its buildings and its motor vehicles. Policy B4564 on the building was purchased on July 1, 1995, for $9,600. The policy has a term of 3 years. Policy A2958 on the vehicles was purchased on January 1, 1996, for $4,800. This policy has a term of 2 years.
2. Unearned Subscription Revenue $49,000. The company began selling magazine subscriptions in 1996 on an annual basis. The selling price of a subscription is $50. A review of subscription contracts reveals the following:

Subscription Date	Number of Subscriptions
October 1	200
November 1	300
December 1	480
	980

3. Notes Payable, $50,000. This balance consists of a note for 6 months at an annual interest rate of 9%, dated September 1.
4. Salaries Payable $0. There are eight salaried employees. Salaries are paid every Friday for the current week. Five employees receive a salary of $600 each per week, and three employees earn $700 each per week. December 31 is a Wednesday. Employees do not work weekends. All employees worked the last 3 days of December.

Instructions
Prepare the adjusting entries at December 31, 1996.

P3–5   On November 1, 1996, the trial balance of Alou Equipment Repair Corp. is as follows:

Journalize transactions and follow through accounting cycle to preparation of financial statements.
(SO 5, 6, 7)

No.	Trial Balance—Accounts	Debit	Credit
101	Cash	$ 2,790	
112	Accounts Receivable	2,510	
126	Supplies	1,000	
153	Equipment	10,000	
154	Accumulated Depreciation		$ 500
201	Accounts Payable		2,100
209	Unearned Service Revenue		400
212	Salaries Payable		500
311	Common Stock		10,000
320	Retained Earnings		2,800
407	Service Revenue		
615	Depreciation Expense		
631	Supplies Expense		
726	Salaries Expense		
729	Rent Expense		
	Totals	$16,300	$16,300

Sal Pay 500
Sal exp 600 ⟵ Nov. 8 Paid $1,100 for salaries due employees, of which $600 is for November and $500 is
Cash   1100

During November the following summary transactions were completed.

Nov. 8 Paid $1,100 for salaries due employees, of which $600 is for November and $500 is
         for October.
     10 Received $1,200 cash from customers on account.
     12 Received $1,400 cash for services performed in November.
     15 Purchased equipment on account $3,000.
     17 Purchased supplies on account $1,500.
     20 Paid creditors on account $2,500.
     22 Paid November rent $300.
     25 Paid salaries $1,000.
     27 Performed services on account and billed customers for services rendered $700.
     29 Received $550 from customers for future service.

Adjustment data consist of:

1. Supplies on hand $1,600.
2. Accrued salaries payable $500.
3. Depreciation for the month is $120.
4. Unearned service revenue of $300 is earned.

Instructions

(a) Enter the November 1 balances in the ledger accounts.
(b) Journalize the November transactions.
(c) Post to the ledger accounts. Use J1 for posting reference and No. 407 Service Reve-
     nue, No. 615 Depreciation Expense, No. 631 Supplies Expense, No. 726 Salaries Ex-
     pense, and No. 729 Rent Expense.
(d) Prepare a trial balance at November 30.
(e) Journalize and post adjusting entries.
(f) Prepare an adjusted trial balance.
(g) Prepare an income statement and a retained earnings statement for November and a
     balance sheet at November 30.

*Prepare adjusting entries,
adjusted trial balance, and
financial statements using
appendix.
(SO 5, 6, 7, 9)*

*P3–6 The Global Graphics Company was organized on January 1, 1996, by Nancy Glover.
At the end of the first 6 months of operations, the trial balance contained the following
accounts:

Debits		Credits	
Cash	$ 9,500	Notes Payable	$ 17,000
Accounts Receivable	14,000	Accounts Payable	9,000
Equipment	45,000	Common Stock	25,000
Insurance Expense	1,800	Graphic Fees Earned	52,100
Salaries Expense	30,000	Consulting Fees Earned	5,000
Supplies Expense	2,700		
Advertising Expense	1,900		
Rent Expense	1,500		
Utilities Expense	1,700		
	$108,100		$108,100

Analysis reveals the following additional data:

1. The $2,700 balance in Supplies Expense represents supplies purchased in January. At
    June 30, there was $1,500 of supplies on hand.
2. The note payable was issued on February 1. It is a 12%, 6-month note.
3. The balance in Insurance Expense is the premium on a one-year policy, dated
    March 1, 1996.
4. Consulting fees are credited to revenue when received. At June 30, consulting fees of
    $1,000 are unearned.
5. Graphic fees earned but unbilled at June 30 total $2,000.
6. Depreciation is $2,000 per year.

Instructions

(a) Journalize the adjusting entries at June 30 (assume adjustments are recorded every 6
     months).

(b) Prepare an adjusted trial balance.
(c) Prepare an income statement and a retained earnings statement for the 6 months ended June 30 and a balance sheet at June 30.

ALTERNATE PROBLEMS

P3–1A The Ortega Security Service Inc. began operations on January 1, 1996. At the end of the first year of operations, the trial balance before adjustment shows the following:

Prepare adjusting entries, post, and prepare an adjusted trial balance.
(SO 5, 6, 7)

ORTEGA SECURITY SERVICE INC.
Trial Balance
December 31, 1996

	Debit	Credit
Cash	$ 12,400	
Accounts Receivable	3,200	
Prepaid Insurance	3,600	
Automobiles	58,000	
Notes Payable		$ 45,000
Unearned Fees		2,500
Common Stock		18,000
Fees Earned		84,000
Salaries Expense	57,000	
Repairs Expense	6,000	
Gas and Oil Expense	9,300	
	$149,500	$149,500

Other data:

1. Fees earned but unbilled $1,500 at December 31.
2. Insurance coverage began on January 1 under a 2-year policy.
3. Automobile depreciation is $15,000 for the year.
4. Interest of $5,400 accrued on notes payable for the year.
5. $1,000 of the unearned fees has been earned.
6. Drivers' salaries total $500 per day. At December 31, 4 days' salaries are unpaid.
7. Repairs to automobiles of $650 have been incurred, but bills have not been received prior to December 31. (Use Accounts Payable.)

Instructions
(a) Journalize the annual adjusting entries at December 31, 1996.
(b) Prepare a ledger using the three-column account form. Enter the trial balance amounts and post the adjusting entries. (Use J15 as the posting reference.)
(c) Prepare an adjusted trial balance at December 31, 1996.

P3–2A The Highland Cove Resort Inc. opened for business on June 1 with eight air-conditioned units. Its trial balance before adjustment on August 31 is as follows:

Prepare adjusting entries, adjusted trial balance, and financial statements.
(SO 5, 6, 7)

HIGHLAND COVE RESORT INC.
Trial Balance
August 31, 1996

	Debit	Credit
Cash	$ 19,600	
Prepaid Insurance	5,400	
Supplies	3,300	
Land	25,000	
Cottages	125,000	
Furniture	26,000	
Accounts Payable		$ 6,500
Unearned Rent Revenue		6,800
Mortgage Payable		80,000

	Debit	Credit
Common Stock		100,000
Dividends	5,000	
Rent Revenue		80,000
Salaries Expense	51,000	
Utilities Expense	9,400	
Repair Expense	3,600	
	$273,300	$273,300

Other data:

1. Insurance expires at the rate of $300 per month.
2. An inventory count on August 31 shows $700 of supplies on hand.
3. Annual depreciation is $4,800 on cottages and $2,400 on furniture.
4. Unearned rent of $5,000 was earned prior to August 31.
5. Salaries of $400 were unpaid at August 31.
6. Rentals of $800 were due from tenants at August 31. (Use Accounts Receivable.)
7. The mortgage interest rate is 12% per year. (The mortgage was taken out on August 1.)

Instructions

(a) Journalize the adjusting entries on August 31 for the 3-month period June 1–August 31.
(b) Prepare a ledger using the three-column form of account. Enter the trial balance amounts and post the adjusting entries. (Use J1 as the posting reference.)
(c) Prepare an adjusted trial balance on August 31.
(d) Prepare an income statement and a retained earnings statement for the 3 months ending August 31 and a balance sheet as of August 31.

Prepare adjusting entries and financial statements.
(SO 5, 6, 7)

P3–3A The Grant Advertising Agency Inc. was founded by Thomas Grant in January of 1992. Presented below are both the adjusted and unadjusted trial balances as of December 31, 1996.

GRANT ADVERTISING AGENCY INC.
Trial Balance
December 31, 1996

	Unadjusted Dr.	Unadjusted Cr.	Adjusted Dr.	Adjusted Cr.
Cash	$ 11,000		$ 11,000	
Accounts Receivable	20,000		21,000	
Art Supplies	8,400		5,000	
Prepaid Insurance	3,350		2,500	
Printing Equipment	60,000		60,000	
Accumulated Depreciation		$ 28,000		$ 35,000
Accounts Payable		5,000		5,000
Interest Payable		0		150
Notes Payable		5,000		5,000
Unearned Advertising Revenue		7,000		5,600
Salaries Payable		0		1,800
Common Stock		20,000		20,000
Retained Earnings		5,500		5,500
Dividends	12,000		12,000	
Advertising Revenue		58,600		61,000
Salaries Expense	10,000		11,800	
Insurance Expense			850	
Interest Expense	350		500	
Depreciation Expense			7,000	
Art Supplies Expense			3,400	
Rent Expense	4,000		4,000	
	$129,100	$129,100	$139,050	$139,050

Instructions
(a) Journalize the annual adjusting entries that were made.
(b) Prepare an income statement and a retained earnings statement for the year ending December 31, 1996, and a balance sheet at December 31.
(c) Answer the following questions:
   (1) If the note has been outstanding 3 months, what is the annual interest rate on that note?
   (2) If the company paid $13,500 in salaries in 1996, what was the balance in Salaries Payable on December 31, 1995?

P3–4A A review of the ledger of Greenberg Company at December 31, 1996, produces the following data pertaining to the preparation of annual adjusting entries.

Prepare adjusting entries.
(SO 5, 6)

1. Salaries Payable $0. There are eight salaried employees. Salaries are paid every Friday for the current week. Five employees receive a salary of $600 each per week, and three employees earn $500 each per week. December 31 is a Tuesday. Employees do not work weekends. All employees worked the last 2 days of December.
2. Unearned Rent Revenue $369,000. The company began subleasing office space in its new building on November 1. Each tenant is required to make a $5,000 security deposit that is not refundable until occupancy is terminated. At December 31, the company had the following rental contracts that are paid in full for the entire term of the lease.

Date	Term (in months)	Monthly Rent	Number of Leases
Nov. 1	6	$4,000	5
Dec. 1	6	$8,500	4

3. Prepaid Advertising $13,200. This balance consists of payments on two advertising contracts. The contracts provide for monthly advertising in two trade magazines. The terms of the contracts are as follows:

Contract	Date	Amount	Number of Magazine Issues
A650	May 1	$6,000	12
B974	Sept. 1	7,200	24

The first advertisement runs in the month in which the contract is signed.

4. Notes Payable $80,000. This balance consists of a note for one year at an annual interest rate of 12%, dated June 1.

Instructions
Prepare the adjusting entries at December 31, 1996. (Show all computations.)

P3–5A On September 1, 1996, the trial balance of Rijo Equipment Repair Corp. is as follows:

Journalize transactions and follow through accounting cycle to preparation of financial statements.
(SO 5, 6, 7)

No.	Trial Balance—Accounts	Debit	Credit
101	Cash	$ 4,880	
112	Accounts Receivable	3,520	
126	Supplies	1,000	
153	Store Equipment	15,000	
154	Accumulated Depreciation		$ 1,500
201	Accounts Payable		3,400
209	Unearned Service Revenue		400
212	Salaries Payable		500
311	Common Stock		10,000
320	Retained Earnings		8,600
407	Service Revenue		
615	Depreciation Expense		
631	Supplies Expense		
726	Salaries Expense		
729	Rent Expense		
	Totals	$24,400	$24,400

During September the following summary transactions were completed.

Sept. 8   Paid $1,100 for salaries due employees, of which $600 is for September and $500 is for August.

10   Received $1,200 cash from customers on account.

12   Received $3,400 cash for services performed in September.

15   Purchased store equipment on account $3,000.

17   Purchased supplies on account $1,500.

20   Paid creditors $4,500 on account.

22   Paid September rent $500.

25   Paid salaries $1,050.

27   Performed services on account and billed customers for services rendered $900.

29   Received $650 from customers for future service.

Adjustment data consist of:

1. Supplies on hand $1,800.
2. Accrued salaries payable $400.
3. Depreciation is $200 per month.
4. Unearned service revenue of $350 is earned.

Instructions
(a) Enter the September 1 balances in the ledger accounts.
(b) Journalize the September transactions.
(c) Post to the ledger accounts. Use J1 for posting reference and No. 407 Service Revenue, No. 615 Depreciation Expense, No. 631 Supplies Expense, No. 726 Salaries Expense, and No. 729 Rent Expense.
(d) Prepare a trial balance at September 30.
(e) Journalize and post adjusting entries.
(f) Prepare an adjusted trial balance.
(g) Prepare an income statement and a retained earnings statement for September and a balance sheet at September 30.

▶*B*roadening *Your Perspective*

*F*INANCIAL REPORTING PROBLEM—PEPSICO, INC.

The financial statements of PepsiCo are presented in Appendix A at the end of this textbook.

Instructions
(a) Using the consolidated income statement and balance sheet, identify items that may result in adjusting entries for prepayments.
(b) Using the consolidated income statement, identify two items that may result in adjusting entries for accruals.
(c) Using the Notes to Consolidated Financial Statements section, what was the amount of depreciation expense for 1995 and 1994? How was depreciation expense reported in the income statement? Do you have any suggestions for improving PepsiCo's presentation of accumulated depreciation?
(d) Using the Selected Financial Data section, what has been the trend since 1991 for interest expense (net)?
(e) Using the Consolidated Income Statement and the Consolidated Statement of Cash Flows, how much interest was paid in 1995? Where is the remainder presumably reported in the balance sheet?

COMPARATIVE ANALYSIS PROBLEM— COCA-COLA COMPANY VS. PEPSICO, INC.

The financial statements of Coca-Cola Company are presented at the end of Chapter 1, and PepsiCo's financial statements are presented in Appendix A.

Instructions
(a) Based on information contained in these financial statements, determine the following for each company:
  (1) Prepaid expenses (and other assets) at December 31, 1995.
  (2) Total accrued expenses at December 31, 1995 (include all accrued items, and assume Coca-Cola had $897 of accrued expenses included in the accounts payable and accrued expenses amount of $2,894).
  (3) Depreciation expense for 1995. (See the notes to Consolidated Financial Statements for PepsiCo's depreciation expense.)
  (4) Interest expense for 1995.
(b) Prepare the adjusting entry made by each company to record 1995's depreciation expense. Explain what other adjusting entries were likely made by each company during 1995.

INTERPRETATION OF FINANCIAL STATEMENTS

Mini-Case—Smith's Food and Drug Centers, Inc.

Smith's Food and Drug Centers, Inc. is a supermarket and drug store chain that operates 137 stores in the Intermountain and Southwestern regions of the United States. Smith's competes using a strategy of providing one-stop shopping for customers. This requires large inventories and frequent restocking of inventories. To reduce these costs, Smith's owns and operates its own warehouse and distribution facilities. The company's Current Liabilities section of its 1994 balance sheet included the following (dollar amounts are in the thousands):

Trade accounts payable	$235,843
Accured sales and other taxes	44,379
Accrued payroll and related benefits	84,083

Instructions
(a) What kind of companies would you expect to find in the trade accounts payable? Identify at least three types of creditors (suppliers) of Smith's.
(b) Why does the company have accrued payroll and related benefits? Does this mean that the company is behind in paying its employees? Explain.
(c) The company has state-of-the-art scanners at most of its registers. Even at older stores, each cash register computes daily totals for both sales and sales taxes. Why then does the company have accrued sales taxes?

DECISION CASE

The Holiday Travel Court Inc. was organized on April 1, 1995, by Alice Adare. Alice is a good manager but a poor accountant. From the trial balance prepared by a part-time bookkeeper, Alice prepared the following income statement for the quarter that ended March 31, 1996.

HOLIDAY TRAVEL COURT INC.
Income Statement
For the Quarter Ended March 31, 1996

Revenues		
Travel court rental fees		$95,000
Operating expenses		
Advertising	$ 5,200	
Wages	29,800	
Utilities	900	
Depreciation	800	
Repairs	4,000	
Total operating expenses		40,700
Net income		$54,300

Alice knew that something was wrong with the statement because net income had never exceeded $20,000 in any one quarter. Knowing that you are an experienced accountant, she asks you to review the income statement and other data.

You first look at the trial balance. In addition to the account balances reported above in the income statement, the ledger contains the following additional selected balances at March 31, 1996.

Supplies	$ 5,200
Prepaid Insurance	7,200
Notes Payable	12,000

You then make inquiries and discover the following:

1. Travel court rental fees include advanced rentals for summer month occupancy $28,000.
2. There were $1,300 of supplies on hand at March 31.
3. Prepaid insurance resulted from the payment of a one-year policy on January 1, 1996.
4. The mail on April 1, 1996, brought the following bills: advertising for week of March 24, $110; repairs made March 10, $260; and utilities, $180.
5. There are four employees who receive wages totaling $350 per day. At March 31, 2 days' wages have been incurred but not paid.
6. The note payable is a 3-month, 10% note dated January 1, 1996.

Instructions
(a) Prepare a correct income statement for the quarter ended March 31, 1996.
(b) Explain to Alice the generally accepted accounting principles that she did not recognize in preparing her income statement and their effect on her results.

COMMUNICATION ACTIVITY
••

In reviewing the accounts of the Marylee Co. at the end of the year, you discover that adjusting entries have not been made.

Instructions
Write a memorandum to Mary Lee Virgil, the president of Marylee Co., that explains the following: the nature and purpose of adjusting entries, why adjusting entries are needed, and the types of adjusting entries that may be made.

GROUP ACTIVITY
••

The following types of adjusting entries were introduced in this chapter: (1) prepaid expenses, (2) unearned revenues, (3) accrued revenues, and (4) accrued expenses.

Instructions
With the class divided into four groups, each group will choose one type of adjusting entry. Each group is to report to the class on the following: (a) the account relationship that is involved, (b) the status of the accounts before adjustment, (c) the debit/credit effect of the adjusting entry, and (d) the effects on the balance sheet and income statement if the adjusting entry is not made.

ETHICS CASE

Diamond Company is a pesticide manufacturer. Its sales declined greatly this year due to the passage of legislation outlawing the sale of several of Diamond's chemical pesticides. During the coming year, Diamond will have environmentally safe and competitive replacement chemicals to replace these discontinued products. Sales in the next year are expected to greatly exceed any prior year's. The development in sales and profits appears to be a one-year aberration. But even so, the company president believes that a large dip in current year's profits could cause a significant drop in the market price of Diamond's stock and make it a takeover target. To avoid this possibility, the company president urges Carol Denton, controller, in making this period's year-end adjusting entries to accrue every possible revenue and to defer as many expenses as possible. The president says to Carol, "We need the revenues this year, and next year can easily absorb expenses deferred from this year. We can't let our stock price be hammered down!" Carol didn't get around to recording the adjusting entries until January 17, but she dated the entries December 31 as if they were recorded then. Carol also made every effort to comply with the president's request.

Instructions
   (a) Who are the stakeholders in this situation?
   (b) What are the ethical considerations of (1) the president's request and (2) Carol's dating the adjusting entries December 31?
   (c) Can Carol accrue revenues and defer expenses and still be ethical?

RESEARCH ASSIGNMENT

The Enterprise Standard Industrial Classification (SIC) coding scheme, a published classification of firms into separate industries, is commonly used in practice. SIC codes permit identification of company activities on three levels of detail. Two-digit codes designate a "major group," three-digit codes designate an "industry group," while four-digit codes identify a specific "industry." At your library, find the *Standard Industrial Classification Manual* (published by the U.S. Government's Office of Management and Budget in 1987) to answer the following questions.

   (a) On what basis are SIC codes assigned to companies?
   (b) Identify the major group/industry group/industry represented by the following codes: 12, 271, 3571, 7033, 75, and 872.
   (c) Identify the SIC code for the following industries:
       1. Golfing equipment—manufacturing
       2. Worm farms
       3. Felt tip markers—manufacturing
       4. Household appliance stores, electric, or gas—retail
       5. Advertising agencies
   (d) You are interested in examining several companies in the passenger airline industry. Determine the appropriate two-, three-, and four-digit SIC codes. Use *Wards Business Directory of U.S. Private and Public Companies (Vol. 5)* to compile a list of the five largest parent companies (by total sales) in the industry. Note: If Wards is not available, alternative sources include *Standard & Poor's Register of Corporations, Directors, and Executives, Standard & Poor's Industry Surveys,* and the Dun & Bradstreet *Million Dollar Directory.*

CRITICAL THINKING
▸ A Real-World Focus: Laser Recording Systems Incorporated
• •

Laser Recording Systems, founded in 1981, produces laser disks for use in the home market. Sales since 1985 have increased approximately 15 percent per year.

The following is an excerpt from Laser Recording Systems' 1994 financial statements (all dollars in thousands):

Management Discussion

Accrued liabilities increased to $1,642 at January 31, 1994, from $138 at the end of fiscal year 1993. Compensation and related accruals increased $195 due primarily to increases in accruals for severance, vacation, commissions, and relocation expenses. Accrued professional services increased by $137 primarily as a result of legal expenses related to several outstanding contractual disputes. Other expense increased $35, of which $18 was for interest payable.

Instructions

(a) Can you tell from the discussion whether Laser Recording has prepaid their legal expenses and is now making an adjustment to the asset account Prepaid Legal Expenses, or whether they are handling the legal expense via an accrued expense adjustment?

(b) Identify each of the adjustments Laser Recording is discussing as one of the four types of possible adjustments discussed in the chapter. How is net income ultimately affected by each of the adjustments?

(c) What journal entry did Laser Recording make to record their accrued interest?

Answers to Self-Study Questions

1. c   2. a   3. d   4. d   5. c   6. a   7. b   8. b   9. c   10. d   11. a

Before studying this chapter you should know or, if necessary, review:

a. *How to apply the revenue recognition and matching principles. (Ch. 3, pp. 99–100)*

b. *How to make adjusting entries. (Ch. 3, pp. 101–112)*

c. *How to prepare an adjusted trial balance. (Ch. 3, p. 115)*

d. *How to prepare a balance sheet, income statement, and retained earnings statement. (Ch. 3, pp. 116–117)*

A Little Knowledge Brings a Lot of Profits

WOODRIDGE, Ill. — Employee training in financial accounting has paid off for Jack Stack at SRC Corporation which rebuilds engines. President and owner of SRC, he was really concerned when his company lost $61,000 on sales of $16 million. He decided that the "only way to turn things around was to get employees to think like owners." But how to do it? He decided to "teach anyone who moved a broom or operated a grinder everything a bank lender would know. That way they would really understand how each nickel saved could make a difference."

Therefore, in 1994 alone SRC spent $300,000 on financial accounting training for its employees. Each week the company stopped its operations for half an hour while its 800 employees broke into small groups to study the latest financial statements. "At first it wasn't easy for everyone to understand the numbers," concedes Craig Highbarger (an employee), "but we've been over the different figures enough times now, if you hand any one of us a financial statement and leave out a few numbers, we can fill them in." Employees now understand how much it costs to copy a document or turn on a light.

Has it made a difference? In 1994 SRC earned $6 million on sales of $100 million. As a result of this turnaround, SRC has handed out $1.4 million in bonuses to its employees, who are now wealthier in both cash and knowledge. ◀

CHAPTER 4

COMPLETION OF THE ACCOUNTING CYCLE

After studying this chapter, you should be able to:

1. *Prepare a work sheet.*
2. *Explain the process of closing the books.*
3. *Describe the content and purpose of a post-closing trial balance.*
4. *State the required steps in the accounting cycle.*
5. *Explain the approaches to preparing correcting entries.*
6. *Identify the sections of a classified balance sheet.*

As was true at SRC Corporation, financial statements can help employees understand what is happening in the business. In Chapter 3, we prepared financial statements directly from the adjusted trial balance. However, with so many details involved in the end-of-period accounting procedures, it is easy to make errors. Locating and correcting errors can cost much time and effort. One way to minimize errors in the records and to simplify the end-of-period procedures is to use a work sheet.

In this chapter we will explain the role of the work sheet in accounting as well as the remaining steps in the accounting cycle, most especially, the closing process, again using Pioneer Advertising Agency as an example. Then we will consider (1) correcting entries and (2) classified balance sheets. The organization and content of the chapter are as follows:

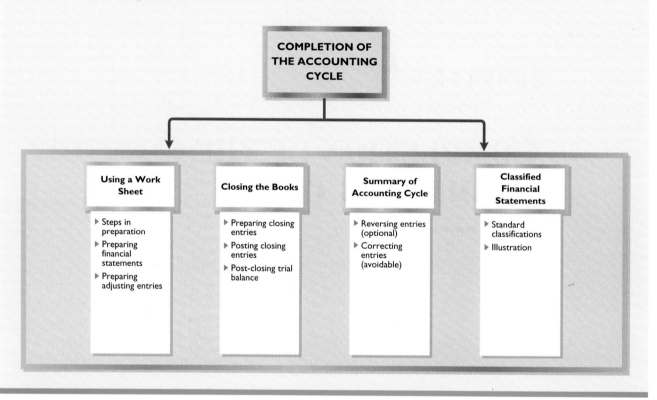

Using a Work Sheet

STUDY OBJECTIVE

1

Prepare a work sheet.

A work sheet is a multiple-column form that may be used in the adjustment process and in preparing financial statements. As its name suggests, the work sheet is a working tool or a supplementary device for the accountant. **A work sheet is not a permanent accounting record;** it is neither a journal nor a part of the general ledger. The work sheet is merely a device used to make it easier to prepare adjusting entries and the financial statements. In small companies with relatively few accounts and adjustments, a work sheet may not be needed. In large companies with numerous accounts and many adjustments, it is almost indispensable.

The basic form of a work sheet and the procedure (5 steps) for preparing a work sheet are shown in Illustration 4-1.

Illustration 4-1

Form and procedure for a work sheet

Work Sheet

Account Titles	Trial Balance		Adjustments		Adjusted Trial Balance		Income Statement		Balance Sheet	
	Dr.	Cr.	Dr.	Cr.	Dr.	Cr.	Dr.	Cr.	Dr.	Cr.

(Ledger account titles)

(Additional account titles for adjustments)

↑ 1. Prepare a trial balance on the work sheet

↑ 2. Enter adjustment data

↑ 3. Enter adjusted balances

↑ 4. Extend adjusted balances to appropriate statement columns

5. Total the statement columns, compute net income, (or net loss), and complete work sheet

Each of the steps in preparing the work sheet must be performed in the pre-scribed sequence.

The use of a work sheet is optional. When a work sheet is used, financial statements are prepared from the work sheet. The adjustments are entered in the work sheet columns and are then journalized and posted after the financial statements have been prepared. Thus, management and other interested parties can receive the financial statements at an earlier date than without a work sheet.

Steps in Preparing a Work Sheet

We will use the October 31 trial balance and adjustment data of Pioneer Advertising in Chapter 3 to illustrate the preparation of a work sheet. Each step of the process is described below and demonstrated in Illustrations 4-2 and 4-3A, B, C, and D following page 150.

Step 1. Prepare a Trial Balance on the Work Sheet. The account title space and trial balance columns are used to prepare a trial balance. The data for the trial balance come directly from the ledger accounts. The trial balance for Pioneer Advertising Agency is entered in the trial balance columns of the work sheet as shown in Illustration 4-2.

Helpful hint A trial balance is *not* prepared separately and then copied onto the work sheet.

Step 2. Enter the Adjustments in the Adjustment Columns. Turn over the **first transparency, Illustration 4-3A.** When a work sheet is used, all adjustments are entered in the adjustment columns. In entering the adjustments, applicable trial balance accounts should be used. If additional accounts are needed, they should be inserted on the lines immediately below the trial balance totals. Each adjustment is indexed and keyed to facilitate the journalizing of the adjusting entry in the general journal. **It is important to recognize that the adjustments are not journalized until after the work sheet is completed and the financial statements have been prepared.**

The adjustments for Pioneer Advertising Agency are the same as the adjustments illustrated on page 113. They are keyed in the adjustment columns of the work sheet as follows:

Helpful hint Careful keying of adjustments will save time and reduce errors when adjusting entries are journalized.

(a) An additional account, Advertising Supplies Expense, is debited $1,500 for the cost of supplies used, and Advertising Supplies is credited $1,500.

(b) An additional account, Insurance Expense, is debited $50 for the insurance that has expired, and Prepaid Insurance is credited $50.

(c) Two additional accounts are needed. Depreciation Expense is debited $40 for the month's depreciation, and Accumulated Depreciation—Office Equipment is credited $40.

(d) Unearned Fees is debited $400 for fees earned, and Fees Earned is credited $400.

(e) An additional account, Accounts Receivable, is debited $200 for fees earned but not billed, and Fees Earned is credited $200.

(f) Two additional accounts are needed. Interest Expense is debited $50 for accrued interest, and Interest Payable is credited $50.

(g) Salaries Expense is debited $1,200 for accrued salaries, and an additional account, Salaries Payable, is credited $1,200.

Note in the Illustration that after all the adjustments have been entered, the adjustment columns are totaled and the equality of the column totals is proved.

Step 3. Enter Adjusted Balances in the Adjusted Trial Balance Columns. Turn over the second transparency, Illustration 4-3B. The adjusted balance of an account is obtained by combining the amounts entered in the first four columns of the work sheet for each account. For example, the Prepaid Insurance account in the trial balance columns has a $600 debit balance. When this is combined with the $50 credit in the adjustment columns, the result is a $550 debit balance recorded in the adjusted trial balance columns. **For each account on the work sheet, the amount in the adjusted trial balance columns is equal to the account balance that will appear in the ledger after the adjusting entries have been journalized and posted.** The balances in these columns are the same as those in the adjusted trial balance in Illustration 3-17 on page 115.

▸*Technology in Action*

The work sheet can be computerized using an electronic spreadsheet program. The LOTUS 1–2–3 supplement for this textbook is one of the most popular versions of such spreadsheet packages. With a program like LOTUS 1–2–3, you can produce any type of work sheet (accounting or otherwise) that you could produce with paper and pencil on a columnar pad. The tremendous advantage of an electronic work sheet over the paper and pencil version is the ability to change selected data. When data are changed, the computer updates the balance of your computations instantly. More specific applications of electronic spreadsheets will be noted as we proceed.

Helpful hint Every adjusted trial balance amount must be extended to one of the four statement columns. Debit amounts go to debit columns and credit amounts go to credit columns.

After the balances of all accounts have been entered in the adjusted trial balance columns, the columns are totaled and their equality is proved. The agreement of the column totals facilitates the completion of the work sheet. If these columns are not in agreement, the statement columns will not balance and the financial statements will be incorrect.

Step 4. Extend Adjusted Trial Balance Amounts to Appropriate Financial Statement Columns. Turn over the third transparency, Illustration 4-3C. This step involves the extension of adjusted trial balance amounts to the last four columns of the work sheet. Balance sheet accounts such as Cash and Notes Payable are entered in the balance sheet debit and credit columns, respectively. The balance in accumulated depreciation is extended to the balance sheet credit column. This results because accumulated depreciation is a contra-asset account with a credit balance.

The balances in Common Stock and Retained Earnings, if any, are extended to the balance sheet credit column. In addition, the balance in Dividends is extended to the balance sheet debit column because it is a stockholders' equity account with a debit balance. The expense and revenue accounts such as Salaries Expense and Fees Earned are entered in the appropriate income statement columns. These extensions are shown in Illustration 4-3C.

Step 5. Total the Statement Columns, Compute the Net Income (or Net Loss), and Complete the Work Sheet. Turn over the fourth transparency, Illustration 4-3D. Each of the statement columns must be totaled. The net income or loss for the period is then found by computing the difference between the totals of the two income statement columns. If total credits exceed total debits, net income has resulted. In such a case, as shown in Illustration 4-3D, the words "net income" are inserted in the account title space. The amount then is entered in the income statement debit column and the balance sheet credit column. **The debit amount balances the income statement columns and the credit amount balances the balance sheet columns.** In addition, the credit in the balance sheet column indicates the increase in stockholders' equity resulting from net income. Conversely, if total debits in the income statement columns exceed total credits, a net loss has occurred. The amount of the net loss is entered in the income statement credit column and the balance sheet debit column.

After the net income or net loss has been entered, new column totals are determined. The totals shown in the debit and credit income statement columns will be identical. The totals shown in the debit and credit balance sheet columns will also be identical. If either the income statement columns or the balance sheet columns are not equal after the net income or net loss has been entered, an error has been made in completing the work sheet. The completed work sheet for Pioneer Advertising Agency is shown in Illustration 4-3D.

Helpful hint All pairs of columns must balance for a work sheet to be complete.

Preparing Financial Statements from a Work Sheet

After a work sheet has been completed, the statement columns contain all the data that are required for the preparation of financial statements. The income statement is prepared from the income statement columns, and the balance sheet and retained earnings statement are prepared from the balance sheet columns. The financial statements prepared from the work sheet for Pioneer Advertising Agency, Inc. are shown in Illustration 4-4. At this point, adjusting entries have not been journalized and posted. Therefore, the ledger does not support all financial statement amounts.

The amount shown for common stock on the work sheet does not change from the beginning to the end of the period, unless additional stock is issued by the corporation during the period. Because there was no balance in Pioneer's retained earnings, the account is not listed in the work sheet. Only after dividends and net income (or loss) are posted to retained earnings, does this account have a balance at the end of the first year of business.

Using a work sheet, accountants can prepare financial statements before adjusting entries are journalized and posted. **However, the completed work sheet is not a substitute for formal financial statements.** Data in the financial statement columns are not properly arranged for statement purposes. Moreover, as noted above, the financial statement presentation for some accounts differs from their statement columns on the work sheet. **A work sheet is essentially a working tool of the accountant and is not distributed to management and other parties.**

(Note: Text continues on page 152, following acetate overlays.)

Illustration 4-2

Preparing a trial balance

PIONEER ADVERTISING AGENCY
Work Sheet
For the Month Ended October 31, 1996

Account Titles	Trial Balance		Adjustments		Adjusted Trial Balance		Income Statement		Balance Sheet	
	Dr.	Cr.	Dr.	Cr.	Dr.	Cr.	Dr.	Cr.	Dr.	Cr.
Cash	15,200									
Advertising Supplies	2,500									
Prepaid Insurance	600									
Office Equipment	5,000									
Notes Payable		5,000								
Accounts Payable		2,500								
Unearned Fees		1,200								
C. R. Byrd, Capital *Common Stock*		10,000								
C. R. Byrd, Drawing *Dividend*	500									
Fees Earned		10,000								
Salaries Expense	4,000									
Rent Expense	900									
Totals	28,700	28,700								

↑ Include all accounts from ledger with balances.

↑ Trial balance amounts are taken directly from ledger accounts.

Illustration 4-4

Financial statements from a work sheet

PIONEER ADVERTISING AGENCY, INC.
Income Statement
For the Month Ended October 31, 1996

Revenues		
Fees earned		$10,600
Expenses		
Salaries expense	$5,200	
Advertising supplies expense	1,500	
Rent expense	900	
Insurance expense	50	
Interest expense	50	
Depreciation expense	40	
Total expenses		7,740
Net Income		$ 2,860

PIONEER ADVERTISING AGENCY, INC.
Retained Earnings Statement
For the Month Ended October 31, 1996

Retained earnings, October 1	$ –0–
Add: Net income	2,860
	2,860
Less: Dividends	500
Retained earnings, October 31	$2,360

PIONEER ADVERTISING AGENCY, INC.
Balance Sheet
October 31, 1996

Assets

Cash		$15,200
Accounts receivable		200
Advertising supplies		1,000
Prepaid insurance		550
Office equipment	$5,000	
Less: Accumulated depreciation	40	4,960
Total assets		$21,910

Liabilities and Stockholders' Equity

Liabilities	
Notes payable	$ 5,000
Accounts payable	2,500
Interest payable	50
Unearned fees	800
Salaries payable	1,200
Total liabilities	9,550
Stockholders' equity	
Common stock	10,000
Retained earnings	2,360
Total liabilities and stockholders' equity	$21,910

Preparing Adjusting Entries from a Work Sheet

A work sheet is not a journal, and it cannot be used as a basis for posting to ledger accounts. To adjust the accounts, it is necessary to journalize and post the adjustments to the ledger. **The adjusting entries are prepared from the adjustment columns of the work sheet.** The reference letters in the adjustment columns and the explanation of the adjustments that appear at the bottom of the work sheet help identify entries. However, writing the explanation to the adjustments at the bottom of the work sheet is not required. As indicated previously, the journalizing and posting of adjusting entries **follows** the preparation of financial statements when a work sheet is used. The adjusting entries on October 31 for Pioneer Advertising Agency, Inc. are the same as those shown in Illustration 3-15 (page 113).

Before You Go On . . .

▸ *Review It*

1. What are the five steps in preparing a work sheet?
2. How is net income or net loss shown in a work sheet?
3. How does a work sheet relate to preparing financial statements and adjusting entries?

▸ *Do It*

Merlynn Kimmel is preparing a work sheet. Explain to Merlynn how the following adjusted trial balance accounts should be extended to the financial statement columns of the work sheet: Cash; Accumulated Depreciation; Accounts Payable; Dividends; Fees Earned; and Salaries Expense.

   Reasoning: Asset and liability balances are extended to the balance sheet debit and credit columns respectively except for accumulated depreciation which is extended to the balance sheet credit column. The Dividends account and expenses are extended to the income statement debit column. Revenue accounts are extended to the income statement credit column.

   Solution:
   Income statement debit column—Salaries Expense
   Income statement credit column—Fees Earned
   Balance sheet debit column—Cash; Dividends
   Balance sheet credit column—Accumulated Depreciation; Accounts Payable
      As indicated in the Technology in Action box on page 148, the work sheet is an ideal application for electronic spreadsheet software like Microsoft Excel and LOTUS 1–2–3.

Related exercise material: BE4–1, BE4–2, BE4–3, E4–1, E4–2, E4–4, and E4–5.

*C*losing the Books

STUDY OBJECTIVE
2
Explain the process of closing the books.

In Chapter 2, you learned that revenue and expense accounts and the dividends account are subdivisions of retained earnings, which is reported in the stockholders' equity section of the balance sheet. Because revenues, expenses, and dividends relate only to a given accounting period they are considered to be temporary or nominal accounts. In contrast, all balance sheet accounts are considered to be permanent or real accounts because they are carried forward into future accounting periods. Illustration 4-5 identifies the types of accounts in each category.

Illustration 4-5

Temporary versus permanent accounts

Temporary (Nominal)	Permanent (Real)
All revenue accounts	All asset accounts
All expense accounts	All liability accounts
Dividends	Stockholders' equity

Preparing Closing Entries

At the end of the accounting period, the temporary account balances are transferred to the permanent stockholders' equity account, retained earnings, through the preparation of closing entries. Closing entries formally recognize in the ledger the transfer of net income or net loss and dividends to retained earnings as shown in the retained earnings statement. These entries also produce a zero balance in each temporary account so it can be used to accumulate data in the next accounting period separate from the data of prior periods. Permanent accounts are not closed.

Journalizing and posting closing entries is a required step in the accounting cycle. This step is performed after financial statements have been prepared. In contrast to the steps in the cycle that you have already studied, closing entries are generally journalized and posted only at the end of a company's annual accounting period. This practice facilitates the preparation of annual financial statements because all temporary accounts will contain data for the entire year.

In preparing closing entries, each income statement account could be closed directly to retained earnings. However, to do so would result in excessive detail in the retained earnings account. Accordingly, the revenue and expense accounts are closed to another temporary account, Income Summary, and only the net income or net loss is transferred from this account to retained earnings.

Closing entries are journalized in the general journal. A center caption entitled Closing Entries may be inserted in the journal between the last adjusting entry and the first closing entry to identify these entries. Then the closing entries are posted to the ledger accounts. Closing entries may be prepared directly from the adjusted balances in the ledger, from the income statement and balance sheet columns of the work sheet, or from the income and retained earnings statements. Separate closing entries could be prepared for each nominal account, but the following four entries accomplish the desired result more efficiently:

Helpful hint When the work sheet is used, revenue and expense account data are found in the income statement columns, and dividends is in the balance sheet debit column.

1. Debit each revenue account for its balance and credit Income Summary for total revenues.
2. Debit Income Summary for total expenses and credit each expense account for its balance.
3. Debit Income Summary and credit Retained Earnings for the amount of net income.
4. Debit Retained Earnings for the balance in the Dividends account and credit Dividends for the same amount.

The four entries are referenced in the diagram of the closing process shown in Illustration 4-6 and in the journal entries in Illustration 4-7. The posting of closing entries is shown in Illustration 4-8.

Illustration 4-6

Diagram of closing process—corporation

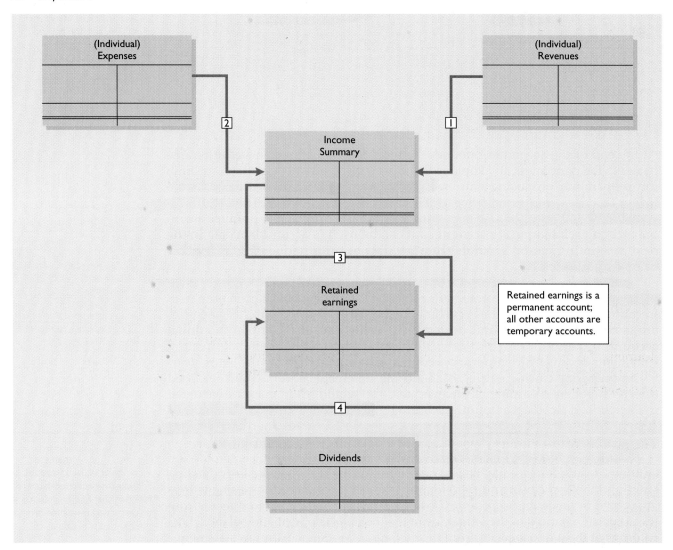

Retained earnings is a permanent account; all other accounts are temporary accounts.

If a net loss has occurred, entry (3) credits Income Summary and debits Retained Earnings.

Closing Entries Illustrated

As explained above, closing entries are generally prepared only at the end of a company's annual accounting period. However, to illustrate the journalizing and posting of closing entries, we will assume that Pioneer Advertising Agency, Inc. closes its books monthly. The closing entries at October 31 are shown in Illustration 4-7.

Illustration 4-7

Closing entries journalized

GENERAL JOURNAL				J3
Date	Account Titles and Explanation	Ref.	Debit	Credit
	Closing Entries			
	(1)			
Oct. 31	Fees Earned	50	10,600	
	Income Summary	49		10,600
	(To close revenue account)			
	(2)			
31	Income Summary	49	7,740	
	Salaries Expense	60		5,200
	Advertising Supplies Expense	61		1,500
	Rent Expense	62		900
	Insurance Expense	63		50
	Interest Expense	64		50
	Depreciation Expense	65		40
	(To close expense accounts)			
	(3)			
31	Income Summary	49	2,860	
	Retained Earnings	40		2,860
	(To close net income to retained earnings)			
	(4)			
31	Retained Earnings	40	500	
	Dividends	41		500
	(To close dividends to retained earnings)			

Helpful hint Income Summary is a very descriptive title: total revenues are closed to Income Summary, total expenses are closed to Income Summary, and the balance in the Income Summary is a net income or net loss.

Note that the amounts for Income Summary in entries (1) and (2) are the totals of the income statement credit and debit columns, respectively, in the work sheet.

A couple of cautions in preparing closing entries: (1) Avoid unintentionally doubling the revenue and expense balances rather than zeroing them. (2) Do not close Dividends through the Income Summary account. **Dividends are not expenses, and they are not a factor in determining net income.**

Posting of Closing Entries

The posting of the closing entries and the ruling of the accounts are shown in Illustration 4-8. Note that all temporary accounts have zero balances. In addition, you should realize that the balance in retained earnings represents the accumulated undistributed earnings of the corporation at the end of the accounting period. This balance is shown on the balance sheet and is the ending amount reported on the retained earnings statement, as shown in Illustration 4-4. **The Income Summary account is used only in closing.** No entries are journalized and posted to this account during the year.

As part of the closing process, the **temporary accounts** (revenues, expenses and dividends) in T-account form are totaled, balanced, and double ruled as shown in Illustration 4-8. The **permanent accounts**—assets, liabilities, and stockholders' equity (common stock and retained earnings)—are not closed. A single rule is drawn beneath the current-period entries and the account balance carried forward to the next period is entered below the single rule, for example, see Retained Earnings.

Helpful hint The balance in Income Summary before it is closed must equal the net income or net loss for the period.

Preparing a Post-Closing Trial Balance

After all closing entries have been journalized and posted, another trial balance, called a post-closing trial balance, is prepared from the ledger. A post-closing

Illustration 4-8

Posting of closing entries

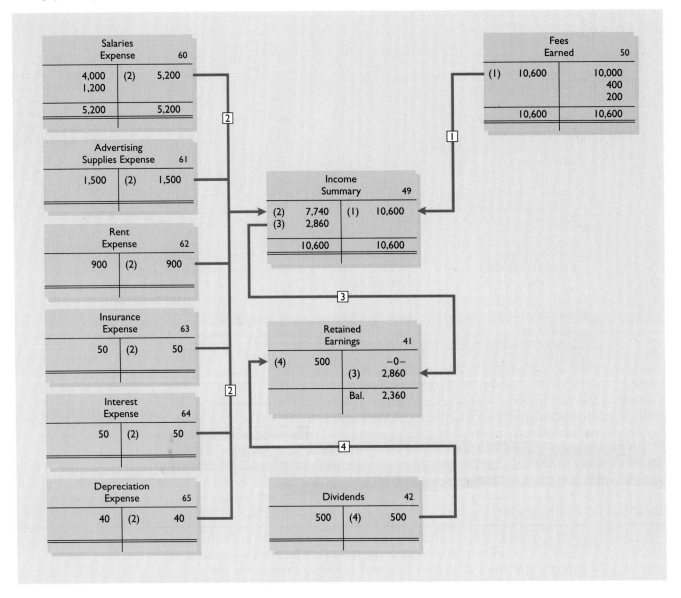

trial balance is a list of permanent accounts and their balances after closing entries have been journalized and posted. **The purpose of this trial balance is to prove the equality of the permanent account balances that are carried forward into the next accounting period.** Since all temporary accounts will have zero balances, the post-closing trial balance will contain only permanent—balance sheet—accounts.

The procedure for preparing a post-closing trial balance again consists entirely of listing the accounts and their balances. These balances are the same as those reported in the company's balance sheet in Illustration 4-4. The post-closing trial balance for Pioneer Advertising Agency, Inc. is shown in Illustration 4-9.

Illustration 4-9

Post-closing trial balance

PIONEER ADVERTISING AGENCY, INC. Post-Closing Trial Balance October 31, 1996		
	Debit	Credit
Cash	$15,200	
Accounts Receivable	200	
Advertising Supplies	1,000	
Prepaid Insurance	550	
Office Equipment	5,000	
Accumulated Depreciation—Office Equipment		$ 40
Notes Payable		5,000
Accounts Payable		2,500
Interest Payable		50
Unearned Fees		800
Salaries Payable		1,200
Common Stock		10,000
Retained Earnings		2,360
	$21,950	$21,950

Helpful hint Will total debits in a post-closing trial balance equal total assets on the balance sheet? Answer: No. Accumulated depreciation is deducted from assets on the balance sheet but added to the credit balance total in a post-closing trial balance.

The post-closing trial balance is prepared from the permanent accounts in the ledger. The permanent accounts of Pioneer Advertising are shown in the general ledger in Illustration 4-10. Because the balance of each account is computed after every posting, no additional work on these accounts is needed as part of the closing process. The remaining accounts in the general ledger are temporary accounts (shown in Illustration 4-11). After the closing entries are posted, each temporary account has a zero balance. These accounts are double-ruled to finalize the closing process.

A post-closing trial balance provides evidence that the journalizing and posting of closing entries has been properly completed. In addition, it shows that the accounting equation is in balance at the end of the accounting period. However, as in the case of the trial balance, it does not prove that all transactions have been recorded or that the ledger is correct. For example, the post-closing trial balance will balance if a transaction is not journalized and posted or if a transaction is journalized and posted twice.

Summary of the Accounting Cycle

The required steps in the accounting cycle are shown graphically in Illustration 4-12 on page 160. From the graphic you can see that the cycle begins with the analysis of business transactions and ends with the preparation of a post-closing trial balance. The steps in the cycle are performed in sequence and are repeated in each accounting period.

Steps 1–3 may occur daily during the accounting period, as explained in Chapter 2. Steps 4–7 are performed on a periodic basis, such as monthly, quarterly, or annually. Steps 8 and 9, closing entries, and a post-closing trial balance, are usually prepared only at the end of a company's **annual** accounting period.

There are also two optional steps in the accounting cycle. As you have seen, a work sheet may be used in preparing adjusting entries and financial statements. In addition, reversing entries may be used as explained in the following section.

STUDY OBJECTIVE
4

State the required steps in the accounting cycle.

Illustration 4-10

General ledger: permanent accounts

(Permanent Accounts Only)

GENERAL LEDGER

Cash   No. 1

Date	Explanation	Ref.	Debit	Credit	Balance
1996					
Oct. 1		J1	10,000		10,000
2		J1	1,200		11,200
3		J1		900	10,300
4		J1		600	9,700
20		J1		500	9,200
26		J1		4,000	5,200
31		J1	10,000		15,200

Accounts Receivable   No. 6

Date	Explanation	Ref.	Debit	Credit	Balance
1996					
Oct. 31	Adj. entry	J2	**200**		200

Advertising Supplies   No. 8

Date	Explanation	Ref.	Debit	Credit	Balance
1996					
Oct. 5		J1	2,500		2,500
31	Adj. entry	J2		**1,500**	**1,000**

Prepaid Insurance   No. 10

Date	Explanation	Ref.	Debit	Credit	Balance
1996					
Oct. 4		J1	600		600
31	Adj. entry	J2		**50**	550

Office Equipment   No. 15

Date	Explanation	Ref.	Debit	Credit	Balance
1996					
Oct. 1		J1	5,000		5,000

Accumulated Depreciation—Office Equipment   No. 16

Date	Explanation	Ref.	Debit	Credit	Balance
1996					
Oct. 31	Adj. entry	J2		**40**	40

Notes Payable   No. 25

Date	Explanation	Ref.	Debit	Credit	Balance
1996					
Oct. 1		J1		5,000	5,000

Accounts Payable   No. 26

Date	Explanation	Ref.	Debit	Credit	Balance
1996					
Oct. 5		J1		2,500	2,500

Interest Payable   No. 27

Date	Explanation	Ref.	Debit	Credit	Balance
1996					
Oct. 31	Adj. entry	J2		**50**	50

Unearned Fees   No. 28

Date	Explanation	Ref.	Debit	Credit	Balance
1996					
Oct. 2		J1		1,200	1,200
31	Adj. entry	J2	**400**		800

Salaries Payable   No. 29

Date	Explanation	Ref.	Debit	Credit	Balance
1996					
Oct. 31	Adj. entry	J2		**1,200**	1,200

Common Stock   No. 40

Date	Explanation	Ref.	Debit	Credit	Balance
1996					
Oct. 1		J1		10,000	10,000

Retained Earnings   No. 41

Date	Explanation	Ref.	Debit	Credit	Balance
1996					
Oct. 1					–0–
31	Closing entry	J3		2,860	**2,860**
31	Closing entry	J3	500		**2,360**

Note: The permanent accounts for Pioneer Advertising Agency, Inc. are shown here; the temporary accounts are shown in Illustration 4-11. Both permanent and temporary accounts are part of the general ledger; they are segregated here to aid in learning.

Illustration 4-11

General ledger: temporary accounts

(Temporary Accounts Only)

GENERAL LEDGER

Dividends — No. 42

Date	Explanation	Ref.	Debit	Credit	Balance
1996					
Oct. 20		J1	500		500
31	Closing entry	J3		500	–0–

Income Summary — No. 49

Date	Explanation	Ref.	Debit	Credit	Balance
1996					
Oct. 31	Closing entry	J3		10,600	10,600
31	Closing entry	J3	7,740		2,860
31	Closing entry	J3	2,860		–0–

Fees Earned — No. 50

Date	Explanation	Ref.	Debit	Credit	Balance
1996					
Oct. 31		J1		10,000	10,000
31	Adj. entry	J2		400	10,400
31	Adj. entry	J2		200	10,600
31	Closing entry	J3	10,600		–0–

Salaries Expense — No. 60

Date	Explanation	Ref.	Debit	Credit	Balance
1996					
Oct. 26		J1	4,000		4,000
31	Adj. entry	J2	1,200		5,200
31	Closing entry	J3		5,200	–0–

Advertising Supplies Expense — No. 61

Date	Explanation	Ref.	Debit	Credit	Balance
1996					
Oct. 31	Adj. entry	J2	1,500		1,500
31	Closing entry	J3		1,500	–0–

Rent Expense — No. 62

Date	Explanation	Ref.	Debit	Credit	Balance
1996					
Oct. 3		J1	900		900
31	Closing entry	J3		900	–0–

Insurance Expense — No. 63

Date	Explanation	Ref.	Debit	Credit	Balance
1996					
Oct. 31	Adj. entry	J2	50		50
31	Closing entry	J3		50	–0–

Interest Expense — No. 64

Date	Explanation	Ref.	Debit	Credit	Balance
1996					
Oct. 31	Adj. entry	J2	50		50
31	Closing entry	J3		50	–0–

Depreciation Expense — No. 65

Date	Explanation	Ref.	Debit	Credit	Balance
1996					
Oct. 31	Adj. entry	J2	40		40
31	Closing entry	J3		40	–0–

Note: The temporary accounts for Pioneer Advertising Agency, Inc. are shown here; the permanent accounts are shown in Illustration 4-10. Both permanent and temporary accounts are part of the general ledger; they are segregated here to aid in learning.

Illustration 4-12

Required steps in the accounting cycle

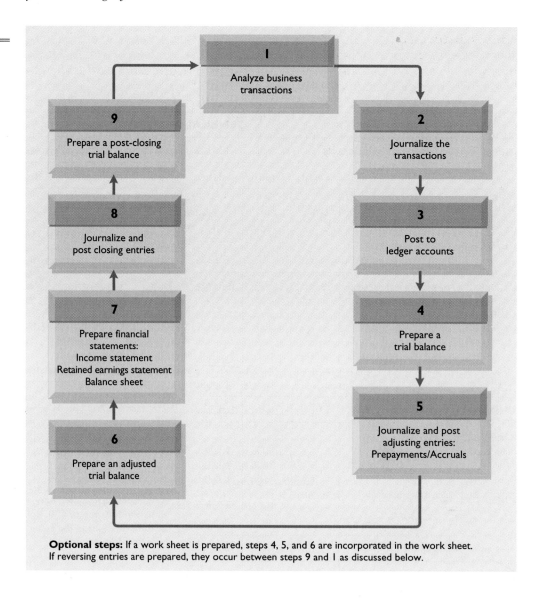

Optional steps: If a work sheet is prepared, steps 4, 5, and 6 are incorporated in the work sheet. If reversing entries are prepared, they occur between steps 9 and 1 as discussed below.

Reversing Entries—An Optional Step

Helpful hint Reversing entries are a bookkeeping matter and not an accounting principle or assumption.

Some accountants prefer to reverse certain adjusting entries at the beginning of a new accounting period. A reversing entry is made at the beginning of the next accounting period and is the exact opposite of the adjusting entry made in the previous period. **The preparation of reversing entries is an optional bookkeeping procedure that is not a required step in the accounting cycle.** Accordingly, we have chosen to cover this topic in an appendix at the end of the chapter.

only reverse accruals

Correcting Entries—An Avoidable Step

STUDY OBJECTIVE

••••••••• 5 •••••••••

Explain the approaches to preparing correcting entries.

If the accounting records are free of errors, no correcting entries are necessary. Unfortunately, errors may occur in the recording process. Errors should be corrected **as soon as they are discovered** by journalizing and posting correcting entries. You should recognize several significant differences between correcting entries and adjusting entries. First, adjusting entries are an integral part of the accounting cycle, whereas correcting entries are unnecessary if the records are free of errors. Second, **adjustments are journalized and posted only at the end of an accounting period; in contrast, correcting entries are made whenever an** error is discovered. Finally, adjusting entries always affect at least one balance sheet account and one income statement account. In contrast, correcting entries may involve any combination of accounts in need of correction. Correcting entries must be posted before closing entries.

To determine the correcting entry, it is useful to compare the incorrect entry with the correct entry. Doing so helps identify the accounts and amounts that should—and should not—be corrected. After comparison, a correcting entry is made to correct the accounts. This approach is illustrated in the following two cases.

Case 1. On May 10, a $50 cash collection on account from a customer is journalized and posted as a debit to Cash $50 and a credit to Fees Earned $50. The error is discovered on May 20, when the customer pays the remaining balance in full.

▶ *Ethics note*

In 1991 Citicorp reported a correcting entry reducing reported revenue by $23 million, while firing 11 employees. Citicorp officials did not specify why the employees had apparently intentionally inflated the revenue figures, although it was noted that their bonuses were tied to their unit's performance.

Incorrect Entry (May 10)			Correct Entry (May 10)		
Cash	50		Cash	50	
Fees Earned		50	Accounts Receivable		50

Illustration 4-13

Comparison of entries

A comparison of the incorrect entry with the correct entry reveals that the debit to Cash $50 is correct. However, the $50 credit to Fees Earned should have been credited to Accounts Receivable. As a result, both Fees Earned and Accounts Receivable are overstated in the ledger. The following correcting entry is required:

	Correcting Entry		
May 20	Fees Earned	50	
	Accounts Receivable		50
	(To correct entry of May 10)		

Illustration 4-14

Correcting entry

Case 2. On May 18, office equipment costing $450 is purchased on account. The transaction is journalized and posted as a debit to Delivery Equipment $45, and a credit to Accounts Payable $45. The error is discovered on June 3, when the monthly statement for May is received from the creditor.

Incorrect Entry (May 18)			Correct Entry (May 18)		
Delivery Equipment	45		Office Equipment	450	
Accounts Payable		45	Accounts Payable		450

Illustration 4-15

Comparison of entries

A comparison of the two entries shows that three accounts are incorrect. Delivery Equipment is overstated $45; Office Equipment is understated $450; and Accounts Payable is understated $405. The correcting entry is:

	Correcting Entry		
June 3	Office Equipment	450	
	Delivery Equipment		45
	Accounts Payable		405
	(To correct May 18 entry)		

Illustration 4-16

Correcting entry

Instead of preparing a correcting entry, **it is possible to reverse the incorrect entry and then prepare the correct entry**. This approach will result in more entries and postings than a correcting entry, but it will accomplish the desired result.

▸Accounting in Action ▸ *Business Insight*

Yale Express, a short-haul trucking firm, turned over much of its cargo to local truckers for delivery completion. Yale collected the entire delivery charge and, when billed by the local trucker, remitted payment for the final phase to the local trucker. Yale used a cutoff period of 20 days into the next accounting period in making its adjusting entries for accrued liabilities. That is, it waited 20 days to receive the local truckers' bills to determine the amount of the unpaid but incurred delivery charges as of the balance sheet date.

On the other hand, Republic Carloading, a nationwide, long-distance freight forwarder, frequently did not receive transportation bills from truckers to whom it passed on cargo until months after the year end. In making its year-end adjusting entries, Republic waited for months in order to include all of these outstanding transportation bills.

When Yale Express merged with Republic Carloading, Yale's vice-president employed the 20-day cutoff procedure for both firms. As a result, millions of dollars of Republic's accrued transportation bills went unrecorded. When the erroneous procedure was detected and correcting entries were made, these and other errors changed a reported profit of $1.14 million into a loss of $1.88 million!

Before You Go On . . .

▸ *Review It*

1. How do permanent accounts differ from temporary accounts?
2. What four different types of entries are required in closing the books?
3. What is the content and purpose of a post-closing trial balance?
4. What are the required and optional steps in the accounting cycle?

▸ *Do It*

The work sheet for Hancock Corporation shows the following in the financial statement columns: Common Stock $98,000, Dividends $15,000, Retained Earnings $42,000, and net income $18,000. Prepare the closing entries at December 31 that affect stockholders' equity.

Reasoning: Closing entries are made in sequence. The first two entries close revenues and expenses. The remaining two entries close net income and dividends to retained earnings.

Solution:

Dec 31	Income Summary	18,000	
	Retained Earnings		18,000
	(To close net income to retained earnings)		
31	Retained Earnings	15,000	
	Dividends		15,000
	(To close dividends to retained earnings)		

Related exercise material: BE4–4, BE4–5, BE4–6, E4–3, E4–6, and E4–8.

Classified Financial Statements

The financial statements illustrated up to this point were purposely kept simple. We classified items as assets, liabilities, and stockholders' equity in the balance sheet, and as revenues and expenses in the income statement. **Financial statements, however, become more useful to management, creditors, and potential investors when the elements are classified into significant subgroups.** In the remainder of this chapter we will introduce you to the primary balance sheet classifications. The classified income statement is presented in Chapter 5. The classified financial statements are what Jack Stack, the president of SRC Corporation, gave to his employees to understand what was happening in the business.

STUDY OBJECTIVE
··········▼6··········

Identify the sections of a classified balance sheet.

Standard Classifications

A classified balance sheet generally contains the following standard classifications:

Assets	Liabilities and Owner's Equity
Current Assets	Current Liabilities
Long-Term Investments	Long-Term Liabilities
Property, Plant, and Equipment	Stockholders' Equity
Intangible Assets	

Illustration 4-17

Standard balance sheet classifications

These sections help the financial statement user to determine such matters as (1) the availability of assets to meet debts as they come due and (2) the claims of short- and long-term creditors on total assets. A classified balance sheet also makes it easier to compare companies in the same industry, such as GM, Ford, and Chrysler in the automobile industry. Each of the sections is explained below, except for stockholders' equity, which has already been discussed.

A complete set of specimen financial statements for PepsiCo, Inc. is shown in Appendix A at the back of the book. The Coca-Cola Company's financial statements are at the end of Chapter 1.

Current Assets

Current assets are cash and other resources that are reasonably expected to be realized in cash or sold or consumed in the business within one year of the balance sheet date or the company's operating cycle, whichever is longer. For example, accounts receivable are included in current assets because they will be realized in cash through collection within one year. In contrast, a prepayment such as supplies is a current asset because of its expected use or consumption in the business within one year.

The operating cycle of a company is the average time that is required to go from cash to cash in producing revenues. The term "cycle" suggests a circular flow, which in this case, starts and ends with cash. For example, in municipal transit companies, the operating cycle would tend to be very short since services are rendered entirely on a cash basis. On the other hand, the operating cycle in public utility companies is longer: they bill customers for services rendered and the collection period may extend for several months. Most companies have operating cycles of less than one year. More will be said about operating cycles in later chapters.

In a service enterprise, it is customary to recognize four types of current assets: (1) cash, (2) marketable securities such as U.S. government bonds held as

▶ *International note*

Other countries use a different format for the balance sheet. In Great Britain, for example, property, plant, and equipment are reported first on the balance sheet; assets and liabilities are netted and grouped into net current and net total assets.

a temporary (short-term) investment, (3) receivables (notes receivable, accounts receivable, and interest receivable), and (4) prepaid expenses (insurance and supplies). **These items are listed in the order of liquidity,** that is, in the order in which they are expected to be converted into cash. This arrangement is illustrated below in the presentation of UAL, Inc. (United Airlines).

Illustration 4-18

Current asset section

UAL, INC. (United Airlines)	
Current assets (in thousands)	
Cash	$ 52,368
Marketable securities	389,862
Receivables	721,479
Aircraft fuel, spare parts, and supplies	178,840
Prepaid expenses	83,662
Total current assets	$1,426,211

A company's current assets are important in assessing the company's short-term debt-paying ability, as explained later in the chapter.

Long-Term Investments

Like current assets, long-term investments are resources that can be realized in cash. However, the conversion into cash is not expected within one year or the operating cycle, whichever is longer. In addition, long-term investments are not intended for use or consumption within the business. This category, often just called "investments," normally includes stocks and bonds of other corporations. Deluxe Check Printers Incorporated reported the following in its balance sheet:

Illustration 4-19

Long-term investment section

DELUXE CHECK PRINTERS INCORPORATED		
Long-term investments		
Investment in stock of Data Card Corporation	$20,468,000	
Other long-term investments	16,961,000	$37,429,000

Property, Plant, and Equipment

Helpful hint Property, plant, and equipment are sometimes referred to as plant assets or fixed assets.

Property, plant, and equipment are tangible resources of a relatively permanent nature that are used in the business and not intended for sale. This category includes land, buildings, machinery and equipment, delivery equipment, and furniture and fixtures. Assets subject to depreciation should be reported at cost less accumulated depreciation. This practice is illustrated in the following presentation of Delta Airlines:

Illustration 4-20

Property, plant, and equipment section

Helpful hint Remember that the $2,812,747 is not the market value of Delta's property, plant, and equipment.

DELTA AIRLINES, INC.			
Property, plant, and equipment (in thousands)			
Flight equipment	$3,985,796		
Less: Accumulated depreciation	1,713,059	$2,272,737	
Ground equipment	865,628		
Less: Accumulated depreciation	325,618	540,010	$2,812,747

Intangible Assets

Intangible assets are noncurrent resources that do not have physical substance. Intangible assets include patents, copyrights, and trademarks or trade names that give the holder **exclusive right** of use for a specified period of time. Their value to a company is generally derived from the rights or privileges granted by governmental authority.

In its balance sheet, Brunswick Corporation reported:

BRUNSWICK CORPORATION	
Intangible assets	
Patents, trademarks, and other intangibles	$10,460,000

Illustration 4-21

Intangible assets section

Current Liabilities

Listed first in the liabilities and stockholders' equity section of the balance sheet are current liabilities. Current liabilities are obligations that are reasonably expected to be paid from existing current assets or through the creation of other current liabilities. As in the case of current assets, the time period for payment is one year or the operating cycle, whichever is longer. Current liabilities include (1) debts related to the operating cycle, such as accounts payable and wages and salaries payable, and (2) other short-term debts, such as bank loans payable, interest payable, taxes payable, and current maturities of long-term obligations (payments to be made within the next year on long-term obligations).

Helpful hint An account payable is still current if it is expected to be "paid" by issuing a short-term note payable.

The arrangement of items within the current liabilities section has evolved through custom rather than from a prescribed rule. Notes payable is usually listed first, followed by accounts payable. Other items are then listed in any order. The current liability section adapted from the balance sheet of UAL, Inc. (United Airlines) is as follows:

UAL, INC. (United Airlines)	
Current liabilities (in thousands)	
Notes payable	$ 297,518
Accounts payable	382,967
Current maturities of long-term obligations	81,525
Unearned ticket revenue	432,979
Salaries and wages payable	435,622
Taxes payable	80,390
Other current liabilities	240,652
Total current liabilities	$1,951,653

Illustration 4-22

Current liabilities section

Users of financial statements look closely at the relationship between current assets and current liabilities. This relationship is important in evaluating a company's liquidity—its ability to pay obligations that are expected to become due within the next year or operating cycle. When current assets exceed current liabilities at the balance sheet date, the likelihood for paying the liabilities is favorable. When the reverse is true, short-term creditors may not be paid, and the company may ultimately be forced into bankruptcy.

Long-Term Liabilities

Helpful hint   Long-term liabilities are also called long-term debt or non-current liabilities.

Obligations expected to be paid after one year are classified as long-term liabilities (or long-term debt). Liabilities in this category include bonds payable, mortgages payable, long-term notes payable, lease liabilities, and obligations under employee pension plans. Many companies report long-term debt maturing after one year as a single amount in the balance sheet and show the details of the debt in the notes that accompany the financial statements. Others list the various sources of long-term liabilities. In its balance sheet, Consolidated Freightways, Inc. reported:

Illustration 4-23

Long-term liabilities section

CONSOLIDATED FREIGHTWAYS, INC.

Long-term liabilities (in thousands)	
Bank notes payable	$10,000
Mortgage payable	2,900
Bonds payable	53,422
Other long-term debt	9,597
Total long-term liabilities	$75,919

Stockholders' (Owners') Equity

The content of the owners' equity section varies with the form of business organization. In a proprietorship, there is one capital account. In a partnership, there is a capital account for each partner. For a corporation, owners' (stockholders') equity is divided into two accounts—Common Stock and Retained Earnings. As previously indicated, investments of capital in the business by the stockholders are recorded in the Common Stock account. Income retained for use in the business is recorded in the Retained Earnings account. These two accounts are combined and reported as stockholders' equity on the balance sheet.

   In its balance sheet, the Americana Corporation reported its stockholders' equity section as follows:

Illustration 4-24

Stockholders' equity section

AMERICANA CORPORATION

Stockholders' equity		
Common stock	$1,000,000	
Retained earnings	200,000	
Total stockholders' equity		$1,200,000

Classified Balance Sheet Illustrated

An unclassified balance sheet of Pioneer Advertising Agency, Inc. was presented in Illustration 3-19 on page 117. Using the same adjusted trial balance accounts for Pioneer at October 31, 1996, we can prepare the classified balance sheet shown in Illustration 4-25. For illustrative purposes, we have assumed that $1,000 of the notes payable is due currently and $4,000 is long-term.

Helpful hint   A recent survey of 600 companies in *Accounting Trends & Techniques* showed that 70% use the report form and 30% use the account form balance sheet.

   The balance sheet is most often presented in **report form**, as in Illustration 4-25, with the assets shown above the liabilities and stockholders' equity. The balance sheet may also be presented in **account form** with the assets section placed on the left and the liabilities and stockholders' equity section on the right.

Illustration 4-25

Classified balance sheet in report form

PIONEER ADVERTISING AGENCY, INC.
Balance Sheet
October 31, 1996

Assets

Current assets		
Cash		$15,200
Accounts receivable		200
Advertising supplies		1,000
Prepaid insurance		550
Total current assets		16,950
Property, plant, and equipment		
Office equipment	$5,000	
Less: Accumulated depreciation	40	4,960
Total assets		$21,910

Liabilities and Stockholders' Equity

Current liabilities	
Notes payable	$ 1,000
Accounts payable	2,500
Interest payable	50
Unearned fees	800
Salaries payable	1,200
Total current liabilities	5,550
Long-term liabilities	
Notes payable	4,000
Total liabilities	9,550
Stockholders' equity	
Common stock	10,000
Retained earnings	2,360
Total liabilities and stockholders' equity	$21,910

Before You Go On . . .

► Review It

1. What are the major sections in a classified balance sheet?
2. What is the difference between the report form and the account form of the classified balance sheet?

► A Look Back at SRC Corporation

Refer to the opening story about SRC Corporation, and answer the following questions:

1. What is the lesson of the SRC story and Jack Stack's innovations?
2. How did Craig Highbarger's knowledge of financial statements, especially the income statement, contribute to his effectiveness as an employee?

Solution:

1. If you give employees equity in the company and provide them with the training and the information to understand the financial consequences of their decisions and actions, they will act more responsibly and make a greater contribution to the sales and income of the company. In other words, they begin to think like owners.
2. By understanding the income statement, he now recognizes the impact of revenues and expenses in arriving at net income—as well as how they affect his bonus.

Summary of Study Objectives

1. *Prepare a work sheet.* The steps in preparing a work sheet are: (a) prepare a trial balance on the work sheet, (b) enter the adjustments in the adjustment columns, (c) enter adjusted balances in the adjusted trial balance columns, (d) extend adjusted trial balance amounts to appropriate financial statement columns, and (e) total the statement columns, compute net income (or net loss), and complete the work sheet.

2. *Explain the process of closing the books.* Closing the books occurs at the end of an accounting period. The process is to journalize and post closing entries and then rule and balance all accounts. In closing the books, separate entries are made to close revenues and expenses to Income Summary, Income Summary to Retained Earnings, and Dividends to Retained Earnings. Only temporary accounts are closed.

3. *Describe the content and purpose of a post-closing trial balance.* A post-closing trial balance contains the balances in permanent accounts that are carried forward to the next accounting period. The purpose of this trial balance is to prove the equality of these balances.

4. *State the required steps in the accounting cycle.* The required steps in the accounting cycle are: (a) analyze business transactions, (b) journalize the transactions, (c) post to ledger accounts, (d) prepare a trial balance, (e) journalize and post adjusting entries, (f) prepare an adjusted trial balance, (g) prepare financial statements, (h) journalize and post closing entries, and (i) prepare a post-closing trial balance.

5. *Explain the approaches to preparing correcting entries.* One approach for determining the correcting entry is to compare the incorrect entry with the correct entry. After comparison, a correcting entry is made to correct the accounts. An alternative to a correcting entry is to reverse the incorrect entry and then prepare the correct entry.

6. *Identify the sections of a classified balance sheet.* In a classified balance sheet, assets are classified as current assets; long-term investments; property, plant, and equipment; or intangibles. Liabilities are classified as either current or long-term. There is also a stockholders' (owners') equity section, which varies with the form of business organization.

APPENDIX ▶ *Reversing Entries*

STUDY OBJECTIVE

After studying this Appendix, you should be able to:

7. *Prepare reversing entries.*

After the financial statements are prepared and the books are closed, it is often helpful to reverse some of the adjusting entries before recording the regular transactions of the next period. Such entries are called reversing entries. **A reversing entry is made at the beginning of the next accounting period and is the exact opposite of the adjusting entry made in the previous period.** The recording of reversing entries is an **optional** step in the accounting cycle.

The purpose of reversing entries is to simplify the recording of a subsequent transaction related to an adjusting entry. In Chapter 3, you may recall, the payment of salaries after an adjusting entry resulted in two debits: one to Salaries Payable and the other to Salaries Expense. With reversing entries, the entire subsequent payment can be debited to Salaries Expense. **The use of reversing entries does not change the amounts reported in the financial statements. It does, however, simplify the recording of subsequent transactions.**

Illustration of Reversing Entries

Reversing entries are most often used to reverse two types of adjusting entries: accrued revenues and accrued expenses. They are seldom made for prepaid expenses and unearned revenues. To illustrate the optional use of reversing entries for accrued expenses, we will use the salaries expense transactions for Pioneer Advertising Agency, Inc. The transaction and adjustment data are as follows:

1. October 26 (initial salary entry): $4,000 of salaries earned between October 15 and October 26 are paid.
2. October 31 (adjusting entry): Salaries earned between October 29 and October 31 are $1,200. These will be paid in the November 9 payroll.
3. November 9 (subsequent salary entry): Salaries paid are $4,000. Of this amount, $1,200 applied to accrued wages payable and $2,800 was earned between November 1 and November 9.

The comparative entries with and without reversing entries are shown in Illustration 4A-1.

Illustration 4A-1

Comparative entries— not reversing vs. reversing

When Reversing Entries Are Not Used (per chapter)				When Reversing Entries Are Used (per appendix)		
Initial Salary Entry				**Initial Salary Entry**		
Oct. 26	Salaries Expense	4,000		Oct. 26	Salaries Expense	4,000
	Cash		4,000		Cash	4,000
Adjusting Entry				**Adjusting Entry**		
Oct. 31	Salaries Expense	1,200		Oct. 31	Salaries Expense	1,200
	Salaries Payable		1,200		Salaries Payable	1,200
Closing Entry				**Closing Entry**		
Oct. 31	Income Summary	5,200		Oct. 31	Income Summary	5,200
	Salaries Expense		5,200		Salaries Expense	5,200
Reversing Entry				**Reversing Entry**		
Nov. 1	No reversing entry is made.			Nov. 1	Salaries Payable	1,200
					Salaries Expense	1,200
Subsequent Salary Entry				**Subsequent Salary Entry**		
Nov. 9	Salaries Payable	1,200		Nov. 9	Salaries Expense	4,000
	Salaries Expense	2,800			Cash	4,000
	Cash		4,000			

The comparative entries show that the first three entries are the same whether or not reversing entries are used. The last two entries, however, are different. The November 1 **reversing entry** eliminates the $1,200 balance in Salaries Payable that was created by the October 31 adjusting entry. The reversing entry also creates a $1,200 credit balance in the Salaries Expense account. As you know, it is unusual for an expense account to have a credit balance. The balance is correct in this instance, though, because it anticipates that the entire amount of the first salary payment in the new accounting period will be debited to Salaries Expense. This debit will eliminate the credit balance, and the resulting debit balance in the expense account will equal the salaries expense incurred in the new accounting period ($2,800 in this example).

►Technology in Action

Using reversing entries in a computerized accounting system is more efficient than in a manual system. The reversing entry saves writing a program to locate the amount accrued from the preceding period and making the more complicated entry in the current period. That is, the computer does not have to be programmed to determine whether any accrued items exist.

When reversing entries are made, all cash payments of expenses can be debited to the expense account. This means that on November 9 (and every payday) Salaries Expense can be debited for the amount paid without regard to the existence of any accrued salaries payable. Being able to make the same entry each time simplifies the recording process. Note that when reversing entries are used, the recording of subsequent transactions is simplified because they can be recorded as if the related adjusting entry had never been made.

The posting of the entries with reversing entries is shown in Illustration 4A-2.

Illustration 4A-2

Postings with reversing entries

Salaries Expense					Salaries Payable			
10/26 Paid	4,000	10/31 Closing	5,200		11/1 Reversing	1,200	10/31 Adjusting	1,200
31 Adjusting	1,200							
	5,200		5,200					
11/9 Paid	4,000	11/1 Reversing	1,200					

Reversing entries may also be made for accrued revenue adjusting entries. For Pioneer Advertising, the adjusting entry was: Accounts Receivable (Dr.) $200 and Fees Earned (Cr.) $200. Thus, the reversing entry on November 1 is:

Nov. 1	Fees Earned	200	
	Accounts Receivable		200
	(To reverse October 31 adjusting entry)		

When the accrued fees are collected, Cash is debited and Fees Earned is credited.

Summary of Study Objective for Chapter 4 Appendix

7. *Prepare reversing entries.* Reversing entries are the direct opposite of the adjusting entry made in the preceding period. They are made at the beginning of a new accounting period to simplify the recording of later transactions related to the adjusting entry. In most cases, only accrued adjusting entries are reversed.

GLOSSARY

Classified balance sheet A balance sheet that contains a number of standard classifications or sections. (p. 163).

Closing entries Entries at the end of an accounting period to transfer the balances of temporary accounts to a permanent stockholders' equity account, Retained Earnings. (p. 153).

Correcting entries Entries to correct errors made in recording transactions. (p. 160).

Current assets Cash and other resources that are reasonably expected to be realized in cash or sold or consumed in the business within one year or the operating cycle, whichever is longer. (p. 163).

Current liabilities Obligations reasonably expected to be paid from existing current assets or through the creation of other current liabilities within the next year or operating cycle, whichever is longer. (p. 165).

Income Summary A temporary account used in closing revenue and expense accounts. (p. 153).

Intangible assets Noncurrent resources that do not have physical substance. (p. 165).

Liquidity The ability of a company to pay obligations that are expected to become due within the next year or operating cycle. (p. 165).

Long-term investments   Resources not expected to be realized in cash within the next year or operating cycle. (p. 164).

Long-term liabilities (Long-term debt)   Obligations expected to be paid after one year. (p. 166).

Operating cycle   The average time required to go from cash to cash in producing revenues. (p. 163).

Permanent (real) accounts   Balance sheet accounts whose balances are carried forward to the next accounting period. (p. 152).

Post-closing trial balance   A list of permanent accounts and their balances after closing entries have been journalized and posted. (p. 155).

Property, plant, and equipment   Assets of a relatively per-

manent nature that are being used in the business and not intended for resale. (p. 164).

Reversing entry   An entry at the beginning of the next accounting period that is the exact opposite of the adjusting entry made in the previous period. (p. 160).

Stockholders' equity   The ownership claim of shareholders on total assets. It is to a corporation what owner's equity is to a proprietorship. (p. 166).

Temporary (nominal) accounts   Revenue, expense, and dividends accounts whose balances are transferred to retained earnings at the end of an accounting period. (p. 152).

Work sheet   A multiple-column form that may be used in the adjustment process and in preparing financial statements. (p. 146).

DEMONSTRATION PROBLEM

At the end of its first month of operations, Watson Answering Service, Inc. has the following unadjusted trial balance:

WATSON ANSWERING SERVICE, INC.
August 31, 1996
Trial Balance

	Debit	Credit
Cash	$ 5,400	
Accounts Receivable	8,800	
Prepaid Insurance	2,400	
Supplies	1,300	
Equipment	60,000	
Notes Payable		$40,000
Accounts Payable		2,400
Common Stock		30,000
Dividends	1,000	
Fees Earned		10,900
Salaries Expense	3,200	
Utilities Expense	800	
Advertising Expense	400	
	$83,300	$83,300

Problem-Solving Strategies

1. In completing the work sheet, be sure to (a) key the adjustments, (b) extend adjusted balances to the correct statement columns, and (c) enter net income (or net loss) in the proper columns.

2. In preparing a classified balance sheet, know the contents of each of the sections.

3. In journalizing closing entries, remember that there are only four entries and that Dividends is closed to Retained Earnings.

Other data consist of the following:

1. Insurance expires at the rate of $200 per month.
2. There are $1,000 of supplies on hand at August 31.
3. Monthly depreciation is $900 on the equipment.
4. Interest of $500 has accrued during August on the notes payable.

Instructions

(a) Prepare a work sheet.
(b) Prepare a classified balance sheet assuming $35,000 of the notes payable are long-term.
(c) Journalize the closing entries.

Solution to Demonstration Problem

(a)

WATSON ANSWERING SERVICE, INC.
Work Sheet
For the Month Ended August 31, 1996

Account Titles	Trial Balance		Adjustments		Adjusted Trial Balance		Income Statement		Balance Sheet	
	Dr.	Cr.	Dr.	Cr.	Dr.	Cr.	Dr.	Cr.	Dr.	Cr.
Cash	5,400				5,400				5,400	
Accounts Receivable	8,800				8,800				8,800	
Prepaid Insurance	2,400			(a) 200	2,200				2,200	
Supplies	1,300			(b) 300	1,000				1,000	
Equipment	60,000				60,000				60,000	
Notes Payable		40,000				40,000				40,000
Accounts Payable		2,400				2,400				2,400
Common Stock		30,000				30,000				30,000
Dividends	1,000				1,000				1,000	
Fees Earned		10,900				10,900		10,900		
Salaries Expense	3,200				3,200		3,200			
Utilities Expense	800				800		800			
Advertising Expense	400				400		400			
Totals	83,300	83,300								
Insurance Expense			(a) 200		200		200			
Supplies Expense			(b) 300		300		300			
Depreciation Expense			(c) 900		900		900			
Accumulated Depreciation—Equipment				(c) 900		900				900
Interest Expense			(d) 500		500		500			
Interest Payable				(d) 500		500				500
Totals			1,900	1,900	84,700	84,700	6,300	10,900	78,400	73,800
Net Income							4,600			4,600
Totals							10,900	10,900	78,400	78,400

Explanation: (a) Insurance expired, (b) Supplies used, (c) Depreciation expensed, (d) Interest accrued.

(b)

WATSON ANSWERING SERVICE, INC.
Balance Sheet
August 31, 1996

Assets

Current assets		
Cash		$ 5,400
Accounts receivable		8,800
Prepaid insurance		2,200
Supplies		1,000
Total current assets		17,400
Property, plant, and equipment		
Equipment	$60,000	
Less: Accumulated depreciation—equipment	900	59,100
Total assets		$76,500

Liabilities and Stockholders' Equity

Current liabilities		
Notes payable		$ 5,000
Accounts payable		2,400
Interest payable		500
Total current liabilities		7,900

Long-term liabilities

Notes payable		35,000
Total liabilities		42,900

Stockholders' equity

Common stock		30,000
Retained earnings		3,600*
Total liabilities and stockholders' equity		$76,500

*Net income of $4,600 less dividends of $1,000.

(c)

Aug. 31	Fees Earned		10,900	
	Income Summary			10,900
	(To close revenue account)			
31	Income Summary		6,300	
	Salaries Expense			3,200
	Depreciation Expense			900
	Utilities Expense			800
	Interest Expense			500
	Advertising Expense			400
	Supplies Expense			300
	Insurance Expense			200
	(To close expense accounts)			
31	Income Summary		4,600	
	Retained Earnings			4,600
	(To close net income to retained earnings)			
31	Retained Earnings		1,000	
	Dividends			1,000
	(To close dividends to retained earnings)			

*Note: All **asterisked** Questions, Exercises, and Problems relate to material contained in the Appendix to each chapter.

SELF-STUDY QUESTIONS

• •

Answers are at the end of the chapter.

(SO 1) 1. Which of the following statements is *incorrect* concerning the work sheet?
   a. The work sheet is essentially a working tool of the accountant.
   b. The work sheet cannot be used as a basis for posting to ledger accounts.
   c. The work sheet is distributed to management and other interested parties.
   d. Financial statements can be prepared directly from the work sheet before journalizing and posting the adjusting entries.

(SO 1) 2. In a work sheet, net income is entered in the following columns:
   a. income statement (Dr) and balance sheet (Dr).
   b. income statement (Dr) and balance sheet (Cr).
   c. income statement (Cr) and balance sheet (Dr).
   d. income statement (Cr) and balance sheet (Cr).

(SO 2) 3. An account that will have a zero balance after closing entries have been journalized and posted is:
   a. Unearned Fees.
   b. Advertising Supplies.
   c. Prepaid Insurance.
   d. Rent Expense.

4. When a net loss has occurred, Income Summary is: (SO 2)
   a. credited and retained earnings is debited.
   b. debited and retained earnings is credited.
   c. debited and common stock is credited.
   d. credited and common stock is debited.

5. The closing process involves separate entries to (SO 2) close (1) expenses, (2) dividends, (3) revenues and (4) net income (or loss). The correct sequencing of the entries is:
   a. (4), (3), (2), (1)
   b. (1), (2), (3), (4)
   c. (3), (2), (1), (4)
   d. (3), (1), (4), (2)

   1. Revenues
   2. Expenses
   3. Net income (In. Sum/Ret. Ear)
   4. Dividends

6. Which types of accounts will appear in the post- (SO 3) closing trial balance?
   a. Temporary (nominal) accounts.
   b. Permanent (real) accounts.

c. Accounts shown in the income statement columns of a work sheet.
d. None of the above.

(SO 4)   7. All of the following are required steps in the accounting cycle *except*:
   a. preparing a work sheet.
   b. journalizing and posting closing entries.
   c. preparing an adjusted trial balance.
   d. preparing a post-closing trial balance.

(SO 5)   8. Cash of $100 received at the time the service was rendered was journalized and posted as a debit to Cash $100 and a credit to Accounts Receivable $100. Assuming the incorrect entry is not reversed, the correcting entry is:
   a. debit Fees Earned $100 and credit Accounts Receivable $100.
   b. debit Cash $100 and credit Fees Earned $100.
   c. debit Accounts Receivable $100 and credit Fees Earned $100.
   d. debit Accounts Receivable $100 and credit Cash $100.

(SO 6)   9. In a classified balance sheet, assets are usually classified as:
   a. current assets; long-term assets; property, plant, and equipment; and intangible assets.

b. current assets; long-term investments; property, plant, and equipment; and other assets.
   c. current assets; long-term investments; property, plant, and equipment; and intangible assets.
   d. current assets; long-term investments; tangible assets; and intangible assets.

10. Current assets are listed: (SO 6)
   a. by importance.
   b. by liquidity.
   c. by longevity.
   d. alphabetically.

*11. On December 31, the Scott Company correctly   (SO 7)
made an adjusting entry to recognize $2,000 of accrued salaries payable. On January 8 of the next year, total salaries of $3,500 were paid. Assuming the correct reversing entry was made on January 1, the entry on January 8 will result in a credit to Cash $3,500, and the following debit(s):
   a. Salaries Payable $3,500.
   b. Salaries Expense $3,500.
   c. Salaries Payable $2,000 and Salaries Expense $1,500.
   d. Salaries Payable $1,500 and Salaries Expense $2,000.

QUESTIONS

1. "A work sheet is a permanent accounting record and its use is required in the accounting cycle." Do you agree? Explain.

2. The use of a work sheet affects two steps of the accounting cycle after preparing the trial balance. What steps are they, and how are they affected by the work sheet?

3. What is the relationship, if any, between the amount shown in the adjusted trial balance column for an account and that account's ledger balance?

4. If a company's revenues are $122,000 and its expenses are $113,000, in which financial statement columns of the work sheet will the net income of $9,000 appear? When expenses exceed revenues, in which columns will the difference appear?

5. Why is it necessary to prepare formal financial statements when all of the data are in the statement columns of the work sheet?

6. Identify the account(s) debited and credited in each of the four closing entries, assuming the company has net income for the year.

7. Describe the nature of the Income Summary account and identify the types of summary data that may be posted to this account.

8. What are the content and purpose of a post-closing trial balance?

9. Which of the following accounts would not appear in the post-closing trial balance? Interest Payable; Equipment; Depreciation Expense; Dividends; Unearned Fees; Accumulated Depreciation—Equipment; and Fees Earned.

10. Distinguish between a reversing entry and an adjusting entry. Are reversing entries required?

11. Indicate, in the sequence in which they are made, the three required steps in the accounting cycle that involve journalizing.

12. Identify, in the sequence in which they are prepared, the three trial balances that are required in the accounting cycle.

13. How do correcting entries differ from adjusting entries?

14. What standard classifications are used in preparing a classified balance sheet?

15. What is meant by the term "operating cycle"?

16. Define current assets. What basis is used for arranging individual items within the current asset section?

17. Distinguish between long-term investments and property, plant, and equipment.

18. How do current liabilities differ from long-term liabilities?

19. (a) What is the term used to describe the owner's equity section of a corporation? (b) Identify the two owner's equity accounts in a corporation and indicate the purpose of each.

20. How does a report form balance sheet differ from an account form balance sheet?

*21. Kimbria Shumway Company prepares reversing entries. If the adjusting entry for interest payable is reversed, what type of an account balance, if any, will there be in Interest Payable and Interest Expense after the reversing entry is posted?

*22. At December 31, accrued salaries payable totaled $4,500. On January 10, total salaries of $7,000 are paid. (a) Assume that reversing entries are made at January 1. Give the January 10 entry and indicate the Salaries Expense account balance after the entry is posted. (b) Repeat part (a) assuming reversing entries are not made.

BRIEF EXERCISES

BE4–1   The steps in using a work sheet are presented in random order below. List the steps in the proper order.

_____ Total the statement columns, compute net income (loss), and complete the work sheet.
_____ Enter adjustment data.
_____ Prepare a trial balance on the work sheet.
_____ Enter adjusted balances.
_____ Extend adjusted balances to appropriate statement columns.

List the steps in preparing a work sheet.
(SO 1)

BE4–2   The ledger of Ingram Company includes the following unadjusted balances: Prepaid Insurance $4,200, Fees Earned $58,000, and Salaries Expense $24,000. Adjusting entries are required for (a) expired insurance $1,600, (b) accrued fees earned $900, and (c) accrued salaries payable $800. Enter the unadjusted balances and adjustments into a work sheet and complete the work sheet for all accounts. Note: You will need to add the following accounts: Accounts Receivable, Salaries Payable, and Insurance Expense.

Prepare partial work sheet.
(SO 1)

BE4–3   The following selected accounts appear in the adjusted trial balance columns of the work sheet for the Khanna Company: Accumulated Depreciation; Depreciation Expense; Common Stock; Dividends; Fees Earned; Supplies; and Accounts Payable. Indicate the financial statement column (income statement Dr., balance sheet Cr., etc.) to which each balance should be extended.

Identify work sheet columns for selected accounts.
(SO 1)

BE4–4   The ledger of the Batan Company contains the following balances: Common Stock $30,000; Dividends $2,000; Fees Earned $41,000; Salaries Expense $26,000; and Supplies Expense $4,000. Prepare the closing entries at December 31.

Prepare closing entries from ledger balances.
(SO 2)

BE4–5   Using the data in BE4–4, enter the balances in T accounts, post the closing entries, and rule and balance the accounts.

Post closing entries and rule and balance T accounts.
(SO 2)

BE4–6   The income statement for the Edgebrook Golf Club for the month ending July 31 shows Green Fees Earned $16,000, Salaries Expense $6,200, Maintenance Expense $2,500, and Net Income $7,300. Prepare the entries to close the revenue and expense accounts. Post the entries to the revenue and expense accounts and complete the closing process for these accounts using the three-column form of account.

Journalize and post closing entries using the three-column form of account.
(SO 2)

BE4–7   Using the data in BE4–3, identify the accounts that would be included in a post-closing trial balance.

Identify post-closing trial balance accounts.
(SO 3)

BE4–8   The required steps in the accounting cycle are listed in random order below. List the steps in proper sequence.

_____ Prepare a post-closing trial balance.
_____ Prepare an adjusted trial balance.
_____ Analyze business transactions.
_____ Prepare a trial balance.
_____ Journalize the transactions.
_____ Journalize and post closing entries.
_____ Prepare financial statements.
_____ Journalize and post adjusting entries.
_____ Post to ledger accounts.

List the required steps in the accounting cycle in sequence.
(SO 4)

Prepare correcting entries.
(SO 5)

BE4–9   At John McKee Company, the following errors were discovered after the transactions had been journalized and posted. Prepare the correcting entries.

1. A collection on account from a customer for $780 was recorded as a debit to Cash $780 and a credit to Fees Earned $780.
2. The purchase of store supplies on account for $1,530 was recorded as a debit to Store Supplies $1,350 and a credit to Accounts Payable $1,350.

Prepare the current asset section of a balance sheet.
(SO 6)

BE4–10   The balance sheet debit column of the work sheet for Ben Alschuler Company includes the following accounts: Accounts Receivable $16,500; Prepaid Insurance $3,600; Cash $18,400; Supplies $5,200, and Marketable Securities $8,200. Prepare the current asset section of the balance sheet listing the accounts in proper sequence.

Prepare reversing entries.
(SO 7)

*BE4–11   At October 31, Frank Voris Company made an accrued expense adjusting entry of $500 for salaries. Prepare the reversing entry on November 1 and indicate the balances in Salaries Payable and Salaries Expense after posting the reversing entry.

EXERCISES

• •

Complete work sheet.
(SO 1)

E4–1   The adjusted trial balance columns of the work sheet for Rey Sanchez Company are as follows:

REY SANCHEZ COMPANY
(Partial) Work Sheet
For the Month Ended April 30, 1996

NI = Revenue − Expenses

BS − A ≠ L + SE

Account Titles	Adjusted Trial Balance Dr.	Cr.	Income Statement Dr.	Cr.	Balance Sheet Dr.	Cr.
Cash	18,052					
Accounts Receivable	7,840					
Prepaid Rent	2,280					
Equipment	23,050					
Accumulated Depreciation		4,921				
Notes Payable		5,700				
Accounts Payable		5,972				
Common Stock		30,000				
Retained Earnings		3,960				
Dividends	3,650					
Fees Earned		12,590				
Salaries Expense	6,840					
Rent Expense	760					
Depreciation Expense	671					
Interest Expense	57					
Interest Payable		57				
Totals	63,200	63,200				

Instructions
Complete the work sheet.

Prepare financial statements from work sheet.
(SO 1, 6)

E4–2   Work sheet data for the Rey Sanchez Company are presented in E4–1.

Instructions
Prepare an income statement, a retained earnings statement, and a classified balance sheet.

Journalize and post closing entries and prepare a post-closing trial balance.
(SO 2, 3)

E4–3   Work sheet data for the Rey Sanchez Company are presented in E4–1.

Instructions
(a) Journalize the closing entries at April 30.
(b) Post the closing entries to Income Summary and stockholders' equity. Use T accounts.
(c) Prepare a post-closing trial balance at April 30.

E4–4 The adjustments columns of the work sheet for Betsy Company are shown below.

Prepare adjusting entries from a work sheet and extend balances to work sheet columns.
(SO 1)

	Adjustments	
Account Titles	Debit	Credit
Accounts Receivable	700	
Prepaid Insurance		400
Accumulated Depreciation		1,000
Salaries Payable		600
Fees Earned		700
Salaries Expense	600	
Insurance Expense	400	
Depreciation Expense	1,000	
	2,700	2,700

Instructions
(a) Prepare the adjusting entries.
(b) Assuming the adjusted trial balance amount for each account is normal, indicate the financial statement column to which each balance should be extended.

E4–5 Selected work sheet data for Nikon Company are presented below.

Derive adjusting entries from work sheet data.
(SO 1)

Account Titles	Trial Balance		Adjusted Trial Balance	
	Dr.	Cr.	Dr.	Cr.
Accounts Receivable	?		34,000	
Prepaid Insurance	24,000		18,000	
Supplies	9,000		?	
Accumulated Depreciation		12,000		?
Salaries Payable		?		7,000
Fees Earned		90,000		94,000
Insurance Expense			?	
Depreciation Expense			10,000	
Supplies Expense			4,000	
Salaries Expense	?		49,000	

Instructions
(a) Fill in the missing amounts.
(b) Prepare the adjusting entries that were made.

E4–6 The adjusted trial balance of Batra Company at the end of its fiscal year on July 31, 1996, is as follows:

Journalize and post closing entries and prepare a post-closing trial balance.
(SO 2, 3)

BATRA COMPANY
Adjusted Trial Balance
July 31, 1996

No.	Account Titles	Debits	Credits
101	Cash	$ 11,940	
112	Accounts Receivable	8,780	
157	Equipment	15,900	
167	Accumulated Depreciation		$ 5,400
201	Accounts Payable		6,220
208	Unearned Rent Revenue		1,800
311	Common Stock		20,000
320	Retained Earnings		25,200
332	Dividends	14,000	
404	Commission Revenue		63,100
429	Rent Revenue		6,500
711	Depreciation Expense	4,000	
720	Salaries Expense	58,700	
732	Utilities Expense	14,900	
		$128,220	$128,220

Instructions

(a) Prepare the closing entries using page J15.
(b) Post to Retained Earnings and No. 350 Income Summary accounts. (Use the three-column form.)
(c) Prepare a post-closing trial balance at July 31.

Prepare financial statements.
(SO 6)

E4–7 The adjusted trial balance for Batra Company is presented in E4–6.

Instructions

(a) Prepare an income statement and a retained earnings statement for the year. There were no issuances of stock during the year.
(b) Prepare a classified balance sheet at July 31.

Prepare closing entries.
(SO 2)

E4–8 Selected accounts for Barb's Beauty Salon Inc. are presented below. All June 30 postings are from closing entries.

Salaries Expense				Fees Earned				Dividends			
6/10	3,200	6/30	7,800	6/30	15,600	6/15	7,200	6/15	1,300	6/30	1,300
6/28	4,600					6/24	8,400				

Common Stock		
	6/1	12,000

Supplies Expense				Rent Expense			
6/12	800	6/30	1,500	6/1	3,500	6/30	3,500
6/24	700						

Retained Earnings		
6/30	1,300	6/30	2,800
		Bal.	1,500

Instructions

(a) Prepare the closing entries that were made.
(b) Post the closing entries to Income Summary.

Prepare correcting entries.
(SO 5)

E4–9 The Choi Company has an inexperienced accountant. During the first 2 weeks on the job, the following errors were made in journalizing transactions. All entries were posted as made.

1. A payment on account to a creditor of $530 was debited to Accounts Payable $350 and credited to Cash $350.
2. The purchase of supplies on account for $500 was debited to Equipment $50 and credited to Accounts Payable $50.
3. A $400 cash dividend was debited to Salaries Expense $400 and credited to Cash $400.

Instructions

Prepare the correcting entries.

Prepare a classified balance sheet.
(SO 6)

E4–10 The adjusted trial balance for Summit's Bowling Alley Inc. at December 31, 1996, contains the following accounts.

Debits		Credits	
Building	$125,800	Common Stock	$100,000
Accounts Receivable	14,520	Retained Earnings	10,000
Prepaid Insurance	4,680	Accumulated Depreciation—Building	45,600
Cash	20,840	Accounts Payable	13,480
Equipment	62,400	Mortgage Payable	93,600
Land	61,200	Accumulated Depreciation—Equipment	18,720
Insurance Expense	780	Interest Payable	2,600
Depreciation Expense	5,360	Bowling Revenues	14,180
Interest Expense	2,600		$298,180
	$298,180		

Instructions

(a) Prepare a classified balance sheet; assume that $13,600 of the mortgage payable will be paid in 1997.
(b) ▭▭▭▭▭▭▷ Comment on the liquidity of the company.

*E4–11 On December 31, the adjusted trial balance of Goode Employment Agency shows the following selected data:

Prepare closing and reversing entries.
(SO 2, 4, 7)

Accounts Receivable	$5,000	Commission Revenue	$97,000
Interest Expense	7,800	Interest Payable	2,000

Analysis shows that adjusting entries were made to (a) accrue $5,000 of commission revenue and (b) accrue $2,000 interest expense.

Instructions
(a) Prepare the closing entries for the temporary accounts at December 31.
(b) Prepare the reversing entries on January 1.
(c) Post the entries in (a) and (b). Rule and balance the accounts. (Use T accounts.)
(d) Prepare the entries to record (1) the collection of the accrued commissions on January 10 and (2) the payment of all interest due ($2,700) on January 15.
(e) Post the entries in (d) to the temporary accounts.

PROBLEMS
••

P4–1 The trial balance columns of the work sheet for Everlast Roofing Inc. at March 31, 1996, are as follows:

Prepare a work sheet, financial statements, and adjusting and closing entries.
(SO 1, 2, 3, 6)

EVERLAST ROOFING INC.
Work Sheet
For the Month Ended March 31, 1996

Account Titles	Trial Balance	
	Dr.	Cr.
Cash	$ 2,700	
Accounts Receivable	1,600	
Roofing Supplies	1,100	
Equipment	6,000	
Accumulated Depreciation—Equipment		$ 1,200
Accounts Payable		1,100
Unearned Fees		300
Common Stock		5,000
Retained Earnings		2,000
Dividends	600	
Fees Earned		3,000
Salaries Expense	500	
Miscellaneous Expense	100	
	$12,600	$12,600

Other data:

1. A physical count reveals only $420 of roofing supplies on hand.
2. Depreciation for March is $200.
3. Unearned fees amounted to $100 after adjustment on March 31.
4. Accrued salaries are $400.

Instructions
(a) Enter the trial balance on a work sheet and complete the work sheet.
(b) Prepare an income statement and retained earnings statement for the month of March and classified balance sheet at March 31.
(c) Journalize the adjusting entries from the adjustments columns of the work sheet.
(d) Journalize the closing entries from the financial statement columns of the work sheet.

Complete work sheet and prepare financial statements, closing entries, and post-closing trial balance.
(SO 1, 2, 3, 6)

P4–2   The adjusted trial balance columns of the work sheet for Diaz Company, owned by Carl Diaz, is as follows:

DIAZ COMPANY
Work Sheet
For the Year Ended December 31, 1996

Account No.	Account Titles	Adjusted Trial Balance Dr.	Adjusted Trial Balance Cr.
101	Cash	14,600	
112	Accounts Receivable	15,400	
126	Supplies	1,500	
130	Prepaid Insurance	2,800	
151	Office Equipment	34,000	
152	Accumulated Depreciation—Office Equipment		8,000
200	Notes Payable		16,000
201	Accounts Payable		6,000
212	Salaries Payable		3,000
230	Interest Payable		500
311	Common Stock		20,000
320	Retained Earnings		5,000
332	Dividends	10,000	
400	Fees Earned		88,000
610	Advertising Expense	14,000	
631	Supplies Expense	5,700	
711	Depreciation Expense	4,000	
722	Insurance Expense	5,000	
726	Salaries Expense	39,000	
905	Interest Expense	500	
		146,500	146,500

Instructions

(a) Complete the work sheet by extending the balances to the financial statement columns.

(b) Prepare an income statement, retained earnings statement, and a classified balance sheet. (Note: $10,000 of the notes payable become due in 1997.)

(c) Prepare the closing entries. Use J14 for the journal page.

(d) Post the closing entries and rule and balance the accounts. Use the three-column form of account. Income Summary is No. 350.

(e) Prepare a post-closing trial balance.

Prepare financial statements, closing entries, and post-closing trial balance.
(SO 1, 2, 3, 6)

P4–3   The completed financial statement columns of the work sheet for Melinda Company are shown below.

MELINDA COMPANY
Work Sheet
For the Year Ended December 31, 1996

Account No.	Account Titles	Income Statement Dr.	Income Statement Cr.	Balance Sheet Dr.	Balance Sheet Cr.
101	Cash			13,600	
112	Accounts Receivable			13,500	
130	Prepaid Insurance			3,500	
157	Equipment			26,000	
167	Accumulated Depreciation				5,600
201	Accounts Payable				13,300
212	Salaries Payable				3,000
311	Common Stock				20,000
320	Retained Earnings				16,000
332	Dividends			12,000	
400	Fees Earned		54,000		
622	Repair Expense	1,800			

711	Depreciation Expense	2,600			
722	Insurance Expense	2,200			
726	Salaries Expense	35,000			
732	Utilities Expense	1,700			
	Totals	43,300	54,000	68,600	57,900
	Net Income	10,700			10,700
		54,000	54,000	68,600	68,600

Instructions

(a) Prepare an income statement, retained earnings statement, and a classified balance sheet.

(b) Prepare the closing entries.

(c) Post the closing entries and rule and balance the accounts. Use T-accounts. Income Summary is No. 350.

(d) Prepare a post-closing trial balance.

P4–4 Porter Management Services Inc. began business on January 1, 1996, with a capital investment of $120,000. The company manages condominiums for owners (Fees Earned) and rents space in its own office building (Rent Revenue). The trial and adjusted trial balance columns of the work sheet at the end of the first year are as follows:

Complete work sheet and prepare classified balance sheet, entries, and post-closing trial balance.
(SO 1, 2, 3, 6)

PORTER MANAGEMENT SERVICES INC.
Work Sheet
For the Year Ended December 31, 1996

Account Titles	Trial Balance Dr.	Trial Balance Cr.	Adjusted Trial Balance Dr.	Adjusted Trial Balance Cr.
Cash	12,500		12,500	
Accounts Receivable	23,600		23,600	
Prepaid Insurance	3,100		1,600	
Land	56,000		56,000	
Building	106,000		106,000	
Equipment	48,000		48,000	
Accounts Payable		10,400		10,400
Unearned Rent Revenue		4,000		1,800
Mortgage Payable		100,000		100,000
Common Stock		90,000		90,000
Retained Earnings		30,000		30,000
Dividends	20,000		20,000	
Fees Earned		75,600		75,600
Rent Revenue		24,000		26,200
Salaries Expense	32,000		32,000	
Advertising Expense	17,000		17,000	
Utilities Expense	15,800		15,800	
Totals	334,000	334,000		
Insurance Expense			1,500	
Depreciation Expense—Building			2,500	
Accumulated Depreciation—Building				2,500
Depreciation Expense—Equipment			3,900	
Accumulated Depreciation—Equipment				3,900
Interest Expense			12,000	
Interest Payable				12,000
Totals			352,400	352,400

Instructions

(a) Prepare a complete work sheet.

(b) Prepare a classified balance sheet. (Note: $10,000 of the mortgage payable is due for payment next year.)

(c) Journalize the adjusting entries.

(d) Journalize the closing entries.

(e) Prepare a post-closing trial balance.

Complete all steps in accounting cycle.
(SO 1, 2, 3, 4, 6)

P4–5   Jan Jansen opened Jan's Window Washing Inc. on July 1, 1996. During July the following transactions were completed.

July   1   Issued $8,000 of common stock for $8,000 cash.

1   Purchased used truck for $6,000, paying $3,000 cash and the balance on account.

3   Purchased cleaning supplies for $900 on account.

5   Paid $1,200 cash on one-year insurance policy effective July 1.

12   Billed customers $2,500 for cleaning services.

18   Paid $1,000 cash on amount owed on truck and $500 on amount owed on cleaning supplies.

20   Paid $1,200 cash for employee salaries.

21   Collected $1,400 cash from customers billed on July 12.

25   Billed customers $3,000 for cleaning services.

31   Paid gas and oil for month on truck $200.

31   Declared and paid $600 cash dividend.

The chart of accounts for Jan's Window Washing Inc. contains the following accounts: No. 101 Cash, No. 112 Accounts Receivable, No. 128 Cleaning Supplies, No. 130 Prepaid Insurance, No. 157 Equipment, No. 158 Accumulated Depreciation—Equipment, No. 201 Accounts Payable, No. 212 Salaries Payable, No. 311 Common Stock, No. 320 Retained Earnings, No. 332 Dividends, No. 350 Income Summary, No. 400 Fees Earned, No. 633 Gas & Oil Expense, No. 634 Cleaning Supplies Expense, No. 711 Depreciation Expense, No. 722 Insurance Expense, No. 726 Salaries Expense.

Instructions

(a) Journalize and post the July transactions. Use page J1 for the journal and the three-column form of account.

(b) Prepare a trial balance at July 31 on a work sheet.

(c) Enter the following adjustments on the work sheet and complete the work sheet.

(1) Earned but unbilled fees at July 31 were $1,100.

(2) Depreciation on equipment for the month was $200.

(3) One-twelfth of the insurance expired.

(4) An inventory count shows $600 of cleaning supplies on hand at July 31.

(5) Accrued but unpaid employee salaries were $400.

(d) Journalize and post adjusting entries. Use page J2 for the journal.

(e) Prepare the income statement and retained earnings statement for July and a classified balance sheet at July 31.

(f) Journalize and post closing entries and complete the closing process. Use page J3 for the journal.

(g) Prepare a post-closing trial balance at July 31.

Analyze errors and prepare correcting entries.
(SO 5)

P4–6   Michael Mears, CPA, was retained by Campus TV Repair Corp. to prepare financial statements for April 1996. Mears accumulated all the ledger balances per Morris's records and found the following:

CAMPUS TV REPAIR CORP.
Trial Balance
April 30, 1996

	Debit	Credit
Cash	$ 5,100	
Accounts Receivable	3,200	
Supplies	800	
Equipment	10,600	
Accumulated Depreciation		$ 1,350
Accounts Payable		2,100
Salaries Payable		500
Unearned Fees		890

Common Stock		10,000
Retained Earnings		3,900
Fees Earned		5,450
Salaries Expense	3,300	
Advertising Expense	400	
Miscellaneous Expense	290	
Depreciation Expense	500	
	$24,190	$24,190

Michael Mears reviewed the records and found the following errors:

1. Cash received from a customer on account was recorded as $650 instead of $560.
2. The purchase, on account, of a typewriter costing $340 was recorded as a debit to supplies and a credit to accounts payable for $340.
3. A payment of $30 for advertising expense was entered as a debit to Miscellaneous Expense $30 and a credit to Cash $30.
4. The first salary payment this month was for $1,900, which included $500 of salaries payable on March 31. The payment was recorded as a debit to Salaries Expense $1,900 and a credit to Cash $1,900. (No reversing entries were made on April 1.)
5. A cash payment of repair expense on equipment for $86 was recorded as a debit to Equipment $68 and a credit to Cash $68.

Instructions
(a) Prepare an analysis of each error showing (1) the incorrect entry, (2) the correct entry, and (3) the correcting entry.
(b) Prepare a correct trial balance.

ALTERNATE PROBLEMS
••

P4–1A Nancy Zarl began operations as a private investigator on January 1, 1996. The trial balance columns of the work sheet for Nancy Zarl Corp. at March 31 are as follows:

Prepare work sheet, financial statements, and adjusting and closing entries.
(SO 1, 2, 3, 6)

NANCY ZARL CORP.
Work Sheet
For the Quarter Ended March 31, 1996

	Trial Balance	
Account Titles	Dr.	Cr.
Cash	$12,400	
Accounts Receivable	5,620	
Supplies	1,050	
Prepaid Insurance	2,400	
Equipment	30,000	
Notes Payable		$10,000
Accounts Payable		12,350
Common Stock		20,000
Dividends	600	
Fees Earned		13,620
Salaries Expense	1,200	
Travel Expense	1,300	
Rent Expense	1,200	
Miscellaneous Expense	200	
	$55,970	$55,970

Other data:

1. Supplies on hand total $750.
2. Depreciation is $400 per quarter.
3. Interest accrued on six months note payable, issued January 1, $300.
4. Insurance expires at the rate of $150 per month.
5. Fees earned but unbilled at March 31 total $750.

Instructions

(a) Enter the trial balance on a work sheet and complete the work sheet.

(b) Prepare an income statement and retained earnings statement for the quarter and a classified balance sheet at March 31.

(c) Journalize the adjusting entries from the adjustments columns of the work sheet.

(d) Journalize the closing entries from the financial statement columns of the work sheet.

Complete work sheet and prepare financial statements, closing entries, and post-closing trial balance.
(SO 1, 2, 3, 6)

P4–2A   The adjusted trial balance columns of the work sheet for Ohno Company is as follows:

OHNO COMPANY
Work Sheet
For the Year Ended December 31, 1996

Account No.	Account Titles	Adjusted Trial Balance Dr.	Cr.
101	Cash	24,800	
112	Accounts Receivable	15,400	
126	Supplies	2,300	
130	Prepaid Insurance	4,800	
151	Office Equipment	44,000	
152	Accumulated Depreciation—Office Equipment		18,000
200	Notes Payable		20,000
201	Accounts Payable		8,000
212	Salaries Payable		3,000
230	Interest Payable		1,000
311	Common Stock		20,000
320	Retained Earnings		16,000
332	Dividends	12,000	
400	Fees Earned		79,000
610	Advertising Expense	12,000	
631	Supplies Expense	3,700	
711	Depreciation Expense	6,000	
722	Insurance Expense	4,000	
726	Salaries Expense	35,000	
905	Interest Expense	1,000	
		165,000	165,000

Instructions

(a) Complete the work sheet by extending the balances to the financial statement columns.

(b) Prepare an income statement, retained earnings statement, and a classified balance sheet. $10,000 of the notes payable become due in 1997.

(c) Prepare the closing entries. Use J14 for the journal page.

(d) Post the closing entries and rule and balance the accounts. Use the three-column form of account. Income Summary is No. 350.

(e) Prepare a post-closing trial balance.

Prepare financial statements, closing entries, and post-closing trial balance.
(SO 1, 2, 3, 6)

P4–3A   The completed financial statement columns of the work sheet for Batavia Company are shown below.

BATAVIA COMPANY
Work Sheet
For the Year Ended December 31, 1996

Account No.	Account Titles	Income Statement Dr.	Cr.	Balance Sheet Dr.	Cr.
101	Cash			8,200	
112	Accounts Receivable			7,500	
130	Prepaid Insurance			1,800	
157	Equipment			28,000	
167	Accumulated Depreciation				8,600

201	Accounts Payable				12,000
212	Salaries Payable				3,000
311	Common Stock				20,000
320	Retained Earnings				14,000
332	Dividends			7,200	
400	Fees Earned		42,000		
622	Repair Expense	3,200			
711	Depreciation Expense	2,800			
722	Insurance Expense	1,200			
726	Salaries Expense	36,000			
732	Utilities Expense	3,700			
	Totals	46,900	42,000	52,700	57,600
	Net Loss		4,900	4,900	
		46,900	46,900	57,600	57,600

Instructions

(a) Prepare an income statement, retained earnings statement, and a classified balance sheet.

(b) Prepare the closing entries.

(c) Post the closing entries and rule and balance the accounts. Use T-accounts. Income Summary is No. 350.

(d) Prepare a post-closing trial balance.

P4–4A Space Amusement Park Inc. has a fiscal year ending on September 30. Selected data from the September 30 work sheet are presented below:

Complete work sheet and prepare classified balance sheet, entries, and post-closing trial balance.

(SO 1, 2, 3, 6)

SPACE AMUSEMENT PARK INC.
Work Sheet
For the Year Ended September 30, 1996

	Trial Balance		Adjusted Trial Balance	
	Dr.	Cr.	Dr.	Cr.
Cash	37,400		37,400	
Supplies	18,600		1,200	
Prepaid Insurance	31,900		3,900	
Land	80,000		80,000	
Equipment	120,000		120,000	
Accumulated Depreciation		36,200		43,000
Accounts Payable		14,600		14,600
Unearned Admissions		2,700		1,700
Mortgage Payable		50,000		50,000
Common Stock		100,000		100,000
Retained Earnings		9,700		9,700
Dividends	14,000		14,000	
Admission Revenue		278,500		279,500
Salaries Expense	109,000		109,000	
Repair Expense	30,500		30,500	
Advertising Expense	9,400		9,400	
Utilities Expense	16,900		16,900	
Property Taxes Expense	18,000		21,000	
Interest Expense	6,000		12,000	
Totals	491,700	491,700		
Insurance Expense			28,000	
Supplies Expense			17,400	
Interest Payable				6,000
Depreciation Expense			6,800	
Property Taxes Payable				3,000
Totals			507,500	507,500

Instructions

(a) Prepare a complete work sheet.
(b) Prepare a classified balance sheet. (Note: $10,000 of the mortgage payable is due for payment in the next fiscal year.)
(c) Journalize the adjusting entries using the work sheet as a basis.
(d) Journalize the closing entries using the work sheet as a basis.
(e) Prepare a post-closing trial balance.

Complete all steps in accounting cycle.
(SO 1, 2, 3, 4, 6)

P4–5A   Helga Kohl opened Helga's Carpet Cleaners Inc. on March 1. During March, the following transactions were completed.

Mar 1 Issued $10,000 of common stock for $10,000 cash.
1 Purchased used truck for $6,000, paying $4,000 cash and the balance on account.
3 Purchased cleaning supplies for $1,200 on account.
5 Paid $1,800 cash on one-year insurance policy effective March 1.
14 Billed customers $2,800 for cleaning services.
18 Paid $1,500 cash on amount owed on truck and $500 on amount owed on cleaning supplies.
20 Paid $1,500 cash for employee salaries.
21 Collected $1,600 cash from customers billed on July 14.
28 Billed customers $3,200 for cleaning services.
31 Paid gas and oil for month on truck $200.
31 Declared and paid $900 cash dividend.

The chart of accounts for Helga's Carpet Cleaners Inc. contains the following accounts: No. 101 Cash, No. 112 Accounts Receivable, No. 128 Cleaning Supplies, No. 130 Prepaid Insurance, No. 157 Equipment, No. 158 Accumulated Depreciation—Equipment, No. 201 Accounts Payable, No. 212 Salaries Payable, No. 311 Common Stock, No. 320 Retained Earnings, No. 332 Dividends, No. 350 Income Summary, No. 400 Fees Earned, No. 633 Gas & Oil Expense, No. 634 Cleaning Supplies Expense, No. 711 Depreciation Expense, No. 722 Insurance Expense, No. 726 Salaries Expense.

Instructions

(a) Journalize and post the March transactions. Use page J1 for the journal and the three-column form of account.
(b) Prepare a trial balance at March 31 on a work sheet.
(c) Enter the following adjustments on the work sheet and complete the work sheet.
    (1) Earned but unbilled fees at March 31 were $600.
    (2) Depreciation on equipment for the month was $250.
    (3) One-twelfth of the insurance expired.
    (4) An inventory count shows $400 of cleaning supplies on hand at March 31.
    (5) Accrued but unpaid employee salaries were $500.
(d) Journalize and post adjusting entries. Use page J2 for the journal.
(e) Prepare the income statement and retained earnings statement for March and a classified balance sheet at March 31.
(f) Journalize and post closing entries and complete the closing process. Use page J3 for the journal.
(g) Prepare a post-closing trial balance at July 31.

▼*B*roadening Your Perspective

*F*INANCIAL REPORTING PROBLEM—PEPSICO, INC.

The financial statements of PepsiCo, Inc. are presented in Appendix A at the end of this textbook.

Instructions
Answer the following questions using the Consolidated Balance Sheet and the Notes to Consolidated Financial Statements section.

1. What were PepsiCo's total current assets at December 30, 1995, and December 31, 1994?
2. Are assets included in current assets listed in proper order? Explain.
3. How are PepsiCo's assets classified?
4. What are "cash equivalents"?
5. What were PepsiCo's total current liabilities at December 30, 1995, and December 31, 1994?
6. What was the composition of the company's short-term borrowing balance at December 30, 1995?

*C*OMPARATIVE ANALYSIS PROBLEM—
THE COCA-COLA COMPANY VS. PEPSICO, INC.

The financial statements of Coca-Cola Company are presented at the end of Chapter 1 and PepsiCo's financial statements are presented in Appendix A.

Instructions
(a) Based on the information contained in these financial statements, determine each of the following for each company at December 31, 1995:
    1. Total current assets.
    2. Net amount of property, plant, and equipment.
    3. Total current liabilities.
    4. Total stockholders' (shareholders') equity.
(b) What conclusions concerning the companies' respective financial position can be drawn from these data?

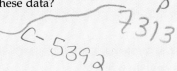

*I*NTERPRETATION OF FINANCIAL STATEMENTS

Mini-Case—Case Corporation
Case Corporation, based in Racine, Wisconsin, manufactures farm tractors, farm equipment, and light- and medium-sized construction equipment. The company's products are distributed through both independent and company-owned distributing companies, which are located throughout the world. Case Corporation's 1995 partial income statement is shown below. Dollar amounts are in millions.

Revenues	
Net sales	$ 4,937
Interest income and other	168
	5,105

Costs and Expenses

Cost of goods sold	3,779
Selling, general, and administrative	553
Research, development, and engineering	156
Interest expense	174
Other, net	16
	4,678
Income from operations before taxes	$ 427

Instructions

Assume that the partial income statement above was prepared before all adjusting entries had been made, and that the internal audit staff identified the following items that require adjustments:

1. Depreciation on the administrative offices of $13 million needs to be recorded.
2. A physical inventory determined that $1 million in office supplies had been used in 1995.
3. $4 million in salaries have been earned but not recorded, and half this amount is for the salaries of the engineering staff; the other half is for the administrative staff.
4. $3 million in annual insurance premiums were prepaid on May 1.
5. $7 million in prepaid rent has expired at year end.
6. Cost of goods sold of $2 million was recorded in error as interest expense.
   (a) Make the adjusting journal entries required. Use standard account titles with pre-payments having been recorded as assets.
   (b) Which of the entries is not a routine adjusting entry? Explain your answer.
   (c) For each of the accounts in these adjusting entries that will be posted to Case's general ledger, tell which item on the income statement will be increased or decreased.
   (d) Recast the partial income statement based on the adjusting entries prepared.

DECISION CASE

• •

Moody Janitorial Service Inc. was started 2 years ago by Pat Moody. Because business has been exceptionally good, Pat decided on July 1, 1996, to expand operations by acquiring an additional truck and hiring two more assistants. To finance the expansion, Pat obtained on July 1, 1996, a $25,000, 10% bank loan, payable $10,000 on July 1, 1997, and the balance on July 1, 1998. The terms of the loan require the borrower to have $10,000 more current assets than current liabilities at December 31, 1996. If these terms are not met, the bank loan will be refinanced at 15% interest.

At December 31, 1996, the accountant for Moody Janitorial Service Inc. prepared the following balance sheet:

MOODY JANITORIAL SERVICE INC.
Balance Sheet
December 31, 1996

Assets

Current assets		
Cash		$ 6,500
Accounts receivable		9,000
Janitorial supplies		5,200
Prepaid insurance		4,800
Total current assets		25,500
Property, plant, and equipment		
Cleaning equipment (net)	$22,000	
Delivery trucks (net)	34,000	56,000
Total assets		$81,500

Liabilities and Stockholders' Equity

Current liabilities
Notes payable	$10,000
Accounts payable	2,500
Total current liabilities	12,500

Long-term liability
Notes payable	15,000
Total liabilities	27,500

Stockholders' equity
Common stock	30,000
Retained earnings	24,000
Total liabilities and stockholders' equity	$81,500

Pat presented the balance sheet to the bank's loan office on January 2, 1997, confident that the company had met the terms of the loan. The loan officer was not impressed. She said, "We need financial statements audited by a CPA."

A CPA was hired and immediately realized that the balance sheet had been prepared from a trial balance and not from an adjusted trial balance. The adjustment data at the balance sheet date consisted of the following:

1. Earned but unbilled janitorial services were $2,400.
2. Janitorial supplies on hand were $3,500.
3. Prepaid insurance was a three-year policy dated January 1, 1996.
4. December expenses incurred but unpaid at December 31, $250.
5. Interest on the bank loan was not recorded.
6. The amounts for plant assets were net of accumulated depreciation of $4,000 for cleaning equipment and $5,000 for delivery trucks as of January 1, 1996. Depreciation for 1996 was $2,000 for cleaning equipment and $5,000 for delivery trucks.

Instructions
(a) Prepare a correct balance sheet.
(b) Were the terms of the bank loan met? Explain.

COMMUNICATION ACTIVITY

The accounting cycle is important in understanding the accounting process.

Instructions
Write a memorandum to your instructor which lists the required steps in the order in which they should be completed. Complete your memorandum with a paragraph that explains the optional steps in the accounting cycle.

GROUP ACTIVITY

A classified balance sheet has the following sections: current assets; property, plant, and equipment; long-term investments; intangible assets; current liabilities; long-term liabilities; and stockholders' equity.

Instructions
With the class divided into seven groups, each group should choose one section of the classified balance sheet. Each group is to explain its section and illustrate the section using an example from a published annual report.

ETHICS CASE

• •

As the controller of Breathless Perfume Company, you discover a significant misstatement that overstated net income in the prior year's financial statements. The misleading financial statements are contained in the company's annual report which was issued to banks and other creditors less than a month ago. After much thought about the consequences of telling the president, Eddy Kadu, about this misstatement, you gather your courage to inform him. Eddy says, "Hey! What they don't know won't hurt them. But, just so we set the record straight, we'll adjust this year's financial statements for last year's misstatement. We can absorb that misstatement better in this year than in last year anyway! Just don't make that kind of mistake again."

Instructions
   (a) Who are the stakeholders in this situation?
   (b) What are the ethical issues in this situation?
   (c) What would you do as a controller in this situation?

RESEARCH ASSIGNMENT

• •

The March 1995 issue of *Management Review* includes an article by Barbara Ettorre, entitled "How Motorola Closes Its Books in Two Days." Read the article and answer the following questions.
   (a) How often does Motorola close its books? How long did the process used to take?
   (b) What was the major change Motorola initiated to shorten the closing process?
   (c) What incentive does Motorola offer to ensure accurate and timely information?
   (d) In a given year, how many journal entry lines does Motorola process?
   (e) Provide an example of an external force that prevents Motorola from closing faster than a day-and-a-half.
   (f) According to Motorola's corporate vice president and controller, how do external financial statement users perceive companies that release information early?

CRITICAL THINKING
▸ *A Real-World Focus: Bethlehem Corporation*

• •

*Located in Easton, Pennsylvania, **Bethlehem Corp.** was established in 1856. Today it offers contract services for industrial products, rebuilding and remanufacturing industrial and military equipment per customer specifications and designs. The company also manufactures and sells a line of equipment used in the chemical, environmental, and food industries.*

Bethlehem Corporation has a net loss for 1994 of $239,251. One reason for the loss is that Bethlehem established an accrual to provide for expenses and costs associated with certain legal proceedings against Bethlehem.

Instructions
   (a) Indicate how the net loss would be shown in Bethlehem's 1994 work sheet.
   (b) Where in the general ledger would you expect to find the two accounts related to the accrual for expenses and costs associated with legal proceedings?
   (c) Identify the financial statement columns to which the balances of the two accounts in part (b) would be extended on the work sheet.

─────────

Answers to Self-Study Questions
1. c   2. b   3. d   4. a   5. d   6. b   7. a   8. c   9. c   10. b   11. b

Concepts for Review

Before studying this chapter, you should know or, if necessary, review:

a. *How to prepare a work sheet. (Ch. 4, pp. 146–150)*
b. *How to close revenue, expense, and dividends accounts. (Ch. 4, pp. 152–155)*
c. *The steps in the accounting cycle. (Ch. 4, p. 160)*

Dropped Courses Produce Bookstore Headaches

PULLMAN, Wash. — Larry Martin is in charge of ordering textbooks for the Washington State University bookstore in Pullman, Washington. The bookstore sells about $4 million in textbooks each year. The average inventory at any point in time is 2,500 titles.

Mr. Martin's big challenge is to order enough books to satisfy demand—but not to order too many. For example, say a course historically has sold 75 books; he'll order 85 to be on the safe side. The reason: if he orders short, he'll have to order additional books by second-day air express—which is expensive and cuts into profits. However, if Martin orders too many, the publisher won't accept for return more than 20% of his original order.

Of course, returns occur all the time, especially when students drop

courses during the first week of class. If the returned books are in "new and resalable" condition, the publisher will accept the return of such books and issue Martin a credit memo.

Washington State University starts its fall term before Labor Day. The busy book selling and return

period lasts three to four weeks. Therefore, Martin waits until the end of September to take the inventory and determine his returns. That count verifies the accuracy of his computerized perpetual inventory accounting system. At that point, he is ready to order more books. ◀

CHAPTER · **5**

ACCOUNTING FOR MERCHANDISING OPERATIONS

▶ **STUDY OBJECTIVES** ◀

After studying this chapter, you should be able to:

1. *Identify the differences between a service enterprise and a merchandising company.*
2. *Explain the entries for purchases under a perpetual inventory system.*
3. *Explain the entries for sales revenues under a perpetual inventory system.*
4. *Explain the computation and importance of gross profit.*
5. *Identify the unique features of the income statement for a merchandising company.*
6. *Explain the steps in the accounting cycle for a merchandising company.*
7. *Distinguish between a multiple-step and a single-step income statement.*

As indicated in the opening story, Washington State University Bookstore earns a profit by selling goods to customers rather than performing services. Merchandising companies that purchase and sell directly to consumers—such as Kmart, Washington State Bookstore, Safeway, and Toys "R" Us—are called **retailers**. In contrast, merchandising companies that sell to retailers are known as **wholesalers**. For example, retailer Walgreens might buy goods from wholesaler McKesson & Robbins; Office Depot might buy office supplies from wholesaler United Stationers.

The steps in the accounting cycle for a merchandising company are the same as the steps for a service enterprise. However, merchandising companies use additional accounts and entries which are required in recording merchandising transactions. The content and organization of this chapter are as follows:

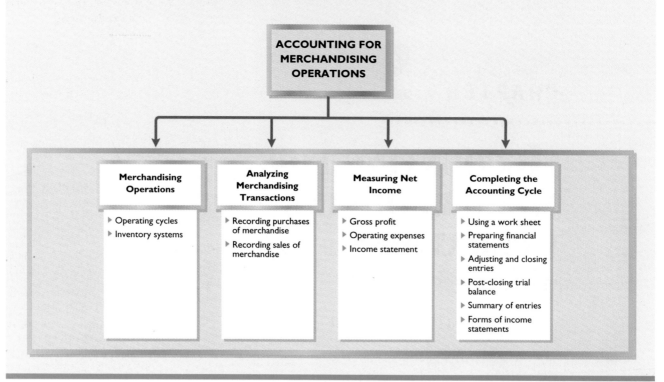

Merchandising Operations

STUDY OBJECTIVE

1

Identify the differences between a service enterprise and a merchandising company.

Helpful hint For most merchandising companies, cost of goods sold is the largest expense incurred.

Measuring net income for a merchandising company is conceptually the same as for a service enterprise. That is, net income (or loss) results from the matching of expenses with revenues. In a merchandising company, the primary source of revenues is the sale of merchandise, often referred to simply as sales revenue or sales. Unlike expenses for a service company, expenses for a merchandising company are divided into two categories: (1) the cost of goods sold and (2) operating expenses.

The cost of goods sold is the total cost of merchandise sold during the period. This expense is directly related to the revenue recognized from the sale of the goods.

Sales revenue less cost of goods sold is called gross profit (or gross margin) on sales. For example, when a pocket calculator costing $15 is sold for $25, the gross profit is $10. Merchandising companies customarily report gross profit on sales in the income statement.

After gross profit is calculated, operating expenses are deducted to determine net income (or loss). Operating expenses are expenses incurred in the process of earning sales revenue. Examples of operating expenses are sales salaries, advertising expense, and insurance expense. The operating expenses of a merchandising company include many of the expenses found in a service enterprise.

The income measurement process for a merchandising company may be diagrammed as shown in Illustration 5-1. The items in the two blue boxes are peculiar to a merchandising company; they are not used by a service company.

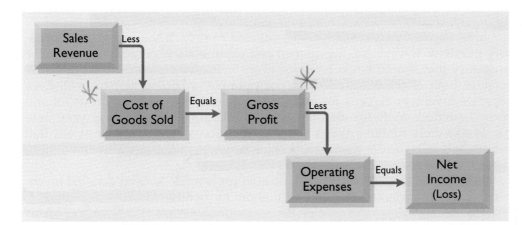

Illustration 5-1

Income measurement process for a merchandising company

Operating Cycles

While measuring income for a merchandising company is conceptually the same as for a service company, their operating cycles differ. The normal operating cycle of a merchandising company ordinarily is longer than that of a service company.

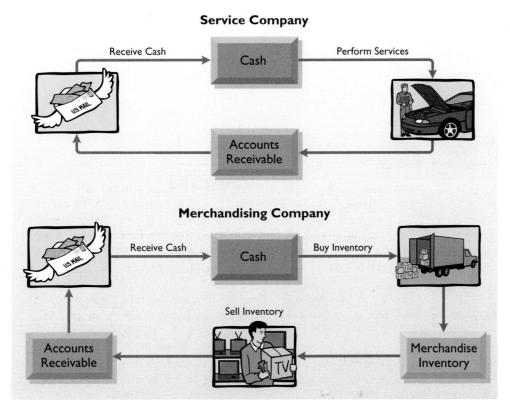

Illustration 5-2

Operating cycles for a service company and a merchandising company

The purchase of merchandise inventory and its eventual sale lengthens the cycle. Graphically, the operating cycles of service and merchandising companies can be contrasted as shown in Illustration 5-2. Note that the added asset account for a merchandising company is an **inventory** account (usually entitled Merchandise Inventory). Merchandise inventory is reported as a current asset on the balance sheet.

Inventory Systems

Either of two systems may be used in accounting for merchandising transactions: (1) a **perpetual inventory system** or (2) a **periodic inventory system**.

In a perpetual inventory system, detailed records of the cost of each inventory purchase and sale are maintained and continuously (perpetually) show the inventory that should be on hand for every item. A perpetual inventory keeps track of both **quantities and costs**. For example, a Ford dealership will have separate inventory records for each automobile, truck, and van on its lot and showroom floor. With the use of bar codes and optical scanners, a grocery store can keep a daily running record of every box of cereal and every jar of jelly that it buys and sells. **Under a perpetual inventory system the cost of goods sold is determined and recorded each time a sale occurs.**

In a periodic inventory system, no attempt is made to keep detailed inventory records of the goods on hand throughout the period. **The cost of goods sold is determined only at the end of the accounting period when a physical inventory count is taken to determine the cost of goods on hand.**

To determine the cost of goods sold under a periodic inventory system, it is necessary to (1) record purchases of merchandise, (2) determine the cost of goods purchased, and (3) determine the cost of goods on hand at the beginning and end of the accounting period.

Illustration 5-3 graphically compares the sequence of activities and the timing of the cost of goods sold computation under the two inventory systems.

Illustration 5-3

Comparing perpetual to periodic inventory

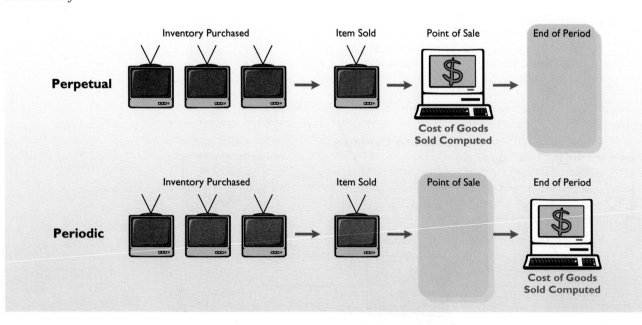

Some businesses employ the periodic system because they can control merchandise and manage day-to-day operations without detailed inventory records. In addition, perpetual systems are in many cases more expensive.

Under a perpetual inventory system, inventory shrinkage and lost or stolen goods are more readily determined. Also, reorder decisions are more accurately made under a perpetual system because exact inventory levels are known constantly. Because the perpetual inventory system is growing in popularity and use, we illustrate it in this chapter. The periodic system, still widely used, is described in Chapter 9.

▼SECTION *1* ▸ *Analyzing Merchandising Transactions*

Recording merchandising transactions requires the analysis of purchases and sales of merchandise. Related to both purchases and sales are returns and allowances, discounts, and transportation costs.

▼Recording Purchases of Merchandise

STUDY OBJECTIVE
•••••••••2••••••••••
Explain the entries for purchases under a perpetual inventory system.

Purchases may be made for cash or on account (credit). Purchases are normally recorded when the goods are received from the supplier. Every purchase should be supported by business documents that provide written evidence of the transaction. Cash purchases should be supported by canceled checks or cash register receipts indicating the items purchased and amounts paid. Credit purchases should be supported by an invoice, like the one shown in Illustration 5-4, that indicates the items purchased and the total purchase price.

Illustration 5-4 shows a sales invoice prepared by Highpoint Electronic, Inc. to document a sale to Chelsea Video. Chelsea Video will use this as a purchase invoice to document the purchase from Highpoint. Chelsea will make the following entry to record the purchase of merchandise from Highpoint:

May 4	Merchandise Inventory	3,800	
	Accounts Payable		3,800
	(To record goods purchased on account, terms 2/10, n/30, from Highpoint Electronic)		

Under the perpetual inventory system, purchases of merchandise for sale are recorded in the Merchandise Inventory account. Thus, Larry Martin, as manager of the Washington State University Bookstore, would **debit Merchandise Inventory for books purchased for resale to students**. However, not all purchases are debited to Merchandise Inventory. Purchases of assets acquired for use and not for resale, such as supplies, equipment, and similar items, should be **debited to specific asset accounts rather than to Merchandise Inventory**. For example, Larry Martin would debit Supplies for the supplies he buys to make shelf signs and labels that identify which books are for which courses.

Purchases Returns and Allowances

A purchaser may be dissatisfied with the merchandise received because the goods are damaged or defective, of inferior quality, or not in accord with the

Illustration 5-4

Invoice

Helpful hint To better understand the contents of this invoice, identify the:
(1) Seller.
(2) Invoice date.
(3) Purchaser.
(4) Salesperson.
(5) Credit terms.
(6) Freight terms.
(7) Goods sold:
   Catalogue no.
   Description.
   Quantity.
   Price per unit.
(8) Total invoice amount.

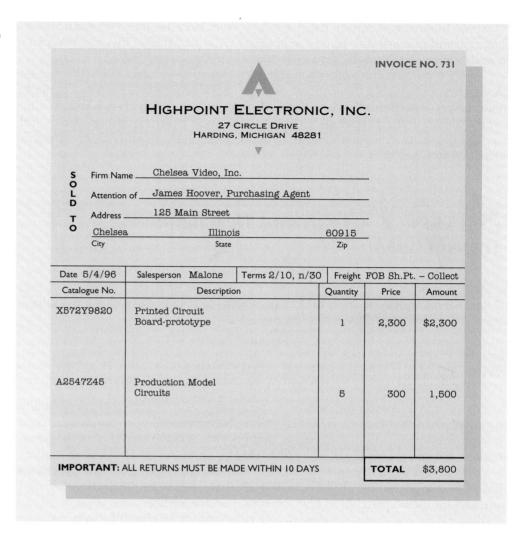

INVOICE NO. 731

HIGHPOINT ELECTRONIC, INC.
27 CIRCLE DRIVE
HARDING, MICHIGAN 48281

SOLD TO:
Firm Name ___ Chelsea Video, Inc.
Attention of ___ James Hoover, Purchasing Agent
Address ___ 125 Main Street
Chelsea   Illinois   60915
City   State   Zip

Date 5/4/96	Salesperson Malone	Terms 2/10, n/30	Freight FOB Sh.Pt. – Collect		
Catalogue No.	Description		Quantity	Price	Amount
X572Y9820	Printed Circuit Board-prototype		1	2,300	$2,300
A2547Z45	Production Model Circuits		5	300	1,500

IMPORTANT: ALL RETURNS MUST BE MADE WITHIN 10 DAYS   **TOTAL** $3,800

purchaser's specifications. In such cases, the purchaser may return the goods to the supplier for credit if the sale was made on credit, or for a cash refund if the purchase was originally for cash. This transaction is known as a **purchase return**. Alternatively, the purchaser may choose to keep the merchandise if the supplier is willing to grant an allowance (deduction) from the purchase price. This transaction is known as a **purchase allowance**.

The purchaser initiates the request for a reduction of the balance due through the issuance of a debit memorandum. A debit memorandum is a document issued by a purchaser to inform a supplier that a debit has been made to the supplier's account on the purchaser's books. The original copy of the memorandum is sent to the supplier and one copy is retained by the purchaser. The information contained in a debit memorandum is shown on the next page in Illustration 5-5; it relates to the sales invoice shown in Illustration 5-4.

The entry by Chelsea Video for the merchandise returned to Highpoint Electronic on May 8 is:

Merchandise Returned →

May 8	Accounts Payable	300	
	Merchandise Inventory		300
	(To record return of inoperable goods received from Highpoint Electronic, DM No. 126)		

Illustration 5-5

Debit memorandum

```
                                                    DEBIT-DM126

                         CHELSEA VIDEO
                            125 MAIN STREET
                          CHELSEA, IL  60915
  Purchased
  From:
         Firm Name ___ Highpoint Electronic _____

         Attention of ___ Susan Malone, Sales Representative ___

         Address ___ 27 Circle Drive _____

         Harding              MI              48281
         City                State           Zip
```

Date 5/8/96	Salesperson Malone	Invoice No. 731	Invoice Date 5/4/96	Approved Reid

Catalogue No.	Description	Quantity	Price	Amount
A2547Z45	Production Model Circuits (Inoperative)	1	300	$300

Cash Refund ☐   Debit Account ☒   Other ☐

Helpful hint Note that the debit memorandum is pre-numbered to help ensure that all are accounted for.

Because Merchandise Inventory was debited when the goods were received, Merchandise Inventory is credited when the goods are returned.

Purchase Discounts

The credit terms of a purchase on account may permit the purchaser to claim a cash discount for the prompt payment of a balance due. The purchaser calls this cash discount a purchase discount. This incentive offers advantages to both parties: The purchaser saves money, and the supplier is able to convert the accounts receivable into cash earlier.

The **credit terms** specify the amount and time period for the cash discount. They also indicate the length of time in which the purchaser is expected to pay the full invoice price. In the sales invoice in Illustration 5-4, credit terms are 2/10, n/30, which is read "two-ten, net thirty." This means that a 2% cash discount may be taken on the invoice price (less any returns or allowances) if payment is made within 10 days of the invoice date (the **discount period**); otherwise, the invoice price less any returns or allowances is due 30 days from the invoice date. Alternatively, the discount period may extend to a specified number of days following the month in which the sale occurs. For example, 1/10 EOM (end-of-

Helpful hint The term "net" in "net 30" means the remaining amount due after subtracting any purchase returns and allowances and partial payments.

month) means that a 1% discount is available if the invoice is paid within the first 10 days of the next month.

When the supplier elects not to offer a cash discount for prompt payment, credit terms will specify only the maximum time period for paying the balance due. For example, the time period may be stated as n/30, n/60, or n/10 EOM.

When an invoice is paid within the discount period, the amount of the discount is credited to Merchandise Inventory. To illustrate, assume Chelsea Video pays the balance due of $3,500 (gross invoice price of $3,800 less purchase returns and allowances of $300) on May 14, the last day of the discount period. The cash discount is $70 ($3,500 × 2%), and the amount of cash paid by Chelsea Video is $3,430 ($3,500 − $70). The entry to record the May 14 payment by Chelsea Video is as follows:

CASH DISCOUNT

May 14	Accounts Payable	3,500	
	Cash		3,430
	Merchandise Inventory		70
	(To record payment within discount period)		

If Chelsea Video had failed to take the discount and full payment is made on June 3, Chelsea would have made the following entry:

NO DISCOUNT

June 3	Accounts Payable	3,500	
	Cash		3,500
	(To record payment with no discount taken)		

▶ Accounting in Action ▸ *Business Insight*

In the early 1990s, Sears wielded its retail clout by telling its suppliers that, rather than pay its obligations in the standard 30-day period, it would now pay in 60 days. This practice is often adopted by firms that are experiencing financial distress from a shortage of cash. A Sears spokesperson insisted, however, that Sears did not have cash problems, but, rather, was simply utilizing "vendor-financed inventory methods to improve its return on investment." Supplier trade groups have been outspoken critics of Sears' new policy, and have suggested that consumers will be the ultimate victims, because the financing costs will eventually be passed on to them.

Source: The Wall Street Journal, August 15, 1991.

A buyer usually should take all available discounts. For example, if Chelsea Video takes the discount, it pays $70 less in cash. Conversely, if it forgoes the discount and invests the $3,500 in a bank savings account for 20 days at 10% interest, it will earn only $19.44 in interest. The savings obtained by taking the discount is computed as follows:

Illustration 5-6

Savings obtained by taking purchase discount

Discount of 2% on $3,500	$70.00
Interest received on $3,500 (for 20 days at 10%)	19.44
Savings by taking the discount	**$50.56**

Alternatively, passing up the discount may be viewed as **paying an interest rate of 2%** for the use of $3,500 for 20 days. This is the equivalent of an annual interest rate of 36.5% (2% × 365/20). Obviously, it would be better for Chelsea Video to borrow at prevailing bank interest rates of 8–12% than to lose the discount.

Freight Costs

The sales agreement should indicate whether the seller or the buyer is to pay the cost of transporting the goods to the buyer's place of business. When a common carrier such as a railroad, trucking company, or airline is used, the transportation company prepares a freight bill (often called a bill of lading) in accordance with the sales agreement. Freight terms are expressed as either **FOB shipping point** or **FOB destination**. The letters FOB mean **free on board**. Thus, FOB shipping point means that goods are placed free on board the carrier by the seller, and the buyer pays the freight costs. Conversely, FOB destination means that the goods are placed free on board at the buyer's place of business, and the seller pays the freight. For example, the sales invoice in Illustration 5-4 on page 198 indicates that freight is FOB shipping point. Thus, the buyer (Chelsea Video) pays the freight charges.

When the purchaser directly incurs the freight costs, the account Merchandise Inventory is debited. For example, if upon delivery of the goods on May 6, Chelsea Video pays Acme Freight Company $150 for freight charges, the entry on Chelsea's books is:

May 6	Merchandise Inventory	150	
	Cash		150
	(To record payment of freight, terms FOB		
	shipping point)		

In contrast, **freight costs incurred by the seller on outgoing merchandise are an operating expense to the seller.** These costs are debited to Freight-out or Delivery Expense. For example, if the freight terms on invoice no. 731 in Illustration 5-4 had specified FOB destination and Highpoint Electronic paid the $150 freight charges, the entry by Highpoint would be:

May 4	Freight-out (Delivery Expense)	150	
	Cash		150
	(To record payment of freight on goods		
	sold FOB destination)		

When the freight charges are paid by the seller, the seller will usually establish a higher invoice price for the goods, to cover the expense of shipping.

Alternative Accounting for Returns and Allowances, Discounts, and Freight Costs

A business manager may want to keep detailed records of returns and allowances, discounts, and freight costs related to purchases of merchandise. For example, if management wishes to know the amount saved through cash discounts on purchases of merchandise, the amount of discounts taken can be accumulated in a separate Purchase Discounts account. Or, if management wishes to keep track of the purchase returns and allowances due to defective, inferior quality, or damaged goods, a special account, Purchase Returns and Allowances, may be credited to serve as a running record of such transactions. And, Freight-in could be debited for transportation costs on purchased merchandise. In order to

Helpful hint So as no miss purchase discounts, paid invoices should be file due dates. For example, Chelsea Video should have a file dated May 14 in which all bills to be paid on this date are filed. This procedure helps the purchaser remember the discount date, prevents early payment of bills, and maximizes the time that cash can be used for other purposes.

Helpful hint Freight terms may be stated by location. A Chicago seller may use "FOB Chicago" for FOB shipping point and the buyer's city for FOB destination.

Helpful hint The freight cost under the terms FOB shipping point and paid by Chelsea does not enter into the computation of the discount shown above.

report Merchandise Inventory at total cost in the financial statements, these separate accounts may be combined with the amount in Merchandise Inventory as follows:

[handwritten: Sales Discount contra Sales Act]

Merchandise Inventory		$XXXX
Less: Purchase Returns and Allowances	$XXX	
Purchase Discounts	XXX	XXX
Net purchases of merchandise inventory		XXXX
Add: Freight-in		XXX
Total cost of merchandise inventory		$XXXX

Before You Go On . . .

▸ Review It

1. How do the components used in measuring net income in a merchandising company differ from those in a service enterprise?
2. In what ways is a perpetual inventory system different from a periodic inventory system?
3. What entries are made to record purchases of inventory, purchases returns and allowances, purchases discounts, and freight-in under a perpetual inventory system?
4. What is an alternative method of accounting for purchases returns and allowances, discounts, and freight costs?

◤ Recording Sales of Merchandise

Sales revenues, like service revenues, are recorded when earned. This is in accordance with the revenue recognition principle. Typically, sales revenues are earned when the goods are transferred from the seller to the buyer. At this point, the sales transaction is completed and the sales price is established.

Sales may be made on credit or for cash. Every sales transaction should be supported by a **business document** that provides written evidence of the sale. **Cash register tapes** provide evidence of cash sales. A sales invoice, like the one shown in Illustration 5-4, provides support for a credit sale. The original copy of the invoice goes to the customer, and a copy is kept by the seller for use in recording the sale. The invoice shows the date of sale, customer name, total sales price, and other relevant information.

For cash sales, the Cash account is debited and the Sales account is credited; and, under the perpetual inventory system, the **cost of the merchandise sold** and the **reduction in merchandise inventory** are also recorded. Therefore, two entries are made for each sale, one at the selling price of the goods and the other at the cost of the goods sold. For example, assume that on May 4 Highpoint Electronic has cash sales of $2,200 from merchandise having a cost of $1,400. The entries to record the day's cash sales are as follows:

May 4	Cash	2,200	
	Sales		2,220
	(To record daily cash sales)		
4	Cost of Goods Sold	1,400	
	Merchandise Inventory		1,400
	(To record cost of merchandise sold for cash)		

For credit sales, Accounts Receivable is debited and Sales is credited; and, Cost of Goods Sold is debited and Merchandise Inventory is credited. In this way, under a perpetual inventory system, the Merchandise Inventory account will show at all times the amount of inventory that should be on hand. To illustrate a credit sales transaction, Highpoint Electronic's sales of $3,800 per invoice No. 731 (Illustration 5-4) of May 4 to Chelsea Video would be recorded as follows (assume the merchandise cost Highpoint $2,400):

Helpful hint Credit sales are sometimes referred to as charge sales or sales on account.

May 4	Accounts Receivable	3,800	
	Sales		3,800
	(To record credit sale to Chelsea Video per invoice #731)		
4	Cost of Goods Sold	2,400	
	Merchandise Inventory		2,400
	(To record cost of merchandise sold on invoice #731 to Chelsea Video)		

Merchandising companies may use more than one sales account. For example, Highpoint Electronic may decide to keep separate sales accounts for its sales of television sets, videocassette recorders, and microwave ovens. Because sales are the principal source of revenue for a merchandising company, the amount and trend of sales are of critical importance. For example, an increase in sales from the preceding year signifies a growing business and often leads to higher net income. A decrease in sales may suggest an unfavorable trend, and, therefore, lower future earnings.

Helpful hint The Sales account is credited only for sales of goods held for resale. Sales of assets not held for resale, such as equipment or land, are credited directly to the asset account.

►Accounting in Action ► *Ethics Insight*

Inventory losses can be substantial. Shoplifting is a big crime in the United States, with a cost of more than $18 billion annually, or 5% of retail sales, not including thefts by store employees. Shoplifting losses have led to the demise of many companies. For example, Dayton-Hudson closed its landmark store in downtown Detroit, in part, because of excessive shoplifting losses. Many department stores are trying to reduce shoplifting losses by use of electronic tags on merchandise and by continuous surveillance of customers on closed circuit television.

Sales have Credit Bal

Sales Returns and Allowances *have Debit balances*

A purchase return and allowance on the purchaser's books is recorded as a **sales return and allowance** on the books of the seller. To grant the customer a sales return or allowance, the seller normally prepares a credit memorandum. This document informs a customer that a credit has been made to the customer's account receivable for a sales return or allowance. The information contained in a credit memorandum is similar to the information found in the debit memorandum in Illustration 5-5 (p. 199). The original copy of the credit memorandum is sent to the customer, and a copy is kept by the seller as evidence of the transaction. Highpoint's entries to record a credit memorandum for returned goods involve (1) a debit to Sales Returns and Allowances and a credit to Accounts Receivable at the $300 selling price, and (2) a debit to Merchandise Inventory (assume a $140 cost) and a credit to Cost of Goods Sold as follows:

May 8	Sales Returns and Allowances	300	
	Accounts Receivable		300
	(To record return of inoperable goods delivered to Chelsea Video, per credit memorandum)		
8	Merchandise Inventory	140	
	Cost of Goods Sold		140
	(To record cost of goods returned per credit memorandum)		

When a sales allowance for damaged goods is granted on a **credit sale**, no entry to inventory and cost of goods sold is necessary because the supplier receives no returned goods from the customer. As shown in the first entry above, the supplier debits Sales Returns and Allowances and credits Accounts Receivable for the damaged goods allowance.

When goods are returned or an allowance is made on a **cash sale**, the supplier normally provides a cash refund and debits Sales Returns and Allowances and credits Cash. If the supplier **receives returned merchandise** in good condition, a second entry is made debiting Merchandise Inventory and crediting Cost of Goods Sold at cost. If the supplier grants an allowance and the **merchandise is not returned**, no entry affecting inventory and cost of goods sold is necessary by the supplier.

Helpful hint Most retailers do disclose their customer returns. When returns are substantial, failure to disclose is inappropriate.

Sales Returns and Allowances is a contra revenue account to Sales with a normal debit balance. A contra account is used, instead of debiting Sales, to disclose the amount of sales returns and allowances in the accounts and in the income statement because disclosure of this information is important to management. Excessive returns and allowances suggest inferior merchandise, inefficiencies in filling orders, errors in billing customers, and mistakes in delivery or shipment of the goods. Moreover, a debit directly to Sales would obscure the relative importance of sales returns and allowances as a percentage of sales and could distort comparisons between total sales in different accounting periods.

▸Accounting in Action ▸ *Business Insight*

How high is too high? Returns can become so high that it is questionable whether sales revenue should have been recognized in the first place. An example of high returns is Florafax International Inc., a floral supply company, which was alleged to ship its product without customer authorization on 10 holiday occasions, including 8,562 shipments of its product to customers for Mother's Day and 6,575 for Secretary's Day. The return rate on these shipments went as high as 69% of sales. As one employee noted: "products went out the front door and came in the back door."

An offshoot of high returns is "channel stuffing." In channel stuffing, the seller "sells" its product by providing substantial inducements to buy. Although this helps the sellers' revenue in the short run, the long term can be devastating when the merchandise bought remains on the purchasers' shelves for a long period of time.

Sales Discounts

As mentioned in our discussion of purchase transactions, the seller may offer the customer a cash discount, called by the seller a sales discount, for the prompt payment of the balance due. Like a purchase discount, a sales discount is based on the invoice price less returns and allowances, if any. Sales Discounts is debited

for the cash discounts that are taken. The entry by Highpoint to record the cash receipt on May 14 from Chelsea Video within the discount period is as follows:

May 14	Cash	3,430	
	Sales Discounts	70	
	Accounts Receivable		3,500
	(To record collection within 2/10, n/30		
	discount period from Chelsea Video)		

Like Sales Returns and Allowances, Sales Discounts is a **contra revenue account** to Sales. Its normal balance is a debit. This account is used, instead of debiting sales, to accumulate the amount of cash discounts taken by customers. If the discount is not taken, Highpoint Electronic debits Cash for $3,500 and credits Accounts Receivable for $3,500 at the date of the collection.

Helpful hint Contra account balances are the opposite of the accounts to which they relate.

Statement Presentation of Sales

As contra revenue accounts, sales returns and allowances and sales discounts are deducted from sales in the income statement to arrive at net sales. The sales revenues section of the income statement based on assumed data for Highpoint Electronic is as follows:

HIGHPOINT ELECTRONIC, INC.
Partial Income Statement

Sales revenues		
Sales		$480,000
Less: Sales returns and allowances	$12,000	
Sales discounts	8,000	20,000
Net sales		$460,000

Illustration 5-7

Statement presentation of sales revenues section

Helpful hint PepsiCo (see specimen financial statements in Appendix A), like many other companies, just reports Net Sales in its income statement.

This presentation discloses the significant aspects of the company's principal revenue producing activities.

Measuring Net Income

Gross Profit

From Illustration 5-1, you learned that cost of goods sold is deducted from sales revenue to determine **gross profit**. Sales revenue used for this computation is **net sales** (which takes into account sales returns and allowances and sales discounts). On the basis of the sales data presented in Illustration 5-7 (net sales of $460,000) and the cost of goods sold, accumulated under the perpetual inventory system (assume a balance of $316,000), the gross profit for Highpoint Electronic is $144,000, computed as follows:

STUDY OBJECTIVE ◄ 4 ►

Explain the computation and importance of gross profit.

Net sales	$460,000
Cost of goods sold	316,000
Gross profit	**$144,000**

Illustration 5-8

Computation of gross profit

Helpful hint Gross profit is sometimes referred to as merchandising profit or gross margin.

A company's gross profit may also be expressed as a percentage by dividing the amount of gross profit by net sales. For Highpoint Electronic the gross profit rate is 31.3% ($144,000 ÷ $460,000). The gross profit rate is generally considered to be more useful than the gross profit amount because it expresses a more meaningful (qualitative) relationship between net sales and gross profit. For example, a gross profit of $1,000,000 may be impressive. But, if it is the result of a gross profit rate of only 7%, it is not so impressive. The gross profit rate tells how many cents of each sales dollar go to gross profit.

Gross profit represents the **merchandising profit** of a company. It is not a measure of the overall profitability of a company, because operating expenses have not been deducted. Nevertheless, the amount and trend of gross profit is closely watched by management and other interested parties. Comparisons of current gross profit with amounts reported in past periods, and comparisons of gross profit rates of competitors and with industry averages provide information about the effectiveness of a company's purchasing function and the soundness of its pricing policies.

▸Accounting in Action ▸ *Business Insight*

In a recent year, Woolworth Corporation reported a gross profit rate of 32%; J.C. Penney, 31%; Kmart, 24%; and Wal-Mart, 20%. Gross profit is critical. "If you don't have someone monitoring it," says one business consultant, "you are asking for instant death." A decline should trigger a search for the cause. The drop could be due to an increase in cost of goods sold or a decrease in sales revenue, either of which needs prompt attention. The change may be temporary and easily reversed, or it may signal the beginning of a bad trend.

Operating Expenses

Operating expenses are the third component in measuring net income for a merchandising company. As indicated earlier, these expenses are similar in merchandising and service enterprises. At Highpoint Electronic, operating expenses were $114,000. The firm's net income is determined by subtracting operating expenses from gross profit. Thus, net income is $30,000 as shown below:

Illustration 5-9

Operating expenses in computing net income

Gross profit	$144,000
Operating expenses	114,000
Net income	$ 30,000

The net income amount is the "bottom line" of a company's income statement.

STUDY OBJECTIVE

▪▪▪▪▪▪▪▪▪▪ 5 ▪▪▪▪▪▪▪▪▪▪

Identify the unique features of the income statement for a merchandising company.

Income Statement

The income statement for retailers and wholesalers contains three features not found in the income statement of a service enterprise. These features are: (1) a sales revenue section, (2) a cost of goods sold section, and (3) gross profit. Using assumed data for specific operating expenses, the income statement for Highpoint Electronic, Inc. is shown in Illustration 5-10.

Illustration 5-10

Income statement for a merchandising company

HIGHPOINT ELECTRONIC, INC. Income Statement For the Year Ended December 31, 1996		
Sales revenues		
Sales		$480,000
Less: Sales returns and allowances	$ 12,000	
Sales discounts	8,000	20,000
Net sales		460,000
Cost of goods sold		316,000
Gross profit		144,000
Operating expenses		
Store salaries expense	45,000	
Rent expense	19,000	
Utilities expense	17,000	
Advertising expense	16,000	
Depreciation expense—store equipment	8,000	
Freight-out	7,000	
Insurance expense	2,000	
Total operating expenses		114,000
Net income		$ 30,000

Helpful hint What is and is not disclosed?
1. Did company sell on credit? Yes, had sales discounts.
2. Did company ship FOB destination? Yes, had freight-out.
3. Did company take all purchase discounts? Don't know; purchase discounts taken are not reported.

Before You Go On . . .

▶ *Review It*

1. What entries are made to record sales, sales returns and allowances, and sales discounts?
2. How are sales and contra revenue accounts reported in the income statement?
3. What is the significance of gross profit?

▼ SECTION 2 ▸ *Completing the Accounting Cycle*

Up to this point, we have been primarily concerned with measuring net income in a merchandising company. We have also illustrated the basic entries in recording transactions relating to purchases and sales in a perpetual inventory system. Now it is time to consider the remaining steps in the accounting cycle that were identified in Chapter 4.

Each of the required steps in the cycle applies to a merchandising company. Again, a work sheet is an optional step. To illustrate the steps in the cycle, we will assume that Highpoint Electronic uses a work sheet.

STUDY OBJECTIVE
•••••••••• 6 ••••••••••

Explain the steps in the accounting cycle for a merchandising company.

◤ Using a Work Sheet

As indicated in Chapter 4, a work sheet enables financial statements to be prepared before the adjusting entries are journalized and posted. The steps in preparing a work sheet for a merchandising company are the same as they are for a service enterprise (see pp. 147–49). The work sheet for Highpoint Electronic,

Illustration 5-11

Work sheet for merchandising company

Inc. shown in Illustration 5-11, contains all the income statement data explained above plus other data. The unique accounts for a merchandising company, using a perpetual inventory system, are shown in capital letters in red.

HIGHPOINT ELECTRONIC, INC.
Work Sheet
For the Year Ended December 31, 1996

	Trial Balance Dr.	Trial Balance Cr.	Adjustments Dr.	Adjustments Cr.	Adjusted Trial Balance Dr.	Adjusted Trial Balance Cr.	Income Statement Dr.	Income Statement Cr.	Balance Sheet Dr.	Balance Sheet Cr.
Cash	9,500				9,500				9,500	
Accounts Receivable	16,100				16,100				16,100	
MERCHANDISE INVENTORY	40,000				40,000				40,000	
Prepaid Insurance	3,800			(a) 2,000	1,800				1,800	
Store Equipment	80,000				80,000				80,000	
Accumulated Depreciation		16,000		(b) 8,000		24,000				24,000
Accounts Payable		20,400				20,400				20,400
Common Stock		50,000				50,000				50,000
Retained Earnings		33,000				33,000				33,000
Dividends	15,000				15,000				15,000	
SALES		480,000				480,000		480,000		
SALES RETURNS AND ALLOWANCES	12,000				12,000		12,000			
SALES DISCOUNTS	8,000				8,000		8,000			
COST OF GOODS SOLD	316,000				316,000		316,000			
Freight-out	7,000				7,000		7,000			
Advertising Expense	16,000				16,000		16,000			
Rent Expense	19,000				19,000		19,000			
Store Salaries Expense	40,000		(c) 5,000		45,000		45,000			
Utilities Expense	17,000				17,000		17,000			
Totals	599,400	599,400								
Insurance Expense			(a) 2,000		2,000		2,000			
Depreciation Expense			(b) 8,000		8,000		8,000			
Salaries Payable				(c) 5,000		5,000				5,000
Totals			15,000	15,000	612,400	612,400	450,000	480,000	162,400	132,400
Net Income							30,000			30,000
Totals							480,000	480,000	162,400	162,400

Key: (a) Insurance expired, (b) Depreciation expensed, (c) Salaries accrued.

Trial Balance Columns

Data for the trial balance are obtained from the ledger balances of Highpoint Electronic at December 31. The amount shown for Merchandise Inventory, $40,000, is the year-end inventory amount which results from the application of a perpetual inventory system.

Adjustments Columns

A merchandising company generally has the same types of adjustments as a service company. As you see in the work sheet, adjustments (a), (b), and (c) are for insurance, depreciation, and salaries. These adjustments were also required for Pioneer Advertising Agency, as illustrated in Chapters 3 and 4.

After all adjustment data are entered on the work sheet, the equality of the adjustment column totals is established. The balances in all accounts are then extended to the adjusted trial balance columns.

Adjusted Trial Balance

The adjusted trial balance shows the balance of all accounts after adjustment at the end of the accounting period.

Income Statement Columns

The accounts and balances that affect the income statement are transferred from the adjusted trial balance columns to the income statement columns. For Highpoint Electronic, Sales of $480,000 is shown in the credit column whereas the contra revenue accounts, Sales Returns and Allowances of $12,000 and Sales Discounts of $8,000, are shown in the debit column. Thus, the difference of $460,000 is the net sales shown on the income statement (Illustration 5-10).

Finally, all the credits in the income statement column should be totaled and compared to the total of all the debits in the income statement column. If the credits exceed the debits, then the company has net income. In Highpoint Electronic's case there was net income of $30,000. Conversely if the debits exceed the credits, the company would report a net loss.

Balance Sheet Columns

The major difference between the balance sheets of a service company and a merchandising company is inventory. For Highpoint Electronic, the ending inventory amount of $40,000 is shown in the balance sheet debit column. Note also that the information to prepare the retained earnings statement is also found in these columns. That is, the retained earnings account beginning balance is $33,000. The dividends are $15,000. The total of the debit column exceeds the total of the credit column in the balance sheet columns of the work sheet because net income was earned. Conversely, the total of the credits exceeds the total of the debit balances because a net loss occurred. These three amounts comprise the contents of the retained earnings statement.

Preparing Financial Statements

As is true in a service enterprise, financial statements for a merchandising company are prepared from the financial statement columns of the work sheet. The income statement for Highpoint Electronic has already been illustrated (see Illustration 5-10).

The retained earnings statement is as follows:

Illustration 5-12

Retained earnings statement

HIGHPOINT ELECTRONIC, INC.
Retained Earnings Statement
For the Year Ended December 31, 1996

Retained earnings, January 1	$ 33,000
Add: Net income	30,000
	63,000
Less: Dividends	15,000
Retained earnings, December 31	$ 48,000

The classified balance sheet, then, is as follows:

Illustration 5-13

Classified balance sheet

Helpful hint   The $40,000 is the cost of the inventory on hand, not its expected selling price.

HIGHPOINT ELECTRONIC, INC.		
Balance Sheet		
December 31, 1996		
Assets		
Current assets		
Cash		$ 9,500
Accounts receivable		16,100
Merchandise inventory		40,000
Prepaid insurance		1,800
Total current assets		67,400
Property, plant, and equipment		
Store equipment	$80,000	
Less: Accumulated depreciation—store equipment	24,000	56,000
Total assets		$123,400
Liabilities and Stockholders' Equity		
Current liabilities		
Accounts payable		$ 20,400
Salaries payable		5,000
Total current liabilities		25,400
Stockholders' equity		
Common stock		50,000
Retaining earnings		48,000
Total liabilities and stockholders' equity		$123,400

Helpful hint   Merchandise inventory is a current asset because it is expected to be sold within one year or the operating cycle, whichever is longer.

In the balance sheet, merchandise inventory is reported as a current asset immediately below accounts receivable. Recall that items are listed under current assets in the order of liquidity. Merchandise inventory is less liquid than accounts receivable because the goods must first be sold and then collection must be made from the customer.

▶Accounting in Action ▸ *Ethics Insight*

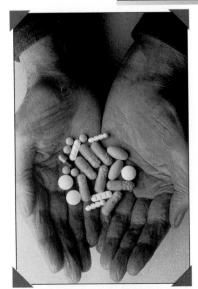

Phar Mor was one of the largest and fastest growing retail dry goods and pharmacy chains in the United States until a massive fraud was discovered in 1992 by the company's auditors, Coopers and Lybrand. Dry goods were Phar Mor's business, but some of its executives had a taste for raisin cookies. Schemers in Phar Mor's executive suite kept two sets of records, an official ledger that they sometimes manipulated with false entries, and another, nicknamed the "cookies," where they kept track of the false entries, called "raisins." They would refer to their ledger domain as "putting raisins in the cookies."

Based on reports in *The Wall Street Journal*, the assets of the company were overstated by more than $400 million, or about one-third of Phar Mor's gross revenue. Most of this overstatement pertained to fake or overvalued merchandise inventories at various store locations, and was perpetrated by the company's top financial managers.

Adjusting Entries and Closing Entries

Adjusting entries are journalized from the adjustment columns of the work sheet. Because the journalizing and posting of the entries are the same as they are for a service enterprise, they are not illustrated here.

For a merchandising company, like a service enterprise, all accounts that affect the determination of net income are closed to Income Summary. Data for the preparation of closing entries may be obtained from the income statement columns of the work sheet. In journalizing, all debit column amounts are credited, and all credit column amounts are debited, as shown below for Highpoint Electronic. Cost of goods sold is a new account that must be closed to Income Summary.

Dec. 31	Sales	480,000	
	Income Summary		480,000
	(To close income statement accounts with credit balances)		
31	Income Summary	450,000	
	Sales Returns and Allowances		12,000
	Sales Discounts		8,000
	Cost of Goods Sold		316,000
	Store Salaries Expense		45,000
	Rent Expense		19,000
	Freight-out		7,000
	Advertising Expense		16,000
	Utilities Expense		17,000
	Depreciation Expense		8,000
	Insurance Expense		2,000
	(To close income statement accounts with debit balances)		
31	Income Summary	30,000	
	Retained Earnings		30,000
	(To close net income to retained earnings)		
31	Retained Earnings	15,000	
	Dividends		15,000
	(To close dividends to retained earnings)		

Helpful hint The easiest way to prepare the first two closing entries is to identify the temporary accounts by their balances and then prepare one entry for the credits and one for the debits.

[handwritten: Ret / net income - Rev / Exp]

After the closing entries are posted, all temporary accounts have zero balances. In addition, Retained Earnings has a credit balance of $48,000: beginning balance + net income − drawings ($33,000 + $30,000 − $15,000).

Preparing the Post-Closing Trial Balance

After the closing entries are posted, the post-closing trial balance is prepared. The only new account in the post-closing trial balance is Merchandise Inventory. The post-closing trial balance for Highpoint Electronic at December 31, 1996, is shown in Illustration 5-14.

Illustration 5-14

Post-closing trial balance

HIGHPOINT ELECTRONIC, INC. Post-Closing Trial Balance December 31, 1996		
	Debit	Credit
Cash	$ 9,500	
Accounts receivable	16,100	
Merchandise inventory	40,000	
Prepaid insurance	1,800	
Store equipment	80,000	
Accumulated depreciation		$ 24,000
Accounts payable		20,400
Salaries payable		5,000
Common stock		50,000
Retained earnings		48,000
	$147,400	$147,400

◣Summary of Merchandising Entries

The entries for the merchandising accounts using a perpetual inventory system are summarized in Illustration 5-15.

Illustration 5-15

Daily recurring and closing entries

Transactions	Daily Recurring Entries	Dr.	Cr.
Selling merchandise to customers	Cash or Accounts Receivable	XX	
	Sales		XX
	Cost of Goods Sold	XX	
	Merchandise Inventory		XX
Granting sales returns or allowances to customers	Sales Returns and Allowances	XX	
	Cash or Accounts Receivable		XX
Paying freight costs on sales; FOB destination	Freight-out	XX	
	Cash		XX
Receiving payment from customers within discount period	Cash	XX	
	Sales Discounts	XX	
	Accounts Receivable		XX
Purchasing merchandise for resale	Merchandise Inventory	XX	
	Cash or Accounts Payable		XX
Paying freight costs on merchandise purchased; FOB shipping point	Merchandise Inventory	XX	
	Cash		XX
Receiving purchase returns or allowances from suppliers	Cash or Accounts Payable	XX	
	Merchandise Inventory		XX
Paying suppliers within discount period	Accounts Payable	XX	
	Merchandise Inventory		XX
	Cash		XX

Illustration 5-15

Continued

Events	Closing Entries		
Closing accounts with credit balances	Sales	XX	
	Income Summary		XX
Closing accounts with debit balances	Income Summary	XX	
	Sales Returns and Allowances		XX
	Sales Discounts		XX
	Cost of Goods Sold		XX
	Freight-out		XX
	Expenses		XX

Before You Go On . . .

▶ Review It

1. How does a work sheet for a merchandising company differ from a work sheet for a service company? In what ways is the work sheet similar for a merchandising company and a service company?
2. In what columns of the work sheet will (a) merchandise inventory and (b) cost of goods sold be shown?
3. What merchandising account(s) will appear in the post-closing trial balance?

▶ Do It

The trial balance of Revere Clothing Company at December 31 shows Merchandise Inventory $25,000, Sales $162,400, Sales Returns and Allowances $4,800, Sales Discounts $3,600, Cost of Goods Sold $110,000, Rental Revenue $6,000, Freight-out $1,800, Rent Expense $8,800, and Salaries and Wages Expense $22,000. Prepare the closing entries for the above accounts.

Reasoning: The first closing entry for a merchandising company closes temporary accounts with credit balances. The second closing entry closes temporary accounts with debit balances.

Solution: The two closing entries are:

Dec. 31	Sales	162,400	
	Rental Revenue	6,000	
	Income Summary		168,400
	(To close accounts with credit balances)		
Dec. 31	Income Summary	151,000	
	Cost of Goods Sold		110,000
	Sales Returns and Allowances		4,800
	Sales Discounts		3,600
	Freight-out		1,800
	Rent Expense		8,800
	Salaries and Wages Expense		22,000
	(To close accounts with debit balances)		

Related exercise material: BE5–7 and E5–4.

Forms of Income Statements

Two forms of the income statement are widely used by merchandising companies. These income statements are explained on the next page.

STUDY OBJECTIVE

7

Distinguish between a multiple-step and a single-step income statement.

Multiple-Step Income Statement

The multiple-step income statement is so named because it shows the numerous steps in determining net income (or net loss). The Highpoint Electronic income statement in Illustration 5-10 is an example. It shows two steps: (1) cost of goods sold was subtracted from net sales, and (2) operating expenses were deducted from gross profit. These steps pertain to the company's principal operating activities. A multiple-step statement provides users with more information about a company's income performance by distinguishing between **operating** and **nonoperating activities**. The statement also highlights intermediate components of income and shows subgroupings of expenses.

▶ *International note*

When the owner of a Russian business was recently asked, "What is net income?" he responded, "We don't have that concept here." Then, after consulting his colleagues, he explained that although he thinks he understands the concept, he isn't comfortable with it. The conversation highlights the difficulties that countries like Russia face in attempting to develop a market-based economy.

Nonoperating Activities

Nonoperating activities consist of (1) revenues and expenses that result from secondary or auxiliary operations and (2) gains and losses that are unrelated to the company's operations. The results of nonoperating activities are shown in two sections: Other revenues and gains and Other expenses and losses. For a merchandising company, these sections will typically include the following items:

Illustration 5-16

Items reported in nonoperating sections

Helpful hint Nonoperating items are expected to be significantly less than income from operations.

Other Revenues and Gains	Other Expenses and Losses
Interest revenue from notes receivable and marketable securities	Interest expense on notes and loans payable
Dividend revenue from investments in capital stock	Casualty losses from recurring causes such as vandalism and accidents
Rent revenue from subleasing a portion of the store	Loss from the sale or abandonment of property, plant, and equipment
Gain from the sale of property, plant, and equipment	Loss from strikes by employees and suppliers

The nonoperating sections are reported in the income statement immediately after the sections that pertain to the company's primary operating activities. These sections are illustrated in Illustration 5-17 using assumed data for Highpoint Electronic.

▶Accounting in Action ▶ *Business Insight*

The distinction between operating and nonoperating activities is crucial to many external users of financial data. The reason is that operating income is viewed as sustainable and therefore long-term, and nonoperating is viewed as nonrecurring and therefore short-term. For example, it was reported that a large cinema chain in North America was selling some of its assets and counting the gains as part of operating income. As a result, operating losses were being offset by these gains. Because of unfavorable press reaction to this practice, the company revised its financial statements. By not counting its nonrecurring items as part of operating income, its first quarter results changed from $24.9 million operating income to a $22.6 million loss. Although the net income figure didn't change, investors were able to see that income was derived from selling assets rather than from selling movie tickets. Thus, with this new information, investors were able to make a more informed decision about the company's earnings.

HIGHPOINT ELECTRONIC, INC. Income Statement For the Year Ended December 31, 1996			
Sales revenues			
Sales			$480,000
Less: Sales returns and allowances		$ 12,000	
Sales discounts		8,000	20,000
Net sales			460,000
Cost of goods sold			316,000
Gross profit			144,000
Operating expenses			
Selling expenses			
Store salaries expense	$ 45,000		
Advertising expense	16,000		
Depreciation expense—store equipment	8,000		
Freight-out	7,000		
Total selling expenses		76,000	
Administrative expenses			
Rent expense	19,000		
Utilities expense	17,000		
Insurance expense	2,000		
Total administrative expenses		38,000	
Total operating expenses			114,000
Income from operations			30,000
Other revenues and gains			
Interest revenue	3,000		
Gain on sale of equipment	600	3,600	
Other expenses and losses			
Interest expense	1,800		
Casualty loss from vandalism	200	2,000	1,600
Net income			$ 31,600

Illustration 5-17

Multiple-step income statement—nonoperating sections and subgrouping of operating expenses

Helpful hint What are the steps in arriving at each of the three profit (income) amounts reported in the statement?
Answer:
1. Gross profit—Net sales less cost of goods sold.
2. Income from operations—Gross profit less operating expenses.
3. Net income—Income from operations plus other revenues and gains and less other expenses and losses.

Helpful hint Operating income relates to the sale of primary goods in the ordinary course of business.

► *Ethics note*

How would *you* account for this expense? At the end of a celebratory lunch the employees of a sales department each gave the manager $10, and the manager paid the bill with his charge card. During the next week you notice that the manager reported the full amount of the lunch bill on his expense report (and requested reimbursement). When this question was posed to the CEO of Intel, he suggested that an appropriate action would be to report the problem anonymously to the internal audit staff for investigation.

When the two nonoperating sections are included, the label Income from operations (or Operating income) precedes them. It clearly identifies the results of the company's normal operations. Income from operations is determined by subtracting cost of goods sold and operating expenses from net sales.

Observe that the results of the two nonoperating sections are netted. The difference is added to or subtracted from income from operations to determine net income. Finally, within the nonoperating sections, items are generally reported at the net amount. Thus, if a company received a $2,500 insurance settlement on vandalism losses of $2,700, the loss is reported at $200. It is not uncommon for companies to combine these two nonoperating sections into a single "Other Revenues and Expenses" section.

Subgrouping of Operating Expenses

In larger companies, operating expenses are often subdivided into selling expenses and administrative expenses, as illustrated in the income statement in Illustration 5-17. Selling expenses are those associated with making sales. They include sales promotional expenses as well as expenses of completing the sale, such as delivery and shipping expenses. Administrative expenses (sometimes called general expenses) relate to general operating activities such as personnel management, accounting, and store security.

When subgroupings are made, some expenses may have to be pro-rated, e.g., 70% to selling and 30% to administrative expenses. For example, if a store building is used for both selling and general functions, building expenses such as depreciation, utilities, and property taxes will need to be allocated.

Any reasonable classification of expenses that serves to inform those who use the statement is satisfactory. For example, the present tendency in statements prepared for management is to present in considerable detail expense data grouped along lines of responsibility.

Single-Step Income Statement

Helpful hint Note that income tax expense when a corporation is involved is usually reported in a separate section. Income tax expense is reported separately whether a multiple-step or single-step income statement is used.

Another format for income statement presentation is the single-step income statement. The statement is so named because only one step, subtracting total expenses from total revenues, is required in determining net income (or net loss).

In a single-step statement, all data are classified under two categories: (1) **Revenues**, which includes both operating revenues and other revenues and gains, or (2) **Expenses**, which includes cost of goods sold, operating expenses, and other expenses and losses. A condensed single-step statement for Highpoint Electronic is illustrated in Illustration 5-18.

Illustration 5-18

Single-step income statement

HIGHPOINT ELECTRONIC, INC. Income Statement For the Year Ended December 31, 1996		
Revenues		
Net sales		$460,000
Interest revenue		3,000
Gain on sale of equipment		600
Total revenues		463,600
Expenses		
Cost of goods sold	$316,000	
Selling expenses	76,000	
Administrative expenses	38,000	
Interest expense	1,800	
Casualty loss from vandalism	200	
Total expenses		432,000
Net income		$ 31,600

Helpful hint Walgreen Co., Munsingwear, Inc., and Black and Decker are among many companies that use the multiple-step form of income statement. Companies that use the single-step include General Electric and Goodyear Tire & Rubber. The PepsiCo income statement is illustrated in Appendix A at the end of this textbook.

There are two primary reasons for using the single-step form: (1) A company does not realize any type of profit or income until total revenues exceed total expenses, so it makes sense to divide the statement into these two categories. (2) The form is simpler and easier to read than the multiple-step form. For homework problems, the single-step form of income statement should be used only when it is specifically requested.

Before You Go On . . .

▸ *Review It*

1. What are nonoperating activities and how are they reported in the income statement?
2. How does a single-step income statement differ from a multiple-step income statement?

▶ *A Look Back at Washington State University Bookstore*

● ●

Refer to the opening story about the Washington State University bookstore, and answer the following questions:

1. What entry, if any, would the WSU bookstore make when ordering books? When books are received? When returning books? When allowing the students to return books? When purchasing used books from students?

2. How often is it necessary for Larry Martin to take a physical inventory? Why is it necessary to take an inventory? For the inventory taken in September, does Larry need both quantities and costs? Explain.

Solution

1. No entry is made at the time books are ordered. Probably an open purchase order file or memo record is maintained for keeping track of open (unfilled) purchase orders. When books are received, the bookstore would record the purchases at invoice cost as follows:

Merchandise Inventory		
Accounts Payable		
(To record goods purchased on account)		

When books are returned to the publisher, the WSU bookstore would prepare a debit memo from which the following entry is made:

Accounts Payable		
Merchandise Inventory		
(To record books returned to publisher)		

When the bookstore gives a refund for a returned book (not a used book purchase), the following entry would be made at the book's selling price:

Sales Returns and Allowances		
Cash		
(To record payment to customer for returned book)		

And the following entry would be made at the book's cost :

Merchandise Inventory		
Cost of goods sold		
(To record cost of book returned)		

When used books are bought from students, the bookstore would record the following entry:

Inventory of Used Books		
Cash		
(To record purchase of used goods)		

2. Larry Martin waits about 4 weeks after the school term, when the busy book selling and return period ends, to take a physical inventory of books. He does that each school term. In addition Larry takes a physical inventory when the financial statements are prepared at least once a year.

It is necessary for Larry to take accurate inventory counts in order to insure the accuracy of the perpetual inventory records. He needs accurate records to make good ordering and return decisions. Accurate ordering coupled with efficient return practices is a must for profitable bookstore operations.

Larry uses the September inventory balances for ordering books. Thus, only quantities—not costs—are needed by Larry.

Summary of Study Objectives

1. *Identify the differences between a service enterprise and a merchandising company.* Because of the presence of inventory, a merchandising company has sales revenue, cost of goods sold, and gross profit. To account for inventory, a merchandising company must choose between a perpetual inventory system and a periodic inventory system.

2. *Explain the entries for purchases under a perpetual inventory system.* The Merchandise Inventory account is debited for all purchases of merchandise, for freight-in and other costs, and it is credited for purchase discounts and purchase returns and allowances.

3. *Explain the entries for sales revenues under a perpetual inventory system.* When inventory is sold, Accounts Receivable (or Cash) is debited and Sales is credited for the **selling price** of the merchandise. At the same time, Cost of Goods Sold is debited and Merchandise Inventory is credited for the **cost** of the inventory items sold.

4. *Explain the computation and importance of gross profit.* Gross profit is computed by subtracting cost of goods sold from net sales. Gross profit represents the merchandising profit of a company, and the amount and trend of gross profit is closely watched by management and other interested parties.

5. *Identify the unique features of the income statement for a merchandising company.* The income statement for a merchandising company contains three sections: sales revenues, cost of goods sold, and operating expenses.

6. *Explain the steps in the accounting cycle for a merchandising company.* Each of the required steps in the accounting cycle for a service enterprise applies to a merchandising company. A work sheet is again an optional step.

7. *Distinguish between a multiple-step and a single-step income statement.* A multiple-step income statement shows numerous steps in determining net income including nonoperating sections. In a single-step income statement all data are classified under two categories, revenues or expenses, and net income is determined by one step.

Glossary

Administrative expenses   Expenses relating to general operating activities such as personnel management, accounting, and store security. (p. 215).

Contra revenue account   An account that is offset against a revenue account on the income statement. (p. 204).

Cost of goods sold   The total cost of merchandise sold during the period. (p. 194).

Credit memorandum   A document issued by a seller to inform a customer that a credit has been made to the customer's account receivable for a sales return or allowance. (p. 203).

Debit memorandum   A document issued by a buyer to inform a seller that a debit has been made to the seller's account because of unsatisfactory merchandise. (p. 198).

FOB destination   Freight terms indicating that the goods will be placed free on board at the buyer's place of business, and the seller pays the freight costs. (p. 201).

FOB shipping point   Freight terms indicating that goods are placed free on board the carrier by the seller, and the buyer pays the freight costs. (p. 201).

Gross profit   The excess of net sales over the cost of goods sold. (p. 194).

Income from operations   Income from a company's principal operating activity determined by subtracting cost of goods sold and operating expenses from net sales. (p. 215).

Invoice   A document that provides support for a credit purchase. (p. 197).

Multiple-step income statement   An income statement that shows numerous steps in determining net income (or net loss). (p. 214).

Net sales   Sales less sales returns and allowances and sales discounts. (p. 205).

Operating expenses   Expenses incurred in the process of earning sales revenues that are deducted from gross profit in the income statement. (p. 195).

Other expenses and losses   A nonoperating section of the income statement that shows expenses from auxiliary operations and losses unrelated to the company's operations. (p. 214).

Other revenues and gains   A nonoperating section of the income statement that shows revenues from auxiliary operations and gains unrelated to the company's operations. (p. 214).

Periodic inventory system   An inventory system in which detailed records are not maintained and the cost of goods sold is determined only at the end of an accounting period. (p. 196).

Perpetual inventory system   A detailed inventory system in which the cost of each inventory item is maintained and the records continuously show the inventory that should be on hand. (p. 196).

Purchase discount   A cash discount claimed by a buyer for prompt payment of a balance due. (p. 199).

Sales discount   A reduction given by a seller for prompt payment of a credit sale. (p. 204).

Sales invoice   A document that provides support for credit sales. (p. 202).

Sales revenue   Primary source of revenue in a merchandising company. (p. 194).

Selling expenses   Expenses associated with the making of sales. (p. 215).

Single-step income statement   An income statement that shows only one step in determining net income (or net loss). (p. 216).

DEMONSTRATION PROBLEM

The adjusted trial balance columns of the work sheet for the year ended December 31, 1998, for Dykstra Company are as follows:

Debit		Credit	
Cash	$ 14,500	Accumulated Depreciation	$ 18,000
Accounts Receivable	11,100	Notes Payable	25,000
Merchandise Inventory	29,000	Accounts Payable	10,600
Prepaid Insurance	2,500	Common Stock	70,000
Store Equipment	95,000	Retained Earnings	11,000
Dividends	12,000	Sales	536,800
Sales Returns and Allowances	6,700	Interest Revenue	2,500
Sales Discounts	5,000		$673,900
Cost of Goods Sold	363,400		
Freight-out	7,600		
Advertising Expense	12,000		
Store Salaries Expense	56,000		
Utilities Expense	18,000		
Rent Expense	24,000		
Depreciation Expense	9,000		
Insurance Expense	4,500		
Interest Expense	3,600		
	$673,900		

Instructions

(a)   Enter the adjusted trial balance data on a work sheet. Complete the work sheet.

(b)   Prepare an income statement assuming Dykstra Company does not use subgroupings for operating expenses.

Solution to Demonstration Problem

(a)

DYKSTRA COMPANY
Work Sheet
For the Year Ended December 31, 1998

Account Titles	Adjusted Trial Balance		Income Statement		Balance Sheet	
	Dr.	Cr.	Dr.	Cr.	Dr.	Cr.
Cash	14,500				14,500	
Accounts Receivable	11,100				11,100	
Merchandise Inventory	29,000				29,000	
Prepaid Insurance	2,500				2,500	
Store Equipment	95,000				95,000	

Problem-Solving Strategies

1. Make sure in the adjusted trial balance that debits and credits are equal before transferring amounts to the income statement and balance sheet columns.

2. Transfer all amounts in the adjusted trial balance to either the income statement or balance sheet columns.

3. The net income or net loss is the reconciling item in both the income statement and the balance sheet columns.

Accumulated Depreciation		18,000				18,000
Notes Payable		25,000				25,000
Accounts Payable		10,600				10,600
Common Stock		70,000				70,000
Retained Earnings		11,000				11,000
Dividends	12,000				12,000	
Sales		536,800		536,800		
Sales Returns and Allowances	6,700		6,700			
Sales Discounts	5,000		5,000			
Cost of Goods Sold	363,400		363,400			
Freight-out	7,600		7,600			
Advertising Expense	12,000		12,000			
Store Salaries Expense	56,000		56,000			
Utilities Expense	18,000		18,000			
Rent Expense	24,000		24,000			
Depreciation Expense	9,000		9,000			
Insurance Expense	4,500		4,500			
Interest Expense	3,600		3,600			
Interest Revenue		2,500		2,500		
Totals	673,900	673,900	509,800	539,300	164,100	134,600
Net Income			29,500			29,500
Totals			539,300	539,300	164,100	164,100

(b)

DYKSTRA COMPANY
Income Statement
For the Year Ended December 31, 1998

Sales revenues			
Sales			$536,800
Less: Sales returns and allowances		$ 6,700	
Sales discounts		5,000	11,700
Net sales			525,100
Cost of goods sold			363,400
Gross profit			161,700
Operating expenses			
Store salaries expense		56,000	
Rent expense		24,000	
Utilities expense		18,000	
Advertising expense		12,000	
Depreciation expense		9,000	
Freight-out		7,600	
Insurance expense		4,500	
Total operating expenses			131,100
Income from operations			30,600
Other revenues and gains			
Interest revenue		2,500	
Other expenses and losses			
Interest expense		3,600	1,100
Net income			$ 29,500

Problem-Solving Strategies

1. In preparing the income statement, remember that the key components are net sales, cost of goods sold, gross profit, total operating expenses, and net income (loss). These components are reported in the right-hand column of the income statement.
2. Nonoperating items follow income from operations.

*Note: All **asterisked** Questions, Exercises, and Problems relate to material contained in the appendixes to this chapter.

SELF-STUDY QUESTIONS

Answers are at the end of the chapter.

(SO 1) 1. Gross profit will result if:
  a. operating expenses are less than net income.
  b. sales revenues are greater than operating expenses.
  c. sales revenues are greater than cost of goods sold.
  d. operating expenses are greater than cost of goods sold.

(SO 2) 2. Under a perpetual inventory system, when goods are purchased for resale by a company:
  a. purchases on account are debited to Merchandise Inventory.
  b. purchases on account are debited to Purchases.
  c. purchase returns are debited to Purchase Returns and Allowances.
  d. freight costs are debited to Freight-out.

(SO 3) 3. The sales accounts that normally have a debit balance are:
  a. sales discounts.
  b. sales returns and allowances.
  c. Both (a) and (b).
  d. Neither (a) nor (b).

(SO 3) 4. A credit sale of $750 is made on June 13, terms 2/10, net/30, on which a return of $50 is granted on June 16. The amount received as payment in full on June 23 is:
  a. $700.
  b. $686.
  c. $685.
  d. $650.

(SO 3) 5. Which of the following accounts will normally appear in the ledger of a merchandising company that uses a perpetual inventory system?
  a. Purchases.
  b. Freight-in.
  c. Cost of Goods Sold.
  d. Purchase Discounts.

(SO 4) 6. If sales revenues are $400,000, cost of goods sold is $310,000, and operating expenses are $60,000, the gross profit is:
  a. $30,000.
  b. $90,000.
  c. $340,000.
  d. $400,000.

(SO 5) 7. The income statement for a merchandising company shows each of the following features *except*:
  a. gross profit.
  b. cost of goods sold.
  c. a sales revenue section.
  d. operating income section.

(SO 6) 8. In a work sheet, merchandise inventory is shown in the following columns:
  a. Adjusted trial balance debit and balance sheet debit.
  b. Income statement debit and balance sheet debit.
  c. Income statement credit and balance sheet debit.
  d. Income statement credit and adjusted trial balance debit.

(SO 7) 9. In a single-step income statement:
  a. gross profit is reported.
  b. cost of goods sold is not reported.
  c. sales revenues and other revenues and gains are reported in the revenues section of the income statement.
  d. operating income is separately reported.

(SO 7) 10. Which of the following appear on both a single-step and multiple-step income statement?
  a. sales.
  b. gross profit.
  c. income from operations.
  d. cost of goods sold.

QUESTIONS

1. (a) "The steps in the accounting cycle for a merchandising company are different from the accounting cycle for a service enterprise." Do you agree or disagree? (b) Is the measurement of net income in a merchandising company conceptually the same as in a service enterprise? Explain.

2. (a) How do the components of revenues and expenses differ between a merchandising company and a service enterprise? (b) Explain the income measurement process in a merchandising company.

3. How does income measurement differ between a merchandising company and a service company?

4. When is cost of goods sold determined in a perpetual inventory system?

5. Distinguish between FOB shipping point and FOB destination. Identify the freight terms that will result in a debit to Merchandise Inventory by the purchaser and a debit to Freight-out by the seller.

6. Explain the meaning of the credit terms 2/10, n/30.

7. Goods costing $1,600 are purchased on account on July 15 with credit terms of 2/10, n/30. On July 18 a $100 credit memo is received from the supplier for damaged goods. Give the journal entry on July 24 to record payment of the balance due within the

discount period using a perpetual inventory system.

8. Joan Hollins believes revenues from credit sales may be earned before they are collected in cash. Do you agree? Explain.

9. (a) What is the primary source document for recording (1) cash sales, (2) credit sales, and (3) sales returns and allowances? (b) Using XXs for amounts, give the journal entry for each of the transactions in part (a).

10. A credit sale is made on July 10 for $900, terms 2/10, n/30. On July 12, $100 of goods are returned for credit. Give the journal entry on July 19 to record the receipt of the balance due within the discount period.

11. Chuck Rudy Co. has sales revenue of $100,000, cost of goods sold of $70,000, and operating expenses of $20,000. What is its gross profit?

12. Anna Ford Company reports net sales of $800,000, gross profit of $580,000, and net income of $300,000. What are its operating expenses?

13. Identify the distinguishing features of an income statement for a merchandising company.

14. Indicate the columns of the work sheet in which (a) merchandise inventory, and (b) cost of goods sold will be shown.

15. Why is the normal operating cycle for a merchandising company likely to be longer than for a service company?

16. Prepare the closing entries for the Sales account, assuming a balance of $200,000 and the Cost of Goods Sold account which has a $120,000 balance.

17. What merchandising account(s) will appear in the post-closing trial balance?

18. Identify the sections of a multiple-step income statement that relate to (a) operating activities, and (b) nonoperating activities.

19. Distinguish between the types of functional groupings of operating expenses. What problem is created by these groupings?

20. How does the single-step form of income statement differ from the multiple-step form?

BRIEF EXERCISES

Compute missing amounts in determining net income.
(SO 1)

BE5–1 Presented below are the components in Sang Nam Company's income statement. Determine the missing amounts.

	Sales	−	Cost of Goods Sold	=	Gross Profit	−	Operating Expenses	=	Net Income
(a)	$75,000		31500		$43,500		?		$10,800
(b)	$108,000		$65,000		43000		13500		29,500
(c)	181500		$71,900		$109,600		$39,500		70100

Journalize perpetual inventory entries.
(SO 2, 3)

BE5–2 Keo Company buys merchandise on account from Mayo Company. The selling price of the goods is $900, and the cost of the goods is $600. Both companies use perpetual inventory systems. Journalize the transaction on the books of both companies.

Journalize sales transactions.
(SO 3)

BE5–3 Prepare the journal entries to record the following transactions on H. Hunt Company's books using a perpetual inventory system.

(a) On March 2, H. Hunt Company sold $900,000 of merchandise to B. Streisand Company, terms 2/10, n/30. The cost of the merchandise sold was $600,000.

(b) On March 6, B. Streisand Company returned $120,000 of the merchandise purchased on March 2 because it was defective. The cost of the returned merchandise was $80,000.

(c) On March 12, H. Hunt Company received the balance due from B. Streisand Company.   764400

Journalize purchases transactions.
(SO 2)

BE5–4 From the information in BE5–3, prepare the journal entries to record these transactions on B. Streisand Company's books under a perpetual inventory system.

Prepare sales revenue section of income statement.
(SO 3)

BE5–5 A. Cosby Company provides the following information for the month ended October 31, 1998: Sales on credit $300,000, Cash sales $100,000, Sales discounts $5,000, Sales returns and allowances $20,000. Prepare the sales revenues section of the income statement based on this information.

BE5–6 Presented below is the format of the work sheet presented in the chapter.

Trial Balance		Adjustments		Adjusted Trial Balance		Income Statement		Balance Sheet	
Dr.	Cr.	Dr.	Cr.	Dr.	Cr.	Dr.	Cr.	Dr.	Cr.

Indicate where the following items will appear on the work sheet: (a) cash, (b) merchandise inventory, (c) sales, (d) cost of goods sold.
Example:
    Cash: Trial balance debit column; Adjusted trial balance debit column; and Balance sheet debit column.

BE5–7 Pema Company has the following merchandise account balances: Sales $180,000, Sales Discounts $2,000, Cost of Goods Sold $100,000, and Merchandise Inventory $40,000. Prepare the entries to record the closing of these items to Income Summary.

BE5–8 Explain where each of the following items would appear on (1) a multiple-step income statement and on (2) a single-step income statement: (a) gain on sale of equipment, (b) casualty loss from vandalism, and (c) cost of goods sold.

BE5–9 Assume Bicknell Company has the following account balances: Sales $500,000, Sales Returns and Allowances $15,000, Cost of Goods Sold $340,000, Selling Expenses $70,000, and Administrative Expenses $40,000. Compute (a) net sales, (b) gross profit, and (c) income from operations.

EXERCISES

E5–1 Presented below is the following information related to Hans Olaf Co.

1. On April 5, purchased merchandise from D. DeVito Company for $18,000 terms 2/10, net/30, FOB shipping point.
2. On April 6 paid freight costs of $900 on merchandise purchased from D. DeVito.
3. On April 7, purchased equipment on account for $26,000.
4. On April 8, returned damaged merchandise to D. DeVito Company and was granted a $3,000 allowance.
5. On April 15 paid the amount due to D. DeVito Company in full.

Instructions
(a) Prepare the journal entries to record these transactions on the books of Hans Olaf Co. under a perpetual inventory system.
(b) Assume that Hans Olaf Co. paid the balance due to D. DeVito Company on May 4 instead of April 15. Prepare the journal entry to record this payment.

E5–2 On September 1, Campus Office Supply had an inventory of 30 deluxe pocket calculators at a cost of $20 each. The company uses a perpetual inventory system. During September, the following transactions occurred.

Sept. 6 Purchased 60 calculators at $19 each from Digital Co. for cash.
     9 Paid freight of $60 on calculators purchased from Digital Co.
    10 Returned 2 calculators to Digital Co. for $38 credit because they did not meet specifications.
    12 Sold 26 calculators costing $20 (including freight-in) for $30 each to Campus Book Store, terms, n/30.
    14 Granted credit of $30 to Campus Book Store for the return of one calculator that was not ordered.
    20 Sold 30 calculators costing $20 for $30 each to Varsity Card Shop, terms, n/30.

Instructions
Journalize the September transactions.

Prepare purchase and sale entries and closing entries.
(SO 2, 3)

E5–3   On June 10, L. Pele Company purchased $5,000 of merchandise from R. Duvall Company FOB shipping point, terms 2/10, n/30. L. Pele pays the freight costs of $300 on June 11. Damaged goods totaling $300 are returned to R. Duvall for credit on June 12. On June 19, L. Pele pays R. Duvall Company in full, less the purchase discount. Both companies ues a perpetual inventory system.

Instructions
(a) Prepare separate entries for each transaction on the books of L. Pele Company.
(b) Prepare separate entries for each transaction for Duvall Company. The merchandise purchased by Pele on June 10 had cost Duvall $2,500.

Journalize sales transactions.
(SO 3)

E5–4   Presented below are the following transactions related to C. Pippen Company.

1. On December 3, C. Pippen Company sold $400,000 of merchandise to I. Thomas Co., terms 2/10, n/30, FOB shipping point. The cost of the merchandise sold was $320,000.
2. On December 8, I. Thomas Co. was granted an allowance of $20,000 for merchandise purchased on December 3.
3. On December 13, C. Pippen Company received the balance due from I. Thomas Co.

Instructions
(a) Prepare the journal entries to record these transactions on the books of C. Pippen Company using a perpetual inventory system.
(b) Assume that C. Pippen Company received the balance due from I. Thomas Co. on January 2 of the following year instead of December 13. Prepare the journal entry to record the receipt of payment on January 2.

Prepare sales revenues section and closing entries.
(SO 3, 5, 6)

E5–5   The adjusted trial balance of Cecilie Company shows the following data pertaining to sales at the end of its fiscal year October 31, 1998: Sales $900,000, Freight-out $12,000, Sales Returns and Allowances $24,000, and Sales Discounts $15,000.

Instructions
(a) Prepare the sales revenues section of the income statement.
(b) Prepare separate closing entries for (1) sales, and (2) the contra accounts to sales.

Prepare closing entries.
(SO 6)

E5–6   Presented is information related to Baja Co. for the month of January 1998.

Cost of Goods Sold	208,000	Salary expense	61,000
Freight-out	7,000	Sales discounts	8,000
Insurance expense	12,000	Sales returns and allowances	13,000
Rent expense	20,000	Sales	342,000

Instructions
Prepare the necessary closing entries.

Complete work sheet.
(SO 6)

E5–7   Presented below are selected accounts for B. Milia Company as reported in the work sheet at the end of May 1998.

Accounts	Adjusted Trial Balance		Income Statement		Balance Sheet	
	Dr.	Cr.	Dr.	Cr.	Dr.	Cr.
Cash	9,000					
Merchandise Inventory	80,000					
Sales		450,000				
Sales Returns and Allowances	10,000					
Sales Discounts	5,000					
Cost of Goods Sold	250,000					

Instructions
Complete the work sheet by extending amounts reported in the adjusted trial balance to the appropriate columns in the work sheet. Do not total individual columns.

E5–8 In its income statement for the year ended December 31, 1998, Chevalier Company reported the following condensed data:

Prepare multiple-step and single-step income statements.
(SO 7)

Administrative expenses	$435,000	Selling expenses	$ 690,000
Cost of goods sold	989,000	Loss on sale of equipment	10,000
Interest expense	70,000	Net sales	2,359,000
Interest revenue	45,000		

Instructions
(a) Prepare a multiple-step income statement.
(b) Prepare a single-step income statement.

E5–9 An inexperienced accountant for Churchill Company made the following errors in recording merchandising transactions:

Prepare correcting entries for sales and purchases.
(SO 2, 3)

1. A $150 refund to a customer for faulty merchandise was debited to Sales $150 and credited to Cash $150.
2. A $250 credit purchase of supplies was debited to Merchandise Inventory $250 and credited to Cash $250.
3. An $80 sales discount was debited to Sales.
4. A cash payment of $30 for freight on merchandise purchases was debited to Freight-out $300 and credited to Cash $300.

Instructions
Prepare separate correcting entries for each error, assuming that the incorrect entry is not reversed. (Omit explanations.)

E5–10 Presented below is financial information for two different companies:

Compute missing amounts.
(SO 3, 4, 5)

	Young Company	Rice Company
Sales	$90,000	(d)
Sales returns	(a)	$ 5,000
Net sales	81,000	95,000
Cost of goods sold	56,000	(e)
Gross profit	(b)	38,000
Operating expenses	15,000	(f)
Net income	(c)	15,000

Instructions
Determine the missing amounts .

PROBLEMS

P5–1 Eagle Hardware Store completed the following merchandising transactions in the month of May. At the beginning of May, the ledger of Eagle showed Cash of $5,000 and Common stock of $5,000.

Journalize, post, and prepare partial income statement.
(SO 2, 3, 4, 5)

May 1 Purchased merchandise on account from Depot Wholesale Supply $5,000, terms 2/10, n/30.

2 Sold merchandise on account $4,000, terms 2/10, n/30. The cost of the merchandise sold was $3,000.

5 Received credit from Depot Wholesale Supply for merchandise returned $200.

9 Received collections in full, less discounts, from customers billed on sales of $4,000 on May 2.

10 Paid Depot Wholesale Supply in full, less discount.

11 Purchased supplies for cash $900.

12 Purchased merchandise for cash $2,400.

15 Received refund for poor quality merchandise from supplier on cash purchase $230.

17 Purchased merchandise from Harlow Distributors $1,900, FOB shipping point, terms 2/10, n/30.

19 Paid freight on May 17 purchase $250.

24 Sold merchandise for cash $6,200. The merchandise sold had a cost of $4,340.

25 Purchased merchandise from Horicon Inc. $1,000, FOB destination, terms 2/10, n/30.

27 Paid Harlow Distributors in full, less discount.

29 Made refunds to cash customers for defective merchandise $100. The returned merchandise had a cost of $70.

31 Sold merchandise on account $1,600, terms n/30. The cost of the merchandise sold was $1,120.

Eagle Hardware's chart of accounts includes the following: No. 101 Cash, No. 112 Accounts Receivable, No. 120 Merchandise Inventory, No. 126 Supplies, No. 201 Accounts Payable, No. 311 Common Stock, No. 401 Sales, No. 412 Sales Returns and Allowances, No. 414 Sales Discounts, No. 501 Cost of Goods Sold.

Instructions
(a) Journalize the transactions using a perpetual inventory system.
(b) Enter the beginning cash and common stock balances and post the transactions. (Use J1 for the journal reference.)
(c) Prepare an income statement through gross profit for the month of May 1998.

Journalize entries under a perpetual inventory system.
(SO 2,3)

P5–2 Presented below are selected transactions for the Norlan Company during September of the current year. Norlan Company uses the perpetual inventory system.

Sept. 2 Purchased delivery equipment on account for $28,000.

4 Purchased merchandise on account from Hillary Company at a cost of $60,000, terms FOB shipping point, 2/10, n/30.

5 Paid freight charges of $2,000 on merchandise purchased from Hillary Company on September 4.

5 Returned damaged goods costing $7,000 received from Hillary Company on September 4.

6 Sold merchandise to Kimmel Company costing $15,000 on account for $21,000, terms 1/10, n/30.

14 Paid Hillary balance due related to September 4 transaction.

15 Purchased supplies costing $4,000 for cash.

16 Received balance due from Kimmel Company.

18 Purchased merchandise for cash $6,000.

22 Sold to Waldo Company on account for $28,000 inventory costing $20,000, terms 1/10, n/30.

Instructions
Journalize the September transactions.

Complete accounting cycle beginning with a work sheet.
(SO 5, 6, 7)

P5–3 The trial balance of Mesa Wholesale Company contained the following accounts at December 31, the end of the company's fiscal year:

MESA WHOLESALE COMPANY
Trial Balance
December 31, 1998

	Debit	Credit
Cash	$ 33,400	
Accounts Receivable	37,600	
Merchandise Inventory	90,000	
Land	92,000	
Buildings	197,000	
Accumulated Depreciation—Buildings		$ 54,000
Equipment	83,500	
Accumulated Depreciation—Equipment		42,400
Notes Payable		50,000
Accounts Payable		37,500

Common Stock		200,000
Retained Earnings		67,800
Dividends	10,000	
Sales		902,100
Sales Discounts	4,600	
Cost of Goods Sold	709,900	
Salaries Expense	69,800	
Utilities Expense	9,400	
Repair Expense	5,900	
Gas and Oil Expense	7,200	
Insurance Expense	3,500	
	$1,353,800	$1,353,800

Adjustment data:

1. Depreciation is $10,000 on buildings and $9,000 on equipment. (Both are administrative expenses.)
2. Interest of $7,000 is due and unpaid on notes payable at December 31.

Other data:

1. Salaries are 80% selling and 20% administrative.
2. Utilities expense, repair expense, and insurance expense are 100% administrative.
3. $15,000 of the notes payable are payable next year.
4. Gas and oil expense is a selling expense.

Instructions

(a) Enter the trial balance on a work sheet and complete the work sheet.
(b) Prepare a multiple-step income statement and retained earnings statement for the year, and a classified balance sheet at December 31, 1998.
(c) Journalize the adjusting entries.
(d) Journalize the closing entries.
(e) Prepare a post-closing trial balance.

P5–4 Metro Department Store is located in midtown Metropolis. During the past several years, net income has been declining because of suburban shopping centers. At the end of the company's fiscal year on November 30, 1998, the following accounts appeared in two of its trial balances:

Prepare financial statements and adjusting and closing entries.
(SO 5, 6, 7)

	Trial Balances	
	Unadjusted	**Adjusted**
Accounts Payable	$ 37,310	$ 37,310
Accounts Receivable	11,770	11,770
Accumulated Depreciation—Delivery Equipment	15,680	19,680
Accumulated Depreciation—Store Equipment	32,300	41,800
Cash	8,000	8,000
Common stock	70,000	70,000
Cost of Goods Sold	633,220	633,220
Delivery Expense	8,200	8,200
Delivery Equipment	57,000	57,000
Depreciation Expense—Delivery Equipment		4,000
Depreciation Expense—Store Equipment		9,500
Dividends	12,000	12,000
Insurance Expense		9,000
Interest Expense	8,000	8,000
Interest Revenue	5,000	5,000
Merchandise Inventory	36,200	36,200
Notes Payable	46,000	46,000
Prepaid Insurance	13,500	4,500
Property Tax Expense		3,500
Property Taxes Payable		3,500
Rent Expense	19,000	19,000
Retained Earnings	14,200	14,200

	Trial Balances	
	Unadjusted	Adjusted
Salaries Expense	120,000	120,000
Sales	860,000	860,000
Sales Commissions Expense	8,000	14,000
Sales Commissions Payable		6,000
Sales Returns and Allowances	10,000	10,000
Store Equipment	125,000	125,000
Utilities Expense	10,600	10,600

Analysis reveals the following additional data:

1. Salaries expense is 70% selling and 30% administrative.
2. Insurance expense is 50% selling and 50% administrative.
3. Rent expense, utilities expense, and property tax expense are administrative expenses.
4. Notes payable are due in 2002.

Instructions
(a) Prepare a multiple-step income statement, a retained earnings statement, and a classified balance sheet.
(b) Journalize the adjusting entries that were made.
(c) Journalize the closing entries that are necessary.

Journalize, post, and prepare trial balance.
(SO 2, 3, 6)

P5–5   Chi Chi Ramos, a former professional golf star, operates Chi Chi's Pro Shop at Bay Golf Course. At the beginning of the current season on April 1, the ledger of Chi Chi's Pro Shop showed Cash $2,500, Merchandise Inventory $3,500, and Common Stock $6,000. The following transactions were completed during April.

Apr. 5   Purchased golf bags, clubs, and balls on account from Balata Co. $1,600, FOB shipping point, terms 2/10, n/60.
     7   Paid freight on Balata purchase $80.
     9   Received credit from Balata Co. for merchandise returned $100.
    10   Sold merchandise on account to members $900, terms n/30. The merchandise sold had a cost of $630.
    12   Purchased golf shoes, sweaters, and other accessories on account from Arrow Sportswear $660, terms 1/10, n/30.
    14   Paid Balata Co. in full.
    17   Received credit from Arrow Sportswear for merchandise returned $60.
    20   Made sales on account to members $700, terms n/30. The cost of the merchandise sold was $490.
    21   Paid Arrow Sportswear in full.
    27   Granted an allowance to members for clothing that did not fit properly $30.
    30   Received payments on account from members $1,100.

The chart of accounts for the pro shop includes the following: No. 101 Cash, No. 112 Accounts Receivable, No. 120 Merchandise Inventory, No. 201 Accounts Payable, No. 311 Common Stock, No. 401 Sales, No. 412 Sales Returns and Allowances, No. 501 Cost of Goods Sold.

Instructions
(a) Journalize the April transactions using a perpetual inventory system.
(b) Enter the beginning balances in the ledger accounts and post the April transactions. (Use J1 for the journal reference.)
(c) Prepare a trial balance on April 30, 1998.

Journalize, post, and prepare a partial income statement.
(SO 2, 3, 4, 5)

ALTERNATE PROBLEMS

••

P5–1A   The Nisson Distributing Company completed the following merchandising transactions in the month of April. At the beginning of April, the ledger of Nisson showed Cash of $9,000 and Common Stock of $9,000.

Apr. 2 Purchased merchandise on account from Kentucky Supply Co. $4,900, terms 2/10, n/30.

4 Sold merchandise on account $5,000, FOB destination, terms 2/10, n/30. The cost of the merchandise sold was $4,000.

5 Paid $200 freight on April 4 sale.

6 Received credit from Kentucky Supply Co. for merchandise returned $300.

11 Paid Kentucky Supply Co. in full, less discount.

13 Received collections in full, less discounts, from customers billed on April 4.

14 Purchased merchandise for cash $4,400.

16 Received refund from supplier on cash purchase of April 14, $500.

18 Purchased merchandise from Pigeon Distributors $4,200, FOB shipping point, terms 2/10, n/30.

20 Paid freight on April 18 purchase $100.

23 Sold merchandise for cash $6,400. The merchandise sold had a cost of $5,120.

26 Purchased merchandise for cash $2,300.

27 Paid Pigeon Distributors in full, less discount.

29 Made refunds to cash customers for defective merchandise $90. The returned merchandise had a cost of $70.

30 Sold merchandise on account $3,700, terms n/30. The cost of the merchandise sold was $3,000.

Nisson Company's chart of accounts includes the following: No. 101 Cash, No. 112 Accounts Receivable, No. 120 Merchandise Inventory, No. 201 Accounts Payable, No. 311 Common Stock, No. 401 Sales, No. 412 Sales Returns and Allowances, No. 414 Sales Discounts, No. 501 Cost of Goods Sold, and No. 644 Freight-out.

Instructions
(a) Journalize the transactions using a perpetual inventory system.
(b) Enter the beginning cash balances, and post the transactions (Use J1 for the journal reference.)
(c) Prepare the income statement through gross profit for the month of April, 1998.

P5–2A Varsity Auto Sales uses a perpetual inventory system. On April 1, the new car inventory records show total inventory of $140,000 consisting of the following:

Journalize transactions under a perpetual inventory system.
(SO 2, 3)

Model	Units	Unit Cost
Custom Sedans	4	$14,000
Convertibles	3	16,000
Recreational Vans	2	18,000

During April, the following purchases and sales were made on account.

April 5 Purchased three custom sedans for $14,000 each.

7 Sold two custom sedans for $18,200 each.

13 Purchased two recreational vans for $18,000 each.

17 Sold one custom sedan for $18,500.

20 Purchased two convertibles for $16,000 each.

22 Returned one convertible purchased on April 20 for $16,000 credit.

24 Sold three recreational vans for $24,000 each.

28 Sold one convertible for $21,000.

Instructions
Journalize the transactions using a perpetual inventory system.

Complete accounting cycle beginning with a work sheet.
(SO 5, 6, 7)

P5–3A The trial balance of Ivanna Fashion Center contained the following accounts at November 30, the end of the company's fiscal year.

IVANNA FASHION CENTER
Trial Balance
November 30, 1998

	Debit	Credit
Cash	$ 16,700	
Accounts Receivable	33,700	
Merchandise Inventory	45,000	
Store Supplies	5,500	
Store Equipment	85,000	
Accumulated Depreciation—Store Equipment		$ 18,000
Delivery Equipment	48,000	
Accumulated Depreciation—Delivery Equipment		6,000
Notes Payable		51,000
Accounts Payable		48,500
Common Stock		80,000
Retained Earnings		30,000
Dividends	12,000	
Sales		757,200
Sales Returns and Allowances	4,200	
Cost of Goods Sold	507,400	
Salaries Expense	140,000	
Advertising Expense	26,400	
Utilities Expense	14,000	
Repair Expense	12,100	
Delivery Expense	16,700	
Rent Expense	24,000	
	$990,700	$990,700

Adjustment data:

1. Store supplies on hand totaled $3,500.
2. Depreciation is $9,000 on the store equipment and $7,000 on the delivery equipment.
3. Interest of $11,000 is accrued on notes payable at November 30.

Other data:

1. Salaries expense is 70% selling and 30% administrative.
2. Rent expense and utilities expense are 80% selling and 20% administrative.
3. $30,000 of notes payable are due for payment next year.
4. Repair expense is 100% administrative.

Instructions

(a) Enter the trial balance on a work sheet and complete the work sheet.
(b) Prepare a multiple-step income statement and retained earnings statement for the year and a classified balance sheet as of November 30, 1998.
(c) Journalize the adjusting entries.
(d) Journalize the closing entries.
(e) Prepare a post-closing trial balance.

Prepare financial statements and adjusting and closing entries.
(SO 5, 6, 7)

P5–4A The N-Mart Department Store is located near the Village shopping mall. At the end of the company's fiscal year on December 31, 1998, the following accounts appeared in two of its trial balances.

	Trial Balances	
	Unadjusted	Adjusted
Accounts Payable	$ 89,300	$ 89,300
Accounts Receivable	50,300	50,300
Accumulated Depreciation—Building	42,100	52,500
Accumulated Depreciation—Equipment	29,600	42,900
Building	190,000	190,000
Cash	23,000	23,000

Common Stock	150,000	150,000
Cost of Goods Sold	412,700	412,700
Depreciation Expense—Building		10,400
Depreciation Expense—Equipment		13,300
Dividends	28,000	28,000
Equipment	110,000	110,000
Insurance Expense		7,200
Interest Expense	3,000	11,000
Interest Payable		8,000
Interest Revenue	4,000	4,000
Merchandise Inventory	75,000	75,000
Mortgage Payable	80,000	80,000
Office Salaries Expense	32,000	32,000
Prepaid Insurance	9,600	2,400
Property Taxes Expense		4,800
Property Taxes Payable		4,800
Retained Earnings	26,600	26,600
Sales Salaries Expense	76,000	76,000
Sales	618,000	618,000
Sales Commissions Expense	11,000	14,500
Sales Commissions Payable		3,500
Sales Returns and Allowances	8,000	8,000
Utilities Expense	11,000	11,000

Analysis reveals the following additional data:

1. Insurance expense and utilities expense are 60% selling and 40% administrative.
2. $20,000 of the mortgage payable is due for payment next year.
3. Depreciation on the building and property tax expense are administrative expenses; depreciation on the equipment is a selling expense.

Instructions
(a) Prepare a multiple-step income statement, a retained earnings statement, and a classified balance sheet.
(b) Journalize the adjusting entries that were made.
(c) Journalize the closing entries that are necessary.

P5–5A Billy Jean Evert, a former professional tennis star, operates B.J.'s Tennis Shop at the Jackson Lake Resort. At the beginning of the current season, the ledger of B.J.'s Tennis Shop showed Cash $2,500, Merchandise Inventory $1,700, and Common Stock $4,200. The following transactions were completed during April:

Journalize, post, and prepare a trial balance.
(SO 2, 3, 6)

Apr. 4 Purchased racquets and balls from Robert Co. $640 FOB shipping point, terms 3/10, n/30.
    6 Paid freight on Robert purchase $40.
    8 Sold merchandise to members $900, terms n/30. The merchandise sold had a cost of $600.
    10 Received credit of $40 from Robert Co. for a damaged racquet that was returned.
    11 Purchased tennis shoes from Niki Sports for cash, $300.
    13 Paid Robert Co. in full.
    14 Purchased tennis shirts and shorts from Martina's Sportswear $700, FOB shipping point, terms 2/10, n/60.
    15 Received cash refund of $50 from Niki Sports for damaged merchandise that was returned.
    17 Paid freight on Martina's Sportswear purchase $30.
    18 Sold merchandise to members, $800, terms n/30. The cost of the merchandise sold was $530.
    20 Received $500 in cash from members in settlement of their accounts.
    21 Paid Martina's Sportswear in full.
    27 Granted an allowance of $30 to members for tennis clothing that did not fit properly.
    30 Received cash payments on account from members, $500.

The chart of accounts for the tennis shop includes the following: No. 101 Cash, No. 112 Accounts Receivable, No. 120 Merchandise Inventory, No. 201 Accounts Payable, No. 311 Common Stock, No. 401 Sales, No. 412 Sales Returns and Allowances, No. 501 Cost of Goods Sold.

Instructions
(a) Journalize the April transactions using a perpetual inventory system.
(b) Enter the beginning balances in the ledger accounts and post the April transactions. (Use J1 for the journal reference.)
(c) Prepare a trial balance on April 30, 1998.

▼*B*roadening *Your Perspective*

*F*INANCIAL REPORTING PROBLEM—PEPSICO, INC.

The financial statements of PepsiCo, Inc. are presented in Appendix A at the end of this textbook.

Instructions
Answer the following questions using the Consolidated Income Statement.
(a) What was the percentage change in sales and in net income from year to year for 1994 and 1995?
(b) What was PepsiCo's gross profit rate in each of the 3 years?
(c) What was PepsiCo's percentage of net income to net sales in each of the 3 years? Comment on any trend in this percentage.

*C*OMPARATIVE ANALYSIS PROBLEM—
THE COCA-COLA COMPANY VS. PEPSICO, INC.

The financial statements of The Coca-Cola Company are presented at the end of Chapter 1 and PepsiCo's financial statements are presented in Appendix A.

Instructions
(a) Based on the information contained in these financial statements, determine each of the following for each company:
   (1) Gross profit for 1995.
   (2) Gross profit rate for 1995.
   (3) Operating Income for 1995.
   (4) Percent change in operating income from 1994 to 1995.
(b) What conclusions concerning the relative profitability of the two companies can be drawn from these data?

*I*NTERPRETATION OF FINANCIAL STATEMENTS

Mini-Case One—Kellogg Company
Kellogg Company has its headquarters in Battle Creek, Michigan. The company manufactures and sells ready-to-eat breakfast cereals and convenience foods including toaster pastries and cereal bars.

Selected data from Kellogg Company's 1994 annual report follows: (dollar amounts and share data in millions)

	1994	1993	1992
Net sales	$6,562.0	$6,295.4	$6,190.6
Cost of goods sold	$2,950.7	$2,989.0	$2,987.7
Selling and administrative expense	$2,448.7	$2,237.5	$2,140.1
Net income	$705.4	$680.7	$431.2

In its 1994 annual report, Kellogg Company outlined its plans for the future, which it described as its six "global strategies." A brief description of these plans follows.

1. Focus on the cereal and convenience food markets that are considered to be core businesses. The company has already divested seven businesses in the past three years that it considered non-core, such as the Mrs. Smith's pie business. In the coming year, Kellogg Company plans to invest more heavily in advertising in order to build brand recognition in the U.S. cereal market.
2. Continue to launch more new products.
3. Continue to be the first to introduce ready-to-eat cereals in countries around the world. Kellogg Company achieved this goal in India and the Soviet Union, and plans to achieve the goal in China.
4. Maintain or reduce present levels of capital expenditures. Kellogg Company plans to achieve this goal by using value-based management and value engineering.
5. Reduce operating costs. This measure is made necessary because of the limited ability to increase sales prices. Kellogg Company reported that cost of goods sold per kilo was virtually flat in 1994.
6. Repurchase shares of its own stock aggressively. This is done partly to improve earnings per share.

Instructions
(a) For each of the six global strategies, describe how gross profit and net income are likely to be affected.
(b) Compute the percentage change in sales, gross profit, operating costs (cost of goods sold plus selling and administrative expenses), and net income from year to year for each of the three years shown. Evaluate Kellogg Company's performance. Which trend seems to be least favorable? Do you think the global strategies described will improve that trend? Explain.

Mini-Case Two—McDonnell Douglas
McDonnell Douglas, based in St. Louis, Missouri, describes itself in its 1994 Annual Report as the world's largest builder of fighter and military transport aircraft, the third largest commercial aircraft maker, and a leading producer of helicopters, missiles, and satellite launch vehicles.

The company's strategy for future growth might be described as "cautiously aggressive," because it aggressively competes in markets in which it believes that it has a competitive advantage, while it evaluates other markets carefully, and then expands its product line or divests, depending upon whether it believes that it can remain or become a leading competitor.

McDonnell Douglas' 1994 income statement is reproduced below. Dollar amounts are in millions.

Revenues	$13,176
Costs and expenses:	
Cost of products, services, and rentals	11,026
General and administrative expenses	684
Research and development	297
Interest expense	249
Total costs and expenses	12,256
Earnings before income taxes	920
Income taxes	322
Net earnings	$ 598

Instructions

(a) What account name appears to represent McDonnell Douglas' cost of goods sold account? Why do you think that company chose the account name that it did? Using that account as cost of goods sold, what is gross profit?

(b) The income statement shown is in summary form. This means that each account title listed is a summary of several other accounts. For example, the Revenue account includes such things as Commercial Aircraft Revenue, Defense Contract Revenue, and so forth, as well as any offsetting accounts such as Sales Discounts. In which summary account from the income statement would the following merchandising accounts be located:
   1. Sales returns and allowances.
   2. Freight-in.
   3. Merchandise inventory increases and decreases.
   4. Sales discounts.

(c) The company is evaluating a divisional plant that builds satellite launch vehicles. The product line presently consists of a single vehicle, which is the only one of its kind, but competitors have built vehicles that can launch smaller satellites. The company is confident that it can produce an expanded product line, which would include both larger and smaller vehicles than the one currently made. The two choices being evaluated are: First, spending approximately $17 million in research and development to expand the product line. This cost would be considered an expense immediately. Revenue of about $100 million would be generated each year, beginning two years after development; it would continue at least five years, but possibly more. Second, sell the assets of the existing business to a competitor. This would generate a gain of $315 million next year. If the choice is made at the end of this year, how will net income be affected under each alternative? How will gross profit change? Which alternative do you recommend? Give reasons for your answer.

DECISION CASE
••

Three years ago, Kathy Webb and her brother-in-law John Utley opened FedCo. Department Store. For the first 2 years, business was good, but the following condensed income results for 1998 were disappointing.

FEDCO. DEPARTMENT STORE
Income Statement
For the Year Ended December 31, 1998

Net sales		$700,000
Cost of goods sold		546,000
Gross profit		154,000
Operating expenses		
Selling expenses	$100,000	
Administrative expenses	25,000	125,000
Net income		$ 29,000

Kathy believes the problem lies in the relatively low gross profit rate (gross profit divided by net sales) of 22%. John believes the problem is that operating expenses are too high.

Kathy thinks the gross profit rate can be improved by making both of the following changes: (1) Increase average selling prices by 17%; this increase is expected to lower sales volume so that total sales will increase only 6%. (2) Buy merchandise in larger quantities and take all purchase discounts; these changes are expected to increase the gross profit rate by 3%. Kathy does not anticipate that these changes will have any effect on operating expenses.

John thinks expenses can be cut by making both of the following changes: (1) Cut 1998 sales salaries of $60,000 in half and give sales personnel a commission of 2% of net sales. (2) Reduce store deliveries to one day per week rather than twice a week; this change will reduce 1998 delivery expenses of $30,000 by 40%. John feels that these changes will not have any effect on net sales.

Kathy and John come to you for help in deciding the best way to improve net income.

Instructions

(a) Prepare a condensed income statement for 1999 assuming (1) Kathy's changes are implemented and (2) John's ideas are adopted.

(b) What is your recommendation to Kathy and John?

(c) Prepare a condensed income statement for 1999 assuming both sets of proposed changes are made.

COMMUNICATION ACTIVITY
••

The following situation is in chronological order:

1. Dexter decides to buy a surfboard.
2. He calls Surfing USA Co. to inquire about their surfboards.
3. Two days later he requests Surfing USA Co. to make him a surfboard.
4. Three days later, Surfing USA Co. sends him a purchase order to fill out.
5. He sends back the purchase order.
6. Surfing USA Co. receives the completed purchase order.
7. Surfing USA Co. completes the surfboard.
8. Dexter picks up the surfboard.
9. Surfing USA Co. bills Dexter.
10. Surfing USA Co. receives payment from Dexter.

Instructions

In a memo to the President of Surfing USA Co., explain the following:

(a) When should Surfing USA Co. record the sale?

(b) Suppose that with his purchase order, Dexter is required to make a down payment. Would that change your answer?

GROUP ACTIVITY
••

The following information is taken from the accounting records of Grant Company:

Sales	$150,000
Sales Discounts	8,000
Cost of Goods Sold	90,000
Operating Expenses	30,000
Interest Expense	3,000
Sales Returns and Allowances	10,000
Merchandise Inventory	8,000
Interesr Revenue	2,000

Instructions

Working in groups of four or five students, determine the following:

(a) Net sales.

(b) Gross profit.

(c) Income from operations.

(d) Net income.

ETHICS CASE
••

Rita Pelzer was just hired as the assistant treasurer of Yorkshire Stores, a specialty chain store company consisting of nine retail stores concentrated in one metropolitan area. Among other things, the payment of all invoices is centralized in one of the departments Rita will manage. Her primary responsibility is to maintain the company's high credit rating by paying all bills when due and to take advantage of all cash discounts. Jamie Caterino, the former assistant treasurer, who has been promoted to treasurer, is training Rita in her new duties. He instructs Rita that she is to continue the practice of preparing all checks "net of discount" and dating the checks the last day of the discount period. "But," Jamie continues, "we always hold the checks at least four days beyond the discount period before mailing them. That way we get another four days of interest on our money. Most of our creditors need our business and don't complain. And, if they scream about our missing the discount period, we blame it on the mail room or the post office. We've only lost one discount out of every hundred we take that way. I think everybody does it. By the way, welcome to our team!"

Instructions
    (a) What are the ethical considerations in this case?
    (b) Who are the stakeholders that are harmed or benefitted in this situation?
    (c) Should Rita continue the practice started by Jamie? Does she have any choice?

RESEARCH ASSIGNMENT
. . . .

The April 1996 issue of the *Journal of Accountancy* includes an article by Dennis R. Beresford, L. Todd Johnson, and Cheri L. Reither, entitled " Is a Second Income Statement Needed?" Read the article and answer the following questions.

    (a) On what basis would the "second income statement" be prepared? Briefly describe this basis.
    (b) Why is there a perceived need for a second income statement?
    (c) Identify three alternatives for reporting the proposed measure of income.

CRITICAL THINKING
▸ A Real-World Focus: A.L. Laboratories
. . . .

A.L. Laboratories is headquartered in Ft. Lee, N.J., and also has operations in Scandinavia and Indonesia. The company develops and produces generic pharmaceuticals, specializing in both over-the-counter and prescription creams and ointments, aerosol inhalants, and liquids such as cough syrups. A significant share of its income is also derived from the development and distribution of animal health products such as food additives for poultry. The company was founded in 1975 and today has over 2,700 employees.

Gross profit at A.L. Laboratories declined in both dollars and as a percentage of revenues. The decline was attributed to lower sales volume, customer credits associated with product recalls, inventory disposals, and the impact of higher inventory costs. In addition to the above, the gross profit percentage declined as a result of lower production volumes.

Instructions
    (a) What account is affected when A.L. Laboratories has a product recall?
    (b) What factors caused gross profit to decline?
    (c) What factors could cause this company to have to dispose of inventory?

Answers to Self-Study Questions
1. c   2. a   3. c   4. b   5. c   6. b   7. d   8. a   9. c   10. d

●●●●●● ▶ **Concepts for Review**

Before studying this chapter, you should know or, if necessary, review:

a. *The two organizations primarily responsible for setting accounting standards. (Ch. 1, pp. 8–9)*

b. *The monetary unit assumption, the economic entity assumption, and the time period assumption. (Chs. 1 and 3, pp. 9, 10, 99)*

c. *The cost principle, the revenue recognition principle, and the matching principle. (Chs. 1 and 3, pp. 9, 99–100)*

d. *The presentation of classified balance sheets (Ch. 4, p. 167) and classified income statements. (Ch. 5, pp. 215)*

Is Online "Off-Track"?

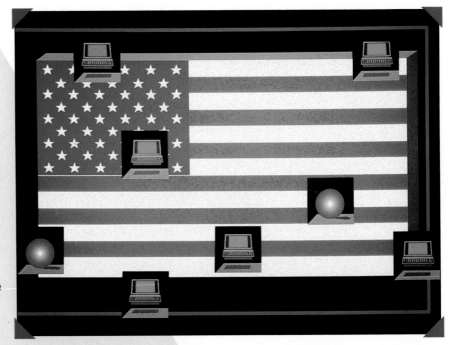

VIENNA, Va. — In the world of interactive media, subscribers pay a monthly fee ($9.95 or so) for limited access to electronic data systems. America Online (AOL) is one of the success stories in this industry. Its stock has increased from $11.50 in 1992, when the company went public, to $71.50 in late 1994. However, an accounting controversy over some of its costs has raised questions about the amount of its earnings.

AOL's biggest expenditure is the cost of attracting subscribers. The company sends out millions of mail solicitations, and works deals to give away a trial subscription with each new computer. Such promotion is expensive; in 1994, subscription-acquisition costs totaled $37 million. Are those an expense against revenue? Or are they an investment undertaken to create an asset?

AOL believes they are the latter. The company capitalizes the costs and amortizes them over 18 months. The other treatment would reduce earnings more: If it had expensed the $37 million as incurred, AOL would have reported a net loss of about $6 million—rather than net income of $6 million. AOL's practice has the FASB's blessing: it considers the cost of obtaining the subscriptions from direct-mail campaigns to be assets. Magazine publishers, similarly, often capitalize such costs.

However, AOL's biggest competitor, CompuServe, takes a more conservative approach by expensing subscriber-acquisition costs as they occur. As CompuServe's controller noted, "We didn't want to taint [our earnings] or dilute them by following [AOL's] accounting."

AOL defends its accounting as a policy of matching expenses with revenues. As its CFO notes, "We're writing these costs off much more rapidly than the ongoing revenue stream." One test of the wisdom of AOL's accounting practice may be the long-term loyalty of subscribers: If they stay with AOL in the face of increasing competition, the subscription-acquisition costs will have created long-term assets. ◀

CHAPTER · **6**

*A*CCOUNTING PRINCIPLES

▶ **STUDY OBJECTIVES** ◀

After studying this chapter, you should be able to:

1. *Explain the meaning of generally accepted accounting principles and identify the key items of the conceptual framework.*

2. *Describe the basic objectives of financial reporting.*

3. *Discuss the qualitative characteristics of accounting information and elements of financial statements.*

4. *Identify the basic assumptions used by accountants.*

5. *Identify the basic principles of accounting.*

6. *Identify the two constraints in accounting.*

7. *Understand and analyze classified financial statements.*

8. *Explain the accounting principles used in international operations.*

As indicated in the opening story, it is important that general guidelines be available to resolve accounting issues such as that faced by America Online. Without these basic guidelines, each enterprise would have to develop its own set of accounting practices. If this happened, we would have to become familiar with every company's peculiar accounting and reporting rules in order to understand their financial statements. Thus, it would be difficult, if not impossible, to compare the financial statements of different companies.

This chapter explores the basic accounting principles followed in developing specific accounting guidelines. The content and organization of the chapter are as follows:

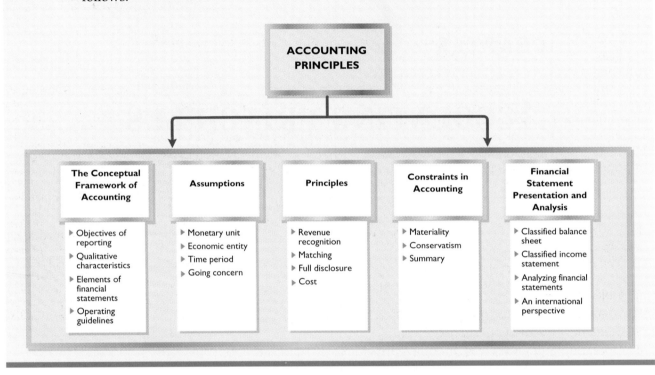

*T*he Conceptual Framework of Accounting

STUDY OBJECTIVE

· · · · · · · · · · **1** · · · · · · · · ·

Explain the meaning of generally accepted accounting principles and identify the key items of the conceptual framework.

The accounting profession has established a set of standards and rules that are recognized as a general guide for financial reporting purposes. This recognized set of standards, called generally accepted accounting principles (GAAP), was discussed briefly in Chapter 1. "Generally accepted" means that these principles must have "substantial authoritative support." Such support usually comes from two standard-setting bodies: the Financial Accounting Standards Board (FASB) and the Securities and Exchange Commission (SEC).[1]

Since the early 1970s the business and governmental communities have given the FASB the responsibility for developing accounting principles in this country.

---

[1]The SEC is an agency of the U.S. government that was established in 1933 to administer laws and regulations relating to the exchange of securities and the publication of financial information by U.S. businesses. The agency has the authority to mandate generally accepted accounting principles for companies under its jurisdiction. However, throughout its history, the SEC has been willing to accept the principles set forth by the FASB and similar bodies.

►Accounting in Action ► *International Insight*

You should recognize that different political and cultural influences affect the accounting that occurs in foreign countries. For example, in the Near East, Islamic accounting is presently being considered. If adopted, the changes would introduce religious tenets into accounting practice. In Sweden, accounting is considered an instrument to be used to shape fiscal policy. In Europe, more emphasis is given to social reporting (more information on employment statistics, health of workers, and so on) because employees and their labor organizations are strong and demand that type of information from management.

This job is an ongoing process in which accounting principles change to reflect changes in the business environment and in the needs of users of accounting information.

Prior to the establishment of the FASB, accounting principles were developed on a problem-by-problem basis. Thus, rule-making bodies developed and issued accounting rules and methods to solve specific problems. Critics charged that the problem-by-problem approach led to inconsistent rules and practices over time. Unfortunately, no clearly developed conceptual framework of accounting existed for the accounting rule makers to refer to in solving problems.

In response to these criticisms, the FASB developed a conceptual framework to serve as the basis for resolving accounting and reporting problems. The FASB spent considerable time and effort on this project. The Board views its conceptual framework as "... a constitution, a coherent system of interrelated objectives and fundamentals."[2]

The FASB's conceptual framework consists of the following four items:

1. Objectives of financial reporting.
2. Qualitative characteristics of accounting information.
3. Elements of financial statements.
4. Operating guidelines (assumptions, principles, and constraints).

We will discuss each of these items on the following pages.

Helpful hint In the history of accounting standard setting, the following facts are relevant: (1) The first official accounting pronouncements were called Accounting Research Bulletins (51 of them were issued between 1939 and 1959 by the Committee on Accounting Procedure); (2) The Accounting Principles Board (APB) replaced the CAP and issued 31 APB Opinions between 1959 and 1973; (3) The FASB replaced the APB in 1973 and has since issued over 120 Statements of Financial Accounting Standards.

Objectives of Financial Reporting

In developing the conceptual framework, the FASB concluded that the first level of study was to determine the objectives of financial reporting. Determining these objectives required answers to such basic questions as: Who uses financial statements? Why? What information do they need? How knowledgeable about business and accounting are the users of financial statements? How should financial information be reported so that it is best understood?

In answering these questions, the FASB concluded that the objectives of financial reporting are to provide information that:

1. Is useful to those making investment and credit decisions.
2. Is helpful in assessing future cash flows.
3. Identifies the economic resources (assets), the claims to those resources (liabilities), and the changes in those resources and claims.

STUDY OBJECTIVE
••••••••••▼2▼••••••••••
Describe the basic objectives of financial reporting.

---

[2]"Conceptual Framework for Financial Accounting and Reporting: Elements of Financial Statements and Their Measurement," *FASB Discussion Memorandum* (Stamford, Conn.: 1976), p. 1.

The FASB then undertook to describe the characteristics that make accounting information useful.

Qualitative Characteristics of Accounting Information

STUDY OBJECTIVE
•••••••••▾3▾•••••••••
Discuss the qualitative characteristics of accounting information and elements of financial statements.

How does a company like Microsoft decide on the amount of financial information to disclose? In what format should its financial information be presented? How should assets, liabilities, revenues, and expenses be measured? **The FASB concluded that the overriding criterion by which such accounting choices should be judged is decision usefulness.** The accounting practice selected or the policy adopted should be the one that generates the most useful financial information for making a decision. To be useful, information should possess the following qualitative characteristics: relevance, reliability, comparability, and consistency.

Relevance

Helpful hint What makes accounting information relevant? Answer: Relevant accounting information provides feedback, serves as a basis for predictions, and is timely (current).

Accounting information is **relevant** if it makes a difference in a decision. Relevant information has either predictive or feedback value or both. **Predictive value** helps users forecast future events. For example, when Exxon issues financial statements, the information in the statements is considered relevant because it provides a basis for forecasting (predicting) future earnings. **Feedback value** confirms or corrects prior expectations. When Exxon issues financial statements, in addition to helping predict future events, it confirms or corrects prior expectations about the financial health of the company.

In addition, for accounting information to be relevant it must be **timely**. That is, it must be available to decision makers before it loses its capacity to influence decisions. If Exxon reported its financial information only every 5 years, the information would have limited usefulness for decision making purposes.

Reliability

Helpful hint What makes accounting information reliable? Answer: Reliable accounting information is free of error and bias, is factual, verifiable, and neutral.

Reliability of information means that the information is free of error and bias; it can be depended on. To be reliable, accounting information must be **verifiable**—we must be able to prove that it is free of error and bias. The information must be a **faithful representation** of what it purports to be—it must be factual. If Sears, Roebuck's income statement reports sales of $100 billion when it had sales of $51 billion, then the statement is not a faithful representation. Finally, accounting information must be **neutral**—it cannot be selected, prepared, or presented to favor one set of interested users over another. To ensure reliability, certified public accountants audit financial statements, just as the Internal Revenue Service audits tax returns for the same purpose.

Comparability and Consistency

Accounting information about an enterprise is most useful when it can be compared with accounting information about other enterprises. **Comparability** results when different companies use the same accounting principles. For example, Sears, Roebuck, Montgomery Ward, and J.C. Penney all use the cost principle in reporting plant assets on the balance sheet. Moreover, each company uses the revenue recognition and matching principles in determining its net income.

Conceptually, comparability should also extend to the methods used by companies in complying with an accounting principle. Accounting methods include the FIFO and LIFO methods of inventory costing, and various depreciation methods. At this point, comparability of methods is not required, even for companies in the same industry, as the opening story about America Online demonstrates. Thus, Ford, General Motors, and Chrysler may use different inventory costing and depreciation methods in their financial statements. The only accounting requirement is that each company **must disclose** the accounting methods used. From the disclosures, the external user can determine whether the financial information is comparable.

Consistency means that a company uses the same accounting principles and methods from year to year. Thus, if a company selects FIFO as the inventory costing method in the first year of operations, it is expected to continue to use FIFO in succeeding years. When financial information has been reported on a consistent basis, the financial statements permit meaningful analysis of trends within a company.

A company can change to a new method of accounting if management can justify that the new method results in more meaningful financial information. In the year in which the change occurs, the change must be disclosed in the notes to the financial statements so that users of the financial statements are aware of the lack of consistency.

The qualitative characteristics of accounting information are summarized in Illustration 6-1.

Helpful hint When companies were first required to consolidate their finance subsidiaries, it caused substantial increases in total assets. For example, Ford rose 23.7%, and General Motors 89.9%. Thus, it is important to identify changes in accounting methods.

Illustration 6-1

Qualitative characteristics of accounting information

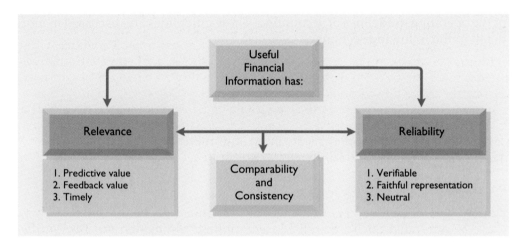

Elements of Financial Statements

An important part of an accounting conceptual framework is a set of definitions that describe the basic terms used in accounting. The FASB refers to this set of definitions as the elements of financial statements. They include such terms as assets, liabilities, equity, revenues, and expenses.

Because these elements are so important, it is imperative that they be precisely defined and universally understood and applied. Finding the appropriate definition for many of these elements is not easy. For example, how should an

▶**A**ccounting in **A**ction ▸ *Business Insight*

There is an old story that professors often tell students about a company looking for an accountant. The company approached the first accountant and asked: "What do you believe our net income will be this year?" The accountant said $4 million dollars. The company asked the second accountant the same question, and the answer was "What would you like it to be?" Guess who got the job? The reason we tell the story here is that, because accounting principles offer flexibility, it is important that a consistent treatment be provided from period to period. Otherwise it would be very difficult to interpret financial statements. Perhaps *no* alternative methods should be permitted in accounting. What do you think?

asset be defined? Should the value of a company's employees be reported as an asset on a balance sheet? Should the death of the company's president be reported as a loss? A good set of definitions should provide answers to these types of questions. Because you have already encountered most of these definitions in earlier chapters, they are not repeated here.

Operating Guidelines

The objectives of financial statements, the qualitative characteristics of accounting information, and the elements of financial statements are very broad. However, because practicing accountants and standard-setting bodies must solve practical problems, more detailed guidelines are needed. In its conceptual framework, the FASB recognized the need for operating guidelines. We have chosen to classify these guidelines as assumptions, principles, and constraints. These guidelines are well-established and accepted in accounting.

Assumptions provide a foundation for the accounting process. **Principles** are specific rules that indicate how economic events should be reported in the accounting process. **Constraints** on the accounting process allow for a relaxation of the principles under certain circumstances. Illustration 6-2 provides a roadmap of the operating guidelines of accounting. These guidelines are discussed in more detail in the following sections.

Illustration 6-2

The operating guidelines of accounting

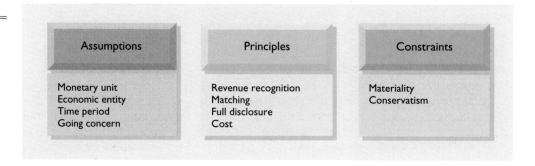

Assumptions	Principles	Constraints
Monetary unit	Revenue recognition	Materiality
Economic entity	Matching	Conservatism
Time period	Full disclosure	
Going concern	Cost	

Before You Go On . . .

▸ *Review It*

1. What are generally accepted accounting principles?
2. What are the basic objectives of financial information?
3. What are the qualitative characteristics that make accounting information useful? Identify two elements of the financial statements.

*A*ssumptions

STUDY OBJECTIVE

4

Identify the basic assumptions used by accountants.

As noted above, assumptions provide a foundation for the accounting process. You have already studied three of the major assumptions in preceding chapters—the monetary unit, economic entity, and time period assumptions. The fourth is called the going concern assumption.

Monetary Unit Assumption

The monetary unit assumption states that only transaction data capable of being expressed in terms of money should be included in the accounting records of the economic entity. For example, the death of a company president would not be reported in a company's financial records as a loss because the event cannot be expressed easily in dollars.

An important corollary to the monetary unit assumption is the added assumption that the unit of measure remains sufficiently constant over time. This point will be discussed in more detail later in this chapter.

Economic Entity Assumption

The economic entity assumption states that economic events can be identified with a particular unit of accountability. For example, it is assumed that the activities of IBM can be distinguished from those of other computer companies such as Apple, Compaq, and Hewlett-Packard.

Time Period Assumption

The time period assumption states that the economic life of a business can be divided into artificial time periods. Thus, it is assumed that the activities of business enterprises such as General Electric, America Online, Exxon, or any enterprise can be subdivided into months, quarters, or a year for meaningful financial reporting purposes.

Going Concern Assumption

The going concern assumption assumes that the enterprise will continue in operation long enough to carry out its existing objectives. Experience indicates that, in spite of numerous business failures, companies have a fairly high continuance rate, and it has proved useful to adopt a going concern assumption for accounting purposes.

The accounting implications of adopting this assumption are critical. If a going concern assumption is not used, then plant assets should be stated at their liquidation value (selling price less cost of disposal)—not at their cost. As a result, depreciation and amortization of these assets would not be needed. Each period these assets would simply be reported at their liquidation value. Also, without this assumption, the current–noncurrent classification of assets and liabilities would have little significance. Labeling anything as fixed or long-term would be difficult to justify.

Acceptance of the going concern assumption gives credibility to the cost principle. If, instead, liquidation were assumed, assets would be better stated at liquidation value than at cost. Only when liquidation appears imminent is the going concern assumption inapplicable.

These basic accounting assumptions are illustrated graphically in Illustration 6-3.

▼ Principles

On the basis of these fundamental assumptions of accounting, the accounting profession has developed principles that dictate how transactions and other economic events should be recorded and reported. In earlier chapters we discussed the cost principle (Chapter 1) and the revenue recognition and matching principles (Chapter 3). We now examine a number of reporting issues related to these principles. In addition, another principle, the full disclosure principle, is discussed.

Helpful hint The dollar as a monetary unit measures both quantity and quality.

▶ *International note*

In a recent action that sent shock-waves through the French business community, the CEO of Alcatel-Alsthom was taken into custody for an apparent violation of the economic entity assumption. Allegedly, the executive improperly used company funds to install an expensive security system in his home.

Helpful hint The going concern concept assumes that the entity will continue at least long enough to recover the cost of its longest lived depreciable asset.

STUDY OBJECTIVE
5

Identify the basic principles of accounting.

Economic Entity

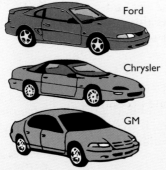

Ford

Chrysler

GM

Economic events can be identified with
a particular unit of accountability.

Monetary Unit

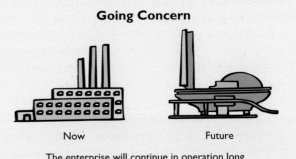

| Measure of employee satisfaction | Salaries paid |
| Total number of employees | Percent of international employees |

Only transaction data capable of being expressed in terms of money
should be included in the accounting records of the economic entity.

Time Period

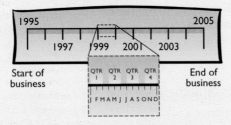

1995   2005

1997   1999   2001   2003

Start of   End of
business   business

QTR 1   QTR 2   QTR 3   QTR 4

J F M A M J J A S O N D

The economic life of a business can be
divided into artificial time periods.

Going Concern

Now   Future

The enterprise will continue in operation long
enough to carry out its existing objectives.

Illustration 6-3

Assumptions used in accounting

Helpful hint Revenue should be recognized in the accounting period in which it is earned, which may not be the period in which the related cash is received. In a retail establishment the point of sale is often the critical point in the process of earning revenue.

Helpful hint For long-term contracts, revenue is recognized on a percentage-of-completion basis during the contract period as the work is being done. And, in transactions where collection is very uncertain, the installment method is implemented by recognizing profit as cash is collected. Coverage of these methods is reserved for more advanced accounting courses.

Revenue Recognition Principle

The revenue recognition principle dictates that revenue should be recognized in the accounting period in which it is earned. Applying this general principle in practice, however, can be difficult. For example, it was reported that Automatic Inc. was improperly recognizing revenue on goods that had not been shipped to customers. Similarly, many questioned the revenue recognition practices of the savings and loan industry, which until recently recorded a large portion of its fees for granting a loan as revenue immediately rather than spreading those fees over the life of the loan.

When a sale is involved, revenue is recognized at the point of sale. The **sales basis** involves an exchange transaction between the seller and buyer, and the sales price provides an objective measure of the amount of revenue realized. There are exceptions to the sales basis for revenue recognition that have become generally accepted. These methods are left for more advanced courses.

Matching Principle (Expense Recognition)

Expense recognition is traditionally tied to revenue recognition: "Let the expense follow the revenue." This practice is referred to as the matching principle: it dictates that expenses be matched with revenues in the period in which efforts are expended to generate revenues. Expenses are not recognized when cash is paid, or when the work is performed, or when the product is produced; they are recognized when the labor (service) or the product actually makes its contribution to revenue.

The problem is that it is sometimes difficult to determine the accounting period in which the expense contributed to the generation of revenues. Several approaches have therefore been devised for matching expenses and revenues on the income statement.

To understand these approaches, it is necessary to examine the nature of expenses. Costs that will generate revenues only in the current accounting period are expensed immediately. They are reported as operating expenses in the income statement. Examples include such costs as advertising, sales salaries, and repairs. These expenses are often called **expired costs**.

Costs that will generate revenues in future accounting periods are recognized as assets. For example, this is the basis on which America Online accounts for its subscription-acquisition costs. Other examples include merchandise inventory, prepaid expenses, and plant assets. These costs represent **unexpired costs**. Unexpired costs become expenses in two ways:

1. **Cost of goods sold.** Costs carried as merchandise inventory are expensed as cost of goods sold in the period when the sale occurs. Thus, there is a direct matching of expenses with revenues.

2. **Operating expenses.** Unexpired costs become operating expenses through use or consumption (as in the case of store supplies) or through the passage of time (as in the case of prepaid insurance and prepaid rent). The cost of plant assets and other long-lived productive resources is expensed through rational and systematic allocation methods which result in periodic depreciation and amortization. Operating expenses contribute to the revenues of the period but their association with revenues is less direct than for cost of goods sold.

These points about expense recognition are illustrated in Illustration 6-4.

Helpful hint Costs are the source of expenses. Costs become expenses when they are charged against revenue.

▶*Ethics note*

Many appear to do it, but few like to discuss it: it's earnings management, and it's a clear violation of the revenue recognition and matching principles. Banks sometimes time the sale of investments or the expensing of bad debts to accomplish earnings objectives. Prominent companies, such as GE, have been accused of matching one-time gains with one-time charge-offs so that current period earnings are not so high that they can't be surpassed next period.

Illustration 6-4

Expense recognition pattern

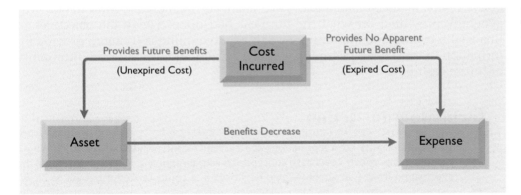

▶Accounting in Action ▸ *Business Insight*

Implementing expense recognition guidelines can be difficult. Consider, for example, Harold's Club (a gambling casino) in Reno, Nevada. How should it report expenses related to the payoff of its progressive slot machines? Progressive slot machines, which generally have no ceiling on their jackpots, are capable of providing a lucky winner with all the money that many losers had previously put in. Payoffs tend to be huge, but infrequent; at Harold's, the progressive slots pay off on average every 4½ months. The basic accounting question is: Can Harold's deduct the millions of dollars sitting in its progressive slot machines from the revenue recognized at the end of the accounting period? One might argue that no, you cannot deduct the money until the "winning handle pull." However, a winning handle pull might not occur for many months or even years. Although admittedly an estimate would have to be used, the better answer is to match these costs with the revenue recognized, assuming that an average 4½ months' payout is well documented. This example demonstrates that the matching principle can be difficult to apply in practice.

Source: Adapted from *Fortune*, July 7, 1986, p. 100.

Full Disclosure Principle

Helpful hint   The full disclosure principle requires that all significant financial facts be disclosed. A reporting entity should disclose all items that make a difference in the decisions and judgments of readers of the financial statements. An easy description of this principle is to simply say, "disclose all items necessary to make the statements complete and not misleading."

Helpful hint   See the specimen financial statements of PepsiCo illustrated in Appendix A for an example of information disclosed in a summary of significant accounting policies.

The **full disclosure principle** requires that circumstances and events that make a difference to financial statement users be disclosed. For example, most accountants would agree that Manville Corporation should have disclosed the 52,000 asbestos liability suits (totaling $2 billion) pending against it so that interested parties were made aware of this contingent loss. Similarly, it is generally agreed that companies should disclose the major provisions of employee pension plans and long-term lease contracts.

Compliance with the full disclosure principle occurs through the data contained in the financial statements and the information in the notes that accompany the statements. The first note in most cases is a **summary of significant accounting policies**. The summary includes, among others, the methods used by the company for inventory costing, depreciation of plant assets, and amortization of intangible assets.

Deciding how much disclosure is enough can be difficult. Accountants could disclose every financial event that occurs and every contingency that exists. However, accounting information must be condensed and combined to make it understandable. Providing additional information entails a cost, and the benefits of providing this information in some cases may be less than the costs. Many companies complain of an accounting standards overload. In addition, they object to requirements that force them to disclose confidential information. Determining where to draw the line on disclosure is not easy.

One thing is certain: financial statements were much simpler years ago, when many companies provided little additional information regarding the financial statements. In 1930, General Electric had no notes to the financial statements; today it has over 10 pages of notes! Why this change? A major reason is that the objectives of financial statements have changed. In the past, information was generally presented on what the business had done. Today the objectives of financial reporting are more future-oriented; accounting is trying to provide information that makes it possible to predict the amount, timing, and uncertainty of future cash flows.

▶*T*echnology in *A*ction

Some accountants are reconsidering the current means of financial reporting. These accountants propose a data base concept of financial reporting. In such a system, all the information from transactions would be stored in a computerized data base to be accessed by various user groups. The main benefit of such a system is the ability to tailor the information requested to the needs of each user.

What makes it controversial? Discussion currently revolves around access and aggregation issues. Questions such as "Who should be allowed to make inquiries of the system?" "What is the lowest/smallest level of information to be provided?" and "Will such a system necessarily improve on the current means of disclosure?" must be answered before such a system can be implemented on a large scale.

Cost Principle

As you know, the **cost principle** dictates that assets are recorded at their cost. Cost is used because it is both relevant and reliable. Cost is **relevant** because it represents the price paid, the assets sacrificed, or the commitment made at date of acquisition. Cost is **reliable** because it is objectively measurable, factual, and verifiable. It is the result of an exchange transaction. Cost is the basis used in preparing financial statements.

The cost principle, however, has come under much criticism. It is criticized by some as irrelevant. Subsequent to acquisition, the argument goes, cost is not equivalent to market value or current value. For that matter, as the purchasing power of the dollar changes, so also does the meaning associated with the dollar that is used as the basis of measurement. Consider the classic story about the individual who went to sleep and woke up 10 years later. Hurrying to a telephone, he got through to his broker and asked what his formerly modest stock portfolio was worth. He was told that he was a multi-millionaire—his General Motors stock was worth $5 million and his AT&T stock was up to $10 million. Elated, he was about to inquire about his other holdings, when the telephone operator cut in with "Your time is up. Please deposit $100,000 for the next 3 minutes."[3]

This story demonstrates that prices can and do change over a period of time, and that one is not necessarily better off when they do. Although the numbers in the story are extreme, consider some more realistic data that compare prices in 1983 with what is expected in 1999, assuming average price increases of 6% and 12% per year.

Helpful hint Although cost is criticized, at the date of acquisition or incurrence it is the best indicator of fair value, current market value, present value, or any other measurement of the values exchanged or obligations assumed. Cost represents something that someone should be held accountable for.

Helpful hint In a recent 50-year period, the price level has increased ninefold! A market basket of goods that cost $11 fifty years ago now costs approximately $100. The average rate of inflation over this period was 4.5%.

Assumed average price increase	1983	1999 6%	1999 12%
Public college, yearly average cost	$ 3,350.00	$ 8,510.00	$ 20,537.00
Average taxi ride, New York City (before tip)	2.95	7.49	18.08
Slice of pizza	.65	1.65	3.98
First-class postage stamp	.15	.38	.92
Run-of-the-mill suburban house, New York City	150,000.00	381,052.00	919,559.00
McDonald's milk shake	.75	1.91	4.60

Illustration 6-5

Example of changing prices

Helpful hint Are you a winner or loser when you hold cash in a period of inflation? Answer: A loser, because the value of the cash declines as inflation climbs.

Despite the inevitability of changing prices during a period of inflation, the accounting profession still follows the stable monetary unit assumption in preparing a company's primary financial statements. While admitting that some changes in prices do occur, the profession believes the unit of measure—the dollar—has remained sufficiently constant over time to provide meaningful financial information.

The basic principles of accounting are summarized in Illustration 6-6.

Constraints in Accounting

Constraints permit a company to modify generally accepted accounting principles without reducing the usefulness of the reported information. The constraints are materiality and conservatism.

Materiality

Materiality relates to an item's impact on a firm's overall financial condition and operations. An item is material when it is likely to influence the decision of a reasonably prudent investor or creditor. It is immaterial if its inclusion or omission has no mpact on a decision maker. In short, if the item does not make a difference, GAAP does not have to be followed. To determine the materiality of

STUDY OBJECTIVE
········ 6 ·········
Identify the two constraints in accounting.

---

[3]Adapted from *Barron's*, January 28, 1980, p. 27.

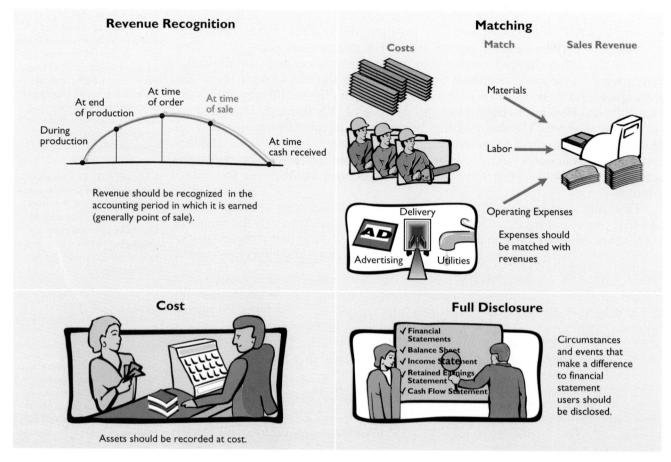

Illustration 6-6

Basic principles used in accounting

Helpful hint An example of the application of materiality is as follows. A wastebasket is purchased for an executive's office at a cost of $18. It is expected to have a useful life of 10 years. The matching principle dictates that the $18 cost be capitalized and depreciated over 10 years. However, because the amount is immaterial, the accountant will give this purchase expedient treatment by expensing the entire $18 cost in the year it is acquired.

an amount, that is, to determine its financial significance, the accountant usually compares it with such items as total assets, total liabilities, and net income.

To illustrate how the constraint of materiality is applied, assume that Rodriguez Co. purchases a number of low-cost plant assets, such as wastepaper baskets. Although the proper accounting would appear to be to depreciate these wastepaper baskets over their useful life, they are usually expensed immediately. This practice is justified because these costs are considered immaterial. Establishing depreciation schedules for these assets is costly and time-consuming and will not make a material difference on total assets and net income. Other applications of the materiality constraint are the expensing of small tools or the expensing of any plant assets under a certain dollar amount.

Conservatism

Conservatism in accounting means that when in doubt the accountant should choose the method that will be least likely to overstate assets and income. It does **not** mean **understating** assets or income. Conservatism gives the accountant a guide in difficult situations, and the guide is a reasonable one: do not overstate assets and income.[4] We shall see several examples of conservatism in practice in succeeding chapters.

The two constraints are graphically depicted in Illustration 6-7.

---

[4]A common application of the conservatism constraint is the use of the lower of cost or market method for inventories. As indicated in Chapter 9, inventories are reported at market value if market value is below cost. This practice results in a higher cost of goods sold and lower net income. In addition, inventory on the balance sheet is stated at a lower amount when market value is below cost. Other examples of conservatism in accounting are the use of the LIFO method for inventory valuation when prices are rising and the use of accelerated depreciation methods for plant assets. Both these methods result in lower asset carrying values and lower net income than alternative methods.

Materiality

Account for under GAAP

If dollar amounts of costs are small, GAAP does not have to be followed.

Conservatism

When in doubt, choose the solution that will be least likely to overstate assets and income.

Illustration 6-7

Constraints in accounting

Summary of Conceptual Framework

As we have seen, the conceptual framework for developing sound reporting practices starts with a set of objectives for financial reporting and follows with the development of qualities that make information useful. In addition, elements of financial statements are defined. Operating guidelines in the form of assumptions and principles are then provided. The conceptual framework also recognizes that important constraints exist on the reporting environment. These points are illustrated graphically in Illustration 6-8:

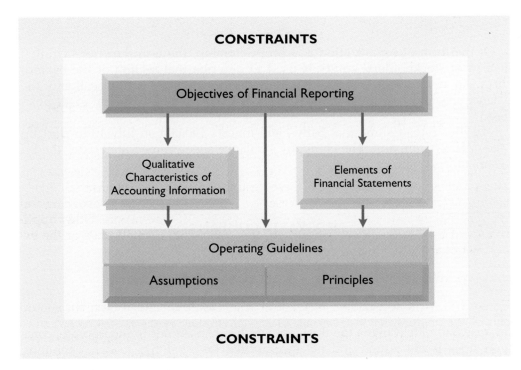

CONSTRAINTS

Objectives of Financial Reporting

Qualitative Characteristics of Accounting Information

Elements of Financial Statements

Operating Guidelines

Assumptions

Principles

CONSTRAINTS

Illustration 6-8

Conceptual framework

Before You Go On . . .

► *Review It*

1. What are the monetary unit assumption, the economic entity assumption, the time period assumption, and the going concern assumption?
2. What are the revenue recognition principle, the matching principle, the full disclosure principle, and the cost principle?
3. What are the materiality constraint and the conservatism constraint?

*F*inancial Statement Presentation and Analysis

STUDY OBJECTIVE

•••••••••• **7** ••••••••••

Understand and analyze classified financial statements.

Financial statements play an important role in attempting to meet the objectives of financial reporting. "Bottom line" information such as total assets and net income are useful to investors, but these single numbers lack sufficient detail for serious analysis. Investors and creditors generally find the parts of a financial statement more useful than the whole. Proper classification within the financial statements is therefore extremely important.

Classified Balance Sheet

The balance sheet is composed of three major elements: assets, liabilities, and stockholders' equity. Additional segregation within these groups, however, is considered useful to financial statement readers. As indicated in Chapter 4, the following classification is generally found.

Illustration 6-9

Standard Classification of Balance Sheet

Assets	Liabilities and Stockholders' Equity
Current assets	Current liabilities
Long-term investments	Long-term liabilities
Property, plant, and equipment	Stockholders' equity
Intangible assets	

If the form of organization is a proprietorship, the term "owner's equity" instead of stockholders' equity is used to describe that section of the balance sheet. An account called capital is reported in the owner's equity section of the balance sheet for a proprietorship. **Capital** is the owner's investment in the business.

To illustrate, assume that Sally Field invests $90,000 on July 10 to start up Med/Waste Company. The company's balance sheet immediately after the investment is as follows:

Illustration 6-10

Proprietorship Balance Sheet

MED/WASTE COMPANY
Balance Sheet
July 10, 1996

Cash	$90,000	Sally Field, Capital	$90,000

Because Sally Field owns the business and has chosen not to incorporate, common stock is not issued and net income (net loss) belongs to her. Therefore, common stock and retained earnings accounts are not needed. Instead, her capital account is increased by investments and net income and is decreased by withdrawals of assets for personal use and net losses. The capital account represents Sally Field's claim to the net assets (assets less liabilities) of the company.

If the form of organization is a partnership, each partner has a separate capital account and the owners' equity section shows the capital accounts of all the partners. For example, assume that A. Roy and B. Siegfried form a partnership on December 11, 1996, at which time Roy and Seigfried each invest $60,000. The balance sheet immediately after their investments is as follows:

Illustration 6-11

Partnership Balance Sheet

ROY AND SEIGFRIED
Balance Sheet
December 11, 1996

Cash	$120,000	A. Roy, Capital	$ 60,000
		B. Seigfried, Capital	60,000
			$120,000

Classified Income Statement

Chapter 5 presented a multiple-step income statement for Highpoint Electronic, Inc. The multiple-step income statement included the following:

Sales revenue section—Presents the sales, discounts, allowances, and other related information to arrive at the net amount of sales revenue.

Cost of goods sold—Indicates the cost of goods sold to produce sales.

Operating expenses—Provides information on both selling and administrative expenses.

Other revenues and gains—Indicates revenues earned or gains resulting from nonoperating transactions.

Other expenses and losses—Indicates expenses or losses incurred from nonoperating transactions.

Two additional items not discussed in Chapter 5 are income tax expense and earnings per share.

Income Tax Expense

Income taxes must be paid and therefore reported for a corporation because a corporation is a legal entity separate and distinct from its owners. Proprietorships and partnerships are not separate legal entities; owners are therefore taxed directly on their business income. Stockholders are taxed only on the dividends they receive.

Corporate **income taxes (or income tax expense)** are reported in a separate section of the income statement before net income. The condensed income statement for Leads Inc. in Illustration 6-12 shows a typical presentation. Note that income before income taxes is reported before income tax expense.

Illustration 6-12

Income statement with income taxes

LEADS INC.
Income Statement
For the Year Ended December 31, 1996

Sales	$800,000
Cost of goods sold	600,000
Gross profit	200,000
Operating expenses	50,000
Income from operations	150,000
Other revenues and gains	10,000
Other expenses and losses	4,000
Income before income taxes	156,000
Income tax expense	46,800
Net income	$109,200

Income tax expense and the related liability for income taxes payable are recorded as part of the adjusting process preceding financial statement preparation. Using the data above for Leads Inc., the adjusting entry for income tax expense at December 31, 1996, would be as follows:

Income Tax Expense	46,800	
Income Taxes Payable		46,800
(To record income taxes for 1996)		

Another example of income tax presentation appears in the income statement of PepsiCo in Appendix A.

Earnings Per Share

Earnings per share data are frequently reported in the financial press and are widely used by stockholders and potential investors in evaluating the profitability of a company. Investors, especially, attempt to link earnings per share to the market price per share.[5] Earnings per share (EPS) indicates the net income earned by each share of outstanding common stock. Thus, **earnings per share is reported only for common stock**. The formula for computing earnings per share when there has been no change in outstanding shares during the year is as follows:

Illustration 6-13

Earnings per share formula—no change in outstanding shares

For example, Leads, Inc. (Illustration 6-12) has net income of $109,200. Assuming that it has 54,600 shares of common stock outstanding for the year, earnings per share is $2 ($109,200 ÷ 54,600).[6]

Because of the importance of earnings per share (EPS), most companies are required to report it on the face of the income statement. Generally this amount is simply reported below net income on the statement. For Leads, Inc. the presentation would be:

Illustration 6-14

Basic earnings per share disclosure

Net income	$109,200
Earnings per share	$ 2.00

A real advantage of earnings per share information is in computing the price-earnings ratio to evaluate the relative richness of the market price of a company's share of stock.

---

[5]The ratio of the market price per share to the earnings per share is referred to as the *price-earnings ratio*. This ratio is reported in *The Wall Street Journal* and other newspapers for common stocks listed on major stock exchanges.

[6]Whenever the number of outstanding shares changes during the year the calculation of EPS becomes more complicated. These computations are shown in Chapter 15.

Analyzing Financial Statements

The financial statements should provide financial information that is useful for helping make sound investing/credit decisions. Presented below are the condensed balance sheet and income statement of Genlyte Inc. for 1996:

Illustration 6-15

*Financial Statements—
Genlyte Inc.*

GENLYTE INC.
Balance Sheet
December 31, 1996

Assets		Liabilities and Stockholders' Equity	
Current assets	$156,000	Current liabilities	$ 70,000
Plant and equipment (net)	74,000	Long-term liabilities	114,000
Intangible assets	14,000	Stockholders' equity	60,000
Total assets	$244,000	Total liabilities and stockholders' equity	$244,000

GENLYTE INC.
Income Statement
For the Year Ended December 31, 1996

Net sales	$430,000
Cost of sales	295,000
Gross Profit	135,000
Selling and administrative expenses	109,000
Income from operations	26,000
Other expenses and losses	5,000
Income before income taxes	21,000
Income tax expense	7,000
Net income	$ 14,000
Earnings per share	$0.35

In analyzing and interpreting financial statement information, three major characteristics are generally evaluated: **liquidity**, **profitability**, and **solvency**. A **short-term debt holder**, for example, is primarily interested in the ability of a borrower to pay obligations when they become due. The liquidity of the borrower in such a case is extremely important in assessing the safety of a loan. A **long-term debt holder**, however, looks to indicators such as profitability and solvency that point to the firm's ability to survive over a long period of time. Long-term debt holders analyze earnings per share, the relationship of income to total assets invested, and the amount of debt in relation to total assets to determine whether money should be lent and at what interest rate. Similarly, **stockholders** are interested in the profitability and solvency of a company when assessing the likelihood of dividends and the growth potential of the common stock.

Liquidity

What is Genlyte's ability to pay its maturing obligations and meet unexpected needs for cash? The relationship between current assets and current liabilities is critical to helping answer this question. These relationships are expressed as a ratio, called the **current ratio**, and as a dollar amount, called **working capital**.

Current Ratio. The current ratio is current assets divided by current liabilities. For Genlyte Inc., the ratio is 2.23:1, computed as follows:

Illustration 6-16

Current ratio formula and computation

Current Assets	÷	Current Liabilities	=	Current Ratio
$156,000	÷	$70,000	=	2.23:1

(Working Capital Ratio)

This ratio means that current assets are more than two times greater than current liabilities. Bankers, other creditors, and agencies such as Dun & Bradstreet use this ratio to determine whether the company is a good credit risk. In many cases, a ratio of 2:1 is considered to be the standard for a good credit rating. With its 2.23:1 ratio, Genlyte's short-term debt-paying ability appears to be very favorable.

From the foregoing, you might at first assume that the higher the current ratio, the better. This is not necessarily true. A very high current ratio may indicate that the company is holding more current assets than it currently needs in the business. It is possible, therefore, that the excess resources might be directed to more profitable investment opportunities.

Working Capital.   The excess of current assets over current liabilities is called **working capital**. For Genlyte Inc., working capital is $86,000, as shown below:

Illustration 6-17

Working capital formula and computation

Current Assets	−	Current Liabilities	=	Working Capital
$156,000	−	$70,000	=	$86,000

The amount of working capital provides some indication of the company's ability to meet its existing current obligations. A large amount of working capital generally means a company can meet its current liabilities as they fall due and pay dividends, if desired. Although no set standards exist for the level of working capital a company should maintain, the general adequacy of a company's working capital is often determined by comparing data from prior periods and from similar companies of comparable size. Genlyte's working capital appears adequate.

Profitability

Profitability ratios measure the income or operating success of an enterprise for a given period of time. Income, or the lack of it, affects the company's ability to obtain debt or equity financing and the company's ability to grow.

Profit Margin Percentage.   One important ratio used to measure profitability is the **profit margin percentage** (or rate of return on sales). It measures the percentage of each dollar of sales that results in net income. It is calculated by dividing net income by net sales for the period. Genlyte Inc.'s profit margin percentage is 3.3 percent, computed as follows:

Illustration 6-18

*Profit margin formula
and computation*

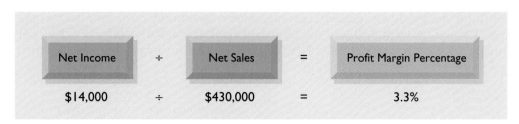

Net Income	÷	Net Sales	=	Profit Margin Percentage
$14,000	÷	$430,000	=	3.3%

This ratio seems low. Much, however, depends on the type of company. High-volume retailers, such as grocery stores (Safeway or Kroger) or discount stores (Wal-Mart or Kmart), generally have a low profit margin.

▲*Accounting in Action* ► *Business Insight*

The type of industry can make a difference in the profit margin percentage investors and creditors expect. Profit margins among service companies—from airlines and banks to telecommunication companies and utilities—have traditionally been lower than those among manufacturers. MCI Communications, for example, showed a profit margin percentage of 4.9 percent for fiscal year 1993, which is high for a telecommunications company. Sprint's rate of return on sales was only 0.5 percent for the same period, and AT&T posted a loss. By contrast, the top three pharmaceutical firms—Johnson & Johnson, Bristol-Meyers Squibb, and Merck—had returns on sales for 1993 of 12.6 percent, 17.2 percent, and 20.6 percent, respectively. Before using a ratio like the profit margin percentage to evaluate company performance, you need to know what is reasonable performance for the industry.

Return on Assets. In making an investment, an investor wants to know what rate of return to expect and what risks are associated with that rate of return. The greater the risk, the higher the rate of return the investor will demand on the investment.

One overall measure of profitability of a company is its **rate of return on assets**. It is calculated by dividing net income by total assets.[7] Genlyte Inc.'s rate of return is 5.7 percent, computed as follows:

Illustration 6-19

*Return on assets formula
and computation*

Net Income	÷	Total Assets	=	Return on Assets
$14,000	÷	$244,000	=	5.7%

The rate of return on assets is relatively low, which suggests that Genlyte may not be using its assets effectively.

Return on Common Stockholders' Equity. Another widely used rate that measures profitability from the common stockholders' viewpoint is **return on**

---

[7]For simplicity, the rate of return calculations are based on end-of-year total amounts. In Chapter 15, the more conceptually correct average total assets and average common stockholders' equity is used.

common stockholders' equity. This rate shows how many dollars of net income were earned for each dollar of owner investment. It is calculated by dividing net income by common stockholders' equity. In Genlyte Inc.'s case, the rate of return is 23.3 percent, computed as follows:

Illustration 6-20

*Return on common stock-
holders' equity formula
and computation*

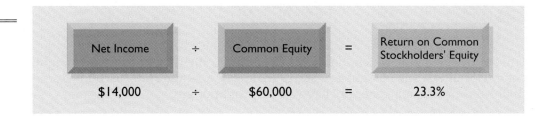

Genlyte's return on common stockholders' equity is quite good. The reason for this high rate of return is that Genlyte's assets are earning a return higher than the borrowing costs the company incurs.

Solvency

Solvency measures the ability of an enterprise to survive over a long period of time. Long-term debt holders and stockholders are interested in a company's ability to pay periodic interest and to repay the face value of the debt at maturity.

Debt to Total Assets.   One useful measure of solvency is the **debt to total assets ratio**. It measures the percentage of total assets that creditors, as opposed to stockholders, provide. It is calculated by dividing total debt (liabilities) by total assets, normally expressed as a percentage. Genlyte Inc.'s debt to total assets ratio is 75.4 percent, computed as follows:

Illustration 6-21

*Debt to total assets formula
and computation*

Debt to total assets of 75.4 percent means that Genlyte's creditors have provided approximately three-quarters of its total assets. The higher the percentage of debt to total assets, the greater the risk that the company may be unable to meet its maturing obligations; the lower the percentage, the greater the "buffer" available to creditors should the company become insolvent. In Genlyte Inc.'s case, unless earnings are positive and very stable, the company may have too much debt.

   These percentage and ratio relationships are often used in comparison with (1) expected results, (2) prior year results, and (3) published results of other companies in the same line of business. Conclusions based on a single year's results are hazardous at best. Chapter 15 provides more detailed consideration of the analysis of financial statements.

Financial Statement Presentation—An International Perspective

World markets are becoming increasingly intertwined. Foreigners use American computers, eat American breakfast cereals, read American magazines, listen to

American rock music, watch American movies and TV shows, and drink American soda. And, Americans drive Japanese cars, wear Italian shoes and Scottish woolens, drink Brazilian coffee and Indian tea, eat Swiss chocolate bars, sit on Danish furniture, and use Arabian oil. The tremendous variety and volume of both exported and imported goods indicates the extensive involvement of U.S. business in international trade. For many U.S. companies, the world is their market.

The following table illustrates the magnitude of foreign sales and type of product sold by U.S. companies.

STUDY OBJECTIVE

•••••••••• **8** ••••••••••

Explain the accounting principles used in international operations.

Company	Foreign Sales as a % of Total	Product
Caterpillar	22.6	Heavy machinery, engines, turbines
Coca-Cola	68.3	Beverages
Eastman Kodak	52.5	Photographic equipment and supplies
E.I. duPont de Nemours	42.1	Specialty chemicals
Exxon	77.4	Petroleum, chemicals
Ford Motor	29.6	Motor vehicles and parts
General Motors	28.4	Motor vehicles and parts
Hewlett-Packard	54.1	Computers, electronics
IBM	62.3	Computers and related equipment
Philip Morris Cos.	30.4	Tobacco, beverages, food products

Illustration 6-22

Foreign sales and type of product

Firms that conduct their operations in more than one country through subsidiaries, divisions, or branches in foreign countries are referred to as **multinational corporations**. The accounting for multinational corporations is complicated because foreign currencies are involved. These international transactions and operations must be translated into U.S. dollars.

Helpful hint Accounting and auditing in the free world is dominated by the large international American public accounting firms and their affiliates. These firms audit companies everywhere in the world.

►Accounting in Action ► *International Insight*

In 1991, for the first time, McDonald's opened more restaurants overseas than in the United States: 427 abroad compared with just 188 in the United States. The top 10 McDonald's restaurants in sales and profits are on foreign soil. The busiest McDonald's are in Moscow, on the Champs-Elysees in Paris, and in central Rome. In 1992 McDonald's opened its first store in Beijing, China. Recently, 37% of McDonald's sales and 40% of the company's operating income came from outside the United States.

Source: The New York Times, April 17, 1992.

Differences in Standards

As the "world economy" is becoming globalized to the point where the United States is only one in a set of major players, many investment and credit decisions require the analysis and interpretation of foreign financial statements. Unfortunately, there is little uniformity in accounting standards from country to country, and there are few recognized worldwide accounting standards. This lack of uniformity is the result of different legal systems, different processes for developing accounting standards, different governmental requirements, and different economic environments.

▶ Accounting in Action ▸ *International Insight*

Research and development costs are an example of different international accounting standards. Compare how four countries account for research and development:

Country	Accounting treatment
United States	Expenditures are expensed.
United Kingdom	Certain expenditures may be capitalized.
Germany	Expenditures are expensed.
Japan	Expenditures may be capitalized and amortized over 5 years.

Thus, a research and development expenditure of $100 million is charged totally to expense in the current period in the United States and Germany. This expense could range from zero to $100 million in the United Kingdom and from $20 million to $100 million in Japan!

Do you believe that accounting principles should be comparable across countries?

Uniformity in Standards

Some efforts have been made to obtain uniformity in international accounting practices. In 1973 the International Accounting Standards Committee (IASC) was formed by agreement of accounting organizations in the United States, the United Kingdom, Canada, Australia, France, Germany, Japan, Mexico, and the Netherlands. More than 80 accounting organizations representing more than 60 countries now participate in the development of international accounting standards.

To date, over 30 International Accounting Standards have been issued for IASC members to introduce to their respective countries. But, because the IASC has no enforcement powers, these standards are by no means universally applied. They are, however, generally followed by the large multinational companies that are audited by international public accounting firms. Thus, the foundation has been laid for considerable progress toward greater uniformity in international accounting.

Before You Go On . . .

▶ Review It

1. What is the major difference in the equity section of the balance sheet between a corporation and proprietorship?
2. Where are income tax expense and earnings per share reported on the income statement? How is earnings per share computed?
3. How are the current ratio, profit margin percentage, return on assets, return on common stockholders' equity, and debt to total assets computed?
4. Explain how these ratios are useful in financial statement analysis.
5. What is the purpose of the International Accounting Standards Committee?

▶ A Look Back at America Online

Refer back to the opening story and answer the following questions.

1. CompuServe expenses its subscriber acquisition costs as incurred; America Online capitalizes these costs and amortizes them over 18 months. Are the concepts of comparability or consistency violated in this situation? Explain.

2. The controller for CompuServe stated, "We consider our earnings strong. We didn't want to taint them or dilute them by following [America Online's] accounting." Explain this statement.

Solution:

1. Comparability results when different companies use the same accounting principles. In this case, comparability does not occur because CompuServe and America Online use different practices to account for subscriber acquisition costs. Consistency means that a company uses the same accounting principles and methods from year to year. Both companies are consistent in that they continue to use the same accounting method from year to year.

2. CompuServe expenses its subscriber acquisition costs as incurred. Its earnings are therefore conservatively reported (often referred to as "high-quality earnings"). That is, earnings may be understated because of the expensing of subscriber acquisition costs.

Summary of Study Objectives

1. *Explain the meaning of generally accepted accounting principles and identify the key items of the conceptual framework.* Generally accepted accounting principles are a set of rules and practices that are recognized as a general guide for financial reporting purposes. Generally accepted means that these principles must have "substantial authoritative support." The key items of the conceptual framework are: (1) objectives of financial reporting; (2) qualitative characteristics of accounting information; (3) elements of financial statements; and (4) operating guidelines (assumptions, principles, and constraints).

2. *Describe the basic objectives of financial reporting.* The basic objectives of financial reporting are to provide information that is (1) useful to those making investment and credit decisions; (2) helpful in assessing future cash flows; and (3) helpful in identifying economic resources (assets), the claims to those resources (liabilities), and the changes in those resources and claims.

3. *Discuss the qualitative characteristics of accounting information and elements of financial statements.* To be judged useful, information should possess the following qualitative characteristics: relevance, reliability, comparability, and consistency. The elements of financial statements are a set of definitions that can be used to describe the basic terms used in accounting.

4. *Identify the basic assumptions used by accountants.* The major assumptions are: monetary unit, economic entity, time period, and going concern.

5. *Identify the basic principles of accounting.* The major principles are revenue recognition, matching, full disclosure, and cost.

6. *Identify the two constraints in accounting.* The major constraints are materiality and conservatism.

7. *Understand and analyze classified financial statements.* We present classified balance sheets and classified income statements in Chapters 4 and 5, respectively. Two new items added to the classified income statement in this chapter are income taxes and earnings per share. Three items used to analyze the balance sheet are the current ratio, working capital, and debt to total assets. Earnings per share, profit margin percentage (return on sales), return on assets, and return on common stockholders' equity are used to analyze profitability.

8. *Explain the accounting principles used in international operations.* There are few recognized worldwide accounting standards. The International Accounting Standards Committee (IASC), of which the United States is a member, is making efforts to obtain conformity in international accounting practices.

GLOSSARY

Comparability Ability to compare accounting information of different companies because they use the same accounting principles. (p. 242).

Conceptual framework A coherent system of interrelated objectives and fundamentals that can lead to consistent standards. (p. 241).

Conservatism The approach of choosing an accounting method when in doubt that will least likely overstate assets and net income. (p. 250).

Consistency Use of the same accounting principles and methods from year to year within a company. (p. 243).

Cost principle Accounting principle that assets should be recorded at their historical cost. (p. 248).

Current ratio A measure that expresses the relationship of current assets to current liabilities by dividing current assets by current liabilities. (p. 255).

Earnings per share (EPS) The net income earned by each share of outstanding common stock. (p. 254).

Economic entity assumption   Accounting assumption that economic events can be identified with a particular unit of accountability. (p. 245).

Elements of financial statements   Definitions of basic terms used in accounting. (p. 243).

Full disclosure principle   Accounting principle that circumstances and events that make a difference to financial statement users should be disclosed. (p. 248).

Generally accepted accounting principles (GAAP)   A set of rules and practices, having substantial authoritative support, that are recognized as a general guide for financial reporting purposes. (p. 240).

Going concern assumption   The assumption that the enterprise will continue in operation long enough to carry out its existing objectives and commitments. (p. 245).

Matching principle   Accounting principle that expenses should be matched with revenues in the period when efforts are expended to generate revenues. (p. 246).

Materiality   The constraint of determining if an item is important enough to likely influence the decision of a reasonably prudent investor or creditor. (p. 249).

Monetary unit assumption   Accounting assumption that only transaction data capable of being expressed in monetary terms should be included in accounting records. (p. 244).

Relevance   The quality of information that indicates the information makes a difference in a decision. (p. 242).

Reliability   The quality of information that gives assurance that it is free of error and bias. (p. 242).

Revenue recognition principle   Accounting principle that revenue should be recognized in the accounting period in which it is earned (generally at the point of sale). (p. 246).

Time period assumption   Accounting assumption that the economic life of a business can be divided into artificial time periods. (p. 245).

DEMONSTRATION PROBLEM I

Presented below are a number of operational guidelines and practices that have developed over time. Identify the accounting assumption, accounting principle, or reporting constraint that most appropriately justifies these procedures and practices. Use only one item per description.

Helpful hint

1. The four principles are cost, revenue recognition, matching, and full disclosure.
2. The two constraints are materiality and conservatism.
3. Full disclosure relates generally to the item; materiality to the amount. The better answer for 6 is full disclosure.
4. Try to find the concept that best describes the situation.

1. The first note, "Summary of Significant Accounting Policies," presents information on the subclassification of plant assets and discusses the company's depreciation methods.

2. The local hamburger restaurant expenses all spatulas, french fry baskets, and other cooking utensils when purchased.

3. Price-level changes are not recognized in the accounting records. (Do not use monetary unit assumption.)

4. Retailers recognize revenue at the point of sale.

5. Green-Grow Lawn Mowers, Inc., includes an estimate of warranty expense in the year in which it sells its lawn mowers, which carry a two-year warranty.

6. Companies present financial information so that creditors and reasonably prudent investors will not be misled.

7. Companies listed on U.S. stock exchanges report audited financial information annually and report unaudited information quarterly.

8. Beach Resorts, Inc., does not record the 1997 value of $1.5 million for a piece of beachfront property it purchased in 1979 for $500,000.

9. Office Systems, Inc., takes a $32,000 loss on a number of older microcomputers in its inventory; it paid the manufacturer $107,000 for them but can only sell them for $75,000.

10. Pizza Hut is a wholly owned subsidiary of PepsiCo, Inc., and Pizza Hut's operating results and financial condition are included in the consolidated financial statements of PepsiCo (do not use full disclosure).

Solution to Demonstration Problem I

1. *Full disclosure principle*

2. *Materiality constraint*

3. *Cost principle*

4. *Revenue recognition principle*

5. *Matching principle*

6. *Full disclosure principle*

7. *Time period assumption*

8. *Cost principle*

9. *Conservatism constraint*

10. *Economic entity assumption*

DEMONSTRATION PROBLEM 2

Presented below is financial information related to José Perez Corporation for the year 1997. All balances are ending balances unless stated otherwise.

Accounts payable	$ 868,000	
Accounts receivable	700,000	
Accumulated depreciation—equipment	100,000	
Administrative expenses	280,000	
Bonds payable	1,600,000	
Cash	800,000	
Common stock	500,000	
Cost of goods sold	1,600,000	
Dividends	60,000	
Equipment	1,100,000	
Income tax expense	83,000	
Interest expense	60,000	
Interest revenue	120,000	
Inventories	500,000	
Loss on the sale of equipment	35,000	
Marketable (trading) securities	400,000	
Net sales	2,400,000	
Notes payable (short-term)	800,000	
Other long-term debt	387,000	
Patents and other intangibles	900,000	
Prepaid expenses	200,000	
Retained earnings (January 1, 1997)	80,000	
Selling expenses	220,000	
Taxes payable	83,000	

José Perez Corporation had 88,000 shares of common stock outstanding for the entire year.

Instructions:

(a) Prepare a multiple-step income statement.

(b) Prepare a single-step income statement.

(c) Prepare a retained earnings statement.

(d) Prepare a classified balance sheet.

(e) Compute the following balance sheet relationships:
  (1) current ratio,
  (2) the amount of working capital, and
  (3) debt to total assets ratio.
  What insights do these relationships provide to the reader of the financial statements?

(f) Compute three measures of profitability from the income statement and balance sheet information. What insights do these relationships provide to the reader of the financial statements?

Helpful hint

1. Review the format in Chapter 5, page 215 for a multiple-step income statement. Note the multiple-step income statement reports gross profit, and income from operations. A single-step income statement does not report these items.

2. Income tax expense is reported immediately after income before income tax for both a multiple-step and single-step income statement.

3. Earnings per share must be reported on both a multiple-step and a single-step income statement.

4. A retained earnings statement reports net income and dividends.

5. Refer to Chapter 4, p. 167 for an example of a classified balance sheet.

Solution to Demonstration Problem 2

(a) Multiple-step income statement

JOSÉ PEREZ CORPORATION
Income Statement
For the Year Ended December 31, 1997

Net sales		$2,400,000
Cost of goods sold		1,600,000
Gross profit		800,000
Selling expenses	$220,000	
Administrative expenses	280,000	500,000
Income from operations		300,000
Other revenues and gains		
Interest revenue		120,000
Other expenses and losses		
Loss on sale of equipment	35,000	
Interest expense	60,000	95,000
Income before income taxes		325,000
Income tax expense		83,000
Net income		$ 242,000
Earnings per share		$2.75

(b) Single-step income statement

JOSÉ PEREZ CORPORATION
Income Statement
For the Year Ended December 31, 1997

Revenues		
Net sales		$2,400,000
Interest revenue		120,000
Total revenues		2,520,000
Expenses		
Cost of goods sold	$1,600,000	
Selling expenses	220,000	
Administrative expenses	280,000	
Interest expense	60,000	
Loss on the sale of equipment	35,000	2,195,000
Income before income taxes		325,000
Income tax expense		83,000
Net income		$ 242,000
Earnings per share		$2.75

(c) Retained earnings statement

JOSÉ PEREZ CORPORATION
Retained Earnings Statement
For the Year Ended December 31, 1997

Retained earnings, January 1	$ 80,000
Add: Net income	242,000
	322,000
Less: Dividends	60,000
Retained earnings, December 31	$262,000

(d) Classified balance sheet

JOSÉ PEREZ CORPORATION
Balance Sheet
December 31, 1997

Current assets		
Cash		$ 800,000
Marketable (trading) securities		400,000
Accounts receivable		700,000
Inventories		500,000
Prepaid Expenses		200,000
		2,600,000
Property, plant, and equipment		
Equipment	$1,100,000	
Less: Accumulated depreciation	100,000	1,000,000
Intangible assets		
Patents and other intangible assets		900,000
Total assets		$4,500,000
Current liabilities		
Notes payable		$ 800,000
Accounts payable		868,000
Taxes payable		83,000
		1,751,000
Long-term liabilities		
Bonds payable	$1,600,000	
Other long-term debt	387,000	1,987,000
Total liabilities		3,738,000
Stockholders' equity		
Common stock		500,000
Retained earnings		262,000
Total liabilities and stockholders' equity		$4,500,000

(e) Balance sheet relationships

(1) Current ratio $= \dfrac{\text{Current assets}}{\text{Current liabilities}} = \dfrac{\$2,600,000}{\$1,751,000} = 1.48 : 1$

(2) Working capital $=$ Current assets $-$ Current liabilities

Current assets	$2,600,000
Current liabilities	1,751,000
Working capital	$ 849,000

(3) Debt to total assets $= \dfrac{\text{Debt}}{\text{Total assets}} = \dfrac{\$3,738,000}{\$4,500,000} = 83.07\%$

Perez's liquidity does not look good. The current ratio is not substantial. Its working capital looks healthy but will not cover the accounts payable due; and its debt to total assets, at well over 80%, is too high. Given the company's relatively low profitability (see below), its creditors should be concerned.

(f) Profitability relationships

$$\dfrac{\text{Net income}}{\text{Net sales}} = \dfrac{\$242,000}{\$2,400,000} = 10.08\%$$

$$\dfrac{\text{Net income}}{\text{Total assets}} = \dfrac{\$242,000}{\$4,500,000} = 5.38\%$$

$$\dfrac{\text{Net income}}{\text{Common stockholders' equity}} = \dfrac{\$242,000}{\$762,000} = 31.76\%$$

The profit margin percentage (return on sales) for Perez seems adequate. Given the company's large asset base, however, it should probably generate a higher profit. The company's overall financial picture, then, could be better.

SELF-STUDY QUESTIONS

Answers are at the end of the chapter.

(SO 1)   1. Generally accepted accounting principles are:
   a. a set of standards and rules that are recognized as a general guide for financial reporting.
   b. usually established by the Internal Revenue Service.
   c. the guidelines used to resolve ethical dilemmas.
   d. fundamental truths that can be derived from the laws of nature.

(SO 2)   2. Which of the following is *not* an objective of financial reporting?
   a. Provide information that is useful in investment and credit decisions.
   b. Provide information about economic resources, claims to those resources, and changes in them.
   c. Provide information that is useful in assessing future cash flows.
   d. Provide information on the liquidation value of a business.

(SO 3)   3. The primary criterion by which accounting information can be judged is:
   a. consistency.
   b. predictive value.
   c. decision-usefulness.
   d. comparability.

(SO 3)   4. Verifiable is an ingredient of:

	Reliability	Relevance
a.	Yes	Yes
b.	No	No
c.	Yes	No
d.	No	Yes

(SO 4, 5, 6)   5. Valuing assets at their liquidation value rather than their cost is *inconsistent* with the:
   a. time period assumption.
   b. matching principle.
   c. going concern assumption.
   d. materiality constraint.

(SO 4)   6. The accounting constraint that refers to the tendency of accountants to resolve uncertainty in favor of understating assets and revenues is known as (the):
   a. matching principle.
   b. materiality.
   c. conservatism.
   d. monetary unit assumption.

(SO 7)   7. Mark Enterprises has current assets of $80,000 and current liabilities of $20,000. It's current ratio and working capital are:
   a. .25:1; $60,000
   b. 4:1; $60,000
   c. .25:1; $80,000
   d. 4:1; $80,000

(SO 7)   8. Hernandez Company has a retained earnings balance of $162,000 at the beginning of the period. At the end of the period, the retained earnings balance was $220,000. Assuming a dividend of $25,000 was declared and paid during the period, the net income for the period was:
   a. $33,000
   b. $58,000
   c. $83,000
   d. $187,000

(SO 7)   9. The basic formula for computing earnings per share is net income divided by:
   a. common shares authorized
   b. common shares issued
   c. common shares outstanding
   d. common stock purchased

(SO 7)   10. Atmel Corp. has total liabilities of $1,400,000, total stockholders' equity of $2,800,000, current assets of $600,000, and current liabilities of $400,000. Atmel's total debt to total assets ratio is:
   a. 50%
   b. 41.2%
   c. 33.3%
   d. 28.6%

QUESTIONS

1. (a) What are generally accepted accounting principles (GAAP)? (b) What bodies provide authoritative support for GAAP?

2. What elements comprise the FASB's conceptual framework?

3. (a) What are the objectives of financial reporting? (b) Identify the qualitative characteristics of accounting information.

4. Ray Aldag, the president of Raynard Company, is pleased. Raynard substantially increased its net income in 1995 while keeping the number of **units** in its inventory relatively the same. Tom Erhardt, chief accountant, cautions Aldag, however. Erhardt says that since Raynard changed its method of inventory **valuation**, there is a consistency problem and it would be difficult to determine if Raynard is better off. Is Erhardt correct? Why?

5. What is the distinction between comparability and consistency?

6. Why is it necessary for accountants to assume that an economic entity will remain a going concern?

7. When should revenue be recognized? Why has the date of sale been chosen as the point at which to recognize the revenue resulting from the entire producing and selling process?

8. Distinguish between expired costs and unexpired costs.

9. (a) Where does the accountant disclose information about an entity's financial position, operations, and cash flows? (b) The full disclosure principle recognizes that the nature and amount of information included in financial reports reflects a series of judgmental trade-offs. What are the objectives of these trade-offs?

10. Sue Leonard is the president of Better Books. She has no accounting background. Leonard cannot understand why current cost is not used as the basis for accounting measurement and reporting. Explain what basis is used and why.

11. Describe the two constraints inherent in the presentation of accounting information.

12. In February 1996, Richard Holland invested an additional $5,000 in his business, Holland's Pharmacy, which is organized as a corporation. Holland's accountant, Donna Havaci, recorded this receipt as an increase in cash and revenues. Is this treatment appropriate? Why or why not?

13. Identify three financial relationships that are useful in analyzing the profitability of a company. Why might we want more than one measure of profitability?

14. Ann Schmitt Company has current assets of $50,000 and current liabilities of $20,000. What is its (a) working capital and (b) current ratio?

15. If current assets are less than current liabilities, will working capital be positive or negative? Will the current ratio be greater than or less than 1:1?

16. Whitehurst Inc.'s debt to total assets stands at 62 percent. If you were a banker, would you be comfortable about extending additional credit to Whitehurst? Why or why not?

17. Your roommate believes that international accounting standards are uniform throughout the world. Is your roommate correct? Explain.

18. What organization establishes international accounting standards?

BRIEF EXERCISES

BE6–1 Indicate whether each of the following statements is true or false.

1. ____ GAAP is a set of rules and practices established by the accounting profession to serve as a general guide for financial reporting purposes.
2. ____ Substantial authoritative support for GAAP usually comes from two standard-setting bodies: the FASB and the IRS.
3. ____ "Generally accepted" means that these principles must have "substantial authoritative support."

Generally accepted accounting principles.
(SO 1)

BE6–2 Indicate which of the following items is(are) included in the FASB's conceptual framework. (Use "Yes" or "No" to answer this question.)

1. ____ Analysis of financial statement ratios.
2. ____ Objectives of financial reporting.
3. ____ Qualitative characteristics of accounting information.

Items included in conceptual framework.
(SO 1)

BE6–3 According to the FASB's conceptual framework, which of the following are objectives of financial reporting? (Use "Yes" or "No" to answer this question.)

1. ____ Provide information that is helpful in assessing past cash flows and stock prices.
2. ____ Provide information that is useful to those making investment and credit decisions.
3. ____ Provide information that identifies the economic resources (assets), the claims to those resources (liabilities), and the changes in those resources and claims.

Objectives of financial reporting.
(SO 2)

BE6–4 Presented below is a chart of the qualitative characteristics of accounting information. Fill in the blanks from (a) to (e).

Qualitative characteristics.
(SO 3)

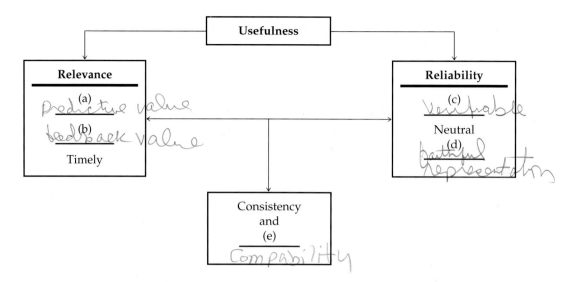

Qualitative characteristics.
(SO 3)

BE6–5　Given the *qualitative characteristics* of accounting established by the FASB's conceptual framework, complete each of the following statements:

1. ____ For information to be ____, it should have predictive or feedback value, and it must be presented on a timely basis.
2. ____ is the quality of information that gives assurance that it is free of error and bias; it can be depended on.
3. ____ means using the same accounting principles and methods from year to year within a company.

Qualitative characteristics.
(SO 3)

BE6–6　Presented below is a set of qualitative characteristics of accounting information.

(a) Predictive value　　　(c) Verifiable
(b) Neutral　　　　　　　(d) Timely

　　Match these qualitative characteristics to the following statements, using letters a through d.

1. ____ Accounting information should help users make predictions about the outcome of past, present, and future events.
2. ____ Accounting information cannot be selected, prepared, or presented to favor one set of interested users over another.
3. ____ Accounting information must be proved to be free of error and bias.
4. ____ Accounting information must be available to decision makers before it loses its capacity to influence their decisions.

Operating guidelines.
(SO 4, 5, 6)

BE6–7　Presented below are four concepts discussed in this chapter.

(a) Time period assumption　　　(c) Full disclosure principle
(b) Cost principle　　　　　　　(d) Conservatism

　　Match these concepts to the following accounting practices. Each letter can be used only once.

1. ____ Recording inventory at its purchase price.
2. ____ Using notes and supplementary schedules in the financial statements.
3. ____ Preparing financial statements on an annual basis.
4. ____ Using the lower of cost or market method for inventory valuation.

Identify the constraints that have been violated.
(SO 6)

BE6–8　The Emelda Company uses the following accounting practices:

1. Inventory is reported at cost when market value is lower.
2. Expenses are overstated in order to avoid reporting a higher net income.
3. Small tools are recorded as plant assets and depreciated.
4. The income statement shows paper clips expense of $10.

Indicate the accounting constraint, if any, that has been violated by each practice.

BE6–9 The following data are taken from the balance sheet of Kellogg Company. The data are arranged in alphabetical order.

Accounts payable	$43,000	Other current liabilities	$12,000
Accounts receivable	68,000	Retained earnings	86,000
Cash	55,000	Wages payable	27,000

Compute Kellogg's (a) current ratio and (b) working capital.

BE6–10 The following information, presented in alphabetical order, is taken from the financial statements of Glassgow Inc.:

Gross profit	$895,000	Other revenues and gains	$ 36,000
Income before income taxes	276,000	Net income	179,400
Income from operations	240,000	Net sales	1,652,000

Compute Glassgow's (a) operating expenses and (b) income tax expense for the period.

BE6–11 Additional information for Glassgow Inc. (BE6-10) is as follows:

Common shares outstanding		Dividends on common stock	
for the entire year	46,000	paid during the year	$34,500

Given the information above and in BE6-10, compute Glassgow's earnings per share.

EXERCISES

E6–1 A number of accounting reporting situations are described below.

1. Tercek Company recognizes revenue at the end of the production cycle, but before sale. The price of the product, as well as the amount that can be sold, is not certain.
2. In preparing its financial statements, Seco Company omitted information concerning its method of accounting for inventories.
3. Jan Way Corp. charges the entire premium on a two-year insurance policy to the first year.
4. Ravine Hospital Supply Corporation reports only current assets and current liabilities on its balance sheet. Property, plant, and equipment and bonds payable are reported as current assets and current liabilities, respectively. Liquidation of the company is unlikely.
5. Barton Inc. is carrying inventory at its current market value of $100,000. Inventory had an original cost of $110,000.
6. Bonilla Company is in its fifth year of operation and has yet to issue financial statements. (Do not use full disclosure principle.)
7. Watts Company has inventory on hand that cost $400,000. Watts reports inventory on its balance sheet at its current market value of $425,000.
8. Steph Wolfson, president of the Classic Music Company, bought a computer for her personal use. She paid for the computer by using company funds and debited the "computers" account.

Instructions
For each of the above, list the assumption, principle, or constraint that has been violated, if any. List only one term for each case.

E6–2 Presented below are some business transactions that occurred during 1996 for Marietta Co.

(a) Merchandise inventory with a cost of $208,000 is reported at its market value of $260,000. The following entry was made:

Merchandise Inventory	52,000	
Gain		52,000

(b) Equipment worth $90,000 was acquired at a cost of $72,000 from a company that had water damage in a flood. The following entry was made:

Equipment	90,000	
Cash		72,000
Gain		18,000

(c) The president of Marietta Corp., George Winston, purchased a truck for personal use and charged it to his expense account. The following entry was made:

Travel Expense	18,000	
Cash		18,000

(d) An electric pencil sharpener costing $50 is being depreciated over 5 years. The following entry was made:

Depreciation Expense—Pencil Sharpener	10	
Accumulated Depreciation—Pencil Sharpener		10

Instructions

In each of the situations above, identify the assumption, principle, or constraint that has been violated, if any, and discuss the appropriateness of the journal entries. Give the correct journal entry, if necessary.

Identify accounting assumptions, principles, and constraints to different situations.
(SO 4, 5, 6)

E6–3 Presented below are the assumptions, principles, and constraints discussed in this chapter:

(a) Economic entity assumption
(b) Going concern assumption
(c) Monetary unit assumption
(d) Time period assumption
(e) Cost principle

(f) Matching principle
(g) Full disclosure principle
(h) Revenue recognition principle
(i) Materiality
(j) Conservatism

Instructions

Identify by letter the accounting assumption, principle, or constraint that describes each situation below. Do not use a letter more than once.

1. Is the rationale for why plant assets are not reported at liquidation value. (Do not use historical cost principle.)
2. Indicates that personal and business record-keeping should be separately maintained.
3. Ensures that all relevant financial information is reported.
4. Assumes that the dollar is the "measuring stick" used to report on financial performance.
5. Requires that the operational guidelines be followed for all significant items.
6. Separates financial information into time periods for reporting purpose.
7. Requires recognition of expenses in the same period as related revenues.
8. Indicates that market value changes subsequent to purchase are not recorded in the accounts.

Determine the amount of revenue to be recognized.
(SO 5)

E6–4 Consider the following transactions of Kokomo Company for 1996.

1. Sold a 6-month insurance policy to Taylor Corporation for $9,000 on March 1.
2. Leased office space to Excel Supplies for a 1-year period beginning September 1. The rent of $36,000 was paid in advance.
3. A sales order for merchandise costing $9,000 that had a sales price of $12,000 was received on December 28 from Warfield Company. The goods were shipped FOB shipping point on December 31 and Warfield received them on January 3, 1997.
4. Merchandise inventory on hand at year-end amounted to $160,000. Kokomo expects to sell the inventory in 1997 for $180,000.

Instructions

For each item above, indicate the amount of revenue Kokomo should recognize in calendar year 1996. Explain.

Compute earnings per share.
(SO 7)

E6–5 The ledger of Geneva Corporation at December 31, 1997 contains the following summary information:

Administrative expenses	$112,000	Other expenses and losses	$34,700
Cost of goods sold	409,200	Other revenues and gains	17,500
Net sales	682,000	Selling expenses	98,600

The income tax rate for all items is 30%. Geneva had 10,000 shares of common stock outstanding throughout the year, and the company paid $15,000 in dividends during 1997.

Instructions
Compute earnings per share for 1997.

E6–6 Presented below, in alphabetical order, is information related to the Pritt Corporation for the year 1997:

Prepare an income statement and calculate related information.
(SO 7)

Ret Eain E Cost of goods sold	$1,499,900
Dividends on common stock	140,000
R Gain on the sale of equipment	110,000
E Income tax expense	150,000
Interest expense	90,000
R Interest revenue	300,000
R Net sales	2,142,800
E Selling and administrative expenses	340,750

Pritt had 35,000 shares outstanding for the entire year.

Instructions
(a) Prepare in good form a single-step income statement for Pritt Corporation for 1997.
(b) Assuming a multiple-step income statement was prepared instead, compute
   (1) gross profit,
   (2) income from operations, and
   (3) net income.
(c) Calculate Pritt Corporation's profit margin percentage (return on sales).

E6–7 Net sales, net income, total assets, and total common stockholders' equity information for fiscal year 1996 is available for the following three companies:

Calculate and analyze profitability and solvency relationships.
(SO 7)

Company	Net Sales (in millions)	Net Income (in millions)	Total Assets (in millions)	Total Common Equity (in millions)
Intel	$ 8,782.0	$2,295.0	$11,344.0	$7,500.0
MCI Communications	11,921.0	582.0	11,276.0	4,713.0
Pacific Gas & Electric	10,582.4	1,065.5	27,165.5	9,254.0

Instructions
(a) Compute the following relationships for each company:
   (1) Debt to total assets ratio
   (2) Return on sales (profit margin percentage)
   (3) Return on assets
   (4) Return on common stockholders' equity
(b) What reasons might there be for the differing relationships among these three companies? In your answer, consider the different kinds of industries these companies represent. Do any similarities or differences in the type of business help account for the differences you see?

E6–8 Net sales, net income, total assets, and total common stockholders' equity information for fiscal year 1996 is available for the following three companies:

Calculate and analyze profitability and solvency relationships.
(SO 7)

Company	Net Sales (in millions)	Net Income (in millions)	Total Assets (in millions)	Total Common Equity (in millions)
Ford Motor Company	$108,521.0	$2,529.0	$198,938.0	$15,574.0
Exxon	97,825.0	5,280.0	84,145.0	34,792.0
Sears Roebuck	54,873.4	2,374.4	90,807.8	11,664.1

Instructions
(a) Compute the following relationships for each company:
   (1) Debt to total assets ratio
   (2) Return on sales (profit margin percentage)
   (3) Return on assets
   (4) Return on common stockholders' equity
(b) What reasons might there be for the differing relationships among these three companies? In your answer, consider the different kinds of industries these companies

represent. Do any similarities or differences in the type of business help account for the differences you see?

Use balance sheet relationships to prepare a balance sheet.
(SO 7)

E6–9 As of December 31, 1996, Yosemite Corporation has a current ratio of 2.6:1 and working capital of $600,000. Yosemite's total debt is 60% of its total assets. All of Yosemite's long-term assets, which are exactly half of total assets, are properly categorized as property, plant, and equipment.

Instructions

Prepare a summary classified balance sheet for Yosemite Corporation at year-end 1996. (*Hint:* First calculate Yosemite's current asset and current liability amounts.)

Restate foreign financial statements.
(SO 8)

E6–10 Presented below, is partial balance sheet information related to Bato Ltd., a United Kingdom company. All financial information has been translated from pounds to dollars.

BATO LTD.
Partial Balance Sheet
December 31, 1996
(in thousands)

Fixed assets		
Tangible assets		$1,200,000
Current assets		
Stocks (inventory)	$300,000	
Debtors	121,000	
Investments	53,000	
Cash	62,000	
	536,000	
Creditors		
Amount falling due within one year	110,000	
Net current assets		426,000
Total assets less current liabilities		1,626,000
Creditors		
Amounts falling due after one year		230,000
Total net assets		$1,396,000

Instructions

(a) Restate the asset side of the balance sheet in accordance with generally accepted accounting principles in the United States.
(b) What is total stockholders' equity?

PROBLEMS

....

Analyze transactions to identify the accounting principle or assumption violated and preparation of correct entries.
(SO 4, 5)

P6–1 Garner and Simon are accountants for Desktop Computers. They are having disagreements concerning the following transactions that occurred during the calendar year 1996.

1. A 1-year insurance policy was purchased by Desktop on September 1, 1996 for $12,000. Garner believes that the following entry should be made on September 1:

Insurance Expense	12,000	
Cash		12,000

2. Desktop purchased equipment for $35,000 at a going-out-of-business sale. The equipment was worth $45,000. Garner believes that the following entry should be made:

Equipment	45,000	
Cash		35,000
Gain		10,000

3. Land costing $60,000 was appraised at $90,000. Garner suggests the following journal entry:

Land	30,000	
Gain on Appreciation of Land		30,000

4. Depreciation for the year was $18,000. Since net income is expected to be lower this year, Garner suggests deferring depreciation to a year when there is more net income.
5. Desktop bought a custom-made piece of equipment for $18,000. This equipment has a useful life of 6 years. Desktop depreciates equipment using the straight-line method. "Since the equipment is custom-made, it will have no resale value and, therefore, shouldn't be depreciated but instead expensed immediately," argues Garner. "Besides, it provides for lower net income."
6. Garner suggests that equipment should be reported on the balance sheet at its liquidation value, which is $15,000 less than its cost.

Simon disagrees with Garner on each of the above situations.

Instructions
For each transaction, indicate why Simon disagrees. Identify the accounting principle or assumption that Garner would be violating if his suggestions were used. Prepare the correct journal entry for each transaction, if any.

P6–2 Presented below are a number of business transactions that occurred during the current year for Hialeah, Inc.

Determine the appropriateness of journal entries in terms of generally accepted accounting principles or assumptions.
(SO 4, 5)

1. Because the general level of prices increased during the current year, Hialeah, Inc. determined that there was a $20,000 understatement of depreciation expense on its equipment and decided to record it in its accounts. The following entry was made:

Depreciation Expense	20,000	
Accumulated Depreciation		20,000

2. Materials were purchased on March 31 for $65,000 and this amount was entered in the Materials account. On December 31, the materials would have cost $85,000, so the following entry was made:

Inventory	20,000	
Gain on Inventories		20,000

3. An order for $30,000 has been received from a customer for products on hand. This order is to be shipped on January 9 next year. The following entry was made:

Accounts Receivable	30,000	
Sales		30,000

4. The president of Hialeah, Inc. used his expense account to purchase a new Saab 9000 solely for personal use. The following entry was made:

Miscellaneous Expense	34,000	
Cash		34,000

5. Because of a "flood sale," equipment obviously worth $230,000 was acquired at a cost of $150,000. The following entry was made:

Equipment	230,000	
Cash		150,000
Gain on Purchase of Equipment		80,000

Instructions
◄▬▬► In each of the situations above, discuss the appropriateness of the journal entries in terms of generally accepted accounting principles.

P6–3 Presented below are the assumptions, principles, and constraints used in this chapter.

Identify accounting assumptions, principles, and constraints.
(SO 4, 5, 6)

(a) Economic entity assumption
(b) Going concern assumption
(c) Monetary unit assumption
(d) Time period assumption
(e) Full disclosure principle
(f) Revenue recognition principle
(g) Matching principle
(h) Cost principle
(i) Materiality
(j) Conservatism

Identify by letter the accounting assumption, principle, or constraint that describes each situation below. Do not use a letter more than once.

1. Repair tools are expensed when purchased. (Do not use conservatism)
2. Allocates expenses to revenues in proper period.

3. Assumes that the dollar is the measuring stick used to report financial information.
4. Separates financial information into time periods for reporting purposes.
5. Market value changes subsequent to purchase are not recorded in the accounts. (Do not use revenue recognition principle.)
6. Indicates that personal and business record keeping should be separately maintained.
7. Ensures that all relevant financial information is reported.
8. Lower of cost or market is used to value inventories.

Prepare a classified balance sheet and analyze financial position.
(SO 7)

P6–4 The adjusted trial balance of Bresnehan Bottle and Glass, Inc., as of June 30, 1997 (its year-end) contains the following information:

Accounts payable	$ 478,000
Accounts receivable	420,000
Accumulated depreciation—Buildings	180,000
Accumulated depreciation—Equipment	577,500
Bonds payable	1,750,000
Buildings—Manufacturing plant and offices	680,000
Cash	79,000
Common stock	500,000
Equipment	1,650,000
Income taxes payable	45,000
Interest payable	70,000
Interest receivable	21,000
Inventories	845,000
Investment in Todd, Inc., bonds (held-to-maturity—long-term)	600,000
Land	200,000
Mortgage payable (on manufacturing plant—long-term)	310,000
Notes payable (short-term)	200,000
Prepaid advertising	9,500
Prepaid insurance	19,000
Retained earnings (June 30, 1997)	447,000
Supplies	34,000

Instructions
(a) Prepare in good form a classified balance sheet for Bresnehan Bottle & Glass.
(b) Calculate the following balance sheet relationships: current ratio, debt-to-total assets ratio, and working capital.
(c) Assume that Bresnehan has come to you, as vice president of Neighborhood National Bank, seeking a $450,000 loan to help defray the costs of upgrading some of its bottling machinery. Would you be willing to approve the loan? Is there any additional information you would like to have before making your decision?

Prepare a multiple-step income statement and analyze profitability.
(SO 7)

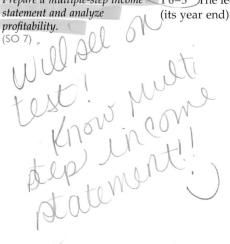

P6–5 The ledgers of Lee's Leathers Inc. contain the following balances as of January 31, 1997 (its year end):

Advertising expense	$ 126,000
Depreciation expense	53,000
Gain on the sale of equipment	8,500
Insurance expense	54,000
Interest expense	13,900
Interest revenue	7,300
Inventory, February 1	296,400
Inventory, January 31	303,400
Managerial salaries	129,800
Miscellaneous administrative expenses	22,200
Miscellaneous selling expenses	39,000
Net Purchases	1,697,000
Net Sales	2,647,000
Rent expense	84,000
Sales staff wages	159,000
Transportation in	27,900

| Transportation out | 6,800 |
| Utilities expense | 30,300 |

Income taxes are calculated at 30 percent of income; Lee's had 84,000 shares of common stock outstanding for the entire year. Total assets amounted to $5,460,000 and common stockholders' equity was $1,966,200 at year end.

Instructions

(a) Prepare in good form a multiple-step income statement for Lee's Leathers Inc.

(b) Calculate three measures of profitability and one ratio of solvency.

(c) Assume that you are considering supplying Lee's Leathers with a line of wallets, key holders, and other small leather goods for sale in its two stores. Is this a company for which you would like to be a supplier? What additional information would you like to have before deciding to become a supplier for Lee's Leathers?

[handwritten notes in right margin:]
N/A
profit margin
6%
rate of return assets
2.91
return on equity
8.08
Debt to total assets
N/A   63.99

ALTERNATE PROBLEMS

••

P6–1A Ava and Brad are accountants for Qwik Printers. They are having disagreements concerning the following transactions that occurred during the year.

Analyze transactions to identify accounting principle or assumption violated and preparation of correct entries.
(SO 4, 5)

1. Qwik bought equipment for $30,000, including installation costs. The equipment has a useful life of 5 years. Qwik depreciates equipment using the straight-line method. "Since the equipment as installed into our system cannot be removed without considerable damage, it will have no resale value, and therefore should not be depreciated but instead expensed immediately," argues Ava. "Besides, it lowers net income."

2. Depreciation for the year was $26,000. Since net income is expected to be lower this year, Ava suggests deferring depreciation to a year when there is more net income.

3. Qwik purchased equipment at a fire sale for $21,000. The equipment was worth $26,000. Ava believes that the following entry should be made:

Equipment	26,000	
Cash		21,000
Gain		5,000

4. Ava suggests that Qwik should carry equipment on the balance sheet at its liquidation value, which is $20,000 less than its cost.

5. Qwik rented office space for 1 year starting October 1, 1995. The total amount of $24,000 was paid in advance. Ava believes that the following entry should be made on October 1:

Rent Expense	24,000	
Cash		24,000

6. Land costing $41,000 was appraised at $49,000. Ava suggests the following journal entry:

Land	8,000	
Gain on Appreciation of Land		8,000

Brad disagrees with Ava on each of the situations above.

Instructions

For each transaction, indicate why Brad disagrees. Identify the accounting principle or assumption that Ava would be violating if her suggestions were used. Prepare the correct journal entry for each transaction, if any.

P6–2A Presented below are a number of business transactions that occurred during the current year for Chita, Inc.

Determine the appropriateness of journal entries in terms of generally accepted accounting principles or assumptions.
(SO 4, 5)

1. An order for $70,000 has been received from a customer for products on hand. This order is to be shipped on January 9 next year. The following entry was made:

Accounts Receivable	70,000	
Sales		70,000

2. Because of a "flood sale," equipment obviously worth $300,000 was acquired at a cost of $250,000. The following entry was made:

Equipment	300,000	
Cash		250,000
Gain on Purchase of Equipment		50,000

3. Because the general level of prices increased during the current year, Chita, Inc. determined that there was a $40,000 understatement of depreciation expense on its equipment and decided to record it in its accounts. The following entry was made:

Depreciation Expense	40,000	
Accumulated Depreciation		40,000

4. The president of Chita, Inc. used his expense account to purchase a pre-owned Mercedes-Benz 190 solely for personal use. The following entry was made:

Miscellaneous Expense	28,000	
Cash		28,000

5. Land was purchased on April 30 for $200,000 and this amount was entered in the Land account. On December 31, the land would have cost $230,000, so the following entry was made:

Land	30,000	
Gain on Land		30,000

Instructions

In each of the situations above, discuss the appropriateness of the journal entries in terms of generally accepted accounting principles.

Identify accounting assumptions, principles, and constraints.
(SO 4, 5, 6)

P6–3A Presented below are the assumptions, principles, and constraints used in this chapter.

(a) Economic entity assumption	(f) Revenue recognition principle
(b) Going concern assumption	(g) Matching principle
(c) Monetary unit assumption	(h) Cost principle
(d) Time period assumption	(i) Materiality
(e) Full disclosure principle	(j) Conservatism

Identify by letter the accounting assumption, principle, or constraint that describes each situation below. Do not use a letter more than once.

1. Assets are not stated at their liquidation value. (Do not use cost principle.)
2. The death of the president is not recorded in the accounts.
3. Pencil sharpeners are expensed when purchased.
4. Depreciation is recorded in the accounts over the life of an asset. (Do not use the going concern assumption.)
5. Each entity is kept as a unit distinct from its owner or owners.
6. Reporting must be done at defined intervals.
7. Revenue is recorded at the point of sale.
8. When in doubt, it is better to understate rather than overstate net income.
9. All important information related to inventories is presented in the footnotes or in the financial statements.

Prepare a classified balance sheet and analyze financial position.
(SO 7)

P6–4A The adjusted trial balance of North Shore Outfitters Inc., as of October 31, 1997 (its year-end) contains the following information:

Accounts payable	$162,000
Accounts receivable	15,000
Accumulated depreciation—Buildings	144,000
Accumulated depreciation—Equipment	715,000
Bonds payable	600,000
Buildings—Offices and cabins	660,000
Cash	36,000
Common stock	300,000
Equipment	840,000
Income taxes payable	56,250
Interest payable	30,000

Inventories	480,000
Investment in the Superior Trading Post, Inc. (trading—short-term)	140,000
Land	650,000
Mortgage payable (on fishing cabins—long-term)	247,750
Notes payable (short-term)	160,000
Prepaid advertising	17,000
Prepaid insurance	9,000
Retained earnings (October 31, 1997)	444,000
Supplies	12,000

Instructions

(a) Prepare in good form a classified balance sheet for North Shore Outfitters.

(b) Calculate the following balance sheet relationships: current ratio, debt-to-total assets ratio, and working capital.

(c) Assume that North Shore Outfitters has come to you, as the senior loan officer of Lake Shore Credit Union, seeking a $500,000 loan to help defray the costs of replacing much of its rental camping gear and canoes. Would you be willing to approve the loan? Is there any additional information you would like to have before making your decision?

P6–5A The ledgers of Inigo Jones Galleries Inc. contain the following balances as of December 31, 1997:

Prepare a multiple-step income statement and analyze profitability
(SO 7)

Advertising expense	$ 126,000
Commissions expense on art sales	1,200,000
Depreciation expense	98,000
Dividend revenue	44,000
Insurance expense	600,000
Interest expense	98,000
Inventory, January 1	1,650,000
Inventory, December 31	1,424,000
Loss on the sale of office equipment	23,300
Miscellaneous administrative expenses	53,200
Miscellaneous selling expenses	39,000
Net Purchases	3,500,000
Net Sales	9,675,000
Rent expense	805,000
Transportation in	232,000
Transportation out	82,500
Utilities expense	117,000
Wages and salaries	1,264,000

Income taxes are calculated at 30 percent of income; the galleries had 90,000 shares of common stock outstanding for the entire year. Total assets amounted to $7,509,000 and common stockholders' equity was $3,975,400.

Instructions

(a) Prepare in good form a multistep income statement for Inigo Jones Galleries.

(b) Calculate three measures of profitability and one ratio of solvency.

(c) Assume that you are considering supplying Inigo Jones Galleries with a line of miniature replicas of fine arts sculptures for sale in its gift shops. Is this a company for which you would like to be a supplier? What additional information would you like to have before deciding to become a major supplier for Inigo Jones Galleries?

COMPREHENSIVE PROBLEM

Presented below is financial information related to Do-Re-Mi Corporation for the year 1997. Unless otherwise stated, all balances are ending balances.

Accounts payable	$ 874,200
Accounts receivable	1,000,800
Accumulated depreciation—equipment	1,560,000
Administrative expenses	420,000
Bonds payable	3,400,000
Cash	125,000
Common stock	2,200,000
Cost of goods sold	2,285,000
Dividends	290,000
Equipment	5,894,000
Gain on the sale of land	87,000
Interest expense	108,000
Interest revenue	94,000
Inventories	984,000
Marketable securities (short-term)	1,175,000
Net sales	3,670,000
Notes payable (short-term)	1,136,500
Other long-term debt	401,300
Patents and other intangibles	1,250,100
Prepaid expenses	356,100
Retained earnings (January 1, 1997)	833,000
Selling expenses	368,000

Do-Re-Mi Corporation had 88,000 shares of common stock outstanding for the entire year. Its effective income tax rate for state and federal income taxes combined is 35 percent.

Instructions:
(a) Prepare a multiple-step income statement
(b) Prepare a single-step income statement
(c) Prepare a retained earnings statement
(d) Prepare a classified balance sheet
(e) Compute the following balance sheet relationships:
  (1) current ratio,
  (2) the amount of working capital, and
  (3) debt-to-total-assets ratio.
  What insights do these relationships provide to the reader of the financial statements?
(f) Compute three measures of profitability. What insights do these relationships provide to the reader of the financial statements?
(g) Compare the results for Do-Re-Mi, calculated here, and the results for Perez in the demonstration problem. As an investor, which corporation seems more attractive to you? Why?

▶*B*roadening Your Perspective

*F*INANCIAL REPORTING PROBLEM

••

Sue Federco has successfully completed her first accounting course during the spring semester and is now working as a management trainee for First Arizona Bank during the summer. One of her fellow management trainees, Bill Harlow, is taking the same accounting course this summer and has been having a "lot of trouble." On the second examination, for example, Bill became confused about inventory valuation methods and completely missed all the points on a problem involving LIFO and FIFO.

Bill's instructor recently indicated that the third examination will probably have a number of essay questions dealing with accounting principle issues. Bill is quite concerned about the third examination for two reasons. First, he has never taken an accounting examination where essay answers were required. Second, Bill feels he has to do well on this examination to get an acceptable grade in the course.

Bill has therefore asked Sue to help him prepare for the next examination. Sue agrees, and suggests that Bill develop a set of possible questions on the accounting principles material that they might discuss.

Instructions
Answer the following questions that were developed by Bill.

(a) What is a conceptual framework?
(b) Why is there a need for a conceptual framework?
(c) What are the objectives of financial reporting?
(d) If you had to explain generally accepted accounting principles to a nonaccountant, what essential characteristics would you include in your explanation?
(e) What are the qualitative characteristics of accounting? Explain each one.
(f) Identify the basic assumptions used in accounting.
(g) What are two major constraints involved in financial reporting? Explain both of them.

COMPARATIVE ANALYSIS PROBLEM— THE COCA-COLA COMPANY VS. PEPSICO, INC.

The financial statements of the Coca-Cola Company are presented at the end of Chapter 1, and PepsiCo's financial statements are presented in Appendix A.

Instructions:
(a) Based on the information contained in these financial statements, compute the following 1995 ratios for each company:

1. Current ratio	4. Return on assets
2. Working capital	5. Return on common stockholders' equity
3. Profit margin percentage	6. Debt to total assets ratio

(b) Compare the liquidity, profitability, and solvency of the two companies.

INTERPRETATION OF FINANCIAL STATEMENTS

Mini-Case One—The North Face, Inc.
The North Face, Inc. is a leader in high-quality technical outerwear, mountaineering equipment, skiwear, and sports apparel. Its products are sold through independent retailers, as well as eleven of its own retail outlets. Recently the company issued shares to the public. While these shares may represent a good investment, potential investors should be aware that, in the company's own words "in the late 1980s, the Company's financial performance deteriorated for a variety of reasons." In fact, in 1993, the parent company that used to own The North Face filed for bankruptcy protection (although The North Face did not). In deciding whether it would be wise to invest or loan money to The North Face, one would want to investigate some relationships in the following summarized financial statement information:

(all dollars in thousands) Current Assets	1994	1995
Cash and cash equivalents	$ 826	$ 2,823
Accounts receivable, net	13,486	16,582
Inventories	12,068	21,048
Other current assets	2,883	3,391
Total current assets	$29,263	$43,844
Total assets	$66,549	$84,508
Current liabilities	$15,074	$21,176
Total liabilities	$49,370	$63,940

Instructions:

(a) Evaluate the liquidity of The North Face, Inc. for 1994 and 1995 using the current ratio and working capital. Discuss whether the company's liquidity appears to be improving. Comment on any concerns you might have in relying on these measures.

(b) Evaluate the solvency of The North Face, Inc. using the ratio of debt to assets.

Mini-Case Two—RJR Nabisco and Phillip Morris

The results of RJR Nabisco and Phillip Morris Companies, Inc. are frequently compared since the two are fierce competitors in the world of cigarettes. RJR Nabisco makes Winston, Camel, and Salem cigarettes, while Phillip Morris makes Marlboro and L&M cigarettes. Both companies also have significant operations in other product lines—RJR Nabisco makes Oreo cookies, Ritz crackers, and Planters nuts, while Phillip Morris makes Post cereals, Maxwell House coffee, and Miller beer. The following information is provided in order to compare the profitability of these two companies in 1995.

(all dollars in millions)	RJR Nabisco	Phillip Morris
Net sales	$16,008	$66,071
Net income	611	5,450
Total assets	31,508	53,811
Common stockholders' equity	12,153	13,985

Instructions:

(a) Compare the profitability of these two companies using each of the following measures. In each case describe what the ratio is intended to measure.
1. Profit margin percentage.
2. Return on assets.
3. Return on common stockholders' equity.

(b) Comment on any problems or challenges incurred by comparing the two companies in this fashion.

DECISION CASE
• •

Presented below are key figures and relationships from the financial statements of a prominent company in each of three different industries for two recent fiscal years:*

	Manufacturing (3M)		Mining/Oil (Chevron)		Merchandising (Dayton Hudson)	
	19X0	19X1	19X0	19X1	19X0	19X1
From the Balance Sheets:						
Total Assets (millions)	$11,079	$11,083	$33,884	$35,089	$ 8,524	$ 9,485
Current Ratio	1.72	1.73	1.14	1.12	1.51	1.56
Working Capital (millions)	$ 2,390	$ 2,349	$ 1,037	$ 1,072	$ 1,236	$ 1,452
Debt-to-Total-Assets Ratio	0.45	0.43	0.59	0.58	0.72	0.72
Profitability:						
Total Sales (millions)	$13,021	$13,340	$31,916	$41,540	$14,739	$16,115
Profit Margin Percentage	10.0%	8.7%	0.8%	5.2%	2.8%	1.9%
Return on Assets	11.8%	10.4%	0.7%	6.1%	4.8%	3.2%
Return on Common Equity	21.4%	18.3%	1.8%	15.0%	20.1%	13.5%
Earnings per Common Share	$5.91	$5.26	$0.73	$6.10	$5.20	$3.72
From the annual reports:						
End-of-year Stock Price	$67.75	$72.63	$85.75	$95.25	$56.50	$62.00

*Numbers in the table adapted from the annual reports of 3M, Chevron, and Dayton-Hudson.

Instructions:

(a) The benchmark for the current ratio is generally 2:1. None of these companies has a ratio that high, yet all three are well regarded firms. Why might a current ratio less than 2:1 NOT signal a problem?

(b) Dayton Hudson acquired the Marshall Field department stores just prior to 19X0. Apart from such major acquisitions, what else might contribute to differing debt-to-total-asset ratios? Consider industry-specific as well as company-specific considerations.

(c) For all three companies, the ratio of debt to total assets changed little from 19X0 to 19X1 yet for two of the three companies return on common stockholders' equity decreased. What might cause this pattern?

(d) The profitability relationships and earnings per share for both 3M and Dayton Hudson decreased from 19X0 to 19X1, yet the price per share of stock for each company increased. Why might investors be willing to pay more for 3M and Dayton Hudson in 19X1?

COMMUNICATION ACTIVITY

If you go on to advanced accounting courses, you'll study the differences between accounting in the business world and university accounting. You'll find that there's one major similarity: both depend heavily on the matching principle.

At Long Beach City College, a two-year community college with 30,000 students, most of the revenues come from the state of California and the federal government. As a condition of receiving these grants, "we must match expenses against revenues in the right fiscal year," says Catalina Cruz, accounting manager.

For example, the college receives federal funding under the Job Training Partnership Act. "We receive funding from the federal government, which allows us to offer classes to students for job preparation. The government specifies the grant periods, for instance, from July 1 to June 30. We therefore have to ensure that all transactions for that project are completed within that fiscal year." Another project is the amnesty program, the federal government's legalization of foreign nationals. Expenses to offset the grant money are mostly teaching salaries and instructional materials.

By year-end, the goal is to break even. Excess funds, if any, have to be returned. But program managers do not want a deficit, either, because these projects are accountable to the college administration and any overspending will come from the college's general fund.

Instructions
Write a letter to your instructor covering the following points:

1. Why is the matching principle important in accounting for government grants?
2. Give some examples of grant or special programs to which the matching principle might be applied at your college or university.
3. What are some examples of costs that Long Beach Community College might properly charge to its grant or special programs?

GROUP ACTIVITY

Assume that the FASB has decided to address the problem of information overload. It has agreed to eliminate one of the principles, assumptions, constraints, or qualitative characteristics listed below. This concept will be deleted from all textbooks and will no longer be considered important in accounting literature.

Instructions
With the class divided into groups, each group will be assigned one or more of the following:

Relevance	Revenue recognition
Reliability	Matching
Comparability and consistency	Full disclosure
Economic entity	Cost
Monetary unit	Materiality
Time period	Conservatism

(a) Discuss within your group why your specific concept(s) should *not* be eliminated.
(b) Pick a group leader who will present to the class the group's reasons why the FASB should not delete the group's concept(s).
(c) At the end of all presentations, the class should vote on which concept to delete.

ETHICS CASE

When the Financial Accounting Standards Board issues new standards, the required implementation date is usually 12 months or more from the date of issuance, with early implementation encouraged. Kathy Johnston, accountant at Redondo Corporation, discusses with her financial vice-president the need for early implementation of a recently issued standard that would result in a much fairer presentation of the company's financial condition and earnings. When the financial vice-president determines that early implementation of the standard will adversely affect reported net income for the year, he strongly discourages Kathy from implementing the standard until it is required.

Instructions
(a) Who are the stakeholders in this situation?
(b) What, if any, are the ethical considerations in this situation?
(c) What does Kathy have to gain by advocating early implementation? Who might be affected by the decision against early implementation?

RESEARCH ASSIGNMENT

During the years 1978–85, the Financial Accounting Standards Board (FASB) issued six *Statements of Financial Accounting Concepts* (SFACs). From the library, obtain copies of SFAC No. 2 (*Qualitative Characteristics of Accounting Information*) and SFAC No. 3 (*Elements of Financial Statements of Business Enterprises*) and use them to answer the following questions.

(a) Your textbook indicates that "an item is material when it is likely to influence the decision of a reasonably prudent investor or creditor." SFAC No. 2 identifies a number of examples in which specific quantitative guidelines are provided to accountants and auditors. Identify two of these examples. Do you think that materiality guidelines should be quantified? Why or why not?
(b) SFAC No. 3 discusses the concept of "articulation" between financial statement elements. Briefly summarize the meaning of this term and how it relates to an entity's financial statements.

CRITICAL THINKING
▸ *A Real-World Focus: Weyerhaeuser Company*

Weyerhaeuser Company is one of the world's largest growers and producers of forest and lumber products. It has assets of $14 billion and annual sales of over $12 billion. Weyerhaeuser employs over 38,000 workers and has as its most significant assets its many acres of prime timberland.

Presented below is a statement that appeared about Weyerhaeuser Company in a financial magazine.

> The land and timber holdings are now carried on the company's books at a mere $422 million. The value of the timber alone is variously estimated at $3 billion to $7 billion and is rising all the time. "The understatement of the company is pretty severe," conceded Charles W. Bingham, a senior vice-president. Adds Robert L. Schuyler, another senior vice-president: "We have a whole stream of profit nobody sees and there is no way to show it on our books."

Instructions
   (a) What does Schuyler mean when he says that "we have a whole stream of profit nobody sees and there is no way to show it on our books"?
   (b) If the understatement of the company's assets is severe, why does accounting not report this information?

————————

Answers to Self-Study Questions
1. a   2. d   3. c   4. c   5. c   6. c   7. b   8. c   9. c   10. c

Before studying this chapter, you should know or, if necessary, review:

a. *How cash transactions are recorded.*
(Ch. 2, pp. 58–59, 65–69,)
b. *How cash is classified on a balance sheet.*
(Ch. 4, p. 163–65)
c. *The role ethics plays in proper financial reporting.*
(Ch. 1, p. 8–9)

No Free Lunch

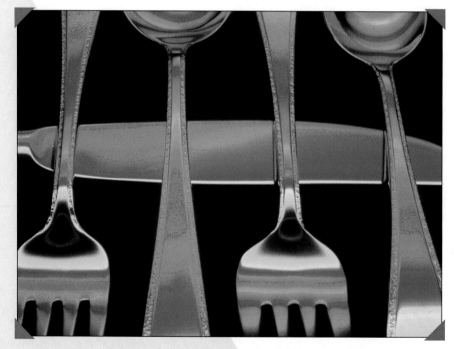

NEW YORK, NY — At Columbia University, thousands of dollars in cash changes hands between students and dining facility cashiers. Making sure that all of the money received by cashiers gets to where it's supposed to go requires various control measures. In accounting, these measures are called internal control.

One control measure used in the cafeteria at Columbia is that the register tape that records the sale and the amount of cash received must reconcile with the amount of cash in the cash drawer at the end of the day. "We see if there are significant overages or shortages at the end of each day for each register," says Susan McLaughlin, director of Columbia's dining facilities. Do cash differences happen very often? "No, because the cashier knows that if there are repeated or significant shortages, disciplinary action will be taken," she says. "There should not be a variance of more than $5, either over or under, at any given time—or else it indicates poor cash handling."

If a student buying a meal at a register sees that a sale isn't rung up or if the student doesn't get a receipt, there is a possibility that the cashier is stealing. "We know that taking the receipt is an annoyance," says Ms. McLaughlin, "but issuing receipts is an absolutely mandatory control for us." ◀

CHAPTER 7

INTERNAL CONTROL AND CASH

▶ STUDY OBJECTIVES ◀

After studying this chapter, you should be able to:

1. *Define internal control.*
2. *Identify the principles of internal control.*
3. *Explain the applications of internal control principles to cash receipts.*
4. *Describe the applications of internal control principles to cash disbursements.*
5. *Explain the operation of a petty cash fund.*
6. *Indicate the control features of a bank account.*
7. *Prepare a bank reconciliation.*
8. *Explain the reporting of cash.*

As the story about the dining facilities at Columbia University indicates, control of cash is important. Similarly, controls are needed to safeguard other types of assets. For example, Columbia University undoubtedly has controls to prevent the theft of food served in the cafeteria and controls to prevent the theft of computer equipment and supplies from its computer laboratories.

In this chapter, we explain the essential features of an internal control system and then describe how those controls apply to cash. The applications include some controls with which you may be already familiar. Toward the end of the chapter, we describe the use of a bank and explain how cash is reported on the balance sheet. The organization and content of Chapter 7 are as follows:

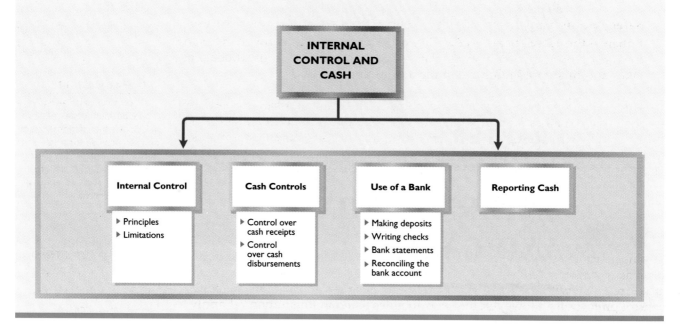

Internal Control

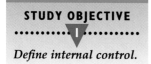

STUDY OBJECTIVE
········ **1** ··········

Define internal control.

Could there be dishonest employees in the business that you own or manage? Unfortunately, the answer sometimes is Yes. For example, the financial press recently reported the following:

A bookkeeper in a small company diverted $750,000 of bill payments to a personal bank account over a 3-year period.

A shipping clerk with 28 years of service shipped $125,000 of merchandise to himself.

A computer operator embezzled $21 million from Wells Fargo Bank over a 2-year period.

A church treasurer "borrowed" $150,000 of church funds to finance a friend's business dealings.

These situations emphasize the need for a good system of internal control.

►*Technology in Action*

Good internal control must be designed into computerized systems. The starting point is usually flow charts that graphically depict each component of a firm's operations. The assembled flow charts serve as the basis for writing detailed programs. An example of flow charting is given in this chapter. When attempts to automate or improve accounting systems fail, it is often due to the absence of such well-documented procedures.

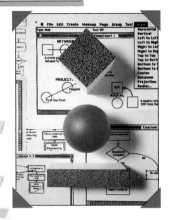

Internal control consists of the plan of organization and all the related methods and measures adopted within a business to:

1. **Safeguard its assets** from employee theft, robbery, and unauthorized use.
2. **Enhance the accuracy and reliability of its accounting records** by reducing the risk of errors (unintentional mistakes) and irregularities (intentional mistakes and misrepresentations) in the accounting process.

Under the Foreign Corrupt Practices Act of 1977, all major U.S. corporations are required to maintain an adequate system of internal control. Companies that fail to comply are subject to fines, and company officers may be imprisoned. Also, the National Commission on Fraudulent Financial Reporting concluded that all companies whose stock is publicly traded should maintain internal controls that can provide reasonable assurance that fraudulent financial reporting will be prevented or subject to early detection.[1]

► *International note*

U.S. companies also adopt model business codes that guide their international operations to provide for a safe and healthy workplace, avoid child and forced labor, abstain from bribes, and follow sound environmental practices.

Principles of Internal Control

To safeguard its assets and enhance the accuracy and reliability of its accounting records, a company follows specific control principles. Of course, internal control measures vary with the size and nature of the business and with management's control philosophy. However, the six principles listed in Illustration 7-1 apply to most enterprises:

STUDY OBJECTIVE
·········· **2** ··········

Identify the principles of internal control.

Illustration 7-1

Principles of internal control

► *Ethics note*

Fundamental to internal control systems is the assumption that employees are honest and ethical and will not commit wrongdoing. As a result, most control measures are more effective in preventing and detecting errors than irregularities.

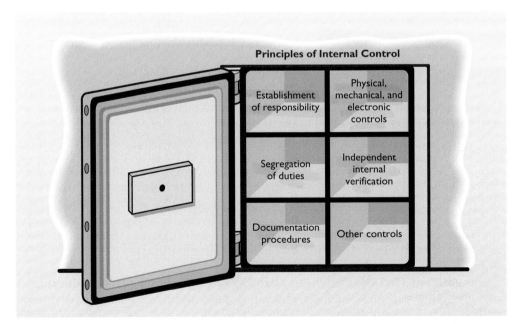

Principles of Internal Control

Establishment of responsibility	Physical, mechanical, and electronic controls
Segregation of duties	Independent internal verification
Documentation procedures	Other controls

---

[1]*Report of the National Commission on Fraudulent Financial Reporting*, October 1987, p. 11.

Each principle is explained in the following sections.

Establishment of Responsibility

Helpful hint You may have noticed in a supermarket that when a cashier comes on duty, the tray is inserted in the register. At the end of the shift, the tray is removed and the cash is counted by a supervisor. The cash count is compared to the cash register total.

An essential characteristic of internal control is the assignment of responsibility to specific individuals. **Control is most effective when only one person is responsible for a given task.** To illustrate, assume that the cash on hand at the end of the day in a Safeway supermarket is $10 short of the cash rung up on the cash register. If only one person has operated the register, responsibility for the shortage can be assessed quickly. However, if two or more individuals have worked the register, it may be impossible to determine who is responsible for the error unless each person is assigned a separate cash drawer and register key. The principle of establishing responsibility was followed by Columbia University's dining services (in the opening story) by assigning a cashier to a cash register and keeping each cashier's cash drawer separate from others.

Establishing responsibility includes the authorization and approval of transactions. For example, the vice-president of sales should have the authority to establish policies for making credit sales. The policies ordinarily will require written credit department approval of credit sales.

Segregation of Duties

Helpful hint Without good internal control, companies are asking for trouble. To some extent the victims have themselves to blame. A company with shoddy internal controls or badly trained internal auditors practically begs employees to steal.

This principle (also identified as separation of functions or division of work) is indispensable in a system of internal control. There are two common applications of this principle:

1. The responsibility for related activities should be assigned to different individuals.
2. The responsibility for establishing the accountability (keeping the records) for an asset should be separate from the physical custody of that asset.

The rationale for segregation of duties is that the work of one employee should, without a duplication of effort, provide a reliable basis for evaluating the work of another employee.

Related Activities. Related activities that should be assigned to different individuals arise in both the purchasing and selling areas. **When one individual is responsible for all of the related activities, the potential for errors and irregularities is increased.** Related purchasing activities include ordering the merchandise, receiving the goods, and paying (or authorizing payment) for the merchandise. In purchasing, for example, orders could be placed with friends or with suppliers who give kickbacks. Similarly, only a cursory count and inspection could be made upon receiving the goods, which could lead to errors and poor quality merchandise. In addition, payment might be authorized without a careful review of the invoice, or even worse, fictitious invoices might be approved for payment. When the responsibility for ordering, receiving, and paying are assigned to different individuals or departments, the risk of such abuses is minimized.

Similarly, related sales activities should be assigned to different individuals. Related selling activities include making a sale, shipping (or delivering) the goods to the customer, and billing the customer. When one person is responsible for related sales transactions, a salesperson could make sales at unauthorized prices to increase sales commissions; a shipping clerk could ship goods to himself, as indicated at the beginning of the chapter; a billing clerk could understate

►**A**ccounting in **A**ction ▸ *Ethics Insight*

A former electronic data processing employee of Texaco, Inc., and his wife were indicted for stealing thousands of dollars from the company in an accounts payable-type fraud. The employee instructed Texaco's computer to pay his wife rent for land she allegedly leased to Texaco by assigning her an alphanumeric code as a lessor and then ordering that payments be made. The lesson here is simple: "*never* allow the same person to both authorize and pay for goods and services." Doing otherwise violates the segregation-of-duties principle of internal control.

the amount billed for sales made to friends and relatives. These abuses are reduced when salespersons make the sale, shipping department employees ship the goods on the basis of the sales order, and billing department employees prepare the sales invoice after comparing the sales order with the report of goods shipped.

Accountability for Assets. If accounting is to provide a valid basis of accountability for an asset, the accountant should have neither physical custody of the asset nor access to it. Moreover, the custodian of the asset should not maintain or have access to the accounting records. When one employee maintains the record of the asset that should be on hand, and a different employee has physical custody of the asset, the custodian of the asset is not likely to convert the asset to personal use. The separation of accounting responsibility from the custody of assets is especially important for cash and inventories because these assets are very vulnerable to unauthorized use or misappropriation.

Documentation Procedures

Documents provide evidence that transactions and events have occurred. In the Columbia University cafeteria, the cash register tape was the university's documentation for the sale and the amount of cash received. Similarly, the shipping document indicates that the goods have been shipped, and the sales invoice indicates that the customer has been billed for the goods. By adding signatures (or initials) to the documents, the individual(s) responsible for the transaction or event can be identified. Documentation of transactions should be made when the transaction occurs. Documentation of events, such as those leading to adjusting entries, is generally developed when the adjustments are made.

Several procedures should be established for documents. First, whenever possible, **documents should be prenumbered and all documents should be accounted for.** Prenumbering helps to prevent a transaction from being recorded more than once, or conversely, to prevent the transactions from not being recorded. Second, documents that are **source documents for accounting entries should be promptly forwarded to the accounting department to help ensure timely recording of the transaction and event**. Thus, this control measure contributes directly to the accuracy and reliability of the accounting records.

Helpful hint An important corollary to prenumbering is that voided documents be kept until all documents are accounted for.

Physical, Mechanical, and Electronic Controls

Use of physical, mechanical, and electronic controls is essential. Physical controls relate primarily to the safeguarding of assets. Mechanical and electronic controls safeguard assets and enhance the accuracy and reliability of the accounting records. Examples of these controls are shown in Illustration 7-2.

Helpful hint At the gas pumps, the customer is part of the control by watching the amount registered on the pump. The locked-in total prevents the attendant/cashier from covering up a shortage by altering the tape.

Illustration 7-2

Physical, mechanical, and electronic controls

Physical Controls

Safes, vaults, and safety deposit boxes for cash and business papers

Locked warehouses and storage cabinets for inventories and records

Computer facilities with pass key access

Mechanical and Electronic Controls

Alarms to prevent break-ins

Television monitors and garment sensors to deter theft

Time clocks for recording time worked

Independent Internal Verification

Helpful hint This principle is also called independent check.

Most systems of internal control provide for independent internal verification. This principle involves the review, comparison, and reconciliation of data prepared by one or several employees. To obtain maximum benefit from independent internal verification:

1. The verification should be made periodically or on a surprise basis.
2. The verification should be done by an employee who is independent of the personnel responsible for the information.
3. Discrepancies and exceptions should be reported to a management level that can take appropriate corrective action.

▶ Accounting in Action ▸ *Business Insight*

John Patterson, a young Ohio merchant, couldn't understand why his retail business didn't show a profit. There were lots of customers, but the money just seemed to disappear.

Patterson suspected pilferage and sloppy bookkeeping by store clerks. Frustrated, he placed an order with a Dayton, Ohio, company for two rudimentary cash registers. A year later, Patterson's store was in the black.

"What is a good thing for this little store is a good thing for every retail store in the world," he observed. A few months later, in 1884, John Patterson and his brother, Frank, bought the tiny cash register maker for $6,500. The word around Dayton was that the Patterson boys got stung.

In the following 37 years, John Patterson built National Cash Register Co. into a corporate giant. Patterson died in 1922, the year in which NCR sold its two millionth cash register.

Source: Wall Street Journal. January 28, 1989.

Independent internal verification is especially useful in comparing recorded accountability with existing assets. The reconciliation of the cash register tape with the cash in the register in the Columbia University dining facility is an example of this internal control principle. Another common example is the reconciliation by an independent person of the cash balance per books with the cash balance per bank. The relationship between this principle and the segregation of duties principle is shown graphically in Illustration 7-3.

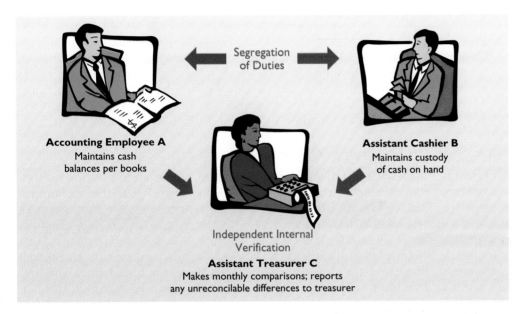

Illustration 7-3

Comparison of segregation of duties principle with independent internal verification principle

In large companies, independent internal verification is often assigned to internal auditors. Internal auditors are employees of the company who evaluate on a continuous basis the effectiveness of the company's system of internal control. They periodically review the activities of departments and individuals to determine whether prescribed internal controls are being followed and to make recommendations for improvement. The importance of this function is illustrated by the number of internal auditors employed by companies. In a recent year, AT&T had 350 internal auditors, Exxon had 395, and IBM had 142.

Helpful hint Internal auditing is a professional activity within a company, often with direct access to the board of directors.

►*T*echnology in *A*ction

Program controls are controls built into the computer to prevent intentional or unintentional errors or unauthorized access. To prevent unauthorized access, the computer system may require that passwords be entered and random personal questions be correctly answered before system access is allowed. Once access has been allowed, other program controls identify data having a value higher or lower than a predetermined amount (limit checks), validate computations (math checks), and detect improper processing order (sequence checks).

A crucial consideration in programming computerized systems is building in controls that limit unauthorized or unintentional tampering. Entire books and movies have been produced with computer system tampering as a major theme. Most programmers would agree that tamper proofing and debugging programs are the most difficult and time-consuming phases of their jobs.

Other Controls

Other control measures include the following:

1. **Bonding of employees who handle cash.** Bonding involves obtaining insurance protection against misappropriation of assets by dishonest employees. This measure contributes to the safeguarding of cash in two ways: First, the insurance company carefully screens all individuals before adding them to the policy and may reject risky applicants. Second, bonded employees know that the insurance company will vigorously prosecute all offenders.

2. **Rotating employees' duties and requiring employees to take vacations.** These measures are designed to deter employees from attempting any thefts since they will not be able to permanently conceal their improper actions. Many bank embezzlements, for example, have been discovered when the perpetrator has been on vacation or assigned to a new position.

Limitations of Internal Control

A company's system of internal control is generally designed to provide reasonable assurance that assets are properly safeguarded and that the accounting records are reliable. **The concept of reasonable assurance rests on the premise that the costs of establishing control procedures should not exceed their expected benefit.** To illustrate, consider shoplifting losses in retail stores. Such losses could be completely eliminated by having a security guard stop and search customers as they leave the store. Store managers have concluded, however, that the negative effects of adopting such a procedure cannot be justified. Instead, stores have attempted to "control" shoplifting losses by less costly procedures such as: (1) posting signs saying, "We reserve the right to inspect all packages," and "All shoplifters will be prosecuted," (2) using hidden TV cameras and store detectives to monitor customer activity, and (3) using sensoring equipment at exits.

The **human element** is also an important factor in every system of internal control. A good system can become ineffective as a result of employee fatigue, carelessness, or indifference. For example, a receiving clerk may not bother to count goods received or may just "fudge" the counts. Occasionally, two or more individuals may work together to get around prescribed controls. Such **collusion** can significantly impair the effectiveness of a system, because it eliminates the protection anticipated from segregation of duties. If a supervisor and a cashier collaborate to understate cash receipts, the system of internal control may be negated (at least in the short run). No system of internal control is perfect.

The size of the business may impose limitations on internal control. In a small company, for example, it may be difficult to apply the principles of segregation of duties and independent internal verification.

▸**T**echnology in **A**ction

 Unfortunately, computer-related frauds have become a major concern. On the basis of known cases, the average computer fraud loss is $650,000, compared with an average loss of only $19,000 resulting from other types of white-collar crime.

Computer fraud can be perpetrated almost invisibly and done with electronic speed. Psychologically, stealing with impersonal computer tools can seem far less criminal. Therefore, the moral threshold to commit computer fraud is far lower than in fraud involving person-to-person contact.

Preventing and detecting computer fraud represents a major challenge. One of the best ways for a company to minimize the likelihood of computer fraud is to have a good system of internal control that allows the benefits of computerization to be gained without opening the possibility for rampant fraud.

Before You Go On . . .

► Review It

1. What are the two primary objectives of internal control?
2. Identify and describe the principles of internal control.
3. What are the limitations of internal control?

► Do It

Li Song owns a small retail store. Li wants to establish good internal control procedures but is confused about the difference between segregation of duties and independent internal verification. Explain the differences to Li.

Reasoning: In order to help Li, you need to thoroughly understand each principle. From this knowledge, and a study of Illustration 7-3, it should be possible to explain the differences between the two principles.

Solution: Segregation of duties pertains to the assignment of responsibility so that the work of one employee will permit the evaluation of the work of another employee. Segregation of duties occurs daily in executing and recording transactions. In contrast, independent internal verification involves reviewing, comparing, and reconciling data prepared by one or several employees. Independent internal verification occurs after the fact, as in the case of reconciling cash register totals at the end of the day with cash on hand.

Related exercise material: BE7–1, BE7–2, E7–1, E7–2, and E7–3.

Cash Controls

Just as cash is the beginning of a company's operating cycle, it is usually the starting point for a company's system of internal control. Cash is the one asset that is readily convertible into any other type of asset; it is easily concealed and transported; and it is highly desired. Because of these characteristics, cash is the asset most susceptible to improper diversion and use. Moreover, because of the large volume of cash transactions, numerous errors may occur in executing and recording cash transactions. To safeguard cash and to assure the accuracy of the accounting records for cash, effective internal control over cash is imperative.

Cash consists of coins, currency (paper money), checks, money orders, and money on hand or on deposit in a bank or similar depository. The general rule is that if the bank will accept it for deposit, it is cash. Items such as postage stamps and postdated checks (checks payable in the future) are not cash. Stamps are a prepaid expense; the postdated checks are accounts receivable. The application of internal control principles to cash receipts and cash disbursements is explained in the following sections.

Helpful hint Without cash controls, a company may find cash going out as fast as it comes in.

► International note

Other countries also have control problems. For example, a judge in France has issued a 36-page "book" detailing many of the scams that are widespread, such as kickbacks in public-works contracts, the skimming of development aid money to Africa, and bribes on arms sales.

► Accounting in Action ► Business Insight

In 1891 James C. Fargo, president of American Express Co., gave one of his managers a challenge: Devise a piece of paper that will be accepted as money around the world.
Mr. Fargo, just back from a long trip in Europe, was frustrated by cumbersome bank letters of credit and confusing exchange rates. He asked Marcellus Fleming Berry, a manager, to come up with a negotiable instrument secure against loss, theft, counterfeit, fraud, and forgery. Mr. Berry created the "Travelers Cheque," using the British spelling.

The checks were a small sideline for American Express, whose principal business then was forwarding freight. But American Express kept its early lead. In 1891 the company sold checks with a face amount of $9,120, or about $122,000 in today's dollars. Not too long ago, American Express sold a record $22 billion in checks, giving it more than half of what has become a $40-billion-a-year market.

Source: Wall Street Journal, January 13, 1989.

STUDY OBJECTIVE

· · · · · · · · · · ▼ 3 · · · · · · · · ·

Explain the applications of internal control principles to cash receipts.

Internal Control over Cash Receipts

Cash receipts may result from a variety of sources: cash sales; collections on account from customers; the receipt of interest, rents, and dividends; investments by stockholders; bank loans; and proceeds from the sale of noncurrent assets. The internal control principles explained earlier apply to cash receipts transactions as shown in Illustration 7-4:

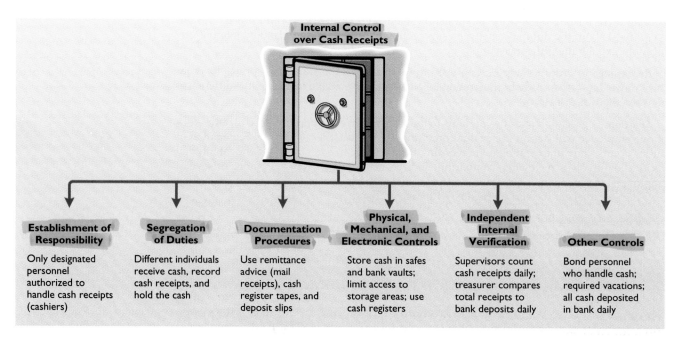

Establishment of Responsibility	Segregation of Duties	Documentation Procedures	Physical, Mechanical, and Electronic Controls	Independent Internal Verification	Other Controls
Only designated personnel authorized to handle cash receipts (cashiers)	Different individuals receive cash, record cash receipts, and hold the cash	Use remittance advice (mail receipts), cash register tapes, and deposit slips	Store cash in safes and bank vaults; limit access to storage areas; use cash registers	Supervisors count cash receipts daily; treasurer compares total receipts to bank deposits daily	Bond personnel who handle cash; required vacations; all cash deposited in bank daily

Illustration 7-4

Application of internal control principles to cash receipts

Helpful hint The cashier registers a cash sale manually by punching the appropriate keys on the register or electronically by using electronic scanning equipment.

▶ *Ethics note*

In terms of cash receipts, most American car dealerships do not have adequate internal controls in parts sales. According to a recent study, this lack of controls can cost the average dealership between $40,000 and $65,000 per year in theft and lost profits.

As might be expected, companies vary considerably in how they apply these principles. To illustrate internal control over cash receipts, we will examine control measures for a retail store with both over-the-counter and mail receipts.

Over-the-Counter Receipts

Control of over-the-counter receipts in retail businesses is centered on cash registers that are visible to customers. In supermarkets and variety stores such as Kmart, cash registers are placed in check-out lines near the exit(s). In Sears, Roebuck & Co. and J. C. Penney stores each department has its own cash register. When a cash sale occurs, the sale is "rung up" on a cash register **with the amount clearly visible to the customer.** This measure prevents the cashier from ringing up a lower amount and pocketing the difference. The customer receives an itemized cash register receipt slip and is expected to count the change received. A cash register tape, which is locked into the register until removed by a supervisor or manager, accumulates the daily transactions and totals. When the tape is removed, the supervisor compares the total with the amount of cash in the register. It should show all registered receipts accounted for. The supervisor's findings are reported on a cash count sheet that is signed by both the cashier and supervisor. The cash count sheet used by Alrite Food Mart is shown in Illustration 7-5.

The count sheets, register tapes, and cash are then given to the head cashier. This individual prepares a daily cash summary showing the total cash received and the amount from each source, such as cash sales and collections on account.

Illustration 7-5

Cash count sheet

Store No. ___8___	Date ___March 8, 1996___
1. Opening cash balance	$ 50.00
2. Cash sales per tape (attached)	6,956.20
3. Total cash to be accounted for	7,006.20
4. Cash on hand (see list)	6,996.10
5. Cash (short) or over	$ (10.10)
6. Ending cash balance	$ 50.00
7. Cash for deposit (Line 4 – Line 6)	$6,946.10

Cashier *J. Cruse*   Supervisor *M. Braun*

The head cashier sends one copy of the summary to the accounting department for entry into the cash receipts journal. The other copy goes to the treasurer's office for subsequent comparison with the daily bank deposit. Next, the head cashier prepares a deposit slip (see Illustration 7-9 on page 301) and makes the bank deposit. The total amount deposited should be equal to the total receipts on the daily cash summary. This will assure that all receipts have been placed in the custody of the bank. In accepting the bank deposit, the bank stamps (authenticates) the duplicate deposit slip and sends it to the company treasurer, who makes the comparison with the daily cash summary. The foregoing measures for cash sales are graphically presented in Illustration 7-6. The activities of the sales department are shown separate from those of the cashier's department to indicate the segregation of duties in handling cash.

Mail Receipts

Because of your experience as an individual customer, you may be more familiar with over-the-counter receipts than with mail receipts. However, mail receipts resulting from billings and credit sales are by far the most common way cash is received by the greatest variety of businesses. Think, for example, of the number of checks received through the mail daily by a national retailer such as Land's End or L.L. Bean.

All mail receipts should be received in the presence of two mail clerks. These receipts are generally in the form of checks or money orders and frequently are accompanied by a remittance advice stating the purpose of the check. Each check should be promptly endorsed "For Deposit Only" by use of a company stamp. This **restrictive endorsement** reduces the likelihood that the check will be diverted to personal use because banks will not give an individual any cash under this type of endorsement.

A list of the checks received each day should be prepared in duplicate showing the name of the issuer of the check, the purpose of the payment, and the amount of the check. Each mail clerk should sign the list to establish responsibility for the data. The original copy of the list, along with the checks and remittance advices, are then sent to the cashier's department, where they are added to over-the-counter receipts (if any) in preparing the daily cash summary and in making the daily bank deposit. In addition, a copy of the list is sent to the trea-

Helpful hint In billing customers many companies state: Pay by check, do not send cash. This is designed to reduce the risk that cash receipts will be misappropriated when received.

Illustration 7-6

Executing over-the-counter cash sales

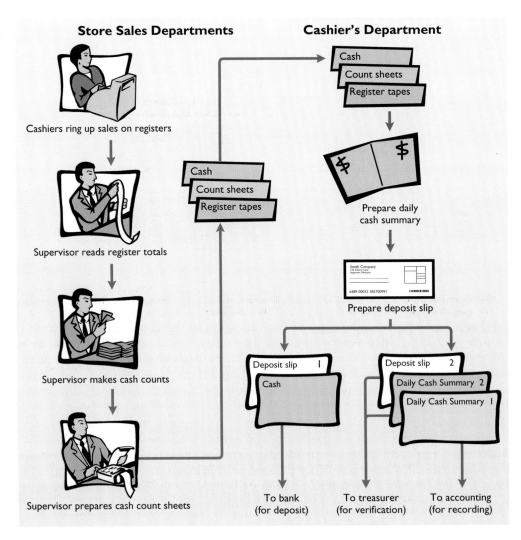

Store Sales Departments

Cashiers ring up sales on registers

Supervisor reads register totals

Supervisor makes cash counts

Supervisor prepares cash count sheets

Cashier's Department

Cash
Count sheets
Register tapes

Cash
Count sheets
Register tapes

Prepare daily cash summary

Smith Company
123 Cherry Lane
Anytown, Montana

6489 00032 385700991

Prepare deposit slip

Deposit slip 1
Cash

Deposit slip 2
Daily Cash Summary 2
Daily Cash Summary 1

To bank
(for deposit)

To treasurer
(for verification)

To accounting
(for recording)

Helpful hint Flowcharts enhance the understanding of the flow of documents, the processing steps, and the internal control procedures.

surer's office for comparison with the total mail receipts shown on the daily cash summary, to assure that all mail receipts have been included.

Internal Control over Cash Disbursements

STUDY OBJECTIVE
••••••••• **4** •••••••••
Describe the applications of internal control principles to cash disbursements.

Cash may be disbursed for a variety of reasons, such as to pay expenses and liabilities, or to purchase assets. **Generally, internal control over cash disbursements is more effective when payments are made by check, rather than by cash, except for incidental amounts that are paid out of petty cash.**[2] Payment by check generally occurs only after specified control procedures have been followed. In addition, the "paid" check provides proof of payment. Principles of internal control apply to cash disbursements as shown in Illustration 7-7 on the next page.

Electronic Funds Transfer (EFT) System

To account for and control cash is an expensive and time-consuming process. For example, it was estimated recently that the cost to process a check through

---

[2]The operation of a petty cash fund is explained on pages 297–300.

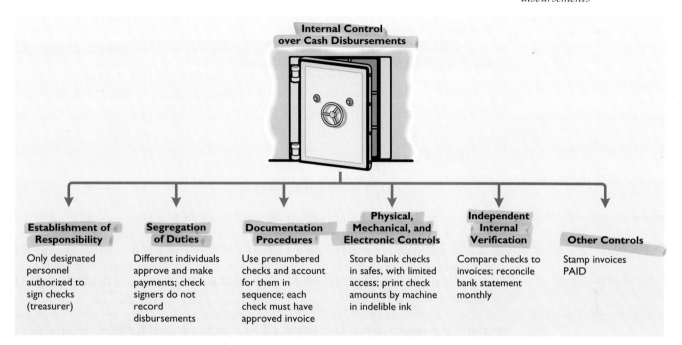

Internal Control over Cash Disbursements

Establishment of Responsibility	Segregation of Duties	Documentation Procedures	Physical, Mechanical, and Electronic Controls	Independent Internal Verification	Other Controls
Only designated personnel authorized to sign checks (treasurer)	Different individuals approve and make payments; check signers do not record disbursements	Use prenumbered checks and account for them in sequence; each check must have approved invoice	Store blank checks in safes, with limited access; print check amounts by machine in indelible ink	Compare checks to invoices; reconcile bank statement monthly	Stamp invoices PAID

a bank system ranges from $0.55 to $1.00 and is increasing. It is not surprising, therefore, that new approaches are being developed to transfer funds among parties without the use of paper (deposit tickets, checks, etc.). Such a procedure is called an electronic funds transfer (EFT). EFT is a disbursement system that uses wire, telephone, telegraph, or computer to transfer cash from one location to another. Use of EFT is quite common. For example, the authors receive no formal payroll checks from their universities, which simply send magnetic tapes to the appropriate banks for deposit. Regular payments such as those for house, car, or utilities are frequently made by EFT.

Petty Cash Fund

As you learned earlier in the chapter, better internal control over cash disbursements is possible when payments are made by check. However, using checks to pay such small amounts as those for postage due, employee lunches, and taxi fares is both impractical and a nuisance. A common way of handling such pay-

STUDY OBJECTIVE
·········· 5 ··········
Explain the operation of a petty cash fund.

▶Technology in Action

The development of EFT will continue. Already it is estimated that 80% of the total volume of bank transactions in the United States is performed using EFT. The computer technology is available to create a "checkless" society. The only major barriers appear to be the individual's concern for privacy and protection and certain legislative constraints. It should be noted that numerous safeguards have been built into EFT systems. However, the possibility of errors and fraud still exists because only a limited number of individuals are involved in the transfers, which may prevent appropriate segregation of duties.

ments, while maintaining satisfactory control, is to use a petty cash fund. A petty cash fund is a cash fund used to pay relatively small amounts. The operation of a petty cash fund, often called an **imprest system,** involves (1) establishing the fund, (2) making payments from the fund, and (3) replenishing the fund.[3]

Establishing the Fund.   Two essential steps in establishing a petty cash fund are (1) appointing a petty cash custodian who will be responsible for the fund and (2) determining the size of the fund. Ordinarily, the amount is expected to cover anticipated disbursements for a 3- to 4-week period. When the fund is established, a check payable to the petty cash custodian is issued for the stipulated amount. If the Laird Company decides to establish a $100 fund on March 1, the entry in general journal form is:

Mar. 1	Petty Cash	100.00	
	Cash		100.00
	(To establish a petty cash fund)		

The check is then cashed and the proceeds are placed in a locked petty cash box or drawer. Most petty cash funds are established on a fixed amount basis. Moreover, no additional entries will be made to the Petty Cash account unless the stipulated amount of the fund is changed. For example, if Laird Company decides on July 1 to increase the size of the fund to $250, it would debit Petty Cash $150 and credit Cash $150.

Making Payments from the Fund.   The custodian of the petty cash fund has the authority to make payments from the fund that conform to prescribed management policies. Usually, management limits the size of expenditures that may be made and does not permit use of the fund for certain types of transactions (such as making short-term loans to employees). Each payment from the fund must be documented on a prenumbered petty cash receipt (or petty cash voucher), as shown in Illustration 7-8. Note that the signatures of both the custodian and the individual receiving payment are required on the receipt. If other supporting documents such as a freight bill or invoice are available, they should be attached to the petty cash receipt.

Illustration 7-8

Petty cash receipt

Helpful hint From the standpoint of internal control, the receipt satisfies two principles: (1) establishing responsibility (signature of custodian) and (2) documentation procedures.

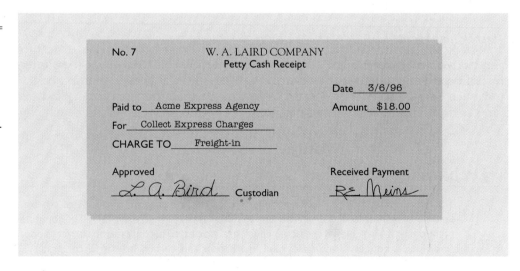

---

[3]The term "imprest" means an advance of money for a designated purpose.

The receipts are kept in the petty cash box until the fund is replenished. As a result, the sum of the petty cash receipts and money in the fund should equal the established total at all times. This means that surprise counts can be made at any time by an independent person, such as an internal auditor, to determine whether the fund is being maintained intact.

No accounting entry is made to record a payment at the time it is made from petty cash. It is considered to be both inexpedient and unnecessary to do so. Instead, the accounting effects of each payment are recognized when the fund is replenished.

Replenishing the Fund. When the money in the petty cash fund reaches a minimum level, the fund is replenished. The request for reimbursement is initiated by the petty cash custodian. This individual prepares a schedule (or summary) of the payments that have been made and sends the schedule, supported by petty cash receipts and other documentation, to the treasurer's office. The receipts and supporting documents are examined in the treasurer's office to verify that they were proper payments from the fund. The treasurer then approves the request and a check is prepared to restore the fund to its established amount. At the same time, all supporting documentation is stamped "paid" so that it cannot be submitted again for payment.

To illustrate, assume that on March 15 the petty cash custodian requests a check for $87. The fund contains $13 cash and petty cash receipts for postage $44, freight-in $38, and miscellaneous expenses $5. The entry, in general journal form, to record the check is:

Helpful hint Replenishing involves three internal control procedures: segregation of duties, documentation procedures, and independent internal verification.

Mar. 15	Postage Expense	44	
	Freight-in	38	
	Miscellaneous Expense	5	
	Cash		87
	(To replenish petty cash fund)		

Note that the Petty Cash account is not affected by the reimbursement entry. Replenishment changes the composition of the fund by replacing the petty cash receipts with cash, but it does not change the balance in the fund.

It may be necessary in replenishing a petty cash fund to recognize a cash shortage or overage. To illustrate, assume in the example above that the custodian had only $12 in cash in the fund plus the receipts as listed. The request for reimbursement would, therefore, have been for $88, and the following entry would be made:

Mar. 15	Postage Expense	44	
	Freight-in	38	
	Miscellaneous Expense	5	
	Cash Over and Short	1	
	Cash		88
	(To replenish petty cash fund)		

Conversely, if the custodian had $14 in cash, the reimbursement request would have been for $86 and Cash Over and Short would have been credited for $1. A debit balance in Cash Over and Short is reported in the income statement as miscellaneous expense; a credit balance is reported as miscellaneous revenue. Cash Over and Short is closed to Income Summary at the end of the year.

A petty cash fund should be replenished at the end of the accounting period regardless of the cash in the fund. Replenishment at this time is necessary in order to recognize the effects of the petty cash payments on the financial statements.

Internal control over a petty cash fund is strengthened by (1) having a supervisor make surprise counts of the fund to ascertain whether the paid vouchers and fund cash equal the imprest amount and (2) canceling or mutilating the paid vouchers so they cannot be resubmitted for reimbursement.

Before You Go On . . .

▸ *Review It*

1. How do the principles of internal control apply to cash receipts?
2. How do the principles of internal control apply to cash disbursements?
3. When are entries required in a petty cash system?

▸ *Do It*

L. R. Cortez is concerned about the control over cash receipts in his fast-food restaurant, Big Cheese. The restaurant has two cash registers. At no time do more than two employees take customer orders and ring up sales. Work shifts for employees range from 4 to 8 hours. Cortez asks your help in installing a good system of internal control over cash receipts.

Reasoning: Cortez needs to understand the principles of internal control, especially the principles of establishing responsibility, the use of electronic controls, and independent internal verification. Using this knowledge, an effective system of control over cash receipts can be designed and implemented.

Solution: Cortez should assign a cash register to each employee at the start of each work shift, with register totals set at zero. Each employee should be instructed to use only the assigned register and to ring up all sales. At the end of each work shift, Cortez or a supervisor/manager should total the register and make a cash count to see whether all cash is accounted for.

Related exercise material: BE7–3 and E7–2.

◢ **U**se of a Bank

....

STUDY OBJECTIVE
▸▸▸▸▸▸▸▸▸ ◢**6**◣ ▸▸▸▸▸▸▸▸▸▸

Indicate the control features of a bank account.

Helpful hint The counterpart to a cash register for cash receipts is the use of a bank account for cash disbursements.

The use of a bank contributes significantly to good internal control over cash. A company can safeguard its cash by using a bank as a depository and clearing house for checks received and checks written. Use of a bank minimizes the amount of currency that must be kept on hand. In addition, the use of a bank facilitates the control of cash because a double record is maintained of all bank transactions—one by the business and the other by the bank. The asset account, Cash, maintained by the depositor is the reciprocal of the bank's liability account for each depositor. It should be possible to **reconcile these accounts** (make them agree) at any time.

Opening a bank checking account is a relatively simple procedure. Typically, the bank makes a credit check on the new customer and the depositor is required to sign a **signature card**. The card should contain the signatures of each person authorized to sign checks on the account. The signature card is used by bank employees to validate signatures on the checks.

As soon as possible after an account is opened, the bank will provide the depositor with a book of serially numbered checks and deposit slips imprinted

▶ Technology in Action

The first big consumer business on the information highway is shaping up as a set of financial household chores: balancing the checkbook, paying bills, and saving for retirement. Several major U.S. banks now offer electronic home banking. For customers, the new capabilities mean more convenient service, more up-to-date information about their finances, and more control over their money. Several hundred thousand households now do a substantial amount of their money management electronically from home, and this number is expected to increase significantly.

with the depositor's name and address. Each check and deposit slip is imprinted with both a bank and a depositor identification number in magnetic ink to permit computer processing of the transaction.

Many companies have more than one bank account. For efficiency of operations and better control, national retailers like Wal-Mart Stores and Kmart may have regional bank accounts. Similarly, a company such as Exxon with more than 150,000 employees may have a payroll bank account, as well as one or more general bank accounts. In addition, a company may maintain several bank accounts in order to have more than one source for obtaining short-term loans when needed.

Making Bank Deposits

Bank deposits should be made by an authorized employee, such as the head cashier. Each deposit must be documented by a deposit slip (ticket), as shown in Illustration 7-9.

Bank code numbers

Front side

Reverse side

DEPOSIT TICKET

W.A. LAIRD COMPANY
77 West Central Avenue,
Midland, Michigan 48654

DATE _____ April 19 19 96

NB National Bank & Trust
Midland, Michigan 48654

⑈⑆O⑈24⑆0497⑆: 457 923⑈"02 75

CHECKS AND OTHER ITEMS ARE RECEIVED FOR DEPOSIT SUBJECT TO THE PROVISIONS OF THE UNIFORM COMMERCIAL CODE OR ANY APPLICABLE COLLECTION AGREEMENT

CASH	CURRENCY	462	10
	COIN		
LIST CHECKS SINGLY			
TOTAL FROM OTHER SIDE		1116	80
TOTAL		1578	90
TOTAL FROM OTHER SIDE			
NET DEPOSIT		1578	90

74—102/724

USE OTHER SIDE FOR ADDITIONAL LISTINGS

BE SURE EACH ITEM IS PROPERLY ENDORSED

CHECKS LIST SINGLY	DOLLARS	CENTS
1 74 – 331/724	175	40
2 61 – 157/220	292	60
3 19 – 401/710	337	55
4 22 – 815/666	165	72
5 15 – 360/011	145	53
6		
7		
8		
9		
10		
11		
12		
13		
14		
15		
16		
17		
18		
19		
TOTAL	1116	80
ENTER TOTAL ON THE FRONT OF THIS TICKET		

Illustration 7-9

Deposit slip

Helpful hint In addition to validating the deposit slip, banks provide a machine-prepared deposit receipt that shows the depositor's account number and the date and amount of the deposit.

Deposit slips are prepared in duplicate. The original is retained by the bank; the duplicate, machine stamped by the bank to establish its authenticity, is retained by the depositor.

Writing Checks

A **check** is a written order signed by the depositor directing the bank to pay a specified sum of money to a designated recipient. Thus, there are three parties to a check: the **maker** (or drawer) who issues the check, the **bank** (or payer) on which the check is drawn, and the **payee** to whom the check is payable. A check is a negotiable instrument that can be transferred to another party by endorsement. Each check should be accompanied by an explanation of its purposes. In many businesses, this is done by attaching a remittance advice to the check, as shown in Illustration 7-10.

Illustration 7-10

Check with remittance advice

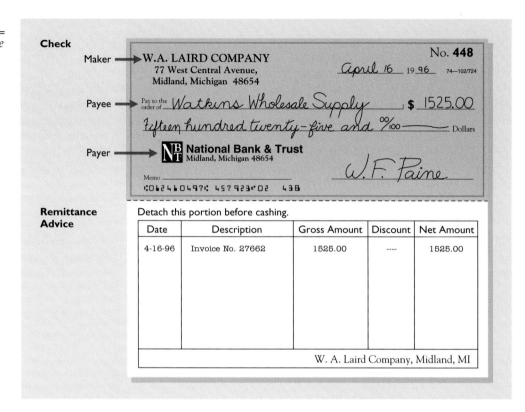

For both individuals and businesses, it is important to know the balance in the checking account at all times. To keep the balance current, each deposit and check should be entered on running balance memorandum forms provided by the bank or on the check stubs contained in the checkbook.

Bank Statements

Helpful hint Essentially, the bank statement is a copy of the bank's records sent to the customer for periodic review.

Each month, the depositor receives a bank statement from the bank. A **bank statement** shows the depositor's bank transactions and balances. For example, the statement, like the one in Illustration 7-11, shows (1) checks paid and other debits that reduce the balance in the depositor's account, (2) deposits and other credits that increase the balance in the depositor's account, and (3) the account balance after each day's transactions.

Most banks offer depositors the option of receiving "paid" checks with their bank statements. For those who decline, the bank keeps a record of each check on microfilm. Irrespective of the depositor's choice, all "paid" checks are listed in numerical sequence on the bank statement along with the date the check was paid and its amount. Upon paying a check, the bank stamps the check "paid"; a paid check is sometimes referred to as a **canceled** check. In addition, the bank

Illustration 7-11

Bank statement

National Bank & Trust
Midland, Michigan 48654   Member FDIC

ACCOUNT STATEMENT

W. A. LAIRD COMPANY
77 WEST CENTRAL AVENUE
MIDLAND, MICHIGAN 48654

Statement Date/Credit Line Closing Date

April 30, 1996

457923

ACCOUNT NUMBER

Balance Last Statement	Deposits and Credits		Checks and Debits		Balance This Statement
	No.	Total Amount	No.	Total Amount	
13,256.90	20	34,805.10	26	32,154.55	15,907.45

CHECKS AND DEBITS			DEPOSITS AND CREDITS		DAILY BALANCE	
Date	No.	Amount	Date	Amount	Date	Amount
4–2	435	644.95	4–2	4,276.85	4–2	16,888.80
4–5	436	3,260.00	4–3	2,137.50	4–3	18,249.65
4–4	437	1,185.79	4–5	1,350.47	4–4	17,063.86
4–3	438	776.65	4–7	982.46	4–5	15,154.33
4–8	439	1,781.70	4–8	1,320.28	4–7	14,648.89
4–7	440	1,487.90	4–9 CM	1,035.00	4–8	11,767.47
4–8	441	2,420.00	4–11	2,720.00	4–9	12,802.47
4–11	442	1,585.60	4–12	757.41	4–11	13,936.87
4–12	443	1,226.00	4–13	1,218.56	4–12	13,468.28
4–29	NSF	425.60	4–27	1,545.57	4–27	13,005.45
4–29	459	1,080.30	4–29	2,929.45	4–29	14,429.00
4–30	DM	30.00	4–30	2,128.60	4–30	15,907.45
4–30	461	620.15				

Symbols:	**CM** Credit Memo	**EC** Error Correction	**NSF** Not Sufficient Funds	Reconcile Your Account Promptly
	DM Debit Memo	**INT** Interest Earned	**SC** Service Charge	

Helpful hint Every deposit received by the bank is *credited* to the customer's account. The reverse occurs when the bank "pays" a check issued by a company on its checking account balance: Payment reduces the bank's liability and is therefore *debited* to the customer's account with the bank.

includes with the bank statement memoranda explaining other debits and credits made by the bank to the depositor's account.

Debit Memorandum

Banks charge a monthly fee for the use of their services. Often the fee is charged only when the average monthly balance in a checking account falls below a specified amount. The fee, called a bank service charge, is often identified on the bank statement by a code symbol such as SC. A debit memorandum explaining the charge is included with the bank statement. Separate debit memoranda may also be issued for other bank services such as the cost of printing checks, issuing traveler's checks, and wiring funds to other locations. The symbol DM is often used for such charges.

A debit memorandum is used by the bank when a previously deposited customer's check "bounces" because of insufficient funds. In such a case, the check is marked NSF (not sufficient funds) by the customer's bank and is returned to the depositor's bank. The bank then debits the depositor's account, as shown by the symbol NSF on the bank statement in Illustration 7-11, and sends the NSF check and debit memorandum to the depositor as notification of the charge. The NSF check creates an accounts receivable for the depositor and reduces cash in the bank account.

Helpful hint The debit memorandum is so named because the bank debits (decreases) the depositor's account which is a liability on the bank's books.

Helpful hint The average fee charged by banks for an NSF check was $19.92 in 1994.

▶Accounting in Action ▸ *Business Insight*

As copying machines have become ever more sophisticated, check counterfeiting has flourished. For example, in the second quarter of a recent fiscal year, the Woolworth Corporation had a $5 million loss from bad checks. Most of the total occurred in the Foot Locker division of the company, a spokesperson said. In the U.S. business community as a whole, some $10 billion worth of bad checks are written every year.

Checkmate Electronic Inc. thinks it has at least a partial answer to this problem. It makes electronic devices that read the magnetic ink used to print account and routing numbers on checks. By identifying the magnetic frequencies as well as the precise shape and size of the numbers, the machine can determine if a check is a fake. Checkmate has a machine small enough to be installed beside cash registers, and it is now in use by such retailers as J.C. Penney, Neiman-Marcus, and Pier 1 Imports.

Source: Wall Street Journal, March 31, 1994, p. C2; and Business Week, May 23, 1994, p. 9.

Credit Memorandum

Helpful hint On your personal bank statement there will be symbols for ATM withdrawals and deposits.

A depositor may ask the bank to collect its notes receivable. In such a case, the bank will credit the depositor's account for the cash proceeds of the note, as illustrated on the bank statement by the symbol CM. It will issue a credit memorandum which is sent with the statement to explain the entry. Many banks also offer interest on checking accounts. The interest earned may be indicated on the bank statement by the symbol CM or INT.

Reconciling the Bank Account

STUDY OBJECTIVE
.... **7** ....

Prepare a bank reconciliation.

Because the bank and the depositor maintain independent records of the depositor's checking account, you might assume that the respective balances will always agree. In fact, the two balances are seldom the same at any given time, and it is necessary to make the balance per books agree with the balance per bank—a process called **reconciling the bank account**. The lack of agreement between the two balances is due to:

1. **Time lags** that prevent one of the parties from recording the transaction in the same period.
2. **Errors** by either party in recording transactions.

Time lags occur frequently. For example, several days may elapse between the time a check is mailed to a payee and the date the check is paid by the bank.

▶Accounting in Action ▸ *Ethics Insight*

Some firms have used time lags to their advantage. For example, E. F. Hutton managers at one time overdrew their accounts by astronomical amounts—on some days the overdrafts totaled $1 billion—creating interest-free loans they could invest. The loans lasted as long as it took for the covering checks to be collected. Although not technically illegal at the time, Hutton's actions were wrong because it did not have bank permission to do so.

Similarly, when the depositor uses the bank's night depository to make its deposits, there will be a difference of one day between the time the receipts are recorded by the depositor and the time they are recorded by the bank. A time lag also occurs whenever the bank mails a debit or credit memorandum to the depositor.

▶Technology in Action

A malfunctioning computer software program doubled all withdrawals and transfers made at Chemical Bank automatic teller machines (ATMs) in New York state for about 12 hours. The printed record of transactions spit out by the ATM was accurate, but the computerized posting of the transactions was automatically doubled. The bank corrected all errors, which in the aggregate may have been $15 million.

Source: Denver Post, February 19, 1994.

The incidence of errors depends on the effectiveness of the internal controls maintained by the depositor and the bank. Bank errors are infrequent. However, either party could inadvertently record a $450 check as $45 or $540. In addition, the bank might mistakenly charge a check drawn by C. D. Berg to the account of C. D. Burg.

Reconciliation Procedure

To obtain maximum benefit from a bank reconciliation, the reconciliation should be prepared by an employee who has no other responsibilities pertaining to cash. When the internal control principle of independent internal verification is not followed in preparing the reconciliation, cash embezzlements may escape unnoticed. For example, a cashier who prepares the reconciliation can embezzle cash and conceal the embezzlement by misstating the reconciliation. Thus, the bank accounts would reconcile and the embezzlement would not be detected.

In reconciling the bank account, it is customary to reconcile the balance per books and balance per bank to their adjusted (correct or true) cash balances. The reconciliation schedule is divided into two sections, as shown in Illustration 7-12. The starting point in preparing the reconciliation is to enter the balance per bank statement and balance per books on the schedule. The following steps should reveal all the reconciling items that cause the difference between the two balances.

Helpful hint For maximum internal control, the bank statement should be sent by the bank directly to the reconciler to prevent tampering with the contents of the bank statement by the cashier.

1. Compare the individual deposits on the bank statement with deposits in transit from the preceding bank reconciliation and with the deposits per company records or copies of duplicate deposit slips. Deposits recorded by the depositor that have not been recorded by the bank represent **deposits in transit** and are added to the balance per bank.

2. Compare the paid checks shown on the bank statement or the paid checks returned with the bank statement with (a) checks outstanding from the preceding bank reconciliation and (b) checks issued by the company as recorded in the cash payments journal. Issued checks recorded by the company that have not been paid by the bank represent **outstanding checks** that are deducted from the balance per the bank.

3. Note any **errors** discovered in the foregoing steps and list them in the appropriate section of the reconciliation schedule. For example, if a paid check correctly written by the company for $195 was mistakenly recorded by the company for $159, the error of $36 is deducted from the balance per books. All errors made by the depositor are reconciling items in determining the adjusted cash balance per books. In contrast, all errors made by the bank are reconciling items in determining the adjusted cash balance per the bank.

Helpful hint Deposits in transit and outstanding checks are reconciling items because of time lags.

4. Trace **bank memoranda** to the depositor's records. Any unrecorded memoranda should be listed in the appropriate section of the reconciliation schedule. For example, a $5 debit memorandum for bank service charges is deducted from the balance per books, and $32 of interest earned is added to the balance per books.

Bank Reconciliation Illustrated

The bank statement for the Laird Company is shown in Illustration 7-11. It shows a balance per bank of $15,907.45 on April 30, 1996. On this date the balance of cash per books is $11,589.45. From the foregoing steps, the following reconciling items are determined.

<table>
<tr><td>**Helpful hint** Note in the bank statement that checks No. 459 and 461 have been paid but check No. 460 is not listed. Thus, this check is outstanding. If a complete bank statement were provided, checks No. 453 and 457 would also not be listed. The amounts for these three checks are obtained from the company's cash payments records.</td></tr>
</table>

1. **Deposits in transit:** April 30 deposit (received by bank on May 1). $2,201.40

2. **Outstanding checks:** No. 453 $3,000.00; No. 457 $1,401.30; No. 460 $1,502.70.   5,904.00

3. **Errors:** Check No. 443 was correctly written by Laird for $1,226.00 and was correctly paid by the bank. However, it was recorded for $1,262.00 by Laird Company.   36.00

4. **Bank memoranda:**
   a. Debit—NSF check from J. R. Baron for $425.60   425.60
   b. Debit—Printing company checks charge, $30.00   30.00
   c. Credit—Collection of note receivable for $1,000 plus interest
   earned $50, less bank collection fee $15.00   1,035.00

The bank reconciliation is as follows:

Illustration 7-12

Bank reconciliation

LAIRD COMPANY
Bank Reconciliation
April 30, 1996

Cash balance per bank statement		$15,907.45
Add: Deposits in transit		2,201.40
		18,108.85
Less: Outstanding checks		
No. 453	$3,000.00	
No. 457	1,401.30	
No. 460	1,502.70	5,904.00
Adjusted cash balance per bank		$12,204.85
Cash balance per books		$11,589.45
Add: Collection of note receivable, $1,000 plus interest		
earned $50, less collection fee $15	$1,035.00	
Error in recording check No. 443	36.00	1,071.00
		12,660.45
Less: NSF check	425.60	
Bank service charge	30.00	455.60
Adjusted cash balance per books		$12,204.85

Helpful hint The terms *adjusted balance*, *true cash balance*, and *correct cash balance* may be used interchangeably.

►*A*ccounting in *A*ction ► *Business Insight*

Imagine reconciling a bank statement when you have an employee like Billie Hurst. She worked as a librarian at Southwest Missouri State University for 30 years, yet she never got around to cashing paychecks totaling more than $100,000 because she didn't need the money.

The 72-year-old woman got the money anyway when State Treasurer Wendell Bailey presented an $88,100.85 check to Hurst's cousin and guardian, Frances Jane Gleghorn, after a special act of the Legislature made it possible to pay checks more than 5 years old.

Bailey's office said it already had re-issued checks amounting to $20,024.53 for uncashed checks not more than 5 years old, bringing the total reimbursement to $108,125.38.

Hurst occasionally cashed a paycheck, Gleghorn said, but co-workers tried for years to get her to cash the rest of the checks.

Source: Bay City Times, March 24, 1989.

Helpful hint Did the reissue of the checks restore the librarian's cash position? Answer: No. Thousands of dollars in interest were lost, investment opportunities were lost, and there was a loss in the purchasing power of the dollar over the years.

Entries from Bank Reconciliation

Each reconciling item in determining the **adjusted cash balance per books** should be recorded by the depositor. If these items are not journalized and posted, the Cash account will not show the correct balance. The entries for the Laird Company on April 30 are as follows:

Collection of Note Receivable. This entry involves four accounts. Assuming that the interest of $50 has not been accrued and the collection fee is charged to Miscellaneous Expense, the entry is:

Apr. 30	Cash	1,035.00	
	Miscellaneous Expense	15.00	
	Notes Receivable		1,000.00
	Interest Revenue		50.00
	(To record collection of notes receivable by bank)		

Helpful hint These entries are adjusting entries. In prior chapters, Cash was an account that did not require adjustment because a bank reconciliation had not been explained.

Book Error. An examination of the cash disbursements journal shows that check No. 443 was a payment on account to Andrea Company, a supplier. The correcting entry is:

Apr. 30	Cash	36.00	
	Accounts Payable—Andrea Company		36.00
	(To correct error in recording check No. 443)		

NSF Check. As indicated earlier, an NSF check becomes an accounts receivable to the depositor. The entry is:

Apr. 30	Accounts Receivable—J. R. Baron	425.60	
	Cash		425.60
	(To record NSF check)		

Bank Service Charges. Check printing charges (DM) and other bank service charges (SC) are debited to Miscellaneous Expense because they are usually nominal in amount. The entry is:

Apr. 30	Miscellaneous Expense	30.00	
	Cash		30.00
	(To record charge for printing company checks)		

The foregoing entries could also be combined into one compound entry. After the entries are posted, the cash account will show the following:

Illustration 7-13

Adjusted balance in cash account

	Cash		
Apr. 30 Bal.	11,589.45	Apr. 30	425.60
30	1,035.00		30.00
30	36.00		
Apr. 30 Bal.	12,204.85		

The adjusted cash balance in the ledger should agree with the adjusted cash balance per books in the bank reconciliation in Illustration 7-12.

What entries does the bank make? If any bank errors are discovered in preparing the reconciliation, the bank should be notified so it can make the necessary corrections on its records. The bank does not make any entries for deposits in transit or outstanding checks. Only when these items reach the bank will the bank record these items.

Before You Go On . . .

▶ Review It

1. Why is it necessary to reconcile a bank account?
2. What steps are involved in the reconciliation procedure?
3. What information is included in a bank reconciliation?

▶ Do It

Sally Kist owns Linen Kist Fabrics. Sally asks you to explain how the following reconciling items should be treated in reconciling the bank account at December 31: (1) a debit memorandum for an NSF check, (2) a credit memorandum for a note collected by the bank, (3) outstanding checks, and (4) a deposit in transit.

Reasoning: Sally needs to understand that one cause of a reconciling item is time lags. Items (1) and (2) are reconciling items because Linen Kist Fabrics has not yet recorded the memoranda. Items (3) and (4) are reconciling items because the bank has not recorded the transactions.

Solution: In reconciling the bank account, the reconciling items are treated as follows:

NSF check: Deducted from balance per books.
Collection of note: Added to balance per books.
Outstanding checks: Deducted from balance per bank.
Deposit in transit: Added to balance per bank.

Related exercise material: BE7–6, BE7–7, BE7–8, BE7–9, E7–7, E7–8, E7–9, and E7–10.

◤Reporting Cash

STUDY OBJECTIVE

••••••••• 8 •••••••••

Explain the reporting of cash.

Cash on hand, cash in banks, and petty cash are often combined and reported simply as **Cash**. Because it is the most liquid asset owned by a company, cash is listed first in the current asset section of the balance sheet. Some companies use the designation "cash and cash equivalents" in reporting cash as illustrated by the following:

Illustration 7-14

Presentation of cash and cash equivalents

EASTMAN KODAK COMPANY		
	1994	1993
Current assets (in millions)		
Cash and cash equivalents	$2,020	$1,635

Cash equivalents are highly liquid investments, with maturities of 3 months or less when purchased, that can be converted into a specific amount of cash. They include money market funds, money market savings certificates, bank certificates of deposit, and U.S. Treasury bills and notes.

Helpful hint Highly liquid investments with maturities of 3 to 12 months are considered to be temporary investments and are listed immediately below cash in the balance sheet.

A company may have cash that is restricted for a special purpose. Examples include a payroll bank account for paying salaries and wages, and plant expansion fund cash for financing new construction. If the restricted cash is expected to be used within the next year, the amount should be reported as a current asset. However, when this is not the case, the restricted funds should be reported as a noncurrent asset. Since a payroll bank account will be used as early as the next payday for employees, it is reported as a current asset. In contrast, unless the new construction will begin within the next year, plant expansion fund cash is classified as a noncurrent asset.

In making loans to depositors, it is common for banks to require the borrowers to maintain minimum cash balances. These minimum balances, called **compensating balances**, provide the bank with support for the loans. Compensating balances are a restriction on the use of cash that may affect a company's liquidity. Accordingly, compensating balances should be disclosed in the financial statements.

Before You Go On . . .

► *Review It*

1. What is generally reported as cash on a company's balance sheet?
2. What is meant by cash equivalents and compensating balances?

► *A Look Back at Columbia University*

Refer to the opening story about Columbia University, and answer the following questions:

1. Does Susan McLaughlin have a valid basis for establishing responsibility for overages or shortages? Why or why not?
2. What internal control principles are applicable to reconciling cash register tapes and the amount of cash in the cash drawer at the end of the day?
3. What internal control principle is involved in seeing that a student gets a receipt when buying a meal at a register? How does this requirement contribute to good internal control?
4. Do you think the cashiers are, or should be, bonded?

Solution

1. Establishing responsibility for overages or shortages is made only at the end of the day. This will provide a valid basis for evaluation only if one person worked the register for the entire day. If more than one person works the register during the day, the single count will not provide a valid basis for establishing who is responsible for the overage or shortage.
2. Applicable internal control principles are: (a) Segregation of duties—the cashier(s) should not be involved in performing the reconciliation. (b) Documentation

procedures—the cash register tape provides the documentation for total receipts for the day. (c) Independent internal verification—a supervisor should perform the reconciliation.

3. The internal control principle of documentation procedures is involved. The control does not reside in the receipt itself. For example, there will not be any subsequent reconciliation of cash register receipts with cash at the end of the day. The control is forcing the cashier to ring up each sale so that a receipt is produced. Each receipt is recorded on the cash register tape. At the end of the day, the tape is used in determining overages or shortages.

4. If the dining facility has nonstudent employees who work as cashiers, they may be bonded. However, if students work part-time as cashiers, it is doubtful that they are bonded. From the employer's standpoint, bonding is protection against major embezzlements. The risk of this occurring with student help is relatively low.

Summary of Study Objectives

1. *Define internal control.* Internal control is the plan of organization and related methods and procedures adopted within a business to safeguard its assets and to enhance the accuracy and reliability of its accounting records.

2. *Identify the principles of internal control.* The principles of internal control are: establishment of responsibility; segregation of duties; documentation procedures; physical, mechanical, and electronic controls; independent internal verification; and other controls.

3. *Explain the applications of internal control principles to cash receipts.* Internal controls over cash receipts include: (a) designating only personnel such as cashiers to handle cash; (b) assigning the duties of receiving cash, recording cash, and custody of cash to different individuals; (c) obtaining remittance advices for mail receipts, cash register tapes for over-the-counter receipts, and deposit slips for bank deposits; (d) using company safes and bank vaults to store cash with access limited to authorized personnel, and using cash registers in executing over-the-counter receipts; (e) making independent daily counts of register receipts and daily comparisons of total receipts with total deposits; and (f) bonding personnel that handle cash and requiring them to take vacations.

4. *Describe the applications of internal control principles to cash disbursements.* Internal controls over cash disbursements include: (a) having only specified individuals such as the treasurer authorized to sign checks; (b) assigning the duties of approving items for payment, paying the items, and recording the payment to different individuals; (c) using

prenumbered checks and accounting for all checks, with each check supported by an approved invoice; (d) storing blank checks in a safe or vault with access restricted to authorized personnel, and using a checkwriter to imprint amounts on checks; (e) comparing each check with the approved invoice before issuing the check, and making monthly reconciliations of bank and book balances; and (f) after payment, stamping each approved invoice "paid."

5. *Explain the operation of a petty cash fund.* In operating a petty cash fund, it is necessary to establish the fund, make payments from the fund, and replenish the fund.

6. *Indicate the control features of a bank account.* A bank account contributes to good internal control by providing physical controls for the storage of cash, minimizing the amount of currency that must be kept on hand, and creating a double record of a depositor's bank transactions.

7. *Prepare a bank reconciliation.* In reconciling the bank account, it is customary to reconcile the balance per books and balance per bank to their adjusted balances. The steps in determining the reconciling items are to ascertain deposits in transit, outstanding checks, errors by the depositor or the bank, and unrecorded bank memoranda.

8. *Explain the reporting of cash.* Cash is listed first in the current assets section of the balance sheet. In some cases, cash is reported together with cash equivalents. Cash restricted for a special purpose is reported separately as a current asset or as a noncurrent asset depending on when the cash is expected to be used.

Glossary

Bank service charge A fee charged by a bank for the use of its services. (p. 303).

Bank statement A statement received monthly from the bank that shows the depositor's bank transactions and balances. (p. 302).

Cash Resources that consist of coins, currency, checks, money orders, and money on hand or on deposit in a bank or similar depository. (p. 293).

Cash equivalents Highly liquid investments, with maturities of three months or less when purchased, that can be converted to a specific amount of cash. (p. 309).

Check A written order signed by the depositor directing the bank to pay a specified sum of money to a designated recipient. (p. 302).

Compensating balances Minimum cash balances required by a bank in support of bank loans. (p. 309).

Deposits in transit Deposits recorded by the depositor that have not been recorded by the bank. (p. 305).

Electronic funds transfer (EFT) A disbursement system that uses wire, telephone, telegraph, or computer to transfer cash from one location to another. (p. 297).

Internal auditors Company employees who evaluate on a continuous basis the effectiveness of the company's system of internal control. (p. 291).

Internal control The plan of organization and all the related methods and measures adopted within a business to safeguard its assets and enhance the accuracy and reliability of its accounting records. (p. 287).

NSF check A check that is not paid by a bank because of insufficient funds in a customer's bank account. (p. 303).

Outstanding checks Checks issued and recorded by a company that have not been paid by the bank. (p. 305).

Petty cash fund A cash fund used to pay relatively small amounts. (p. 298).

DEMONSTRATION PROBLEM

Trillo Company's bank statement for May 1996 shows the following data:

Balance 5/1	$12,650	Balance 5/31	$14,280
Debit memorandum:		Credit memorandum:	
NSF check	$ 175	Collection of note receivable	$ 505

The cash balance per books at May 31 is $13,319. Your review of the data reveals the following:

1. The NSF check was from Hup Co., a customer.
2. The note collected by the bank was a $500, three-month, 12% note. The bank charged a $10 collection fee. No interest has been accrued.
3. Outstanding checks at May 31 total $2,410.
4. Deposits in transit at May 31 total $1,752.
5. A Trillo Company check for $352 dated May 10 cleared the bank on May 25. This check, which was a payment on account, was journalized for $325.

Instructions
(a) Prepare a bank reconciliation at May 31.
(b) Journalize the entries required by the reconciliation.

Solution to Demonstration Problem

(a)

TRILLO COMPANY
Bank Reconciliation
May 31, 1996

Cash balance per bank statement		$14,280
Add: Deposits in transit		1,752
		16,032
Less: Outstanding checks		2,410
Adjusted cash balance per bank		$13,622
Cash balance per books		$13,319
Add: Collection of note receivable $500, plus $15 interest less collection fee $10		505
		13,824
Less: NSF check	$175	
Error in recording check	27	202
Adjusted cash balance per books		$13,622

Problem-Solving Strategies
1. Follow the four steps used in reconciling items (pp. 305–6).
2. Work carefully to minimize mathematical errors in the reconciliation.
3. All entries are based on reconciling items per books.
4. Make sure the cash ledger balance after posting the reconciling entries agrees with the adjusted cash balance per books.

(b)

May 31	Cash	505	
	Miscellaneous Expense	10	
	Notes Receivable		500
	Interest Revenue		15
	(To record collection of note by bank)		
31	Accounts Receivable—Hup Co.	175	
	Cash		175
	(To record NSF check from Hup Co.)		
31	Accounts Payable	27	
	Cash		27
	(To correct error in recording check)		

SELF-STUDY QUESTIONS

Answers are at the end of the chapter.

(SO 1) 1. Internal control is used in a business to enhance the accuracy and reliability of its accounting records and to:
   a. safeguard its assets.
   b. prevent fraud.
   c. produce correct financial statements.
   d. deter employee dishonesty.

(SO 2) 2. The principles of internal control do not include:
   a. establishment of responsibility.
   b. documentation procedures.
   c. management responsibility.
   d. independent internal verification.

(SO 2) 3. Physical controls do not include:
   a. safes and vaults to store cash.
   b. independent bank reconciliations.
   c. locked warehouses for inventories.
   d. bank safety deposit boxes for important papers.

(SO 3) 4. Which of the following items in a cash drawer at November 30 is not cash?
   a. Money orders.
   b. Coins and currency.
   c. A customer check dated December 1.
   d. A customer check dated November 28.

(SO 3) 5. Permitting only designated personnel such as cashiers to handle cash receipts is an application of the principle of:
   a. segregation of duties.
   b. establishment of responsibility.
   c. independent check.
   d. other controls.

(SO 4) 6. The use of prenumbered checks in disbursing cash is an application of the principle of:
   a. establishment of responsibility.
   b. segregation of duties.
   c. physical, mechanical, and electronic controls.
   d. documentation procedures.

(SO 5) 7. A check is written to replenish a $100 petty cash fund when the fund contains receipts of $94 and $3 in cash. In recording the check,
   a. Cash Over and Short should be debited for $3.
   b. Petty Cash should be debited for $94.
   c. Cash should be credited for $94.
   d. Petty Cash should be credited for $3.

(SO 6) 8. The control features of a bank account do not include:
   a. having bank auditors verify the correctness of the bank balance per books.
   b. minimizing the amount of cash that must be kept on hand.
   c. providing a double record of all bank transactions.
   d. safeguarding cash by using a bank as a depository.

(SO 7) 9. In a bank reconciliation, deposits in transit are:
   a. deducted from the book balance.
   b. added to the book balance
   c. added to the bank balance.
   d. deducted from the bank balance.

(SO 7) 10. The reconciling item in a bank reconciliation that will result in an adjusting entry by the depositor is:
   a. outstanding checks.
   b. deposit in transit.
   c. a bank error.
   d. bank service charges.

(SO 8) 11. The statement that correctly describes the reporting of cash is:
   a. Cash cannot be combined with cash equivalents.
   b. Restricted cash funds may be combined with Cash.
   c. Cash is listed first in the current asset section.
   d. Restricted cash funds cannot be reported as a current asset.

QUESTIONS

1. "Internal control is concerned only with enhancing the accuracy of the accounting records." Do you agree? Explain.

2. What principles of internal control apply to most business enterprises?

3. In the corner grocery store, all sales clerks make change out of one cash register drawer. Is this a violation of internal control? Why?

4. J. Duma is reviewing the principle of segregation of duties. What are the two common applications of this principle?

5. How do documentation procedures contribute to good internal control?

6. What internal control objectives are met by physical, mechanical, and electronic controls?

7. (a) Explain the control principle of independent internal verification. (b) What practices are important in applying this principle?

8. The management of Cobo Company asks you, as the company accountant, to explain (a) the concept of reasonable assurance in internal control and (b) the importance of the human factor in internal control.

9. Midwest Inc. owns the following assets at the balance sheet date:

Cash in bank-savings account	$ 5,000
Cash on hand	850
Cash refund due from the IRS	1,000
Checking account balance	12,000
Postdated checks	500

What amount should be reported as cash in the balance sheet?

10. What principle(s) of internal control is (are) involved in making daily cash counts of over-the-counter receipts?

11. Dent Department Stores has just installed new electronic cash registers in its stores. How do cash registers improve internal control over cash receipts?

12. In Allen Wholesale Company, two mail clerks open all mail receipts. How does this strengthen internal control?

13. "To have maximum effective internal control over cash disbursements, all payments should be made by check." Is this true? Explain.

14. Handy Company's internal controls over cash disbursements provide for the treasurer to sign checks imprinted by a checkwriter after comparing the check with the approved invoice. Identify the internal control principles that are present in these controls.

15. How do the principles of (a) physical, mechanical, and electronic controls and (b) other controls apply to cash disbursements?

16. What is the essential feature of an electronic funds transfer (EFT) procedure?

17. (a) Identify the three activities that pertain to a petty cash fund, and indicate an internal control principle that is applicable to each activity. (b) When are journal entries required in the operation of a petty cash fund?

18. "The use of a bank contributes significantly to good internal control over cash." Is this true? Why?

19. Paul Pascal is confused about the lack of agreement between the cash balance per books and the balance per the bank. Explain the causes for the lack of agreement to Paul, and give an example of each cause.

20. What are the four steps involved in finding differences between the balance per books and balance per banks?

21. Mary Mora asks your help concerning an NSF check. Explain to Mary (a) what an NSF check is, (b) how it is treated in a bank reconciliation, and (c) whether it will require an adjusting entry per bank.

22. (a) "Cash equivalents are the same as cash." Do you agree? Explain. (b) How should restricted cash funds be reported on the balance sheet?

BRIEF EXERCISES

BE7–1 Gina Milan is the new owner of Liberty Parking. She has heard about internal control but is not clear about its importance for her business. Explain to Gina the two purposes of internal control and give her one application of each purpose for Liberty Parking.

Explain the importance of internal control.
(SO 1)

BE7–2 The internal control procedures in Marion Company provide that:

(a) Employees who have physical custody of assets do not have access to the accounting records.

Identify internal control principles.
(SO 2)

(b) Each month the assets on hand are compared to the accounting records by an internal auditor.

(c) A prenumbered shipping document is prepared for each shipment of goods to customers.

Identify the principles of internal control that are being followed.

Identify the internal control principles applicable to cash receipts.
(SO 3)

BE7–3 The Tene Company has the following internal control procedures over cash receipts. Identify the internal control principle that is applicable to each procedure.

1. All over-the-counter receipts are registered on cash registers.
2. All cashiers are bonded.
3. Daily cash counts are made by cashier department supervisors.
4. The duties of receiving cash, recording cash, and custody of cash are assigned to different individuals.
5. Only cashiers may operate cash registers.

Identify the internal control principle applicable to cash disbursements.
(SO 4)

BE7–4 Hills Company has the following internal control procedures over cash disbursements. Identify the internal control principle that is applicable to each procedure.

1. Company checks are prenumbered. *documentation*
2. The bank statement is reconciled monthly by an internal auditor. *indep. inter. verific.*
3. Blank checks are stored in a safe in the treasurer's office. *physical control*
4. Only the treasurer or assistant treasurer may sign checks. *est. of respons.*
5. Check signers are not allowed to record cash disbursement transactions. *seg. of duties*

Prepare entry to replenish a petty cash fund.
(SO 5)

BE7–5 On March 20, Gimbal's petty cash fund of $100 is replenished when the fund contains $12 in cash and receipts for postage $52, freight-in $26, and travel expense $10. Prepare the journal entry to record the replenishment of the petty cash fund.

Identify the control features of a bank account.
(SO 6)

BE7–6 T. J. Boad is uncertain about the control features of a bank account. Explain the control benefits of (a) a signature card, (b) a check, and (c) a bank statement.

Indicate location of reconciling items in a bank reconciliation.
(SO 7)

BE7–7 The following reconciling items are applicable to the bank reconciliation for Ashley Company: (1) outstanding checks, (2) bank debit memorandum for service charge, (3) bank credit memorandum for collecting a note for the depositor, (4) deposit in transit. Indicate how each item should be shown on a bank reconciliation.

Identify reconciling items that require adjusting entries.
(SO 7)

BE7–8 Using the data in BE7–7, indicate (a) the items that will result in an adjustment to the depositor's records and (b) why the other items do not require adjustment.

Prepare partial bank reconciliation.
(SO 7)

BE7–9 At July 31, Dana Company has the following bank information: cash balance per bank, $7,420, outstanding checks $762, deposits in transit $1,700, and a bank service charge $20. Determine the adjusted cash balance per bank at July 31.

Prepare partial bank reconciliation.
(SO 7)

BE7–10 At August 31, Kahn Company has a cash balance per books of $9,200 and the following additional data from the bank statement: charge for printing Kahn Company checks $35, interest earned on checking account balance $40, and outstanding checks $800. Determine the adjusted cash balance per books at August 31.

Explain the statement presentation of cash balances.
(SO 8)

BE7–11 Tijuana Company has the following cash balances: Cash in Bank $12,742, Payroll Bank Account $6,000, and Plant Expansion Fund Cash $25,000. Explain how each balance should be reported on the balance sheet.

EXERCISES

Identify the principles of internal control.
(SO 2)

E7–1 Joe Marino is the owner of Marino's Pizza. Marino's is operated strictly on a carryout basis. Customers pick up their orders at a counter where a clerk exchanges the pizza for cash. While at the counter, the customer can see other employees making the pizzas and the large ovens in which the pizzas are baked.

Instructions

Identify the six principles of internal control and give an example of each principle that you might observe when picking up your pizza. (Note: It may not be possible to observe all the principles.)

E7–2 The following control procedures are used in the Tolan Company for over-the-counter cash receipts.

List internal control weaknesses over cash receipts and suggest improvements.
(SO 2, 3)

1. Cashiers are experienced; thus they are not bonded.
2. All over-the-counter receipts are registered by three clerks who use a cash register with a single cash drawer.
3. To minimize the risk of robbery, cash in excess of $100 is stored in an unlocked attaché case in the stock room until it is deposited in the bank.
4. At the end of each day, the total receipts are counted by the cashier on duty and reconciled to the cash register total.
5. The company accountant makes the bank deposit and then records the day's receipts.

Instructions
(a) For each procedure, explain the weakness in internal control and identify the control principle that is violated.
(b) For each weakness, suggest a change in procedure that will result in good internal control.

E7–3 The following control procedures are used in Ann's Botique Shoppe for cash disbursements.

List internal control weaknesses over cash disbursements and suggest improvements.
(SO 2, 4)

1. Each week, Ann leaves 100 company checks in an unmarked envelope on a shelf behind the cash register.
2. The store manager personally approves all payments before signing and issuing checks.
3. The company checks are unnumbered.
4. After payment, bills are "filed" in a paid invoice folder.
5. The company accountant prepares the bank reconciliation and reports any discrepancies to the owner.

Instructions
(a) For each procedure, explain the weakness in internal control and identify the internal control principle that is violated.
(b) For each weakness, suggest a change in the procedure that will result in good internal control.

E7–4 In the O'Malley Company, checks are not prenumbered because both the purchasing agent and the treasurer are authorized to issue checks. Each signer has access to unissued checks kept in an unlocked file cabinet. The purchasing agent pays all bills pertaining to goods purchased for resale. Prior to payment, the purchasing agent determines that the goods have been received and verifies the mathematical accuracy of the vendor's invoice. After payment, the invoice is filed by vendor, and the purchasing agent records the payment in the cash disbursements journal. The treasurer pays all other bills following approval by authorized employees. After payment, the treasurer stamps all bills PAID, files them by payment date, and records the checks in the cash disbursements journal. Webber Company maintains one checking account that is reconciled by the treasurer.

Identify internal control weaknesses for cash disbursements and make recommendations for improvement.
(SO 4)

Instructions
(a) List the weaknesses in internal control over cash disbursements.
(b) ▭▭▭▶ Write a memo to your boss indicating your recommendations for improvement.

E7–5 Ramona Company uses an imprest petty cash system. The fund was established on March 1 with a balance of $100. During March the following petty cash receipts were found in the petty cash box:

Prepare journal entries for a petty cash fund.
(SO 5)

Date	Receipt No.	For	Amount
3/5	1	Stamp Inventory	$38
7	2	Freight-in	19
9	3	Miscellaneous Expense	12
11	4	Travel Expense	24
14	5	Miscellaneous Expense	5

There was no cash over or short. The fund was replenished on March 15. On March 20, the amount in the fund was increased to $150.

Instructions
Journalize the entries in March that pertain to the operation of the petty cash fund.

Prepare bank reconciliation and adjusting entries.
(SO 7)

E7–6   Ono LoKo is unable to reconcile the bank balance at January 31. Ono's reconciliation is as follows:

Cash balance per bank	$3,560.20
Add: NSF check	530.00
Less: Bank service charge	25.00
Adjusted balance per bank	$4,065.20
Cash balance per books	$3,875.20
Less: Deposits in transit	490.00
Add: Outstanding checks	730.00
Adjusted balance per books	$4,115.20

Instructions
(a) Prepare a correct bank reconciliation.
(b) Journalize the entries required by the reconciliation.

Determine outstanding checks.
(SO 7)

E7–7   On April 30, the bank reconciliation of Drofo Company shows three outstanding checks: No. 254 $650, No. 255 $820, and No. 257 $410. The May bank statement and the May cash payments journal show the following:

Bank Statement			Cash Payments Journal		
Checks Paid			Checks Issued		
Date	Check No.	Amount	Date	Check No.	Amount
5/4	254	650	5/2	258	159
5/2	257	410	5/5	259	275
5/17	258	159	5/10	260	925
5/12	259	275	5/15	261	500
5/20	261	500	5/22	262	750
5/29	263	480	5/24	263	480
5/30	262	750	5/29	264	360

Instructions
Using step 2 in the reconciliation procedure, list the outstanding checks at May 31.

Prepare bank reconciliation and adjusting entries.
(SO 7)

E7–8   The following information pertains to Mohammed Company.
1. Cash balance per bank, July 31, $7,463.
2. July bank service charge not recorded by the depositor $15.
3. Cash balance per books, July 31, $7,190.
4. Deposits in transit, July 31, $1,700.
5. Note for $1,200 collected for Mohammed in July by the bank, plus interest $36 less fee $20. The collection has not been recorded by Mohammed, and no interest has been accrued.
6. Outstanding checks, July 31, $772.

Instructions
(a) Prepare a bank reconciliation at July 31.
(b) Journalize the adjusting entries at July 31 on the books of Mohammed Company.

Prepare bank reconciliation and adjusting entries.
(SO 7)

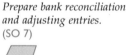

E7–9   The information below relates to the Cash account in the ledger of Reston Company.

Balance September 1—$17,150; Cash deposited—$64,000.
Balance September 30—$17,404; Checks written—$63,746.

The September bank statement shows a balance of $16,422 on September 30 and the following memorandum:

Credits		Debits	
Collection of $1,500 note plus interest $30	$1,530	NSF check: J. Hower	$410
Interest earned on checking account	$45	Safety deposit box rent	$30

At September 30, deposits in transit were $4,500 and outstanding checks totaled $2,383.

Instructions

(a) Prepare the bank reconciliation at September 30.

(b) Prepare the adjusting entries at September 30, assuming (1) the NSF check was from a customer on account, and (2) no interest had been accrued on the note.

E7–10 The cash records of Kuwait Company show the following:

1. The June 30 bank reconciliation indicated that deposits in transit total $850. During July the general ledger account Cash shows deposits of $15,750, but the bank statement indicates that only $15,600 in deposits were received during the month.

2. The June 30 bank reconciliation also reported outstanding checks of $920. During the month of July, Kuwait Company books show that $17,200 of checks were issued, yet the bank statement showed that $16,400 of checks cleared the bank in July.

3. In September, deposits per the bank statement totaled $26,700, deposits per books were $25,400, and deposits in transit at September 30 were $2,400.

4. In September, cash disbursements per books were $23,700, checks clearing the bank were $25,000, and outstanding checks at September 30 were $2,100.

There were no bank debit or credit memoranda, and no errors were made by either the bank or Kuwait Company.

Compute deposits in transit and outstanding checks for two bank reconciliations.
(SO 7)

Instructions

Answer the following questions:

(a) In situation (1), what were the deposits in transit at July 31?

(b) In situation (2), what were the outstanding checks at July 31?

(c) In situation (3), what were the deposits in transit at August 31?

(d) In situation (4), what were the outstanding checks at August 31?

PROBLEMS

P7–1 Red River Theater is located in the Red River Mall. A cashier's booth is located near the entrance to the theater. Two cashiers are employed. One works from 1–5 P.M., the other from 5–9 P.M. Each cashier is bonded. The cashiers receive cash from customers and operate a machine that ejects serially numbered tickets. The rolls of tickets are inserted and locked into the machine by the theater manager at the beginning of each cashier's shift.

Identify internal control weaknesses over cash receipts.
(SO 2, 3)

After purchasing a ticket, the customer takes the ticket to a doorperson stationed at the entrance of the theater lobby some 60 feet from the cashier's booth. The doorperson tears the ticket in half, admits the customer, and returns the ticket stub to the customer. The other half of the ticket is dropped into a locked box by the doorperson.

At the end of each cashier's shift, the theater manager removes the ticket rolls from the machine and makes a cash count. The cash count sheet is initialed by the cashier. At the end of the day, the manager deposits the receipts in total in a bank night deposit vault located in the mall. In addition, the manager sends copies of the deposit slip and the initialed cash count sheets to the theater company treasurer for verification and to the company's accounting department. Receipts from the first shift are stored in a safe located in the manager's office.

Instructions

(a) Identify the internal control principles and their application to the cash receipts transactions of the Red River Theater.

(b) If the doorperson and cashier decide to collaborate to misappropriate cash, what actions might they take?

P7–2 MTR Company maintains a petty cash fund for small expenditures. The following transactions occurred over a 2-month period:

Journalize and post petty cash fund transactions.
(SO 5)

July 1 Established petty cash fund by writing a check on Metro Bank for $200.

 15 Replenished the petty cash fund by writing a check for $195.00. On this date the fund consisted of $5.00 in cash and the following petty cash receipts: Freight-in $94.00, postage expense $43.00, entertainment expense $46.00, and miscellaneous expense $11.00.

 31 Replenished the petty cash fund by writing a check for $192.00. At this date, the fund consisted of $8.00 in cash and the following petty cash receipts: Freight-in

$82.00, charitable contributions expense $30.00, postage expense $48.00, and miscellaneous expense $32.00.

Aug. 15   Replenished the petty cash fund by writing a check for $188.00. On this date, the fund consisted of $12.00 in cash and the following petty cash receipts: Freight-in $75.00, entertainment expense $43.00, postage expense $34.00, and miscellaneous expense $38.00.

16   Increased the amount of the petty cash fund to $300 by writing a check for $100.

31   Replenished petty cash fund by writing a check for $283.00. On this date, the fund consisted of $17 in cash and the following petty cash receipts: Postage expense $145.00, entertainment expense $91.00, and freight-in $44.00.

Instructions
(a) Journalize the petty cash transactions.
(b) Post to the Petty Cash account.
(c) What internal control features exist in a petty cash fund?

Prepare a bank reconciliation and adjusting entries.
(SO 7)

P7–3   On July 31, 1996, Lori Company had a cash balance per books of $6,815.00. The statement from Tri-County Bank on that date showed a balance of $7,076.00. A comparison of the bank statement with the cash account revealed the following facts:

1. The bank service charge for July was $25.
2. The bank collected a note receivable of $1,200 for Lori Company on July 15, plus $48 of interest. The bank made a $10 charge for the collection. Lori has not accrued any interest on the note.
3. The July 31 receipts of $1,820 were not included in the bank deposits for July. These receipts were deposited by the company in a night deposit vault on July 31.
4. Company check No. 2480 issued to J. Brokaw, a creditor, for $492 that cleared the bank in July was incorrectly entered in the cash payments journal on July 10 for $429.
5. Checks outstanding on July 31 totaled $1,481.
6. On July 31, the bank statement showed an NSF charge of $550 for a check received by the company from R. Close, a customer, on account.

Instructions
(a) Prepare the bank reconciliation as of July 31.
(b) Prepare the necessary adjusting entries at July 31.

Prepare a bank reconciliation and adjusting entries from detailed data.
(SO 7)

P7–4   The bank portion of the bank reconciliation for London Company at October 31, 1996, was as follows:

LONDON COMPANY
Bank Reconciliation
October 31, 1996

Cash balance per bank		$12,367.90
Add: Deposits in transit		1,530.20
		13,898.10
Less: Outstanding checks		

Check Number	Check Amount	
2451	$1,260.40	
2470	720.10	
2471	844.50	
2472	426.80	
2474	1,050.00	4,301.80

Adjusted cash balance per bank		$ 9,596.30

The adjusted cash balance per bank agreed with the cash balance per books at October 31.

The November bank statement showed the following checks and deposits:

		Bank Statement		
Checks			**Deposits**	
Date	Number	Amount	Date	Amount
11-1	2470	$ 720.10	11-1	$ 1,530.20
11-2	2471	844.50	11-4	1,211.60
11-5	2474	1,050.00	11-8	990.10
11-4	2475	1,640.70	11-13	2,575.00
11-8	2476	2,830.00	11-18	1,472.70
11-10	2477	600.00	11-21	2,945.00
11-15	2479	1,750.00	11-25	2,567.30
11-18	2480	1,330.00	11-28	1,650.00
11-27	2481	695.40	11-30	1,186.00
11-30	2483	575.50	Total	$16,127.90
11-29	2486	900.00		
	Total	$12,936.20		

The cash records per books for November showed the following:

		Cash Payments Journal					Cash Receipts Journal	
Date	Number	Amount	Date	Number	Amount		Date	Amount
11-1	2475	$1,640.70	11-20	2483	$ 575.50		11-3	$ 1,211.60
11-2	2476	2,830.00	11-22	2484	829.50		11-7	990.10
11-2	2477	600.00	11-23	2485	974.80		11-12	2,575.00
11-4	2478	538.20	11-24	2486	900.00		11-17	1,472.70
11-8	2479	1,570.00	11-29	2487	398.00		11-20	2,954.00
11-10	2480	1,330.00	11-30	2488	800.00		11-24	2,567.30
11-15	2481	695.40	Total		$14,294.10		11-27	1,650.00
11-18	2482	612.00					11-29	1,186.00
							11-30	1,225.00
							Total	$15,831.70

The bank statement contained two bank memoranda:

1. A credit of $2,105.00 for the collection of a $2,000 note for London Company plus interest of $120 and less a collection fee of $15. London Company has not accrued any interest on the note.
2. A debit for the printing of additional company checks, $50.00.

At November 30 the cash balance per books was $11,123.90, and the cash balance per the bank statement was $17,604.60. The bank did not make any errors, but two errors were made by London Company.

Instructions
(a) Using the four steps in the reconciliation procedure described on pages 305–6, prepare a bank reconciliation at November 30.
(b) Prepare the adjusting entries based on the reconciliation. (*Note:* The correction of any errors pertaining to recording checks should be made to Accounts Payable. The correction of any errors relating to recording cash receipts should be made to Accounts Receivable.)

Prepare a bank reconciliation and adjusting entries.
(SO 7)

P7–5   Mayo Company's bank statement from Lane National Bank at August 31, 1996, shows the following information:

Balance, August 1	$17,400	Bank credit memorandum:	
August deposits	73,000	Collection of note	
Checks cleared in August	68,660	receivable plus $90	
Balance, August 31	24,850	interest	$3,090
		Interest earned	45
		Bank debit memorandum	
		Safety deposit box rent	25

A summary of the Cash account in the ledger for August shows: Balance, August 1, $16,900; receipts $77,000; disbursements $73,570; and balance, August 31, $20,330. Analysis reveals that the only reconciling items on the July 31 bank reconciliation were a deposit in transit for $4,000 and outstanding checks of $4,500. The deposit in transit was the first deposit recorded by the bank in August. In addition, you determine that there were two errors involving company checks drawn in August: (1) a check for $400 to a creditor on account that cleared the bank in August was journalized and posted for $420, and (2) a salary check to an employee for $275 was recorded by the bank for $285.

Instructions
(a) Prepare a bank reconciliation at August 31.
(b) Journalize the adjusting entries to be made by Mayo Company at August 31. Assume the interest on the note has been accrued by the company.

ALTERNATE PROBLEMS

P7–1A   Segal Office Supply Company recently changed its system of internal control over cash disbursements. The system includes the following features.

Identify internal control principles over cash disbursements.
(SO 2, 4)

   Instead of being unnumbered and manually prepared, all checks must now be pre-numbered and written by using the new checkwriter purchased by the company. Before a check can be issued, each invoice must have the approval of Cindy Morris, the purchasing agent, and Ray Mills, the receiving department supervisor. Checks must be signed by either Frank Malone, the treasurer, or Mary Arno, the assistant treasurer. Before signing a check, the signer is expected to compare the amounts of the check with the amounts on the invoice.

   After signing a check, the signer stamps the invoice PAID and inserts within the stamp, the date, check number, and amount of the check. The "paid" invoice is then sent to the accounting department for recording.

   Blank checks are stored in a safe in the treasurer's office. The combination to the safe is known only by the treasurer and assistant treasurer. Each month, the bank statement is reconciled with the bank balance per books by the assistant chief accountant.

Instructions
Identify the internal control principles and their application to cash disbursements of Segal Office Supply Company.

P7–2A   Dockers Company maintains a petty cash fund for small expenditures. The following transactions occurred over a 2-month period:

Journalize and post petty cash fund transactions.
(SO 5)

July 1   Established petty cash fund by writing a check on Metro Bank for $200.
     15   Replenished the petty cash fund by writing a check for $195.00. On this date the fund consisted of $5.00 in cash and the following petty cash receipts: Freight-in $94.00, postage expense $43.00, entertainment expense $46.00, and miscellaneous expense $11.00.
     31   Replenished the petty cash fund by writing a check for $192.00. At this date, the fund consisted of $8.00 in cash and the following petty cash receipts: Freight-in $82.00, charitable contributions expense $40.00, postage expense $28.00, and miscellaneous expense $42.00.

Aug. 15 Replenished the petty cash fund by writing a check for $187.00. On this date, the fund consisted of $13.00 in cash and the following petty cash receipts: Freight-in $75.00, entertainment expense $43.00, postage expense $33.00, and miscellaneous expense $37.00.

 16 Increased the amount of the petty cash fund to $300 by writing a check for $100.

 31 Replenished petty cash fund by writing a check for $283.00. On this date, the fund consisted of $17 in cash and the following petty cash receipts: Postage expense $140.00, travel expense $95.00, and freight-in $46.00.

Instructions
 (a) Journalize the petty cash transactions.
 (b) Post to the Petty Cash account.
 (c) What internal control features exist in a petty cash fund?

P7–3A On May 31, 1996, Maloney Company had a cash balance per books of $5,781.00. The bank statement from Community Bank on that date showed a balance of $6,806.00. A comparison of the statement with the cash account revealed the following facts:

Prepare a bank reconciliation and adjusting entries.
(SO 7)

1. The statement included a debit memo of $40 for the printing of additional company checks.
2. Cash sales of $836.00 on May 12 were deposited in the bank. The cash receipts journal entry and the deposit slip were incorrectly made for $846.00. The bank credited Maloney Company for the correct amount.
3. Outstanding checks at May 31 totaled $1,278.00, and deposits in transit were $936.00.
4. On May 18, the company issued check No. 1181 for $685 to M. Helms, on account. The check, which cleared the bank in May, was incorrectly journalized and posted by Maloney Company for $658.
5. A $2,000 note receivable was collected by the bank for Maloney Company on May 31 plus $80 interest. The bank charged a collection fee of $20. No interest has been accrued on the note.
6. Included with the cancelled checks was a check issued by Teller Company to P. Jonet for $600 that was incorrectly charged to Maloney Company by the bank.
7. On May 31, the bank statement showed an NSF charge of $700 for a check issued by W. Hoad, a customer, to Maloney Company on account.

Instructions
 (a) Prepare the bank reconciliation at May 31, 1996.
 (b) Prepare the necessary adjusting entries for Maloney Company at May 31, 1996.

P7–4A The bank portion of the bank reconciliation for Sandra Company at November 30, 1996, was as follows:

Prepare a bank reconciliation and adjusting entries from detailed data.
(SO 7)

SANDRA COMPANY
Bank Reconciliation
November 30, 1996

Cash balance per bank		$14,367.90
Add: Deposits in transit		2,530.20
		16,898.10

Less: Outstanding checks

Check Number	Check Amount	
3451	$2,260.40	
3470	720.10	
3471	844.50	
3472	1,426.80	
3474	1,050.00	6,301.80
Adjusted cash balance per bank		$10,596.30

The adjusted cash balance per bank agreed with the cash balance per books at November 30.

The December bank statement showed the following checks and deposits:

Bank Statement				
Checks			Deposits	
Date	Number	Amount	Date	Amount
12-1	3451	$ 2,260.40	12-1	$ 2,530.20
12-2	3471	844.50	12-4	1,211.60
12-7	3472	1,426.80	12-8	2,365.10
12-4	3475	1,640.70	12-16	2,672.70
12-8	3476	1,300.00	12-21	2,945.00
12-10	3477	2,130.00	12-26	2,567.30
12-15	3479	3,080.00	12-29	2,836.00
12-27	3480	600.00	12-30	1,025.00
12-30	3482	475.50	Total	$18,152.90
12-29	3483	1,140.00		
12-31	3485	540.80		
	Total	$15,438.70		

The cash records per books for December showed the following:

Cash Payments Journal							Cash Receipts Journal	
Date	Number	Amount	Date	Number	Amount		Date	Amount
12-1	3475	$1,640.70	12-20	3482	$ 475.50		12-3	$ 1,211.60
12-2	3476	1,300.00	12-22	3483	1,140.00		12-7	2,365.10
12-2	3477	2,130.00	12-23	3484	832.00		12-15	2,672.70
12-4	3478	538.20	12-24	3485	450.80		12-20	2,954.00
12-8	3479	3,080.00	12-30	3486	1,389.50		12-25	2,567.30
12-10	3480	600.00	Total		$14,384.10		12-28	2,836.00
12-17	3481	807.40					12-30	1,025.00
							12-31	1,190.40
							Total	$16,822.10

The bank statement contained two memoranda:

1. A credit of $2,145 for the collection of a $2,000 note for Sandra Company plus interest of $160 and less a collection fee of $15.00. Sandra Company has not accrued any interest on the note.
2. A debit of $547.10 for an NSF check written by A. Jordan, a customer. At December 31, the check had not been redeposited in the bank.

At December 31 the cash balance per books was $13,034.30, and the cash balance per the bank statement was $18,680.00. The bank did not make any errors, but two errors were made by Sandra Company.

Instructions
(a) Using the four steps in the reconciliation procedure, prepare a bank reconciliation at December 31.
(b) Prepare the adjusting entries based on the reconciliation. (*Note:* The correction of any errors pertaining to recording checks should be made to Accounts Payable. The correction of any errors relating to recording cash receipts should be made to Accounts Receivable.)

P7–5A Palmeiro Company maintains a checking account at the Marine City Bank. At July 31, selected data from the ledger balance and the bank statement are as follows:

Prepare a bank reconciliation and adjusting entries.
(SO 7)

	Cash in Bank	
	Per Books	Per Bank
Balance, July 1	$17,600	$19,200
July receipts	82,000	
July credits		80,070
July disbursements	76,900	
July debits		74,740
Balance, July 31	$22,700	$24,530

Analysis of the bank data reveals that the credits consist of $78,000 of July deposits and a credit memorandum of $2,070 for the collection of a $2,000 note plus interest revenue of $70. The July debits per bank consist of checks cleared, $74,700 and a debit memorandum of $40 for printing additional company checks.

You also discover the following errors involving July checks: (1) a check for $230 to a creditor on account that cleared the bank in July was journalized and posted as $320, and (2) a salary check to an employee for $255 was recorded by the bank for $155.

The June 30 bank reconciliation contained only two reconciling items: deposits in transit $5,000 and outstanding checks of $6,600.

Instructions
(a) Prepare a bank reconciliation at July 31.
(b) Journalize the adjusting entries to be made by Palmeiro Company at July 31, 1996. Assume that the interest on the note has been accrued.

P7–6A Acura Company is a very profitable small business. It has not, however, given much consideration to internal control. For example, in an attempt to keep clerical and office expenses to a minimum, the company has combined the jobs of cashier and bookkeeper. As a result, Rob Rowe handles all cash receipts, keeps the accounting records, and prepares the monthly bank reconciliations.

Prepare comprehensive bank reconciliation with defalcation and internal control deficiencies.
(SO 2, 3, 4, 7)

The balance per the bank statement on October 31, 1996, was $18,380. Outstanding checks were: No. 62 for $126.75, No. 183 for $150, No. 284 for $253.25, No. 862 for $190.71, No. 863 for $226.80, and No. 864 for $165.28. Included with the statement was a credit memorandum of $200 indicating the collection of a note receivable for the Acura Company by the bank on October 25. This memorandum has not been recorded by Acura Company.

The company's ledger showed one cash account with a balance of $21,892.72. The balance included undeposited cash on hand. Because of the lack of internal controls, Rowe took for personal use all of the undeposited receipts in excess of $3,795.51. He then prepared the following bank reconciliation in an effort to conceal his theft of cash.

Cash balance per books, October 31		$21,892.72
Add: Outstanding checks		
No. 862	$190.71	
No. 863	226.80	
No. 864	165.28	482.79
		22,375.51
Less: Undeposited receipts		3,795.51
Unadjusted balance per bank, October 31		18,580.00
Less: Bank credit memorandum		200.00
Cash balance per bank statement, October 31		$18,380.00

Instructions
(a) Prepare a correct bank reconciliation. (*Hint:* Deduct the amount of the theft from the adjusted balance per books.)
(b) Indicate the three ways that Rowe attempted to conceal the theft and the dollar amount pertaining to each method.
(c) What principles of internal control were violated in this case?

▼*Broadening Your Perspective*

*F*INANCIAL REPORTING PROBLEM—PEPSICO, INC.
● ●

The financial statements of PepsiCo, Inc. are presented in Appendix A of this textbook together with two reports: (1) a management report, Management's Responsibility for Financial Statements, and (2) an auditor's report, Report of Independent Auditors.

Instructions
Using the financial statements and reports, answer the following questions about PepsiCo's internal controls and cash.

1. What comments, if any, concerning the company's system of internal control are included in each report?
2. What reference, if any, is made to internal auditors in each report?
3. What comments, if any, are made about cash in the report of the independent auditors?
4. What data about cash and cash equivalents are shown in the consolidated balance sheet (statement of financial condition)?
5. What activities are identified in the consolidated statement of cash flows as being responsible for the changes in cash during 1995?
6. How are cash equivalents defined under the Notes to Consolidated Financial Statements?

*C*OMPARATIVE ANALYSIS PROBLEM— THE COCA-COLA COMPANY VS. PEPSICO, INC.
● ●

The financial statements of The Coca-Cola Company are presented at the end of Chapter 1, and PepsiCo's financial statements are presented in Appendix A.

Instructions:
(a) Based on the information contained in these financial statements, determine each of the following for each company:
   1. Cash and cash equivalents balance at December 31, 1995.
   2. Increase (decrease) in cash and cash equivalents from 1994 to 1995.
   3. Cash provided by operating activities during 1995 (from Statement of Cash Flows).
(b) What conclusions concerning the management of cash can be drawn from these data?

*I*NTERPRETATION OF FINANCIAL STATEMENTS
● ●

Case—Microsoft, Inc.
Microsoft is the leading developer of software in the world. To continue to be successful Microsoft must generate new products. Generating new products requires significant amounts of cash. Shown below is the current assets section of Microsoft's June 30, 1995, balance sheet and excerpts from a footnote describing the first item listed in the balance sheet, "cash and short-term investments." Below Microsoft is the current asset section of Oracle, another major software developer.

(all dollar amounts in millions)
Microsoft

Current assets:	1994	1995
Cash and short-term investments (1)	$3,614	$4,750
Accounts receivable—net of allowances of $92 and $139	475	581
Inventories	102	88
Other	121	201
Total current assets	$4,312	$5,620
Total current liabilities	$ 913	$1,347

(1) From Microsoft's "Notes to Financial Statements" the following breakdown is available.

	1994	1995
Cash and equivalents	$1,477	$1,962
Short-term investments	2,137	2,788
Cash and short-term investments	$3,614	$4,750

Oracle

Current assets	1994	1995
Cash and cash equivalents	$ 409	$ 480
Short-term cash investments	60	106
Receivables	516	846
Other current assets	95	185
Total current assets	$1,080	$1,617
Current liabilities	$ 682	$1,055

Instructions:
(a) What is the definition of a cash equivalent? Give some examples of cash equivalents. How do cash equivalents differ from other types of short-term investments?
(b) Comment on Microsoft's presentation of cash in its balance sheet.
(c) What problems might this presentation of cash pose for a user of Microsoft's financial statements?
(d) Compare the liquidity of Microsoft and Oracle for 1995.
(e) Is it possible to have too many liquid assets?

DECISION CASE

The board of trustees of a local church is concerned about the internal accounting controls pertaining to the offering collections made at weekly services. They ask you to serve on a three-person audit team with the internal auditor of the university and a CPA who has just joined the church.

At a meeting of the audit team and the board of trustees you learn the following:

1. The church's board of trustees has delegated responsibility for the financial management and audit of the financial records to the finance committee. This group prepares the annual budget and approves major disbursements but is not involved in collections or record keeping. No audit has been made in recent years because the same trusted employee has kept church records and served as financial secretary for 15 years. The church does not carry any fidelity insurance.

2. The collection at the weekly service is taken by a team of ushers who volunteer to serve one month. The ushers take the collection plates to a basement office at the rear of the church. They hand their plates to the head usher and return to the church service. After all plates have been turned in, the head usher counts the cash received. The head usher then places the cash in the church safe along with a notation of the amount counted. The head usher volunteers to serve for 3 months.

3. The next morning the financial secretary opens the safe and recounts the collection. The secretary withholds $150–$200 in cash, depending on the cash expenditures expected for the week, and deposits the remainder of the collections in the bank. To facilitate the deposit, church members who contribute by check are asked to make their checks payable to "cash."
4. Each month, the financial secretary reconciles the bank statement and submits a copy of the reconciliation to the board of trustees. The reconciliations have rarely contained any bank errors and have never shown any errors per books.

Instructions
(a) Indicate the weaknesses in internal accounting control over the handling of collections.
(b) List the improvements in internal control procedures that you plan to make at the next meeting of the audit team for (1) the ushers, (2) the head usher, (3) the financial secretary, and (4) the finance committee.
(c) What church policies should be changed to improve internal control?

COMMUNICATION ACTIVITY

As a new auditor for the CPA firm of Rawls, Keoto, and Landry you have been assigned to review the internal controls over mail cash receipts of Adirondack Company. Your review reveals the following: Checks are promptly endorsed "For Deposit Only," but no list of the checks is prepared by the person opening the mail. The mail is opened either by the cashier or by the employee who maintains the accounts receivable records. Mail receipts are deposited in the bank weekly by the cashier.

Instructions
Write a letter to L. S. Osman, owner of the Adirondack Company, explaining the weaknesses in internal control and your recommendations for improving the system.

GROUP ACTIVITY

From your employment or personal experiences, identify situations in which cash was received or disbursed.

Instructions
In groups of five or six students:
(a) Identify the internal control principles used for cash receipts.
(b) Identify the internal control principles used for cash disbursements.
(c) Identify any weaknesses in internal control related to cash receipts and disbursements.

ETHICS CASE

You are the assistant controller in charge of general ledger accounting at Lemon Twist Bottling Company. Your company has a large loan from an insurance company. The loan agreement requires that the company's cash account balance be maintained at $200,000 or more as reported monthly. At June 30 the cash balance is $80,000, which you report to Sam Williams, the financial vice-president. Sam excitedly instructs you to keep the cash receipts book open for one additional day for purposes of the June 30 report to the insurance company. Sam says, "If we don't get that cash balance over $200,000, we'll default on our loan agreement. They could close us down, put us all out of our jobs!" Sam continues, "I talked to Grochum Distributors (one of Lemon Twist's largest customers) this morning and they said they sent us a check for $150,000 yesterday. We should receive it tomorrow. If we include just that one check in our cash balance, we'll be in the clear. It's in the mail!"

Instructions
    (a) Who will suffer negative effects if you do not comply with Sam Williams' instructions? Who will suffer if you do comply?
    (b) What are the ethical considerations in this case?
    (c) What alternatives do you have?

RESEARCH ASSIGNMENT

The "Fortune 500" issue of *Fortune* magazine can serve as a useful reference. This annual issue of *Fortune*, generally appearing in late April or early May, contains a great deal of information regarding the largest U.S. industrial and service companies. Examine the most recent edition and answer the following questions.

    (a) Identify the three largest U.S. corporations in terms of revenues, profits, assets, market value, and employees.
    (b) Identify the largest corporation headquartered (or operating, if needed) in your state (by total revenue). How does this corporation rank in terms of revenues, profits, assets, market value, and number of employees?

CRITICAL THINKING
► *A Real-World Focus: Alternative Distributor Corp.*

Alternative Distributor Corp., a distributor of groceries and related products, is headquartered in Medford, Massachusetts. It was founded in 1980 and today has seven employees, with a total sales of $7 million.

During its audit, the Alternative Distributor Corp. was advised that previously existing internal controls necessary for the company to develop reliable financial statements were inadequate. The audit report stated that the current system of accounting for sales, receivables, and cash receipts constituted a material weakness.

    Among other items, the report focused on non-timely deposit of cash receipts, exposing Alternative Distributor to potential loss or misappropriation; excessive past due accounts receivable due to lack of collection efforts; disregard of advantages offered by vendors for prompt payment of invoices; absence of appropriate segregation of duties by personnel consistent with appropriate control objectives; inadequate procedures for applying accounting principles; lack of qualified management personnel; lack of supervision by an outside board of directors; and overall poor recordkeeping.

Instructions
Identify the principles of internal control violated by Alternative Distributor Corporation.

Answers to Self-Study Questions
1. a   2. c   3. b   4. c   5. b   6. d   7. a   8. a   9. c   10. d   11. c

Before studying this chapter, you should know or, if necessary, review:

a. *How to record sales transactions (Ch. 5, pp. 202–05)*
b. *Why adjusting entries are made (Ch. 3, p. 101)*
c. *How to compute interest (Ch. 3, p. 110)*

How Long Should the Check Be in the Mail?

RALEIGH, N.C. — Take a look at your campus newspaper. Read the advertisements—the nearby pizza parlor, a local clothing merchant, maybe a review course for the Law School Admission Test. In many cases these advertisers set up accounts with the campus paper and pay their bills 30 days after the ad runs. The paper keeps track of these accounts and bills them on a timely basis.

For more than 70 years, the North Carolina State University newspaper, the *Technician*, has published stories by student writers and run ads by local merchants. "Eighty-five percent of our $400,000 annual operating budget comes from advertising," says Tim Ellington, General Manager—a graduate of NC State. "The rest comes from student fees."

Ellington says that the paper requires prepayment from new advertising accounts. After a trial period, the advertiser will be granted a 30-day payment period. From time to time, however, advertisers don't pay on time. "When it comes to bill paying time, our bill often gets put on the bottom of the pile," says Ellington. "If they are going to anger somebody, they'll anger us before they do a supplier."

The newspaper follows a series of steps in trying to collect late accounts: Once a bill is 30 days past due, the advertiser is sent a letter that says, nicely, "If you haven't sent your payment, please do." At 45 days, the letter isn't as nice: "If we don't receive payment in 30 days, then we could pursue it through small claims court." At 75 days, the newspaper files a small claims suit. ◄

CHAPTER · **8**

ACCOUNTING FOR RECEIVABLES

► **STUDY OBJECTIVES** ◄

After studying this chapter, you should be able to:

1. *Identify the different types of receivables.*
2. *Explain how accounts receivable are recognized in the accounts.*
3. *Distinguish between the methods and bases used to value accounts receivable.*
4. *Describe the entries to record the disposition of accounts receivable.*
5. *Compute the maturity date of, and interest on, notes receivable.*
6. *Explain how notes receivable are recognized in the accounts.*
7. *Describe how notes receivable are valued.*
8. *Describe the entries to record the disposition of notes receivable.*
9. *Explain the statement presentation and analysis of receivables.*

As you read this chapter, you will learn what journal entries the *Technician* makes when it sells its ad space, when it collects the cash for those sales, and when it writes off an uncollectible account. The types of entries the *Technician* makes are typical of most businesses, because our economy depends heavily on the use of credit, which takes the form of accounts and notes receivable.

The content and organization of this chapter are as follows:

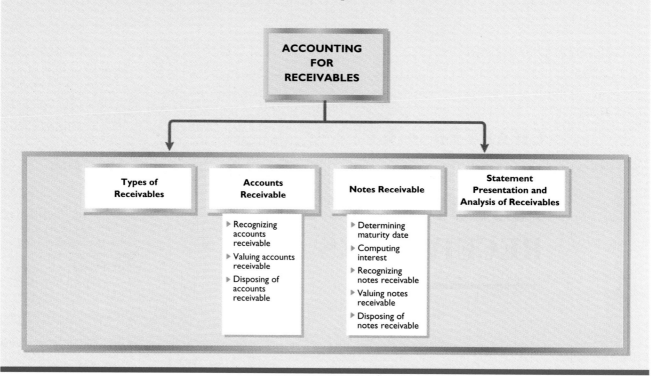

Types of Receivables

The term "receivables" refers to amounts due from individuals and other companies. Receivables are claims that are expected to be collected in cash. Receivables are frequently classified as (1) accounts, (2) notes, and (3) other.

Accounts receivable are amounts owed by customers on account. They result from the sale of goods and services. These receivables generally are expected to be collected within 30 to 60 days. They are the most significant type of claim held by a company.

Notes receivable represent claims for which formal instruments of credit are issued as evidence of the debt. The credit instrument normally requires the debtor to pay interest and extends for time periods of 60–90 days or longer. Notes and accounts receivable that result from sales transactions are often called trade receivables.

Other receivables include nontrade receivables such as interest receivable, loans to company officers, advances to employees, and income taxes refundable. These are unusual; therefore, they are generally classified and reported as separate items in the balance sheet.

Accounts Receivable

The three primary accounting problems associated with accounts receivable are:

1. **Recognizing** accounts receivable.
2. **Valuing** accounts receivable.
3. **Disposing of** accounts receivable.

Recognizing Accounts Receivable

Recognizing accounts receivable is relatively straightforward. In Chapter 5 we saw how accounts receivable are affected by the sale of merchandise. To illustrate, assume that Jordache Co. on July 1, 1996, sells merchandise on account to Polo Company for $1,000, terms 2/10, n/30. On July 5, merchandise having a selling price of $100 is returned to Jordache Co. On July 11, payment is received from Polo Company for the balance due. The journal entries to record the receivables element of these transactions on the books of Jordache Co. are as follows:

July 1	Accounts Receivable	1,000	
	Sales		1,000
	(To record sales on account)		
July 5	Sales Returns and Allowances	100	
	Accounts Receivable		100
	(To record merchandise returned)		
July 11	Cash ($900 − $18)	882	
	Sales Discounts ($900 × .02)	18	
	Accounts Receivable		900
	(To record collection of accounts receivable)		

The opportunity to receive a cash discount usually occurs when a manufacturer sells to a wholesaler or a wholesaler sells to a retailer. A discount is given in these situations either to encourage prompt payment or for competitive reasons.

On the other hand, retailers rarely grant cash discounts to customers. For example, we would be surprised if you ever received a cash discount in purchasing goods from any well-known retailer, such as Kmart, Sears, Wal-Mart, and so on. In these situations, most sales are either cash or credit card sales. In fact, when you use a retailer's credit card (J. C. Penney or Sears, for example), instead of giving a discount, the retailer charges interest on the balance due if not paid within a specified period (usually 25–30 days).

To illustrate, assume that you charge on your J. C. Penney credit card a new outfit with a selling price of $300. J. C. Penney will make the following receivables entry at the date of sale:

Accounts Receivable	300	
Sales		300
(To record sale of merchandise)		

J. C. Penney will then send you a monthly statement of this transaction and any others that have occurred during the month. If you fail to pay in full within 30 days, J. C. Penney adds an interest (financing) charge to the balance due. Although interest rates vary from state to state and from time to time (depending in part on federal monetary policy), a common rate for retailers is 18% per year or 1.5% per month.

STUDY OBJECTIVE
2

Explain how accounts receivable are recognized in the accounts.

Helpful hint These entries are the same as those described in Chapter 5. For simplicity, inventory and cost of goods sold are omitted from this set of journal entries.

Helpful hint A recent survey indicated that the annual charge per credit card is approximately $1,250, which is double what it was 10 years earlier.

When financing charges are added, the seller recognizes interest revenue. Assuming that you owe $300 at the end of the month, and J. C. Penney charges 1.5% per month on the balance due, the entry to record interest revenue of $4.50 ($300 × 1.5%) is as follows:

Accounts Receivable	4.50	
Interest Revenue		4.50
(To record interest on amount due)		

Interest revenue is often substantial for many retailers.

▶ Accounting in Action ▸ *Business Insight*

Interest rates on most credit cards are quite high, averaging approximately 18.8%. As a result, consumers are often looking for companies that charge lower rates. But be careful—some companies offer lower interest rates but have eliminated the standard 25-day grace period before finance charges are incurred. Other companies encourage consumers to get more in debt by advertising that only a $1 minimum payment is due on a $1,000 account balance! They, of course, earn more interest! Chase Manhattan Corp. markets a credit card that allows cardholders to skip a payment twice a year. However, the outstanding balance continues to incur interest. Other credit card companies calculate finance charges initially on two-month, rather than one-month averages, a practice which often translates into higher interest charges. In short, read the fine print. Because of rising competition among banks to issue MasterCard and VISA credit cards, interest rates in 1994 ranged between 9.5% with annual fees (of $18 to $35) to 21% with no annual fees.

Source: Wall Street Journal, February 21, 1992, and Fortune, November 28, 1994.

Valuing Accounts Receivable

STUDY OBJECTIVE
•••••••••▼**3**▼•••••••••

Distinguish between the methods and bases used to value accounts receivable.

Once receivables are recorded in the accounts, the next question is: How should these receivables be reported on the balance sheet? Determining the amount to report as an asset is important because some receivables will become uncollectible. To ensure that receivables are not overstated on the balance sheet, they are stated at their cash (net) realizable value. Cash (net) realizable value is the net amount expected to be received in cash. The cash realizable value excludes amounts that the company estimates it will not be able to collect. Receivables are therefore reduced by estimated uncollectible receivables on the balance sheet.

The income statement also is affected by the amount of uncollectibles. An expense for estimated uncollectibles is recorded to make certain that expenses are not understated and are matched with related sales revenue. This expense is reported as **bad debts expense** on the income statement.

Uncollectible Accounts Receivable

Although each customer must satisfy the credit requirements of the seller before the credit sale is approved, inevitably some accounts receivable become uncollectible. For example, a company may experience a decline in sales because of a downturn in the economy. Similarly, individuals may be laid off from their jobs or be faced with unexpected hospital bills.

Helpful hint Bad debts are quite normal—even the best companies will have them.

In accounting, credit losses are debited to Bad Debts Expense (or Uncollectible Accounts Expense). Such losses are considered a normal and necessary risk of doing business on a credit basis. In fact, from a management point of view, a reasonable amount of uncollectible accounts is evidence of a sound credit policy. When bad debts are abnormally low, the company may be losing profitable business by following a credit policy that is too strict. Of course, abnormally high bad debts indicate a credit policy that is too lenient.

Two methods are used in accounting for uncollectible accounts: (1) the allowance method and (2) the direct write-off method. Each of these methods is explained in the following sections.

Allowance Method. The allowance method is required for financial reporting purposes when bad debts are material in amount. Its essential features are:

1. Uncollectible accounts receivable are estimated and matched against sales in the same accounting period in which the sales occurred.
2. Estimated uncollectibles are debited to Bad Debts Expense and credited to Allowance for Doubtful Accounts through an adjusting entry at the end of each period.
3. Actual uncollectibles are debited to Allowance for Doubtful Accounts and credited to Accounts Receivable at the time the specific account is written off.

> **Helpful hint** In this context, *material* means significant or important.

Recording Estimated Uncollectibles. To illustrate the allowance method, assume that Hampson Furniture has credit sales of $1,200,000 in 1996, of which $200,000 remain uncollected at December 31. The credit manager **estimates** that $12,000 of these sales will prove uncollectible. The adjusting entry to record the estimated uncollectibles is:

Dec. 31	Bad Debts Expense	12,000	
	Allowance for Doubtful Accounts		12,000
	(To record estimate of uncollectible accounts)		

Bad Debts Expense is reported in the income statement as an operating expense (usually as a selling expense). Thus, the estimated uncollectibles are **matched** with sales in 1996 because the expense is recorded in the same year the sales are made.

Allowance for Doubtful Accounts is a contra asset account that shows the claims on customers that are expected to become uncollectible in the future. A contra account is used instead of a direct credit to Accounts Receivable because we do not know which customers will not pay. The credit balance in this account will absorb the specific write-offs when they occur. **Allowance for Doubtful Accounts is not closed at the end of the fiscal year.** It is deducted from Accounts Receivable in the current asset section of the balance sheet as follows:

> **Helpful hint** Bad debts expense is also called uncollectible accounts expense.

> **Helpful hint** Allowance for doubtful accounts is also called allowance for uncollectibles or allowance for bad debts.

Current assets		
Cash		$ 14,800
Accounts receivable	$200,000	
Less: Allowance for doubtful accounts	12,000	188,000
Merchandise inventory		310,000
Prepaid expense		25,000
Total current assets		$537,800

> **Illustration 8-1**
>
> *Presentation of allowance for doubtful accounts*

> ▶ **International note**
>
> The Finance Ministry in Japan recently noted that financial institutions should make better disclosure of bad loans. This disclosure would help depositors pick healthy banks.

The amount of $188,000 represents the expected **cash realizable value** of the accounts receivable at the statement date.

Recording the Write-off of an Uncollectible Account. Companies use various methods of collecting past-due accounts, such as the sequence of letters, calls, and legal action described by Tim Ellington of the NCSU *Technician* in the opening story. When all means of collecting a past-due account have been exhausted and collection appears impossible, the account should be written off. To prevent premature write-offs, each write-off should be formally approved in writing by authorized management personnel.

Assume, for example, that the vice-president of finance of Hampson Furniture authorizes the write-off of the $500 balance owed by R. A. Ware on March 1, 1997. The entry to record the write-off is:

Mar. 1	Allowance for Doubtful Accounts	500	
	Accounts Receivable—R. A. Ware		500
	(Write-off of R. A. Ware account)		

Bad Debts Expense is not debited when the write-off occurs. **Under the allowance method, every bad debt write-off is debited to the allowance account and not to Bad Debts Expense.** A debit to Bad Debts Expense would be incorrect, because the expense is recognized when the adjusting entry is made for estimated bad debts. After posting, the general ledger accounts will show:

Illustration 8-2

General ledger balances after write-off

Accounts Receivable					Allowance for Doubtful Accounts				
1/1/97 Bal.	200,000	3/1/97	500		3/1/97	500	1/1/97 Bal.	12,000	
3/1/97 Bal.	199,500						3/1/97	11,500	

A write-off affects only balance sheet accounts. The write-off of the account reduces both Accounts Receivable and the Allowance for Doubtful Accounts. Cash realizable value in the balance sheet, therefore, remains the same as illustrated below.

Illustration 8-3

Cash realizable value comparison

	Before Write-off	After Write-off
Accounts receivable	$200,000	$199,500
Allowance for doubtful accounts	12,000	11,500
Cash realizable value	$188,000	$188,000

Recovery of an Uncollectible Account. Occasionally, a company collects from a customer after the account has been written off as uncollectible. Two entries are required to record the recovery of a bad debt: (1) The entry made in writing off the account is reversed to reinstate the customer's account. (2) The collection is journalized in the usual manner. To illustrate, assume that on July 1, R. A. Ware pays the $500 amount that had been written off on March 1. The entries are:

(1)

July	1	Accounts Receivable—R. A. Ware	500	
		Allowance for Doubtful Accounts		500
		(To reverse write-off of R. A. Ware account)		

(2)

	1	Cash	500	
		Accounts Receivable—R. A. Ware		500
		(To record collection from R. A. Ware)		

Note that the recovery of a bad debt, like the write-off of a bad debt, affects only balance sheet accounts. The net effect of the two entries above is a debit to Cash and a credit to Allowance for Doubtful Accounts for $500. Accounts Receivable is debited and the Allowance for Doubtful Accounts is credited for two reasons: First, the company made an error in judgment when it wrote off the account receivable. Second, R. A. Ware did pay, and therefore the Accounts Receivable account should show this collection for possible future credit purposes.

Helpful hint Like the write-off, a recovery does not involve the income statement.

Bases Used for Allowance Method. To simplify the preceding explanation, the amount of the expected uncollectibles was given. However, in "real life" companies must estimate that amount if they use the allowance method. Two bases are used to determine this amount: **(1) percentage of sales**, and **(2) percentage of receivables**. Both bases are generally accepted in accounting. The choice is a management decision. It depends on the relative emphasis that management wishes to give to expenses and revenues on the one hand or to cash realizable value of the accounts receivable on the other. The choice is whether to emphasize income statement or balance sheet relationships. Illustration 8-4 compares the two bases.

Helpful hint Both bases are GAAP. The choice is a management decision.

Illustration 8-4

Comparison of bases of estimating uncollectibles

The percentage of sales basis results in a better matching of expenses with revenues—an income statement viewpoint. In contrast, the percentage of receivables basis produces the better estimate of cash realizable value—a balance sheet viewpoint. Under both bases, it is necessary to determine the company's past experience with bad debt losses.

Percentage of Sales. In the percentage of sales basis, management establishes a percentage relationship between the amount of credit sales and expected losses from uncollectible accounts. The percentage is based on past experience and anticipated credit policy.

The percentage is usually applied to either total credit sales or net credit sales of the current year. To illustrate, assume that Gonzalez Company elects to use the percentage of sales basis and concludes that 1% of net credit sales will become uncollectible. If net credit sales for 1996 are $800,000, the estimated bad debts expense is $8,000 (1% × $800,000). The adjusting entry is:

Helpful hint Because of matching, the balance in the allowance account is *never* involved in computing the amount of the adjustment.

Dec. 31	Bad Debts Expense	8,000	
	Allowance for Doubtful Accounts		8,000
	(To record estimated bad debts for year)		

This basis of estimating uncollectibles emphasizes the matching of expenses with revenues. As a result, Bad Debts Expense will show a direct percentage relationship to the sales base on which it is computed. **When the adjusting entry is made, the existing balance in the Allowance for Doubtful Accounts is disregarded.** The adjusted balance in this account should result in a reasonable approximation of the realizable value of the receivables. If actual write-offs differ significantly from the amount estimated, the percentage for future years should be modified.

Percentage of Receivables.   Under the percentage of receivables basis, management establishes a percentage relationship between the amount of receivables and expected losses from uncollectible accounts. A schedule (often called an **aging schedule**) is prepared, in which customer balances are classified by the length of time they have been unpaid. Because of its emphasis on time, the analysis is often called aging the accounts receivable.

After the accounts are aged, the expected bad debt losses are determined by applying percentages based on past experience to the totals of each category. The longer a receivable is past due, the less likely it is to be collected. As a result, the estimated percentage of uncollectible debts increases as the number of days past due increases. An aging schedule for Dart Company is shown in Illustration 8-5. Note the increasing percentages from 2% to 40%.

Illustration 8-5

Aging schedule

Helpful hint The higher percentages are used for the older categories because the longer an account is past due, the more susceptible it is to being uncollectible.

Customer	Total	Not Yet Due	Number of Days Past Due			
			1–30	31–60	61–90	Over 90
T. E. Adert	$ 600		$ 300		$ 200	$ 100
R. C. Bortz	300	$ 300				
B. A. Carl	450		200	$ 250		
O. L. Diker	700	500			200	
T. O. Ebbet	600			300		300
Others	36,950	26,200	5,200	2,450	1,600	1,500
	$39,600	$27,000	$5,700	$3,000	$2,000	$1,900
Estimated Percentage Uncollectible			2%	4%	10%	20%	40%
Total Estimated Bad Debts	$ 2,228	$ 540	$ 228	$ 300	$ 400	$ 760

Total uncollectibles for Dart Company ($2,228) represent the amount of existing customer claims expected to become uncollectible in the future. Thus, this amount represents the **required balance** in Allowance for Doubtful Accounts at the balance sheet date. Accordingly, **the amount of the bad debt adjusting entry**

▶**Technology in Action**

  The aging schedule is another example of output that can be obtained from a computerized accounts receivable system. Manually, preparation of this schedule is an onerous and time-consuming task. However, the schedule can be done in minutes on computer systems.

is the difference between the required balance and the existing balance in the allowance account. If the trial balance shows Allowance for Doubtful Accounts with a credit balance of $528, an adjusting entry for $1,700 ($2,228 − $528) is necessary, as shown below:

Dec. 31	Bad Debts Expense	1,700	
	Allowance for Doubtful Accounts		1,700
	(To adjust allowance account to total		
	estimated uncollectibles)		

After the adjusting entry is posted, the accounts of the Dart Company will show:

Bad Debts Expense		Allowance for Doubtful Accounts	
12/31 Adj. **1,700**		Bal. 528	
		12/31 Adj. **1,700**	
		Bal. **2,228**	

Illustration 8-6

Bad debt accounts after posting

Occasionally the allowance account will have a **debit balance** prior to adjustment, because write-offs during the year have exceeded previous provisions for bad debts. In such a case **the debit balance is added to the required balance** when the adjusting entry is made. Thus, if there had been a $500 debit balance in the allowance account before adjustment, the adjusting entry would have been for $2,728 ($2,228 + $500) to arrive at a credit balance of $2,228.

The percentage of receivables method will normally result in the better approximation of cash realizable value. This method, however, will not result in the better matching of expenses with revenues if some customers' accounts are from sales of a prior period. Under such circumstances, bad debts expense for the current period would include amounts applicable to the sales of a prior period.

Direct Write-off Method. Under the direct write-off method, bad debt losses are not estimated and no allowance account is used. When an account is determined to be uncollectible, the loss is charged to Bad Debts Expense. Assume, for example, that Warden Co. writes off M. E. Doran's $200 balance as uncollectible on December 12. The entry is:

Dec. 12	Bad Debts Expense	200	
	Accounts Receivable—M. E. Doran		200
	(To record write-off of M. E. Doran		
	account)		

When this method is used, bad debts expense will show only actual losses from uncollectibles. Accounts receivable will be reported at its gross amount.

Under the direct write-off method, bad debts expense is often recorded in a period different from the period in which the revenue was recorded. Thus, no attempt is made to match bad debts expense to sales revenues in the income statement or to show the cash realizable value of the accounts receivable in the balance sheet. **Consequently, unless bad debt losses are insignificant, the direct write-off method is not acceptable for financial reporting purposes.** The direct write-off method is, however, used for tax purposes. The Internal Revenue Service allows a tax deduction for uncollectible accounts only when specific accounts receivable are deemed uncollectible.

Disposing of Accounts Receivable

STUDY OBJECTIVE

••••••••• **4** •••••••••

Describe the entries to record the disposition of accounts receivable.

In the normal course of events, accounts receivable are collected in cash and removed from the books. However, as credit sales and receivables have grown in size and significance, the "normal course of events" has changed. In order to accelerate the receipt of cash from receivables, companies frequently sell the receivables to another company for cash, thereby shortening the cash-to-cash operating cycle.

There are several reasons for the sale of receivables. **First, for competitive reasons, sellers** (retailers, wholesalers, and manufacturers) **often must provide financing to purchasers of their goods.** For example, in the sale of durable goods, such as automobiles, trucks, industrial and farm equipment, computers, and appliances, a majority of the sales are on a credit basis. Many major companies in these industries have therefore created companies that accept responsibility for accounts receivable financing. General Motors has General Motors Acceptance Corp. (GMAC), Sears has Sears Roebuck Acceptance Corp. (SRAC), Ford has Ford Motor Credit Corp. (FMCC), and Chrysler has Chrysler Finance Corporation (CFC). These companies are referred to as captive finance companies because they are wholly owned by the company making the product. The purpose of captive financing companies is to encourage the sale of their product by assuring financing to buyers.

Helpful hint Two common expressions apply here:
1. Time is money; i.e., waiting for the normal collection process costs money.
2. A bird in the hand is worth two in the bush; i.e., getting the cash now is better than getting it later.

▸*A*ccounting in *A*ction ▸ *Business Insight*

For example, consider the local car dealer. Most local dealers simply do not have the financial resources to finance the sale of cars because most loans today are quite large in relationship to the cost of the car. Recently, the percentage of the price financed by the Big Three automobile manufacturers in the United States was 93% of the selling price of the automobile. In addition, the average length of the loan was 53.5 months, compared to 35 months a decade ago. It is no wonder, therefore, that a captive finance subsidiary like General Motors Acceptance Corporation, if it were a bank, would rank third in total assets behind Citicorp and Chase Manhattan.

Second, receivables may be sold because they may be the only reasonable source of cash. When money is tight, companies may not be able to borrow money in the usual credit markets. If money is available, the cost of borrowing may be prohibitive. A final reason for selling receivables is that **billing and collection are often time consuming and costly**. As a result, it is often easier for a retailer to sell the receivable to another party with expertise in billing and collection matters. Credit card companies such as MasterCard, VISA, American Express, and Diners Club specialize in billing and collecting accounts receivable.

Sale of Receivables

A common sale of receivables is a sale to a factor. A factor is a finance company or bank that buys receivables from businesses for a fee and then collects the payments directly from the customers. Factoring was traditionally associated with the textiles, apparel, footwear, furniture, and home furnishing industries. It has now spread to many other types of businesses and is a multibillion dollar business. For example, Sears, Roebuck and Co. recently sold $14.8 billion of customer accounts receivable.

►*Accounting in Action* ► *Business Insight*

"They're the devil in disguise," is how CEO Barry Weinstein describes factors. Unable to raise capital from bankers or outside investors, Weinstein turned to factoring receivables. The arrangement was pricey: the factor charged interest of 5% a month, to a maximum of 13% of the total invoice, on any uncollected invoices that were factored. The deal became an endless cycle. Soon Weinstein was factoring all new invoices to get the cash to pay the interest on the older factored invoices.

Source: Inc., July 1994, p. 97.

Factoring arrangements vary widely, but typically the factor (purchaser of the receivables) charges a commission. It ranges from 1% to 3% of the amount of receivables purchased. To illustrate, assume that Hendredon Furniture factors $600,000 of receivables to Federal Factors, Inc. Federal Factors assesses a service charge of 2% of the amount of receivables sold. The journal entry to record the sale by Hendredon Furniture is as follows:

Helpful hint The seller can usually earn more than the commission by (1) taking advantage of 2–3% purchase discounts, (2) investing in short-term securities, or (3) reinvesting the money in productive assets.

Cash	588,000	
Service Charge Expense (2% × $600,000)	12,000	
Accounts Receivable		600,000
(To record the sale of accounts receivable)		

If the company usually sells its receivables, the service charge expense incurred by Hendredon Furniture is recorded as selling expense. If receivables are sold infrequently, this amount may be reported in the Other Expenses and Losses section of the income statement.

Credit Card Sales

Approximately 1 billion credit cards were estimated to be in use recently—more than three credit cards for every man, woman, and child in this country. A common type of credit card is a national credit card such as VISA, MasterCard, and American Express. Three parties are involved when national credit cards are used in making retail sales: (1) the credit card issuer, who is independent of the retailer, (2) the retailer, and (3) the customer. A retailer's acceptance of a national credit card is another form of selling (factoring) the receivable.

The major advantages of these national credit cards to the retailer are shown in Illustration 8-7.

In exchange for these advantages, the retailer pays the credit card issuer a fee of 2–6% of the invoice price for its services.

Helpful hint The millions of cards in use translate to more sales with zero bad debts. Both are powerful reasons for a retailer to accept national credit cards.

VISA and MasterCard Sales. Sales resulting from the use of VISA and MasterCard are considered cash sales by the retailer. These cards are issued by banks. Upon receipt of credit card sales slips from a retailer, the bank immediately adds the amount to the seller's bank balance. These credit card sales slips are therefore recorded in the same manner as checks deposited from a cash sale. Banks generally charge a fee of 2–4% of the credit card sales slips for this service. To illustrate, Anita Ferreri purchases a number of compact discs for her restaurant from Karen Kerr Music Co. for $1,000 using her VISA First Bank Card. The

Helpful hint Our most used credit cards as a percentage of market share in a recent year are: VISA 45.6%; MasterCard 26.3%; American Express 20.5%; Discover 5.5%; and Diner's Club 2.1%.

Illustration 8-7

Advantages of credit cards to the retailer

service fee that First Bank charges is 3%. The entry to record this transaction by Karen Kerr Music is as follows:

Cash	970	
Service Charge Expense	30	
Sales		1,000
(To record Visa credit card sales)		

Helpful hint How do the entries for company credit card sales such as J. C. Penney differ from American Express card sales? Answer:
1. In recording the sale, individual customers must be identified in company credit card sales whereas only American Express is identified for their sales.
2. Company credit card sales may result in additional revenue in the form of interest, whereas American Express sales will result in additional expense; i.e., Service Charge Expense.

American Express Sales. Sales using American Express cards are reported as credit sales, not cash sales. Conversion into cash does not occur until American Express remits the net amount to the seller. To illustrate, assume that Four Seasons restaurant accepts an American Express card for a $300 bill. The entry for the sale by Four Seasons (assuming a 5% fee) is:

Accounts Receivable—American Express	285	
Service Charge Expense	15	
Sales		300
(To record American Express credit card sales)		

Thus American Express will subsequently pay the restaurant $285 which the restaurant will record as follows:

Cash	285	
Accounts Receivable—American Express		285
(To record redemption of credit card billings)		

Service Charge Expense is reported as a selling expense in the income statement by the restaurant.

►*Accounting in Action* ► *Business Insight*

Many *are* leaving home without it! Despite long-standing advertisements that urge customers not to leave home without it, two million users cut up their AmEx (American Express) cards between 1991 and 1993 and went in search of better bargains in credit cards. Now AmEx is staking its future on a new set of twelve different types of credit cards. All will offer revolving credit at rates comparable to AmEx's principal rivals, Visa and MasterCard. The U.S. market is saturated with 1 *billion* cards issued by 6,500 companies. Competition is fierce because the pool of potential new customers is shrinking at the same time America's plastic habit is growing. The industry average for bad debt losses on credit cards is 5%.

Source: Time, September 12, 1994, p. 60.

Before You Go On . . .

►*Review It*

1. How are accounts receivable recognized in the accounts?
2. What are the essential features of the allowance method?
3. Explain the difference between the percentage of sales and the percentage of receivables methods.
4. Why do companies sell their receivables?
5. What is the journal entry when a company sells its receivables to a factor?

►*Do It*

Peter M. Dell Wholesalers Co. has been expanding faster than it can raise capital and, according to its local banker, the company has reached its debt ceiling. Dell's customers are slow in paying (60–90 days), but its suppliers (creditors) are demanding 30-day payment. Dell has a cash flow problem.

Dell needs to raise $120,000 in cash to safely cover next Friday's employee payroll. Dell's present balance of outstanding receivables totals $750,000. What might Dell do to alleviate this cash crunch? Record the entry that Dell would make when it raises the needed cash.

Reasoning: One source of immediate cash at a competitive cost is the sale of receivables to a factor. Rather than waiting until it can collect receivables, Dell may raise immediate cash by selling its receivables. The last thing Dell (or any employer) wants to do is miss a payroll.

Solution: Assuming that Dell Co. factors $125,000 of its accounts receivable at a 1% service charge, the following entry would be made:

Cash	123,750	
Service Charge Expense	1,250	
Accounts Receivable		125,000
(To record sale of receivables to factor)		

Related exercise material: BE8–9 and E8–5.

❋*Notes Receivable*

Credit may also be granted in exchange for a formal credit instrument known as a **promissory note**. A promissory note is a written promise to pay a specified amount of money on demand or at a definite time. Promissory notes may be used (1) when individuals and companies lend or borrow money, (2) when the amount of the transaction and the credit period exceed normal limits, and (3) in settlement of accounts receivable.

Helpful hint Note the similarities and differences between a note and a check. *Similarities:* Both are instruments (documents that are readily transferable by endorsement). Both have a maker and a payee. *Differences:* A check is a cash instrument that does not bear interest. A note is a credit instrument that may bear interest.

In a promissory note, the party making the promise to pay is called the maker; the party to whom payment is to be made is called the payee. The payee may be specifically identified by name or may be designated simply as the bearer of the note. In the note shown in Illustration 8-8, Brent Company is the maker and Wilma Company is the payee. To the Wilma Company, the promissory note is a note receivable; to the Brent Company, the note is a note payable.

Illustration 8-8

Promissory note

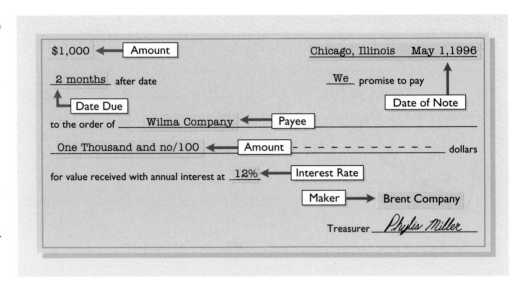

Helpful hint   Who are the two key parties to a note, and what entry does each party make when the note is issued? Answer:
1. The maker, Brent Company, credits Notes Payable.
2. The payee, Wilma Company, debits Notes Receivable.

Notes receivable gives the holder a stronger legal claim to assets than accounts receivable. Like accounts receivable, notes receivable can be readily sold to another party. Promissory notes are negotiable instruments (as are checks), which means that, when sold they can be transferred to another party by endorsement.

Notes receivable are frequently accepted from customers who need to extend the payment of an outstanding account receivable and are often required from high-risk customers. In some industries (e.g., the pleasure and sport boat industry) all credit sales are supported by notes. The majority of notes, however, originate from lending transactions. The basic issues in accounting for notes receivable are the same as those for accounts receivable.

1. **Recognizing** notes receivable.
2. **Valuing** notes receivable.
3. **Disposing of** notes receivable.

On the following pages, we will look at each of these issues. Before we do, though, we need to consider two issues that did not apply to accounts receivable: the maturity date and the computation of interest.

Determining the Maturity Date

STUDY OBJECTIVE
·········▼ 5 ·········
Compute the maturity date of, and interest on, notes receivable.

When the life of a note is expressed in terms of months, the due date is found by counting the months from the date of issue. For example, the maturity date of a 3-month note dated May 1 is August 1. A note drawn on the last day of a month matures on the last day of a subsequent month; that is, a July 31 note due in 2 months matures on September 30. When the due date is stated in terms of days, it is necessary to count the exact number of days to determine the maturity date. In counting, **the date the note is issued is omitted but the due date is**

included. For example, the maturity date of a 60-day note dated July 17 is September 15, computed as follows:

Illustration 8-9

Computation of maturity date

Term of note		60
July (31 – 17)	14	
August	31	45
Maturity date, September		15

The due date (maturity date) of a promissory note may be stated in one of three ways, as shown in Illustration 8-10.

Illustration 8-10

Maturity date of different notes

On demand

On a stated date

At the end of a stated period of time

Computing Interest

As indicated in Chapter 3, the basic formula for computing interest on an interest-bearing note is:

Illustration 8-11

Formula for computing interest

Face Value of Note × Annual Interest Rate × Time in Terms of One Year = Interest

The interest rate specified on the note is an **annual** rate of interest. The time factor in the computation above expresses the fraction of a year that the note is outstanding. When the maturity date is stated in days, the time factor is frequently the number of days divided by 360. When the due date is stated in months, the time factor is the number of months divided by 12. The computation of interest is shown in Illustration 8-12.

Illustration 8-12

Computation of interest

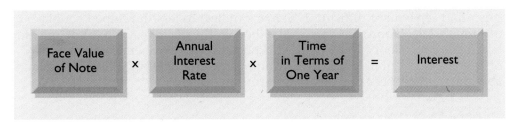

Terms of Note	Interest Computation
	Face × Rate × Time = Interest
$ 730, 18%, 120 days	$ 730 × 18% × 120/360 = $ 43.80
$1,000, 15%, 6 months	$1,000 × 15% × 6/12 = $ 75.00
$2,000, 12%, 1 year	$2,000 × 12% × 1/1 = $240.00

There are many different ways to calculate interest. For example, the computation above assumed the total days to be used for the year are 360. Many financial institutions use 365 days to compute interest. It is more profitable, though, to use 360 days because the holder of the note receives more interest than if 365 days are used. For homework problems, assume 360 days.

Recognizing Notes Receivable

STUDY OBJECTIVE
·········· 6 ··········

Explain how notes receivable are recognized in the accounts.

To illustrate the basic entry for notes receivable, we will use the $1,000, 2-month, 12% promissory note on page 342. Assuming that the note was written to settle an open account, the entry for the receipt of the note by Wilma Company is:

May 1	Notes Receivable	1,000	
	Accounts Receivable—Brent Company		1,000
	(To record acceptance of Brent Company note)		

Observe that the note receivable is recorded at its **face value**, the value shown on the face of the note. No interest revenue is reported when the note is accepted because the revenue recognition principle does not recognize revenue until earned. Interest is earned (accrued) as time passes.

If a note is exchanged for cash, the entry is a debit to Notes Receivable and a credit to Cash in the amount of the loan.

Valuing Notes Receivable

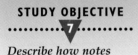

STUDY OBJECTIVE
·········· 7 ··········

Describe how notes receivable are valued.

Helpful hint The use of percentage of sales should be based on the company's experience with uncollectible notes that originated from sales transactions.

Like accounts receivable, short-term notes receivable are reported at their **cash (net) realizable value**. The notes receivable allowance account is Allowance for Doubtful Accounts. Valuing short-term notes receivable is the same as valuing accounts receivable. The computations and estimations involved in determining cash realizable value and in recording the proper amount of bad debt expense and related allowance are similar.

Long-term notes receivable, however, pose additional estimation problems. As an example, we need only look at the problems a number of large U.S. banks are having in collecting their receivables. Loans to less-developed countries are particularly worrisome. Developing countries need loans for development but often find repayment difficult. U.S. loans (notes) to less-developed countries at one time totaled approximately $135 billion. In Brazil alone, Citibank at one time had loans equivalent to 80% of its stockholders' equity; Chemical Bank had 77% of its equity lent out in Mexico. Determining the proper allowance is understandably difficult for these types of long-term receivables.

Disposing of Notes Receivable

STUDY OBJECTIVE
·········· 8 ··········

Describe the entries to record the disposition of notes receivable.

Notes may be held to their maturity date, at which time the face value plus accrued interest is due. In some situations, the maker of the note defaults and appropriate adjustment must be made. In other situations, similar to accounts receivable, the holder of the note speeds up the conversion to cash by selling the receivables. The entries for honoring and dishonoring notes are illustrated below.

Honor of Notes Receivable

A note is **honored** when it is paid in full at its maturity date. For each interest-bearing note, the amount due at maturity is the face value of the note plus interest for the length of time specified on the note.

To illustrate, assume that Wolder Co. lends Higly Inc. $10,000 on June 1, accepting a 4-month, 9% interest note. In this situation, interest is $300 ($10,000 ×

9% × 4/12); the amount due, the maturity value, is $10,300. To obtain payment, Wolder (the payee) must present the note either to Higly Inc. (the maker) or to the maker's duly appointed agent, such as a bank. Assuming that Wolder presents the note to Higly Inc. on October 1, the maturity date, the entry by Wolder to record the collection is:

Oct. 1	Cash	10,300	
	Notes Receivable		10,000
	Interest Revenue		300
	(To record collection of Higly Inc. note)		

Helpful hint How many days of interest should be accrued at September 30 for a 90-day note issued on August 16?
Answer: 45 days (15 days in August plus 30 days in September).

If Wolder Co. prepares financial statements as of September 30, it would be necessary to accrue interest. In this case, the adjusting entry by Wolder would be for 4 months, or $300, as shown below:

Sept. 30	Interest Receivable	300	
	Interest Revenue		300
	(To accrue four months' interest)		

When interest has been accrued, it is necessary to credit Interest Receivable at maturity. The entry by Wolder to record the honoring of the Higly note on October 1 is:

Oct. 1	Cash	10,300	
	Notes Receivable		10,000
	Interest Receivable		300
	(To record collection of note at maturity)		

In this case, Interest Receivable is credited because the receivable was established in the adjusting entry.

▶ Accounting in Action ▸ *International Insight*

Varied plans have been proposed to solve the international debt problem. These plans range from encouraging more lending to reducing or forgiving the debt. At one time, this debt burden to banks worldwide exceeded $1.3 trillion. (As an aside, a trillion is a lot of money—enough money to give every man, woman, and child in the world approximately $250 each. Why were these loans made in the first place? The reasons are numerous, but the three major ones are: (1) to provide stability to these governments and thereby increase trade, (2) the belief that governments would never default on payment, and (3) the desire by banks to increase their income by lending to these countries.

Dishonor of Notes Receivable

A dishonored note is a note that is not paid in full at maturity. A dishonored note receivable is no longer negotiable. However, the payee still has a claim against the maker of the note. Therefore the Notes Receivable account is usually transferred to an Account Receivable.

To illustrate, assume that Higly Inc. on October 1 indicates that it cannot pay at the present time. The entry to record the dishonor of the note depends on whether eventual collection is expected. If Wolder Co. expects eventual collection, the amount due (face value and interest) on the note is debited to Accounts Receivable. Wolder Co. would make the following entry at the time the note is dishonored (assuming no previous accrual of interest):

Oct. 1	Accounts Receivable—Higly Inc.	10,300	
	Notes Receivable		10,000
	Interest Revenue		300
	(To record the dishonor of the note)		

If there is no hope of collection, the face value of the note should be written off by debiting the Allowance for Doubtful Accounts. No interest revenue would be recorded because collection will not occur.

Sale of Notes Receivable

The accounting for the sales of notes receivable is recorded in a manner similar to the sale of accounts receivable. The Accounting in Action discussion that follows demonstrates how notes receivable are sold and resold. The accounting entries for the sale of notes receivable are left for a more advanced course.

Before You Go On . . .

▶ Review It

1. What is the basic formula for computing interest?
2. At what value are notes receivable reported on the balance sheet?
3. Explain the difference between honoring and dishonoring a note receivable.

▶ Do It

Gambit Stores accepts from Leonard Co. a $3,400, 90-day, 12% note dated May 10 in settlement of Leonard's overdue open account. What is the maturity date of the note? What is the entry made by Gambit at the maturity date, assuming Leonard pays the note and interest in full at that time?

Reasoning: When the due date is stated in terms of days, it is necessary to count the exact number of days to determine the maturity date. In counting, the date the note is issued is omitted, but the due date is included. The entry to record interest at maturity in this solution assumes that no interest is accrued on this note.

Solution: The maturity date is August 8, computed as follows:

Term of note:		90 days
May (31 – 10)	21	
June	30	
July	31	82
Maturity date, August		8

The interest payable at maturity date is $102, computed as follows:

$$\text{Face} \times \text{Rate} \times \text{Time} = \text{Interest}$$
$$\$3,400 \times 12\% \times 90/360 = \$102$$

The entry recorded by Gambit Stores at the maturity date is:

Cash	3,502	
Notes Receivable		3,400
Interest Revenue		102
(To record collection of Leonard note)		

Related exercise material: BE8–8, BE8–10, E8–8, and E8–9.

►Accounting in Action ► *Business Insight*

How One Receivable Crisscrossed the U.S.

Consider how the following note receivable of $120,000 was sold and resold in different markets in the United States and abroad.

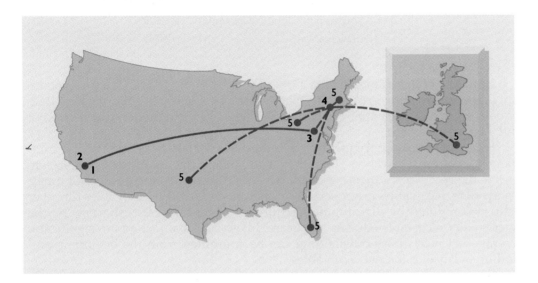

Step 1   *September 1987.* Jim and Erica Vogel bought a four-bedroom house in San Dimas, Calif. They got a $120,000 loan from First Federal S&L of San Gabriel.

Step 2   *December 1987.* First Federal sold the Vogels' receivable to the Federal Home Loan Mortgage Corp., known as Freddie Mac.

Step 3   *December 1987.* In Reston, Va., Freddie Mac put the Vogels' receivable into a giant pool with more than 6,000 other receivables.

Step 4   *May 1988.* Part of that pool was bought by First Boston Corp. in New York. The pool went into a $550 million pool.

Step 5   *May/June 1988.* In Hartford, Conn., Cigna Investments Inc. bought $10 million of this pool for its pension accounts.

   May/June 1988. In El Reno, Okla., Globe Savings Bank bought $66 million of the pool to expand its receivable portfolio.

   May/June 1988. In Florida an S&L bought $40 million of the pool as an interest rate hedge.

   May/June 1988. Other buyers of the pool ranged from a Pittsburgh S&L, to a London commercial bank.

Source: Wall Street Journal, August 17, 1988.

Statement Presentation and Analysis of Receivables

Each of the major types of receivables should be identified in the balance sheet or in the notes to the financial statements. Short-term receivables are reported within the current asset section of the balance sheet below temporary investments. Temporary investments appear before short-term receivables, because these investments are more liquid, or nearer to cash. Both the gross amount of receivables and the allowance for doubtful accounts should be reported. Illus-

STUDY OBJECTIVE
••••••••••9••••••••••

Explain the statement presentation and analysis of receivables.

tration 8-13 shows the current asset presentation of receivables for Microsoft Corporation at December 31, 1995.

Illustration 8-13

Balance sheet presentation of receivables

MICROSOFT CORPORATION	
Accounts receivable (in millions)	$720
Less: Allowance for doubtful accounts	139
Net receivables	$581

In the income statement, Bad Debts Expense and Service Charge Expense are reported as selling expenses in the Operating Expenses section. Interest Revenue is shown under Other Revenues and Gains in the nonoperating section of the income statement.

Financial ratios are frequently computed to evaluate the liquidity of a company's accounts receivable. The ratio used to assess the liquidity of the receivables is the receivables turnover ratio. This ratio measures the number of times, on average, receivables are collected during the period. The receivables turnover ratio is computed by dividing net credit sales (net sales less cash sales) by the average net receivables during the year. Unless seasonal factors are significant, average net receivables outstanding can be computed from the beginning and ending balance of the net receivables.

For example, in 1995 Microsoft Corporation had net credit sales of $5,937 million for the year and a beginning net accounts receivable balance of $475 million, its accounts receivable turnover ratio is computed as follows:

Illustration 8-14

Accounts receivable turnover ratio and computation

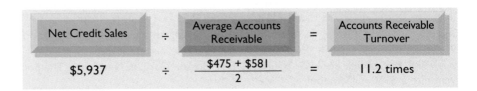

The result indicates an accounts receivable turnover ratio of 11.2 times per year for Microsoft Corporation. The higher the turnover ratio the more liquid the company's receivables.

Another variant of the receivables turnover ratio that makes the liquidity even more evident is the conversion of it into an **average collection period** in terms of days. This is done by dividing the turnover ratio into 365 days. For example, Microsoft's turnover of 11.2 times is divided into 365 days as follows to obtain approximately 33 days:

Illustration 8-15

Average collection period for receivables formula and computation

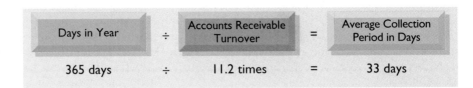

This means that Microsoft's average collection period for receivables is 33 days. This average collection period is frequently used to assess the effectiveness of a company's credit and collection policies. The general rule is that the collection period should not greatly exceed the credit term period (i.e., the time allowed for payment).

Before You Go On . . .

► Review It

1. Explain where accounts and notes receivable are reported on the balance sheet.
2. Where are bad debts expense, service charge expense, and interest revenue reported on the income statement?
3. How may the liquidity of receivables be analyzed?

► A Look Back at North Carolina State University

Refer back to the story about the North Carolina State University newspaper at the beginning of the chapter, and answer the following questions:

1. If you had sold advertising space to a tardy paying client, how would you persuade them to pay?
2. At what point would you recommend that the newspaper write-off uncollectible receivables?
3. Indicate the accounts to be debited and credited for each of the following transactions of the newspaper: (a) ad space is sold on account; (b) ad space is sold and prepaid; (c) cash is collected on account; (d) the ad is run for the advertiser who prepaid; (e) an uncollectible account is written off.

Solution:

1. The collection process used by the newspaper: a friendly letter at the end of 30 days, a less-than-friendly letter at the end of 45 days, and the filing of a suit in small claims court at the end of 75 days. In addition, a tactful, persuasive telephone call might be added to the attempts to collect.
2. An unpaid receivable should be written off when it is determined that it is uncollectible. Past experience with small unpaid ad bills will usually dictate the appropriate point at which bills are deemed uncollectible. With the limited information given in this case, the write-off would seem proper at the conclusion of an unsuccessful court claim.
3. (a) Debit Accounts Receivable, credit Advertising Revenue.
   (b) Debit Cash, credit Unearned Advertising Revenue.
   (c) Debit Cash, credit Accounts Receivable.
   (d) Debit Unearned Advertising Revenue, credit Advertising Revenue.
   (e) Debit Allowance for Doubtful Accounts, credit Accounts Receivable.

Summary of Study Objectives

1. *Identify the different types of receivables.* Receivables are frequently classified as (1) accounts, (2) notes, and (3) other. Accounts receivable are amounts owed by customers on account. Notes receivable represent claims that are evidenced by formal instruments of credit. Other receivables include nontrade receivables such as interest receivable, loans to company officers, advances to employees, and income taxes refundable.

2. *Explain how accounts receivable are recognized in the accounts.* Accounts receivable are recorded at invoice price. They are reduced by Sales Returns and Allowances. Cash discounts reduce the amount received on accounts receivable. When interest is charged on a past due receivable, this interest is added to the accounts receivable balance and is recognized as interest revenue.

3. *Distinguish between the methods and bases used to value accounts receivable.* There are two methods of accounting for uncollectible accounts: (1) the allowance method and (2) the direct write-off method. Either the percentage of sales or the percentage of receivables basis may be used to estimate uncollectible accounts using the allowance method. The percentage of sales basis emphasizes the matching principle. The percentage of receivables basis emphasizes the cash realizable value of the accounts receivable. An aging schedule is frequently used with this basis.

4. *Describe the entries to record the disposition of accounts receivable.* When an account receivable is collected, Accounts Receivable is credited. When an account receivable is sold, a service charge expense is charged which reduces the amount collected.

5. *Compute the maturity date of, and interest on, notes receivable.* The maturity date of a note must be computed unless the due date is specified or the note is payable on demand. For a note stated in months, the maturity date is found by counting the months from the date of issue. For a note stated in days, the number of days is counted, omitting the issue date and counting the due date. The formula for computing interest is face value × interest rate × time.

6. *Explain how notes receivable are recognized in the accounts.* Notes receivable are recorded at face value. In some cases, it is necessary to accrue interest prior to maturity. In this case, Interest Receivable is debited and Interest Revenue is credited.

7. *Describe how notes receivable are valued.* Like accounts receivable, notes receivable are reported at their cash (net) realizable value. The notes receivable allowance account is the Allowance for Doubtful Accounts. The computation and estimations involved in valuing notes receivables at cash realizable value, and in recording the proper amount of bad debt expense and related allowance are similar to accounts receivable.

8. *Describe the entries to record the disposition of notes receivable.* Notes can be held to maturity, at which time the face value plus accrued interest is due and the note is removed from the accounts. However, in many cases, similar to accounts receivable, the holder of the note speeds up the conversion by selling the receivable to another party. In some situations, the maker of the note dishonors the note (defaults), and the note is written off.

9. *Explain the statement presentation and analysis of receivables.* Each major type of receivable should be identified in the balance sheet or in the notes to the financial statements. Short-term receivables are considered current assets. The gross amount of receivables and allowance for doubtful accounts should be reported. Bad debts and service charge expenses are reported in the income statement as operating (selling) expenses, and interest revenue is shown as other revenues and gains in the nonoperating section of the statement. Accounts receivable may be evaluated for liquidity by computing a turnover ratio and an average collection period.

GLOSSARY
••

Aging of accounts receivable   The analysis of customer balances by the length of time they have been unpaid. (p. 336).

Cash (net) realizable value   The net amount expected to be received in cash. (p. 332).

Dishonored note   A note that is not paid in full at maturity. (p. 345).

Factor   A finance company or bank that buys receivables from businesses for a fee and then collects the payments directly from the customers. (p. 338).

Maker   The party in a promissory note who is making the promise to pay. (p. 342).

Payee   The party to whom payment of a promissory note is to be made. (p. 342).

Percentage of receivables basis   Management establishes a percentage relationship between the amount of receivables and the expected losses from uncollectible accounts. (p. 336).

Percentage of sales basis   Management establishes a percentage relationship between the amount of credit sales and expected losses from uncollectible accounts. (p. 335).

Promissory note   A written promise to pay a specified amount of money on demand or at a definite time. (p. 341).

Receivables turnover ratio   A measure of the liquidity of receivables, computed by dividing net credit sales by average net receivables. (p. 348)

Trade receivables   Notes and accounts receivable that result from sales transactions. (p. 330).

••

DEMONSTRATION PROBLEM

Presented below are selected transactions related to B. Dylan Corp.

Mar. 1   Sold $20,000 of merchandise to Potter Company, terms 2/10, n/30.

11   Received payment in full from Potter Company for balance due.

12   Accepted Juno Company's $20,000 6-month, 12% note for balance due.

13   Made Dylan Corp. credit card sales for $13,200.

15   Made American Express credit sales totaling $6,700. A 5% service fee is charged by American Express.

30   Received payment in full from American Express Company less 5% service charge.

Apr. 11   Sold accounts receivable of $8,000 to Harcot Factor. Harcot Factor assesses a service charge of 2% of the amount of receivables sold.

13   Received collections of $8,200 on Dylan Corp. credit card sales and added finance charges of 1.5% to the remaining balances.

May 10   Wrote off as uncollectible $16,000 of accounts receivable. Dylan uses the percentage of sales basis to estimate bad debts.

June 30   Credit sales for the first six months total $2,000,000 and the bad debt percentage is 1%. At June 30, the balance in the allowance account is $3,500.

July 16   One of the accounts receivable written off in May pays the amount due, $4,000, in full.

Instructions

Prepare the journal entries for the transactions.

Solution to Demonstration Problem

Mar. 1	Accounts Receivable—Potter	20,000	
	Sales		20,000
	(To record sales on account)		
Mar. 11	Cash	19,600	
	Sales Discounts (2% × $20,000)	400	
	Accounts Receivable—Potter		20,000
	(To record collection of accounts receivable)		
Mar. 12	Notes Receivable	20,000	
	Accounts Receivable—Juno		20,000
	(To record acceptance of Juno Company note)		
Mar. 13	Accounts Receivable	13,200	
	Sales		13,200
	(To record company credit card sales)		
Mar. 15	Accounts Receivable—American Express	6,365	
	Service Charge Expense (5% × $6,700)	335	
	Sales		6,700
	(To record credit card sales)		
Mar. 30	Cash	6,365	
	Accounts Receivable—American Express		6,365
	(To record redemption of credit card billings)		
Apr. 11	Cash	7,840	
	Service Charge Expense (2% × $8,000)	160	
	Accounts Receivable		8,000
	(To record sale of receivables to factor)		
Apr. 13	Cash	8,200	
	Accounts Receivable		8,200
	(To record collection of accounts receivable)		
	Accounts Receivable [($13,200 − $8,200) × 1.5%]	75	
	Interest Revenue		75
	(To record interest on amount due)		
May 10	Allowance for Doubtful Accounts	16,000	
	Accounts Receivable		16,000
	(To record write-off of accounts receivable)		

Problem-Solving Strategies

1. Accounts receivable are generally recorded at invoice price.
2. Sales returns and allowances and cash discounts reduce the amount received on accounts receivable.
3. When accounts receivable are sold, a service charge expense is incurred by the seller.
4. Bad debts expense is an adjusting entry.
5. Percentage of sales basis ignores any balance in the allowance account. Percentage of receivables basis does not ignore this balance.
6. Write-offs of accounts receivable affect only balance sheet accounts.

June 30	Bad Debts Expense ($2,000,000 × 1%)	20,000	
	Allowance for Doubtful Accounts		20,000
	(To record estimate of uncollectible accounts)		
July 16	Accounts Receivable	4,000	
	Allowance for Doubtful Accounts		4,000
	(To reverse write-off of accounts receivable)		
	Cash	4,000	
	Accounts Receivable		4,000
	(To record collection of accounts receivable)		

SELF-STUDY QUESTIONS

Answers are at the end of the chapter.

(SO 2)   1. Jones Company on June 15 sells merchandise on account to Bullock Co. for $1,000 terms 2/10, n/30. On June 20, Bullock Co. returns merchandise worth $300 to Jones Company. On June 24, payment is received from Bullock Co. for the balance due. What is the amount of cash received?
   a. $700.
   b. $680.
   c. $686.
   d. None of the above.

(SO 3)   2. Which of the following approaches for bad debts is best described as a balance sheet method?
   a. Percentage of receivables basis.
   b. Direct write-off method.
   c. Percentage of sales basis. - *Income Statement*
   d. Both a and b.

(SO 3)   3. Net credit sales for the month are $800,000 and bad debts are expected to be 1.5% of net credit sales. The company uses the percentage of sales basis. If the Allowance for Doubtful Accounts has a credit balance of $15,000 before adjustment, what is the balance after adjustment?
   a. $15,000.
   b. $27,000.
   c. $23,000.
   d. $31,000.

(SO 3)   4. In 1996, D. H. Lawrence Company had net credit sales of $750,000. On January 1, 1996, Allowance for Doubtful Accounts had a credit balance of $18,000. During 1996, $30,000 of uncollectible accounts receivable were written off. Past experience indicates that 3% of net credit sales become uncollectible. What should be the adjusted balance of Allowance for Doubtful Accounts at December 31, 1996?
   a. $10,050.
   b. $10,500.
   c. $22,500.
   d. $40,500.

(SO 3)   5. An analysis and aging of the accounts receivable of Machiavelli Company at December 31 reveals the following data:

Accounts Receivable	$800,000
Allowance for Doubtful Accounts per books before adjustment	50,000
Amounts expected to become uncollectible	65,000

   The cash realizable value of the accounts receivable at December 31, after adjustment, is:
   a. $685,000.
   b. $750,000.
   c. $800,000.
   d. $735,000.

(SO 6)   6. One of the following statements about promissory notes is incorrect. The incorrect statement is:
   a. The party making the promise to pay is called the maker.
   b. The party to whom payment is to be made is called the payee.
   c. A promissory note is not a negotiable instrument.
   d. A promissory note is more liquid than an accounts receivable.

(SO 4)   7. Which of the following statements about VISA credit card sales is incorrect?
   a. The credit card issuer makes the credit investigation of the customer.
   b. The retailer is not involved in the collection process.
   c. Two parties are involved.
   d. The retailer receives cash more quickly than it would from individual customers.

(SO 4)   8. Morgan Retailers accepted $50,000 of Citibank VISA credit card charges for merchandise sold on July 1. Citibank charges 4% for its credit card use. The entry to record this transaction by Morgan Retailers will include a credit to sales of $50,000 and

a debit(s) to:
a. Cash $48,000
   and Service Charge Expense $2,000
b. Accounts Receivable $48,000
   and Service Charge Expense $2,000
c. Cash $50,000
d. Accounts Receivable $50,000

(SO 6) 9. Sorenson Co. accepts a $1,000, 3-month, 12% promissory note in settlement of an account with Parton Co. The entry to record this transaction is as follows:
a. Notes Receivable 1,030
   Accounts Receivable 1,030
b. Notes Receivable 1,000
   Accounts Receivable 1,000
c. Notes Receivable 1,000
   Sales 1,000

d. Notes Receivable 1,020
   Accounts Receivable 1,020

(SO 8) 10. Schlicht Co. holds Osgrove Inc.'s $10,000, 120-day, 9% note. The entry made by Schlicht Co. when the note is collected, assuming no interest has been accrued, is
a. Cash 10,300
   Notes Receivable 10,300
b. Cash 10,000
   Notes Receivable 10,000
c. Accounts Receivable 10,300
   Notes Receivable 10,000
   Interest Revenue 300
d. Cash 10,300
   Notes Receivable 10,000
   Interest Revenue 300

QUESTIONS

1. What is the difference between an account receivable and a note receivable?

2. What are some common types of receivables other than accounts receivable or notes receivable?

3. Texaco Oil Company issues its own credit cards. Assume that Texaco charges you $50 on an unpaid balance. Prepare the journal entry that Texaco makes to record this revenue.

4. What are the essential features of the allowance method of accounting for bad debts?

5. Soo Eng cannot understand why cash realizable value does not decrease when an uncollectible account is written off under the allowance method. Clarify this point for Soo Eng.

6. Distinguish between the two bases that may be used in estimating uncollectible accounts.

7. Kersee Company has a credit balance of $3,200 in Allowance for Doubtful Accounts. The estimated bad debts expense under the percentage of sales basis is $4,100, and the total estimated uncollectibles under the percentage of receivables basis is $5,800. Prepare the adjusting entry under each basis.

8. How are bad debts accounted for under the direct write-off method? What are the disadvantages of this method?

9. Allmar Company accepts both its own credit cards and national credit cards. What are the advantages of accepting both types of cards?

10. An article recently appeared in *The Wall Street Journal* indicating that companies are selling their receivables at a record rate. Why are companies selling their receivables?

11. Southern Textiles decides to sell $700,000 of its accounts receivable to First Central Factors Inc. First Central Factors assesses a service charge of 2% of the amount of receivables sold. Prepare the journal entry that Southern Textiles makes to record this sale.

12. Your roommate is uncertain about the advantages of a promissory note. Compare the advantages of a note receivable with those of an accounts receivable.

13. How may the maturity date of a promissory note be stated?

14. Indicate the maturity date of each of the following promissory notes:

Date of Note	Terms
(a) March 13	one year after date of note
(b) May 4	3 months after date
(c) June 10	30 days after date
(d) July 2	60 days after date

15. Compute the missing amounts for each of the following notes:

	Principal	Annual Interest Rate	Time	Total Interest
(a)	?	9%	120 days	$360
(b)	$30,000	10%	3 years	?
(c)	$60,000	?	5 months	$2,500
(d)	$50,000	11%	?	$1,375

16. In determining interest revenue, some financial institutions use 365 days per year whereas others use 360 days. Why might a financial institution use 360 days?

17. May Company dishonors a note at maturity. What actions by May may occur with the dishonoring of the note?

18. Paula Company has accounts receivable and notes receivable. How should the receivables be reported on the balance sheet?

19. If the receivables turnover ratio is 7.15 and average net receivables during the period is $210,000, what is the amount of net credit sales for the period?

BRIEF EXERCISES

Different types of receivables
(SO 1)

BE8–1 Presented below are three receivable transactions. Indicate whether these receivables are reported as accounts receivable, notes receivable, or other receivables on a balance sheet.

1. Advanced $10,000 to an employee.
2. Received a promissory note of $57,000 for services performed.
3. Sold merchandise on account for $60,000 to a customer.

Basic accounts receivable transactions
(SO 2)

BE8–2 Record the following transactions on the books of Essex Co.

1. On July 1, Essex Co. sold merchandise on account to Cambridge Inc. for $14,000, terms 2/10, n/30.
2. On July 8, Cambridge Inc. returned merchandise worth $3,800 to Essex Co.
3. On July 11, Cambridge Inc. paid for the merchandise.

Entries for allowance method and classifications
(SO 3, 9)

BE8–3 During its first year of operations, Wendy Company had credit sales of $3,000,000, of which $600,000 remained uncollected at year-end. The credit manager estimates that $40,000 of these receivables will become uncollectible. (a) Prepare the journal entry to record the estimated uncollectibles. (b) Prepare the current asset section of the balance sheet for Wendy Company, assuming that in addition to the receivables it has cash of $90,000, merchandise inventory of $130,000, and prepaid expenses of $13,000.

Entries for write-off and determining cash realizable value
(SO 3)

BE8–4 At the end of 1996, Searcy Co. has accounts receivable of $700,000 and an allowance for doubtful accounts of $54,000. On January 24, 1997, it is learned that the company's receivable from Hutley Inc. is not collectible and therefore management authorizes a write-off of $8,000. (a) Prepare the journal entry to record the write-off. (b) What is the cash realizable value of the accounts receivable (1) before the write-off and (2) after the write-off?

Entries for collection of bad debt write-off
(SO 3)

BE8–5 Assume the same information as BE8–4 and that on March 4, 1997, Searcy Co. receives payment of $8,000 in full from Hutley Co. Prepare the journal entries to record this transaction.

Entry using percentage of sales method
(SO 3)

BE8–6 Alex Co. elects to use the percentage of sales basis in 1996 to record bad debts expense and concludes that 2% of net credit sales will become uncollectible. Credit sales are $700,000 for 1996, sales returns and allowances are $50,000, and the allowance for doubtful accounts has a credit balance of $12,000. Prepare the adjusting entry to record bad debts expense in 1996.   *14,000*

Entry using percentage of receivables method
(SO 3)

BE8–7 Massey Co. uses the percentage of accounts receivable basis to record bad debt expense, and concludes that 1% of accounts receivable will become uncollectible. Accounts receivable are $500,000 at the end of the year, and the allowance for doubtful accounts has a credit balance of $3,000. (a) Prepare the adjusting journal entry to record bad debt expense for the year. (b) If the allowance for doubtful accounts had a debit balance of $800 instead of credit balance of $3,000, determine the amount to be reported for bad debt expense.

Compute maturity date and interest on note.
(SO 5)

BE8–8 Presented below are three promissory notes. Determine the missing amounts.

Date of Note	Terms	Maturity Date	Principal	Annual Interest Rate	Total Interest
(a) April 1	60 days	? *May 31*	$900,000	10%	? *15,000*
(b) July 2	30 days	? *Aug 1*	79,000	? *9*	$592.50
(c) March 7	6 months	? *Sep 7*	56,000	12%	? *3360*

BE8–9 Presented below are the following transactions.

1. St. Pierre Restaurant accepted a Visa card in payment of a $100 lunch bill. The bank charges a 3% fee. What entry should St. Pierre make?
2. Mayfield Company sold its accounts receivable of $70,000. What entry should May-field make, given a service charge of 3% on the amount of receivables sold?

Disposition of accounts receivable
(SO 4)

BE8–10 On January 10, 1995, Raja Co. sold merchandise on account to R. Opal for $12,000, n/30. On February 9, R. Opal gave Raja Co. a 10% promissory note in settlement of this account. Prepare the journal entry to record the sale and the settlement of the accounts receivable.

Notes receivable exchanged for accounts receivable
(SO 6)

BE8–11 The financial statements of Minnesota Mining and Manufacturing Company (3M) report net sales of $9.4 billion. Accounts receivable are $1.6 billion at the beginning of the year and $1.4 billion at the end of the year. Compute 3M's accounts receivable turnover ratio. Compute 3M's average collection period for accounts receivable in days.

Accounts receivable analysis.
(SO 9)

EXERCISES

••

E8–1 Presented below are two independent situations that occurred during the year.

1. On January 6, Nicklaus Co. sells merchandise on account to Watson Inc. for $4,000, terms 2/10, n/30. On January 16, Watson pays the amount due. Prepare the entries on Nicklaus' books to record the sale and related collection.
2. On January 10, Margaret Giger uses her Salizar Co. credit card to purchase merchandise from Salizar Co. for $11,000. On February 10, Giger is billed for the amount due of $11,000. On February 12, Giger pays $5,000 on the balance due. On March 10, Giger is billed for the amount due, including interest at 2% per month on the unpaid balance as of February 12. Prepare the entries on Salizar Co.'s books related to the transactions that occurred on January 10, February 12, and March 10.

Journalize entries for recognizing accounts receivable.
(SO 2)

E8–2 The ledger of the Patillo Company at the end of the current year shows Accounts Receivable $80,000, Credit Sales $940,000, and Sales Returns and Allowances $40,000.

Journalize entries to record allowance for doubtful accounts using two different bases.
(SO 3)

Instructions

(a) If Allowance for Doubtful Accounts has a credit balance of $800 in the trial balance, journalize the adjusting entry at December 31, assuming bad debts are expected to be (1) 1% of net credit sales, and (2) 10% of accounts receivable.
(b) If Allowance for Doubtful Accounts has a debit balance of $500 in the trial balance, journalize the adjusting entry at December 31, assuming bad debts are expected to be (1) .75% of net credit sales and (2) 8% of accounts receivable.

E8–3 Grevina Company has accounts receivable of $92,500 at March 31. An analysis of the accounts shows the following:

Determine bad debts expense and prepare the adjusting entry for bad debts expense.
(SO 3)

Month of Sale	Balance, March 31
March	$65,000
February	12,600
December and January	8,500
November and October	6,400
	$92,500

Credit terms are 2/10, n/30. At March 31, there is a $1,600 credit balance in Allowance for Doubtful Accounts prior to adjustment. The company uses the percentage of receivables basis for estimating uncollectible accounts. The company's estimate of bad debts are as follows:

Age of Accounts	Estimated Percentage Uncollectible
Current	2.0%
1–30 days past due	10.0%
31–90 days past due	30.0%
Over 90 days	50.0%

Instructions
(a) Determine the total estimated uncollectibles.
(b) Prepare the adjusting entry at March 31 to record bad debts expense.

Percentage of sales basis, write-off, recovery.
(SO 3)

E8–4   On December 31, 1996, Lisa Ceja Co. estimates that 2% of its net credit sales of $300,000 will become uncollectible and records this amount as an addition to Allowance for Doubtful Accounts. On May 11, 1997, Lisa Ceja Co. determined that Robert Worthy's account was uncollectible and wrote off $900. On June 12, 1997, Worthy paid the amount previously written off.

Instructions
Prepare the journal entries on December 31, 1996, May 11, 1997, and June 12, 1997.

Journalize entries for the sale of accounts receivable.
(SO 4)

E8–5   Presented below are two independent situations:

1. On March 3, Soyka Appliances sells $900,000 of its receivables to Potter Factors Inc. Potter Factors Inc. assesses a finance charge of 3% of the amount of receivables sold. Prepare the entry on Soyka Appliances' books to record the sale of the receivables.
2. On May 10, Monee Company sold merchandise for $3,000 and accepted the customer's First Business Bank MasterCard. At the end of the day, the First Business Bank MasterCard receipts were deposited in the company's bank account. First Business Bank charges a 4% service charge for credit card sales. Prepare the entry on Monee Company's books to record the sale of merchandise.

Journalize entries for credit card sales.
(SO 4)

E8–6   Presented below are two independent situations that occurred during the year.

1. On April 2, P. Zachos uses her J. C. Penney credit card to purchase merchandise from a J. C. Penney store for $1,300. On May 1, Zachos is billed for the $1,300 amount due. Zachos pays $900 on the balance due on May 3. On June 1, Zachos receives a bill for the amount due, including interest at 1.0% per month on the unpaid balance as of May 3. Prepare the entries on J. C. Penney Co.'s books related to the transactions that occurred on April 2, May 3, and June 1.
2. On July 4, Robyn's Restaurant accepts an American Express card for a $300 dinner bill. American Express charges a 5% service fee. On July 10, American Express pays Robyn $285. Prepare the entries on Robyn's books related to the transactions.

Journalize credit card sales and indicate the statement presentation of financing charges and service charge expense.
(SO 4)

E8–7   Kasko Stores accepts both its own and national credit cards. During the year the following selected summary transactions occurred.

Jan. 15   Made Kasko credit card sales totaling $16,000.
    20   Made American Express credit card sales (service charge fee, 5%) totaling $2,800.
    30   Received payment in full from American Express less a 5% service charge.
Feb. 10   Collected $12,000 on Kasko credit card sales.
    15   Added finance charges of 1.5% to Kasko credit card balance.

Instructions
(a) Journalize the transactions for Kasko Stores.
(b) Indicate the statement presentation of the financing charges and the credit card service expense for Kasko Stores.

Journalize entries for notes receivable transactions.
(SO 5, 6)

E8–8   Indiana Supply Co. has the following transactions related to notes receivable during the last 2 months of the year.

Nov. 1   Loaned $24,000 cash to A. Gomez on a 1-year, 10% note.
Dec. 11   Sold goods to R. Wright, Inc., receiving a $3,600, 90-day, 12% note.
    16   Received a $4,000, 6-month, 12% note on account from B. Barnes.
    31   Accrued interest revenue on all notes receivable.

Instructions
Journalize the transactions for Indiana Supply Co.

Journalize entries for notes receivable.
(SO 5, 6)

E8–9   Record the following transactions for the Rather Co. in the general journal:

1996
May 1   Received a $6,000, 1-year, 10% note on account from T. Jones.
Dec. 31   Accrued interest on the Jones' note.
Dec. 31   Closed the interest revenue account.

1997

May 1 Received principal plus interest on the Jones note. (No interest has been accrued in 1997)

E8–10 On May 2, P. Brey Company lends $4,000 to Feingold Inc., issuing a 6-month, 10% note. At the maturity date, November 2, Feingold indicates that it cannot pay.

Journalize entries for dishonor of notes receivable.
(SO 5, 8)

Instructions

(a) Prepare the entry to record the dishonor of the note, assuming that Brey Company expects collection will occur.

(b) Prepare the entry to record the dishonor of the note, assuming that Brey Company does not expect collection in the future.

PROBLEMS

● ●

P8–1 At December 31, 1996, Trisha Underwood Imports reported the following information on its balance sheet:

Prepare journal entries related to bad debt expense and compute turnover ratio.
(SO 2, 3, 9)

Accounts receivable	$1,000,000
Less: Allowance for doubtful accounts	60,000

During the first quarter of 1997, the company had the following transactions related to receivables.

1. Sales on account	$2,600,000
2. Sales returns and allowances	40,000
3. Collections of accounts receivable	2,300,000
4. Write-offs of accounts receivable deemed uncollectible	80,000
5. Recovery of bad debts previously written off as uncollectible	25,000

Instructions

(a) Prepare the journal entries to record each of these five transactions. Assume that no cash discounts were taken on the collections of accounts receivable.

(b) Enter the January 1, 1996, balances in Accounts Receivable and Allowance for Doubtful Accounts, post the entries to the two accounts (use T accounts), and determine the balances.

(c) Prepare the journal entry to record bad debts expense for the first quarter of 1997, assuming that an aging of accounts receivable indicates that estimated bad debts are $70,000.

(d) Compute the accounts receivable turnover ratio for the first quarter.

P8–2 Information related to Aris Company for 1996 is summarized below:

Computation of bad debts amounts
(SO 3)

Total credit sales	$1,800,000
Accounts receivable at December 31	$600,000
Bad debts written off	$26,000

Instructions

(a) What amount of bad debts expense will Aris Company report if it uses the direct write-off method of accounting for bad debts?

(b) Assume that Aris Company decides to estimate its bad debts expense to be 3% of credit sales. What amount of bad debts expense will Aris Company record if Allowance for Doubtful Accounts has a credit balance of $3,000?

(c) Assume that Aris Company decides to estimate its bad debts expense based on 4% of accounts receivable. What amount of bad debts expense will Aris Company record if Allowance for Doubtful Accounts balance has a credit balance of $4,000?

(d) Assume the same facts as in (c), except that there is a $2,000 debit balance in Allowance for Doubtful Accounts. What amount of bad debts expense will Aris record?

(e) ▮▮▮▮▶ What is the weakness of the direct write-off method of reporting bad debts expense?

Journalize entries to record transactions related to bad debts.
(SO 2, 3)

P8–3 Presented below is an aging schedule for Boitano Company.

Customer	Total	Not Yet Due	Number of Days Past Due			
			1–30	31–60	61–90	Over 90
Aber	$ 20,000		$ 9,000	$11,000		
Bohr	30,000	$ 30,000				
Case	50,000	15,000	5,000		$30,000	
Datz	38,000					$38,000
Others	120,000	92,000	15,000	$13,000		
	$258,000	$137,000	$29,000	$24,000	$30,000	$38,000
Estimated Percentage Uncollectible		3%	6%	12%	24%	50%
Total Estimated Bad Debts	$ 34,930	$ 4,110	$ 1,740	$ 2,880	$ 7,200	$19,000

At December 31, 1996, the unadjusted balance in Allowance for Doubtful Accounts is a credit of $9,000.

Instructions

(a) Journalize and post the adjusting entry for bad debts at December 31, 1996.

(b) Journalize and post to the allowance account the following 1997 events and transactions.

(1) March 1, an $800 customer balance originating in 1996 is judged uncollectible.

(2) May 1, a check for $800 is received from the customer whose account was written off as uncollectible on March 1.

(c) Journalize the adjusting entry for bad debts on December 31, 1997, assuming that the unadjusted balance in Allowance for Doubtful Accounts is a debit of $1,100 and the aging schedule indicates that total estimated bad debts will be $27,100.

Journalize entries to record transactions related to bad debts.
(SO 3)

P8–4 Carlo Fassi Co. uses 2% of net sales to determine its bad debts expense for the period. At the beginning of the current period, Fassi had Allowance for Doubtful Accounts of $10,000 (credit). During the period, it had net credit sales of $900,000 and wrote off as uncollectible accounts receivable of $6,000. However, one of the accounts written off as uncollectible in the amount of $3,000 was recovered before the end of the current period.

Instructions

(a) Prepare the entry to record bad debts expense for the current period.

(b) Prepare the entry to record the write-off of uncollectible accounts during the current period.

(c) Prepare the entries to record the recovery of the uncollectible accounts during the current period.

(d) Determine the ending balance in Allowance for Doubtful Accounts.

Prepare entries for various note receivable transactions.
(SO 2, 4, 5, 8, 9)

P8–5 The Bon Ton Company closes its books on July 31. On June 30, the Notes Receivable account balance is $19,800. Notes Receivable include the following:

Date	Maker	Face	Term	Interest
May 21	Alder Inc.	$6,000	60 days	12%
May 25	Dorn Co.	4,800	60 days	11%
June 30	MJH Corp.	9,000	6 months	9%

During July, the following transactions were completed.

July 5 Made sales of $6,200 on Bon Ton credit cards.

14 Made sales of $700 on VISA credit cards. The credit card service charge is 3%.

16 Added $415 to Bon Ton charge customer balances for finance charges on unpaid balances.

20 Received payment in full from Alder Inc. on the amount due.

25 Received notice that Dorn note has been dishonored. (Assume that Dorn is expected to pay in the future.)

Instructions

(a) Journalize the July transactions and the July 31 adjusting entry for accrued interest receivable. (Interest is computed using 360 days.)

(b) Enter the balances at July 1 in the receivable accounts and post the entries to all of the receivable accounts.

(c) Show the balance sheet presentation of the receivable accounts at July 31.

P8–6 On January 1, 1996, Comaneci Company had Accounts Receivable $54,200 and Allowance for Doubtful Accounts $4,700. Comaneci Company prepares financial statements annually. During the year the following selected transactions occurred.

Prepare entries for various receivables transactions.
(SO 2, 4, 5, 6, 7, 8)

Jan. 5 Sold $6,000 of merchandise to Garth Brooks Company, terms n/30.

Feb. 2 Accepted a $6,000, 4-month, 12% promissory note from Garth Brooks Company for balance due.

12 Sold $7,200 of merchandise to Gage Company and accepted Gage's $7,200 two-month, 10% note for the balance due.

26 Sold $5,000 of merchandise to Mathias Co., terms n/10.

Apr. 5 Accepted a $5,000, 3-month, 8% note from Mathias Co. for balance due.

12 Collected Gage Company note in full.

June 2 Collected Garth Brooks Company note in full.

July 5 Mathias Co. dishonors its note of April 5. It is expected that Mathias will eventually pay the amount owed.

15 Sold $3,000 of merchandise to Tritt Inc. and accepted Tritt's $3,000, 3-month, 12% note for the amount due.

Oct. 15 The Tritt Inc. note was dishonored. Tritt Inc. is bankrupt, and there is no hope of future settlement.

Instructions
Journalize the transactions.

ALTERNATE PROBLEMS

P8–1A At December 31, 1996, Bordeaux Inc. reported the following information on its balance sheet.

Prepare journal entries related to bad debts expense and compute turnover ratio.
(SO 2, 3, 4, 9)

Accounts Receivable	$960,000
Less: Allowance for doubtful accounts	70,000

During the first quarter of 1997, the company had the following transactions related to receivables.

1. Sales on account	$3,200,000
2. Sales returns and allowances	50,000
3. Collections of accounts receivable	2,800,000
4. Write-offs of accounts receivable deemed uncollectible	90,000
5. Recovery of bad debts previously written off as uncollectible	35,000

Instructions

(a) Prepare the journal entries to record each of these five transactions. Assume that no cash discounts were taken on the collections of accounts receivable.

(b) Enter the January 1, 1997, balances in Accounts Receivable and Allowance for Doubtful Accounts, post the entries to the two accounts (use T accounts), and determine the balances.

(c) Prepare the journal entry to record bad debts expense for the first quarter of 1997, assuming that an aging of accounts receivable indicates that expected bad debts are $100,000.

(d) Compute the accounts receivable turnover ratio for the first quarter.

Computation of bad debts amounts.
(SO 3)

P8–2A   Information related to Volkov Company for 1996 is summarized below:

Total credit sales	$2,000,000
Accounts receivable at December 31	$800,000
Bad debts written off	$36,000

Instructions

(a) What amount of bad debts expense will Volkov Company report if it uses the direct write-off method of accounting for bad debts?

(b) Assume that Volkov Company decides to estimate its bad debts expense to be 3% of credit sales. What amount of bad debts expense will Volkov Company record if it has an Allowance for Doubtful Accounts credit balance of $4,000?

(c) Assume that Volkov Company decides to estimate its bad debts expense based on 5% of accounts receivable. What amount of bad debts expense will Volkov Company record if it has an Allowance for Doubtful Accounts credit balance of $3,000?

(d) Assume the same facts as in (c), except that there is a $3,000 debit balance in Allowance for Doubtful Accounts. What amount of bad debts expense will Volkov record?

(e) What is the weakness of the direct write-off method of reporting bad debts expense?

Journalize entries to record transactions related to bad debts.
(SO 2, 3)

P8–3A   Presented below is an aging schedule for Deep Canyon Company.

Customer	Total	Not Yet Due	Number of Days Past Due			
			1–30	31–60	61–90	Over 90
Anita	$ 22,000		$10,000	$12,000		
Barry	40,000	$ 40,000				
Chagnon	57,000	16,000	6,000		$35,000	
David	34,000					$34,000
Others	126,000	96,000	16,000	14,000		
	$279,000	$152,000	$32,000	$26,000	35,000	$34,000
Estimated Percentage Uncollectible			4%	7%	13%	25%	50%
Total Estimated Bad Debts	$ 37,450	$ 6,080	$ 2,240	$ 3,380	$ 8,750	$17,000

At December 31, 1996, the unadjusted balance in Allowance for Doubtful Accounts is a credit of $10,000.

Instructions

(a) Journalize and post the adjusting entry for bad debts at December 31, 1996.

(b) Journalize and post to the allowance account the following 1997 events and transactions.

    (1) March 31, an $800 customer balance originating in 1996 is judged uncollectible.

    (2) May 31, a check for $800 is received from the customer whose account was written off as uncollectible on March 31.

(c) Journalize the adjusting entry for bad debts on December 31, 1997, assuming that the unadjusted balance in Allowance for Doubtful Accounts is a debit of $800 and the aging schedule indicates that total estimated bad debts will be $28,300.

Journalize entries to record transactions related to bad debts.
(SO 3)

P8–4A   Huang Co. uses 3% of net credit sales to determine its bad debts expense for the period. At the beginning of the current period, Huang had Allowance for Doubtful Accounts of $9,000 (credit). During the period, it had net sales of $800,000 and wrote off as uncollectible accounts receivable of $7,000. However, one of the accounts written off as uncollectible in the amount of $4,000 was recovered before the end of the current period.

Instructions
(a) Prepare the entry to record bad debts expense for the current period.
(b) Prepare the entry to record the write-off of uncollectible accounts during the current period.
(c) Prepare the entries to record the recovery of the uncollectible account during the current period.
(d) Determine the ending balance in Allowance for Doubtful Accounts.

P8–5A Selica Company closes its books on October 31. On September 30, the Notes Receivable account balance is $23,400. Notes Receivable include the following:

Prepare entries for various note receivable transactions.
(SO 2, 4, 5, 8, 9)

Date	Maker	Face	Term	Interest
Aug. 16	Foran Inc.	$ 8,000	60 days	12%
Aug. 25	Drexler Co.	5,200	2 months	12%
Sept. 30	MGH Corp.	10,200	6 months	9%

Interest is computed using a 360-day year. During October, the following transactions were completed.

Oct. 7 Made sales of $6,900 on Selica credit cards.
12 Made sales of $750 on VISA credit cards. The credit card service charge is 4%.
15 Added $485 to Selica charge customer balances for finance charges on unpaid balances.
15 Received payment in full from Foran Inc. on the amount due.
25 Received notice that Drexler note has been dishonored. (Assume that Drexler is expected to pay in future.)

Instructions
(a) Journalize the October transactions and the October 31 adjusting entry for accrued interest receivable.
(b) Enter the balances at October 1 in the receivable accounts and post the entries to all of the receivable accounts.
(c) Show the balance sheet presentation of the receivable accounts at October 31.

P8–6A On January 1, 1996, Ricardo Company had Accounts Receivable $146,000, Notes Receivable $15,000, and Allowance for Doubtful Accounts $13,200. The note receivable is from the Annabelle Company. It is a 4-month, 12% note dated December 31, 1995. Uptown Company prepares financial statements annually. During the year the following selected transactions occurred.

Prepare entries for various receivable transactions.
(SO 2, 4, 5, 6, 7, 8)

Jan. 5 Sold $12,000 of merchandise to George Company, terms n/15.
20 Accepted George Company's $12,000, 3-month, 9% note for balance due.
Feb. 18 Sold $8,000 of merchandise to Swaim Company and accepted Swaim's $8,000, 6-month, 10% note for the amount due.
Apr. 20 Collected George Company note in full.
30 Received payment in full from Annabelle Company on the amount due.
May 25 Accepted Avery Inc.'s $7,000, 3-month, 8% note in settlement of a past-due balance on account.
Aug. 18 Received payment in full from Swaim Company on note due.
25 The Avery Inc. note was dishonored. Avery Inc. is not bankrupt and future payment is anticipated.
Sept. 1 Sold $10,000 of merchandise to Young Company and accepted a $10,000, 6-month, 10% note for the amount due.

Instructions
Journalize the transactions.

*B*roadening Your Perspective

*F*INANCIAL REPORTING PROBLEM—PEPSICO, INC.

Arvada Company sells office equipment and supplies to many organizations in the city and surrounding area on contract terms of 2/10, n/30. In the past, over 75% of the credit customers have taken advantage of the discount by paying within 10 days of the invoice date.

The number of customers taking the full 30 days to pay has increased within the last year. Current indications are that less than 60% of the customers are now taking the discount. Bad debts as a percentage of gross credit sales have risen from the 1.5% provided in past years to about 4% in the current year.

The controller has responded to a request from the Finance Committee for more information on the collections of accounts receivable with the report reproduced below.

ARVADA COMPANY
Accounts Receivable Collections
May 31, 1997

The fact that some credit accounts will prove uncollectible is normal. Annual bad debt write-offs have been 1.5% of gross credit sales over the past five years. During the last fiscal year, this percentage increased to slightly less than 4%. The current Accounts Receivable balance is $1,400,000. The condition of this balance in terms of age and probability of collection is as follows:

Proportion of Total	Age Categories	Probability of Collection
66%	not yet due	99%
16%	less than 30 days past due	96½%
9%	30 to 60 days past due	95%
5%	61 to 120 days past due	91%
2½%	121 to 180 days past due	75%
1½%	over 180 days past due	20%

The Allowance for Doubtful Accounts had a credit balance of $29,500 on June 1, 1996. Arvada has provided for a monthly bad debts expense accrual during the current fiscal year based on the assumption that 4% of gross credit sales will be uncollectible. Total gross credit sales for the 1996–97 fiscal year amounted to $2,800,000. Write-offs of bad accounts during the year totaled $96,000.

Instructions
  (a) Prepare an accounts receivable aging schedule for Arvada Company using the age categories identified in the controller's report to the Finance Committee showing:
    1. The amount of accounts receivable outstanding for each age category and in total.
    2. The estimated amount that is uncollectible for each category and in total.
  (b) Compute the amount of the year-end adjustment necessary to bring Allowance for Doubtful Accounts to the balance indicated by the age analysis. Then prepare the necessary journal entry to adjust the accounting records.
  (c) In a recessionary environment with tight credit and high interest rates:
    1. Identify steps Arvada Company might consider to improve the accounts receivable situation.
    2. Then evaluate each step identified in terms of the risks and costs involved.

*C*OMPARATIVE ANALYSIS PROBLEM—
THE COCA-COLA COMPANY VS. PEPSICO, INC.

The financial statements of Coca-Cola Company are presented at the end of Chapter 1, and PepsiCo's financial statements are presented in Appendix A.

Instructions:
  (a) Based on the information contained in these financial statements, compute the following 1995 ratios for each company:
      1. Accounts receivable turnover ratio.
      2. Average collection period for receivables.
  (b) What conclusions concerning the management of accounts receivable can be drawn from these data?

INTERPRETATION OF FINANCIAL STATEMENTS

●●●

Mini-Case—Sears Roebuck & Co.

Sears is one of the world's largest retailers. It is also a huge provider of credit through its Sears credit card. Revenue generated from credit operations was $3.9 billion in 1995. The rate of interest Sears earns on outstanding receivables varies from 10 to 21 percent in the United States to up to 28 percent in Canada. Managing these receivables is critical to the performance of the corporation. One aspect of receivables management is that in some instances, to acquire cash when needed, the company will sell its receivables. At December 31, 1995 Sears had sold $4.55 billion of its receivables.

The following information was available in Sears 1995 financial statements.

(in millions of dollars)	1995	1994	1993
Accounts receivable (gross)	$20,949	$19,033	$15,906
Allowance for doubtful accounts	843	832	810
Merchandise sales	31,035	29,451	27,420
Credit revenues	3,890	3,574	3,020
Bad debts expense	826	698	821

Instructions:
  (a) Discuss whether the sale of receivables by Sears represents a significant portion of its receivables. Why might they have sold these receivables? As an investor, what concerns might you have about these sales?
  (b) Calculate and discuss the accounts receivable turnover ratio and average collection period for Sears for 1995 and 1994.
  (c) Do you think Sears provided credit as a revenue generating activity, or as a convenience for its customers?
  (d) Compute the ratio of Bad Debt Expense to Merchandise sales for 1995 and 1994. Did this ratio improve or get worse? What considerations should Sears make in deciding whether it wants to have liberal or conservative policies?

DECISION CASE

●●●

Johanna and Jake Berkvom own Campus Fashions. From its inception Campus Fashions has sold merchandise on either a cash or credit basis, but no credit cards have been accepted. During the past several months, the Berkvoms have begun to question their sales policies. First, they have lost some sales because of refusing to accept credit cards. Second, representatives of two metropolitan banks have been persuasive in convincing them to accept their national credit cards. One bank, City National Bank, has stated that (1) its credit card fee is 4%, and (2) it pays the retailer 96 cents on each $1 of sales within 3 days of receiving the credit card billings.

The Berkvoms decide that they should determine the cost of carrying their own credit sales. From the accounting records of the past three years they accumulate the following data:

	1996	1995	1994
Net credit sales	$500,000	$600,000	$400,000
Collection agency fees for slow paying customers	2,450	2,500	1,600
Salary of part-time accounts receivable clerk	3,800	3,800	3,800

Credit and collection expenses as a percentage of net credit sales: uncollectible accounts 1.6%, billing and mailing costs 0.5%, and credit investigation fee on new customers 0.15%.

Johanna and Jake also determine that the average accounts receivable balance outstanding during the year is 5% of net credit sales. The Berkvoms estimate that they could earn an average of 10% annually on cash invested in other business opportunities.

Instructions

(a) Prepare a tabulation showing for each year total credit and collection expenses in dollars and as a percentage of net credit sales.

(b) Determine the net credit and collection expense in dollars and as a percentage of sales after considering the revenue not earned from other investment opportunities. (*Note:* The income lost on the cash held by the bank for 3 days is considered to be immaterial.)

(c) Discuss both the financial and nonfinancial factors that are relevant to the decision.

COMMUNICATION ACTIVITY

Lois, a friend of yours who knows little about accounting, asks you to help make sense of a discussion she overheard at work about changes her employer wants to make in accounting for uncollectible accounts. Specifically, she asks you to explain the differences between the percentage of sales, percentage of receivables, and the direct write-off methods for uncollectible accounts.

Instructions

In a letter of one page (or less), explain to Lois the three methods of accounting for uncollectibles. Be sure to discuss differences among these methods.

GROUP ACTIVITY

Sherie Mitchell, controller for S & J Mitchell Co., provides you with the following list of accounts receivable that were written off during the current year.

Date	Customer	Amount
February 26	Kadlec Corp.	$ 8,700
April 17	Lois Hamilton Shops	13,219
June 30	Ilsa Kosinski Co.	5,500
October 4	Eleanor Schewe	3,187

S & J Mitchell Co. follows the policy of debiting Bad Debts Expense as accounts are written off. Sherie Mitchell maintains that this practice is appropriate for financial statement purposes because the Internal Revenue Service will not accept other methods for recognizing bad debts.

All of S & J Mitchell's sales are on a 30-day credit basis. Sales for the current year total $2,470,000. Experience has determined that bad debt losses approximate 2% of sales.

Instructions

In groups of four or five students, answer the following questions.

(a) Do you agree or disagree with S & J Mitchell's policy concerning recognition of bad debts? Why or why not?

(b) By what amount would net income differ if bad debts expense were computed using the percentage of sales approach?

ETHICS CASE

Shirt Co. is a subsidiary of Clothes Corp. The controller believes that the yearly allowance for doubtful accounts for Shirt Co. should be 2% of net credit sales. The president of Shirt Co., nervous that the parent company might expect the subsidiary to sustain its 10% growth rate, suggests that the controller increase the allowance for doubtful accounts to 4%. The president thinks that the lower net income, which reflects a 6% growth rate, will be a more sustainable rate for Shirt Co.

Instructions
(a) Who are the stakeholders in this case?
(b) Does the president's request pose an ethical dilemma for the controller?
(c) Should the controller be concerned with Shirt Co.'s growth rate in estimating the allowance? Explain your answer.

RESEARCH ASSIGNMENT

The May 6, 1996, issue of *Forbes* magazine includes an article by Matthew Schifrin and Howard Rudnitsky, entitled "Rx for receivables." Read the article and answer the following questions.

(a) Why has the pharmacy business moved from a cash-based business to a receivables-based business?
(b) What is the economic motivation for pharmacies to sell their receivables?
(c) What is the economic motivation for the Pharmacy Fund to purchase the receivables?

CRITICAL THINKING
▸ A Real-World Focus: Art World Industries, Inc.

Art World Industries, Inc. was incorporated in 1986 in Delaware, though it is located in Los Angeles. The company employs 25 people to print, publish, and sell limited edition graphics and reproductive prints in the wholesale market.

The operating expenses for the year ended August 1994 for Art World Industries, Inc., include bad debts expense of $6,715.50. The balance sheet shows an allowance for doubtful accounts of $175,477. The allowance was set up against certain Japanese accounts receivable which average over one year in age. The Japanese acknowledge the amount due, but with the slow economy in Japan lack the resources to pay at this time.

Instructions
(a) Which basis for estimating uncollectible accounts does Art World Industries use?
(b) When Art World makes its adjusting entry to record bad debts expense must it consider a previous existing balance in the Allowance for Doubtful Accounts?
(c) Explain the difference between the percentage of sales and percentage of receivables methods. In applying either of these methods, based on Art World's disclosure above, what important factor would you have to consider in arriving at appropriate percentages to apply?

Answers to Self-Study Questions
1. c   2. a   3. b   4. b   5. d   6. c   7. c   8. a   9. b   10. d

Before studying this chapter, you should know or, if necessary, review:

a. *The cost principle (Ch. 1, p. 9) and matching principle of accounting. (Ch. 3, p. 100)*

b. *How to record purchases, sales, and cost of goods sold under a perpetual inventory system. (Ch. 5, pp. 197–206)*

c. *How to prepare financial statements for a merchandising company. (Ch. 5, pp. 209–215)*

Keeping the Books on the Books

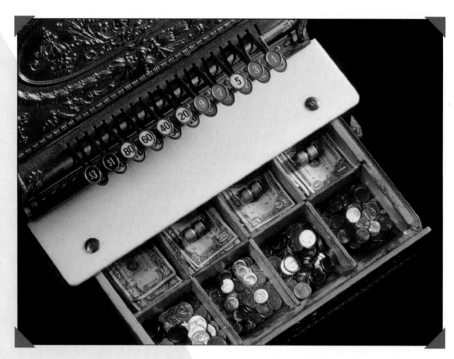

BUFFALO, N.Y. — If you go to a large college or university, chances are that your bookstore or student union has state-of-the-art computer technology for tracking inventories. In an instant, the clerk at the checkout stand "wooshes" your purchases over a scanning machine that automatically rings up the price and deducts the item from inventory.

Not all schools have such state-of-the-art technology. Some bookstores are even small enough that the person managing it can take a "mom-and-pop corner grocery" approach. One such bookstore is at Erie Community College in Buffalo, New York, which produces annual sales of $500,000 per year. Instead of using "point-of-sale" computer technology, the bookstore uses an old-fashioned cash register. The inventory of textbooks, notebooks, art supplies, and so on is counted every month by Joel Damiani, manager. Because the quantity of inventory is relatively small, Damiani, or his two assistants, can specifically

identify each item when sold. A larger bookstore would have too much inventory to use that approach; instead, they would use inventory costing methods that do not specifically match the cost of inventory to the actual sale of goods.

Damiani is candid, too, about some problems at his store. For one thing, the accounting records were in disarray when he took the

job. "They told me it was going to be a challenge," he says. "And I like challenges." His challenges have included working with the school's accountant to produce a monthly balance sheet and income statement for the bookstore and making sure he has enough inventory of books and supplies on hand for the start of classes. "Sometimes, students say we're not quick enough." ◀

CHAPTER · **9**

INVENTORIES

After studying this chapter, you should be able to:

1. Describe the steps in determining inventory quantities.
2. Prepare the entries for purchases and sales of inventory under a periodic inventory system.
3. Determine cost of goods sold under a periodic inventory system.
4. Identify the unique features of the income statement for a merchandising company using a periodic inventory system.
5. Explain the basis of accounting for inventories and describe the inventory cost flow methods.
6. Explain the financial statement and tax effects of each of the inventory cost flow methods.
7. Explain the lower of cost or market basis of accounting for inventories.
8. Indicate the effects of inventory errors on the financial statements.

As indicated in the opening story about the bookstore at Erie Community College, accounting for inventory can be time-consuming and complex. In this chapter we will explain the procedures for determining inventory quantities and the methods used in determining the cost of inventory on hand at the balance sheet date. In addition, we will discuss differences in periodic and perpetual inventory systems, and the effects of inventory errors on a company's financial statements. The content and organization of this chapter are as follows:

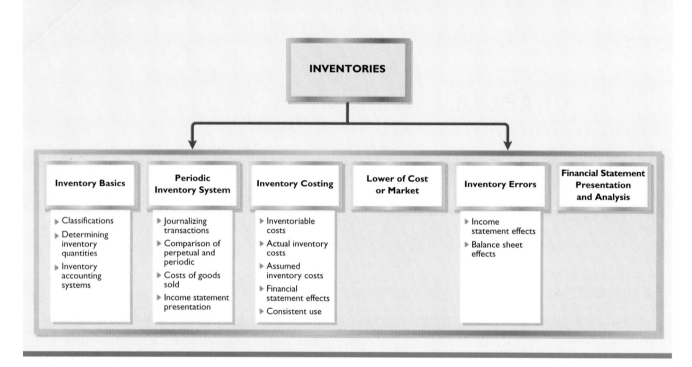

▼ *I*nventory Basics

Helpful hint In general, inventory levels have been reduced because of new methods of inventory control. These control measures are: point-of-sale computers which give retailers up-to-the-minute data; computer aided manufacturing, which reduces reorder time; and air freight, which can minimize inventories all through the production and distribution chain.

In our economy, inventories are an important barometer of business activity. The U.S. Commerce Department, for example, publishes monthly combined inventory data for retailers, wholesalers, and manufacturers. The amount of inventories and the time required to sell the goods on hand are two indicators that are closely watched. During downturns in the economy, there is an initial build-up of inventories, as the length of time needed to sell existing quantities increases. The reverse effects are generally associated with an upturn in business activity. A delicate balance must be maintained between too little inventory and too much. A merchandiser or manufacturer with too little inventory to meet demand will have dissatisfied customers and sales personnel. One with too much inventory will be burdened with unnecessary carrying costs.

Inventories affect both the balance sheet and the income statement. In the **balance sheet** of merchandising companies, inventory is frequently the most significant current asset. Of course, its amount and relative importance can vary, even for enterprises in the same industry. For example, Wal-Mart reported inventory of $14 billion, representing 90% of total current assets, whereas for the same period, J.C. Penney Company reported $3.9 billion of inventory, representing 41% of total current assets. In the **income statement**, inventory is vital in determining the results of operations for a particular period. Moreover, gross profit (net sales less cost of goods sold) is closely watched by management, owners, and other interested parties (as explained in Chapter 5).

Classifying Inventory

How a company classifies its inventory depends on whether the firm is a merchandiser or a manufacturer. In a **merchandising enterprise**, inventory consists of many different items. For example, in a grocery store, canned goods, dairy products, meats, and produce are just a few of the inventory items on hand. These items have two common characteristics: (1) they are owned by the company, and (2) they are in a form ready for sale to customers in the ordinary course of business. Thus, only one inventory classification, **merchandise inventory**, is needed to describe the many different items that make up the total inventory.

In a **manufacturing enterprise**, inventories are also owned by the company, but some goods may not yet be ready for sale. As a result, inventory is usually classified into three categories: finished goods, work in process, and raw materials. For example, General Motors classifies automobiles completed and ready for sale as **finished goods**. The automobiles on the assembly line in various stages of production are classified as **work in process**. The steel, glass, upholstery, and other components that are on hand waiting to be used in the production of automobiles are identified as **raw materials**.

The accounting principles and concepts discussed in this chapter apply to inventory classifications of both merchandising and manufacturing companies. In this chapter we will focus on merchandise inventory.

Determining Inventory Quantities

Many businesses take a physical inventory count on the last day of the year. Businesses using the periodic inventory system are required to take an end-of-the-period physical inventory to determine the inventory on hand at the balance sheet date and to compute cost of goods sold. Even businesses using a perpetual inventory system must take a physical inventory at some time during the year.

Determining inventory quantities consists of two steps: (1) taking a physical inventory of goods on hand, and (2) determining the ownership of goods.

Taking a Physical Inventory

Taking a physical inventory involves actually counting, weighing, or measuring each kind of inventory on hand. In many companies, taking an inventory is a formidable task. Retailers, such as Kmart, True Value Hardware, or your favorite music store have thousands of different inventory items. An inventory count is generally more accurate when goods are not being sold or received during the counting. Consequently, companies often "take inventory" when the business is closed or when business is slow. Many retailers, for example, close early on a chosen day in January—after the holiday sales and returns—to count their inventory.

To minimize errors in taking the inventory, a company should adopt the following procedures to adhere to **internal control** principles that safeguard inventory:

1. The counting should be done by employees who do not have custodial responsibility for the inventory. (Segregation of duties)
2. Each counter should establish the authenticity of each inventory item, e.g., each box does contain a 25-inch television set, and each storage tank does contain gasoline. (Establishment of responsibility)

Helpful hint An important inventory management concept is inventory turnover. Inventory that turns means sales and profit; inventory that doesn't turn means costs and losses.

Helpful hint Regardless of the classification, all inventories are reported under Current Assets on the balance sheet.

STUDY OBJECTIVE ⋯⋯⋯⋯**1**⋯⋯⋯⋯ *Describe the steps in determining inventory quantities.*

Helpful hint Many retailers, like Woolworth Corporation, take a physical inventory at January 31 (the common year end for retailers) when post-holiday season buying is in a lull and most holiday returns have been made.

3. There should be a second count by another employee. (Independent internal verification)
4. Prenumbered inventory tags should be used, and all inventory tags should be accounted for. (Documentation procedures)
5. A designated supervisor should ascertain at the conclusion of the count that all inventory items are tagged and that no items have more than one tag. (Independent internal verification)

After the physical inventory is taken, the quantity of each kind of inventory is listed on **inventory summary sheets**. To assure the accuracy of the summary sheets, the listing should be verified by a second employee or supervisor. Subsequently, unit costs will be applied to the quantities in order to determine a total cost of the inventory—which is the topic of later sections.[1]

▶Accounting in Action ▸ *Business Insight*

Failure to observe the foregoing internal control procedures contributed to the Great Salad Oil Swindle. In this case, management intentionally overstated its salad oil inventory, which was stored in large holding tanks. Three procedures contributed to overstating the oil inventory: (1) Water added to the bottom of the holding tanks caused the oil to float to the top. Inventory-taking crews who viewed the holding tanks from the top observed only salad oil, when, in fact, as much as 37 out of 40 feet of many of the holding tanks contained water. (2) The company's inventory records listed more holding tanks than it actually had. The company repainted numbers on the tanks after inventory crews examined them, so the crews counted the same tanks twice. (3) Underground pipes pumped oil from one holding tank to another during the inventory taking; therefore, the same salad oil was counted more than once. Although the salad oil swindle was unusual, it demonstrates the complexities involved in assuring that inventory is properly counted.

Determining Ownership of Goods

Before we can begin to calculate the cost of inventory, we need to consider the ownership of goods: specifically, we need to be sure that we have not included in the inventory any goods that do not belong to the company.

Goods in Transit.   Goods are considered to be **in transit** when they are in the hands of a public carrier, such as a railroad, trucking, or airline company at the statement date. Goods in transit should be included in the inventory of the party that has legal title to the goods. Legal title is determined by the terms of sale, as shown in Illustration 9-1 and described below:

1. When the terms are **FOB (free on board) shipping point**, ownership of the goods passes to the buyer when the public carrier accepts the goods from the seller.
2. When the terms are **FOB destination**, legal title to the goods remains with the seller until the goods reach the buyer.

---

[1]To arrive at an estimate of the cost of inventory when a physical inventory cannot be taken (the inventory is destroyed) or when it is inconvenient (during interim periods), estimating methods are applied. These methods (gross profit method and retail inventory method) are discussed in Appendix 9A.

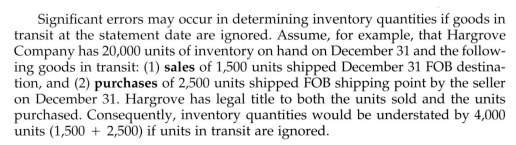

FOB Shipping Point | FOB Destination

Ownership passes to buyer here

Seller — P**C**c Public Carrier Co. → Buyer

Seller → P**C**c Public Carrier Co.

Ownership passes to buyer here

Buyer

Illustration 9-1

Terms of sale

►*T*echnology in *A*ction

Many companies have invested large amounts of time and money in automated inventory systems. One of the most sophisticated is Federal Express' Digitally Assisted Dispatch System (DADS). This system uses hand-held "SuperTrackers" to transmit data about the packages and documents to the firm's computer system. Based on bar codes, the system allows the firm to know where any package is at any time to prevent losses and to fulfill the firm's delivery commitments. More recently, FedEx's newly developed software enables customers to track shipments on their own PCs.

Significant errors may occur in determining inventory quantities if goods in transit at the statement date are ignored. Assume, for example, that Hargrove Company has 20,000 units of inventory on hand on December 31 and the following goods in transit: (1) **sales** of 1,500 units shipped December 31 FOB destination, and (2) **purchases** of 2,500 units shipped FOB shipping point by the seller on December 31. Hargrove has legal title to both the units sold and the units purchased. Consequently, inventory quantities would be understated by 4,000 units (1,500 + 2,500) if units in transit are ignored.

Consigned Goods. In some lines of business, it is customary to acquire merchandise on consignment. Under a consignment arrangement, the holder of the goods (called the *consignee*) does not own the goods. Ownership remains with the shipper of the goods (called the *consignor*) until the goods are actually sold to a customer. Because consigned goods are not owned by the consignee, they should not be included in the consignee's physical inventory count. Conversely, the consignor should include merchandise held by the consignee as part of its inventory.

Inventory Accounting Systems

One of two basic systems of accounting for inventories may be used: **(1) the perpetual inventory system, or (2) the periodic inventory system.** Chapter 5 of this textbook discussed and illustrated the characteristics of the perpetual inventory system. This chapter discusses and illustrates the periodic inventory system and provides a comparison of it with the perpetual inventory system; Appendix B to this chapter continues coverage of the perpetual inventory system.

Some businesses find it either unnecessary or uneconomical to invest in a computerized perpetual inventory system that maintains up-to-date records of merchandise on hand and cost of goods sold. Many small merchandising business managers especially still feel a perpetual inventory system costs more than it is worth. These managers can control merchandise and manage day-to-day operations without detailed inventory records. They use a periodic inventory system.

Before You Go On . . .

▸ *Review It*

1. What steps are involved in determining inventory quantities?
2. How is ownership determined for goods in transit at the balance sheet date?
3. Who has title to consigned goods?
4. Name two basic systems of accounting for inventories.

▸ *Do It*

Hasbeen Corporation completed its inventory count, arriving at a total value for inventory of $200,000. You have been informed of the information listed below. Discuss how this information affects the reported cost of inventory.

1. Goods held on consignment for Falls Corp., costing $15,000, were included in the inventory.
2. Purchased goods of $10,000 which were in transit (terms: FOB shipping point) were not included in the count.
3. Sold inventory with a cost of $12,000 which was in transit (terms: FOB shipping point) was not included in the count.

   Reasoning: For goods in transit, ownership is determined by the freight terms. For consigned goods, ownership rests with the consignor until the goods are sold by the consignee.

   Solution: The goods held on consignment of $15,000 should be deducted from the inventory count. The goods of $10,000 purchased FOB shipping point should be added to the inventory count. Sold goods of $12,000 which were in transit FOB shipping point should not be included in the ending inventory.

   Related exercise material: BE9-4, E9-1, E9-4

▶ *P*eriodic Inventory System

STUDY OBJECTIVE
••••••••••**2**••••••••••
Prepare the entries for purchases and sales of inventory under a periodic inventory system.

In a **periodic inventory system**, revenues from the sale of merchandise are recorded when sales are made in the same way as in a perpetual system. But, no attempt is made on the date of sale to record the cost of the merchandise sold. Instead, a physical inventory count is taken at the end of the period to determine (1) the cost of the merchandise then on hand and (2) the cost of the goods sold during the period. And, under a periodic system, purchases of merchandise are recorded in a Purchases account rather than a Merchandise Inventory account. Also, under a periodic system, it is customary to record purchase returns and allowances, purchase discounts, and freight-in on purchases in separate accounts so that the accumulated amounts for each are known.

Recording Merchandise Transactions Under a Periodic Inventory System

To illustrate the recording of merchandise transactions under a periodic inventory system, we will use the purchase/sale transactions between Highpoint Electronic Inc. and Chelsea Video, Inc. as illustrated under the perpetual inventory system in Chapter 5.

Recording Purchases of Merchandise

On the basis of the sales invoice (Illustration 5-4) shown on page 198 and receipt of the merchandise ordered from Highpoint Electronic, Chelsea Video records the $3,800 purchase as follows:

May 4	Purchases	3,800	
	Accounts Payable		3,800
	(To record goods purchased on account, terms 2/10, n/30		

Purchases is a temporary account whose normal balance is a debit.

Purchase Returns and Allowances

Because $300 of merchandise received from Highpoint Electronic is inoperable, Chelsea Video returns the goods, issues the debt memorandum (Illustration 5-5) shown on page 199, and prepares the following entry to recognize the purchase:

May 8	Accounts Payable	300	
	Purchase Returns and Allowances		300
	(To record return of inoperable goods purchased from Highpoint Electronic)		

Purchases Returns and Allowances is a temporary account whose normal balance is a credit.

Freight Costs

When the purchaser directly incurs the freight costs, the account Freight-in (or Transportation-in) is debited. For example, if upon delivery of the goods on May 6, Chelsea pays Acme Freight Company $150 for freight charges on its purchase from Highpoint Electronic, the entry on Chelsea's books is:

May 9	Freight-in (Transportation-in)	150	
	Cash		150
	(To record payment of freight, terms FOB shipping point)		

Like Purchases, Freight-in is a temporary account whose normal balance is a debit. **Freight-in is part of cost of goods purchased.** The reason is that cost of goods purchased should include any freight charges necessary to bring the goods to the purchaser. Freight costs are not subject to a purchase discount. Purchase discounts apply on the invoice cost of the merchandise.

Purchase Discounts

On May 14 Chelsea Video pays the balance due on account to Highpoint Electronic taking the 2% cash discount allowed by Highpoint for payment within 10 days. The payment and discount are recorded by Chelsea Video as follows:

May 14	Accounts Payable	3,500	
	Purchase Discounts		70
	Cash		3,430
	(To record payment to Highpoint Electronic within the discount period)		

Purchase Discounts is a temporary account whose normal balance is a credit.

Recording Sales of Merchandise

The sale of $3,800 of merchandise to Chelsea Video on May 4 (sales invoice No. 731, Illustration 5-4) is recorded by the seller, Highpoint Electronic, as follows:

May 4	Accounts Receivable	3,800	
	Sales		3,800
	(To record credit sales per invoice #731 to Chelsea Video)		

Sales Returns and Allowances

Based on the debit memorandum (Illustration 5-5, page 199) received from Chelsea Video on May 8 for returned goods, Highpoint Electronic records the $300 sales return as follows:

May 8	Sales Returns and Allowances	300	
	Accounts Receivable		300
	(To record return of goods from Chelsea Video)		

Sales Discounts

On May 15, Highpoint Electronic receives payment of $3,430 on account from Chelsea Video. Highpoint honors the 2% cash discount and records the payment of Chelsea's account receivable in full as follows:

May 15	Cash	3,430	
	Sales Discount	70	
	Accounts Receivable		3,500
	(To record collection from Chelsea Video within 2/10, n/30 discount period)		

Comparison of Entries—Perpetual vs. Periodic

The periodic inventory system entries above are shown in Illustration 9-2 next to those that were illustrated in Chapter 5 (pages 197–205) under the perpetual inventory system for both Highpoint Electronic and Chelsea Video.

Illustration 9-2

Comparison of journal entries under perpetual and periodic inventory systems

ENTRIES ON CHELSEA VIDEO'S BOOKS					
Transaction	Perpetual Inventory System		Periodic Inventory System		
May 4 Purchase of merchandise on credit.	Merchandise Inventory 3,800		Purchases 3,800		
	Accounts Payable	3,800	Accounts Payable	3,800	
May 8 Purchase returns and allowances.	Accounts Payable 300		Accounts Payable 300		
	Merchandise Inventory	300	Purchase Returns and Allowances	300	
May 9 Freight costs on purchases.	Merchandise Inventory 150		Freight-in 150		
	Cash	150	Cash	150	
May 14 Payment on account with a discount.	Accounts Payable 3,500		Accounts Payable 3,500		
	Cash	3,430	Cash	3,430	
	Merchandise Inventory	70	Purchase Discounts	70	

Illustration 9-2

Continued

ENTRIES ON HIGHPOINT ELECTRONIC'S BOOKS

	Transaction	Perpetual Inventory System		Periodic Inventory System	
May 4	Sale of merchandise on credit.	Accounts Receivable	3,800	Accounts Receivable	3,800
		Sales Revenue	3,800	Sales Revenue	3,800
		Cost of Goods Sold	2,400	No entry for cost of	
		Merchandise Inventory	2,400	goods sold	
May 8	Return of merchandise sold.	Sales Returns and		Sales Returns and	
		Allowances	300	Allowances	300
		Accounts Receivable	300	Accounts Receivable	300
		Merchandise Inventory	140	No entry	
		Cost of Goods Sold	140		
May 15	Cash received on account with a discount.	Cash	3,430	Cash	3,430
		Sales Discounts	70	Sales Discounts	70
		Accounts Receivable	3,500	Accounts Receivable	3,500

Cost of Goods Sold

As noted from the entries above, under a periodic inventory system, a running account of the changes in inventory is not recorded as either purchases or sales transactions occur. Neither the daily amount of inventory of merchandise on hand is known nor is the cost of goods sold. To determine the cost of goods sold under a periodic inventory system, it is necessary to (1) record purchases of merchandise (as shown above), (2) determine the cost of goods purchased, and (3) determine the cost of goods on hand at the beginning and end of the accounting period. The cost of goods on hand must be determined by a physical inventory count and application of the cost to the items counted in the inventory.

STUDY OBJECTIVE
••••••••••• 3 •••••••••••
Determine cost of goods sold under a periodic inventory system.

Determining Cost of Goods Purchased

We used four accounts to record the purchase of inventory under a periodic inventory system. These accounts are:

Account	Normal Balance
Purchases	Debit
Purchase Returns and Allowances	Credit
Purchase Discounts	Credit
Freight-in	Debit

Illustration 9-3

Normal balances: cost of goods purchased accounts

All of these accounts are temporary accounts because they are used to determine the cost of goods sold which is an expense disclosed on the income statement. Therefore, the balances in these accounts must be reduced to zero at the end of each accounting period so that information about cost of goods sold can be accumulated in the next accounting period. The procedure for determining the cost of goods purchased is as follows:

1. The accounts with credit balances (Purchase Returns and Allowances and Purchase Discounts) are subtracted from Purchases to produce net purchases.

2. Freight-in is then added to net purchases to produce cost of goods purchased.

To illustrate, assume that Highpoint Electronic shows the following balances for the accounts above: Purchases $325,000; Purchase Returns and Allowances $10,400; Purchase Discounts $6,800; and Freight-in $12,200. Net purchases and cost of goods purchased are $307,800 and $320,000, respectively, as computed in Illustration 9-4:

Illustration 9-4

Computation of net purchases and cost of goods purchased

	Purchases		$325,000
(1)	Less: Purchase returns and allowances	$10,400	
	Purchase discounts	6,800	17,200
	Net purchases		307,800
(2)	Add: Freight-in		12,200
	Cost of goods purchased		$320,000

Determining Cost of Goods on Hand

To **determine the cost of inventory on hand, it is necessary to take a physical inventory**. As explained earlier in this chapter, taking a physical inventory involves:

1. Counting the units on hand for each item of inventory.

2. Applying unit costs to the total units on hand for each item of inventory.

3. Aggregating the costs for each item of inventory to determine the total cost of goods on hand.

A physical inventory should be taken at or near the balance sheet date. To improve the accuracy of the count, many businesses suspend operations while inventory is being taken.

The account Merchandise Inventory is used to record the cost of inventory on hand at the balance sheet date. This amount becomes the beginning inventory for the next accounting period. For Highpoint Electronic, the balance in Merchandise Inventory at December 31, 1995, is $36,000. This amount is also the January 1, 1996, balance in Merchandise Inventory. During 1996, **no entries are made to Merchandise Inventory**. At December 31, 1996, entries are made to eliminate the beginning inventory and to record the ending inventory, which we will assume is $40,000.

Computing Cost of Goods Sold

We have now reached the point where we can compute cost of goods sold. Doing so involves two steps:

1. Add the cost of goods purchased to the cost of goods on hand at the beginning of the period (beginning inventory) to obtain the cost of goods available for sale.

2. Subtract the cost of goods on hand at the end of the period (ending inventory) from the cost of goods available for sale to arrive at the cost of goods sold.

For Highpoint Electronic the cost of goods available for sale and the cost of goods sold are $356,000 and $316,000, respectively, as shown below.

Illustration 9-5

Computation of cost of goods available for sale and cost of goods sold

	Beginning inventory	$ 36,000
(1)	Add: Cost of goods purchased	320,000
	Cost of goods available for sale	356,000
(2)	Less: Ending inventory	40,000
	Cost of goods sold	$316,000

Gross profit, operating expenses, and net income are computed and reported in a periodic inventory system in the same manner as they are under a perpetual inventory system as discussed in Chapter 5, page 207, and shown in Illustration 9-6.

Income Statement Presentation

As under a perpetual inventory system, the income statement for retailers and wholesalers under a periodic inventory system contains three features not found in the income statement of a service enterprise. These features are: (1) a sales revenue section, (2) a cost of goods sold section, and (3) gross profit. But, under a periodic inventory system, the cost of goods sold section generally will contain

STUDY OBJECTIVE
•••••••••**4**•••••••••

Identify the unique features of the income statement for a merchandising company using a periodic inventory system.

Illustration 9-6

Income statement for a merchandising company using a periodic inventory system

HIGHPOINT ELECTRONIC INC.
Income Statement
For the Year Ended December 31, 1996

Sales revenues			
Sales			$480,000
Less: Sales returns and allowances		$ 12,000	
Sales discounts		8,000	20,000
Net sales			460,000
Cost of goods sold			
Inventory, January 1		36,000	
Purchases	$325,000		
Less: Purchases returns and allowances	$10,400		
Purchase discounts	6,800	17,200	
Net purchases		307,800	
Add: Freight-in		12,200	
Cost of goods purchased		320,000	
Cost of goods available for sale		356,000	
Inventory, December 31		40,000	
Cost of goods sold			316,000
Gross profit			144,000
Operating expenses			
Store salaries expense		45,000	
Rent expense		19,000	
Utilities expense		17,000	
Advertising expense		16,000	
Depreciation expense—store equipment		8,000	
Freight-out		7,000	
Insurance expense		2,000	
Total operating expenses			114,000
Net income			$ 30,000

Helpful hint The far right column identifies the major subdivisions of the income statement. The next column identifies the primary items comprising cost of goods sold of $316,000 and operating expenses of $114,000; in addition, contra revenue items of $20,000 are reported. The third column explains cost of goods purchased of $320,000. The fourth column reports contra purchase items of $17,200.

more detail. Using assumed data for specific operating expenses, the income statement for Highpoint Electronic Inc. using a periodic inventory system is shown in Illustration 9-6. Whether the periodic or the perpetual inventory system is used, merchandise inventory is reported at the same amount in the current asset section.

Before You Go On . . .

▸ Review It

1. Identify the three steps in determining cost of goods sold.
2. What accounts are used in determining the cost of goods purchased?
3. What is included in cost of goods available for sale?

▸ Do It

Aerosmith Company's accounting records show the following at year-end: Purchase Discounts $3,400; Freight-in $6,100; Sales $240,000; Purchases $162,500; Beginning Inventory $18,000; Ending Inventory $20,000; Sales Discounts $10,000; Purchase Returns $5,200; and Operating Expenses $57,000. Compute the following amounts for Aerosmith Company: net sales, cost of goods purchased, cost of goods sold, gross profit, and net income.

Reasoning: To compute the required amounts, it is important to know the relationships in measuring net income for a merchandising company. For example, it is necessary to know the difference between the following: sales and net sales, goods available for sale and cost of goods sold, and gross profit and net income.

Solution:
Net sales: $240,000 − $10,000 = $230,000.
Cost of goods purchased: $162,500 − $5,200 − $3,400 + $6,100 = $160,000.
Cost of goods sold: $18,000 + $160,000 − $20,000 = $158,000.
Gross profit: $230,000 − $158,000 = $72,000.
Net income: $72,000 − $57,000 = $15,000.

Related exercise material: BE9-2, BE9-3, E9-2, E9-3

Inventory Costing Under a Periodic Inventory System

STUDY OBJECTIVE
5

Explain the basis of accounting for inventories and describe the inventory cost flow methods.

All expenditures necessary to acquire the goods and to make them ready for sale are included as inventoriable costs. Inventoriable costs may be regarded as a pool of costs that consists of two elements: (1) the cost of the beginning inventory and (2) the cost of goods purchased during the year. The sum of these two elements equals the cost of goods available for sale. Conceptually, the costs of the purchasing, receiving, and warehousing departments (whose efforts make the goods available for sale) should also be included in inventoriable costs. However, because of the practical difficulties in allocating these costs to inventory, they are generally accounted for as **operating expenses** in the period in which they are incurred.

Helpful hint Under a perpetual inventory system, described in Chapter 5, the allocation is continuously recognized as purchases and sales are made.

Inventoriable costs are allocated to ending inventory and to cost of goods sold. Under a periodic inventory system, the allocation is made at the end of the accounting period. First, the costs assignable to the ending inventory are determined. Second, the cost of the ending inventory is subtracted from the cost of goods available for sale to determine the cost of goods sold. Cost of goods sold is then deducted from sales revenues in accordance with the matching principle.

To illustrate, assume that General Suppliers Inc. has a cost of goods available for sale of $120,000, based on a beginning inventory of $20,000 and cost of goods purchased of $100,000. The physical inventory indicates that 5,000 units are on hand. The costs applicable to the units are $3.00 per unit. The allocation of the pool of costs is shown in Illustration 9-7. As shown, the $120,000 of goods available for sale are allocated $15,000 to ending inventory and $105,000 to cost of goods sold.

Pool of Costs

Cost of Goods Available for Sale

Beginning inventory	$ 20,000
Cost of goods purchased	100,000
Cost of goods available for sale	$120,000

Illustration 9-7

Allocation (matching) of pool of costs

Step 1			**Step 2**	
Ending Inventory			**Cost of Goods Sold**	
Units	Unit Cost	Total Cost	Cost of goods available for sale	$120,000
			Less: Ending inventory	15,000
5,000	$3.00	$15,000	Cost of goods sold	$105,000

Using Actual Physical Flow Costing—Specific Identification

Costing of the inventory is complicated because the units on hand for a specific item of inventory may have been purchased at different prices. For example, in a period of rising prices, a company may experience several increases in the cost of identical goods within a given year. Alternatively, unit costs may decline. Under such circumstances, how should the different unit costs in the cost of goods available for sale be allocated between the ending inventory and cost of goods sold?

One answer is to use specific identification of the units purchased. This method tracks the **actual physical flow** of the goods. **Each item of inventory is marked, tagged, or coded with its "specific" unit cost.** Items still in inventory at the end of the year are specifically costed to arrive at the total cost of the ending inventory. Assume, for example, that Southland Music Company purchases three 46-inch television sets at costs of $700, $750, and $800, respectively. During the year, two sets are sold at $1,200 each. At December 31, the company determines that the $750 set is still on hand. Accordingly, the ending inventory is $750 and the cost of goods sold is $1,500 ($700 + $800).

Specific identification is possible when a company sells a limited variety of high-unit cost items that can be clearly identified from the time of purchase through the time of sale. Examples of such companies are automobile dealerships (cars, trucks, and vans), music stores (pianos and organs), and antique shops (tables and cabinets). Although the bookstore at Erie Community College uses specific identification, it is somewhat unusual to do so for that type of business.

Ordinarily, however, the identity of goods purchased at a specific cost is lost between the date of purchase and the date of sale. For example, drug, grocery, and hardware stores sell thousands of relatively low unit-cost items of inventory. These items are often indistinguishable from one another, making it impossible or impractical to track each item's cost.

When feasible, specific identification seems to be the ideal method of allocating cost of goods available for sale. Under this method, the ending inventory is reported at actual cost and the actual cost of goods sold is matched against sales revenue. This method, however, may enable management to manipulate net income. For example, assume that a music store has three identical Steinway grand pianos that were purchased at different costs. When selling one piano, management could maximize its net income by selecting the piano with the lowest cost to match with revenues. Alternatively, it could minimize net income by selecting the highest-cost piano.

Using Assumed Cost Flow Methods—FIFO, LIFO, and Average Cost

Because specific identification is often impractical, other cost flow methods are allowed. These differ from specific identification in that they assume flows of costs that may be unrelated to the physical flow of goods. For this reason we call them **assumed cost flow methods** or **cost flow assumptions**. They are:

1. First-in, first-out (FIFO).
2. Last-in, first-out (LIFO).
3. Average cost.

▶ *International note*

A survey of accounting standards in 21 major industrial countries found that all three methods were permissible. In Ireland and the U.K., LIFO is permitted only in extreme circumstances.

There is no accounting requirement that the cost flow assumption be consistent with the physical movement of the goods. The selection of the appropriate cost flow assumption (method) is made by management. The management of companies in the same industry may reach different conclusions as to the most appropriate method.

To illustrate these three inventory cost flow methods, we will assume that Bow Valley Electronics uses a periodic inventory system and has the information shown below for its Z202 Astro condenser.

Illustration 9-8

Inventoriable units and costs

BOW VALLEY ELECTRONICS
Z202 Astro Condensers

Date	Explanation	Units	Unit Cost	Total Cost
1/1	Beginning inventory	100	$10	$ 1,000
4/15	Purchase	200	11	2,200
8/24	Purchase	300	12	3,600
11/27	Purchase	400	13	5,200
	Total	1,000		$12,000

During the year, 550 units were sold and 450 units are on hand at December 31.

First-in, First-out (FIFO)

The **FIFO method** assumes that the **earliest goods** purchased are the first to be sold. FIFO often parallels the actual physical flow of merchandise because it generally is good business practice to sell the oldest units first. Under the FIFO method, therefore, the **costs** of the earliest goods purchased are the first to be recognized as cost of goods sold. The allocation of the cost of goods available for sale at Bow Valley Electronics under FIFO is shown in Illustration 9-9.

Pool of Costs

Cost of Goods Available for Sale

Date	Explanation	Units	Unit Cost	Total Cost
1/1	Beginning inventory	100	$10	$ 1,000
4/15	Purchase	200	11	2,200
8/24	Purchase	300	12	3,600
11/27	Purchase	400	13	5,200
	Total	1,000		$12,000

Illustration 9-9

Allocation of costs—FIFO method

Helpful hint Note the sequencing of the allocation: (1) compute ending inventory and (2) determine cost of goods sold.

	Step 1			**Step 2**	
	Ending Inventory			**Cost of Goods Sold**	
Date	Units	Unit Cost	Total Cost		
11/27	400	$13	$5,200	Cost of goods available for sale	$12,000
8/24	50	12	600	Less: Ending inventory	5,800
Total	450		$5,800	Cost of goods sold	$ 6,200

Helpful hint Cost of goods sold is often referred to as cost of sales.

Note that the ending inventory is based on the latest units purchased. That is, **the cost of the ending inventory is obtained by taking the unit cost of the most recent purchase and working backward until all units of inventory have been costed**.

We can verify the accuracy of the cost of goods sold by recognizing that the **first units acquired are the first units sold**. The computations for the 550 units sold are shown in Illustration 9-10.

Helpful hint Note that ending inventory of $5,800 and the cost of goods sold of $6,200 equals cost of goods available for sale.

Date	Units		Unit Cost		Total Cost
1/1	100	×	$10	=	$1,000
4/15	200	×	11	=	2,200
8/24	250	×	12	=	3,000
Total	550				$6,200

Illustration 9-10

Proof of cost of goods sold

Last-in, First-out (LIFO)

The **LIFO method** assumes that the **latest goods** purchased are the first to be sold. LIFO seldom coincides with the actual physical flow of inventory. Under the LIFO method, the **costs** of the latest goods purchased are the first to be recognized as cost of goods sold. The allocation of the cost of goods available for sale at Bow Valley Electronics under LIFO is shown in Illustration 9-11.

Pool of Costs
Cost of Goods Available for Sale

Date	Explanation	Units	Unit Cost	Total Cost
1/1	Beginning inventory	100	$10	$ 1,000
4/15	Purchase	200	11	2,200
8/24	Purchase	300	12	3,600
11/27	Purchase	400	13	5,200
	Total	1,000		$12,000

Helpful hint The costs allocated to ending inventory ($5,000) plus the costs allocated to CGS ($7,000) must equal CGAS ($12,000).

	Step 1				Step 2	
	Ending Inventory				**Cost of Goods Sold**	
Date	Units	Unit Cost	Total Cost			
1/1	100	$10	$1,000	Cost of goods available for sale		$12,000
4/15	200	11	2,200	Less: Ending inventory		5,000
8/24	150	12	1,800	Cost of goods sold		$ 7,000
Total	450		$5,000			

Under the LIFO method, **the cost of the ending inventory is obtained by taking the unit cost of the earliest goods available for sale and working forward until all units of inventory are costed**. As a result, the first costs assigned to ending inventory are the costs of the beginning inventory. Proof of the costs allocated to cost of goods sold is shown in Illustration 9-12.

Date	Units		Unit Cost		Total Cost
11/27	400	×	$13	=	$5,200
8/24	150	×	12	=	1,800
Total	550				$7,000

Note that the cost of the **last** goods in are the **first** to be assigned to cost of goods sold. Under a periodic inventory system, which we are using here, **all goods purchased during the period are assumed to be available for the first sale, regardless of the date of purchase.**

Average Cost

The average cost method assumes that the goods available for sale are homogeneous. Under this method, the allocation of the cost of goods available for sale is made on the basis of the **weighted average unit cost** incurred. The formula and a sample computation of the weighted average unit cost are:

Illustration 9-13

Formula for weighted average unit cost

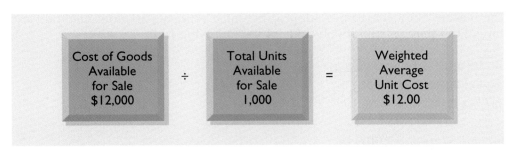

Helpful hint Both factors in the formula are totals; hence a weighted average unit cost.

The weighted average unit cost is then applied to the units on hand to determine the cost of the ending inventory. The allocation of the cost of goods available for sale at Bow Valley Electronics using average cost is shown in Illustration 9-14.

Illustration 9-14

Allocation of costs—average cost method

Pool of Costs

Cost of Goods Available for Sale

Date	Explanation	Units	Unit Cost	Total Cost
1/1	Beginning inventory	100	$10	$ 1,000
4/15	Purchase	200	11	2,200
8/24	Purchase	300	12	3,600
11/27	Purchase	400	13	5,200
	Total	1,000		$12,000

Step 1			Step 2	
Ending Inventory			**Cost of Goods Sold**	
$12,000 ÷	1,000 =	$12.00	Cost of goods available for sale	$12,000
	Unit	Total	Less: Ending inventory	5,400
Units	Cost	Cost	Cost of goods sold	$ 6,600
450	× $12.00 =	$5,400		

We can verify the cost of goods sold under this method by multiplying the units sold by the weighted average unit cost (550 × $12 = $6,600). Note that this method does not use the average of the unit costs. That average is $11.50 ($10 + $11 + $12 + $13 = $46; $46 ÷ 4). The average cost method instead uses the average **weighted** by the quantities purchased at each unit cost.

Financial Statement Effects of Cost Flow Methods

Each of the three cost flow methods is acceptable. For example, Black and Decker Manufacturing Company and Wendy's International currently use the FIFO method of inventory costing. Campbell Soup Company, Krogers, and Walgreen Drugs use LIFO for part or all of their inventory. Bristol-Myers and Motorola use the average cost method. A company may also use more than one cost flow method at the same time. Del Monte Corporation, for example, uses LIFO for domestic inventories and FIFO for foreign inventories. Illustration 9-15 shows the use of the three cost flow methods in the 600 largest companies in the U.S.

STUDY OBJECTIVE
••••••••• **6** •••••••••

Explain the financial statement and tax effects of each of the inventory cost flow methods.

Illustration 9-15

Use of cost flow methods in major U.S. companies

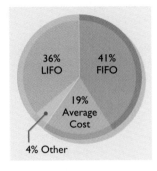

The reasons why companies adopt different inventory cost flow methods are varied, but they usually involve one of the following factors:

1. Income statement effects
2. Balance sheet effects
3. Tax effects

Income Statement Effects

To understand why companies might choose a particular cost flow method, let's examine the effects of the different flow assumptions on the financial statements of Bow Valley Electronics. The condensed income statements in Illustration 9-16 assume that Bow Valley sold its 550 units for $11,500, its operating expenses were $2,000, and its income tax rate is 30%.

Illustration 9-16

Comparative effects of cost flow methods

BOW VALLEY ELECTRONICS Condensed Income Statements			
	FIFO	LIFO	Average Cost
Sales	$11,500	$11,500	$11,500
Beginning inventory	1,000	1,000	1,000
Purchases	11,000	11,000	11,000
Cost of goods available for sale	12,000	12,000	12,000
Ending inventory	5,800	5,000	5,400
Cost of goods sold	6,200	7,000	6,600
Gross profit	5,300	4,500	4,900
Operating expenses	2,000	2,000	2,000
Income before income taxes[2]	3,300	2,500	2,900
Income tax expense (30%)	990	750	870
Net income	$ 2,310	$ 1,750	$ 2,030

Although the cost of goods available for sale ($12,000) is the same under each of the three inventory cost flow methods, both the ending inventories and cost of goods sold are different. This difference is due to the unit costs that are allocated to cost of goods sold and to ending inventory. Each dollar of difference in ending inventory results in a corresponding dollar difference in income before income taxes. For Bow Valley, there is an $800 difference between FIFO and LIFO. In a period of inflation, FIFO produced a higher net income because the lower unit costs of the first units purchased are matched against revenues. In a period of rising prices (as is the case here), FIFO reports the highest net income ($2,310) and LIFO the lowest ($1,750); average cost falls in the middle ($2,030). If prices are falling, the results from the use of FIFO and LIFO are reversed. FIFO will report the lowest net income and LIFO the highest. To management, higher net income is an advantage: it causes external users to view the company more favorably. In addition, if management bonuses are based on net income, FIFO will provide the basis for higher bonuses.

Some argue that the use of LIFO in a period of inflation enables the company to avoid reporting **paper or phantom profit** as economic gain. To illustrate, assume that Kralik Company buys 200 XR492s at $20 per unit on January 10 and

---

[2]It is assumed that Bow Valley is a corporation, and corporations are required to pay income taxes.

200 more on December 31 at $24 each. During the year, 200 units are sold at $30 each. The results under FIFO and LIFO are shown in Illustration 9-17.

	FIFO		**LIFO**	
Sales (200 × $30)	$6,000		$6,000	
Cost of goods sold	4,000	(200 × $20)	4,800	(200 × $24)
Gross profit	$2,000		$1,200	

Illustration 9-17

Income statement effects compared

Under LIFO, the company has recovered the current replacement cost ($4,800) of the units sold. Thus, the gross profit in economic terms is real. However, under FIFO, the company has recovered only the January 10 cost ($4,000). To replace the units sold, it must reinvest $800 (200 × $4) of the gross profit. Thus, $800 of the gross profit is said to be phantom or illusory. As a result, reported net income is also overstated in real terms.

Helpful hint The $800 is also referred to as a holding gain that is deferred under LIFO until the goods are sold.

Balance Sheet Effects

A major advantage of the FIFO method is that in a period of inflation, the costs allocated to ending inventory will approximate their current cost. For example, for Bow Valley, 400 of the 450 units in the ending inventory are costed at the November 27 unit cost of $13.

Conversely, a major shortcoming of the LIFO method is that in a period of inflation, the costs allocated to ending inventory may be significantly understated in terms of current cost. This is true for Bow Valley, where the cost of the ending inventory includes the $10 unit cost of the beginning inventory. The understatement becomes greater over prolonged periods of inflation if the inventory includes goods purchased in one or more prior accounting periods.

Tax Effects

We have seen that both inventory on the balance sheet and net income on the income statement are higher when FIFO is used in a period of inflation. Yet, many companies have switched to LIFO. The reason is that LIFO results in the lowest income taxes (because of lower net income) during times of rising prices. For example, at Bow Valley Electronics, income taxes are $750 under LIFO, compared to $990 under FIFO. The tax saving of $240 makes more cash available for use in the business.

LIFO is for car dealership

►Accounting in Action ► *Business Insight*

Most small firms use the FIFO method. But fears of rising inflation often cause many firms to switch to LIFO. For example, Chicago Heights Steel Co. in Illinois boosted cash "by 5% to 10% by lowering income taxes" when it switched to LIFO. Electronic games distributor Atlas Distributing Inc., Chicago, considered a switch "because the costs of our games, made in Japan, are rising 15% a year," says Joseph Serpico, treasurer. When inflation heats up, "the number of companies electing LIFO will rise dramatically," says William Spiro of BDO Seidman, New York.

Using Inventory Cost Flow Methods Consistently

Whatever cost flow method a company chooses, it should be used consistently from one accounting period to another. Consistent application enhances the comparability of financial statements over successive time periods. In contrast, using

Helpful hint As you learned in Chapter 6, consistency is one of the important characteristics of accounting information.

the FIFO method in one year and the LIFO method in the next year would make it difficult to compare the net incomes of the two years.

Although consistent application is preferred, it does not mean that a company may *never* change its method of inventory costing. When a company adopts a different method, the change and its effects on net income should be disclosed in the financial statements. A typical disclosure is shown in Illustration 9-18, using information from recent financial statements of the Quaker Oats Company.

Illustration 9-18

Disclosure of change in cost flow method

Notes to the Financial Statements:

Note 1   Effective July 1, the Company adopted the LIFO cost flow assumption for valuing the majority of U.S. Grocery Products inventories. The Company believes that the use of the LIFO method better matches current costs with current revenues. The effect of this change on the current year was to decrease net income by $16.0 million.

▸Accounting in Action ▸ *International Insight*

U.S. companies typically choose between LIFO and FIFO. Many choose LIFO because it reduces inventory profits and taxes. However, the international community recently considered rules that would ban LIFO entirely and force companies to use FIFO. This proposed rule was defeated, but the issue will not go away.

The issue is sensitive. As John Wulff, controller for Union Carbide noted, "We were in support of the international effort up until the proposal to eliminate LIFO." Wulff says that if Union Carbide had been suddenly forced to switch from LIFO to FIFO recently, its reported $632 million pretax income would have jumped by $300 million. That would have increased Carbide's income tax bill by as much as $120 million.

Do you believe that accounting principles and rules should be the same around the world?

Before You Go On . . .

▸ *Review It*

1. How do the cost and matching principles apply to inventoriable costs?
2. How are the three assumed cost flow methods applied in allocating inventoriable costs?
3. What factors should be considered by management in selecting an inventory cost flow method?
4. Which inventory cost flow method produces (a) the highest net income in a period of rising prices, and (b) the lowest income taxes?

▸ *Do It*

The accounting records of Shumway Ag Implement show the following data:

Beginning inventory	4,000 units at $3
Purchases	6,000 units at $4
Sales	5,000 units at $12

Determine the cost of goods sold during the period under a periodic inventory system using (a) the FIFO method, (b) the LIFO method, and (c) the average cost method.

Reasoning: Because the units of inventory on hand and available for sale may have been purchased at different prices, a systematic method must be adopted to allocate the costs between the goods sold and the goods on hand (ending inventory).

Solution:

(a) FIFO: (4,000 @ $3) + (1,000 @ $4) = $12,000 + $4,000 = $16,000.

(b) LIFO: 5,000 @ $4 = <u>$20,000</u>
(c) Average cost: [(4,000 @ $3) + (6,000 @ $4)] ÷ 10,000 = ($12,000 + $24,000) ÷ 10,000 = $3.60 per unit; 5,000 @ $3.60 = <u>$18,000</u>.

Related exercise material: BE9-6, BE9-7, E9-5, E9-6, E9-7.

Valuing Inventory at the Lower of Cost or Market (LCM)

When the value of inventory is lower than its cost, the inventory is written down to its market value. This is accomplished by valuing the inventory at the **lower of cost or market (LCM)** in the period in which the price decline occurs. LCM is an example of the accounting concept of conservatism. **Conservatism** means that when choosing among accounting alternatives, the best choice is to select the method that is least likely to overstate assets and net income.

Under the LCM basis, market is defined as current replacement cost, not selling price. For a merchandising company, market is the cost of purchasing the same goods at the present time from the usual suppliers in the usual quantities. Current replacement cost is used because a decline in the replacement cost of an item usually leads to a decline in the selling price of the item.

The lower of cost or market basis may be applied to individual items of inventory, major categories of inventory, or total inventory. For example, assume that Len's TV has the following lines of merchandise with costs and market values as indicated. LCM produces the following three results:

STUDY OBJECTIVE

7

Explain the lower of cost or market basis of accounting for inventories.

	Cost	Market	Lower of Cost or Market by:		
			Individual Items	Major Categories	Total Inventory
Television sets					
Consoles	$ 60,000	$ 55,000	$ 55,000		
Portables	45,000	52,000	45,000		
Total	105,000	107,000		$105,000	
Video equipment					
Recorders	48,000	45,000	45,000		
Movies	15,000	14,000	14,000		
Total	63,000	59,000		59,000	
Total inventory	$168,000	$166,000	$159,000	$164,000	$166,000

Illustration 9-19

Alternative lower of cost or market results

The amount entered in the individual items column is the lower of the cost or market amount for **each item**. For the major categories column, the amount is the lower of the total cost or total market for **each category**. Finally, the amount for the total inventory column is the lower of the cost or market for the **entire inventory**. The common practice is to use individual items in determining the LCM valuation. This approach gives the most conservative valuation for balance sheet purposes and also the lowest net income. LCM should be applied consistently from period to period.

LCM is applied to the items in inventory after one of the costing methods (specific identification, FIFO, LIFO, or average cost) has been applied to determine cost.

*I*nventory Errors

STUDY OBJECTIVE

8

Indicate the effects of inventory errors on the financial statements.

Unfortunately, errors occasionally occur in taking or costing inventory. In some cases, errors are caused by failure to count or price the inventory correctly. In other cases, errors occur because proper recognition is not given to the transfer of legal title to goods that are in transit. When errors occur, they affect both the income statement and the balance sheet.

Income Statement Effects

As you know, both the beginning and ending inventories are part of the computation of net income. The ending inventory of one period automatically becomes the beginning inventory of the next period. Inventory errors affect the determination of cost of goods sold and net income.

The effects on cost of goods sold can be determined by entering the incorrect data in the following formula and then substituting the correct data.

Illustration 9-20

Formula for cost of goods sold

▸ *Ethics note*

Inventory fraud increases during recessions. Such fraud includes pricing inventory at amounts in excess of their actual value, or claiming to have inventory when no inventory exists. Inventory fraud is usually done to overstate ending inventory, thereby understating cost of goods sold and creating higher income.

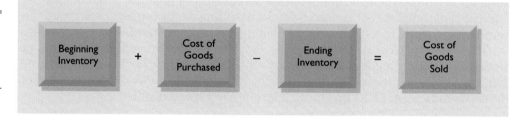

If beginning inventory is understated, cost of goods sold will be understated. On the other hand, an understatement of ending inventory will overstate cost of goods sold. The effects of inventory errors on the current year's income statement are shown in Illustration 9-21.

Illustration 9-21

Effects of inventory errors on current year's income statement

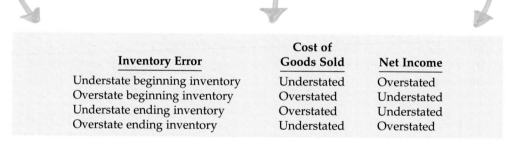

Inventory Error	Cost of Goods Sold	Net Income
Understate beginning inventory	Understated	Overstated
Overstate beginning inventory	Overstated	Understated
Understate ending inventory	Overstated	Understated
Overstate ending inventory	Understated	Overstated

An error in ending inventory of the current period will have a **reverse effect on net income of the next accounting period**. This is shown in Illustration 9-22. Note that the understatement of ending inventory in 1996 results in an understatement of beginning inventory in 1997 and an overstatement of net income in 1997.

Illustration 9-22

Effects of inventory errors on 2 years' income statements

Condensed Income Statement								
	1996				**1997**			
	Incorrect		Correct		Incorrect		Correct	
Sales		$80,000		$80,000		$90,000		$90,000
Beginning inventory	$20,000		$20,000		$12,000		$15,000	
Cost of goods purchased	40,000		40,000		68,000		68,000	
Cost of goods available for sale	60,000		60,000		80,000		83,000	
Ending inventory	12,000		15,000		23,000		23,000	
Cost of goods sold		48,000		45,000		57,000		60,000
Gross profit		32,000		35,000		33,000		30,000
Operating expenses		10,000		10,000		20,000		20,000
Net income		$22,000		$25,000		$13,000		$10,000

($3,000)
Net income
understated

$3,000
Net income
overstated

Total income for
2 years correct

Over the 2 years, total net income is correct because the errors offset one another. Notice that total income using incorrect data is $35,000 ($22,000 + $13,000), which is the same as the total income of $35,000 ($25,000 + $10,000) using correct data. Also note in this example that an error in the beginning inventory does not result in a corresponding error in the ending inventory for that period. The correctness of the ending inventory depends entirely on the accuracy of taking and costing the inventory at the balance sheet date.

Balance Sheet Effects

The effect of ending inventory errors on the balance sheet can be determined by using the basic accounting equation: assets equal liabilities plus stockholders' equity. Errors in the ending inventory have the following effects on these components:

Illustration 9-23

Ending inventory error— balance sheet effects

Ending Inventory Error	Assets	Liabilities	Stockholders' Equity
Overstated	Overstated	None	Overstated
Understated	Understated	None	Understated

The effect of an error in ending inventory on the subsequent period was shown in Illustration 9-22. Recall that if the error is not corrected, total net income for the two periods would be correct. Thus, total stockholders' equity reported on the balance sheet at the end of 1997 will also be correct.

Helpful hint Assume ending inventory is overstated at the end of Year I by $15,000. Explain the effects on the following:
(1) Year I net income;
(2) Year 2 net income;
(3) Year I stockholders' equity; (4) Year 2 stockholders' equity. Answers:
(1) Overstated;
(2) understated;
(3) overstated; (4) no effect.

![F]inancial Statement Presentation and Analysis

As indicated in an earlier chapter, inventory is classified as a current asset after receivables in the balance sheet, and cost of goods sold is subtracted from sales in the income statement. In addition, there should be disclosure of (1) the major inventory classifications, (2) the basis of accounting (cost or lower of cost or market), and (3) the costing method (FIFO, LIFO, or average).

Colgate-Palmolive Company, for example, reported inventory of $616,067,000 under current assets in a recent balance sheet. The accompanying notes to the financial statements, as shown in Illustration 9-24, disclosed the following information:

Illustration 9-24

Inventory disclosures

Colgate-Palmolive Company

Note 1. Inventories
Inventories are valued at the lower of cost or market. The last-in, first-out (LIFO) method is used to value substantially all inventories in the U.S. as well as in certain overseas locations. The remaining inventories are valued using the first-in, first-out (FIFO) method.

The amount of inventory carried by a company has significant economic consequences. And, inventory management is a double-edged sword that requires constant attention. On the one hand, management wants to have a great variety and quantity on hand so customers have the greatest selection and inventory items always in stock. But, such an inventory policy may incur excessive carrying costs (e.g., investment, storage, insurance, taxes, obsolescence, and damage). On the other hand, low inventory levels lead to stockouts, lost sales, and disgruntled customers. Common ratios used in the management and evaluation of inventory levels are inventory turnover and a related measure, average days to sell the inventory.

The inventory turnover ratio measures the number of times on average the inventory is sold during the period. Its purpose is to measure the liquidity of the inventory. The inventory turnover is computed by dividing cost of goods sold by the average inventory during the period. Unless seasonal factors are significant, average inventory can be computed from the beginning and ending inventory balances. For example, assume that Colgate-Palmolive Company, discussed above, has a beginning inventory of $576,803,000, and cost of goods sold for the year of $2,803,244,500; its inventory turnover formula and computation are shown below:

Illustration 9-25

Inventory turnover formula and computation

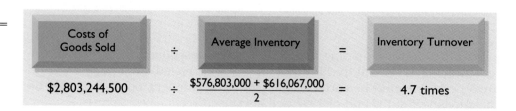

A variant of the inventory turnover ratio is the **average days to sell inventory**. For example, the inventory turnover for Colgate-Palmolive Company of 4.7 times divided into 365 is approximately 78 days. There are typical levels of inventory in every industry. However, companies that are able to keep their inventory at lower levels and higher turnovers and still satisfy customer needs are the most successful.

Before You Go On . . .

▶ *Review It*

1. Why is it appropriate to report inventories at the lower of cost or market?
2. How do inventory errors affect financial statements?

▸ *A Look Back at Erie Community College*

Refer to the opening story concerning the bookstore at Erie Community College, and answer the following questions.

1. Why might a small bookstore use specific identification to determine inventory?
2. If the inventory is overstated at the end of the month, what effect does this error have on the balance sheet and the income statement?

Solution:

1. A small bookstore, as opposed to a large bookstore, might use specific identification because of:
   a. A smaller number of any one book in inventory.
   b. Fewer different books in inventory.
   c. The familiarity of the owner/manager (who handles sales) with the books being sold.
2. An end-of-month, inventory overstatement will result in overstated inventory in the balance sheet along with overstated stockholders' equity, due to overstated net income on the income statement. Cost of goods sold will be understated on the income statement. The next month's income statement will have overstated beginning inventory and understated net income.

Summary of Study Objectives

1. *Describe the steps in determining inventory quantities.* The steps in determining inventory quantities are (1) taking a physical inventory of goods on hand and (2) determining the ownership of goods in transit.

2. *Prepare the entries for purchases and sales of inventory under a periodic inventory system.* In recording purchases, entries are required for (a) cash and credit purchases, (b) purchase returns and allowances, (c) purchase discounts, and (d) freight costs. In recording sales, entries are required for (a) cash and credit sales, (b) sales returns and allowances, and (c) sales discounts.

3. *Determine cost of goods sold under a periodic inventory system.* The steps in determining cost of goods sold are (a) recording the purchase of merchandise, (b) determining the cost of goods purchased, and (c) determining the cost of goods on hand at the beginning and end of the accounting period.

4. *Identify the unique features of the income statement for a merchandising company using a periodic inventory system.* The income state for a merchandising company contains three sections: sales revenue, cost of goods sold, and operating expenses. The cost of goods sold section under a periodic inventory system generally shows more detail by reporting beginning and ending inventory, net purchases, and total goods available for sale.

5. *Explain the basis of accounting for inventories and describe the inventory cost flow methods.* The primary basis of accounting for inventories is cost. Cost includes all expenditures necessary to acquire goods and place them in condition ready for sale. Inventoriable costs include (1) cost of beginning inventory and (2) the cost of goods purchased. The inventory cost flow methods are: specific identification, FIFO, LIFO, and average cost.

6. *Explain the financial statement and tax effects of each of the inventory cost flow methods.* The cost of goods available for sale may be allocated to cost of goods sold and ending inventory by specific identification or by a method based on an assumed cost flow. These methods have different effects on financial statements during periods of changing prices. When prices are rising, the first-in, first-out method (FIFO) results in lower cost of goods sold and higher net income than the average and the last-in, first-out (LIFO) methods. The reverse is true when prices are falling. In the balance sheet, FIFO results in an ending inventory that is closest to current value, whereas the inventory under LIFO is the farthest from current value. LIFO results in the lowest income taxes (because of lower net income).

7. *Explain the lower of cost or market basis of accounting for inventories.* The lower of cost or market basis (LCM) may be used when the current replacement cost (market) is less than cost. Under LCM, the loss is recognized in the period in which the price decline occurs. LCM may be applied to individual inventory items, major categories of inventory, or to total inventory.

8. *Indicate the effects of inventory errors on the financial statements.* In the income statement of the current year: (a) an error in beginning inventory will have a reverse effect on net income (overstatement of inventory results in understatement of net income) and (b) an error in ending inventory will have a similar effect on net income (overstatement of inventory results in overstatement of net income). If ending inventory errors are not corrected in the following period, their effect on net income for that period is reversed, and total net income for the two years will be correct. In the balance sheet, ending inventory errors will have the same effect on total assets and total stockholders' equity and no effect on liabilities.

▶**A**PPENDIX *9A* ▸ *Estimating Inventories*

STUDY OBJECTIVE
••••••••••▾**9**••••••••••

After studying this Appendix, you should be able to:

9. Describe the two methods of estimating inventories.

We have assumed throughout the chapter that a company would be able to do a physical count of its inventory. But what if it cannot, as in the example of the lumber inventory destroyed by fire? In that case, we would use an estimate.

Two circumstances explain the reasons for estimating rather than counting inventories. First, management may want monthly or quarterly financial statements but a physical inventory is taken only annually. Second, a casualty such as fire, flood, or earthquake may make it impossible to take a physical inventory. The need for estimating inventories is associated primarily with a periodic inventory system because of the absence of detailed inventory records.

There are two widely used methods of estimating inventories: (1) the gross profit method and (2) the retail inventory method.

▸**G**ross Profit Method

The **gross profit method** estimates the cost of ending inventory by applying a gross profit rate to net sales. It is used in preparing monthly financial statements under a periodic system when physical inventories are not taken. This method is a relatively simple but effective estimation technique. Accountants, auditors, and managers frequently use the gross profit method to test the reasonableness of the ending inventory amount. This method will detect large errors. To use this method, a company needs to know its net sales, cost of goods available for sale, and gross profit rate. The company then uses the gross profit rate to estimate its gross profit for the accounting period. The formulas for using the gross profit method are given in Illustration 9A-1.

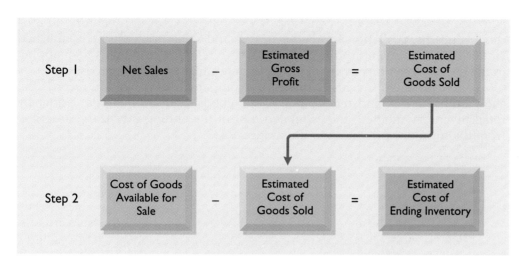

To illustrate, assume that Williams Company wishes to prepare an income statement for the month of January, when its records show net sales $200,000; beginning inventory $40,000; and cost of goods purchased $120,000. In the preceding year, the company realized a 30% gross profit rate, and it expects to earn the same rate this year. Given these facts and assumptions, the estimated cost of the ending inventory at January 31 under the gross profit method is $20,000, computed as follows:

Step 1:

Net sales	$200,000
Less: Estimated gross profit (30% × $200,000)	60,000
Estimated cost of goods sold	$140,000

Step 2:

Beginning inventory	$ 40,000
Cost of goods purchased	120,000
Cost of goods available for sale	160,000
Less: Estimated cost of goods sold	140,000
Estimated cost of ending inventory	$ 20,000

The gross profit method is based on the assumption that the rate of gross profit will remain constant from one year to the next. It may not remain constant, though, because of a change either in merchandising policies or in market conditions. In such cases, the rate of the prior period should be adjusted to reflect current operating conditions. In some cases, a more accurate estimate may be obtained by applying this method on a department or product-line basis.

The gross profit method should not be used in preparing a company's financial statements at the end of the year. These statements should be based on a physical inventory count.

Helpful hint Question: What is the estimated cost of ending inventory if the gross profit rate is (a) 25% and (b) 35%? Answer: (a) CGS = $150,000 [$200,000 − ($200,000 × 25%)]. EI = $10,000 ($160,000 − $150,000). (b) CGS = $130,000 [$200,000 − ($200,000 × 35%)]. EI = $30,000 ($160,000 − $130,000).

Retail Inventory Method

A retail store such as Kmart, Ace Hardware, or Wal-Mart has thousands of different types of merchandise at low unit costs. In such cases the application of unit costs to inventory quantities is difficult and time-consuming. An alternative

Helpful hint In determining inventory at retail, selling prices on the units are used, and tracing actual unit costs to invoices is unnecessary.

is to use the **retail inventory method** to estimate the cost of inventory. In most retail concerns, a relationship between cost and sales price can be established. Under the retail inventory method, the cost to retail percentage is then applied to the ending inventory at retail prices to determine inventory at cost.

To use the retail inventory method, a company must maintain records that show both the cost and retail value of the goods available for sale. Under the retail inventory method, the estimated cost of the ending inventory is derived from the formulas presented in Illustration 9A-3.

Illustration 9A-3

Retail inventory method formulas

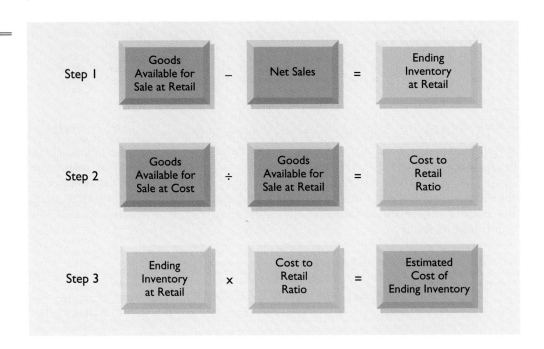

Helpful hint   Question: What are the answers for (1), (2), and (3) if cost of goods available for sale at retail is $120,000? Answer: (1) $50,000 ($120,000 − $70,000). (2) 62.5% ($75,000 ÷ $120,000). (3) $31,250 ($50,000 × 62.5%).

The logic of the retail method can be demonstrated by using unit cost data. Assume that 10 units purchased at $7.00 each are marked to sell for $10 per unit. Thus, the cost to retail ratio is 70% ($70 ÷ $100). If 4 units remain unsold, their retail value is $40 and their cost is $28 ($40 × 70%), which agrees with the total cost of goods on hand on a per unit basis (4 × $7).

The application of the retail method based on the accounting records and supplementary data for Lacy Co. is shown in Illustration 9A-4. Note that it is not necessary to take a physical inventory to determine the estimated cost of goods on hand at any given time.

Illustration 9A-4

Example of retail inventory method

	At Cost	At Retail
Beginning inventory	$14,000	$ 21,500
Goods purchased	61,000	78,500
Goods available for sale	$75,000	100,000
Net sales		70,000
(1) Ending inventory at retail		$ 30,000

(2) Cost to retail ratio = ($75,000 ÷ $100,000) = 75%
(3) Estimated cost of ending inventory = ($30,000 × 75%) $22,500

The retail inventory method also facilitates taking a physical inventory at the end of year. With this method, the goods on hand can be valued at the prices marked on the merchandise. The cost to retail ratio is then applied to the goods actually on hand at retail to determine the ending inventory at cost.

The major disadvantage of the retail method is that it is an averaging technique. It may produce an incorrect inventory valuation if the mix of the ending inventory is not representative of the mix in the goods available for sale. Assume, for example, that the cost to retail ratio of 75% in the Lacy Co. consists of equal proportions of inventory items that have cost to retail ratios of 70%, 75%, and 80%, respectively. If the ending inventory contains only items with a 70% ratio, an incorrect inventory cost will result. This problem can be minimized by applying the retail method on a departmental or product-line basis.

Summary of Study Objective for Chapter 9 Appendix A

9. *Describe the two methods of estimating inventories.* The two methods of estimating inventories are the gross profit method and the retail inventory method. Under the gross profit method, a gross profit rate is applied to net sales to determine estimated cost of goods sold. Estimated cost of goods sold is then subtracted from cost of goods available for sale to determine the estimated cost of the ending inventory. Under the retail inventory method, a cost to retail ratio is computed by dividing the cost of goods available for sale by the retail value of the goods available for sale. This ratio is then applied to the ending inventory at retail to determine the estimated cost of the ending inventory.

APPENDIX 9B ► Inventory Cost Flow Methods in Perpetual Inventory Systems

Each of the inventory cost flow methods described in the chapter for a periodic inventory system may be used in a perpetual inventory system. To illustrate the application of the three assumed cost flow methods (FIFO, LIFO, and average cost), we will use the data shown below and in this chapter for Bow Valley Electronic's product Z202 Astro Condenser.

STUDY OBJECTIVE

••••••••••**10**••••••••••

After studying this Appendix, you should be able to:

10. Apply the inventory cost flow methods to perpetual inventory records.

BOW VALLEY ELECTRONICS
Z202 Astro Condensers

Date	Explanation	Units	Unit Cost	Total Cost	Balance in Units
1/1	Beginning inventory	100	$10	$1,000	100
4/15	Purchases	200	11	2,200	300
8/24	Purchases	300	12	3,600	600
9/10	Sale	550			50
11/27	Purchases	400	13	5,200	450
				$12,000	

Illustration 9B-1

Inventoriable units and costs

First-In, First-Out (FIFO)

Under FIFO, the cost of the earliest goods on hand prior to each sale is charged to cost of goods sold. Therefore, the cost of goods sold on September 10 consists of the units on hand January 1 and the units purchased April 15 and August 24. The inventory on a FIFO method perpetual system is shown in Illustration 9B-2.

Illustration 9B-2

Perpetual system—FIFO

Date	Purchases	Sales	Balance
January 1			(100 @ $10) $1,000
April 15	(200 @ $11) $2,200		(100 @ $10) ⎱ $3,200 (200 @ $11) ⎰
August 24	(300 @ $12) $3,600		(100 @ $10) ⎫ (200 @ $11) ⎬ $6,800 (300 @ $12) ⎭
September 10		(100 @ $10) (200 @ $11) (250 @ $12) —————— $6,200	(50 @ $12) $ 600
November 27	(400 @ $13) $5,200		(50 @ $12) ⎱ $5,800 (400 @ $13) ⎰

The ending inventory in this situation is $5,800 and the cost of goods sold is $6,200 [(100 @ $10) + (200 @ $11) + (250 @ $12)].

The results under FIFO in a perpetual system are the **same as in a periodic system** (see Illustration 9-9 on page 381 where similarly the ending inventory is $5,800 and cost of goods sold in $6,200). Regardless of the system, the first costs in are the costs assigned to cost of goods sold.

Last-In, First-Out (LIFO)

Under the LIFO method using a perpetual system, the cost of the most recent purchase prior to sale is allocated to the units sold. Therefore, the cost of the goods sold on September 10 consists of all the units from the August 24 and April 15 purchases and 50 of the units in beginning inventory. The ending inventory on a LIFO method is computed in Illustration 9B-3.

Illustration 9B-3

Perpetual system—LIFO

Date	Purchases	Sales	Balance
January 1			(100 @ $10) $1,000
April 15	(200 @ $11) $2,200		(100 @ $10) ⎱ $3,200 (200 @ $11) ⎰
August 24	(300 @ $12) $3,600		(100 @ $10) ⎫ (200 @ $11) ⎬ $6,800 (300 @ $12) ⎭
September 10		(300 @ $12) (200 @ $11) (50 @ $10) —————— $6,300	(50 @ $10) $ 500
November 27	(400 @ $13) $5,200		(50 @ $10) ⎱ $5,700 (400 @ $13) ⎰

The use of LIFO in a perpetual system will usually produce cost allocations that differ from using LIFO in a periodic system. In a perpetual system, the latest units incurred prior to each sale are allocated to cost of goods sold. In contrast, in a periodic system, the latest units incurred during the period are allocated to cost of goods sold. Thus, when a purchase is made after the last sale, the LIFO periodic system will apply this purchase to the previous sale. See Illustration 9-11 on page 382 where the proof shows the 400 units @ $13 purchased on November 27 applied to the sale of 550 units on September 10.

As shown above under the LIFO perpetual system, the 400 units @ $13 purchased on November 27 are all applied to the ending inventory.

The ending inventory in this LIFO perpetual illustration is $5,700 and cost of goods sold is $6,300 as compared to the LIFO periodic illustration where the ending inventory is $5,000 and cost of goods sold is $7,000.

Average Cost

The average cost method in a perpetual inventory system is called the **moving average method**. Under this method a new average is computed **after each purchase**. The average cost is computed by dividing the cost of goods available for sale by the units on hand. The average cost is then applied to: (1) the units sold, to determine the cost of goods sold, and (2) the remaining units on hand, to determine the ending inventory amount. The application of the average cost method by Bow Valley Electronics is shown in Illustration 9B-4.

Date	Purchases		Sales	Balance	
January 1				(100 @ $10)	$1,000
April 15	(200 @ $11)	$2,200		(300 @ $10.667)	$3,200
August 24	(300 @ $12)	$3,600		(600 @ $11.333)	$6,800
September 10			(550 @ $11.333) $6,233	(50 @ $11.333)	$ 567
November 27	(400 @ $13)	$5,200		(450 @ $12.816)	$5,767

Illustration 9B-4

Perpetual system—average cost method

As indicated above, **a new average is computed each time a purchase is made**. On April 15, after 200 units are purchased for $2,200, a total of 300 units costing $3,200 ($1,000 + $2,200) are on hand. The average unit cost is $10.667 ($3,200 ÷ 300). On August 24, after 300 units are purchased for $3,600, a total of 600 units costing $6,800 ($1,000 + $2,200 + $3,600) are on hand at an average cost per unit of $11.333 ($6,800 ÷ 600). This unit cost of $11.333 is used in costing sales until another purchase is made, when a new unit cost is computed. Accordingly, the unit cost of the 550 units sold on September 10 is $11.333, and the total cost of goods sold is $6,233. On November 27, following the purchase of 400 units for $5,200, there are 450 units on hand costing $5,767 ($567 + $5,200) with a new average cost of $12.816 ($5,767 ÷ 450).

This moving average cost under the perpetual inventory system should be compared to Illustration 9-14 showing the weighted average method under a periodic inventory system.

Summary of Study Objective for Chapter 9 Appendix B

10. Apply the inventory cost flow methods to perpetual inventory records. Under FIFO, the cost of the earliest goods on hand prior to each sale is charged to cost of goods sold. Under LIFO, the cost of the most recent purchase prior to sale is charged to cost of goods sold. Under the average cost method, a new average cost is computed after each purchase.

GLOSSARY

Average cost method   An inventory costing method that assumes that the goods available for sale are homogeneous. (p. 382).

Consigned goods   Goods shipped by a consignor, who retains ownership, to another party called the consignee. (p. 371).

Cost of goods available for sale   The sum of the beginning merchandise inventory plus the cost of goods purchased. (p. 376).

Cost of goods purchased   The sum of net purchases plus freight-in. (p. 376).

Cost of goods sold   The total cost of merchandise sold during the period, determined by subtracting ending inventory from the cost of goods available for sale. (p. 376).

Current replacement cost   The current cost to replace an inventory item. (p. 387).

First-in, first-out method (FIFO)   An inventory costing method that assumes that the costs of the earliest goods acquired are the first to be recognized as cost of goods sold. (p. 380).

Gross profit method   A method for estimating the cost of the ending inventory by applying a gross profit rate to net sales. (p. 392).

Inventoriable costs   The pool of costs that consists of two elements: (1) the cost of the beginning inventory and (2) the cost of goods purchased during the period. (p. 378).

Inventory turnover ratio   A ratio that measures the number of times on average the inventory sold during the period. It is computed by dividing cost of goods sold by the average inventory during the period. (p. 390).

Last-in, first-out method (LIFO)   An inventory costing method that assumes that the costs of the latest units purchased are the first to be allocated to cost of goods sold. (p. 381).

Lower of cost or market basis (LCM) (inventories)   A basis whereby inventory is stated at the lower of cost or market (current replacement cost). (p. 387).

Net purchases   Purchases less purchase returns and allowances and purchase discounts. (p. 375).

Periodic inventory system   An inventory system in which inventoriable costs are allocated to ending inventory and cost of goods sold at the end of the period. Cost of goods sold is computed at the end of the period by subtracting the ending inventory (costs are assigned to a physical count of items on hand) from the cost of goods available for sale. (p. 372).

Retail inventory method   A method used to estimate the cost of the ending inventory by applying a cost to retail ratio to the ending inventory at retail. (p. 394).

Specific identification method   An actual physical flow costing method in which items still in inventory are specifically costed to arrive at the total cost of the ending inventory. (p. 379).

DEMONSTRATION PROBLEM

Gerald D. Englehart Company has the following inventory, purchases, and sales data for the month of March:

Inventory, March 1	200 units @ $4.00	$ 800
Purchases:		
	March 10	500 units @ $4.50	2,250
	March 20	400 units @ $4.75	1,900
	March 30	300 units @ $5.00	1,500
Sales:		
	March 15	500 units
	March 25	400 units

The physical inventory count on March 31 shows 500 units on hand.

Instructions

(a)   Under a **periodic inventory system**, determine the cost of inventory on hand at March 31 and the cost of goods sold for March under the (a) first-in, first-out (FIFO) method, (b) last-in, first-out (LIFO) method, and (c) average cost method.

*(b)   Under a **perpetual inventory system**, determine the cost of inventory on hand at March 31 and the cost of goods sold for March under the (a) first-in, first-out (FIFO) method, (b) last-in, first-out (LIFO) method, and (c) average cost method.

Solution to Demonstration Problem

The cost of goods available for sale is $6,450:

Inventory	200 units @ $4.00	$ 800	
Purchases:			
March 10	500 units @ $4.50	2,250	
March 20	400 units @ $4.75	1,900	
March 30	300 units @ $5.00	1,500	
Total cost of goods available for sale		$6,450	

(a) PERIODIC INVENTORY SYSTEM

FIFO Method

Ending Inventory:

Date	Units	Unit Cost	Total Cost	
March 30	300	$5.00	$1,500	
March 20	200	4.75	950	$2,450

Cost of goods sold: $6,450 − $2,450 = $4,000

LIFO Method

Ending Inventory:

Date	Units	Unit Cost	Total Cost	
March 1	200	$4.00	$ 800	
March 10	300	4.50	1,350	$2,150

Cost of goods sold: $6,450 − $2,150 = $4,300

Weighted Average Cost Method

Weighted average unit cost: $6,450 ÷ 1,400 = $4.607
Ending inventory: 500 × $4.607 = $2,303.50

Cost of goods sold: $6,450 − $2,303.50 = $4,146.50

*(b) PERPETUAL INVENTORY SYSTEM

FIFO Method

Date	Purchases	Sales	Balance
March 1			(200 @ $4.00) $ 800
March 10	(500 @ $4.50) $2,250		(200 @ $4.00) (500 @ $4.50) } $3,050
March 15		(200 @ $4.00) (300 @ $4.50) $2150	(200 @ $4.50) $ 900
March 20	(400 @ $4.75) $1,900		(200 @ $4.50) (400 @ $4.75) } $2,800
March 25		(200 @ $4.50) (200 @ $4.75) $1,850	(200 @ $4.75) $ 950
March 30	(300 @ $5.00) $1,500		(200 @ $4.75) (300 @ $5.00) } $2,450

Ending inventory, $2,450. Cost of goods sold: $6,450 − $2,450 = $4,000

LIFO Method

Date	Purchases		Sales		Balance	
March 1					(200 @ $4.00)	$ 800
March 10	(500 @ $4.50)	$2,250			(200 @ $4.00)⎱ (500 @ $4.50)⎰	$3,050
March 15			(500 @ $4.50)	$2,250	(200 @ $4.00)	$ 800
March 20	(400 @ $4.75)	$1,900			(200 @ $4.00)⎱ (200 @ $4.75)⎰	$2,700
March 25			(400 @ $4.75)	$1,900	(200 @ $4.00)	$ 800
March 30	(300 @ $5.00)	$1,500			(200 @ $4.00)⎱ (300 @ $5.00)⎰	$2,300

Ending inventory, $2,300. Cost of goods sold: $6,450 − $2,300 = $4,150

Moving Average Cost Method

Date	Purchases		Sales		Balance	
March 1					(200 @ $4.00)	$ 800
March 10	(500 @ $4.50)	$2,250			(700 @ $4.357)	$3,050
March 15			(500 @ $4.357)	$2,179	(200 @ $4.357)	$ 871
March 20	(400 @ $4.75)	$1,900			(600 @ $4.618)	$2,771
March 25			(400 @ $4.618)	$1,847	(200 @ $4.618)	$ 924
March 30	(300 @ $5.00)	$1,500			(500 @ $4.848)	$2,424

Ending inventory, $2,424. Cost of goods sold: $6,450 − $2,424 = $4,026

*Note: All **asterisked** Questions, Exercises, and Problems relate to material contained in the appendix to the chapter.

SELF-STUDY QUESTIONS

Answers are at the end of the chapter.

(SO 2) 1. When goods are purchased for resale by a company using a periodic inventory system:
  a. purchases on account are debited to Merchandise Inventory.
  b. purchases on account are debited to Purchases.
  c. purchase returns are debited to Purchase Returns and Allowances.
  d. freight costs are debited to Purchases.

(SO 3) 2. In determining cost of goods sold:
  a. purchases discounts are deducted from net purchases.
  b. freight-out is added to net purchases.
  c. purchase returns and allowances are deducted from net purchases.
  d. freight-in is added to net purchases.

(SO 3) 3. If beginning inventory is $60,000, cost of goods purchased is $380,000, and ending inventory is $50,000, cost of goods sold is:
  a. $390,000.
  b. $370,000.
  c. $330,000.
  d. $420,000.

(SO 1) 4. Which of the following should *not* be included in the physical inventory of a company?
  a. Goods held on consignment from another company.
  b. Goods shipped on consignment to another company.
  c. Goods in transit from another company shipped FOB shipping point.
  d. None of the above.

(SO 5) 5. Inventoriable costs consist of two elements: beginning inventory and
  a. ending inventory.
  b. cost of goods purchased.
  c. cost of goods sold.
  d. cost of goods available for sale.

(SO 5) 6. Kam Company has the following:

	Units	Unit Cost
Inventory, Jan. 1	8,000	$11
Purchase, June 19	13,000	12
Purchase, Nov. 8	5,000	13

If 9,000 units are on hand at December 31, the cost of the ending inventory under FIFO is:
a. $99,000. *(Bottom up)*
b. $108,000.
c. $113,000.
d. $117,000.

(SO 5) 7. Using the data in (6) above, the cost of the ending inventory under LIFO is: *(Top ↓)*
a. $113,000.
b. $108,000.
c. $99,000.
d. $100,000.

(SO 6) 8. In periods of rising prices, LIFO will produce:
a. higher net income than FIFO.
b. the same net income as FIFO.
c. lower net income than FIFO.
d. higher net income than average costing.

(SO 6) 9. Factors that affect the selection of an inventory costing method do *not* include:
a. tax effects.
b. balance sheet effects.
c. income statement effects.
d. perpetual vs. periodic inventory system.

(SO 7) 10. The lower of cost or market basis may be applied to:
a. categories of inventories.
b. individual items of inventories.
c. total inventory.
d. all of the above.

*11. Somers Company has sales of $150,000 and cost of (SO 9) goods available for sale of $135,000. If the gross profit rate is 30%, the estimated cost of the ending inventory under the gross profit method is:
a. $15,000.
b. $30,000.
c. $45,000.
d. $75,000.

12. In Fran Company, ending inventory is understated (SO 8) $4,000. The effects of this error on the current year's cost of goods sold and net income, respectively, are:
a. understated, overstated.
b. overstated, understated.
c. overstated, overstated.
d. understated, understated.

*13. In a perpetual inventory system, (SO 10)
a. LIFO cost of goods sold will be the same as in a periodic inventory system.
b. average costs are based entirely on unit cost averages.
c. a new average is computed under the average cost method after each sale.
d. FIFO cost of goods sold will be the same as in a periodic inventory system.

QUESTIONS

1. Goods costing $1,600 are purchased on account on July 15 with credit terms of 2/10, n/30. On July 18 a $100 credit memo is received from the supplier for damaged goods. Give the journal entry on July 24 to record payment of the balance due within the discount period.

2. Identify the accounts that are added to or deducted from purchases to determine the cost of goods purchased. For each account, indicate (a) whether it is added or deducted and (b) its normal balance.

3. In the following separate mini cases, using a periodic inventory system, identify the item(s) designated by letter.
   (a) Purchases − X − Y = Net purchases.
   (b) Cost of goods purchased − Net purchases = X.
   (c) Beginning inventory + X = Cost of goods available for sale.
   (d) Cost of goods available for sale − Cost of goods sold = X.

4. "The key to successful business operations is effective inventory management." Do you agree? Explain.

5. An item must possess two characteristics to be classified as inventory. What are these two characteristics?

6. Your friend Tom Wetzel has been hired to help take the physical inventory in Casey's Hardware Store. Explain to Tom Wetzel what this job will entail.

7. (a) Janine Company ships merchandise to Laura Corporation on December 30. The merchandise reaches the buyer on January 5. Indicate the terms of sale that will result in the goods being included in (1) Janine's December 31 inventory, and (2) Laura's December 31 inventory.
   (b) Under what circumstances should Janine Company include consigned goods in its inventory?

8. Mary Ann's Hat Shop received a shipment of hats for which it paid the wholesaler $2,940. The price of the hats was $3,000, but Mary Ann's was given a $60 cash discount and required to pay freight charges of $70. In addition, Mary Ann's paid $100 to cover the travel expenses of an employee who negotiated the purchase of the hats. What amount should Mary Ann's include in inventory? Why?

9. What is the primary basis of accounting for inventories? What is the major objective in accounting for inventories? What accounting principles are involved here?

10. Identify the distinguishing features of an income statement for a merchandising company.

11. Dave Wier believes that the allocation of inventoriable costs should be based on the actual physical flow of the goods. Explain to Dave why this may be both impractical and inappropriate.

12. What is a major advantage and a major disadvantage of the specific identification method of inventory costing?

13. "The selection of an inventory cost flow method is a decision made by accountants." Do you agree? Explain. Once a method has been selected, what accounting requirement applies?

14. Which assumed inventory cost flow method:
    (a) usually parallels the actual physical flow of merchandise?
    (b) assumes that goods available for sale during an accounting period are homogeneous?
    (c) assumes that the latest units purchased are the first to be sold?

15. In a period of rising prices, the inventory reported in Plato Company's balance sheet is close to the current cost of the inventory, whereas York Company's inventory is considerably below its current cost. Identify the inventory cost flow method being used by each company. Which company has probably been reporting the higher gross profit?

16. Shaunna Corporation has been using the FIFO cost flow method during a prolonged period of inflation. During the same time period, Shaunna has been paying out all of its net income as dividends. What adverse effects may result from this policy?

17. Lucy Ritter is studying for the next accounting midterm examination. What should Lucy know about (a) departing from the cost basis of accounting for inventories and (b) the meaning of "market" in the lower of cost or market method?

18. Rock Music Center has 5 CD players on hand at the balance sheet date that cost $400 each. The current replacement cost is $320 per unit. Under the lower of cost or market basis of accounting for inventories, what value should be reported for the CD players on the balance sheet? Why?

19. What methods may be used under the lower of cost or market basis of accounting for inventories? Which method will produce the lowest inventory value?

*20. When is it necessary to estimate inventories?

*21. Both the gross profit method and the retail inventory method are based on averages. For each method, indicate the average used, how it is determined, and how it is applied.

*22. Pat Voga Company has net sales of $400,000 and cost of goods available for sale of $300,000. If the gross profit rate is 30%, what is the estimated cost of the ending inventory? Show computations.

*23. Miller Shoe Shop had goods available for sale in 1998 with a retail price of $120,000. The cost of these goods was $84,000. If sales during the period were $90,000, what is the ending inventory at cost using the retail inventory method?

24. Mila Company discovers in 1998 that its ending inventory at December 31, 1997, was $5,000 understated. What effect will this error have on (a) 1997 net income, (b) 1998 net income, and (c) the combined net income for the 2 years?

25. Maureen & Nathan Company's balance sheet shows Inventories $162,800. What additional disclosures should be made?

*26. "When perpetual inventory records are kept, the results under the FIFO and LIFO methods are the same as they would be in a periodic inventory system." Do you agree? Explain.

*27. How does the average method of inventory costing differ between a perpetual inventory system and a periodic inventory system?

BRIEF EXERCISES

• •

Journalize purchases transactions.
(SO 2)

BE9–1   Prepare the journal entries to record the following transactions on H. Hunt Company's books using a periodic inventory system.

(a) On March 2, H. Hunt Company purchased $900,000 of merchandise from B. Streisand Company, terms 2/10, n/30.

(b) On March 6, H. Hunt company returned $130,000 of the merchandise purchased on March 2 because it was defective.

(c) On March 12, H. Hunt Company paid the balance due to B. Streisand Company.

Compute net purchases and cost of goods purchased.
(SO 3)

BE9–2   Assume that K. Bassing Company uses a periodic inventory system and has the following account balances: Purchases $400,000, Purchase Returns and Allowances $11,000, Purchase Discounts $8,000, and Freight-in $16,000. Determine (a) net purchases and (b) cost of goods purchased.

Compute cost of goods sold and gross profit.
(SO 3)

BE9–3   Assume the same information as in BE9–2, and also that K. Bassing Company has beginning inventory of $60,000, ending inventory of $90,000, and net sales of $630,000. Determine the amounts to be reported for cost of goods sold and gross profit.

BE9–4 Ginger Helgeson Company identifies the following items for possible inclusion in the taking of a physical inventory. Indicate whether each item should be included or excluded from the inventory taking.

Identify items to be included in taking a physical inventory.
(SO 1)

1. Goods shipped on consignment by Helgeson to another company.
2. Goods in transit from a supplier shipped FOB destination.
3. Goods sold but being held for customer pickup.
4. Goods held on consignment from another company.

BE9–5 The ledger of Wharton Company includes the following items: (1) Freight-in, (2) Purchase Returns and Allowances, (3) Purchases, (4) Sales Discounts, (5) Purchase Discounts. Identify which items are included in inventoriable costs.

Identify the components of inventoriable costs.
(SO 5)

BE9–6 In its first month of operations, Quilt Company made three purchases of merchandise in the following sequence: (1) 300 units at $6, (2) 400 units at $7, and (3) 300 units at $8. Assuming there are 400 units on hand, compute the cost of the ending inventory under the (1) FIFO method and (2) LIFO method. Quilt uses a periodic inventory system.

Compute ending inventory using FIFO and LIFO.
(SO 5)

BE9–7 Data for Quilt Company are presented in BE9–6. Compute the cost of the ending inventory under the average cost method, assuming there are 400 units on hand.

Compute the ending inventory using average costs.
(SO 5)
Determine the LCM valuation using inventory categories.
(SO 7)

BE9–8 Hawkeye Appliance Center accumulates the following cost and market data at December 31:

Inventory Categories	Cost Data	Market Data
Cameras	$12,000	$10,200
Camcorders	9,000	9,500
VCRs	14,000	12,800

Compute the lower of cost or market valuation using categories.

*BE9–9 At May 31, Jansen Company has net sales of $300,000 and cost of goods available for sale of $210,000. Compute the estimated cost of the ending inventory assuming the gross profit rate is 40%.

Apply the gross profit method.
(SO 9)

*BE9–10 On June 30, Faber's Fabrics has the following data pertaining to the retail inventory method: Goods available for sale: at cost $35,000, at retail $50,000; net sales $30,000, and ending inventory at retail $20,000. Compute the estimated cost of the ending inventory using the retail inventory method.

Apply the retail inventory method.
(SO 9)

BE9–11 Creole Company reports net income of $90,000 in 1998. However, ending inventory was understated $7,000. What is the correct net income for 1998? What effect, if any, will this error have on total assets as reported in the balance sheet at December 31, 1998?

Determine correct income statement amounts.
(SO 8)

*BE9–12 Graf Department Store uses a perpetual inventory system. Data for product XX include the following purchases:

Apply cost flow methods to records.
(SO 10)

Date	Number of Units	Unit Price
May 5	50	$10
July 29	30	15

On June 1 Graf sold 30 units, and on August 27, 33 more units. Prepare the perpetual inventory card for the above transactions using (1) FIFO, (2) LIFO, and (3) average cost.

EXERCISES

E9–1 Presented below is the following information related to Hans Olaf Co.

Journalize purchases transactions.
(SO 2)

1. On April 5, purchased merchandise from D. DeVito Company for $18,000 terms 2/10, net/30, FOB shipping point. buyer pays
2. On April 6 paid freight costs of $900 on merchandise purchased from D. DeVito.
3. On April 7, purchased equipment on account for $26,000.
4. On April 8, returned damaged merchandise to D. DeVito Company and was granted a $3,000 allowance.
5. On April 15 paid the amount due to D. DeVito Company in full.

Instructions

(a) Prepare the journal entries to record these transactions on the books of Hans Olaf Co. using a periodic inventory system.

(b) Assume that Hans Olaf Co. paid the balance due to D. DeVito Company on May 4 instead of April 15. Prepare the journal entry to record this payment.

Prepare cost of goods sold section.
(SO 3)

E9–2   The trial balance of G. Garbo Company at the end of its fiscal year, August 31, 1998, includes the following accounts: Merchandise Inventory $17,200, Purchases $142,400, Sales $190,000, Freight-in $4,000, Sales Returns and Allowances $3,000, Freight-out $1,000, and Purchase Returns and Allowances $2,000. The ending merchandise inventory is $26,000.

Instructions
Prepare a cost of goods sold section for the year ending August 31.

Prepare an income statement.
(SO 4)

E9–3   Presented is information related to Baja Co. for the month of January 1998.

Freight-in	$10,000	Rent expense	20,000
Freight-out	7,000	Salary expense	61,000
Insurance expense	12,000	Sales discounts	8,000
Purchases	200,000	Sales returns and allowances	13,000
Purchase discounts	3,000	Sales	312,000
Purchase returns and allowances	6,000		

Beginning merchandise inventory was $42,000 and ending inventory was $63,000.

Instructions
Prepare an income statement using the format presented on page 377. Operating expenses should not be segregated into selling and administrative expenses.

Determine the correct inventory amount.
(SO 1)

E9–4   First Bank and Trust is considering giving Novotna Company a loan. Before doing so, they decide that further discussions with Novotna's accountant may be desirable. One area of particular concern is the inventory account, which has a year-end balance of $295,000. Discussions with the accountant reveal the following:

1. Novotna sold goods costing $35,000 to Moghul Company FOB shipping point on December 28. The goods are not expected to arrive in India until January 12. The goods were not included in the physical inventory because they were not in the warehouse.
2. The physical count of the inventory did not include goods costing $95,000 that were shipped to Novotna FOB destination on December 27, and were still in transit at year-end.
3. Novotna received goods costing $25,000 on January 2. The goods were shipped FOB shipping point on December 26 by Cellar Co. The goods were not included in the physical count.
4. Novotna sold goods costing $40,000 to Sterling of Canada FOB destination on December 30. The goods were received in Canada on January 8. They were not included in Novotna's physical inventory.
5. Novotna received goods costing $44,000 on January 2 that were shipped FOB destination on December 29. The shipment was a rush order that was supposed to arrive December 31. This purchase was included in the ending inventory of $295,000.

Instructions
Determine the correct inventory amount on December 31.

Compute inventory and cost of goods sold using FIFO and LIFO.
(SO 5)

E9–5   Mawmey Inc. uses a periodic inventory system. Its records show the following for the month of May, in which 78 units were sold.

		Units	Unit Cost	Total Cost
May 1	Inventory	30	$ 8	$240
15	Purchases	25	10	250
24	Purchases	35	12	420
	Totals	90		$910

Instructions
Compute the ending inventory at May 31 using the FIFO and LIFO methods. Prove the amount allocated to cost of goods sold under each method.

E9–6 In June, Dakota Company reports the following for the month of June.

Compute inventory and cost of goods sold using FIFO and LIFO.
(SO 5, 6)

		Units	Unit Cost	Total Cost
June 1	Inventory	200	$5	$1,000
12	Purchases	300	6	1,800
23	Purchases	500	7	3,500
30	Inventory	180		

Instructions

(a) Compute the cost of the ending inventory and the cost of goods sold under (1) FIFO and (2) LIFO.

(b) Which costing method gives the higher ending inventory? Why?

(c) Which method results in the higher cost of goods sold? Why?

E9–7 Inventory data for Dakota Company are presented in E9–6.

Compute inventory and cost of goods sold using average costs.
(SO 5, 6)

Instructions

(a) Compute the cost of the ending inventory and the cost of goods sold using the average cost method.

(b) Will the results in (a) be higher or lower than the results under (1) FIFO and (2) LIFO?

(c) Why is the average unit cost not $6?

E9–8 Cody Camera Shop uses the lower of cost or market basis for its inventory. The following data are available at December 31:

Determine ending inventory under lower of cost or market inventory method.
(SO 7)

Item	Units	Unit Cost	Market
Cameras			
Minolta	5	$175	$160
Canon	7	150	152
Light Meters			
Vivitar	12	125	110
Kodak	10	115	135

Instructions

Determine the amount of the ending inventory by applying the lower of cost or market basis to (a) individual items, (b) inventory categories, and (c) the total inventory.

*E9–9 The inventory of Susan Company was destroyed by fire on March 1. From an examination of the accounting records, the following data for the first 2 months of the year are obtained: Sales $51,000, Sales Returns and Allowances $1,000, Purchases $28,200, Freight-in $1,200, and Purchase Returns and Allowances $1,400.

Determine merchandise lost using the gross profit method of estimating inventory.
(SO 9)

Instructions

Determine the merchandise lost by fire, assuming:

(a) A beginning inventory of $20,000 and a gross profit rate of 30% on net sales.

(b) A beginning inventory of $25,000 and a gross profit rate of 25% on net sales.

*E9–10 Sharp Shoe Store uses the retail inventory method for its two departments: Women's Shoes and Men's Shoes. The following information for each department is obtained:

Determine ending inventory at cost using retail method.
(SO 9)

Item	Women's Department	Men's Department
Beginning inventory at cost	$ 32,000	$ 46,450
Cost of goods purchased at cost	148,000	137,300
Net sales	185,000	195,000
Beginning inventory at retail	45,000	60,000
Cost of goods purchased at retail	180,000	185,000

Instructions

Compute the estimated cost of the ending inventory for each department under the retail inventory method.

Determine effects of inventory errors.
(SO 8)

E9–11   Seles Hardware reported cost of goods sold as follows:

	1998	1999
Beginning inventory	$ 20,000	$ 30,000
Cost of goods purchased	150,000	175,000
Cost of goods available for sale	170,000	205,000
Ending inventory	26,000 ~~30,000~~	~~35,000~~ 38,000
Cost of goods sold	$140,000	$170,000

Seles made two errors: (1) 1998 ending inventory was overstated $4,000 and (2) 1999 ending inventory was understated $3,000.

Instructions
Compute the correct cost of goods sold for each year.

Prepare correct income statements.
(SO 8)

E9–12   Aruba Company reported the following income statement data for a 2-year period.

	1998	1999
Sales	$210,000	$250,000
Cost of goods sold		
Beginning inventory	32,000	40,000
Cost of goods purchased	173,000	202,000
Cost of goods available for sale	205,000	242,000
Ending inventory	40,000	52,000
Cost of goods sold	165,000	190,000
Gross profit	$ 45,000	$ 60,000

Aruba uses a periodic inventory system. The inventories at January 1, 1998, and December 31, 1999, are correct. However, the ending inventory at December 31, 1998, was overstated $6,000.

Instructions
(a) Prepare correct income statement data for the 2 years.
(b) What is the cumulative effect of the inventory error on total gross profit for the 2 years?
(c) ▭▭▭▶ Explain in a letter to the president of Aruba Company what has happened—i.e., the nature of the error and its effect on the financial statements.

Apply cost flow methods to perpetual records.
(SO 10)

*E9–13   Stracka Appliance uses a perpetual inventory system. For its model B47 television sets, the January 1 inventory was four sets at $600 each. During January, the following purchase was made: Jan. 10, 6 units at $640 each. That month, the company had the following sales: Jan. 8, 2 units and Jan. 15, 4 units.

Instructions
Compute the ending inventory under (1) FIFO, (2) LIFO, and (3) average cost.

PROBLEMS

Journalize, post, and prepare trial balance and partial income statement.
(SO 2, 3, 4)

P9–1   Chi Chi Ramos, a former professional golf star, operates Chi Chi's Pro Shop at Bay Golf Course. At the beginning of the current season on April 1, the ledger of Chi Chi's Pro Shop showed Cash $2,500, Merchandise Inventory $3,500, and Common Stock $6,000. The following transactions were completed during April.

Apr. 5   Purchased golf bags, clubs, and balls on account from Balata Co. $1,600, FOB shipping point, terms 2/10, n/60.
        7   Paid freight on Balata purchase $80.
        9   Received credit from Balata Co. for merchandise returned $100.
      10   Sold merchandise on account to members $900, terms n/30.
      12   Purchased golf shoes, sweaters, and other accessories on account from Arrow Sportswear $660, terms 1/10, n/30.

14 Paid Balata Co. in full.

17 Received credit from Arrow Sportswear for merchandise returned $60.

20 Made sales on account to members $700, terms n/30.

21 Paid Arrow Sportswear in full.

27 Granted credit to members for clothing that did not fit $30.

30 Made cash sales $600.

30 Received payments on account from members $1,100.

The chart of accounts for the pro shop includes the following: No. 101 Cash, No. 112 Accounts Receivable, No. 120 Merchandise Inventory, No. 201 Accounts Payable, No. 311 Common Stock, No. 401 Sales, No. 412 Sales Returns and Allowances, No. 510 Purchases, No. 512 Purchase Returns and Allowances, No. 514 Purchase Discounts, No. 516 Freight-in.

Instructions

(a) Journalize the April transactions using a periodic inventory system.

(b) Enter the beginning balances in the ledger accounts and post the April transactions. (Use J1 for the journal reference.)

(c) Prepare a trial balance on April 30, 1998.

(d) Prepare an income statement through gross profit, assuming merchandise inventory on hand at April 30 is $4,200.

P9–2 Metro Department Store is located in midtown Metropolis. During the past several years, net income has been declining because of suburban shopping centers. At the end of the company's fiscal year on November 30, 1998, the following accounts appeared in its adjusted trial balance:

Prepare an income statement. (SO 3, 4)

Accounts Payable	$ 37,310
Accounts Receivable	11,770
Accumulated Depreciation—Delivery Equipment	19,680
Accumulated Depreciation—Store Equipment	41,800
Cash	8,000
Delivery Expense	8,200
Delivery Equipment	57,000
Depreciation Expense—Delivery Equipment	4,000
Depreciation Expense—Store Equipment	9,500
Freight-in	5,060
Common Stock	70,000
Retained Earnings	17,200
Dividends	12,000
Insurance Expense	9,000
Merchandise Inventory	34,360
Notes Payable	46,000
Prepaid Insurance	4,500
Property Tax Expense	3,500
Purchases	640,000
Purchase Discounts	7,000
Purchase Returns and Allowances	3,000
Rent Expense	19,000
Salaries Expense	120,000
Sales	860,000
Sales Commissions Expense	14,000
Sales Commissions Payable	6,000
Sales Returns and Allowances	10,000
Store Equipment	125,000
Property Taxes Payable	3,500
Utilities Expense	10,600

Analysis reveals the following additional data:

1. Salaries expense is 70% selling and 30% administrative.
2. Insurance expense is 50% selling and 50% administrative.
3. Merchandise inventory at November 30, 1998, is $36,200.
4. Rent expense, utilities expense, and property tax expense are administrative expenses.

Instructions
Prepare an income statement for the year ended November 30, 1998.

Determine cost of goods sold and ending inventory, using FIFO, LIFO, and average cost with analysis.
(SO 5, 6)

P9–3 Kane Company had a beginning inventory on January 1 of 100 units of Product SXL at a cost of $20 per unit. During the year, the following purchases were made.

Mar. 15	300 units at $24	Sept. 4	300 units at $28
July 20	200 units at 25	Dec. 2	100 units at 30

850 units were sold. Kane Company uses a periodic inventory system.

Instructions
(a) Determine the cost of goods available for sale.
(b) Determine (1) the ending inventory, and (2) the cost of goods sold under each of the assumed cost flow methods (FIFO, LIFO, and average). Prove the accuracy of the cost of goods sold under the FIFO and LIFO methods.
(c) Which cost flow method results in (1) the highest inventory amount for the balance sheet and (2) the highest cost of goods sold for the income statement?

Compute ending inventory, prepare income statements, and answer questions using FIFO and LIFO.
(SO 5, 6)

P9–4 The management of Tumatoe Inc. asks your help in determining the comparative effects of the FIFO and LIFO inventory cost flow methods. For 1998, the accounting records show the following data:

Inventory, January 1 (10,000 units)	$ 35,000
Cost of 110,000 units purchased	460,000
Selling price of 95,000 units sold	665,000
Operating expenses	120,000

Units purchased consisted of 40,000 units at $4.00 on May 10; 50,000 units at $4.20 on August 15; and 20,000 units at $4.50 on November 20. Income taxes are 30%.

Instructions
(a) Prepare comparative condensed income statements for 1998 under FIFO and LIFO. (Show computations of ending inventory.)
(b) ▱▱▱◤▭▭▭▷ Answer the following questions for management in the form of a business letter:
  (1) Which inventory cost flow method produces the most meaningful inventory amount for the balance sheet? Why?
  (2) Which inventory cost flow method produces the most meaningful net income? Why?
  (3) Which inventory cost flow method is most likely to approximate actual physical flow of the goods? Why?
  (4) How much additional cash will be available for management under LIFO than under FIFO? Why?
  (5) How much of the gross profit under FIFO is illusionary in comparison with the gross profit under LIFO?

Compute gross profit rate and inventory loss using gross profit method.
(SO 9)

*P9–5 M. Chang Company lost all of its inventory in a fire on December 28, 1998. The accounting records showed the following gross profit data for November and December.

	November	December (to 12/28)
Net sales	$400,000	$300,000
Beginning inventory	22,100	29,100
Purchases	314,975	236,000
Purchase returns and allowances	11,800	4,000
Purchase discounts	8,577	6,000
Freight-in	4,402	3,700
Ending inventory	29,100	?

M. Chang is fully insured for fire losses but must prepare a report for the insurance company.

Instructions
(a) Compute the gross profit rate for November.
(b) Using the gross profit rate for November, determine the estimated cost of the inventory lost in the fire.

*P9–6 Barker's Book Store uses the retail inventory method to estimate its monthly ending inventories. The following information is available for two of its departments at October 31, 1998.

	Hardcovers		Paperbacks	
	Cost	Retail	Cost	Retail
Beginning inventory	$ 260,000	$ 400,000	$ 63,000	$ 90,000
Purchases	1,180,000	1,800,000	268,000	380,000
Freight-in	5,000		2,000	
Purchase discounts	15,000		4,000	
Net sales		1,810,000		363,000

At December 31, Barker's Book Store takes a physical inventory at retail. The actual retail values of the inventories in each department are: Hardcovers $400,000 and Paperbacks $100,000.

Instructions
(a) Determine the estimated cost of the ending inventory for each department at **October 31**, 1998, using the retail inventory method.
(b) Compute the ending inventory at cost for each department at **December 31**, assuming the cost to retail ratios for the year are 65% for hardcovers and 70% for paperbacks.

*P9–7 Save-Mart Center began operations on July 1. It uses a perpetual inventory system. During July the company had the following purchases and sales:

	Purchases		
Date	Units	Unit Cost	Sales Units
July 1	5	$90	
July 6			3
July 11	4	$99	
July 14			3
July 21	3	$106	
July 27			4

Instructions
(a) Determine the inventory under a perpetual inventory system using (1) FIFO, (2) average cost, and (3) LIFO.
(b) Which costing method produces the highest ending inventory valuation?

ALTERNATE PROBLEMS

P9–1A Billy Jean Evert, a former professional tennis star, operates B.J.'s Tennis Shop at the Jackson Lake Resort. At the beginning of the current season, the ledger of B.J.'s Tennis Shop showed Cash $2,500, Merchandise Inventory $1,700, and Common Stock $4,200. The following transactions were completed during April:

Apr. 4 Purchased racquets and balls from Robert Co. $640 FOB shipping point, terms 3/10, n/30.
   6 Paid freight on Robert purchase $40.
   8 Sold merchandise to members $900, terms n/30.
  10 Received credit of $40 from Robert Co. for a damaged racquet that was returned.
  11 Purchased tennis shoes from Niki Sports for cash, $300.
  13 Paid Robert Co. in full.
  14 Purchased tennis shirts and shorts from Martina's Sportswear $700, FOB shipping point, terms 2/10, n/60.
  15 Received cash refund of $50 from Niki Sports for damaged merchandise that was returned.
  17 Paid freight on Martina's Sportswear purchase $30.

18   Sold merchandise to members, $800, terms n/30.
20   Received $500 in cash from members in settlement of their accounts.
21   Paid Martina's Sportswear in full.
27   Granted credit of $30 to members for tennis clothing that did not fit.
30   Sold merchandise to members $900, terms n/30.
30   Received cash payments on account from members, $500.

The chart of accounts for the tennis shop includes the following: No. 101 Cash, No. 112 Accounts Receivable, No. 120 Merchandise Inventory, No. 201 Accounts Payable, No. 311 Common Stock, No. 401 Sales, No. 412 Sales Returns and Allowances, No. 510 Purchases, No. 512 Purchase Returns and Allowances, No. 514 Purchase Discounts, No. 516 Freight-in.

Instructions
(a) Journalize the April transactions using a periodic inventory system.
(b) Enter the beginning balances in the ledger accounts and post the April transactions. (Use J1 for the journal reference.)
(c) Prepare a trial balance on April 30, 1998.
(d) Prepare an income statement through gross profit, assuming merchandise inventory on hand at April 30 is $1,800.

Prepare an income statement.
(SO 3, 4)

P9–2A   The N-Mart Department Store is located near the Village shopping mall. At the end of the company's fiscal year on December 31, 1998, the following accounts appeared in its adjusted trial balance:

Accounts Payable	$ 89,300
Accounts Receivable	50,300
Accumulated Depreciation—Building	52,500
Accumulated Depreciation—Equipment	42,900
Building	190,000
Cash	23,000
Depreciation Expense—Building	10,400
Depreciation Expense—Equipment	13,300
Equipment	110,000
Freight-in	3,600
Insurance Expense	7,200
Merchandise Inventory	40,500
Mortgage Payable	80,000
Office Salaries Expense	32,000
Prepaid Insurance	2,400
Property Taxes Payable	4,800
Purchases	462,000
Purchase Discounts	12,000
Purchase Returns and Allowances	6,400
Sales Salaries Expense	76,000
Sales	618,000
Sales Commissions Expense	14,500
Sales Commissions Payable	3,500
Sales Returns and Allowances	8,000
Common Stock	150,000
Retained Earnings	27,600
Dividends	28,000
Property Taxes Expense	4,800
Utilities Expense	11,000

Analysis reveals the following additional data:

1. Merchandise inventory on December 31, 1998, is $75,000.
2. Insurance expense and utilities expense are 60% selling and 40% administrative.
3. Depreciation on the building and property tax expense are administrative expenses; depreciation on the equipment is a selling expense.

Instructions
Prepare an income statement for the year ended December 31, 1998.

P9–3A Steward Company had a beginning inventory of 400 units of Product MLN at a cost of $8.00 per unit. During the year, purchases were:

Determine cost of goods sold and ending inventory, using FIFO, LIFO, and average cost. (SO 5, 6)

Feb. 20	700 units at $9.00	Aug. 12	300 units at $11.00
May 5	500 units at $10.00	Dec. 8	100 units at $12.00

Steward Company uses a periodic inventory system. Sales totaled 1,550 units.

Instructions
(a) Determine the cost of goods available for sale.
(b) Determine (1) the ending inventory, and (2) the cost of goods sold under each of the assumed cost flow methods (FIFO, LIFO, and average). Prove the accuracy of the cost of goods sold under the FIFO and LIFO methods.
(c) Which cost flow method results in (1) the lowest inventory amount for the balance sheet, and (2) the lowest cost of goods sold for the income statement?

P9–4A The management of Real Novelty Inc. is reevaluating the appropriateness of using its present inventory cost flow method, which is average cost. They request your help in determining the results of operations for 1998 if either the FIFO method or the LIFO method had been used. For 1998, the accounting records show the following data:

Compute ending inventory, prepare income statements, and answer questions using FIFO and LIFO. (SO 5, 6)

Inventories		Purchases and Sales	
Beginning (15,000 units)	$34,000	Total net sales (225,000 units)	$865,000
Ending (20,000 units)		Total cost of goods purchased	
		(230,000 units)	578,500

Purchases were made quarterly as follows:

Quarter	Units	Unit Cost	Total Cost
1	60,000	$2.30	$138,000
2	50,000	2.50	125,000
3	50,000	2.60	130,000
4	70,000	2.65	185,500
	230,000		$578,500

Operating expenses were $147,000, and the company's income tax rate is 30%.

Instructions
(a) Prepare comparative condensed income statements for 1998 under FIFO and LIFO. (Show computations of ending inventory.)
(b) ▭▭▭▷ Answer the following questions for management:
   (1) Which cost flow method (FIFO or LIFO) produces the more meaningful inventory amount for the balance sheet? Why?
   (2) Which cost flow method (FIFO or LIFO) produces the more meaningful net income? Why?
   (3) Which cost flow method (FIFO or LIFO) is more likely to approximate actual physical flow of the goods? Why?
   (4) How much additional cash will be available for management under LIFO than under FIFO? Why?
   (5) Will gross profit under the average cost method be higher or lower than (a) FIFO and (b) LIFO? (*Note:* It is not necessary to quantify your answer.)

*P9–5A** Vanessa Company lost 80% of its inventory in a fire on March 23, 1998. The accounting records showed the following gross profit data for February and March.

Estimate inventory loss using gross profit method. (SO 9)

	February	March (to 3/23)
Net sales	$270,000	$260,000
Net purchases	200,800	191,000
Freight-in	2,900	3,500
Beginning inventory	16,500	20,400
Ending inventory	20,400	?

Vanessa Company is fully insured for fire losses but must prepare a report for the insurance company.

Instructions

(a) Compute the gross profit rate for the month of February.

(b) Using the gross profit rate for February, determine both the estimated total inventory and inventory lost in the fire in March.

Compute ending inventory and cost of inventory lost using retail method.
(SO 9)

*P9–6A   Martinez Department Store uses the retail inventory method to estimate its monthly ending inventories. The following information is available for two of its departments at August 31, 1998.

	Sporting Goods		Jewelry and Cosmetics	
	Cost	Retail	Cost	Retail
Net sales		$1,020,000		$1,160,000
Purchases	$670,000	1,066,000	$731,000	1,158,000
Purchase returns	(26,000)	(40,000)	(12,000)	(20,000)
Purchase discounts	(15,360)	—	(9,440)	—
Freight-in	6,000	—	8,000	—
Beginning inventory	47,360	74,000	38,440	62,000

At December 31, Martinez Department Store takes a physical inventory at retail. The actual retail values of the inventories in each department are: Sporting Goods $75,000, and Jewelry and Cosmetics $44,000.

Instructions

(a) Determine the estimated cost of the ending inventory for each department on August 31, 1998, using the retail inventory method.

(b) Compute the ending inventory at cost for each department at December 31, assuming the cost-to-retail ratios are 60% for Sporting Goods and 65% for Jewelry and Cosmetics.

Prepare subsidiary ledger records under a perpetual inventory system.
(SO 10)

*P9–7A   The Family Home Appliance Mart begins operations on May 1. It uses a perpetual inventory system. During May the company had the following purchases and sales for its Model 25 Sureshot camera.

	Purchases		Sales
Date	Units	Unit Cost	Units
May 1	7	$150	
4			5
8	8	$170	
12			5
15	5	$180	
20			4
25			3

Instructions

(a) Determine the inventory under a perpetual inventory system using (1) FIFO, (2) average cost, and (3) LIFO.

(b) Which costing method produces (1) the highest ending inventory valuation and (2) the lowest ending inventory valuation?

*B*roadening *Your Perspective*

FINANCIAL REPORTING PROBLEM
• •

The notes that accompany a company's financial statements provide informative details that would clutter the amounts and descriptions presented in the statements. Refer to the financial statements of PepsiCo and the Notes to Consolidated Financial Statements in Appendix A.

Instructions

Answer the following questions. Complete the requirements in millions of dollars, as shown in PepsiCo's annual report.

(a) What did PepsiCo report for the amount of inventories in its Consolidated Balance Sheet at December 30, 1995? December 31, 1994?

(b) Compute the dollar amount of change and the percentage change in inventories between 1994 and 1995. Compute inventory as a percentage of current assets for 1995.

(c) How does PepsiCo value its inventories? Which inventory cost flow method does PepsiCo use?

(d) What two categories of inventories are classified in the note on "Inventories"? Briefly explain what you think is contained in each category.

(e) What is the cost of sales (cost of goods sold) reported by PepsiCo for 1995, 1994, and 1993? Compute the percentage of cost of sales to net sales in 1995.

COMPARATIVE ANALYSIS PROBLEM— THE COCA-COLA COMPANY VS. PEPSICO, INC.

The financial statements of Coca-Cola Company are presented at the end of Chapter 1, and PepsiCo's financial statements are presented in Appendix A.

Instructions

(a) Based on the information contained in these financial statements, compute the following 1995 ratios for each company:
   1. Inventory turnover ratio
   2. Average days to sell inventory

(b) What conclusions concerning the management of the inventory can be drawn from these data?

INTERPRETATION OF FINANCIAL STATEMENTS

Mini-Case One—Morrow Snowboards

Snowboarding is a rapidly growing sport in the United States. Morrow Snowboards, located in Salem, Oregon, is a significant player in snowboard manufacture and sales. In 1995 Morrow announced it was going to sell shares to the public. In its prospectus (an information-filled document that must be provided by all publicly traded U.S. firms the first time they issue shares to the public), it disclosed the following information:

> *Uncertain Ability to Manage Growth:* Since inception, the Company has experienced rapid growth in its sales, production and employee base. These increases have placed significant demands on the Company's management, working capital and financial and management control systems. The Company's independent auditors issued management letters in connection with their audit of the fiscal years ended December 31, 1993 and 1994 and the nine-month period ended September 30, 1995 that identified certain significant deficiencies in the Company's accounting systems, procedures and controls. To address these growth issues, the Company has, in the past 18 months, relocated its facilities and expanded production capacity, implemented a number of financial accounting control systems, and hired experienced finance, accounting, manufacturing and marketing personnel. In the accounting area, the Company has begun implementing or improving a perpetual inventory system, a cost accounting system, written accounting policies and procedures and a comprehensive annual capital expenditure budget. Until the Company develops a reliable perpetual inventory system, it intends to perform physical inventories on a quarterly basis. Although the Company is continuously evaluating and improving its facilities, management and financial control systems, there can be no assurance that such improvements will meet the demands of future growth. Any inadequacies in these areas could have a material adverse effect on the Company's business, financial condition, and results of operations.

Instructions

    (a) What implications does this disclosure have for someone interested in investing in Morrow Snowboards?

    (b) Do you think that the price of Morrow's stock will suffer because of these admitted deficiencies in its internal controls, including its controls over inventory?

    (c) Why do you think Morrow decided to disclose this negative information about itself?

    (d) List the steps that Morrow has taken to improve its control systems.

    (e) Do you think that these weaknesses are unusual for a rapidly growing company?

Mini-Case Two—Nike/Reebok

Nike and Reebok compete head-to-head in the sport shoe and sport apparel business. For both companies, inventory is a significant portion of their total assets. The following information was taken from each company's financial statements and notes to those financial statements.

Nike inventory footnote

Inventories are stated at the lower of cost or market. Cost is determined using the last-in, first-out (LIFO) method for substantially all U.S. inventories. International inventories are valued on a first-in, first-out (FIFO) basis.

Inventories by major classification are as follows:
(in thousands)

May 31,	1995	1994
Finished goods	$618,521	$465,065
Work-in-process	9,064	2,915
Raw materials	2,157	2,043

Other information for Nike:

	1995	1994
Inventory	629,742	470,023
Cost of goods sold	2,865,280	2,301,423

Reebok inventory footnote

Inventory, substantially all finished goods, is recorded at the lower of cost (first-in, first-out method) or market.

Other information for Reebok:

	1995	1994
Inventory	635,012	624,625
Cost of goods sold	2,114,084	1,966,138

Instructions

Address each of the following questions which deal with how these two companies manage their inventory.

    (a) What problems of inventory management face Nike and Reebok in the international sport apparel industry?

    (b) What inventory cost flow assumptions does each company use? Why might Nike use a different approach for U.S. operations versus international operations? What are the implications of their respective cost flow assumptions for their financial statements?

    (c) Nike provides more detail regarding the nature of its inventory (e.g., raw materials, work-in-process, and finished goods) than does Reebok. How might this additional information be useful in evaluating Nike?

    (d) Calculate and interpret the inventory turnover ratio and average days to sell inventory for each company. Comment on how the use of different inventory methods by the two companies impacts your ability to compare their ratios.

DECISION CASE

On April 10, 1998, fire damaged the office and warehouse of Gibson Company. Most of the accounting records were destroyed but the following account balances were determined as of March 31, 1998: Merchandise Inventory, January 1, 1998, $80,000; Sales (January 1–March 31, 1998), $150,000; Purchases (January 1–March 31, 1998), $84,000.

The company's fiscal year ends on December 31, and it uses a periodic inventory system.

From an analysis of the April bank statement you discover cancelled checks of $4,200 during the period April 1–10 for cash purchases. Deposits during the same period totaled $18,500 of which 60% were collections on accounts receivable and the balance was cash sales.

Correspondence with the company's principal suppliers revealed $12,400 of purchases on account from April 1 to April 10 of which $1,800 was for merchandise in transit on April 10 that was shipped FOB destination.

Correspondence with the company's principal customers produced acknowledgments of credit sales totaling $28,000 from April 1 to April 10. It was estimated that $4,600 of credit sales will never be acknowledged or recovered from customers.

Gibson Company reached an agreement with the insurance company that its fire-loss claim should be based on the average of the gross profit rates for the preceding 2 years. The financial statements for 1996 and 1997 showed the following data:

	1997	1996
Net sales	$600,000	$480,000
Cost of goods purchased	416,000	356,000
Beginning inventory	60,000	40,000
Ending inventory	80,000	60,000

Inventory with a cost of $19,000 was salvaged from the fire.

Instructions

(a) Determine the balances in (1) Sales and (2) Purchases at April 10.
*(b) Determine the average profit rate for the years 1996 and 1997. (*Hint:* Find the gross profit rate for each year and divide the sum by 2.)
*(c) Determine the inventory loss as a result of the fire, using the gross profit method.

COMMUNICATION ACTIVITY

You are the controller of Small Toys Inc. Joe Paisley, the president, recently mentioned to you that he found an error in the 1997 financial statements which he believes has corrected itself. He determined, in discussions with the Purchasing Department, that 1997 ending inventory was overstated by $1 million. Joe says that the 1998 ending inventory is correct, thus he assumes that 1998 income is correct. Joe says to you, "What happened has happened—there's no point in worrying about it anymore."

Instructions

You conclude that Joe is incorrect. Write a brief, tactful memo to Joe, clarifying the situation.

GROUP ACTIVITY

In groups of four or five students, choose one of the following inventory cost flow methods: FIFO periodic, FIFO perpetual (per appendix), LIFO periodic, LIFO perpetual (per appendix), average cost, specific identification.

Instructions

(a) Discuss the inventory methodology and its effects on the financial statements if adopted.
(b) Explain to the class how to implement the method you chose and its effects on the financial statements that you discussed earlier.

ETHICS CASE

Lonergan Wholesale Corp. uses the LIFO method of inventory costing. In the current year, profit at Lonergan is running unusually high. The corporate tax rate is also high this year, but it is scheduled to decline significantly next year. In an effort to lower current year's net income and to take advantage of the changing income tax rate, the president of Lonergan Wholesale instructs the plant accountant to recommend to the purchasing department a large purchase of inventory for delivery 3 days before the end of the year. The price of the inventory to be purchased has doubled during the year and the purchase will represent a major portion of the ending inventory value.

Instructions
   (a) What is the effect of this transaction on this year's and next year's income statement and income tax expense? Why?
   (b) If Lonergan Wholesale had been using the FIFO method of inventory costing, would the president give the same directive?
   (c) Should the plant accountant order the inventory purchase to lower income? What are the ethical implications of this order?

RESEARCH ASSIGNMENT

The September 23, 1994 edition of the *Wall Street Journal* includes an article entitled "CompUSA Auctions Notebook Computers Through Bulk Sale." Read the article and answer the following inventory-related questions.

   (a) At what amount did CompUSA estimate the retail value of the computers? What was the estimate made by one of the bidders?
   (b) What was wrong with the computers?
   (c) What were the rules of the auction as specified by CompUSA?
   (d) CompUSA had just recorded a $3 million inventory writedown in the preceding quarter. Based on the information in the article, does it appear that additional writedowns were called for?

CRITICAL THINKING
▶ *A Real-World Focus: General Motors Corporation*

General Motors is the largest producer of automobiles in the world, as well as the world's biggest industrial enterprise. After stumbling in the early 1990s, GM has enacted numerous cost-cutting measures, including downsizing and renegotiating contracts with suppliers. In addition, it has shifted more of its resources to the hot-selling truck market.

The annual report of General Motors Corporation disclosed the following information about its accounting for inventories:

Note 12.   Inventories
Major Classes of Inventories

(Dollars in millions)	1994	1993
Productive material, work in process, and supplies	$ 5,478.3	$4,671.9
Finished product, service parts, etc.	4,649.5	3,943.2
Total	$10,127.8	$8,615.1
Memo: Increase in LIFO inventories if valued at first-in, first-out (FIFO)	$ 2,535.9	$2,519.0

Inventories are stated generally at cost, which is not in excess of market. The cost of substantially all U.S. inventories other than the inventories of Saturn Corporation (Saturn) and GMHE is determined by the last-in, first-out (LIFO) method. The cost of non-U.S., Saturn, and GMHE inventories is determined generally by FIFO or average cost methods.

Instructions

(a) What is meant by "inventories are stated generally at cost, which is not in excess of market"?

(b) The company uses LIFO for most of its inventory. What impact does this have on reported ending inventory if prices are increasing?

(c) General Motors uses different inventory methods for different types of inventory. Why might it do this?

Answers to Self-Study Questions

1. b   2. d   3. a   4. a   5. b   6. c   7. d   8. c   9. d   10. d   11. b
12. b   *13. d

● ● ● ● ● ● ▶ **Concepts for Review**

Before studying this chapter, you should know or, if necessary, review:

a. *The time period assumption. (Ch. 3, p. 99)*
b. *The cost principle. (Ch. 1, p. 9) and the matching principle (Ch. 3, p. 100)*
c. *What is depreciation? (Ch. 3, p. 105)*
d. *How to make adjustments for depreciation. (Ch. 3, pp. 105–6)*

On the Books, Your Classroom May Be Worthless

PORTLAND, Maine — Take a stroll around your campus. Some of those buildings were built before you were born. How much do you think they cost to build? Are they depreciating? Are they appreciating?

These questions are not merely academic. It costs millions of dollars to construct, maintain, and sometimes demolish these campus buildings. Where does the money come from? Partly your tuition, perhaps tax dollars, perhaps from contributions of wealthy alumni, or from long-term borrowing. How these dollars are allocated can depend upon a reasonable estimate of a building's condition, its remaining life—and of course, how much it would cost to replace (its replacement cost).

At Westbrook College in Portland, Maine, Ms. Betty-Ann Doucette, the school's controller, recently researched the age of cer-

tain buildings on campus. The reason: a recent Financial Accounting Standards Board rule mandates that private colleges report fixed assets and depreciate them. Ms. Doucette found that some of the college's buildings go back to the nineteenth century. In order to value each building, she tried to find original construction costs and periodic renovations costs, as well as current replacement costs.

"For example, the building I'm

in, Goddard Hall, was built in the early part of this century," says Ms. Doucette. "It's now being depreciated over 40 years, and because it's over eighty years old, I show it as fully depreciated." If it is fully depreciated, does that mean it has a zero value? "On the books it says it does," she says. Of course, that doesn't mean it's worthless. An asset can have a zero value on the books yet have a substantial market value. ◀

CHAPTER 10

*P*LANT ASSETS, NATURAL RESOURCES, AND INTANGIBLE ASSETS

► STUDY OBJECTIVES ◄

After studying this chapter, you should be able to:

1. *Describe the application of the cost principle to plant assets.*

2. *Explain the concept of depreciation.*

3. *Compute periodic depreciation using different methods.*

4. *Describe the procedure for revising periodic depreciation.*

5. *Distinguish between revenue and capital expenditures and explain the entries for these expenditures.*

6. *Explain how to account for the disposal of a plant asset through retirement, sale, or exchange.*

7. *Identify the basic accounting issues related to natural resources.*

8. *Contrast the accounting for intangible assets with the accounting for plant assets.*

9. *Indicate how plant assets, natural resources, and intangible assets are reported and analyzed.*

As you can see, the accounting for campus buildings at Westbrook College is complex. In this chapter, we explain the application of the cost principle of accounting to buildings like those at Westbrook, as well as to natural resources and intangible assets such as Westbrook's school logo. We also describe the methods that may be used to allocate an asset's cost over its useful life. In addition, the accounting for expenditures incurred during the useful life of assets is discussed. The organization and content of this chapter are as follows:

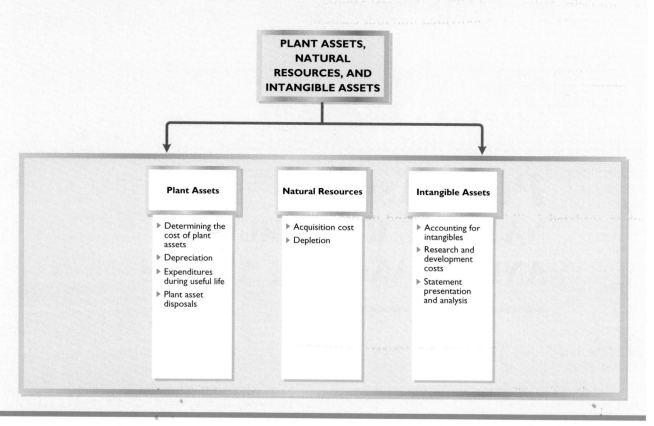

SECTION *1* ► *Plant Assets*

Plant assets are tangible resources that are used in the operations of the business and are not intended for sale to customers. They are also called **property, plant, and equipment; plant and equipment;** or **fixed assets**. These assets are generally long-lived and are expected to provide services to the company for a number of years. Except for land, plant assets decline in service potential over their useful lives.

Many companies have substantial investments in plant assets. In public utility companies, for example, net plant assets (plant assets less accumulated depreciation) often represent more than 75% of total assets. Recently net plant assets were 79% of Consolidated Edison's total assets and 92% of Pennsylvania Power & Light Company's. In other types of companies the percentages of plant assets to total assets were:

McDonald's	86%	Delta Airlines	82%
Marriott Corporation	63%	General Motors Corporation	37%
Caterpillar	26%	Wal-Mart	44%

Illustration 10-1

Percentages of plant assets to total assets

In the income statement, the relationship of depreciation expense and maintenance expense to total operating expenses was 10.4% for Consolidated Edison, 9.6% for Delta Airlines, and 6.2% for General Motors.

Plant assets are often subdivided into four classes:

1. **Land**, such as a building site.
2. **Land improvements**, such as driveways, parking lots, fences, and underground sprinkler systems.
3. **Buildings**, such as stores, offices, factories, and warehouses.
4. **Equipment**, such as store check-out counters, cash registers, coolers, office furniture, factory machinery, and delivery equipment.

Like the purchase of a home by an individual, the acquisition of plant assets is an important decision for a business enterprise. It is also important for a business enterprise to (1) keep the asset in good operating condition, (2) replace worn-out or outdated facilities, and (3) expand its productive resources as needed. The decline of rail travel in the United States can be traced in part to the failure of railroad companies to meet the first two conditions. Conversely, the growth of air travel in this country can be attributed in part to the general willingness of airline companies to observe these essential conditions.

Determining the Cost of Plant Assets

Plant assets are recorded at cost in accordance with the **cost principle** of accounting. Thus the buildings at Westbrook College are recorded at cost. Cost consists of all expenditures necessary to acquire the asset and make it ready for its intended use. For example, the purchase price, freight costs paid by the purchaser, and installation costs are all considered part of the cost of factory machinery.

Cost is measured by the cash paid in a cash transaction or by the cash equivalent price paid when noncash assets are used in payment. **The cash equivalent price is equal to the fair market value of the asset given up or the fair market value of the asset received, whichever is more clearly determinable.** Once cost is established, it becomes the basis of accounting for the plant asset over its useful life. Current market or replacement values are not used after acquisition. The application of the cost principle to each of the major classes of plant assets is explained in the following sections.

STUDY OBJECTIVE

Describe the application of the cost principle to plant assets.

Land

The cost of land includes (1) the cash purchase price, (2) closing costs such as title and attorney's fees, (3) real estate brokers' commissions, and (4) accrued property taxes and other liens on the land assumed by the purchaser. For example, if the cash price is $50,000 and the purchaser agrees to pay accrued taxes of $5,000, the cost of the land is $55,000.

All necessary costs incurred in making land **ready for its intended use** are debited to the Land account. When vacant land is acquired, these costs include

Helpful hint Management's intended use is important in applying the cost principle.

▶ *International note*

The United Kingdom (UK) is more flexible regarding asset valuation. Most companies in the UK make occasional revaluations to fair value when they believe this information is more relevant. Other examples of countries that permit revaluations are Switzerland and the Netherlands.

expenditures for clearing, draining, filling, and grading. Sometimes the land has a building on it that must be removed to make the site suitable for construction of a new building. In this case, all demolition and removal costs less any proceeds from salvaged materials are chargeable to the Land account. To illustrate, assume that Hayes Manufacturing Company acquires real estate at a cash cost of $100,000. The property contains an old warehouse that is razed at a net cost of $6,000 ($7,500 in costs less $1,500 proceeds from salvaged materials). Additional expenditures consist of the attorney's fee, $1,000, and the real estate broker's commission, $8,000. Given these factors, the cost of the land is $115,000, computed as follows:

Illustration 10-2

Computation of cost of land

Land	
Cash price of property	$100,000
Net removal cost of warehouse	6,000
Attorney's fee	1,000
Real estate broker's commission	8,000
Cost of land	$115,000

In recording the acquisition, Land is debited for $115,000 and Cash is credited for $115,000.

Land Improvements

The cost of land improvements includes all expenditures necessary to make the improvements ready for their intended use. For example, the cost of a new company parking lot will include the amount paid for paving, fencing, and lighting. These improvements have limited useful lives and their maintenance and replacement are the responsibility of the company. Thus, these costs are debited to Land Improvements and are depreciated over the useful lives of the improvements.

Buildings

Helpful hint Homeowners can include all renovation costs incurred in making a purchased home suitable for their use as part of the cost basis for income tax purposes.

All necessary expenditures relating to the purchase or construction of a building are charged to the Buildings account. When a building is purchased, such costs include the purchase price, closing costs (attorney's fees, title insurance, etc.), and real estate broker's commission. Costs to make the building ready for its intended use consist of expenditures for remodeling rooms and offices and replacing or repairing the roof, floors, electrical wiring, and plumbing.

When a new building is constructed, such as a new science building by Westbrook College, cost consists of the contract price plus payments made by the owner for architects' fees, building permits, and excavation costs. In addition, interest costs incurred to finance the project are included in the cost of the asset when a significant period of time is required to get the asset ready for use. In these circumstances, interest costs are considered as necessary as materials and labor. The inclusion of interest costs in the cost of a constructed building is **limited to the construction period**. When construction has been completed, subsequent interest payments on funds borrowed to finance the construction are debited to Interest Expense.

Equipment

The cost of equipment consists of the cash purchase price, sales taxes, freight charges, and insurance during transit paid by the purchaser. It also includes expenditures required in assembling, installing, and testing the unit. However, motor vehicle licenses and accident insurance on company trucks and cars are expensed as incurred, because they represent annual recurring expenditures and do not benefit future periods.

Helpful hint Two criteria apply in determining cost here: (1) the frequency of the cost—one-time or recurring, and (2) the benefit period—life of asset or one year.

To illustrate, assume that the Lenard Company purchases a delivery truck at a cash price of $22,000. Related expenditures consist of sales taxes $1,320, painting and lettering $500, motor vehicle license $80, and a 3-year accident insurance policy $1,600. The cost of the delivery truck is $23,820, computed as follows:

Illustration 10-3

Computation of cost of delivery truck

Delivery Truck

Cash price	$22,000
Sales taxes	1,320
Painting and lettering	500
Cost of delivery truck	$23,820

The motor vehicle license is expensed when incurred and the insurance policy is a prepaid asset. Thus, the summary entry to record the purchase of the truck and related expenditures is:

Delivery Truck	23,820	
License Expense	80	
Prepaid Insurance	1,600	
Cash		25,500
(To record purchase of delivery truck and related expenditures)		

For another example, assume the Merten Company purchases factory machinery at a cash price of $50,000. Related expenditures consist of sales taxes $3,000, insurance during shipping $500, and installation and testing $1,000. The cost of the factory machinery is $54,500 computed as follows:

Illustration 10-4

Computation of cost of factory machinery

Factory Machinery

Cash price	$50,000
Sales taxes	3,000
Insurance during shipping	500
Installation and testing	1,000
Cost of factory machinery	$54,500

The summary entry to record the purchase and related expenditures is:

Factory Machinery	54,500	
Cash		54,500
(To record purchase of factory machine)		

Depreciation

As explained in Chapter 3, depreciation is the process of allocating to expense the cost of a plant asset over its useful (service) life in a rational and systematic manner. Cost allocation is designed to provide for the proper matching of expenses with revenues in accordance with the matching principle.

STUDY OBJECTIVE 2

Explain the concept of depreciation.

Helpful hint   Once cost is established, then the matching principle applies under GAAP.

Depreciation is a process of cost allocation, not a process of asset valuation. Accountants make no attempt to measure the change in an asset's market value during ownership, because plant assets are not held for resale. Thus, the **book value** (cost less accumulated depreciation) of a plant asset may differ significantly from its market value. This is why Goddard Hall, in the opening story, can have zero book value and still have substantial market value.

Depreciation applies to three classes of plant assets: land improvements, buildings, and equipment. Each of these classes is considered to be a **depreciable asset**, because the usefulness to the company and revenue-producing ability of each class will decline over the asset's useful life. Depreciation does not apply to land because its usefulness and revenue-producing ability generally remain intact as long as the asset is owned. In fact, in many cases, the usefulness of land is greater over time because of the scarcity of good land sites. Thus, **land is not a depreciable asset**.

Helpful hint   Land does not depreciate because it does not wear out.

During a depreciable asset's useful life its revenue-producing ability will decline because of **wear and tear**. A delivery truck that has been driven 100,000 miles will be less useful to a company than one driven only 800 miles. Similarly, trucks and planes exposed to snow and salt will deteriorate faster than equipment that is not exposed to these elements.

A decline in revenue-producing ability may also occur because of **obsolescence**. Obsolescence is the process of becoming out of date before the asset physically wears out. The rerouting of major airlines from Chicago's Midway Airport to Chicago-O'Hare International Airport because Midway's runways were too short for jumbo jets is an example. Likewise, diesel train engines made coal-burning locomotives obsolete, and municipal buses sent streetcars to the scrap heap.

Helpful hint   Remember that depreciation is the process of allocating cost over the useful life of an asset. It is not a measure of value.

Recognition of depreciation does not result in the accumulation of cash for the replacement of the asset. The balance in Accumulated Depreciation represents the total cost that has been charged to expense; it is not a cash fund.

Factors in Computing Depreciation

Three factors affect the computation of depreciation, as shown in Illustration 10-5.

Illustration 10-5

Three factors in computing depreciation

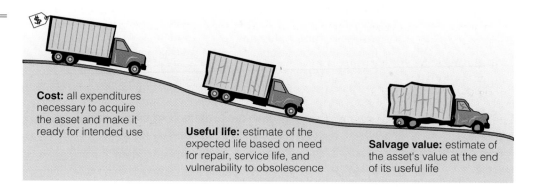

Cost: all expenditures necessary to acquire the asset and make it ready for intended use

Useful life: estimate of the expected life based on need for repair, service life, and vulnerability to obsolescence

Salvage value: estimate of the asset's value at the end of its useful life

1. **Cost.** Considerations affecting the cost of a depreciable asset have been explained earlier in this chapter. You will recall that plant assets are recorded at cost, in accordance with the cost principle of accounting.
2. **Useful life.** Useful life is an estimate of the expected productive life, also called service life, of the asset. Useful life may be expressed in terms of time, units of activity such as machine hours, or in units of output. Like salvage value, useful life is an estimate. In making the estimate, management should

consider such factors as the intended use of the asset, its expected repair and maintenance policies, and its vulnerability to obsolescence. The company's past experience with similar assets is often helpful in deciding on expected useful life.

3. **Salvage value.** Salvage value is an estimate of the asset's value at the end of its useful life. The value may be based on the asset's worth as scrap or salvage or on its expected trade-in value. Salvage value is an estimate. In making the estimate, management should consider how it plans to dispose of the asset and its experience with similar assets.

Helpful hint Another term often used for salvage value is residual value.

▶ Accounting in Action ▸ *Business Insight*

Not all companies use the same useful life for assets. Compare the useful lives used by the Big Three automakers, for example: At one time General Motors depreciated its machinery over 10 years, compared to Ford's 12 years and Chrysler's 11 years. GM also depreciated its buildings over 28 years while Ford used 30 years and Chrysler used 26 years. General Motors also depreciated its dies and equipment used to manufacture car bodies about twice as fast as Ford and three times as fast as Chrysler. Now GM has changed and aligned itself with its principal competitors by applying more liberal depreciation policies that have increased annual income. Should companies in the same industry be required to use the same useful life for the same type of assets?

Before You Go On . . .

▶ *Review It*

1. What are plant assets? What are the major classes of plant assets? How is the cost principle applied to accounting for plant assets?
2. What is the relationship, if any, of depreciation to (a) cost allocation, (b) asset valuation, and (c) cash accumulation?
3. Explain the factors that affect the computation of depreciation.

▶ *Do It*

Assume that a delivery truck is purchased for $15,000 cash, plus sales taxes of $900 and delivery costs to the dealer of $500. The buyer also pays $200 for painting and lettering, $600 for an annual insurance policy, and $80 for a motor vehicle license. Explain how each of these costs would be accounted for.

Reasoning: The cost principle applies to all expenditures made in order to get delivery equipment ready for its intended use. The principle does not apply to operating costs incurred during the useful life of the equipment, such as gas and oil, motor tune-ups, and insurance.

Solution: The first four payments ($15,000, $900, $500, and $200) are considered to be expenditures necessary to make the truck ready for its intended use. Thus, the cost of the truck is $16,600. The payments for insurance and the license are considered to be operating expenses incurred during the useful life of the asset.

Related exercise material: BE10–1, BE10–2, E10–1, E10–2, and E10–3.

Depreciation Methods

Depreciation is generally computed using one of the following methods:

1. Straight-line
2. Units-of-activity
3. Declining-balance

STUDY OBJECTIVE

•••••••••••▼3▼•••••••••••

Compute periodic depreciation using different methods.

Illustration 10-6

Use of depreciation methods in major U.S. companies

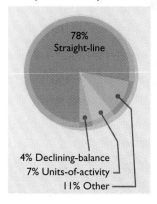

78%
Straight-line

4% Declining-balance
7% Units-of-activity
11% Other

Like the inventory methods discussed in Chapter 9, each method is acceptable under generally accepted accounting principles. Management selects the method or methods it believes to be appropriate in the circumstances. The objective is to select the method that best measures the asset's contribution to revenue over its useful life. Once a method is chosen, it should be applied consistently over the useful life of the asset. Consistency enhances the comparability of financial statements.

Depreciation affects the balance sheet through accumulated depreciation and the income statement through depreciation expense. Illustration 10-6 shows the use of the different depreciation methods in 600 of the largest companies in the United States.

To facilitate the comparison of the three depreciation methods, we will base all computations on the following data applicable to a small delivery truck purchased by Barb's Florists on January 1, 1996:

Illustration 10-7

Delivery truck data

Helpful hint The adjusting entry for depreciation is a debit to Depreciation Expense and a credit to Accumulated Depreciation.

Cost	$13,000
Expected salvage value	$ 1,000
Estimated useful life in years	5
Estimated useful life in miles	100,000

Straight-Line

Under the straight-line method, depreciation is the same for each year of the asset's useful life. It is measured solely by the passage of time. In order to compute depreciation expense, it is necessary to determine depreciable cost. Depreciable cost is the cost of the asset less its salvage value. It is the total amount subject to depreciation. Depreciable cost is then divided by the asset's useful life to determine depreciation expense. The formula and computation of depreciation expense in the first year for Barb's Florists are shown in Illustration 10-8.

Illustration 10-8

Formula for straight-line method

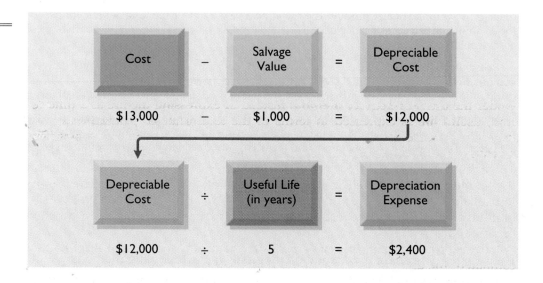

Cost	−	Salvage Value	=	Depreciable Cost
$13,000	−	$1,000	=	$12,000

Depreciable Cost	÷	Useful Life (in years)	=	Depreciation Expense
$12,000	÷	5	=	$2,400

Alternatively, we also can compute an annual rate at which the delivery truck is being depreciated. In this case, the rate is 20% (100% ÷ 5 years). When an annual rate is used under the straight-line method, the percentage rate is applied to the depreciable cost of the asset, as shown in the following **depreciation schedule**:

Illustration 10-9

Straight-line depreciation schedule

BARB'S FLORISTS

Year	Computation — Depreciable Cost	×	Depreciation Rate	=	Annual Depreciation Expense	End of Year — Accumulated Depreciation	Book Value
1996	$12,000		20%		**2,400**	$ 2,400	$10,600*
1997	12,000		20		**2,400**	4,800	8,200
1998	12,000		20		**2,400**	7,200	5,800
1999	12,000		20		**2,400**	9,600	3,400
2000	12,000		20		**2,400**	12,000	**1,000**

*($13,000 − $2,400).

Note that the depreciation expense of $2,400 is the same each year, and that the book value at the end of the useful life is equal to the estimated $1,000 salvage value.

What happens when an asset is purchased **during** the year, rather than on January 1, as in our example? In that case, it is necessary to **prorate the annual depreciation** for the proportion of time used. If Barb's Florists had purchased the delivery truck on April 1, 1996, the depreciation for 1996 would be $1,800 ($12,000 × 20% × 9/12 of a year).

The straight-line method predominates in practice, as shown in Illustration 10-6. For example, such large companies as Campbell Soup, Marriott Corporation, and General Mills use the straight-line method. It is simple to apply, and it matches expenses with revenues appropriately when the use of the asset is reasonably uniform throughout the service life. In the opening story, Westbrook College is probably using the straight-line method of depreciation for its buildings.

Helpful hint Question: What types of assets give equal benefits over useful life? Answer: Assets in which daily use does not affect their productivity. Examples might be office furniture and fixtures, warehouses, and garages for motor vehicles.

Units-of-Activity

Under the units-of-activity method, instead of expressing the life as a time period, useful life is expressed in terms of the total units of production or use expected from the asset. The units-of-activity method is ideally suited to factory machinery: production can be measured in terms of units of output or in terms of machine hours used in operating the machinery. It is also possible to use this method for such items as delivery equipment (miles driven) and airplanes (hours in use). The units-of-activity method is generally not suitable for such assets as buildings or furniture, because depreciation for these assets is more a function of time than of use.

To use this method, the total units of activity for the entire useful life are estimated, the amount is divided into depreciable cost to determine the depreciation cost per unit. The depreciation cost per unit is then applied to the units of activity during the year to determine the annual depreciation. To illustrate, assume that the delivery truck of Barb's Florists is driven 15,000 miles in the first year. The formula and computation of depreciation expense in the first year are:

Helpful hint Another term often used is the units-of-production method.

Helpful hint Depreciation stops when the asset's book value equals expected salvage value.

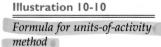

Illustration 10-10

Formula for units-of-activity method

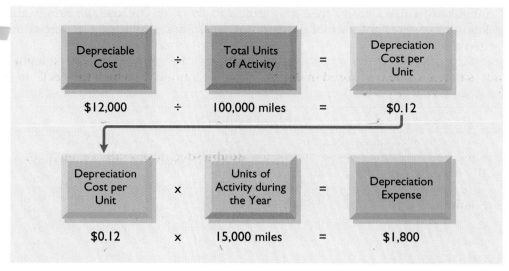

The depreciation schedule, using assumed mileage data, is as follows:

Illustration 10-11

Units-of-activity depreciation schedule

	Computation		Annual	End of Year	
Year	Units of Activity	× Depreciation Cost/Unit	= Depreciation Expense	Accumulated Depreciation	Book Value
1996	15,000	$.12	**$1,800**	$ 1,800	$11,200*
1997	30,000	.12	**3,600**	5,400	7,600
1998	20,000	.12	**2,400**	7,800	5,200
1999	25,000	.12	**3,000**	10,800	2,200
2000	10,000	.12	**1,200**	12,000	**1,000**

BARB'S FLORISTS

*($13,000 − $1,800).

The units-of-activity method is not nearly as popular as the straight-line method (see, for example, Illustration 10-6), primarily because it is often difficult to make a reasonable estimate of total activity. However, this method is used by some very large companies, such as Standard Oil Company of California and Boise Cascade Corporation. When the productivity of the asset varies significantly from one period to another, the units-of-activity method results in the best matching of expenses with revenues. This method is easy to apply when assets are purchased during the year. In such a case, the productivity of the asset for the partial year is used in computing the depreciation.

Declining-Balance

The declining-balance method produces a decreasing annual depreciation expense over the useful life of the asset. The method is so named because the computation of periodic depreciation is based on a **declining book value** (cost less accumulated depreciation) of the asset. Annual depreciation expense is computed by multiplying the book value at the beginning of the year by the declining-balance depreciation rate. **The depreciation rate remains constant from year to year, but the book value to which the rate is applied declines each year.**

Book value for the first year is the cost of the asset, because the balance in accumulated depreciation at the beginning of the asset's useful life is zero. In subsequent years, book value is the difference between cost and accumulated depreciation at the beginning of the year. **Unlike the other depreciation methods, salvage value is ignored in determining the amount to which the declining balance rate is applied.** Salvage value, however, does limit the total depreciation that can be taken. Depreciation stops when the asset's book value equals expected salvage value.

A common declining-balance rate is double the straight-line rate. As a result, the method is often referred to as the **double-declining-balance method.** If Barb's Florists uses the double-declining-balance method, the depreciation rate is 40% (2 × the straight-line rate of 20%). The formula and computation of depreciation for the first year on the delivery truck are:

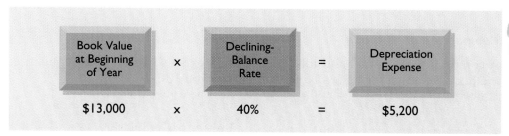

Illustration 10-12

Formula for declining-balance method

The depreciation schedule under this method is as follows:

BARB'S FLORISTS

Year	Computation Book Value Beginning of Year	×	Depreciation Rate	=	Annual Depreciation Expense	End of Year Accumulated Depreciation	Book Value
1996	$13,000		40%		**$5,200**	$ 5,200	$7,800
1997	7,800		40		**3,120**	8,320	4,680
1998	4,680		40		**1,872**	10,192	2,808
1999	2,808		40		**1,123**	11,315	1,685
2000	1,685		40		**685***	12,000	**1,000**

*Computation of $674 ($1,685 × 40%) is adjusted to $685 in order for book value to equal salvage value.

Illustration 10-13

Double-declining-balance depreciation schedule

Helpful hint Book value is variable and the depreciation rate is constant for this method.

You can see that the delivery equipment is 69% depreciated ($8,320 ÷ $12,000) at the end of the second year. Under the straight-line method it would be depreciated 40% ($4,800 ÷ $12,000) at that time. Because the declining-balance method produces higher depreciation expense in the early years than in the later years, it is considered an accelerated-depreciation method. The declining-balance method is compatible with the matching principle. The higher depreciation expense in early years is matched with the higher benefits received in these years. Conversely, lower depreciation expense is recognized in later years when the asset's contribution to revenue is less. Also, some assets lose usefulness rapidly because of obsolescence. In these cases, the declining-balance method provides a more appropriate depreciation amount.

When an asset is purchased during the year, it is necessary to prorate the declining-balance depreciation in the first year on a time basis. For example, if Barb's Florists had purchased the delivery equipment on April 1, 1996, depre-

Helpful hint The method to be used for an asset that is expected to be more productive in the first half of its useful life is the declining-balance method.

ciation for 1996 would become $3,900 ($13,000 × 40% × 9/12). The book value for computing depreciation in 1997 then becomes $9,100 ($13,000 − $3,900), and the 1997 depreciation is $3,640 ($9,100 × 40%).

▶Accounting in Action ▸ *Business Insight*

Why does Gingiss Formal Wear have 70 depreciation accounts and use the units-of-activity method for its tuxedos? The reason is that Gingiss wants to track wear and tear on each of its 16,000 dinner jackets individually. So each tuxedo has a bar code, like a box of cereal at the supermarket. When a tux is rented, a clerk runs its code across an electronic scanner. At year-end, the computer adds up the total rentals for each of 15 styles, then divides by expected total use to compute the rate. For instance, on one dolphin-gray tux, Gingiss expects a life of 30 rentals. In a recent year the tux was rented 13 times. So depreciation that period was 43% (13 ÷ 30) of the total cost.

Comparison of Methods

A comparison of annual and total depreciation expense under each of the three methods is shown for Barb's Florists in Illustration 10-14.

Illustration 10-14

Comparison of depreciation methods

Year	Straight-Line	Units-of-Activity	Declining-Balance
1996	$ 2,400	$ 1,800	$ 5,200
1997	2,400	3,600	3,120
1998	2,400	2,400	1,872
1999	2,400	3,000	1,123
2000	2,400	1,200	685
	$12,000	$12,000	$12,000

Observe that periodic depreciation varies considerably among the methods, but total depreciation is the same for the 5-year period. Each method is acceptable in accounting, because each recognizes the decline in service potential of the asset in a rational and systematic manner. The depreciation expense pattern under each method is presented graphically in Illustration 10-15.

Depreciation and Income Taxes

Helpful hint Depreciation per GAAP usually will be different from depreciation per IRS rules.

The Internal Revenue Service (IRS) allows corporate taxpayers to deduct depreciation expense when computing taxable income. However, the tax regulations of the IRS do not require the taxpayer to use the same depreciation method on the tax return that is used in preparing financial statements. Consequently, many large corporations use straight-line depreciation in their financial statements to

▶*Technology in Action*

Software packages to account for plant assets exist for both large and small computer systems. Though varying in complexity, even the least sophisticated packages can maintain a control and subsidiary ledger for plant assets and make the necessary depreciation computations and adjusting entries. Many packages also maintain separate depreciation schedules for both financial statement and income tax purposes, with reconciliations made for any differences. Even spreadsheet packages contain embedded formulas or functions for calculating depreciation using a variety of methods.

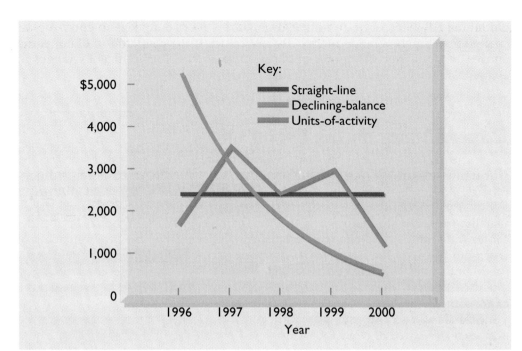

Illustration 10-15

Patterns of depreciation

maximize net income, and at the same time, a special accelerated-depreciation method is generally used on their tax returns to minimize their income taxes. For tax purposes, taxpayers must use on their tax returns either the straight-line method or a special accelerated-depreciation method called **Modified Accelerated Cost Recovery System** (MACRS).

▶ *International note*

In Germany, tax laws have a strong influence on financial accounting. Depreciation expense determined by the tax code must also be used for preparing financial statements.

Revising Periodic Depreciation

Depreciation is one example of the estimation procedures that are part of the accounting process. Annual depreciation expense should be reviewed periodically by management. If wear and tear or obsolescence indicate that annual depreciation is inadequate or excessive, a change in the amount should be made.

When a change in an estimate is required, the change is made in **current and future years but not to prior periods.** Thus, when a change is made, (1) there is no correction of previously recorded depreciation expense, and (2) depreciation expense for current and future years is revised. The rationale for this treatment is that continual restatement of prior periods would adversely affect the reader's confidence in financial statements.

To determine the new annual depreciation expense, we compute the asset's depreciable cost at the time of the revision and divide it by remaining useful life. To illustrate, assume that Barb's Florists decides on January 1, 1999, to extend the useful life of the truck one year because of its excellent condition. The company has used the straight-line method to depreciate the asset to date, and book value is $5,800 ($13,000 − $7,200). The new annual depreciation is $1,600, computed as follows:

STUDY OBJECTIVE
••••••••••4••••••••••

Describe the procedure for revising periodic depreciation.

Book value, 1/1/99	$5,800	
Less: Salvage value	1,000	
Depreciable cost	$4,800	
Remaining useful life	3 years	(1999–2001)
Revised annual depreciation ($4,800 ÷ 3)	$1,600	

Illustration 10-16

Revised depreciation computation

On January 1, 1999, or at any other time, Barb's Florists makes no entry for the change in estimate. On December 31, 1999, during the preparation of adjusting entries, it would record depreciation expense of $1,600. Significant changes in estimates must be described in the financial statements.

Expenditures during Useful Life

During the useful life of a plant asset a company may incur costs for ordinary repairs, additions, and improvements. Ordinary repairs are expenditures to maintain the operating efficiency and expected productive life of the unit. They usually are fairly small amounts that occur frequently throughout service life. Motor tune-ups and oil changes, the painting of buildings, and the replacing of worn-out gears on factory machinery are examples. They are debited to Repair (or Maintenance) Expense as incurred. Because they are immediately charged against revenues as an expense, these costs are often referred to as revenue expenditures.

Revenue Expend.

Additions and improvements are costs incurred to increase the operating efficiency, productive capacity, or expected useful life of the plant asset. These expenditures are usually material in amount and occur infrequently during the period of ownership. Expenditures for additions and improvements increase the company's investment in productive facilities and are generally debited to the plant asset affected. Accordingly, they are often referred to as capital expenditures. Most major U.S. corporations disclose the amount of their annual capital expenditures. In a recent year, both IBM and General Motors reported capital expenditures slightly in excess of $6 billion. The accounting for capital expenditures varies depending on the nature of the expenditure.

▸Accounting in Action ▸ *Business Insight*

Northwest Airlines is spending $120 million to spruce up forty DC9–30 jets. The improvements are designed to extend the lives of the planes, meet stricter government noise limits, and save money. The capital expenditure will extend the life of the jets by 10 to 15 years and save about $560 million over the cost of buying new planes. The DC9 jets now have an average age of 24 years.

Source: Ann Arbor News, August 9, 1994.

Plant Asset Disposals

Plant assets of various types may be disposed of in three ways, as shown in Illustration 10-17. Whatever the method of disposal, at the time of disposal it is necessary to determine the book value of the plant asset. The book value is the difference between the cost of the plant asset and the accumulated depreciation to date. If the disposal occurs at any time during the year, depreciation for the fraction of the year to the date of disposal must be recorded. The book value is then eliminated by debiting Accumulated Depreciation for the total depreciation to the date of disposal and crediting the asset account for the cost of the asset.

In this section we will examine the accounting for each of the three methods of plant asset disposal.

Retirement	Sale	Exchange
Equipment is scrapped or discarded.	Equipment is sold to another party.	Existing equipment is traded for new equipment.

Illustration 10-17

Methods of plant asset disposal

Retirement of Plant Assets

To illustrate the accounting for a retirement of plant assets, assume that Hobart Enterprises retires its computer printers, which cost $32,000. The accumulated depreciation on these printers is also $32,000; the equipment, therefore, is fully depreciated (zero book value). The entry to record this retirement is as follows:

Accumulated Depreciation—Printing Equipment	32,000	
Printing Equipment		32,000
(To record retirement of fully depreciated equipment)		

What happens if a fully depreciated plant asset is still useful to the company? In this case, the plant asset and the related accumulated depreciation continue to be reported on the balance sheet without further depreciation or adjustment until the asset is retired. Reporting the asset and related accumulated depreciation on the balance sheet informs the reader of the financial statements that the asset is still being used by the company. However, once an asset is fully depreciated, even if it is still being used, no additional depreciation should be taken. In no situation can the accumulated depreciation on the plant asset exceed its cost.

If a plant asset is retired before it is fully depreciated, and no scrap or salvage value is received, a loss on disposal occurs. For example, assume that Sunset Company discards delivery equipment that cost $18,000 and has accumulated depreciation of $14,000 at the date of retirement. The entry is as follows:

Accumulated Depreciation—Delivery Equipment	14,000	
Loss on Disposal	4,000	
Delivery Equipment		18,000
(To record retirement of delivery equipment at a loss)		

Helpful hint When a plant asset is disposed of, all amounts related to the asset must be removed from the accounts. This includes the original cost in the asset account and the total depreciation to date in the accumulated depreciation account.

The loss on disposal is reported in the Other Expenses and Losses section of the income statement.

Sale of Plant Assets

In a disposal by sale, the book value of the asset is compared with the proceeds received from the sale. If the proceeds of the sale exceed the book value of the plant asset, a **gain on disposal** occurs. If the proceeds of the sale are less than the book value of the plant asset sold, a **loss on disposal** occurs.

Only by coincidence will the book value and the fair market value of the asset be the same at the time the asset is sold. Gains and losses on sales of plant assets are, therefore, quite common. As an example, Delta Airlines, Inc. reported a $94,343,000 gain on the sale of five Boeing B-727-200 aircraft and five Lockheed L-1011-1 aircraft.

Gain on Disposal

To illustrate a gain, assume that on July 1, 1996, Wright Company sells office furniture for $16,000 cash. The office furniture originally cost $60,000 and as of January 1, 1996, had accumulated depreciation of $41,000. Depreciation for the first 6 months of 1996 is $8,000. The entry to record depreciation expense and update accumulated depreciation to July 1 is as follows:

July 1	Depreciation Expense	8,000	
	Accumulated Depreciation—Office Furniture		8,000
	(To record depreciation expense for the first		
	six months of 1996)		

After the accumulated depreciation balance is updated, a gain on disposal of $5,000 is computed:

Illustration 10-18

Computation of gain on disposal

Cost of office furniture	$60,000
Less: Accumulated depreciation ($41,000 + $8,000)	49,000
Book value at date of disposal	11,000
Proceeds from sale	16,000
Gain on disposal	$ 5,000

The entry to record the sale and the gain on disposal is as follows:

July 1	Cash	16,000	
	Accumulated Depreciation—Office Furniture	49,000	
	Office Furniture		60,000
	Gain on Disposal		5,000
	(To record sale of office furniture at a gain)		

The gain on disposal is reported in the Other Revenues and Gains section of the income statement.

Loss on Disposal

Assume that instead of selling the office furniture for $16,000, Wright sells it for $9,000. In this case, a loss of $2,000 is computed:

Illustration 10-19

Computation of loss on disposal

Cost of office furniture	$60,000
Less: Accumulated depreciation	49,000
Book value at date of disposal	11,000
Proceeds from sale	9,000
Loss on disposal	$ 2,000

The entry to record the sale and the loss on disposal is as follows:

July 1	Cash	9,000	
	Accumulated Depreciation—Office Furniture	49,000	
	Loss on Disposal	2,000	
	Office Furniture		60,000
	(To record sale of office furniture at a loss)		

The loss on disposal is reported in the Other Expenses and Losses section of the income statement.

Exchanges of Plant Assets

Plant assets may also be disposed of through exchange. Exchanges can be for either similar or dissimilar assets. Because exchanges of similar assets are more common, they are discussed here.

An exchange of similar assets involves assets of the same type. This occurs, for example, when old delivery equipment is exchanged for new delivery equipment or when old office furniture is exchanged for new office furniture. In an exchange of similar assets, the new asset performs the **same function** as the old asset.

In exchanges of similar plant assets, it is necessary to determine (1) the cost of the asset acquired and (2) the gain or loss on the asset given up. Because a noncash asset is given up in the exchange, cost is equal to the **cash equivalent price** paid. Cost, therefore, is the fair market value of the asset given up plus the cash paid. The gain or loss on disposal is the **difference between the fair market value and the book value of the asset given up**. These determinations and the resulting accounting entries are explained and illustrated below.

Loss Treatment

When a loss occurs on the exchange of similar assets, it is recognized immediately. To illustrate the accounting for a loss, assume that Roland Company exchanged old office equipment for similar new office equipment. The book value of the old office equipment is $26,000 (cost $70,000 less accumulated depreciation $44,000), its fair market value is $10,000, and cash of $81,000 is paid. The cost of the new office equipment, $91,000, is computed as follows:

Helpful hint As indicated earlier, immediate recognition of the loss also occurs in disposals by retirement and sale.

Fair market value of old office equipment	$10,000
Cash	81,000
Cost of new office equipment	$91,000

Illustration 10-20

Computation of cost of new office equipment

Through this exchange, a loss on disposal of $16,000 is incurred. A loss results when the book value is greater than the fair market value of the asset given up. The computation is as follows:

Book value of old office equipment ($70,000 − $44,000)	$26,000
Fair market value of old office equipment	10,000
Loss on disposal	$16,000

Illustration 10-21

Computation of loss on disposal

In recording an exchange at a loss it is necessary to (1) eliminate the book value of the asset given up, (2) record the cost of the asset acquired, and (3) recognize the loss on disposal. The entry for the Roland Company is as follows:

Office Equipment (new)	91,000	
Accumulated Depreciation—Office Equipment (old)	44,000	
Loss on Disposal	16,000	
Office Equipment (old)		70,000
Cash		81,000
(To record exchange of old office equipment for similar new equipment)		

Helpful hint If the loss were deferred, the cost of the new office equipment would be $107,000 ($91,000 + $16,000), which is higher than the fair market value of the new asset—an unacceptable result.

Gain Treatment

When a gain occurs on the exchange of similar assets, it is not recognized immediately. Instead, the gain is deferred by reducing the cost basis of the new asset. Thus, in determining the cost of the asset acquired, it is necessary to compute the **cost before deferral of the gain** and then the **cost after deferral of the gain**.

To illustrate the accounting for similar assets, assume that Mark's Express Delivery decides to exchange its old delivery equipment plus cash of $3,000 for new delivery equipment. At this time, the book value of the old delivery equipment is $12,000 (cost $40,000 less accumulated depreciation $28,000). In addition, it is determined that the fair market value of the old delivery equipment is $19,000.

The cost of the new asset received (before deferral of the gain) is equal to the **fair market value of the old asset exchanged plus any cash or other consideration given up**. The cost of the new delivery equipment (before deferral of the gain) is $22,000, computed as follows:

Illustration 10-22

Cost of new equipment (before deferral of gain)

Fair market value of old delivery equipment	$19,000
Cash	3,000
Cost of new delivery equipment (before deferral of gain)	**$22,000**

A gain results when the fair market value is greater than the book value of the asset given up. For Mark's Express, there is a gain of $7,000, computed as follows, on the disposal:

Illustration 10-23

Computation of gain on disposal

Fair market value of old delivery equipment	$19,000
Book value of old delivery equipment ($40,000 − $28,000)	12,000
Gain on disposal	**$ 7,000**

The $7,000 gain on disposal is then offset against the $22,000 cost of the new delivery equipment. The result is a $15,000 cost of the new delivery equipment, after deferral of the gain, as shown in Illustration 10-24.

Illustration 10-24

Cost of new delivery equipment (after deferral of gain)

Cost of new delivery equipment (before deferral of gain)	$22,000
Less: Gain on disposal	7,000
Cost of new delivery equipment (after deferral of gain)	**$15,000**

The entry to record the exchange is as follows:

Delivery Equipment (new)	15,000	
Accumulated Depreciation—Delivery Equipment (old)	28,000	
Delivery Equipment (old)		40,000
Cash		3,000
(To record exchange of old delivery equipment for similar new delivery equipment)		

This entry does not eliminate the gain; it just postpones or defers it to future periods. The deferred gain of $7,000 reduces the $22,000 cost to $15,000. As a result, net income in future periods increases because depreciation expense on the newly acquired delivery equipment is less by $7,000.

Summarizing, the rules for accounting for exchanges of similar assets are as follows:

Illustration 10-25

Accounting rules for plant exchanges

Type of Event	Recognition
Loss	Recognize immediately by debiting Loss on Disposal
Gain	Defer and reduce cost of new asset

Before You Go On . . .

▶ Review It

1. What are the formulas for computing annual depreciation under each of the depreciation methods?
2. How do the methods differ in terms of their effects on annual depreciation over the useful life of the asset?
3. Are revisions of periodic depreciation made to prior periods? Explain.
4. How does a capital expenditure differ from a revenue expenditure?
5. What is the proper accounting for the retirement and sale of plant assets?
6. What is the proper accounting for the exchange of similar plant assets?

▶ Do It

Overland Trucking has an old truck that cost $30,000, has accumulated depreciation of $16,000, and a fair value of $17,000. It has a choice of either selling the truck for cash of $17,000 or exchanging the old truck and $4,000 cash for a new truck. What is the entry that Overland Trucking would record under each option?

Reasoning: Gains and losses on the sale or exchange of plant assets are determined by the difference between the book value and the fair value of the company's asset. Gains on the exchange of similar assets are deferred.

Solution:
Sale of truck for cash:

Cash	17,000	
Accumulated Depreciation—Truck (old)	16,000	
Truck (old)		30,000
Gain on Disposal [$17,000 − ($30,000 − $16,000)]		3,000
(To record sale of truck at a gain)		

Exchange of old truck and cash for new truck:

Truck (new)*	18,000	
Accumulated Depreciation—Truck (old)	16,000	
Truck (old)		30,000
Cash		4,000
(To record exchange of old truck for similar new truck)		
*($20,000 + $4,000 − $3,000)		

If the old truck is exchanged for the new truck, the $3,000 gain is deferred, and the recorded cost of the new truck is reduced by $3,000.

Related exercise material: BE10–8, BE10–9, BE10–10, BE10–11, E10–10, E10–11, E10–12, E10–13, and E10–14.

▼SECTION *2* ▸ *Natural Resources*

Helpful hint On a balance sheet, natural resources may be described as Timberlands, Mineral Deposits, Oil Reserves, and so on.

Natural resources consist of standing timber and underground deposits of oil, gas, and minerals. Such resources include the much-publicized offshore oil deposits of major petroleum companies and the oil deposits for which the Alaskan pipeline was built. These long-lived productive assets have two distinguishing characteristics: (1) they are physically extracted in operations (such as mining, cutting, or pumping), and (2) they are replaceable only by an act of nature. Because of these characteristics, natural resources are frequently called **wasting assets**.

▼Acquisition Cost

STUDY OBJECTIVE
•••••••••• **7** ••••••••••
Identify the basic accounting issues related to natural resources.

The acquisition cost of a natural resource is the cash or cash equivalent price necessary to acquire the resource and prepare it for its intended use. For an already discovered resource, such as an existing coal mine, cost is the price paid for the property.

Determining acquisition cost becomes a problem when exploration is involved. For example, some argue that the costs of unsuccessful exploration as well as successful exploration should be capitalized. They believe that, using an oil well as an example, the cost of drilling the dry holes is a cost that is needed to find the commercially profitable wells. As a result, both successful and unsuccessful explorations are capitalized, and the costs are written off to expense over the useful life of the successful wells. This method is often referred to as the **full-cost approach**.

Others disagree, arguing that the costs of only successful projects should be capitalized and unsuccessful projects should be expensed. They maintain that if only one of ten exploratory wells becomes commercially viable, it is inappropriate to assign the costs of the nine unsuccessful wells to the cost of the successful well. This method is referred to as the successful efforts approach. At present, both approaches are used in accounting for natural resources. For example, such companies as American Petrofina, DuPont, Callahan Mining, and Copperweld use full costing, whereas Texaco, Mobil, and Gulf use successful efforts.

▶Accounting in Action ▸ *Business Insight*

Should both full cost and successful efforts be permitted in accounting? Views are particularly strong on this subject. As one financial expert, commenting on the full-cost method, noted: "It lets them call a dry hole an asset, and as far as I am concerned, any company that uses full-cost accounting is guilty until proven innocent." On the other hand, companies using the full-cost method argue that "it enables us to undertake risky exploration projects without having sharp swings in reported earnings." Or as one writer noted: "Forcing companies to use successful efforts accounting would retard domestic oil and gas exploration and imperil national security." The debate raises an interesting question—should accounting be concerned with national security, or should it "tell it like it is"?

Depletion

The process of allocating the cost of natural resources to expense in a rational and systematic manner over the resource's useful life is called depletion. **The units-of-activity method is generally used to compute depletion, because periodic depletion generally is a function of the units extracted during the year.** Under this method, the total cost of the natural resource minus salvage value, if any, is divided by the number of units estimated to be in the resource. The result is a depletion cost per unit of product. The depletion cost per unit is then multiplied by the number of units extracted and sold, to compute the depletion expense. The formula is as follows:

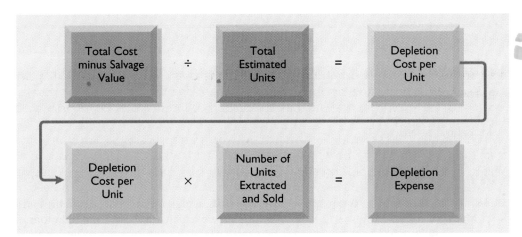

Illustration 10-26

Formula to compute depletion expense

Helpful hint The computation for depletion is similar to the computation for depreciation using the units-of-activity method of depreciation.

To illustrate, assume that the Lane Coal Company invests $5 million in a mine estimated to have 10 million tons of coal and no salvage value. In the first year, 800,000 tons of coal are extracted and sold. Using the formulas above, the computations are as follows:

$$\$5,000,000 \div 10,000,000 = \$.50 \text{ depletion cost per ton}$$

$$\$.50 \times 800,000 = \$400,000 \text{ depletion expense}$$

The entry to record depletion expense for the first year of operation is as follows:

Dec. 31	Depletion Expense	400,000	
	Accumulated Depletion		400,000
	(To record depletion expense on coal deposits)		

The account Depletion Expense is reported as a part of the cost of producing the product. Accumulated Depletion, a contra asset account similar to accumulated depreciation, is deducted from the cost of the natural resource in the balance sheet as follows:

Helpful hint Natural resources are generally reported as part of Property, Plant, and Equipment on the balance sheet.

Illustration 10-27

Statement presentation of accumulated depletion

Coal mine	$5,000,000	
Less: Accumulated depletion	400,000	$4,600,000

However, in many companies an Accumulated Depletion account is not used, and the amount of depletion is credited directly to the natural resource account.

Sometimes, natural resources extracted in one accounting period will not be sold until a later period. In this case, depletion is not expensed until the resource is sold. The amount not sold is reported in the Current Asset section as inventory.

▶Technology in Action

Firms in the oil and gas industry maintain extensive computerized data bases on their natural resources. Depletion amounts (in both monetary and physical units) are constantly monitored by these systems. Revisions in cost projections are automatically updated as new deposits are located or as estimates on existing deposits are changed. We all see the end result of this accounting at the gas pump.

Before You Go On . . .

▶ *Review It*

1. What is the difference between the full-cost and successful efforts methods in accounting for natural resources?
2. How is depletion expense computed?

▶ *Do It*

Explain the method used in computing depletion and show the computation, assuming Hard Rock Mining Corporation invests $12 million in a mine estimated to have 10 million tons of ore and a $2 million salvage value. In the first year 40,000 tons of ore are mined and sold.

Reasoning: There are many similarities between depreciation and depletion. In computing depletion expense, the units-of-activity method is generally used.

Solution: Under the units-of-activity method, a depletion cost per unit is determined by dividing total cost minus salvage value by the total estimated units. The computation is as follows:

$$($12,000,000 - $2,000,000) \div 10,000,000 = $1 \text{ depletion cost per ton}$$

The cost per unit is then multiplied by the number of units extracted and sold to determine depletion expense. Depletion expense for Hard Rock is $40,000 ($1 × 40,000).

Related exercise material: BE10–12 and E10–15.

▼SECTION 3 ▸ *Intangible Assets*

Intangible assets are rights, privileges, and competitive advantages that result from the ownership of long-lived assets that do not possess physical substance. Evidence of intangibles may exist in the form of contracts, licenses, and other documents. Intangibles may arise from:

1. Government grants such as patents, copyrights, franchises, trademarks, and trade names.
2. Acquisition of another business in which the purchase price includes a payment for goodwill.

3. Private monopolistic arrangements arising from contractual agreements, such as franchises and leases.

Some widely known intangibles are the patents of Polaroid, the franchises of McDonald's, the trade name of Col. Sander's Kentucky Fried Chicken, and the trademark 3M of Minnesota Mining and Manufacturing Company.

Accounting for Intangible Assets

In general, accounting for intangible assets parallels the accounting for plant assets. That is, **intangible assets are recorded at cost**, and this cost is expensed **over the useful life of the intangible asset in a rational and systematic manner**. At disposal, the book value of the intangible asset is eliminated, and a gain or loss, if any, is recorded.

There are, however, differences between accounting for intangible assets and accounting for plant assets. First, the term used to describe the allocation of the cost of an intangible asset to expense is amortization, rather than depreciation. To record amortization of an intangible, an amortization expense is debited and the specific intangible asset is credited. An alternative is to credit an accumulated amortization account, similar to accumulated depreciation. Most companies, however, choose simply to reduce the cost of the intangible asset.

There is also a difference in determining cost. For plant assets, cost includes both the purchase price of an asset and the costs incurred by a company in designing and constructing the plant asset. In contrast, cost for an intangible asset includes only the purchase price. Costs incurred in developing an intangible asset are expensed as incurred.

A third difference is that **the amortization period of an intangible asset cannot be longer than 40 years**. For example, even if the useful life of an intangible asset is 60 years, it must be written off over 40 years. Conversely, if the useful life is less than 40 years, the useful life is used. This rule ensures that all intangibles, especially those with indeterminable lives, will be written off in a reasonable period of time.

Unlike plant assets, intangible assets are typically amortized on a straight-line basis. The widespread use of this method adds comparability in accounting for intangible assets.

STUDY OBJECTIVE
8
Contrast the accounting for intangible assets with the accounting for plant assets.

Helpful hint The 40-year rule was adopted to ensure that companies at least write their intangibles off against revenues. Prior to this guideline, some companies maintained that intangibles had indeterminable lives.

Patents

A patent is an exclusive right issued by the United States Patent Office that enables the recipient to manufacture, sell, or otherwise control an invention for a period of 17 years from the date of the grant. A patent is nonrenewable, but the legal life of a patent may be extended beyond its original term by obtaining new patents for improvements and other changes in the basic design. **The initial cost of a patent is the cash or cash equivalent price paid to acquire the patent.** It should be noted that the saying, "A patent is only as good as the money you're prepared to spend defending it," is very true. Most patents are subject to some type of litigation by competitors. A well-known example is the patent infringement suit won by Polaroid against Eastman Kodak in protecting its patent on instant cameras. If the owner incurs legal costs in successfully defending the patent in an infringement suit, such costs are considered necessary to establish the validity of the patent. Thus, **they are added to the Patent account and amortized over the remaining life of the patent**.

Helpful hint The cost of a patent is comprised of two items generally. The first is the price paid (if any) and the second is legal fees to defend the patent. Costs incurred initially to develop a patent are not capitalized.

The cost of a patent should be amortized over its 17-year legal life or its useful life, whichever is shorter. In determining useful life, obsolescence, inadequacy, and other factors should be considered; these may cause a patent to become economically ineffective before the end of its legal life. To illustrate the computation of patent expense, assume that National Labs purchases a patent at a cost of $60,000. If the useful life of the patent is 8 years, the annual amortization expense is $7,500 ($60,000 ÷ 8). The entry to record the annual amortization is:

Dec. 31	Patent Expense	7,500	
	Patents		7,500
	(To record patent amortization)		

Patent Expense is classified as an **operating expense** in the income statement.

Copyrights

Copyrights are granted by the federal government, giving the owner the exclusive right to reproduce and sell an artistic or published work. Copyrights extend for the life of the creator plus 50 years. The cost of the copyright consists of the **cost of acquiring and defending it**. The cost may be only the $10 fee paid to the U.S. Copyright office, or it may amount to a great deal more if a copyright infringement suit is involved.

The useful life of a copyright generally is significantly shorter than its legal life. Similar to other intangible assets, the maximum write-off is 40 years. However, because of the difficulties of determining the period over which benefits are to be received, copyrights usually are amortized over a relatively short period of time.

▶Accounting in Action ▸ *International Insight*

One of the significant new items copyrighted today is computer software. Lotus Development Corporation (Lotus 1-2-3), Microsoft (Windows), and WordPerfect Corporation (WordPerfect) are some examples. These intangible assets—copyrights, in this case—are one of the most valuable assets of these corporations. To illustrate how important copyrights are, consider that in China only $1 million in computer software was sold in two recent years because China had no copyright law to discourage software piracy. Now an agreement has been reached with the Chinese that will provide protection against unlicensed copying of software. As one software maker observed, "If copyrights are protected, the value of the computer-software market in China will skyrocket."

Trademarks and Trade Names

A trademark or trade name is a word, phrase, jingle, or symbol that distinguishes or identifies a particular enterprise or product. Trade names like Wheaties, Trivial Pursuit, Sunkist, Kleenex, Coca-Cola, Big Mac, and Cadillac create immediate product identification and generally enhance the sale of the product. The creator or original user may obtain exclusive legal right to the trademark or trade name by registering it with the U.S. Patent Office. Such registration provides 20 years' protection and may be renewed indefinitely as long as the trademark or trade name is in use.

If the trademark or trade name is purchased, the cost is the purchase price. If it is developed by the enterprise itself, the cost includes attorney's fees, registration fees, design costs, successful legal defense costs, and other expenditures directly related to securing it.

As with other intangibles, the cost of trademarks and trade names must be amortized over the shorter of its useful life or 40 years. Because of the uncertainty involved in estimating the useful life, the cost is frequently amortized over a much shorter period.

►Accounting in Action ► *Business Insight*

Consider the trademarks that Kohlberg, Kravis, Roberts and Company (KKR) received when it purchased RJR Nabisco. First RJR Nabisco owned 30% of the cigarette market, with such trade names as Camel, Salem, Doral, and Vantage. In the food area, RJR Nabisco owned Oreo, Ritz, Chips Ahoy, Premium Saltines (crackers), Fleischmann's and Blue Bonnet (margarine), Grey Poupon (mustard), Milk Bone, Ortega (Mexican foods), Shredded Wheat, Peek Freans (cookies), Hawaiian Punch, Del Monte, Planters, Life Savers, Baby Ruth, and Butterfinger. It is no wonder that KKR paid approximately $25 billion for the company!

Franchises and Licenses

When you drive down the street in your Trans-Am purchased from a General Motors dealer, fill up your tank at the corner Standard Oil station, eat lunch at Wendy's, and vacation at a Club Med resort, you are dealing with franchises. A franchise is a contractual arrangement under which the franchisor grants the franchisee the right to sell certain products, to render specific services, or to use certain trademarks or trade names, usually within a designated geographical area.

Another type of franchise is that entered into between a governmental body (commonly municipalities) and a business enterprise. This type of franchise permits the enterprise to use public property in performing its services. Examples are the use of city streets for a bus line or taxi service, use of public land for telephone and electric lines, and the use of airwaves for radio or TV broadcasting. Such operating rights are referred to as licenses.

Franchises and licenses may be granted for a definite period of time, an indefinite period, or perpetual. **When costs can be identified with the acquisition of the franchise or license, an intangible asset should be recognized.** In the case of a limited life, the cost of a franchise (or license) should be amortized as operating expense over the useful life. If the life is indefinite or perpetual, the cost may be amortized over a reasonable period not to exceed 40 years. Annual payments made under a franchise agreement should be recorded as **operating expenses** in the period in which they are incurred.

► *Ethics note*

A pharmaceutical company was growing rapidly by buying unwanted drug licensing rights held by larger companies. These licensing rights, reported as intangible assets, represented over 70% of the company's total assets. At first considered a "hot stock" because of its quick growth in profits, it sustained a 50% drop in value when the market realized the rights were being amortized over 40 years. If a more reasonable life had been used to amortize the rights, the company's reported profits would, instead, have been huge losses.

►Accounting in Action ► *Business Insight*

King World's most valuable asset is the right to license television shows such as "Wheel of Fortune," "Jeopardy," "The Oprah Winfrey Show," and "Inside Edition." Almost 90% of its $396.4 million in a recent year came from the fees associated with the rights to license agreements on these intangible assets.

Goodwill

Usually, the largest intangible asset that appears on a company's balance sheet is goodwill. Goodwill is the value of all favorable attributes that relate to a business enterprise. These include exceptional management, desirable location, good customer relations, skilled employees, high-quality products, fair pricing policies, and harmonious relations with labor unions. Some view goodwill as expected earnings in excess of normal earnings. Goodwill is, therefore, unusual: unlike other assets such as investments, plant assets, and other intangibles that can be sold individually in the marketplace, goodwill can be identified only with the business as a whole.

If goodwill can be identified only with the business as a whole, how can it be determined? Certainly, many of the factors above (exceptional management, desirable location, and so on) are present in many business enterprises. However, to determine the amount of goodwill in these types of situations would be too difficult and very subjective. In other words, to recognize goodwill without an exchange transaction would lead to subjective valuations that do not contribute to the reliability of financial statements. **Therefore, goodwill is recorded only when there is an exchange transaction that involves the purchase of an entire business. When an entire business is purchased, goodwill is the excess of cost over the fair market value of the net assets (assets less liabilities) acquired.**

In recording the purchase of a business, the net assets are shown at their fair market values, goodwill is recorded at its cost, and cash is credited for the purchase price. Subsequently, goodwill is written off over its useful life, not to exceed 40 years. The amortization entry generally results in a debit to Goodwill Expense and a credit to Goodwill. Goodwill is reported in the balance sheet under Intangible Assets.

Helpful hint Goodwill is recorded only when it has been purchased along with tangible and identifiable intangible assets of a business. Internally created goodwill must be expensed as incurred.

▶Accounting in Action ▸ *International Insight*

Does the amortization requirement for goodwill create a disadvantage for U.S. companies? British companies, for example, do not have to amortize goodwill against earnings. Rather, they bypass the income statement completely and charge goodwill directly to stockholders' equity. For example, Pillsbury was purchased by Grand Met, a British firm. Many complained that U.S. companies were reluctant to bid for Pillsbury because it would mean that they would have to record a large amount of goodwill, which would substantially depress income in the future. What should be done when accounting practices are different among countries and perhaps give one country a competitive edge?

Research and Development Costs

Research and development costs are not intangible costs, but because these expenditures may lead to patents and copyrights, they are discussed in this section. Many companies spend considerable sums of money on research and development in an ongoing effort to develop new products or processes. For example, in a recent year IBM spent over $2.5 billion on research and development, an amount greater than the total expenditure budget of many state governments.

Research and development costs present accounting problems: (1) it is sometimes difficult to assign the costs to specific projects, and (2) there are uncertainties in identifying the extent and timing of future benefits. As a result, research and development costs are **usually recorded as an expense when incurred**, whether the research and development is successful or not.

To illustrate, assume that Laser Scanner Company spent $3 million on research and development. These research and development costs resulted in the development of two highly successful patents. The R&D costs, however, cannot be included in the cost of the patent. Rather, they are recorded as an expense when incurred.

▶ *International note*

Many factors, including differences in accounting treatment of R&D, contribute to differences in R&D expenditures across nations. R&D as a percentage of gross domestic product in 1994 was 2.6% in the United States, 2.4% in France, 2.5% in Germany, 3% in Japan, and 1.8% in Korea.

Many disagree with this accounting approach. They argue that to expense these costs leads to understated assets and net income. Others, however, argue that capitalizing these costs will lead only to highly speculative assets on the balance sheet. Who is right is difficult to determine. The controversy, however, illustrates how difficult it is to establish proper guidelines for financial reporting.

Statement Presentation and Analysis

Usually plant assets and natural resources are combined under Property, Plant, and Equipment, and intangibles are shown separately under Intangible Assets. Either within the balance sheet or in the notes, there should be disclosure of the balances of the major classes of assets, such as land, buildings, and equipment, and accumulated depreciation by major classes or in total. In addition, the depreciation and amortization methods used should be described and the amount of depreciation and amortization expense for the period disclosed.

Illustration 10-28 is an excerpt from Owens-Illinois' balance sheet. The notes to the financial statements of Owens-Illinois identify the major classes of property, plant, and equipment. They also indicate that depreciation is by the straight-line method, depletion is by the units-of-activity method, and amortization is by the straight-line method.

STUDY OBJECTIVE 9

Indicate how plant assets, natural resources, and intangible assets are reported and analyzed.

OWENS-ILLINOIS, INC.
Partial Balance Sheet
(In millions of dollars)

Property, plant, and equipment		
Timberlands, at cost, less accumulated depletion		$ 95.4
Buildings and equipment, at cost	$2,207.1	
Less: Accumulated depreciation	1,229.0	978.1
Total property, plant, and equipment		$1,073.5
Intangibles		
Patents		410.0
Total		$1,483.5

Illustration 10-28

Presentation of property, plant, and equipment and intangible assets

Because the original cost, the accumulated depreciation, and the current period's depreciation expense for property, plant, and equipment are reported in the financial statements, it is possible to analyze the lives and ages of these assets (especially for companies that use the straight-line method of depreciation). A measure of the **average life** and the **average age** of these assets can be computed using the following formulas and the data above from Owens-Illinois, Inc. (depreciation expense for the year is $180.5 million):

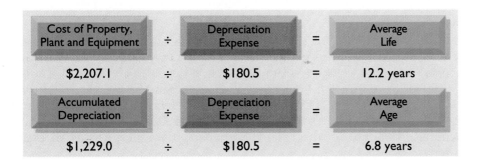

Illustration 10-29

Average life and average age formulae and computations

These averages are only rough estimates and possess all the weaknesses of averages. The actual lives of the individual assets that are contained in these averages range from 3 years (tools and office machines) to 35 years (buildings). However, the usefulness of these averages may come from a comparison with averages of other companies in the same industry.

The turnover of assets may be used in analyzing the productivity of a company's assets. That is, the **asset turnover ratio** is computed to measure how efficiently a company uses its assets to generate sales. This ratio is computed by dividing net sales by average total assets for the period, as shown in the formula below:

Illustration 10-30

Asset turnover formula and computation

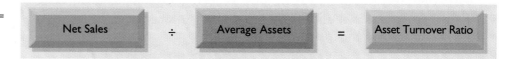

This ratio shows the dollars of sales produced for each dollar invested in assets. If a company is using its assets efficiently, each dollar of assets will create a high amount of sales. This ratio varies greatly among different industries—from those that are asset intensive (utility) to those that are not (services).

Before You Go On . . .

▸*Review It*

1. What are the main differences between accounting for intangible assets and plant assets?
2. Identify the major types of intangibles and the proper accounting for them.
3. Explain the accounting for research and development costs.
4. What ratios may be computed to analyze property, plant, and equipment?

▸*A Look Back at Westbrook College*

Refer back to the opening story about Westbrook College, and answer the following questions:

1. Why should Westbrook College depreciate its buildings?
2. How can Westbrook College have a building with a zero book value yet a substantial market value?
3. Give some examples of intangibles other than a trademark that you might find on your college campus.
4. Give some examples of company or product trademarks or trade names. Are trade names and trademarks reported on a company's balance sheet? Explain.

Solution:

1. Westbrook College should depreciate its buildings because depreciation is necessary in order to allocate the cost of the buildings to the periods in which they are used.
2. A building can have a zero book value if it has no salvage value and it is fully depreciated—that is, if it has been used for a period longer than its expected life. Because depreciation is used to allocate cost rather than to reflect actual value, it is not at all unlikely that a building could have a low or zero book value, but a positive market value.

3. Examples of other intangibles that might be found on a college campus are franchise of a bookstore chain, license to operate a radio station, patents developed by professors, and a permit to operate a bus service.
4. Typical company or product trade names are:
    Clothes—Gap, Gitano, Dockers, Calvin Klein, Chaus, Guess.
    Perfume—Passion, Ruffles, Chanel No. 5, Diamonds.
    Cars—TransAm, Nova, Prelude, Coupe DeVille, Eclipse.
    Shoes—Nike, Florsheim, L.A. Gear, Adidas.
    Breakfast cereals—Cheerios, Wheaties, Frosted Mini-Wheats, Rice Krispies.

Trade names and trademarks are reported on a balance sheet if there is a cost attached to them. If the trade name or trademark is purchased, the cost is the purchase price. If it is developed by the enterprise, the cost includes attorney's fees, registration fees, design costs, successful legal defense costs, and other expenditures directly related to securing the trade name or trademark.

Summary of Study Objectives

1. *Describe the application of the cost principle to plant assets.* The cost of plant assets includes all expenditures necessary to acquire the asset and make it ready for its intended use. Cost is measured by the cash or cash equivalent price paid.

2. *Explain the concept of depreciation.* Depreciation is the process of allocating to expense the cost of a plant asset over its useful (service) life in a rational and systematic manner. Depreciation is not a process of valuation, and it is not a process that results in an accumulation of cash. Depreciation is caused by wear and tear and by obsolescence.

3. *Compute periodic depreciation using different methods.* There are three depreciation methods:

Method	Effect on Annual Depreciation	Formula
Straight-line	Constant amount	Depreciable cost ÷ useful life (in years)
Units-of-activity	Varying amount	Depreciation cost per unit × units of activity during the year
Declining-balance	Decreasing amount	Book value at beginning of year × declining-balance rate

4. *Describe the procedure for revising periodic depreciation.* Revisions of periodic depreciation are made in present and future periods, not retroactively. The new annual depreciation is determined by dividing the depreciable cost at the time of the revision by the remaining useful life.

5. *Distinguish between revenue and capital expenditures and explain the entries for these expenditures.* Revenue expenditures are incurred to maintain the operating efficiency and expected productive life of the asset. These expenditures are debited to Repair Expense as incurred. Capital expenditures increase the operating efficiency, productive capacity, or expected useful life of the asset. These expenditures are generally debited to the plant asset affected.

6. *Explain how to account for the disposal of a plant asset through retirement, sale, or exchange.* The accounting for disposal of a plant asset through retirement or sale is as follows:
(a) Eliminate the book value of the plant asset at the date of disposal.
(b) Record cash proceeds, if any.
(c) Account for the difference between the book value and the cash proceeds as a gain or loss on disposal.

In accounting for exchanges of similar assets:
(a) Eliminate the book value of the old asset at the date of the exchange.
(b) Record the acquisition cost of the new asset.
(c) Account for the loss or gain, if any, on the old asset.
    1. If a loss, recognize it immediately.
    2. If a gain, defer and reduce the cost of the new asset.

7. *Identify the basic accounting issues related to natural resources.* The basic accounting issues related to natural resources are whether exploration costs on unsuccessful explorations should be capitalized or expensed. Under the full-cost approach, both successful and unsuccessful explorations are capitalized and the costs amortized to expense over the useful life of the successful wells. The other approach is to capitalize only the costs of successful explorations. This is referred to as the successful efforts approach.

8. *Contrast the accounting for intangible assets with the accounting for plant assets.* The accounting for intangible assets and plant assets is much the same. One difference is that the term used to describe the write-off of an intangible asset is amortization, rather than depreciation. In addition, the amortization of the intangible asset cannot be longer than 40 years. The straight-line method is normally used for amortizing intangible assets.

9. *Indicate how plant assets, natural resources, and intangible assets are reported and analyzed.* Usually plant assets and natural resources are combined under Property, Plant, and Equipment; intangibles are shown separately under Intangible Assets. Either within the balance sheet or in the notes, the balances of the major classes of assets, such as land, buildings, and equipment, and accumulated depreciation by major classes or in total should be disclosed. Also, the depreciation and amortization methods used should be described, and the amount of depreciation and amortization expense for the period should be disclosed. Assets may be analyzed to measure average life, average age, and turnover.

GLOSSARY

Accelerated-depreciation method A depreciation method that produces higher depreciation expense in the early years than in the later years. (p. 429).

Additions and improvements Costs incurred to increase the operating efficiency, productive capacity, or expected useful life of a plant asset. (p. 432).

Amortization The allocation of the cost of an intangible asset to expense. (p. 441).

Capital expenditures Expenditures that increase the company's investment in productive facilities. (p. 432).

Cash equivalent price An amount equal to the fair market value of the asset given up or the fair market value of the asset received, whichever is more clearly determinable. (p. 421).

Copyright An exclusive right granted by the federal government allowing the owner to reproduce and sell an artistic or published work. (p. 442).

Declining-balance method A depreciation method that applies a constant rate to the declining book value of the asset and produces a decreasing annual depreciation expense over the useful life of the asset. (p. 428).

Depletion The process of allocating the cost of a natural resource to expense in a rational and systematic manner over the resource's useful life. (p. 439).

Depreciable cost The cost of a plant asset less its salvage value. (p. 426).

Franchise (license) A contractual arrangement under which the franchisor grants the franchisee the right to sell certain products, to render specific services, or to use certain trademarks or trade names, usually within a designated geographical area. (p. 443).

Full-cost approach Method in which both successful and unsuccessful exploration costs are included in the cost of a natural resource and the costs are written off to expense over the useful life of the successful wells. (p. 438).

Goodwill The value of all favorable attributes that relate to a business enterprise. (p. 443).

Intangible assets Rights, privileges, and competitive advantages that result from the ownership of long-lived assets that do not possess physical substance. (p. 440).

Licenses Operating rights to use public property, granted by a governmental agency to a business enterprise. (p. 443).

Natural resources Assets that consist of standing timber and underground deposits of oil, gas, and minerals. Also called *wasting assets*. (p. 438).

Ordinary repairs Expenditures to maintain the operating efficiency and expected productive life of the unit. (p. 432).

Patent An exclusive right issued by the U.S. Patent Office that enables the recipient to manufacture, sell, or otherwise control an invention for a period of 17 years from the date of the grant. (p. 441).

Plant assets Tangible resources that are used in the operations of the business and are not intended for sale to customers. (p. 420).

Research and development costs Expenditures that may lead to patents, copyrights, new processes, and products. (p. 444).

Revenue expenditures Expenditures that are immediately charged against revenues as an expense. (p. 432).

Straight-line method A method in which periodic depreciation is the same for each year of the asset's useful life. (p. 426).

Successful efforts approach Method in which only the costs of successful exploration are included in the cost of a natural resource. (p. 438).

Trademark (trade name) A word, phrase, jingle, or symbol that distinguishes or identifies a particular enterprise or product. (p. 442).

Units-of-activity method A depreciation method in which useful life is expressed in terms of the total units of production or use expected from the asset. (p. 427).

DEMONSTRATION PROBLEM 1

DuPage Company purchases a factory machine at a cost of $18,000 on January 1, 1996. The machine is expected to have a salvage value of $2,000 at the end of its 4-year useful life.

During its useful life, the machine is expected to be used 160,000 hours. Actual annual hourly use was: Year 1, 40,000; Year 2, 60,000; Year 3, 35,000; and Year 4, 25,000.

Instructions

Prepare depreciation schedules for the following methods: (a) the straight-line, (b) units-of-activity, and (c) declining-balance using double the straight-line rate.

Solution to Demonstration Problem

(a)

Straight-Line Method

Year	Depreciable Cost	×	Depreciation Rate	=	Annual Depreciation Expense	Accumulated Depreciation (End of Year)	Book Value (End of Year)
1996	$16,000		25%		$4,000	$ 4,000	$14,000*
1997	16,000		25%		4,000	8,000	10,000
1998	16,000		25%		4,000	12,000	6,000
1999	16,000		25%		4,000	16,000	2,000

*$18,000 − $4,000.

(b)

Units-of-Activity Method

Year	Units of Activity (Computation)	×	Depreciation Cost/Unit (Computation)	=	Annual Depreciation Expense	Accumulated Depreciation (End of Year)	Book Value (End of Year)
1996	40,000		$.10		$4,000	$ 4,000	$14,000
1997	60,000		.10		6,000	10,000	8,000
1998	35,000		.10		3,500	13,500	4,500
1999	25,000		.10		2,500	16,000	2,000

(c)

Declining-Balance Method

Year	Book Value Beginning of Year	×	Depreciation Rate	=	Annual Depreciation Expense	Accumulated Depreciation (End of Year)	Book Value (End of Year)
1996	$18,000		50%		$9,000	$ 9,000	$9,000
1997	9,000		50%		4,500	13,500	4,500
1998	4,500		50%		2,250	15,750	2,250
1999	2,250		50%		250*	16,000	2,000

*Adjusted to $250 because ending book value should not be less than expected salvage value.

Problem-Solving Strategies

1. Under the straight-line method, the depreciation rate is applied to depreciable cost.

2. Under the units-of-activity method, depreciation cost per unit is computed by dividing depreciable cost by total units of activity.

3. Under the declining-balance method, the depreciation rate is applied to **book value** at the beginning of the year.

DEMONSTRATION PROBLEM 2

On January 1, 1994, the Skyline Limousine Co. purchased a limousine at an acquisition cost of $28,000. The vehicle has been depreciated by the straight-line method using a 4-year service life and a $4,000 salvage value. The company's fiscal year ends on December 31.

Instructions

Prepare the journal entry or entries to record the disposal of the limousine assuming that it was:

(1) Retired and scrapped with no salvage value on January 1, 1998.

(2) Sold for $5,000 on July 1, 1997.

(3) Traded in on a new limousine on January 1, 1997. The fair market value of the old vehicle was $9,000 and $22,000 was paid in cash.

(4) Traded in on a new limousine on January 1, 1997. The fair market value of the old vehicle was $11,000 and $2,000 was paid in cash.

Solution to Demonstration Problem

Problem-Solving Strategies

1. At the time of disposal, determine the book value of the asset.

2. Recognize any gain or loss from disposal of the asset.

3. Remove the book value of the asset from the records by debiting accumulated depreciation for the total depreciation to date of disposal and crediting the asset account for the cost of the asset.

(1)	1/1/98	Accumulated Depreciation—Limousine	24,000	
		Loss on Disposal	4,000	
		Limousine		28,000
		(To record retirement of limousine)		
(2)	7/1/97	Depreciation Expense	3,000	
		Accumulated Depreciation—Limousine		3,000
		(To record depreciation to date of disposal)		
		Cash	5,000	
		Accumulated Depreciation—Limousine	21,000	
		Loss on Disposal	2,000	
		Limousine		28,000
		(To record sale of limousine)		
(3)	1/1/97	Limousine (new)	31,000	
		Accumulated Depreciation—Limousine	18,000	
		Loss on Disposal	1,000	
		Limousine		28,000
		Cash		22,000
		(To record exchange of limousines)		
(4)	1/1/97	Limousine (new)*	12,000	
		Accumulated Depreciation—Limousine (old)	18,000	
		Limousine (old)		28,000
		Cash		2,000
		(To record exchange of limousines)		
		*($11,000 + $2,000 − $1,000)		

SELF-STUDY QUESTIONS

• •

(SO 1)   Answers are at the end of the chapter.

1. Corrieten Company purchased equipment and the following costs were incurred:

Cash price	$24,000
Sales taxes	1,200
Insurance during transit	200
Installation and testing	400
Total costs	$25,800

What amount should be recorded as the cost of the equipment?
a. $24,000.
b. $25,200.
c. $25,400.
d. $25,800.

2. Depreciation is a process of: (SO 2)
a. valuation.
b. cost allocation.
c. cash accumulation.
d. appraisal.

3. Cuso Company purchased equipment on January   (SO 3)
1, 1995, at a total invoice cost of $400,000. The equipment has an estimated salvage value of $10,000 and an estimated useful life of 5 years. The amount of accumulated depreciation at December 31, 1996, if the straight-line method of depreciation is used is:
a. $80,000.
b. $160,000.
c. $78,000.
d. $156,000.

(SO 3) 4. Kant Enterprises purchased a truck for $11,000 on January 1, 1995. The truck will have an estimated salvage value of $1,000 at the end of 5 years. Using the units-of-activity method, the balance in accumulated depreciation at December 31, 1996, can be computed by the following formula:
   a. ($11,000 ÷ Total estimated activity) × Units of activity for 1996.
   b. ($10,000 ÷ Total estimated activity) × Units of activity for 1996.
   c. ($11,000 ÷ Total estimated activity) × Units of activity for 1995 and 1996.
   d. ($10,000 ÷ Total estimated activity) × Units of activity for 1995 and 1996.

(SO 4) 5. When there is a change in estimated depreciation:
   a. previous depreciation should be corrected.
   b. current and future years' depreciation should be revised.
   c. only future years' depreciation should be revised.
   d. None of the above.

(SO 5) 6. Additions are:
   a. revenue expenditures.
   b. debited to a Repair Expense account.
   c. debited to a Purchases account.
   d. capital expenditures.

(SO 6) 7. Schopenhauer Company exchanged an old machine, with a book value of $39,000 and a fair market value of $35,000, and paid $10,000 cash for a similar new machine. At what amount should the machine acquired in the exchange be recorded on the books of Schopenhauer?
   a. $45,000.
   b. $46,000.
   c. $49,000.
   d. $50,000.

(SO 6) 8. In exchanges of similar assets:
   a. neither gains nor losses are recognized immediately.
   b. gains, but not losses, are recognized immediately.
   c. losses, but not gains, are recognized immediately.
   d. both gains and losses are recognized immediately.

(SO 7) 9. Averroes Company expects to extract 20 million tons of coal from a mine that cost $12 million. If no salvage value is expected, and 2 million tons are mined and sold in the first year, the entry to record depletion will include a:
   a. debit to Accumulated Depletion of $2,000,000.
   b. credit to Depletion Expense of $1,200,000.
   c. debit to Depletion Expense of $1,200,000.
   d. credit to Accumulated Depletion of $2,000,000.

(SO 8, 9) 10. Pierce Company incurred $150,000 of research and development costs in its laboratory to develop a patent granted on January 2, 1995. On July 31, 1995, Pierce paid $35,000 for legal fees in a successful defense of the patent. The total amount debited to Patents through July 31, 1995, should be:
   a. $150,000.
   b. $35,000.
   c. $185,000.
   d. some other amount.

(SO 9) 11. Indicate which of the following statements is *true*.
   a. Since intangible assets lack physical substance they need be disclosed only in the notes to the financial statements.
   b. Goodwill should be reported as a contra-account in the Stockholder's Equity section.
   c. Totals of major classes of assets can be shown in the balance sheet, with asset details disclosed in the notes to the financial statements.
   d. Intangible assets are typically combined with plant assets and natural resources and then shown in the Property, Plant, and Equipment section.

QUESTIONS

1. Susan Dey is uncertain about the applicability of the cost principle to plant assets. Explain the principle to Susan.

2. How is cost for a plant asset measured in (a) a cash transaction, and (b) a noncash transaction?

3. Jamie Company acquires the land and building owned by Smitt Company. What types of costs may be incurred to make the asset ready for its intended use if Jamie Company wants to use (a) only the land, and (b) both the land and the building?

4. In a recent newspaper release, the president of Lawsuit Company asserted that something has to be done about depreciation. The president said, "Depreciation does not come close to accumulating the cash needed to replace the asset at the end of its useful life." What is your response to the president?

5. Cecile is studying for the next accounting examination. She asks your help on two questions: (a) What is salvage value? (b) Is salvage value used in determining depreciable cost under each depreciation method? Answer Cecile's questions.

6. Contrast the straight-line method and the units-of-activity method as to (a) useful life, and (b) the pattern of periodic depreciation over useful life.

7. Contrast the effects of the three depreciation methods on annual depreciation expense.

8. In the fourth year of an asset's 5-year useful life, the company decides that the asset will have a 6-year service life. How should the revision of depreciation be recorded? Why?

9. Distinguish between revenue expenditures and capital expenditures during useful life.

10. How is a gain or loss on the sale of a plant asset computed?

11. Ewing Corporation owns a machine that is fully depreciated but is still being used. How should Ewing account for this asset and report it in the financial statements?

12. When similar assets are exchanged, how is the gain or loss on disposal computed?

13. Ice-Master Refrigeration Company trades in an old machine on a new model when the fair market value of the old machine is greater than its book value. Should Ice-Master recognize a gain on disposal? If the fair market value of the old machine is less than its book value, should Ice-Master recognize a loss on disposal?

14. Hakeem Company experienced a gain on disposal when exchanging similar machines. In accordance with generally accepted accounting principles, the gain was not recognized. How will Hakeem's future financial statements be affected by not recognizing the gain?

15. What are natural resources, and what are their distinguishing characteristics?

16. Sandy Shaw and Jo Koehn are arguing about the full-cost approach and the successful efforts approach. Shaw says that the full-cost approach will provide a greater reported asset value, while Koehn says that the successful efforts approach would. Who is correct?

17. What are the similarities and differences between the terms depreciation, depletion, and amortization?

18. Heflin Company hires an accounting intern who says that intangible assets should always be amortized over their legal lives. Is the intern correct? Explain.

19. Goodwill has been defined as the value of all favorable attributes that relate to a business enterprise. What types of attributes could result in goodwill?

20. Bob Leno, a business major, is working on a case problem for one of his classes. In this case problem, the company needs to raise cash to market a new product it developed. Saul Cain, an engineering major, takes one look at the company's balance sheet and says, "This company has an awful lot of goodwill. Why don't you recommend that they sell some of it to raise cash?" How should Bob respond to Saul?

21. Under what conditions is goodwill recorded?

22. Often research and development costs provide companies with benefits that last a number of years. (For example, these costs can lead to the development of a patent that will increase the company's income for many years.) However, generally accepted accounting principles require that such costs be recorded as an expense when incurred. Why?

23. McDonald's Corporation reports total average assets of $14.5 billion and net sales of $9.8 billion. What is McDonald's asset turnover ratio?

BRIEF EXERCISES

Determine the cost of land.
(SO 1)

BE10–1 The following expenditures were incurred by Gene Shumway Company in purchasing land. Cash price $50,000, accrued taxes $3,000, attorneys' fees $2,500, real estate broker's commission, $2,000, and clearing and grading $3,500. What is the cost of the land?

Determine the cost of a truck.
(SO 1)

BE10–2 Shirley Basler Company incurs the following expenditures in purchasing a truck: cash price $18,000, accident insurance $2,000, sales taxes $900, motor vehicle license $100, and painting and lettering $400. What is the cost of the truck?

Compute straight-line depreciation.
(SO 3)

BE10–3 Joy Cunningham Company acquires a delivery truck at a cost of $22,000. The truck is expected to have a salvage value of $2,000 at the end of its 4-year useful life. Compute annual depreciation for the first and second years using the straight-line method.

Compute declining-balance depreciation.
(SO 3)

BE10–4 Depreciation information for Joy Cunningham Company is given in BE10–3. Assuming the declining-balance depreciation rate is double the straight-line rate, compute annual depreciation for the first and second years under the declining-balance method.

Compute depreciation using the units-of-activity method.
(SO 3)

BE10–5 Jerry Englehart Taxi Service uses the units-of-activity method in computing depreciation on its taxicabs. Each cab is expected to be driven 120,000 miles. Taxi No. 10 cost $24,500 and is expected to have a salvage value of $500. Taxi No. 10 is driven 30,000 miles in Year 1 and 20,000 miles in Year 2. Compute the depreciation for each year.

BE10–6 On January 1, 1997, the Asler Company ledger shows Equipment $32,000 and Accumulated Depreciation $12,000. The depreciation resulted from using the straight-line method with a useful life of 10 years and salvage value of $2,000. On this date, the company concludes that the equipment has only a remaining useful life of 4 years with the same salvage value. Compute the revised annual depreciation.

Compute revised depreciation. (SO 4)

BE10–7 Prepare journal entries to record the following:

(a) Ruiz Company retires its delivery equipment, which cost $41,000. Accumulated depreciation is also $41,000 on this delivery equipment. No salvage value is received.

(b) Assume the same information as (a), except that accumulated depreciation for Ruiz Company is $35,000, instead of $41,000.

Disposal by retirement (SO 6)

BE10–8 Wiley Company sells office equipment on September 30, 1996, for $21,000 cash. The office equipment originally cost $72,000 and as of January 1, 1996, had accumulated depreciation of $42,000. Depreciation for the first 9 months of 1996 is $6,250. Prepare the journal entries to (a) update depreciation to September 30, 1996, and (b) record the sale of the equipment.

Disposal by sale (SO 6)

BE10–9 Concord Company exchanges old delivery equipment for similar new delivery equipment. The book value of the old delivery equipment is $31,000 (cost $61,000 less accumulated depreciation $30,000), its fair market value is $19,000, and cash of $3,000 is paid. Prepare the entry to record the exchange.

Disposal by exchange (SO 6)

BE10–10 Assume the same information as BE10–9, except that the fair market value of the old delivery equipment is $42,000. Prepare the entry to record the exchange.

Disposal by exchange (SO 6)

BE10–11 Sunshine Mining Co. purchased for $7 million a mine which is estimated to have 28 million tons of ore and no salvage value. In the first year, 4 million tons of ore are extracted and sold. (a) Prepare the journal entry to record depletion expense for the first year. (b) Show how this mine is reported on the balance sheet at the end of the first year.

Accounting for natural resources (SO 7)

BE10–12 Popper Company purchases a patent for $180,000 on January 2, 1996. Its estimated useful life is 10 years. (a) Prepare the journal entry to record patent expense for the first year. (b) Show how this patent is reported on the balance sheet at the end of the first year.

Accounting for intangibles— patents (SO 8)

BE10–13 Presented below is information related to plant assets, natural resources and intangibles at the end of 1996 for Joker Company: buildings $800,000; accumulated depreciation— buildings $650,000; goodwill $410,000; coal mine $200,000; accumulated depletion—coal mine $108,000. Prepare a partial balance sheet of Joker Company for these items.

Classification of long-lived assets on balance sheet (SO 9)

BE10–14 In its 1995 Annual Report McDonald's Corporation report beginning total assets of $13.6 billion; ending total assets of $15.4 billion; property, plant and equipment (at cost) of $17.1 billion; accumulated depreciation of $4.3 billion; depreciation expense of $620 million; and net sales of $9.8 billion. (a) Compute the average life of McDonald's property, plant, and equipment. (b) Compute the average age of McDonald's property, plant, and equipment. (c) Compute McDonald's asset turnover ratio.

Analysis of long-lived assets. (SO 9)

Exercises

• •

E10–1 The following expenditures relating to plant assets were made by John Kosinski Company during the first 2 months of 1996.

Determine cost of plant acquisitions. (SO 1)

1. Paid $250 to have company name and advertising slogan painted on new delivery truck. *Delivery Expense Equipment*
2. Paid $75 motor vehicle license fee on the new truck. *License Expense*
3. Paid $850 sales taxes on new delivery truck. *Delivery Equip*
4. Paid $17,500 for parking lots and driveways on new plant site. *land improvement*
5. Paid $5,000 of accrued taxes at time plant site was acquired. *land*
6. Paid $8,000 for installation of new factory machinery. *Factory machinery*
7. Paid $900 for one-year accident insurance policy on new delivery truck. *Prepaid Expense Ins.*
8. Paid $200 insurance to cover possible accident loss on new factory machinery while the machinery was in transit. *Factory Machinery*

Instructions

(a) Explain the application of the cost principle in determining the acquisition cost of plant assets.

(b) List the numbers of the foregoing transactions, and opposite each indicate the account title to which each expenditure should be debited.

Determine acquisition costs on land.
(SO 1)

E10–2   On March 1, 1996, Roy Orbis Company acquired real estate, on which they planned to construct a small office building, by paying $100,000 in cash. An old warehouse on the property was razed at a cost of $6,600; the salvaged materials were sold for $1,700. Additional expenditures before construction began included $1,100 attorney's fee for work concerning the land purchase, $4,000 real estate broker's fee, $7,800 architect's fee, and $14,000 to put in driveways and a parking lot.

Instructions

(a) Determine the amount to be reported as the cost of the land.

(b) For each cost not used in part (a), indicate the account to be debited.

Compute depreciation under units-of-activity method.
(SO 3)

E10–3   Interstate Bus Lines uses the units-of-activity method in depreciating its buses. One bus was purchased on January 1, 1996, at a cost of $108,000. Over its 4-year useful life, the bus is expected to be driven 100,000 miles. Salvage value is expected to be $8,000.

Instructions

(a) Compute the depreciation cost per unit.

(b) Prepare a depreciation schedule assuming actual mileage was: 1996, 28,000; 1997, 30,000; 1998, 25,000; and 1999, 17,000.

Determine depreciation for partial periods.
(SO 3)

E10–4   Elvis Costello Company purchased a new machine on October 1, 1996, at a cost of $96,000. The company estimated that the machine will have a salvage value of $12,000. The machine is expected to be used for 84,000 working hours during its 6-year life.

Instructions

Compute the depreciation expense under the following methods for the year indicated: (1) straight-line for 1996, (2) units-of-activity for 1996, assuming machine usage was 1,700 hours, and (3) declining-balance using double the straight-line rate for 1996 and 1997.

Compute revised annual depreciation.
(SO 3, 4)

E10–5   Lindy Weink, the new controller of the Waterloo Company, has reviewed the expected useful lives and salvage values of selected depreciable assets at the beginning of 1996. Her findings are as follows:

Type of Asset	Date Acquired	Cost	Accumulated Depreciation 1/1/96	Useful Life in Years		Salvage Value	
				Old	Proposed	Old	Proposed
Building	1/1/90	$800,000	$114,000	40	45	$40,000	$62,000
Warehouse	1/1/93	100,000	11,400	25	20	5,000	3,600

All assets are depreciated by the straight-line method. Waterloo Company uses a calendar year in preparing annual financial statements. After discussion, management has agreed to accept Lindy's proposed changes.

Instructions

(a) Compute the revised annual depreciation on each asset in 1996. (Show computations.)

(b) Prepare the entry (or entries) to record depreciation on the building in 1996.

Journalize entries for disposal of plant assets.
(SO 6)

E10–6   Presented below are selected transactions at Beck Company for 1996.

Jan. 1   Retired a piece of machinery that was purchased on January 1, 1986. The machine cost $62,000 on that date, and had a useful life of 10 years with no salvage value.

June 30   Sold a computer that was purchased on January 1, 1993. The computer cost $35,000, and had a useful life of 7 years with no salvage value. The computer was sold for $28,000.

Dec. 31   Discarded a delivery truck that was purchased on January 1, 1990. The truck cost $27,000 and was depreciated based on an 8-year useful life with a $3,000 salvage value.

Instructions

Journalize all entries required on the above dates, including entries to update depreciation, where applicable, on assets disposed of. Beck Company uses straight-line depreciation. (Assume depreciation is up to date as of December 31, 1995.)

E10-7 Presented below are two independent transactions:

1. Noyes Co. exchanged trucks (cost $64,000 less $22,000 accumulated depreciation) plus cash of $17,000 for new trucks. The old trucks had a fair market value of $36,000. Prepare the entry to record the exchange of similar assets by Noyes Co.
2. Greg Inc. trades its used accounting machine (cost $12,000 less $4,000 accumulated depreciation) for a new accounting machine. In addition to exchanging the old accounting machine (which had a fair market value of $9,000), Greg also paid cash of $2,000. Prepare the entry to record the exchange of similar assets by Greg Inc.

Journalize entries for exchange of similar assets.
(SO 6)

E10-8 Mueller Company exchanges similar equipment with the Logan Company. Also Evert Company exchanges similar equipment with Flader Company. The following information pertains to these two exchanges:

Journalize entries for the exchange of similar plant assets.
(SO 6)

	Mueller Co.	**Evert Co.**
Equipment (cost)	$28,000	$22,000
Accumulated depreciation	20,000	5,000
Fair market value of equipment	12,000	15,000
Cash paid	3,000	–0–

Instructions

Prepare the journal entries to record the exchange on the books of Mueller Company and Evert Company.

E10-9 Abner's Delivery Company and Wainwright's Express Delivery exchanged similar delivery trucks on January 1, 1996. Abner's truck cost $18,000, had accumulated depreciation of $13,000, and has a fair market value of $3,000. Wainwright's truck cost $10,000, had accumulated depreciation of $8,000, and has a fair market value of $3,000.

Journalize entries for the exchange of similar plant assets.
(SO 6)

Instructions

(a) Journalize the exchange for Abner's Delivery Company.
(b) Journalize the exchange for Wainwright's Express Delivery.

E10-10 On July 1, 1996, Phillips Inc. invested $360,000 in a mine estimated to have 600,000 tons of ore of uniform grade. During the last 6 months of 1996, 100,000 tons of ore were mined and sold.

Journalize entries for natural resources depletion.
(SO 7)

Instructions

(a) Prepare the journal entry to record depletion expense.
(b) Assume that the 100,000 tons of ore were mined, but only 80,000 units were sold. How are the costs applicable to the 20,000 unsold units reported?

E10-11 The following are selected 1996 transactions of Graf Corporation.

Prepare adjusting entries for amortization.
(SO 8)

Jan. 1 Purchased a small company and recorded goodwill of $120,000. The goodwill has a useful life of 55 years.

May 1 Purchased a patent with an estimated useful life of 5 years and a legal life of 17 years for $15,000.

Instructions

Prepare all adjusting entries at December 31 to record amortization required by the events above.

E10-12 Collins Company, organized in 1996, has the following transactions related to intangible assets.

Prepare entries to set up appropriate accounts for different intangibles; amortize intangible assets.
(SO 8)

1/2/96	Purchased patent (7-year life)	$350,000
4/1/96	Goodwill purchased (indefinite life)	360,000
7/1/96	10-year franchise; expiration date 7/1/2006	450,000
9/1/96	Research and development costs	185,000

Instructions

Prepare the necessary entries to record these intangibles. All costs incurred were for cash. Make the entries as of December 31, 1996, recording any necessary amortization and indicating what the balances should be on December 31, 1996.

PROBLEMS

Determine acquisition costs of land and building.
(SO 1)

P10–1   Jay Weiseman Company was organized on January 1. During the first year of operations, the following plant asset expenditures and receipts were recorded in random order.

Debits

1. Cost of real estate purchased as a plant site (land $100,000 and building $25,000)	$125,000
2. Installation cost of fences around property	4,000
3. Cost of demolishing building to make land suitable for construction of new building	13,000
4. Excavation costs for new building	20,000
5. Accrued real estate taxes paid at time of purchase of real estate	2,000
6. Cost of parking lots and driveways	12,000
7. Architect's fees on building plans	10,000
8. Real estate taxes paid for the current year on land	3,000
9. Full payment to building contractor	600,000
	$789,000

Credits

10. Proceeds from salvage of demolished building	$ 2,500

Instructions

Analyze the foregoing transactions using the following tabular arrangement. Insert the number of each transaction in the Item space and insert the amounts in the appropriate columns. For amounts entered in the Other Accounts column also indicate the account title.

Item	Land	Building	Other Accounts

Compute depreciation under different methods.
(SO 3)

P10–2   In recent years, Wind Company has purchased three machines. Because of heavy turnover in the accounting department, a different accountant was in charge of selecting the depreciation method for each machine, and various methods have been selected. Information concerning the machines is summarized below:

Machine	Acquired	Cost	Salvage Value	Useful Life in Years	Depreciation Method
1	1/1/93	$ 86,000	$ 6,000	10	Straight-line
2	1/1/94	100,000	10,000	8	Declining-balance
3	11/1/96	78,000	6,000	6	Units-of-activity

For the declining-balance method, Wind Company uses the double-declining rate. For the units-of-activity method, total machine hours are expected to be 24,000. Actual hours of use in the first 3 years were: 1996, 4,000; 1997, 4,500; and 1998, 5,000.

Instructions

(a) Compute the amount of accumulated depreciation on each machine at December 31, 1996.

(b) If machine 2 was purchased on April 1 instead of January 1, what is the depreciation expense for this machine in (1) 1994 and (2) 1995?

Compute depreciation under different methods.
(SO 3, 4)

P10–3   Keith Whitley Corporation purchased machinery on January 1, 1996, at a cost of $100,000. The estimated useful life of the machinery is 4 years, with an estimated residual value at the end of that period of $10,000. The company is considering different depreciation methods that could be used for financial reporting purposes.

Instructions

(a) Prepare separate depreciation schedules for the machinery using the straight-line method, and the declining-balance method using double the straight-line rate. Round to the nearest dollar.

(b) Which method would result in the higher reported 1996 income? In the highest total reported income over the 4-year period?

(c) Which method would result in the lower reported 1996 income? In the lowest total reported income over the 4-year period?

P10–4 At December 31, 1996, Jerry Hamsmith Corporation reported the following as plant assets:

Land		$ 3,000,000
Buildings	$26,500,000	
Less: Accumulated depreciation—buildings	12,100,000	14,400,000
Equipment	40,000,000	
Less: Accumulated depreciation—equipment	5,000,000	35,000,000
Total plant assets		$52,400,000

Journalize a series of equipment transactions related to purchase, sale, retirement, and depreciation.
(SO 6, 9)

During 1997, the following selected cash transactions occurred:

April 1 Purchased land for $2,200,000.

May 1 Sold equipment that cost $600,000 when purchased on January 1, 1993. The equipment was sold for $350,000.

June 1 Sold land purchased on June 1, 1987 for $1,800,000. The land cost $500,000.

July 1 Purchased equipment for $1,200,000.

Dec. 31 Retired equipment that cost $500,000 when purchased on December 31, 1987. No salvage value was received.

Instructions

(a) Journalize the above transactions. (Hint: You may wish to set up "T" accounts, post beginning balances and then post 1996 transactions.) Hamsmith uses straight-line depreciation for buildings and equipment. The buildings are estimated to have a 40-year useful life and no salvage value; the equipment is estimated to have a 10-year useful life and no salvage value. Update depreciation on assets disposed of at the time of sale or retirement.

(b) Record adjusting entries for depreciation for 1997.

(c) Prepare the plant asset section of Hamsmith's balance sheet at December 31, 1997.

P10–5 Express Co. has delivery equipment that cost $48,000 and that has been depreciated $20,000. Record the disposal under the following assumptions:

(a) It was scrapped as having no value.

(b) It was sold for $31,000.

(c) It was sold for $18,000.

(d) It was exchanged for similar delivery equipment. The old delivery equipment has a fair market value of $12,000 and $32,000 was paid.

(e) It was exchanged for similar delivery equipment. The old delivery equipment has a fair market value of $35,000 and $9,000 was paid.

Journalize a series of transactions related to disposals of plant assets.
(SO 6)

P10–6 The intangible asset section of Roberts Corporation at December 31, 1996, is presented below:

Patent ($60,000 cost less $6,000 amortization)	$54,000
Copyright ($36,000 cost less $14,400 amortization)	21,600
Total	$75,600

Prepare entries to record transactions related to acquisition and amortization of intangibles; prepare the intangible asset section.
(SO 8, 9)

The patent was acquired in January of 1996 and has a useful life of 10 years. The copyright was acquired in January of 1993 and also has a useful life of 10 years. The following cash transactions may have affected intangible assets during 1997:

Jan. 2 Paid $9,000 legal costs to successfully defend the patent against infringement by another company.

Jan.–June   Developed a new product incurring $140,000 in research and development costs. A patent was granted for the product on July 1, and its useful life is equal to its legal life.

Sept. 1   Paid $60,000 to a quarterback to appear in commercials advertising the company's products. The commercials will air in September and October.

Oct. 1   Acquired a copyright for $100,000. The copyright has a useful life of 50 years.

Instructions
(a) Prepare journal entries to record the transactions above.
(b) Prepare journal entries to record the 1997 amortization expense for intangible assets.
(c) Prepare the intangible asset section of the balance sheet at December 31, 1997.
(d) ▭▭▭▶ Prepare the note to the financials on Roberts' intangibles as of December 31, 1997.

Prepare entries to correct errors made in recording and amortizing intangible assets.
(SO 8)

P10–7   Due to rapid turnover in the accounting department, a number of transactions involving intangible assets were improperly recorded by Riley Corporation in 1997.

1. Riley developed a new manufacturing process, incurring research and development costs of $102,000. The company also purchased a patent for $37,400. In early January, Riley capitalized $139,400 as the cost of the patents. Patent amortization expense of $8,200 was recorded based on a 17-year useful life.

2. On July 1, 1997, Riley purchased a small company and as a result acquired goodwill of $60,000. Riley recorded a half-year's amortization in 1997, based on a 50-year life ($600 amortization).

Instructions
Prepare all journal entries necessary to correct any errors made during 1997. Assume the books have not yet been closed for 1997.

ALTERNATE PROBLEMS

Determine acquisition costs of land and building.
(SO 1)

P10–1A   Jule Kadlec Company was organized on January 1. During the first year of operations, the following plant asset expenditures and receipts were recorded in random order.

Debits

1. Cost of real estate purchased as a plant site (land $100,000 and building $45,000)	$145,000
2. Accrued real estate taxes paid at time of purchase of real estate	2,000
3. Cost of demolishing building to make land suitable for construction of new building	12,000
4. Cost of filling and grading the land	4,000
5. Excavation costs for new building	20,000
6. Architect's fees on building plans	10,000
7. Full payment to building contractor	700,000
8. Cost of parking lots and driveways	14,000
9. Real estate taxes paid for the current year on land	5,000
	$912,000

Credits

10. Proceeds for salvage of demolished building	$ 3,500

Instructions
Analyze the foregoing transactions using the following tabular arrangement. Insert the number of each transaction in the Item space and insert the amounts in the appropriate columns. For amounts entered in the Other Accounts column, also indicate the account titles.

Item	Land	Building	Other Accounts

P10–2A In recent years, Rapid Transportation purchased three used buses. Because of frequent turnover in the accounting department, a different accountant selected the depreciation method for each bus, and various methods have been selected. Information concerning the buses is summarized below:

Bus	Acquired	Cost	Salvage Value	Useful Life in Years	Depreciation Method
1	1/1/94	$ 96,000	$ 6,000	5	Straight-line
2	1/1/94	120,000	10,000	4	Declining-balance
3	1/1/95	80,000	8,000	5	Units-of-activity

For the declining balance method, Rapid Transportation uses the double-declining rate. For the units-of-activity method, total miles are expected to be 120,000. Actual miles of use in the first 3 years were: 1995, 24,000; 1996, 34,000; and 1997, 30,000.

Instructions
(a) Compute the amount of accumulated depreciation on each bus at December 31, 1996.
(b) If Bus No. 2 was purchased on April 1 instead of January 1, what is the depreciation expense for this bus in (1) 1994 and (2) 1995?

P10–3A Scott Piper Corporation purchased machinery on January 1, 1996, at a cost of $243,000. The estimated useful life of the machinery is 5 years, with an estimated residual value at the end of that period of $12,000. The company is considering different depreciation methods that could be used for financial reporting purposes.

Instructions
(a) Prepare separate depreciation schedules for the machinery using the straight-line method, and the declining-balance method using double the straight-line rate.
(b) Which method would result in the higher reported 1996 income? In the highest total reported income over the 5-year period?
(c) Which method would result in the lower reported 1996 income? In the lowest total reported income over the 5-year period?

P10–4A At December 31, 1996, Yount Corporation reported the following as plant assets:

Land		$ 4,000,000
Buildings	$28,500,000	
Less: Accumulated depreciation—buildings	12,100,000	16,400,000
Equipment	48,000,000	
Less: Accumulated depreciation—equipment	5,000,000	43,000,000
Total plant assets		$63,400,000

During 1997, the following selected cash transactions occurred:

April 1 Purchased land for $2,630,000.
May 1   Sold equipment that cost $600,000 when purchased on January 1, 1993. The equipment was sold for $370,000.
June 1 Sold land purchased on June 1, 1987, for $1,800,000. The land cost $200,000.
July 1 Purchased equipment for $1,200,000.
Dec. 31 Retired equipment that cost $500,000 when purchased on December 31, 1987. No salvage value was received.

Instructions
(a) Journalize the above transactions. Yount uses straight-line depreciation for buildings and equipment. The buildings are estimated to have a 40-year life and no salvage value; the equipment is estimated to have a 10-year useful life and no salvage value. Update depreciation on assets disposed of at the time of sale or retirement.
(b) Record adjusting entries for depreciation for 1997.
(c) Prepare the plant asset section of Yount's balance sheet at December 31, 1997.

P10–5A Walker Co. has office furniture that cost $80,000 and that has been depreciated $47,000. Record the disposal under the following assumptions:

(a) It was scrapped as having no value.
(b) It was sold for $21,000.

(c) It was sold for $61,000.

(d) It was exchanged for similar office furniture. The old office furniture has a fair market value of $46,000 and $8,000 was paid.

(e) It was exchanged for similar office furniture. The old office furniture has a fair market value of $25,000 and $29,000 was paid.

Prepare entries to record transactions related to acquisition and amortization of intangibles; prepare the intangible asset section.
(SO 8, 9)

P10–6A The intangible asset section of Eikel Company at December 31, 1996, is presented below:

Patent ($70,000 cost less $7,000 amortization)	$63,000
Copyright ($48,000 cost less $19,200 amortization)	28,800
Total	$91,800

The patent was acquired in January of 1996 and has a useful life of 10 years. The copyright was acquired in January of 1993 and also has a useful life of 10 years. The following cash transactions may have affected intangible assets during 1997:

Jan. 2   Paid $9,000 legal costs to successfully defend the patent against infringement by another company.

Jan.–June   Developed a new product incurring $140,000 in research and development costs. A patent was granted for the product on July 1, and its useful life is equal to its legal life.

Sept. 1   Paid $80,000 to an extremely large defensive lineman to appear in commercials advertising the company's products. The commercials will air in September and October.

Oct. 1   Acquired a copyright for $80,000. The copyright has a useful life of 50 years.

Instructions

(a) Prepare journal entries to record the transactions above.

(b) Prepare journal entries to record the 1997 amortization expense.

(c) Prepare the intangible asset section of the balance sheet at December 31, 1997.

Prepare entries to correct for errors made in recording and amortizing intangible assets.
(SO 8)

P10–7A Due to rapid turnover in the accounting department, a number of transactions involving intangible assets were improperly recorded by the Glover Company in 1997.

1. Glover developed a new manufacturing process, incurring research and development costs of $136,000. The company also purchased a patent for $39,100. In early January, Glover capitalized $175,100 as the cost of the patents. Patent amortization expense of $10,300 was recorded based on a 17-year useful life.

2. On July 1, 1997, Glover purchased a small company and as a result acquired goodwill of $76,000. Glover recorded a half-year's amortization in 1997, based on a 50-year life ($760 amortization).

Instructions

Prepare all journal entries necessary to correct any errors made during 1997. Assume the books have not yet been closed for 1997.

▼*B*roadening *Your Perspective*

*F*INANCIAL REPORTING PROBLEM

Refer to the financial statements and the Notes to Consolidated Financial Statements of PepsiCo, Inc. in Appendix A, and answer the following questions:

(a) What was the total cost and book value of property, plant, and equipment at December 30, 1995?

(b) What method or methods of depreciation are used by PepsiCo for financial reporting purposes?

(c) What was the amount of depreciation expense for each of the three years 1993–1995?
(d) Using the Statement of Cash Flows, what is the amount of property, plant, and equipment purchased (capital spending) in 1995 and 1994?
(e) Identify the primary reason why PepsiCo has goodwill and other intangibles.
(f) What was the amortization for goodwill and other intangibles in 1995, and where was it reported in the income statement? Was it more or less than 1994? What useful life was used to amortize goodwill and other intangibles?
(g) What was the amount of research and development expenses PepsiCo incurred in 1995?

COMPARATIVE ANALYSIS PROBLEM— THE COCA-COLA COMPANY VS. PEPSICO, INC.
••

The financial statements of Coca-Cola Company are presented at the end of Chapter 1, and PepsiCo's financial statements are presented in Appendix A.

Instructions
(a) Based on the information contained in thess financial statements, compute the following 1995 ratios for each company:
1. Average life of plant assets. Assume Coca-Cola's 1995 depreciation expense was $421,000,000.
2. Average age of plant assets.
3. Asset turnover ratio.
(b) What conclusions concerning the management of assets can be drawn from these data?

INTERPRETATION OF FINANCIAL STATEMENTS
••

Mini-Case One—Microsoft vs. Oracle
As noted in the chapter, most expenditures for research and development must be expensed. One exception is that computer software companies are allowed to capitalize some software development costs and record them as assets on their books. Any capitalized software costs are then amortized over the life of the software. The implementation of this rule differs across companies, with some capitalizing many costs, while others expense nearly all of their costs. For example, in 1995 Microsoft incurred research and development costs of $860 million, and capitalized none of these costs. Oracle incurred research and development costs of $301 million, and capitalized $48 million during 1995.

The following additional facts are also available for 1995.

(all dollars in millions)	Company Microsoft	Oracle
Total revenue	$5,937	$2,966
Net income	$1,453	$ 442

Instructions
(a) If you are evaluating the performance of Microsoft versus that of Oracle, what implications does their different policy on capitalization of software development expenditures have on your analysis?
(b) Which company spends a greater percentage of its revenue on developing new products? What implications might this have for the future performance of the companies?
(c) SoftKey International Inc., headquartered in Cambridge, Massachusetts, noted in its 1994 report that, beginning in 1994, it changed the estimated life of its computer software for amortization purposes from a 3 year life to a 12 year life. What implications does this have for analysis of Softkey's results?

Mini-Case Two—Merck and Johnson & Johnson

Merck and Co., Inc. and Johnson and Johnson are two leading producers of health care products. Each has considerable assets, as well as expending considerable funds each year toward the development of new products. The development of a new health care product is ofter very expensive, and risky. New products frequently must undergo considerable testing before approval for distribution to the public. For example, it took Johnson and Johnson 4 years and $200 million to develop its 1-DAY ACUVUE contact lenses. Below are some basic data complied from the 1994 financial statements of these two companies.

(all dollars in millions)	Johnson and Johnson	Merck
Total assets	$15,668	$21,857
Total revenue	15,734	14,970
Net income	2,006	2,997
Research and development expense	1,278	1,230
Intangible assets	2,403	7,212

Instructions

(a) What kinds of intangible assets might a health care products company have? Does the composition of these intangible matter to investors—that is, would it be perceived differently if all of Merck's intangibles were goodwill, than if all of its intangibles were patents?

(b) By employing the total asset turnover ratio, determine which company is using its assets more effectively. (Note, 1993 total assets were $19,928 million for Merck and $12,242 million for Johnson and Johnson.)

(c) Suppose the president of Merck has come to you for advice. He has noted that by eliminating research and development expenditures the company could have reported $1.3 billion more in net income in 1994. He is frustrated because much of the research never results in a product, or the products take years to develop. He says shareholders are eager for higher returns, so he is considering eliminating research and development expenditures for at least a couple of years. What would you advise?

(d) The notes to Merck's financial statements note that Merck has goodwill of $4.1 billion. Where does recorded goodwill come from? Is it necessarily a good thing to have a lot of goodwill on your books?

Mini-Case Three—Boeing vs. McDonnell Douglas

Boeing and McDonnell Douglas are two leaders in the manufacture of aircraft. In 1996 Boeing announced intentions to acquire McDonnell Douglas and create one huge corporation. Its competitors, primarily Airbus of Europe, are very concerned that they will not be able to compete with such a huge rival. In addition, customers are concerned that this will reduce the number of suppliers to a point where Boeing will be able to dictate prices. Provided below are figures taken from the 1995 financial statements of Boeing and McDonnell Douglas which allow a comparison of the operations of the two corporations prior to their proposed merger.

(in millions of dollars)	Boeing	McDonnell Douglas
Total revenue	$19,515	$14,322
Net income (loss)	393	(416)
Total assets	22,098	10,466
Land	404	91
Buildings and fixtures	5,791	1,647
Machinery and equipment	7,251	2,161
Total property, plant, and equipment (at cost)	13,744	3,899
Accumulated depreciation	7,288	2,541
Depreciation expense	976	196

Instructions

(a) Which company has older assets?

(b) Which company used a longer average estimated useful life for its assets?

(c) Based on the total asset turnover ratio, which company uses its assets more effectively to generate sales?

(d) Besides an increase in size, what other factors might be motivating this merger?

DECISION CASE

Tammy Company and Hamline Company are two proprietorships that are similar in many respects except that Tammy Company uses the straight-line method and Hamline Company uses the declining-balance method at double the straight-line rate. On January 2, 1994, both companies acquired the following depreciable assets.

Asset	Cost	Salvage Value	Useful Life
Building	$320,000	$20,000	40 years
Equipment	110,000	10,000	10 years

Including the appropriate depreciation charges, annual net income for the companies in the years 1994, 1995, and 1996 and total income for the 3 years were as follows:

	1994	1995	1996	Total
Tammy Company	$84,000	$88,400	$90,000	$262,400
Hamline Company	68,000	76,000	85,000	229,000

At December 31, 1996, the balance sheets of the two companies are similar except that Hamline Company has more cash than Tammy Company.

Dawna Tucci is interested in buying one of the companies, and she comes to you for advice.

Instructions
(a) Determine the annual and total depreciation recorded by each company during the 3 years.
(b) Assuming that Hamline Company also uses the straight-line method of depreciation instead of the declining-balance method as in (a), prepare comparative income data for the 3 years.
(c) Which company should Mrs. Tucci buy? Why?

COMMUNICATION ACTIVITY

The following was published with the financial statements to American Exploration Company:

> **Property, Plant and Equipment**—The Company accounts for its oil and gas exploration and production activities using the successful efforts method of accounting. Under this method, acquisition costs for proved and unproved properties are capitalized when incurred. . . . The costs of drilling exploratory wells are capitalized pending determination of whether each well has discovered proved reserves. If proved reserves are not discovered, such drilling costs are charged to expense. . . . Depletion of the cost of producing oil and gas properties is computed on the units-of-activity method.

Instructions
Write a brief memo to your instructor discussing American Exploration Company's footnote regarding property, plant and equipment. Your memo should address what is meant by the "successful efforts method" and "units-of-activity method."

GROUP ACTIVITY

With the class divided into three groups, each group should be assigned one of the following depreciation methods: straight-line, units-of-activity, declining-balance.

Instructions
(a) Think of an example using the methodology assigned. Calculate depreciation for the first 2 years of useful life.
(b) Present your example to the class. Include necessary journal entries.

ETHICS CASE

Imporia Container Company is suffering declining sales of its principal product, nonbiodegradeable plastic cartons. The president, Benny Benson, instructs his controller, John Straight, to lengthen asset lives to reduce depreciation expense. A processing line of automated plastic extruding equipment, purchased for $2.7 million in January 1996 was originally estimated to have a useful life of 8 years and a salvage value of $300,000. Depreciation has been recorded for 2 years on that basis. Benny wants the estimated life changed to 12 years total, and the straight-line method continued. John is hesitant to make the change, believing it is unethical to increase net income in this manner. Benny says, "Hey, the life is only an estimate, and I've heard that our competition uses a 12-year life on their production equipment."

Instructions
(a) Who are the stakeholders in this situation?
(b) Is the change in asset life unethical or simply a good business practice by an astute president?
(c) What is the effect of Benny Benson's proposed change on income before taxes in the year of change?

RESEARCH ASSIGNMENT

The December 18, 1995 issue of *Forbes* includes an article by Rita Koselka, entitled "Tall Story." Read the article and answer the following questions.

(a) What is the biggest expense in running a video rental store?
(b) Over how long a period does Hollywood Entertainment Corp. depreciate its video tapes? How did the author arrive at this figure?
(c) The author asserts that, once a store is fully stocked, depreciation expense should be approximately equal to the cost of new tapes. Calculate and compare the ratio of depreciation expense to new purchases for Hollywood and Blockbuster.
(d) If Hollywood can open a new store for $400,000 or buy an existing store for $1.2 million, why might investors value Hollywood at an average of $3 million per store?

CRITICAL THINKING
▶ *A Real-World Focus: Clark Equipment Company*

Clark Equipment Company was originally formed in 1902 as a general manufacturing company. During its history it has specialized in the manufacture of drills, gears, towing tractors, and truck transmissions. Today the company operates throughout the U.S. and Europe in the design, manufacture, and sale of skid steer loaders, construction machinery, and transmissions for on-highway trucks and for off-highway equipment. It also is involved in a 50–50 joint venture with Volvo in the manufacture of construction equipment.

The following information relates to the plant assets of Clark Equipment:

	(All amounts in millions)	
	1993	**1994**
Land	$ 7.4	$ 13.2
Land improvements	5.9	8.8
Buildings	77.3	126.0
Machinery and equipment	398.4	451.7
Totals	489.0	599.7
Accumulated depreciation	272.8	315.9
Total plant assets	$216.2	$283.8

Instructions
   (a) What type of costs would Clark Equipment capitalize in the land category of plant assets?
   (b) Cite several possible types of land improvements that Clark Equipment might have made.
   (c) What is the book value of Clark Equipment's plant assets?

_____

Answers to Self-Study Questions
1. d   2. b   3. d   4. d   5. b   6. d   7. a   8. c   9. c   10. b   11. c

• • • • • • ▶

Concepts for Review

UK Builds with Bonds

LEXINGTON, Ky. — Every year, hundreds of college campuses around the country build new buildings. Where do most schools get the money for these expensive projects? From long-term bonds, which are obligations in which the issuer of the bond promises to repay the loan amount plus interest on or before a specified date.

The University of Kentucky (UK) has issued "revenue" bonds to build buildings on the 23,000-student Lexington campus, and on 14 community colleges throughout the state. These bonds pledge the school's revenues as collateral to guarantee payment of the bonds. Recently the outstanding debt on the Lexington campus buildings was $137 million. The total debt on the community college buildings equaled $121 million. The interest rates on the bonds range from 3% (issued in 1970 and guaranteed by a federal program) to 9% (issued in 1983). The bonds generally have maturities ranging from 10 to 20 years.

Additional "guarantees" for bond purchasers are the ratings given the bonds by professional rating agencies. "Our bonds are rated AA − by Standard & Poor's Corp.," says Henry Clay Owen, UK's treasurer. "That's well above investment grade," he says. "We always have a very good market for our bonds. People in Kentucky identify very closely with the university. Even though the bonds are rated AA −, they trade at AAA [the top bond rating] because they're so easy to sell."

One advantage for investors: the bonds are exempt from federal income tax and from state tax for in-state investors. So, an issue offering 6% is the equivalent of 10% to those individuals in the top tax bracket. "I would feel very comfortable buying UK bonds because it's inconceivable to me that there would ever be a default," says Owen. ◄

CHAPTER · 11

*L*IABILITIES

► STUDY OBJECTIVES ◄

After studying this chapter, you should be able to:

1. *Explain a current liability and identify the major types of current liabilities.*
2. *Describe the accounting for notes payable.*
3. *Explain the accounting for other current liabilities.*
4. *Explain why bonds are issued and identify the types of bonds.*
5. *Prepare the entries for the issuance of bonds and interest expense.*
6. *Describe the entries when bonds are redeemed or converted.*
7. *Describe the accounting for long-term notes payable.*
8. *Identify the methods for the financial statement presentation and analysis of long-term liabilities.*

In Chapter 4, we defined liabilities as "creditors' claims on total assets" and as "existing debts and obligations." These claims, debts, and obligations must be settled or paid at some time in the **future** by the transfer of assets or services. The future date on which they are due or payable (maturity date) is a significant feature of liabilities. This "future date" feature gives rise to two basic classifications of liabilities: (1) current liabilities and (2) long-term liabilities. Thus, our discussion of liabilities in this chapter is divided into these two classifications.

The University of Kentucky, as you can tell from our opening story, has chosen to issue long-term bonds to fund its building projects. The University's bonds are classified as *long-term liabilities* because they are obligations that are expected to be paid off more than one year in the future. The content and organization of the chapter are as follows:

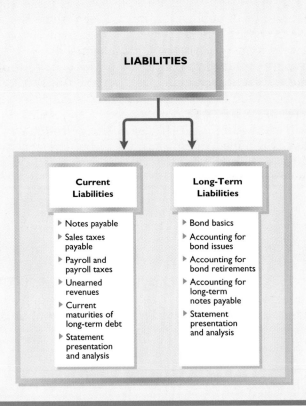

LIABILITIES

Current Liabilities	Long-Term Liabilities
▸ Notes payable	▸ Bond basics
▸ Sales taxes payable	▸ Accounting for bond issues
▸ Payroll and payroll taxes	▸ Accounting for bond retirements
▸ Unearned revenues	▸ Accounting for long-term notes payable
▸ Current maturities of long-term debt	▸ Statement presentation and analysis
▸ Statement presentation and analysis	

▼ **SECTION 1 ► Current Liabilities**

▼ **What Is a Current Liability?**

As explained in Chapter 4, a **current liability** is a debt that can reasonably be expected to be paid (1) from existing current assets or through the creation of other current liabilities, and (2) within one year or the operating cycle, whichever is longer. Debts that do not meet both criteria are classified as long-term liabilities. In most companies, current liabilities are paid within one year out of current assets, rather than through the creation of other liabilities.

Companies must carefully monitor the relationship of current liabilities to current assets. This relationship is critical in evaluating a company's liquidity, or short-term debt paying ability. A company that has more current liabilities than current assets is usually the subject of some concern because the company may not be able to meet its current obligations when they become due.

Current liabilities include notes payable, accounts payable, unearned revenues, and accrued liabilities such as taxes, salaries and wages, and interest payable. The entries for accounts payable and adjusting entries for some current liabilities have been explained in previous chapters. Other types of current liabilities that are frequently encountered in practice are discussed in the following sections.

Helpful hint Assessment of a company's liquidity is important to investors and particularly to creditors. The current liability section gives creditors a good idea of what obligations are coming due.

Notes Payable

Obligations in the form of written promissory notes are recorded as notes payable. Notes payable are often used instead of accounts payable. Doing so gives the lender written documentation of the obligation in case legal remedies are needed to collect the debt. Notes payable usually require the borrower to pay interest and frequently are issued to meet short-term financing needs.

STUDY OBJECTIVE
•••••••••• **2** ••••••••••
Describe the accounting for notes payable.

Notes are issued for varying periods. **Those due for payment within one year of the balance sheet date are usually classified as current liabilities.** Most notes are interest bearing. To illustrate the accounting for notes payable, assume that First National Bank agrees to lend $100,000 on March 1, 1998, if Cole Williams Co. signs a $100,000, 12%, 4-month note. With an interest-bearing promissory note, the amount of assets received upon issuance of the note generally equals the note's face value. Cole Williams Co. therefore will receive $100,000 cash and will make the following journal entry:

Mar. 1	Cash	100,000	
	Notes Payable		100,000
	(To record issuance of 12%, 4-month note to		
	First National Bank)		

Interest accrues over the life of the note and must be recorded periodically. If Cole Williams Co. prepares financial statements semiannually, an adjusting entry is required to recognize interest expense and interest payable of $4,000 ($100,000 × 12% × 4/12) at June 30. The adjusting entry is:

June 30	Interest Expense	4,000	
	Interest Payable		4,000
	(To accrue interest for 4 months on First		
	National Bank note)		

In the June 30 financial statements, the current liability section of the balance sheet will show notes payable $100,000 and interest payable $4,000. In addition, interest expense of $4,000 will be reported under Other Expenses and Losses in the income statement. If Cole Williams Co. prepared financial statements monthly, the adjusting entry at the end of each month would have been $1,000 ($100,000 × 12% × 1/12).

At maturity (July 1), Cole Williams Co. must pay the face value of the note ($100,000) plus $4,000 interest ($100,000 × 12% × 4/12). The entry to record payment of the note and accrued interest is as follows:

July 1	Notes Payable	100,000	
	Interest Payable	4,000	
	Cash		104,000
	(To record payment of First National Bank		
	interest-bearing note and accrued interest at		
	maturity)		

Sales Taxes Payable

STUDY OBJECTIVE
··········▼3··········

*Explain the accounting
for other current
liabilities.*

Helpful hint   Watch how
sales are rung up at local
retailers, to see whether
the sales tax is computed
separately.

As consumers, we are well aware that many of the products we purchase at retail stores are subject to sales taxes. The tax is expressed as a stated percentage of the sales price. The retailer (or selling company) collects the tax from the customer when the sale occurs, and periodically (usually monthly) remits the collections to the state's department of revenue.

Under most state sales tax laws, the amount of the sale and the amount of the sales tax collected must be rung up separately on the cash register. (Gasoline sales are a major exception.) The cash register readings are then used to credit Sales and Sales Taxes Payable. For example, assuming that the March 25 cash register readings for Cooley Grocery show sales of $10,000 and sales taxes of $600 (sales tax rate of 6%), the entry is:

Mar. 25	Cash	10,600	
	Sales		10,000
	Sales Taxes Payable		600
	(To record daily sales and sales taxes)		

When the taxes are remitted to the taxing agency, Sales Taxes Payable is debited and Cash is credited. The company does not report sales taxes as an expense; it simply forwards the amount paid by the customer to the government. Thus, Cooley Grocery serves only as a **collection agent** for the taxing authority.

When sales taxes are not rung up separately on the cash register, total receipts are divided by 100% plus the sales tax percentage to determine sales. To illustrate, assume in the above example that Cooley Grocery "rings up" total receipts, which are $10,600. Because the amount received from the sale is equal to the sales price 100% plus 6% of sales, or 1.06 times the sales total, we can compute sales as follows:

$$\$10,600 \div 1.06 = \$10,000.$$

Thus, the sales tax amount of $600 is found either by (1) subtracting sales from total receipts ($10,600 − $10,000) or (2) multiplying sales by the sales tax rate ($10,000 × 6%).

▸**A**ccounting in **A**ction ▸ *Business Insight*

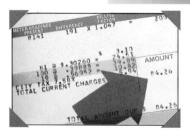

Sales taxes do not apply exclusively to retail companies. They also apply to manufacturing companies, service companies, and public utilities, and the extent of the taxes is increasing. There are now over 9,000 state and local sales taxes. "Compliance is becoming much more complex as states expand their sales taxes," says an American Telephone and Telegraph (AT&T) tax attorney. They are also becoming more costly. AT&T employs 76 people to file the company's sales tax returns each year. They also handle the 200 sales tax audits AT&T is presently undergoing.

Source: Forbes, September 30, 1991.

Payroll and Payroll Taxes Payable

Every employer incurs liabilities relating to employees' salaries and wages. One is the amount of wages and salaries owed to employees—**wages and salaries payable**. Another is the amount required by law to be withheld from employees' gross pay. Until these **withholding taxes** (federal and state income taxes, and social security taxes) are remitted to the governmental taxing authorities, they

are credited to appropriate liability accounts. For example, if a corporation withholds taxes from its employees' wages and salaries, accrual and payment of a
$100,000 payroll would be recorded as follows:

March 7	Salaries and Wages Expense	100,000	
	FICA Taxes Payable[1]		7,250
	Federal Income Taxes Payable		21,864
	State Income Taxes Payable		2,922
	Salaries and Wages Payable		67,964
	(To record payroll and withholding taxes for the week ending March 7)		
	Salaries and Wages Payable	67,964	
	Cash		67,964
	(To record payment of the March 7 payroll)		

Illustration 11-1 summarizes the types of payroll deductions.

Illustration 11-1

Payroll deductions

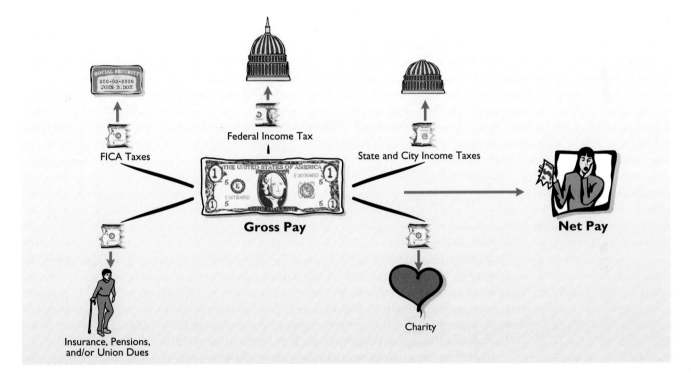

Also, with every payroll, the employer incurs liabilities to pay various **payroll taxes** levied upon the employer. These payroll taxes include the employer's
share of social security taxes and the state and federal unemployment taxes.
Based on the $100,000 payroll in the previous example, the following entry would
be made to record the employer's expense and liability for these payroll taxes.

March 7	Payroll Tax Expense	13,450	
	FICA Taxes Payable		7,250
	Federal Unemployent Taxes Payable		800
	State Unemployment Taxes Payable		5,400
	(To record employer's payroll taxes on March 7 payroll)		

---

[1]Social security taxes are commonly referred to as FICA taxes. In 1937, Congress enacted the Federal
Insurance Contribution Act (FICA). This act and other payroll issues are discussed in greater detail
in Appendix C.

The payroll and payroll tax liability accounts are classified as current liabilities because they must be paid to employees or remitted to taxing authorities periodically and near term. Taxing authorities impose substantial fines and penalties on employers if the withholding and payroll taxes are not computed correctly and paid on time.

Unearned Revenues

A magazine publisher such as Sports Illustrated may receive a customer's check when magazines are ordered, and an airline company, such as American Airlines, often receives cash when it sells tickets for future flights. How do these companies account for unearned revenues that are received before goods are delivered or services are rendered?

1. When the advance is received, Cash is debited, and a current liability account identifying the source of the unearned revenue is credited.
2. When the revenue is earned, the unearned revenue account is debited, and an earned revenue account is credited.

To illustrate, assume that Superior University sells 10,000 season football tickets at $50 each for its five-game home schedule. The entry for the sale of season tickets is:

Aug. 6	Cash	500,000	
	Unearned Football Ticket Revenue		500,000
	(To record sale of 10,000 season tickets)		

As each game is completed, the following entry is made:

Sept. 7	Unearned Football Ticket Revenue	100,000	
	Football Ticket Revenue		100,000
	(To record football ticket revenues earned)		

Unearned Football Ticket Revenue is, therefore, unearned revenue and is reported as a current liability in the balance sheet. As revenue is earned, a transfer from unearned revenue to earned revenue occurs. Unearned revenue is material for some companies: In the airline industry, tickets sold for future flights represent almost 50% of total current liabilities. At United Air Lines, unearned ticket revenue is the largest current liability, recently amounting to over $1 billion.

Illustration 11-2 shows specific unearned and earned revenue accounts used in selected types of businesses.

Illustration 11-2

Unearned and earned revenue accounts

Type of Business	Account Title	
	Unearned Revenue	**Earned Revenue**
Airline	Unearned Passenger Ticket Revenue	Passenger Revenue
Magazine publisher	Unearned Subscription Revenue	Subscription Revenue
Hotel	Unearned Rental Revenue	Rental Revenue

Current Maturities of Long-Term Debt

Companies often have a portion of long-term debt that comes due in the current year. For example, assume that Wendy Construction issues a 5-year interest-bearing $25,000 note on January 1, 1998. This note specifies that each January 1, starting January 1, 1999, $5,000 of the note should be paid. When financial statements are prepared on December 31, 1998, $5,000 should be reported as a current liability and $20,000 as a long-term liability. Current maturities of long-term debt are often identified on the balance sheet as **long-term debt due within one year**.

It is not necessary to prepare an adjusting entry to recognize the current maturity of long-term debt. The proper statement classification of each balance sheet account is recognized when the balance sheet is prepared.

Financial Statement Presentation and Analysis

As indicated in Chapter 4, current liabilities are the first category under liabilities on the balance sheet. Each of the principal types of current liabilities is listed separately within the category. In addition, the terms of notes payable and other pertinent information concerning the individual items are disclosed in the notes to the financial statements.

Current liabilities are seldom listed in the order of maturity because of the varying maturity dates that may exist for specific obligations such as notes payable. A more common, and entirely satisfactory, method of presenting current liabilities is to list them by **order of magnitude**, with the largest obligations first. Many companies, as a matter of custom, show current maturities of long-term debt first, regardless of amount. The following adapted excerpt from a recent balance sheet of NIKE, Inc. illustrates this practice.

Helpful hint For another example of a current liability section refer to the PepsiCo balance sheet in Appendix A.

Illustration 11-3

Balance sheet presentation of current liabilities

NIKE, Inc.
Balance Sheet
May 31, 1994

Assets

Current assets	$1,770,431
Property, plant, and equipment (net)	405,845
Identifiable intangible assets and goodwill	197,539
Total assets	$2,373,815

Liabilities and Stockholders' Equity

Current liabilities	
Current portion of long-term debt	$ 3,857
Notes payable	127,378
Accounts payable	210,576
Accrued liabilities	181,889
Income taxes payable	38,287
Total current liabilities	561,987
Noncurrent liabilities	70,879
Stockholders' equity	1,740,949
Total liabilities and stockholders' equity	$2,373,815

Classifying both assets and liabilities into current and noncurrent allows a company's liquidity to be analyzed and evaluated. Liquidity refers to the ability of a company to pay its maturing obligations and meet unexpected needs for cash. As discussed in Chapter 6, the relationship of current assets and current liabilities is critical in analyzing liquidity. This relationship is expressed as a dollar amount called working capital and as a ratio called the current ratio.

The excess of current assets over current liabilities is **working capital**. The formula for the computation of NIKE's working capital is shown in Illustration 11-4.

Illustration 11-4

Working capital formula and computation

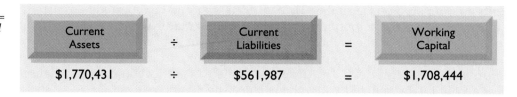

Current Assets	÷	Current Liabilities	=	Working Capital
$1,770,431	÷	$561,987	=	$1,708,444

As an absolute dollar amount, working capital is limited in its informational value. For example $1 million of working capital may be far more than needed for a small company but be inadequate for a large corporation. And, $1 million of working capital may be adequate for a company at one time but be inadequate at another time. The current ratio permits us to compare the liquidity of different sized companies and of a single company at different times. The current ratio is current assets divided by current liabilities. This ratio is expressed graphically below along with its computation using NIKE's current asset and current liability data:

Illustration 11-5

Current ratio and computation

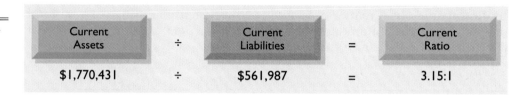

Current Assets	÷	Current Liabilities	=	Current Ratio
$1,770,431	÷	$561,987	=	3.15:1

For many companies a ratio of 2:1 is considered to be the standard for a good credit rating. With a 3.15:1 current ratio, NIKE's liquidity appears to be very favorable.

Before You Go On . . .

▶ ***Review It***

1. What are the two criteria for classifying a debt as a current liability?
2. What entries are made for an interest-bearing note payable?
3. How are sales taxes recorded by a retailer? Identify three unearned revenues.
4. What are the three taxes generally withheld from employees' wages or salaries?
5. How may the liquidity of a company be analyzed?

▶ ***Do It***

You and several classmates are studying for the next accounting examination. They ask you to answer the following questions: (1) How is the sales tax amount determined when the cash register total includes sales taxes? (2) What is the amount of taxes to be withheld from an employee's payroll check?

Reasoning: To answer the first question, you must remove the sales taxes from the total sales. To answer the second question, you need to know the employee's gross pay, the number of exemptions claimed by the employee, the maximum taxable earnings, the employee's accumulated earnings, and the tax rates.

Solution:

(1) First, divide the total proceeds by 100% plus the sales tax percentage to find the sales amount; second, subtract the sales amount from the total proceeds to determine the sales taxes.

(2) The taxable FICA earnings are multiplied by the FICA tax rate. Both the Federal and state income tax withheld are determined by multiplying the applicable tax rate times the amount of current earnings.

Related exercise material: BE11–3, BE11–4, E11–1, E11–2, and E11–3.

SECTION 2 ► *Long-Term Liabilities*

Long-term liabilities are obligations that are expected to be paid after one year. In this section we will explain the accounting for the principal types of obligations reported in the long-term liability section of the balance sheet. These obligations often are in the form of bonds or long-term notes.

Bond Basics

Bonds are a form of interest bearing notes payable issued by corporations, universities, and governmental agencies. Bonds, like common stock, are sold in small denominations (usually a thousand dollars or multiples of a thousand dollars). As a result, bonds attract many investors.

STUDY OBJECTIVE

4

Explain why bonds are issued and identify the types of bonds.

Why Issue Bonds?

A corporation may use long-term financing other than bonds, such as notes payable and leasing. However, these other forms of financing involve one individual, one company, or a financial institution. Notes payable and leasing are therefore seldom sufficient to furnish the funds needed for plant expansion and major projects like new buildings. To obtain **large amounts of long-term capital**, corporate management usually must decide whether to issue bonds or to use equity financing (common stock).

From the standpoint of the corporation seeking long-term financing, bonds offer the following advantages over common stock:

Illustration 11-6

Advantages of bond financing over common stock

Bond Financing	Advantages
	1. **Stockholder control is not affected.** Bondholders do not have voting rights, so current owners (stockholders) retain full control of the company.
	2. **Tax savings result.** Bond interest is deductible for tax purposes; dividends on stock are not.
	3. **Earnings per share on common stock may be higher.** Although bond interest expense reduces net income, earnings per share on common stock often is higher under bond financing because no additional shares of common stock are issued.

To illustrate the potential effect on earnings per share, assume that Microsystems, Inc., is considering two plans for financing the construction of a new $5 million plant: Plan A involves issuance of 200,000 shares of common stock at the current market price of $25 per share. Plan B involves issuance of $5 million, 12% bonds at face value. Income before interest and taxes on the new plant will be $1.5 million; income taxes are expected to be 30%. Microsystems currently has 100,000 shares of common stock outstanding. The alternative effects on earnings per share are shown in Illustration 11-7.

Illustration 11-7

Effects on earnings per share—stocks vs. bonds

Helpful hint Most corporations have both stock and bonds outstanding.

▸ *International note*
The priority of bondholders' versus stockholders' rights varies across countries. In Japan, Germany, and France stockholders and employees are given priority, with liquidation of the firm to pay creditors seen as a last resort. In Britain creditors interests are put first—the courts are quick to give control of the firm to creditors.

	Plan A Issue stock	Plan B Issue bonds
Income before interest and taxes	$1,500,000	$1,500,000
Interest (12% × $5,000,000)	—	600,000
Income before income taxes	1,500,000	900,000
Income tax expense (30%)	450,000	270,000
Net income	$1,050,000	$ 630,000
Outstanding shares	300,000	100,000
Earnings per share	$ 3.50	$ 6.30

Note that net income is $420,000 ($1,050,000 − $630,000) less with long-term debt financing (bonds). However, earnings per share is higher because there are 200,000 fewer shares of common stock outstanding.

The major disadvantages resulting from the use of bonds are that interest must be paid on a periodic basis and the principal (face value) of the bonds must be paid at maturity. A company with fluctuating earnings and a relatively weak cash position may experience great difficulty in meeting interest requirements in periods of low earnings.

▸Accounting in Action ▸ *Business Insight*

Our discussion of long-term liability in this chapter is relatively traditional. However, it is important to understand that we saw in the late 1980s the leveraging (debt financing) of corporate America. A spectacular group of characters invented ways to take over some of the largest and most prestigious companies in America through the use of debt. Names such as Boone Pickens, Ivan Boesky, Michael Milken, and Carl Icahn became familiar to all those involved in high finance. An obscure firm at one time, Kohlberg Kravis Roberts & Co. (KKR) learned the intricacies of leveraged buyouts (in which management or a third party takes over a company, financing it with debt) so well that it now routinely is involved in takeovers of some of the country's largest corporations.

Why the use of debt? The approach is relatively simple—buy a company's stock using debt, sell off assets to pay off the debt, and then after this procedure issue new stock, and, hopefully, reap a bonanza. Consider the example of Beatrice Cos.: KKR bought Beatrice for a premium of approximately 50% over its initial stock price. What KKR saw in Beatrice was a group of well-known brand names—Playtex undergarments, Samsonite luggage, Tropicana orange juice, La Choy Chinese food, and Hunt's catsup. It then sold off some of these companies and then resold the restructured company to the public at a handsome profit. Although this strategy sometimes works, in other cases what has happened is that the acquired company is saddled with an enormous debt load that has been difficult to pay off from operations. Indeed, as a result, the 1990s have found many companies conserving cash in order to pay these interest costs. Unfortunately conserving cash has led to layoffs, dividend reductions, and in some cases massive restructurings.

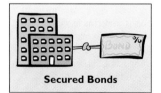

Secured Bonds

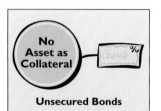

Unsecured Bonds

Types of Bonds

Bonds may have many different features. Some types of bonds commonly issued are described in the following sections:

Secured and Unsecured Bonds

Secured bonds have specific assets of the issuer pledged as collateral for the bonds. A bond secured by real estate, for example, is called a mortgage bond. A bond secured by specific assets set aside to retire the bonds is called a sinking fund bond. Unsecured bonds are issued against the general credit of the borrower. These bonds, called debenture bonds, are used extensively by large corporations with good credit ratings. For example, in a recent annual report, DuPont reported over $2 billion of debenture bonds outstanding.

Term and Serial Bonds

Bonds that are due for payment (mature) at a single specified future date are called term bonds. In contrast, bonds that mature in installments are called serial bonds. For example, Caterpillar Inc. debentures due in 2007 are term bonds, and their debentures due between 1996 and 2007 are serial bonds.

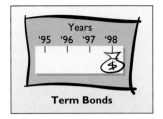

Term Bonds

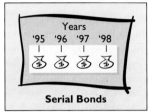

Serial Bonds

Registered and Bearer Bonds

Bonds issued in the name of the owner are called registered bonds; interest payments on registered bonds are made by check to bondholders of record. Bonds not registered are called bearer (or coupon) bonds; holders are required to send in coupons to receive interest payments. Coupon bonds may be transferred directly to another party. In contrast, the transfer of registered bonds requires cancellation of the bonds by the corporation and the issuance of new bonds. With minor exceptions, most bonds issued today are registered bonds.

Registered Bonds

Bearer Bonds

Convertible and Callable Bonds

Bonds that can be converted into common stock at the bondholder's option are called convertible bonds. Bonds subject to retirement at a stated dollar amount prior to maturity at the option of the issuer are known as callable bonds.

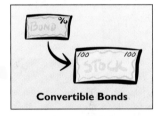

Convertible Bonds

Issuing Procedures

State laws grant corporations the power to issue bonds. Within the corporation, formal approval by both the board of directors and stockholders is usually required before bonds can be issued. **In authorizing the bond issue, the board of directors must stipulate the total number of bonds to be authorized, total face value, and the contractual interest rate**. The total bond authorization often exceeds the number of bonds originally issued. This is done intentionally to help ensure that the corporation will have the flexibility it needs to meet future cash requirements.

The face value is the amount of principal due at the maturity date. The contractual interest rate, often referred to as the **stated rate**, is the rate used to determine the amount of cash interest the borrower pays and the investor receives. Usually the contractual rate is stated as an annual rate, and interest is generally paid semiannually.

The terms of the bond issue are set forth in a legal document called a bond indenture. In addition to the terms, the indenture summarizes the respective rights and privileges of the bondholders and their trustees, as well as the obligations and commitments of the issuing company. The **trustee** (usually a financial institution) keeps records of each bondholder, maintains custody of unissued bonds, and holds conditional title to pledged property.

After the bond indenture is prepared, **bond certificates** are printed. The indenture and the certificate are separate documents. As shown in Illustration 11-8, a bond certificate provides information such as the following: name of the issuer, the face value of the bonds, the contractual interest rate, and the maturity date of the bonds. Bonds are generally sold through an investment company that specializes in selling securities. In most cases, the issue is underwritten by the investment company. Under an underwriting arrangement, the company sells the bonds to the investment company, which, in turn, sells the bonds to individual investors.

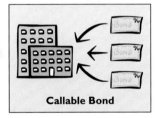

Callable Bond

Helpful hint Do not confuse the terms *indenture* and *debenture*. Indenture refers to the formal bond document (contract). Debenture bonds are unsecured bonds.

Illustration 11-8

Bond certificate

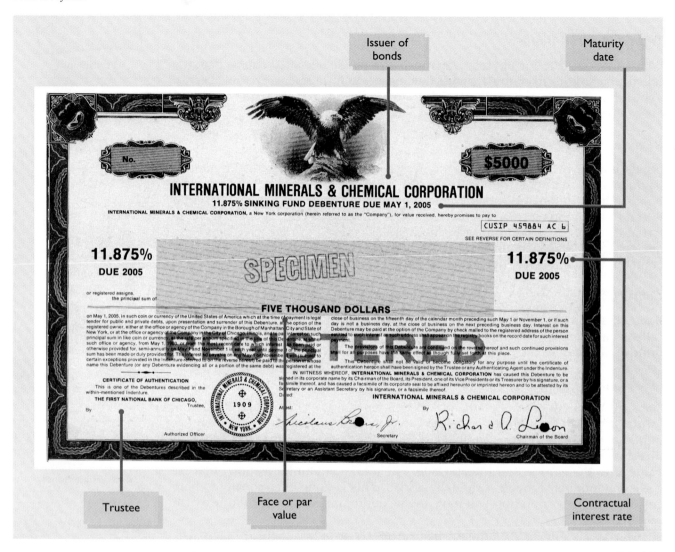

▸**A**ccounting in **A**ction ▸ *Business Insight*

Although bonds are generally secured by solid, substantial assets like land, buildings, and equipment, exceptions occur. For example Trans World Airlines Inc. (TWA) at one time decided to issue $300 million of high-yielding 5-year bonds. TWA's bonds would be secured by a grab bag of assets, including some durable spare parts, but also a lot of disposable items that TWA has in its warehouses, such as light bulbs and gaskets. Some are calling the planned TWA bonds "light bulb bonds." As one financial expert noted: "You've got to admit that some security is better than none." However, another noted, "They're digging pretty far down the barrel."

Source: Wall Street Journal, June 2, 1989.

Bond Trading

Corporate bonds, like capital stock, are traded on national securities markets. Thus, bondholders have the opportunity to convert their holdings into cash at any time by selling the bonds at the current market price.

Bond prices are quoted as a percentage of the face value of the bond, which is usually $1,000. Thus, a $1,000 bond with a quoted price of 97 means that the selling price of the bond is 97% of face value, or $970 in this case. Bond prices and trading activity are published daily in newspapers and the financial press, as illustrated by the following:

Bonds	Current Yield	Volume	Close	Net Change
Kmart 8⅜ 17	8.4	35	100¼	+⅞

Illustration 11-9

Market information for bonds

The information in Illustration 11-9 indicates that Kmart Corporation has outstanding 8⅜%, $1,000 bonds maturing in 2017 and currently yielding an 8.4% return. In addition, 35 bonds were traded on this day; and at the close of trading, the price was 100¼% of face value, or $1,002.50. The net change column indicates the difference between the day's closing price and the previous day's closing price.

Transactions between a bondholder and other investors **are not journalized by the issuing corporation**. If Tom Smith sells bonds that are bought by Faith Jones, the issuing corporation does not journalize the transaction (although it does keep records of the names of bondholders in the case of registered bonds). A corporation makes journal entries only when it issues or buys back bonds, and when bondholders convert bonds into common stock.

Determining the Market Value of Bonds

If you were an investor interested in purchasing a bond, how would you determine how much to pay? To be more specific, assume that Coronet, Inc., issues a zero-interest bond (pays no interest) with a face value of $1,000,000 due in 20 years. For this bond, the only cash you receive is a million dollars at the end of 20 years. Would you pay a million dollars for this bond? We hope not, because a million dollars received 20 years from now is not the same as a million dollars received today. The reason you would not pay a million dollars relates to what is called the **time value of money**. If you had a million dollars today, you would invest it and earn interest such that at the end of 20 years, your investment would be worth much more than a million dollars. Thus, if someone is going to pay you a million dollars 20 years from now, you would want to find its equivalent today, or its **present value**. In other words, you would want to determine how much must be invested today at current interest rates to have a million dollars in 20 years.

The market value (present value) of a bond is, therefore, a function of three factors: (1) the dollar amounts to be received, (2) the length of time until the amounts are received, and (3) the market rate of interest. The market interest rate is the rate investors demand for loaning funds to the corporation. The process of finding the present value is referred to as **discounting** the future amounts.

To illustrate, assume that Acropolis Company on January 1, 1998, issues $100,000 of 9% bonds, due in 5 years, with interest payable annually at year-end. The purchaser of the bonds would receive the following two cash payments: (1) **principal** $100,000 to be paid at maturity, and (2) five $9,000 **interest pay-**

Same dollars at different times are not equal.

Helpful hint The face value of most marketable bonds is $1,000, but it can be any value, such as $100 or $5,000 or $10,000.

ments ($100,000 × 9%) over the term of the bonds. The time diagram depicting both cash flows is shown below:

Illustration 11-10

Time diagram depicting cash flows

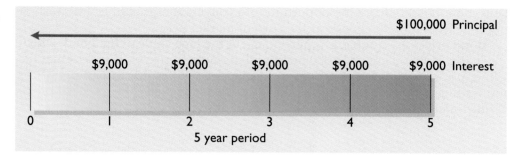

The present values of these amounts are as shown in Illustration 11-11.

Illustration 11-11

Computing the market price of bonds

Present value of $100,000 received in 5 years	$ 64,993
Present value of $9,000 received annually for 5 years	35,007
Market price of bonds	$100,000

Helpful hint The market value of a bond is equal to the present value of all the future cash payments promised by the bond.

Tables are available to provide the present value numbers to be used, or these values can be determined mathematically.[2] Further discussion of the concepts and the mechanics of the time value of money computations is provided in Appendix B near the end of the book.

Before You Go On . . .

▸ Review It

1. What are the advantages of bond versus stock financing?
2. What are secured versus unsecured bonds, term versus serial bonds, registered versus bearer bonds, and callable versus convertible bonds?
3. Explain the terms face value, contractual interest rate, and bond indenture.
4. Explain why you would prefer to receive $1 million today rather than 5 years from now.

Accounting for Bond Issues

Bonds may be issued at face value, below face value (discount), or above face value (premium). They also are sometimes issued between interest dates.

Issuing Bonds at Face Value

STUDY OBJECTIVE
· · · · · · · · · 5 · · · · · · · · · ·

Prepare the entries for the issuance of bonds and interest expense.

To illustrate the accounting for bonds, assume that Devor Corporation issues 1,000, 10-year, 9%, $1,000 bonds dated January 1, 1998, at 100 (100% of face value). The entry to record the sale is:

Jan. 1	Cash	1,000,000	
	Bonds Payable		1,000,000
	(To record sale of bonds at face value)		

---

[2]For those knowledgeable in the use of present value tables, the computations in this example are: $100,000 × .64993 = $64,993 and $9,000 × 3.88965 = $35,007 (rounded).

Bonds payable are reported in the long-term liability section of the balance sheet because the maturity date is January 1, 2008 (more than one year away).

Over the term (life) of the bonds, entries are required for bond interest. Interest on bonds payable is computed in the same manner as interest on notes payable, as explained on page 469. Assuming that interest is payable semiannually on January 1 and July 1 on the bonds described above, interest of $45,000 ($1,000,000 × 9% × 6/12) must be paid on July 1, 1998. The entry for the payment, assuming no previous accrual of interest, is:

July 1	Bond Interest Expense	45,000	
	Cash		45,000
	(To record payment of bond interest)		

At December 31, an adjusting entry is required to recognize the $45,000 of interest expense incurred since July 1. The entry is:

Dec. 31	Bond Interest Expense	45,000	
	Bond Interest Payable		45,000
	(To accrue bond interest)		

Bond interest payable is classified as a current liability, because it is scheduled for payment within the next year. When the interest is paid on January 1, 1999, Bond Interest Payable is debited and Cash is credited for $45,000.

Discount or Premium on Bonds

The previous illustrations assumed that the interest rate paid on bonds, often referred to as the contractual (stated) interest rate and the market (effective) interest rate were the same. The contractual interest rate is the rate applied to the face (par) value to arrive at the interest paid in a year. The market interest rate is the rate investors demand for loaning funds to the corporation. When the contractual interest rate and the market interest rate are the same, bonds sell at face value.

However, market interest rates change daily. They are influenced by the type of bond issued, the state of the economy, current industry conditions and the company's individual performance. As a result, the contractual and market interest rates often differ and therefore bonds sell below or above face value.

To illustrate, suppose that investors have one of two options: purchase bonds that have a market rate of interest of 10% or purchase bonds that have a contractual rate of interest of 8%. Assuming that the bonds are of equal risk, investors will select the 10% investment. To make the investments equal, investors will demand a rate of interest higher than the contractual interest rate on the 8% bonds. Because investors cannot change the contractual interest rate, they will pay less than the face value for the bonds. By paying less for the bonds, they can obtain the market rate of interest. In these cases, **bonds sell at a discount**.

Conversely, if the market rate of interest is **lower** than the contractual interest rate, investors will have to pay more than face value for the bonds. That is, if the market rate of interest is 8%, but the contractual interest rate is 9%, the issuer will require more funds from the investor. In these cases, **bonds sell at a premium**. These relationships are shown graphically in Illustration 11-12.

Issuance of bonds at an amount different from face value is quite common. By the time a company prints the bond certificates and markets the bonds, it will be a coincidence if the market rate and the contractual rate are the same. Thus, the issuance of bonds at a discount does not mean that the financial strength of the issuer is suspect. Conversely, the sale of bonds at a premium does not indicate that the financial strength of the issuer is exceptional.

► *International note*
The use of debt financing varies considerably across countries. The amount of debt borrowed by governments can affect a country's ability to borrow funds. One measure of the degree of debt financing is the ratio of national debt to gross national product. In a 1995 survey, this ratio was 49.7%, 13%, 106.2%, and 17.1% in the U.S., Australia, Belgium, and Brazil, respectively.

Helpful hint Bond prices vary inversely with changes in the market interest rate. As market interest rate declines, bond prices will increase. When a bond is issued, if the market interest rate is below the contractual rate, the price will be higher than the face value. In the Candlestick example on the next page, the market rate is greater than the 10% and therefore the bonds sell at a discount.

Illustration 11-12

Interest rates and bond prices

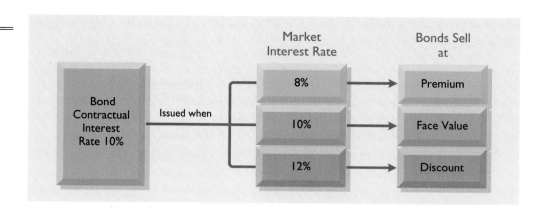

Issuing Bonds at a Discount

To illustrate the issuance of bonds at a discount, assume that on January 1, 1998, Candlestick, Inc. sells $1 million, 5-year, 10% bonds at 98 (98% of face value) with interest payable on July 1 and January 1. The entry to record the issuance is:

Jan. 1	Cash	980,000	
	Discount on Bonds Payable	20,000	
	Bonds Payable		1,000,000
	(To record sale of bonds at a discount)		

Although Discount on Bonds Payable has a debit balance, **it is not an asset.** Rather it is a **contra account,** which is **deducted from bonds payable** on the balance sheet, as illustrated below:

Illustration 11-13

Statement presentation of discount on bonds payable

Long-term liabilities		
Bonds payable	$1,000,000	
Less: Discount on bonds payable	20,000	$980,000

Helpful hint Carrying value (book value) of bonds issued at a discount is determined by subtracting the balance of the discount account from the balance of the Bonds Payable account.

The $980,000 represents the **carrying (or book) value** of the bonds. On the date of issue this amount equals the market price of the bonds.

    The issuance of bonds below face value causes the total cost of borrowing to differ from the bond interest paid. That is, at maturity the issuing corporation must pay not only the contractual interest rate over the term of the bonds, but also the face value (rather than the issuance price). Therefore, the difference between the issuance price and face value of the bonds—the discount—is an **additional cost of borrowing that should be recorded as bond interest expense over the life of the bonds.** The total cost of borrowing $980,000 for Candlestick, Inc., is $520,000, computed as follows:

Illustration 11-14

Total cost of borrowing— bonds issued at discount

Bonds Issued at a Discount	
Semiannual interest payments	
($1,000,000 × 10% × ½ = $50,000; $50,000 × 10)	$500,000
Add: Bond discount ($1,000,000 − $980,000)	20,000
Total cost of borrowing	$520,000

Alternatively, the total cost of borrowing can be determined as follows:

Illustration 11-15

Alternative computation of total cost of borrowing— bonds issued at discount

Bonds Issued at a Discount	
Principal at maturity	$1,000,000
Semiannual interest payments ($50,000 × 10)	500,000
Cash to be paid to bondholders	1,500,000
Cash received from bondholders	980,000
Total cost of borrowing	$ 520,000

Amortizing Bond Discount

To comply with the matching principle, it follows that bond discount should be allocated systematically to each accounting period benefiting from the use of the cash proceeds.

One method, the straight-line method of amortization, allocates the same amount to interest expense in each interest period.[3] The amount is determined as shown in Illustration 11-16:

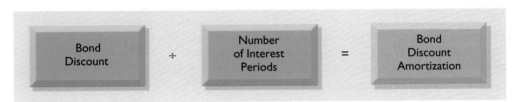

Illustration 11-16

Formula for straight-line method of bond discount amortization

In this example, the bond discount amortization is $2,000 ($20,000 ÷ 10). The entry to record the payment of bond interest and the amortization of bond discount on the first interest date (July 1, 1998) is:

July 1	Bond Interest Expense	52,000	
	Discount on Bonds Payable		2,000
	Cash		50,000
	(To record payment of bond interest and amortization of bond discount)		

At December 31, the adjusting entry is:

Dec. 31	Bond Interest Expense	52,000	
	Discount on Bonds Payable		2,000
	Bond Interest Payable		50,000
	(To record accrued bond interest and amortization of bond discount)		

Helpful hint Note the effects of this entry: expenses increase (which reduces net income and owners' equity) by $52,000, assets decrease by $50,000, and liabilities increase by $2,000 (because the balance in the contra account decreases).

Over the term of the bonds, the balance in Discount on Bonds Payable will decrease annually by the same amount until it has a zero balance at the maturity date of the bonds. Thus, the carrying value of the bonds at maturity will be equal to the face value of the bonds.

Helpful hint The amount in the Discount on Bonds Payable account is often referred to as Unamortized Discount on Bonds Payable.

---

[3]Another method, the effective-interest method, is discussed in the appendix at the end of this chapter.

Preparing a bond discount amortization schedule as shown in Illustration 11-17 is useful to determine interest expense, discount amortization and the carrying value of the bond. As indicated, the interest expense recorded each period is $52,000. Also note that the carrying value of the bond increases $2,000 each period until it reaches its face value $1,000,000 at the end of period 10.

Illustration 11-17

Bond discount amortization schedule

Semiannual Interest Periods	(A) Interest to Be Paid (5% × $1,000,000)	(B) Interest Expense to Be Recorded (A) + (C)	(C) Discount Amortization ($20,000 ÷ 10)	(D) Unamortized Discount (D) − (C)	(E) Bond Carrying Value ($1,000,000 − D)
Issue date				$20,000	$ 980,000
1	$ 50,000	$ 52,000	$ 2,000	18,000	982,000
2	50,000	52,000	2,000	16,000	984,000
3	50,000	52,000	2,000	14,000	986,000
4	50,000	52,000	2,000	12,000	988,000
5	50,000	52,000	2,000	10,000	990,000
6	50,000	52,000	2,000	8,000	992,000
7	50,000	52,000	2,000	6,000	994,000
8	50,000	52,000	2,000	4,000	996,000
9	50,000	52,000	2,000	2,000	998,000
10	50,000	52,000	2,000	–0–	1,000,000
	$500,000	$520,000	$20,000		

Column (A) remains constant because the face value of the bonds ($1,000,000) is multiplied by the semiannual contractual interest rate (5%) each period.

Column (B) is computed as the interest paid (Column A) plus the discount amortization (Column C).

Column (C) indicates the discount amortization each period.

Column (D) decreases each period by the same amount until it reaches zero at maturity.

Column (E) increases each period by the amount of discount amortization until it equals the face value at maturity.

Helpful hint Both a discount and a premium account are valuation accounts. A valuation account is one that is needed to value properly the item to which it relates. A discount account is a contra-type valuation account (its balance is deducted from Bonds Payable), whereas a premium account is an adjunct-type valuation account (its balance is added to the balance of Bonds Payable).

Issuing Bonds at a Premium

The issuance of bonds at a premium can be illustrated by assuming the Candlestick, Inc. bonds described above are sold at 102 (102% of face value) rather than at 98.

The entry to record the sale is:

Jan. 1	Cash	1,020,000	
	Bonds Payable		1,000,000
	Premium on Bonds Payable		20,000
	(To record sale of bonds at a premium)		

Premium on bonds payable is **added to bonds payable** on the balance sheet, as shown below:

Illustration 11-18

Statement presentation of bond premium

Long-term liabilities

| Bonds payable | $1,000,000 | |
| Add: Premium on bonds payable | 20,000 | $1,020,000 |

The sale of bonds above face value causes the total cost of borrowing to be **less than the bond interest paid**, because the borrower is not required to pay the bond premium at the maturity date of the bonds. Thus, the premium is considered to be **a reduction in the cost of borrowing** that should be credited to Bond Interest Expense over the life of the bonds. The total cost of borrowing $1,020,000 for Candlestick, Inc., is $480,000, computed as follows:

Illustration 11-19

Total cost of borrowing— bonds issued at a premium

Bonds Issued at a Premium	
Semiannual interest payments ($1,000,000 × 10% × ½ = $50,000; $50,000 × 10)	$500,000
Less: Bond premium ($1,020,000 − $1,000,000)	20,000
Total cost of borrowing	$480,000

Alternatively, the cost of borrowing can be computed as follows:

Illustration 11-20

Alternative computation of total cost of borrowing— bonds issued at a premium

Bonds Issued at a Premium	
Principal at maturity	$1,000,000
Semiannual interest payments ($50,000 × 10)	500,000
Cash to be paid to bondholders	1,500,000
Cash received from bondholders	1,020,000
Total cost of borrowing	$ 480,000

Amortizing Bond Premium

The formula for determining bond premium amortization under the straight-line method is: bond premium divided by the number of interest periods. Thus, the premium amortization for each interest period is $2,000 ($20,000 ÷ 10). The entry to record the first payment of interest on July 1 is:

July 1	Bond Interest Expense	48,000	
	Premium on Bonds Payable	2,000	
	Cash		50,000
	(To record payment of bond interest and amortization of bond premium)		

At December 31, the adjusting entry is:

Dec. 31	Bond Interest Expense	48,000	
	Premium on Bonds Payable	2,000	
	Bond Interest Payable		50,000
	(To record accrued bond interest and amortization of bond premium)		

Helpful hint What are the effects of this entry? Answer: Total expenses increase $48,000 (so net income and owners' equity decrease), assets decrease $50,000, and total liabilities decrease $2,000 (because of the reduction in the premium account balance).

Over the term of the bonds, the balance in Premium on Bonds Payable will decrease annually by the same amount until it has a zero balance at maturity.

Preparing a bond premium amortization schedule as shown in Illustration 11-21 is useful to determine interest expense, premium amortized, and the carrying value of the bond. As indicated, the interest expense recorded each period is $48,000. Also note that the carrying value of the bond decreases $2,000 each period until it reaches its face value $1,000,000 at the end of period 10.

Illustration 11-21

Bond premium amortization schedule

Semiannual Interest Periods	(A) Interest to Be Paid (5% × $1,000,000)	(B) Interest Expense to Be Recorded (A) − (C)	(C) Premium Amortization ($20,000 ÷ 10)	(D) Unamortized Premium (D) − (C)	(E) Bond Carrying Value ($1,000,000 + D)
Issue date				$20,000	$1,020,000
1	$ 50,000	$ 48,000	$ 2,000	18,000	1,018,000
2	50,000	48,000	2,000	16,000	1,016,000
3	50,000	48,000	2,000	14,000	1,014,000
4	50,000	48,000	2,000	12,000	1,012,000
5	50,000	48,000	2,000	10,000	1,010,000
6	50,000	48,000	2,000	8,000	1,008,000
7	50,000	48,000	2,000	6,000	1,006,000
8	50,000	48,000	2,000	4,000	1,004,000
9	50,000	48,000	2,000	2,000	1,002,000
10	50,000	48,000	2,000	–0–	1,000,000
	$500,000	$480,000	$20,000		

Column (A) remains constant because the face value of the bonds ($1,000,000) is multiplied by the semiannual contractual interest rate (5%) each period.

Column (B) is computed as the interest paid (Column A) less the premium amortization (Column C).

Column (C) indicates the premium amortization each period.

Column (D) decreases each period by the same amount until it reaches zero at maturity.

Column (E) decreases each period by the amount of premium amortization until it equals the face value at maturity.

Issuing Bonds between Interest Dates

Bonds are often issued between interest payment dates. **When this occurs, the issuer requires the investor to pay the market price for the bonds plus accrued interest since the last interest date.** At the next interest date, the corporation will return the accrued interest to the investor by paying the full amount of interest due on outstanding bonds.

To illustrate, assume that Deer Corporation sells $1,000,000, 9% bonds at face value plus accrued interest on March 1. Interest is payable semiannually on July 1 and January 1. The accrued interest is $15,000 ($1,000,000 × 9% × 2/12). The total proceeds on the sale of the bonds, therefore, are $1,015,000, and the entry to record the sale is:

Mar. 1	Cash	1,015,000	
	Bonds Payable		1,000,000
	Bond Interest Payable		15,000
	(To record sale of bonds at face value plus accrued interest)		

At the first interest date, it is necessary to eliminate the bond interest payable balance and to recognize interest expense for the 4 months (March 1–June 30) the bonds have been outstanding. Interest expense in this example is, therefore, $30,000 ($1,000,000 × 9% × 4/12). The entry on July 1 for the $45,000 interest payment is:

July 1	Bond Interest Payable	15,000	
	Bond Interest Expense	30,000	
	Cash		45,000
	(To record payment of bond interest)		

Why does Deer Corporation collect interest at the time of issuance and then return this interest at the time of payment? The rationale: Collection of accrued interest at the issuance date allows the company to pay a full period's interest to all bondholders at the next interest payment date. Deer Corporation does not have to determine the individual amount of interest due each holder based on the time each bond has been outstanding during the interest period.

In other words, if bonds are not sold "with accrued interest," Deer Corporation would have to keep track of the purchaser and the dates that the bonds were purchased. This procedure would be necessary to ensure that each bondholder received the correct amount of interest. By selling the bonds "with accrued interest," Deer does not have to maintain detailed records and cost savings occur.

Before You Go On . . .

► Review It

1. What entry is made to record the issuance of bonds payable of $1 million at 100? at 96? at 102?
2. Why do bonds sell at a discount? at a premium? at face value?
3. Explain the accounting for bonds sold between interest dates.

► Do It

A bond amortization table shows (a) interest to be paid $50,000, (b) interest expense to be recorded $52,000, and (c) amortization $2,000. Answer the following questions: (1) Were the bonds sold at a premium or a discount? (2) After recording the interest expense, will the bond carrying value increase or decrease?

Reasoning: To answer the questions you need to know the effects that the amortization of bond discount and bond premium have on bond interest expense and on the carrying value of the bonds. Bond discount amortization increases both bond interest expense and the carrying value of the bonds. Bond premium amortization has the reverse effect.

Solution: The bond amortization table indicates that interest expense is $2,000 greater than the interest paid. This difference is equal to the amortization amount. Thus, the bonds were sold at a discount. The interest entry will decrease Discount on Bonds Payable and increase the carrying value of the bonds.

Related exercise material: BE11–6, BE11–7, BE11–8, BE11–9, E11–5, E11–6, E11–7, and E11–8.

Accounting for Bond Retirements

Bonds may be retired either when they are purchased (redeemed) by the issuing corporation or when they are converted into common stock by bondholders. The appropriate entries for these transactions are explained in the following sections.

Redeeming Bonds at Maturity

Regardless of the issue price of bonds, the book value of the bonds at maturity will equal their face value. This can be seen in Illustrations 11-17 and 11-21 where the carrying value of the bonds at the end of their 10-year life ($1 million) is equal to the face value of the bonds.

STUDY OBJECTIVE 6

Describe the entries when bonds are redeemed or converted.

Assuming that the interest for the last interest period is paid and recorded separately, the entry to record the redemption of the Candlestick bonds at maturity is:

Bonds Payable	1,000,000	
Cash		1,000,000
(To record redemption of bonds at maturity)		

Redeeming Bonds before Maturity

Helpful hint Question: If a bond is redeemed prior to its maturity date and its carrying value exceeds its redemption price, will the retirement result in a gain or a loss on redemption? Answer: Gain.

Bonds may be redeemed before maturity. A company may decide to retire bonds before maturity to reduce interest cost and remove debt from its balance sheet. A company should retire debt early only if it has sufficient cash resources. When bonds are retired before maturity, it is necessary to: (1) eliminate the carrying value of the bonds at the redemption date, (2) record the cash paid, and (3) recognize the gain or loss on redemption. The carrying value of the bonds is the face value of the bonds less unamortized bond discount or plus unamortized bond premium at the redemption date.

To illustrate, assume at the end of the eighth period Candlestick, Inc. (having sold its bonds at a premium, per Illustration 11-21) retires its bonds at 103 after paying the semiannual interest. The carrying value of the bonds at the redemption date, as shown in the bond premium amortization schedule, is $1,004,000. The entry to record the redemption at the end of the eighth interest period (January 1, 2002) is:

Jan. 1	Bonds Payable	1,000,000	
	Premium on Bonds Payable	4,000	
	Loss on Bond Redemption	26,000	
	Cash		1,030,000
	(To record redemption of bonds at 103)		

Note that the loss of $26,000 is the difference between the cash paid of $1,030,000 and the carrying value of the bonds of $1,004,000. Losses (gains) on bond redemption are reported in the income statement as extraordinary items as required by the accounting profession.

Converting Bonds into Common Stock

Convertible bonds have features that are attractive both to bondholders and to the issuer. The conversion often gives bondholders an opportunity to benefit if the market price of the common stock increases substantially. Furthermore, until conversion, the bondholder receives interest on the bond. For the issuer, the bonds sell at a higher price and pay a lower rate of interest than comparable debt securities that do not have a conversion option. Many corporations, such as USAir, USX Corp., and Chrysler Corporation, have convertible bonds outstanding.

Helpful hint The method of recording this conversion of bonds to stock is called the *book value method* because the amount of the book value of the bonds is removed from the liability accounts and recorded as common stock and related paid-in capital.

When bonds are converted into common stocks and the conversion is recorded, the current market prices of the bonds and the stock are ignored. Instead, the **carrying value** of the bonds is transferred to paid-in capital accounts, and **no gain or loss is recognized**. To illustrate, assume that on July 1 Saunders Associates converts $100,000 bonds sold at face value into 2,000 shares of $10 par value common stock. Both the bonds and the common stock have a market value of $130,000. The entry to record the conversion is:

July 1	Bonds Payable	100,000	
	Common Stock		20,000
	Paid-in Capital in Excess of Par Value		80,000
	(To record bond conversion)		

Note that the current market price of the bonds and stocks ($130,000) is not considered in making the entry. This method of recording the bond conversion is often referred to as the **carrying (or book) value method**.

►Accounting in Action ► *International Insight*

 Now that you have read about bonds, you may be beginning to realize how significant bond financing can be. A dramatic example of bond financing—which literally changed the course of history—is seen in Britain's struggle for supremacy in the eighteenth and nineteenth centuries. With only a fraction of the population and wealth of France, Britain ultimately humbled its mightier foe through the use of bonds. Because of its effective central bank and a fair system of collecting taxes, Britain developed the capital markets that enabled its government to issue bonds. Britain was able to borrow money at almost half the cost paid by France, and was able to incur more debt as a proportion of the economy than could France. Britain thus could more than match the French navy, raise an army of its own, and lavishly subsidize other armies, eventually destroying Napoleon and his threat to Europe.

Source: "How British Bonds Beat Back Bigger France," *Forbes*, March 13, 1995.

Before You Go On . . .

► *Review It*

1. Explain the accounting for redemption of bonds at maturity and before maturity by payment in cash.
2. How is the conversion of bonds into common stock accounted for?

► *Do It*

R & B Inc. issued $500,000, 10-year bonds at a premium. Prior to maturity, when the carrying value of the bonds is $508,000, the company retires the bonds at 102. Prepare the entry to record the redemption of the bonds.

Reasoning: In recording the redemption of bonds before maturity, it is necessary to (1) eliminate the carrying value of the bonds, (2) recognize the cash paid, and (3) recognize the gain or loss equal to the difference between (1) and (2).

Solution: There is a loss on redemption because the cash paid, $510,000 ($500,000 × 102), is greater than the carrying value of $508,000. The entry is:

Bonds Payable	500,000	
Premium on Bonds Payable	8,000	
Loss on Bond Redemption	2,000	
Cash		510,000
(To record redemption of bonds at 102)		

Related exercise material: BE11–10, E11–6, E11–7, and E11–9.

►Accounting for Long-Term Notes Payable

The use of notes payable in long-term debt financing is quite common. Long-term notes payable are similar to short-term interest-bearing notes payable except that the terms of the notes exceed one year. In periods of unstable interest rates, the interest rate on long-term notes may be tied to changes in the market

STUDY OBJECTIVE
········· **7** ·········

Describe the accounting for long-term notes payable.

490 CHAPTER 11 ▸ Liabilities

rate for comparable loans. Examples are the 8.03% adjustable rate notes issued by General Motors and the floating rate notes issued by American Express Company.

A long-term note may be secured by a document called a **mortgage** that pledges title to specific assets as security for a loan. Mortgage notes payable are widely used in the purchase of homes by individuals and in the acquisition of plant assets by many small and some large companies. For example, approximately 18% of McDonald's long-term debt relates to mortgage notes on land, buildings, and improvements. Like other long-term notes payable, the mortgage loan terms may stipulate either a fixed or an adjustable interest rate. Typically, the terms require the borrower to make installment payments over the term of the loan. Each payment consists of (1) interest on the unpaid balance of the loan, and (2) a reduction of loan principal. The interest decreases each period, while the portion applied to the loan principal increases.

Mortgage notes payable are recorded initially at face value, and entries are required subsequently for each installment payment. To illustrate, assume that Augustana Technology Inc. issues a $500,000, 12%, 20-year mortgage note on December 31, 1998, to obtain needed financing for the construction of a new research laboratory. The terms provide for semiannual installment payments of $33,231 (not including real estate taxes and insurance). The installment payment schedule for the first 2 years is as follows:

Illustration 11-22

Mortgage installment payment schedule

Semiannual Interest Period	(A) Cash Payment	(B) Interest Expense (D) × 6%	(C) Reduction of Principal (A) − (B)	(D) Principal Balance (D) − (C)
Issue date				$500,000
1	$33,231	$30,000	$3,231	496,769
2	33,231	29,806	3,425	493,344
3	33,231	29,601	3,630	489,714
4	33,231	29,383	3,848	485,866

The entries to record the mortgage loan and first installment payment are as follows:

Dec. 31	Cash	500,000	
	Mortgage Notes Payable		500,000
	(To record mortgage loan)		
June 30	Interest Expense	30,000	
	Mortgage Notes Payable	3,231	
	Cash		33,231
	(To record semiannual payment on		
	mortgage)		

In the balance sheet, the reduction in principal for the next year is reported as a current liability, and the remaining unpaid principal balance is classified as a long-term liability. At December 31, 1999, the total liability is $493,344 of which $7,478 ($3,630 + $3,848) is current, and $485,866 ($493,344 − $7,478) is long-term.

Statement Presentation and Analysis of Long-Term Liabilities

STUDY OBJECTIVE

·········▼·········
8

Identify the methods for the financial statement presentation and analysis of long-term liabilities.

Long-term liabilities are reported in a separate section of the balance sheet immediately following current liabilities, as shown below.

Illustration 11-23

Balance sheet presentation of long-term liabilities

Long-term liabilities		
Bonds payable 10% due in 2009	$1,000,000	
Less: Discount on bonds payable	80,000	$ 920,000
Mortgage notes payable, 11%, due in 2015 and secured by plant assets		500,000
Total long-term liabilities		$1,420,000

Alternatively, summary data may be presented in the balance sheet with detailed data (such as interest rates, maturity dates, conversion privileges, and assets pledged as collateral) shown in a supporting schedule. The current maturities of long-term debt should be reported under current liabilities if they are to be paid from current assets.

Long-term creditors and stockholders are interested in a company's long-run solvency, particularly its ability to pay interest as it comes due and to repay the face value of the debt at maturity. Debt to total assets and times interest earned are two ratios that provide information about debt-paying ability and long-run solvency.

The debt to total assets ratio measures the percentage of the total assets provided by creditors. It is computed as shown in the following formula by dividing total debt (both current and long-term liabilities) by total assets. The higher the percentage of debt to total assets, the greater the risk that the company may be unable to meet its maturing obligations.

The times interest earned ratio provides an indication of the company's ability to meet interest payments as they come due. It is computed by dividing income before interest expense and income taxes by interest expense.

To illustrate these ratios, we will use data from Hershey Foods Company's 1995 Annual Report which disclosed total liabilities of $1,748 million, total assets of $2,831 million, interest expense of $44,833 million, income taxes of $184,034 million, and net income of $281,919 million. Hershey Food's debt to total assets ratio and the times interest earned ratio are shown graphically below along with their computations.

Illustration 11-24

Debt to total assets and times interest earned ratios with computations

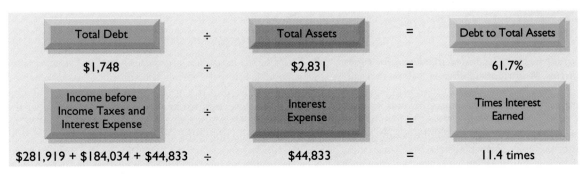

Total Debt	÷	Total Assets	=	Debt to Total Assets
$1,748	÷	$2,831	=	61.7%
Income before Income Taxes and Interest Expense	÷	Interest Expense		Times Interest Earned
$281,919 + $184,034 + $44,833	÷	$44,833	=	11.4 times

Even though Hershey Food's has a relatively high debt to total assets percentage of 61.7%, its interest coverage of 11.4 times appears very safe.

Before You Go On . . .

▶ *Review It*

1. Explain the accounting for long-term mortgage notes payable.
2. Where are current maturities of long-term debt reported in the financial statements?
3. What ratios may be computed to analyze a company's long-run solvency?

▶ *A Look Back at the University of Kentucky*

Refer to the opening story and answer the following questions:

1. The University of Kentucky's bonds are rated AA − by Standard & Poor's and A1 by Moody's Investor Service. Why is it important to the University of Kentucky that its bonds have a high bond rating?
2. Explain the meaning of the tax-exempt status of the University of Kentucky bonds. What does it mean to say that "a recent issue offering 6% is the equivalent of 10% to those individuals in the top tax bracket"?
3. Why does the state use bonds to finance the buildings rather than taking the funds out of general revenues?

Solution:

1. Having a high (good) bond rating is as important to a university as it is to a business corporation. A high bond rating indicates that the bonds are less risky, and thus more attractive, to purchasers of the bonds. Hence a lower interest rate results, and the cost to the issuer of the bonds is less.
2. Because the University of Kentucky bonds are tax exempt, holders of the bonds do not have to pay federal income tax on the interest received on the bonds. To earn an after-tax return of 6%, a person in the maximum tax bracket would have to receive interest equal to approximately 10% on taxable bonds [10% − (40% × 10%)].
3. Financing the buildings through the issuance of bonds spreads the cost of the buildings over many years and more equitably distributes the costs to a broader base of taxpayers. Future taxpayers pay for the buildings as the buildings are used, rather than the taxpayers of one year absorbing the total cost out of general revenues in the year of construction.

▼*Summary of Study Objectives*

1. *Explain a current liability and identify the major types of current liabilities.* A current liability is a debt that can reasonably be expected to be paid (1) from existing current assets or through the creation of other current liabilities, and (2) within one year or the operating cycle, whichever is longer. The major types of current liabilities are notes payable, accounts payable, sales taxes payable, unearned revenues, and accrued liabilities such as taxes, salaries and wages, and interest payable.

2. *Describe the accounting for notes payable.* When a promissory note is interest-bearing, the amount of assets received upon the issuance of the note is generally equal to the face value of the note, and interest expense is accrued over the life of the note. At maturity, the amount paid is equal to the face value of the note plus accrued interest.

3. *Explain the accounting for other current liabilities.* Sales taxes payable are recorded at the time the related sales occur. The company serves as a collection agent for the taxing authority. Sales taxes are not an expense to the company. Until employee withholding taxes are remitted to the governmental taxing authorities, they are credited to appropriate liability accounts. Unearned revenues are initially recorded in an unearned revenue account. As the revenue is earned, a transfer from unearned revenue to earned revenue occurs. The current maturities of long-term debt should be reported as a current liability in the balance sheet.

4. *Explain why bonds are issued and identify the types of bonds.* Bonds may be sold to many investors, and they offer the following advantages over common stock: (a) stockholder control is not affected, (b) tax savings result, (c) earnings per share of common stock may be higher. The following different types of bonds may be issued: secured and unsecured, term and serial bonds, registered and bearer bonds, convertible and callable bonds.

5. *Prepare the entries for the issuance of bonds and interest expense.* When bonds are issued, Cash is debited for the cash proceeds and Bonds Payable is credited for the face value of the bonds. In addition, Bond Interest Payable is credited if there is accrued interest, and the accounts Premium on Bonds Payable and Discount on Bonds Payable are used to show the bond premium and bond discount. Bond discount and bond premium are amortized by the straight-line method.

6. *Describe the entries when bonds are redeemed or converted.* When bonds are redeemed at maturity, Cash is credited and Bonds Payable is debited for the face value of the bonds. When bonds are redeemed before maturity, it is necessary to (a) eliminate the carrying value of the bonds at the redemption date, (b) record the cash paid, and (c) recognize the gain or loss on redemption. When bonds are converted to common stock, the carrying (or book) value of the bonds is transferred to appropriate paid-in capital accounts, and no gain or loss is recognized.

7. *Describe the accounting for long-term notes payable.* Each payment consists of (1) interest on the unpaid balance of the loan, and (2) a reduction of loan principal. The interest decreases each period, while the portion applied to the loan principal increases each period.

8. *Identify the methods for the financial statement presentation and analysis of long-term liabilities.* The nature and amount of each long-term debt should be reported in the balance sheet or in schedules in the notes accompanying the statements. The long-run solvency of a company may be analyzed by computing the debt to total assets and the times interest earned ratios.

◤APPENDIX ▸ *Effective-Interest Amortization*

The straight-line method of amortization that you studied in the chapter has a conceptual deficiency: It does not completely satisfy the matching principle. Under the straight-line method, interest expense as a percentage of the carrying value of the bonds varies each interest period. This can be seen by using data from the first three interest periods of the bond amortization schedule shown in Illustration 11-17:

Semiannual Interest Period	Interest Expense to Be Recorded (A)	Bond Carrying Value (B)	Interest Expense as a Percentage of Carrying Value (A) ÷ (B)
1	$52,000	$980,000	5.31%
2	52,000	982,000	5.29%
3	52,000	984,000	5.27%

Illustration 11A-1

Interest percentage rates under straight-line method

Note that interest expense as a percentage of carrying value declines in each interest period. However, to completely comply with the matching principle, interest expense as a percentage of carrying value should not change over the life of the bonds. This percentage, referred to as the effective-interest rate, is established when the bonds are issued and remains constant in each interest period. The effective-interest method of amortization accomplishes this result.

Under the effective-interest method, the amortization of bond discount or bond premium results in periodic interest expense equal to a constant percentage of the carrying value of the bonds. The effective-interest method results in varying amounts of amortization and interest expense per period but a constant percentage rate; the straight-line method results in constant amounts of amortization and interest expense per period but a varying percentage rate.

The following steps are required under the effective-interest method:

1. Compute the **bond interest expense** by multiplying the carrying value of the bonds at the beginning of the interest period by the effective-interest rate.
2. Compute the **bond interest paid** (or accrued) by multiplying the face value of the bonds by the contractual interest rate.
3. Compute the **amortization amount** by determining the difference between the amounts computed in steps (1) and (2).

These steps are graphically depicted in Illustration 11A-2.

Illustration 11A-2

Computation of amortization—effective-interest method

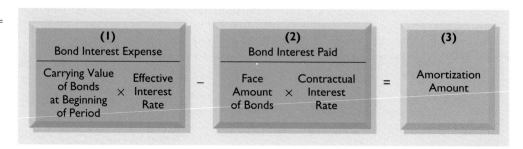

Helpful hint Note that the amount of periodic interest expense increases over the life of the bonds when the effective-interest method is used for bonds issued at a discount. The reason is that a constant percentage is applied to an increasing bond carrying value to compute interest expense. The carrying value is increasing because of the amortization of the discount.

Both the straight-line and effective-interest methods of amortization result in the same total amount of interest expense over the term of the bonds. Furthermore, interest expense each interest period is generally comparable in amount. However, **when the amounts are materially different, the effective-interest method is required under generally accepted accounting principles (GAAP).**

Amortizing Bond Discount

To illustrate the effective-interest method of bond discount amortization, assume that Wrightway Corporation issues $100,000 of 10%, 5-year bonds on January 1, 1998, with interest payable each July 1 and January 1. The bonds sell for $92,639 (92.639% of face value), which results in bond discount of $7,361 ($100,000 − $92,639) and an effective-interest rate of 12%. (Note that the $92,639 can be proven as shown in Appendix B at the end of this book.) Preparing a bond discount amortization schedule as shown in Illustration 11A-3 facilitates the recording of interest expense and the discount amortization.

WRIGHTWAY CORPORATION
Bond Discount Amortization
Effective-Interest Method—Semiannual Interest Payments
10% Bonds Issued at 12%

Semiannual Interest Periods	(A) Interest to Be Paid (5% × $100,000)	(B) Interest Expense to Be Recorded (6% × Preceding Bond Carrying Value)	(C) Discount Amortization (B) − (A)	(D) Unamortized Discount (D) − (C)	(E) Bond Carrying Value ($100,000 − D)
Issue date				$7,361	$ 92,639
1	$ 5,000	$ 5,558 (6% × $92,639)	$ 558	6,803	93,197
2	5,000	5,592 (6% × $93,197)	592	6,211	93,789
3	5,000	5,627 (6% × $93,789)	627	5,584	94,416
4	5,000	5,665 (6% × $94,416)	665	4,919	95,081
5	5,000	5,705 (6% × $95,081)	705	4,214	95,786
6	5,000	5,747 (6% × $95,786)	747	3,467	96,533
7	5,000	5,792 (6% × $96,533)	792	2,675	97,325
8	5,000	5,840 (6% × $97,325)	840	1,835	98,165
9	5,000	5,890 (6% × $98,165)	890	945	99,055
10	5,000	5,945* (6% × $99,055)	945	–0–	100,000
	$50,000	$57,361	$7,361		

Column (A) remains constant because the face value of the bonds ($100,000) is multiplied by the semiannual contractual interest rate (5%) each period.

Column (B) is computed as the preceding bond carrying value times the semiannual effective-interest rate (6%).

Column (C) indicates the discount amortization each period.

Column (D) decreases each period until it reaches zero at maturity.

Column (E) increases each period until it equals face value at maturity.

*$2 difference due to rounding.

Illustration 11A-3

Bond discount amortization schedule

Note that interest expense as a percentage of carrying value remains constant at 6%.

For the first interest period, the computations of bond interest expense and the bond discount amortization are as follows:

Illustration 11A-4

Computation of bond discount amortization

Bond interest expense ($92,639 × 6%)	$5,558
Contractual interest ($100,000 × 5%)	5,000
Bond discount amortization	$ 558

As a result, the entry to record the payment of interest and amortization of bond discount by Wrightway Corporation on July 1, 1998, is:

July 1	Bond Interest Expense	5,558	
	Discount on Bonds Payable		558
	Cash		5,000
	(To record payment of bond interest and amortization of bond discount)		

For the second interest period, bond interest expense will be $5,592 ($93,197 × 6%), and the discount amortization will be $592. At December 31, the following adjusting entry is made:

Dec. 31	Bond Interest Expense	5,592	
	Discount on Bonds Payable		592
	Bond Interest Payable		5,000
	(To record accrued interest and amortization of bond discount)		

Total bond interest expense for 1998 is $11,150 ($5,558 + $5,592). On January 1, payment of the interest is recorded by a debit to Bond Interest Payable and a credit to Cash.

Amortizing Bond Premium

The amortization of bond premium by the effective-interest method is similar to the procedures described for bond discount. As an example, assume that Wrightway Corporation issues $100,000, 10%, 5-year bonds on January 1, 1998, with interest payable on July 1 and January 1. In this case, the bonds sell for $108,111, which results in bond premium of $8,111 and an effective-interest rate of 8%. The bond premium amortization schedule is shown in Illustration 11A-5.

Illustration 11A-5

Bond premium amortization schedule

WRIGHTWAY CORPORATION
Bond Premium Amortization
Effective-Interest Method—Semiannual Interest Payments
10% Bonds Issued at 8%

Semiannual Interest Periods	(A) Interest to Be Paid (5% × $100,000)	(B) Interest Expense to Be Recorded (4% × Preceding Bond Carry Value)	(C) Premium Amortization (A) − (B)	(D) Unamortized Premium (D) − (C)	(E) Bond Carrying Value ($100,000 + D)
Issue date				$8,111	$108,111
1	$ 5,000	$ 4,324 (4% × $108,111)	$ 676	7,435	107,435
2	5,000	4,297 (4% × $107,435)	703	6,732	106,732
3	5,000	4,269 (4% × $106,732)	731	6,001	106,001
4	5,000	4,240 (4% × $106,001)	760	5,241	105,241
5	5,000	4,210 (4% × $105,241)	790	4,451	104,451
6	5,000	4,178 (4% × $104,451)	822	3,629	103,629
7	5,000	4,145 (4% × $103,629)	855	2,774	102,774
8	5,000	4,111 (4% × $102,774)	889	1,885	101,885
9	5,000	4,075 (4% × $101,885)	925	960	100,960
10	5,000	4,040* (4% × $100,960)	960	–0–	100,000
	$50,000	$41,889	$8,111		

Column (A) remains constant because the face value of the bonds ($100,000) is multiplied by the semiannual contractual interest rate (5%) each period.

Column (B) is computed as the carrying value of the bonds times the semiannual effective-interest rate (4%).

Column (C) indicates the premium amortization each period.

Column (D) decreases each period until it reaches zero at maturity.

Column (E) decreases each period until it equals face value at maturity.

*$2 difference due to rounding.

For the first interest period, the computations of bond interest expense and the bond premium amortization are:

Illustration 11A-6

Computation of bond premium amortization

Bond interest expense ($108,111 × 4%)	$4,324
Contractual interest ($100,000 × 5%)	5,000
Bond premium amortization	$ 676

The entry on the first interest date is:

July 1	Bond Interest Expense	4,324	
	Premium on Bonds Payable	676	
	Cash		5,000
	(To record payment of bond interest and amortization of bond premium)		

For the second interest period, interest expense will be $4,297, and the premium amortization will be $703. Total bond interest expense for 1998 is $8,621 ($4,324 + $4,297).

Helpful hint Note that the amount of periodic interest expense decreases over the life of the bond when the effective-interest method is applied to bonds issued at a premium. The reason is that a constant percentage is applied to a decreasing bond carrying value to compute interest expense. The carrying value is decreasing because of the amortization of the premium.

►*T*echnology in *A*ction

The amortization schedule is an excellent example of an accounting computation efficiently and effectively performed by an electronic spreadsheet. Once the selling price, face amount, contractual rate of interest, effective rate of interest, and number of interest periods are determined and entered into the spreadsheet, all of the computations until maturity can be performed by the computer. Note that all data needed for the adjusting entries can be taken directly from the amortization schedule.

▼*S*ummary of Study Objective for Chapter 11 Appendix

9. *Contrast the effects of the straight-line and effective-interest methods of amortizing bond discount and bond premium.* The straight-line method of amortization results in a constant amount of amortization and interest expense per period but a varying percentage rate. In contrast, the effective-interest method results in varying amounts of amortization and interest expense per period but a constant percentage rate of interest. The effective-interest method generally results in a better matching of expenses with revenues. When the difference between the straight-line and effective-interest method is material, the use of the effective-interest method is required under GAAP.

G**LOSSARY**

Bearer (coupon) bonds Bonds not registered. (p. 477).

Bond certificate A legal document that indicates the name of the issuer, the face value of the bonds, and such other data as the contractual interest rate and maturity date of the bonds. (p. 477).

Bond indenture A legal document that sets forth the terms of the bond issue. (p. 477).

Bonds A form of interest bearing notes payable issued by corporations, universities, and governmental entities. (p. 475).

Callable bonds Bonds that are subject to retirement at a stated dollar amount prior to maturity at the option of the issuer. (p. 477).

Convertible bonds Bonds that permit bondholders to convert them into common stock at their option. (p. 477).

Contractual interest rate Rate used to determine the amount of interest the borrower pays and the investor receives. (p. 477).

Debenture bonds Bonds issued against the general credit of the borrower. Also called unsecured bonds. (p. 477).

Effective-interest method of amortization A method of amortizing bond discount or bond premium that results in periodic interest expense equal to a constant percentage of the carrying value of the bonds. (p. 494).

Effective-interest rate Rate established when bonds are issued that remains constant in each interest period. (p. 493).

Face value Amount of principal due at the maturity date of the bond. (p. 477).

Long-term liabilities Obligations expected to be paid more than one year in the future. (p. 475).

Market interest rate The rate investors demand for loaning funds to the corporation. (p. 479).

Mortgage bond A bond secured by real estate. (p. 476).

Mortgage note payable A long-term note secured by a mortgage that pledges title to specific units of property as security for the loan. (p. 490).

Registered bonds   Bonds issued in the name of the owner. (p. 477).

Secured bonds   Bonds that have specific assets of the issuer pledged as collateral. (p. 476).

Serial bonds   Bonds that mature in installments. (p. 477).

Sinking fund bonds   Bonds secured by specific assets set aside to retire them. (p. 476).

Straight-line method of amortization   A method of amortizing bond discount or bond premium that allocates the same amount to interest expense in each interest period. (p. 483).

Term bonds   Bonds that mature at a single specified future date. (p. 477).

Unsecured bonds   Bonds issued against the general credit of the borrower. Also called debenture bonds. (p. 476).

DEMONSTRATION PROBLEM 1

Snyder Software Inc. has successfully developed a new spreadsheet program. However, to produce and market the program, the company needed $2.0 million of additional financing. On December 31, 1996, Snyder borrowed money as follows:

1. Snyder issued $500,000, 11%, 10-year convertible bonds. The bonds sold at face value and pay semiannual interest on January 1 and July 1. Each $1,000 bond is convertible into 30 shares of Snyder's $20 par value common stock.
2. Snyder issued $1.0 million, 10%, 10-year bonds for $885,301. Interest is payable semiannually on January 1 and July 1. Snyder uses the straight-line method of amortization.
3. Snyder also issued a $500,000, 12%, 15-year mortgage note payable. The terms provide for semiannual installment payments of $36,324 on June 30 and December 31.

Instructions

1. For the convertible bonds, prepare journal entries for:
   (a) the issuance of the bonds on January 1, 1997.
   (b) interest expense on July 1 and December 31, 1997.
   (c) the payment of interest on January 1, 1998.
   (d) the conversion of all bonds into common stock on January 1, 1998, when the market value of the common stock was $67 per share.
2. For the 10 year, 10% bonds:
   (a) journalize the issuance of the bonds on January 1, 1997.
   (b) prepare a bond discount amortization schedule for the first six interest periods.
   (c) prepare the journal entries for interest expense and amortization of bond discount in 1997.
   (d) prepare the entry for the redemption of the bonds at 101 on January 1, 2000, after paying the interest due on this date.
3. For the mortgage note payable:
   (a) prepare the entry for the issuance of the note on December 31, 1996.
   (b) prepare a payment schedule for the first four installment payments.
   (c) indicate the current and noncurrent amounts for the mortgage note payable at December 31, 1997.

Solution to Demonstration Problem 1

1. (a) 1997

Jan. 1	Cash		500,000	
	Bonds Payable			500,000
	(To record issue of 11%, 10-year convertible bonds at face value)			

(b) 1997

July 1	Bond Interest Expense		27,500	
	Cash ($500,000 × 0.055)			27,500
	(To record payment of semiannual interest)			
Dec. 31	Bond Interest Expense		27,500	
	Bond Interest Payable			27,500
	(To record accrual of semiannual bond interest)			

(c) 1998

Jan. 1	Bond Interest Payable		27,500	
	Cash			27,500
	(To record payment of accrued interest)			
(d) Jan. 1	Bonds Payable		500,000	
	Common Stock			300,000*
	Paid-in Capital in Excess of Par Value			200,000
	(To record conversion of bonds into common stock)			
	*($500,000 ÷ $1,000 = 500 bonds;			
	500 × 30 = 15,000 shares;			
	15,000 × $20 = $300,000)			

Problem-Solving Strategies

1. Interest is usually paid semi-annually. Be careful to use only 6 months' interest in your computations.

2. Upon conversion, the book (carrying) value of the bonds is removed from the liability accounts and recorded as common stock and related paid-in capital.

2. (a) 1997

Jan. 1	Cash		885,301	
	Discount on Bonds Payable		114,699	
	Bonds Payable			1,000,000
	(To record issuance of bonds at a discount)			

(b)

Semiannual Interest Period	Interest to Be Paid	Interest Expense to Be Recorded	Discount Amortization	Unamortized Discount	Bond Carrying Value
Issue date				$114,699	$885,301
1	$50,000	$55,735	$5,735	108,964	891,036
2	50,000	55,735	5,735	103,229	896,771
3	50,000	55,735	5,735	97,494	902,506
4	50,000	55,735	5,735	91,759	908,241
5	50,000	55,735	5,735	86,024	913,976
6	50,000	55,735	5,735	80,289	919,711

(c) 1997

July 1	Bond Interest Expense		55,735	
	Discount on Bonds Payable			5,735
	Cash			50,000
	(To record payment of semiannual interest and amortization of bond discount)			
Dec. 31	Bond Interest Expense		55,735	
	Discount on Bonds Payable			5,735
	Bond Interest Payable			50,000
	(To record accrual of semiannual interest and amortization of bond discount)			

Problem-Solving Strategies

1. Discount on bonds payable is a contra liability account.

2. Amortization of bond discount increases bond interest expense.

3. Bond interest expense is the same each period when the straight-line method is used.

4. Loss on bond redemption occurs when the cash paid is greater than the bond carrying value.

(d) 2000

Jan. 1	Bonds Payable	1,000,000		
	Loss on Bond Redemption	90,289*		
	Discount on Bonds Payable		80,289	
	Cash		1,010,000	
	(To record redemption of bonds at			
	101)			
	*($1,010,000 − $919,711)			

3. (a) 1996

Dec. 31	Cash	500,000		
	Mortgage Notes Payable		500,000	
	(To record issuance of mortgage note			
	payable)			

Problem-Solving Strategies

1. Interest expense decreases each period because the principal is decreasing each period.
2. Each payment consists of (1) interest on the unpaid loan balance and (2) a reduction of the loan principal.

(b)

Semiannual Interest Period	Cash Payment	Interest Expense	Reduction of Principal	Principal Balance
Issue date				$500,000
1	$36,324	$30,000	$6,324	493,676
2	36,324	29,621	6,703	486,973
3	36,324	29,218	7,106	479,867
4	36,324	28,792	7,532	472,335

(c) Current liability $14,638 ($7,106 + $7,532)
     Long-term liability $472,335.

DEMONSTRATION PROBLEM 2 (Appendix Problem)

Gardner Corporation issues $1,750,000, 10-year, 12% bonds on January 1, 1998, at $1,970,000 to yield 10%. The bonds pay semiannual interest July 1 and January 1. Gardner uses the effective-interest method of amortization.

Instructions

(a) Prepare the journal entry to record the issuance of the bonds.
(b) Prepare the journal entry to record the payment of interest on July 1, 1998.

Solution to Demonstration Problem 2

Problem-Solving Strategies

1. Bond carrying value at beginning of period times effective-interest rate equals interest expense.
2. Credit to cash (or bond interest payable) is computed by multiplying the face value of the bonds by the contractual interest rate.
3. Bond premium or discount amortization is the difference between (1) and (2).
4. Interest expense increases when the effective-interest method is used for bonds issued at a discount. The reason is that a constant percentage is applied to an increasing book value to compute interest expense.

(a) 1998

Jan. 1	Cash	1,970,000		
	Premium on Bonds Payable		220,000	
	Bonds Payable		1,750,000	
	(To record issuance of bonds at a premium)			
1998 July 1	Bond Interest Expense	98,500*		
	Premium on Bonds Payable	6,500**		
	Cash		105,000	
	(To record payment of semiannual interest			
	and amortization of bond premium)			
	*($1,970,000 × 5%)			
	**($105,000 − $98,500)			

SELF-STUDY QUESTIONS

Answers are at the end of the chapter.

(SO 1) 1. The time period for classifying a liability as current is one year or the operating cycle, whichever is:
   a. longer.
   b. shorter.
   c. probable.
   d. possible.

(SO 1) 2. To be classified as a current liability, a debt must be expected to be paid:
   a. out of existing current assets.
   b. by creating other current liabilities.
   c. within two years.
   d. both (a) and (b).

(SO 2) 3. Julie Gilbert Company borrows $88,500 on September 1, 1997 from the Sandwich State Bank by signing an $88,500 12%, one-year note. What is the accrued interest at December 31, 1997?
   a. $2,655.
   b. $3,540.
   c. $4,425.
   d. $10,620.

(SO 3) 4. Reeves Company has total proceeds from sales of $4,515. If the proceeds include sales taxes of 5%, the amount to be credited to Sales is:
   a. $4,000.
   b. $4,300.
   c. $4,289.25.
   d. No correct answer given.

(SO 4) 5. The term used for bonds that are unsecured is:
   a. callable bonds.
   b. indenture bonds.
   c. debenture bonds.
   d. bearer bonds.

(SO 5) 6. Karson Inc. issues 10-year bonds with a maturity value of $200,000. If the bonds are issued at a premium, this indicates that:
   a. the contractual interest rate exceeds the market interest rate.
   b. the market interest rate exceeds the contractual interest rate.
   c. the contractual interest rate and the market interest rate are the same.
   d. no relationship exists between the two rates.

(SO 5) 7. On January 1, Hurley Corporation issues $500,000, 5-year, 12% bonds at 96 with interest payable on July 1 and January 1. The entry on July 1 to record payment of bond interest and the amortization of bond discount using the straight-line method will include a:
   a. debit to Interest Expense, $30,000.
   b. debit to Interest Expense, $60,000.
   c. credit to Discount on Bonds Payable, $4,000.
   d. credit to Discount on Bonds Payable, $2,000.

(SO 5) 8. For the bonds issued in question 3, above, what is the carrying value of the bonds at the end of the third interest period?
   a. $486,000.
   b. $488,000.
   c. $472,000.
   d. $464,000.

(SO 5) 9. Gester Corporation retires its $100,000 face value bonds at 105 on January 1, following the payment of semiannual interest. The carrying value of the bonds at the redemption date is $103,745. The entry to record the redemption will include a:
   a. credit of $3,745 to Loss on Bond Redemption.
   b. debit of $3,745 to Premium on Bonds Payable.
   c. credit of $1,255 to Gain on Bond Redemption.
   d. debit of $5,000 to Premium on Bonds Payable.

(SO 6) 10. Colson Inc. converts $600,000 of bonds sold at face value into 10,000 shares of common stock, par value $1. Both the bonds and the stock have a market value of $760,000. What amount should be credited to Paid-in Capital in Excess of Par as a result of the conversion?
   a. $10,000
   b. $160,000
   c. $600,000
   d. $590,000

(SO 7) 11. Andrews Inc. issues a $497,000, 10% 3-year mortgage note on January 1. The note will be paid in three annual installments of $200,000, each payable at the end of the year. What is the amount of interest expense that should be recognized by Andrews Inc. in the second year?
   a. $16,567
   b. $49,740
   c. $34,670
   d. $347,600

(SO 9) *12. On January 1, Besalius Inc. issued $1,000,000, 9% bonds for $939,000. The market rate of interest for these bonds is 10%. Interest is payable annually on December 31. Besalius uses the effective interest method of amortizing bond discount. At the end of the first year, Besalius should report unamortized bond discount of:
   a. $54,900.
   b. $57,100.
   c. $51,610.
   d. $51,000.

(SO 9) *13. On January 1, Dias Corporation issued $1,000,000, 14%, 5-year bonds with interest payable on July 1 and January 1. The bonds sold for $1,098,540. The market rate of interest for these bonds was 12%. On the first interest date, using the effective-interest method, the debit entry to Bond Interest Expense is for:
   a. $60,000.
   b. $76,898.
   c. $65,912.
   d. $131,825.

QUESTIONS

••

1. Li Feng believes a current liability is a debt that can be expected to be paid in one year. Is Li correct? Explain.

2. Rio Grande Company obtains $25,000 in cash by signing a 9%, 6-month $25,000 note payable to First Bank on July 1. Rio Grande's fiscal year ends on September 30. What information should be reported for the note payable in the annual financial statements?

3. (a) Your roommate says, "Sales taxes are reported as an expense in the income statement." Do you agree? Explain.
   (b) Hard Walk Cafe has cash proceeds from sales of $10,400. This amount includes $400 of sales taxes. Give the entry to record the proceeds.

4. Aurora University sold 10,000 season football tickets at $90 each for its five-game home schedule. What entries should be made (a) when the tickets were sold and (b) after each game?

5. Identify three taxes commonly withheld by the employer from an employee's gross pay.

6. Identify three taxes commonly paid by employers on employee's salaries and wages. Where in the financial statements does the employer report taxes withheld from employee's pay?

7. (a) What are long-term liabilities? Give two examples. (b) What is a bond?

8. (a) As a source of long-term financing, what are the major advantages of bonds over common stock? (b) What are the major disadvantages in using bonds for long-term financing?

9. Contrast the following types of bonds: (a) secured and unsecured, (b) term and serial, (c) registered and bearer, and (d) convertible and callable.

10. The following terms are important in issuing bonds: (a) face value, (b) contractual interest rate, (c) bond indenture, and (d) bond certificate. Explain each of these terms.

11. Describe the two major obligations incurred by a company when bonds are issued.

12. Assume that Stoney Inc. sold bonds with a par value of $100,000 for $104,000. Was the market interest rate equal to, less than, or greater than the bonds' contractual interest rate? Explain.

13. Barbara Secord and Jack Dalton are discussing how the market price of a bond is determined. Barbara believes that the market price of a bond is solely a function of the amount of the principal

payment at the end of the term of a bond. Is she right? Discuss.

14. If a 10%, 10-year, $600,000 bond is issued at par and interest is paid semiannually, what is the amount of the interest payment at the end of the first semiannual period?

15. If the Bonds Payable account has a balance of $900,000 and the Discount on Bonds Payable account has a balance of $40,000, what is the carrying value of the bonds?

16. Explain the straight-line method of amortizing discount and premium on bonds payable.

17. Jennifer Brent Corporation issues $200,000 of 8%, 5-year bonds on January 1, 1998, at 104. Assuming that the straight-line method is used to amortize the premium, what is the total amount of interest expense for 1998?

18. Which accounts are debited and which are credited if a bond issue originally sold at a premium is redeemed before maturity at 97 immediately following the payment of interest?

19. Li Su Corporation is considering issuing a convertible bond. What is a convertible bond? Discuss the advantages of a convertible bond from the standpoint of (a) the bondholders and (b) the issuing corporation.

20. Doug Wisdom, a friend of yours, has recently purchased a home for $125,000, paying $25,000 down and the remainder financed by a 10.5%, 20-year mortgage, payable at $998.38 per month. At the end of the first month, Doug receives a statement from the bank indicating that only $123.38 of principal was paid during the month. At this rate, he calculates that it will take over 67 years to pay off the mortgage. Is he right? Discuss.

21. In general, what are the requirements for the financial statement presentation of long-term liabilities? What ratios may be computed to evaluate a company's liquidity and solvency?

*22. Julia Amant is discussing the advantages of the effective-interest method of bond amortization with her accounting staff. What do you think Julia is saying?

*23. Summit Corporation issues $400,000 of 9%, 5-year bonds on January 1, 1998, at 104. If Summit uses the effective-interest method in amortizing the premium, will the annual interest expense increase or decrease over the life of the bonds? Explain.

Note: All **asterisked** Questions, Exercises, and Problems relate to material contained in the appendix to each chapter.

BRIEF EXERCISES
•••

BE11–1 Fresno Company has the following obligations at December 31: (a) a note payable for $100,000 due in 2 years, (b) a 10-year mortgage payable of $200,000 payable in 10 $20,000 annual payments, (c) interest payable of $15,000 on the mortgage, and (d) accounts payable of $60,000. For each obligation, indicate whether it should be classified as a current liability.

Identify whether obligations are current liabilities.
(SO 1)

BE11–2 Romez Company borrows $60,000 on July 1 from the bank by signing a $60,000 10%, one-year note payable. Prepare the journal entries to record (a) the proceeds of the note and (b) accrued interest at December 31, assuming adjusting entries are made only at the end of the year.

Prepare entries for an interest-bearing note payable.
(SO 2)

BE11–3 Grandy Auto Supply does not segregate sales and sales taxes at the time of sale. The register total for March 16 is $9,975. All sales are subject to a 5% sales tax. Compute sales taxes payable and make the entry to record sales taxes payable and sales.

Compute and record sales taxes payable.
(SO 3)

BE11–4 Outstanding University sells 3,000 season basketball tickets at $60 each for its 12-game home schedule. Give the entry to record (a) the sale of the season tickets and (b) the revenue earned by playing the first home game.

Prepare entries for unearned revenues.
(SO 3)

BE11–5 Olga Inc. is considering two alternatives to finance its construction of a new $2 million plant:

Comparison of bond versus stock financing.
(SO 4)

(a) Issuance of 200,000 shares of common stock at the market price of $10 per share.
(b) Issuance of $2 million, 8% bonds at par.

Complete the following table and indicate which alternative is preferable.

	Issue Stock	Issue Bond
Income before interest and taxes	$1,000,000	$1,000,000
Interest expense from bonds		
Income before income taxes	$	$
Income tax expense (30%)		
Net income	$	$
Outstanding shares		700,000
Earnings per share		

BE11–6 Keystone Corporation issued 1,000, 9%, 5-year, $1,000 bonds dated January 1, 1996, at 100. (a) Prepare the journal entry to record the sale of these bonds on January 1, 1996. (b) Prepare the journal entry to record the first interest payment on July 1, 1996 (interest payable semiannually), assuming no previous accrual of interest. (c) Prepare the adjusting journal entry on December 31, 1996, to record interest expense.

Journal entries for bonds issued at face value.
(SO 5)

BE11–7 Dominic Company issues $2 million, 10 year, 9% bonds at 98, with interest payable on July 1 and January 1. The straight-line method is used to amortize bond discount. (a) Prepare the journal entry to record the sale of these bonds on January 1, 1996. (b) Prepare the journal entry to record interest expense and bond discount amortization on July 1, 1996, assuming no previous accrual of interest.

Journal entries for bonds issued at a discount.
(SO 5)

BE11–8 Hercules Inc. issues $5 million, 5-year, 10% bonds at 103, with interest payable on July 1 and January 1. The straight-line method is used to amortize bond premium. (a) Prepare the journal entry to record the sale of these bonds on January 1, 1996. (b) Prepare the journal entry to record interest expense and bond premium amortization on July 1, 1996, assuming no previous accrual of interest.

Journal entries for bonds issued at a premium.
(SO 5)

BE11–9 Goodland Inc. has outstanding $1 million, 10-year, 12% bonds with interest payable on July 1 and January 1. The bonds were dated January 1, 1996, but were issued on May 1, 1996, at face value plus accrued interest. (a) Prepare the journal entry to record the sale of the bonds on May 1, 1996. (b) Prepare the journal entry to record the interest payment on July 1, 1996.

Journal entries for bonds issued between interest dates.
(SO 5)

Redemption of bonds.
(SO 6)

BE11–10 The balance sheet for Hathaway Company reports the following information on July 1, 1996:

Long-term liabilities

Bonds payable	$1,000,000	
Less: Discount on bonds payable	60,000	$940,000

Hathaway decides to redeem these bonds at 102 after paying semiannual interest. Prepare the journal entry to record the redemption on July 1, 1996.

Accounting for long-term notes payable.
(SO 7)

BE11–11 Escobar Inc. issues a $300,000, 10%, 10-year mortgage note on December 31, 1996, to obtain financing for a new building. The terms provide for semiannual installment payments of $24,073. Prepare the entry to record the mortgage loan on December 31, 1996, and the first installment payment.

Financial statement presentation of long-term liabilities.
(SO 8)

BE11–12 Presented below are long-term liability items for Warner Company at December 31, 1996. Prepare the long-term liabilities section of the balance sheet for Warner Company.

Bonds payable, due 2001	$900,000
Notes payable, due 2003	80,000
Discount on bonds payable	45,000

Analysis of Liquidity and Solvency
(SO 8)

BE11–13 Motorola's 1995 financial statements contain the following selected data (in millions):

Current assets	$10,510	Interest expense	$ 149
Total assets	22,801	Income taxes	1,001
Current liabilities	7,791	Net income	1,781
Total liabilities	11,753		

Compute the following ratios:

(a) Working capital   (c) Debt to total assets ratio
(b) Current ratio   (d) Times interest earned ratio

Effective interest method of bond amortization.
(SO 9)

*BE11–14 Presented below is the partial bond discount amortization schedule for Lodge Corp. Lodge uses the effective-interest method of amortization.

Semiannual Interest Periods	Interest to Be Paid	Interest Expense to Be Recorded	Discount Amortization	Unamortized Discount	Bond Carrying Value
Issue date				$62,311	$937,689
1	$45,000	$46,884	$1,884	60,427	939,573
2	45,000	46,979	1,979	58,448	941,552

Instructions

(a) Prepare the journal entry to record the payment of interest and the discount amortization at the end of period 1.
(b) ▭▭▭► Explain why interest expense is greater than interest paid.
(c) ▭▭▭► Explain why interest expense will increase each period.

EXERCISES

Prepare entries for interest-bearing notes.
(SO 2)

E11–1 Cairo Company on June 1 borrows $50,000 from First Bank on a 6-month, $50,000, 12% note.

Instructions

(a) Prepare the entry on June 1.
(b) Prepare the adjusting entry on June 30.
(c) Prepare the entry at maturity (December 1), assuming monthly adjusting entries have been made through November 30.
(d) What was the total financing cost (interest expense)?

E11–2 In providing accounting services to small businesses, you encounter the following situations pertaining to cash sales:

Journalize sales and related taxes.
(SO 3)

1. Nash Company rings up sales and sales taxes separately on its cash register. On April 10, the register totals are sales $25,000 and sales taxes $1,500.
2. Pontiac Company does not segregate sales and sales taxes. Its register total for April 15 is $13,780, which includes a 6% sales tax.

Instructions
Prepare the entry to record the sales transactions and related taxes for each client.

E11–3 Westland Company publishes a monthly sports magazine, *Fishing Preview*. Subscriptions to the magazine cost $24 per year. During November 1996, Westwood sells 6,000 subscriptions beginning with the December issue. Westwood prepares financial statements quarterly and recognizes subscription revenue earned at the end of the quarter. The company uses the accounts Unearned Subscription Revenue and Subscription Revenue.

Journalize unearned subscription revenue.
(SO 3)

Instructions
(a) Prepare the entry in November for the receipt of the subscriptions.
(b) Prepare the adjusting entry at December 31, 1996, to record subscription revenue earned in December of 1996.
(c) Prepare the adjusting entry at March 31, 1997, to record subscription revenue earned in the first quarter of 1997.

E11–4 Sundown Airlines is considering two alternatives for the financing of a purchase of a fleet of airplanes. These two alternatives are:

Compare two alternatives of financing—issuance of common stock vs. issuance of bonds.
(SO 4)

1. Issue 60,000 shares of common stock at $45 per share. (Cash dividends have not been paid nor is the payment of any contemplated.)
2. Issue 13%, 10-year bonds at face value for $2,700,000.

It is estimated that the company will earn $900,000 before interest and taxes as a result of this purchase. The company has an estimated tax rate of 30% and has 90,000 shares of common stock outstanding prior to the new financing.

Instructions
Determine the effect on net income and earnings per share for these two methods of financing.

E11–5 On January 1, Laramie Company issued $90,000, 10%, 10-year bonds at face value. Interest is payable semiannually on July 1 and January 1. Interest is not accrued on June 30.

Journal entries for issuance of bonds and payment and accrual of bond interest.
(SO 5)

Instructions
Present journal entries to record:

(a) The issuance of the bonds.
(b) The payment of interest on July 1.
(c) The accrual of interest on December 31.

E11–6 Pueblo Company issued $240,000, 9%, 20-year bonds on January 1, 1996, at 103. Interest is payable semiannually on July 1 and January 1. Pueblo uses straight-line amortization for bond premium or discount. Interest is not accrued on June 30.

Journal entries to record issuance of bonds, payment of interest, amortization of premium, and redemption at maturity.
(SO 5, 6)

Instructions
Prepare the journal entries to record:

(a) The issuance of the bonds.
(b) The payment of interest and the premium amortization on July 1, 1996.
(c) The accrual of interest and the premium amortization on December 31, 1996.
(d) The redemption of the bonds at maturity, assuming interest for the last interest period has been paid and recorded.

E11–7 Cotter Company issued $180,000, 11%, 10-year bonds on December 31, 1995, for $172,000. Interest is payable semiannually on June 30 and December 31. Cotter uses the straight-line method to amortize bond premium or discount.

Journal entries to record issuance of bonds, payment of interest, amortization of discount, and redemption at maturity.
(SO 5, 6)

Instructions
Prepare the journal entries to record:

(a) The issuance of the bonds.
(b) The payment of interest and the discount amortization on June 30, 1996.

(c) The payment of interest and the discount amortization on December 31, 1996.
(d) The redemption of the bonds at maturity, assuming interest for the last interest period has been paid and recorded.

Journal entries to record issuance of bonds between interest dates, and payment and accrual of interest.
(SO 5)

accrued interest for 3 months 1800

E11–8   On April 1, Virginia Company issued $72,000, 10%, 10-year bonds dated January 1 at face value plus accrued interest. Interest is payable semiannually on July 1 and January 1.

Instructions
Present journal entries to record:

(a) The issuance of the bonds.
(b) The payment of interest on July 1. Interest is not accrued on June 30.
(c) The accrual of interest on December 31.   *Bond Interest Exp 3600*
Bond Int. Payable   3600

Journal entries for redemption of bonds and conversion of bonds into common stock.
(SO 6)

E11–9   Presented below are three independent situations:

1. Ernst Corporation retired $120,000 face value, 12% bonds on June 30, 1996, at 102. The carrying value of the bonds at the redemption date was $107,500. The bonds pay semi-annual interest and the interest payment due on June 30, 1996, has been made and recorded.
2. Young, Inc. retired $150,000 face value, 12.5% bonds on June 30, 1996, at 98. The carrying value of the bonds at the redemption date was $151,000. The bonds pay semi-annual interest and the interest payment due on June 30, 1996, has been made and recorded.
3. Lybrand Company has $80,000, 8%, 12-year convertible bonds outstanding. These bonds were sold at face value and pay semiannual interest on June 30 and December 31 of each year. The bonds are convertible into 30 shares of Jefferson $2 par value common stock for each $1,000 worth of bonds. On December 31, 1996, after the bond interest has been paid, $20,000 face value bonds were converted. The market value of Jefferson common stock was $44 per share on December 31, 1996.

Instructions
For each independent situation above, prepare the appropriate journal entry for the redemption or conversion of the bonds.

Journal entries to record mortgage note and installment payments.
(SO 7)

E11–10   Peyton Co. receives $110,000 when it issues a $110,000, 10%, mortgage note payable to finance the construction of a building at December 31, 1996. The terms provide for semi-annual installment payments of $7,500 on June 30 and December 31.

Instructions
Prepare the journal entries to record the mortgage loan and the first two installment payments.

Statement presentation of long-term liabilities.
(SO 8)

Long term Liab.
Bonds Payable Due 2007   120,000
Prem. on Bonds Pay-   32,000
Mortgage Note Pay

E11–11   The adjusted trial balance for Viola Corporation at the end of the current year contained the following accounts: *current liabilities*

Bond interest payable	$ 9,000
Mortgage note payable liability	59,500
Bonds payable, due 2007	120,000
Premium on bonds payable	32,000

152,000
59,500   211,500

Instructions
(a) Prepare the long-term liabilities section of the balance sheet.
(b) Indicate the proper balance sheet classification for the account(s) listed above that do not belong in the long-term liabilities section.

Journal entries for issuance of bonds payment of interest, and amortization of discount using effective-interest method.
(SO 9)

*E11–12   Quebec Corporation issued $260,000, 9%, 10-year bonds on January 1, 1996, for $243,799. This price resulted in an effective interest rate of 10% on the bonds. Interest is payable semiannually on July 1 and January 1. Quebec uses the effective-interest method to amortize bond premium or discount. Interest is not accrued on June 30.

Instructions
Prepare the journal entries to record (round to the nearest dollar):

(a) The issuance of the bonds.
(b) The payment of interest and the discount amortization on July 1, 1996.
(c) The accrual of interest and the discount amortization on December 31, 1996.

MToR

*E11–13 Cleveland Company issued $180,000, 11%, 10-year bonds on January 1, 1996, for $191,216. This price resulted in an effective interest rate of 10% on the bonds. Interest is payable semiannually on July 1 and January 1. Cleveland uses the effective-interest method to amortize bond premium or discount. Interest is not accrued on June 30.

Journal entries for issuance of bonds, payment of interest, and amortization of premium using effective-interest method.
(SO 9)

Instructions
Prepare the journal entries (rounded to the nearest dollar) to record:

   (a) The issuance of the bonds.
   (b) The payment of interest and the premium amortization on July 1, 1996.
   (c) The accrual of interest and the premium amortization on December 31, 1996.

PROBLEMS

• •

P11–1 On January 1, 1996, the ledger of Calcutta Company contains the following liability accounts.

Prepare current liability entries, adjusting entries, and current liability section.
(SO 1, 2, 3)

Accounts Payable	$42,500
Sales Taxes Payable	5,600
Unearned Service Revenue	15,000

During January the following selected transactions occurred:

Jan. 1 Borrowed $15,000 in cash from Midland Bank on a 4-month, 10%, $15,000 note.
    5 Sold merchandise for cash totaling $7,800 which includes 4% sales taxes.
   12 Provided services for customers who had made advance payments of $8,000. (Credit Service Revenue.)
   14 Paid state treasurer's department for sales taxes collected in December 1995 $5,600.
   20 Sold 500 units of a new product on credit at $52 per unit, plus 4% sales tax.
   25 Sold merchandise for cash totaling $11,440, which includes 4% sales taxes.

Instructions

   (a) Journalize the January transactions.
   (b) Journalize the adjusting entries at January 31 for the outstanding note payable.
   (c) Prepare the current liability section of the balance sheet at January 31, 1996. Assume no change in Accounts Payable.

P11–2 The following are selected transactions of Eldorado Company. Eldorado prepares financial statements *quarterly*.

Journalize and post note transactions and show balance sheet presentation.
(SO 2)

Jan. 2 Purchased merchandise on account from McCoy Company, $15,000, terms 2/10, n/30.
Feb. 1 Issued a 10%, 2-month, $15,000 note to McCoy in payment of account.
Mar. 31 Accrued interest for 2 months on McCoy note.
Apr. 1 Paid face value and interest on McCoy note.
July 1 Purchased equipment from Scottie Equipment paying $11,000 in cash and signing a 10%, 3-month, $24,000 note.
Sept. 30 Accrued interest for 3 months on Scottie note.
Oct. 1 Paid face value and interest on Scottie note.
Dec. 1 Borrowed $10,000 from the Federation Bank by issuing a 3-month, 9%-interest-bearing note with a face value of $10,000.
Dec. 31 Recognized interest expense for 1 month on Federation Bank note.

Instructions

   (a) Prepare journal entries for the above transactions and events.
   (b) Post to the accounts, Notes Payable, Interest Payable, and Interest Expense.
   (c) Show the balance sheet presentation of notes payable at December 31.
   (d) What is total interest expense for the year?

Prepare journal entries to record issuance of bonds, interest accrual, and amortization for 2 years.
(SO 5, 8)

P11–3 Moriarity Company sold $4,000,000, 9%, 20-year bonds on January 1, 1996. The bonds were dated January 1, 1996, and pay interest on January 1 and July 1. Moriarity Company uses the straight-line method to amortize bond premium or discount. The bonds were sold at 97. Assume no interest is accrued on June 30.

Instructions

(a) Prepare the journal entry to record the issuance of the bonds on January 1, 1996.
(b) Prepare a bond discount amortization schedule for the first four interest periods.
(c) Prepare the journal entries for interest and the amortization of the discount in 1996 and 1997.
(d) Show the balance sheet presentation of the bond liability at December 31, 1997.

Prepare journal entries to record issuance of bonds, interest, and amortization of bond premium and discount.
(SO 5, 8)

P11–4   Beatrice Corporation sold $1,500,000, 8%, 10-year bonds on January 1, 1996. The bonds were dated January 1, 1996, and pay interest on July 1 and January 1. Beatrice Corporation uses the straight-line method to amortize bond premium or discount. Assume no interest is accrued on June 30.

Instructions

(a) Prepare all the necessary journal entries to record the issuance of the bonds and bond interest expense for 1996, assuming that the bonds sold at 102.
(b) Prepare journal entries as in part (a) assuming that the bonds sold at 97.
(c) Show balance sheet presentation for each bond issue at December 31, 1996.

Prepare journal entries to record interest payments, discount amortization, and redemption of bonds.
(SO 5, 8)

P11–5   The following is taken from Bermuda Corp. balance sheet at December 31, 1996:

Current liabilities		
Bond interest payable (for 6 months from July 1 to December 31)		$132,000
Long-term liabilities		
Bonds payable, 11%, due January 1, 2007	$2,400,000	
Less: Discount on bonds payable	84,000	$2,316,000

Interest is payable semiannually on January 1 and July 1. The bonds are callable on any semi-annual interest date. Bermuda uses straight-line amortization for any bond premium or discount. From December 31, 1996, the bonds will be outstanding for an additional 10 years or 120 months. Assume no interest is accrued on June 30.

Instructions
(Round all computations to the nearest dollar.)

(a) Journalize the payment of bond interest on January 1, 1997.
(b) Prepare the entry to amortize bond discount and to pay the interest due on July 1, 1997.
(c) Assume on July 1, 1997, after paying interest that Bermuda Corp. calls bonds having a face value of $800,000. The call price is 102. Record the redemption of the bonds.
(d) Prepare the adjusting entry at December 31, 1997, to amortize bond discount and to accrue interest on the remaining bonds.

Prepare installment payments schedule and journal entries for a mortgage note payable.
(SO 7)

P11–6   Nankin Electronics issues a $900,000, 10%, 10-year mortgage note on December 31, 1995, to help finance a plant expansion program. The terms provide for semiannual installment payments, not including real estate taxes and insurance of $72,218. Payments are due June 30 and December 31.

Instructions

(a) Prepare an installment payments schedule for the first 2 years.
(b) Prepare the entries for (1) the mortgage loan and (2) the first two installment payments.
(c) Show how the total mortgage liability should be reported on the balance sheet at December 31, 1996.

Prepare journal entries to record issuance of bonds, payment of interest, and amortization of bond discount using effective-interest method.
(SO 9)

*P11–7   On July 1, 1996, Global Satellites issued $1,200,000 face value, 9%, 10-year bonds at $1,125,227. This price resulted in an effective-interest rate of 10% on the bonds. Global uses the effective-interest method to amortize bond premium or discount. The bonds pay semi-annual interest July 1 and January 1.

Instructions
(Round all computations to the nearest dollar.)

(a) Prepare the journal entry to record the issuance of the bonds on July 1, 1996.

(b) Prepare an amortization table through December 31, 1997 (three interest periods) for this bond issue.
(c) Prepare the journal entry to record the accrual of interest and the amortization of the discount on December 31, 1996.
(d) Prepare the journal entry to record the payment of interest and the amortization of the discount on July 1, 1997.
(e) Prepare the journal entry to record the accrual of interest and the amortization of the discount on December 31, 1997.

*P11–8   On July 1, 1996, Saudi Chemical Company issued $2,000,000 face value, 12%, 10-year bonds at $2,249,245. This price resulted in a 10% effective-interest rate on the bonds. Saudi uses the effective-interest method to amortize bond premium or discount. The bonds pay semiannual interest on each July 1 and January 1.

Prepare journal entries to record issuance of bonds, payment of interest, and amortization of premium using effective-interest method. In addition, answer questions.
(SO 9)

Instructions
(a) Prepare the journal entries to record the following transactions:
(1) The issuance of the bonds on July 1, 1996.
(2) The accrual of interest and the amortization of the premium on December 31, 1996.
(3) The payment of interest and the amortization of the premium on July 1, 1997.
(4) The accrual of interest and the amortization of the premium on December 31, 1997.
(b) Show the proper balance sheet presentation for the liability for bonds payable on the December 31, 1997, balance sheet.
(c) ◼▭▭▭▷ Provide the answers to the following questions in letter form.
(1) What amount of interest expense is reported for 1997?
(2) Would the bond interest expense reported in 1997 be the same as, greater than, or less than the amount that would be reported if the straight-line method of amortization were used?
(3) Determine the total cost of borrowing over the life of the bond.
(4) Would the total bond interest expense be greater than, the same as, or less than the total interest expense if the straight-line method of amortization were used?

ALTERNATE PROBLEMS

• •

P11–1A   On January 1, 1996, the ledger of El Paso Company contains the following liability accounts:

Prepare current liability entries, adjusting entries, and current liability section.
(SO 1, 2, 3)

Accounts Payable	$52,000
Sales Taxes Payable	7,500
Unearned Service Revenue	16,000

During January the following selected transactions occurred:

Jan. 5   Sold merchandise for cash totaling $16,632, which includes 8% sales taxes.
   12   Provided services for customers who had made advance payments of $9,000. (Credit Service Revenue)
   14   Paid state revenue department for sales taxes collected in December 1995 ($7,500).
   20   Sold 500 units of a new product on credit at $50 per unit, plus 8% sales tax.
   21   Borrowed $18,000 from Midland Bank on a 3-month, 10%, $18,000 note.
   25   Sold merchandise for cash totaling $11,340, which includes 8% sales taxes.

Instructions
(a) Journalize the January transactions.
(b) Journalize the adjusting entries at January 31 for the outstanding notes payable.
(c) Prepare the current liability section of the balance sheet at January 31, 1996. Assume no change in accounts payable.

P11–2A   Montego Electric sold $3,000,000, 10%, 10-year bonds on January 1, 1996. The bonds were dated January 1 and pay interest July 1 and January 1. Montego Electric uses the straight-line method to amortize bond premium or discount. The bonds were sold at 104. Assume no interest is accrued on June 30.

Prepare journal entries to record issuance of bonds, interest accrual, and amortization for 2 years.
(SO 5, 8)

Instructions
(a) Prepare the journal entry to record the issuance of the bonds on January 1, 1996.
(b) Prepare a bond premium amortization schedule for the first four interest periods.
(c) Prepare the journal entries for interest and the amortization of the premium in 1996 and 1997.
(d) Show the balance sheet presentation of the bond liability at December 31, 1997.

Prepare journal entries to record issuance of bonds, interest, and amortization of bond premium and discount.
(SO 5, 8)

P11–3A   San Diego Company sold $1,500,000, 12%, 10-year bonds on July 1, 1996. The bonds were dated July 1, 1996, and pay interest July 1 and January 1. San Diego Company uses the straight-line method to amortize bond premium or discount. Assume no interest is accrued on June 30.

Instructions
(a) Prepare all the necessary journal entries to record the issuance of the bonds and bond interest expense for 1996, assuming that the bonds sold at 102.
(b) Prepare journal entries as in part (a) assuming that the bonds sold at 94.
(c) Show balance sheet presentation for each bond issue at December 31, 1996.

Prepare journal entries to record interest payments, premium amortization, and redemption of bonds.
(SO 5, 6)

P11–4A   The following is taken from the Walenda Oil Company balance sheet at December 31, 1996:

Current liabilities		
Bond interest payable (for 6 months		
from July 1 to December 31)		$ 216,000
Long-term liabilities		
Bonds payable, 12% due January 1, 2007	$3,600,000	
Add: Premium on Bonds Payable	300,000	$3,900,000

Interest is payable semiannually on January 1 and July 1. The bonds are callable on any semi-annual interest date. Walenda uses straight-line amortization for any bond premium or discount. From December 31, 1996, the bonds will be outstanding for an additional 10 years (120 months). Assume no interest is accrued on June 30.

Instructions
(a) Journalize the payment of bond interest on January 1, 1997.
(b) Prepare the entry to amortize bond premium and to pay the interest due on July 1, 1997.
(c) Assume on July 1, 1997, after paying interest, that Walenda Company calls bonds having a face value of $1,800,000. The call price is 101. Record the redemption of the bonds.
(d) Prepare the adjusting entry at December 31, 1997, to amortize bond premium and to accrue interest on the remaining bonds.

Prepare installment schedule and journal entries for a mortgage note payable.
(SO 7)

P11–5A   Elite Electronics issues an $800,000, 12%, 10-year mortgage note on December 31, 1995. The proceeds from the note are to be used in financing a new research laboratory. The terms of the note provide for semiannual installment payments, exclusive of real estate taxes and insurance, of $69,748. Payments are due June 30 and December 31.

Instructions
(a) Prepare an installment payments schedule for the first 2 years.
(b) Prepare the entries for (1) the loan and (2) the first two installment payments.
(c) Show how the total mortgage liability should be reported on the balance sheet at December 31, 1996.

Prepare journal entries to record issuance of bonds, payment of interest, and amortization of bond premium using effective-interest method.
(SO 5, 9)

*P11–6A   On July 1, 1996, Mt. Vernon Corporation issued $1,500,000 face value, 12%, 10-year bonds at $1,686,934. This price resulted in an effective-interest rate of 10% on the bonds. Mt. Vernon uses the effective-interest method to amortize bond premium or discount. The bonds pay semiannual interest July 1 and January 1.

Instructions
(Round all computations to the nearest dollar.)
(a) Prepare the journal entry to record the issuance of the bonds on July 1, 1996.

(b) Prepare an amortization table through December 31, 1997 (three interest periods) for this bond issue.

(c) Prepare the journal entry to record the accrual of interest and the amortization of the premium on December 31, 1996.

(d) Prepare the journal entry to record the payment of interest and the amortization of the premium on July 1, 1997.

(e) Prepare the journal entry to record the accrual of interest and the amortization of the premium on December 31, 1997.

*P11–7A On July 1, 1996, Cherokee Company issued $2,200,000 face value, 10%, 10-year bonds at $1,947,651. This price resulted in an effective-interest rate of 12% on the bonds. Cherokee uses the effective-interest method to amortize bond premium or discount. The bonds pay semiannual interest July 1 and January 1.

Prepare journal entries to record issuance of bonds, payment of interest, and amortization of discount using effective-interest method. In addition, answer questions. (SO 5, 9)

Instructions

(a) Prepare the journal entries to record the following transactions.
   (1) The issuance of the bonds on July 1, 1996.
   (2) The accrual of interest and the amortization of the discount on December 31, 1996.
   (3) The payment of interest and the amortization of the discount on July 1, 1997.
   (4) The accrual of interest and the amortization of the discount on December 31, 1997.

(b) Show the proper balance sheet presentation for the liability for bonds payable on the December 31, 1997, balance sheet.

(c) ▭▭▭▷ Provide the answers to the following questions in letter form.
   (1) What amount of interest expense is reported for 1997?
   (2) Would the bond interest expense reported in 1997 be the same as, greater than, or less than the amount that would be reported if the straight-line method of amortization were used?
   (3) Determine the total cost of borrowing over the life of the bond.
   (4) Would the total bond interest expense be greater than, the same as, or less than the total interest expense that would be reported if the straight-line method of amortization were used?

▶B*roadening Your Perspective*

F*INANCIAL* REPORTING PROBLEM
••

A. Refer to the financial statements of PepsiCo, Inc., and the Notes to Consolidated Financial Statements in Appendix A.

Instructions

Answer the following questions about current and contingent liabilities and payroll costs:

(a) What were PepsiCo's total current liabilities at December 30, 1995? What was the increase/decrease in PepsiCo's total current liabilities from the prior year?

(b) How much were the "short-term borrowings" at December 30, 1995?

(c) What were the components of total current liabilities on December 30, 1995 (other than "short-term borrowings" already discussed in b above)?

B. Presented below is the long-term debt portion of the notes to the financial statements of Didde Industries, Inc.

Long-Term Debt
Long-term debt is summarized as follows (000s omitted):

	December 31, 1998
Unsecured variable interest rate note (weighted average interest rate of 9.3% and 9.6% at December 31, 1998 and 1997, respectively) due in quarterly installments through 2000	$ 4,000
9.75% first mortgage bonds secured by a lien on phosphate rock reserves, due $7.0 million annually through 2003	40,000
8.625% to 9.875% mortgage notes secured by various distribution facilities, due monthly through 2010	13,023
Total long-term debt	57,023
Less current portion	15,574
	$41,449

Certain borrowings are collateralized by property, plant and equipment. Maintenance of specified minimum working capital (current assets less liabilities) and stockholders' equity levels, specified maximum debt ratios and investments are also required.

Long-term debt maturities for the four years succeeding December 31, 1999 are $8.7 million in 2000, $8.0 million in 2001, $8.0 million in 2002 and $8.2 million in 2003.

Instructions
(a) Indicate how much long-term debt is outstanding and what are the different types of debt Didde Industries reports.
(b) Why do you think the loan agreement contains debt covenants requiring minimum working capital and stockholders' equity levels, and specified maximum debt ratios and investments?

COMPARATIVE ANALYSIS PROBLEM— THE COCA-COLA COMPANY VS. PEPSICO, INC.

The financial statements of Coca-Cola Company are presented at the end of Chapter 1, and PepsiCo's financial statements are presented in Appendix A.

Instructions
(a) Based on the information contained in these financial statements, compute the following 1995 ratios for each company:
   (1) Debt to total assets ratio
   (2) Times interest earned ratio
(b) What conclusions concerning the companies' long-run solvency can be drawn from these data?

INTERPRETATION OF FINANCIAL STATEMENTS

Mini-Case One—Texas Instruments
Texas Instruments designs and produces devices that use semiconductor technology. You may have one of their calculators sitting on your desk. Because it is in a high-tech industry, it must constantly invest in new technology. This requires considerable financing. During 1995, Texas Instruments' current liabilities and its long-term liabilities both increased by about $1 billion each. Provided below is additional information from Texas Instruments' 1995 annual report.

(All dollars in millions)	1995	1994
Current assets	$5,518	$4,017
Total assets	9,215	6,980
Current liabilities	3,188	2,199
Total liabilities	5,120	3,950
Stockholders' equity	4,095	3,030
Sales revenue	13,128	10,315
Income taxes	531	351
Interest expense	48	45
Net income	1,088	691

Maturities of long-term debt due during the four years subsequent to December 31, 1996:

	Millions of dollars
1997	$ 14
1998	18
1999	168
2000	19

Instructions

Address each of the following questions related to the liabilities of Texas Instruments.

(a) Using both working capital and the current ratio as indicators, evaluate the change in its liquidity from 1994 to 1995.
(b) Using both the debt to assets ratio, and times interest earned, evaluate the change in its solvency from 1994 to 1995.
(c) What are the implications of the information provided about the maturities of the company's long-term debt?

Mini-Case Two—Northland Cranberries

Despite only being a publicly traded company since 1987, Northland Cranberries, of Wisconsin Rapids, Wisconsin, is the world's largest cranberry grower. During its short life as a publicly traded corporation, it has engaged in an aggressive growth strategy. As a consequence, the company has taken on significant amounts of both short-term and long-term debt. The following information is taken from recent annual reports of the company.

	1995	1994
Current assets	$ 6,745,759	$ 5,598,054
Total assets	107,744,751	83,074,339
Current liabilities	10,168,685	4,484,687
Total liabilities	73,118,204	49,948,787
Stockholders' equity	34,626,547	33,125,552
Net sales	21,783,966	18,051,355
Cost of goods sold	13,057,275	8,751,220
Interest expense	3,654,006	2,393,792
Income tax expense	1,051,000	1,917,000
Net income	1,581,707	2,942,954

Instructions

(a) Evaluate the company's liquidity by calculating and analyzing working capital and the current ratio.
(b) The following discussion of the company's liquidity was provided by the company in the Management Discussion and Analysis section of the company's 1995 annual report. Comment on whether you agree with management's statements, and what might be done to remedy the situation.

The lower comparative current ratio at March 31, 1995 was due to $3 million of short-term borrowing then outstanding which was incurred to fund the Company's September 1994 Yellow River Marsh acquisitions. As a result of the extreme seasonality of its business, the company does not believe that its current ratio or its underlying stated working capital at its March 31, 1995 fiscal year end is a meaningful indication of the Company's liquidity. As of March 31 of each fiscal year, the Company has historically carried no significant amounts of inventories and by such date all of the Company's accounts receivable from its crop sold for processing under the supply agreements have been paid in cash, with the resulting cash received from such payments used to reduce indebtedness. The Company utilizes its revolving bank credit facility, together with cash generated from operations, to fund its working capital requirements throughout its growing season.

(c) Evaluate the company's solvency using the debt to assets ratio and times interest earned ratio.

DECISION CASE

On January 1, 1993, Jerry Mall Corporation issued $1,200,000 of 5-year, 8% bonds at 97; the bonds pay interest semiannually on July 1 and January 1. By January 1, 1995, the market rate of interest for bonds of risk similar to those of Jerry Mall Corporation had risen. As a result the market value of these bonds was $1,000,000 on January 1, 1995—below their carrying value. Jerry Mall, president of the company suggests repurchasing all of these bonds in the open market at the $1,000,000 price. But, to do so the company will have to issue $1,000,000 (face value) of new 10-year, 12% bonds at par. The president asks you as controller, "What is the feasibility of my proposed repurchase plan?"

Instructions
  (a) What is the carrying value of the outstanding Mall Corporation 5-year bonds on January 1, 1995 (assume straight-line amortization)?
  (b) Prepare the journal entry to retire the 5-year bonds on January 1, 1995. Prepare the journal entry to issue the new 10-year bonds.
  (c) Prepare a short memo to the president in response to his request for advice. List the economic factors that you believe should be considered for his repurchase proposal.

COMMUNICATION ACTIVITY

Finn Berge, president of the Blue Marlin, is considering the issuance of bonds to finance an expansion of his business. He has asked you to (1) discuss the advantages of bonds over common stock financing, (2) indicate the type of bonds he might issue, and (3) explain the issuing procedures used in bond transactions.

Instructions
Write a memorandum to the president, answering his request.

GROUP ACTIVITY 1

There are six topics in the section on Accounting for Current Liabilities: notes payable, sales taxes payable, payroll and payroll taxes payable, unearned revenues, current maturities of long-term debt, and financial statement presentation.

Instructions

With the class divided into six groups, each group should choose one topic and prepare a presentation to explain to the class the key points about the assigned topic.

GROUP ACTIVITY 2

The text explains that bonds may be issued at (1) face value, (2) a discount, (3) a premium, and (4) a date that is between interest dates.

Instructions

With the class divided into four groups, each group should choose one type of bond issue. Your group is to explain, using dollar amounts different from those used in the text: (a) the entry to record the sale of the bonds, (b) the entry at the end of the first interest period after the sale, and (c) the financial statement presentation of the bonds and interest expense at the end of the first interest period.

ETHICS CASE

Andy Vicks is the president, founder, and majority owner of Custom Medical Corporation, an emerging medical technology products company. Custom is in dire need of additional capital to keep operating and to bring several promising products to final development, testing, and production. Andy, as owner of 51% of the outstanding stock, manages the company's operations. He places heavy emphasis on research and development and long-term growth. The other principal stockholder is Jill Caterino who, as a nonemployee investor, owns 40% of the stock. Jill would like to deemphasize the R&D functions and emphasize the marketing function to maximize short-run sales and profits from existing products. She believes this strategy would raise the market price of Custom's stock.

All of Andy's personal capital and borrowing power is tied up in his 51% stock ownership. He knows that any offering of additional shares of stock will dilute his controlling interest because he won't be able to participate in such an issuance. But, Jill has money and would likely buy enough shares to gain control of Custom. She then would dictate the company's future direction, even if it meant replacing Andy as president and CEO.

The company already has considerable debt. Raising additional debt will be costly, will adversely affect Custom's credit rating, and will increase the company's reported losses due to the growth in interest expense. Jill and the other minority stockholders express opposition to the assumption of additional debt, fearing the company will be pushed to the brink of bankruptcy. Wanting to maintain his control and to preserve the direction of "his" company, Andy is doing everything to avoid a stock issuance and is contemplating a large issuance of bonds, even if it means the bonds are issued with a high effective-interest rate.

Instructions

   (a) Who are the stakeholders in this situation?
   (b) What are the ethical issues in this case?
   (c) What would you do if you were Andy?

RESEARCH ASSIGNMENT

The November 6, 1995 edition of *The Wall Street Journal* includes an article by Linda Sandler, entitled "Kmart Is Pressured Over Obscure Bond 'Puts', Which Stir Worries Amid Tough Retail Times." Read the article and answer the following questions.

   (a) What is the total dollar amount of the bond issue in question? Who purchased these bonds?
   (b) What right does the "put option" give to bondholders?
   (c) What amount is available under Kmart's bank lines? Why can't Kmart borrow under these lines to purchase the bonds? What is the most likely solution to the problem?
   (d) Were the terms of the put bonds adequately disclosed?

CRITICAL THINKING
▸ *A Real-World Focus: Apache Corporation*
....

Apache Corporation is an international, independent energy enterprise engaged in the exploration, development, production, gathering, processing, and marketing of natural gas and crude oil. Its corporate headquarters are located in Houston, Texas, and it has operations in 18 states of the U.S. as well as Australia, the Congo, France, Myanmar, and Indonesia.

The 1994 annual report of Apache Corporation disclosed the following information in its management discussion section:

> In May 1994, Apache issued 9.25% bonds due 2002 in the principal amount of $100 million. The proceeds of $99 million from the offering were used to reduce bank debt, to pay off the 9.5% convertible debentures due 1996, and for general corporate purposes. In December 1994, the company privately placed 3.93% convertible notes due 1997 in the principal amount of $75 million. The notes are not redeemable before maturity and are convertible into Apache common stock at the option of the holders at any time prior to maturity, at a conversion price of $27 per share. Proceeds from the sale of the notes were used for the repayment of bank debt.

Instructions
(a) Identify the face amount, contractual interest rate, and selling price of the newly issued bonds due in 2002. Explain whether the bonds sold at a premium or a discount.
(b) For what purposes has Apache Corporation been incurring more debt?

Answers to Self-Study Questions
1. a   2. d   3. b   4. b   5. c   6. a   7. d   8. a   9. b   10. d   11. c
*12. b   *13. c

●●●●●▶ **Concepts for Review**

Before studying this chapter, you should know or, if necessary, review:

a. *The content of the stockholders' equity section of a balance sheet.* (Ch. 4, p. 166)

b. *How to prepare closing entries for a corporation (Ch. 4, pp. 152–56).*

c. *What is the difference between paid-in capital and retained earnings.* (Ch. 1, p. 12–13)

"Have You Driven a Ford Lately?"

DETROIT, Mich. — A company that has produced such renowned successes as the Model T and the Mustang, and such a dismal failure as the Edsel, would have some interesting tales to tell. Henry Ford was a defiant visionary from the day Ford Motor Company was formed in 1903. His goal from day one was to design a car he could mass-produce and sell at a price that was affordable to the masses. In short order he accomplished this goal, and by 1920 60 percent of all vehicles on American roads were Fords.

Henry Ford was intolerant of anything that stood between himself and success. In the early years Ford issued shares to the public in order to finance the company's exponential growth. In 1916 he decided that, to retain funds to finance expansion, the company would skip a dividend payment to its shareholders. The shareholders sued. Henry Ford's reaction was swift and direct: if the shareholders didn't see things his way, he would get rid of them. In 1919 the Ford family purchased 100 percent of the outstanding shares of

Ford, eliminating any outside "interference." It was over 35 years before shares were again issued to the public.

Ford Motor Company has continued to evolve over the years while at the same time it sometimes has appeared to become even more like the company Henry Ford originally dreamed of. Today there are nearly a billion shares of publicly traded Ford stock outstanding, and the President and Chief Executive is not a member of the Ford family.

However, the Ford family still retains a significant stake in Ford. In 1994, in a move Henry Ford might have supported, top management decided to centralize decision-making—that is, to have more key decisions made by top management, rather than by division managers. And, reminiscent of Henry Ford's most famous car, the company is attempting to make a "global car"—a mass-produced car that can be sold around the world with only minor changes. ◄

CORPORATIONS: ORGANIZATION, STOCK TRANSACTIONS, DIVIDENDS, AND RETAINED EARNINGS

► STUDY OBJECTIVES ◄

After studying this chapter, you should be able to:

1. Identify and discuss the major characteristics of a corporation.
2. Record the issuance of common stock.
3. Explain the accounting for treasury stock.
4. Differentiate preferred stock from common stock.
5. Prepare the entries for cash dividends and stock dividends.
6. Identify the items that are reported in a retained earnings statement.
7. Prepare a comprehensive stockholders' equity section.

Corporations like Ford Motor Company have substantial resources. In fact, the corporation is the dominant form of business organization in the United States in terms of dollar volume of sales, earnings, and employees. All of the 500 largest companies in the United States are corporations. In this chapter we will explain the essential features of a corporation, the accounting for a corporation's capital stock transactions, dividends and retained earnings. The content and organization of this chapter are as follows:

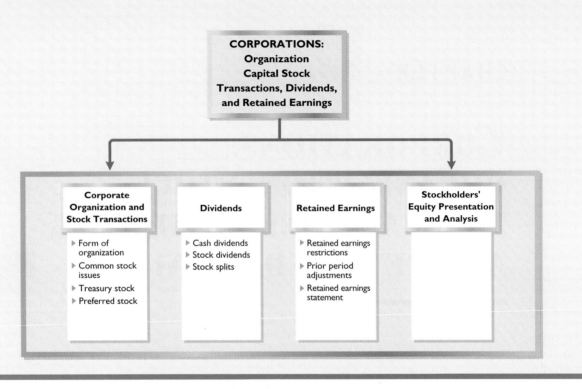

►SECTION 1 ► The Corporate Form of Organization

Helpful hint A corporation is a separate entity for both accounting and legal purposes.

A corporation is created by law, and its continued existence depends upon the corporate statutes of the state in which it is incorporated. As a legal entity, a corporation has most of the rights and privileges of a person. The major exceptions relate to privileges that can be exercised only by a living person, such as the right to vote or to hold public office. Similarly, a corporation is subject to the same duties and responsibilities as a person, e.g., it must abide by the laws and it must pay taxes.

Corporations may be classified in a variety of ways. Two common bases are by purpose and by ownership. A corporation may be organized for the **purpose** of making a **profit**, or it may be **nonprofit**. Corporations for profit include such well-known companies as McDonald's, General Motors, and Apple Computer. Nonprofit corporations are organized for charitable, medical, and educational purposes and include the Salvation Army, the American Cancer Society, and the Ford Foundation.

Classification by **ownership** distinguishes between publicly held and privately held corporations. A publicly held corporation may have thousands of stockholders, and its stock is regularly traded on a national securities market such as the New York Stock Exchange. Most of the largest U.S. corporations are publicly held. Examples of publicly held corporations are International Business Machines, Caterpillar Inc., and General Electric. In contrast, a privately held corporation, often referred to as a closely held corporation, usually has only a few stockholders, and does not offer its stock for sale to the general public. Privately held companies are generally much smaller than publicly held companies.

Characteristics of a Corporation

A number of characteristics distinguish a corporation from proprietorships and partnerships. The most important of these characteristics are explained below.

Separate Legal Existence

As an entity separate and distinct from its owners, the corporation acts under its own name rather than in the name of its stockholders. A corporation may buy, own, and sell property, borrow money, and enter into legally binding contracts in its own name. It may also sue or be sued, and it pays its own taxes.

In contrast to a partnership, in which the acts of the owners (partners) bind the partnership, the acts of the owners (stockholders) do not bind the corporation unless such owners are duly appointed agents of the corporation. For example, if you owned shares of Ford Motor Company stock, you would not have the right to purchase automobile parts for the company unless you were appointed as an agent of the corporation.

Legal existence separate from owners

Limited Liability of Stockholders

Since a corporation is a separate legal entity, creditors ordinarily have recourse only to corporate assets to satisfy their claims. The liability of stockholders is normally limited to their investment in the corporation, and creditors have no legal claim on the personal assets of the owners unless fraud has occurred. Thus, even in the event of bankruptcy of the corporation, stockholders' losses are generally limited to their capital investment in the corporation.

Limited liability of stockholders

Transferable Ownership Rights

Ownership of a corporation is shown in shares of capital stock, which are transferable units. Stockholders may dispose of part or all of their interest in a corporation simply by selling their stock. In contrast to the transfer of an ownership interest in a partnership, which requires the consent of each owner, the transfer of stock is entirely at the discretion of the stockholder. It does not require the approval of either the corporation or other stockholders. The transfer of ownership rights between stockholders normally has no effect on the operating activities of the corporation or on a corporation's assets, liabilities, and total ownership equity. That is, the enterprise does not participate in the transfer of these ownership rights after it issues the capital stock.

Transferable ownership rights

Ability to Acquire Capital

It generally is relatively easy for a corporation to obtain capital through the issuance of stock. Buying stock in a corporation is often more attractive to an investor than investing in a partnership because a stockholder has limited liability and shares of stock are readily transferable. Moreover, many individuals can become stockholders by investing small amounts of money. In sum, the ability of a successful corporation to obtain capital is virtually unlimited.

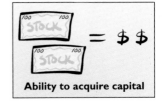

Ability to acquire capital

Continuous Life

Continuous life

The life of a corporation is stated in its charter; it may be perpetual or it may be limited to a specific number of years. If it is limited, the period of existence can be extended through renewal of the charter. Since a corporation is a separate legal entity, the life of a corporation and its continuance as a going concern are not affected by the withdrawal, death, or incapacity of a stockholder, employee, or officer. As a result, a successful enterprise can have a continuous and perpetual life.

Corporation Management

Although stockholders legally own the corporation, as in Ford Motor Company, they manage the corporation indirectly through a board of directors they elect. The board, in turn, formulates the operating policies for the company and selects officers, such as a president and one or more vice-presidents, to execute policy and to perform daily management functions.

A typical organization chart showing the delegation of responsibility is shown in Illustration 12-1. The **president** is the chief executive officer (CEO) with direct responsibility for managing the business. As the organization chart shows, the president delegates responsibility to other officers. The chief accounting officer is the **controller**. The controller's responsibilities include (1) maintaining the accounting records, (2) maintaining an adequate system of internal control, and (3) preparing financial statements, tax returns, and internal reports. The **treasurer** has custody of the corporation's funds and is responsible for maintaining the company's cash position.

Illustration 12-1

Corporation organization chart

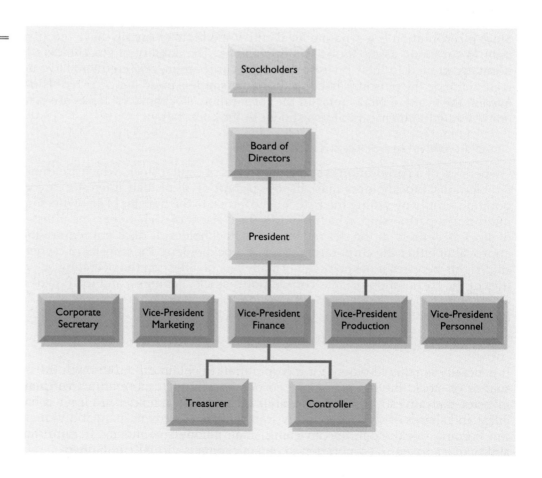

►*A*ccounting in *A*ction ► *Business Insight*

An interesting question is: Who runs a corporation—the stockholders or the board of directors? This issue has taken on increased importance because stockholders and boards of directors are often on the opposite sides of the fence these days when potential takeovers occur.

A classic example is the unfriendly takeover bid made by Paramount Communication Inc. for Time Inc. Paramount bid up Time's stock price substantially; many stockholders said sell—but Time's board of directors had other plans. They were in the process of trying to make a friendly deal with Warner Communications. Some stockholders said, "Let's vote on what we should do." But Time decided to proceed without a stockholders' vote, even though the board of directors knew the Warner deal would depress Time's stock price in the short term. They figured that many stockholders would prefer to accept the Paramount bid. The stockholders sued to overturn the deal with Warner Communications but lost. The judge wrote: "Corporation law does not operate on the theory that directors, in exercising their powers to manage the firm, are obligated to follow the wishes of a majority of stockholders. In fact, the directors, not the stockholders, are charged with the duty to manage the firm."

►*Ethics note*

The separation of ownership from management caused by the corporation form of organization can create an ethical dilemma for management. Managers are often compensated based upon the performance of the firm, and thus may be tempted to exaggerate firm performance by inflating income figures.

The organizational structure of a corporation enables a company to hire professional managers to run the business. On the other hand, the separation of ownership and management prevents owners from having an active role in managing the company, which some owners like to have.

Government Regulations

A corporation is subject to numerous state and federal regulations. For example, state laws usually prescribe the requirements for issuing stock, the distributions of earnings permitted to stockholders, and the effects of retiring stock, as well as other procedures and restrictions. Similarly, federal securities laws govern the sale of capital stock to the general public. Also, most publicly held corporations are required to make extensive disclosure of their financial affairs to the Securities and Exchange Commission through quarterly and annual reports. In addition, when a corporate stock is listed and traded on organized securities markets, the corporation must comply with the reporting requirements of these exchanges.

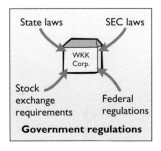

Government regulations

Government regulations are designed to protect the owners of the corporation. Unlike the owners of most proprietorships and partnerships, most stockholders do not participate in the day-to-day management of the company.

Additional Taxes

Neither proprietorships nor partnerships pay income taxes. The owner's share of these organizations' earnings is reported on his or her personal income tax return. Taxes are then paid by the individual on this amount. Corporations, on the other hand, must pay federal and state income taxes as a separate legal entity. These taxes are substantial: they can amount to as much as 40% of taxable income.

Additional taxes

In addition, stockholders are required to pay taxes on cash dividends, which are pro rata distributions of net income. Thus, many argue that corporate income is **taxed twice (double taxation)**, once at the corporate level, and again at the individual level.

From the foregoing, we can identify the following advantages and disadvantages of a corporation compared to a proprietorship and partnership:

Illustration 12-2

Advantages and disadvantages of a corporation

Advantages	Disadvantages
Separate legal existence	Corporation management—separation of
Limited liability of stockholders	ownership and management
Transferable ownership rights	Government regulations
Ability to acquire capital	Additional taxes
Continuous life	
Corporation management—professional	
managers	

Forming a Corporation

Upon receipt of its charter from the state of incorporation, by-laws[1] must be established for conducting the affairs of the corporation. Regardless of the number of states in which a corporation has operating divisions, it is incorporated in only one state. It is the company's advantage to incorporate in a state whose laws are favorable to the corporate form of business organization. General Motors, for example, is incorporated in Delaware, whereas USX Corp. is a New Jersey corporation. In fact, some corporations have increasingly been incorporating in states with rules favorable to existing management. For example, Gulf Oil changed its state of incorporation to Delaware to thwart possible unfriendly takeovers. There, certain defensive tactics against takeovers can be approved by the board of directors alone, without a vote by shareholders.

▶ Accounting in Action ▶ *Business Insight*

It is not necessary for a corporation to have an office in the state in which it incorporates. In fact, more than 50% of the Fortune 500 corporations are incorporated in Delaware. A primary reason is the Delaware courts' long-standing "business judgment rule." The rule provides that as long as directors exercise "due care" in the interests of stockholders (who have the right to sue directors), their actions will not be second-guessed by the courts. The rule has enabled directors to reject hostile takeover offers, even with hefty premiums, or to spurn takeovers simply because they did not want to sell the company. However, new interpretations of the rule appear to be emerging. In a recent case, the state court ruled for the company that made a hostile takeover bid. On appeal, the Delaware Supreme Court ruled for the directors but gave the following guideline to the state courts: "Was the board's response reasonable in the light of the threat posed?"

Corporations engaged in interstate commerce must obtain a license from each state in which they do business. The license subjects the corporation's operating activities to the general corporation laws of the state. Costs incurred in the formation of a corporation are called **organization costs**. These costs include fees to underwriters for handling stock and bond issues, legal fees, state incorporation fees, and promotional expenditures involved in the organization of the business.

These organization costs are capitalized by debiting an intangible asset entitled Organization Costs. It may be argued that organization costs have an asset life equal to the life of the corporation. Many companies, however, **amortize these costs** over an arbitrary period of time, up to a maximum of 40 years. Because income tax regulations require the amortization of organization costs over

---

[1]Following approval by two-thirds of the stockholders, the by-laws become binding upon all stockholders, directors, and officers. Legally, a corporation is regulated first by the laws of the state, second by its charter, and third by its by-laws. Care must be exercised to ensure that the provisions of the by-laws are not in conflict with either state laws or the charter.

a period of at least five years, some companies prefer to use the same period of amortization for accounting purposes. Determining the amount to be recorded when capital stock is used to pay for organization costs is explained later in the chapter.

◣orporate Capital
••

Owners' equity in a corporation is identified as **stockholders' equity, shareholders' equity**, or **corporate capital**. The stockholders' equity section of a corporation's balance sheet consists of: (1) paid-in (contributed) capital, and (2) retained earnings (earned capital). The distinction between paid-in capital and retained earnings is important from both a legal and an economic point of view. Legally, dividends can be declared out of retained earning in all states but in many states dividends cannot be declared out of paid-in capital. Economically, management, stockholders, and others look to earnings for the continued existence and growth of the corporation.

Ownership Rights of Stockholders

When chartered, the corporation may begin selling ownership rights in the form of shares of stock. When a corporation has only one class of stock, it is identified as **common stock**. Each share of common stock gives the stockholder the ownership rights pictured in Illustration 12-3. The ownership rights of a share of stock are stated in the articles of incorporation or in the by-laws.

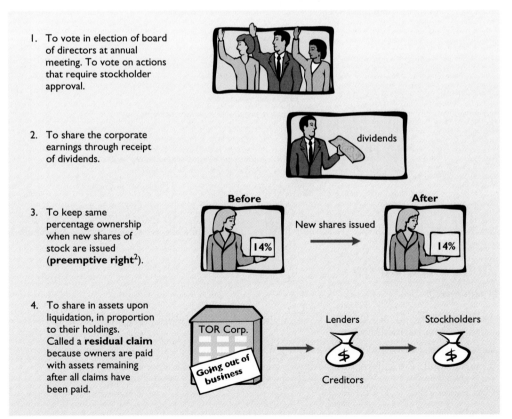

1. To vote in election of board of directors at annual meeting. To vote on actions that require stockholder approval.

2. To share the corporate earnings through receipt of dividends.

3. To keep same percentage ownership when new shares of stock are issued **(preemptive right²)**.

4. To share in assets upon liquidation, in proportion to their holdings. Called a **residual claim** because owners are paid with assets remaining after all claims have been paid.

Illustration 12-3

Ownership rights of stockholders

---

²A number of companies have eliminated the preemptive right, because they believe it makes an unnecessary and cumbersome demand on management. For example, IBM, by stockholder approval, has dropped its preemptive right for stockholders.

▶**A**ccounting in **A**ction ▸ *International Insight*

Illustration 12-4

A stock certificate

In Japan, stockholders are considered to be far less important to a corporation than employees, customers, and suppliers. Stockholders are rarely asked to vote on an issue, and the notion of bending corporate policy to favor stockholders borders on the heretical in Japan. This attitude toward stockholders appears to be slowly changing, however, as influential Japanese are advocating listening to investors, raising the extremely low dividends paid by Japanese corporations, and improving disclosure of financial information.

Proof of stock ownership is evidenced by a printed or engraved form known as a **stock certificate**. As shown in Illustration 12-4, the face of the certificate shows the name of the corporation, the stockholder's name, the class and special features of the stock, the number of shares owned, and the signatures of duly authorized corporate officials. Certificates are prenumbered to facilitate their accountability; they may be issued for any quantity of shares.

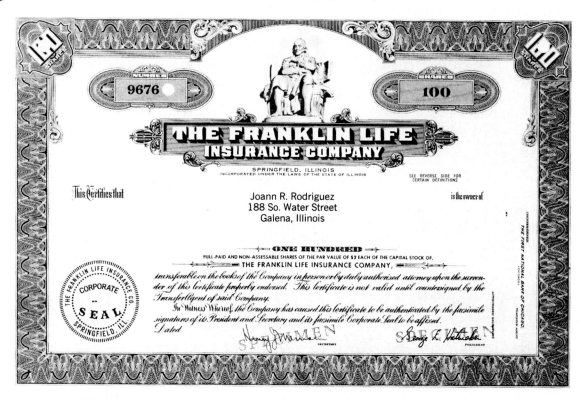

Before You Go On . . .

▶ *Review It*

1. What are the advantages and disadvantages of a corporation compared to a proprietorship and a partnership?
2. Identify the principal steps in forming a corporation.
3. What rights are inherent in owning a share of stock in a corporation?

Stock Issue Considerations

In considering the issuance (or sale) of stock, a corporation must resolve a number of basic questions: How many shares should be authorized for sale? How should the stock be issued? At what price should the shares be issued? What value should be assigned to the stock? These questions are answered in the following sections.

Authorized Stock

The amount of stock that a corporation is **authorized** to sell is indicated in its charter. The total amount of authorized stock at the time of incorporation normally anticipates both initial and subsequent capital needs of a company. As a result, the number of total shares authorized generally exceeds the number of shares initially sold. If all authorized stock is sold, a corporation must obtain consent of the state to amend its charter before it can issue additional shares.

The authorization of capital stock does not result in a formal accounting entry, since the event has no immediate effect on either corporate assets or stockholders' equity. However, disclosure of the number of shares of authorized stock is required in the stockholders' equity section. To determine the number of unissued shares that can be issued without amending the charter, the total shares issued are subtracted from the total authorized. For example, if Advanced Micro was authorized to sell 100,000 shares of common stock and issued 80,000 shares, 20,000 shares would remain unissued.

Issuance of Stock

A corporation has the choice of issuing common stock **directly** to investors or **indirectly** through an investment banking firm (brokerage house) that specializes in bringing securities to the attention of prospective investors. Direct issue is typical in closely held companies, whereas indirect issue is customary for a publicly held corporation.

In an indirect issue, the investment banking firm may agree to **underwrite** the entire stock issue. Under this arrangement, the investment banker buys the stock from the corporation at a stipulated price and resells the shares to investors. The corporation avoids any risk of being unable to sell the shares, and it obtains immediate use of the cash received from the underwriter. The investment banking firm, in turn, assumes the risk of reselling the shares in return for an underwriting fee—the profits expected to be realized from a sales price to the public higher than the price paid to the corporation.[3] For example, Kolff Medical, maker of the Jarvik artificial heart, used an underwriter to help it issue common stock to the public. The underwriter charged a 6.6% underwriting fee on Kolff Medical's approximate $20 million public offering.

How does a corporation set the price for a new issue of stock? Among the factors to be considered are (1) the company's anticipated future earnings, (2) its expected dividend rate per share, (3) its current financial position, (4) the current state of the economy, and (5) the current state of the securities market. The calculation can be complex and is properly the subject of a finance course.

Market Value of Stock

The stock of publicly held companies is traded on organized exchanges at dollar prices per share established by the interaction between buyers and sellers. In general, the prices set by the marketplace tend to follow the trend of a company's earnings and dividends. However, factors beyond a company's control, such as

> ▶ **International note**
>
> U.S. and U.K. corporations raise most of their capital through millions of outside shareholders and bondholders. In contrast, companies in Germany, France, and Japan acquire financing from large banks or other institutions. Consequently, in the latter environment, shareholders are less important, and external reporting and auditing receive less emphasis.

---

[3]Alternatively, the investment banking firm may agree only to enter into a **best efforts** contract with the corporation. In such cases, the banker agrees to sell as many shares as possible at a specified price, and the corporation bears the risk of unsold stock. Under a best efforts arrangement, the banking firm is paid a fee or commission for its services.

Helpful hint U.S. stock exchanges include the New York Stock Exchange, the American Stock Exchange, and 13 regional exchanges. Stock may also be traded on the over-the-counter (OTC) telecommunication network through NASDAQ.

the imposition of an oil embargo, changes in interest rates, and the outcome of a presidential election, may cause day-to-day fluctuations in market prices.

The volume of trading on national and international exchanges is heavy. Shares in excess of 400 million are often traded daily on the New York Stock Exchange alone. For each listed security the financial press reports the highs and lows of the stock during the year, the total volume of stock traded for a given day, the high and low price for the day, and the closing market price, with the net change for the day. A recent listing for Boeing Aircraft is shown below:

Illustration 12-5

Stock market price information

| Stock | 52 Weeks | | Sales 3/14 | High | Low | Close | Net Change |
	High	Low					
Boeing	114½	74⅛	27785	103	100⅛	102⅞	+2⅛

Helpful hint The United States has the largest market capitalization, $3.7 trillion, followed by Japan, $2.3 trillion; Britain, $1 trillion; Germany, $389 billion; France, $384 billion; and Hong Kong, $171 billion.

These numbers indicate that the high and low market prices for the last 52 weeks have been 114½ and 74½; the trading volume for March 14 was 2,778,500 shares; the high, low, and closing prices for that date were 103, 100½, and 102⅞, respectively; and the net change for the day was an increase of 2⅛ or $2.125 per share.

The trading of capital stock on securities exchanges involves the transfer of **already issued shares** from an existing stockholder to another investor. Consequently, these transactions have no impact on a corporation's stockholders' equity section.

▸*T*echnology in *A*ction

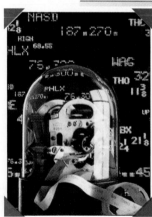

The giant, publicly held corporation could not exist without the organized stock markets, and the stock markets could not exist without massive computerization. Not too many years ago, the NYSE "ticker" would run behind, or trading would even be halted, when sales exceeded 30 million shares or so. Now, with sales sometimes in excess of 500 million shares, the NYSE and its companion exchanges throughout the country operate efficiently with computer technology. Technology has also made possible extended trading hours. An investor in New York, for example, can trade electronically at 3:30 A.M., which is the time in New York when the London Stock Exchange opens. Some predict that 24-hour-trading is not far off.

Par and No-Par Value Stocks

Par value stock is capital stock that has been assigned a value per share in the corporate charter. The par value may be any amount selected by the corporation. Generally, the amount of par value is quite low, because states often levy a tax on the corporation based on par value. For example, International Business Machines has a par of $1.25, Ford Motor Company, $1 par, General Motors Corporation, $1.67, and PepsiCo has 1⅔ cents.

Par value is not indicative of the worth or market value of the stock. As indicated above, IBM has a par value of $1.25, but its recent market price was $145 per share. **The significance of par value is a legal matter.** Par value represents the legal capital per share that must be retained in the business for the protection of corporate creditors. That is, it is not available for withdrawal by stockholders. Thus, most states require the corporation to sell its shares at par or above.

No-par value stock is capital stock that has not been assigned a value in the corporate charter. No-par value stock is often issued because some confusion still exists concerning par value and fair market value. If shares have no par value, the questionable treatment of using par value as a basis for fair market value never arises. The major disadvantage of no-par stock is that some states levy a high tax on the shares issued.

No-par value stock is quite common today. For example, Procter & Gamble and North American Van Lines both have no-par stock. In many states the board of directors is permitted to assign a stated value to the no-par shares, which becomes the legal capital per share. The stated value of no-par stock may be changed at any time by action of the directors. Stated value, like par value, is not indicative of the market value of the stock. When there is no assigned stated value, the entire proceeds received upon issuance of the stock is considered to be legal capital.

The relationship of par and no-par value to legal capital is shown below.

Helpful hint Legal capital per share always establishes the credit to the capital stock account.

Stock	Legal Capital per Share
Par value ————————————————→	Par value
No-par value with stated value ——————→	Stated value
No-par value without stated value ————→	Entire proceeds

Illustration 12-6

Relationship of par and no-par value stock to legal capital

As will be explained later, a common stock account is credited for the legal capital per share each time stock is issued.

Before You Go On . . .

▶ *Review It*

1. Of what significance to a corporation is the amount of authorized stock?
2. What alternative approaches may a corporation use in issuing stock?
3. Distinguish between par value and fair market value.

▶ *Do It*

At the end of its first year of operation, Doral Corporation has $750,000 of common stock and net income of $122,000. Prepare (a) the closing entry for net income (as illustrated in Chapter 4, pp. 153–56) and (b) the stockholders' equity section at year end.

Reasoning: Net income is recorded in Retained Earnings by a closing entry in which Income Summary is debited and Retained Earnings is credited. The stockholders' equity section consists of (1) paid-in capital and (2) retained earnings.

Solution:

(a) Income Summary	122,000	
Retained Earnings		122,000
(To close income summary and transfer net income to retained earnings)		

(b) Stockholders' equity

Paid-in capital		
Common stock	$750,000	
Retained earnings	122,000	
Total stockholders' equity		$872,000

Related exercise material: BE12–12, E12–13, and E12–15.

Accounting for Common Stock Issues

Let's now look at how to account for issues of common stock. The primary objectives in accounting for the issuance of common stock are to (1) identify the specific sources of paid-in capital and (2) maintain the distinction between paid-in capital and retained earnings. As shown below, **the issue of common stock affects only paid-in capital accounts.**

Issuing Par Value Common Stock for Cash

As discussed earlier, par value does not indicate a stock's market value. Therefore, the cash proceeds from issuing par value stock may be equal to, greater than, or less than par value. When the issuance of common stock for cash is recorded, the par value of the shares is credited to Common Stock, and the portion of the proceeds that is above or below par value is recorded in a separate paid-in capital account.

To illustrate, assume that Hydro-Slide, Inc. issues 1,000 shares of $1 par value common stock at par for cash. The entry to record this transaction is:

Cash	1,000	
Common Stock		1,000
(To record issuance of 1,000 shares of $1 par common stock at par)		

If Hydro-Slide, Inc., issues an additional 1,000 shares of the $1 par value common stock for cash at $5 per share, the entry is:

Cash	5,000	
Common Stock		1,000
Paid-in Capital in Excess of Par Value		4,000
(To record issuance of 1,000 shares of common stock in excess of par)		

Helpful hint Paid-in Capital in Excess of Par is also called Premium on Stock.

The total paid-in capital from these two transactions is $6,000, and the legal capital is $2,000. If Hydro-Slide, Inc. has retained earnings of $27,000, the stockholders' equity section is as follows:

Illustration 12-7

Stockholders' equity—paid-in capital in excess of par value

Stockholders' equity	
Paid-in capital	
Common stock	$ 2,000
Paid-in capital in excess of par value	4,000
Total paid-in capital	6,000
Retained earnings	27,000
Total stockholders' equity	$33,000

Helpful hint Paid-in Capital in Excess of Par Value is not reported in the income statement. It is not a gain.

When stock is issued for less than par value, the account Paid-in Capital in Excess of Par Value is debited, if a credit balance exists in this account. If a credit balance does not exist, then the amount less than par is debited to Retained Earnings. This situation occurs only rarely: The sale of common stock below par value is not permitted in most states, because stockholders may be held personally liable for the difference between the price paid upon original sale and par value.

Issuing No-Par Common Stock for Cash

When no-par common stock has a stated value, the entries are similar to those illustrated for par value stock. The stated value represents legal capital and therefore is credited to Common Stock. In addition, when the selling price of no-par stock exceeds stated value, the excess is credited to Paid-in Capital in Excess of Stated Value. For example, assume that instead of $1 par value stock, Hydro-Slide, Inc. has $5 stated value no-par stock and that it issues 5,000 shares at $8 per share for cash. The entry is:

Cash	40,000	
Common Stock		25,000
Paid-in Capital in Excess of Stated Value		15,000
(To record issue of 5,000 shares of $5 stated value no-par stock)		

Paid-in Capital in Excess of Stated Value is reported as part of paid-in capital in the stockholders' equity section.

When no-par stock does not have a stated value, the entire proceeds from the issue become legal capital and are credited to Common Stock. Thus, if Hydro-Slide does not assign a stated value to its no-par stock, the issuance of the 5,000 shares at $8 per share for cash is recorded as follows:

Cash	40,000	
Common Stock		40,000
(To record issue of 5,000 shares of no-par stock)		

The amount of legal capital for Hydro-Slide with a $5 stated value is $25,000; without a stated value, it is $40,000.

Issuing Common Stock for Services or Noncash Assets

Stock may be issued for services (compensation to attorneys, consultants, and others) or for noncash assets (land, buildings, and equipment). In such cases, a question arises as to the cost that should be recognized in the exchange transaction. To comply with the **cost principle** in a noncash transaction, **cost is the cash equivalent price.** Thus, **cost is either the fair market value of the consideration given up or the fair market value of the consideration received,** whichever is more clearly determinable.

To illustrate, assume that the attorneys for The Jordan Company agree to accept 4,000 shares of $1 par value common stock in payment of their bill of $5,000 for services performed in helping the company to incorporate. At the time of the exchange, there is no established market price for the stock. In this case, the market value of the consideration received, $5,000, is more clearly evident. Accordingly, the entry is:

Organization Costs	5,000	
Common Stock		4,000
Paid-in Capital in Excess of Par Value		1,000
(To record issuance of 4,000 shares of $1 par value stock to attorneys)		

As explained on page 524, organization costs are classified as an intangible asset in the balance sheet.

In contrast, assume that Athletic Research Inc. is a publicly held corporation whose $5 par value stock is actively traded at $8 per share. The company issues 10,000 shares of stock to acquire land recently advertised for sale at $90,000. On the basis of these facts the most clearly evident value is the market price of the consideration given, $80,000. Thus, the transaction is recorded as follows:

Land		80,000	
Common Stock			50,000
Paid-in Capital in Excess of Par Value			30,000
(To record issuance of 10,000 shares of $5 par value			
stock for land)			

As illustrated in these examples, **the par value of the stock is never a factor in determining the cost of the assets received**. This is also true of the stated value of no-par stock.

Before You Go On . . .

▶ Review It

1. Explain the accounting for par and no-par common stock issued for cash.
2. Explain the accounting for the issuance of stock for services or noncash assets.

▶ Do It

Cayman Corporation begins operations on March 1 by issuing 100,000 shares of $10 par value common stock for cash at $12 per share. On March 15, it issues 5,000 shares of common stock to attorneys in settlement of their bill of $50,000 for organization costs. Journalize the issuance of the shares assuming the stock is not publicly traded.

Reasoning: In issuing shares for cash, common stock is credited for par value per share and any additional proceeds are credited to a separate paid-in capital account. When stock is issued for services, the cash equivalent price should be used. In this case, this price is the value of the attorneys' services.

Solution:

Mar. 1	Cash	1,200,000	
	Common Stock		1,000,000
	Paid-in Capital in Excess of Par Value		200,000
	(To record issuance of 100,000 shares at $12		
	per share)		
Mar. 15	Organization Costs	50,000	
	Common Stock		50,000
	(To record issuance of 5,000 shares for		
	attorneys' fees)		

Related exercise material: BE12–2, BE12–3, BE12–4, E12–1, E12–2, E12–3, and E12–7.

Accounting for Treasury Stock

STUDY OBJECTIVE

•••••••••• 3 ••••••••••

Explain the accounting for treasury stock.

Treasury stock is a corporation's own stock that has been issued, fully paid for, and reacquired by the corporation but not retired. A corporation may acquire treasury stock for the reasons listed below.

1. Reissue the shares to officers and employees under bonus and stock compensation plans.
2. Increase trading of the company's stock in the securities market in the hopes of enhancing its market value.

3. Have additional shares available for use in the acquisition of other companies.
4. Reduce the number of shares outstanding and thereby increase earnings per share.

Helpful hint Treasury stock is so named because the company often holds the shares in its treasury for safekeeping.

Another infrequent reason for purchasing treasury shares, as illustrated in the Ford Motor Company opening story, is that management may want to eliminate hostile shareholders.

Many corporations have treasury stock. For example, one survey of 600 companies in the United States found that 62% have treasury stock.[4] Specifically, Kellogg Company recently reported 82.3 million treasury shares, PepsiCo 73.2 million, and Bristol-Meyers Squibb 20.8 million.

Purchase of Treasury Stock

The cost method is generally used in accounting for treasury stock. This method derives its name from the fact that the Treasury Stock account is maintained at the cost of shares purchased. Under the cost method, **Treasury Stock is debited at the price paid to reacquire the shares, and the same amount is credited to Treasury Stock when the shares are sold.** To illustrate, assume that on January 1, 1996, the stockholders' equity section of Mead, Inc. has 100,000 shares of $5 par value common stock outstanding (all issued at par value) and Retained Earnings of $200,000.

The stockholders' equity section before purchase of treasury stock is as follows:

Helpful hint Everything about treasury stock under the cost method is based on cost. None of the values (par, stated, or legal) are involved in recording treasury stock transactions.

Illustration 12-8

Stockholders' equity with no treasury stock

Stockholders' equity
  Paid-in capital
    Common stock, $5 par value, 100,000 shares issued and
      outstanding $500,000
  Retained earnings   200,000
    Total stockholders' equity $700,000

On February 1, 1996, Mead acquires 4,000 shares of its stock at $8 per share. The entry is:

Feb. 1	Treasury Stock	32,000	
	Cash		32,000
	(To record purchase of 4,000 shares of treasury stock at $8 per share)		

Helpful hint Treasury stock is a permanent account. It is not closed at the end of the year.

►Accounting in Action ► *Business Insight*

Philip Morris will spend $6 billion over the next three years to buy back a massive amount of stock from its shareholders. The repurchase is second in size to General Electric's $10 billion in the late 1980s. Buying back stock, which tends to increase the value of remaining shares, is not new to Philip Morris; it has at other times bought back stock, because it had few good places to reinvest the cash that it generated. The company also announced it will boost its cash dividend nearly 20%, from 69 cents up to 82½ cents per share.

Source: USA Today, September 1, 1994, p. B1.

[4]*Accounting Trends & Techniques 1996* (New York: American Institute of Certified Public Accountants).

Note that Treasury Stock is debited for the cost of the shares purchased. The original paid-in capital account, Common Stock, is not affected because the number of issued shares does not change. Treasury stock is deducted from total paid-in capital and retained earnings in the stockholders' equity section.

The stockholders' equity section of Mead, Inc., after purchase of treasury stock is as follows:

Illustration 12-9

Stockholders' equity with treasury stock

Stockholders' equity	
Paid-in capital	
Common stock, $5 par value, 100,000 shares issued and 96,000 shares outstanding	$500,000
Retained earnings	200,000
Total paid-in capital and retained earnings	700,000
Less: Treasury stock (4,000 shares)	32,000
Total stockholders' equity	$668,000

Thus, the acquisition of treasury stock reduces stockholders' equity.

Both the number of shares issued (100,000) and the number in the treasury (4,000) are disclosed. The difference is the number of shares of stock outstanding (96,000). The term outstanding stock means the number of shares of issued stock that are being held by stockholders.

Some maintain that treasury stock should be reported as an asset because it can be sold for cash. Under this reasoning, unissued stock should also be shown as an asset, clearly an erroneous conclusion. Rather than being an asset, treasury stock reduces stockholder claims on corporate assets. This effect is correctly shown by reporting treasury stock as a deduction from total paid-in capital and retained earnings.

Disposal of Treasury Stock

Treasury stock is usually sold or retired. The accounting for its sale is different when treasury stock is sold above cost than when it is sold below cost.

Sale of Treasury Stock above Cost

If the selling price of the treasury shares is equal to cost, the sale of the shares is recorded by a debit to Cash and a credit to Treasury Stock. When the selling price of the shares is greater than cost, the difference is credited to Paid-in Capital from Treasury Stock. To illustrate, assume that 1,000 shares of treasury stock of Mead, Inc., previously acquired at $8 per share, are sold at $10 per share on July 1. The entry is as follows:

July 1	Cash	10,000	
	Treasury Stock		8,000
	Paid-in Capital from Treasury Stock		2,000
	(To record sale of 1,000 shares of treasury stock above cost)		

The $2,000 credit in the entry is **not** made to Gain on Sale of Treasury Stock for two reasons: (1) Gains on sales occur when assets are sold and treasury stock is not an asset. (2) A corporation does not realize a gain or suffer a loss from stock transactions with its own stockholders. Thus, paid-in capital arising from the sale of treasury stock should not be included in the measurement of net income. Paid-in Capital from Treasury Stock is listed separately on the balance sheet as a part of paid-in capital.

Sale of Treasury Stock below Cost

When treasury stock is sold below its cost, the excess of cost over selling price is usually debited to Paid-in Capital from Treasury Stock. Thus, if Mead, Inc. sells an additional 800 shares of treasury stock on October 1 at $7 per share, the entry is as follows:

Oct. 1	Cash	5,600	
	Paid-in Capital from Treasury Stock	800	
	Treasury Stock		6,400
	(To record sale of 800 shares of treasury		
	stock below cost)		

Observe from the two sales entries that (1) Treasury Stock is credited at cost in each entry, (2) Paid-in Capital from Treasury Stock is used for the difference between the cost and resale price of the shares, and (3) The original paid-in capital account, Common Stock, again is not affected. **The sale of treasury stock increases both total assets and total stockholders' equity.**

After posting the foregoing entries, the treasury stock accounts will show the following balances on October 1:

Treasury Stock					**Paid-in Capital from Treasury Stock**			
Feb. 1	32,000	July 1	8,000		Oct. 1	800	July 1	2,000
		Oct. 1	6,400					
							Oct. 1 Bal.	1,200
Oct. 1 Bal.	17,600							

Illustration 12-10

Treasury stock accounts

When the credit balance in Paid-in Capital from Treasury Stock is eliminated, any additional excess of cost over selling price is debited to Retained Earnings. To illustrate, assume that Mead, Inc., sells its remaining 2,200 shares at $7 per share on December 1. The excess of cost over selling price is $2,200 [2,200 × ($8 − $7)]. In this case, $1,200 of the excess is debited to Paid-in Capital from Treasury Stock, and the remainder is debited to Retained Earnings. The entry is:

Dec. 1	Cash	15,400	
	Paid-in Capital from Treasury Stock	1,200	
	Retained Earnings	1,000	
	Treasury Stock		17,600
	(To record sale of 2,200 shares of treasury		
	stock at $7 per share)		

▾Preferred Stock

To appeal to a larger segment of potential investors, a corporation may issue a class of stock in addition to common stock, called preferred stock. Preferred stock has contractual provisions that give it a preference or priority over common stock in certain areas. Typically, preferred stockholders have a priority as to (1) dividends and (2) assets in the event of liquidation. However, they generally do not have voting rights.

STUDY OBJECTIVE

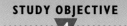

▾4

Differentiate preferred stock from common stock.

Helpful hint A recent edition of *Accounting Trends & Techniques* shows that 152 of 600 companies have one or more classes of preferred stock.

Like common stock, preferred stock may be issued for cash or for noncash assets. The entries for these transactions are similar to the entries for common stock. When a corporation has more than one class of stock, each paid-in capital account title should identify the stock to which it relates (e.g., Preferred Stock, Common Stock, Paid-in Capital in Excess of Par Value—Preferred Stock, and Paid-in Capital in Excess of Par Value—Common Stock). Assume that Stine Corporation issues 10,000 shares of $10 par value preferred stock for $12 cash per share. The entry to record the issuance is:

Cash	120,000	
Preferred Stock		100,000
Paid-in Capital in Excess of Par Value—Preferred Stock		20,000
(To record the issuance of 10,000 shares of $10 par value preferred stock)		

Preferred stock may have either a par value or no-par value. For example, Walgreen Drug Co. has $0.50 par value preferred and General Motors has three classes of no-par preferred stock, each with a stated value of $100. In the stockholders' equity section, preferred stock is shown first because of its dividend and liquidation preferences over common stock.

Dividend Preferences

Helpful hint A corporation does not have a contractual obligation to pay dividends.

As indicated before, **preferred stockholders have the right to share in the distribution of corporate income before common stockholders.** For example, if the dividend rate on preferred stock is $5 per share, common shareholders will not receive any dividends in the current year until preferred stockholders have received $5 per share. The first claim to dividends does not, however, guarantee dividends. Dividends depend on many factors, such as adequate retained earnings and availability of cash.

The per share dividend amount is stated as a percentage of the par value of preferred stock or as a specified amount. For example, the Crane Company specifies 3¾% dividend on its $100 par value preferred ($100 × 3¾% = $3.75 per share), whereas DuPont has both a $4.50 and a $3.50 series of no-par preferred stock.

Cumulative Dividend

Preferred stock contracts often contain a cumulative dividend feature. This right means that preferred stockholders must be paid both current-year dividends and any unpaid prior-year dividends before common stockholders receive dividends. When preferred stock is cumulative, preferred dividends not declared in a given period are called **dividends in arrears**. To illustrate, assume that Scientific-Leasing has 5,000 shares of 7%, $100 par value cumulative preferred stock outstanding. The annual dividend is $35,000 (5,000 × $7 per share). If dividends are 2 years in arrears, preferred stockholders are entitled to receive the following dividends in the current year before any distribution is made to common stockholders:

Illustration 12-11

Computation of total dividends to preferred stock

Dividends in arrears ($35,000 × 2)	$ 70,000
Current-year dividends	35,000
Total preferred dividends	**$105,000**

Dividends in arrears are not considered a liability. No obligation exists until a dividend is declared by the board of directors. However, the amount of dividends in arrears should be disclosed in the notes to the financial statements. Doing so enables investors to assess the potential impact of this commitment on the corporation's financial position.

Dividends cannot be paid on common stock while any dividend on preferred stock is in arrears. The cumulative feature is often critical in investor acceptance of a preferred stock issue. When preferred stock is noncumulative, a dividend passed in any year is lost forever. Companies that are unable to meet their dividend obligations are not looked upon favorably by the investment community. As a financial officer noted in discussing one company's failure to pay its cumulative preferred dividend for a period of time, "Not meeting your obligations on something like that is a major black mark on your record."

►Accounting in Action ► *Business Insight*

Dividends in arrears can extend for fairly long periods of time. Long Island Lighting Company's directors voted at one time to make up some $390 million in preferred dividends that had been in arrears since 1984 and to resume normal quarterly preferred payments. The announcement resulted from an agreement between the company and New York State to abandon a nuclear power plant in exchange for sizable rate increases over the next 10 years.

Liquidation Preference

Most preferred stocks have a preference on corporate assets if the corporation fails. This feature provides security for the preferred stockholder. The preference to assets may be for the par value of the shares or for a specified liquidating value. For example, Commonwealth Edison issued preferred stock that entitles the holders to receive $31.80 per share, plus accrued and unpaid dividends, in the event of involuntary liquidation. The liquidation preference is used in litigation pertaining to bankruptcy lawsuits involving the respective claims of creditors and preferred stockholders.

Before You Go On . . .

► *Review It*

1. What is treasury stock, and why do companies acquire it?
2. How is treasury stock recorded?
3. Where is treasury stock reported in the financial statements? Does a company record gains and losses on treasury stock transactions? Explain.
4. Preferred stock has what preferences over common stock?
5. Why are dividends in arrears on preferred stock not considered a liability?

► *Do It*

Caroline Anne Remmers Inc. purchases 3,000 shares of its $50 par value common stock for $180,000 cash on July 1. The shares are to be held in the treasury until resold. On November 1, the corporation sells 1,000 shares of treasury stock for cash at $70 per share. Journalize the treasury stock transactions.

Reasoning: The purchase of treasury stock is recorded at cost. When treasury stock is sold, the excess of the selling price over cost is credited to Paid-in Capital from Treasury Stock.

Solution:

July 1	Treasury Stock	180,000	
	Cash		180,000
	(To record the purchase of 3,000 shares at $60 per share)		
Nov. 1	Cash	70,000	
	Treasury Stock		60,000
	Paid-in Capital from Treasury Stock		10,000
	(To record the sale of 1,000 shares at $70 per share)		

Related exercise material: BE12–5, E12–2, E12–4, E12–7, and E12–8.

SECTION 2 ▸ Dividends

STUDY OBJECTIVE

5

Prepare the entries for cash dividends and stock dividends.

A dividend **is a distribution by a corporation to its stockholders on a pro rata (equal) basis.** Potential buyers and sellers of a corporation's stock are very interested in a company's dividend policies and practices. Dividends can take four forms: cash, property, scrip (promissory note to pay cash), or (capital) stock. Cash dividends, which predominate in practice, and stock dividends, which are declared with some frequency, will be the focus of discussion in this chapter.

Dividends may be expressed as a percentage of the par or stated value of the stock or as a dollar amount per share. In the financial press, **dividends are generally reported quarterly as a dollar amount per share.** For example, Dow Chemical Company's quarterly dividend rate is 65 cents a share, J.C. Penney Company's is 42 cents, and PepsiCo's is 20 cents.

Cash Dividends

Helpful hint A regular dividend is declared out of retained earnings whereas a liquidating dividend is declared out of paid-in capital.

A cash dividend is a pro rata distribution of cash to stockholders. For a cash dividend to occur, a corporation must have:

1. **Retained earnings.** The legality of a cash dividend depends on the laws of the state in which the company is incorporated. In general, cash dividends based on retained earnings are legal, and distributions based on common stock (legal capital) are illegal. Statutory provisions vary considerably with respect to cash dividends based on paid-in capital in excess of par or stated value. Many states permit such dividends. A dividend declared out of paid-in capital is termed a liquidating dividend, because the amount originally paid in by stockholders is being reduced or "liquidated."

2. **Adequate cash.** The legality of a dividend does not indicate a company's ability to pay a dividend. For example, a company such as PepsiCo, with a cash balance of $382 million and retained earnings of $8,730 million, could legally declare a dividend of $8,730 million. However, if it attempted to pay the dividend, it would need to raise additional cash through the sale of other

assets or through additional financing. It follows that before declaring a cash dividend, the board of directors must carefully consider both current and future demands on the company's cash resources. In some cases, current liabilities may make a cash dividend inappropriate; in other cases, a major plant expansion program may warrant only a relatively small dividend.

3. **Declared dividends.** The board of directors has full authority to determine the amount of income to be distributed in the form of a dividend and the amount to be retained in the business. Dividends do not accrue like interest on a note payable, and they are not a liability until declared.

Helpful hint Announcements of cash dividends in the financial press often say XYZ paid a 50¢ per share dividend out of retained earnings. This mistakenly implies that retained earnings is cash.

Helpful hint The board of directors is not obligated or even obliged to declare dividends.

The amount and timing of a dividend are important issues for management to consider. The payment of a large cash dividend could lead to liquidity problems for the enterprise. Conversely, a small dividend or a missed dividend may cause unhappiness among stockholders who expect to receive a reasonable cash payment from the company on a periodic basis. Many companies declare and pay cash dividends quarterly.

▶*A*ccounting in *A*ction ▸ *Business Insight*

In order to remain in business, companies must honor their interest payments to creditors, bankers, and bondholders. But the payment of dividends to stockholders is another matter. Many companies can survive, even thrive, without such payouts. In fact, managements might consider dividend payments unnecessary, even harmful to the company. Pay your creditors, by all means. But, fork over perfectly good cash to stockholders as dividends? "Why give money to those strangers?" is the response of one company president.

Investors must keep an eye on the company's dividend policy. For most companies, regular boosts in the face of irregular earnings can be a warning signal. So can the refusal of management to lower dividends when earnings fall or capital requirements rise. Companies with high dividends and rising debt may be borrowing money to pay shareholders. For investors who are seeking high returns on their stock investments, low dividends may mean high returns through market appreciation.

Entries for Cash Dividends

Three dates are important in connection with dividends: (1) the declaration date, (2) the record date, and (3) the payment date. Normally, there is a time span of two to four weeks between each date. Accounting entries are required on two of the dates—the declaration date and the payment date.

On the declaration date, the board of directors formally declares (authorizes) the cash dividend and announces it to stockholders. The declaration of a cash dividend **commits the corporation to a binding legal obligation** that cannot be rescinded. Thus, an entry is required to recognize the decrease in retained earnings and the increase in the liability, Dividends Payable. To illustrate, assume that on December 1, 1996, the directors of Media General declare a 50¢ per share cash dividend on 100,000 shares of $10 par value common stock. The dividend is $50,000 (100,000 × 50¢), and the entry to record the declaration is:

Declaration Date

Dec. 1	Retained Earnings	50,000	
	Dividends Payable		50,000
	(To record declaration of cash dividend)		

Dividends Payable is a current liability because it will normally be paid within the next several months. Instead of debiting Retained Earnings, the account Dividends may be debited. This account provides additional information in the ledger. For example, a company may have separate dividend accounts for each class of stock. When a dividend account is used, its balance is transferred to Retained Earnings at the end of the year by a closing entry. Consequently, the effect of the declaration is the same: retained earnings is decreased and a current liability is increased. For homework problems, you should use the Retained Earnings account for recording dividend declarations.

The record date marks the time when ownership of the outstanding shares is determined for dividend purposes. The stockholders' records maintained by the corporation supply this information. The time interval between the declaration date and the record date enables the corporation to update its stock ownership records. Between the declaration date and record date, the number of shares outstanding should remain the same. Thus, the purpose of the record date is to identify the persons or entities that will receive the dividend, not to determine the amount of the dividend liability. For Media General, the record date is December 22. No entry is required on this date because the corporation's liability recognized on the declaration date is unchanged:

Record Date

| Dec. 22 | No entry necessary | | |

▸Technology in Action

A casual glance at *The Wall Street Journal* reveals the vast amount of stock traded on the national and regional stock exchanges. Thousands of shares of a single company's stock may change hands each day. Companies must rely on computers to keep track of the volume of transactions for both ownership and dividend purposes. With dividends, a review of the computer records on the record date would reveal which parties should receive dividend distributions in a timely fashion.

On the payment date, dividend checks are mailed to the stockholders and the payment of the dividend is recorded. Assuming that the payment date is January 20 for Media General, the entry on that date is:

Payment Date

Jan. 20	Dividends Payable	50,000	
	Cash		50,000
	(To record payment of cash dividend)		

Note that payment of the dividend reduces both current assets and current liabilities but has no effect on stockholders' equity. The cumulative effect of the **declaration and payment** of a cash dividend on a company's financial statements is to **decrease both stockholders' equity and total assets**.

Allocating Cash Dividends between Preferred and Common Stock

As explained on page 536, preferred stock has priority over common stock in regard to dividends. That is, cash dividends must be paid to preferred stockholders before common stockholders are paid any dividends.

To illustrate, assume that IBR Inc. has 1,000 shares of 8%, $100 par value cumulative preferred stock and 50,000 shares of $10 par value common stock outstanding at December 31, 1996. The dividend per share for preferred stock is $8 ($100 par value × 8%), and the required annual dividend for preferred stock is $8,000 (1,000 × $8). At December 31, 1996, the directors declare a $6,000 cash dividend. In this case, the entire dividend amount goes to preferred stockholders because of their dividend preference. The entry to record the declaration of the dividend is:

Dec. 31	Retained Earnings	6,000	
	Dividends Payable		6,000
	(To record $6 per share cash dividend to preferred stockholders)		

Because of the cumulative feature, dividends of $2 per share are in arrears on preferred stock for 1996. These dividends must be paid to preferred stockholders before any future dividends can be paid to common stockholders. As explained on page 537, dividends in arrears should be disclosed in the financial statements.

At December 31, 1997, IBR declares a $50,000 cash dividend. The allocation of the dividend to the two classes of stock is as follows:

Total dividend		$50,000
Allocated to preferred stock		
Dividends in arrears, 1996 (1,000 × $2)	$2,000	
1997 dividend (1,000 × $8)	8,000	10,000
Remainder allocated to common stock		$40,000

Illustration 12-12

Allocating dividends to preferred and common stock

The entry to record the declaration of the dividend is:

Dec. 31	Retained Earnings	50,000	
	Dividends Payable		50,000
	(To record declaration of cash dividends of $10,000 to preferred stock and $40,000 to common stock)		

If the preferred stock were not cumulative, preferred stockholders would have received only $8,000 in dividends in 1997 and common stockholders would have received $42,000.

Stock Dividends

A stock dividend is a pro rata distribution of the corporation's own stock to stockholders. Whereas a cash dividend is paid in cash, a stock dividend is paid in stock. **A stock dividend results in a decrease in retained earnings and an increase in paid-in capital.** Unlike a cash dividend, a stock dividend does not decrease total stockholders' equity or total assets.

To illustrate a stock dividend, assume that you have a 2% ownership interest in Cetus Inc. by virtue of owning 20 of its 1,000 shares of common stock. In a 10% stock dividend, 100 shares (1,000 × 10%) of stock would be issued. You

Helpful hint The declaration and distribution of a stock dividend will have no effect on total stockholders' equity or total assets.

would receive two shares (2% × 100), but your ownership interest would remain at 2% (22 ÷ 1,100). **You now own more shares of stock but your ownership interest has not changed.** Moreover, no cash is disbursed, and no liabilities have been assumed by the corporation.

What then are the purposes and benefits of a stock dividend? Corporations issue stock dividends generally for one or more of the following reasons:

1. To satisfy stockholders' dividend expectations without spending cash.
2. To increase the marketability of its stock by increasing the number of shares outstanding and thereby decreasing the market price per share. Decreasing the market price of the stock makes it easier for smaller investors to purchase the shares.
3. To emphasize that a portion of stockholders' equity has been permanently reinvested in the business and therefore is unavailable for cash dividends.

The size of the stock dividend and the value to be assigned to each dividend share are determined by the board of directors when the dividend is declared. The per share amount must be at least equal to the par or stated value in order to meet legal requirements.

The accounting profession distinguishes between a **small stock dividend** (less than 20–25% of the corporation's issued stock) and a **large stock dividend** (greater than 20–25%). It recommends that the directors assign the **fair market value per share** for small stock dividends. The recommendation is based on the assumption that a small stock dividend will have little effect on the market price of the shares previously outstanding. Thus, many stockholders consider small stock dividends to be distributions of earnings equal to the fair market value of the shares distributed. The amount to be assigned for a large stock dividend is not specified by the accounting profession. However, **par or stated value per share** is normally assigned. Small stock dividends predominate in practice. Thus, we will illustrate only the entries for small stock dividends.

Entries for Stock Dividends

To illustrate the accounting for stock dividends, assume that Medland Corporation has a balance of $300,000 in retained earnings and declares a 10% stock dividend on its 50,000 shares of $10 par value common stock. The current fair market value of its stock is $15 per share. The number of shares to be issued is 5,000 (10% × 50,000) and the total amount to be debited to Retained Earnings is $75,000 (5,000 × $15). The entry to record this transaction at the declaration date is as follows:

Retained Earnings	75,000	
Common Stock Dividends Distributable		50,000
Paid-in Capital in Excess of Par Value		25,000
(To record declaration of 10% stock dividend)		

Note that Retained Earnings is debited for the fair market value of the stock issued; Common Stock Dividends Distributable is credited for the par value of the dividend shares (5,000 × $10); and the excess over par (5,000 × $5) is credited to an additional paid-in capital account.

Common Stock Dividends Distributable is a stockholders' equity account; it is not a liability because assets will not be used to pay the dividend. If a balance sheet is prepared before the dividend shares are issued, the distributable account is reported in paid-in capital as an addition to common stock issued, as shown below:

Paid-in capital		
Common stock	$500,000	
Common stock dividends distributable	50,000	$550,000

When the dividend shares are issued, Common Stock Dividends Distributable is debited and Common Stock is credited as follows:

Common Stock Dividends Distributable	50,000	
Common Stock		50,000
(To record issuance of 5,000 shares in a stock dividend)		

Effects of Stock Dividends

How do stock dividends affect stockholders' equity? They **change the composition of stockholders' equity** because a portion of retained earnings is transferred to paid-in capital. However, **total stockholders' equity remains the same**. Stock dividends also have no effect on the par or stated value per share, but the number of shares outstanding increases. These effects are shown below for Medland Corporation.

Illustration 12-14

Stock dividend effect

Stockholders' equity	Before Dividend	After Dividend
Paid-in capital		
Common stock, $10 par	$500,000	$550,000
Paid-in capital in excess of par value	—	25,000
Total paid-in capital	500,000	575,000
Retained earnings	300,000	225,000
Total stockholders' equity	$800,000	$800,000
Outstanding shares	50,000	55,000

In this example, total paid-in capital is increased by $75,000 and retained earnings is decreased by the same amount. Note also that total stockholders' equity remains unchanged at $800,000.

Stock Splits

A stock split, like a stock dividend, involves the issuance of additional shares of stock to stockholders according to their percentage ownership. However, **a stock split results in a reduction in the par or stated value per share.** The purpose of a stock split is to increase the marketability of the stock by lowering its market value per share. This, in turn, makes it easier for the corporation to issue additional stock. The effect of a split on market value is generally inversely proportional to the size of the split. For example, after a 4-for-1 stock split, the market value of IBM stock fell from $284 to approximately $71. In announcing the split, the chief executive of IBM said, "We want to make our stock more attractive to the small investor."

In a stock split, the number of shares is increased in the same proportion that par or stated value per share is decreased. For example, in a 2-for-1 split, one share of $10 par value stock is exchanged for two shares of $5 par value stock. **A stock split does not have any effect on total paid-in capital, retained earnings, and total stockholders' equity.** However, the number of shares outstanding increases. These effects are shown in Illustration 12-15 for Medland Corporation, assuming that instead of a 10% stock dividend, Medland splits its 50,000 shares of common stock on a 2-for-1 basis.

Helpful hint A stock split changes the par value per share but does not affect any balances in stockholders' equity.

Illustration 12-15

Stock split effects

	Before Stock Split	After Stock Split
Stockholders' equity		
Paid-in capital		
Common stock	$500,000	$500,000
Paid-in capital in excess of par value	–0–	–0–
Total paid-in capital	500,000	500,000
Retained earnings	300,000	300,000
Total stockholders' equity	$800,000	$800,000
Outstanding shares	50,000	100,000

Because a stock split does not affect the balances in any stockholders' equity accounts, **it is not necessary to journalize a stock split.** Significant differences between stock splits and stock dividends are shown in Illustration 12-16:

Illustration 12-16

Effects of stock splits and stock dividends differentiated

Item	Stock Split	Stock Dividend
Total paid-in capital	No change	Increase
Total retained earnings	No change	Decrease
Total par value (common stock)	No change	Increase
Par value per share	Decrease	No change

Before You Go On . . .

▸ *Review It*

1. What entries are made for cash dividends on (a) the declaration date, (b) the record date, and (c) the payment date?
2. Distinguish between a small and large stock dividend and indicate the basis for valuing each kind of dividend.
3. Contrast the effects of a small stock dividend and a 2 for 1 stock split on (a) stockholders' equity, and (b) outstanding shares.

▸ *Do It*

Due to 5 years of record earnings at Sing CD Corporation, the market price of its 500,000 shares of $2 par value common stock tripled from $15 per share to $45. During this period, paid-in capital remained the same at $2,000,000, but retained earnings increased from $1,500,000 to $10,000,000. President Joan Elbert is considering either (1) a 10% stock dividend or (2) a 2-for-1 stock split. She asks you to show the before and after effects of each option on retained earnings.

Reasoning: A stock dividend decreases retained earnings and increases paid-in capital, but total stockholders' equity remains the same. A stock split only changes par value per share and the number of shares outstanding. Thus, this event has no effect on the retained earnings balance.

Solution:

(a) (1) The stock dividend amount is $2,250,000 [(500,000 × 10%) × $45]. The new balance in retained earnings is $7,750,000 ($10,000,000 − $2,250,000).

(2) The retained earnings balance after the stock split is the same as it was before the split: $10,000,000.

(b) The effects on shares outstanding are as follows:

	Original Balances	After Dividend	After Split
Paid-in capital	$ 2,000,000	$ 4,250,000	$ 2,000,000
Retained earnings	10,000,000	7,750,000	10,000,000
Total stockholders' equity	$12,000,000	$12,000,000	$12,000,000
Shares outstanding	500,000	550,000	1,000,000

Related exercise material: BE12–8, BE12–9, E12–9, E12–10, E12–11, and E12–12.

SECTION 3 ▸ Retained Earnings

Retained earnings is net income that is retained in the business. The balance in retained earnings is part of the stockholders' claim on the total assets of the corporation. It does not, however, represent a claim on any specific asset. Nor can the amount of retained earnings be associated with the balance of any asset account. For example, a $100,000 balance in retained earnings does not mean that there should be $100,000 in cash. The reason is that the cash resulting from the excess of revenues over expenses may have been used to purchase buildings, equipment, and other assets. Illustration 12-17 shows the relationship of cash to retained earnings in selected companies.

STUDY OBJECTIVE
•••••••••••• 6 ••••••••••••

Identify the items that are reported in a retained earnings statement.

Illustration 12-17

Retained earnings and cash balances

Company	(In Millions) Retained Earnings	Cash
Amoco Corp.	$12,223	$ 168
Sears, Roebuck and Co.	8,163	1,864
Bob Evans Farms, Inc.	211	6
The Liposome Company, Inc.	(75)	5

When expenses exceed revenues, a **net loss** results. In contrast to net income, a net loss is debited to Retained Earnings in preparing closing entries. This is done even if a debit balance results in Retained Earnings. **Net losses are not debited to paid-in capital accounts.** To do so would destroy the distinction between paid-in and earned capital. A debit balance in retained earnings is identified as a **deficit** and is reported as a deduction in the stockholders' equity section, as shown below:

Illustration 12-18

Stockholders' equity with deficit

Stockholders' equity		
Paid-in capital		
Common stock		$800,000
Retained earnings (deficit)		(50,000)
Total stockholders' equity		$750,000

▸*R*etained Earnings Restrictions

The balance in retained earnings is generally available for dividend declarations. Some companies state this fact. For example, in the notes to its financial statements, Martin Marietta Corporation states:

> At December 31, retained earnings were unrestricted and available for dividend payments.

In some cases, however, there may be retained earnings restrictions that make a portion of the balance currently unavailable for dividends. Restrictions result from one or more of the following causes: legal, contractual, or voluntary.

1. **Legal restrictions.** Many states require a corporation to restrict retained earnings for the cost of treasury stock purchased. The restriction serves to keep intact the corporation's legal capital that is temporarily being held as treasury stock. When the treasury stock is sold, the restriction is lifted.

2. **Contractual restrictions.** Long-term debt contracts may impose a restriction on retained earnings as a condition for the loan. The restriction limits the use of corporate assets for the payment of dividends. Thus, it enhances the likelihood that the corporation will be able to meet required loan payments.

3. **Voluntary restrictions.** The board of directors of a corporation may voluntarily create retained earnings restrictions for specific purposes. For example, the board may authorize a restriction for the purpose of future plant expansion. By reducing the amount of retained earnings available for dividends, more cash may be available for the planned expansion.

Helpful hint *Accounting Trends & Techniques* reported in a recent year that 71% of the 600 companies have restrictions, with the majority being contractual in nature.

Retained earnings restrictions are generally disclosed in the notes to the financial statements. For example, Pratt & Lambert, a leading producer of architectural finishes (paint) has the following note in a recent financial statement:

Illustration 12-19

Disclosure of restriction

PRATT & LAMBERT

Note D Long-term Debt and Retained Earnings
    Loan agreements contain, among other covenants, a restriction on the payment of dividends, which limits future dividend payments to $20,565,000 plus 75% of future net income.

Prior Period Adjustments

Suppose that after the books have been closed and the financial statements have been issued, a corporation discovers that a material error has been made in reporting net income of a prior year. How should this situation be recorded in the accounts and reported in the financial statements? The correction of an error in previously issued financial statements is known as a **prior period adjustment**. The correction is made directly to Retained Earnings because the effect of the error is now in this account; the net income for the prior period has been recorded in retained earnings through the journalizing and posting of closing entries.

To illustrate, assume that General Microwave discovers in 1998 that it understated depreciation expense in 1997 by $300,000 as a result of computational errors. These errors overstated net income for 1997, and the current balance in retained earnings is also overstated. The entry for the prior period adjustment, assuming all tax effects are ignored, is as follows:

Retained Earnings	300,000	
Accumulated Depreciation		300,000
(To adjust for understatement of depreciation in a prior period)		

A debit to an income statement account in 1998 would be incorrect because the error pertains to a prior year.

Prior period adjustments are reported in the retained earnings statement.[5] They are added (or deducted) from the beginning retained earnings balance to show the adjusted beginning balance. Assuming General Microwave has a beginning balance of $800,000 in retained earnings, the prior period adjustment is reported as follows:

Illustration 12-20

Statement presentation of prior period adjustments

(Partial) Retained Earnings Statement	
Balance, January 1, as reported	$800,000
Correction for overstatement of net income in prior period (depreciation error)	300,000
Balance, January 1, as adjusted	$500,000

Reporting the correction in the current year's income statement would be incorrect because it applies to a prior year's income statement.

Helpful hint Normally, any errors made in a given year are discovered and corrected before the financial statements for the year are issued. Thus, prior period adjustments occur infrequently.

Retained Earnings Statement

The **retained earnings statement** shows the changes in retained earnings during the year. The statement is prepared from the Retained Earnings account. Transactions and events that affect retained earnings are tabulated in account form as shown in Illustration 12-21.

---

[5]A complete retained earnings statement is shown in Illustration 12-22 on page 548.

Illustration 12-21

Debits and credits to retained earnings

Retained Earnings	
1. Net loss	1. Net income
2. Prior period adjustments for overstatement of net income	2. Prior period adjustments for understatement of net income
3. Cash and stock dividends	
4. Some disposals of treasury stock	

As indicated, net income increases retained earnings, and a net loss decreases retained earnings. Prior period adjustments may either increase or decrease retained earnings, whereas both cash and stock dividends decrease retained earnings. The circumstances when treasury stock transactions decrease retained earnings are explained on page 535. The retained earnings statement for Graber Inc., based on assumed data, is as follows:

Illustration 12-22

Retained earnings statement

GRABER INC.
Retained Earnings Statement
For the Year Ended December 31, 1996

Balance, January 1, as reported		$1,050,000
Correction for understatement of net income in prior period (inventory error)		50,000
Balance, January 1, as adjusted		1,100,000
Add: Net income		360,000
		1,460,000
Less: Cash dividends	$100,000	
Stock dividends	200,000	300,000
Balance, December 31		$1,160,000

Before You Go On . . .

▶ Review It

1. How are retained earnings restrictions generally reported?
2. What is a prior period adjustment and how is it reported?
3. What are the principal sources of debits and credits to Retained Earnings?
4. How are stock dividends distributable reported in the stockholders' equity section?

▶ Do It

Vega Corporation has retained earnings of $5,130,000 on January 1, 1997. During the year, the company earns $2,000,000 of net income and it declares and pays a $250,000 cash dividend. In 1997, Vega records an adjustment of $180,000 that pertains to the understatement of 1996 depreciation expense due to a mathematical error. Prepare a retained earnings statement for 1997.

Reasoning: The $180,000 correction of 1996 depreciation is a prior period adjustment. It should be reported as a deduction from the beginning retained earnings balance. Net income is shown as an addition in the statement and dividends are deducted in the statement.

Solution:

VEGA CORPORATION
Retained Earnings Statement
For the Year Ended December 31, 1997

Balance, January 1, as reported	$5,130,000
Correction for overstatement of net income in prior period (depreciation error)	180,000
Balance, January 1, as adjusted	4,950,000
Add: Net income	2,000,000
	6,950,000
Less: Cash dividends	250,000
Balance, December 31	$6,700,000

Related exercise material: BE12–10, BE12–11, E12–12, and E12–15.

Stockholders' Equity Presentation and Analysis

In the stockholders' equity section of the balance sheet, paid-in capital and retained earnings are reported, and the specific sources of paid-in capital are identified.

Within paid-in capital, two classifications are recognized:

1. **Capital stock**, which consists of preferred and common stock. Preferred stock is shown before common stock because of its preferential rights. Information

GRABER INC.
Partial Balance Sheet

Stockholders' equity			
Paid-in capital			
Capital stock			
9% Preferred stock, $100 par value, cumulative, callable at $120, 10,000 shares authorized, 6,000 shares issued and outstanding		$ 600,000	
Common stock, no par, $5 stated value, 500,000 shares authorized, 400,000 shares issued and 390,000 outstanding	$2,000,000		
Common stock dividends distributable	50,000	2,050,000	
Total capital stock		2,650,000	
Additional paid-in capital			
In excess of par value—preferred stock	30,000		
In excess of stated value—common stock	1,050,000		
Total additional paid-in capital		1,080,000	
Total paid-in capital		3,730,000	
Retained earnings (see Note R)		1,160,000	
Total paid-in capital and retained earnings		4,890,000	
Less: Treasury stock—common (10,000 shares)		80,000	
Total stockholders' equity		$4,810,000	

Note R: Retained earnings is restricted for the cost of treasury stock, $80,000.

Illustration 12-23

Comprehensive stockholders' equity section

▶ **International note**

In Switzerland, there are no specific disclosure requirements for shareholders' equity. However, companies typically disclose separate categories of capital on the balance sheet.

as to the par value, shares authorized, shares issued, and shares outstanding is reported for each class of stock.

2. **Additional paid-in capital**, which includes the excess of amounts paid in over par or stated value and paid-in capital from treasury stock.

Illustrations

The stockholders' equity section of the balance sheet of Graber Inc. is presented in Illustration 12-23. Note that (1) Common Stock Dividends Distributable is shown under capital stock in paid-in capital, and (2) a retained earnings restriction is disclosed in the notes.

The stockholders' equity section of Graber Inc. shown in Illustration 12-23 includes most of the accounts discussed in this chapter. The disclosures pertaining to Graber's common stock indicate that 400,000 shares are issued, 100,000 shares are unissued (500,000 authorized less 400,000 issued), and 390,000 shares are outstanding (400,000 issued less 10,000 shares in treasury).

In published annual reports, subclassifications within the stockholders' equity section are seldom presented. Moreover, the individual sources of additional paid-in capital are often combined and reported as a single amount as shown in Illustration 12-24.

Illustration 12-24

Published stockholders' equity section

KNIGHT-RIDDER INC.	
Stockholders' equity (in millions)	
Common stock, $.02½ par value; shares authorized—250,000,000; shares issued—45,720,000	$ 1,143
Additional paid-in capital	342,201
Retained earnings	899,825
Total stockholders' equity	$1,243,169

In practice, the term "capital surplus" is sometimes used in place of additional paid-in capital and "earned surplus" in place of retained earnings. The use of the term "surplus" suggests that an excess amount of funds is available. Such is not necessarily the case, which is why **the term surplus should not be employed in accounting**. Unfortunately, a number of financial statements still include these terms.

Instead of presenting a detailed stockholders' equity section in the balance sheet and a retained earnings statement, many companies prepare a stockholders' equity statement. This statement shows the changes in each stockholders' equity account and in total stockholders' equity that have occurred during the year. An example of a stockholders' equity statement is illustrated in an appendix to this chapter and in PepsiCo's financial statements in Appendix A.

Analysis

A widely used ratio that measures profitability from the common stockholder's viewpoint is return on common stockholders' equity. This ratio shows how many dollars of net income were earned for each dollar invested by the owners. It is computed by dividing net income by average stockholders' equity. For example, assuming that Graber Inc's. beginning of the year common stockholders' equity was $3,900,000, the return on common stockholders' equity ratio is shown graphically and computed as follows:

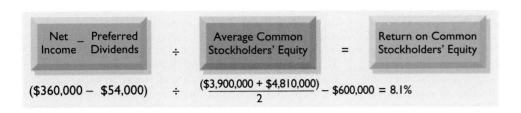

Illustration 12-25

Return on common stock-holders' equity ratio and computation

($360,000 − $54,000)   ÷ $\frac{(\$3,900,000 + \$4,810,000)}{2}$ − $600,000 = 8.1%

As evidenced above, because preferred stock is present, **preferred dividend** requirements of $54,000 ($600,000 × .09) are deducted from net income to compute income available to common stockholders. Similarly, the par value of preferred stock, $600,000, is deducted from total average stockholders' equity to arrive at the amount of common stock equity used in this ratio.

Before You Go On . . .

► *Review It*

1. Identify the classifications within the paid-in capital section and the totals that are stated in the stockholders' equity section of a balance sheet.
2. Explain the return on common stockholders' equity ratio.

► *A Look Back at Ford Motor Company*

Refer back to the opening story about Ford Motor Company, and answer the following questions.

1. Why did Henry Ford originally choose to form a corporation rather than a sole proprietorship?
2. Why did the Ford Motor Company repurchase all of its shares?
3. What advantages and disadvantages of being organized as a corporation are illustrated by Ford?

Solution:

1. Henry Ford wanted to take full advantage of mass-production. This would require large factories and many employees, which would in turn require considerable funds. The most efficient way to raise these funds was to issue stock.
2. Ford Motor Company initiated a massive treasury stock purchase when Henry Ford's vision was not consistent with the wishes of the shareholders.
3. The history of Ford Motor Company illustrates a number of the strengths and weaknesses of being formed as a corporation. Forming a corporation allowed for more efficient access to funds, and thus more rapid expansion. This was critical because, in the early 1900s, many companies were trying to build cars for the American market. However, by issuing shares, Henry Ford relinquished his control over the firm. This led to a collision in 1916 when the founder believed that it was in the company's best interest to retain funds in the firm rather than to pay dividends. To the extent that outside shareholders are not as well informed as a corporation's managers, the shareholders may force management to do things that hinder the firm's success.

Summary of Study Objectives

1. *Identify and discuss the major characteristics of a corporation.* The major characteristics of a corporation are separate legal existence, limited liability of stockholders, transferable ownership rights, ability to acquire capital, continuous life, corporation management, government regulations, and additional taxes.

2. *Record the issuance of common stock.* When the issuance of common stock for cash is recorded, the par value of the shares is credited to Common Stock and the portion of the proceeds that is above or below par value is recorded in a separate paid-in capital account. When no-par common stock has a stated value, the entries are similar to those for par value stock. When no-par does not have a stated value, the entire proceeds from the issue become legal capital and are credited to Common Stock.

3. *Explain the accounting for treasury stock.* The cost method is generally used in accounting for treasury stock. Under this approach, Treasury Stock is debited at the price paid to reacquire the shares, and the same amount is credited to Treasury Stock when the shares are sold. The difference between the sales price and cost is recorded in stockholders' equity accounts, not in income statement accounts.

4. *Differentiate preferred stock from common stock.* Preferred stock has contractual provisions that give it priority over common stock in certain areas. Typically, preferred stockholders have a preference as to (1) dividends and (2) assets in the event of liquidation. However, they usually do not have voting rights.

5. *Prepare the entries for cash dividends and stock dividends.* Entries for both cash and stock dividends are required at the declaration date and the payment date. At the declaration date the entries are: Cash dividend—debit Retained Earnings and credit Dividends Payable; small stock dividend—debit Retained Earnings, credit Paid-in Capital in Excess of Par (or Stated) Value and credit Common Stock Dividends Distributable. At the payment date, the entries for cash and stock dividends, respectively, are debit Dividends Payable and credit Cash, and debit Common Stock Dividends Distributable and credit Common Stock.

6. *Identify the items that are reported in a retained earnings statement.* Each of the individual debits and credits to retained earnings should be reported in the retained earnings statement. Additions consist of net income and prior period adjustments to correct understatements of prior years' net income. Deductions consist of net loss, adjustments to correct overstatements of prior years' net income, cash and stock dividends, and some disposals of treasury stock.

7. *Prepare a comprehensive stockholders' equity section.* In the stockholders' equity section, paid-in capital and retained earnings are reported and specific sources of paid-in capital are identified. Within paid-in capital, two classifications are shown: capital stock and additional paid-in capital. If a corporation has treasury stock, the cost of treasury stock is deducted from total paid-in capital and retained earnings to obtain total stockholders' equity.

APPENDIX 12A ▸ Stockholders' Equity Statement

STUDY OBJECTIVE
8

After studying this appendix, you should be able to:

8. Describe the use and content of the stockholders' equity statement.

When balance sheets and income statements are presented by a corporation, changes in the separate accounts comprising stockholders' equity should also be disclosed. Disclosure of such changes is necessary to make the financial statements sufficiently informative for users. The disclosures may be made in an additional statement or in the notes to the financial statements.

Many corporations make the disclosures in a stockholders' equity statement. The statement shows the changes in **each** stockholders' equity account and in **total** stockholders' equity during the year. As shown in Illustration 12A-1 the stockholders' equity statement is prepared in columnar form, with columns for each account and for total stockholders' equity. The transactions are then identified and their effects are shown in the appropriate columns.

In practice, additional columns are usually provided to show the number of shares of issued stock and treasury stock. The stockholders' equity statement for PepsiCo, Inc., for a three-year period is shown in Appendix A. **When this statement is presented, a retained earnings statement is not necessary** because the retained earnings column explains the changes in this account.

	Common Stock ($5 Par)	Paid-in Capital in Excess of Par	Retained Earnings	Treasury Stock	Total
HAMPTON CORPORATION Stockholders' Equity Statement For the Year Ended December 31, 1996					
Balance January 1	$300,000	$200,000	$650,000	$(34,000)	$1,116,000
Issued 5,000 shares of common stock at $15	25,000	50,000			75,000
Declared a $40,000 cash dividend			(40,000)		(40,000)
Purchased 2,000 shares for treasury at $16				(32,000)	(32,000)
Net income for year			240,000		240,000
Balance December 31	$325,000	$250,000	$850,000	$(66,000)	$1,359,000

Summary of Study Objective for Chapter 12 Appendix A

8. *Describe the use and content of the stockholders' equity statement.* Corporations must disclose changes in stockholders' equity accounts and may choose to do so by issuing a separate stockholders' equity statement. This statement, prepared in columnar form, shows changes in each stockholders' equity account and in total stockholders' equity during the accounting period. When this statement is presented, a retained earnings statement is not necessary.

APPENDIX *12B* ▸ Book Value—Another Per Share Amount

You have learned about a number of per share amounts in this chapter. Another per share amount of some importance is book value per share. This per share amount represents **the equity a common stockholder has in the net assets of the corporation** from owning one share of stock. Since the net assets of a corporation must be equal to total stockholders' equity, the formula for computing book value per share when a company has only one class of stock outstanding is:

STUDY OBJECTIVE

· · · · · · · · · 9 · · · · · · · · · ·

After studying this appendix, you should be able to:
9. Compute book value per share.

Illustration 12B-1

Book value per share formula

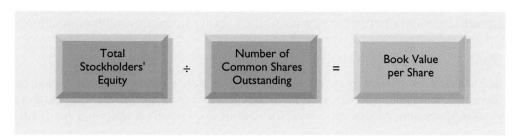

Total Stockholders' Equity ÷ Number of Common Shares Outstanding = Book Value per Share

Thus, if the Marlo Corporation has total stockholders' equity of $1,500,000 (Common Stock $1,000,000 and Retained Earnings $500,000) and 50,000 shares of common stock outstanding, book value per share is $30 ($1,500,000 ÷ 50,000).

When a company has both preferred and common stock, the computation of book value is more complex. Since preferred stockholders have a prior claim on net assets over common stockholders, their equity must be deducted from total stockholders' equity to determine the stockholders' equity that applies to the common stock. The computation of book value per share involves the following steps:

1. Compute the preferred stock equity. This equity is equal to the sum of the call price of preferred stock plus any cumulative dividends in arrears. If the preferred stock does not have a call price, the par value of the stock is used.
2. Determine the common stock equity by subtracting the preferred stock equity from total stockholders' equity.
3. Divide common stock equity by shares of common stock outstanding to determine book value per share.

Illustration

We will use the stockholders' equity section of Graber Inc. shown in Illustration 12-23. Graber's preferred stock is callable at $120 per share and cumulative. Assume that dividends on Graber's preferred stock were in arrears for one year, $54,000 (6,000 × $9). The computation of preferred stock equity is:

Illustration 12B-2

Computation of preferred stock equity (Step 1)

Call price (6,000 shares × $120)	$720,000
Dividends in arrears (6,000 shares × $9)	54,000
Preferred stock equity	$774,000

The computation of book value is as follows:

Illustration 12B-3

Computation of book value per share with preferred stock (Steps 2 and 3)

Total stockholders' equity	$4,810,000
Less Preferred stock equity	774,000
Common stock equity	$4,036,000
Shares of common stock outstanding	390,000
Book value per share ($4,036,000 ÷ 390,000)	$10.35

The call price of $120 was used instead of the par value of $100. Note also that the paid-in capital in excess of par value of preferred stock, $30,000, **is not assigned to the preferred stock equity**. Preferred stockholders ordinarily do not have a right to amounts paid-in in excess of par value. Accordingly, such amounts are assigned to the common stock equity in computing book value.

Helpful hint Book value can obscure real value. Companies that have real estate, brand names, licenses, or other properties worth more than the GAAP numbers are closely watched; therefore, the market value of the stock often reflects these "hidden" values.

Book Value versus Market Value

Book value per share may not equal market value. Book value is based on recorded costs; market value reflects the subjective judgment of thousands of stockholders and prospective investors about a company's potential for future earnings and dividends. Market value per share may exceed book value per share, but that fact does not necessarily mean that the stock is overpriced. The correlation between book value and the annual range of a company's market value per share is often remote, as indicated by the following recent data:

Company	Book Value (year-end)	Market Range (for year)
McDonnell Douglas	$86.84	$47.88–$118.38
Callaway Golf	$ 6.90	$17.19–$65.25
Eastman Kodak	$ 8.85	$40.38–$64.75

Illustration 12B-4

Book and market values compared

Book value per share **is** useful in determining the trend of a stockholder's per share equity in a corporation. It is also significant in many contracts and in court cases where the rights of individual parties are based on cost information.

Summary of Study Objective for Chapter 12 Appendix B

9. *Compute book value per share.* Book value per share represents the equity a common stockholder has in the net assets of a corporation from owning one share of stock. When there is only common stock outstanding, the formula for computing book value is: Total Stockholders' Equity ÷ Number of Common Shares Outstanding = Book Value per Share.

GLOSSARY

Authorized stock The amount of stock that a corporation is authorized to sell as indicated in its charter. (p. 527).

Book value per share The equity a common stockholder has in the net assets of the corporation from owning one share of stock. (p. 553).

Cash dividend A pro rata distribution of cash to stockholders. (p. 538).

Cumulative dividend A feature of preferred stock entitling the stockholder to receive current and unpaid prior-year dividends before common stockholders receive any dividends. (p. 536).

Declaration date The date the board of directors formally declares the dividend and announces it to stockholders. (p. 539).

Deficit A debit balance in retained earnings. (p. 546).

Dividend A distribution by a corporation to its stockholders on a pro rata (equal) basis. (p. 538).

Legal capital The amount per share of stock that must be retained in the business for the protection of corporate creditors. (p. 528).

Liquidating dividend A dividend declared out of paid-in capital. (p. 538).

No-par value stock Capital stock that has not been assigned a value in the corporate charter. (p. 528).

Organization costs Costs incurred in the formation of a corporation. (p. 524).

Outstanding stock Capital stock that has been issued and is being held by stockholders. (p. 534).

Par value stock Capital stock that has been assigned a value per share in the corporate charter. (p. 528).

Payment date The date dividend checks are mailed to stockholders. (p. 540).

Preferred stock Capital stock that has contractual preferences over common stock in certain areas. (p. 535).

Prior period adjustment   The correction of an error in previously issued financial statements. (p. 547).

Privately held corporation   A corporation that has only a few stockholders and whose stock is not available for sale to the general public. (p. 520).

Publicly held corporation   A corporation that may have thousands of stockholders and whose stock is regularly traded on a national securities market. (p. 520).

Record date   The date when ownership of outstanding shares is determined for dividend purposes. (p. 540).

Retained earnings   Net income that is retained in the business. (p. 545).

Retained earnings restrictions   Circumstances that make a portion of retained earnings currently unavailable for dividends. (p. 546).

Retained earnings statement   A financial statement that shows the changes in retained earnings during the year. (p. 547).

Return on common stockholders' equity ratio   A ratio that measures profitability from the stockholders' point of view. It is computed by dividing net income by average stockholders' equity. (p. 550).

Stated value   The amount per share assigned by the board of directors to no-par stock that becomes legal capital per share. (p. 529).

Stock dividend   A pro rata distribution of the corporation's own stock to stockholders. (p. 541).

Stock split   The issuance of additional shares of stock to stockholders accompanied by a reduction in the par or stated value per share. (p. 543).

Stockholders' equity statement   A statement that shows the changes in each stockholders' equity account and in total stockholders' equity during the year. (p. 550).

Treasury stock   A corporation's own stock that has been issued, fully paid for, and reacquired by the corporation but not retired. (p. 532).

DEMONSTRATION PROBLEM

The Rolman Corporation is authorized to issue 1,000,000 shares of $5 par value common stock. In its first year, the company has the following stock transactions:

Jan. 10   Issued 400,000 shares of stock at $8 per share.

July 1   Issued 100,000 shares of stock for land. The land had an asking price of $900,000. The stock is currently selling on a national exchange at $8.25 per share.

Sept. 1   Purchased 10,000 shares of common stock for the treasury at $9.00 per share.

Dec. 1   Sold 4,000 shares of the treasury stock at $10 per share.

Dec. 24   Declared a cash dividend of 10¢ per share.

Instructions

(a) Journalize the transactions.

(b) Prepare the stockholders' equity section assuming the company had retained earnings of $150,600 at December 31.

Problem-Solving Strategies

1. When common stock has a par value, Common Stock is always credited for par value.

2. In a noncash transaction, fair market value should be used.

3. The Treasury Stock account is debited and credited at cost.

4. Differences between the cost and selling price of treasury stock are recorded in stockholders' equity accounts, not as gains or losses.

Solution to Demonstration Problem

(a) Jan. 10   Cash   3,200,000
            Common Stock   2,000,000
            Paid-in Capital in Excess of Par Value   1,200,000
                (To record issuance of 400,000 shares of $5
                par value stock)

    July 1   Land   825,000
            Common Stock   500,000
            Paid-in Capital in Excess of Par Value   325,000
                (To record issuance of 100,000 shares of $5
                par value stock for land)

    Sept. 1   Treasury Stock   90,000
            Cash   90,000
                (To record purchase of 10,000 shares of
                treasury stock at cost)

Dec. 1 Cash	40,000	
Treasury Stock		36,000
Paid-in Capital from Treasury Stock		4,000
(To record sale of 4,000 shares of treasury		
stock above cost)		
Dec. 24 Retained Earnings	49,400	
Dividends Payable		49,400
(To record declaration of 10¢ per share cash		
dividend)		

(b) Stockholders' equity

Paid-in capital		
Capital Stock		
Common stock, $5 par value, 1,000,000 shares		
authorized, 500,000 shares issued, 494,000 shares		
outstanding		$2,500,000
Additional paid-in capital		
In excess of par value	$1,525,000	
From treasury stock	4,000	
Total additional paid-in capital		1,529,000
Total paid-in capital		4,029,000
Retained earnings		150,600
Total paid-in capital and retained earnings		4,179,600
Less: Treasury stock (6,000 shares)		54,000
Total stockholders' equity		$4,125,600

SELF-STUDY QUESTIONS

Answers are at the end of the chapter.

(SO 1) 1. Which of the following is *not* a major advantage of a corporation?
  a. Separate legal existence.
  b. Continuous life.
  c. Government regulations.
  d. Transferable ownership rights.

(SO 1) 2. A major disadvantage of a corporation is:
  a. limited liability of stockholders.
  b. additional taxes.
  c. transferable ownership rights.
  d. none of the above.

(SO 2) 3. Which of the following statements is *false*?
  a. Ownership of common stock gives the owner a voting right.
  b. The stockholders' equity section begins with paid-in capital.
  c. The authorization of capital stock does not result in a formal accounting entry.
  d. Legal capital per share applies to par value stock but not to no-par value stock.

(SO 2) 4. ABC Corporation issues 1,000 shares of $10 par value common stock at $12 per share. In recording the transaction, credits are made to:
  a. Common Stock $10,000 and Paid-in Capital in Excess of Stated Value, $2,000.
  b. Common Stock $12,000.

  c. Common Stock $10,000 and Paid-in Capital in Excess of Par Value $2,000.
  d. Common Stock $10,000 and Retained Earnings $2,000.

(SO 3) 5. XYZ, Inc., sells 100 shares of $5 par value treasury stock at $13 per share. If the cost of acquiring the shares was $10 per share, the entry for the sale should include credits to:
  a. Treasury Stock $1,000 and Paid-in Capital from Treasury Stock $300.
  b. Treasury Stock $500 and Paid-in Capital from Treasury Stock $800.
  c. Treasury Stock $1,000 and Retained Earnings $300.
  d. Treasury Stock $500 and Paid-in Capital in Excess of Par Value $800.

(SO 3) 6. In the stockholders' equity section, the cost of treasury stock is deducted from:
  a. Total paid-in capital and retained earnings.
  b. Retained earnings.
  c. Total stockholders' equity.
  d. Common stock in paid-in capital.

(SO 4) 7. Preferred stock may have priority over common stock *except* in:
  a. dividends.
  b. assets in the event of liquidation.
  c. conversion.
  d. voting.

(SO 5) 8. Entries for cash dividends are required on the:
a. declaration date and the record date.
b. record date and the payment date.
c. declaration date, record date, and payment date.
d. declaration date and the payment date.

(SO 5) 9. Which of the following statements about small stock dividends is true?
a. A debit to Retained Earnings for the par value of the shares issued should be made.
b. Market value per share should be assigned to the dividend shares.
c. A stock dividend decreases total stockholders' equity.
d. A stock dividend ordinarily will have no effect on book value per share of stock.

(SO 6) 10. All *but one* of the following is reported in a retained earnings statement. The exception is:
a. cash and stock dividends.
b. net income and net loss.
c. some disposals of treasury stock below cost.
d. sales of treasury stock above cost.

(SO 6) 11. A prior period adjustment is:
a. reported in the income statement as a nontypical item.

b. a correction of an error that is made directly to retained earnings.
c. reported directly in the stockholders' equity section.
d. reported in the retained earnings statement as an adjustment of the ending balance of retained earnings.

*12. When a stockholders' equity statement is presented, it is not necessary to prepare a(an):   (SO 8)
a. retained earnings statement.
b. balance sheet.
c. income statement.
d. none of the above.

*13. The ledger of JFK, Inc., shows common stock, common treasury stock, and no preferred stock. For this company, the formula for computing book value per share is: (SO 9)
a. Total paid-in capital and retained earnings divided by the number of shares of common stock issued.
b. Common stock divided by the number of shares of common stock issued.
c. Total stockholders' equity divided by the number of shares of common stock outstanding.
d. Total stockholders' equity divided by the number of shares of common stock issued.

QUESTIONS

••

1. Pat Kabza, a student, asks your help in understanding the following characteristics of a corporation: (a) separate legal existence, (b) limited liability of stockholders, and (c) transferable ownership rights. Explain these characteristics to Pat.

2. (a) Your friend T.R. Cedras cannot understand how the characteristic of corporation management is both an advantage and a disadvantage. Clarify this problem for T.R.
(b) Identify and explain two other disadvantages of a corporation.

3. Cary Brant believes a corporation must be incorporated in the state in which its headquarters office is located. Is Cary correct? Explain.

4. What are the basic ownership rights of common stockholders in the absence of restrictive provisions?

5. A corporation has been defined as an entity separate and distinct from its owners. In what ways is a corporation a separate legal entity?

6. What are the two principal components of stockholders' equity?

7. The corporate charter of Letterman Corporation allows the issuance of a maximum of 100,000 shares of common stock. During its first two years of operations, Letterman sold 60,000 shares to shareholders and reacquired 7,000 of these shares. After

these transactions, how many shares are authorized, issued, and outstanding?

8. Which is the better investment—common stock with a par value of $5 per share or common stock with a par value of $20 per share?

9. What factors help determine the market value of stock?

10. Why is common stock usually not issued at a price that is less than par value?

11. Land appraised at $80,000 is purchased by issuing 1,000 shares of $20 par value common stock. The market price of the shares at the time of the exchange, based on active trading in the securities market, is $90 per share. Should the land be recorded at $20,000, $80,000, or $90,000? Explain.

12. For what reasons might a company like IBM repurchase some of its stock (treasury stock)?

13. Wilmor, Inc., purchases 1,000 shares of its own previously issued $5 par common stock for $11,000. Assuming the shares are held in the treasury, what effect does this transaction have on (a) net income, (b) total assets, (c) total paid-in capital, and (d) total stockholders' equity?

14. The treasury stock purchased in question 14, above, is resold by Wilmor, Inc., for $12,500. What effect does this transaction have on (a) net income,

(b) total assets, (c) total paid-in capital, and (d) total stockholders' equity?

15. (a) What are the principal differences between common stock and preferred stock?
    (b) Preferred stock may be cumulative. Discuss this feature.
    (c) How are dividends in arrears presented in the financial statements?

16. Identify the events that result in credits and debits to retained earnings.

17. Indicate how each of the following accounts should be classified in the stockholders' equity section.
    (a) Common stock
    (b) Paid-in capital in excess of par value
    (c) Retained earnings
    (d) Treasury stock
    (e) Paid-in capital from treasury stock
    (f) Paid-in capital in excess of stated value
    (g) Preferred stock

18. What are the three conditions that must exist before a cash dividend is paid?

19. Three dates associated with Galena Company's cash dividend are May 1, May 15, and May 31. Discuss the significance of each date and give the entry at each date.

20. Contrast the effects of a cash dividend and a stock dividend on a corporation's balance sheet.

21. Jill Sims asks, "Since stock dividends don't change anything, why declare them?" What is your answer to Jill?

22. The Bella Corporation has 10,000 shares of $15 par value common stock outstanding when they announce a 2 for 1 split. Before the split, the stock had a market price of $140 per share. After the split, how many shares of stock will be outstanding, and what will be the approximate market price per share?

23. The board of directors is considering a stock split or a stock dividend. They understand that total stockholders' equity will remain the same under either action. However, they are not sure of the different effects of the two types of actions on other aspects of stockholders' equity. Explain the differences to the directors.

24. What is a prior period adjustment, and how is it reported in the financial statements?

25. What is the purpose of a retained earnings restriction? Identify the possible causes of retained earnings restrictions.

*26. WAT, Inc.'s common stock has a par value of $1, a book value of $29, and a current market value of $15. Explain why these amounts are all different.

*27. What is the formula for computing book value per share when a corporation has only common stock?

BRIEF EXERCISES

BE12–1 Tracy Bono is studying for her accounting midterm examination. Identify for Tracy the advantages and disadvantages of the corporate form of business organization.

Advantages and disadvantages of a corporation.
(SO 1)

BE12–2 On May 10, Armada Corporation issues 1,000 shares of $10 par value common stock for cash at $14 per share. Journalize the issuance of the stock.

Issuance of par value common stock.
(SO 2)

BE12–3 On June 1, Eagle Inc. issues 2,000 shares of no-par common stock at a cash price of $7 per share. Journalize the issuance of the shares assuming the stock has a stated value of $1 per share.

Issuance of no-par value common stock.
(SO 2)

BE12–4 Spiro Inc.'s $10 par value common stock is actively traded at a market value of $14 per share. Spiro issues 5,000 shares to purchase land advertised for sale at $80,000. Journalize the issuance of the stock in acquiring the land.

Issuance of stock in a noncash transaction.
(SO 2)

BE12–5 On July 1, ARB Corporation purchases 500 shares of its $5 par value common stock for the treasury at a cash price of $7 per share. On September 1, it sells 300 shares of the treasury stock for cash at $10 per share. Journalize the two treasury stock transactions.

Treasury stock transactions.
(SO 3)

BE12–6 Ozark Inc. issues 5,000 shares of $100 par value preferred stock for cash at $112 per share. Journalize the issuance of the preferred stock.

Issuance of preferred stock.
(SO 4)

BE12–7 The Seabee Corporation has 10,000 shares of common stock outstanding. It declares a $1 per share cash dividend on November 1 to stockholders of record on December 1. The dividend is paid on December 31. Prepare the entries on the appropriate dates to record the declaration and payment of the cash dividend.

Prepare entries for a cash dividend.
(SO 5)

BE12–8 Satina Corporation has 100,000 shares of $10 per value common stock outstanding. It declares a 10% stock dividend on December 1 when the market value per share is $12. The

Prepare entries for a stock dividend.
(SO 5)

dividend shares are issued on December 31. Prepare the entries for the declaration and payment of the stock dividend.

Show before and after effects of a stock dividend.
(SO 5)

BE12–9 The stockholders' equity section of the Desi Corporation consists of common stock ($10 par) $1,000,000 and retained earnings $400,000. A 10% stock dividend (10,000 shares) is declared when the market value per share is $12. Show the before and after effects of the dividend on (a) the components of stockholders' equity, and (b) shares outstanding.

Prepare a retained earnings statement.
(SO 6)

BE12–10 For the year ending December 31, 1996, Maddy Inc. reports net income $182,000 and dividends $85,000. Prepare the retained earnings statement for the year assuming the balance in retained earnings on January 1, 1996, was $220,000.

Prepare retained earnings statement.
(SO 6)

BE12–11 The balance in retained earnings on January 1, 1997 for Julio Cortez Inc. was $800,000. During the year, the corporation paid cash dividends of $90,000 and distributed a stock dividend of $8,000. In addition, the company determined that it had understated its depreciation expense in prior years by $50,000. Net income for 1997 was $150,000. Prepare the retained earnings statement for 1997.

Stockholders' equity section.
(SO 7)

BE12–12 Anita Corporation has the following accounts at December 31: Common Stock, $10 par, 5,000 shares issued, $50,000; Paid-in Capital in Excess of Par Value $10,000; Retained Earnings $29,000; and Treasury Stock—Common, 500 shares, $7,000. Prepare the stockholders' equity section of the balance sheet.

Book value per share.
(SO 9)

*BE12–13 The balance sheet for Loren Inc. shows the following: total paid-in capital and retained earnings $860,000, total stockholders' equity $840,000, common stock issued 44,000 shares, and common stock outstanding 40,000 shares. Compute the book value per share.

EXERCISES

Journalize issuance of common stock.
(SO 2)

E12–1 During its first year of operations, the Bevis Corporation had the following transactions pertaining to its common stock.

Jan. 10 Issued 80,000 shares for cash at $5 per share.

July 1 Issued 30,000 shares for cash at $7 per share.

Instructions
(a) Journalize the transactions, assuming that the common stock has a par value of $5 per share.
(b) Journalize the transactions, assuming that the common stock is no-par with a stated value of $1 per share.

Entries for issuance of common and preferred stock and purchase of treasury stock.
(SO 2, 3, 4)

E12–2 Santiago Co. had the following transactions during the current period:

Mar. 2 Issued 5,000 shares of $1 par value common stock to attorneys in payment of a bill for $27,000 for services rendered in helping the company to incorporate.

June 12 Issued 60,000 shares of $1 par value common stock for cash of $375,000.

July 11 Issued 1,000 shares of $100 par value preferred stock for cash at $105 per share.

Nov. 28 Purchased 2,000 shares of treasury stock for $80,000.

Instructions
Journalize the transactions.

Journalize noncash common stock transactions.
(SO 2)

E12–3 As an auditor for the CPA firm of Bell and Heft, you encounter the following situations in auditing different clients:

1. The Ruth Corporation is a closely held corporation whose stock is not publicly traded. On December 5, the corporation acquired land by issuing 5,000 shares of its $20 par value common stock. The owners' asking price for the land was $120,000, and the fair market value of the land was $110,000.
2. The Hand Corporation is a publicly held corporation whose common stock is traded on the securities markets. On June 1, it acquired land by issuing 20,000 shares of its $10 par value stock. At the time of the exchange, the land was advertised for sale at $250,000, and the stock was selling at $12 per share.

Instructions
Prepare the journal entries for each of the situations above.

E12–4 On January 1, 1996, the stockholders' equity section of the Margo Corporation shows: Common stock ($5 par value) $1,500,000; Paid-in capital in excess of par value $1,000,000; and Retained earnings $1,200,000. During the year, the following treasury stock transactions occurred:

Journalize treasury stock transactions.
(SO 3)

Mar. 1   Purchased 50,000 shares for cash at $14 per share.

July 1   Sold 10,000 treasury shares for cash at $16 per share.

Sept. 1   Sold 8,000 treasury shares for cash at $13 per share.

Instructions
(a) Journalize the treasury stock transactions.

(b) Restate the entry for September 1, assuming the treasury shares were sold at $11 per share.

E12–5 Talley Corporation is authorized to issue both preferred and common stock. The par value of the preferred is $50. During the first year of operations, the company had the following events and transactions pertaining to its preferred stock:

Journalize preferred stock transactions and indicate statement presentation.
(SO 4, 7)

Feb. 1   Issued 30,000 shares for cash at $53 per share.

July 1   Issued 10,000 shares for cash at $57 per share.

Instructions
(a) Journalize the transactions.

(b) Post to the stockholders' equity accounts.

(c) Indicate the statement presentation of the accounts.

E12–6 The stockholders' equity section of Kimbria Shumway Corporation at December 31 is as follows:

Answer questions about stockholders' equity section.
(SO 2, 3, 4, 7)

Paid-in capital

Preferred stock, cumulative, 10,000 shares authorized, 6,000 shares issued and outstanding	$ 600,000
Common stock, no par, 750,000 shares authorized, 600,000 shares issued	1,800,000
Total paid-in capital	2,400,000
Retained earnings	1,158,000
Total paid-in capital and retained earnings	3,558,000
Less: Treasury stock (10,000 common shares)	(64,000)
Total stockholders' equity	$3,494,000

Instructions
▯▯▷ From a review of the stockholders' equity section, answer the following questions.

(a) How many shares of common stock are outstanding?

(b) Assuming there is a stated value, what is the stated value of the common stock?

(c) What is the par value of the preferred stock?

(d) If the annual dividend on preferred stock is $48,000, what is the dividend rate on preferred stock?

(e) If dividends of $96,000 were in arrears on preferred stock, what would be the balance reported for Retained Earnings?

E12–7 Anita Ferreri Corporation recently hired a new accountant with extensive experience in accounting for partnerships. Because of the pressure of the new job, the accountant was unable to review what he had learned earlier about corporation accounting. During the first month, the accountant made the following entries for the corporation's capital stock:

Prepare correct entries for capital stock transactions.
(SO 2, 3, 4)

May 2	Cash	144,000	
	Capital Stock		144,000
	(Issued 12,000 shares of $5 par value common stock at $12 per share)		
10	Cash	600,000	
	Capital Stock		600,000
	(Issued 10,000 shares of $50 par value preferred stock at $60 per share)		

15	Capital Stock	14,000	
	Cash		14,000
	(Purchased 1,000 shares of common stock for the		
	treasury at $14 per share)		
31	Cash	7,500	
	Capital Stock		2,500
	Gain on Sale of Stock		5,000
	(Sold 500 shares of treasury stock at $15 per share)		

Instructions

On the basis of the explanation for each entry, prepare the entry that should have been made for the capital stock transactions.

Journalize cash dividends and indicate statement presentation.
(SO 5)

E12–8   On January 1, Tarow Corporation had 75,000 shares of no-par common stock issued and outstanding. The stock has a stated value of $5 per share. During the year, the following occurred:

Apr. 1   Issued 5,000 additional shares of common stock.

June 15   Declared a cash dividend of $1 per share to stockholders of record on June 30.

July 10   Paid the $1 cash dividend.

Dec. 1   Issued 2,000 additional shares of common stock.

     15   Declared a cash dividend on outstanding shares of $1.20 per share to stockholders of record on December 31.

Instructions

(a) Prepare the entries, if any, on each of the three dividend dates.

(b) How are dividends and dividends payable reported in the financial statements prepared at December 31?

Journalize stock dividends.
(SO 5)

E12–9   On January 1, 1997, the Keyes Corporation had $1,500,000 of common stock outstanding that was issued at par and retained earnings of $750,000. The company issued 50,000 shares of common stock at par on July 1 and earned net income of $400,000 for the year.

Instructions

Journalize the declaration of a 10% stock dividend on December 10, 1997, for the following independent assumptions:

(1) Par value is $10 and market value is $15.

(2) Par value is $5 and market value is $20.

Compare effects of a stock dividend and a stock split.
(SO 5)

E12–10   On October 31, the stockholders' equity section of the Sarah Lane Company consists of common stock $800,000 and retained earnings $400,000. Sarah is considering the following two courses of action: (1) declaring a 10% stock dividend on the 80,000 $10 par value shares outstanding or (2) effecting a 2-for-1 stock split that will reduce par value to $5 per share. The current market price is $15 per share.

Instructions

Prepare a tabular summary of the effects of the alternative actions on the components of stockholders' equity, outstanding shares, and book value per share. Use the following column headings: Before Action, After Stock Dividend, and After Stock Split.

Prepare correcting entries for dividends and a stock split.
(SO 5)

E12–11   Before preparing financial statements for the current year, the chief accountant for Phil, Chris, and Caroline Company discovered the following errors in the accounts:

1. The declaration and payment of $25,000 cash dividend was recorded as a debit to Interest Expense $25,000 and a credit to Cash $25,000.

2. A 10% stock dividend (1,000 shares) was declared on the $10 par value stock when the market value per share was $17. The only entry made was: Retained Earnings (Dr.) $10,000 and Dividend Payable (Cr.) $10,000. The shares have not been issued.

3. A 4-for-1 stock split involving the issue of 400,000 shares of $5 par value common stock for 100,000 shares of $20 par value common stock was recorded as a debit to Retained Earnings $2,000,000 and a credit to Common Stock $2,000,000.

Instructions

Prepare the correcting entries at December 31.

E12–12   On January 1, 1996, Waikiki Corporation had Retained Earnings of $580,000. During the year, Waikiki had the following selected transactions:

1. Declared cash dividends $120,000.
2. Corrected overstatement of 1995 net income because of depreciation error $20,000.
3. Earned net income $310,000.
4. Declared stock dividends $60,000.

Prepare a retained earnings statement.
(SO 6)

Instructions
Prepare a retained earnings statement for the year.

E12–13   The ledger of Mintur Corporation contains the following accounts: Common Stock, Preferred Stock, Treasury Stock—Common, Paid-in Capital in Excess of Par Value—Preferred Stock, Paid-in Capital in Excess of Stated Value—Common Stock, Paid-in Capital from Treasury Stock, and Retained Earnings.

Classify stockholders' equity accounts.
(SO 7)

Instructions
Classify each account using the following tabular alignment:

	Paid-in Capital			
Account	Capital Stock	Additional	Retained Earnings	Other

E12–14   The following accounts appear in the ledger of Ozabal Inc. after the books are closed at December 31.

Prepare a stockholders' equity section.
(SO 7)

Common Stock, no par, $1 stated value, 400,000 shares authorized; 300,000 shares issued	$ 300,000
Common Stock Dividends Distributable	75,000
Paid-in Capital in Excess of Stated Value—Common Stock	1,200,000
Preferred Stock, $5 par value, 8%, 40,000 shares authorized; 30,000 shares issued	150,000
Retained Earnings	900,000
Treasury Stock (10,000 common shares)	60,000
Paid-in Capital in Excess of Par Value—Preferred Stock	244,000

Instructions
Prepare stockholders' equity section at December 31, assuming retained earnings is restricted for plant expansion in the amount of $100,000.

*E12–15   In a recent year, the stockholders' equity section of the Aluminum Company of America (Alcoa) showed the following (in alphabetical order): Additional (paid-in) Capital $680.5, Common stock $88.3, Preferred stock $66.0, and Retained earnings $3,750.2. All dollar data are in millions.

Prepare a stockholders' equity section and compute book value.
(SO 7, 9)

The preferred stock has 660,000 shares authorized with a par value of $100 and an annual $3.75 per share cumulative dividend preference. At December 31, all authorized preferred stock is issued and outstanding. There are 300 million shares of $1 par value common stock authorized of which 88.3 million are outstanding at December 31.

Instructions
(a) Prepare the stockholders' equity section, including disclosure of all relevant data.
(b) Compute the book value per share of common stock, assuming there are no preferred dividends in arrears. (Round to two decimals.)

*E12–16   At December 31, Kilgora Corporation has total stockholders' equity of $3,000,000. Included in this total are Preferred stock $500,000 and Paid-in capital in excess of par value—Preferred stock $50,000. There are 10,000 shares of $50 par value 10% cumulative preferred stock outstanding. At year end, 200,000 shares of common stock are outstanding.

Compute book value per share with preferred stock.
(SO 4, 9)

Instructions
Compute the book value per share of common stock, under each of the following assumptions:

(a) There are no preferred dividends in arrears, and the preferred stock does not have a call price.

(b) Preferred dividends are one year in arrears, and the preferred stock has a call price of $60 per share.

Compute book value per share and indicate account balances after a stock dividend.
(SO 5, 7, 9)

*E12–17   On October 1, 1997, Valentine Corporation's stockholders' equity is as follows:

Common stock $10 par value	$200,000
Paid-in capital in excess of par value	25,000
Retained earnings	175,000
Total stockholders' equity	$400,000

On October 1, Valentine declares and distributes a 10% stock dividend when the market value of the stock is $15 per share.

Instructions
(a) Compute the book value per share (1) before the stock dividend and (2) after the stock dividend. (Round to two decimals.)
(b) Indicate the balances in the three stockholders' equity accounts after the stock dividend shares have been distributed.

PROBLEMS

Journalize stock transactions, post, and prepare paid-in capital section.
(SO 2, 4, 7)

P12–1   Jackie Remmers Corporation was organized on January 1, 1996. It is authorized to issue 20,000 shares of 6%, $50 par value preferred stock, and 500,000 shares of no-par common stock with a stated value of $1 per share. The following stock transactions were completed during the first year:

Jan. 10   Issued 100,000 shares of common stock for cash at $3 per share.
Mar. 1   Issued 10,000 shares of preferred stock for cash at $51 per share.
Apr. 1   Issued 25,000 shares of common stock for land. The asking price of the land was $90,000; the fair market value of the land was $85,000.
May 1   Issued 75,000 shares of common stock for cash at $4 per share.
Aug. 1   Issued 10,000 shares of common stock to attorneys in payment of their bill for $50,000 pertaining to services rendered in helping the company organize.
Sept. 1   Issued 5,000 shares of common stock for cash at $6 per share.
Nov. 1   Issued 2,000 shares of preferred stock for cash at $53 per share.

Instructions
(a) Journalize the transactions.
(b) Post to the stockholders' equity accounts. (Use J1 as the posting reference.)
(c) Prepare the paid-in capital section of stockholders' equity at December 31, 1996.

Journalize treasury stock transactions, post, and prepare stockholders' equity section.
(SO 3, 7)

P12–2   Cole William Sondgeroth Corporation had the following stockholders' equity accounts on January 1, 1996: Common Stock ($1 par) $400,000, Paid-in Capital in Excess of Par Value $500,000, and Retained Earnings $100,000. In 1996, the company had the following treasury stock transactions:

Mar. 1   Purchased 5,000 shares at $8 per share.
June 1   Sold 1,000 shares at $10 per share.
Sept. 1   Sold 2,000 shares at $9 per share.
Dec. 1   Sold 1,000 shares at $6 per share.

Cole William Sondgeroth Corporation uses the cost method of accounting for treasury stock. In 1996, the company reported net income of $50,000.

Instructions
(a) Journalize the treasury stock transactions, and prepare the closing entry at December 31, 1996, for net income.
(b) Open accounts for (1) Paid-in Capital from Treasury Stock, (2) Treasury Stock, and (3) Retained Earnings. Post to these accounts using J12 as the posting reference.
(c) Prepare the stockholders' equity section for Cole William Sondgeroth Corporation at December 31, 1996.

P12–3   The stockholders' equity accounts of Chung Corporation on January 1, 1996, were as follows:

Journalize and post transactions, prepare stockholders' equity section, and compute book value.
(SO 2, 3, 4, 7, 9)

Preferred Stock (10%, $100 par noncumulative, 5,000 shares authorized)	$ 300,000
Common Stock ($5 stated value, 300,000 shares authorized)	1,000,000
Paid-in Capital in Excess of Par Value—Preferred Stock	15,000
Paid-in Capital in Excess of Stated Value—Common Stock	400,000
Retained Earnings	488,000
Treasury Stock—Common (5,000 shares)	40,000

During 1996, the corporation had the following transactions and events pertaining to its stockholders' equity:

Feb. 1   Issued 4,000 shares of common stock for $25,000.
Mar. 20   Purchased 1,000 additional shares of common treasury stock at $8 per share.
June 14   Sold 4,000 shares of treasury stock—common for $34,000.
Sept. 3   Issued 2,000 shares of common stock for a patent valued at $13,000.
Dec. 31   Determined that net income for the year was $215,000.

Instructions
(a) Journalize the transactions and the closing entry for net income.
(b) Enter the beginning balances in the accounts and post the journal entries to the stockholders' equity accounts. (Use J1 as the posting reference.)
(c) Prepare a stockholders' equity section at December 31, 1996.
*(d) Compute the book value per share of common stock at December 31, 1996, assuming the preferred stock does not have a call price.

P12–4   On December 31, 1996, V. Conway Company had 1,500,000 shares of $10 par common stock issued and outstanding. The stockholders' equity accounts at December 31, 1996 have the following balances.

Prepare a retained earnings statement and the stockholders' equity section.
(SO 6, 7)

Common stock	$15,000,000
Additional paid-in capital	1,500,000
Retained earnings	900,000

Transactions during 1997 and other information related to stockholders' equity accounts were as follows:

1. On January 10, 1997, Conway issues at $110 per share 100,000 shares of $100 par value, 8% cumulative preferred stock.
2. On February 8, 1997, Conway reacquired 10,000 shares of its common stock for $16 per share.
3. On June 8, 1997, Conway declared a cash dividend of $1 per share on the common stock outstanding, payable on July 10, 1997, to stockholders of record on July 1, 1997.
4. On December 15, 1997, Conway declared the yearly cash dividend on preferred stock, payable January 10, 1998 to stockholders of record on December 15, 1997.
5. Net income for the year is $3,600,000.
6. It was discovered that depreciation expense had been overstated in 1996 by $100,000.

Instructions
(a) Prepare a retained earnings statement for the year ended December 31, 1997.
(b) Prepare the stockholders' equity section of Conway's balance sheet at December 31, 1997.

Prepare retained earnings statement and stockholders' equity section.
(SO 5, 6, 7)

P12–5   The ledger of Reno Corporation at December 31, 1996, after the books have been closed, contains the following stockholders' equity accounts:

Preferred Stock (10,000 shares issued)	$1,000,000
Common Stock (400,000 shares issued)	2,000,000
Paid-in Capital in Excess of Par Value—Preferred	200,000
Paid-in Capital in Excess of Par Value—Common	1,200,000
Common Stock Dividends Distributable	100,000
Retained Earnings	2,540,000

A review of the accounting records reveals the following:

1. No errors have been made in recording 1996 transactions or in preparing the closing entry for net income.
2. Preferred stock is 10% $100 par value, non-cumulative, and callable at $125. Since January 1, 1995, 10,000 shares have been outstanding; 20,000 shares are authorized.
3. Common stock is no-par with a stated value of $5 per share; 600,000 shares are authorized.
4. The January 1 balance in Retained Earnings was $2,200,000.
5. On October 1, 100,000 shares of common stock were sold for cash at $8 per share.
6. A cash dividend of $400,000 was declared and properly allocated to preferred and common stock on November 1. No dividends were paid to preferred stockholders in 1995.
7. On December 31, a 5% common stock dividend was declared out of retained earnings on common stock when the market price per share was $7.
8. Net income for the year was $880,000.
9. On December 31, 1996, the directors authorized disclosure of a $100,000 restriction of retained earnings for plant expansion. (Use Note A.)

Instructions
(a) Reproduce the retained earnings account (T account) for the year.
(b) Prepare a retained earnings statement for the year.
(c) Prepare a stockholders' equity section at December 31.

Prepare entries for stock transactions and stockholders' equity section.
(SO 2, 3, 4, 7)

P12–6   Largent Corporation has been authorized to issue 20,000 shares of $100 par value, 10%, noncumulative preferred stock and 1,000,000 shares of no-par common stock. The corporation assigned a $2.50 stated value to the common stock. At December 31, 1996, the ledger contained the following balances pertaining to stockholders' equity:

Preferred Stock	$ 120,000
Paid-in Capital in Excess of Par Value—Preferred	24,000
Common Stock	1,000,000
Paid-in Capital in Excess of Stated Value—Common	2,850,000
Treasury Stock—Common (1,000 shares)	12,000
Paid-in Capital from Treasury Stock	1,000
Retained earnings	82,000

The preferred stock was issued for land having a fair market value of $144,000. All common stock issued was for cash. In November, 1,500 shares of common stock were purchased for the treasury at a per share cost of $12. In December, 500 shares of treasury stock were sold for $14 per share. No dividends were declared in 1996.

Instructions
(a) Prepare the journal entries for the:
   (1) Issuance of preferred stock for land.
   (2) Issuance of common stock for cash.
   (3) Purchase of common treasury stock for cash.
   (4) Sale of treasury stock for cash.
(b) Prepare the stockholders' equity section at December 31, 1996.

P12–7 On January 1, 1997, Wirth Corporation had the following stockholders' equity accounts:

Common Stock ($10 par value, 80,000 shares issued and outstanding)	$800,000
Paid-in Capital in Excess of Par Value	200,000
Retained Earnings	540,000

During the year, the following transactions occurred:

Jan. 15 Declared a $1 cash dividend per share to stockholders of record on January 31, payable February 15.

Feb. 15 Paid the dividend declared in January.

Apr. 15 Declared a 10% stock dividend to stockholders of record on April 30, distributable May 15. On April 15, the market price of the stock was $13 per share.

May 15 Issued the shares for the stock dividend.

July 1 Announced a 2-for-1 stock split. The market price per share prior to the announcement was $15. (The new par value is $5.)

Dec. 1 Declared a $.50 per share cash dividend to stockholders of record on December 15, payable January 10, 1996.

31 Determined that net income for the year was $220,000.

Instructions
(a) Journalize the transactions and the closing entry for net income.
(b) Enter the beginning balances and post the entries to the stockholders' equity accounts. (*Note:* Open additional stockholders' equity accounts as needed.)
(c) Prepare a stockholders' equity section at December 31.

*P12–8 The following stockholders' equity accounts arranged alphabetically are in the ledger of Dublin Corporation at December 31, 1996:

Common Stock ($10 stated value)	$1,500,000
Paid-in Capital from Treasury Stock	6,000
Paid-in Capital in Excess of Stated Value—Common Stock	900,000
Paid-in Capital in Excess of Par Value—Preferred Stock	280,000
Preferred Stock (8%, $100 par, noncumulative)	400,000
Retained Earnings	1,134,000
Treasury Stock—Common (8,000 shares)	88,000

Instructions
(a) Prepare a stockholders' equity section at December 31, 1996.
(b) Compute the book value per share of the common stock, assuming the preferred stock has a call price of $110 per share.

*P12–9 On January 1, 1996, Cedeno Inc. had the following stockholders' equity balances:

Common Stock (500,000 shares issued)	$1,000,000
Paid-in Capital in Excess of Par Value	500,000
Stock Dividends Distributable	100,000
Retained Earnings	600,000

During 1996, the following transactions and events occurred:

1. Issued 50,000 shares of $2 par value common stock as a result of 10% stock dividend declared on December 15, 1995.
2. Issued 30,000 shares of common stock for cash at $5 per share.
3. Purchased 20,000 shares of common stock for the treasury at $6 per share.
4. Declared and paid a cash dividend of $100,000.
5. Sold 5,000 shares of treasury stock for cash at $6 per share.
6. Earned net income of $300,000.

Instructions
Prepare a stockholders' equity statement for the year.

ALTERNATE PROBLEMS

Journalize stock transactions, post, and prepare paid-in capital section.
(SO 2, 4, 7)

P12–1A   The Wetland Corporation was organized on January 1, 1996. It is authorized to issue 10,000 shares of 8%, $100 par value preferred stock, and 500,000 shares of no-par common stock with a stated value of $2 per share. The following stock transactions were completed during the first year:

Jan. 10   Issued 80,000 shares of common stock for cash at $3 per share.
Mar. 1   Issued 5,000 shares of preferred stock for cash at $104 per share.
Apr. 1   Issued 24,000 shares of common stock for land. The asking price of the land was $90,000; the fair market value of the land was $80,000.
May 1   Issued 80,000 shares of common stock for cash at $4 per share.
Aug. 1   Issued 10,000 shares of common stock to attorneys in payment of their bill of $50,000 for services rendered in helping the company organize.
Sept. 1   Issued 10,000 shares of common stock for cash at $5 per share.
Nov. 1   Issued 1,000 shares of preferred stock for cash at $108 per share.

Instructions
(a) Journalize the transactions.
(b) Post to the stockholders' equity accounts. (Use J5 as the posting reference.)
(c) Prepare the paid-in capital section of stockholders' equity at December 31, 1996.

Journalize treasury stock transactions, post, and prepare stockholders' equity section.
(SO 3, 7)

P12–2A   Rena Rhoda Corporation had the following stockholders' equity accounts on January 1, 1996: Common Stock ($5 par) $500,000, Paid-in Capital in Excess of Par Value $200,000, and Retained Earnings $100,000. In 1996, the company had the following treasury stock transactions:

Mar. 1   Purchased 5,000 shares at $9 per share.
June 1   Sold 1,000 shares at $12 per share.
Sept. 1   Sold 2,000 shares at $10 per share.
Dec. 1   Sold 1,000 shares at $8 per share.

Rena Rhoda Corporation uses the cost method of accounting for treasury stock. In 1996, the company reported net income of $50,000.

Instructions
(a) Journalize the treasury stock transactions and prepare the closing entry at December 31, 1996, for net income.
(b) Open accounts for (1) Paid-in Capital from Treasury Stock, (2) Treasury Stock, and (3) Retained Earnings. Post to these accounts using J10 as the posting reference.
(c) Prepare the stockholders' equity section for Rena Rhoda Corporation at December 31, 1996.

Journalize and post transactions, prepare stockholders' equity section, and compute book value.
(SO 2, 3, 4, 7, 9)

P12–3A   The stockholders' equity accounts of the Capozza Corporation on January 1, 1996, were as follows:

Preferred Stock (12%, $50 par cumulative, 10,000 shares authorized)	$ 400,000
Common Stock ($1 stated value, 2,000,000 shares authorized)	1,000,000
Paid-in Capital in Excess of Par Value—Preferred Stock	80,000
Paid-in Capital in Excess of Stated Value—Common Stock	1,400,000
Retained Earnings	1,816,000
Treasury Stock—Common (10,000 shares)	40,000

During 1996, the corporation had the following transactions and events pertaining to its stockholders' equity:

Feb. 1   Issued 20,000 shares of common stock for $100,000.
Apr. 14   Sold 6,000 shares of treasury stock—common for $28,000.
Sept. 3   Issued 5,000 shares of common stock for a patent valued at $25,000.
Nov. 10   Purchased 1,000 shares of common stock for the treasury at a cost of $6,000.
Dec. 31   Determined that net income for the year was $377,000.

No dividends were declared during the year.

Instructions

(a) Journalize the transactions and the closing entry for net income.

(b) Enter the beginning balances in the accounts and post the journal entries to the stockholders' equity accounts. (Use J5 for the posting reference.)

(c) Prepare a stockholders' equity section at December 31, 1996, including the disclosure of the preferred dividends in arrears.

*(d) Compute the book value per share of common stock at December 31, 1996. (Round to two decimals.)

P12–4A On January 1, 1997, the Casey Stengel Corporation had the following stockholders' equity accounts:

Prepare dividend entries and stockholders' equity section.
(SO 5, 7)

Common Stock ($20 par value, 60,000 shares issued and outstanding)	$1,200,000
Paid-in Capital in Excess of Par Value	200,000
Retained Earnings	500,000

During the year, the following transactions occurred:

Feb. 1 Declared a $1 cash dividend per share to stockholders of record on February 15, payable March 1.

Mar. 1 Paid the dividend declared in February.

Apr. 1 Announced a 4 for 1 stock split. Prior to the split, the market price per share was $36.

July 1 Declared a 5% stock dividend to stockholders of record on July 15, distributable July 31. On July 1, the market price of the stock was $10 per share.

   31 Issued the shares for the stock dividend.

Dec. 1 Declared a $.50 per share dividend to stockholders of record on December 15, payable January 5, 1996.

   31 Determined that net income for the year was $325,000.

Instructions

(a) Journalize the transactions and closing entries.

(b) Enter the beginning balances and post the entries to the stockholders' equity accounts. (*Note:* Open additional stockholders' equity accounts as needed.)

(c) Prepare a stockholders' equity section at December 31.

P12–5A On December 31, 1996, K. Schipper Company had 1,000,000 shares of $1 par common stock issued and outstanding. The stockholders' equity accounts at December 31, 1996 have the following balances:

Prepare a retained earnings statement and the stockholders' equity section.
(SO 6, 7)

Common stock	1,000,000
Additional paid in capital	500,000
Retained earnings	700,000

Transactions during 1997 and other information related to stockholders' equity accounts were as follows:

1. On January 9, 1997, Schipper issues at $6 per share 100,000 shares of $5 par value, 8% cumulative preferred stock.

2. On February 8, 1997, Schipper reacquired 10,000 shares of its common stock for $12 per share.

3. On June 10, 1997, Schipper declared a cash dividend of $1 per share on the common stock outstanding, payable on July 10, 1997, to stockholders' of record on July 1, 1997.

4. On December 15, 1997, Schipper declared the yearly cash dividend on preferred stock, payable January 10, 1998 to stockholders of record on December 15, 1997.

5. Net income for the year is $2,400,000.

6. It was discovered that depreciation expense had been overstated in 1996 by $100,000.

Instructions

(a) Prepare a retained earnings statement for the year ended December 31, 1997.

(b) Prepare the stockholders' equity section of Schipper's balance sheet at December 31, 1997.

Prepare retained earnings statement and stockholders' equity section.
(SO 6, 7)

P12–6A   The post-closing trial balance of Maggio Corporation at December 31, 1996, contains the following stockholders' equity accounts:

Preferred Stock (15,000 shares issued)	$ 750,000
Common Stock (250,000 shares issued)	2,500,000
Paid-in Capital in Excess of Par Value—Preferred	250,000
Paid-in Capital in Excess of Par Value—Common	500,000
Common Stock Dividends Distributable	200,000
Retained Earnings	743,000

A review of the accounting records reveals the following:

1. No errors have been made in recording 1996 transactions or in preparing the closing entry for net income.
2. Preferred stock is $50 par, 10%, and cumulative. 15,000 shares have been outstanding since January 1, 1995.
3. Authorized stock is 20,000 shares of preferred, 500,000 shares of common with a $10 par value.
4. The January 1 balance in Retained Earnings was $920,000.
5. On July 1, 20,000 shares of common stock were sold for cash at $16 per share.
6. On September 1, the company discovered an understatement error of $60,000 in computing depreciation in 1995. The net of tax effect of $42,000 was properly debited directly to Retained Earnings.
7. A cash dividend of $250,000 was declared and properly allocated to preferred and common stock on October 1. No dividends were paid to preferred stockholders in 1995.
8. On December 31, an 8% common stock dividend was declared out of retained earnings on common stock when the market price per share was $16.
9. Net income for the year was $435,000.
10. On December 31, 1996, the directors authorized disclosure of a $200,000 restriction of retained earnings for plant expansion. (Use Note X.)

Instructions
   (a) Reproduce the retained earnings account for the year.
   (b) Prepare a retained earnings statement for the year.
   (c) Prepare a stockholders' equity section at December 31.

Prepare stockholders' equity section and compute book value.
(SO 7, 9)

*P12–7A   The following stockholders' equity accounts arranged alphabetically are in the ledger of Shirley Denson Corporation at December 31, 1996:

Common Stock ($5 stated value)	$2,500,000
Paid-in Capital from Treasury Stock	10,000
Paid-in Capital in Excess of Stated Value—Common Stock	1,500,000
Paid-in Capital in Excess of Par Value—Preferred Stock	692,000
Preferred Stock (8%, $50 par, noncumulative)	800,000
Retained Earnings	1,958,000
Treasury Stock—Common (10,000 shares)	130,000

Instructions
   (a) Prepare a stockholders' equity section at December 31, 1996.
   (b) Compute the book value per share of the common stock, assuming the preferred stock has a call price of $60 per share.

▼*B*roadening Your Perspective

*F*INANCIAL REPORTING PROBLEM

The stockholders' equity section for PepsiCo, Inc. is shown in the Consolidated Balance Sheet in Appendix A. You will also find data relative to this problem on other pages of the appendix.

Instructions
Answer the following questions.

(a) What is the par or stated value per share of PepsiCo's common stock?
(b) What percentage of PepsiCo's authorized common stock was issued at December 30, 1995? (Round to nearest full percentage.)
(c) How many shares of common stock were outstanding at December 30, 1995, and at December 31, 1994?
(d) What was book value per share at December 30, 1995, and at December 31, 1994? (Note: The currency translation adjustment is part of stockholders' equity.) Compare your answers with the amounts reported in the Selected Financial Data.
(e) What were the growth rates for book value (shareholders' equity) per share for 1, 5, and 10 years as shown in Selected Financial Data?
(f) What was the closing market price per share at December 30, 1995, and at December 31, 1994, as reported under Selected Financial Data?
(g) What was the low and high quarterly cash dividend during 1995 and 1994? What significant historical facts are stated concerning PepsiCo's dividend policy?

*C*OMPARATIVE ANALYSIS PROBLEM— THE COCA-COLA COMPANY VS. PEPSICO, INC.

The financial statements of Coca-Cola Company are presented at the end of Chapter 1, and PepsiCo's financial statements are presented in Appendix A.

Instructions
(a) Based on the information contained in these financial statements, compute the 1995 return on common stockholders' equity for each company.
(b) What conclusions concerning the companies' profitability can be drawn from this ratio?

*I*NTERPRETATION OF FINANCIAL STATEMENTS

Mini-Case—Kellogg Corporation
Kellogg Corporation is the world's leading producer of ready-to-eat cereal products. In recent years the company has taken numerous steps aimed at improving its profitability and earnings per share. Included in these steps was the lay-off of 2,000 employees, roughly 13% of Kellogg's workforce. In addition, in 1995, 1994, and 1993 the company repurchased 5,684,864, 6,194,500, and 9,487,508 of its own shares, and announced plans for significant additional repurchases in the coming year. During 1995, 1994, and 1993 amounts expended for share repurchases were $380 million, $327 million, and $548 million—that's nearly $1.3 billion dollars over a three-year period. Total amounts expended for new property during this same period was $1.1 billion, thus the company spent more money repurchasing stock than building the company. Also during this period the company issued $400 million in new debt.

Presented below are some basic facts for the Kellogg Corporation.

(all dollars in millions)	1995	1994
Net sales	$7,003	$6,562
Net income	490	705
Total assets	3,801	4,467
Total liabilities	2,824	2,659
Common stock, $.25 par value	78	78
Capital in excess of par value	105	69
Retained earnings	3,963	3,801
Treasury stock, at cost	2,361	1,981
Preferred stock	0	0
Number of shares outstanding (in millions)	217	222

Instructions

(a) What are some of the reasons that management purchases its own stock?

(b) What was the approximate impact on earnings per share of the common stock re-purchases during this three-year period—that is, calculate earnings per share after the share repurchases and before the repurchases for 1995. (Use the total repurchases during the three-year period—21,366,872 shares—rounded to 21 million).

(c) Calculate the ratio of debt to total assets for 1994 and 1995 and discuss the implications of the change.

Decision case

The stockholders' meeting for Mantle Corporation has been in progress for some time. The chief financial officer for Mantle is presently reviewing the company's financial statements and is explaining the items that comprise the stockholders' equity section of the balance sheet for the current year. The stockholders' equity section of Mantle Corporation at December 31, 1996, is as follows:

Paid-in capital		
Capital stock		
Preferred stock, authorized 1,000,000 shares		
cumulative, $100 par value, $8 per share, 6,000		
shares issued and outstanding		$ 600,000
Common stock, authorized 5,000,000 shares, $1 par		
value, 3,000,000 shares issued, and 2,700,000		
outstanding		3,000,000
Total capital stock		3,600,000
Additional paid-in capital		
In excess of par value-preferred stock	$ 50,000	
In excess of par value-common stock	25,000,000	
Total additional paid-in capital		25,050,000
Total paid-in capital		28,650,000
Retained earnings		900,000
Total paid-in capital and retained earnings		29,550,000
Less: Common treasury stock (300,000 shares)		9,300,000
Total stockholders' equity		$20,250,000

A number of questions regarding the stockholders' equity section of Mantle Corporation's balance sheet have been raised at the meeting.

Instructions

Answer the following questions as if you were the chief financial officer for Mantle Corporation.

(a) "What does the cumulative provision related to the preferred stock mean?"

(b) "I thought the common stock was presently selling at $29.75, and yet the company has the stock stated at $1 per share. How can that be?"

(c) "Why is the company buying back its common stock? Furthermore, the treasury stock has a debit balance because it is subtracted from stockholders' equity. Why is treasury stock not reported as an asset if it has a debit balance?"

(d) "Why is it necessary to show additional paid-in capital? Why not just show common stock at the total amount paid in?"

COMMUNICATION ACTIVITY

Louis P. Brady, your uncle, is an inventor who has decided to incorporate. Uncle Lou knows that you are an accounting major at U.N.O. In a recent letter to you, he ends with the question, "I'm filling out a state incorporation application; can you tell me the difference in the following terms: (1) authorized stock, (2) issued stock, (3) outstanding stock, (4) preferred stock?"

Instructions
In a brief note, differentiate for Uncle Lou among the four different stock terms. Write the letter to be friendly, yet professional.

GROUP ACTIVITY

You are employed as an auditor for the firm of Honest and Accurate. On the last two engagements you encountered the following situations:

1. Larry D. Beaty Corporation is a closely held corporation whose stock is not publicly traded. On May 15 the corporation acquired property (land and building) by issuing 20,000 shares of its $10 par value common stock. The day before the exchange, the property was advertised for sale at $260,000. This listing was based somewhat on a qualified independent appraisal of $240,000 (fair market value), with $50,000 allocable to land and $190,000 to the building.

2. Jea Nea B. Wood Corporation is a publicly held corporation whose common stock is traded on the American Stock Exchange. On September 10, it acquired land by issuing 8,000 shares of $5 par value stock. At the date of the exchange, the land was listed with a real estate firm at an advertised selling price of $175,000, and the stock was selling at $20 a share.

Instructions
In groups of five or six people:
(a) Discuss the approach that should be taken or the basis used when recording the above situations.
(b) Prepare the journal entry for each situation.

ETHICS CASES

Case A
The R & D division of Simplex Chemical Corp. has just developed a chemical for sterilizing the vicious Brazilian "killer bees" which are invading Mexico and the southern states of the United States. The president of Simplex is anxious to get the chemical on the market because Simplex's profits need a boost—his job is in jeopardy because of decreasing sales and profits. Simplex has an opportunity to sell this chemical in Central American countries, where the laws are much more relaxed than in the United States.

The director of Simplex's R & D division strongly recommends further testing in the laboratory for side effects of this chemical on other insects, birds, animals, plants, and even humans. He cautions the president, "We could be sued from all sides if the chemical has tragic side effects that we didn't even test for in the labs." The president answers, "We can't wait an additional year for your lab tests. We can avoid losses from such lawsuits by establishing a separate wholly owned corporation to shield Simplex Corp. from such lawsuits. We can't lose any more than our investment in the new corporation, and we'll invest just the patent covering this chemical. We'll reap the benefits if the chemical works and is safe, and avoid the losses from lawsuits if it's a disaster." The following week Simplex creates a new wholly owned corporation called Zoebee Inc., sells the chemical patent to it for $10, and watches the spraying begin.

Instructions
   (a) Who are the stakeholders in this situation?
   (b) Are the president's motives and actions ethical?
   (c) Can Simplex shield itself against losses of Zoebee Inc.?

Case B
Flambeau Corporation has paid 60 consecutive quarterly cash dividends (15 years). The last six months, however, have been a real cash drain on the company as profit margins have been greatly narrowed by increasing competition. With a cash balance only sufficient to meet only day-to-day operating needs, the president, Vince Ramsey, has decided that a stock dividend instead of a cash dividend should be declared. He tells Flambeau's financial vice-president, Janice Rahn, to issue a press release stating that the company is extending its consecutive dividend record with the issuance of a 5% stock dividend. "Write the press release convincing the stockholders that the stock dividend is just as good as a cash dividend," he orders. "Just watch our stock rise when we announce the stock dividend; it must be a good thing if that happens."

Instructions
   (a) Who are the stakeholders in this situation?
   (b) Is there anything unethical about President Ramsey's intentions or actions?
   (c) What is the effect of a stock dividend on a corporation's stockholders' equity accounts? Which would you rather receive as a stockholder—a cash dividend or a stock dividend? Why?

RESEARCH ASSIGNMENT

The September 4, 1995 issue of *Fortune* includes an article by Richard D. Hylton, entitled "Stock Buybacks Are Hot—Here's How You Can Cash In." Read the article and answer the following questions.

   (a) What was the total amount of announced intentions to repurchase shares of stock in 1994? What was this figure during the first six months of 1995?
   (b) The goal of many of these repurchase programs was to increase the price of the remaining outstanding shares. Identify the three factors which will determine the impact of repurchases on share price.
   (c) What did Microsoft do with the shares it repurchased? Why might they use repurchased shares for this purpose rather than issuing new shares?

CRITICAL THINKING
▸ *A Real-World Focus: Diebold, Inc.*

Diebold, Incorporated, is a world leader in financial self-service transaction systems, security products, and customer service. The company develops, manufactures, sells, and services automated teller machines (ATMs), electronic and physical security systems, and bank facility equipment. It also designs and markets related application software and integrated systems for global financial and commercial markets. Headquartered in Canton, Ohio, Diebold has offices in five countries and manufacturing facilities in the United States and in China.

The following note related to stockholders' equity was recently reported in Diebold's annual report:

On February 1, 1994, the Board of Directors declared a 3-for-2 stock split, distributed on February 22, 1994, to shareholders of record on February 10, 1994. Accordingly, all numbers of common shares, except authorized shares and treasury shares, and all per share data have been restated to reflect this stock split in addition to the 3-for-2 stock split declared on January 27, 1993, distributed on February 26, 1993, to shareholders of record on February 10, 1993.

On the basis of amounts declared and paid, the annualized quarterly dividends per share were $0.80 in 1993, $0.75 in 1992, and $0.71 in 1991.

Instructions
- (a) What is the significance of the date of record and the date of distribution?
- (b) Why might Diebold have declared a 3-for-2 stock split?
- (c) What impact does Diebold's stock split have on (1) total stockholders' equity; (2) total par value; (3) outstanding shares, and (4) book value per share?

► *A Real-World Focus: Barrister Information Systems Corporation*

Barrister Information Systems Corp. *develops, assembles, markets, and services computer systems and local area networks for law firms. Headquartered in Buffalo, N.Y., it has offices in 19 U.S. cities.*

Barrister Information Systems has two classes of preferred stock—A and C—in addition to its common stock. The 1,300 shares of Series A preferred stock are nonvoting, have a 12% cumulative dividend, have liquidation preference rights over the Series C preferred stock and the common stock, and are callable by the company at any time for $1,000 per share plus cumulative unpaid dividends. Each share of Series A preferred stock is convertible into 500 shares of common stock. As of March 31, 1993, the cumulative unpaid dividends on the Series A preferred stock totaled $254,000.

Instructions
- (a) Should the $254,000 in dividends not paid be reported as a liability on the balance sheet?
- (b) If the par value of the Class A preferred stock is $100 per share, what dollar amount in dividends can the shareholders expect annually on the Class A preferred stock?

Answers to Self-Study Questions
1. c   2. b   3. d   4. c   5. a   6. a   7. d   8. d   9. b   10. d   11. b
12. a   13. c

Before studying this chapter, you should know or, if necessary, review:

a. *How to record the issuance of bonds. (Ch. 11, pp. 480–87)*
b. *How to compute and record interest. (Ch. 3, pp. 110–11, Ch. 8, pp. 343–4, and Ch. 11, pp. 479–81 and 490)*
c. *How to record amortization of bond discount and bond premium using the straight-line method. (Ch. 11, pp. 483–86)*
d. *Where temporary and long-term investments are classified on a balance sheet. (Ch. 4, pp. 163–64)*

They Play the Market for Fun, Profit, and an Education

BEARDSTOWN, Ill. — By day she's a trust officer at the local bank; in her free time Betty Sinnock is the financial planner for the Beardstown Ladies—a fifteen-woman investment club whose success has earned it national attention and air time on "Donahue" and "20/20." The club has attained the public spotlight by earning an average annual return of 23.4% on its investments over the last decade—a return many highly paid mutual fund managers did not come close to equaling during the same period. The National Association of Investors Corporation has six times ranked the group near the top of the 11,000 investment clubs that it follows.

Do these women post a collection of impressive graduate degrees? No—this group of women (twelve of whom are past age 60) is largely self-educated in the ways of Wall Street. The secrets to their investment success are spelled out in a best-selling book, *The Beardstown Ladies Common-Sense Investment Guide.* A central theme of the book

is this: "Women need to gain financial information—whether they be young, middle-aged, or old"; they must not "rely on others."

The group's stock-picking methodology combines sound fundamental analysis of financial data with an eye toward innovative products or services. They rely heavily on the information provided by the *Value Line Investment Survey* to determine whether a stock meets their criteria for safety, industry rank, and volatility. But they also look to the products that they purchase themselves:

If they think a new product shows promise, they analyze the company as a possible investment.

The fund's investments themselves have made none of the women rich, since each member contributes only $25 a month to the fund. But the women unanimously agree that participation in the club has been "fun" and has allowed them to have confidence in running their own personal financial affairs. As one member put it, she considers the monthly $25 as tuition toward her financial education. ◀

CHAPTER · **13**

....

*I*NVESTMENTS

▶ **STUDY OBJECTIVES** ◀

....

After studying this chapter, you should be able to:

1. *Distinguish between temporary and long-term investments.*
2. *Explain the accounting for debt investments.*
3. *Explain the accounting for stock investments.*
4. *Describe the purpose and usefulness of consolidated financial statements.*
5. *Indicate how debt and stock investments are valued and reported on the financial statements.*

....

Investment clubs, such as the Beardstown Ladies, represent just one of a vast assortment of ways that investments can be purchased. Investments also can be made by individuals, mutual funds, banks, pension funds, and corporations. In addition, investments can be purchased for a short or a long period of time, as a passive investment, or with the intent to control the firm. As you will see in this chapter, the way in which a company accounts for its investments is determined by a number of factors. The content and organization of this chapter are as follows:

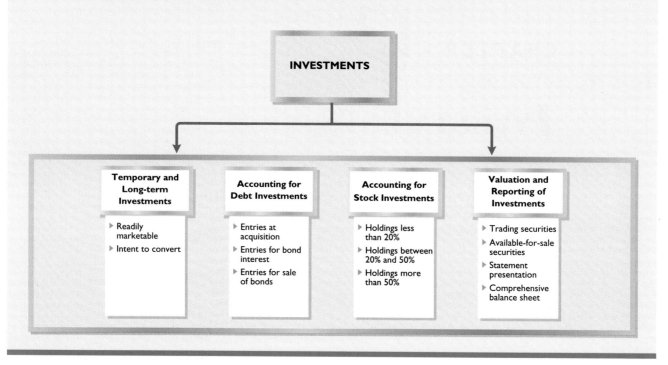

Temporary and Long-Term Investments

Many companies experience seasonal fluctuations in sales. A Cape Cod marina will have higher sales in the spring and summer than in the fall and winter, whereas the reverse will be true for an Aspen ski shop. Thus, at the end of their operating cycles, many companies may have cash on hand that is temporarily idle pending the start of another operating cycle. Until the cash is needed in operations, these companies may invest the excess funds to earn interest and dividends. The relationship of temporary investments to the operating cycle is graphically depicted in Illustration 13-1.

Illustration 13-1

Temporary investments and the operating cycle

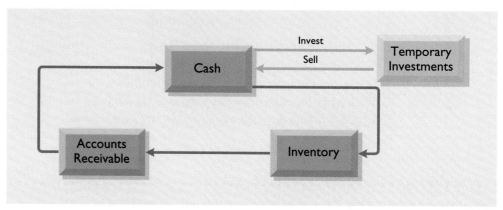

Temporary investments are securities, held by a company, that are (1) **readily marketable** and (2) **intended to be converted into cash** within the next year or operating cycle, whichever is longer. Investments that do not meet **both** criteria are classified as long-term investments.

Readily Marketable

An investment is readily marketable when it can be sold easily whenever the need for cash arises. Short-term paper[1] meets this criterion because it can be sold readily to other investors. Stocks and bonds traded on organized securities markets, such as the New York Stock Exchange, are readily marketable because they can be bought and sold daily. In contrast, there may be only a limited market for the securities issued by small corporations and no market for the securities of a privately held company.

Intent to Convert

Intent to convert means that management intends to sell the investment within the next year or operating cycle, whichever is longer. Generally, this criterion is satisfied when the investment is considered a resource that will be used whenever the need for cash arises. For example, an Aspen ski resort may invest idle cash during the summer months with the intent to sell the securities to buy supplies and equipment shortly before the next winter season. This investment is considered temporary even if lack of snow cancels the next ski season and eliminates the need to convert the securities into cash as intended.

Accounting for Debt Investments

Debt investments are investments in government and corporation bonds. In accounting for debt investments, entries are required to record (1) the acquisition, (2) the interest revenue, and (3) the sale. **At acquisition, the cost principle applies.** Cost includes all expenditures necessary to acquire these investments, such as the price paid plus brokerage fees (commissions), if any. The entries for debt investments are illustrated below.

STUDY OBJECTIVE
········ **2** ········
Explain the accounting for debt investments.

Entries at Acquisition

Assume that Kuhl Corporation acquires 50 Doan Inc. 12%, 10-year, $1,000 bonds on January 1, 1996, for $54,000, including brokerage fees of $1,000. The entry to record the investment is:

Jan. 1	Debt Investments	54,000	
	Cash		54,000
	(To record purchase of 50 Doan Inc. bonds)		

Entries for Bond Interest

The bonds pay interest of $3,000 semiannually on July 1 and January 1 ($50,000 × 12% × ½). The entry for the receipt of interest on July 1 is:

July 1	Cash	3,000	
	Interest Revenue		3,000
	(To record receipt of interest on Doan Inc. bonds)		

---

[1]Short-term paper includes (1) certificates of deposits (CDs) issued by banks, (2) money market certificates issued by banks and savings and loan associations, (3) Treasury bills issued by the U.S. government, and (4) commercial paper issued by corporations with good credit ratings.

If Kuhl Corporation's fiscal year ends on December 31, it is necessary to accrue the interest of $3,000 earned since July 1. The adjusting entry is:

Dec. 31	Interest Receivable	3,000	
	Interest Revenue		3,000
	(To accrue interest on Doan Inc. bonds)		

Interest Receivable is reported as a current asset in the balance sheet; Interest Revenue is reported under Other Revenues and Gains in the income statement. When the interest is received on January 1, the entry is:

Jan. 1	Cash	3,000	
	Interest Receivable		3,000
	(To record receipt of accrued interest)		

A credit to Interest Revenue at this time is incorrect because the interest revenue was earned and accrued in the preceding accounting period.

Entries for Sale of Bonds

When the bonds are sold, it is necessary to credit the investment account for the cost of the bonds. Any difference between the net proceeds (sales price less brokerage fees) from sale and the cost of the bonds is recorded as a gain or loss. Assume, for example, that Kuhl Corporation receives net proceeds of $58,000 on the sale of the Doan Inc. bonds on January 1, 1997, after receiving the interest due. Since the securities cost $54,000, a gain of $4,000 has been realized. The entry to record the sale is:

Jan. 1	Cash	58,000	
	Debt Investments		54,000
	Gain on Sale of Debt Investments		4,000
	(To record sale of Doan Inc. bonds)		

The gain on sale of debt investments is reported under Other Revenues and Gains in the income statement.

Helpful hint The entries by the investor are not the exact reverse of the entries made by the issuer in Chapter 11. A major difference is that separate discount and premium accounts are normally not used by the investor.

The accounting for temporary debt investments and for long-term debt investments is similar. The major exception is when bonds are purchased at a premium or discount. For temporary investments, the bond premium or discount is not amortized to interest revenue because the bonds are held for a short period of time and a misstatement of interest revenue for such a period is not considered material. For long-term investments, however, any bond premium or discount is amortized to interest revenue over the remaining term of the bonds. Like the issuer of the bonds, the investor uses either the straight-line or the effective-interest method of amortization. The effective-interest method is required under generally accepted accounting principles when the annual amounts of the two amortization methods are materially different.

Before You Go On . . .

▸ Review It

1. What criteria must be met to classify an investment as temporary?
2. What entries are required in accounting for debt investments?
3. How does the accounting for a temporary debt investment differ from that for a long-term debt investment?

► Do It

The Waldo Corporation had the following transactions pertaining to debt investments:

Jan. 1   Purchased 30 10%, $1,000 Hillary Co. bonds for $30,000 plus brokerage fees of $900. Interest is payable semiannually on July 1 and January 1.

July 1   Received semiannual interest on Hillary Co. bonds.

July 1   Sold 15 Hillary Co. bonds for $15,000 less $400 brokerage fees.

(a) Journalize the transactions, and (b) prepare the adjusting entry for the accrual of interest on December 31.

Reasoning: Bond investments are recorded at cost. Interest is recorded when received and/or accrued. When bonds are sold, the investment account is credited for the cost of the bonds. Any difference between the cost and the net proceeds is recorded as a gain or loss.

Solution:

(a) Jan. 1	Debt Investments	30,900	
	Cash		30,900
	(To record purchase of 30 Hillary Co. bonds)		
July 1	Cash	1,500	
	Interest Revenue ($30,000 × .10 × 6/12)		1,500
	(To record receipt of interest on Hillary Co. bonds)		
July 1	Cash	14,600	
	Loss on Sale of Debt Investments	850	
	Debt Investments ($30,900 ÷ 15/30)		15,450
	(To record sale of 15 Hillary Co. bonds)		
(b) Dec. 31	Interest Receivable	750	
	Interest Revenue ($15,000 × .10 × 6/12)		750
	(To accrue interest on Hillary Co. bonds)		

Related exercise material: BE13–1 and E13–1.

Accounting for Stock Investments

Stock investments are investments in the capital stock of corporations. When a company holds stock (or debt) of several different corporations, the group of securities is identified as an investment portfolio. The accounting for investments in common stock is based on the extent of the investor's influence over the operating and financial affairs of the issuing corporation (commonly called the **investee**) as shown in Illustration 13-2. In some cases, depending on the degree of investor influence, net income of the investee is considered to be income to the investor.

The presumed influence may be negated by extenuating circumstances. For example, a company that acquires a 25% interest in another company in a "hostile" takeover may not have any significant influence over the investee.[2] In other

STUDY OBJECTIVE

•••••••••**3**••••••••••

Explain the accounting for stock investments.

▶ *International note*

A recent study demonstrated the peril of investing overseas. For the same company under different reporting systems, income was $84,600, $260,600, $240,600, and $10,402 in the United States, the United Kingdom, Australia, and West Germany, respectively.

---

[2]Among the factors that should be considered in determining an investor's influence are whether (1) the investor has representation on the investee's board of directors, (2) the investor participates in the investee's policy-making process, (3) there are material transactions between the investor and investee, and (4) the common stock held by other stockholders is concentrated or dispersed.

Illustration 13-2

Accounting guidelines for stock investments

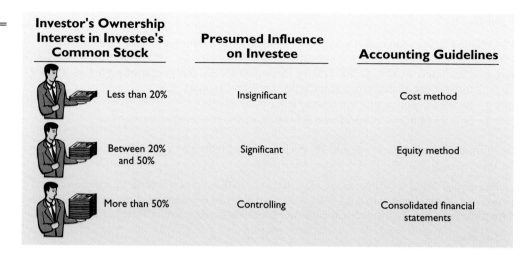

Investor's Ownership Interest in Investee's Common Stock	Presumed Influence on Investee	Accounting Guidelines
Less than 20%	Insignificant	Cost method
Between 20% and 50%	Significant	Equity method
More than 50%	Controlling	Consolidated financial statements

words, companies are required to use judgment instead of blindly following the guidelines. On the following pages we will explain and illustrate the application of each guideline.

▶Accounting in Action ▸ *Business Insight*

A corporation may have a variety of motives in purchasing the capital stock of another corporation. Usually, however, the primary reason is to increase its own net income. This may be achieved through (1) the receipt of dividends, (2) appreciation in the market value of the stock, or (3) use of the investment for expanding or diversifying its own operations. For example, at one time Gulf & Western Industries, Inc., had the following investments in common stock that affected its operations:

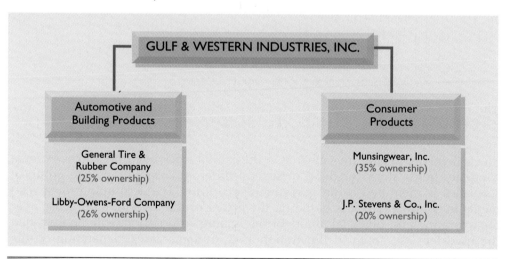

GULF & WESTERN INDUSTRIES, INC.

Automotive and Building Products

General Tire & Rubber Company (25% ownership)

Libby-Owens-Ford Company (26% ownership)

Consumer Products

Munsingwear, Inc. (35% ownership)

J.P. Stevens & Co., Inc. (20% ownership)

Holdings Less Than 20%

In accounting for stock investments of less than 20%, the cost method is used. Under the cost method, the investment is recorded at cost and revenue is recognized only when cash dividends are received. At acquisition, the cost principle applies. Cost includes all expenditures necessary to acquire these investments, such as the price paid plus brokerage fees (commissions), if any. The entries for stock investments are illustrated on the next page.

Entries at Acquisition

The starting point in accounting for stock investments is cost. Assume, for example, that on July 1, 1996, Sanchez Corporation acquires 1,000 shares (10% ownership) of Beal Corporation common stock at $40 per share plus brokerage fees of $500. The entry for the purchase is:

July 1	Stock Investments	40,500	
	Cash		40,500
	(To record purchase of 1,000 shares of Beal Corporation common stock)		

Entries for Dividends

During the time the stock is held, entries are required for any cash dividends received. Thus, if a $2.00 per share dividend is received by Sanchez Corporation on December 31, the entry is:

Dec. 31	Cash (1,000 × $2)	2,000	
	Dividend Revenue		2,000
	(To record receipt of a cash dividend)		

Dividend Revenue is reported under Other Revenues and Gains in the income statement. Unlike interest on notes and bonds, dividends do not accrue. Therefore, adjusting entries are not made to accrue dividends.

Helpful hint Dividend revenue may be recognized at the date of the declaration. In this case, Dividends Receivable is debited and Dividend Revenue credited. Typically, the investor uses a Dividends Receivable account only when financial statements are prepared between the declaration date and the payout date.

Entries for Sale of Stock

When stock is sold, the difference between the net proceeds (sales price less brokerage fees) from the sale and the cost of the stock is recognized as a gain or a loss. Assume, for instance, that Sanchez Corporation receives net proceeds of $39,500 on the sale of its Beal stock on February 10, 1997. Because the stock cost $40,500, a loss of $1,000 has been incurred. The entry to record the sale is:

Feb. 10	Cash	39,500	
	Loss on Sale of Stock Investments	1,000	
	Stock Investments		40,500
	(To record sale of Beal common stock)		

The loss account is reported under Other Expenses and Losses in the income statement, whereas a gain on sale is shown under Other Revenues and Gains.

Holdings between 20% and 50%

When an investor owns between 20% and 50% of the common stock of a corporation, it is generally presumed that the investor has significant influence over the financial and operating activities of the investee. **As a result, the investor should record its share of the net income of the investee in the year when it is earned.** To delay recognizing the investor's share of net income until a cash dividend is declared ignores the fact that the investor is better off by the investee's earned income.

This type of investment in common stock requires the use of the equity method. Under the equity method, the investment in common stock is initially recorded at cost, and the investment account is adjusted annually to show the investor's equity in the investee. Each year, the investor (1) debits the investment account and credits revenue for its share of the investee's net income[3] and

Helpful hint The entries for investments in common stock also apply to investments in preferred stock.

Helpful hint By exerting influence, an investor could force a dividend payment from the investee even when the investee reports a net loss. Using dividends as a basis for recognizing income would not properly indicate the economics of the situation.

---

[3]Conversely, the investor debits a loss account and credits the investment account for its share of the investee's net loss.

(2) credits dividends received to the investment account. The investment account is reduced for dividends received, because the net assets of the investee are decreased when a dividend is paid.

Entries at Acquisition

Assume that Milar Corporation acquires 30% of the common stock of Beck Company for $120,000 on January 1, 1996. The entry to record this transaction is:

Jan. 1	Stock Investments		120,000	
	Cash			120,000
	(To record purchase of Beck common stock)			

Entries for Revenue and Dividends

For 1996, Beck reports net income of $100,000 and declares and pays a $40,000 cash dividend. Milar is required to record (1) its share of Beck's income, $30,000 (30% × $100,000) and (2) the reduction in the investment account for the dividends received, $12,000 ($40,000 × 30%). The entries are:

(1)

Dec. 31	Stock Investments		30,000	
	Revenue from Investment in Beck Company			30,000
	(To record 30% equity in Beck's 1996 net income)			

(2)

Dec. 31	Cash		12,000	
	Stock Investments			12,000
	(To record dividends received)			

After posting the transactions for the year, the investment and revenue accounts will show the following:

Illustration 13-3

Investment and revenue accounts after posting

Stock Investments				Revenue from Investment in Beck Company	
Jan. 1	120,000	Dec. 31	12,000		
Dec. 31	30,000			Dec. 31	30,000
Dec. 31 Bal. 138,000					

During the year, the investment account has increased by $18,000. This $18,000 is Milar's 30% equity in the $60,000 increase in Beck's retained earnings ($100,000 − $40,000). In addition, Milar will report $30,000 of revenue from its investment, which is 30% of Beck's net income of $100,000. Note that the difference between reported income under the cost method and reported revenue under the equity method can be significant. For example, Milar would report only $12,000 of dividend revenue (30% × $40,000) if the cost method were used.

STUDY OBJECTIVE

•••••••• 4 ••••••••

Describe the purpose and usefulness of consolidated financial statements.

Holdings of More Than 50%

A company that owns more than 50% of the common stock of another entity is known as the **parent company**. The entity whose stock is owned by the parent company is called the **subsidiary (affiliated) company**. Because of its stock ownership, the parent company has a **controlling interest** in the subsidiary company.

When a company owns more than 50% of the common stock of another company, consolidated financial statements are usually prepared. **Consolidated financial statements** present the assets and liabilities controlled by the parent company and the aggregate profitability of the subsidiary companies. They are prepared in addition to the financial statements for each of the individual parent and subsidiary companies. **Consolidated statements are especially useful to the stockholders, board of directors, and management of the parent company.** Moreover, consolidated statements inform creditors, prospective investors, and regulatory agencies as to the magnitude and scope of operations of the companies operating under common control. For example, regulators and the courts undoubtedly used the consolidated statements of AT&T to determine whether a breakup of AT&T was in the public interest. Provided below are examples of two companies that prepare consolidated statements and some of the companies they have owned.

Helpful hint If parent (A) has three wholly owned subsidiaries (B, C, & D), there are four separate legal entities, but only one economic entity from the viewpoint of the shareholders of the parent company.

Helpful hint The operating relationship between a parent company and a subsidiary is similar to the operating relationship between parents and their teenagers. The parent may exercise tight or relatively little control.

Beatrice Foods	**American Brands, Inc.**
Tropicana Frozen Juices	American Tobacco Company
Switzer Candy Company	Master Lock Company
Samsonite Corporation	Pinkerton's Security Service
Dannon Yogurt Company	Titleist Golf Company

The accounting for consolidated financial statements is discussed in the appendix to this chapter.

►Accounting in Action ► *Business Insight*

Philip Morris, Inc., for example, owns 100% of the common stock of Kraft General Foods Corporation. The common stockholders of Philip Morris elect the board of directors of the company, who, in turn, select the officers and managers of the company. The board of directors will control the property owned by the corporation, which includes the common stock of Kraft General Foods. Thus, they are in a position to elect the board of directors of Kraft General Foods and, in effect, control its operations. These relationships are graphically illustrated below:

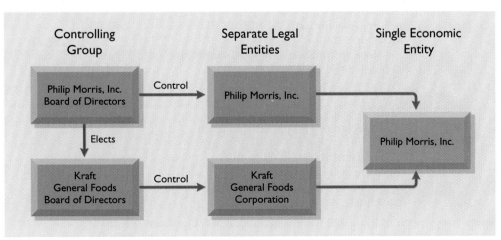

Before You Go On . . .

▶ *Review It*

1. What are the accounting entries for investments in stock for which ownership is less than 20%?
2. What entries are made under the equity method when (a) the investor receives a cash dividend from the investee and (b) the investee reports net income for the year?
3. What is the purpose of consolidated financial statements?

▶ *Do It*

Presented below are two independent situations:

1. Rho Jean Inc. acquired 5% of the 400,000 shares of common stock of Stillwater Co. at a total cost of $6 per share on May 18, 1996. On August 30, Stillwater declared and paid a $75,000 dividend. On December 31, Stillwater reported net income of $244,000 for the year.
2. Debbie, Inc., obtained significant influence over North Sails by buying 40% of North Sails' 60,000 outstanding shares of common stock at a cost of $12 per share on January 1, 1996. On April 15, North Sails declared and paid a cash dividend of $45,000. On December 31, North Sails reported a net income of $120,000 for the year.

Prepare all necessary journal entries for 1996 for (1) Rho Jean Inc. and (2) Debbie, Inc.

Reasoning: When an investor owns less than 20% of the common stock of another corporation, it is presumed that the investor has relatively little influence over the investee. As a result, net income earned by the investee is not considered a proper basis for recognizing income from the investment by the investor. For investments of 20%–50%, significant influence is presumed and therefore the investor's share of the net income of the investee should be recorded.

Solution:

(1) May 18	Stock Investments (20,000 × $6)	120,000	
	Cash		120,000
	(To record purchase of 20,000 shares of Stillwater Co. stock)		
Aug. 30	Cash	3,750	
	Dividend Revenue ($75,000 × 5%)		3,750
	(To record receipt of cash dividend)		
(2) Jan. 1	Stock Investments (60,000 × 40% × $12)	288,000	
	Cash		288,000
	(To record purchase of 24,000 shares of North Sails' stock)		
Apr. 15	Cash	18,000	
	Stock Investments ($45,000 × 40%)		18,000
	(To record receipt of cash dividend)		
Dec. 31	Stock Investments ($120,000 × 40%)	48,000	
	Revenue from Investment in North Sails		48,000
	(To record 40% equity in North Sails' net income)		

Related exercise material: BE13–2, BE13–3, E13–1, E13–2, E13–3, E13–4, and E13–5.

Valuation and Reporting of Investments

The value of debt and stock investments may fluctuate greatly during the time they are held. The Dow-Jones Industrial Average of common stocks illustrates the volatile nature of stock prices. This average, which is based on the stock prices of 30 large companies, may drop drastically with unfavorable economic developments and may jump dramatically with favorable economic events. In light of such price fluctuations, how should investments be valued at the balance sheet date? Valuation could be at cost, at fair value (market value), or at the lower of cost or market value. Fair value offers the best approach because it represents the expected cash realizable value of the securities. Fair value is the amount for which a security could be sold in a normal market.

For purposes of valuation and reporting at a financial statement date, debt and stock investments are classified into three categories of securities, as follows:

> Trading securities are securities bought and held primarily for sale in the near term to generate income on short-term price differences.
> Available-for-sale securities are securities that may be sold in the future.
> Held-to-maturity securities are debt securities that the investor has the intent and ability to hold to maturity.[4]

The valuation guidelines for these securities are as follows:

STUDY OBJECTIVE 5

Indicate how debt and stock investments are valued and reported on the financial statements.

Illustration 13-4

Valuation guidelines

The guidelines apply to all debt securities and all stock investments where the holdings are less than 20%.

Trading Securities

Trading securities are held with the intention of selling them in a short period of time (generally less than a month). Trading means frequent buying and selling. As indicated in Illustration 13-4, trading securities are reported at fair value, and changes from cost are reported as part of net income. The changes are reported as **unrealized gains or losses** because the securities have not been sold. The unrealized gain or loss is the difference between the **total cost** of the securities in the category and their **total fair value**.

---

[4]This category is provided for completeness. The accounting and valuation issues related to held-to-maturity securities are discussed in more advanced accounting courses.

To illustrate, assume that on December 31, 1996, Plano Corporation has the following costs and fair values for its investments classified as trading securities:

Illustration 13-5

Valuation of trading securities

Trading Securities, December 31, 1996			
Investments	Cost	Fair Value	Unrealized Gain (Loss)
Yorkville Company bonds	$ 50,000	$ 48,000	$(2,000)
Kodak Company stock	90,000	99,000	9,000
Total	$140,000	$147,000	$ 7,000

Helpful hint An unrealized gain or loss is reported in the income statement because of the likelihood that the securities will be sold at fair value since they are a short-term investment.

Plano Corporation has an unrealized gain of $7,000 because total fair value ($147,000) is $7,000 greater than total cost ($140,000).

Fair value and the unrealized gain or loss are recorded through an adjusting entry at the time financial statements are prepared. In the entry, a valuation allowance account, Market Adjustment—Trading, is used to record the difference between the total cost and total fair value of the securities. The adjusting entry for Plano Corporation is:

Dec. 31	Market Adjustment—Trading	7,000	
	Unrealized Gain—Income		7,000
	(To record unrealized gain on trading securities)		

The use of a Market Adjustment—Trading account enables the company to maintain a record of the investment cost. Actual cost is needed to determine the gain or loss realized when the securities are sold. The Market Adjustment—Trading balance is added to the cost of the investments to arrive at a fair value for the trading securities.

The fair value of the securities is the amount reported on the balance sheet. The unrealized gain is reported on the income statement in the Other Revenues and Gains section. The term income is used in the account title to indicate that the gain affects net income. When the total cost of the trading securities is greater than total fair value, an unrealized loss has occurred. In such a case, the adjusting entry is a debit to Unrealized Loss—Income and a credit to Market Adjustment—Trading. The unrealized loss is reported under Other Expenses and Losses in the income statement.

The market adjustment account is carried forward into future accounting periods. No entries are made to this account during the period. At the end of each reporting period, the balance in the account is adjusted to the difference between cost and fair value. The Unrealized Gain or Loss—Income account is closed at the end of the reporting period.

Available-for-Sale Securities

▸ Ethics note

Some managers appear to hold their available-for-sale securities that have experienced losses, while selling those that have gains, thus increasing income. Do you think this is ethical?

As indicated earlier, available-for-sale securities are held with the intent of selling them sometime in the future. If the intent is to sell the securities within the next year or operating cycle, the securities are classified as current assets in the balance sheet. Otherwise, they are classified as long-term assets in the investments section of the balance sheet.

Available-for-sale securities are also reported at fair value. The procedure for determining fair value and the unrealized gain or loss for these securities is the same as for trading securities. To illustrate, assume that Elbert Corporation has two securities that are classified as available-for-sale. Illustration 13-6 provides information on cost, fair value, and the amount of the unrealized gain or loss.

Illustration 13-6

Valuation of available-for-sale securities

Available-for-Sale Securities, December 31, 1996			
Investments	**Cost**	**Fair Value**	**Unrealized Gain (Loss)**
Campbell Soup Corporation 8% bonds	$ 93,537	$103,600	$ 10,063
Hersey Corporation stock	200,000	180,400	(19,600)
Total	$293,537	$284,000	$ (9,537)

For Elbert Corporation, there is an unrealized loss of $9,537 because total cost ($293,537) is $9,537 more than total fair value ($284,000).

Both the adjusting entry and the reporting of the unrealized gain or loss from available-for-sale securities differ from those illustrated for trading securities. The differences result because these securities are not going to be sold in the near term. Thus, prior to actual sale there is a much greater likelihood of changes in fair value that may reverse either unrealized gains or losses. Accordingly, an unrealized gain or loss is not reported in the income statement. Instead, it is reported as a separate component of stockholders' equity. In the adjusting entry, the market adjustment account is identified with available-for-sale securities, and the unrealized gain or loss account is identified with stockholders' equity. The adjusting entry for Elbert Corporation to record the unrealized loss of $9,537 is as follows:

Dec. 31	Unrealized Gain or Loss—Equity	9,537	
	Market Adjustment—Available-for-Sale		9,537
	(To record unrealized loss on available-for-sale securities)		

Helpful hint The entry is the same regardless of whether the securities are considered temporary or long-term.

If total fair value exceeds total cost, the adjusting entry would have a debit to the market adjustment account and a credit to the unrealized gain or loss account. For available-for-sale securities, the unrealized gain or loss account is carried forward to future periods. At each future balance sheet date, it is adjusted with the market adjustment account to show the difference between cost and fair value at that time.

Financial Statement Presentation

Because of their high liquidity, temporary investments are listed immediately below cash in the current asset section of the balance sheet. Temporary investments are reported at fair value. For example, Plano Corporation, as shown in Illustration 13-5 above, would report its trading securities as follows:

Current assets	
Cash	$ xx,xxx
Temporary investments, at fair value	147,000

Long-term investments are generally reported in a separate section of the balance sheet immediately below current assets, as shown in Illustration 13-9 on page 591. In this section, long-term investments in available-for-sale securities are reported at fair value, and investments in common stock accounted for under the equity method are reported at equity.

In the income statement, the following items are reported in the nonoperating section:

Illustration 13-7

Nonoperating items related to investments

Other Revenue and Gains	Other Expenses and Losses
Interest Revenue	Loss on Sale of Investments
Dividend Revenue	Unrealized Loss—Income
Gain on Sale of Investments	
Unrealized Gain—Income	

Helpful hint   Interest revenue is also called interest income, and dividend revenue may be called dividend income.

As indicated earlier, an unrealized gain or loss on available-for-sale securities is reported as a separate component of stockholders' equity. To illustrate, assume that Dawson Inc. has common stock of $3,000,000, retained earnings of $1,500,000 and an unrealized loss on available-for-sale securities of $100,000. The statement presentation of the unrealized loss is as follows:

Illustration 13-8

Unrealized loss in stock-holders' equity section

[handwritten note: Net income - closed in Ret Earn]

Stockholders' equity	
Common stock	$3,000,000
Retained earnings	1,500,000
Total paid-in capital and retained earnings	4,500,000
Less: Unrealized loss on available-for-sale securities	(100,000)
Total stockholders' equity	$4,400,000

Note that the presentation of the loss is similar to the presentation of the cost of treasury stock in the stockholders' equity section. An unrealized gain is added in the section. Reporting the unrealized gain or loss in the stockholders' equity section serves two important purposes: (1) It reduces the volatility of net income due to fluctuations in fair value, and (2) it still informs the financial statement user of the gain or loss that would occur if the securities were sold at fair value.

Comprehensive Balance Sheet

Numerous examples of sections of classified balance sheets have been presented in this and preceding chapters. The balance sheet shown in Illustration 13-9 for Pace Corporation includes such topics from previous chapters as the issuance of par value common stock, organization costs, restrictions of retained earnings, issuance of long-term bonds, and bond sinking funds.[5] From this chapter, the statement includes (highlighted in red) temporary and long-term investments. The investments in temporary securities are considered trading securities; the long-term investments in stock of less than 20% owned companies are considered available-for-sale securities. Illustration 13-9 also includes a long-term investment reported at equity and descriptive notations within the statement such as the basis for valuing merchandise and two notes to the statement.

---

[5]A **sinking fund** is cash or other assets set aside to retire debt. It is like a savings account that is used to pay back bondholders. A sinking fund makes bonds more attractive to investors because it enhances the likelihood that the bonds will be redeemed at maturity. In other words, it is like a savings account that is used to pay back bondholders. The bond sinking fund is reported as a single amount in the investment section of the balance sheet.

Illustration 13-9

*Comprehensive balance sheet;
investment related items in
red.*

PACE CORPORATION
Balance Sheet
December 31, 1996

Assets

Current assets		
Cash		$ 21,000
Temporary investments, at fair value		60,000
Accounts receivable	$ 84,000	
Less: Allowance for doubtful accounts	4,000	80,000
Merchandise inventory, at FIFO cost		130,000
Prepaid insurance		23,000
Total current assets		314,000
Investments		
Bond sinking fund	100,000	
Investments in stock of less than 20% owned companies, at fair value	50,000	
Investment in stock of 20–50% owned company, at equity	150,000	
Total investments		300,000
Property, plant, and equipment		
Land	200,000	
Buildings	$800,000	
Less: Accumulated depreciation	200,000	600,000
Equipment	180,000	
Less: Accumulated depreciation	54,000	126,000
Total property, plant, and equipment		926,000
Intangible assets		
Goodwill (Note 1)	100,000	
Organization costs	70,000	
Total intangible assets		170,000
Total assets		$1,710,000

Liabilities and Stockholders' Equity

Current liabilities		
Accounts payable		$185,000
Bond interest payable		10,000
Federal income taxes payable		60,000
Total current liabilities		255,000
Long-term liabilities		
Bonds payable, 10%, due 2010	$ 300,000	
Less: Discount on bonds	10,000	
Total long-term liabilities		290,000
Total liabilities		545,000
Stockholders' equity		
Paid-in capital		
Common stock, $10 par value, 200,000 shares authorized, 80,000 shares issued and outstanding	800,000	
Paid-in capital in excess of par value	100,000	
Total paid-in capital	900,000	
Retained earnings (Note 2)	255,000	
Total paid-in capital and retained earnings	1,155,000	
Add: Unrealized gain on available-for-sale securities	10,000	
Total stockholders' equity		1,165,000
Total liabilities and stockholders' equity		$1,710,000

Note 1. Goodwill is amortized by the straight-line method over 40 years.

Note 2. Retained earnings of $100,000 is restricted for plant expansion.

Before You Go On . . .

▶ *Review It*

1. What is the proper valuation and reporting of trading and available-for-sale securities on a balance sheet?
2. Explain how the unrealized gain or loss for both trading and available-for-sale securities is reported.
3. Explain where temporary and long-term investments are reported on a balance sheet.

▸ *A Look Back at the Beardstown Ladies*

Use the opening story about the Beardstown Ladies to answer the following questions:

1. The Beardstown Ladies have averaged a 23.4% annual return over the last decade. Is it more likely that this return has been earned from dividends or from appreciation in share value? Why?
2. Assume that the Beardstown Ladies invest only in stock. If they want to make their investment income look good, what choices might they make in terms of choosing which securities to sell and which to hold?
3. What investment strategies do the Beardstown Ladies employ?

Solution:

1. Firms could not consistently pay anywhere near a 23.4% dividend; thus most of the Beardstown Ladies' return must be coming from appreciation in share value.
2. Unrealized losses on available-for-sale securities are not reported in income. In order to maximize reported income the Beardstown Ladies could choose at year-end to sell all securities in the available-for-sale category that have experienced gains, and to hold all such securities that have unrealized losses.
3. They use financial information from *Value Line* to evaluate a security's safety, industry rank, and volatility. In addition, they use good, sound common sense by looking for new products that they think have promising futures.

◣ *Summary of Study Objectives*

1. *Distinguish between temporary and long-term investments.* Temporary investments are securities, held by a company, that are readily marketable and intended to be converted to cash within the next year or operating cycle, whichever is longer. Investments that do not meet both criteria are classified as long-term investments.

2. *Explain the accounting for debt investments.* Entries for investments in debt securities are required when the bonds are purchased, interest is received or accrued, and the bonds are sold. The accounting for long-term investments in bonds is the same as for temporary investments in bonds, except that bond premium and bond discount must be amortized.

3. *Explain the accounting for stock investments.* Entries for investments in common stock are required when the stock is purchased, dividends are received, and stock is sold. When ownership is less than 20%, the cost method is used. When ownership is between 20% and 50%, the equity

method should be used. When ownership is more than 50%, consolidated financial statements should be prepared.

4. *Describe the purpose and usefulness of consolidated financial statements.* When a company owns more than 50% of the common stock of another company, consolidated financial statements are usually prepared. These statements are especially useful to the stockholders, board of directors, and management of the parent company.

5. *Indicate how debt and stock investments are valued and reported on the financial statements.* Investments in debt and stock securities are classified as trading, available-for-sale, or held-to-maturity securities for valuation and reporting purposes. Trading securities are reported in current assets at fair value with changes from cost reported in net income. Available-for-sale securities are also reported at fair value with the changes from cost reported in stockholders' equity. Available-for-sale securities are classified as temporary or long-term depending on their expected realization.

APPENDIX ▸ *Preparing Consolidated Financial Statements*

Preparing a Consolidated Balance Sheet

Consolidated balance sheets are prepared from the individual balance sheets of the affiliated companies. They are not prepared from ledger accounts kept by the consolidated entity because only the separate legal entities maintain accounting records.

All items in the individual balance sheets are included in the consolidated balance sheet except amounts that pertain to transactions between the affiliated companies. Transactions between the affiliated companies are identified as **intercompany transactions**. The process of excluding these transactions in preparing consolidated statements is referred to as **intercompany eliminations**. These eliminations are necessary to avoid overstating assets, liabilities, and stockholders' equity in the consolidated balance sheet. For example, amounts owed by a subsidiary to a parent company and the related receivable reported by the parent company would be eliminated. The objective in a consolidated balance sheet is to show only obligations to and receivables from parties who are not part of the affiliated group of companies.

To illustrate, assume that on January 1, 1996, Powers Construction Company pays $150,000 in cash for 100% of Serto Brick Company's common stock. Powers Company records the investment at cost, as required by the cost principle. The separate balance sheets of the two companies immediately after the purchase, together with combined and consolidated data, are presented in Illustration 13A-1.[1] The balances in the "combined" column are obtained by adding the items

Illustration 13A-1

Combined and consolidated data

	Powers Company	Serto Company	Combined Data	Consolidated Data
POWERS COMPANY AND SERTO COMPANY Balance Sheets January 1, 1996				
Assets				
Current assets	$ 50,000	$ 80,000	$130,000	$130,000
Investment in Serto Company common stock	150,000		150,000	–0–
Plant and equipment (net)	325,000	145,000	470,000	470,000
Total assets	$525,000	$225,000	$750,000	$600,000
Liabilities and Stockholders' Equity				
Current liabilities	$ 50,000	$ 75,000	$125,000	$125,000
Common stock	300,000	100,000	400,000	300,000
Retained earnings	175,000	50,000	225,000	175,000
Total liabilities and stockholders' equity	$525,000	$225,000	$750,000	$600,000

[1]Condensed data will be used throughout this material to keep details at a minimum.

in the separate balance sheets of the affiliated companies. The combined totals do not represent a consolidated balance sheet, because there has been a double counting of assets and owners' equity in the amount of $150,000.

The Investment in Serto Company common stock that appears on the balance sheet of Powers Company represents an interest in the net assets of Serto. As a result, there has been a double counting of assets. Similarly, there has been a double counting in stockholders' equity, because the common stock of Serto Company is completely owned by the stockholders of Powers Company.

The balances in the consolidated data column are the amounts that should appear in the consolidated balance sheet. The double counting has been eliminated by showing Investment in Serto Company at zero and by reporting only the common stock and retained earnings of Powers Company as stockholders' equity.

Use of a Work Sheet—Cost Equal to Book Value

STUDY OBJECTIVE

•••••••••▼6•••••••••

Describe the content of a work sheet for a consolidated balance sheet.

The preparation of consolidated balance sheets is usually facilitated by the use of a work sheet. As shown in Illustration 13A-2, the work sheet for a consolidated balance sheet contains columns for (1) the balance sheet data for the separate legal entities, (2) intercompany eliminations, and (3) consolidated data. All data in the work sheet relate to the preceding example in which Powers Company acquires 100% ownership of Serto Company for $150,000. In this case, the cost of the investment, $150,000, is equal to the book value $150,000 ($225,000 − $75,000) of the subsidiary's net assets. The intercompany elimination results in a credit to the Investment account maintained by Powers Company for its balance, $150,000, and debits to the Common Stock and Retained Earnings accounts of Serto Company for their respective balances, $100,000 and $50,000.

Illustration 13A-2

Work sheet—Cost equals book value

POWERS COMPANY AND SUBSIDIARY
Work Sheet—Consolidated Balance Sheet
January 1, 1996 (Acquisition Date)

Assets	Powers Company	Serto Company	Eliminations Dr.	Eliminations Cr.	Consolidated Data
Current assets	50,000	80,000			130,000
Investment in Serto Company common stock	150,000			150,000	–0–
Plant and equipment (net)	325,000	145,000			470,000
Totals	525,000	225,000			600,000
Liabilities and Stockholders' Equity					
Current liabilities	50,000	75,000			125,000
Common stock—Powers Company	300,000				300,000
Common stock—Serto Company		100,000	100,000		–0–
Retained earnings—Powers Company	175,000				175,000
Retained earnings—Serto Company		50,000	50,000		–0–
Totals	525,000	225,000	150,000	150,000	600,000

Helpful hint As in the case of the work sheets explained earlier in this textbook, consolidated work sheets are also optional.

It is important to recognize that intercompany eliminations are made solely on the work sheet to present correct consolidated data. They are not journalized or posted by either of the affiliated companies and therefore do not affect the ledger accounts. Powers Company's investment account and Serto Company's common stock and retained earnings accounts are reported by the separate entities in preparing their own financial statements.

►Technology in Action

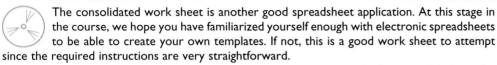

The consolidated work sheet is another good spreadsheet application. At this stage in the course, we hope you have familiarized yourself enough with electronic spreadsheets to be able to create your own templates. If not, this is a good work sheet to attempt since the required instructions are very straightforward.

However, computer programs are available that can merge multiple general ledgers for consolidated entities. All you need to do is supply the eliminating information, enter a few command keystrokes, and the consolidated financial statements will come off the printer, ready for distribution.

Use of a Work Sheet—Cost Above Book Value

The cost of acquiring the common stock of another company may be above or below its book value. The management of the parent company may pay more than book value because it believes (1) the fair market values of identifiable assets such as land, buildings, and equipment are higher than their recorded book values, or (2) the subsidiary's future earnings prospects warrant a payment for goodwill.

To illustrate, assume the same data used above, except that Powers Company pays $165,000 in cash for 100% of Serto's common stock. The excess of cost over book value is $15,000 ($165,000 − $150,000). This amount is separately recognized in eliminating the parent company's investment account, as shown in Illustration 13A-3.

Total assets and total liabilities and stockholders' equity are the same as in the preceding example ($600,000). However, in this case, total assets include $15,000 of Excess of Cost Over Book Value of Subsidiary. The disposition of the excess is explained in the next section.

Illustration 13A-3

Work sheet—Cost above book value

POWERS COMPANY AND SUBSIDIARY
Work Sheet—Consolidated Balance Sheet
January 1, 1996 (Acquisition Date)

Assets	Powers Company	Serto Company	Eliminations Dr.	Eliminations Cr.	Consolidated Data
Current assets	35,000	80,000			115,000
Investment in Serto Company common stock	165,000			165,000	–0–
Plant and equipment (net)	325,000	145,000			470,000
EXCESS OF COST OVER BOOK VALUE OF SUBSIDIARY			15,000		15,000
Totals	525,000	225,000			600,000
Liabilities and Stockholders' Equity					
Current liabilities	50,000	75,000			125,000
Common stock—Powers Company	300,000				300,000
Common stock—Serto Company		100,000	100,000		–0–
Retained earnings—Powers Company	175,000				175,000
Retained earnings—Serto Company		50,000	50,000		–0–
Totals	525,000	225,000	165,000	165,000	600,000 ·

Note that a separate line is added to the work sheet for the excess of cost over book value of subsidiary.

Content of a Consolidated Balance Sheet

To illustrate a consolidated balance sheet, we will use the work sheet shown in Illustration 13A-3. This work sheet shows an excess of cost over book value of $15,000. In the consolidated balance sheet, this amount is first allocated to specific assets, such as inventory and plant equipment, if their fair market values on the acquisition date exceed their book values. Any remainder is considered to be goodwill. For Serto Company, assume that the fair market value of property and equipment is $155,000. Thus, $10,000 of the excess of cost over book value is allocated to property and equipment, and the remainder, $5,000, is allocated to goodwill.

The condensed consolidated balance sheet of Powers Company is shown in Illustration 13A-4. As explained in Chapter 10, goodwill would be amortized by the straight-line method over the period benefited, but not in excess of 40 years.

Illustration 13A-4

Consolidated balance sheet

POWERS COMPANY		
Consolidated Balance Sheet		
January 1, 1996		
Assets		
Current assets		$115,000
Plant and equipment (net)		480,000
Goodwill		5,000
Total assets		$600,000
Liabilities and Stockholders' Equity		
Current liabilities		$125,000
Stockholders' equity		
Common stock	$300,000	
Retained earnings	175,000	475,000
Total liabilities and stockholders' equity		$600,000

▸*A*ccounting in *A*ction ▸ *Business Insight*

Through innovative financial restructuring, the Coca-Cola Company at one time eliminated a substantial amount of non-intercompany debt. It sold to the public 51% of two bottling companies. The "49% solution," as insiders call the strategy, enabled Coca-Cola to keep effective control over the businesses and it swept $3 billion of debt from its consolidated balance sheet. (It no longer consolidated the two bottling companies.) At the same time the new companies obtained independent access to equity markets to satisfy their own voracious appetites for capital.

*C*onsolidated Income Statement

A consolidated income statement is also prepared for affiliated companies. This statement shows the results of operations of affiliated companies as though they are one economic unit. This means that the statement shows only revenue and expense transactions between the consolidated entity and companies and individuals who are outside the affiliated group. Consequently, all intercompany revenue and expense transactions must be eliminated. Intercompany transactions such as sales between affiliates and interest on loans charged by one affiliate to another must be eliminated. A work sheet facilitates the preparation of consolidated income statements in the same manner as it does for the balance sheet.

Before You Go On . . .

► *Review It*

1. Why are eliminations needed in preparing consolidated financial statements?
2. What eliminations are made for the parent company's investment in the common stock of a subsidiary company?
3. How may the excess of cost over book value be reported in a consolidated balance sheet?

Summary of Study Objectives for Chapter 13 Appendix

6. Describe the content of a work sheet for a consolidated balance sheet. The work sheet for a consolidated balance sheet contains columns for (a) the balance sheet data for the separate entities, (b) intercompany eliminations, and (c) consolidated data.

7. Explain the form and content of consolidated financial statements. Consolidated financial statements are similar in form and content to the financial statements of an individual corporation. A consolidated balance sheet shows the assets and liabilities controlled by the parent company. A consolidated income statement shows the results of operations of affiliated companies as though they are one economic unit.

*Note: All **asterisked** glossary entries, Questions, Exercises, and Problems relate to material contained in the appendix to the chapter.

GLOSSARY

Available-for-sale securities Securities that may be sold in the future. (p. 587)

Consolidated financial statements Financial statements that present the assets and liabilities controlled by the parent company and the aggregate profitability of the affiliated companies. (p. 585)

Controlling interest Ownership of more than 50% of the common stock of another entity. (p. 584)

Cost method An accounting method in which the investment in common stock is recorded at cost and revenue is recognized only when cash dividends are received. (p. 582)

Debt investments Investments in government and corporation bonds. (p. 579)

Equity method An accounting method in which the investment in common stock is initially recorded at cost, and the investment account is then adjusted annually to show the investor's equity in the investee. (p. 583)

Fair value Amount for which a security could be sold in a normal market. (p. 587)

Held-to-maturity securities Debt securities which the investor has the intent and ability to hold to their maturity date. (p. 587)

*Intercompany eliminations** Eliminations made to exclude

the effects of intercompany transactions in preparing consolidated statements. (p. 593)

*Intercompany transactions** Transactions between affiliated companies. (p. 593)

Investment portfolio A group of stocks in different corporations held for investment purposes. (p. 581)

Long-term investments Investments that are not readily marketable or that management does not intend to convert into cash within the next year or operating cycle, whichever is longer. (p. 579)

Parent company A company that owns more than 50% of the common stock of another entity. (p. 584)

Stock investments Investments in the capital stock of corporations. (p. 581)

Subsidiary (affiliated) company A company in which more than 50% of its stock is owned by another company. (p. 584)

Temporary investments Investments that are readily marketable and intended to be converted into cash within the next year or operating cycle, whichever is longer. (p. 579)

Trading securities Securities bought and held primarily for sale in the near term to generate income on short-term price differences. (p. 587)

DEMONSTRATION PROBLEM

In its first year of operations, the DeMarco Company had the following selected transactions in stock investments which are considered trading securities:

June 1   Purchased for cash 600 shares of Sanburg common stock at $24 per share plus $300 brokerage fees.

July 1   Purchased for cash 800 shares of Cey common stock at $33 per share plus $600 brokerage fees.

Sept. 1   Received a $1 per share cash dividend from Cey Corporation.

Nov. 1   Sold 200 shares of Sanburg common stock for cash at $27 per share less $150 brokerage fees.

Dec. 15   Received a $.50 per share cash dividend on Sanburg common stock.

At December 31, the fair values per share were: Sanburg $25 and Cey $30.

Instructions

(a) Journalize the transactions.

(b) Prepare the adjusting entry at December 31 to report the securities at fair value.

Problem-Solving Strategies

1. Cost includes the price paid plus brokerage fees.

2. Gain or loss on sales is determined by the difference between net selling price and the cost of the securities.

3. The adjustment to fair value is based on the total difference between cost and fair value of the securities.

Solution to Demonstration Problem

(a) June	1	Stock Investments		14,700	
		Cash			14,700
		(To record purchase of 600 shares of Sanburg common stock)			
July	1	Stock Investments		27,000	
		Cash			27,000
		(To record purchase of 800 shares of Cey common stock)			
Sept.	1	Cash		800	
		Dividend Revenue			800
		(To record receipt of $1 per share cash dividend from Cey Corporation)			
Nov.	1	Cash		5,250	
		Stock Investments			4,900
		Gain on Sale of Stock Investments			350
		(To record sale of 200 shares of Sanburg common stock)			
Dec.	15	Cash		200	
		Dividend Revenue			200
		(To record receipt of $.50 per share dividend from Sanburg Corporation)			
(b) Dec.	31	Unrealized Loss—Income		2,800	
		Market Adjustment—Trading			2,800
		(To record unrealized loss on trading securities)			

Investment	Cost	Fair Value	Unrealized Gain (Loss)
Sanburg common stock	$ 9,800	$10,000	$ 200
Cey common stock	27,000	24,000	(3,000)
Totals	$36,800	$34,000	$(2,800)

SELF-STUDY QUESTIONS

Answers are at the end of the chapter.

(SO 1) 1. Temporary debt investments must be readily marketable and be expected to be sold within:
a. 3 months from the date of purchase.
b. the next year or operating cycle, whichever is shorter.
c. the next year or operating cycle, whichever is longer.
d. the operating cycle.

(SO 2) 2. Debt investments are initially recorded at:
a. cost.
b. cost plus accrued interest.
c. fair value.
d. None of the above.

(SO 2) 3. Hanes Company sells debt investments costing $26,000 for $28,000 plus accrued interest that has been recorded. In journalizing the sale, credits are:
a. Debt Investments and Loss on Sale of Debt Investments.
b. Debt Investments, Gain on Sale of Debt Investments, and Bond Interest Receivable.
c. Stock Investments and Bond Interest Receivable.
d. No correct answer given.

(SO 3) 4. Pryor Company receives net proceeds of $42,000 on the sale of stock investments that cost $39,500. This transaction will result in reporting in the income statement a:
a. loss of $2,500 under Other Expenses and Losses.
b. loss of $2,500 under Operating Expenses.
c. gain of $2,500 under Other Revenues and Gains.
d. gain of $2,500 under Operating Revenues.

(SO 3) 5. The equity method of accounting for long-term investments in stock should be used when the investor has significant influence over an investee and owns:
a. between 20% and 50% of the investee's common stock.
b. 20% or more of the investee's common stock.
c. more than 50% of the investee's common stock.
d. less than 20% of the investee's common stock.

(SO 4) 6. Which of the following statements is *not true*? Consolidated financial statements are useful to:
a. determine the profitability of specific subsidiaries.
b. determine the aggregate profitability of enterprises under common control.
c. determine the breadth of a parent company's operations.
d. determine the full extent of aggregate obligations of enterprises under common control.

(SO 5) 7. At the end of the first year of operations, the total cost of the trading securities portfolio is $120,000, and total fair value is $115,000. The financial statements should show:

a. a reduction of an asset of $5,000 and a realized loss of $5,000.
b. a reduction of an asset of $5,000 and an unrealized loss of $5,000 in the stockholders' equity section.
c. a reduction of an asset of $5,000 in the current asset section and an unrealized loss in Other Expenses and Losses of $5,000.
d. a reduction of an asset of $5,000 in the current asset section and a realized loss of $5,000 in Other Expenses and Losses.

8. In the balance sheet, Unrealized Loss—Equity is (SO 5) reported as a:
a. contra asset account.
b. contra stockholders' equity account.
c. loss in the income statement.
d. loss in the retained earnings statement.

*9. Pate Company pays $175,000 for 100% of Sinko's (SO 6) common stock when Sinko's stockholders' equity consists of Common Stock $100,000 and Retained Earnings $60,000. In the work sheet for the consolidated balance sheet, the eliminations will include a:
a. credit to Investment in Sinko Common Stock $160,000.
b. credit to Excess of Book Value over Cost of Subsidiary $15,000.
c. debit to Retained Earnings $75,000.
d. debit to Excess of Cost over Book Value of Subsidiary $15,000.

*10. Which of the following statements about intercompany eliminations is *true*? (SO 6)
a. They are not journalized or posted by any of the subsidiaries.
b. They do not affect the ledger accounts of any of the subsidiaries.
c. Intercompany eliminations are made solely on the work sheet to arrive at correct consolidated data.
d. All of these statements are true.

*11. Which one of the following statements about consolidated income statements is *false*? (SO 7)
a. A work sheet facilitates the preparation of the statement.
b. The consolidated income statement shows the results of operations of affiliated companies as a single economic unit.
c. All revenue and expense transactions between parent and subsidiary companies are eliminated.
d. When a subsidiary is wholly owned, the form and content of the statement will differ from the income statement of an individual corporation.

QUESTIONS

1. Kirk Wholesale Supply owns stock in Xerox Corporation, which it intends to hold indefinitely because of some negative tax consequences if sold. Should the investment in Xerox be classified as a temporary investment? Why?

2. (a) What is the cost of an investment in bonds?
   (b) When is interest on bonds recorded?

3. Ann Adler is confused about losses and gains on the sale of debt investments. Explain to Ann (a) how the gain or loss is computed, and (b) the statement presentation of the gains and losses.

4. Clio Company sells Cross's bonds costing $40,000 for $45,000, including $3,000 of accrued interest. In recording the sale, Clio books a $5,000 gain. Is this correct? Explain.

5. What is the cost of an investment in stock?

6. To acquire Mega Corporation stock, R. L. Duran pays $65,000 in cash plus $1,500 broker's fees. What entry should be made for this investment, assuming the stock is readily marketable?

7. (a) When should a long-term investment in common stock be accounted for by the equity method?
   (b) When is revenue recognized under this method?

8. Malon Corporation uses the equity method to account for its ownership of 35% of the common stock of Flynn Packing. During 1996 Flynn reported a net income of $80,000 and declares and pays cash dividends of $10,000. What recognition should Malon Corporation give to these events?

9. What constitutes "significant influence" when an investor's financial interest is below the 50% level?

10. Distinguish between the cost and equity methods of accounting for investments in stocks.

11. What are consolidated financial statements?

12. What are the valuation guidelines for investments at a balance sheet date?

13. Wendy Walner is the controller of G-Products, Inc. At December 31, the company's investments in trading securities cost $74,000 and have a fair value of $70,000. Indicate how Wendy would report these data in the financial statements prepared on December 31.

14. Using the data in question 13, how would Wendy report the data if the investment were long-term and the securities were classified as available-for-sale?

15. Reo Company's investments in available-for-sale securities at December 31 shows total cost of $192,000 and total fair value of $210,000. Prepare the adjusting entry.

16. Using the data in question 15, prepare the adjusting entry assuming the securities are classified as trading securities.

17. What is the proper statement presentation of the account Unrealized Loss—Equity?

18. What purposes are served by reporting Unrealized Gains (Losses)—Equity in the stockholders' equity section?

*19. (a) What asset and stockholders' equity balances are eliminated in preparing a consolidated balance sheet for a parent and a wholly owned subsidiary? (b) Why are they eliminated?

*20. Weller Company pays $320,000 to purchase all the outstanding common stock of Wood Corporation. At the date of purchase the net assets of Wood have a book value of $290,000. Weller's management allocates $20,000 of the excess cost to undervalued land on the books of Wood. What should be done with the rest of the excess?

BRIEF EXERCISES

Journalize entries for debt investments.
(SO 2)

BE13–1   Phelps Corporation purchased debt investments for $41,500 on January 1, 1996. On July 1, 1996, Phelps received cash interest of $2,075. Journalize the purchase and the receipt of interest. Assume that no interest has been accrued.

Journalize entries for stock investments.
(SO 3)

BE13–2   On August 1, McLain Company buys 1,000 shares of ABC common stock for $35,000 cash plus brokerage fees of $600. On December 1, the stock investments are sold for $38,000 in cash. Journalize the purchase and sale of the common stock.

Record transactions under the equity method of accounting.
(SO 3)

BE13–3   Harmon Company owns 30% of Hook Company. For the current year Hook reports net income of $150,000 and declares and pays a $50,000 cash dividend. Record Harmon's equity in Hook's net income and the receipt of dividends from Hook.

Prepare adjusting entry using fair value.
(SO 5)

BE13–4   Cost and fair value data for the trading securities of Michele Company at December 31, 1996, are $62,000 and $59,000, respectively. Prepare the adjusting entry to record the securities at fair value.

BE13–5 For the data presented in BE13–4, show the financial statement presentation of the trading securities and related accounts.

Indicate statement presentation using fair value.
(SO 5)

BE13–6 Duggen Corporation holds available-for-sale stock securities costing $72,000 as a long-term investment. At December 31, 1996, the fair value of the securities is $65,000. Prepare the adjusting entry to record the securities at fair value.

Prepare adjusting entry using fair value.
(SO 5)

BE13–7 For the data presented in BE13–6, show the financial statement presentation of the available-for-sale securities and related accounts. Assume the available-for-sale securities are noncurrent.

Indicate statement presentation using fair value.
(SO 5)

BE13–8 Saber Corporation has the following long-term investments: common stock of Sword Co. (10% ownership) held as available-for-sale securities, cost $108,000, fair value $113,000; common stock of Epee Inc. (30% ownership), cost $210,000, equity $250,000; and a bond sinking fund of $150,000. Prepare the investments section of the balance sheet.

Prepare investment section of balance sheet.
(SO 5)

*BE13–9 Provo Company acquires 100% of the common stock of Stanton Company for $180,000 cash. On the acquisition date, Stanton's ledger shows Common Stock $120,000 and Retained Earnings $60,000. Complete the work sheet for the following accounts: Provo— Investment in Stanton Common Stock, Stanton—Common Stock, and Stanton—Retained Earnings.

Prepare partial consolidated work sheet when cost equals book value.
(SO 6, 7)

*BE13–10 Data for the Provo and Stanton companies are given in BE13–9. Instead of paying $180,000, assume that Provo pays $200,000 to acquire the 100% interest in Stanton Company. Complete the work sheet for the accounts identified in BE13–9 and for the excess of cost over book value.

Prepare partial consolidated work sheet when cost exceeds book value.
(SO 6, 7)

EXERCISES

E13–1 Piper Corporation had the following transactions pertaining to debt investments:

Journalize debt investment transactions and accrue interest.
(SO 2)

Jan. 1 Purchased 60 10%, $1,000 Harris Co. bonds for $60,000 cash plus brokerage fees of $900. Interest is payable semiannually on July 1 and January 1.

July 1 Received semiannual interest on Harris Co. bonds.

July 1 Sold 30 Harris Co. bonds for $32,000 less $400 brokerage fees.

Instructions
(a) Journalize the transactions.
(b) Prepare the adjusting entry for the accrual of interest at December 31.

E13–2 Malea Company had the following transactions pertaining to stock investments:

Journalize stock investment transactions.
(SO 3)

Feb. 1 Purchased 800 shares of ABC common stock (2%) for $8,200 cash plus brokerage fees of $200.

July 1 Received cash dividends of $1 per share on ABC common stock.

Sept. 1 Sold 300 shares of ABC common stock for $4,000 less brokerage fees of $100.

Dec. 1 Received cash dividends of $1 per share on ABC common stock.

Instructions
(a) Journalize the transactions.
(b) Explain how dividend revenue and the gain (loss) on sale should be reported in the income statement.

E13–3 McCormick Inc. had the following transactions pertaining to investments in common stock:

Journalize transactions for investments in stocks.
(SO 3)

Jan. 1 Purchased 1,000 shares of Starr Corporation common stock (5%) for $70,000 cash plus $1,400 broker's commission.

July 1 Received a cash dividend of $9 per share.

Dec. 1 Sold 500 shares of Starr Corporation common stock for $37,000 cash less $800 broker's commission.

Dec. 31 Received a cash dividend of $9 per share.

Instructions
Journalize the transactions.

Journalize and post transactions under the equity method.
(SO 3)

E13–4   On January 1 Ranier Corporation purchased a 25% equity in Bellingham Corporation for $150,000. At December 31 Bellingham declared and paid a $60,000 cash dividend and reported net income of $200,000.

Instructions
(a) Journalize the transactions.
(b) Determine the amount to be reported as an investment in Bellingham stock at December 31.

Journalize entries under cost and equity methods.
(SO 3)

E13–5   Presented below are two independent situations:

1. Karen Cosmetics acquired 10% of the 200,000 shares of common stock of Bell Fashion at a total cost of $12 per share on March 18, 1996. On June 30, Bell declared and paid a $75,000 dividend. On December 31, Bell reported net income of $122,000 for the year. At December 31, the market price of Bell Fashion was $15 per share. The stock is classified as available-for-sale.
2. Barb, Inc., obtained significant influence over Diner Corporation by buying 30% of Diner's 30,000 outstanding shares of common stock at a total cost of $9 per share on January 1, 1996. On June 15, Diner declared and paid a cash dividend of $35,000. On December 31, Diner reported a net income of $80,000 for the year.

Instructions
Prepare all the necessary journal entries for 1996 for (a) Karen Cosmetics and (b) Barb, Inc.

Prepare adjusting entry to record fair value and indicate statement presentation.
(SO 5)

E13–6   At December 31, 1996, the trading securities for Nielson, Inc., are as follows:

Security	Cost	Fair Value
A	$17,500	$15,000
B	12,500	14,000
C	23,000	21,000
	$53,000	$50,000

Instructions
(a) Prepare the adjusting entry at December 31, 1996, to report the securities at fair value.
(b) Show the balance sheet and income statement presentation at December 31, 1996, after adjustment to fair value.

Prepare adjusting entry to record fair value and indicate statement presentation.
(SO 5)

E13–7   Data for investments in stock classified as trading securities are presented in E13–6. Assume instead that the investments are classified as available-for-sale securities with the same cost and fair value data. The securities are considered to be a long-term investment.

Instructions
(a) Prepare the adjusting entry at December 31, 1996, to report the securities at fair value.
(b) Show the statement presentation at December 31, 1996, after adjustment to fair value.
(c) ▥▭▭▭▷ J. Arnet, a member of the board of directors, does not understand the reporting of the unrealized gains or losses. Write a letter to Mr. Arnet explaining the reporting and the purposes that it serves.

Prepare adjusting entries for fair value and indicate statement presentation for two classes of securities.
(SO 5)

E13–8   Felipe Company has the following data at December 31, 1996:

Securities	Cost	Fair Value
Trading	$120,000	$125,000
Available-for-sale	100,000	90,000

The available-for-sale securities are held as a long-term investment.

Instructions
(a) Prepare the adjusting entries to report each class of securities at fair value.
(b) Indicate the statement presentation of each class of securities and the related unrealized gain (loss) accounts.

*E13–9 On January 1, Swiss Corporation acquires 100% of Arco Inc. for $200,000 in cash. The condensed balance sheets of the two corporations immediately following the acquisition are as follows:

	Swiss Corporation	Arco Inc.
Current assets	$ 60,000	$ 40,000
Investment in Arco Inc. common stock	200,000	
Plant and equipment (net)	300,000	210,000
	$560,000	$250,000
Current liabilities	$180,000	$ 50,000
Common stock	225,000	75,000
Retained earnings	155,000	125,000
	$560,000	$250,000

Instructions
Prepare a work sheet for a consolidated balance sheet.

*E13–10 Data for the Swiss and Arco corporations are presented in E13–9. Assume that instead of paying $200,000 in cash for Arco Inc., Swiss Corporation pays $215,000 in cash. Thus, at the acquisition date, the assets of Swiss Corporation are: Current assets $45,000, Investment in Arco Inc. Common Stock $215,000, and Plant and Equipment (net) $300,000.

Instructions
Prepare a work sheet for a consolidated balance sheet.

PROBLEMS

P13–1 The following transactions related to long-term bonds occurred for Lund Corporation:

1996
Jan. 1   Purchased $50,000 RAM Corporation 10% bonds for $50,000.
July 1   Received interest on RAM bonds.
Dec. 31   Accrued interest on RAM bonds.

1997
Jan. 1   Received interest on RAM bonds.
Jan. 1   Sold $25,000 RAM bonds for $27,500.
July 1   Received interest on RAM bonds.

Instructions
(a) Journalize the transactions.
(b) Assume that the fair value of the bonds at December 31, 1996, was $57,000. These bonds are classified as available-for-sale securities. Prepare the adjusting entry to record these bonds at fair value.
(c) Show the balance sheet presentation of the bonds and interest receivable at December 31, 1996, and indicate where any unrealized gain or loss is reported in the financial statements.

P13–2 In January 1996, the management of Reed Company concludes that it has sufficient cash to purchase some temporary investments in debt and stock securities. During the year, the following transactions occurred:

Feb. 1   Purchased 800 shares of IBF common stock for $32,000 plus brokerage fees of $800.
Mar. 1   Purchased 500 shares of RST common stock for $15,000 plus brokerage fees of $500.
Apr. 1   Purchased 60 $1,000, 12% CRT bonds for $60,000 plus $1,200 brokerage fees. Interest is payable semiannually on April 1 and October 1.
July 1   Received a cash dividend of $.60 per share on the IBF common stock.
Aug. 1   Sold 200 shares of IBF common stock at $42 per share less brokerage fees of $350.
Sept. 1   Received a $1 per share cash dividend on the RST common stock.

Oct. 1   Received the semiannual interest on the CRT bonds.

Oct. 1   Sold the CRT bonds for $63,000 less $1,000 brokerage fees.

At December 31, the fair value of the IBF and RST common stocks were $39 and $30 per share, respectively.

Instructions

(a) Journalize the transactions and post to the accounts Debt Investments and Stock Investments. (Use the T-account form.)
(b) Prepare the adjusting entry at December 31, 1996, to report the investments at fair value. All securities are considered to be trading securities.
(c) Show the balance sheet presentation of investment securities at December 31, 1996.
(d) Identify the income statement accounts and give the statement classification of each account.

Journalize transactions and adjusting entry for stock investments.
(SO 3, 5)

P13–3   On December 31, 1995, Harmon Associates owned the following securities that are held as long-term investments:

Common Stock	Shares	Cost
A Co.	1,000	$50,000
B Co.	6,000	36,000
C Co.	1,200	24,000

On this date, the total fair value of the securities was equal to its cost. The securities are not held for influence or control over the investees. In 1996, the following transactions occurred:

July 1   Received $1 per share semiannual cash dividend on B Co. common stock.

Aug. 1   Received $.50 per share cash dividend on A Co. common stock.

Sept. 1   Sold 500 shares of B Co. common stock for cash at $8 per share less brokerage fees of $100.

Oct. 1   Sold 400 shares of A Co. common stock for cash at $54 per share less brokerage fees of $600.

Nov. 1   Received $1 per share cash dividend on C Co. common stock.

Dec. 15   Received $.50 per share cash dividend on A Co. common stock.

     31   Received $1 per share semiannual cash dividend on B Co. common stock.

At December 31, the fair values per share of the common stocks were: A Co. $47, B Co. $6, and C Co. $18.

Instructions

(a) Journalize the 1996 transactions and post to the account Stock Investments. (Use the T-account form.)
(b) Prepare the adjusting entry at December 31, 1996, to show the securities at fair value. The stock should be classified as available-for-sale securities.
(c) Show the balance sheet presentation of the investments and the unrealized gain (loss) at December 31, 1996. At this date, Harmon Associates has common stock $2,000,000 and retained earnings $1,200,000.

Prepare entries at cost and at equity and prepare memorandum.
(SO 3)

P13–4   Cardinal Concrete acquired 20% of the outstanding common stock of Edra, Inc., on January 1, 1996, by paying $1,200,000 for 50,000 shares. Edra declared and paid an $0.80 per share cash dividend on June 30 and again on December 31, 1996. Edra reported net income of $700,000 for the year.

Instructions

(a) Prepare the journal entries for Cardinal Concrete for 1996 assuming Cardinal cannot exercise significant influence over Edra. (Use the cost method.)
(b) Prepare the journal entries for Cardinal Concrete for 1996, assuming Cardinal can exercise significant influence over Edra. (Use the equity method).
(c) ▭▭▭▷ The board of directors of Cardinal Concrete is confused about the differences between the cost and equity methods. Prepare a memorandum for the board that (1) explains each method and (2) shows, in tabular form, the account balances under each method at December 31, 1996.

P13–5 The following are in Hi-Tech Company's portfolio of long-term available-for-sale securities at December 31, 1995:

Journalize stock transactions and show statement presentation.
(SO 3, 5)

	Cost
500 shares of Awixa Corporation common stock.	$26,000
700 shares of HAL Corporation common stock.	42,000
400 shares of Renda Corporation preferred stock.	16,800

On December 31, the total cost of the portfolio equaled total fair value. Hi-Tech had the following transactions related to the securities during 1996:

Jan. 7 Sold 500 shares of Awixa Corporation common stock at $56 per share less brokerage fees of $700.

Jan. 10 Purchased 200 shares, $70 par value common stock of Mintor Corporation at $78 per share, plus brokerage fees of $240.

26 Received a cash dividend of $1.15 per share on HAL Corporation common stock.

Feb. 2 Received cash dividends of $.40 per share on Renda Corporation preferred stock.

10 Sold all 400 shares of Renda Corporation preferred stock at $28.00 per share less brokerage fees of $180.

July 1 Received a cash dividend of $1.00 per share on HAL Corporation common stock.

Sept. 1 Purchased an additional 400 shares of the $70 par value common stock of Mintor Corporation at $82 per share, plus brokerage fees of $400.

Dec. 15 Received a cash dividend of $1.50 per share on Mintor Corporation common stock.

At December 31, 1996, the fair values of the securities were:

HAL Corporation common stock	$64 per share
Mintor Corporation common stock	$70 per share

Hi-Tech uses separate account titles for each investment, such as Investment in HAL Corporation Common Stock.

Instructions
(a) Prepare journal entries to record the transactions.
(b) Post to the investment accounts. (Use T accounts.)
(c) Prepare the adjusting entry at December 31, 1996, to report the porfolio at fair value.
(d) Show the balance sheet presentation at December 31, 1996.

P13–6 The following data, presented in alphabetical order, are taken from the records of Oklahoma Corporation.

Prepare a balance sheet.
(SO 5)

Accounts payable	$ 240,000
Accounts receivable	110,000
Accumulated depreciation—building	180,000
Accumulated depreciation—equipment	52,000
Allowance for doubtful accounts	6,000
Bonds payable (10%, due 2012)	400,000
Bond sinking fund	360,000
Buildings	900,000
Cash	92,000
Common stock ($5 par value; 500,000 shares authorized, 300,000 shares issued)	1,500,000
Discount on bonds payable	20,000
Dividends payable	50,000
Equipment	275,000
Goodwill	200,000
Income taxes payable	120,000

Investment in Houston Inc, stock (30% ownership), at equity	240,000
Land	500,000
Temporary stock investment, at fair value	185,000
Merchandise inventory	170,000
Notes payable (due 1997)	70,000
Organization costs	50,000
Paid-in capital in excess of par value	200,000
Prepaid insurance	16,000
Retained earnings	300,000

Instructions

Prepare a balance sheet at December 31, 1996.

Prepare consolidated work sheet and balance sheet when cost exceeds book value. (SO 6, 7)

*P13–7 Neal Company purchased all the outstanding common stock of Wheaton Company on December 31, 1996. Just before the purchase, the condensed balance sheets of the two companies were as follows:

	Neal Company	Wheaton Company
Current assets	$1,476,000	$379,000
Plant and equipment (net)	1,882,000	353,000
	$3,358,000	$732,000
Current liabilities	$ 868,000	$ 92,000
Common stock	1,947,000	360,000
Retained earnings	543,000	280,000
	$3,358,000	$732,000

Neal used current assets of $726,000 to acquire the stock of Wheaton. The excess of this purchase price over the book value of Wheaton's net assets is determined to be attributable $30,000 to Wheaton's plant and equipment and the remainder to goodwill.

Instructions

(a) Prepare the entry for Neal Company's acquisition of Wheaton Company stock.

(b) Prepare a consolidated work sheet at December 31, 1996.

(c) Prepare a consolidated balance sheet at December 31, 1996.

ALTERNATE PROBLEMS

Journalize transactions and show financial statement presentation. (SO 2, 5)

P13–1A The following transactions related to long-term bonds occurred for Givarz Corporation.

1996

Jan. 1   Purchased $100,000 Leslye Corporation 9% bonds for $100,000.

July 1   Received interest on Leslye bonds.

Dec. 31   Accrued interest on Leslye bonds.

1997

Jan. 1   Received interest on Leslye bonds.

Jan. 1   Sold $25,000 Leslye bonds for $30,500.

July 1   Received interest on Leslye bonds.

Instructions

(a) Journalize the transactions.

(b) Assume that the fair value of the bonds at December 31, 1996, was $97,000. These bonds are classified as available-for-sale securities. Prepare the adjusting entry to record these bonds at fair value.

(c) Show the balance sheet presentation of the bonds and interest receivable at December 31, 1996, and indicate where any unrealized gain or loss is reported in the financial statements.

P13–2A In January, 1996, the management of the Mead Company concludes that it has sufficient cash to permit some temporary investments in debt and stock securities. During the year, the following transactions occurred:

Journalize investment transactions, prepare adjusting entry, and show statement presentation.
(SO 1, 2, 3, 5)

Feb. 1   Purchased 600 shares of CBF common stock for $31,800 plus brokerage fees of $600.

Mar. 1   Purchased 800 shares of RSD common stock for $20,000 plus brokerage fees of $400.

Apr. 1   Purchased 50 $1,000, 12% MRT bonds for $50,000 plus $1,000 brokerage fees. Interest is payable semiannually on April 1 and October 1.

July 1   Received a cash dividend of $.60 per share on the CBF common stock.

Aug. 1   Sold 200 shares of CBF common stock at $56 per share less brokerage fees of $200.

Sept. 1   Received a $1 per share cash dividend on the RSD common stock.

Oct. 1   Received the semiannual interest on the MRT bonds.

Oct. 1   Sold the MRT bonds for $51,000 less $1,000 brokerage fees.

At December 31, the fair value of the CBF and RSD common stocks were $55 and $24 per share, respectively.

Instructions

(a) Journalize the transactions and post to the accounts Debt Investments and Stock Investments. (Use the T-account form.)

(b) Prepare the adjusting entry at December 31, 1996, to report the investment securities at fair value. All securities are considered to be trading securities.

(c) Show the balance sheet presentation of investment securities at December 31, 1996.

(d) Identify the income statement accounts and give the statement classification of each account.

P13–3A On December 31, 1996, Karen Associates owned the following securities that are held as a long-term investment. The securities are not held for influence or control of the investee.

Journalize transactions and adjusting entry for stock investments.
(SO 3, 5)

Common Stock	Shares	Cost
X Co.	2,000	$90,000
Y Co.	5,000	45,000
Z Co.	1,500	30,000

On this date, the total fair value of the securities was equal to its cost. In 1997, the following transactions occurred.

July 1   Received $1 per share semiannual cash dividend on Y Co. common stock.

Aug. 1   Received $.50 per share cash dividend on X Co. common stock.

Sept. 1   Sold 700 shares of Y Co. common stock for cash at $8 per share less brokerage fees of $200.

Oct. 1   Sold 600 shares of X Co. common stock for cash at $54 per share less brokerage fees of $500.

Nov. 1   Received $1 per share cash dividend on Z Co. common stock.

Dec. 15   Received $.50 per share cash dividend on X Co. common stock.

31   Received $1 per share semiannual cash dividend on Y Co. common stock.

At December 31, the fair values per share of the common stocks were: X Co. $48, Y Co. $8, and Z Co. $17.

Instructions

(a) Journalize the 1997 transactions and post to the account Stock Investments. (Use the T-account form.)

(b) Prepare the adjusting entry at December 31, 1997, to show the securities at fair value. The stock should be classified as available-for-sale securities.

(c) Show the balance sheet presentation of the investments and the unrealized gain (loss) at December 31, 1997. At this date, Karen Associates has common stock $1,500,000 and retained earnings $1,000,000.

Prepare entries under the cost and equity methods and tabulate differences.
(SO 3)

P13–4A DFM Services acquired 30% of the outstanding common stock of BNA Company on January 1, 1996, by paying $800,000 for the 40,000 shares. BNA declared and paid $0.20 per share cash dividends on March 15, June 15, September 15, and December 15, 1996. BNA reported net income of $350,000 for the year.

Instructions
(a) Prepare the journal entries for DFM Services for 1996 assuming DFM cannot exercise significant influence over BNA. (Use the cost method.)
(b) Prepare the journal entries for DFM Services for 1996, assuming DFM can exercise significant influence over BNA. (Use the equity method.)
(c) In tabular form, indicate the investment and income statement account balances at December 31, 1996, under each method of accounting.

Prepare a balance sheet.
(SO 5)

P13–5A The following data, presented in alphabetical order, are taken from the records of Alameda Corporation:

Accounts payable	$ 250,000
Accounts receivable	120,000
Accumulated depreciation—building	180,000
Accumulated depreciation—equipment	52,000
Allowance for doubtful accounts	6,000
Bonds payable (10%, due 2010)	500,000
Bond sinking fund	150,000
Buildings	950,000
Cash	92,000
Common stock ($10 par value; 500,000 shares authorized, 150,000 shares issued)	1,500,000
Dividends payable	80,000
Equipment	275,000
Goodwill	200,000
Income taxes payable	120,000
Investment in Dodge common stock (10% ownership), at cost	278,000
Investment in Huston common stock (30% ownership), at equity	230,000
Land	500,000
Market adjustment—available-for-sale securities (Dr)	8,000
Merchandise inventory	170,000
Notes payable (due 1997)	70,000
Organization costs	50,000
Paid-in capital in excess of par value	200,000
Premium on bonds payable	40,000
Prepaid insurance	16,000
Retained earnings	213,000
Temporary stock investment, at fair value	180,000
Unrealized gain—available-for-sale securities	8,000

The investment in Dodge common stock is considered to be a long-term available-for-sale security.

Instructions
Prepare a balance sheet at December 31, 1996.

Prepare consolidated work sheet and balance sheet when cost exceeds book value.
(SO 6, 7)

*P13–6A Linger Corporation purchased all the outstanding common stock of Chrissy Foods, Inc. on December 31, 1996. Just before the purchase, the condensed balance sheets of the two companies appeared as follows:

	Linger Corporation	Chrissy Foods, Inc.
Current assets	$1,480,000	$ 439,500
Plant and equipment (net)	2,100,000	672,000
	$3,580,000	$1,111,500
Current liabilities	$ 578,000	$ 92,500
Common stock	1,950,000	525,000
Retained earnings	1,052,000	494,000
	$3,580,000	$1,111,500

Linger used current assets of $1,200,000 to acquire the stock of Chrissy Foods. The excess of this purchase price over the book value of Chrissy Foods' net assets is determined to be attributable $81,000 to Chrissy Foods' plant and equipment and the remainder to goodwill.

Instructions
   (a) Prepare the entry for Linger's acquisition of Chrissy Foods, Inc. stock.
   (b) Prepare a consolidated work sheet at December 31, 1996.
   (c) Prepare a consolidated balance sheet at December 31, 1996.

▼*B*roadening *Your Perspective*

*F*INANCIAL REPORTING PROBLEM—
PEPSICO, INC.
....

The annual report of PepsiCo, Inc. is presented in Appendix A.

Instructions
Answer the following questions.

   (a) What information about investments is reported in the consolidated balance sheet?
   (b) Based on the information under Assets in Management's Analysis of Consolidated Financial Condition (page A17), what is the nature of PepsiCo, Inc.'s short-term investments?
   (c) Using the information under Interest Expense in Management's Analysis of the Results of Operations (page A14), what effect did investments have on Income Before Income Taxes in 1995?
   (d) Using the Statement of Cash Flows, did cash flows from investing activities increase or decrease in 1995, and by how much?
   (e) Based on the information under Investing Activities in Management's Analysis of Consolidated Cash Flows (page A16), what types of investments have been made in (1) recent years and (2) 1995? Does management expect investing activity to increase or decrease in 1996? How much?

*C*OMPARATIVE ANALYSIS PROBLEM—
THE COCA-COLA COMPANY VS. PEPSICO, INC.
....

The financial statements of Coca-Cola Company are presented at the end of Chapter 1, and PepsiCo's financial statements are presented in Appendix A.

Instructions
   (a) Based on the information contained in these financial statements, determine each of the following for each company:
      (1) Cash used in (for) investing activities during 1995 (from the Statement of Cash Flows).
      (2) Cash used for acquisitions and investments in unconsolidated affiliates (or principally bottling companies) during 1995.
      (3) Total investments in unconsolidated affiliates (or investments and other assets) at December 31, 1995.
   (b) What conclusions concerning the management of investments can be drawn from these data?

INTERPRETATION OF FINANCIAL STATEMENTS

•••

Mini-Case—KeyCorp

KeyCorp is a Ohio bank holding company (meaning that it is a corporation that owns banks). It manages $66 billion in assets, the largest of which is its loan portfolio of $47 billion. In addition to its loan portfolio, however, like other banks it has significant debt and stock investments. The nature of these investments varies from short-term in nature to long-term in nature, and as a consequence, consistent with the requirements of accounting rules, KeyCorp reports its investments in three different categories—trading, available-for-sale, and held-to-maturity. In its balance sheet it uses different terminology for these categories, however, calling them short-term investments, securities available for sale, and investment securities, respectively. The following facts were found in KeyCorp's 1995 Annual Report:

(all dollars in millions)	Amortized Cost	Gross Unrealized Gains	Gross Unrealized Losses	Fair Value
Short-term investments	—	—	—	$ 682
Securities available for sale	$7,994	$112	$ 46	8,060
Investment securities	1,688	51	1	1,738
Net income				825
Net securities gains (losses)				41

Instructions

(a) Why do you suppose KeyCorp purchases investments, rather than simply making loans? Why do they purchase investments that vary in nature both in terms of their maturities and in type (debt versus stock)?

(b) How must KeyCorp account for its investments in each of the three categories?

(c) In what ways does classifying investments into three different categories assist investors in evaluating the profitability of a company like KeyCorp?

(d) Suppose that the management of KeyCorp was not happy with its 1995 net income. What step could it have taken with its investment portfolio that would have definitely increased 1995 reported profit? How much could they have increased reported profit? Why do you suppose they chose not to do this?

DECISION CASE

•••

At the beginning of the question and answer portion of the annual stockholders' meeting of Revell Corporation, stockholder Carol Finstrom asks, "Why did management sell the holdings in AHM Company at a loss when this company has been very profitable during the period its stock was held by Revell?"

Since president Larry Wisdom has just concluded his speech on the recent success and bright future of Revell, he is taken aback by this question and responds, "I remember we paid $1,100,000 for that stock some years ago, and I am sure we sold that stock at a much higher price. You must be mistaken."

Finstrom retorts, "Well, right here in footnote number 7 to the annual report it shows that 240,000 shares, a 30% interest in AHM, was sold on the last day of the year. Also, it states that AHM earned $550,000 this year and paid out $150,000 in cash dividends. Further, a summary statement indicates that in past years, while Revell held AHM stock, AHM earned $1,240,000 and paid out $440,000 in dividends. Finally, the income statement for this year shows a loss on the sale of AHM stock of $180,000. So, I doubt that I am mistaken."

Red-faced, president Wisdom turns to you.

Instructions

What dollar amount did Revell receive upon the sale of the AHM stock? Explain why both stockholder Finstrom and president Wisdom are correct.

COMMUNICATION ACTIVITY

Chapperal Corporation has purchased two securities for its portfolio. The first is a stock investment in Sting Ray Corporation, one of its suppliers. Chapperal purchased 10% of Sting Ray with the intention of holding it for a number of years, but has no intention of purchasing more shares. The second investment was a purchase of debt securities. Chapperal purchased the debt securities because its analysts believe that changes in market interest rates will cause these securities to increase in value in a short period of time. Chapperal intends to sell the securities as soon as they have increased in value.

Instructions

Write a memo to Gils Stiles, the Chief Financial Officer, explaining how to account for each of these investments, and what the implications for reported income are from this accounting treatment.

GROUP ACTIVITY

Finland Corporation holds a portfolio of debt and equity investments. Although some of the securities in the portfolio have declined in value, the total value of the portfolio is above its total cost. Finn Berge, Finland Corporation's president, has decided to classify all securities in the portfolio that have decreased in value as available-for-sale (the stock investments) or as held-to-maturity (the debt investments). He will classify all securities that have increased in value as trading securities.

Instructions

In groups of four or five discuss the following:

   (a) What impact will this classification approach have on Finland Corporation's reported results?
   (b) Is this an appropriate approach for classifying these securities?
   (c) What are the implications of this approach for subsequent years?

ETHICS CASE

Scott Kreiter Financial Services Company holds a large portfolio of debt and stock securities as an investment. The total fair value of the portfolio at December 31, 1996, is greater than total cost, with some securities having increased in value and others having decreased. Vicki Lemke, the financial vice-president, and Ula Greenwood, the controller, are in the process of classifying for the first time the securities in the portfolio.

Lemke suggests classifying the securities that have increased in value as trading securities in order to increase net income for the year. She also wants to classify the securities that have decreased in value as long-term available-for-sale securities so that the decreases in value will not affect 1996 net income.

Greenwood disagrees. She recommends classifying the securities that have decreased in value as trading securities and those that have increased in value as long-term available-for-sale securities. Greenwood argues that the company is having a good earnings year and that recognizing the losses now will help to smooth income for this year. Moreover, for future years, when the company may not be as profitable, the company will have built-in gains.

Instructions

   (a) Will classifying the securities as Lemke and Greenwood suggest actually affect earnings as each says it will?
   (b) Is there anything unethical in what Lemke and Greenwood propose? Who are the stakeholders affected by their proposals?

(c) Assume that Lemke and Greenwood properly classify the portfolio. Assume, at year-end, that Lemke proposes to sell the securities that will increase 1996 net income, and that Greenwood proposes to sell the securities that will decrease 1996 net income. Is this unethical?

RESEARCH ASSIGNMENT

The July 6, 1995 edition of *The Wall Street Journal* includes an article by Jim Carlton and David P. Hamilton, entitled "Packard Bell Sells 20% Stake to NEC for $170 Million; Deal Gives Japanese Firm Unprecedented Access to the U.S. PC Market." Read the article and answer the following questions.

(a) Why did Packard Bell sell shares to NEC?
(b) Identify a similar transaction between two other computer companies.
(c) Under U.S. GAAP, how would NEC account for its investment in Packard Bell?
(d) Packard Bell was considering a sale of common shares to the general public. Why didn't it select this option?

CRITICAL THINKING
▶ *A Real-World Focus: SPS Technologies, Inc.*

SPS Technologies, Inc., was formed in 1903 as Standard Pressed Steel. Today the company is engaged in the design, manufacture, and marketing of high-strength mechanical fasteners, superalloys, and magnetic materials for the aerospace, automotive, and off-highway equipment industries. The company owns plants in the United States, United Kingdom, Ireland, Australia, and Spain, and has minority interests in facilities in Brazil and India.

The following note to the financial statements appears in a recent SPS annual report:

Investments: The Company's investments in affiliates consist of a 16.75% interest in Precision Fasteners Ltd., Bombay, India; a 46.49% interest in Metalac S.A. Industria e Comercio, Sao Paulo, Brazil; a 51.0% interest in Pacific Products Limited, Guernsey, Channel Islands, United Kingdom; and a 51.0% interest in National-Arnold Magnetics Company, Adelanto, California, United States. Dividends received from these companies were $42,000, $44,000, and $66,000 in 1993, 1992 and 1991, respectively.

Instructions
(a) Does the investment in these companies represent short- or long-term investments? Are these investments in stocks or in bonds of these companies?
(b) The ownership percentages in these companies vary. Based upon the information given, which accounting method would appear appropriate for each company? What other information would you like to know before deciding how to account for each investment?
(c) What is the most likely method used to account for dividends received from Precision Fasteners? From National-Arnolds Magnetics Company?

Answers to Self-Study Questions
1. c   2. a   3. b   4. c   5. a   6. a   7. c   8. b   9. d   10. d   11. d

"Cash Is Cash, and Everything Else Is Accounting"

SIOUX FALLS, S.D. — For Gerald Biby, vice president and chief financial officer of Kilian Community College in Sioux Falls, South Dakota, the statement of cash flows was the difference between being able to refinance a mortgage and being turned down by six local banks. "We recently wanted to refinance a $125,000 mortgage on a piece of property that we own," he says. "It was the statement of cash flows that finally showed our lender that we had the cash flow to service the debt."

As he explains, the traditional financial statement for a not-for-profit, educational institution shows revenues and all expenditures, even the capital expenditures. According to this format, which the banks focused on initially, Kilian Community College was just breaking even. "In the business world, if we had spent $250,000 on a computer system, then we would have put that on a depreciation schedule. But in the non-profit arena, it's typical that the entire $250,000 is written off as an expense against the general fund." The statement of cash flows showed the bankers that one of the uses of funds was really the purchase of computer equipment that had several years of life.

The college's statement of cash flows has over 30 classifications including tuition, fees, bookstore revenues, and so on. The school has 250 students, charges $70 a credit hour (12 hours is a full-time schedule), and has five terms each year.

The bankers granted the refinancing when they saw that the college's sources of funds exceeded the loan repayments, including principal and interest, by a ratio of 3-to-1. Not only did the school get the loan, but it did so at a favorable rate. "We were able to cut the mortgage rate to prime plus 1% from prime plus 3%." ◄

CHAPTER · **14**

*T*HE STATEMENT OF CASH FLOWS

► STUDY OBJECTIVES ◄

After studying this chapter, you should be able to:

1. *Indicate the primary purpose of the statement of cash flows.*
2. *Distinguish among operating, investing, and financing activities.*
3. *Prepare a statement of cash flows using the indirect method.*
4. *Prepare a statement of cash flows using the direct method.*

As the story about Kilian Community College indicates, the balance sheet, income statement, and retained earnings statement do not always show the whole picture of the financial condition of a company or institution. In fact, looking at the three traditional financial statements of some well-known companies, a thoughtful investor might have questions like the following: How did Eastman Kodak finance cash dividends of $649 million in a year in which it earned only $17 million? How could Delta Airlines purchase new planes costing $900 million in a year in which it reported a net loss of $86 million? How did Kohlberg Kravis Roberts finance its record-shattering $25 billion purchase of RJR Nabisco? Answers to these and similar questions can be found in this chapter, which presents the **statement of cash flows**. The content and organization of this chapter are as follows:

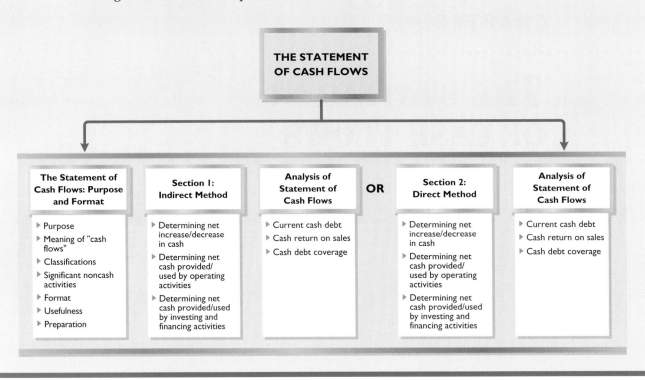

THE STATEMENT OF CASH FLOWS

The Statement of Cash Flows: Purpose and Format	Section 1: Indirect Method	Analysis of Statement of Cash Flows	OR	Section 2: Direct Method	Analysis of Statement of Cash Flows
▶ Purpose ▶ Meaning of "cash flows" ▶ Classifications ▶ Significant noncash activities ▶ Format ▶ Usefulness ▶ Preparation	▶ Determining net increase/decrease in cash ▶ Determining net cash provided/ used by operating activities ▶ Determining net cash provided/used by investing and financing activities	▶ Current cash debt ▶ Cash return on sales ▶ Cash debt coverage		▶ Determining net increase/decrease in cash ▶ Determining net cash provided/ used by operating activities ▶ Determining net cash provided/used by investing and financing activities	▶ Current cash debt ▶ Cash return on sales ▶ Cash debt coverage

*T*he Statement of Cash Flows: Purpose and Format

Helpful hint The statement of cash flows is a relatively new basic financial statement resulting from the 1987 *FASB Statement No. 95* and was first required in practice in 1988.

The three basic financial statements we've studied so far present only limited and fragmentary information about a company's cash flows (cash receipts and cash payments). For example, comparative balance sheets show the increase in property, plant, and equipment during the year, but they do not show how the additions were financed or paid for. The income statement shows net income, but it does not indicate the amount of cash generated by operating activities. Similarly, the retained earnings statement shows cash dividends declared but not the cash dividends paid during the year. None of these statements presents a detailed summary of the net change in cash as a result of operating, investing, and financing activities during the period.

▶**A**ccounting in **A**ction ▸ *Business Insight*

Libby-Owens-Ford (LOF) Company's mission statement in its annual report emphasizes the importance of cash flow as follows: "LOF stresses the importance of cash flow measurement and performance. Individual companies must analyze the cash flow effects of running their business. Where cash comes from and what cash is used for must be simply and clearly set forth."

Purpose of the Statement of Cash Flows

The primary purpose of the statement of cash flows is to provide information about the cash receipts and cash payments of an entity during a period. A secondary objective is to provide information about the operating, investing, and financing activities of the entity during the period.[1] The **statement of cash flows** reports the cash receipts, cash payments, and net change in cash resulting from the operating, investing, and financing activities of an enterprise during a period in a format that reconciles the beginning and ending cash balances.

Reporting the causes of changes in cash is considered useful because investors, creditors, and other interested parties want to know what is happening to a company's most liquid resource—its cash. As the opening story about Kilian Community College demonstrates, a statement of cash flows helps us understand what is happening. It provides answers to the following simple, but important, questions about the enterprise:

1. Where did the cash come from during the period?
2. What was the cash used for during the period?
3. What was the change in the cash balance during the period?

STUDY OBJECTIVE

••••••••• 1 •••••••••

Indicate the primary purpose of the statement of cash flows.

Meaning of "Cash Flows"

The statement of cash flows is generally prepared using "**cash and cash equivalents**" as its basis. Cash equivalents are short-term, highly liquid investments that are both:

1. Readily convertible to known amounts of cash, and
2. So near their maturity that their market value is relatively insensitive to changes in interest rates.

Generally, only investments with original maturities of three months or less qualify under this definition. Examples of cash equivalents are Treasury bills, commercial paper (short-term corporate notes), and money market funds. All typically are purchased with cash that is in excess of immediate needs. Note that since cash and cash equivalents are viewed as the same, transfers between cash and cash equivalents are not treated as cash receipts and cash payments—i.e., they are not reported in the statement of cash flows. The term "cash" when used in this chapter includes cash and cash equivalents.

Classification of Cash Flows

The statement of cash flows classifies cash receipts and cash payments by operating, investing, and financing activities. Transactions and other events characteristic of each kind of activity are as follows:

STUDY OBJECTIVE

••••••••• 2 •••••••••

Distinguish among operating, investing, and financing activities.

---

[1]"Statement of Cash Flows," *Statement of Financial Accounting Standards No. 95* (Stamford, Conn.: FASB, 1987).

1. **Operating activities** include the cash effects of transactions that create revenues and expenses and thus enter into the determination of net income.
2. **Investing activities** include (a) acquiring and disposing of investments and productive long-lived assets, and (b) lending money and collecting the loans.
3. **Financing activities** include (a) obtaining cash from issuing debt and repaying the amounts borrowed, and (b) obtaining cash from stockholders and providing them with a return on their investment.

Helpful hint You determine what classification a transaction is by looking to see if it is in the list of investing activities or financing activities. If it is in neither of these lists, it is an operating activity.

The category of operating activities is the most important because it shows the cash provided by company operations. This source of cash is generally considered to be the best measure of a company's ability to generate sufficient cash to continue as a going concern.

Illustration 14-1 lists typical cash receipts and cash payments within each of the three classifications. Study the list carefully. It will prove very useful in solving homework exercises and problems.

Illustration 14-1

Typical receipts and payments classified by activity

Helpful hint Operating activities generally relate to changes in current assets and current liabilities. Investing activities generally relate to changes in noncurrent assets. Financing activities relate to changes in noncurrent liabilities and stockholders' equity accounts.

Types of Cash Inflows and Outflows

Operating activities
Cash inflows:
From sale of goods or services.
From returns on loans (interest received) and on equity securities (dividends received).
Cash outflows:
To suppliers for inventory.
To employees for services.
To government for taxes.
To lenders for interest.
To others for expenses.

Investing activities
Cash inflows:
From sale of property, plant, and equipment.
From sale of debt or equity securities of other entities.
From collection of principal on loans to other entities.
Cash outflows:
To purchase property, plant, and equipment.
To purchase debt or equity securities of other entities.
To make loans to other entities.

Financing activities
Cash inflows:
From sale of equity securities (company's own stock).
From issuance of debt (bonds and notes).
Cash outflows:
To stockholders as dividends.
To redeem long-term debt or reacquire capital stock.

As you can see, some cash flows relating to investing or financing activities are classified as operating activities. For example, receipts of investment revenue (interest and dividends) and payments of interest to lenders are classified as operating activities because these items are reported in the income statement.

Note that, generally, (1) operating activities involve income determination (income statement) items, (2) investing activities involve cash flows resulting from changes in investments and long-term asset items, and (3) financing activities involve cash flows resulting from changes in long-term liability and stockholders' equity items.

Significant Noncash Activities

Not all of a company's significant activities involve cash. Examples of significant noncash activities are:

1. Issuance of common stock to purchase assets.
2. Conversion of bonds into common stock.
3. Issuance of debt to purchase assets.
4. Exchanges of plant assets.

Significant financing and investing activities that do not affect cash are not reported in the body of the statement of cash flows. However, these activities are reported in either a separate schedule at the bottom of the statement of cash flows or in a separate note or supplementary schedule to the financial statements.

The reporting of these activities in a separate note or supplementary schedule satisfies the **full disclosure principle** because it identifies significant noncash investing and financing activities of the enterprise. In solving homework assignments you should present significant noncash investing and financing activities in a separate schedule at the bottom of the statement of cash flows. (See lower section of Illustration 14-2 for an example.)

Helpful hint Do not include noncash investing and financing activities in the body of the statement of cash flows. Report this information in a separate schedule at the bottom of the statement.

Format of the Statement of Cash Flows

The three activities discussed above—operating, investing, and financing—plus the significant noncash investing and financing activities constitute the general format of the statement of cash flows. A widely used form of the statement of cash flows is shown in Illustration 14-2.

COMPANY NAME
Statement of Cash Flows
Period Covered

Cash flows from operating activities		
(List of individual items)	XX	
Net cash provided (used) by operating activities		XXX
Cash flows from investing activities		
(List of individual inflows and outflows)	XX	
Net cash provided (used) by investing activities		XXX
Cash flows from financing activities		
(List of individual inflows and outflows)	XX	
Net cash provided (used) by financing activities		XXX
Net increase (decrease) in cash		XXX
Cash at beginning of period		XXX
Cash at end of period		XXX
Noncash investing and financing activities		
(List of individual noncash transactions)		XXX

Illustration 14-2

Format of statement of cash flows

Helpful hint Indicate the classification in the statement of cash flows for each of the following: (1) Proceeds from the sale of an investment. (2) Disbursement for the purchase of treasury stock. (3) Loan to another corporation. (4) Proceeds from an insurance policy because a building was destroyed by fire. (5) Proceeds from winning a lawsuit. (6) Receipt of interest from an investment in bonds. (7) Payment of dividends. (8) Sale of merchandise for cash. Answers:
(1) Investing. (2) Financing.
(3) Investing. (4) Investing.
(5) Operating. (6) Operating.
(7) Financing. (8) Operating.

As illustrated, the cash flows from operating activities section always appears first, followed by the investing activities and the financing activities sections. Also, **the individual inflows and outflows from investing and financing activities are reported separately**. Thus, cash outflow for the purchase of property, plant, and equipment is reported separately from the cash inflow from the sale of property, plant, and equipment. Similarly, the cash inflow from the issuance

▸Accounting in Action ▸ *Business Insight*

 Differences between net income and net cash provided by operating activities are illustrated by the following results from recent annual reports for the same fiscal year (all data are in millions of dollars):

Company	Net Income	Net Cash from Operations
Kmart Corporation	$ 296	$ 76
Wal-Mart Stores, Inc.	2,681	2,906
Woolworth Corporation	47	(340)
J.C. Penney Company, Inc.	1,057	738
Sears Roebuck & Co.	1,454	1,930
The May Department Stores Company	782	999

Note the wide disparity among the companies that engaged in similar types of retail merchandising.

of debt securities is reported separately from the cash outflow for the retirement of debt. If a company did not report the inflows and outflows separately, it would obscure the investing and financing activities of the enterprise and thus make it more difficult to assess future cash flows.

The reported operating, investing, and financing activities result in either net cash **provided or used** by each activity. The net cash provided or used by each activity is totaled to show the net increase (decrease) in cash for the period. The net increase (decrease) in cash for the period is then added to or subtracted from the beginning-of-the-period cash balance to obtain the end-of-the-period cash balance. Finally, any significant noncash investing and financing activities are reported in a separate schedule at the bottom of the statement.

Usefulness of the Statement of Cash Flows

The information in a statement of cash flows should help investors, creditors, and others assess various aspects of the firm's financial position:

1. **The entity's ability to generate future cash flows.** By examining relationships between such items as sales and net cash provided by operating activities, or cash provided by operations and increases or decreases in cash, investors and others can make predictions of the amounts, timing, and uncertainty of future cash flows better than from accrual basis data.

2. **The entity's ability to pay dividends and meet obligations.** Simply put, if a company does not have adequate cash, employees cannot be paid, debts settled, or dividends paid. Employees, creditors, stockholders, and customers should be particularly interested in this statement, because it alone shows the flows of cash in a business.

3. **The reasons for the difference between net income and net cash provided (used) by operating activities.** Net income is important, because it provides information on the success or failure of a business enterprise. However, some are critical of accrual basis net income because it requires many estimates; as a result, the reliability of the number is often challenged. Such is not the case with cash. Thus, many readers of the financial statement want to know the reasons for the difference between net income and net cash provided by operating activities. Then they can assess for themselves the reliability of the income number.

4. **The cash investing and financing transactions during the period.** By examining a company's investing activities and its financing transactions, a

▸*Ethics note*

Many investors believe that "Cash is cash and everything else is accounting"—that is, cash flow is less susceptible to management manipulation and fraud than traditional accounting measures such as net income. Though we would suggest that reliance on cash flows to the exclusion of accrual accounting is inappropriate, comparing cash from operations to net income can reveal important information about the "quality" of reported net income—that is, the extent to which net income provides a good measure of actual performance.

Helpful hint Income from operations and cash flow from operating activities are different. Income from operations is based on accrual accounting; cash flow from operating activities is prepared on a cash basis.

financial statement reader can better understand why assets and liabilities increased or decreased during the period. In summary, the information in the statement of cash flows is useful in answering the following questions:

How did cash increase when there was a net loss for the period?

How were the proceeds of the bond issue used?

How was the expansion in the plant and equipment financed?

Why were dividends not increased?

How was the retirement of debt accomplished?

How much money was borrowed during the year?

Is cash flow greater or less than net income?

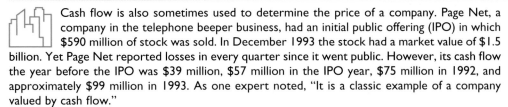
Accounting in Action ▸ *Business Insight*

Cash flow is also sometimes used to determine the price of a company. Page Net, a company in the telephone beeper business, had an initial public offering (IPO) in which $590 million of stock was sold. In December 1993 the stock had a market value of $1.5 billion. Yet Page Net reported losses in every quarter since it went public. However, its cash flow the year before the IPO was $39 million, $57 million in the IPO year, $75 million in 1992, and approximately $99 million in 1993. As one expert noted, "It is a classic example of a company valued by cash flow."

Preparing the Statement of Cash Flows

The statement of cash flows is prepared differently from the three other basic financial statements. First, it is not prepared from an adjusted trial balance. Because the statement requires detailed information concerning the changes in account balances that occurred between two periods of time, an adjusted trial balance will not provide the necessary data for the statement. Second, the statement of cash flows deals with cash receipts and payments. As a result, **the accrual concept is not used in the preparation of a statement of cash flows**.

The information to prepare this statement usually comes from three sources:

Comparative balance sheet. Information in this statement indicates the amount of the changes in assets, liabilities, and stockholders' equities from the beginning to the end of the period.

Current income statement. Information in this statement helps the reader determine the amount of cash provided by or used by operations during the period.

Additional information. Additional information includes transaction data that are needed to determine how cash was provided or used during the period.

Preparing the statement of cash flows from these data sources involves three major steps, explained in Illustration 14-3 on page 622.

Indirect and Direct Methods

In order to perform step 2, the operating activities section of the statement of cash flows **must be converted from an accrual basis to a cash basis**. This conversion may be done by either of two methods: (1) the indirect method or (2) the direct method. **Both methods arrive at the same total amount** for "Net cash provided by operating activities," but they differ in disclosing the items that comprise the total amount. Note that the two different methods only impact the

Step 1: Determine the net increase/decrease in cash.

The difference between the beginning and ending cash balances can be easily computed from comparative balance sheets.

Step 2: Determine net cash provided/used by operating activities.

This step involves analyzing not only the current year's income statement but also comparative balance sheets and selected additional data.

Step 3: Determine net cash provided/used by investing and financing activities.

This step involves analyzing comparative balance sheet data and selected additional information for their effects on cash.

Illustration 14-3

Three major steps in preparing the statement of cash flows

operating activities section; the investing activities and financing activities sections are not affected by the choice of method.

The indirect method is used extensively in practice, as shown in Illustration 14-4.[2] Companies favor the indirect method for two reasons: (1) it is easier to prepare, and (2) it focuses on the differences between net income and net cash flow from operating activities.

Illustration 14-4

Usage of indirect and direct methods

▶ *International note*

International accounting requirements are quite similar in most respects with regard to the cash flow statement. Some interesting exceptions: In Japan, operating and investing activities are combined; in Australia, the direct method is mandatory; in Spain, the indirect method is mandatory. Also, in a number of European and Scandinavian countries a cash flow statement is not required at all, although in practice most publicly traded firms provide one.

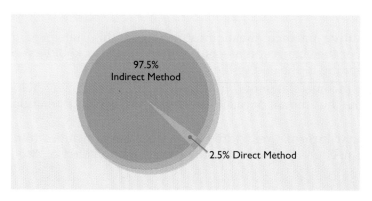

Others, however, favor the direct method. The direct method shows operating cash receipts and payments. Thus, it is more consistent with the objective of a statement of cash flows. The FASB has expressed a preference for the direct method, but allows the use of either method. However, when the direct method is used, the net cash flow from operating activities as computed using the indirect method must also be reported in a separate schedule.

---

[2]*Accounting Trends and Techniques–1996* (New York: American Institute of Certified Public Accountants, 1996).

Section 1 of this chapter illustrates the indirect method; Section 2 illustrates the direct method. These sections are independent of each other; only one or the other need be covered in order to understand and prepare the statement of cash flows.

Before You Go On . . .

► *Review It*

1. What is the primary purpose of a statement of cash flows?
2. What are the major classifications of cash flows on the statement of cash flows?
3. What are the three major steps in the preparation of a statement of cash flows?
4. Why is the statement of cash flows useful? What key information does it convey?

► *Do It*

During its first week of existence, Plano Molding Company had the following transactions:

1. Issued 100,000 shares of $5 par value common stock for $800,000 cash.
2. Borrowed $200,000 from Sandwich State Bank, signing a 5-year note bearing 8% interest.
3. Purchased two semi-trailer trucks for $170,000 cash.
4. Paid employees $12,000 for salaries and wages.
5. Collected $20,000 cash for services rendered.

Classify by type of cash flow activity each of these transactions.

Reasoning: All cash flows are classified into three types of activities for purposes of reporting cash inflows and outflows: operating activities, investing activities, and financing activities. Operating activities include the cash effects of transactions that create revenues and expenses and thus enter into the determination of net income. Investing activities include (a) acquiring and disposing of investments and productive long-lived assets, and (b) lending money and collecting the loans. Financing activities include (a) obtaining cash from issuing debt and repaying the amounts borrowed, and (b) obtaining cash from stockholders and providing them with a return on their investment.

Solution:

1. Financing activity.
2. Financing activity.
3. Investing activity.
4. Operating activity.
5. Operating activity.

Related exercise material: BE14–3, BE14–5, E14–1, and E14–6.

▼ SECTION *1* ► *Statement of Cash Flows— Indirect Method*

To explain and illustrate the indirect method, we will use the transactions of the Computer Services Company for two years—1996 and 1997. Annual statements of cash flows will be prepared. Basic transactions will be used in the first year with additional transactions added in the second year.

STUDY OBJECTIVE

•••••••••• **3** ••••••••••

Prepare a statement of cash flows using the indirect method.

First Year of Operations—1996

Computer Services Company started on January 1, 1996, when it issued 50,000 shares of $1.00 par value common stock for $50,000 cash. The company rented its office space and furniture and performed consulting services throughout the first year. The comparative balance sheets at the beginning and end of 1996, showing increases or decreases, appear in Illustration 14-5.

Illustration 14-5

Comparative balance sheet, 1996, with increases and decreases

COMPUTER SERVICES COMPANY
Comparative Balance Sheet

Assets	Dec. 31, 1996	Jan. 1, 1996	Change Increase/Decrease
Cash	$34,000	$ –0–	$34,000 Increase
Accounts receivable	30,000	–0–	30,000 Increase
Equipment	10,000	–0–	10,000 Increase
Total	$74,000	$ –0–	
Liabilities and Stockholders' Equity			
Accounts payable	$ 4,000	$ –0–	$ 4,000 Increase
Common stock	50,000	–0–	50,000 Increase
Retained earnings	20,000	–0–	20,000 Increase
Total	$74,000	$ –0–	

Helpful hint Note that although each of the balance sheet items of Computer Services increased, their individual effects are not the same. Some of these increases are cash inflows, and some are cash outflows.

The income statement and additional information for Computer Services Company are shown in Illustration 14-6.

Illustration 14-6

Income statement and additional information, 1996

COMPUTER SERVICES COMPANY
Income Statement
For the Year Ended December 31, 1996

Revenues	$85,000
Operating expenses	40,000
Income before income taxes	45,000
Income tax expense	10,000
Net income	$35,000

Additional information:
(a) Examination of selected data indicates that a dividend of $15,000 was declared and paid during the year.
(b) The equipment was purchased at the end of 1996. No depreciation was taken in 1996.

Determining the Net Increase/Decrease in Cash (Step 1)

To prepare a statement of cash flows, the first step is **determining the net increase or decrease in cash**. This is a simple computation. For example, Computer Services Company had no cash on hand at the beginning of 1996, but had $34,000 on hand at the end of 1996. Thus, the change in cash for 1996 was an increase of $34,000.

Determining Net Cash Provided/Used by Operating Activities (Step 2)

Helpful hint You may wish to insert the beginning and ending cash balances and the increase/decrease in cash necessitated by these balances immediately into the statement of cash flows. The net increase/decrease is the target amount. The net cash flows from the three classes of activity must equal the target amount.

To determine net cash provided by operating activities under the indirect method, **net income is adjusted for items that did not affect cash**. A useful starting point in determining net cash provided by operating activities is to understand **why** net income must be converted. Under generally accepted accounting principles, most companies use the accrual basis of accounting. As you have learned, this basis requires that revenue be recorded when earned and that expenses be recorded when incurred. Earned revenues may include credit sales that have not been collected in cash and expenses incurred that may not have been paid in cash. Thus, under the accrual basis of accounting, net income does not indicate the net cash provided by operating activities. Therefore, under the indirect method, net income must be adjusted to convert certain items to the cash basis.

The indirect method (or reconciliation method) starts with net income and converts it to net cash provided by operating activities. In other words, **the indirect method adjusts net income for items that affected reported net income but did not affect cash**, as shown in Illustration 14-7. That is, noncash charges in the income statement are added back to net income and noncash credits are deducted to compute net cash provided by operating activities. A useful starting point in identifying the adjustments to net income is the current asset and current liability accounts other than cash. Those accounts—receivables, payables, prepayments, and inventories—should be analyzed for their effects on cash.

Helpful hint The presentation of the computation of net cash provided by operating activities by use of the indirect method explains the differences between the accrual based net income figure and the amount of cash generated by operations.

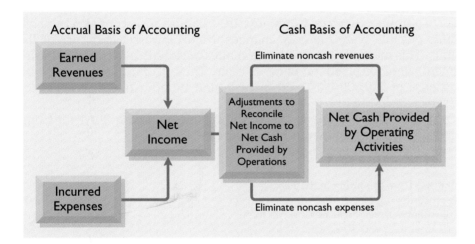

Illustration 14-7

Net income versus net cash provided by operating activities

Increase in Accounts Receivable. When accounts receivable increase during the year, revenues on an accrual basis are higher than revenues on a cash basis. In other words, operations of the period led to increased revenues, **but not all of these revenues resulted in an increase in cash**; some of the increase in revenues resulted in an increase in accounts receivable.

Illustration 14-8 shows that Computer Services Company had $85,000 in revenues, but it collected only $55,000 in cash. Therefore, to convert net income to net cash provided by operating activities, the increase of $30,000 in accounts receivable must be deducted from net income.

ACCOUNTS RECEIVABLE			
1/1/96	Balance	–0–	Receipts from customers 55,000
	Revenues	85,000	
12/31/96	Balance	30,000	

Illustration 14-8

Analysis of accounts receivable

Increase in Accounts Payable. In the first year, operating expenses incurred on account were credited to Accounts Payable. When accounts payable increase during the year, operating expenses on an accrual basis are higher than they are on a cash basis. For Computer Services, operating expenses reported in the income statement were $40,000. However, since Accounts Payable increased $4,000, only $36,000 ($40,000 − $4,000) of the expenses were paid in cash. To adjust net income to net cash provided by operating activities, the increase of $4,000 in accounts payable must be added to net income.

A T-account analysis also indicates that payments to creditors are less than operating expenses.

Illustration 14-9

Analysis of accounts payable

ACCOUNTS PAYABLE				
Payments to creditors	36,000	1/1/96	Balances	–0–
			Operating expenses	40,000
		12/31/96	Balance	4,000

For Computer Services Company, the changes in accounts receivable and accounts payable were the only changes in current asset and current liability accounts. This means that any other revenues or expenses reported in the income statement were received or paid in cash. Thus, Computer Services' income tax expense of $10,000 was paid in cash, and no adjustment of net income is necessary.

The operating activities section of the statement of cash flows for Computer Services Company is shown in Illustration 14-10.

Illustration 14-10

Presentation of net cash provided by operating activities, 1996—indirect method

Cash flows from operating activities		
Net income		$35,000
Adjustments to reconcile net income to net cash provided		
by operating activities:		
Increase in accounts receivable	$(30,000)	
Increase in accounts payable	4,000	(26,000)
Net cash provided by operating activities		$ 9,000

Determining Net Cash Provided/Used by Investing and Financing Activities (Step 3)

The third and final step in preparing the statement of cash flows begins with a study of the balance sheet to determine changes in noncurrent accounts. The changes in each noncurrent account are then analyzed using selected transaction data to determine the effect, if any, the changes had on cash.

In Computer Services Company, the three noncurrent accounts are Equipment, Common Stock, and Retained Earnings, and all three have increased during the year. What caused these increases? No transaction data are given for the increases in Equipment of $10,000 and Common Stock of $50,000. In solving your homework, you can conclude that **any unexplained differences in noncurrent accounts involve cash**. Thus, the increase in equipment is assumed to be a purchase of equipment for $10,000 cash. This purchase is reported as a cash outflow in the investing activities section. The increase in common stock is assumed to result from the issuance of common stock for $50,000 cash. It is reported as an inflow of cash in the financing activities section of the statement of cash flows.

The reasons for the net increase of $20,000 in the Retained Earnings account are determined by analysis. First, net income increased retained earnings by

$35,000. Second, the additional information provided below the income statement in Illustration 14-6 indicates that a cash dividend of $15,000 was declared and paid. The $35,000 increase due to net income is reported in the operating activities section. The cash dividend paid is reported in the financing activities section.

This analysis can also be made directly from the Retained Earnings account in the ledger of Computer Services Company as shown in Illustration 14-11:

RETAINED EARNINGS				
12/31/96 Cash dividend	15,000	1/1/96 Balance	–0–	
		12/31/96 Net income	35,000	
		12/31/96 Balance	20,000	

Illustration 14-11

Analysis of retained earnings

The $20,000 increase in Retained Earnings in 1996 is a **net** change. When a net change in a noncurrent balance sheet account has occurred during the year, it generally is necessary to report the causes of the net change separately in the statement of cash flows.

Statement of Cash Flows—1996

Having completed the three steps above, we can prepare the statement of cash flows. The statement starts with the operating activities section, followed by the investing activities section, and then the financing activities section. The 1996 statement of cash flows for Computer Services is shown in Illustration 14-12.

COMPUTER SERVICES COMPANY Statement of Cash Flows For the Year Ended December 31, 1996		
Cash flows from operating activities		
Net income		$35,000
Adjustments to reconcile net income to net cash provided by operating activities:		
Increase in accounts receivable	$(30,000)	
Increase in accounts payable	4,000	(26,000)
Net cash provided by operating activities		9,000
Cash flows from investing activities		
Purchase of equipment	(10,000)	
Net cash used by investing activities		(10,000)
Cash flows from financing activities		
Issuance of common stock	50,000	
Payment of cash dividends	(15,000)	
Net cash provided by financing activities		35,000
Net increase in cash		34,000
Cash at beginning of period		–0–
Cash at end of period		$34,000

Illustration 14-12

Statement of cash flows, 1996—indirect method

Computer Services' statement of cash flows for 1996 shows that operating activities **provided** $9,000 cash; investing activities **used** $10,000 cash; and financing activities **provided** $35,000 cash. The increase in cash of $34,000 reported in the statement of cash flows agrees with the increase of $34,000 shown as the change in the cash account in the comparative balance sheet.

Second Year of Operations—1997

Presented in Illustrations 14-13 and 14-14 is information related to the second year of operations for Computer Services Company.

Illustration 14-13

Comparative balance sheet, 1997, with increases and decreases

COMPUTER SERVICES COMPANY
Comparative Balance Sheet
December 31

Assets	1997	1996	Change Increase/Decrease
Cash	$ 56,000	$34,000	$ 22,000 Increase
Accounts receivable	20,000	30,000	10,000 Decrease
Prepaid expenses	4,000	–0–	4,000 Increase
Land	130,000	–0–	130,000 Increase
Building	160,000	–0–	160,000 Increase
Accumulated depreciation—building	(11,000)	–0–	11,000 Increase
Equipment	27,000	10,000	17,000 Increase
Accumulated depreciation—equipment	(3,000)	–0–	3,000 Increase
Total	$383,000	$74,000	
Liabilities and Stockholders' Equity			
Accounts payable	$ 59,000	$ 4,000	$ 55,000 Increase
Bonds payable	130,000	–0–	130,000 Increase
Common stock	50,000	50,000	–0–
Retained earnings	144,000	20,000	124,000 Increase
Total	$383,000	$74,000	

Illustration 14-14

Income statement and additional information, 1997

COMPUTER SERVICES COMPANY
Income Statement
For the Year Ended December 31, 1997

Revenues		$507,000
Operating expenses (excluding depreciation)	$261,000	
Depreciation expense	15,000	
Loss on sale of equipment	3,000	279,000
Income from operations		228,000
Income tax expense		89,000
Net income		$139,000

Additional information:
(a) In 1997, the company declared and paid a $15,000 cash dividend.
(b) The company obtained land through the issuance of $130,000 of long-term bonds.
(c) A building costing $160,000 was purchased for cash; equipment costing $25,000 was also purchased for cash.
(d) During 1997, the company sold equipment with a book value of $7,000 (cost $8,000, less accumulated depreciation $1,000) for $4,000 cash.

Determining the Net Increase/Decrease in Cash (Step 1)

To prepare a statement of cash flows from this information, the first step is to **determine the net increase or decrease in cash**. As indicated from the information presented, cash increased $22,000 ($56,000 − $34,000).

Determining Net Cash Provided/Used by Operating Activities (Step 2)

As in step 2 in 1996, net income on an accrual basis must be adjusted to arrive at net cash provided/used by operating activities. Explanations for the adjustments to net income for Computer Services in 1997 are as follows:

Decrease in Accounts Receivable. Accounts receivable decreases during the period because cash receipts are higher than revenues reported on an accrual basis. To adjust net income to net cash provided by operating activities, the decrease of $10,000 in accounts receivable must be added to net income.

Increase in Prepaid Expenses. Prepaid expenses increase during a period because cash paid for expenses is higher than expenses reported on an accrual basis. Cash payments have been made in the current period, but expenses (as charges to the income statement) have been deferred to future periods. To adjust net income to net cash provided by operating activities, the increase of $4,000 in prepaid expenses must be deducted from net income. An increase in prepaid expenses results in a decrease in cash during the period.

Increase in Accounts Payable. Like the increase in 1996, the 1997 increase of $55,000 in accounts payable must be added to net income to convert to net cash provided by operating activities.

Depreciation Expense. During 1997, Computer Services Company reported depreciation expense of $15,000. Of this amount, $11,000 related to the building and $4,000 to the equipment. These two amounts were determined by analyzing the accumulated depreciation accounts.

Increase in Accumulated Depreciation—Building. As shown in Illustration 14-13, accumulated depreciation increased $11,000. This change represents the depreciation expense on the building for the year. **Because depreciation expense is a noncash charge, it is added back to net income** in order to arrive at net cash provided by operating activities.

Increase in Accumulated Depreciation—Equipment. The increase in the Accumulated Depreciation—Equipment account was $3,000. This amount does not represent depreciation expense for the year because the additional information indicates that this account was decreased (debited $1,000) as a result of the sale of some equipment. Thus depreciation expense for 1997 was $4,000 ($3,000 + $1,000). This amount is added to net income to determine net cash provided by operating activities. The T-account below provides information about the changes that occurred in this account in 1997.

ACCUMULATED DEPRECIATION—EQUIPMENT			
Accumulated depreciation on equipment sold	1,000	1/1/97 Balance	–0–
		Depreciation expense	**4,000**
		12/31/97 Balance	3,000

Illustration 14-15

Analysis of accumulated depreciation—equipment

Depreciation expense on the building of $11,000 plus depreciation expense on the equipment of $4,000 equals the depreciation expense of $15,000 reported on the income statement.

Helpful hint Whether the indirect or direct method (Section 2) is used, net cash provided by operating activities will be the same.

Helpful hint **Decrease in accounts receivable:** Indicates that cash collections were greater than sales. **Increase in accounts receivable:** Indicates that sales were greater than cash collections. **Increase in prepaid expenses:** Indicates that the amount paid for the prepayments exceeded the amount that was recorded as an expense. **Decrease in prepaid expenses:** Indicates that the amount recorded as an expense exceeded the amount of cash paid for the prepayments. **Increase in accounts payable:** Indicates that expenses incurred exceed the cash paid for expenses that period.

Helpful hint Depreciation is similar to any other expense in that it reduces net income. It differs in that it does not involve a current cash outflow; that is why it must be added back to net income to arrive at cash provided by operations.

Other charges to expense that do not require the use of cash, such as the amortization of intangible assets and depletion expense, are treated in the same manner as depreciation. Depreciation and similar noncash charges are frequently listed in the statement of cash flows as the first adjustments to net income.

Loss on Sale of Equipment.   On the income statement, Computer Services Company reported a $3,000 loss on the sale of equipment (book value $7,000, less cash proceeds $4,000). The loss reduced net income but **did not reduce cash**. Thus the loss is **added to net income** in determining net cash provided by operating activities.[3]

As a result of the previous adjustments, net cash provided by operating activities is $218,000 as computed in Illustration 14-16.

Illustration 14-16

Presentation of net cash provided by operating activities, 1997—indirect method

Cash flows from operating activities		
Net income		$139,000
Adjustments to reconcile net income to net cash provided by operating activities:		
Depreciation expense	$15,000	
Loss on sale of equipment	3,000	
Decrease in accounts receivable	10,000	
Increase in prepaid expenses	(4,000)	
Increase in accounts payable	55,000	79,000
Net cash provided by operating activities		$218,000

Determining Net Cash Provided/Used by Investing and Financing Activities (Step 3)

Helpful hint   The investing and financing activities are measured and reported the same under both the direct and indirect method.

After finding net cash provided by operating activities, the next step involves analyzing the remaining changes in balance sheet accounts to determine net cash provided (used) by investing and financing activities.

Increase in Land.   As indicated from the change in the land account, land of $130,000 was purchased through the issuance of long-term bonds. Although the issuance of bonds payable for land has no effect on cash, it is a significant noncash investing and financing activity that merits disclosure. As indicated earlier, these activities are disclosed in a separate schedule at the bottom of the statement of cash flows.

Increase in Building.   As indicated in the additional data, an office building was acquired using cash of $160,000. This transaction is a cash outflow reported in the investing section.

Increase in Equipment.   The equipment account increased $17,000. Based on the additional information, this was a net increase that resulted from two transactions: (1) a purchase of equipment of $25,000 and (2) the sale of equipment costing $8,000 for $4,000. These transactions are classified as investing activities, and each transaction should be reported separately. Thus the purchase of equipment should be reported as an outflow of cash for $25,000 and the sale should

---

[3]If a gain on sale occurs, a different situation results. To allow a gain to flow through to net cash provided by operating activities would be double-counting the gain—once in net income and again in the investing activities section as part of the cash proceeds from sale. As a result, a gain is deducted from net income in reporting net cash provided by operating activities.

be reported as an inflow of cash for $4,000. The T-account below shows the reasons for the change in this account during the year.

Illustration 14-17

Analysis of equipment

EQUIPMENT			
1/1/97 Balance	10,000	Cost of equipment sold	8,000
Purchase of equipment	25,000		
12/31/97 Balance	27,000		

Increase in Bonds Payable. The bonds payable account increased $130,000. As shown in the additional information, land was acquired from the issuance of these bonds. As indicated earlier, this noncash transaction is reported in a separate schedule at the bottom of the statement.

Increase in Retained Earnings. Retained earnings increased $124,000 during the year. This increase can be explained by two factors: (1) net income of $139,000 increased retained earnings and (2) dividends of $15,000 decreased retained earnings. Net income is adjusted to net cash provided by operating activities in the operating activities section. Payment of the dividends is a **cash outflow that is reported as a financing activity**.

Helpful hint When stocks or bonds are issued for cash, it is the amount of the issuance price (proceeds) that will appear on the statement of cash flows as a financing inflow (rather than the amount of par value of the stocks or face value of bonds).

Helpful hint It is the **payment** of dividends, not the declaration, that appears on the cash flow statement.

Statement of Cash Flows—1997

Combining the previous items, we obtain a statement of cash flows for 1997 for Computer Services Company as presented in Illustration 14-18.

Illustration 14-18

Statement of cash flows, 1997—indirect method

COMPUTER SERVICES COMPANY Statement of Cash Flows For the Year Ended December 31, 1997		
Cash flows from operating activities		
Net income		$139,000
Adjustments to reconcile net income to net cash provided by operating activities:		
Depreciation expense	$ 15,000	
Loss on sale of equipment	3,000	
Decrease in accounts receivable	10,000	
Increase in prepaid expenses	(4,000)	
Increase in accounts payable	55,000	79,000
Net cash provided by operating activities		218,000
Cash flows from investing activities		
Purchase of building	$(160,000)	
Purchase of equipment	(25,000)	
Sale of equipment	4,000	
Net cash used by investing activities		(181,000)
Cash flows from financing activities		
Payment of cash dividends	(15,000)	
Net cash used by financing activities		(15,000)
Net increase in cash		22,000
Cash at beginning of period		34,000
Cash at end of period		$ 56,000
Noncash investing and financing activities		
Issuance of bonds payable to purchase land		$130,000

Helpful hint Note that in the investing and financing activities sections, positive numbers indicate cash inflows (receipts) and negative numbers indicate cash outflows (payments).

Summary of Conversion to Net Cash Provided by Operating Activities—Indirect Method

As shown in the previous illustrations, the statement of cash flows prepared by the indirect method starts with net income and adds (or deducts) items not affecting cash to arrive at net cash provided by operating activities. The additions and deductions consist of (1) changes in specific current assets and current liabilities and (2) noncash charges reported in the income statement. A summary of the adjustments for current assets and current liabilities is provided in Illustration 14-19.

Illustration 14-19

Adjustments for current assets and current liabilities

Current Assets and Current Liabilities	Adjustments to Convert Net Income to Net Cash Provided by Operating Activities	
	Add to Net Income	Deduct from Net Income
Accounts receivable	Decrease	Increase
Inventory	Decrease	Increase
Prepaid expenses	Decrease	Increase
Accounts payable	Increase	Decrease
Accrued expenses payable	Increase	Decrease

Adjustments for the noncash charges reported in the income statement are made as shown in Illustration 14-20.

Illustration 14-20

Adjustments for noncash charges

Noncash Charges	Adjustments to Convert Net Income to Net Cash Provided by Operating Activities
Depreciation expense	Add
Patent amortization expense	Add
Depletion expense	Add
Loss on sale of asset	Add

Analysis of the Statement of Cash Flows

The statement of cash flows provides information about a company's financial health that is not evident from analysis of the balance sheet or the income statement. Bankers, creditors, and other users of the statement of cash flows are as concerned with cash flow from operations as they are with net income because they are interested in a company's ability to pay its bills. Does accrual accounting conceal cash flow problems? What can be learned about Computer Services Company and its management from the statement of cash flows?

As with the balance sheet and the income statement, ratio analysis of the statement of cash flows can evaluate Computer Services Company's liquidity, profitability, and solvency. Three cash flow ratios that contribute to these evaluations are (a) the current cash debt coverage ratio, (b) the cash return on sales ratio, and (c) the cash debt coverage ratio. Each of these ratios uses net cash provided by operating activities as the numerator.

Current Cash Debt Coverage Ratio

A disadvantage of the current ratio is that it employs year-end balances of current asset and current liability accounts. These year-end balances may not be representative of what the company's current position was during most of the year. A ratio which partially corrects for this problem is the ratio of net cash provided by operating activities to average current liabilities, referred to as the current cash debt coverage ratio. Because it uses net cash provided by operating activities during the period, rather than a balance at a point in time, it may provide a better representation of **liquidity**. Using Computer Services Company 1997 financial data, the current cash debt coverage ratio is computed as follows:

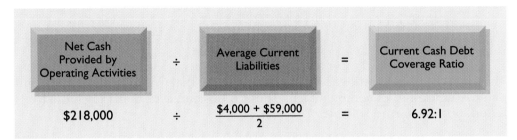

Illustration 14-21

Current Cash Debt Coverage Ratio

This ratio indicates that for every dollar of debt due during the year, $6.92 of cash was generated from operations to pay that debt.

Cash Return on Sales Ratio

In Chapter 6 you were introduced to three accrual based ratios measuring **profitability**: profit margin percentage, return on assets, and return on common stockholders' equity. The cash based ratio that is the counter-part of the profit margin percentage is the cash return on sales ratio (sometimes referred to as "cash flow margin"), computed by dividing net cash provided by operating activities by net sales. For Computer Services Company, this ratio is computed as follows:

Illustration 14-22

Cash Return on Sales Ratio

This ratio indicates the company's ability to turn sales into cash. A significant difference between the profit margin percentage and this ratio needs to be evaluated to assure that cash collection on sales and profit margin on sales over time are similar.

Cash Debt Coverage Ratio

In Chapter 6 we introduced the debt to total assets ratio as one measure of long-term **solvency**. The cash basis measure of solvency is the cash debt coverage ratio—the ratio of net cash provided by operating activities to average total liabilities. This ratio demonstrates a company's ability to repay its liabilities from net cash provided by operating activities, without having to liquidate the assets employed in its operations. Computer Services Company's cash debt coverage ratio is computed as follows:

Illustration 14-23

Cash Debt Coverage Ratio

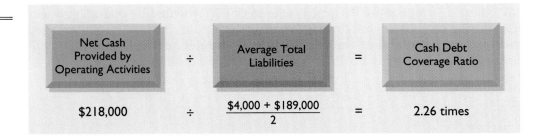

The three cash-based ratios illustrated above show that Computer Services Company is efficiently generating cash. These ratios indicate that the company is liquid, profitable, and solvent.

Before You Go On . . .

▸ *Review It*

1. What is the format of the operating activities section of the statement of cash flows using the indirect method?
2. Where is depreciation expense shown on a statement of cash flows using the indirect method?
3. Where are significant noncash investing and financing activities shown in a statement of cash flows? Give some examples.
4. What cash basis ratios may be prepared to evaluate liquidity, profitability, and solvency?

▸ *Do It*

Presented below is information related to Reynolds Company. Use it to prepare a statement of cash flows using the indirect method.

REYNOLDS COMPANY
Comparative Balance Sheet
December 31

Assets	1997	1996	Change Increase/Decrease
Cash	$ 54,000	$ 37,000	$ 17,000 Increase
Accounts receivable	68,000	26,000	42,000 Increase
Inventories	54,000	–0–	54,000 Increase
Prepaid expenses	4,000	6,000	2,000 Decrease
Land	45,000	70,000	25,000 Decrease
Buildings	200,000	200,000	–0–
Accumulated depreciation—buildings	(21,000)	(11,000)	10,000 Increase
Equipment	193,000	68,000	125,000 Increase
Accumulated depreciation—equipment	(28,000)	(10,000)	18,000 Increase
Totals	$569,000	$386,000	

Liabilities and Stockholders' Equity

Accounts payable	$ 23,000	$ 40,000	$ 17,000 Decrease
Accrued expenses payable	10,000	–0–	10,000 Increase
Bonds payable	110,000	150,000	40,000 Decrease
Common stock ($1 par)	220,000	60,000	160,000 Increase
Retained earnings	206,000	136,000	70,000 Increase
Totals	$569,000	$386,000	

REYNOLDS COMPANY
Income Statement
For the Year Ended December 31, 1997

Revenues		$890,000
Cost of goods sold	$465,000	
Operating expenses	221,000	
Interest expense	12,000	
Loss on sale of equipment	2,000	700,000
Income from operations		190,000
Income tax expense		65,000
Net income		$125,000

Additional information:

(a) Operating expenses include depreciation expense of $33,000 and charges from prepaid expenses of $2,000.

(b) Land was sold at its book value for cash.

(c) Cash dividends of $55,000 were declared and paid in 1997.

(d) Interest expense of $12,000 was paid in cash.

(e) Equipment with a cost of $166,000 was purchased for cash. Equipment with a cost of $41,000 and a book value of $36,000 was sold for $34,000 cash.

(f) Bonds of $10,000 were redeemed at their book value for cash; bonds of $30,000 were converted into common stock.

(g) Common stock ($1 par) of $130,000 was issued for cash.

(h) Accounts payable pertain to merchandise suppliers.

Reasoning: As you have learned, the balance sheet and the income statement are prepared from an adjusted trial balance of the general ledger. The statement of cash flows is prepared from an analysis of the content and changes in the balance sheet and the income statement.

Solution:

REYNOLDS COMPANY
Statement of Cash Flows
For the Year Ended December 31, 1997

Cash flows from operating activities			
Net income			$125,000
Adjustments to reconcile net income to net cash provided by operating activities:			
Depreciation expense		$ 33,000	
Increase in accounts receivable		(42,000)	
Increase in inventories		(54,000)	
Decrease in prepaid expenses		2,000	
Decrease in accounts payable		(17,000)	
Increase in accrued expenses payable		10,000	
Loss on sale of equipment		2,000	(66,000)
Net cash provided by operating activities			59,000
Cash flows from investing activities			
Sale of land		25,000	
Sale of equipment		34,000	
Purchase of equipment		(166,000)	
Net cash used by investing activities			(107,000)

Helpful hint To prepare the statement of cash flows:
1. Determine the net increase/decrease in cash.
2. Determine net cash provided/used by operating activities.
3. Determine net cash provided/used by investing and financing activities.
4. Operating activities generally relate to changes in current assets and current liabilities.
5. Investing activities generally relate to changes in non-current assets.
6. Financing activities generally relate to changes in non-current liabilities and stockholders' equity accounts.

Cash flows from financing activities		
Redemption of bonds	(10,000)	
Sale of common stock	130,000	
Payment of dividends	(55,000)	
Net cash provided by financing activities		65,000
Net increase in cash		17,000
Cash at beginning of period		37,000
Cash at end of period		$ 54,000
Noncash investing and financing activities		
Conversion of bonds into common stock		$ 30,000

Helpful hint You may wish to insert the beginning and ending cash balances and the increase/decrease in cash necessitated by these balances immediately into the statement of cash flows. The net increase/decrease is the target amount. The net cash flows from the three classes of activities must equal the target amount.

Related exercise material: BE14–1, BE14–2, BE14–4, E14–2, E14–3, E14–4, and E14–5.

Section 2 ▸ Statement of Cash Flows— Direct Method

To explain and illustrate the direct method, we will use the transactions of Juarez Company for two years, 1996 and 1997. Annual statements of cash flow will be prepared. Basic transactions will be used in the first year with additional transactions added in the second year.

First Year of Operations—1996

STUDY OBJECTIVE

· · · · · · · · · · 4 · · · · · · · · · ·

Prepare a statement of cash flows using the direct method.

Juarez Company began business on January 1, 1996, when it issued 300,000 shares of $1 par value common stock for $300,000 cash. The company rented office and sales space along with equipment. The comparative balance sheet at the beginning and end of 1996 and the changes in each account are shown in Illustration 14-24. The income statement and additional information for Juarez Company are shown in Illustration 14-25.

Illustration 14-24

Comparative balance sheet, 1996, with increases and decreases

JUAREZ COMPANY
Comparative Balance Sheet

Assets	Dec. 31, 1996	Jan. 1, 1996	Change Increase/Decrease
Cash	$159,000	$-0-	$159,000 Increase
Accounts receivable	15,000	-0-	15,000 Increase
Inventory	160,000	-0-	160,000 Increase
Prepaid expenses	8,000	-0-	8,000 Increase
Land	80,000	-0-	80,000 Increase
Total	$422,000	$-0-	
Liabilities and Stockholders' Equity			
Accounts payable	$ 60,000	$-0-	$ 60,000 Increase
Accrued expenses payable	20,000	-0-	20,000 Increase
Common stock	300,000	-0-	300,000 Increase
Retained earnings	42,000	-0-	42,000 Increase
Total	$422,000	$-0-	

Illustration 14-25

Income statement and additional information, 1996

JUAREZ COMPANY Income Statement For the Year Ended December 31, 1996	
Revenues from sales	$780,000
Cost of goods sold	450,000
Gross profit	330,000
Operating expenses	170,000
Income before income taxes	160,000
Income tax expense	48,000
Net income	$112,000

Additional information:
(a) Dividends of $70,000 were declared and paid in cash.
(b) The accounts payable increase resulted from the purchase of merchandise.

The three steps cited on page 622 for preparing the statement of cash flows are used in the direct method.

Determining the Net Increase/Decrease in Cash (Step 1)

The comparative balance sheet for Juarez Company shows a zero cash balance at January 1, 1996, and a cash balance of $159,000 at December 31, 1996. Thus, the change in cash for 1996 was a net increase of $159,000.

Determining the Net Cash Provided/Used by Operating Activities (Step 2)

Under the direct method, net cash provided by operating activities is computed by **adjusting each item in the income statement** from the accrual basis to the cash basis. To simplify and condense the operating activities section, **only major classes of operating cash receipts and cash payments are reported**. The difference between these major classes of cash receipts and cash payments is the net cash provided by operating activities as shown in Illustration 14-26.

    An efficient way to apply the direct method is to analyze the revenues and expenses reported in the income statement in the order in which they are listed. Cash receipts and cash payments related to these revenues and expenses are then determined. The direct method adjustments for Juarez Company in 1996 to determine net cash provided by operating activities are presented in the following sections.

Cash Receipts from Customers.   The income statement for Juarez Company reported revenues from customers of $780,000. To determine cash receipts from customers, it is necessary to consider the change in accounts receivable during the year. When accounts receivable increase during the year, revenues on an accrual basis are higher than cash receipts from customers. In other words, operations led to increased revenues, but not all of these revenues resulted in cash receipts. To determine the amount of cash receipts, the increase in accounts receivable is deducted from sales revenues. Conversely, a decrease in accounts receivable is added to sales revenues, because cash receipts from customers then exceed sales revenues.

Illustration 14-26

Major classes of cash receipts and payments

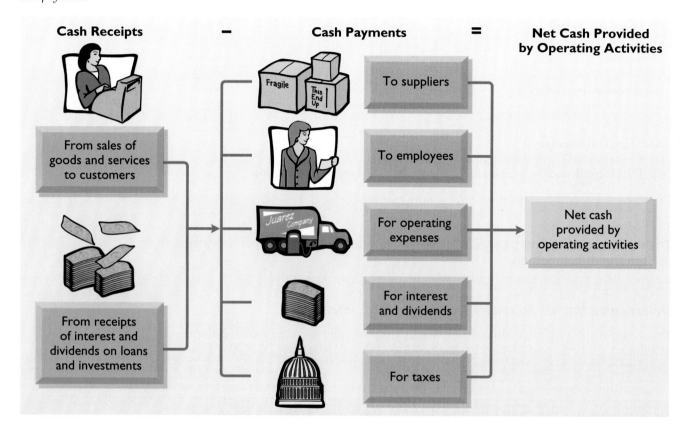

For Juarez Company, accounts receivable increased $15,000. Thus, cash receipts from customers were $765,000, computed as follows:

Illustration 14-27

Computation of cash receipts from customers

Revenues from sales	$780,000
Deduct: Increase in accounts receivable	15,000
Cash receipts from customers	**$765,000**

Cash receipts from customers may also be determined from an analysis of the Accounts Receivable account as shown in Illustration 14-28.

Illustration 14-28

Analysis of accounts receivable

ACCOUNTS RECEIVABLE				
1/1/96	Balance	–0–	**Receipts from customers**	**765,000**
	Revenues from sales	780,000		
12/31/96	Balance	15,000		

Helpful hint The T-account shows that revenue less increase in receivables equals cash receipts.

The relationships between cash receipts from customers, revenues from sales, and changes in accounts receivable are shown in Illustration 14-29.

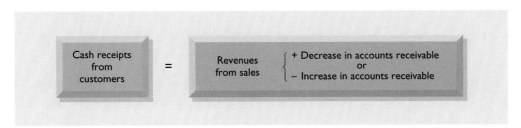

Illustration 14-29

Formula to compute cash receipts from customers—direct method

Cash Payments to Suppliers. Juarez Company reported cost of goods sold on its income statement of $450,000. To determine cash payments to suppliers, it is first necessary to find purchases for the year. To find purchases, cost of goods sold is adjusted for the change in inventory. When inventory increases during the year, it means that purchases this year exceed cost of goods sold. As a result, the increase in inventory is added to cost of goods sold to arrive at purchases.

In 1996, Juarez Company's inventory increased $160,000. Purchases, therefore, are computed as follows:

Cost of goods sold	$450,000
Add: Increase in inventory	160,000
Purchases	$610,000

Illustration 14-30

Computation of purchases

After purchases are computed, cash payments to suppliers are determined by adjusting purchases for the change in accounts payable. When accounts payable increase during the year, purchases on an accrual basis are higher than they are on a cash basis. As a result, an increase in accounts payable is deducted from purchases to arrive at cash payments to suppliers. Conversely, a decrease in accounts payable is added to purchases because cash payments to suppliers exceed purchases. Cash payments to suppliers were $550,000, computed as follows:

Purchases	$610,000
Deduct: Increase in accounts payable	60,000
Cash payments to suppliers	$550,000

Illustration 14-31

Computation of cash payments to suppliers

Cash payments to suppliers may also be determined from an analysis of the Accounts Payable account as shown in Illustration 14-32.

ACCOUNTS PAYABLE				
Payments to suppliers	550,000	1/1/96	Balance	–0–
			Purchases	610,000
		12/31/96	Balance	60,000

Illustration 14-32

Analysis of accounts payable

The relationship between cash payments to suppliers, cost of goods sold, changes in inventory, and changes in account payable is shown in the following formula:

Helpful hint The T-account shows that purchases less increase in accounts payable equals payments to suppliers.

Illustration 14-33

Formula to compute cash payments to suppliers— direct method

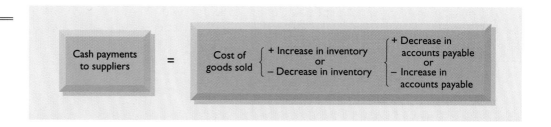

Cash Payments for Operating Expenses. Operating expenses of $170,000 were reported on Juarez's income statement. To determine the cash paid for operating expenses, this amount must be adjusted for any changes in prepaid expenses and accrued expenses payable. For example, when prepaid expenses increased $8,000 during the year, cash paid for operating expenses was $8,000 higher than operating expenses reported on the income statement. To convert operating expenses to cash payments for operating expenses, the increase of $8,000 must be added to operating expenses. Conversely, if prepaid expenses decrease during the year, the decrease must be deducted from operating expenses.

Operating expenses must also be adjusted for changes in accrued expenses payable. When accrued expenses payable increase during the year, operating expenses on an accrual basis are higher than they are in a cash basis. As a result, an increase in accrued expenses payable is deducted from operating expenses to arrive at cash payments for operating expenses. Conversely, a decrease in accrued expenses payable is added to operating expenses because cash payments exceed operating expenses.

Juarez Company's cash payments for operating expenses were $158,000, computed as follows:

Illustration 14-34

Computation of cash payments for operating expenses

Operating expenses	$170,000
Add: Increase in prepaid expenses	8,000
Deduct: Increase in accrued expenses payable	(20,000)
Cash payments for operating expenses	$158,000

The relationships among cash payments for operating expenses, changes in prepaid expenses, and changes in accrued expenses payable are shown in the following formula:

Illustration 14-35

Formula to compute cash payments for operating expenses—direct method

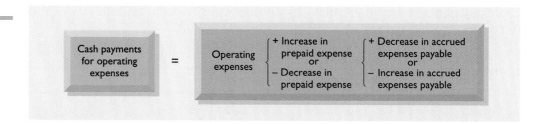

Cash Payments for Income Taxes. The income statement for Juarez shows income tax expense of $48,000. This amount equals the cash paid because the comparative balance sheet indicated no income taxes payable at either the beginning or end of the year.

All of the revenues and expenses in the 1996 income statement have now been adjusted to a cash basis. The operating activities section of the statement of cash flows is as follows:

Cash flows from operating activities		
Cash receipts from customers		$765,000
Cash payments:		
To suppliers	$550,000	
For operating expenses	158,000	
For income taxes	48,000	756,000
Net cash provided by operating activities		$ 9,000

Illustration 14-36

Operating activities section—direct method

Helpful hint Whether the direct or indirect method (Section 1) is used, net cash provided by operating activities will be the same.

Determining Net Cash Provided/Used by Investing and Financing Activities (Step 3)

Preparing the investing and financing activities sections of the statement of cash flows begins with a determination of the changes in noncurrent accounts reported in the comparative balance sheet. The change in each account is then analyzed using the additional information to determine the effect, if any, the change had on cash.

Helpful hint This is the same procedure used under the indirect method; the investing and financing activities are measured and reported the same under both methods.

Increase in Land. No additional information is given for the increase in land. In such case, you should assume that the increase affected cash. You should also make the same assumption in solving homework problems when the cause of a change in a noncurrent account is not explained. The purchase of land is an investing activity. Thus, an outflow of cash of $80,000 for the purchase of land should be reported in the investing activities section.

Increase in Common Stock. As indicated earlier, 300,000 shares of $1 par value stock were sold for $300,000 cash. The issuance of common stock is a financing activity. Thus, a cash inflow of $300,000 from the issuance of common stock is reported in the financing activities section.

Increase in Retained Earnings. For the Retained Earnings account, the reasons for the net increase of $42,000 are determined by analysis. First, net income increased retained earnings by $112,000. Second, the additional information section indicates that a cash dividend of $70,000 was declared and paid. The adjustment of revenues and expenses to arrive at net cash provided by operations was done in step 2 above. The cash dividend paid is reported as an outflow of cash in the financing activities section.

This analysis can also be made directly from the Retained Earnings account in the ledger of Juarez Company as shown in Illustration 14-37.

Helpful hint It is the **payment** of dividends, not the declaration, that appears on the cash flow statement.

RETAINED EARNINGS				
12/31/96	Cash dividend	70,000	1/1/96 Balance	–0–
			12/31/96 Net income	112,000
			12/31/96 Balance	42,000

Illustration 14-37

Analysis of retained earnings

The $42,000 increase in Retained Earnings in 1996 is a net change. When a net change in a noncurrent balance sheet account has occurred during the year, it generally is necessary to report the individual items that cause the net change.

Statement of Cash Flows—1996

The statement of cash flows can now be prepared. The operating activities section is reported first, followed by the investing and financing activities sections. The statement of cash flows for Juarez Company for 1996 is shown in Illustration 14-38.

Illustration 14-38

Statement of cash flows, 1996—direct method

Helpful hint Note that in the investing and financing activities sections, positive numbers indicate cash inflows (receipts) and negative numbers indicate cash outflows (payments).

JUAREZ COMPANY
Statement of Cash Flows
For the Year Ended December 31, 1996

Cash flows from operating activities		
Cash receipts from customers		$765,000
Cash payments:		
To suppliers	$550,000	
For operating expenses	158,000	
For income taxes	48,000	756,000
Net cash provided by operating activities		9,000
Cash flows from investing activities		
Purchase of land	(80,000)	
Net cash used by investing activities		(80,000)
Cash flows from financing activities		
Issuance of common stock	300,000	
Payment of cash dividend	(70,000)	
Net cash provided by financing activities		230,000
Net increase in cash		159,000
Cash at beginning of period		–0–
Cash at end of period		$159,000

The statement of cash flows shows that operating activities provided $9,000 of the net increase in cash of $159,000. Financing activities **provided** $230,000 of cash, and investing activities **used** $80,000 of cash. The net increase in cash for the year of $159,000 agrees with the increase in cash of $159,000 reported in the comparative balance sheet.

Second Year of Operations—1997

Illustration 14-39 and 14-40 present the comparative balance sheet, the income statement, and additional information pertaining to the second year of operations for Juarez Company.

JUAREZ COMPANY
Comparative Balance Sheet
December 31

Assets	1997	1996	Change Increase/Decrease
Cash	$191,000	$159,000	$ 32,000 Increase
Accounts receivable	12,000	15,000	3,000 Decrease
Inventory	130,000	160,000	30,000 Decrease
Prepaid expenses	6,000	8,000	2,000 Decrease
Land	180,000	80,000	100,000 Increase
Equipment	160,000	–0–	160,000 Increase
Accumulated depreciation—equipment	(16,000)	–0–	16,000 Increase
Total	$663,000	$422,000	
Liabilities and Stockholders' Equity			
Accounts payable	$ 52,000	$ 60,000	$ 8,000 Decrease
Accrued expenses payable	15,000	20,000	5,000 Decrease
Income taxes payable	12,000	–0–	12,000 Increase
Bonds payable	90,000	–0–	90,000 Increase
Common stock	400,000	300,000	100,000 Increase
Retained earnings	94,000	42,000	52,000 Increase
Total	$663,000	$422,000	

Illustration 14-40

Income statement and additional information, 1997

JUAREZ COMPANY
Income Statement
For the Year Ended December 31, 1997

Revenues from sales		$975,000
Cost of goods sold	$660,000	
Operating expenses (excluding depreciation)	176,000	
Depreciation expense	18,000	
Loss on sale of store equipment	1,000	855,000
Income before income taxes		120,000
Income tax expense		36,000
Net income		$ 84,000

Additional information:
(a) In 1997, the company declared and paid a $32,000 cash dividend.
(b) Bonds were issued at face value for $90,000 in cash.
(c) Equipment costing $180,000 was purchased for cash.
(d) Equipment costing $20,000 was sold for $17,000 cash when the book value of the equipment was $18,000.
(e) Common stock of $100,000 was issued to acquire land.

Determining the Net Increase/Decrease in Cash (Step 1)

The comparative balance sheet shows a beginning cash balance of $159,000 and an ending cash balance of $191,000. Thus, there was a net increase in cash in 1997 of $32,000.

Determining Net Cash Provided/Used in Operating Activities (Step 2)

Cash Receipts from Customers. Revenues from sales were $975,000. Since accounts receivable decreased $3,000, cash receipts from customers were greater than sales revenues. Cash receipts from customers were $978,000, computed as follows:

Illustration 14-41

Computation of cash receipts from customers

Revenues from sales	$975,000
Add: Decrease in accounts receivable	3,000
Cash receipts from customers	**$978,000**

Cash Payments to Suppliers.   The conversion of cost of goods sold to purchases and purchases to cash payments to suppliers is similar to the computations made in 1996. For 1997, purchases are computed using cost of goods sold of $660,000 from the income statement and the decrease in inventory of $30,000 from the comparative balance sheet. Purchases are then adjusted by the decrease in accounts payable of $8,000. Cash payments to suppliers were $638,000, computed as follows:

Illustration 14-42

Computation of cash payments to suppliers

Cost of goods sold	$660,000
Deduct: Decrease in inventory	30,000
Purchases	630,000
Add: Decrease in accounts payable	8,000
Cash payments to suppliers	**$638,000**

Cash Payments for Operating Expenses.   Operating expenses (exclusive of depreciation expense) for 1997 were reported at $176,000. This amount is then adjusted for changes in prepaid expenses and accrued expenses payable to arrive at cash payments for operating expenses.

As indicated from the comparative balance sheet, prepaid expenses decreased $2,000 during the year. This means that $2,000 was allocated to operating expenses (thereby increasing operating expenses), but cash payments did not increase by that $2,000. To arrive at cash payments for operating expenses, the decrease in prepaid expenses is deducted from operating expenses.

Accrued operating expenses decreased $5,000 during the period. As a result, cash payments were higher by $5,000 than the amount reported for operating expenses. The decrease in accrued expenses payable is added to operating expenses. Cash payments for operating expenses were $179,000, computed as follows:

Illustration 14-43

Computation of cash payments for operating expenses

Operating expenses, exclusive of depreciation	$176,000
Deduct: Decrease in prepaid expenses	(2,000)
Add: Decrease in accrued expenses payable	5,000
Cash payments for operating expenses	**$179,000**

Depreciation Expense and Loss on Sale of Equipment.   Operating expenses are shown exclusive of depreciation. Depreciation expense in 1997 was $18,000. Depreciation expense is not shown on a statement of cash flows because it is a noncash charge. If the amount for operating expenses includes depreciation expense, operating expenses must be reduced by the amount of depreciation to determine cash payments for operating expenses.

The loss on sale of equipment of $1,000 is also a noncash charge. The loss on sale of equipment reduces net income, but it does not reduce cash. Thus, the loss on sale of equipment is not reported on a statement of cash flows.

Other charges to expense that do not require the use of cash, such as the amortization of intangible assets and depletion expense, are treated in the same manner as depreciation.

Cash Payments for Income Taxes. Income tax expense reported on the income statement was $36,000. Income taxes payable, however, increased $12,000 which means that $12,000 of the income taxes have not been paid. As a result, income taxes paid were less than income taxes reported on the income statement. Cash payments for income taxes were, therefore, $24,000 as shown below.

Income tax expense	$36,000
Deduct: Increase in income taxes payable	12,000
Cash payments for income taxes	**$24,000**

Illustration 14-44

Computation of cash payments for income taxes

The relationships of cash payments for income taxes, income tax expense, and changes in income taxes payable are shown in the following formula:

Illustration 14-45

Formula to compute cash payments for income taxes—direct method

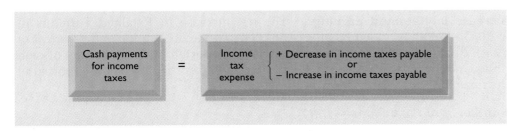

Determining Net Cash Provided/Used by Investing and Financing Activities (Step 3)

Increase in Land. Land increased $100,000. The additional information section indicates that common stock was issued to purchase the land. Although the issuance of common stock for land has no effect on cash, it is a **significant noncash investing and financing transaction**. This transaction requires disclosure in a separate schedule at the bottom of the statement of cash flows.

Increase in Equipment. The comparative balance sheet shows that equipment increased $160,000 in 1997. The additional information in Illustration 14-40 indicates that the increase resulted from two investing transactions: (1) equipment costing $180,000 was purchased for cash, and (2) equipment costing $20,000 was sold for $17,000 cash when its book value was $18,000. The relevant data for the statement of cash flows is the cash paid for the purchase and the cash proceeds from the sale. For Juarez Company, the investing activities section will show: Purchase of equipment $180,000, as an outflow of cash; and sale of equipment $17,000, as an inflow of cash. The two amounts **should not be netted** because one is an outflow of cash and the other is an inflow of cash; **both flows should be shown**.

The analysis of the changes in equipment should include the related Accumulated Depreciation account. These two accounts for Juarez Company are shown in Illustration 14-46.

EQUIPMENT					
1/1/97	Balance	–0–	Cost of equipment sold		20,000
	Cash purchase	180,000			
12/31/97	Balance	160,000			

ACCUMULATED DEPRECIATION—EQUIPMENT					
Sale of equipment	2,000	1/1/97	Balance	–0–	
			Depreciation expense	18,000	
		12/31/97	Balance	16,000	

Increase in Bonds Payable. Bonds Payable increased $90,000. The additional information in Illustration 14-40 indicates that bonds with a face value of $90,000 were issued for $90,000 cash. The issuance of bonds is a financing activity. For Juarez Company, there is an inflow of cash of $90,000 from the issuance of bonds.

Increase in Common Stock. The Common Stock account increased $100,000. As indicated from the additional information, land was acquired from the issuance of common stock. This transaction is a **significant noncash investing and financing transaction** that should be reported in a separate schedule at the bottom of the statement.

Increase in Retained Earnings. The net increase in Retained Earnings of $52,000 resulted from net income of $84,000 and the declaration and payment of a cash dividend of $32,000. **Net income is not reported in the statement of cash flows under the direct method.** Cash dividends paid of $32,000 are reported in the financing activities section as an outflow of cash.

Statement of Cash Flows—1997

The statement of cash flows for Juarez Company is shown in Illustration 14-47.

Illustration 14-47

Statement of cash flows, 1997—direct method

JUAREZ COMPANY			
Statement of Cash Flows			
For the Year Ended December 31, 1997			
Cash flows from operating activities			
Cash receipts from customers			$978,000
Cash payments:			
To suppliers		$638,000	
For operating expenses		179,000	
For income taxes		24,000	841,000
Net cash provided by operating activities			137,000
Cash flows from investing activities			
Purchase of equipment		(180,000)	
Sale of equipment		17,000	
Net cash used by investing activities			(163,000)
Cash flows from financing activities			
Issuance of bonds payable		90,000	
Payment of cash dividends		(32,000)	
Net cash provided by financing activities			58,000
Net increase in cash			32,000
Cash at beginning of period			159,000
Cash at end of period			$191,000
Noncash investing and financing activities			
Issuance of common stock to purchase land			$100,000

Analysis of the Statement of Cash Flows

The statement of cash flows provides information about a company's financial health that is not evident from analysis of the balance sheet or the income statement. Bankers, creditors, and other users of the statement of cash flows are as concerned with cash flow from operations as they are with net income because they are interested in a company's ability to pay its bills. Does accrual accounting conceal cash flow problems? What can be learned about Juarez Company and its management from the statement of cash flows?

As with the balance sheet and the income statement, ratio analysis of the statement of cash flows can evaluate Juarez Company's liquidity, profitability, and solvency. Three cash flow ratios that contribute to these evaluations are (a) the current cash debt coverage ratio, (b) the cash return on sales ratio, and (c) the cash debt coverage ratio. Each of these ratios uses net cash provided by operating activities as the numerator.

Current Cash Debt Coverage Ratio

A disadvantage of the current ratio is that it employs year-end balances of current asset and current liability accounts. These year-end balances may not be representative of what the company's current position was during most of the year. A ratio which partially corrects for this problem is the ratio of net cash provided by operating activities to average current liabilities, referred to as the current cash debt coverage ratio. Because it uses net cash provided by operating activities during the period, rather than a balance at a point in time, it may provide a better representation of **liquidity**. Using Juarez Company 1997 financial data, the current cash debt coverage ratio is computed as follows:

Illustration 14-48

Current Cash Debt Coverage Ratio

This ratio indicates that for every dollar of debt due during the year, $1.72 of cash was generated from operations to pay that debt.

Cash Return on Sales Ratio

In Chapter 6 you were introduced to three accrual based ratios measuring **profitability**: profit margin percentage, return on assets, and return on common stockholders' equity. The cash based ratio that is the counter-part of the profit margin percentage is the cash return on sales ratio (sometimes referred to as "cash flow margin"), computed by dividing net cash provided by operating activities by net sales. For Juarez Company, this ratio is computed as follows:

Illustration 14-49

Cash Return on Sales Ratio

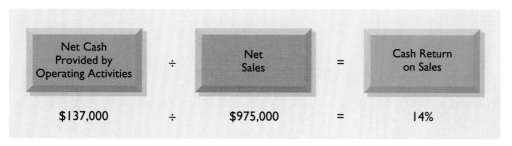

This ratio indicates the company's ability to turn sales into cash. A significant difference between the profit margin percentage and this ratio needs to be evaluated to assure that cash collection on sales and profit margin on sales over time are similar.

Cash Debt Coverage Ratio

In Chapter 6 we introduced the debt to total assets ratio as one measure of long-term **solvency**. The cash basis measure of solvency is the cash debt coverage ratio—the ratio of net cash provided by operating activities to average total liabilities. This ratio demonstrates a company's ability to repay its liabilities from net cash provided by operating activities, without having to liquidate the assets employed in its operations. Juarez Company's cash debt coverage ratio is computed as follows:

Illustration 14-50

Cash Debt Coverage Ratio

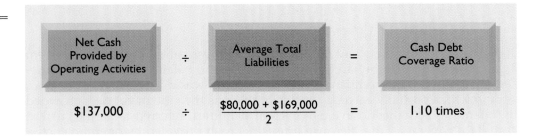

The three cash-based ratios illustrated above show that Juarez Company is efficiently generating cash. These ratios indicate that the company is liquid, profitable, and solvent.

Before You Go On . . .

▸ *Review It*

1. What is the format of the operating activities section of the statement of cash flows using the direct method?
2. Where is depreciation expense shown on a statement of cash flows using the direct method?
3. Where are significant noncash investing and financing activities shown on a statement of cash flows? Give some examples.
4. What cash basis ratios may be prepared to evaluate liquidity, profitability, and solvency?

▸ *Do It*

Presented below is information related to Reynolds Company. Use it to prepare a statement of cash flows using the direct method.

REYNOLDS COMPANY
Comparative Balance Sheet
December 31

Assets	1997	1996	Change Increase/Decrease
Cash	$ 54,000	$ 37,000	$ 17,000 Increase
Accounts receivable	68,000	26,000	42,000 Increase
Inventories	54,000	–0–	54,000 Increase
Prepaid expenses	4,000	6,000	2,000 Decrease

Land	45,000	70,000	25,000 Decrease
Buildings	200,000	200,000	–0–
Accumulated depreciation—buildings	(21,000)	(11,000)	10,000 Increase
Equipment	193,000	68,000	125,000 Increase
Accumulated depreciation—equipment	(28,000)	(10,000)	18,000 Increase
Totals	$569,000	$386,000	

Liabilities and Stockholders' Equity

Accounts payable	$ 23,000	$ 40,000	$ 17,000 Decrease
Accrued expenses payable	10,000	–0–	10,000 Increase
Bonds payable	110,000	150,000	40,000 Decrease
Common stock ($1 par)	220,000	60,000	160,000 Increase
Retained earnings	206,000	136,000	70,000 Increase
Totals	$569,000	$386,000	

REYNOLDS COMPANY
Income Statement
For the Year Ended December 31, 1997

Revenues		$890,000
Cost of goods sold	$465,000	
Operating expenses	221,000	
Interest expense	12,000	
Loss on sale of equipment	2,000	700,000
Income from operations		190,000
Income tax expense		65,000
Net income		$125,000

Additional information:

(a) Operating expenses include depreciation expense of $33,000 and charges from prepaid expenses of $2,000.

(b) Land was sold at its book value for cash.

(c) Cash dividends of $55,000 were declared and paid in 1997.

(d) Interest expense of $12,000 was paid in cash.

(e) Equipment with a cost of $166,000 was purchased for cash. Equipment with a cost of $41,000 and a book value of $36,000 was sold for $34,000 cash.

(f) Bonds of $10,000 were redeemed at their book value for cash; bonds of $30,000 were converted into common stock.

(g) Common stock ($1 par) of $130,000 was issued for cash.

(h) Accounts payable pertain to merchandise suppliers.

Reasoning: The indirect and the direct methods differ primarily in their presentation of the cash flows from the operating activities. The direct method reports cash receipts less cash payments to arrive at net cash provided by operating activities.

Solution:

REYNOLDS COMPANY
Statement of Cash Flows
For the Year Ended December 31, 1997

Cash flows from operating activities		
Cash receipts from customers		$848,000ª
Cash payments:		
To suppliers	$536,000ᵇ	
For operating expenses	176,000ᶜ	
For interest expense	12,000	
For income taxes	65,000	789,000
Net cash provided by operating activities		59,000

Helpful hint To prepare the statement of cash flows:

1. Determine the net increase/decrease in cash.

2. Determine net cash provided/used by operating activities.

3. Determine net cash provided/used by investing and financing activities.

4. Operating activities generally relate to changes in
current assets and current
liabilities.
5. Investing activities generally
relate to changes in non-
current assets.
6. Financing activities generally
relate to changes in non-
current liabilities and stockholders' equity accounts.

Cash flows from investing activities			
Sale of land		25,000	
Sale of equipment		34,000	
Purchase of equipment		(166,000)	
Net cash used by investing activities			(107,000)
Cash flows from financing activities			
Redemption of bonds		(10,000)	
Sale of common stock		130,000	
Payment of dividends		(55,000)	
Net cash provided by financing activities			65,000
Net increase in cash			17,000
Cash at beginning of period			37,000
Cash at end of period			$ 54,000
Noncash investing and financing activities			
Conversion of bonds into common stock			$ 30,000

Computations:
ª$848,000 = $890,000 − $42,000
ᵇ$536,000 = $465,000 + $54,000 + $17,000
ᶜ$176,000 = $221,000 − $33,000 − $2,000 − $10,000
Technically, an additional schedule reconciling net income to net cash provided by
operating activities should be presented as part of the statement of cash flows when using
the direct method.

Related exercise material: BE14–6, BE14–7, BE14–8, E14–7, E14–8, E14–9, and E14–10.

▸ A Look Back at Kilian Community College

Refer to the opening story of Gerald Biby's attempt to refinance Kilian Community College's mortgage, and answer the following questions:

1. How was the purchase of the $250,000 computer system presented on the "traditional
   educational institution financial statement" so that it negatively affected Biby's ability
   to refinance the mortgage?
2. How was the purchase of the $250,000 computer system presented on the statement
   of cash flows? How did the preparation of the statement of cash flows aid Biby in
   securing the refinancing of the mortgage?

Solution:

1. A traditional financial statement for a not-for-profit, educational institution reports
   receipts as revenues and expenses all expenditures, even capital expenditures such
   as the $250,000 computer system. That is, the traditional financial statement reported
   the entire $250,000 as an expense in one year, making it look like the college was just
   breaking even.
2. When the computer purchase was classified as an investing activity, the statement of
   cash flows showed the bankers that one of the uses of funds was really the purchase
   of computer equipment that had several years of life. In addition, the bankers noted
   from the statement of cash flows "that the college's sources of funds exceeded the
   loan repayments, including principal and interest, by a ratio of 3-to-1."

◣ Summary of Study Objectives

1. *Indicate the primary purpose of the statement of cash
flows.* The primary purpose of the statement of cash flows
is to provide information about the cash receipts and cash
payments of an entity during a period. A secondary objective is to provide information about the operating, investing,
and financing activities of the entity during the period.

2. *Distinguish among operating, investing, and financing activities.* Operating activities include the cash effects of transactions that enter into the determination of net income. Investing activities involve cash flows resulting from changes in investments and long-term asset items. Financing activities involve cash flows resulting from changes in long-term liability and stockholders' equity items.

3. *Prepare a statement of cash flows using the indirect method.* The preparation of a statement of cash flows involves three major steps: (1) determine the net increase or decrease in cash; (2) determine net cash provided (used) by operating activities; and (3) determine net cash flows pro-

vided (used) by investing and financing activities. Under the indirect method, accrual basis net income is adjusted to net cash provided by operating activities.

4. *Prepare a statement of cash flows using the direct method.* The preparation of the statement of cash flows involves three major steps: (1) determine the net increase or decrease in cash; (2) determine net cash provided (used) by operating activities; and (3) determine net cash flows provided (used) by investing and financing activities. The direct method reports cash receipts less cash payments to arrive at net cash provided by operating activities.

▼ ◢APPENDIX ► *Using a Work Sheet for Preparing the Statement of Cash Flows—Indirect Method*

When numerous adjustments of net income are necessary, **a work sheet is often used to assemble and classify the data that will appear on the statement of cash flows.** The work sheet is merely a device that aids in the preparation of the statement; its use is optional. The skeleton format of the work sheet for preparation of the statement of cash flows is shown in Illustration 14A-1.

STUDY OBJECTIVE

•••••••••▼5••••••••••

After studying this appendix, you should be able to:

5. Explain the guidelines and procedural steps in using a work sheet to prepare the statement of cash flows.

XYZ COMPANY
Work Sheet
Statement of Cash Flows
For the Year Ended . . .

Balance Sheet Accounts	End of Last Year Balances	Reconciling Items		End of Current Year Balances
		Debits	Credits	
Debit balance accounts	XX	XX	XX	XX
	XX	XX	XX	XX
Totals	XXX			XXX
Credit balance accounts	XX	XX	XX	XX
	XX	XX	XX	XX
Totals	XXX			XXX
Statement of Cash Flows Effects				
Operating activities				
Net income		XX		
Adjustments		XX	XX	
Investing activities				
Receipts and payments		XX	XX	
Financing activities				
Receipts and payments		XX	XX	
Totals		XXX	XXX	
Increase (decrease) in cash		(XX)	XX	
Totals		XXX	XXX	

Illustration 14A-1

Format of work sheet

The following guidelines are important in using a work sheet:

1. In the balance sheet accounts section, **accounts with debit balances are listed separately from those with credit balances**. This means, for example, that Accumulated Depreciation is listed under credit balances and not as a contra account under debit balances. The beginning and ending balances of each account are entered in the appropriate columns. The transactions that caused the change in the account balance during the year are entered as reconciling items in the two middle columns. After all reconciling items have been entered, each line pertaining to a balance sheet account should "foot across." That is, the beginning balance plus or minus the reconciling item(s) must equal the ending balance. When this agreement exists for all balance sheet accounts, all changes in account balances have been reconciled.

2. The bottom portion of the work sheet consists of the operating, investing, and financing activities sections. Accordingly, it provides the information necessary to prepare the formal statement of cash flows. **Inflows of cash are entered as debits in the reconciling columns, and outflows of cash are entered as credits in the reconciling columns.** Thus, in this section, the sale of equipment for cash at book value is entered as a debit under investing activities. Similarly, the purchase of land for cash is entered as a credit under investing activities.

3. **The reconciling items shown in the work sheet are not entered in any journal or posted to any account.** They do not represent either adjustments or corrections of the balance sheet accounts. They are used only to facilitate the preparation of the statement of cash flows.

▶ Preparing the Work Sheet

As in the case of work sheets illustrated in earlier chapters, the preparation of a work sheet involves a series of prescribed steps. The steps in this case are:

1. Enter in the balance sheet accounts section the balance sheet accounts and their beginning and ending balances.
2. Enter in the reconciling columns of the work sheet the data that explain the changes in the balance sheet accounts other than cash and their effects on the statement of cash flows.
3. Enter on the cash line and at the bottom of the work sheet the increase or decrease in cash. This entry should enable the totals of the reconciling columns to be in agreement.

To illustrate the preparation of a work sheet, we will use the 1997 data for Computer Services Company. Your familiarity with these data should help you understand the use of a work sheet. For ease of reference, the comparative balance sheets, income statement, and selected data for 1997 are presented in Illustrations 14A-2 and 14A-3.

Illustration 14A-2

Comparative balance sheet, 1997, with increases and decreases

COMPUTER SERVICES COMPANY
Comparative Balance Sheet
December 31

Assets	1997	1996	Change Increase/Decrease
Cash	$ 56,000	$34,000	$ 22,000 Increase
Accounts receivable	20,000	30,000	10,000 Decrease
Prepaid expenses	4,000	–0–	4,000 Increase
Land	130,000	–0–	130,000 Increase
Building	160,000	–0–	160,000 Increase
Accumulated depreciation—building	(11,000)	–0–	11,000 Increase
Equipment	27,000	10,000	17,000 Increase
Accumulated depreciation—equipment	(3,000)	–0–	3,000 Increase
Totals	$383,000	$74,000	
Liabilities and Stockholders' Equity			
Accounts payable	$ 59,000	$ 4,000	55,000 Increase
Bonds payable	130,000	–0–	130,000 Increase
Common stock	50,000	50,000	–0–
Retained earnings	144,000	20,000	124,000 Increase
Totals	$383,000	$74,000	

Illustration 14A-3

Income statement and additional information, 1997

COMPUTER SERVICES COMPANY
Income Statement
For the Year Ended December 31, 1997

Revenues		$507,000
Operating expenses (excluding depreciation)	$261,000	
Depreciation expense	15,000	
Loss on sale of equipment	3,000	279,000
Income from operations		228,000
Income tax expense		89,000
Net income		$139,000

Additional information:
(a) In 1997, the company declared and paid a $15,000 cash dividend.
(b) The company obtained land through the issuance of $130,000 of long-term bonds.
(c) A building costing $160,000 was purchased for cash; equipment costing $25,000 was also purchased for cash.
(d) During 1997, the company sold equipment with a book value of $7,000 (cost $8,000, less accumulated depreciation $1,000) for $4,000 cash.

Determining the Reconciling Items

Several approaches may be used to determine the reconciling items. For example, the changes affecting net cash provided by operating activities could be completed first and then the effects of financing and investing transactions could be determined. Alternatively, the balance sheet accounts can be analyzed in the order in which they are listed on the work sheet. We will follow this latter approach for Computer Services, except for cash. As indicated above, **cash is handled last**.

Accounts Receivable. The decrease of $10,000 in accounts receivable means that cash collections from revenues are higher than the revenues reported in the income statement. To convert net income to net cash provided by operating activities, the decrease of $10,000 is added to net income. The entry in the reconciling columns of the work sheet is:

(a)	Operating—Decrease in Accounts Receivable	10,000	
	Accounts Receivable		10,000

Prepaid Expenses. An increase of $4,000 in prepaid expenses means that expenses deducted in determining net income are less than expenses that were paid in cash. Thus, the increase of $4,000 must be deducted from net income in determining net cash provided by operating activities. The work sheet entry is:

(b)	Prepaid Expenses	4,000	
	Operating—Increase in Prepaid Expenses		4,000

Helpful hint These amounts are asterisked in the work sheet to indicate that they result from a significant noncash transaction.

Land. The increase in land of $130,000 resulted from a purchase through the issuance of long-term bonds. This transaction should be reported as a significant noncash investing and financing activity. The work sheet entry is:

(c)	Land	130,000	
	Bonds Payable		130,000

Building. The cash purchase of a building for $160,000 is an investing activity cash outflow. The entry in the reconciling columns of the work sheet is:

(d)	Building	160,000	
	Investing—Purchase of Building		160,000

Equipment. The increase in equipment of $17,000 resulted from a cash purchase of $25,000 and the sale of equipment costing $8,000. The book value of the equipment was $7,000, the cash proceeds were $4,000, and a loss of $3,000 was recorded. The work sheet entries are:

(e)	Equipment	25,000	
	Investing—Purchase of Equipment		25,000

(f)	Investing—Sale of Equipment	4,000	
	Operating—Loss on Sale of Equipment	3,000	
	Accumulated Depreciation—Equipment	1,000	
	Equipment		8,000

Accounts Payable. The increase of $55,000 in accounts payable must be added to net income to obtain net cash provided by operating activities. The following work sheet entry is made:

(g)	Operating—Increase in Accounts Payable	55,000	
	Accounts Payable		55,000

Bonds Payable. The increase of $130,000 in this account resulted from the issuance of bonds for land. This is a significant noncash investing and financing activity. Work sheet entry (c) above is the only entry necessary.

Accumulated Depreciation—Building and Accumulated Depreciation—Equipment. The increases in these accounts of $11,000 and $4,000, respectively, resulted from depreciation expense. Depreciation expense is a **noncash charge that must be added to net income** in determining net cash provided by operating activities. The work sheet entries are:

(h)	Operating—Depreciation Expense—Building	11,000	
	Accumulated Depreciation—Building		11,000
(i)	Operating—Depreciation Expense—Equipment	4,000	
	Accumulated Depreciation—Equipment		4,000

Retained Earnings. The $124,000 increase in retained earnings resulted from net income of $139,000 and the declaration of a $15,000 cash dividend that was paid in 1997. Net income is included in net cash provided by operating activities and the dividends are a financing activity cash outflow. The entries in the reconciling columns of the work sheet are:

(j)	Operating—Net Income	139,000	
	Retained Earnings		139,000
(k)	Retained Earnings	15,000	
	Financing—Payment of Dividends		15,000

Disposition of Change in Cash. The firm's cash increased $22,000 in 1997. The final entry on the work sheet, therefore, is:

(l)	Cash	22,000	
	Increase in cash		22,000

As shown in the work sheet, the increase in cash is entered in the reconciling credit column as a **balancing** amount. This entry should complete the reconciliation of the changes in the balance sheet accounts. In addition, it should permit the totals of the reconciling columns to be in agreement. When all changes have been explained and the reconciling columns are in agreement, the reconciling columns are ruled to complete the work sheet. The completed work sheet for Computer Services Company is shown in Illustration 14A-4.

Preparing the Statement

The statement of cash flows is prepared primarily from the data that appear in the work sheet under Statement of Cash Flows Effects. The reconciling columns should also be scanned for any asterisked items that designate significant noncash activities. The formal statement was shown in Illustration 14-18.

Illustration 14A-4

Completed work sheet—
indirect method

COMPUTER SERVICES COMPANY
Work Sheet
Statement of Cash Flows
For the Year Ended December 31, 1997

Balance Sheet Accounts	Balance 12/31/96	Reconciling Items Debit	Reconciling Items Credit	Balance 12/31/97
Debits				
Cash	34,000	(l) 22,000		56,000
Accounts receivable	30,000		(a) 10,000	20,000
Prepaid expenses	–0–	(b) 4,000		4,000
Land	–0–	(c) 130,000*		130,000
Building	–0–	(d) 160,000		160,000
Equipment	10,000	(e) 25,000	(f) 8,000	27,000
Total	74,000			397,000
Credits				
Accounts payable	4,000		(g) 55,000	59,000
Bonds payable	–0–		(c) 130,000*	130,000
Accumulated depreciation—building	–0–		(h) 11,000	11,000
Accumulated depreciation—equipment	–0–	(f) 1,000	(i) 4,000	3,000
Common stock	50,000			50,000
Retained earnings	20,000	(k) 15,000	(j) 139,000	144,000
Total	74,000			397,000
Statement of Cash Flows Effects				
Operating activities				
Net income		(j) 139,000		
Decrease in accounts receivable		(a) 10,000		
Increase in prepaid expenses			(b) 4,000	
Increase in accounts payable		(g) 55,000		
Depreciation expense—building		(h) 11,000		
Depreciation expense—equipment		(i) 4,000		
Loss on sale of equipment		(f) 3,000		
Investing activities				
Purchase of building			(d) 160,000	
Purchase of equipment			(e) 25,000	
Sale of equipment		(f) 4,000		
Financing activities				
Payment of dividends			(k) 15,000	
Totals		583,000	561,000	
Increase in cash			(l) 22,000	
Totals		583,000	583,000	

*Significant noncash investing and financing activity.

Summary of Study Objective for Chapter 14 Appendix

5. *Explain the guidelines and procedural steps in using a* *work sheet to prepare the statement of cash flows.* When there are numerous adjustments, a work sheet can be a help-ful tool in preparing the statement of cash flows. Key guide-lines for using a work sheet are: (1) list accounts with debit balances separately from those with credit balances; (2) in the reconciling columns in the bottom portion of the work sheet, show cash inflows as debits and cash outflows as credits; (3) do not enter reconciling items in any journal or account but use them only to help prepare the statement of cash flows.

The steps in preparing the work sheet are: (1) enter beginning and ending balances of balance sheet accounts; (2) enter debits and credits in reconciling columns; (3) enter the increase or decrease in cash in two places as a balancing amount.

GLOSSARY

Cash debt coverage ratio   A cash basis ratio used to evaluate solvency by dividing net cash provided by operating activities by average total liabilities. (pp. 634 and 648)

Cash return on sales ratio   A cash basis ratio used to evaluate profitability by dividing net cash provided by operating activities by sales. (pp. 633 and 647)

Current cash debt coverage ratio   A cash basis ratio used to evaluate liquidity by dividing net cash provided by operating activities by average current liabilities. (pp. 633 and 647)

Direct method   A method of determining the "net cash provided by operating activities" by adjusting each item in the income statement from the accrual basis to the cash basis. (p. 637)

Financing activities   Cash flow activities that include (a) obtaining cash from issuing debt and repaying the amounts borrowed and (b) obtaining cash from stockholders and providing them with a return on their investment. (p. 618)

Indirect method   A method of preparing a statement of cash flows in which net income is adjusted for items that did not affect cash, to determine net cash provided by operating activities. (p. 625)

Investing activities   Cash flow activities that include (a) acquiring and disposing of investments and productive long-lived assets and (b) lending money and collecting on those loans. (p. 618)

Operating activities   Cash flow activities that include the cash effects of transactions that create revenues and expenses and thus enter into the determination of net income. (p. 618)

Statement of cash flows   A basic financial statement that provides information about the cash receipts and cash payments of an entity during a period, classified as operating, investing, and financing activities, in a format that reconciles the beginning and ending cash balances. (p. 617)

DEMONSTRATION PROBLEM

The income statement for the year ended December 31, 1996, for John Kosinski Manufacturing Company contains the following condensed information:

Revenues		$6,583,000
Operating expenses (excluding depreciation)	$4,920,000	
Depreciation expense	880,000	5,800,000
Income before income taxes		783,000
Income tax expense		353,000
Net income		$ 430,000

Included in operating expenses is a $24,000 loss resulting from the sale of machinery for $270,000 cash. Machinery was purchased at a cost of $750,000. The following balances are reported on Kosinski's comparative balance sheet at December 31:

	1996	1995
Cash	$672,000	$130,000
Accounts receivable	775,000	610,000
Inventories	834,000	867,000
Accounts payable	521,000	501,000

Income tax expense of $353,000 represents the amount paid in 1996. Dividends declared and paid in 1996 totaled $200,000.

Instructions
(a) Prepare the statement of cash flows using the indirect method.
(b) Prepare the statement of cash flows using the direct method.

Solution to Demonstration Problem

JOHN KOSINSKI MANUFACTURING COMPANY
Statement of Cash Flows
For the Year Ended December 31, 1996

(a)   (Indirect Method)

Cash flows from operating activities		
Net income		$ 430,000
Adjustments to reconcile net income to net cash provided by operating activities:		
Depreciation expense	$880,000	
Loss on sale of machinery	24,000	
Increase in accounts receivable	(165,000)	
Decrease in inventories	33,000	
Increase in accounts payable	20,000	792,000
Net cash provided by operating activities		1,222,000
Cash flows from investing activities		
Sale of machinery	270,000	
Purchase of machinery	(750,000)	
Net cash used by investing activities		(480,000)
Cash flows from financing activities		
Payment of cash dividends		(200,000)
Net increase in cash		542,000
Cash at beginning of period		130,000
Cash at end of period		$672,000

(b)   (Direct Method)

Cash flows from operating activities	
Cash collections from customers	$6,418,000 *
Cash payments for operating expenses	4,843,000 **
Income before income taxes	1,575,000
Cash payment for income taxes	353,000
Net cash provided by operating activities	1,222,000

Cash flows from investing activities		
Sale of machinery	$270,000	
Purchase of machinery	(750,000)	
Net cash used by investing activities		(480,000)
Cash flows from financing activities		
Payment of cash dividends		(200,000)
Net increase in cash		542,000
Cash at beginning of period		130,000
Cash at end of period		$ 672,000

Direct Method Computations

*   Computation of cash collections from customers:

Revenues per the income statement	$6,583,000
Less increase in accounts receivable	165,000
Cash collections from customers	$6,418,000

**   Computation of cash payments for operating expenses:

Operating expenses per the income statement	$4,920,000
Deduct loss from sale of machinery	(24,000)
Deduct decrease in inventories	(33,000)
Deduct increase in accounts payable	(20,000)
Cash payments for operating expenses	$4,843,000

Note: All **asterisked** Questions, Exercises, and Problems relate to material contained in the appendix to the chapter.

SELF-STUDY QUESTIONS

Answers are at the end of the chapter.

(SO 1) 1. Which of the following is *incorrect* about the statement of cash flows?
   a. It is a fourth basic financial statement.
   b. It provides information about cash receipts and cash payments of an entity during a period.
   c. It reconciles the ending cash account balance to the balance per the bank statement.
   d. It provides information about the operating, investing, and financing activities of the business.

(SO 2) 2. The statement of cash flows classifies cash receipts and cash payments by the following activities:
   a. operating and nonoperating.
   b. investing, financing, and operating.
   c. financing, operating, and nonoperating.
   d. investing, financing, and nonoperating.

(SO 2) 3. An example of a cash flow from an operating activity is:
   a. payment of cash to lenders for interest.
   b. receipt of cash from the sale of capital stock.
   c. payment of cash dividends to the company's stockholders.
   d. none of the above.

(SO 2) 4. An example of a cash flow from an investing activity is:
   a. receipt of cash from the issuance of bonds payable.
   b. payment of cash to repurchase outstanding capital stock.
   c. receipt of cash from the sale of equipment.
   d. payment of cash to suppliers for inventory.

(SO 2) 5. Cash dividends paid to stockholders are classified on the statement of cash flows as:
   a. operating activities.
   b. investing activities.
   c. a combination of the above.
   d. financing activities.

(SO 2) 6. An example of a cash flow from a financing activity is:
   a. receipt of cash from sale of land.
   b. issuance of debt for cash.
   c. purchase of equipment for cash.
   d. none of the above.

(SO 2) 7. Which of the following about the statement of cash flows is **incorrect**?
   a. The direct method may be used to report cash provided by operations.
   b. The statement shows the cash provided (used) for three categories of activity.

   c. The operating section is the last section of the statement.
   d. The indirect method may be used to report cash provided by operations.

Questions 8 and 9 apply only to the indirect method.

(SO 3) 8. Net income is $132,000, accounts payable increased $10,000 during the year, inventory decreased $6,000 during the year, and accounts receivable increased $12,000 during the year. Under the indirect method, net cash provided by operations is:
   a. $102,000.
   b. $112,000.
   c. $124,000.
   d. $136,000.

(SO 3) 9. Noncash charges that are added back to net income in determining cash provided by operations under the indirect method do **not** include:
   a. depreciation expense.
   b. an increase in inventory.
   c. amortization expense.
   d. loss on sale of equipment.

Questions 10 and 11 apply only to the direct method.

(SO 4) 10. The beginning balance in accounts receivable is $44,000, and the ending balance is $42,000. Sales during the period are $129,000. Cash receipts from customers is:
   a. $127,000.
   b. $129,000.
   c. $131,000.
   d. $141,000.

(SO 4) 11. Which of the following items is reported on a cash flow statement prepared by the direct method?
   a. loss on sale of building.
   b. increase in accounts receivable.
   c. depreciation expense.
   d. cash payments to suppliers.

(SO 3) 12. The statement of cash flows should **not** be used to evaluate an entity's ability to:
   a. earn net income.
   b. generate future cash flows.
   c. pay dividends.
   d. meet obligations.

(SO 5) *13. In a work sheet for the statement of cash flows, a decrease in accounts receivable is entered in the reconciling columns as a credit to Accounts Receivable and a debit in the:
   a. investing activities section.
   b. operating activities section.
   c. financing activities section.
   d. none of the above.

QUESTIONS

1. (a) What is the statement of cash flows? (b) Alice Weiseman maintains that the statement of cash flows is an optional financial statement. Do you agree? Explain.

2. What questions about cash are answered by the statement of cash flows?

3. What are "cash equivalents"? How do cash equivalents affect the statement of cash flows?

4. Distinguish among the three types of activities reported in the statement of cash flows.

5. What are the major sources (inflows) of cash in a statement of cash flows? What are the major uses (outflows) of cash?

6. Why is it important to disclose certain noncash transactions? How should they be disclosed?

7. Wilma Flintstone and Barny Kublestone were discussing the presentation format of the statement of cash flows of Rock Candy Co. At the bottom of Rock Candy's statement of cash flows was a separate section entitled "Noncash investing and financing activities." Give three examples of significant noncash transactions that would be reported in this section.

8. Why is it necessary to use comparative balance sheets, a current income statement, and certain transaction data in preparing a statement of cash flows?

9. Contrast the advantages and disadvantages of the direct and indirect methods. Are both methods acceptable? Which method is preferred by the FASB? Which method is more popular?

10. When the total cash inflows exceed the total cash outflows in the statement of cash flows, how and where is this excess identified?

11. Describe the indirect method for determining net cash provided by operating activities.

12. Why is it necessary to convert accrual based net income to cash basis income when preparing a statement of cash flows?

13. The president of Aerosmith Company is puzzled. During the last year, the company experienced a net loss of $800,000, yet its cash increased $300,000 during the same period of time. Explain to the president how this situation could occur.

14. Identify five items that are adjustments to reconcile net income to net cash provided by operating activities under the indirect method.

15. Why and how is depreciation expense reported in a statement prepared using the indirect method?

16. Why is the statement of cash flows useful?

17. During 1996, Johnny Carson Company converted $1,700,000 of its total $2,000,000 of bonds payable into common stock. Indicate how the transaction would be reported on a statement of cash flows, if at all.

18. Describe the direct method for determining net cash provided by operating activities.

19. Give the formulas under the direct method for computing (a) cash receipts from customers and (b) cash payments to suppliers.

20. Cindy Crawford Inc. reported sales of $2 million for 1996. Accounts receivable decreased $100,000 and accounts payable increased $300,000. Compute cash receipts from customers, assuming that the receivable and payable transactions related to operations.

21. Why is depreciation expense not reported in the direct method cash flow from operating activities section?

*22. Why is it advantageous to use a work sheet when preparing a statement of cash flows? Is a work sheet required to prepare a statement of cash flows?

BRIEF EXERCISES

Compute cash provided by operating activities—indirect method.
(SO 3)

BE14–1   Crystal, Inc., reported net income of $2.5 million in 1996. Depreciation for the year was $260,000, accounts receivable decreased $350,000, and accounts payable decreased $310,000. Compute net cash provided by operating activities using the indirect approach.

Compute cash provided by operating activities—indirect method.
(SO 3)

BE14–2   The net income for Sterling Engineering Co. for 1996 was $280,000. For 1996, depreciation on plant assets was $60,000, and the company incurred a loss on sale of plant assets of $9,000. Compute net cash provided by operating activities under the indirect method.

Indicate statement presentation of selected transactions.
(SO 2)

BE14–3   Each of the following items must be considered in preparing a statement of cash flows for Murphy Co. for the year ended December 31, 1996. For each item, state how it should be shown in the statement of cash flows for 1996.

(a) Issued bonds for $200,000 cash.

(b) Purchased equipment for $150,000 cash.

(c) Sold land costing $20,000 for $20,000 cash.

(d) Declared and paid a $50,000 cash dividend.

BE14–4 The comparative balance sheet for the Rolex Company shows the following changes in noncash current asset accounts: accounts receivable decrease $80,000, prepaid expenses increase $12,000, and inventories increase $30,000. Compute net cash provided by operating activities using the indirect method assuming that net income is $200,000.

Compute net cash provided by operating activities using indirect method.
(SO 3)

BE14–5 Classify the following items as an operating, investing, or financing activity. Assume all items involve cash unless there is information to the contrary.

Classify items by activities.
(SO 2)

(a) Purchase of equipment.

(b) Sale of building.

(c) Redemption of bonds.

(d) Depreciation.

(e) Payment of dividends.

(f) Issuance of capital stock.

BE14–6 Billy Idol Corporation has accounts receivable of $14,000 at 1/1/96 and $24,000 at 12/31/96. Sales revenues were $480,000 for the year 1996. What is the amount of cash receipts from customers in 1996?

Compute receipts from customers using direct method.
(SO 5)

BE14–7 Depeche Mode Corporation reported income taxes of $70,000 on its 1996 income statement and income taxes payable of $12,000 at December 31, 1995, and $9,000 at December 31, 1996. What amount of cash payments were made for income taxes during 1996?

Compute cash payments for income taxes using direct method.
(SO 5)

BE14–8 Excel Corporation reports operating expenses of $90,000 excluding depreciation expense of $15,000 for 1996. During the year prepaid expenses decreased $6,600 and accrued expenses payable increased $4,400. Compute the cash payments for operating expenses in 1996.

Compute cash payments for operating expenses using direct method.
(SO 5)

BE14–9 The T-accounts for Equipment and the related Accumulated Depreciation for Cindy Trevis Company at the end of 1996 are as follows:

Determine cash received in sale of equipment.
(SO 3, 5)

Equipment					Accumulated Depreciation			
Beg. bal.	80,000	Disposals	22,000		Disposals	5,500	Beg. bal.	44,500
Acquisitions	41,600						Depr.	12,000
End. bal.	99,600						End. bal.	51,000

In addition, Cindy Trevis Company's income statement reported a loss on the sale of equipment of $6,700. What amount was reported on the statement of cash flows as "cash flow from sale of equipment"?

BE14–10 The following T-account is a summary of the cash account of Anita Baker Company.

Identify financing activity transactions.
(SO 2)

Cash (Summary Form)

Balance, 1/1/96	8,000		
Receipts from customers	364,000	Payments for goods	200,000
Dividends on stock investments	6,000	Payments for operating expenses	140,000
Proceeds from sale of equipment	36,000	Interest paid	10,000
Proceeds from issuance of bonds		Taxes paid	8,000
payable	100,000	Dividends paid	40,000
Balance, 12/31/96	116,000		

For Anita Baker Company what amount of net cash provided (used) by financing activities should be reported in the statement of cash flows?

*BE14–11 Using the data in BE14–8, indicate how the changes in prepaid expenses and accrued expenses payable should be entered in the reconciling columns of a work sheet. Assume that beginning balances were: prepaid expenses, $18,600 and accrued expenses payable, $8,200.

Indicate entries in work sheet.
(SO 6)

EXERCISES

Classify transactions by type of activity.
(SO 2)

E14–1 Li Eng Corporation had the following transactions during 1996:

1. Purchased a machine for $30,000, giving a long-term note in exchange.
2. Issued $50,000 par value common stock for cash.
3. Collected $16,000 of accounts receivable.
4. Declared and paid a cash dividend of $25,000.
5. Sold a long-term investment with a cost of $15,000 for $15,000 cash.
6. Issued $200,000 par value common stock upon conversion of bonds having a face value of $200,000.
7. Paid $18,000 on accounts payable.

Instructions
Analyze the transactions above and indicate whether each transaction resulted in a cash flow from (a) operating activities, (b) investing activities, (c) financing activities, or (d) noncash investing and financing activities.

Prepare the operating activities section—indirect method.
(SO 3)

E14–2 Joe Pesci Company reported net income of $195,000 for 1996. Pesci also reported depreciation expense of $35,000, and a loss of $5,000 on the sale of equipment. The comparative balance sheet shows an increase in accounts receivable of $15,000 for the year, an $8,000 increase in accounts payable, and a decrease in prepaid expenses $4,000.

Instructions
Prepare the operating activities section of the statement of cash flows for 1996. Use the indirect method.

Prepare the operating activities section—indirect method.
(SO 3)

E14–3 The current sections of Barth Inc.'s balance sheets at December 31, 1995 and 1996, are presented below.

	1996	1995
Current assets		
Cash	$105,000	$ 99,000
Accounts receivable	110,000	89,000
Inventory	171,000	186,000
Prepaid expenses	27,000	32,000
Total current assets	$413,000	$406,000
Current liabilities		
Accrued expenses payable	$ 15,000	$ 5,000
Accounts payable	$ 85,000	$ 92,000
Total current liabilities	$100,000	$ 97,000

Barth's net income for 1996 was $122,000. Depreciation expense was $24,000.

Instructions
Prepare the net cash provided by operating activities section of Barth Inc.'s statement of cash flows for the year ended December 31, 1996 using the indirect method.

Prepare partial statement of cash flows—indirect method.
(SO 3)

E14–4 Presented below are three accounts that appear in the general ledger of Roberta Dupre Corp. during 1996:

Equipment

Date		Debit	Credit	Balance
Jan. 1	Balance			160,000
July 31	Purchase of equipment	70,000		230,000
Sept. 2	Cost of equipment constructed	53,000		283,000
Nov. 10	Cost of equipment sold		45,000	238,000

Accumulated Depreciation—Equipment

Date		Debit	Credit	Balance
Jan. 1	Balance			71,000
Nov. 10	Accumulated depreciation on equipment sold	30,000		41,000
Dec. 31	Depreciation for year		24,000	65,000

Retained Earnings

Date		Debit	Credit	Balance
Jan. 1	Balance			105,000
Aug. 23	Dividends (cash)	14,000		91,000
Dec. 31	Net income		47,000	138,000

Instructions
From the postings in the accounts above, indicate how the information is reported on a statement of cash flows using the indirect method. The loss on sale of equipment was $6,000. Hint: Purchase of equipment is reported in the investing activities section as a decrease in cash of $70,000.

E14–5 A comparative balance sheet for Oprah Winfrey Company is presented below.

Prepare a statement of cash flows—indirect method.
(SO 3, 4)

December 31

Assets	1996	1995
Cash	$ 63,000	$ 22,000
Accounts receivable	85,000	76,000
Inventories	180,000	189,000
Land	75,000	100,000
Equipment	260,000	200,000
Accumulated depreciation	(66,000)	(42,000)
Total	$597,000	$545,000

Liabilities and Stockholders' Equity

	1996	1995
Accounts payable	$ 34,000	$ 47,000
Bonds payable	150,000	200,000
Common stock ($1 par)	214,000	164,000
Retained earnings	199,000	134,000
Total	$597,000	$545,000

Additional information:

1. Net income for 1996 was $105,000.
2. Cash dividends of $40,000 were declared and paid.
3. Bonds payable amounting to $50,000 were redeemed for cash $50,000.
4. Common stock was issued for $50,000 cash.
5. Sales for 1996 are $978,000.

Instructions
(a) Prepare a statement of cash flows for 1996 using the indirect method.
(b) Compute the following cash-basis ratios:
    (1) Current cash debt coverage ratio.
    (2) Cash return on sales ratio.
    (3) Cash debt coverage ratio.

E14–6 An analysis of comparative balance sheets, the current year's income statement and the general ledger accounts of Pierce Brosnan Corp. uncovered the following items. Assume all items involve cash unless there is information to the contrary.

Classify transactions by type of activity.
(SO 2)

(a) Purchase of land.
(b) Payment of dividends.
(c) Sale of building at book value.
(d) Exchange of land for patent.
(e) Depreciation.
(f) Redemption of bonds.

(g) Receipt of interest on notes receivable.   (k) Payment of interest on notes payable.
(h) Issuance of capital stock.   (l) Conversion of bonds into common stock.
(i) Amortization of patent.   (m) Loss on sale of land.
(j) Issuance of bonds for land.   (n) Receipt of dividends on investment in stock.

Instructions
Indicate how the above items should be classified in the statement of cash flows using the following four major classifications: operating activity (indirect method), investing activity, financing activity, and significant noncash investing and financing activity.

Compute cash provided by operating activities—direct method.
(SO 5)

E14–7   Kelly McGillis Company has just completed its first year of operations on December 31, 1996. Its initial income statement showed that Kelly McGillis had revenues of $157,000 and operating expenses of $78,000. Accounts receivable and accounts payable at year end were $42,000 and $33,000, respectively. Assume that accounts payable related to operating expenses. Ignore income taxes.

Instructions
Compute net cash provided by operating activities using the direct method.

Compute cash payments—direct method.
(SO 5)

E14–8   The income statement for the Garcia Company shows cost of goods sold $355,000 and operating expenses (exclusive of depreciation) $230,000. The comparative balance sheet for the year shows that inventory increased $6,000, prepaid expenses decreased $6,000, accounts payable (merchandise suppliers) decreased $8,000, and accrued expenses payable increased $8,000.

Instructions
Using the direct method, compute (a) cash payments to suppliers and (b) cash payments for operating expenses.

Compute cash flow from operating activities—direct method
(SO 2, 5)

E14–9   The 1997 accounting records of Flypaper Airlines reveal the following transactions and events.

Payment of interest	$ 6,000	Collection of accounts receivable	$180,000
Cash sales	48,000	Payment of salaries and wages	68,000
Receipt of dividend revenue	14,000	Depreciation expense	16,000
Payment of income taxes	16,000	Proceeds from sale of aircraft	812,000
Net income	38,000	Purchase of equipment for cash	22,000
Payment of accounts payable for		Loss on sale of aircraft	3,000
merchandise	90,000	Payment of dividends	14,000
Payment for land	74,000	Payment of operating expenses	20,000

Instructions
Prepare the cash flows from operating activities section using the direct method. (Not all of the above items will be used.)

Calculate cash flows—direct method
(SO 5)

E14–10   The following information is taken from the 1997 general ledger of Joan Robinson Company:

Rent	Rent expense	$ 31,000
	Prepaid rent, January 1	5,900
	Prepaid rent, December 31	3,000
Salaries	Salaries expense	$ 54,000
	Salaries payable, January 1	5,000
	Salaries payable, December 31	8,000
Sales	Revenue from sales	$180,000
	Accounts receivable, January 1	12,000
	Accounts receivable, December 31	9,000

Instructions
In each of above cases, compute the amount that should be reported in the operating activities section of the statement of cash flows applying the direct method.

Prepare a work sheet.
(SO 6)

*****E14–11**

Instructions
Refer to Exercise E14–5 (Oprah Winfrey Company) and use these data to prepare a work sheet for a statement of cash flows for 1996. Enter the reconciling items directly on the work sheet, identifying the entries alphabetically.

PROBLEMS

P14–1 The income statement of Breckenridge Company is shown below:

Prepare the operating activities section—indirect method.
(SO 3)

BRECKENRIDGE COMPANY
Income Statement
For the Year Ended November 30, 1996

Sales		$6,900,000
Cost of goods sold		
Beginning inventory	$1,900,000	
Purchases	4,400,000	
Goods available for sale	6,300,000	
Ending inventory	1,600,000	
Cost of goods sold		4,700,000
Gross profit		2,200,000
Operating expenses		
Selling expenses	450,000	
Administrative expenses	700,000	1,150,000
Net income		$1,050,000

Additional information:

1. Accounts receivable decreased $300,000 during the year.
2. Prepaid expenses increased $150,000 during the year.
3. Accounts payable to suppliers of merchandise decreased $300,000 during the year.
4. Accrued expenses payable decreased $100,000 during the year.
5. Administrative expenses include depreciation expense of $60,000.

Instructions
Prepare the operating activities section of the statement of cash flows for the year ended November 30, 1996, for Breckenridge Company, using the indirect method.

P14–2 Data for the Breckenridge Company are presented in P14–1.

Prepare operating activities section—direct method.
(SO 5)

Instructions
Prepare the operating activities section of the statement of cash flows using the direct method.

P14–3 Vail Company's income statement for the year ended December 31, 1996, contained the following condensed information:

Prepare the operating activities section—direct method.
(SO 5)

Revenue from fees		$840,000
Operating expenses (excluding depreciation)	$624,000	
Depreciation expense	60,000	
Loss on sale of equipment	26,000	710,000
Income before income taxes		130,000
Income tax expense		40,000
Net income		$ 90,000

Vail's balance sheet contained the following comparative data at December 31:

	1996	1995
Accounts receivable	$47,000	$55,000
Accounts payable	41,000	33,000
Income taxes payable	4,000	9,000

(Accounts payable pertains to operating expenses.)

Instructions
Prepare the operating activities section of the statement of cash flows using the direct method.

Prepare the operating activities section—indirect method
(SO 3)

P14–4

Instructions
Using the data from Problem 14–3, prepare the operating activities section of the statement of cash flows using the indirect method.

Prepare a statement of cash flows—indirect method.
(SO 3, 4)

P14–5   The financial statements of Patrick Swayze Company appear below:

PATRICK SWAYZE COMPANY
Comparative Balance Sheet
December 31

Assets	1996	1995
Cash	$ 29,000	$ 13,000
Accounts receivable	28,000	14,000
Merchandise inventory	25,000	35,000
Property, plant, and equipment	60,000	78,000
Accumulated depreciation	(20,000)	(24,000)
Total	$122,000	$116,000

Liabilities and Stockholders' Equity		
Accounts payable	$ 29,000	$ 23,000
Income taxes payable	5,000	8,000
Bonds payable	27,000	33,000
Common stock	18,000	14,000
Retained earnings	43,000	38,000
Total	$122,000	$116,000

PATRICK SWAYZE COMPANY
Income Statement
For the Year Ended December 31, 1996

Sales		$220,000
Cost of goods sold		180,000
Gross profit		40,000
Selling expenses	$18,000	
Administrative expenses	6,000	24,000
Income from operations		16,000
Interest expense		2,000
Income before income taxes		14,000
Income tax expense		4,000
Net income		$ 10,000

The following additional data were provided:

1. Dividends declared and paid were $5,000.
2. During the year equipment was sold for $8,500 cash. This equipment cost $18,000 originally and had a book value of $8,500 at the time of sale.
3. All depreciation expense is in the selling expense category.
4. All sales and purchases are on account.

Instructions
(a) Prepare a statement of cash flows using the indirect method.
(b) Compute the following cash basis ratios:
    (1) Current cash debt coverage ratio.
    (2) Cash return on sales ratio.
    (3) Cash debt coverage ratio.

Prepare a statement of cash flows—direct method.
(SO 4, 5)

P14–6   Data for the Patrick Swayze Company are presented in P14–5. Further analysis reveals the following:

1. Accounts payable pertain to merchandise suppliers.
2. All operating expenses except for depreciation were paid in cash.

Instructions

(a) Prepare a statement of cash flows for Patrick Swayze Company using the direct method.

(b) Compute the following cash-basis ratios:
   (1) Current cash debt coverage ratio.
   (2) Cash return on sales ratio.
   (3) Cash debt coverage ratio.

P14–7 Condensed financial data of Fern Galenti, Inc. appear below.

Prepare a statement of cash flows—indirect method.
(SO 3)

FERN GALENTI, INC.
Comparative Balance Sheet
December 31

Assets	1996	1995
Cash	$ 97,800	$ 38,400
Accounts receivable	90,800	33,000
Inventories	112,500	102,850
Prepaid expenses	18,400	16,000
Investments	108,000	94,000
Plant assets	270,000	242,500
Accumulated depreciation	(50,000)	(52,000)
	$647,500	$474,750

Liabilities and Stockholders' Equity		
Accounts payable	$ 92,000	$ 67,300
Accrued expenses payable	16,500	17,000
Bonds payable	85,000	110,000
Common stock	220,000	175,000
Retained earnings	234,000	105,450
	$647,500	$474,750

FERN GALENTI, INC.
Income Statement Data
For the Year Ended December 31, 1996

Sales		$342,780
Less:		
Cost of goods sold	$115,460	
Operating expenses (excluding depreciation)	12,410	
Depreciation expense	46,500	
Income taxes	7,280	
Interest expense	2,730	
Loss on sale of plant assets	7,500	191,880
Net income		$150,900

Additional information:

1. New plant assets costing $85,000 were purchased for cash during the year.
2. Old plant assets having an original cost of $57,500 were sold for $1,500 cash.
3. Bonds matured and were paid off at face value for cash.
4. A cash dividend of $22,350 was declared and paid during the year.

Instructions
Prepare a statement of cash flows using the indirect method.

P14–8 Data for Fern Galenti, Inc., are presented in P14–7. Further analysis reveals that accounts payable pertains to merchandise creditors.

Prepare a statement of cash flows—direct method.
(SO 5)

Instructions
Prepare a statement of cash flows for Fern Galenti, Inc., using the direct method.

P14–9 Presented below is the comparative balance sheet for Cousin Tommy's Toy Company as of December 31:

Prepare a statement of cash flows—indirect method.
(SO 3)

COUSIN TOMMY'S TOY COMPANY
Comparative Balance Sheet
December 31

Assets	1996	1995
Cash	$ 41,000	$ 45,000
Accounts receivable	47,500	52,000
Inventory	151,450	142,000
Prepaid expenses	16,780	21,000
Land	100,000	130,000
Equipment	228,000	155,000
Accumulated depreciation—equipment	(45,000)	(35,000)
Building	200,000	200,000
Accumulated depreciation—building	(60,000)	(40,000)
	$679,730	$670,000

Liabilities and Stockholders' Equity		
Accounts payable	$ 43,730	$ 40,000
Bonds payable	250,000	300,000
Common stock, $1 par	200,000	150,000
Retained earnings	186,000	180,000
	$679,730	$670,000

Additional information:

1. Operating expenses include depreciation expense of $42,000 and charges from prepaid expenses of $4,220.
2. Land was sold for cash at book value.
3. Cash dividends of $32,000 were paid.
4. Net income for 1996 was $38,000.
5. Equipment was purchased for $95,000 cash. In addition, equipment costing $22,000 with a book value of $10,000 was sold for $8,100 cash.
6. Bonds were converted at face value by issuing 50,000 shares of $1 par value common stock.

Instructions
Prepare a statement of cash flows for the year ended December 31, 1996, using the indirect method.

Prepare a work sheet.
(SO 6)

*P14–10

Instructions
Refer to Problem 14–7 (Fern Galenti, Inc.) and use these data to prepare a work sheet for a statement of cash flows for 1996. Enter the reconciling entries directly on the work sheet, identifying the entries alphabetically.

ALTERNATE PROBLEMS
••

Prepare the operating activities section—indirect method.
(SO 3)

P14–1A   The income statement of Tina Maria Company is shown below:

TINA MARIA COMPANY
Income Statement
For the Year Ended December 31, 1996

Sales		$7,100,000
Cost of goods sold		
Beginning inventory	$1,700,000	
Purchases	5,430,000	
Goods available for sale	7,130,000	
Ending inventory	1,920,000	

Cost of goods sold		5,210,000
Gross profit		1,890,000
Operating expenses		
Selling expenses	400,000	
Administrative expense	525,000	
Depreciation expense	75,000	
Amortization expense	30,000	1,030,000
Net income		$ 860,000

Additional information:

1. Accounts receivable increased $510,000 during the year.
2. Prepaid expenses increased $170,000 during the year.
3. Accounts payable to merchandise suppliers increased $50,000 during the year.
4. Accrued expenses payable decreased $180,000 during the year.

Instructions
Prepare the operating activities section of the statement of cash flows for the year ended December 31, 1996, for Tina Maria Company, using the indirect method.

P14–2A Data for the Tina Maria Company are presented in P14–1A.

Prepare the operating activities section—direct method.
(SO 5)

Instructions
Prepare the operating activities section of the statement of cash flows using the direct method.

P14–3A The income statement of Hanalei International Inc. for the year ended December 31, 1996, reported the following condensed information:

Prepare the operating activities section—direct method.
(SO 5)

Revenue from fees	$430,000
Operating expenses	280,000
Income from operations	150,000
Income tax expense	47,000
Net income	$103,000

Hanalei's balance sheet contained the following comparative data at December 31:

	1996	1995
Accounts receivable	$50,000	$40,000
Accounts payable	30,000	41,000
Income taxes payable	6,000	4,000

Hanalei has no depreciable assets. Accounts payable pertains to operating expenses.

Instructions
Prepare the operating activities section of the statement of cash flows using the direct method.

P14–4A

Prepare the operating activities section—indirect method.
(SO 3)

Instructions
Using the data from Problem 14–3A, prepare the operating activities section of the statement of cash flows using the indirect method.

P14–5A The financial statements of Sean Seymor Company appear below:

Prepare a statement of cash flows—indirect method.
(SO 3, 4)

SEAN SEYMOR COMPANY
Comparative Balance Sheet
December 31

Assets		1996		1995
Cash		$ 26,000		$ 13,000
Accounts receivable		18,000		14,000
Merchandise inventory		38,000		35,000
Property, plant, and equipment	$70,000		$78,000	
Less accumulated depreciation	(30,000)	40,000	(24,000)	54,000
Total		$122,000		$116,000

Liabilities and Stockholders' Equity

Accounts payable	$ 29,000	$ 33,000
Income taxes payable	15,000	20,000
Bonds payable	20,000	10,000
Common stock	25,000	25,000
Retained earnings	33,000	28,000
Total	$122,000	$116,000

SEAN SEYMOR COMPANY
Income Statement
For the Year Ended December 31, 1996

Sales		$240,000
Cost of goods sold		180,000
Gross profit		60,000
Selling expenses	$28,000	
Administrative expenses	6,000	34,000
Income from operations		26,000
Interest expense		2,000
Income before income taxes		24,000
Income tax expense		7,000
Net income		$ 17,000

The following additional data were provided:

1. Dividends of $12,000 were declared and paid.
2. During the year equipment was sold for $10,000 cash. This equipment cost $15,000 originally and had a book value of $10,000 at the time of sale.
3. All depreciation expense, $11,000, is in the selling expense category.
4. All sales and purchases are on account.
5. Additional equipment was purchased for $7,000 cash.

Instructions
(a) Prepare a statement of cash flows using the indirect method.
(b) Compute the following cash basis ratios:
   (1) Current cash debt coverage ratio.
   (2) Cash return on sales ratio.
   (3) Cash debt coverage ratio.

Prepare a statement of cash flows—direct method.
(SO 4, 5)

P14–6A Data for the Sean Seymor Company are presented in P14–5A. Further analysis reveals the following:

1. Accounts payable pertains to merchandise creditors.
2. All operating expenses except for depreciation are paid in cash.

Instructions
(a) Prepare a statement of cash flows using the direct method.
(b) Compute the following cash basis ratios:
   (1) Current cash debt coverage ratio.
   (2) Cash return on sales ratio.
   (3) Cash debt coverage ratio.

Prepare a statement of cash flows—indirect method.
(SO 3)

P14–7A Condensed financial data of Norway Company appear below:

NORWAY COMPANY
Comparative Balance Sheet
December 31

	1996	1995
Assets		
Cash	$ 96,700	$ 47,250
Accounts receivable	86,800	57,000
Inventories	121,900	102,650

Investments	84,500	87,000
Plant assets	250,000	205,000
Accumulated depreciation	(49,500)	(40,000)
	$590,400	$458,900

Liabilities and Stockholders' Equity

Accounts payable	$ 52,700	$ 48,280
Accrued expenses payable	12,100	18,830
Bonds payable	100,000	70,000
Common stock	250,000	200,000
Retained earnings	175,600	121,790
	$590,400	$458,900

NORWAY COMPANY
Income Statement Data
For the Year Ended December 31, 1996

Sales		$297,500
Gain on sale of plant assets		8,750
		306,250
Less:		
Cost of goods sold	$99,460	
Operating expenses (excluding depreciation expense)	14,670	
Depreciation expense	49,700	
Income taxes	7,270	
Interest expense	2,940	174,040
Net income		$132,210

Additional information:

1. New plant assets costing $92,000 were purchased for cash during the year.
2. Investments were sold at cost.
3. Plant assets costing $47,000 were sold for $15,550, resulting in a gain of $8,750.
4. A cash dividend of $78,400 was declared and paid during the year.

Instructions
Prepare a statement of cash flows using the indirect method.

P14–8A Data for Norway Company are presented in P14–7A. Further analysis reveals that accounts payable pertains to merchandise creditors.

Prepare a statement of cash flows—direct method.
(SO 5)

Instructions
Prepare a statement of cash flows for Norway Company using the direct method.

P14–9A Presented below is the comparative balance sheet for Cortina Company at December 31:

Prepare a statement of cash flows—indirect method.
(SO 3)

CORTINA COMPANY
Comparative Balance Sheet
December 31

	1996	1995
Cash	$ 40,000	$ 57,000
Accounts receivable	77,000	64,000
Inventory	132,000	140,000
Prepaid expenses	12,140	16,540
Land	125,000	150,000
Equipment	200,000	175,000
Accumulated depreciation—equipment	(60,000)	(42,000)
Building	250,000	250,000
Accumulated depreciation—building	(75,000)	(50,000)
	$701,140	$760,540

Accounts payable	$ 33,000	$ 45,000
Bonds payable	235,000	265,000
Common stock, $1 par	280,000	250,000
Retained earnings	153,140	200,540
	$701,140	$760,540

Additional information:

1. Operating expenses include depreciation expense $70,000 and charges from prepaid expenses of $4,400.
2. Land was sold for cash at cost.
3. Cash dividends of $74,290 were paid.
4. Net income for 1996 was $26,890.
5. Equipment was purchased for $65,000 cash. In addition, equipment costing $40,000 with a book value of $13,000 was sold for $14,000 cash.
6. Bonds were converted at face value by issuing 30,000 shares of $1 par value common stock.

Instructions
Prepare a statement of cash flows for 1996 using the indirect method.

Prepare a work sheet
(SO 6)

*P14–10A

Instructions
Refer to Problem 14–7A (Norway Company) and use these data to prepare a work sheet for a statement of cash flows. Enter the reconciling items directly in the work sheet columns, identifying the debit and credit amounts alphabetically.

▶B*roadening Your Perspective*

F*INANCIAL REPORTING PROBLEM—* PEPSICO, INC.
....

Refer to the financial statements of PepsiCo, Inc., presented in Appendix A and answer the following questions:

(a) What was the amount of net cash provided by operating activities for the year ended December 30, 1995? For the year ended December 31, 1994?
(b) What was the amount of increase or decrease in cash and cash equivalents for the year ended December 30, 1995? For the year ended December 31, 1994?
(c) Which method of computing net cash provided by operating activities does PepsiCo use?
(d) From your analysis of the 1995 statement of cash flows, was the change in notes and accounts receivable a decrease or an increase? Was the change in inventories a decrease or an increase? Was the change in accounts payable a decrease or an increase?
(e) What was the total (net) outflow of cash for investing activities for 1995?
(f) What was the amount of interest paid in 1995? What was the amount of income taxes paid in 1995?
(g) What significant noncash investing and financing activities did PepsiCo complete in 1995?

C*OMPARATIVE ANALYSIS PROBLEM—* THE COCA-COLA COMPANY VS. PEPSICO, INC.
....

The financial statements of Coca-Cola are presented at the end of Chapter 1, and PepsiCo's financial statements are presented in Appendix A.

Instructions

(a) Based on the information contained in these financial statements, compute the following 1995 ratios for each company:

(1) Current cash debt coverage ratio

(2) Cash return on sales ratio

(3) Cash debt coverage ratio

(b) What conclusions concerning the management of cash can be drawn from these data?

INTERPRETATION OF FINANCIAL STATEMENTS

Mini-Case One—Mattel Corporation

Mattel Corporation makes toys—some very famous toys. Among these are Barbie, Fisher-Price, Disney toys (such as Pocahontas), and hot wheels. In 1994 the company had a great year; in fact at that point it was the best year in its history. A review of the company's balance sheet, however, reveals that the company's cash dropped from $506 million to $239 million. This drop of $267 million represented a 53% decrease in cash. The following additional information was also available from the financial statements.

	1994	1993
Cash	$ 237,002	$ 506,113
Marketable securities	20,581	17,468
Accounts receivable (net)	762,024	580,313
Inventories	339,143	219,993
Prepaid expenses and other current assets	182,675	146,863
Total current assets	1,543,523	1,470,750
Total current liabilities	915,881	783,329
Cash provided (used) by operations	343,439	303,344
Cash provided (used) by investing	(526,497)	(88,804)
Cash provided (used) by financing	(86,053)	(16,369)

Instructions

(a) Discuss whether Mattel has suffered a significant reduction in its liquidity as a result of this decline in cash on hand. Use the current ratio and the current cash debt coverage ratio to support your position. (Note: assume that current liabilities at December 31, 1992 were $529,389.)

(b) Using the data provided, provide an explanation as to why cash declined, and discuss whether this should be a concern to the company and its investors.

Mini-Case Two—Vermont Teddy Bear Co.

Founded in the early 1980s, the Vermont Teddy Bear Co. designs and manufactures American-made teddy bears and markets them primarily as gifts called Bear-Grams or Teddy Bear-Grams. Bear-Grams are personalized teddy bears delivered directly to the recipient for special occasions such as birthdays and anniversaries. The Shelburne Vermont company's primary markets are New York, Boston, and Chicago. Sales have jumped dramatically in recent years, from $351,000 to $20,561,000 in 1994. Such dramatic growth has significant implications for cash flows. Provided below are the cash flow statements for 1993 and 1994 for the company.

	1994	1993
Cash flows from operating activities:		
Net income	$ 17,523	$ 838,955
Adjustments to reconcile net income to net cash provided by operating activities		
Deferred income taxes	(69,524)	(146,590)
Depreciation and amortization	316,416	181,348
Changes in assets and liabilities:		
Accounts receivable, trade	(38,267)	(25,947)
Inventories	(1,599,014)	(1,289,293)

Prepaid and other current assets	(444,794)	(113,205)
Deposit and other assets	(24,240)	(83,044)
Accounts payable	2,017,059	(284,567)
Accrued expenses	61,321	170,755
Accrued interest payable, debentures	—	(58,219)
Other	—	(8,960)
Income taxes payable	—	117,810
Net cash provided by (used for) operating activities	236,480	(700,957)
Net cash used for investing activities	(2,102,892)	(4,422,953)
Net cash (used for) provided by financing activities	(315,353)	9,685,435
Net change in cash and cash equivalents	(2,181,765)	4,561,525

Other information

	1994	1993
Current liabilities	$ 4,055,465	$ 1,995,600
Total liabilities	4,620,085	2,184,386
Net sales	20,560,566	17,025,856

Instructions

(a) Note that net income in 1994 was only $17,523 compared to 1993 income of $838,955, but cash flow from operations was $236,480 in 1994 and a negative $700,957 in 1993. Explain the causes of this apparent paradox.

(b) Evaluate Vermont Teddy Bear's liquidity, solvency, and profitability for 1994 using cash flow-based ratios.

DECISION CASE
••

Greg Rhoda and Debra Sondgeroth are examining the following statement of cash flows for L.L. Bean Trading Company for the year ended January 31, 1997.

L.L. BEAN TRADING COMPANY
Statement of Cash Flows
For the Year Ended January 31, 1997

Sources of cash	
From sales of merchandise	$370,000
From sale of capital stock	420,000
From sale of investment (purchased below)	80,000
From depreciation	55,000
From issuance of note for truck	20,000
From interest on investments	6,000
Total sources of cash	951,000
Uses of cash	
For purchase of fixtures and equipment	340,000
For merchandise purchased for resale	258,000
For operating expenses (including depreciation)	160,000
For purchase of investment	75,000
For purchase of truck by issuance of note	20,000
For purchase of treasury stock	10,000
For interest on note payable	3,000
Total uses of cash	866,000
Net increase in cash	$ 85,000

Greg claims that L.L. Bean's statement of cash flows is an excellent portrayal of a superb first year with cash increasing $85,000. Debra replies that it was not a superb first year, that the year was an operating failure, that the statement was incorrectly presented, and that $85,000 is not the actual increase in cash. The cash balance at the beginning of the year was $140,000.

Instructions
    (a) With whom do you agree, Greg or Debra? Explain your position.
    (b) Using the data provided, prepare a statement of cash flows in proper form using the indirect method. The only noncash items in the income statement are depreciation and the gain from the sale of the investment.

COMMUNICATION ACTIVITY

Arnold Byte, the owner-president of Computer Services Company, is unfamiliar with the statement of cash flows which you, as his accountant, prepared. He asks for further explanation.

Instructions
Write him a brief memo explaining the form and content of the statement of cash flows as shown in Illustration 14-12 on page 627.

GROUP ACTIVITY

In groups of four or five, discuss the following questions: What would you expect to observe in the operating, investing, and financing sections of a statement of cash flows of:

    (a) a severely financially troubled firm?
    (b) a recently formed firm which is experiencing rapid growth?

ETHICS CASE

Puebla Corporation is a medium-sized wholesaler of automotive parts. It has ten stockholders that have been paid a total of $1 million in cash dividends for 8 consecutive years. The Board of Director's policy requires that in order for this dividend to be declared, net cash provided by operating activities as reported in Puebla's current year's statement of cash flows must be in excess of $1 million. President and CEO Phil Monat's job is secure so long as he produces annual operating cash flows to support the usual dividend.

At the end of the current year, controller Rick Rodgers presents President Monat with some disappointing news—the net cash provided by operating activities is calculated by the indirect method to be only $970,000. The president says to Rick, "We must get that amount above $1 million. Isn't there some way to increase operating cash flow by another $30,000?" Rick answers, "These figures were prepared by my assistant. I'll go back to my office and see what I can do." The president replies, "I know you won't let me down, Rick."

Upon close scrutiny of the statement of cash flows, Rick concludes that he can get the operating cash flows above $1 million by reclassifying a $60,000, 2-year note payable listed in the financing activities section as "Proceeds from bank loan—$60,000." He will report the note instead as "Increase in payables—$60,000" and treat it as an adjustment of net income in the operating activities section. He returns to the president saying, "You can tell the Board to declare their usual dividend. Our net cash flow provided by operating activities is $1,030,000." "Good man, Rick! I knew I could count on you," exults the president.

Instructions
    (a) Who are the stakeholders in this situation?
    (b) Was there anything unethical about the president's actions? Was there anything unethical about the controller's actions?
    (c) Are the Board members or anyone else likely to discover the misclassification?

RESEARCH ASSIGNMENT

The March 25, 1996 issue of *Barron's* includes an article by Harry B. Ernst and Jeffrey D. Fotta, entitled "Weary Bull." Read the article and answer the following questions.

(a) The article describes a cash flow-based model used by investors. Identify the model and briefly describe its purpose.
(b) How does the model classify a firm's cash flows?
(c) Identify one way in which the cash flow classifications described in the article differ from those under GAAP.
(d) How can the model be used to predict stock prices?

CRITICAL THINKING
▸ A Real-World Focus: Praxair Incorporated
•••

Praxair was founded in 1907 as Linde-Air Products Company and was a pioneer in separating oxygen from air. It was purchased and run as a subsidiary of Union Carbide. In 1992 Praxair became an independent public company. Today, the company is one of the top three largest suppliers of industrial gases worldwide. Praxair has operations in all regions of the world, with a majority of its sales occurring outside of the United States.

The following management discussion was included in Praxair's 1994 annual report:

> **Liquidity, Capital Resources and Other Financial Data**—In 1994, Praxair changed its presentation of the Statement of Cash Flows to the direct method to report major classes of cash receipts and payments from operations. Praxair believes the direct method more clearly presents its operating cash flows. Prior years' cash flow information has been reclassified to conform to the current year presentation.

Instructions
(a) What method has Praxair changed from?
(b) What will the newly prepared cash flow statement show that the former one did not?
(c) Will the cash flows from investing and financing appear any differently under the new method of preparation than they did under the old method?

Answers to Self-Study Questions
1. c   2. b   3. a   4. c   5. d   6. b   7. c   8. d   9. b   10. c   11. d
12. a   13. b

SAT Scores Help Bring in Loans

CHICAGO, Ill. — When big banks and insurance companies lend millions of dollars to colleges and universities, the lenders understandably want to know that their money is secure. That's why they demand that the schools provide certain financial statement ratios.

At the University of Chicago, John R. Kroll is responsible for putting together some 40 different ratios—ranging from measures of liquidity to qualitative factors such as student SAT scores.

One balance sheet ratio measures the relationship of equity to debt. Kroll says: "A ratio of 1-to-1 says that if a calamity strikes, you could liquidate your net assets and pay off your debt. Your 'A'-rated institutions, as measured by Standard & Poor's, a New York rating agency, have a ratio of 2-to-1. 'AAA' institutions—the highest ranking, have a 4-to-1 ratio. We have a 5.5-to-1 ratio."

Kroll says the good equity-to-debt ratio helped the university bor-row $100 million recently for two new buildings. "Buildings are financed in one of two ways," he says. "Either people give money to build the building, or you have to go out and borrow cash and pay it off over a long period of time."

Another key ratio is the endowment ratio—the ratio of endowment gifts the university has received to the number of students. The more endowment a school has, the less pressure it has to find money from other sources.

Lenders are even interested in SAT scores. The reason: "The stronger the student, the more demand there is to attend your institution," which translates to a healthy financial condition, says Kroll. ◄

*F*INANCIAL STATEMENT ANALYSIS

If you had excess cash which you wanted to invest, what would you do with it? One of the most popular forms of investments is in stocks or bonds. If stocks are your choice, should you invest in conservative public utility company stocks such as Pacific Gas & Electric Company or in speculative research or high-tech stocks such as Genetic Inc. or Satellite Communications Corp.? If you choose to buy bonds, should you invest in General Electric's quality bonds, which generally have greater stability, less risk, and lower yields, or in Sunshine Mining bonds that offer higher rates of return but are less stable and of greater risk? To answer these types of questions, it is helpful for you to understand how to analyze financial statement information.

Financial statement analysis, the topic of this chapter, enhances the usefulness of published financial statements in making decisions about a company. The content and organization of this chapter are shown below.

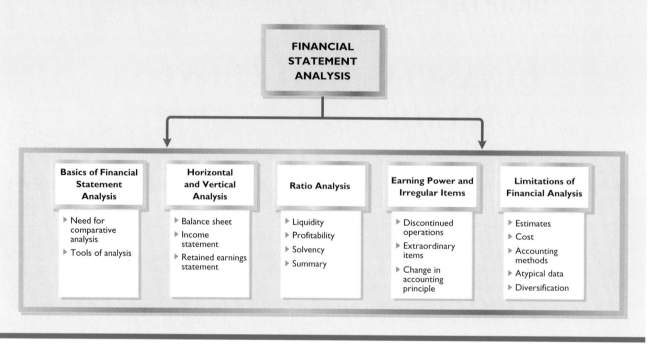

*B*asics of Financial Statement Analysis

Analyzing financial statements involves evaluating three characteristics of a company: its liquidity, its profitability, and its solvency. For example, a **short-term creditor**, such as a bank, is primarily interested in the ability of the borrower to pay obligations when they come due. The liquidity of the borrower in such a case is extremely important in evaluating the safety of a loan. A **long-term creditor**, such as a bondholder, however, looks to indicators such as profitability and solvency that indicate the firm's ability to survive over a long period of time. Long-term creditors consider such measures as the amount of debt in the company's capital structure and the ability to meet interest payments. Similarly, **stockholders** are interested in the profitability and solvency of the enterprise when they assess the likelihood of dividends and the growth potential of the stock.

Need for Comparative Analysis

Every item reported in a financial statement has significance. For example, when Xerox Corporation reports cash of $35 million on its balance sheet, we know the company had that amount of cash on the balance sheet date. However, we do not know whether the amount represents an increase over prior years or whether the amount is adequate in relation to the company's need for cash. To obtain this information, it is necessary to compare the amount of cash with other financial statement data.

Comparisons can be made on a number of different bases—three are illustrated in this chapter:

1. **Intracompany basis.** This basis compares an item or financial relationship **within a company** in the current year with the same item or relationship in one or more prior years. For example, a comparison of Xerox's cash balance at the end of the current year with last year's balance will show the amount of the increase or decrease. Likewise, Xerox can compare the percentage of cash to current assets at the end of the current year with the percentage in one or more prior years. Intracompany comparisons are useful in detecting changes in financial relationships and significant trends.

2. **Industry averages.** This basis compares an item or financial relationship of a company with **industry averages** (or **norms**) published by financial ratings organizations such as Dun & Bradstreet, Moody's, and Standard & Poor's. For example, Xerox's net income can be compared with the average net income of all companies in the copy-equipment industry. Comparisons with industry averages provide information as to a company's relative performance within the industry.

3. **Intercompany basis.** This basis compares an item or financial relationship of one company with the same item or relationship in **one or more competing companies**. The comparisons are made on the basis of the published financial statements of the individual companies. For example, Xerox's total sales for the year can be compared with the total sales of its major competitors such as Canon or Savin. Intercompany comparisons are useful in determining a company's competitive position.

Tools of Financial Statement Analysis

Various tools are used to evaluate the significance of financial statement data. Three commonly used tools are these:

Horizontal analysis is a technique for evaluating a series of financial statement data over a period of time.

Vertical analysis is a technique for evaluating financial statement data that expresses each item in a financial statement in terms of a percent of a base amount.

Ratio analysis expresses the relationship among selected items of financial statement data.

Horizontal analysis is used primarily in intracompany comparisons. Two features in published financial statements facilitate this type of comparison: First, each of the basic financial statements is presented on a comparative basis for a minimum of two years. Second, a summary of selected financial data is presented for a series of 5 to 10 years or more. Vertical analysis is used in both intra- and intercompany comparisons. Ratio analysis is used in all three types of comparisons. In the following sections, we will explain and illustrate each of the three types of analysis.

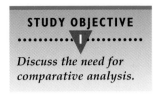

STUDY OBJECTIVE
•••••••••**1**•••••••••
Discuss the need for comparative analysis.

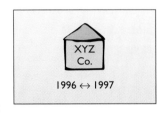

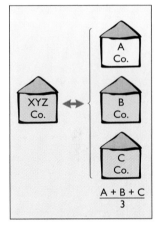

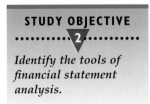

STUDY OBJECTIVE
•••••••••**2**•••••••••
Identify the tools of financial statement analysis.

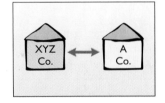

Helpful hint In its annual report, PepsiCo, Inc., presents 11 years of comparative data involving 25 financial statement items to assist stockholders and other interested parties in making intracompany comparisons (see Appendix A).

Horizontal Analysis

Horizontal analysis, also called **trend analysis**, is a technique for evaluating a series of financial statement data over a period of time. Its purpose is to determine the increase or decrease that has taken place, expressed as either an amount or a percentage. For example, the recent net sales figures of Kellogg Company are as follows:

Illustration 15-1

Kellogg's net sales

KELLOGG COMPANY (Net Sales Stated in Millions)				
1994	1993	1992	1991	1990
$6,562.8	$6,295.4	$6,190.6	$5,786.6	$5,181.4

If we assume that 1990 is the base year, we can measure all percentage increases or decreases from this base period amount as follows:

$$\frac{\text{Current year amount} - \text{Base year amount}}{\text{Base year amount}}$$

For example, we can determine that net sales for Kellogg Company increased approximately 11.7% [($5,786.6 − $5,181.4) ÷ $5,181.4] from 1990 to 1991. Similarly, we can determine that net sales increased over 26.7% [($6,562.8 − $5,181.4) ÷ $5,181.4] from 1990 to 1994. The percentage of the base period for each of the 5 years, assuming 1990 as the base period, is shown in Illustration 15-2.

Illustration 15-2

Horizontal analysis of Kellogg's net sales

Helpful hint The percentage expressions are more meaningful than the dollar amounts.

KELLOGG COMPANY (Net Sales Stated in Millions) Base Period 1990				
1994	1993	1992	1991	1990
$6,562.8	$6,295.4	$6,190.6	$5,786.6	$5,181.4
127%	121%	119%	112%	100%

Balance Sheet

To further illustrate horizontal analysis, we will use the financial statements of Quality Department Store Inc., a downtown full-line department store in a southeastern city of 55,000 population. Its 2-year condensed balance sheets for 1996 and 1995 showing dollar and percentage changes are presented in Illustration 15-3.

The comparative balance sheet in Illustration 15-3 shows that a number of significant changes have occurred in Quality Department Store's financial structure from 1995 to 1996. In the asset section, plant assets (net) increased $167,500, or 26.5%. In the liabilities section, current liabilities increased $41,500, or 13.7%. In the stockholders' equity section, we find that retained earnings increased $202,600, or 38.6%. This suggests that the company expanded its asset base during 1996 and financed this expansion primarily by retaining income in the business rather than assuming additional long-term debt.

QUALITY DEPARTMENT STORE INC. Condensed Balance Sheet December 31				
			Increase or (Decrease) during 1996	
	1996	1995	Amount	Percentage
Assets				
Current assets	$1,020,000	$ 945,000	$ 75,000	7.9%
Plant assets (net)	800,000	632,500	167,500	26.5%
Intangible assets	15,000	17,500	(2,500)	(14.3%)
Total assets	$1,835,000	$1,595,000	$240,000	15.0%
Liabilities				
Current liabilities	$ 344,500	$ 303,000	$ 41,500	13.7%
Long-term liabilities	487,500	497,000	(9,500)	(1.9%)
Total liabilities	832,000	800,000	32,000	4.0%
Stockholders' Equity				
Common stock, $1 par	275,400	270,000	5,400	2.0%
Retained earnings	727,600	525,000	202,600	38.6%
Total stockholders' equity	1,003,000	795,000	208,000	26.2%
Total liabilities and stockholders' equity	$1,835,000	$1,595,000	$240,000	15.0%

Illustration 15-3

Horizontal analysis of a balance sheet

Helpful hint It is difficult to comprehend the significance of a change when only the dollar amount of change is examined. When the change is expressed in percentage form, it is easier to grasp the true magnitude of the change.

Income Statement

Presented in Illustration 15-4 is a 2-year comparative income statement of Quality Department Store Inc. for the years 1996 and 1995 in a condensed format.

QUALITY DEPARTMENT STORE INC. Condensed Income Statement For the Years Ended December 31				
			Increase or (Decrease) during 1996	
	1996	1995	Amount	Percentage
Sales	$2,195,000	$1,960,000	$235,000	12.0%
Sales returns and allowances	98,000	123,000	(25,000)	(20.3%)
Net sales	2,097,000	1,837,000	260,000	14.2%
Cost of goods sold	1,281,000	1,140,000	141,000	12.4%
Gross profit	816,000	697,000	119,000	17.1%
Selling expenses	253,000	211,500	41,500	19.6%
Administrative expenses	104,000	108,500	(4,500)	(4.1%)
Total operating expenses	357,000	320,000	37,000	11.6%
Income from operations	459,000	377,000	82,000	21.8%
Other revenues and gains				
Interest and dividends	9,000	11,000	(2,000)	(18.2%)
Other expenses and losses				
Interest expense	36,000	40,500	(4,500)	(11.1%)
Income before income taxes	432,000	347,500	84,500	24.3%
Income tax expense	168,200	139,000	29,200	21.0%
Net income	$ 263,800	$ 208,500	$ 55,300	26.5%

Illustration 15-4

Horizontal analysis of an income statement

Helpful hint Note that while the amount column is additive (the total is $55,300), the percentage column is not additive (the total is not 26.5%). A separate percentage has been calculated for each item.

Horizontal analysis of the income statements shows the following changes:

1. Net sales increased $260,000, or 14.2% ($260,000 ÷ $1,837,000).
2. Cost of goods sold increased $141,000, or 12.4% ($141,000 ÷ $1,140,000).
3. Total operating expenses increased $37,000, or 11.6% ($37,000 ÷ $320,000).

Overall, gross profit and net income were up substantially. Gross profit, for example, increased 17.1% and net income 26.5%. It appears, therefore, that Quality's profit trend is favorable.

Retained Earnings Statement

Quality Department Store's comparative retained earnings statement for the years 1996 and 1995 is presented in Illustration 15-5. Analyzed horizontally, net income increased $55,300, or 26.5%, whereas dividends on the common stock increased only $1,200, or 2%. Ending retained earnings, as shown in the horizontal analysis of the balance sheet, increased 38.6%. As indicated earlier, Quality Department Store Inc. retained a significant portion of its net income to finance expenditures for additional plant facilities.

Illustration 15-5

Horizontal analysis of a retained earnings statement

Helpful hint When using horizontal analysis, both dollar amount changes and percentage changes need to be examined. It is not necessarily bad if a company's earnings are growing at a declining rate. The amount of increase may be the same as or more than the base year. The percentage change may be less because the base is greater each year.

QUALITY DEPARTMENT STORE INC.
Retained Earnings Statement
For the Years Ended December 31

	1996	1995	Increase or (Decrease) during 1996 Amount	Increase or (Decrease) during 1996 Percentage
Retained earnings, Jan. 1	$525,000	$376,500	$148,500	39.4%
Add: Net income	263,800	208,500	55,300	26.5%
	788,800	585,000	203,800	
Deduct: Dividends	61,200	60,000	1,200	2.0%
Retained earnings, Dec. 31	$727,600	$525,000	$202,600	38.6%

The measurement of changes from period to period in terms of percentages is relatively straightforward and is quite useful. However, complications can result in making the computations. For example, if an item has no value in a base year or preceding year and a value in the next year, no percentage change can be computed. Similarly, if a negative amount appears in the base or preceding period and a positive amount exists the following year, or vice versa, no percentage change can be computed.

Vertical Analysis

STUDY OBJECTIVE

••••••••• 4 •••••••••

Describe and apply vertical analysis.

Vertical analysis, sometimes referred to as **common size analysis**, is a technique for evaluating financial statement data that expresses each item within a financial statement in terms of a percent of a base amount. For example, on a balance sheet we might say that current assets are 22% of total assets (total assets being the base amount). Or on an income statement, we might say that selling expenses are 16% of net sales (net sales being the base amount).

Balance Sheet

Presented in Illustration 15-6 is the comparative balance sheet of Quality Department Store Inc. for 1996 and 1995, analyzed vertically. The base for the asset items is **total assets**, and the base for the liability and stockholders' equity items is **total liabilities and stockholders' equity**.

Illustration 15-6

Vertical analysis of a balance sheet

QUALITY DEPARTMENT STORE INC. Condensed Balance Sheet December 31				
	1996		1995	
	Amount	Percent	Amount	Percent
Assets				
Current assets	$1,020,000	55.6%	$ 945,000	59.2%
Plant assets (net)	800,000	43.6%	632,500	39.7%
Intangible assets	15,000	.8%	17,500	1.1%
Total assets	$1,835,000	100.0%	$1,595,000	100.0%
Liabilities				
Current liabilities	$ 344,500	18.8%	$ 303,000	19.0%
Long-term liabilities	487,500	26.5%	497,000	31.2%
Total liabilities	832,000	45.3%	800,000	50.2%
Stockholders' Equity				
Common stock, $1 par	275,400	15.0%	270,000	16.9%
Retained earnings	727,600	39.7%	525,000	32.9%
Total stockholders' equity	1,003,000	54.7%	795,000	49.8%
Total liabilities and stockholders' equity	$1,835,000	100.0%	$1,595,000	100.0%

Helpful hint The formula for calculating these balance sheet percentages is:

$$\frac{\text{Each item on B/S}}{\text{Total assets}} = \%$$

In addition to showing the relative size of each category on the balance sheet, vertical analysis may show the **percentage change** in the individual asset, liability, and stockholders' equity items. In this case, even though current assets increased $75,000 from 1995 to 1996, they decreased from 59.2% to 55.6% of total assets. Plant assets (net) have increased from 39.7% to 43.6% of total assets, and retained earnings have increased from 32.9% to 39.7% of total liabilities and stockholders' equity. These results reinforce the earlier observations that Quality is choosing to finance its growth through retention of earnings rather than through the issuance of additional debt.

Income Statement

Vertical analysis of the comparative income statements of Quality, shown in Illustration 15-7, reveals that cost of goods sold as a percentage of net sales declined 1% (62.1% vs. 61.1%) and total operating expenses declined 0.4% (17.4% vs. 17.0%). As a result, it is not surprising to see net income as a percent of net sales increase from 11.4% to 12.6%. As indicated from the horizontal analysis, Quality appears to be a profitable enterprise that is becoming even more successful.

Illustration 15-7

Vertical analysis of an income statement

QUALITY DEPARTMENT STORE INC. Condensed Income Statement For the Years Ended December 31				
	1996		1995	
	Amount	Percent	Amount	Percent
Sales	$2,195,000	104.7%	$1,960,000	106.7%
Sales returns and allowances	98,000	4.7%	123,000	6.7%
Net sales	2,097,000	100.0%	1,837,000	100.0%
Cost of goods sold	1,281,000	61.1%	1,140,000	62.1%
Gross profit	816,000	38.9%	697,000	37.9%
Selling expenses	253,000	12.0%	211,500	11.5%
Administrative expenses	104,000	5.0%	108,500	5.9%
Total operating expenses	357,000	17.0%	320,000	17.4%
Income from operations	459,000	21.9%	377,000	20.5%
Other revenues and gains Interest and dividends	9,000	0.4%	11,000	0.6%
Other expenses and losses Interest expense	36,000	1.7%	40,500	2.2%
Income before income taxes	432,000	20.6%	347,500	18.9%
Income tax expense	168,200	8.0%	139,000	7.5%
Net income	$ 263,800	12.6%	$ 208,500	11.4%

Helpful hint The formula for calculating these income statement percentages is:

$$\frac{\text{Each item on Inc. St.}}{\text{Net sales}} = \%$$

An associated benefit of vertical analysis is that it enables you to compare companies of different sizes. For example, Quality's main competitor is a J.C. Penney store in a nearby town. Using vertical analysis, the condensed income statements of the small local retail enterprise, Quality Department Store Inc., can be more meaningfully compared with the income statement of a giant international retailer, J.C. Penney Company, as shown in Illustration 15-8.

Illustration 15-8

Intercompany income statement comparison

Helpful hint Questions: (1) For each $1.00 of net sales made by Quality Department Store, how much was net income? (2) For each $1.00 of net sales made by J.C. Penney, how much was net income? Answers: (1) 12.6 cents (2) 5.2 cents.

CONDENSED INCOME STATEMENTS				
	Quality Department Store Inc.		J.C. Penney Company	
(in thousands)	Dollars	Percent	Dollars	Percent
Net sales	$2,097	100.0%	$20,380,000	100.0%
Cost of goods sold	1,281	61.1%	13,970,000	68.5%
Gross profit	816	38.9%	6,410,000	31.5%
Selling and administrative expenses	357	17.0%	4,783,000	23.5%
Income from operations	459	21.9%	1,627,000	8.0%
Other expenses and revenues (including income taxes)	195	9.3%	570,000	2.8%
Net income	$ 264	12.6%	$ 1,057,000	5.2%

Although J.C. Penney's net sales are 9,719 times greater than the net sales of relatively tiny Quality Department Store, vertical analysis eliminates this difference in size. The percentages show that Quality's and Penney's gross profit rates were somewhat comparable at 38.9% and 31.5%, although the percentages related to income from operations were significantly different at 21.9% and 8.0%. This disparity can be attributed to Quality's selling and administrative expense percentage (17%) which is much lower than Penney's (23.5%). Although Penney earned net income more than 4,000 times larger than Quality's, Penney's net income as a **percent of each sales dollar** (5.2%) is only 41% of Quality's (12.6%).

Before You Go On . . .

▶ Review It

1. What are the different tools that might be used to compare financial information?
2. What is horizontal analysis?
3. What is vertical analysis?

▶ Do It

Summary financial information for Rosepatch Company is as follows:

	December 31, 1996	December 31, 1995
Current assets	$234,000	$180,000
Plant assets (net)	756,000	420,000
Total assets	$990,000	$600,000

Compute the amount and percentage changes in 1996 using horizontal analysis, assuming 1995 is the base year.

Reasoning: Since 1995 is the base year, the percentage change is found by dividing the amount of the increase by the 1995 amount.

Solution:

	Increase in 1996	
	Amount	Percentage
Current assets	$ 54,000	30% [($234,000 − $180,000) ÷ $180,000]
Plant assets (net)	336,000	80% [($756,000 − $420,000) ÷ $420,000]
Total assets	$390,000	65% [($990,000 − $600,000) ÷ $600,000]

Related exercise material: BE15–1, BE15–3, BE15–4, BE15–6, E15–1, E15–3, and E15–4.

Ratio Analysis

Ratio analysis expresses the relationship among selected items of financial statement data. A ratio expresses the mathematical relationship between one quantity and another. The relationship is expressed in terms of either a percentage, a rate, or a simple proportion. To illustrate, recently IBM Corporation had current assets of $41,338 million and current liabilities of $29,226 million. The relationship is determined by dividing current assets by current liabilities. The alternative means of expression are:

Percentage: Current assets are 141% of current liabilities.
Rate: Current assets are 1.41 times greater than current liabilities.
Proportion: The relationship of current assets to liabilities is 1.41:1.

STUDY OBJECTIVE 5

Identify and compute ratios and describe their purpose and use in analyzing a firm's liquidity, profitability, and solvency.

Helpful hint Each of these is illustrated in the following sections.

▶Technology in Action

Many general ledger accounting programs include the generation of financial ratios as routine output. All the ratio computations presented in this chapter can be done with electronic spreadsheets as well. There are also many programs written specifically for financial statement analysis. These packages are written for both general purpose use and use in specific industries. For example, financial institutions routinely use over 60 ratios geared specifically to the banking industry.

For analysis of the primary financial statements, ratios can be classified as follows:

Illustration 15-9

Financial ratio classifications

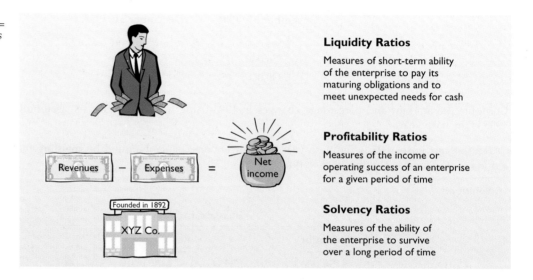

Liquidity Ratios

Measures of short-term ability of the enterprise to pay its maturing obligations and to meet unexpected needs for cash

Profitability Ratios

Measures of the income or operating success of an enterprise for a given period of time

Solvency Ratios

Measures of the ability of the enterprise to survive over a long period of time

Ratios can provide clues to underlying conditions that may not be apparent from inspection of the individual components of a particular ratio. However, a single ratio by itself is not very meaningful. Accordingly, in the following discussion we will use:

1. **Intracompany comparisons** covering 2 years for the Quality Department Store.
2. **Industry average comparisons** based on Dun & Bradstreet's median ratios for department stores and Robert Morris Associates' median ratios for department stores.
3. **Intercompany comparisons** based on the J.C. Penney Company, Inc. as Quality Department Store's principal competitor.

Liquidity Ratios

Liquidity ratios measure the short-term ability of the enterprise to pay its maturing obligations and to meet unexpected needs for cash. Short-term creditors such as bankers and suppliers are particularly interested in assessing **liquidity**. The ratios that can be used to determine the enterprise's short-term debt-paying ability are the current ratio, the acid-test ratio, current debt coverage ratio, receivables turnover, and inventory turnover.

1. *Current Ratio*

The current ratio is a widely used measure for evaluating a company's liquidity and short-term debt-paying ability. The ratio is computed by dividing current assets by current liabilities. It is sometimes referred to as the **working capital ratio** because **working capital** is the excess of current assets over current liabilities. The current ratio is a more dependable indicator of liquidity than working capital. Two companies with the same amount of working capital may have significantly different current ratios. The 1996 and 1995 current ratios for Quality Department Store and comparative data are shown in Illustration 15-10.

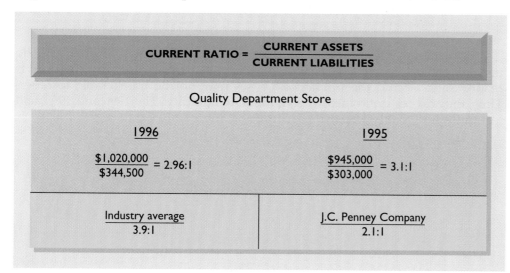

Illustration 15-10

Current ratio

What does the ratio actually mean? The 1996 ratio of 2.96:1 means that for every dollar of current liabilities, Quality has $2.96 of current assets. Quality's current ratio has decreased in the current year. However, compared to the industry average of 3.9:1, and J.C. Penney Company's 2.1:1 current ratio, Quality appears to be reasonably liquid.

The current ratio is only one measure of liquidity. It does not take into account the composition of the current assets. For example, a satisfactory current ratio does not disclose the fact that a portion of the current assets may be tied up in slow-moving inventory. A dollar of cash is more readily available to pay the bills than is a dollar of slow-moving inventory.

Helpful hint Can any corporation operate successfully without working capital? Yes, if it has very predictable cash flows and solid earnings. A surprising number of companies, including Whirlpool, American Standard, and Campbell's Soup, are pursuing this goal. The rationale: Less money tied up in working capital means more money to invest in the business.

2. *Acid-Test Ratio*

The acid-test ratio is a measure of a company's immediate short-term liquidity, computed by dividing the sum of cash, marketable securities, and net receivables by current liabilities. Thus, it is an important complement to the current ratio. For example, assume that the current assets of Quality Department Store for 1996 and 1995 consist of the following items:

Helpful hint The acid-test ratio is also called the quick ratio.

	1996	1995
Current assets		
Cash	$ 100,000	$155,000
Marketable securities	20,000	70,000
Receivables (net)	230,000	180,000
Inventory	620,000	500,000
Prepaid expenses	50,000	40,000
Total current assets	$1,020,000	$945,000

Illustration 15-11

Current assets of Quality Department Store

▶*Accounting in Action* ▸ *Business Insight*

The apparent simplicity of the current ratio can have real world limitations because an addition of equal amounts to both the numerator and the denominator causes the ratio to decrease. Assume, for example, that a company has $2,000,000 of current assets and $1,000,000 of current liabilities; its current ratio is 2:1. If it purchases $1,000,000 of inventory on account, it will have $3,000,000 of current assets and $2,000,000 of current liabilities; its current ratio will decrease to 1.5:1. If, instead, the company pays off $500,000 of its current liabilities, it will have $1,500,000 of current assets and $500,000 of current liabilities, and its current ratio will increase to 3:1. Thus, any trend analysis should be done with care, since the ratio is susceptible to quick changes and is easily influenced by management.

Cash, marketable securities (short-term), and receivables (net) are highly liquid compared to inventory and prepaid expenses. The inventory may not be readily saleable and the prepaid expenses may not be transferable to others. Thus, the acid-test ratio measures **immediate** liquidity. The 1996 and 1995 acid-test ratios for Quality Department Store and comparative data are as follows:

Illustration 15-12

Acid-test ratio

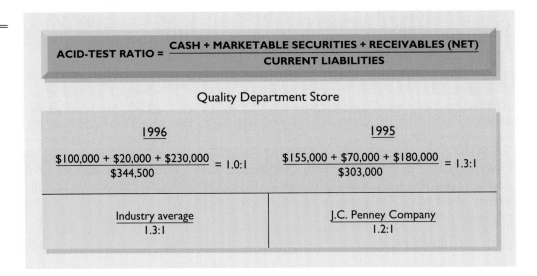

$$\text{ACID-TEST RATIO} = \frac{\text{CASH + MARKETABLE SECURITIES + RECEIVABLES (NET)}}{\text{CURRENT LIABILITIES}}$$

Quality Department Store

1996	1995
$\frac{\$100,000 + \$20,000 + \$230,000}{\$344,500} = 1.0{:}1$	$\frac{\$155,000 + \$70,000 + \$180,000}{\$303,000} = 1.3{:}1$
Industry average 1.3:1	J.C. Penney Company 1.2:1

Is an acid-test ratio of 1.0:1 adequate? The ratio has declined in 1996. However, when compared with the industry median of 1.3:1 and J.C. Penney's 1.2:1, Quality's acid-test ratio seems adequate.

3. Current Cash Debt Coverage Ratio

A disadvantage of the current and acid-test ratios is that they employ year-end balances of current asset and current liability accounts. These year-end balances may not be representative of what the company's current position was during most of the year. A ratio which partially corrects for this problem is the ratio of net cash provided by operating activities to average current liabilities, referred to as the current cash debt coverage ratio. Because it uses net cash provided by operating activities rather than a balance at a point in time, it may provide a better representation of liquidity.

To illustrate the computation of this ratio, assume that Quality Department Store's statement of cash flows shows net cash flows provided by operating activities of $404,000 in 1996 and $340,000 in 1995 and that current liabilities at January 1, 1995 are $290,000.

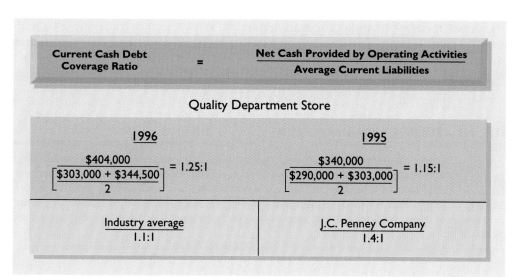

Illustration 15-13

Current cash debt coverage ratio

The ratio has increased in 1996. Is the coverage adequate? Probably so, Quality's operating cash flow coverage of average current liabilities is slightly greater than the industry average and slightly below J.C. Penney's coverage.

4. *Receivables Turnover*

Liquidity may be measured by how quickly certain assets can be converted to cash. How liquid, for example, are the receivables? The ratio used to assess the liquidity of the receivables is the receivables turnover ratio. This ratio measures the number of times, on average, receivables are collected during the period. The receivables turnover ratio is computed by dividing net credit sales (net sales less cash sales) by the average net receivables during the year. Unless seasonal factors are significant, average net receivables outstanding can be computed from the beginning and ending balance of the net receivables.[1]

Assuming that all sales are credit sales and the balance of accounts receivable (net) at the beginning of 1995 is $200,000, the receivables turnover ratio for Qual-

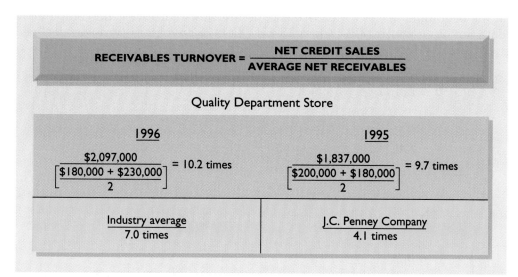

Illustration 15-14

Receivables turnover

---

[1] If seasonal factors are significant, the average receivables balance might be determined by using monthly amounts.

ity Department Store and comparative data are shown in Illustration 15-14. Quality's receivables turnover improved in 1996. The turnover of 10.2 times compares quite favorably with J.C. Penney's 4.1 times and the department store industry's median of 7.0 times.

▸Accounting in Action ▸ *Business Insight*

In some cases, receivable turnover may be misleading. Some companies, especially large retail chains, encourage credit and revolving charge sales, and they slow collections in order to earn a healthy return on the outstanding receivables in the form of interest at rates of 18% to 22%. This may explain why J.C. Penney's turnover is only 4.1 times. In general, however, the faster the turnover, the greater the reliance that can be placed on the current and acid-test ratios for assessing liquidity.

A popular variant of the receivables turnover ratio is to convert it into an **average collection period** in terms of days. This is done by dividing the turnover ratio into 365 days. For example, the receivable turnover in 1996 of 10.2 times is divided into 365 days to obtain approximately 35.8 days. This means that the average collection period for receivables is 36 days, or approximately every 5 weeks. The average collection period is frequently used to assess the effectiveness of a company's credit and collection policies. The general rule is that the collection period should not greatly exceed the credit term period (i.e., the time allowed for payment).

5. Inventory Turnover

The inventory turnover ratio measures the number of times on average the inventory is sold during the period. Its purpose is to measure the liquidity of the inventory. The inventory turnover is computed by dividing cost of goods sold by the average inventory during the period. Unless seasonal factors are significant, average inventory can be computed from the beginning and ending inventory balances. Assuming that the inventory balance for Quality Department Store at the beginning of 1995 was $450,000, its inventory turnover and comparative data are as shown in Illustration 15-15. Quality's inventory turnover declined

Illustration 15-15

Inventory turnover

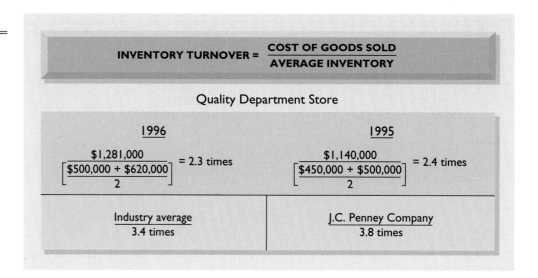

$$\text{INVENTORY TURNOVER} = \frac{\text{COST OF GOODS SOLD}}{\text{AVERAGE INVENTORY}}$$

Quality Department Store

1996	1995
$\dfrac{\$1,281,000}{\left[\dfrac{\$500,000 + \$620,000}{2}\right]} = 2.3 \text{ times}$	$\dfrac{\$1,140,000}{\left[\dfrac{\$450,000 + \$500,000}{2}\right]} = 2.4 \text{ times}$
Industry average 3.4 times	J.C. Penney Company 3.8 times

slightly in 1996. The turnover ratio of 2.3 times is relatively low compared with the industry average of 3.4 and J.C. Penney's 3.8. Generally, the faster the inventory turnover, the less cash that is tied up in inventory and the less the chance of inventory obsolescence.

A variant of the inventory turnover ratio is to compute the **average days to sell the inventory**. For example, the inventory turnover in 1996 of 2.3 times divided into 365 is approximately 159 days. An average selling time of 159 days is also relatively high compared with the industry average of 107 days (365 ÷ 3.4) and J.C. Penney Company's 96 days (365 ÷ 3.8).

►Accounting in Action ► *Business Insight*

Inventory turnover ratios vary considerably among industries. For example, grocery store chains have a turnover of 10 times and an average selling period of 37 days. In contrast, jewelry stores have an average turnover of 1.3 times and an average selling period of 281 days. Within a company there may be significant differences in inventory turnover among different types of products. Thus, in a grocery store the turnover of perishable items such as produce, meats, and dairy products will be faster than the turnover of soaps and detergents.

Profitability Ratios

Profitability ratios measure the income or operating success of an enterprise for a given period of time. Income, or the lack of it, affects the company's ability to obtain debt and equity financing, the company's liquidity position, and the company's ability to grow. As a consequence, creditors and investors alike are interested in evaluating earning power (profitability). Profitability is frequently used as the ultimate test of management's operating effectiveness.

6. Profit Margin

The profit margin ratio is a measure of the percentage of each dollar of sales that results in net income. It is computed by dividing net income by net sales for the period. Quality Department Store's profit margin ratios and comparative data are shown in Illustration 15-16.

Helpful hint The profit margin ratio is also called the rate of return on sales.

Illustration 15-16

Profit margin ratio

Helpful hint How does the profit margin ratio differ from the gross margin ratio? Answer: The profit margin ratio is computed by dividing net income by net sales, and the gross margin ratio is computed by dividing gross profit by net sales.

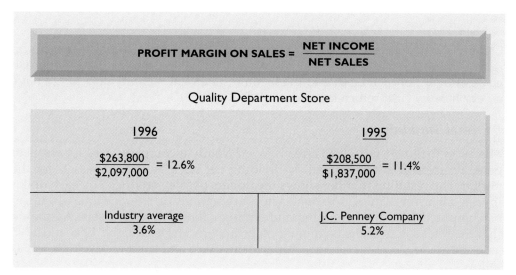

$$\text{PROFIT MARGIN ON SALES} = \frac{\text{NET INCOME}}{\text{NET SALES}}$$

Quality Department Store

1996	1995
$\frac{\$263,800}{\$2,097,000} = 12.6\%$	$\frac{\$208,500}{\$1,837,000} = 11.4\%$
Industry average 3.6%	J.C. Penney Company 5.2%

Quality experienced an increase in its profit margin from 1995 to 1996. Its profit margin is unusually high in comparison with the industry average of 3.6% and J.C. Penney Company's 5.2%.

High-volume (high inventory turnover) enterprises such as grocery stores (Safeway or Kroger) and discount stores (Kmart or Wal-Mart) generally experience low profit margins, whereas low-volume enterprises such as jewelry stores (Tiffany & Co.) or airplane manufacturers (Boeing Aircraft) have high profit margins.

7. Cash Return on Sales Ratio

The profit margin ratio discussed above is an accrual based ratio using net income as the numerator. The cash basis counter-part to that ratio is the cash return on sales ratio which uses net cash provided by operating activities as the numerator and net sales as the denominator. The difference between these two ratios should be explainable as differences between accrual accounting and cash basis accounting, i.e., differences in the timing of revenue and expense recognition. Using net cash provided by operating activities of $404,000 in 1996 and $340,000 in 1995, Quality Department Store's cash return on sales ratios are computed as follows:

Illustration 15-17

Cash return on sales ratio

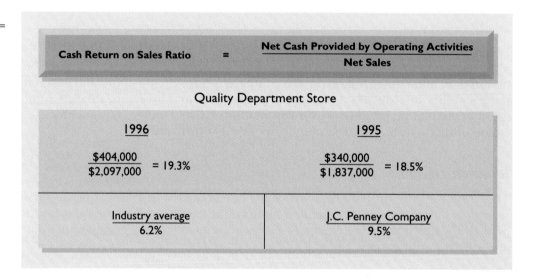

Quality's cash return on sales is considerably higher than its profit margin on sales. The difference of 6.7% (19.3%–12.6%) in 1996 is due to excess noncash charges over noncash credits to the income statement. Quality appears to have a very healthy cash return on sales.

8. Asset Turnover

The asset turnover ratio measures how efficiently a company uses its assets to generate sales. It is determined by dividing net sales by average assets for the period. The resulting number shows the dollars of sales produced by each dollar invested in assets. Unless seasonal factors are significant, average total assets can be computed from the beginning and ending balance of total assets. Assuming that the total assets at the beginning of 1995 were $1,446,000, the 1996 and 1995 asset turnover ratios for Quality Department Store and comparative data are as follows:

Illustration 15-18

Asset turnover

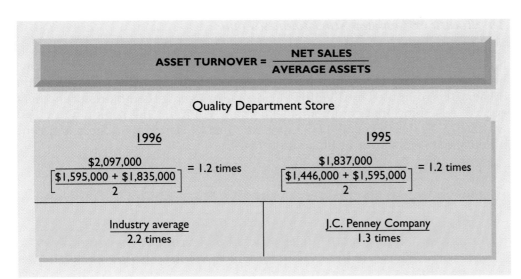

The asset turnover ratio shows that Quality generated sales of $1.22 in 1996 for each dollar it had invested in assets. The ratio changed little from 1995 to 1996. Quality's asset turnover ratio is below the industry median of 2.2 times and J.C. Penney's ratio of 1.3 times.

Asset turnover ratios vary considerably among industries. For example, a large utility company like Union Electric Company (St. Louis) has a ratio of 0.36 times, and the large grocery chain Great Atlantic and Pacific Tea (A&P) has a ratio of 3.6 times.

9. Return on Assets Ratio

An overall measure of profitability is the return on assets ratio. This ratio is computed by dividing net income by average assets. The 1996 and 1995 return on assets for Quality Department Store and comparative data are shown below.

Illustration 15-19

Return on assets

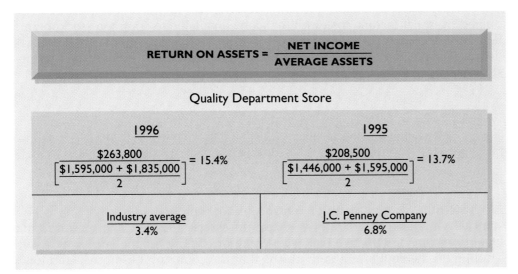

Quality's return on assets improved from 1995 to 1996. Its return of 15.4% is very high, compared with the department store industry median of 3.4% and J.C. Penney Company's 6.8%.

10. Return on Common Stockholders' Equity

Another widely used ratio that measures profitability from the common stock-holder's viewpoint is return on common stockholders' equity. This ratio shows how many dollars of net income were earned for each dollar invested by the owners. It is computed by dividing net income by average common stockholders' equity. Assuming that common stockholders' equity at the beginning of 1995 was $667,000, the 1996 and 1995 ratios for Quality Department Store and comparative data are shown in Illustration 15-20.

Illustration 15-20

Return on common stock-holders' equity

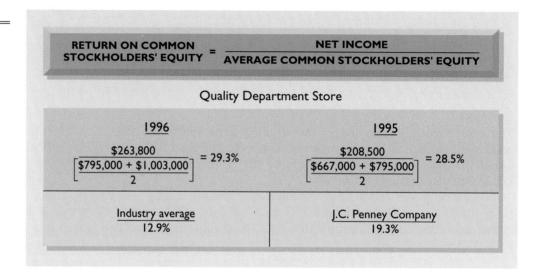

Quality's rate of return on common stockholders' equity is unusually high at 29.3%, considering an industry average of 12.9% and a rate of 19.3% for J.C. Penney Company.

When preferred stock is present, **preferred dividend** requirements are deducted from net income to compute income available to common stockholders. Similarly, the par value of preferred stock (or call price, if applicable) must be deducted from total stockholders' equity to arrive at the amount of common stock equity used in this ratio. The ratio then appears as follows:

Illustration 15-21

Return on common stock-holders' equity with pre-ferred stock

$$\text{Rate of return on common stockholders' equity} = \frac{\text{Net income} - \text{Preferred dividends}}{\text{Average common stockholders' equity}}$$

Note that Quality's rate of return on stockholders' equity (29.3%) is substantially higher than its rate of return on assets (15.38%). The reason is that Quality has made effective use of leverage or trading on the equity at a gain. Trading on the equity at a gain means that the company has borrowed money through the issuance of bonds or notes at a lower rate of interest than it is able to earn by using the borrowed money. Leverage is simply trying to use money supplied by nonowners to increase the return to the owners. A comparison of the rate of return on total assets with the rate of interest paid for borrowed money indicates the profitability of trading on the equity. Note that trading on the equity is a two-way street: for example, if you borrow money at 11% and earn only 8% on it, you are trading on the equity at a loss. Quality Department Store earns more on its borrowed funds than it has to pay in the form of interest. Thus the return to stockholders exceeds the return on the assets, benefiting from the positive leveraging.

Helpful hint Trading on the equity is also called leveraging.

11. Earnings Per Share (EPS)

Earnings per share of stock is a measure of the net income earned on each share of common stock. It is computed by dividing net income by the number of weighted average common shares outstanding during the year. Stockholders usually think in terms of the number of shares they own or plan to buy or sell. Reducing net income earned to a per share basis provides a useful perspective for determining profitability. Assuming that there is no change in the number of outstanding shares during 1995 and that the 1996 increase occurred midyear, the net income per share for Quality Department Store for 1996 and 1995 is computed as shown in Illustration 15-22.

Helpful hint Is earnings per share quoted for common stock or preferred stock, or both? Answer: Only for common stock.

Illustration 15-22

Earnings per share

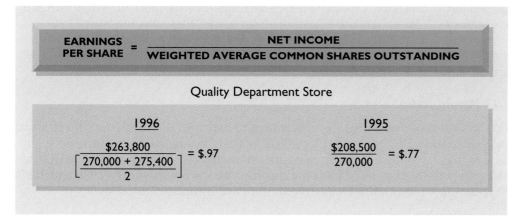

Note that no industry or J.C. Penney data are presented. Such comparisons are not meaningful because of the wide variations in the number of shares of outstanding stock among companies. Quality's earnings per share increased 20 cents per share in 1996. This represents a 26% increase over the 1995 earnings per share of 77 cents.

When the term "net income per share" or "earnings per share" is used, it refers to the amount of net income applicable to each share of **common stock**. Therefore, in computing net income per share, if there are preferred dividends declared for the period, they must be deducted from net income to arrive at income available to the common stockholders.

12. Price-Earnings Ratio

The price-earnings ratio is an oft-quoted statistic that measures the ratio of the market price of each share of common stock to the earnings per share. The price-earnings (PE) ratio reflects investors' assessments of a company's future earnings. It is computed by dividing the market price per share of the stock by earnings per share. Assuming that the market price of Quality Department Store Inc. stock is $8 in 1995 and $12 in 1996, the price-earnings ratio is computed as follows:

Illustration 15-23

Price-earnings ratio

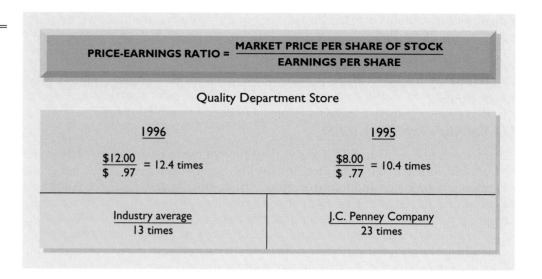

In 1996 each share of Quality's stock sold for 12.4 times the amount that was earned on each share. Quality's price-earnings ratio is less than the industry average of 13 times, and it is significantly lower than the ratio of 23 for J.C. Penney Company. The average price-earnings ratio for the stocks that constitute the Dow-Jones industrial average on the New York Stock Exchange in May 1995 was an unusually high 22 times.

13. Payout Ratio

The payout ratio measures the percentage of earnings distributed in the form of cash dividends. It is computed by dividing cash dividends by net income. Companies that have high growth rates are characterized by low payout ratios because they reinvest most of their net income into the business. The 1996 and 1995 payout ratios for Quality Department Store are computed as follows:

Illustration 15-24

Payout ratio

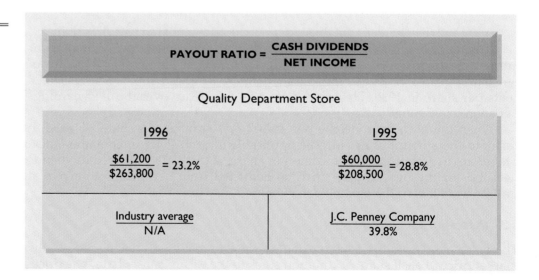

Quality's payout ratio is comparatively low when compared with J.C. Penney's payout ratio of 39.8%. As indicated earlier, the company has apparently decided to fund its purchase of plant assets through retention of earnings.

▶*A*ccounting in *A*ction ▸ *Business Insight*

For the stock of some companies, investors are willing to pay over 20 times the current per-share earnings because they feel the future growth in earnings will provide an adequate return on the investment. Examples of companies with price-earnings ratios over 20 are Microsoft (51), Coca-Cola (42), and Gillette Co. (46). Examples of companies with low price-earnings ratios are Ford Motor (9), General Motors (9), and UAL Inc. (12).

Solvency Ratios

Solvency ratios measure the ability of the enterprise to survive over a long period of time. Long-term creditors and stockholders are interested in a company's long-run solvency, particularly its ability to pay interest as it comes due and to repay the face value of the debt at maturity. Debt to total assets, times interest earned, and cash debt coverage ratio are three ratios that provide information about debt-paying ability.

▶*A*ccounting in *A*ction ▸ *Business Insight*

Many companies with stable earnings have high payout ratios. For example, Pennsylvania Power & Light has had an 86% payout ratio over the last 5 years, and Woolworth Corporation's dividends exceeded net income over the same period. Conversely, companies that are expanding rapidly, such as Toys 'R' Us, Microsoft, and Telecommunications Inc. have never paid a cash dividend.

14. Debt to Total Assets Ratio

The debt to total assets ratio measures the percentage of the total assets provided by creditors (this ratio indicates the degree of leveraging). It is computed by dividing total debt (both current and long-term liabilities) by total assets. This ratio provides some indication of the company's ability to withstand losses without impairing the interests of creditors. The higher the percentage of debt to total assets, the greater the risk that the company may be unable to meet its maturing obligations. The 1996 and 1995 ratios for Quality Department Store and comparative data are as follows:

Illustration 15-25

Debt to total assets

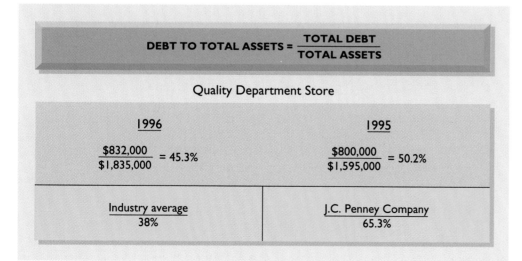

$$\text{DEBT TO TOTAL ASSETS} = \frac{\text{TOTAL DEBT}}{\text{TOTAL ASSETS}}$$

Quality Department Store

1996	1995
$\dfrac{\$832,000}{\$1,835,000} = 45.3\%$	$\dfrac{\$800,000}{\$1,595,000} = 50.2\%$
Industry average 38%	J.C. Penney Company 65.3%

▸Accounting in Action ▸ *Business Insight*

Examples of debt to total assets ratios for selected companies are:

	Total Debt to Total Assets As a Percent
Advanced Micro Devices	29%
General Motors Corporation	93%
Roberts Pharmaceutical	23%
Callaway Golf Company	19%
Sears Roebuck & Company	64%
Eastman Kodak Company	83%

Another means used in practice to measure this same leverage phenomenon is the "debt to equity ratio." It shows the relative use of borrowed funds (total liabilities) as compared to resources invested by the owners. Because this ratio may be computed in several ways, care should be taken when making comparisons. Debt may be defined to include only the noncurrent portion of the liabilities, and intangible assets may be excluded from owners' equity (resulting in tangible net worth).

Helpful hint A variation of this ratio is the **equity to debt ratio**. This is the ratio used by the University of Chicago in the opening vignette. It is computed by dividing total stockholders' equity by total liabilities. The higher this ratio, the more protection creditors have in a period of financial distress.

A ratio of 45.3% means that creditors have provided 45.3% of Quality Department Store's total assets. Quality's 45.3% is above the industry average of 38%, but it is considerably below the 65.3% ratio of J.C. Penney Company. The lower the ratio, the more equity "buffer" there is available to the creditors if the company becomes insolvent. Thus, from the creditors' point of view, a low ratio of debt to total assets is usually desirable.

The adequacy of this ratio is often judged in the light of the company's earnings. Generally, companies with relatively stable earnings, such as public utilities, have higher debt to total assets ratios than cyclical companies with widely fluctuating earnings, such as many high-tech companies. (See Accounting in Action above for examples of debt to total assets ratios for selected companies.)

15. Times Interest Earned Ratio

The times interest earned ratio provides an indication of the company's ability to meet interest payments as they come due. It is computed by dividing income before interest expense and income taxes by interest expense. The 1996 and 1995

Helpful hint The times interest earned ratio is also called the interest coverage ratio.

Illustration 15-26

Times interest earned

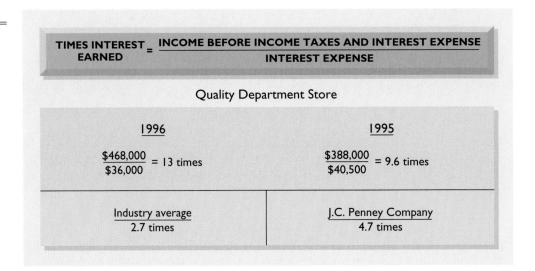

TIMES INTEREST EARNED	=	INCOME BEFORE INCOME TAXES AND INTEREST EXPENSE
		INTEREST EXPENSE

Quality Department Store

1996	1995
$\dfrac{\$468,000}{\$36,000} = 13$ times	$\dfrac{\$388,000}{\$40,500} = 9.6$ times
Industry average 2.7 times	J.C. Penney Company 4.7 times

ratios for Quality Department Store and comparative data are shown in Illustration 15-26. Note that the times interest earned ratio uses income before income taxes and interest expense, because this amount represents the amount available to cover interest. For Quality Department Store the 1996 amount of $468,000 is computed by taking the income before income taxes of $432,000 and adding back the $36,000 of interest expense. The interest expense of Quality is well covered at 13 times relative to the industry average of 2.7 times and J.C. Penney Company's 4.7 times.

▶*T*echnology in *A*ction

In terms of the types of financial information that are available and the ratios used by various industries, you should be aware that what can be practically covered in this textbook gives you only the "Titanic approach." That is, you are seeing only the tip of the iceberg compared to the vast data bases and different types of ratio analysis that are available on computers. The availability of information is not a problem. The real trick is to be discriminating enough to perform relevant analysis and to select pertinent comparative data.

16. Cash Debt Coverage Ratio

The ratio of net cash provided by operating activities to average total liabilities, referred to as the cash debt coverage ratio, is a cash basis measure of **solvency**. This ratio demonstrates a company's ability to repay its liabilities from cash generated from operating activities, without having to liquidate the assets employed in its operations. Using Quality's net cash provided by operating activities of $404,000 in 1996 and $340,000 in 1995 and assuming total liabilities of $740,000 on January 1, 1995, the cash debt coverage ratios are computed as follows:

Illustration 15-27

Cash debt coverage ratio

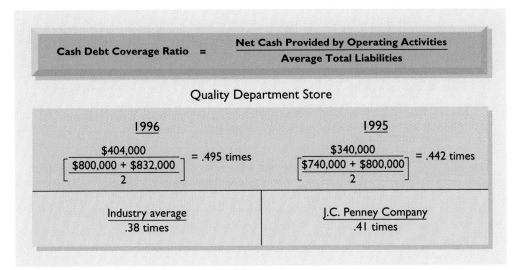

Based on net cash generated from operations in 1996, it would take Quality approximately 2 years to generate enough cash to pay off all its liabilities (assuming all of the net cash generated were used for that purpose only). Its ratio is also superior to that of the retail industry and J.C. Penney's.

Summary of Ratios

A summary of the ratios discussed in the chapter is presented in Illustration 15-28. The summary includes the formula and purpose or use of each ratio.

Illustration 15-28

Summary of liquidity, profit-ability, and solvency ratios

Ratio	Formula	Purpose or Use
Liquidity Ratios		
1. Current ratio	$\dfrac{\text{Current assets}}{\text{Current liabilities}}$	Measures short-term debt-paying ability.
2. Acid-test or quick ratio	$\dfrac{\text{Cash + marketable securities + receivables (net)}}{\text{Current liabilities}}$	Measures immediate short-term liquidity.
3. Current cash debt coverage ratio	$\dfrac{\text{Net cash provided by operating activities}}{\text{Average current liabilities}}$	Measures short-term debt-paying ability (cash basis).
4. Receivables turnover	$\dfrac{\text{Net credit sales}}{\text{Average net receivables}}$	Measures liquidity of receivables.
5. Inventory turnover	$\dfrac{\text{Cost of goods sold}}{\text{Average inventory}}$	Measures liquidity of inventory.
Profitability Ratios		
6. Profit margin	$\dfrac{\text{Net income}}{\text{Net sales}}$	Measures net income generated by each dollar of sales.
7. Cash return on sales ratio	$\dfrac{\text{Net cash provided by operating activities}}{\text{Net sales}}$	Measures the net cash flow generated by each dollar of sales.
8. Asset turnover	$\dfrac{\text{Net sales}}{\text{Average assets}}$	Measures how efficiently assets are used to generate sales.
9. Return on assets	$\dfrac{\text{Net income}}{\text{Average assets}}$	Measures overall profitability of assets.
10. Return on common stockholders' equity	$\dfrac{\text{Net income}}{\text{Average common stockholders' equity}}$	Measures profitability of owners' investment.
11. Earnings per share	$\dfrac{\text{Net income}}{\text{Weighted average common shares outstanding}}$	Measures net income earned on each share of common stock.
12. Price-earnings ratio	$\dfrac{\text{Market price per share of stock}}{\text{Earnings per share}}$	Measures the ratio of the market price per share to earnings per share.
13. Payout ratio	$\dfrac{\text{Cash dividends}}{\text{Net income}}$	Measures percentage of earnings distributed in the form of cash dividends.
Solvency Ratios		
14. Debt to total assets	$\dfrac{\text{Total debt}}{\text{Total assets}}$	Measures the percentage of total assets provided by creditors.
15. Times interest earned	$\dfrac{\text{Income before income taxes and interest expense}}{\text{Interest expense}}$	Measures ability to meet interest payments as they come due.
16. Cash debt coverage ratio	$\dfrac{\text{Net cash provided by operating activities}}{\text{Average total liabilities}}$	Measures the long-term debt paying ability (cash basis).

Before You Go On . . .

► *Review It*

1. What are liquidity ratios? Explain the current ratio, acid-test ratio, current cash debt coverage ratio, receivables turnover ratio, and inventory turnover ratio.
2. What are profitability ratios? Explain the profit margin ratio, cash return on sales ratio, asset turnover ratio, return on assets ratio, return on common stockholders' equity ratio, earnings per share, price-earnings ratio, and payout ratio.
3. What are solvency ratios? Explain the debt to total assets ratio, times interest earned ratio, and cash debt coverage ratio.

► *Do It*

Selected financial data for Drummond Company at December 31, 1996, are as follows: cash $60,000; receivables (net) $80,000; inventory $70,000; current liabilities $140,000. Compute the current and acid-test ratios.

Reasoning: The formula for the current ratio is: current assets ÷ current liabilities. The formula for the acid-test ratio is: cash + marketable securities + receivables (net) ÷ current liabilities.

Solution: The current ratio is 1.5:1 ($210,000 ÷ $140,000). The acid-test ratio is 1:1 ($140,000 ÷ $140,000).

Related exercise material: BE15–7, BE15–8, BE15–9, BE15–10, BE15–11, E15–5, E15–6, and E15–7.

*E*arning Power and Irregular Items

Users of financial statements are interested in the concept of "earning power." Earning power means the normal level of income to be obtained in the future. Earning power differs from actual net income by the amount of irregular revenues, expenses, gains, and losses. Users are interested in earning power because it helps them derive an estimate of future earnings without the "noise" of irregular items.

For users of financial statements to determine "earning power" or regular income, the irregular items are separately identified on the income statement. Three types of irregular items are reported:
1. Discontinued operations,
2. Extraordinary items, and
3. Changes in accounting principle.

All these irregular items are reported net of income taxes. That is, the applicable income tax expense or tax savings is shown for income before income taxes and for each of the listed irregular items. The general concept is "let the tax follow income or loss."

> **STUDY OBJECTIVE**
> ··········▾**6**··········
> *Understand the concept of earning power and indicate how material items not typical of regular operations are presented.*

Discontinued Operations

To downsize its operations, General Dynamics Corp. sold its missile business to Hughes Aircraft Co. for $450 million. In its income statement, General Dynamics was required to report the sale in a separate section entitled "discontinued operations."

Discontinued operations refers to the disposal of a **significant segment** of a business, such as the cessation of an entire activity or the elimination of a major class of customers. Thus, Kmart's decision to terminate its interest in four business activities including PACE Membership Warehouse, Inc., and PayLess Drug

Stores Northwest, Inc., were reported as discontinued operations. On the other hand, the phasing out of a model such as the GM Chevette or part of a line of business is not considered to be a disposal of a segment.

When the disposal of a significant segment occurs, the income statement should report both income from continuing operations and income (or loss) from discontinued operations. **The income (loss) from discontinued operations consists of the income (loss) from operations and the gain (loss) on disposal of the segment.** To illustrate, assume that Acro Energy Inc. has revenues of $2.5 million and expenses of $1.7 million from continuing operations in 1996. The company, therefore, has income before income taxes of $800,000. During 1996 the company discontinued and sold its unprofitable chemical division. The loss in 1996 from chemical operations (net of $60,000 taxes) was $140,000, and the loss on disposal of the chemical division (net of $30,000 taxes) was $70,000. Assuming a 30% tax rate on income before income taxes, the income statement presentation is shown below.

Illustration 15-29

Statement presentation of discontinued operations

Helpful hint Observe the dual disclosures: (1) the results of operations of the discontinued division must be eliminated from the results of continuing operations, and (2) the disposal of the operation.

ACRO ENERGY INC. Partial Income Statement For the Year Ended December 31, 1996		
Income before income taxes		$800,000
Income tax expense		240,000
Income from continuing operations		560,000
Discontinued operations		
Loss from operations of chemical division, net of $60,000 income tax saving	$140,000	
Loss from disposal of chemical division, net of $30,000 income tax saving	70,000	210,000
Net income		$350,000

Note that the caption "Income from continuing operations" is used and that a section "Discontinued operations" is added. **Within the new section, both the operating loss and the loss on disposal are reported net of applicable income taxes.** This presentation clearly indicates the separate effects of continuing operations and discontinued operations on net income.

Extraordinary Items

Extraordinary items are events and transactions that meet two conditions: they are (1) **unusual in nature** and (2) **infrequent in occurrence**. To be considered unusual, the item should be abnormal and be only incidentally related to the customary activities of the entity. To be regarded as infrequent, the event or transaction should not be reasonably expected to recur in the foreseeable future. Both criteria must be evaluated in terms of the environment in which the entity operates. Thus, Weyerhaeuser Co. reported the $36 million in damages to its timberland caused by the volcanic eruption of Mount St. Helens as an extraordinary item because the event was both unusual and infrequent. In contrast, Florida Citrus Company does not report frost damage to its citrus crop as an extraordinary item because frost damage is not viewed as infrequent. Illustration 15-30 shows the appropriate classification of extraordinary and ordinary items.

Extraordinary items

1. Effects of major casualties (acts of God), if rare in the area.

2. Expropriation (takeover) of property by a foreign government.

3. Effects of a newly enacted law or regulation, such as a condemnation action.

Ordinary items

1. Effects of major casualties (acts of God), frequent in the area.

2. Write-down of inventories or write-off of receivables.

3. Losses attributable to labor strikes.

4. Gains or losses from sales of property, plant, or equipment.

Illustration 15-30

Examples of extraordinary and ordinary items

Extraordinary items are reported net of taxes in a separate section of the income statement immediately below discontinued operations. To illustrate, assume that in 1996 a revolutionary foreign government expropriated property held as an investment by Acro Energy Inc. If the loss is $70,000, before applicable income taxes of $21,000, the income statement presentation will show a deduction of $49,000 as shown in Illustration 15-31.

Illustration 15-31

Statement presentation of extraordinary items

ACRO ENERGY INC. Partial Income Statement For the Year Ended December 31, 1996		
Income before income taxes		$800,000
Income tax expense		240,000
Income from continuing operations		560,000
Discontinued operations		
Loss from operations of chemical division, net of $60,000 income tax saving	$140,000	
Loss from disposal of chemical division, net of $30,000 income tax saving	70,000	210,000
Income before extraordinary item		350,000
Extraordinary item		
Expropriation of investment, net of $21,000 income tax saving		49,000
Net income		$301,000

Helpful hint Ordinary gains and losses are reported at pretax amounts in arriving at income before income taxes. For example, gains in item 4 are reported under other revenues and gains.

▸Accounting in Action ▸ *Business Insight*

In the recession of the early 1990s, many companies closed some of their plants and reduced the size of their work forces. The costs incurred in these activities, called plant restructuring costs, are reported as other expenses and losses in the income statement. These costs are not considered to be an extraordinary item because plant closings are neither unusual nor infrequent in many industries. Plant restructuring costs often have a significant effect on net income as illustrated by the following:

Union Pacific Corp. $585 million after-tax charge, of which $492 million applies to the disposal of 7,100 miles of the Union Pacific Railroad.

Borden, Inc. $71.6 million before-tax charge for business reorganization costs as well as severance, relocation, and other employee-related expenses.

As illustrated, the caption "Income before extraordinary item" is added immediately before the section for the extraordinary item. This presentation clearly indicates the effect of the extraordinary item on net income. If there are no discontinued operations, the third line of the income statement in Illustration 15-31 would be labeled "Income before extraordinary item."

If a transaction or event meets one (but not both) of the criteria for an extraordinary item, it is reported under either "Other revenues and gains" or "Other expenses and losses" at its gross amount (not net of tax). This is true, for example, of gains (losses) resulting from the sale of property, plant, and equipment, as explained in Chapter 5.

Change in Accounting Principle

For ease of comparison, financial statements are expected to be prepared on a basis **consistent** with that used for the preceding period. That is, where a choice of accounting principles is available, the principle initially chosen should be consistently applied from period to period. A change in an accounting principle occurs when the principle used in the current year is different from the one used in the preceding year. A change is permitted, when (1) management can show that the new principle is preferable to the old principle, and (2) the effects of the change are clearly disclosed in the income statement. Examples of a change in accounting principle include a change in depreciation methods (e.g., declining-balance to straight-line) and a change in inventory costing methods (e.g., FIFO to average cost). The effect of a change in an accounting principle on net income may be significant.

When a change in an accounting principle has occurred,

1. The new principle should be used in reporting the results of operations of the current year.
2. The cumulative effect of the change on all prior year income statements should be disclosed net of applicable taxes in a special section immediately preceding net income.

To illustrate, we will assume that at the beginning of 1996, Acro Energy Inc. changes from the straight-line method of depreciation to the declining-balance method for equipment purchased on January 1, 1993. The cumulative effect on prior year income statements (statements for 1993–1995) is to increase depreciation expense and decrease income before income taxes by $24,000. Assuming a 30% tax rate, the net of tax effect of the change is $16,800 ($24,000 × 70%). The income statement presentation is shown in Illustration 15-32.

ACRO ENERGY INC. Partial Income Statement For the Year Ended December 31, 1996		
Income before income taxes		$800,000
Income tax expense		240,000
Income from continuing operations		560,000
Discontinued operations		
Loss from operations of chemical division, net of		
$60,000 income tax saving	$140,000	
Loss from disposal of chemical division, net of		
$30,000 income tax saving	70,000	210,000
Income before extraordinary item and cumulative effect of		
change in accounting principle		350,000
Extraordinary item		
Expropriation of investment, net of $21,000 income tax		
saving		49,000
Cumulative effect of change in accounting principle		
Effect on prior years of change in depreciation method,		
net of $7,200 income tax saving		16,800
Net income		$284,200

Illustration 15-32

Statement presentation of cumulative effect of change in accounting principle

Helpful hint Study this illustration carefully for sequencing, labeling, descriptions, and amounts.

▶ *Ethics note*

Changes in accounting principles should result in financial statements that are more informative for statement users. They should not be used to artificially improve the reported performance and financial position of the corporation.

The income statement for Acro Energy will also show depreciation expense for the current year. The amount is based on the new depreciation method. In this case the caption "Income before extraordinary item and cumulative effect of change in accounting principle" is inserted immediately following the effects of discontinued operations. This presentation clearly indicates the cumulative effect of the change on prior years' income. If a company does not have either discontinued operations or extraordinary items, the label, "Income before cumulative effect of change in accounting principle" is used in place of "Income from continuing operations." A complete income statement showing all material items not typical of regular operations is illustrated in the second demonstration problem (pp. 712–13).

▶Accounting in Action ▸ *Business Insight*

Sometimes a change in accounting principle is mandated by the Financial Accounting Standards Board. An example is the change in accounting for interperiod income taxes required by Statement of Financial Accounting Standards 109. Such changes can significantly affect net income. For example, in its 1993 income statement, Consolidated Natural Gas Company reported an increase to income of $17,422,000 under "Cumulative Effect of Accounting Change." An accompanying note explained that the increase in income resulted from a required "change from the deferred method to an asset and liability approach for accounting for and reporting of income taxes."

Limitations of Financial Analysis

Significant business decisions are frequently made using one or more of the three analytical tools illustrated in this chapter. However, you should be aware of some of the limitations of these tools and of the financial statements on which they are based.

STUDY OBJECTIVE

········· **7** ·········

Recognize the limitations of financial statement analysis.

Estimates

Financial statements contain numerous estimates. Estimates, for example, are used in determining the allowance for uncollectible receivables, periodic depreciation, the costs of warranties, and contingent losses. To the extent that these estimates are inaccurate, the financial ratios and percentages are inaccurate.

Cost

Traditional financial statements are based on cost and are not adjusted for price-level changes. Comparisons of unadjusted financial data from different periods may be rendered invalid by significant inflation or deflation. For example, a 5-year comparison of J.C. Penney's revenues might show a growth of 21%. But this growth trend would be misleading if the general price-level had increased significantly during the same 5-year period.

Alternative Accounting Methods

▸ *International note*

In many industries competition is global: To evaluate a firm's standing, an investor or analyst must make comparisons to firms from other countries. However, given the many differences in accounting practices, these comparisons can be both difficult and misleading.

Variations among companies in the application of generally accepted accounting principles may hamper comparability. For example, one company may use the FIFO method of inventory costing, whereas another company in the same industry may use LIFO. If inventory is a significant asset to both companies, it is unlikely that their current ratios are comparable. For example, if General Motors Corporation had used FIFO instead of LIFO in valuing its inventories, its inventories would have been 26% higher, significantly affecting the current ratio (and other ratios as well). In addition to differences in inventory costing methods, differences also exist in reporting such items as depreciation, depletion, and amortization. Although these differences in accounting methods might be detectable from reading the notes to the financial statements, adjusting the financial data to compensate for the different methods is difficult, if not impossible in some cases.

Atypical Data

Fiscal year-end data may not be typical of the financial condition during the year. Firms frequently establish a fiscal year-end that coincides with the low point in operating activity or in inventory levels. Therefore, certain account balances (cash, receivables, payables, and inventories) may not be representative of the balances in the accounts during the year.

▸ *Ethics note*

When investigating diversified firms, investors are often most interested to learn about the results of particular divisions. Firms are required to disclose the results of distinct lines of business separately if they are a material part of operations. Unfortunately, shifting revenues and expenses across divisions to achieve desired results reduces the usefulness of this information for financial statement analysis.

Diversification of Firms

Diversification in American industry also limits the usefulness of financial analysis. Many firms today are so diversified that they cannot be classified by industry. Others appear to be comparable but are not. You might think that PepsiCo, Inc., and Coca-Cola Company would be comparable as soft drink industry competitors. But are they comparable when PepsiCo, in addition to producing Pepsi-Cola, owns Pizza Hut, KFC, Taco Bell, and Frito-Lay; and Coca-Cola, in addition to producing Coke, owns Hi-C (fruit drinks), and Minute Maid (frozen concentrate)?

Before You Go On . . .

▸ *Review It*

1. What are some limitations of financial analysis?
2. Give examples of alternative accounting methods that hamper compatibility.
3. In what way does diversification limit the usefulness of financial statement analysis?

▶ *A Look Back at the University of Chicago*

Refer to the opening story and answer the following questions:

1. What financial ratio(s) helped John R. Kroll of the university receive financing for the school? What other ratios or data are provided by a university when borrowing funds? What relevant information is provided by these ratios or data?
2. What are the sources of funds for a private university?
3. How are educational institutions rated and what equity to debt ratio applies to these ratings? What is the University of Chicago's equity to debt ratio?

Solution:

1. John R. Kroll said that its good equity to debt ratio helped the University of Chicago borrow $100 million to build two new buildings. Other ratios or data discussed in the opening story are the endowment ratio and student SAT scores. The endowment ratio is the ratio of gifts the university has received to the number of students; the larger its endowment, the less pressure a school has to generate money from other sources. The higher the SAT scores, the more demand there is to attend that institution.
2. A private university obtains funds from tuition; contributions, gifts, and bequests from alumni, friends, and corporations; grants from foundations, government agencies, and companies; earnings from endowment investments and operating funds; and borrowings.
3. Standard & Poor's ranks educational institutions, as it does corporations, with credit and bond ratings. "A"-rated institutions have a 2:1 equity to debt ratio; "AAA"-institutions—the highest rating—have a 4:1 ratio. The University of Chicago has a 5.5:1 equity to debt ratio.

◢ Summary of Study Objectives

1. *Discuss the need for comparative analysis.* There are three bases of comparison: (1) Intracompany, which compares an item or financial relationship with other data within a company. (2) Industry, which compares company data with industry averages. (3) Intercompany, which compares an item or financial relationship of a company with data of one or more competing companies.

2. *Identify the tools of financial statement analysis.* Financial statements may be analyzed horizontally, vertically, and with ratios.

3. *Explain and apply horizontal (trend) analysis.* Horizontal analysis is a technique for evaluating a series of data over a period of time to determine the increase or decrease that has taken place, expressed as either an amount or a percentage.

4. *Describe and apply vertical analysis.* Vertical analysis is a technique that expresses each item within a financial statement in terms of a percentage of a relevant total or a base amount.

5. *Identify and compute ratios and describe their purpose and use in analyzing a firm's liquidity, profitability, and solvency.* The formula and purpose of each ratio is presented in Illustration 15-28.

6. *Understand the concept of earning power and indicate how material items not typical of regular operations are presented.* Earning power refers to a company's ability to sustain its profits from operations. Irregular items—discontinued operations, extraordinary items, and changes in accounting principles—are presented net of tax below income from continuing operations to highlight their unusual nature.

7. *Recognize the limitations of financial statement analysis.* The usefulness of analytical tools is limited by the use of estimates, the cost basis, the application of alternative accounting methods, atypical data at year-end, and the diversification of firms.

GLOSSARY

Acid-test ratio A measure of a company's immediate short-term liquidity, computed by dividing the sum of cash, marketable securities, and (net) receivables by current liabilities. (p. 689).

Asset turnover ratio A measure of how efficiently a company uses its assets to generate sales, computed by dividing net sales by average assets. (p. 694).

Cash debt coverage ratio   A cash-basis measure used to evaluate solvency. (p. 701).

Cash return on sales ratio   A measure of the cash generated by every dollar of sales. (p. 694).

Change in accounting principle   Use of an accounting principle in the current year different from the one used in the preceding year. (p. 706).

Current cash debt coverage ratio   A cash-basis measure of the short-term debt paying ability. (p. 690).

Current ratio   A measure used to evaluate a company's liquidity and short-term debt-paying ability, computed by dividing current assets by current liabilities. (p. 689).

Debt to total assets ratio   Measures the percentage of total assets provided by creditors, computed by dividing total debt by total assets. (p. 699).

Discontinued operations   The disposal of a significant segment of a business. (p. 703).

Earnings per share   The net income earned by each share of common stock, computed by dividing net income by the weighted average common shares outstanding. (p. 697).

Extraordinary items   Events and transactions that meet two conditions: (1) unusual in nature, and (2) infrequent in occurrence. (p. 704).

Horizontal analysis   A technique for evaluating a series of financial statement data over a period of time to determine the increase (decrease) that has taken place, expressed as either an amount or a percentage. (p. 682).

Inventory turnover ratio   A measure of the liquidity of inventory, computed by dividing cost of goods sold by average inventory. (p. 692).

Liquidity ratios   Measures of the short-term ability of the enterprise to pay its maturing obligations and to meet unexpected needs for cash. (p. 688).

Payout ratio   Measures the percentage of earnings distributed in the form of cash dividends, computed by dividing cash dividends by net income. (p. 698).

Price-earnings ratio   Measures the ratio of the market price

of each share of common stock to the earnings per share, computed by dividing the market price of the stock by earnings per share. (p. 697).

Profitability ratios   Measures of the income or operating success of an enterprise for a given period of time. (p. 693).

Profit margin ratio   Measures the percentage of each dollar of sales that results in net income, computed by dividing net income by net sales. (p. 693).

Ratio   An expression of the mathematical relationship between one quantity and another. The relationship may be expressed either as a percentage, a rate, or a simple proportion. (p. 687).

Ratio analysis   A technique for evaluating financial statements that expresses the relationship among selected financial statement data. (p. 687).

Receivables turnover ratio   A measure of the liquidity of receivables, computed by dividing net credit sales by average net receivables. (p. 691).

Return on assets ratio   An overall measure of profitability, computed by dividing net income by average assets. (p. 695).

Return on common stockholders' equity   Measures the dollars of net income earned for each dollar invested by the owners, computed by dividing net income by average common stockholders' equity. (p. 696).

Solvency ratios   Measures of the ability of the enterprise to survive over a long period of time. (p. 699).

Times interest earned ratio   Measures a company's ability to meet interest payments as they come due, computed by dividing income before interest expense and income taxes by interest expense. (p. 700).

Trading on the equity (leverage)   Borrowing money at a lower rate of interest than can be earned by using the borrowed money. (p. 696).

Vertical analysis   A technique for evaluating financial statement data that expresses each item within a financial statement in terms of a percent of a base amount. (p. 684).

DEMONSTRATION PROBLEM 1

The condensed financial statements of Kellogg Company for the years 1994 and 1993 are presented below:

KELLOGG COMPANY
Balance Sheet
December 31

Assets

	(In millions)	
	1994	1993
Current assets		
Cash and short-term investments	$ 266.3	$ 98.1
Accounts receivable (net)	564.5	536.8

Inventories	396.3	403.1
Prepaid expenses and other current assets	206.4	207.1
Total current assets	1,433.5	1,245.1
Property, plant, and equipment (net)	2,892.8	2,768.4
Intangibles and other assets	141.0	223.6
Total assets	$4,467.3	$4,237.1

Liabilities and Stockholders' Equity

Current liabilities	$1,185.2	$1,214.6
Long-term liabilities	1,474.6	1,309.1
Stockholders' equity—common	1,807.5	1,713.4
Total liabilities and stockholders' equity	$4,467.3	$4,237.1

KELLOGG COMPANY
Income Statement
For the Year Ended December 31

	(In millions)	
	1994	1993
Revenues	$6,562.0	$6,295.4
Cost and expenses		
Cost of goods sold	2,950.7	2,989.0
Selling and administrative expenses	2,448.7	2,237.5
Interest expense	32.6	34.8
Total costs and expenses	5,432.0	5,261.3
Income before income taxes	1,130.0	1,034.1
Income tax expense	424.6	353.4
Net income	$ 705.4	$ 680.7

Instructions
Compute the following ratios for Kellogg for 1994 and 1993.

(a) Current ratio.
(b) Inventory turnover (Inventory 12/31/92, $416.4).
(c) Profit margin ratio.
(d) Return on assets (Assets 12/31/92, $4,015.0).
(e) Return on common stockholders' equity (Equity 12/31/92, $1,945.2).
(f) Debt to total assets.
(g) Times interest earned.

Solution to Demonstration Problem 1

	1994	1993
(a) Current ratio:		
$1,433.5 ÷ $1,185.2 =	1.2:1	
$1,245.1 ÷ $1,214.6 =		1.0:1
(b) Inventory turnover:		
$2,950.7 ÷ [($396.3 + $403.1) ÷ 2] =	7.4 times	
$2,989.0 ÷ [($403.1 + $416.4) ÷ 2] =		7.3 times
(c) Profit margin:		
$705.4 ÷ $6,562.0 =	10.7%	
$680.7 ÷ $6,295.4 =		10.8%
(d) Return on assets:		
$705.4 ÷ [($4,467.3 + $4,237.1) ÷ 2] =	16.2%	
$680.7 ÷ [($4,237.1 + $4,015.0) ÷ 2] =		16.5%

Problem-Solving Strategies

1. Remember that the current ratio includes all current assets; acid-test ratio uses only cash, marketable securities, and net receivables.
2. Use average balances for turnover ratios like inventory, receivables, and assets.
3. Return on assets is greater or smaller than return on common stockholders' equity depending on cost of debt.

(e) Return on common stockholders' equity:

$705.4 ÷ [($1,807.5 + $1,713.4) ÷ 2] =   40.1%

$680.7 ÷ [($1,713.4 + $1,945.2) ÷ 2] =   37.2%

(f) Debt to total assets:

$2,659.8 ÷ $4,467.3 =   59.5%

$2,523.7 ÷ $4,237.1 =   59.6%

(g) Times interest earned:

($705.4 + $424.6 + $32.6) ÷ $32.6 =   35.7 times

($680.7 + $353.4 + $34.8) ÷ $34.8 =   30.7 times

DEMONSTRATION PROBLEM 2

The events and transactions of the Dever Corporation for the year ending December 31, 1997, resulted in the following data:

Cost of goods sold	$2,600,000
Net sales	4,400,000
Other expenses and losses	9,600
Other revenues and gains	5,600
Selling and administrative expenses	1,100,000
Income from operations of plastics division	70,000
Gain on sale of plastics division	500,000
Loss from tornado disaster (extraordinary loss)	600,000
Cumulative effect of changing from the straight-line depreciation to double-declining-balance (increase in depreciation expense)	300,000

Analysis reveals that

1. All items are before the applicable income tax rate of 30%.
2. The plastics division was sold on July 1.
3. All operating data for the plastics division have been segregated.

Instructions

Prepare an income statement for the year, excluding the presentation of earnings per share.

Solution to Demonstration Problem 2

Helpful hints

1. Remember that material items not typical of operations are reported in separate sections net of taxes.

2. Income taxes should be associated with the item that affects the taxes.

3. A corporation income statement will have income tax expense when there is income before income tax.

4. All data presented in determining income before income taxes is the same as for unincorporated companies.

DEVER CORPORATION
Income Statement
For the Year Ended December 31, 1997

Net sales		$4,400,000
Cost of goods sold		2,600,000
Gross profit		1,800,000
Selling and administrative expenses		1,100,000
Income from operations		700,000
Other revenues and gains	$ 5,600	
Other expenses and losses	9,600	4,000
Income before income taxes		696,000
Income tax expense ($696,000 × 30%)		208,800

Income from continuing operations		487,200
Discontinued operations		
Income from operations of plastics division, net of $21,000 income taxes ($70,000 × 30%)	49,000	
Gain on sale of plastics division, net of $150,000 income taxes ($500,000 × 30%)	350,000	399,000
Income before extraordinary item and cumulative effect of change in accounting principle		886,200
Extraordinary item		
Tornado loss, net of income tax saving $180,000 ($600,000 × 30%)		420,000
Cumulative effect of change in accounting principle		
Effect on prior years of change in depreciation method, net of $90,000 income tax saving ($300,000 × 30%)		210,000
Net income		$ 256,200

SELF-STUDY QUESTIONS

Answers are at the end of the chapter.

(SO 1) 1. Comparisons of data within a company are an example of the following comparative basis:
a. Industry averages.
b. Intracompany.
c. Intercompany.
d. Both (b) and (c).

(SO 2) 2. In horizontal analysis, each item is expressed as a percentage of the:
a. net income amount.
b. stockholders' equity amount.
c. total assets amount.
d. base year amount.

(SO 4) 3. In vertical analysis, the base amount for depreciation expense is generally:
a. net sales.
b. depreciation expense in a previous year.
c. gross profit.
d. fixed assets.

(SO 4) 4. The following schedule is a display of what type of analysis?

	Amount	Percent
Current assets	$200,000	25%
Property, plant, and equipment	600,000	75%
Total assets	$800,000	

a. Horizontal analysis.
b. Differential analysis.
c. Vertical analysis.
d. Ratio analysis.

(SO 3) 5. Leland Corporation reported net sales of $300,000, $330,000, and $360,000 in the years 1994, 1995, and 1996, respectively. If 1994 is the base year, what is the trend percentage for 1996?
a. 77%.
b. 108%.
c. 120%.
d. 130%.

(SO 5) 6. Which of the following measures is an evaluation of a firm's ability to pay current liabilities?
a. Acid-test ratio.
b. Current ratio.
c. Both (a) and (b).
d. None of the above.

(SO 5) 7. A measure useful in evaluating the efficiency in managing inventories is:
a. inventory turnover ratio.
b. average days to sell inventory.
c. Both (a) and (b).
d. None of the above.

(SO 5) 8. Which of the following is *not* a liquidity ratio?
a. Current ratio.
b. Asset turnover.
c. Inventory turnover.
d. Receivables turnover.

(SO 5) 9. Plano Corporation reported net income $24,000, net sales $400,000, and average assets $600,000 for 1996. The 1996 profit margin was:
a. 6%.
b. 12%.
c. 40%.
d. 200%.

(SO 6) 10. In reporting discontinued operations, the income statement should show in a special section:
a. gains and losses on the disposal of the discontinued segment.
b. gains and losses from operations of the discontinued segment.
c. Neither (a) nor (b).
d. Both (a) and (b).

(SO 6) 11. The Candy Stick Corporation has income before taxes of $400,000 and an extraordinary loss of $100,000. If the income tax rate is 25% on all items, the income statement should show income before

extraordinary items and extraordinary items, respectively, of
a. $325,000 and $100,000.
b. $325,000 and $75,000.
c. $300,000 and $100,000.
d. $300,000 and $75,000.

12. Which of the following is generally not considered (SO 7)
to be a limitation of financial analysis?
a. Use of ratio analysis.
b. Use of estimates.
c. Use of cost.
d. Use of alternative accounting methods.

QUESTIONS

1. (a) Tia Kim believes that the analysis of financial statements is directed at two characteristics of a company: liquidity and profitability. Is Tia correct? Explain.
   (b) Are short-term creditors, long-term creditors, and stockholders interested primarily in the same characteristics of a company? Explain.

2. (a) Distinguish among the following bases of comparison: (1) intracompany, (2) industry averages, and (3) intercompany.
   (b) Give the principal value of using each of the three bases of comparison.

3. Two popular methods of financial statement analysis are horizontal analysis and vertical analysis. Explain the difference between these two methods.

4. (a) If Roe Company had net income of $540,000 in 1996 and it experienced a 24.5% increase in net income for 1997, what is its net income for 1997?
   (b) If six cents of every dollar of Roe's revenue is net income in 1996, what is the dollar amount of 1996 revenue?

5. What is a ratio? What are the different ways of expressing the relationship of two amounts? What information does a ratio provide?

6. Name the major ratios useful in assessing (a) liquidity and (b) solvency.

7. Tony Robins is puzzled. His company had a profit margin of 10% in 1996. He feels that this is an indication that the company is doing well. Joan Graham, his accountant, says that more information is needed to determine the firm's financial well-being. Who is correct? Why?

8. What do the following classes of ratios measure? (a) Liquidity ratios. (b) Profitability ratios. (c) Solvency ratios.

9. What is the difference between the current ratio and the acid-test ratio?

10. Gerry Bullock Company, a retail store, has a receivables turnover ratio of 4.5 times. The industry

average is 12.5 times. Does Bullock have a collection problem with its receivables?

11. Which ratios should be used to help answer the following questions?
   (a) How efficient is a company in using its assets to produce sales?
   (b) How near to sale is the inventory on hand?
   (c) How many dollars of net income were earned for each dollar invested by the owners?
   (d) How able is a company to meet interest charges as they fall due?

12. The price-earnings ratio of McDonnell Douglas (aircraft builder) was 5, and the price-earnings ratio of Microsoft (computer software) was 43. Which company did the stock market favor? Explain.

13. What is the formula for computing the payout ratio? Would you expect this ratio to be high or low for a growth company?

14. Holding all other factors constant, indicate whether each of the following changes generally signals good or bad news about a company:
   (a) Increase in profit margin.
   (b) Decrease in inventory turnover.
   (c) Increase in the current ratio.
   (d) Decrease in earnings per share.
   (e) Increase in price-earnings ratio.
   (f) Increase in debt to total assets ratio.
   (g) Decrease in times interest earned.
   (h) Increase in book value per share.

15. The return on total assets for Windsor Corporation is 7.6%. During the same year Windsor's return on common stockholders' equity is 12.8%. What is the explanation for the difference in the two rates?

16. Which two ratios do you think should be of greatest interest to:
   (a) A pension fund considering the purchase of 20-year bonds?
   (b) A bank contemplating a short-term loan?
   (c) A common stockholder?

17. (a) What is meant by trading on the equity?
    (b) How would you determine the profitability of trading on the equity?

18. Khris Inc. has net income of $270,000, weighted average shares of common stock outstanding of 50,000, and preferred dividends for the period of $40,000. What is Khris's earnings per share of common stock? Phil Remmers, the president of Khris Inc., believes the computed EPS of the company is high. Comment.

19. Identify five limitations of financial analysis.

20. Explain how the choice of one of the following accounting methods over the other raises or lowers a company's net income during a period of continuing inflation:
    (a) Use of FIFO instead of LIFO for inventory costing.
    (b) Use of a 6-year life for machinery instead of a 9-year life.
    (c) Use of straight-line depreciation instead of accelerated declining-balance depreciation.

21. Explain "earning power." What relationship does this concept have to the treatment of irregular items on the income statement?

22. Indicate which of the following items would be reported as an extraordinary item on Fine & Fancy Food Corporation's income statement?

(a) Loss from damages caused by a volcano eruption.
(b) Loss from the sale of temporary investments.
(c) Loss attributable to a labor strike.
(d) Loss caused when the Food and Drug Administration prohibited the manufacture and sale of a product line.
(e) Loss of inventory from flood damage because a warehouse is located on a flood plain that floods every five to ten years.
(f) Loss on the write-down of outdated inventory.
(g) Loss from a foreign government's expropriation of a production facility.
(h) Loss from damage to a warehouse in southern California from a minor earthquake.

23. Iron Ingots Inc. reported 1997 earnings per share of $3.26 and had no extraordinary items. In 1998, earnings per share on income before extraordinary items was $2.99, and earnings per share on net income was $3.49. Do you consider this trend to be favorable? Why or why not?

24. Rodger Robotics Inc. has been in operation for three years. All of its manufacturing equipment, which has a useful life of 10 to 12 years, has been depreciated on a straight-line basis. During the 4th year, Rodger Robotics changes to an accelerated depreciation method for all of its equipment.
    (a) Will Rodger Robotics post a gain or a loss on this change?
    (b) How will this change be reported?

BRIEF EXERCISES*

BE15-1 Using the following data from the comparative balance sheet of All-State Company, illustrate horizontal analysis:

Prepare horizontal analysis. (SO 3)

	December 31, 1997	December 31, 1996
Accounts receivable	$ 600,000	$ 400,000
Inventory	$ 780,000	$ 600,000
Total assets	$3,220,000	$2,800,000

BE15-2 Using the same data presented above in BE15-1 for All-State Company, illustrate vertical analysis.

Prepare vertical analysis. (SO 4)

BE15-3 Net income was $500,000 in 1995, $420,000 in 1996, and $504,000 in 1997. What is the percentage of change from (1) 1995 to 1996 and (2) 1996 to 1997? Is the change an increase or a decrease?

Calculate percentage of change. (SO 3)

BE15-4 If Cavalier Company had net income of $672,300 in 1997 and it experienced a 25% increase in net income over 1996, what was its 1996 net income?

Calculate net income. (SO 3)

BE15-5 Vertical analysis (common size) percentages for Waubons Company's sales, cost of goods sold, and expenses are shown below:

Calculate change in net income. (SO 4)

Vertical Analysis	1997	1996	1995
Sales	100.0	100.0	100.0
Cost of goods sold	59.2	62.4	64.5
Expenses	25.0	26.6	29.5

*Follow the rounding procedures used in the chapter.

Did Waubons's net income as a percent of sales increase, decrease, or remain unchanged over the 3-year period presented above? Provide numerical support for your answer.

Calculate change in net income.
(SO 3)

BE15–6   Horizontal analysis (trend analysis) percentages for Tilden Company's sales, cost of goods sold, and expenses are shown below:

Horizontal Analysis	1997	1996	1995
Sales	96.2	106.8	100.0
Cost of goods sold	102.0	97.0	100.0
Expenses	110.6	95.4	100.0

Did Tilden's net income increase, decrease, or remain unchanged over the 3-year period presented above?

Calculate liquidity ratios.
(SO 5)

BE15–7   Selected condensed data taken from a recent balance sheet of Bob Evans Farms are as follows:

Cash	$ 8,241,000
Marketable securities	1,947,000
Accounts receivable	12,545,000
Inventories	14,814,000
Other current assets	5,371,000
Total current assets	$42,918,000
Total current liabilities	$44,844,000

What are the (1) working capital, (2) current, and (3) acid-test ratios?

Calculate profitability ratios.
(SO 5)

BE15–8   Boston Patriots Corporation has net income of $15 million and net revenue of $100 million in 1996. Its assets were $12 million at the beginning of the year and $14 million at the end of the year. What are (a) the Patriots' asset turnover ratio and (b) profit margin ratio? (Round to two decimals.)

Evaluate collection of accounts receivable.
(SO 5)

BE15–9   The following data are taken from the financial statements of Diet-Mite Company:

	1997	1996
Accounts receivable (net), end of year	$ 560,000	$ 540,000
Net sales on account	5,500,000	4,100,000
Terms for all sales are 1/10, n/45.		

Compute for each year (1) the receivables turnover and (2) the average collection period. What conclusions about the management of accounts receivable can be drawn from these data? At the end of 1995, accounts receivable (net) was $490,000.

Evaluate management of inventory.
(SO 5)

BE15–10   The following data were taken from the income statements of Linda Shumway Company:

	1997	1996
Sales	$6,420,000	$6,240,000
Beginning inventory	980,000	837,000
Purchases	4,640,000	4,661,000
Ending inventory	1,020,000	980,000

Calculate profitability ratios.
(SO 5)

Compute for each year (1) the inventory turnover ratio and (2) the average days to sell the inventory. What conclusions concerning the management of the inventory can be drawn from these data?

BE15–11   Haymark Products Company has owners' equity of $400,000 and net income of $50,000. It has a payout ratio of 20% and a rate of return on assets of 16%. How much did Haymark Products pay in cash dividends, and what were its average assets?

BE15–12 On June 30, the Osborn Corporation discontinued its operations in Mexico. During the year, the operating loss was $400,000 before taxes. On September 1, Osborn disposed of the Mexico facility at a pretax loss of $150,000. The applicable tax rate is 30%. Show the discontinued operations section of Osborn's income statement.

Prepare a discontinued operations section of an income statement.
(SO 6)

BE15–13 An inexperienced accountant for the Lima Corporation showed the following in Lima's income statement: Income before income taxes, $300,000; Income tax expense, $72,000; Extraordinary loss from flood (before taxes), $60,000; and Net income, $168,000. The extraordinary loss and taxable income are both subject to a 30% tax rate. Prepare a corrected income statement beginning with "Income before income taxes."

Prepare a corrected income statement with an extraordinary item.
(SO 6)

BE15–14 On January 1, 1995, Shirli, Inc. changed from the straight-line method of depreciation to the declining-balance method. The cumulative effect of the change was to increase prior years' depreciation by $40,000 and 1995 depreciation by $8,000. Show the change in accounting principle section of the 1995 income statement, assuming the tax rate is 30%.

Prepare change in accounting principles section of an income statement.
(SO 6)

BE15–15 Selected data taken from the 1996 financial statements of Shirley Denison Manufacturing Company are as follows:

Net sales for 1996	$6,860,000
Current liabilities, January 1, 1996	180,000
Current liabilities, December 31, 1996	240,000
Net cash provided by operating activities	760,000
Total liabilities, January 1, 1996	1,500,000
Total liabilities, December 31, 1996	1,300,000

Calculate cash-basis liquidity, profitability, and solvency ratios.
(SO 5)

Compute the following ratios at December 31, 1996: (a) the current cash debt coverage ratio, (b) the cash return on sales ratio, and (c) the cash debt coverage ratio.

EXERCISES*

....

E15–1 Financial information for Merchandise Inc. is presented below:

Prepare horizontal analysis.
(SO 3)

	December 31, 1996	December 31, 1995
Current assets	$120,000	$100,000
Plant assets (net)	400,000	330,000
Current liabilities	91,000	70,000
Long-term liabilities	144,000	95,000
Common stock, $1 par	150,000	115,000
Retained earnings	135,000	150,000

Instructions
Prepare a schedule showing a horizontal analysis for 1996 using 1995 as the base year.

E15–2 Operating data for Fleetwood Corporation are presented below:

Prepare vertical analysis.
(SO 4)

	1997	1996
Sales	$800,000	$600,000
Cost of goods sold	472,000	390,000
Selling expenses	120,000	72,000
Administrative expenses	80,000	54,000
Income tax expense	38,400	25,200
Net income	89,600	58,800

Instructions
Prepare a schedule showing a vertical analysis for 1997 and 1996.

---

*Follow the rounding procedures used in the chapter.

Prepare horizontal and vertical analyses.
(SO 3, 4)

E15–3   The comparative balance sheets of Oklahoma Corporation are presented below:

OKLAHOMA CORPORATION
Comparative Balance Sheets
As of December 31

	1997	1996
Assets		
Current assets	$ 72,000	$ 80,000
Property, plant, & equipment (net)	99,000	90,000
Intangibles	24,000	40,000
Total assets	$195,000	$210,000
Liabilities & stockholders' equity		
Current liabilities	$ 40,800	$ 48,000
Long-term liabilities	138,000	150,000
Stockholders' equity	16,200	12,000
Total liabilities & stockholders' equity	$195,000	$210,000

Instructions

(a) Prepare a horizontal analysis of the balance sheet data for Oklahoma Corporation using 1996 as a base. (Show the amount of increase or decrease as well.)

(b) Prepare a vertical analysis of the balance sheet data for Oklahoma Corporation in columnar form for 1997.

Prepare horizontal and vertical analyses.
(SO 3, 4)

E15–4   The comparative income statements of Olympic Corporation are shown below:

OLYMPIC CORPORATION
Comparative Income Statements
For the Years Ended December 31

	1997	1996
Net sales	$550,000	$550,000
Cost of goods sold	440,000	450,000
Gross profit	$110,000	$100,000
Operating expenses	57,200	54,000
Net income	$ 52,800	$ 46,000

Instructions

(a) Prepare a horizontal analysis of the income statement data for Olympic Corporation using 1996 as a base. (Show the amounts of increase or decrease.)

(b) Prepare a vertical analysis of the income statement data for Olympic Corporation in columnar form for both years.

Compute liquidity ratios and compare results.
(SO 5)

E15–5   Nordstrom, Inc., operates department stores in numerous states. Selected financial statement data in millions of dollars for a recent year are as follows:

	End-of-Year	Beginning-of-Year
Cash and cash equivalents	$ 33	$ 91
Receivables (net)	676	586
Merchandise Inventory	628	586
Prepaid expenses	61	52
Total current assets	$1,398	$1,315
Total current liabilities	$690	$627

For the year, net sales were $3,894 and cost of goods sold was $2,600. Net cash provided by operating activities was $800.

Instructions

(a) Compute the five liquidity ratios at the end of the current year.
(b) Using the data in the chapter, compare Nordstrom's liquidity with (1) J.C. Penney and (2) the industry averages for department stores.

E15–6 Firpo Incorporated had the following transactions occur involving current assets and current liabilities during February 1996:

Perform current and acid-test ratio analysis.
(SO 5)

Feb. 3   Accounts receivable of $15,000 are collected.
     7   Equipment is purchased for $25,000 cash.
    11   Paid $3,000 for a 3-year insurance policy.
    14   Accounts payable of $14,000 are paid.
    18   Cash dividends are declared, $6,000.

Additional information:

1. As of February 1, 1996, current assets were $140,000 and current liabilities were $50,000.
2. As of February 1, 1996, current assets included $15,000 of inventory and $5,000 of prepaid expenses.

Instructions

(a) Compute the current ratio as of the beginning of the month and after each transaction.
(b) Compute the acid-test ratio as of the beginning of the month and after each transaction.

E15–7 Georgette Company has the following comparative balance sheet data:

Compute selected ratios.
(SO 5)

	December 31, 1996	December 31, 1995
Cash	$ 20,000	$ 30,000
Receivables (net)	65,000	60,000
Inventories	60,000	50,000
Plant assets (net)	200,000	180,000
	$345,000	$320,000
Accounts payable	$ 50,000	$ 60,000
Mortgage payable (15%)	100,000	100,000
Common stock, $10 par	140,000	120,000
Retained earnings	55,000	40,000
	$345,000	$320,000

Additional information for 1996:

1. Net income was $25,000.
2. Sales on account were $420,000. Sales returns and allowances amounted to $20,000.
3. Cost of goods sold was $198,000.
4. Net cash provided by operating activities was $44,000.

Instructions

Compute the following ratios at December 31, 1996:

(a) Current.
(b) Acid-test.
(c) Receivables turnover.
(d) Inventory turnover.
(e) Cash return on sales.
(f) Cash debt coverage.
(g) Current cash debt coverage.

E15–8 Selected comparative statement data for Mighty Products Company are presented below. All balance sheet data are as of December 31.

Compute selected ratios.
(SO 5)

	1996	1995
Net sales	$800,000	$720,000
Cost of goods sold	480,000	40,000

Interest expense	7,000	5,000
Net income	56,000	42,000
Accounts receivable	120,000	100,000
Inventory	85,000	75,000
Total assets	600,000	500,000
Total common stockholders' equity	450,000	310,000

Instructions
Compute the following ratios for 1996:

(a) Profit margin.
(b) Asset turnover.
(c) Return on assets.
(d) Return on common stockholders' equity.

Compute selected ratios.
(SO 5)

E15–9 The income statement for the year ended December 31, 1996, of Jean LeFay, Inc., appears below.

Sales	$400,000
Cost of goods sold	230,000
Gross profit	170,000
Expenses (including $20,000 interest and $24,000 income taxes)	100,000
Net income	$ 70,000

Additional information:

1. Common stock outstanding January 1, 1996, was 30,000 shares. On July 1, 1996, 10,000 more shares were issued.
2. The market price of Jean LeFay, Inc., stock was $15 in 1996.
3. Cash dividends of $21,000 were paid, $5,000 of which were to preferred stockholders.
4. Net cash provided by operating activities $98,000.

Instructions
Compute the following ratios for 1996.

(a) Earnings per share.   (d) Times interest earned.
(b) Price-earnings.   (e) Cash return on sales.
(c) Payout.

Compute amounts from ratios.
(SO 5)

E15–10 Shaker Corporation experienced a fire on December 31, 1996, in which its financial records were partially destroyed. It has been able to salvage some of the records and has ascertained the following balances:

	December 31, 1996	December 31, 1995
Cash	$ 30,000	$ 10,000
Receivables (net)	72,500	126,000
Inventory	200,000	180,000
Accounts payable	50,000	90,000
Notes payable	30,000	60,000
Common stock, $100 par	400,000	400,000
Retained earnings	113,500	101,000

Additional information:

1. The inventory turnover is 3.6 times.
2. The return on common stockholders' equity is 22%. The company had no additional paid-in capital.
3. The receivables turnover is 9.4 times.
4. The return on assets is 20%.
5. Total assets at December 31, 1995, were $605,000.

Instructions
Compute the following for Shaker Corporation:

(a) Cost of goods sold for 1996.
(b) Net sales for 1996.
(c) Net income for 1996.
(d) Total assets at December 31, 1996.

E15–11 The Davis Company has income from continuing operations of $240,000 for the year ended December 31, 1995. It also has the following items (before considering income taxes): (1) an extraordinary fire loss of $60,000, (2) a gain of $40,000 from the discontinuance of a division, which includes a $110,000 gain from the operation of the division and a $70,000 loss on its disposal, and (3) a cumulative change in accounting principle that resulted in an increase in prior year's depreciation of $30,000. Assume all items are subject to income taxes at a 30% tax rate.

Prepare irregular items portion of an income statement.
(SO 6)

Instructions
Prepare Davis Company's income statement for 1995, beginning with "Income from continuing operations."

E15–12 *The Wall Street Journal* routinely publishes summaries of corporate quarterly and annual earnings reports in a feature called the "Earnings Digest." A typical "digest" report takes the following form:

Evaluate the effects of unusual or irregular items.
(SO 5, 6, 7)

Energy Enterprises (A)

	Quarter ending July 31,	
	1995	1994
Revenues	$2,049,000,000	$1,754,000,000
Net income	97,000,000	(a) 68,750,000
E.P.S.:		
Net income	1.31	.93

	9 months ending July 31,	
	1995	1994
Revenues	$5,578,500,000	$5,065,300,000
Extraord item	(b) 1,900,000	
Net income	102,700,000	(a) 33,250,000
E.P.S.:		
Net income	1.39	.45

(a) Includes a net charge of $26,000,000 from loss on the sale of electrical equipment
(b) Extraordinary gain on Middle East property expropriation

The letter in parentheses following the company name indicates the exchange on which Energy Enterprises' stock is traded—in this case, the American Stock Exchange.

Instructions
Answer the following questions:
(a) How was the loss on the electrical equipment reported on the income statement? Was it reported in the third quarter of 1994? How can you tell?
(b) Why did *The Wall Street Journal* list the extraordinary item separately?
(c) What is the extraordinary item? Was it included in income for the third quarter? How can you tell?
(d) Did Energy Enterprises have an operating loss in any quarter of 1994? Of 1995? How do you know?
(e) Approximately how many shares of stock were outstanding in 1995? Did the number of outstanding shares change from July 31, 1994, to July 31, 1995?
(f) As an investor, what numbers do you think should be used to determine Energy Enterprises' profit margin percentage (return on sales)? Calculate the 9-month profit margin percentage for 1994 and 1995 that you consider most useful. Explain your decision.

PROBLEMS*

•••

Prepare vertical analysis and comment on profitability.
(SO 4, 5)

P15–1 Comparative statement data for Chen Company and Couric Company, two competitors, appear below. All balance sheet data are as of December 31, 1996, and December 31, 1995.

	Chen Company		Couric Company	
	1996	**1995**	**1996**	**1995**
Net sales	$1,549,035		$339,038	
Cost of goods sold	1,080,490		238,006	
Operating expenses	302,275		79,000	
Interest expense	6,800		1,252	
Income tax expense	47,840		7,740	
Current assets	325,975	$312,410	83,336	$ 79,467
Plant assets (net)	521,310	500,000	139,728	125,812
Current liabilities	66,325	75,815	35,348	30,281
Long-term liabilities	108,500	90,000	29,620	25,000
Common stock, $10 par	500,000	500,000	120,000	120,000
Retained earnings	172,460	146,595	38,096	29,998

Instructions

(a) Prepare a vertical analysis of the 1996 income statement data for Chen Company and Couric Company in columnar form.

(b) ▭▭▭▭▷ Comment on the relative profitability of the companies by computing the return on assets and the return on common stockholders' equity ratios for both companies.

Compute ratios from balance sheet and income statement.
(SO 5)

P15–2 The comparative statements of Magic Johnson Company are presented below:

MAGIC JOHNSON COMPANY
Income Statement
For the Year Ended December 31

	1996	1995
Net sales	$1,818,500	$1,750,500
Cost of goods sold	1,005,500	996,000
Gross profit	813,000	754,500
Selling and administrative expense	506,000	479,000
Income from operations	307,000	275,500
Other expenses and losses		
Interest expense	18,000	19,000
Income before income taxes	289,000	256,500
Income tax expense	86,700	77,000
Net income	$ 202,300	$ 179,500

MAGIC JOHNSON COMPANY
Balance Sheet
December 31

	1996	1995
Assets		
Current assets		
Cash	$ 60,100	$ 64,200
Marketable securities	54,000	50,000

*Follow the rounding procedures used in the chapter.

Accounts receivable (net)	107,800	102,800
Inventory	123,000	115,500
Total current assets	344,900	332,500
Plant assets (net)	625,300	520,300
Total assets	$970,200	$852,800

Liabilities and Stockholders' Equity

Current liabilities		
Accounts payable	$150,000	$145,400
Income taxes payable	43,500	42,000
Total current liabilities	193,500	187,400
Bonds payable	210,000	200,000
Total liabilities	403,500	387,400
Stockholders' equity		
Common stock ($5 par)	280,000	300,000
Retained earnings	286,700	165,400
Total stockholders' equity	566,700	465,400
Total liabilities and stockholders' equity	$970,200	$852,800

On April 1, 1996, 4,000 shares were repurchased and canceled. All sales were on account. Net cash provided by operating activities for 1996 was $280,000.

Instructions

Compute the following ratios for 1996:

(a) Earnings per share.

(b) Return on common stockholders' equity.

(c) Return on assets.

(d) Current.

(e) Acid-test.

(f) Receivables turnover.

(g) Inventory turnover.

(h) Times interest earned.

(i) Asset turnover.

(j) Debt to total assets.

(k) Current cash debt coverage.

(l) Cash return on sales.

(m) Cash debt coverage.

P15–3 Condensed balance sheet and income statement data for Pitka Corporation appear below:

Perform ratio analysis.
(SO 5)

PITKA CORPORATION
Balance Sheet
December 31

	1996	1995	1994
Cash	$ 25,000	$ 20,000	$ 18,000
Receivables (net)	50,000	45,000	48,000
Other current assets	90,000	85,000	64,000
Investments	75,000	70,000	45,000
Plant and equipment (net)	400,000	370,000	358,000
	$640,000	$590,000	$533,000
Current liabilities	$ 75,000	$ 80,000	$ 70,000
Long-term debt	80,000	85,000	50,000
Common stock, $10 par	340,000	300,000	300,000
Retained earnings	145,000	125,000	113,000
	$640,000	$590,000	$533,000

PITKA CORPORATION
Income Statement
For the Years Ended December 31

	1996	1995
Sales	$740,000	$700,000
Less: Sales returns and allowances	40,000	50,000
Net sales	700,000	650,000
Cost of goods sold	420,000	400,000
Gross profit	280,000	250,000
Operating expenses (including income taxes)	236,000	218,000
Net income	$ 44,000	$ 32,000

Additional information:

1. The market price of Pitka's common stock was $4.00, $5.00, and $7.95 for 1994, 1995, and 1996, respectively.
2. All dividends were paid in cash.
3. On July 1, 1996, 4,000 shares of common stock were issued.

Instructions

(a) Compute the following ratios for 1995 and 1996:
   (1) Profit margin.
   (2) Asset turnover.
   (3) Earnings per share.
   (4) Price-earnings.
   (5) Payout.
   (6) Debt to total assets.
(b) ▭▭▭▭▷ Based on the ratios calculated, discuss briefly the improvement or lack thereof in financial position and operating results from 1995 to 1996 of Pitka Corporation.

Compute ratios, commenting on overall liquidity and profitability.
(SO 5)

P15–4 Financial information for Caroline Company is presented below:

CAROLINE COMPANY
Balance Sheet
December 31

Assets	1996	1995
Cash	$ 70,000	$ 65,000
Short-term investments	45,000	40,000
Receivables (net)	94,000	90,000
Inventories	130,000	125,000
Prepaid expenses	25,000	23,000
Land	130,000	130,000
Building and equipment (net)	190,000	175,000
	$684,000	$648,000
Liabilities and Stockholders' Equity		
Notes payable	$100,000	$100,000
Accounts payable	45,000	42,000
Accrued liabilities	40,000	40,000
Bonds payable, due 1995	150,000	150,000
Common stock, $10 par	200,000	200,000
Retained earnings	149,000	116,000
	$684,000	$648,000

CAROLINE COMPANY
Income Statement
For the Years Ended December 31

	1996	1995
Sales	$850,000	$790,000
Cost of goods sold	620,000	575,000
Gross profit	230,000	215,000
Operating expenses	194,000	180,000
Net income	$ 36,000	$ 35,000

Additional information:
1. Inventory at the beginning of 1995 was $115,000.
2. Receivables at the beginning of 1995 were $88,000.
3. Total assets at the beginning of 1995 were $630,000.
4. No common stock transactions occurred during 1995 or 1996.
5. All sales were on account.

Instructions
(a) Indicate, by using ratios, the change in liquidity and profitability of Caroline Company from 1995 to 1996. (Note: Not all profitability ratios can be computed nor can cash basis ratios be computed.)
(b) Given below are three independent situations and a ratio that may be affected. For each situation, compute the affected ratio (1) as of December 31, 1996, and (2) as of December 31, 1997, after giving effect to the situation. Net income for 1997 was $40,000. Total assets on December 31, 1997, were $700,000.

Situation	Ratio
1. 18,000 shares of common stock were sold at par on July 1, 1997.	Return on common stockholders' equity
2. All of the notes payable were paid in 1997.	Debt to total assets
3. Market price of common stock was $9 and $12.80 on December 31, 1996, and 1997, respectively.	Price-earnings ratio

P15–5 Selected financial data of two intense competitors in a recent year are presented below in millions of dollars.

Compute selected ratios and compare liquidity, profitability, and solvency for two companies.
(SO 5)

	Kmart Corporation	Wal-Mart Stores, Inc.
Income Statement Data for Year		
Net sales	$34,025	$82,494
Cost of goods sold	25,992	65,586
Selling and administrative expenses	7,701	12,858
Interest expense	494	706
Other income (net)	572	918
Income taxes	114	1,581
Net income	$ 296	$ 2,681
Balance Sheet Data (End-of-Year)		
Current assets	$ 9,187	$15,338
Property, plant, and equipment (net)	7,842	17,481
Total assets	17,029	32,819
Current liabilities	5,626	9,973
Long-term debt	5,371	10,120
Total stockholders' equity	6,032	12,726
Total liabilities and stockholders' equity	$17,029	$32,819
Beginning-of-Year Balances		
Total assets	$17,504	$26,441
Total stockholders' equity	6,093	10,753

Other Data

Average net receivables	$ 1,570	$ 695
Average inventory	7,317	12,539
Net cash provided by operating activities	351	3,106

Instructions

(a) For each company, compute the following ratios:

(1) Current	(7) Return on common stockholders' equity
(2) Receivables turnover	(8) Debt to total assets
(3) Inventory turnover	(9) Times interest earned
(4) Profit margin	(10) Current cash debt
(5) Asset turnover	(11) Cash return on sales
(6) Return on assets	(12) Cash debt coverage

(b) Compare the liquidity, profitability, and solvency of the two companies.

Compute numerous ratios.
(SO 5)

P15–6   The comparative statements of Ultra Vision Company are presented below:

ULTRA VISION COMPANY
Income Statement
For Year Ended December 31

	1996	1995
Net sales (all on account)	$600,000	$520,000
Expenses		
Cost of goods sold	415,000	354,000
Selling and administrative	120,800	114,800
Interest expense	7,200	6,000
Income tax expense	18,000	14,000
Total expenses	561,000	488,800
Net income	$ 39,000	$ 31,200

ULTRA VISION COMPANY
Balance Sheet
December 31

	1996	1995
Assets		
Current assets		
Cash	$ 21,000	$ 18,000
Marketable securities	18,000	15,000
Accounts receivable (net)	92,000	74,000
Inventory	84,000	70,000
Total current assets	215,000	177,000
Plant assets (net)	423,000	383,000
Total assets	$638,000	$560,000
Liabilities and Stockholders' Equity		
Current liabilities		
Accounts payable	$112,000	$110,000
Income taxes payable	23,000	20,000
Total current liabilities	135,000	130,000
Long-term liabilities		
Bonds payable	130,000	80,000
Total liabilities	265,000	210,000
Stockholders' equity		
Common stock ($5 par)	150,000	150,000
Retained earnings	223,000	200,000
Total stockholders' equity	373,000	350,000
Total liabilities and stockholders' equity	$638,000	$560,000

Additional data:
The common stock recently sold at $19.50 per share.

Instructions
Compute the following ratios for 1996:

(a) Current.
(b) Acid-test.
(c) Receivables turnover.
(d) Inventory turnover.
(e) Profit margin.
(f) Asset turnover.
(g) Return on assets.

(h) Return on common stockholders' equity.
(i) Earnings per share.
(j) Price-earnings.
(k) Payout.
(l) Debt to total assets.
(m) Times interest earned.

P15–7 Presented below is an incomplete income statement and an incomplete comparative balance sheet of Vienna Corporation:

Compute missing information given a set of ratios.
(SO 5)

VIENNA CORPORATION
Income Statement
For the Year Ended December 31, 1996

Sales	$11,000,000
Cost of goods sold	?
Gross profit	?
Operating expenses	1,665,000
Income from operations	?
Other expenses and losses	
Interest expense	?
Income before income taxes	?
Income tax expense	560,000
Net income	$?

VIENNA CORPORATION
Balance Sheet
December 31

	1996	1995
Assets		
Current assets		
Cash	$ 450,000	$ 375,000
Accounts receivable (net)	?	950,000
Inventory	?	1,720,000
Total current assets	?	3,045,000
Plant assets (net)	4,620,000	3,955,000
Total assets	$?	$7,000,000
Liabilities and Stockholders' Equity		
Current liabilities	$?	$ 825,000
Long-term notes payable	?	2,800,000
Total liabilities	?	3,625,000
Common stock, $1 par	3,000,000	3,000,000
Retained earnings	400,000	375,000
Total stockholders' equity	3,400,000	3,375,000
Total liabilities and stockholders' equity	$?	$7,000,000

Additional information:

1. The receivables turnover for 1996 is 10 times.
2. All sales are on account.
3. The profit margin for 1996 is 14.5%.
4. Return on assets is 22% for 1996.

5. The current ratio on December 31, 1996, is 3:1.
6. The inventory turnover for 1996 is 4.8 times.

Instructions

Compute the missing information given the ratios above. Show computations. (Note: Start with one ratio and derive as much information as possible from it before trying another ratio. List all missing amounts under the ratio used to find the information.)

ALTERNATE PROBLEMS*

Prepare vertical analysis and comment on profitability.
(SO 4, 5)

P15–1A   Comparative statement data for Brooks Company and Shields Company, two competitors, appear below. All balance sheet data are as of December 31, 1996, and December 31, 1995.

	Brooks Company		Shields Company	
	1996	**1995**	**1996**	**1995**
Net sales	$250,000		$1,200,000	
Cost of goods sold	160,000		720,000	
Operating expenses	51,000		252,000	
Interest expense	3,000		10,000	
Income tax expense	11,000		65,000	
Current assets	130,000	$110,000	700,000	$650,000
Plant assets (net)	305,000	270,000	800,000	750,000
Current liabilities	60,000	52,000	250,000	275,000
Long-term liabilities	50,000	68,000	200,000	150,000
Common stock	260,000	210,000	750,000	700,000
Retained earnings	65,000	50,000	300,000	275,000

Instructions

(a) Prepare a vertical analysis of the 1996 income statement data for Brooks Company and Shields Company in columnar form.

(b) ▭▭▭▭▷ Comment on the relative profitability of the companies by computing the return on assets and the return on common stockholders' equity ratios for both companies.

Compute ratios from balance sheet and income statement.
(SO 5)

P15–2A   The comparative statements of the Marti Rosen Company are presented below:

MARTI ROSEN COMPANY
Income Statement
For the Year Ended December 31

	1996	1995
Net sales	$660,000	$624,000
Cost of goods sold	440,000	405,600
Gross profit	220,000	218,400
Selling and administrative expense	143,880	149,760
Income from operations	76,120	68,640
Other expenses and losses		
Interest expense	7,920	7,200
Income before income taxes	68,200	61,440
Income tax expense	25,300	24,000
Net income	$ 42,900	$ 37,440

*Follow the rounding procedures used in the chapter.

MARTI ROSEN COMPANY
Balance Sheet
December 31

	1996	1995
Assets		
Current assets		
Cash	$ 23,100	$ 21,600
Marketable securities	34,800	33,000
Accounts receivable (net)	106,200	93,800
Inventory	72,400	64,000
Total current assets	236,500	212,400
Plant assets (net)	465,300	459,600
Total assets	$701,800	$672,000
Liabilities and Stockholders' Equity		
Current liabilities		
Accounts payable	$134,200	$132,000
Income taxes payable	25,300	24,000
Total current liabilities	159,500	156,000
Bonds payable	132,000	120,000
Total liabilities	291,500	276,000
Stockholders' equity		
Common stock ($10 par)	140,000	150,000
Retained earnings	270,300	246,000
Total stockholders' equity	410,300	396,000
Total liabilities and stockholders' equity	$701,800	$672,000

On July 1, 1996, 1,000 shares were repurchased and canceled. All sales were on account. Net cash provided by operating activities was $36,000.

Instructions
Compute the following ratios for 1996:

(a) Earnings per share.
(b) Return on common stockholders' equity.
(c) Return on assets.
(d) Current.
(e) Acid-test.
(f) Receivables turnover.
(g) Inventory turnover.

(h) Times interest earned.
(i) Asset turnover.
(j) Debt to total assets.
(k) Current cash debt.
(l) Cash return on sales.
(m) Cash debt coverage.

P15–3A Condensed balance sheet and income statement data for Los Colinas Corporation appear below:

Perform ratio analysis.
(SO 5)

LOS COLINAS CORPORATION
Balance Sheet
December 31

	1996	1995	1994
Cash	$ 40,000	$ 24,000	$ 20,000
Receivables (net)	70,000	45,000	48,000
Other current assets	80,000	75,000	62,000
Investments	90,000	70,000	50,000
Plant and equipment (net)	450,000	400,000	360,000
	$730,000	$614,000	$540,000
Current liabilities	$ 98,000	$ 75,000	$ 70,000
Long-term debt	97,000	75,000	65,000
Common stock, $10 par	400,000	340,000	300,000
Retained earnings	135,000	124,000	105,000
	$730,000	$614,000	$540,000

LOS COLINAS CORPORATION
Income Statement
For the Years Ended December 31

	1996	1995
Sales	$700,000	$750,000
Less: Sales returns and allowances	40,000	50,000
Net sales	660,000	700,000
Cost of goods sold	420,000	400,000
Gross profit	240,000	300,000
Operating expenses (including income taxes)	194,000	237,000
Net income	$ 46,000	$ 63,000

Additional information:

1. The market price of Los Colinas's common stock was $5.00, $4.50, and $2.30 for 1994, 1995, and 1996, respectively.
2. All dividends were paid in cash.
3. On July 1, 1995, 4,000 shares of common stock were issued and on July 1, 1996, 6,000 shares were issued.

Instructions

(a) Compute the following ratios for 1995 and 1996:
   (1) Profit margin.
   (2) Asset turnover.
   (3) Earnings per share.
   (4) Price-earnings.
   (5) Payout.
   (6) Debt to total assets.

(b) ▭▭▭▭▷ Based on the ratios calculated, discuss briefly the improvement or lack thereof in financial position and operating results from 1995 to 1996 of Los Colinas Corporation.

Compute ratios, commenting on overall liquidity and profitability.
(SO 5)

P15–4A   Financial information for Star Track Company is presented below:

STAR TRACK COMPANY
Balance Sheet
December 31

	1996	1995
Assets		
Cash	$ 50,000	$ 42,000
Short-term investments	80,000	100,000
Receivables (net)	100,000	87,000
Inventories	440,000	400,000
Prepaid expenses	25,000	31,000
Land	75,000	75,000
Building and equipment (net)	570,000	500,000
	$1,340,000	$1,235,000
Liabilities and Stockholders' Equity		
Notes payable	$ 125,000	$ 125,000
Accounts payable	160,000	140,000
Accrued liabilities	50,000	50,000
Bonds payable, due 1995	200,000	200,000
Common stock, $5 par	500,000	500,000
Retained earnings	305,000	220,000
	$1,340,000	$1,235,000

STAR TRACK COMPANY
Income Statement
For the Years Ended December 31

	1996	1995
Sales	$1,000,000	$ 940,000
Cost of goods sold	650,000	635,000
Gross profit	350,000	305,000
Operating expenses	235,000	215,000
Net income	$ 115,000	$ 90,000

Additional information:

1. Inventory at the beginning of 1995 was $350,000.
2. Receivables at the beginning of 1995 were $80,000.
3. Total assets at the beginning of 1995 were $1,175,000.
4. No common stock transactions occurred during 1995 or 1996.
5. All sales were on account.

Instructions
(a) Indicate, by using ratios, the change in liquidity and profitability of Star Track Company from 1995 to 1996. (Note: Not all profitability ratios can be computed nor can cash basis ratios be computed.)
(b) Given below are three independent situations and a ratio that may be affected. For each situation, compute the affected ratio (1) as of December 31, 1996, and (2) as of December 31, 1997, after giving effect to the situation. Net income for 1997 was $125,000. Total assets on December 31, 1997, were $1,500,000.

Situation	Ratio
(1) 65,000 shares of common stock were sold at par on July 1, 1997.	Return on common stockholders' equity
(2) All of the notes payable were paid in 1997.	Debt to total assets
(3) Market price of common stock on December 31, 1997, was $6.25. Market price on December 31, 1996, was $5.	Price-earnings ratio

P15–5A Selected financial data of two intense competitors in a recent year are presented below in millions of dollars.

Compute selected ratios and compare liquidity, profitability, and solvency for two companies.
(SO 5)

	Bethlehem Steel Corporation	Inland Steel Company
Income Statement Data for Year		
Net sales	$4,819	$4,497
Cost of goods sold	4,548	3,991
Selling and administrative expenses	137	265
Interest expense	46	72
Other income (net)	7	0
Income taxes	14	62
Net income	$ 81	$ 107
Balance Sheet Data (End-of-Year)		
Current assets	$1,569	$1,081
Property, plant, and equipment (net)	2,759	1,610
Other assets	1,454	662
Total assets	5,782	3,353
Current liabilities	1,011	565
Long-term debt	3,615	2,056
Total stockholders' equity	1,156	732
Total liabilities and stockholders' equity	$5,782	$3,353

Beginning-of-Year Balances

Total assets	$5,877	$3,436
Total stockholders' equity	697	623

Other Data

Average net receivables	$ 511	$ 515
Average inventory	868	403
Net cash provided by operating activities	90	160

Instructions

(a) For each company, compute the following ratios:

(1) Current	(7) Return on common stockholders' equity
(2) Receivables turnover	(8) Debt to total assets
(3) Inventory turnover	(9) Times interest earned
(4) Profit margin	(10) Current cash debt
(5) Asset turnover	(11) Cash return on sales
(6) Return on assets	(12) Cash debt coverage

(b) Compare the liquidity, profitability, and solvency of the two companies.

▶*Broadening Your Perspective*

*F*INANCIAL REPORTING PROBLEM— PEPSICO, INC.

•••

Your parents are considering investing in PepsiCo, Inc., common stock. They ask you, as an accounting expert, to make an analysis of the company for them. Fortunately, excerpts from a current annual report of PepsiCo are presented in Appendix A of this textbook. Note that all amounts omit 000,000's (i.e., all dollar amounts are in millions).

Instructions
(Follow the approach in the chapter for rounding numbers.)

(a) Make a 5-year trend analysis, using 1991 as the base year, of (1) net sales and (2) income from continuing operations. Comment on the significance of the trend results.
(b) Compute for 1995 and 1994 the (1) profit margin, (2) asset turnover, (3) return on assets, and (4) return on common stockholders' equity. How would you evaluate PepsiCo's profitability? Total assets at December 25, 1993, were $23,706, and total stockholders' equity at December 25, 1993, was $6,339.
(c) Compute for 1995 and 1994 the (1) debt to total assets and (2) times interest earned ratio. How would you evaluate PepsiCo's long-term solvency?
(d) What information outside the annual report may also be useful to your parents in making a decision about PepsiCo, Inc.?

*C*OMPARATIVE ANALYSIS PROBLEM— THE COCA-COLA COMPANY VS. PEPSICO, INC.

•••

The financial statements of Coca-Cola Company are presented at the end of Chapter 1, and PepsiCo's financial statements are presented in Appendix A.

Instructions
(a) Based on the information contained in these financial statements, determine each of the following for each company:
1. The percentage increase in (i) net sales and (ii) net income from 1994 to 1995.

2. The percentage increase in (i) total assets and (ii) total stockholders' (shareholders') equity from 1994 to 1995.
3. The earnings per share and price-earnings ratio for 1995.

(b) What conclusions concerning the two companies can be drawn from these data?

INTERPRETATION OF FINANCIAL STATEMENTS

Mini-Case—Manitowoc Company and Caterpillar Corp.

For the Manitowoc Company and Caterpillar Corporation are both producers and sellers of large fixed assets. Caterpillar is substantially larger than Manitowoc. Financial information taken from each company's financial statements is provided below.

| | Caterpillar | | Manitowoc | |
| | (in millions) | | (in thousands) | |
Financial highlights	1995	1994	1995	1994
Cash and short term investments	$ 638	$ 419	$ 16,635	$ 16,163
Accounts receivable	4,285	4,290	51,011	29,500
Inventory	1,921	1,835	52,928	36,793
Other current assets	803	865	14,571	14,082
Current assets	7,647	7,409	135,145	96,538
Total assets	16,830	16,250	324,915	159,465
Current liabilities	6,049	5,498	110,923	54,064
Total liabilities	13,442	13,339	243,254	84,408
Total stockholders' equity	3,388	2,911	81,661	75,057
Sales	15,451		313,149	
Cost of goods sold	12,000		237,679	
Interest expense	191		1,865	
Income tax expense	501		8,551	
Net income	1,136		14,569	
Cash provided from operations	2,190		16,367	

Instructions

(a) Please calculate the following liquidity ratios and provide a discussion of the relative liquidity of the two companies.
 1. Current ratio
 2. Quick or acid test ratio
 3. Current cash debt coverage
 4. Accounts receivable turnover
 5. Inventory turnover

(b) Please calculate the following profitability ratios and provide a discussion of the relative profitability of the two companies.
 1. Asset turnover
 2. Profit margin on sales
 3. Return on assets
 4. Return on common equity

(c) Please calculate the following solvency ratios and provide a discussion of the relative solvency of the two companies.
 1. Debt to assets
 2. Times interest earned

DECISION CASE

As the CPA for J. Martinez Manufacturing Inc., you have been requested to develop some key ratios from the comparative financial statements. This information is to be used to convince creditors that J. Martinez Manufacturing Inc. is solvent and to support the use of going-concern valuation procedures in the financial statements.

The data requested and the computations developed from the financial statements follow:

	1997	1996
Current ratio	3.1 times	2.1 times
Acid-test ratio	.8 times	1.4 times
Asset turnover	2.8 times	2.2 times
Sales to stockholders' equity	2.3 times	2.7 times
Net income	Up 32%	Down 8%
Earnings per share	$3.30	$2.50
Book value per share	Up 8%	Up 11%

Instructions

(a) J. Martinez Manufacturing Inc. asks you to prepare a list of brief comments stating how each of these items supports the solvency and going concern potential of the business. The company wishes to use these comments to support its presentation of data to its creditors. You are to prepare the comments as requested, giving the implications and the limitations of each item separately, and then the collective inference that may be drawn from them about J. Martinez's solvency and going-concern potential.

(b) What warnings should you offer these creditors about the limitations of ratio analysis for the purpose stated here?

COMMUNICATION ACTIVITY

L. R. Stanton is the Chief Executive Officer of Hi-Tech Electronics. Stanton is an expert engineer but a novice in accounting. Stanton asks you, as an accounting major, to explain (1) the bases for comparison in analyzing Hi-Tech's financial statements and (2) the limitations, if any, in financial statement analysis.

Instructions
Write a letter to L. R. Stanton that explains the bases for comparison and the limitations of financial statement analysis.

GROUP ACTIVITY

Three types of analyses are explained in the chapter: horizontal, vertical, and ratio.

Instructions
The class should be divided into five groups. Each group will take one of the following topics: horizontal analysis; vertical analysis; ratio analysis—liquidity; ratio analysis—profitability; and ratio analysis—solvency. For horizontal analysis and vertical analysis, the group should explain the analysis and illustrate its application to the balance sheet and income statement. For each category of ratio analysis, the group should state the formula and purpose of each ratio.

ETHICS CASE

Vern Fairly, president of Fairly Industries, wishes to issue a press release to bolster his company's image and maybe even its stock price, which has been gradually falling. As controller, you have been asked to provide a list of twenty financial ratios along with some other operating statistics relative to Fairly Industries' first quarter financials and operations. Two days after you provide the ratios and data requested, you are asked by Roberto Sanchez, the public relations director of Fairly, to prove the accuracy of the financial and operating data contained in the press release written by the president and edited by Roberto. In the news release, the president highlights the sales increase of 25% over last year's first quarter and the positive change in the current ratio from 1.5:1 last year to 3:1 this year. He also emphasizes that production was up 50% over the prior year's first quarter. You note that the release contains only positive or improved ratios and none of the negative or deteriorated ratios. For instance, no mention is made that the debt to total assets ratio has increased from 35% to 55%, that inventories are up 89%, and that while the current ratio improved, the acid-test ratio fell from 1:1 to .5:1. Nor is there any mention that the reported profit for the quarter would have been a loss had not the estimated lives of Fairly's plant and machinery been increased by 30%. Roberto emphasized, ''The Pres wants this release by early this afternoon.''

Instructions
  (a) Who are the stakeholders in this situation?
  (b) Is there anything unethical in President Fairly's actions?
  (c) Should you as controller remain silent? Does Roberto have any responsibility?

RESEARCH ASSIGNMENT

The chapter stresses the importance of comparing an individual firm's financial ratios to industry norms. Robert Morris Associates (RMA), a national association of bank loan and credit officers, publishes industry-specific financial data in its *Annual Statement Studies*. This publication includes common-size financial statements and various ratios classified by four-digit SIC code. (Note: An alternative source is Dun & Bradstreet's *Industry Norms and Key Business Ratios*.)

Obtain the 1995 edition of *Annual Statement Studies* (covering fiscal years ended 4/1/94 through 3/31/95) and the 1995 or 1996 Annual Report of Wal-Mart Stores, Inc.

Instructions
  (a) Prepare a 1995 common-size balance sheet and income statement for Wal-Mart.
  (b) Calculate those 1995 ratios for Wal-Mart which are covered by RMA. (Note: The specific ratio definitions used by RMA are described in the beginning of the book. Use ending values for balance sheet items.)
  (c) What is Wal-Mart's SIC code? Use your answers from parts (a) and (b) to compare Wal-Mart to the appropriate current industry data. How does Wal-Mart compare to its competitors? (Note: RMA sorts current-year data by firm assets and sales, while five years of historical data are presented on an aggregate basis.)
  (d) How many sets of financial statements did RMA use in compiling the current industry data sorted by sales?

CRITICAL THINKING
► *A Real-World Focus: The Coca-Cola Company*

The Coca-Cola Company provides refreshments to every corner of the world. Four of its brands are among the five best-selling soft drinks in the world, and it ships nearly 11 billion cases of carbonated soft drinks per year. Despite its success, the company believes that great potential still exists—its top 16 markets account for 80% of its sales, but only 20% of the world's population.

The Coca-Cola Company

Selected data from the consolidated financial statements for The Coca-Cola Company are presented below. (All dollars are in millions.)

Total current assets (including cash, accounts receivable, and marketable securities totaling $3,056) at year end	$ 5,205
Total current liabilities at year end	6,177
Net sales	16,172
Cost of goods sold	6,167
Net income	2,554
Average receivables for the year	1,384
Average inventories for the year	1,048
Average total assets	12,947
Average current liabilities	6,763
Average common stockholders' equity	4,910
Net cash provided by operating activities	3,115

Instructions

(a) Compute the five liquidity ratios for The Coca-Cola Company.

(b) Compute the five liquidity ratios for PepsiCo, Inc., using the financial statements in Appendix A.

(c) Comment on the relative liquidity of the two competitors.

(d) Compute the following profitability ratios for the two companies: profit margin, cash return on sales, asset turnover, return on assets, and return on common stockholders' equity.

(e) Comment on the relative profitability of the two competitors.

COMPREHENSIVE FINANCIAL REPORTING PROBLEM

Presented below are the income statements, selected balance sheet information, and selected note disclosures from the Annual Report of Sears, Roebuck and Co. for 1993:

Sears, Roebuck and Co.
Consolidated Statements of Income

millions, except per common share data	1993	1992	1991
Revenues	$50,837.5	$52,344.6	$50,982.9
Expenses			
Costs and Expenses	47,233.7	52,478.3	48,568.2
Restructuring (note 4)		3,108.4	
Interest	1,498.1	1,510.9	1,680.5
Total Expenses	48,731.8	57,097.6	50,248.7
Operating income (loss)	2,105.7	(4,753.0)	734.2
Other income (loss)	206.0	(27.2)	129.6
Gain on the sale of subsidiaries stock	635.1	91.4	
Income (loss) before income taxes (benefit, minority interest, and equity income	2,946.8	(4,688.8)	863.8
Income taxes (benefit)	400.9	(2,114.0)	(38.5)
Minority interest and equity in net income of unconsolidated companies	(136.9)	8.0	13.3
Income (loss) from continuing operations	2,409.1	(2,566.8)	915.6
Discontinued operations (note 3)			
Operating income, less income tax expense of $167.7, $299.2, and $231.0	240.1	507.9	363.3
Loss on disposal, including income tax expense of $22.0	(64.0)		

Year Ended December 31,

Sears, Roebuck and Co.
Consolidated Statements of Income *Cont.*

millions, except per common share data	1993	1992	1991
Income (loss) before extraordinary loss and cumulative effect of accounting changes	2,585.2	(2,058.9)	1,278.9
Extraordinary loss related to the early extinguishment of debt	(210.8)		
Cumulative effect of accounting changes (note 2)		(1,873.4)	
Net income (loss)	$2,374.4	($3,932.3)	$1,278.9
Earnings (loss) per common share, after allowing for dividends on preferred shares			
Income (loss) from continuing operations	$6.22	($7.02)	$2.65
Discontinued operations	0.46	1.37	1.06

Year Ended December 31,

Income (loss) before extraordinary loss and cumulative effect of accounting changes	6.68	(5.65)	3.71
Extraordinary loss	(0.55)		
Cumulative effect of accounting changes		(5.07)	
Net income (loss)	$6.13	($10.72)	$3.71

Selected figures from the Sears balance sheets: December 31

millions	1993	1992
Total assets	$90,807.8	$85,490.6
Retail customer receivables	15,905.6	13,877.6
Inventories	3,518.0	4,047.9
Total liabilities	76,809.7	74,423.2
Common shareholders' equity		
Common shares ($.75 par)	$293.8	$290.6
Capital in excess of par	2,353.8	2,194.6
Retained earnings	8,162.8	8,772.2
Less: Treasury stock (at cost)	(1,703.5)	(1,734.3)
Adjustments	995.9	(311.2)
Total common shareholders' equity	$10,102.8	$9,211.9

Selected information from the notes to Sears' financial statements:

1. Summary of significant accounting policies

   Inventories:

   Inventories . . . are valued primarily at the lower of cost (using the last-in, first-out or LIFO method) or market by application of internally developed price indices to estimate the effects of inflation on inventories. . . . If the first-in, first-out (FIFO) method of inventory valuation had been used instead of the LIFO method, inventories would have been $743.7 and $738.4 million higher at December 31, 1993 and 1992, respectively.

   Property and equipment:

   Property and equipment is stated at cost less accumulated depreciation. Depreciation is provided principally by the straight-line method over the estimated useful lives of the related assets.

2. Accounting changes

   Effective Jan. 1, 1992, the Company adopted SFAS No. 106, "Employers' Accounting for Postretirement Benefits Other than Pensions," and SFAS No. 112, "Employers' Accounting for Postemployment Benefits," for all domestic and foreign postretirement and postemployment benefit plans by immediately recognizing the transition amounts. The Company previously expensed the cost of these benefits, which consist of health care and life insurance, as claims were incurred.

3. Discontinued operations

   In May 1993, the Company entered into separate agreements to sell the Coldwell-Banker Residential business and Sears Mortgage Banking operations. A $64.0 million after-tax loss was recorded in the second quarter of 1993, primarily due to adverse income tax effects related to the sale of Sears Savings Bank. These sales were completed in the fourth quarter of 1993.

4. Restructuring

   The Merchandise Group recorded a pretax charge in the fourth quarter of 1992 of $2.65 billion related to discontinuing its domestic catalog operations, offering a voluntary early retirement program to certain salaried associates, closing unprofitable retail department and specialty stores, streamlining or discontinuing various unprofitable merchandise lines, and the writedown of underutilized assets to market value. Corporate also recorded a $23.8 million pretax charge related to offering termination and early retirement programs to certain associates. Additionally, Homart recorded a $326.6 million pretax writedown of land previously held for office development and selected office properties that were to be sold.

During the first quarter of 1992, the Merchandise Group recorded a $106.0 million pretax charge for severance costs related to cost reduction programs for commission sales and headquarters staff in domestic merchandising.

The Merchandise Group and Corporate restructuring charges and Homart [consolidated subsidiary] property writedowns amounted to a combined after-tax expense of $1.95 billion in 1992.

Instructions

(a) Calculate the following ratios for 1993:
   (1) Profit margin percentage (return on sales) for both income from continuing operations and net income.
   (2) Return on common stockholders' equity.
   (3) Return on assets.
   (4) Times interest earned.

Evaluate Sears' profitability.

(b) Sears showed a loss of $1.65 billion from Hurricane Andrew in 1992. In what category does a loss appear in Sears' 1992 income statement?

(c) Sears' revenues from its merchandising operations were $26.29 billion and its cost of sales was $18.76 billion in 1993.
   (1) Calculate Sears' inventory turnover for 1993.
   (2) Suppose you wanted to compare Sears' inventory turnover ratio with that of a Canadian company, which under Canadian accounting standards must use FIFO. Would you be able to make such a comparison? If so, how?
   (3) Calculate Sears' receivables turnover for 1993.
   (4) Unlike most retailers, whose fiscal year ends a month into the following year, Sears' year-end is December 31. What effect does Sears' year-end have on the inventory turnover and receivables turnover ratios?
   (5) What effect does Sears' nonstandard year-end (for a retailer) have on the comparability of Sears' ratios with those of other large retailers?

(d) Sears sold two business segments in 1993.
   (1) What did it sell and in what quarter were these sales completed?
   (2) Where does the income or loss from these sales appear on Sears' income statement?

Answers to Self-Study Questions

1. b   2. d   3. a   4. c   5. c   6. c   7. c   8. b   9. a   10. d   11. d
12. a

SPECIMEN FINANCIAL STATEMENTS

The Annual Report

Once each year a corporation communicates to its stockholders and other interested parties by issuing a complete set of audited financial statements. The **annual report**, as this communication is called, summarizes the financial results of its operation for the year and its plans for the future. Many such annual reports have become attractive, multicolored, glossy public relations ad pieces containing pictures of corporate officers and directors as well as photos and descriptions of new products and new buildings. Yet the basic function of every annual report is to report financial information, almost all of which is a product of the corporation's accounting system.

The content and organization of corporate annual reports has become fairly standardized. Excluding the public relations part of the report (pictures, products, and propaganda), the following items are the traditional financial portions of the annual report:

Financial Highlights
Letter to the Stockholders
Management's Report
Auditor's Report
Financial Statements (and Management's Analysis)
Notes to the Financial Statements
Supplementary Financial Information

In this appendix we illustrate current financial reporting with a comprehensive set of corporate financial statements that are prepared in accordance with generally accepted accounting principles and audited by an international independent certified public accounting firm. We are grateful for permission to use the actual financial statements and other accompanying financial information from the annual report of a large, publicly held company, PepsiCo, Inc.

▸Financial Highlights

The financial highlights section, called the **Financial Summary** by PepsiCo, is usually presented inside the front cover or on the first two pages of the annual report. This section generally reports the total or per share amounts for five to ten financial items for the current year and one or more previous years. Financial items from the income statement and the balance sheet that typically are presented are sales, income from continuing operations, net income, net income per share, dividends per common share, and the amount of capital expenditures. The financial highlights section from PepsiCo's **Annual Report** is shown below:

PepsiCo, Inc.

Financial Highlights

A Word About the Year's Numbers...

Like a lot of companies, PepsiCo adopted a required new accounting rule in 1995, which caused our "reported" earnings to decline. It didn't involve cash and it didn't keep us from selling record amounts of Pepsi, pizza, tacos, chicken and chips. To understand what actually happened in the business, focus on "ongoing" earnings, which exclude the impact of accounting changes and onetime items.

PepsiCo, Inc. and Subsidiaries ($ in millions except per share amounts)	December 30, 1995 (a)	December 31, 1994 (a)	Percent Change
Statistics			
Year-end market price per share of			
PepsiCo capital stock	$ 55 ⅞	36 ¼	+ 54
Annual return to shareholders	% 56	(12)	
Cash dividends declared per share. . . .	$ 0.78	0.70	+ 11
Summary of Operations			
Net sales	$30,421	28,472	+ 7
Ongoing			
Operating profit	$ 3,507	3,201	+ 10
Income before cumulative effect of			
accounting changes	$ 1,990	1,767	+ 13
Per Share.	$ 2.48	2.20	+ 13
Reported			
Operating profit	$ 2,987	3,201	− 7
Income before cumulative effect of			
accounting changes	$ 1,606	1,784	− 10
Per Share.	$ 2.00	2.22	− 10
Cumulative effect of accounting			
changes	$ −	(32)	
Per Share.	$ −	(0.04)	
Net income	$ 1,606	1,752	− 8
Per Share.	$ 2.00	2.18	− 8
Cash Flows			
Provided by operating activities	$ 3,742	3,716	+ 1
Capital spending.	$ 2,104	2,253	− 7
Purchases of treasury stock.	$ 541	549	− 1
Dividends paid	$ 599	540	+ 11
Acquisitions and investments in			
unconsolidated affiliates	$ 466	316	+ 47

(a)   Fiscal years 1995 and 1994 consisted of 52 and 53 weeks, respectively. The fifty-third week increased 1994 earnings by an estimated $54 ($35 after-tax or $0.04 per share).

As shown above, PepsiCo chose also to present the percent change from last year to the current year for each of the reported items and net sales and operating profits by segments.

Letter to the Stockholders

Nearly every annual report contains a letter to the stockholders from the Chairman of the Board or the President (or both). This letter typically discusses the company's accomplishments during the past year and highlights significant events such as mergers and acquisitions, new products, operating achievements, business philosophy, changes in officers or directors, financing commitments, expansion plans, and future prospects. The letter to the stockholders ("Dear Friends") signed by Wayne Calloway, Chairman of the Board and Chief Executive Officer of PepsiCo, is shown below:

Dear Friends:

It was quite a year. Our stock price soared 54%. Our business prospered. And, most of all, our people flourished, growing personally and professionally, more in touch with the consumer than ever.

It was PepsiCo's thirtieth year as a corporation and my tenth as your chief executive officer. It was also my last full year on the job. I've decided to step down as chief executive officer and turn PepsiCo over to a new generation of terrific leaders.

All of which made me a little philosophical. What have we learned about PepsiCo over the last 30 years, I wondered. What qualities drove our success? What characteristics enabled us to grow, nearly doubling our size every five years?

In other words, what does PepsiCo's relatively brief but extraordinary history tell us about tomorrow?

In thinking about the *heart* of PepsiCo, what struck me most was how *little* has changed. Our values and aspirations today are exactly the same as they were 30 years ago.

In 1965 we were determined to be a great corporation, to grow rapidly through product innovation and a sharp focus on the consumer. We recognized right from the start that the key to success was high performance people working with great freedom and autonomy.

That hasn't changed a bit. If anything, today we value people *more* highly and have an even greater determination to grow.

Reason for Growth

Not long ago I was reminded of just *how* determined we've been when it comes to growth. *Fortune* took a look at the remaining companies of its original list of America's 500 largest industrial corporations, published back in 1954. It found that the sales of one company grew faster than all the rest. PepsiCo.

Fortune reported that our sales grew on average 16% a year for 40 years (back to the days of Pepsi-Cola Company). More impressive, and certainly more important to you, our return to shareholders grew just about as fast – averaging about 16% a year, for 40 years.

With that kind of performance over that period of time, naturally we've become pretty big. We have lots more products and far greater financial strength. But bigness is not the reason we seek growth. In fact, sometimes bigness can get in your way. The reason for growth is something else, something almost spiritual: it produces a winning atmosphere.

Growth is pure oxygen. It creates a vital, enthusiastic corporation where people see genuine personal opportunity. They take bigger chances. They work harder and smarter. In that way growth is more than our single most important financial driver, it's an essential part of our corporate culture. It's why so many talented leaders want to work for PepsiCo rather than lots of other fine corporations.

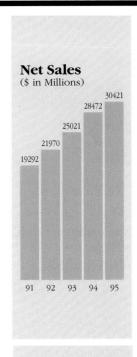

Net Sales
($ in Millions)

19292 — 91
21970 — 92
25021 — 93
28472 — 94
30421 — 95

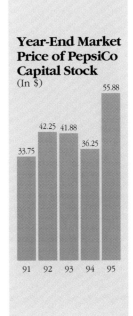

Year-End Market Price of PepsiCo Capital Stock
(In $)

33.75 — 91
42.25 — 92
41.88 — 93
36.25 — 94
55.88 — 95

Cumulative Total Return

(In $. Indexed at 12/31/85)

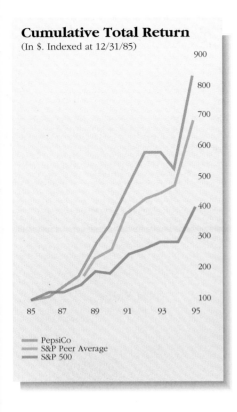

PepsiCo
S&P Peer Average
S&P 500

PepsiCo at 30

So, as I see it, those fundamentals haven't changed at PepsiCo over the last 30 years. But some things certainly have. For one, today we sell more in a week than we did in an entire year back in 1965. In the United States alone, for example, we sell 10 pounds of Lay's potato chips every *second*. That's 600 pounds of Lay's every minute of every day. And, that's only one brand, in one country, in one business. To me, that's powerful stuff.

But not nearly as powerful as the stake our people have in our growth. With 480,000 people, PepsiCo is now the world's third largest corporate employer. Today we employ more people in Australia than we employed worldwide when PepsiCo was formed. And we give almost every full-time employee stock options. That not only lets our people share in our success, it aligns their interests squarely with those of our shareholders. When you get that many people focused on growth, you can make almost anything happen.

So that's how I see PepsiCo at 30 years old: a tradition of outstanding growth, great people and financial success.

Operating Free Cash Flow*

($ In Millions)

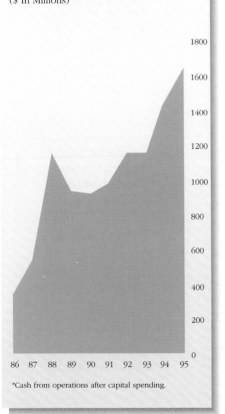

*Cash from operations after capital spending.

Directors

Our long-term success is the result of many things, not the least of which is an excellent board of directors. Let me say just a few words about three wonderful directors who retire this year and a new outside director who joins us:

- Roger Smith is retiring after seven years on our Board. In that short time he's made a terrific contribution and will be missed.
- Robert Stewart, the last of PepsiCo's original Board of Directors, is also retiring. For more than 30 years he has been a source of excellent judgment and wonderful good cheer. We'll certainly miss Bobby.
- Andrall Pearson too is retiring. He's not only been a director for 26 years, he was PepsiCo's president and chief operating officer from 1971 through 1984. Next to our co-founders Don Kendall and Herman Lay, Andy probably had most to do with making PepsiCo the company it is today. Thank you, Andy, for a great contribution.
- Ray Hunt, chairman and chief executive officer of Hunt Oil, joins us as a new director in 1996. Ray is an outstanding executive who brings unique experience and a special viewpoint to our Board.

I've always viewed our Board as one of PepsiCo's greatest assets. And I think today it's as strong as ever.

PepsiCo's Future

A word about the future. In my opinion, PepsiCo has the best young management team in the world of business. They are experienced and aggressive with a powerful record of accomplishment. The Board and I strongly believe it's time to let them lead this corporation.

Roger Enrico, a 24-year PepsiCo veteran, will be the new chief executive officer, and that's great news for shareholders. He's a big star. Equally terrific are three senior executives who have been elected to the Board: Steve Reinemund, Chris Sinclair and Craig Weatherup. Together they'll make a great team.

But, obviously, PepsiCo's management doesn't stop with those four executives. Our restaurant divisions are headed by five of the best leaders you'll ever meet. And under all of our top executives are dozens more bright, talented executives ready to move forward.

If my 10 years as chief executive officer could be remembered for one thing, I hope its the management team I've watched grow and mature during this time. They are the best.

Let me wrap up by saying PepsiCo has great products and huge financial resources. But mostly we have wonderful people, hundreds of thousands of them, who I just can't thank enough. It's hard to generalize about that many folks, but I see them as very special. They do their best to help millions of customers and consumers each day. And while none of us is perfect, we're all working to get better and better.

When you think about it, getting better each day is all we can ask and all we should want. It's the best way I know to guarantee a great future.

Sincerely,

Wayne Calloway

Wayne Calloway
Chairman of the Board and Chief Executive Officer

Segment Capital Spending
Total: $2,085
($ in Millions)

Beverages
$566
27%

Snack Foods
$769
37%

Restaurants
$750
36%

Segment Capital Spending
Total: $2,085
($ in Millions)

U.S.
$1,462
70%

International
$623
30%

Management's Report

A relatively recent addition to corporate annual reports is the statement made by management about its role in and responsibility for the accuracy and integrity of the financial statements. PepsiCo's management letter is entitled **Management's Responsibility for Financial Statements**. In it the Chairman of the Board and Chief Executive Officer along with the Chief Financial Officer and the Controller, on behalf of management: (1) assume primary responsibility for the financial statements and the related notes, (2) outline and assess the company's internal control system, (3) declare the financial statements in conformity with generally accepted accounting principles, and (4) comment on the audit by the certified public accountant and the composition and role of the Audit Committee of the Board of Directors. PepsiCo's management report is presented below:

Management's Responsibility for Financial Statements

To Our Shareholders:

Management is responsible for the reliability of the consolidated financial statements and related notes, which have been prepared in conformity with generally accepted accounting principles and include amounts based upon our estimates and assumptions, as required. The financial statements have been audited and reported on by our independent auditors, KPMG Peat Marwick LLP, who were given free access to all financial records and related data, including minutes of the meetings of the Board of Directors and Committees of the Board. We believe that the representations made to the independent auditors were valid and appropriate.

PepsiCo maintains a system of internal control over financial reporting, designed to provide reasonable assurance as to the reliability of the financial statements, as well as to safeguard assets from unauthorized use on disposition. The system is supported by formal policies and procedures, including an active Code of Conduct program intended to ensure employees adhere to the highest standards of personal and professional integrity. PepsiCo's internal audit function monitors and reports on the adequacy of and compliance with the internal control system, and appropriate actions are taken to address significant control deficiencies and other opportunities for improving the system as they are identified. The Audit Committee of the Board of Directors, which is composed solely of outside directors, provides oversight to our financial reporting process and our controls to safeguard assets through periodic meetings with our independent auditors, internal auditors and management. Both our independent auditors and internal auditors have free access to the Audit Committee.

Although no cost effective internal control system will preclude all errors and irregularities, we believe our controls as of December 30, 1995 provide reasonable assurance that the financial statements are reliable and that our assets are reasonably safeguarded.

Wayne Calloway

Wayne Calloway
Chairman of the Board and Chief Executive Officer

Robert H. Dettmer

Robert G. Dettmer
Executive Vice President and Chief Financial Officer

Robert L. Carleton

Robert L. Carleton
Senior Vice President and Controller

February 6, 1996

Auditor's Report

All publicly held corporations, as well as many other enterprises and organizations (both profit and not-for-profit, large and small) engage the services of independent certified public accountants for the purpose of obtaining an objective, expert report on their financial statements. Based on a comprehensive examination of the company's accounting system and records, and the financial statements, the outside CPA issues the auditor's report.

The standard auditor's report consists of three paragraphs: (1) an introductory paragraph, (2) a scope paragraph, and (3) the opinion paragraph. In the introductory paragraph, the auditor identifies who and what was audited and indicates the responsibilities of management and the auditor relative to the financial statements. In the scope paragraph the auditor states that the audit was conducted in accordance with generally accepted auditing standards and discusses the nature and limitations of the audit. In the opinion paragraph, the auditor expresses an informed opinion as to (1) the fairness of the financial statements and (2) their conformity with generally accepted accounting principles. In this particular report the auditors added a fourth paragraph disclosing PepsiCo's adoption of two very recent "FASB" Statements. The **Report of KPMG Peat Marwick Independent Auditors** appearing in PepsiCo's Annual Report is shown below:

Report of Independent Auditors

Board of Directors and Shareholders
PepsiCo, Inc.

We have audited the accompanying consolidated balance sheet of PepsiCo, Inc. and Subsidiaries as of December 30, 1995 and December 31, 1994, and the related consolidated statements of income, cash flows and shareholders' equity for each of the years in the three-year period ended December 30, 1995. These consolidated financial statements are the responsibility of PepsiCo, Inc.'s management. Our responsibility is to express an opinion on these consolidated financial statements based on our audits.

We conducted our audits in accordance with generally accepted auditing standards. Those standards require that we plan and perform the audit to obtain reasonable assurance about whether the financial statements are free of material misstatement. An audit includes examining, on a test basis, evidence supporting the amounts and disclosures in the financial statements. An audit also includes assessing the accounting principles used and significant estimates made by management, as well as evaluating the overall financial statement presentation. We believe that our audits provide a reasonable basis for our opinion.

In our opinion, the consolidated financial statements referred to above present fairly, in all material respects, the financial position of PepsiCo, Inc. and Subsidiaries as of December 30, 1995 and December 31, 1994, and the results of its operations and its

cash flows for each of the years in the three-year period ended December 30, 1995, in conformity with generally accepted accounting principles.

As discussed in Note 2 to the consolidated financial statements, PepsiCo, Inc. in 1995 adopted the provisions of the Financial Accounting Standards Board's Statement of Financial Accounting Standards No. 121, "Accounting for the Impairment of Long-Lived Assets and for Long-Lived Assets to Be Disposed Of." As discussed in Notes 13 and 14 to the consolidated financial statements, PepsiCo, Inc. in 1994 changed its method for calculating the market-related value of pension plan assets used in the determination of pension expense and adopted the provisions of the Financial Accounting Standards Board's Statement of Financial Accounting Standards No. 112, "Employers' Accounting for Postemployment Benefits," respectively.

KPMG Peat Marwick LLP

New York, New York
February 6, 1996

The auditor's report issued on PepsiCo's financial statements is "unqualified" or "clean"; that is, it contains no qualifications or exceptions. In other words, the auditor conformed completely with generally accepted auditing standards in performing the audit, and the financial statements conformed in all material respects with generally accepted accounting principles.

When the financial statements do not conform with generally accepted accounting principles, the auditor must issue a "qualified" opinion and describe the exception. If the lack of confirmity with GAAP is sufficiently material, the auditor is compelled to issue an "adverse" or negative opinion. An adverse opinion means that the financial statements do not present fairly the company's financial condition and/or the results of the company's operations at the dates and for the periods reported.

In circumstances where the auditor is unable to perform all the auditing procedures necessary to reach a conclusion as to the fairness of the financial statements, a "disclaimer" must be issued. In these rare instances, the auditor must report the reason for failure to reach a conclusion on the fairness of the financial statements.

Companies strive to obtain an unqualified auditor's report. Hence, only infrequently are you likely to encounter anything other than this type of opinion on the financial statements.

*F*inancial Statements and Accompanying Notes

The standard set of financial statements consists of: (1) a comparative income statement for three years, (2) a comparative balance sheet for two years, (3) a comparative statement of cash flows for three years, (4) a statement of retained earnings (or stockholders' equity) for three years, and (5) a set of accompanying notes that are considered an integral part of the financial statements. The auditor's report, unless stated otherwise, covers the financial statements and the accompanying notes. The financial statements and accompanying notes plus some supplementary data and analyses for PepsiCo, Inc., appear on the following pages.

Note to the student: For purposes of consistency PepsiCo uses 52 weeks as its fiscal year in preparing its financial statement. For six years in a row 52 weeks is used; every seventh year a 53-week year (1994 for PepsiCo) is adopted to catch up.

Consolidated Statement of Income

PepsiCo, Inc.

(in millions except per share amounts)
PepsiCo, Inc. and Subsidiaries
Fiscal years ended December 30, 1995, December 31, 1994 and December 25, 1993

	1995 (52 Weeks)	1994 (53 Weeks)	1993 (52 Weeks)
Net Sales	**$30,421**	$28,472	$25,021
Costs and Expenses, net			
Cost of sales	**14,886**	13,715	11,946
Selling, general and administrative expenses	**11,712**	11,244	9,864
Amortization of intangible assets	**316**	312	304
Impairment of long-lived assets	**520**	–	–
Operating Profit	**2,987**	3,201	2,907
Gain on stock offering by an unconsolidated affiliate	**–**	18	–
Interest expense	**(682)**	(645)	(573)
Interest income	**127**	90	89
Income Before Income Taxes and Cumulative Effect of Accounting Changes	**2,432**	2,664	2,423
Provision for Income Taxes	**826**	880	835
Income Before Cumulative Effect of Accounting Changes	**1,606**	1,784	1,588
Cumulative Effect of Accounting Changes			
Postemployment benefits (net of income tax benefit of $29)	**–**	(55)	–
Pension assets (net of income tax expense of $15)	**–**	23	–
Net Income	**$ 1,606**	$ 1,752	$ 1,588
Income (Charge) Per Share			
Before cumulative effect of accounting changes	**$ 2.00**	$ 2.22	$ 1.96
Cumulative effect of accounting changes			
Postemployment benefits	**–**	(0.07)	–
Pension assets	**–**	0.03	–
Net Income Per Share	**$ 2.00**	$ 2.18	$ 1.96
Average shares outstanding	**804**	804	810

See accompanying Notes to Consolidated Financial Statements.

Consolidated Statement of Cash Flows — PepsiCo, Inc.

(in millions)
PepsiCo, Inc. and Subsidiaries
Fiscal years ended December 30, 1995, December 31, 1994 and December 25, 1993

	1995 (52 Weeks)	1994 (53 Weeks)	1993 (52 Weeks)
Cash Flows – Operating Activities			
Income before cumulative effect of accounting changes	$ 1,606	$ 1,784	$ 1,588
Adjustments to reconcile income before cumulative effect of accounting changes to net cash provided by operating activities			
Depreciation and amortization	1,740	1,577	1,444
Impairment of long-lived assets	520	–	–
Deferred income taxes	(111)	(67)	83
Other noncash charges and credits, net	398	391	345
Changes in operating working capital, excluding effects of acquisitions			
Accounts and notes receivable	(434)	(112)	(161)
Inventories	(129)	(102)	(90)
Prepaid expenses, taxes and other current assets	76	1	3
Accounts payable	133	30	143
Income taxes payable	(97)	55	(125)
Other current liabilities	40	159	(96)
Net change in operating working capital	(411)	31	(326)
Net Cash Provided by Operating Activities	3,742	3,716	3,134
Cash Flows – Investing Activities			
Acquisitions and investments in unconsolidated affiliates	(466)	(316)	(1,011)
Capital spending	(2,104)	(2,253)	(1,982)
Sales of property, plant and equipment	138	55	73
Sales of restaurants	165	–	7
Short-term investments, by original maturity			
More than three months-purchases	(289)	(219)	(579)
More than three months-maturities	335	650	846
Three months or less, net	18	(10)	(8)
Other, net	(247)	(268)	(117)
Net Cash Used for Investing Activities	(2,450)	(2,361)	(2,771)
Cash Flows – Financing Activities			
Proceeds from issuances of long-term debt	2,030	1,285	711
Payments of long-term debt	(928)	(1,180)	(1,202)
Short-term borrowings, by original maturity			
More than three months-proceeds	2,053	1,304	3,034
More than three months-payments	(2,711)	(1,728)	(2,792)
Three months or less, net	(747)	114	839
Cash dividends paid	(599)	(540)	(462)
Purchases of treasury stock	(541)	(549)	(463)
Proceeds from exercises of stock options	252	97	69
Other, net	(42)	(43)	(37)
Net Cash Used for Financing Activities	(1,233)	(1,240)	(303)
Effect of Exchange Rate Changes on Cash and Cash Equivalents	(8)	(11)	(3)
Net Increase in Cash and Cash Equivalents	51	104	57
Cash and Cash Equivalents – Beginning of Year	331	227	170
Cash and Cash Equivalents – End of Year	$ 382	$ 331	$ 227
Supplemental Cash Flow Information			
Cash Flow Data			
Interest paid	$ 671	591	550
Income taxes paid	$ 790	663	676
Schedule of Noncash Investing and Financing Activities			
Liabilities assumed in connection with acquisitions	$ 66	224	897
Issuance of treasury stock and debt for acquisitions	$ 9	39	365
Book value of net assets exchanged for investments in unconsolidated affiliates	$ 39	–	61

See accompanying Notes to Consolidated Financial Statements.

Consolidated Balance Sheet

PepsiCo, Inc.

(in millions except per share amount)
PepsiCo, Inc. and Subsidiaries
December 30, 1995 and December 31, 1994

	1995	1994
ASSETS		
Current Assets		
Cash and cash equivalents	$ 382	$ 331
Short-term investments, at cost	1,116	1,157
	1,498	1,488
Accounts and notes receivable, less allowance: $150 in 1995 and $151 in 1994	2,407	2,051
Inventories	1,051	970
Prepaid expenses, taxes and other current assets	590	563
Total Current Assets	5,546	5,072
Investments in Unconsolidated Affiliates	1,635	1,295
Property, Plant and Equipment, net	9,870	9,883
Intangible Assets, net	7,584	7,842
Other Assets	797	700
Total Assets	$25,432	$24,792
LIABILITIES AND SHAREHOLDERS' EQUITY		
Current Liabilities		
Accounts payable	$ 1,556	$ 1,452
Accrued compensation and benefits	815	753
Short-term borrowings	706	678
Accrued marketing	469	546
Income taxes payable	387	672
Other current liabilities	1,297	1,169
Total Current Liabilities	5,230	5,270
Long-term Debt	8,509	8,841
Other Liabilities	2,495	1,852
Deferred Income Taxes	1,885	1,973
Shareholders' Equity		
Capital stock, par value 1⅔¢ per share: authorized 1,800 shares, issued 863 shares	14	14
Capital in excess of par value	1,060	935
Retained earnings	8,730	7,739
Currency translation adjustment and other	(808)	(471)
	8,996	8,217
Less: Treasury stock, at cost: 75 shares and 73 shares in 1995 and 1994, respectively	(1,683)	(1,361)
Total Shareholders' Equity	7,313	6,856
Total Liabilities and Shareholders' Equity	$25,432	$24,792

See accompanying Notes to Consolidated Financial Statements.

Consolidated Statement of Shareholders' Equity

(in millions except per share amounts)
PepsiCo, Inc. and Subsidiaries
Fiscal years ended December 30, 1995, December 31, 1994 and December 25, 1993

PepsiCo, Inc.

	Capital Stock Issued Shares	Capital Stock Issued Amount	Capital Stock Treasury Shares	Capital Stock Treasury Amount	Capital in Excess of Par Value	Retained Earnings	Currency Translation Adjustment and Other	Total
Shareholders' Equity, December 26, 1992 . . .	863	$ 14	(64)	$ (667)	$ 668	$ 5,440	$ (99)	$ 5,356
1993 Net income	–	–	–	–	–	1,588	–	1,588
Cash dividends declared (per share–$0.61)	–	–	–	–	–	(486)	–	(486)
Currency translation adjustment	–	–	–	–	–	–	(77)	(77)
Purchases of treasury stock	–	–	(12)	(463)	–	–	–	(463)
Shares issued in connection with acquisitions	–	–	9	170	165	–	–	335
Stock option exercises, including tax benefits of $23	–	–	3	46	46	–	–	92
Pension liability adjustment, net of deferred taxes of $5	–	–	–	–	–	–	(8)	(8)
Other	–	–	–	1	1	–	–	2
Shareholders' Equity, December 25, 1993	863	$ 14	(64)	$ (913)	$ 880	$ 6,542	$ (184)	$ 6,339
1994 Net income	–	–	–	–	–	1,752	–	1,752
Cash dividends declared (per share–$0.70)	–	–	–	–	–	(555)	–	(555)
Currency translation adjustment	–	–	–	–	–	–	(295)	(295)
Purchases of treasury stock	–	–	(15)	(549)	–	–	–	(549)
Stock option exercises, including tax benefits of $27	–	–	5	81	44	–	–	125
Shares issued in connection with acquisitions	–	–	1	15	14	–	–	29
Pension liability adjustment, net of deferred taxes of $5	–	–	–	–	–	–	8	8
Other	–	–	–	5	(3)	–	–	2
Shareholders' Equity, December 31, 1994	863	$ 14	(73)	$ (1,361)	$ 935	$ 7,739	$ (471)	$ 6,856
1995 Net income	–	–	–	–	–	1,606	–	1,606
Cash dividends declared (per share–$0.78)	–	–	–	–	–	(615)	–	(615)
Currency translation adjustment	–	–	–	–	–	–	(337)	(337)
Purchases of treasury stock	–	–	(12)	(541)	–	–	–	(541)
Stock option exercises, including tax benefits of $91	–	–	10	218	125	–	–	343
Other	–	–	–	1	–	–	–	1
Shareholders' Equity, December 30, 1995 . . .	863	$14	(75)	$(1,683)	$1,060	$8,730	$(808)	$7,313

See accompanying Notes to Consolidated Financial Statements.

Management's Analysis

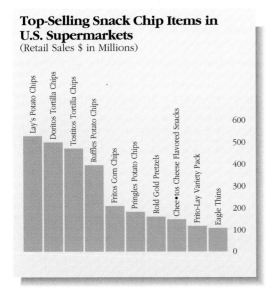

Top-Selling Snack Chip Items in U.S. Supermarkets
(Retail Sales $ in Millions)

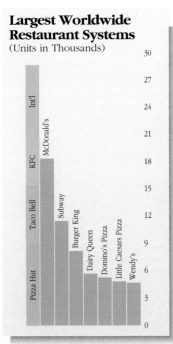

Largest Worldwide Restaurant Systems
(Units in Thousands)

Results of Operations

Consolidated Review

To improve comparability, Management's Analysis identifies the impact, where significant, of beverage and snack food acquisitions, net of operations sold or contributed to joint ventures (collectively, "net acquisitions"). The impact of acquisitions represents the results of the acquired businesses for periods in the current year corresponding to the prior year periods that did not include the results of the businesses. Restaurant units acquired, principally from franchisees, and constructed units are treated the same for purposes of this analysis. These units, net of units closed or sold, principally to franchisees, are collectively referred to as "additional restaurant units."

Net Sales

($ in millions)	1995	1994	1993	% Growth Rates 1995	1994
U.S.	$21,674	$20,246	$18,309	7	11
International.	8,747	8,226	6,712	6	23
	$30,421	$28,472	$25,021	7	14

Worldwide net sales rose $1.9 billion or 7% in 1995. The fifty-third week in 1994 reduced the worldwide, U.S. and international net sales growth by approximately 2 points each. The sales growth benefited from higher effective net pricing, volume gains of $934 million, driven by worldwide snack foods and beverages, and $623 million due to additional restaurant units. The higher effective net pricing reflected increases in international snack foods, driven by Mexico, and U.S. beverages, primarily in response to significantly higher prices for packaging. These benefits were partially offset by the unfavorable currency translation impact of the devaluation of the Mexican peso on international snack foods. Worldwide net sales grew $3.5 billion or 14% in 1994. The fifty-third week favorably affected worldwide, U.S. and international sales growth by about 2 points each. The increase reflected volume gains of $2.2 billion, $934 million due to additional restaurant units and $215 million contributed by net acquisitions.

International net sales grew 6% in 1995 and 23% in 1994 with net acquisitions contributing 1 point in both years. International net sales represented 29%, 29% and 27% of total net sales in 1995, 1994 and 1993, respectively. The unfavorable impact of the devaluation of the Mexican peso beginning in late 1994 through 1995, and its related effects, slowed PepsiCo's trend of an increasing international component of net sales.

Cost of Sales

($ in millions)	1995	1994	1993
Cost of sales.	$14,886	$13,715	$11,946
As a percent of net sales.	48.9%	48.2%	47.7%

The .7 point increase in 1995 was primarily due to worldwide beverages and international snack foods. The increase in worldwide beverages reflected higher packaging prices in the U.S., the effects of which were partially mitigated by increased pricing, and an unfavorable mix shift in international sales from concentrate to packaged products. The international snack foods increase was due to the effect of increased costs, primarily in Mexico, which were partially mitigated by price increases. The .5 point increase in 1994 reflected an unfavorable mix shift in international beverages, from concentrate to packaged products, and in worldwide restaurants, as well as lower net pricing in U.S. beverages. These unfavorable effects were partially offset by a favorable package and product mix shift in international snack foods and manufacturing efficiencies in U.S. snack foods.

Selling, General and Administrative Expensive (S,G&A)

($ in millions)	1995	1994	1993
S,G&A	$11,712	$11,244	$9,864
As a percent of net sales.	38.5%	39.5%	39.4%

S,G&A is comprised of selling and distribution expenses (S&D), advertising and marketing expenses (A&M), and general and administrative expenses (G&A) which include gains on sales of assets as well as other income and expense. S,G&A grew 4% to $11.7 billion in 1995, slower than sales, and 14% to $11.2 billion in 1994, the same rate as sales. In 1995, A&M grew at a substantially slower rate than sales reflecting a slower rate of spending in worldwide beverages and U.S. restaurants. G&A also grew at a substantially slower rate than sales, driven by worldwide beverages and U.S. restaurants. World beverages benefited from international cost containment initiatives, a gain on sale of an international bottling plant, savings in U.S. beverages from a 1994 reorganization as well as benefits of increased pricing in U.S. beverages. U.S. restaurants benefited from a net gain on sales of restaurants in excess of costs of closing other restaurants. S&D grew at a slightly slower rate than sales, in part reflecting the benefits of increased pricing in U.S. beverages and a slower rate of spending in international snack foods.

Amortization of intangible assets increased 1% to $316 million in 1995 and 3% to $312 million in 1994. This noncash expense reduced net income per share by $0.30, $0.29 and $0.28 in 1995, 1994 and 1993, respectively.

Impairment of long-lived assets reflected the initial, noncash charge of $520 million ($384 million after-tax or $0.48 per share) upon adoption of SFAS 121. See Note 2.

Operating Profit

($ in millions)	**1995**	1994	1993	**1995**	1994
				% Growth Rates	
Operating Profit					
Reported	**$2,987**	$3,201	$2,907	**(7)**	10
*Ongoing**	**3,507**	3,201	2,907	**10**	10

*1995 excluded the initial, noncash charge upon adoption of SFAS 121. *See Note 2.*

Reported operating profit declined $214 million or 7% in 1995. Ongoing operating profit increased $306 million or 10% in 1995. The fifty-third week in 1994 reduced the operating profit growth by approximately 2 points. The profit growth was driven by combined segment ongoing operating profit growth of 11%, which benefited from volume growth of $283 million ($430 million excluding the impact of the fifty-third week), driving by U.S. snack foods and worldwide beverages, and $76 million due to additional restaurant units. These advances were partially offset by net unfavorable currency translation impacts, primarily from Mexico. The benefit of higher effective net pricing for all segments combined was almost entirely offset by increased product and operating costs, primarily in Mexico, and higher packaging prices in the U.S. The ongoing operating profit margin increased slightly to 11.5% in 1995. Operating profit increased $294 million or 10% in 1994. The fifty-third week increased the operating profit growth by approximately 2 points. The profit growth was driven by combined segment operating profit growth of 8%, which reflected $850 million from higher volumes ($703 million excluding the impact of the fifty-third week) and $73 million from additional restaurant units, partially offset by higher operating expenses. The profit margin decreased almost one-half point to 11.2% in 1994.

International segment ongoing profit grew 4% in 1995, a slower rate than sales growth, which reflected the adverse effects of the Mexican peso devaluation, particularly in snack foods, partially offset by very strong restaurant performance. International segment ongoing profit represented 18%, 19% and 18% of combined segment ongoing operating profit in 1995, 1994 and 1993, respectively.

Gain on stock offering by an unconsolidated affiliate of $18 million ($17 million after-tax or $0.02 per share) in 1994 related to the public share offering by BAESA, an unconsolidated franchised bottling affiliate in South America. See Note 16.

Interest Expense, net

($ in millions)	**1995**	1994	1993	**1995**	1994
				% Growth Rate	
Interest expense	**$(682)**	$(645)	$(573)	**6**	1:
Interest income	**127**	90	89	**41**	1
Interest expense, net	**$(555)**	$(555)	$(484)	**–**	1:

Interest expense, net in 1995 was even with 1994, reflecting the net impact of higher average interest rates offset by lower average borrowings. The 15% increase in 1994 reflected higher average borrowings, partially offset by higher interest rates on investment balances. Excluding the impact of net acquisitions, interest expense, net decreased 3% in 1995 and increased 10% in 1994.

Provision for Income Taxes

($ in millions)	**1995**	1994	199:
Reported			
Provision for Income Taxes	**$826**	$880	$83:
Effective Tax Rate	**34.0%**	33.0%	34.5%
*Ongoing**			
Provision for Income Taxes	**$962**	$880	$80:
Effective Tax Rate	**32.6%**	33.0%	33.3%

*Excluded the effects of the initial, noncash charge upon adoption of SFAS 121 in 1995 (see Note 2) and the deferred tax charge due to the U.S. tax legislation in 1993 (see Note 11).

The 1995 reported effective tax rate increased 1 point to 34.0%. The 1995 ongoing effective tax rate declined slightly, reflecting a reversal of prior year accruals no longer required and tax refunds, both a result of the current year resolution of certain prior years' audit issues. These benefits were partially offset by a higher foreign effective tax rate, primarily due to a provision in the 1993 U.S. tax legislation that reduced the tax credit associated with beverage concentrate operations in Puerto Rico and became effective for PepsiCo on December 1, 1994 (see Management's Analysis – Significant U.S. Tax Changes Affecting Historical and Future Results on page 15), and a decrease in the proportion of income taxed at lower foreign rates. The 1994 reported effective tax rate declined 1½ points to 33.0%. The slight decline in the ongoing effective tax rate in 1994 reflected a reversal of certain valuation allowances related to deferred tax assets and an increase in the proportion of income taxed at lower foreign rates offset by the absence of a favorable adjustment in 1993 of certain prior years' foreign accruals.

U.S. Soft Drink Industry Volume
% of Total By Distribution Channel

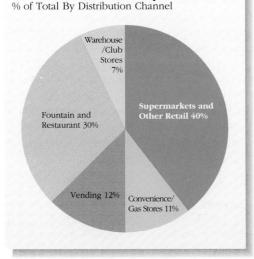

Warehouse/Club Stores 7%
Supermarkets and Other Retail 40%
Fountain and Restaurant 30%
Vending 12%
Convenience/Gas Stores 11%

U.S. Pepsi-Cola Soft Drink Sales to Supermarkets by Package
% of Total From Package

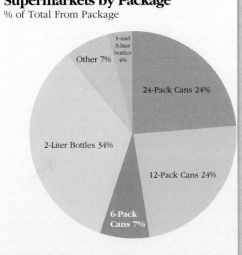

1-and 3-liter bottles 4%
Other 7%
24-Pack Cans 24%
2-Liter Bottles 34%
12-Pack Cans 24%
6-Pack Cans 7%

International Snack Chip Consumption Levels
(Lbs. Per Capita)

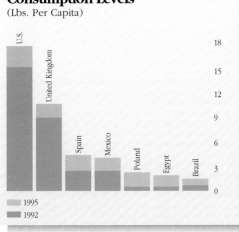

U.S.
United Kingdom
Spain
Mexico
Poland
Egypt
Brazil

1995
1992

Income and Income Per Share Before Cumulative Effect of Accounting Changes

($ in millions except per share amounts)	1995	1994	1993	% Growth Rates 1995	1994
Reported					
Income	$1,606	$1,784	$1,158	(10)	12
Income Per Share	$ 2.00	$ 2.22	$ 1.96	(10)	13
*Ongoing**					
Income	$1,990	$1,767	$1,618	13	9
Income Per Share	$ 2.48	$ 2.20	$ 2.00	13	10

*Excluded the initial, noncash charge upon adoption of SFAS 121 in 1995 (see Note 2), the 1994 BAESA gain (see Note 16) and the deferred tax charge due to the U.S. tax legislation in 1993 (see Note 11).

Growth in ongoing income per share was depressed by estimated dilution from acquisitions of $0.04 or 2 points in 1995 and $0.03 or 2 points in 1994, primarily due to international beverage acquisitions and investments in new unconsolidated affiliates in both years.

Consolidated Cash Flows

Cash flow activity in 1995 reflected strong cash flows from operations of $3.7 billion which were used to fund capital spending of $2.1 billion, dividend payments of $599 million, purchases of treasury stock totaling $541 million and acquisition and investment activity of $466 million.

Net Cash Provided by Operating Activities vs. Capital Spending, Dividends Paid, Acquisitions and Purchases of Treasury Stock
($ in Millions)

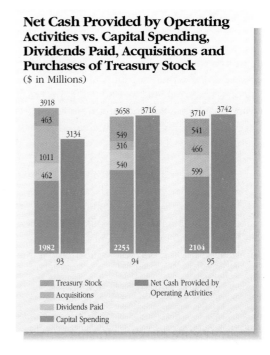

3918
463
1011
462
1982
3134
93

3658
549
316
540
2253
3716
94

3710
541
466
599
2104
3742
95

Treasury Stock
Acquisitions
Dividends Paid
Capital Spending
Net Cash Provided by Operating Activities

One of PepsiCo's most significant financial strengths is its internal cash generation capability. In fact, after capital spending and acquisitions, each of our three industry segments generated positive cash flows in 1995, led by restaurants, which generated nearly $600 million in cash flow compared to marginally positive cash flows in 1994. Net cash flows from PepsiCo's U.S. businesses were partially offset by international uses of cash, reflecting strategies to accelerate growth of international operations.

Cash Flows – Summary of Operating Activities

($ in millions)	1995	1994	1993
Income before cumulative effect of accounting changes	$1,606	$1,784	$1,588
Impairment of long-lived assets. . .	520	–	–
Other noncash charges, net	2,027	1,901	$1,872
Income before noncash charges and credits	4,153	3,685	3,460
Net change in operating working capital.	(411)	31	(326)
Net Cash Provided by Operating Activities	$3,742	$3,716	$3,134

Net cash provided by operating activities in 1995 rose $26 million or 1% over 1994, and in 1994, grew $582 million or 19% over 1993. Income before noncash charges and credits rose 13% in 1995 and 7% in 1994. Increased noncash charges of $646 million in 1995 reflected the $520 million initial, noncash impact of adopting SFAS 121 and increased depreciation and amortization charges of $163 million, partially offset by increased deferred income tax benefits of $44 million, primarily resulting from the adoption of SFAS 121. The $29 million increase in 1994 reflected increased depreciation and amortization charges of $133 million and a decrease of $150 million in the deferred income tax provision, primarily due to the effect in 1994 of converting from premium-based casualty insurance to self-insurance for most of these risks, and adopting SFAS 112 for accounting for postemployment benefits. The working capital net cash outflows of $411 million in 1995 compared to cash inflows of $31 million in 1994 primarily reflected increased growth in accounts and notes receivable, a decrease in income taxes payable in 1995 compared to an increase in 1994 and reduced growth in other current liabilities in 1995 compared to 1994, partially offset by increased growth in accounts payable, led by U.S. beverages, and a reduction in the amounts prefunded in 1995 for employee benefits. The growth in accounts and notes receivable was driven by worldwide beverages, which reflected slower collections and volume growth. The 1994 over 1993 net increase of $357 million reflected normal increases in accrued liabilities across all of our businesses, lapping the effect of higher income tax payments and a lower provision in 1993, and improved trade receivable collections, partially offset by the impact on accounts payable of the timing of a large year-end payment to prefund employee benefits.

Cash Flows – Summary of Investing Activities

($ in millions)	1995	1994	1993
Acquisitions and investments in unconsolidated affiliates	$ (466)	$ (316)	$(1,011)
Capital spending	(2,104)	(2,253)	(1,982)
Sales of restaurants	165	–	7
Net short-term investments	64	421	259
Other investing activities, net. . .	(109)	(213)	(44)
Net Cash Used for Investing Activities	$(2,450)	$(2,361)	$(2,771)

Investing activities over the past three years reflected strategic investments in all three industry segments through capital spending and acquisitions and investments in unconsolidated affiliates. PepsiCo's investments are expected to generate cash returns in excess of its long-term cost of capital, which is estimated to be approximately 10% at year-end 1995. See Note 17 for a discussion of acquisitions and investments in unconsolidated affiliates. About 85% of the total acquisition and investment activity in 1995 represented international transactions compared to 75% in 1994. PepsiCo continues to seek opportunities to strengthen its position in its industry segments, particularly in beverages and snack foods, through strategic acquisitions.

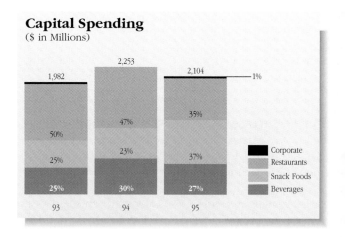

Capital Spending
($ in Millions)

The $149 million decline in capital spending in 1995 reflected substantially reduced spending in restaurants, consistent with our restaurant strategy. Increased U.S. snack food spending, primarily for capacity expansion and new products, was partially offset by a decline in beverages. Increased capital spending of $271 million in 1994 reflected beverage investments in equipment for new packaging and new products in the U.S. and emerging international markets, primarily Eastern Europe. International capital spending represented 29%, 35% and 31% of total segment spending in 1995, 1994 and 1993, respectively. Beverages, snack foods and restaurants represent about 30%, 40% and 30%, respectively, of the $2.5 billion of planned spending in 1996. This reflects the continued shift from restaurants to snack foods. Snack food and beverage 1996 capital spending reflects production capacity expansion for both established and new products, and equipment replacements. Although restaurant spending in 1996 is expected to be about equal to 1995's level, we expect more of the spending in 1996 to be used for refurbishing our existing restaurants and less spent on new store development. Approximately 25% of the planned 1996 capital spending relates to international businesses.

Consistent with management's strategy to improve restaurant returns (see Management's Analysis – Restaurants), proceeds from sales of restaurants in 1995 were $165 million. Although difficult to forecast, management anticipates continued cash flow from this kind of activity over the next few years.

As discussed in Financial Leverage, PepsiCo manages the investment activity in its short-term portfolios, primarily held outside the U.S., as part of its overall financing strategy.

Cash Flows – Summary of Financing Activities

($ in millions)	1995	1994	1993
Net short and long-term debt...	$ (303)	$ (205)	$ 590
Cash dividends paid..........	(599)	(540)	(462)
Purchases of treasury stock....	(541)	(549)	(463)
Proceeds from exercises of stock options.............	252	97	69
Other, net..................	(42)	(43)	(37)
Net Cash Used for Financing Activities	$(1,233)	$(1,240)	$(303)

The net cash flow used for financing activities in 1995 was about even with 1994. In 1995, increased proceeds from exercises of stock options of $155 million were offset by increased net repayments of short and long-term debt of $98 million and higher cash dividends paid of $59 million. The 1994 over 1993 change in cash flows from financing activities was a use of $937 million, primarily reflecting net repayment of short and long-term debt of $205 million compared to net proceeds of $590 million in 1993.

Cash dividends declared were $615 million in 1995 and $555 million in 1994. PepsiCo targets a dividend payout of about one-third of the prior year's income from ongoing operations, thus retaining sufficient earnings to provide financial resources for growth opportunities.

Share repurchase decisions are evaluated considering management's target capital structure and other investment opportunities. PepsiCo expects to repurchase at least 1% to 2% of its outstanding shares each year for the next several years. During 1995, PepsiCo repurchased 1.6% of its shares outstanding at the beginning of 1995, or 12.3 million shares, at a cost of $541 million. Subsequent to year-end, PepsiCo repurchased 1.7 million shares through February 6, 1996 at a cost of $99 million. During 1994, PepsiCo repurchased 1.9% of the shares outstanding at the beginning of 1994, or 15.0 million shares, at a cost of $549 million. Through February 6, 1996, 29.4 million shares have been repurchased under the 50 million share repurchase authority granted by PepsiCo's Board of Directors in July 1993. In February 1996, PepsiCo's Board of Directors replaced the 1993 share repurchase authority with a new authority for 50 million shares.

Consolidated Financial Condition

Assets increased $640 million or 3% to $25.4 billion. The increase reflected the normal growth of the businesses, partially offset by the impact of the initial charge of $520 million upon adoption of SFAS 121 (see Note 2) primarily affecting property, plant and equipment, intangible assets and, to a much lesser extent, investment in unconsolidated affiliates and other noncurrent assets. Increased accounts and notes receivable reflected slower collections and volume advances in worldwide beverages and snack foods. Short-term investments largely represent high-grade marketable securities portfolios held outside the U.S. Our portfolio in Puerto Rico, which totaled $816 million at year-end 1995 and $853 million at year-end 1994, arises from the operating cash flows of a centralized concentrate manufacturing facility that operates under a tax incentive grant. The grant provides that the portfolio funds may be remitted to the U.S. without any additional tax. PepsiCo remitted $792 million of the portfolio to the U.S. in 1995 and

$380 million in 1994. PepsiCo continually reassesses its alternatives to redeploy its maturing investments in this and other portfolios held outside the U.S., considering other investment opportunities and risks, tax consequences and overall financing strategies.

Liabilities rose $183 million or 1% to $18.1 billion. The $643 million increase in other long-term liabilities was partially offset by a $304 million reduction in debt. The increase in other long-term liabilities primarily reflected normal growth and a reclassification of amounts to current liabilities.

At year-end 1995 and 1994, $3.5 billion and $4.5 billion, respectively, of short-term borrowings were classified as long-term, reflecting PepsiCo's intent and ability, through the existence of its unused revolving credit facilities, to refinance these borrowings. PepsiCo's unused credit facilities with lending institutions, which exist largely to support the issuances of short-term borrowings, were $3.5 billion at year-end 1995 and 1994. Effective January 3, 1995, PepsiCo replaced its existing credit facilities with revolving credit facilities aggregating $4.5 billion, of which $1.0 billion was to expire in 1996 and $3.5 billion was to expire in 2000. Effective December 8, 1995, PepsiCo terminated the $1.0 billion due to expire in 1996 based upon a current assessment of the amount of credit facilities required compared to its related cost. The expiration of the remaining credit facilities of $3.5 billion was extended to 2001. Annually, these facilities can be extended an additional year upon the mutual consent of PepsiCo and the lending institutions.

Financial Leverage is measured by PepsiCo on both a market value and historical cost basis. PepsiCo believes that the most meaningful measure of debt is on a net basis, which takes into account its large investment portfolios held outside the U.S. These portfolios are managed as part of PepsiCo's overall financing strategy and are not required to support day-to-day operations. Net debt reflects the pro forma remittance of the portfolios (net of related taxes) as a reduction to total debt. Total debt includes the present value of operating lease commitments.

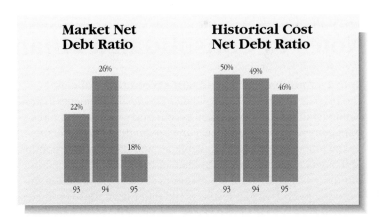

PepsiCo believes that market leverage (defined as net debt as a percent of net debt plus the market value of equity, based on the year-end stock price) is an appropriate measure of PepsiCo's long-term financial leverage. Unlike historical cost measures, the market value of equity primarily reflects the estimated net present value of expected future cash flows that will both support debt and provide returns to shareholders. PepsiCo has established a long-term target range of 20%-25% for its market net debt ratio to optimize its cost of capital.

The market net debt ratio declined 8 points to 18% at year-end 1995 due primarily to a 54% increase in PepsiCo's stock price. The 4 point increase to 26% at year-end 1994 was due to a 13% decline in PepsiCo's stock price as well as an 8% increase in net debt.

As measured on an historical cost basis, the ratio of net debt to net capital employed (defined as net debt, other liabilities, deferred income taxes and shareholders' equity) declined 3 points to 46%, reflecting a 2% decline in net debt and a 4% increase in net capital employed. The 1 point decline to 49% at year-end 1994 was due to a 9% increase in net capital employed, partially offset by the increase in net debt.

Because of PepsiCo's strong cash generating capability and its strong financial condition, PepsiCo has continued access to capital markets throughout the world.

At year-end 1995, about 62% of PepsiCo's net debt portfolio, including the effects of interest rate and currency swaps (see Note 8), was exposed to variable interest rates, compared to about 60% in 1994. In addition to variable rate long-term debt, all net debt with maturities of less than one year is categorized as variable. PepsiCo prefers funding its operations with variable rate debt because it believes that, over the long-term, variable rate debt provides more cost effective financing than fixed rate debt. PepsiCo will issue fixed rate debt if advantageous market opportunities arise. A 1 point change in interest rates on variable rate net debt would impact annual interest expense, net of interest income, by approximately $36 million ($19 million after-tax or $0.02 per share) assuming the level and mix of the December 30, 1995 net debt portfolio were maintained.

PepsiCo's negative operating working capital position, which principally reflects the cash sales nature of its restaurant operations, effectively provides additional capital for investment. Operating working capital, which excludes short-term investments and short-term borrowings, was a negative $94 million and $677 million at year-end 1995 and 1994, respectively. The $583 million decline in negative working capital primarily reflected the reclassification of amounts from long-term to current liabilities, base business growth in the more working capital intensive bottling and snack food operations exceeding the growth in restaurant operations and an increase in prepaid taxes.

Shareholders' Equity increased $457 million or 7% to $7.3 billion. This change reflected a 13% increase in retained earnings due to $1.6 billion in net income less dividends declared of $615 million. This growth was reduced by a $337 million unfavorable change in the currency translation adjustment account (CTA) and a $322 million increase in treasury stock, reflecting repurchases of 12 million shares offset by 10 million shares used for stock option exercises. The CTA change primarily reflected the effects of the Mexican peso devaluation.

Return on Average Shareholders' Equity

Based on income before cumulative effect of accounting changes, PepsiCo's return on average shareholders' equity was 23% and 27% in 1995 and 1994, respectively. Excluding the initial charge upon adoption of SFAS 121 in 1995 (see Note 2) and the 1994 BAESA gain (see Note 16), the return on average shareholders' equity was 27% in 1995 and 1994.

Notes to Consolidated Financial Statements

(tabular dollars in millions except per share amounts)

Note 1 – Summary of Significant Accounting Policies

The preparation of the Consolidated Financial Statements in conformity with generally accepted accounting principles requires management to make estimates and assumptions that affect reported amounts of assets and liabilities and disclosure of contingent assets and liabilities at the date of the financial statements and the reported amounts of revenues and expenses during the reporting period. Actual results could differ from those estimates.

To facilitate the closing process, certain of PepsiCo's international operations close their fiscal year up to one month earlier than PepsiCo's fiscal year.

Certain reclassifications were made to prior year amounts to conform with the 1995 presentation.

Accounting Changes. As discussed below and in Note 2, in 1995 PepsiCo early adopted Statement of Financial Accounting Standards No. 121 (SFAS 121), "Accounting for the Impairment of Long-Lived Assets and for Long-Lived Assets to Be Disposed Of." In 1994, PepsiCo adopted Statement of Financial Accounting Standards No. 112, "Accounting for Postemployment Benefits," (see

Note 14) and a preferred method of calculating the market-related value of plan assets used in determining pension expense (see Note 13).

Statement of Financial Accounting Standards No. 123 (SFAS 123), "Accounting for Stock-Based Compensation," permits stock compensation cost to be measured using either the intrinsic value-based method or the fair value-based method. When adopted in 1996, PepsiCo intends to continue to use the intrinsic value-based method and will provide the expanded disclosures required by SFAS 123.

Principles of Consolidation. The financial statements reflect the consolidated accounts of PepsiCo, Inc. and its controlled affiliates. Intercompany accounts and transactions have been eliminated. Investments in unconsolidated affiliates in which PepsiCo exercises significant influence but not control are accounted for by the equity method and PepsiCo's share of the net income or loss of its affiliates is included in selling, general and administrative expenses.

Fiscal Year. PepsiCo's fiscal year ends on the last Saturday in December and, as a result, a fifty-third week is added every five or six years. The fiscal year ending December 31, 1994 consisted of 53 weeks.

Marketing Costs. Marketing costs are reported in selling, general and administrative expenses and include costs of advertising, marketing and promotional programs. Promotional discounts are expensed as incurred and other marketing costs not deferred at year-end are charged to expense ratably in relation to sales over the year in which incurred. Marketing costs deferred at year-end, which are classified in prepaid expenses in the Consolidated Balance Sheet, consist of media and personal service advertising prepayments, promotional materials in inventory and production costs of future media advertising; these assets are expensed in the year first used.

Promotional discounts to retailers in the beverage segment are classified as a reduction of sales; in the snack food segment, such discounts are generally classified as marketing costs. The difference in classification reflects our view that promotional discounts are so pervasive in the beverage industry, compared to the snack food industry, that they are effectively price discounts and should be classified accordingly. A current survey of the accounting practice of others in the beverage and snack food industries confirmed that our beverage classification is consistent with others in that industry while practice in the snack food industry is mixed.

Advertising expense was $1.8 billion, $1.7 billion and $1.6 billion in 1995, 1994 and 1993, respectively. Prepaid advertising as of year-end 1995 and 1994 was $78 million and $70 million, respectively.

Research and Development Expenses. Research and development expenses, which are expensed as incurred, were $96 million, $152 million and $113 million in 1995, 1994 and 1993, respectively.

Stock-Based Compensation. PepsiCo uses the intrinsic value-based method for measuring stock-based compensation cost which measures compensation cost as the excess, if any, of the quoted market price of PepsiCo's capital stock at the grant date over the amount the employee must pay for the stock. PepsiCo's policy is to grant stock options at fair market value at the date of grant.

Net Income Per Share. Net income per share is computed by dividing net income by the weighted average number of shares and dilutive share equivalents (primarily stock options) outstanding during each year ("average shares outstanding").

Derivative Instruments. PepsiCo's policy prohibits the use of derivative instruments for trading purposes and PepsiCo has procedures in place to monitor and control their use.

PepsiCo enters into interest rate and currency swaps with the objective of reducing borrowing costs. Interest rate and currency swaps are used to effectively change the interest rate and currency of specific debt issuances. In general, the terms of these swaps match the terms of the related debt and the swaps are entered into concurrently with the issuance of the debt they are intended to modify. The interest differential to be paid or received on an interest rate swap is recognized as an adjustment to interest expense as the differential occurs. The interest differential not yet settled in cash is reflected in the Consolidated Balance Sheet as a receivable or payable under the appropriate current asset or lia-

bility caption. If an interest rate swap position was to be terminated, the gain or loss realized upon termination would be deferred and amortized to interest expense over the remaining term of the underlying debt instrument it was intended to modify or would be recognized immediately if the underlying debt instrument was settled prior to maturity. The differential to be paid or received on a currency swap is charged or credited to income as the differential occurs. This is fully offset by the corresponding gain or loss recognized in income on the currency translation of the related non-U.S. dollar denominated debt, as both amounts are based upon the same exchange rates. The currency differential not yet settled in cash is reflected in the Consolidated Balance Sheet under the appropriate current or noncurrent receivable or payable caption. If a currency swap position was to be terminated prior to maturity, the gain or loss realized upon termination would be immediately recognized in income.

A seven-year put option, issued in connection with the formation of a joint venture with the principal shareholder of GEMEX, an unconsolidated franchised bottling affiliate in Mexico (see Note 17), is marked-to-market with gains or losses recognized currently as an adjustment to PepsiCo's share of the net income of unconsolidated affiliates. The offsetting amount adjusts the carrying amount of the put obligation, classified in other liabilities in the Consolidated Balance Sheet.

Gains and losses on futures contracts designated as hedges of future commodity purchases are deferred and included in the cost of the related raw materials when purchased. Changes in the value of futures contracts that PepsiCo uses to hedge commodity purchases are highly correlated to the changes in the value of the purchased commodity. If the degree of correlation between the futures contracts and the purchase contracts were to diminish such that the two were no longer considered highly correlated, subsequent changes in the value of the futures contracts would be recognized in income.

Cash Equivalents. Cash equivalents represent funds temporarily invested (with original maturities not exceeding three months) as part of PepsiCo's management of day-to-day operating cash receipts and disbursements. All other investment portfolios, largely held outside the U.S., are primarily classified as short-term investments.

Inventories. Inventories are valued at the lower of cost (computed on the average, first-in, first-out or last-in, first-out [LIFO] method) or net realizable value.

Property, Plant and Equipment. Property, plant and equipment (PP&E) are stated at cost, except for PP&E that have been impaired, for which the carrying amount is reduced to estimated fair value. Depreciation is calculated principally on a straight-line basis over the estimated useful lives of the assets.

Intangible Assets. Intangible assets are amortized on a straight-line basis over appropriate periods, generally ranging from 20 to 40 years.

Recoverability of Long-Lived Assets to be Held and Used in the Business. As noted above, PepsiCo early adopted SFAS 121 in 1995 for purposes of determining and measuring impairment of certain long-lived assets to be held and used in the business. See Note 2.

PepsiCo reviews most long-lived assets, certain identifiable intangibles and goodwill related to those assets to be held and used in the business for impairment whenever events or changes in circumstances indicate that the carrying amount of an asset or a group of assets may not be recoverable. PepsiCo considers a history of operating losses to be its primary indicator of potential impairment. Assets are grouped and evaluated for impairment at the lowest level for which there are identifiable cash flows that are largely independent of the cash flows of other groups of assets ("Assets"). PepsiCo has identified the appropriate grouping of Assets to be individual restaurants for the restaurant segment and, for each of the snack food and beverage segments, Assets are generally grouped at the country level. PepsiCo deems an Asset to be impaired if a forecast of undiscounted future operating cash flows directly related to the Asset, including disposal value if any, is less than its carrying amount. If an Asset is determined to be impaired, the loss is measured as the amount by which the carrying amount of the Asset exceeds its fair value. Fair value is based on quoted market prices in active markets, if available. If quoted market prices are not available, an estimate of fair value is based on the best information available, including prices for similar assets or the results of valuation techniques such as discounting estimated future cash flows as if the decision to continue to use the impaired Asset was a new investment decision. PepsiCo generally measures fair value by discounting estimated future cash flows. Considerable management judgment is necessary to estimate discounted future cash flows. Accordingly, actual results could vary significantly from such estimates.

Recoverability of other long-lived assets, primarily investments in unconsolidated affiliates and identifiable intangibles and goodwill not identified with impaired Assets covered by the above paragraph, will continue to be evaluated on a recurring basis. The primary indicators of recoverability are current or forecasted profitability over the estimated remaining life of these assets, based on the operating profit of the business directly related to these assets. If recoverability is unlikely based on the evaluation, the carrying amount is reduced by the amount it exceeds the forcasted operating profit and any estimated disposal value.

Note 2 – Impairment of Long-Lived Assets
PepsiCo early adopted Statement of Financial Accounting Standards No. 121 (SFAS 121), "Accounting for the Impairment of Long-Lived Assets and for Long-Lived Assets to Be Disposed Of," as of the beginning of the fourth quarter of 1995. This date was chosen to allow adequate time to collect and analyze data related to the long-lived assets of each of our worldwide operations for purposes of identifying, measuring and reporting any impairment in 1995.

The initial, noncash charge upon adoption of SFAS 121 was $520 million ($384 million after-tax or $0.48 per share), which included $68 million ($49 million after-tax or $0.06 per share) related to restaurants for which closure decisions were made during the fourth quarter. This initial charge resulted from PespiCo grouping assets at a lower level than under its previous accounting policy for evaluating and measuring impairment. Under PepsiCo's previous accounting policy, each of PepsiCo's operating divisions' ("Division") long-lived assets to be held and used by the Division, other than intangible assets, were evaluated as a group for impairment if the Division was incurring operating losses or was expected to incur operating losses in the future. Be-

cause of the strong operating profit history and prospects of each Division, no impairment evaluation had been required for 1994 o 1993 under PepsiCo's previous accounting policy. The initial charge represented a reduction of the carrying amounts of the im paired Assets (as defined in Note 1) to their estimated fair value, as determined by using discounted estimated future cash flows. Considerable management judgment is necessary to estimate discounted future cash flows. Accordingly, actual results could vary significantly from such estimates. This charge affected worldwide restaurants, international beverages and, to a much lesser extent, international snack foods and certain unconsolidated affiliates. See Note 19.

As a result of the reduced carrying amount of the impaired Assets, depreciation and amortization expense for the fourth quarter of 1995 was reduced by $21 million ($15 million after-tax or $0.02 per share) and full-year 1996 depreciation and amortization expense is expected to be reduced by approximately $58 million ($39 million after-tax or $0.05 per share). See Management's Analysis – Restaurants for a discussion of other possible future effects related to this change in accounting.

SFAS 121 also requires, among other provisions, that long-lived assets and certain identifiable intangibles to be disposed of that are not covered by APB Opinion No. 30, "Reporting the Results o Operations – Reporting the Effects of Disposal of a Segment of a Business, and Extraordinary, Unusual and Infrequently Occurring Events and Transactions," be reported at the lower of the asset's carrying amount or its fair value less cost to sell. Under PepsiCo's previous accounting policy, PepsiCo reported an asset to be disposed of at the lower of its carrying amount or its estimated net realizable value. There were no material adjustments to the carrying amounts of assets to be disposed of in 1995, 1994 or 1993 under PepsiCo's previous accounting policy. The impact of adopting SFAS 121 on assets held for disposal during 1995 was immaterial.

Note 3 – Items Affecting Comparability
The effect on comparability of 1995 net gains from sales of restaurants to franchisees in excess of the cost of closing other restaurants is provided under Net Refranchising Gains in Note 19.

The fifty-third week in 1994, as described under Fiscal Year in Note 1, increased 1994 net sales by an estimated $434 million and earnings by approximately $54 million ($35 million after-tax or $0.04 per share). See fiscal year in Note 19 for the estimated impact of the fifty-third week on comparability of segment net sales and operating profit.

The effects of unusual items on comparability of operating profit, primarily restructuring charges and accounting changes, are provided under Unusual Items and Accounting Changes, respectively, in Note 19.

Information regarding the 1994 gain from a public share offering by BAESA, an unconsolidated franchised bottling affiliate in South America, and a 1993 charge to increase net deferred tax liabilities as of the beginning of 1993 for a 1% statutory income tax rate increase due to 1993 U.S. Federal tax legislation is provided in Notes 16 and 11, respectively.

Note 4 – Inventories

	1995	1994
Raw materials and supplies	$ 550	$455
Finished goods	501	515
	$1,051	$970

The cost of 32% of 1995 inventories and 38% of 1994 inventories was computed using the LIFO method. The carrying amount of total LIFO inventories was lower than the approximate current cost of those inventories by $11 million at year-end 1995, but higher by $6 million at year-end 1994.

Note 5 – Property, Plant and Equipment, net

	1995	1994
Land	$ 1,327	$ 1,322
Buildings and improvements	5,668	5,664
Capital leases, primarily buildings.	531	451
Machinery and equipment	8,598	8,208
Construction in progress	627	485
	16,751	16,130
Accumulated depreciation	(6,881)	(6,247)
	$ 9,870	$ 9,883

Depreciation expense in 1995, 1994 and 1993 was $1.3 billion, $1.2 billion and $1.1 billion, respectively. The adoption of SFAS 121 reduced the carrying amount of property, plant and equipment, net by $399 million. See Note 2.

Note 6 – Intangible Assets, net

	1995	1994
Reacquired franchise rights	$3,826	$3,974
Trademarks	711	768
Other identifiable intangibles	286	250
Goodwill.	2,761	2,850
	$7,584	$7,842

Identifiable intangible assets primarily arose from the allocation of purchase prices of businesses acquired and consist principally of reacquired franchise rights and trademarks. Reacquired franchise rights relate to acquisitions of franchised bottling and restaurant operations and trademarks principally relate to acquisitions of international snack food and beverage businesses. Amounts assigned to such identifiable intangibles were based on independent appraisals or internal estimates. Goodwill represents the residual purchase price after allocation to all identifiable net assets.

Accumulated amortization, included in the amounts above, was $1.8 billion and $1.6 billion at year-end 1995 and 1994, respectively. The adoption of SFAS 121 reduced the carrying amount of intangible assets, net by $86 million. See Note 2.

Note 7 – Derivative Financial Instruments

PepsiCo's policy prohibits the use of derivative instruments for trading purposes and PepsiCo has procedures in place to monitor and control their use.

PepsiCo's use of derivative instruments is primarily limited to interest rate and currency swaps, which are entered into with the objective of reducing borrowing costs. PepsiCo enters into interest rate and foreign currency swaps to effectively change the interest rate and currency of specific debt issuances. These swaps are generally entered into concurrently with the issuance of the debt they are intended to modify. The notional amount, interest payment dates and maturity dates of the swaps match the principal, interest payment dates and maturity dates of the related debt. Accordingly, any market impact (risk or opportunity) associated with these swaps is fully offset by the opposite market impact on the related debt. PepsiCo's credit risk related to interest rate and currency swaps is considered low because they are only entered into with strong creditworthy counterparties, are generally settled on a net basis and are of relatively short duration. See Note 8 for the notional amounts, related interest rates and maturities of the interest rate and currency swaps along with the original terms of the related debt and Note 9 for the fair value of these instruments.

In 1995, PepsiCo issued a seven-year put option in connection with the formation of a joint venture with the principal shareholder of GEMEX, an unconsolidated franchised bottling affiliate in Mexico. The put option allows the principal shareholder to sell up to 150 million GEMEX shares to PepsiCo at 66 ⅔¢ per share. PepsiCo accounts for this put option by marking it to market with gains or losses recognized currently. The put option liability, which was valued to $26 million at the date of the original transaction, increased to $30 million by year-end, resulting in a $4 million charge to earnings.

Note 8 – Short-term Borrowings and Long-term Debt

	1995	1994
Short-term Borrowings		
Commercial paper (5.7% and 5.4%) **(A)**	$ 2,006	$ 2,254
Current maturities of long-term dept issuances **(A) (B)**	1,405	988
Notes (6.9% and 5.4%) **(A)**	252	1,492
Other borrowings (7.9% and 6.5%) **(C)**	543	444
Amount reclassified to long-term debt **(D)**	(3,500)	(4,500)
	$ 706	$ 678
Long-term Debt		
Short-term borrowings, reclassified **(D)**	$ 3,500	$ 4,500
Notes due 1996 through 2010 (6.3% and 6.6%) **(A)**	3,886	3,725
Euro notes due 1997 through 1998 (7.5% and 8.0%) **(A)**	550	250
Zero coupon notes, $780 million due 1996 through 2012 (14.4% annual yield to maturity) **(A)**	234	219
Swiss franc perpetual Foreign Interest Payment bonds **(E)**	214	213
Australian dollar 6.3% bonds due 1997 through 1998 with interest payable in Japanese yen **(A) (C)**	212	–
Japanese yen 3.3% bonds due 1997 **(C)**	194	201
Zero coupon notes, $200 million due 1999 (6.4% annual yield to maturity) **(A)**	161	–
Swiss franc 5.0% notes due 1999 **(A) (C)**	108	–
Italian lira 11.4% notes due 1998 **(A) (C)**	95	–
Luxembourg franc 6.6% notes due 1998 **(A) (C)**	68	–
Swiss franc 5¼% bearer bonds due 1995 **(C)**	–	100
Capital lease obligations (See Note 10)	294	298
Other, due 1996-2020 (6.8% and 8.1%)	398	323
	9,914	9,829
Less current maturities of long-term debt issuances **(B)**	(1,405)	(988)
	$ 8,509	$ 8,841

The interest rates in the above table indicate, where applicable, the weighted average of the stated rates at year-end 1995 and 1994, respectively, prior to the effects of any interest rate swaps. See **(A)** below for PepsiCo's weighted average interest rates after giving effect to the impact of the interest rate swaps.

The carrying amount of long-term debt includes any related discount or premium and unamortized debt issuance costs. The debt agreements include various restrictions, none of which are currently significant to PepsiCo.

The annual maturities of long-term debt through 2000, excluding capital lease obligations and the reclassified short-term borrowings, are: 1996-$1.4 billion, 1997-$1.5 billion, 1998-1.5 billion, 1999-$572 million and 2000-$651 million.

See Note 7 for a discussion of PepsiCo's use of interest rate and currency swaps and its management of the inherent credit risk and Note 9 for fair value information related to debt and interest rate and currency swaps.

(A) The following table indicates the notional amount and weighted average interest rates, by category, of interest rate swaps outstanding at year-end 1995 and 1994, respectively. The weighted average variable interest rates that PepsiCo pays, which are primarily indexed to either commercial paper or LIBOR rates, are based on rates as of the respective balance sheet date and are subject to change. Terms of interest rate swaps generally match the terms of the debt they modify and the swaps terminated in 1996 through 2010.

	1995	1994
Receive fixed-pay variable		
Notional amount	$2,657	$1,557
Weighted average receive rate . .	6.8%	5.9%
Weighted average pay rate	5.7%	6.1%
Receive variable-pay variable		
Notional amount	$ 577	$1,009
Weighted average receive rate . .	5.7%	4.9%
Weighted average pay rate	5.8%	6.0%
Receive variable-pay fixed		
Notional amount	$ 215	$ 215
Weighted average receive rate . .	5.8%	6.6%
Weighted average pay rate	8.2%	8.2%

The following table identifies the composition of total debt (excluding capital lease obligations and before the reclassification of amounts from short-term borrowings) after giving effect to the impact of interest rate swaps. All short-term borrowings are considered variable interest rate debt for purposes of this table.

	1995		1994	
	Carrying Amount	Weighted Average Interest Rate	Carrying Amount	Weighted Average Interest Rate
Variable interest rate debt				
Short-term borrowings	$4,177	6.4%	$5,149	6.2%
Long-term debt	2,103	5.8%	937	6.1%
	6,280	6.2%	6,086	6.2%
Fixed interest rate debt	2,641	7.4%	3,135	7.4%
	$8,921	6.6%	$9,221	6.6%

(B) Included certain long-term notes aggregating $248 million which are reasonably expected to be called, without penalty, by PepsiCo in 1996. The expectation is based upon the belief of PepsiCo management that, based upon projected yield curves, our counterparties to interest rate swaps, which were entered into to modify these notes, will exercise their option to early terminate the swaps without penalty. Also included the $214 million carrying amount of the Swiss franc perpetual Foreign Interest Payment bonds (See **(E)** below).

(C) PepsiCo has entered into currency swaps to hedge its foreign currency exposure on non-U.S. dollar denominated debt. At year-end 1995, the aggregate carrying amount of the debt was $696 million and the receivables and payables under related currency swaps were $5 million and $12 million, respectively, resulting in a net effective U.S. dollar liability of $703 million with a weighted average interest rate of 5.8%, including the effects of related interest rate swaps. At year-end 1994, the carrying amount of this debt aggregated $301 million and the receivables and payables under related currency swaps aggregated $50 million and $2 million, respectively, resulting in a net effective U.S. dollar liability of $253 million with a weighted average interest rate of 7.9%, including the effects of related interest rate swaps.

(D) At year-end 1995 and 1994, PepsiCo had unused revolving credit facilities covering potential borrowings aggregating $3.5 billion. Effective January 3, 1995, PepsiCo replaced its existing credit facilities with new revolving credit facilities aggregating $4.5 billion, of which $1.0 billion was to expire in 1996 and $3.5 billion was to expire in 2000. Effective December 8, 1995, PepsiCo terminated the $1.0 billion due to expire in 1996 based upon a current assessment of the amount of credit facilities required compared to its related cost. The expiration of the remaining credit facilities of $3.5 billion was extended to 2001. At year-end 1995 and 1994, $3.5 billion and $4.5 billion, respectively, of short-term borrowings were classified as long-term debt, reflecting PepsiCo's intent and ability, through the existence of the unused credit facilities, to refinance these borrowings. These credit facilities exist largely to support the issuances of short-term borrowings and are available for acquisitions and other general corporate purposes.

(E) The coupon rate of the Swiss franc 400 million perpetual Foreign Interest Payment bonds issued in 1986 is 7 ½% through 1996. The bonds have no stated maturity date. At the end of each 10-year period after the issuance of the bonds, PepsiCo and the bondholders each have the right to cause redemption of the bonds. If not redeemed, the coupon rate will be adjusted based on the prevailing yield of 10-year U.S. Treasury Securities. The principal of the bonds is denominated in Swiss francs. PepsiCo can, and intends to, limit the ultimate redemption amount to the U.S. dollar proceeds at issuance which is the basis of the carrying amount. Interest payments are made in U.S. dollars and are calculated by applying the coupon rate to the original U.S. dollar principal proceeds of $214 million. Although PepsiCo does not currently intend to cause redemption of this dept, this debt has been included in current maturities of long-term debt (see **(B)** above) at year-end 1995 because the bondholders may exercise their right to cause PepsiCo to redeem the debt in 1996 on its 10-year anniversary date. Since the redemption feature is only available on each 10-year anniversary date, the bonds will be reclassified to long-term if redemption does not occur in 1996.

Note 9 – Fair Value of Financial Instruments

	1995		1994	
	Carrying Amount	Fair Value	Carrying Amount	Fair Value
Assets				
Cash and cash equivalents . .	$ 382	$ 382	$ 331	$ 331
Short-term investments	$1,116	$1,116	$1,157	$1,157
Other assets (noncurrent investments)	$ 23	$ 23	$ 48	$ 48
Liabilities				
Debt				
Short-term borrowings and long-term debt, net of capital leases	$8,921	$9,217	$9,221	$9,266
Debt-related derivative instruments				
Open contracts in asset position	(25)	(96)	(52)	(52)
Open contracts in liability position	13	26	8	54
Net debt	$8,909	$9,147	$9,177	$9,268
Other liabilities (GEMEX put option)	$ 30	$ 30	–	–
Guarantees	–	$ 4	–	$ 3

The carrying amounts in the above table are included in the Consolidated Balance Sheet under the indicated captions, except for debt-related derivative instruments (interest rate and currency swaps), which are included in the appropriate current or noncurrent asset or liability caption. Short-term investments consist primarily of debt securities and have been classified as held-to-maturity. Noncurrent investments mature at various dates through 2000.

Because of the short maturity of cash equivalents and short-term investments, the carrying amount approximates fair value. The fair value of noncurrent investments is based upon market quotes. The fair value of debt, debt-related derivative instruments and guarantees is estimated using market quotes, valuation models and calculations based on market rates. The fair value of the GEMEX put option is based upon a valuation model.

See Note 7 for more information regarding PepsiCo's use of derivative instruments and its management of the inherent credit risk related to those instruments.

Note 10 – Leases

PepsiCo has noncancelable commitments under both capital and long-term operating leases, primarily for restaurant units. In addition, PepsiCo is lessee under noncancelable leases covering vehicles, equipment and nonrestaurant real estate. Capital and operating lease commitments expire at various dates through 2088 and, in many cases, provide for rent escalations and renewal options. Most leases require payment of related executory costs, which include property taxes, maintenance and insurance. Sublease income and sublease receivables are insignificant.

Future minimum commitments under noncancelable leases are set forth below:

	Capital	Operating
1996	$ 57	$ 350
1997	49	297
1998	68	269
1999	37	240
2000	38	218
Later years	299	1,170
	$548	$2,544

At year-end 1995, the present value of minimum payments under capital leases was $294 million, after deducting $1 million for estimated executory costs and $253 million representing imputed interest.

The details of rental expense are set forth below:

	1995	1994	1993
Minimum	$439	$433	$392
Contingent	40	32	28
	$479	$465	$420

Contingent rentals are based on sales by restaurants in excess of levels stipulated in the lease agreements.

Note 11 – Income Taxes

The details of the provision for income taxes on income before cumulative effect of accounting changes are set forth below:

		1995	1994	1993
Current:	Federal	$ 706	$642	$467
	Foreign	154	174	196
	State	77	131	89
		937	947	752
Deferred:	Federal	(92)	(64)	78
	Foreign	(18)	(2)	(13)
	State	(1)	(1)	18
		(111)	(67)	83
		$ 826	$880	$835

In 1993, a charge of $30 million ($0.04 per share) was recorded to increase net deferred tax liabilities as of the beginning of 1993 for a 1% statutory income tax rate increase under 1993 U.S. Federal tax legislation.

U.S. and foreign income before income taxes and cumulative effect of accounting changes are set forth below:

	1995	1994	1993
U.S.	$1,792	$1,762	$1,633
Foreign	640	902	790
	$2,432	$2,664	$2,423

PepsiCo operates centralized concentrate manufacturing facilities in Puerto Rico and Ireland under long-term tax incentives. The U.S. amount in the above table included approximately 70% in 1995 and 50% in 1994 and 1993 (consistent with the income subject to U.S. tax) of the income from sales of concentrate manufactured in Puerto Rico. The increase in 1995 reflected the effects of the 1993 Federal income tax legislation, which limited the U.S. Federal tax credit on income earned in Puerto Rico. See Management's Analysis – significant U.S. Tax Changes Affecting Historical and Future Results on page 15 for a discussion of the reduction of the U.S. Federal tax credit associated with beverage concentrate operations in Puerto Rico.

A reconciliation of the U.S. Federal statutory tax rate to PepsiCo's effective tax rate is set forth below:

	1995	1994	1993
U.S. Federal statutory tax rate	35.0%	35.0%	35.0%
State income tax, net of Federal tax benefit	2.0	3.2	2.9
Effect of lower taxes on foreign income (including Puerto Rico and Ireland)	(3.0)	(5.4)	(3.3)
Adjustment to the beginning-of-the-year deferred tax assets valuation allowance	–	(1.3)	
Reduction of prior years' foreign accruals	–	–	(2.0)
Settlement of prior years' audit issues	(4.1)	–	–
Effect of 1993 tax legislation on deferred income taxes	–	–	1.1
Effect of adopting SFAS 121	1.4	–	–
Nondeductible amortization of U.S. goodwill	1.0	0.8	0.8
Other, net	1.7	0.7	–
Effective tax rate	34.0%	33.0%	34.5%

The details of 1995 and deferred tax liabilities (assets) are set forth below:

	1995	1994
Intangible assets other than nondeductible goodwill	$1,631	$1,628
Property, plant and equipment	496	506
Safe harbor leases	165	171
Zero coupon notes	100	111
Other	257	337
Gross deferred tax liabilities	2,649	2,753
Net operating loss carryforwards . . .	(418)	(306)
Postretirement benefits	(248)	(248)
Casualty claims	(119)	(71)
Various accrued liabilities and other	(790)	(637)
Gross deferred tax assets	(1,575)	(1,262)
Deferred tax assets valuation allowance	498	319
Net deferred tax liability	$1,572	$1,810
Included in		
Prepaid expenses, taxes and other current assets	$ (313)	$ (167)
Other current liabilities	–	4
Deferred income taxes	1,885	1,973
	$1,572	$1,810

The valuation allowance related to deferred tax assets increased by $179 million in 1995, primarily resulting from additions related to current year operating losses in a number of state and foreign jurisdictions and the adoption of SFAS 121.

In accordance with generally accepted accounting principles, deferred tax liabilities have not been recognized for bases differences that are essentially permanent in duration related to investments in foreign subsidiaries and joint ventures. These differences, which consist primarily of unremitted earnings intended to be indefinitely reinvested, aggregated approximately $4.5 billion at year-end 1995 and $3.8 billion at year-end 1994, exclusive of amounts that if remitted in the future would result in little or no tax under current tax laws and the Puerto Rico tax incentive grant. Determination of the amount of unrecognized deferred tax liabilities is not practicable.

Net operating loss carryforwards totaling $2.3 billion at year-end 1995 are available to reduce future tax of certain subsidiaries and are related to a number of state and foreign jurisdictions. Of these carryforwards, $16 million expire in 1996, $2.1 billion expire at various times between 1997 and 2010 and $173 million may be carried forward indefinitely.

Tax benefits associated with exercises of stock options of $91 million in 1995, $27 million in 1994 and $23 million in 1993 were credited to shareholders' equity. A change in the functional currency of operations in Mexico from the U.S. dollar to local currency in 1993 resulted in a $19 million decrease in the net deferred foreign tax liability that was credited to shareholders' equity.

Note 12 – Postretirement Benefits Other Than Pensions

PepsiCo provides postretirement health care benefits to eligible retired employees and their dependents, principally in the U.S. Retirees who have 10 years of service and attain age 55 while in service with PepsiCo are eligible to participate in the postretirement benefit plans. The plans are not funded and were largely noncontributory through 1993.

Effective in 1993 and 1994, PepsiCo implemented programs intended to stem rising costs and introduced retiree cost-sharing, including adopting a provision that limits its future obligation to absorb health care cost inflation. These amendments resulted in an unrecognized prior service gain of $191 million, which is being amortized on a straight-line basis over the average remaining employee service period of approximately 10 years as a reduction in postretirement benefit expense beginning in 1993.

The components of postretirement benefit expense for 1995, 1994 and 1993 are set forth below:

	1995	1994	1993
Service cost of benefits earned . . .	$ 13	$ 19	$ 15
Interest cost on accumulated postretirement benefit obligation	46	41	41
Amortization of prior service cost (gain)	(20)	(20)	(20)
Amortization of net (gain) loss . . .	(1)	6	–
	$ 38	$ 46	$ 36

The components of the 1995 and 1994 postretirement benefit liability recognized in the Consolidated Balance Sheet are set forth below:

	1995	1994
Actuarial present value of postretirement benefit obligation		
Retirees	$(344)	$(289)
Fully eligible active plan participants	(96)	(88)
Other active plan participants	(171)	(148)
Accumulated postretirement benefit obligation	(611)	(525)
Unrecognized prior service cost (gain)	(132)	(152)
Unrecognized net loss	68	12
	$(675)	$(665)

The discount rate assumptions used in computing the information above are set forth below:

	1995	1994	1993
Postretirement benefit expense	9.1%	6.8	8.2
Accumulated postretirement benefit obligation	7.7%	9.1	6.8

The year-to-year fluctuations in the discount rate assumptions primarily reflect changes in the U.S. interest rates. The discount rate represents the expected yield on a portfolio of high-grade (AA rated or equivalent) fixed-income investments with cash flow streams sufficient to satisfy benefit obligations under the plans when due.

As a result of the plan amendments discussed above, separate assumed health care cost trend rates are used for employees who retire before and after the effective date of the amendments. The assumed health care cost trend rate for employees who retired before the effective date is 9.0% for 1996, declining gradually to 5.5% in 2005 and thereafter. For employees retiring after the effective date, the trend rate is 7.5% for 1996, declining gradually to 0% in 2001 and thereafter. A 1 point increase in the assumed health care cost trend rate would have increased the 1995 postretirement benefit expense by $2 million and would have increased the 1995 accumulated post-retirement benefit obligation by $24 million.

Note 13 – Pension Plans

PepsiCo sponsors noncontributory defined benefit pension plans covering substantially all full-time U.S. employees as well as contributory and noncontributory defined benefit pension plans covering certain international employees. Benefits generally are based on years of service and compensation or stated amounts for each year of service. PepsiCo funds the U.S. plans in amounts not less than minimum statutory funding requirements nor more than the maximum amount that can be deducted for U.S. income tax purposes. International plans are funded in amounts sufficient to comply with local statutory requirements. The plans' assets consist principally of equity securities, government and corporate debt securities and other fixed income obligations. The U.S. plans' assets included 6.9 billion shares of PepsiCo capital stock for 1995 and 1994, with a market value of $350 million and $227 million, respectively. Dividends on PepsiCo capital stock of $5 million were received by the U.S. plans in both 1995 and 1994.

The components of net pension expense for company-sponsored plans are set forth below:

	U.S. Plans			International Plans		
	1995	1994	1993	1995	1994	1993
Service cost of benefits earned	$ 60	$ 70	$ 57	$ 11	$ 15	$ 12
Interest cost on projected benefit obligation	92	84	76	16	15	15
Return on plan assets						
Actual (gain) loss	(338)	20	(162)	(31)	8	(41)
Deferred gain (loss)	221	(131)	71	6	(32)	21
	(117)	(111)	(91)	(25)	(24)	(20)
Amortization of net transition gain	(19)	(19)	(19)	–	–	–
Net other amortization	5	9	9	–	2	2
	$ 21	$ 33	$ 32	$ 2	$ 8	$ 9

Reconciliations of the funded status of the plans to the pension liability recognized in the Consolidated Balance Sheet are set forth below:

	U.S. Plans				International Plans			
	Assets Exceed Accumulated Benefits		Accumulated Benefits Exceed Assets		Assets Exceed Accumulated Benefits		Accumulated Benefits Exceed Assets	
	1995	1994	1995	1994	1995	1994	1995	1994
Actuarial present value of benefit obligation								
Vested benefits	$ (824)	$ (774)	$(270)	$(22)	$(144)	$(125)	$(34)	$(23)
Nonvested benefits	(110)	(98)	(30)	(1)	(2)	(2)	(1)	(7)
Accumulated benefit obligation	(934)	(872)	(300)	(23)	(146)	(127)	(35)	(30)
Effect of projected compensation increases	(155)	(111)	(78)	(48)	(23)	(24)	(12)	(10)
Projected benefit obligation	(1,089)	(983)	(378)	(71)	(169)	(151)	(47)	(40)
Plan assets at fair value	1,152	1,134	267	3	235	213	18	15

Plan assets in excess of (less than)								
projected benefit obligation	**63**	151	**(111)**	(68)	**66**	62	**(29)**	(25)
Unrecognized prior service cost........	**37**	31	**51**	30	**3**	4	**–**	–
Unrecognized net (gain) loss	**(20)**	(72)	**34**	4	**16**	14	**4**	(3)
Unrecognized net transition (gain) loss...	**(51)**	(73)	**(3)**	–	**(1)**	(2)	**4**	5
Adjustment required to recognize								
minimum liability	**–**	–	**(26)**	–	**–**	–	**(2)**	–
Prepaid (accrued) pension liability	$ **29**	$ 37	$ **(55)**	$(34)	$ **84**	$ 78	**$(23)**	$(23)

The assumptions used to compute the information above were as follows:

	U.S. Plans			International Plans		
	1995	1994	1993	**1995**	1994	1993
Discount rate – pension expense	**9.0%**	7.0	8.2	**9.2%**	7.3	9.0
Expected long-term rate of return on plan assets	**10.0%**	10.0	10.0	**11.3%**	11.3	10.8
Discount rate – projected benefit obligation	**7.7%**	9.0	7.0	**8.8%**	9.3	7.4
Future compensation growth rate.........	**3.3%-6.6%**	3.3-7.0	3.3-7.0	**3.0%-11.8%**	3.0-8.5	3.5-8.5

The discount rates and rates of return for the international plans represent weighted averages.

The year-to-year fluctuations in the discount rate assumptions primarily reflect changes in interest rates. The discount rates represent the expected yield on a portfolio of high-grade (AA rated or equivalent) fixed-income investments with cash flow streams sufficient to satisfy benefit obligations under the plans when due. The lower assumed discount rates used to measure the 1995 projected benefit obligation compared to the assumed discount rates used to measure the 1994 projected benefit obligation changed the funded status of certain plans from overfunded to underfunded.

In 1994, PepsiCo changed the method for calculating the market-related value of plan assets used in determining the return-on-assets components of annual pension expense and the cumulative net unrecognized gain or loss subject to amortization. Under the previous accounting method, the calculation of the market-related value of assets reflected amortization of the actual capital return on assets on a straight-line basis over a five-year period. Under the new method, the calculation of the market-related value of assets reflects the long-term rate of return expected by PepsiCo and amortization of the difference between the actual return (including capital, dividends and interest) and the expected return over a five-year period. PepsiCo believes the new method is widely used in practice and preferred because it results in calculated plan asset values that more closely approximate fair value, while still mitigating the effect of annual market-value fluctuations. Under both methods, only the cumulative net unrecognized gain or loss that exceeds 10% of the greater of the projected benefit obligation or the market-related value of plan assets is subject to amortization. This change resulted in a noncash benefit in 1994 of $38 million ($23 million after-tax or $0.03 per share) representing the cumulative effect of the change related to years prior to 1994 and $35 million in lower pension expense ($22 million after-tax or $0.03 per share) related to 1994 as compared to the previous accounting method. Had this change been applied retroactively, 1993 pension expense would have been reduced by $16 million ($11 million after-tax or $0.01 per share).

Note 14 – Postemployment Benefits Other Than to Retirees

Effective the beginning of 1994, PepsiCo adopted Statement of Financial Accounting Standards No. 112 (SFAS 112), "Employers' Accounting for Postemployment Benefits." SFAS 112 requires PepsiCo to accrue the cost of certain postemployment benefits to be paid to terminated or inactive employees other than retirees. The principal effect to PepsiCo results from accruing severance benefits to be provided to employees of certain business units who are terminated in the ordinary course of business over the expected service lives of the employees. Previously, these benefits were accrued upon the occurrence of an event. Severance benefits resulting from actions not in the ordinary course of business will continue to be accrued when those actions occur. The cumulative effect charge upon adoption of SFAS 112, which relates to years prior to 1994, was $84 million ($55 million after-tax or $0.07 per share). As compared to the previous accounting method, the ongoing impact of adopting SFAS 112 was immaterial to 1994 operating profits. PepsiCo's cash flows have been unaffected by this accounting change as PepsiCo continues to largely fund postemployement benefit costs as incurred.

Note 15 – Employee Stock Options

PepsiCo grants stock options to employees pursuant to three different incentive plans – the SharePower Stock Option Plan (Share-Power), the Long-Term Incentive Plan (LTIP) and the Stock Option Incentive Plan (SOIP). All stock option grants are authorized by the Compensation Committee of PepsiCo's Board of Directors (the Committee), which is comprised of outside directors. In each case, a stock option represents the right to purchase a share of PepsiCo capital stock (Stock) in the future at a price equal to the fair market value of the Stock on the date of the grant.

Under SharePower, approved by the Board of Directors and effective in 1989, essentially all employees, other than executive officers and short-service employees, may be granted stock options annually. The number of options granted is based on each employee's annual earnings. The options generally become exercisable ratably over 5 years from the grant date and must be exercised within 10 years of the grant date. SharePower options of 8 million were granted to approximately 134,000 employees in 1995; 12 million to 128,000 employees in 1994; and 9 million to 118,000 employees in 1993.

The shareholder-approved 1994 Long-Term Incentive Plan succeeds and continues the principal features of the shareholder approved 1987 Long-Term Incentive Plan (the 1987 Plan). PepsiCo ceased making grants under the 1987 Plan at the end of 1994. Together, these plans comprise the LTIP. At year-end 1995 and 1994, there were 74 million and 75 million shares, respectively, available for future grants under the LTIP.

Most LTIP stock options are granted every other year to senior management employees. Most of these options become exercisable after 4 years and must be exercised within 10 years from their grant date. In 1995, 1994, and 1993, 1 million, 16 million and 3 million stock options, respectively, were granted under the LTIP. In addition, the LTIP allows for grants of performance share units (PSUs). The value of a PSU is fixed at the value of a share of Stock at the grant date and vests for payment 4 years from the grant date, contingent upon attainment of prescribed Corporate performance goals. PSUs are not directly granted, as certain stock options granted may be surrendered by employees for a specified number of PSUs within 60 days of the option grant date. At year-end 1995, 1994 and 1993, there were 599,100, 629,200 and 491,200 PSUs outstanding, respectively. Payment of PSUs are made in cash and/or Stock as approved by the Committee. Amounts expensed for PSUs were $5 million, $7 million and $3 million in 1995, 1994 and 1993, respectively.

In 1995, the Committee approved the 1995 Stock Option Incentive Plan for middle management employees, under which a maximum of 25 million stock options may be granted. SOIP stock options are expected to be granted annually and are exercisable after 1 year and must be exercised within 10 years after their grant date. In 1995, 4 million stock options were granted resulting in 21 million shares available for future grants at year-end. In 1994 and 1993, grants similar to those under the SOIP were made under the LTIP to a more limited number of middle management employees.

Stock option activity for 1993, 1994 and 1995 is set forth below:

(options in thousands)	SharePower	LTIP/ SOIP
Outstanding at		
December 26, 1992.	28,796	32,990
Granted	9,121	2,834
Exercised.	(1,958)	(1,412)
Surrendered for PSUs.	–	(96)
Canceled	(2.524)	(966)
Outstanding at		
December 25, 1993.	33,435	33,350
Granted	11,633	16,237
Exercised.	(1,820)	(3,052)
Surrendered for PSUs.	–	(1,541)
Canceled	(3,443)	(2,218)
Outstanding at		
December 31, 1994.	39,805	42,776
Granted	**8,218**	**4,977**
Exercised.	**(5,722)**	**(4,868)**
Surrendered for PSUs.	**–**	**(101)**
Canceled	**(2,939)**	**(1,815)**
Outstanding at		
December 30, 1995.	**39,362**	**40,969**
Exercisable at		
December 30, 1995.	**16,932**	**15,804**
Option prices per share		
Exercised during 1993	$17.58 to $35.75	$4.11 to $36.31
Exercised during 1994	$17.58 to $36.75	$4.11 to $38.75
Exercised during 1995	$17.58 to $46.00	$7.69 to $41.81
Outstanding at year-end 1995	$17.58 to $46.00	$7.69 to $51.19

Note 16 – Stock Offering by an Unconsolidated Affiliate

In 1993, PepsiCo entered into an arrangement with the principal shareholders of Buenos Aires Embotelladora S.A. (BAESA), a franchised bottler which currently has operations in Brazil, Argentina, Chile, Uruguay and Cosa Rica, to form a joint venture. PepsiCo contributed certain assets, primarily bottling operations in Chile and Uruguay, while the principal shareholders contributed all of their shares in BAESA, representing 73% of the voting control and 43% of the ownership interest. Through this arrangement, PepsiCo's beneficial ownership in BAESA, which is accounted for by the equity method, was 26%. Under PepsiCo's partnership agreement with the principal shareholders of BAESA, voting control of BAESA will be transferred to PepsiCo no later than December 31, 1999.

On March 24, 1994, BAESA completed a public offering of 3 million American Depository Shares (ADS) at $34.50 per ADS, which are traded on the New York Stock Exchange. In conjunction with the offering, PepsiCo and certain other shareholders exercised options for the equivalent of 2 million ADS. As a result of these transactions. PepsiCo's ownership in BAESA declined to 24%. The transactions generated cash proceeds for BAESA of $136 million. The resulting onetime, noncash gain to PepsiCo was $18 million ($17 million after-tax or $0.02 per share).

Note 17 – Acquisitions and Investments in Unconsolidated Affiliates

During 1995, PepsiCo completed acquisitions and investments in unconsolidated affiliates aggregating $475 million, principally for cash. In addition, approximately $15 million of debt was assumed in these transactions. This activity included equity investments in international franchised bottling operations, primarily Group Embotellador de Mexico, S.A. (GEMEX) in Mexico, and in Simba, a snack food operation in South Africa. In addition, acquisitions included worldwide restaurant operations, primarily in New Zealand and the buyout of a joint venture partner in Singapore, and worldwide bottling operations.

PepsiCo formed a joint venture with the principal shareholder of GEMEX, an unconsolidated franchised bottling affiliate in Mexico. PepsiCo acquired a 27% interest for $207 million in cash and the contribution of a small company-owned bottling operation and our interest in an existing small franchised bottling joint venture with GEMEX. In addition, PepsiCo provided the principal shareholder of GEMEX a seven-year put option which allows the shareholder to sell up to 150 million GEMEX shares (which represented about 11% of GEMEX's outstanding shares at the date of the transaction) to PepsiCo at 66 ⅔¢ per share, which approximated the market value at the date of the transaction. This is equivalent to 8.3 million GEMEX American Depository Receipts (ADRs) at $12 per ADR. This option was valued at $26 million at the date of the transaction. Under PepsiCo's agreement with the principal shareholder of GEMEX, voting control of GEMEX will be transferred to PepsiCo no later than December 31, 2002.

During 1994, PepsiCo completed acquisitions and investments in unconsolidated affiliates aggregating $355 million, principally for cash. In addition, approximately $41 million of debt was assumed in these transactions, most of which was subsequently retired. This activity included equity investments in international franchised bottling operations, primarily in Thailand and China, and acquisitions of international and U.S. franchised restaurant operations and franchised and independent bottling operations, primarily in India and Mexico.

During 1993, PepsiCo completed acquisitions and investments in unconsolidated affiliates aggregating $1.4 billion, principally comprised of $1.0 billion in cash and $335 million in PepsiCo capital stock. Approximately $307 million of debt was assumed in these transactions, more than half of which was subsequently retired. This activity included acquisitions of U.S. and international franchised restaurant operations, the buyout of PepsiCo's joint venture partners in a franchised bottling operation in Spain and the related acquisition of their fruit-flavored beverage concentrate operation, the acquisition of the remaining 85% interest in a large franchised bottling operation in the Northwestern U.S., the acquisition of Chevys, a regional Mexican-style casual dining restaurant chain in the U.S., and equity investments in certain franchised bottling operations in Argentina and Mexico.

The acquisitions have been accounted for by the purchase method; accordingly, their results are included in the Consolidated Financial Statements from their respective dates of acquisition. The aggregate impact of acquisitions was not material to PepsiCo's net sales, net income or net income per share; accordingly, no related pro forma information is provided.

Note 18 – Contingencies

PepsiCo is subject to various claims and contingencies related to lawsuits, taxes, environmental and other matters arising out of the normal course of business. Management believes that the ultimate liability, if any, in excess of amounts already recognized arising from such claims or contingencies is not likely to have a material adverse effect on PepsiCo's annual results of operations or financial condition. At year-end 1995 and 1994, PepsiCo was contingently liable under guarantees aggregating $283 million and $187 million, respectively. The guarantees are primarily issued to support financial arrangements of certain PepsiCo joint ventures, and bottling and restaurant franchisees. PepsiCo manages the risk associated with these guarantees by performing appropriate credit reviews in addition to retaining certain rights as a joint venture partner or franchisor. See Note 9 for information related to the fair value of the guarantees.

Items Affecting Comparability

Net Refranchising Gains

Restaurant operating profit in 1995 included net gains of $51 million from sales of restaurants to franchisees by Pizza Hut, Taco Bell and International in excess of the cost of closing other restaurants in all of our concepts (net gains at Pizza Hut-$24 million and Taco Bell-$38 million; net losses at KFC-($7) million and International-($4) million).

Fiscal Year

Fiscal year 1994 consisted of 53 weeks and the years 1990 through 1993 and 1995 consisted of 52 weeks. The fifty-third week increased 1994 net sales by an estimated $434 million, increasing beverage, snack food and restaurant net sales by $119 million, $143 million and $172 million, respectively. The estimated impact of the fifty-third week on 1994 operating profit was $65 million, increasing beverage, snack food and restaurant operating profit by $17 million, $26 million and $23 million, respectively, and increasing unallocated expenses, net by $1 million.

Unusual Items

Unusual charges totaled $193 million in 1992 and $170 million in 1991.

These unusual items were as follows:

Beverages – 1992 included $145 million in charges consisting of $115 million and $30 million to reorganize and streamline U.S. and international operations, respectively.

Snack Foods – 1992 included a $40 million charge, principally to consolidate the Walkers businesses in the U.K. 1991 included $127 million in charges consisting of $91 million and $24 million to streamline U.S. and U.K. operations, respectively, and $12 million to dispose of all or part of a small unprofitable business in Japan.

Restaurants – 1991 included $43 million in charges at KFC primarily to streamline operations.

Unallocated expenses, net – 1992 included an $8 million charge to streamline operations of the SVE joint venture.

Accounting Changes

PepsiCo adopted SFAS 121 as of the beginning of the fourth quarter of 1995. See Note 2. The initial, noncash charge upon adoption reduced operating profit as follows:

International Beverages	$ 62
International Snack Foods	4
Restaurants	
Pizza Hut U.S.	68
Taco Bell U.S. (a)	169
KFC U.S.	65
Total U.S. Restaurants	302
International Restaurants	135
Combined Segments	503
Equity (Loss) Income (b)	17
	$520

(a) Hot 'n Now and Chevys incurred $103 of this charge, with Hot 'n Now responsible for almost all of the charge.
(b) Primarily related to CPK.

Included in the initial charge above was $68 million related to restaurants for which closure decisions were made during the fourth quarter (Pizza Hut-$21 million, Taco Bell-$16 million, KFC-$6 million, International-$21 million and equity (loss) income-$4 million). As a result of the reduced carrying amount of certain of PepsiCo's assets used in the business, depreciation and amortization expense for the fourth quarter of 1995 was reduced by $21 million, affecting international beverages by $4 million, restaurants by $16 million and equity (loss) income by $1 million.

In 1994, PepsiCo adopted a preferred method for calculating the market-related value of plan assets used in determining annual pension expense (see Note 13) and extended the depreciable lives on certain Pizza Hut U.S. delivery assets. As compared to the previous accounting methods, these changes increased 1994 operating profit by $49 million, increasing beverage, snack food and restaurant segment operating profit by $12 million, $15 million and $20 million, respectively, and decreasing 1994 unallocated expenses, net by $2 million.

In 1992, PepsiCo adopted Statements of Financial Accounting Standards No. 106 and 109, "Employers' Accounting for Postretirement Benefits Other Than Pensions" and "Accounting for Income Taxes," respectively. As compared to the previous accounting methods, these changes reduced 1992 operating profit by $73 million, decreasing beverage, snack food and restaurant segment operating profit by $22 million, $31 million and $16 million, respectively, and increasing 1992 unallocated expenses, net by $4 million.

Supplementary Financial Information

In addition to the financial statements and the accompanying notes, three items of supplementary financial information typically are presented: business segment information, five- (or ten-) year summary of related financial data, and quarterly financial data, and stock performance information.

Business Segment Information

To help financial statement users assess the performance of diversified companies that operate in several different industries and lines of business, segmented financial information is required. The required information for each significant segment includes: revenues, income from operations, capital expenditures, identifiable assets, and depreciation and amortization. This information is generally included in the form of notes and schedules in the notes accompanying the financial statements. PepsiCo's note summarizing its business segment information is shown below:

Note 19 – Business Segments

PepsiCo operates on a worldwide basis within three industry segments: beverages, snack foods and restaurants.

Beverages

The beverage segment ("Beverages") markets and distributes its Pepsi-Cola, Diet Pepsi, Mountain Dew and other brands worldwide, and 7UP, Diet 7UP, Mirinda, Pepsi Max and other brands internationally. Beverages manufactures concentrates of its brands for sale to franchised bottlers worldwide. Beverages operates bottling plants and distribution facilities located in the U.S. and in various international markets for the production of company-owned and non-company-owned brands. Beverages also manufactures and distributes ready-to-drink Lipton tea products in the U.S. and Canada.

Beverages products are available in 193 countries outside the U.S., including emerging markets such as China, Hungary, India, Poland and Russia. Principal international markets include Argentina, Brazil, Canada, China, Japan, Mexico, Saudi Arabia, Spain, Thailand, the U.K. and Venezuela. Beverages' joint venture ("JV") investments are primarily in franchised bottling and distribution operations. Internationally, the largest JVs are GEMEX (Mexico), BAESA (South America) and Serm Suk (Thailand), as well as the aggregate of several JVs in China. The primary JV in the U.S. is General Bottlers.

Snack Foods

The snack food segment ("Snack Foods") manufactures, distributes and markets salty and sweet snacks worldwide, with Frito-Lay representing the U.S. business. Products manufactured and distributed in the U.S. (primarily salty snacks) include Lay's and Ruffles brand potato chips, Doritos and Tostitos brand tortilla chips, Fritos brand corn chips, Chee•tos brand cheese flavored snacks, Rold Gold brand pretzels, a variety of dips and salsas and other brands. Snack Foods products are available in 39 countries outside the U.S. Principal international markets include Australia, Brazil, Canada, France, Mexico, the Netherlands, Poland, Spain and the U.K. International snack foods manufactures and distributes salty snacks in all countries and sweet snacks in certain countries, primarily in France, Mexico and Poland. Snack Foods has investments in several JVs outside the U.S., the largest of which are Snack Ventures Europe (SVE), a JV with General Mills, Inc., which has operations on most of the European continent, and a recent investment in Simba, a snack food operation in South Africa.

Restaurants

The restaurant segment ("Restaurants") is engaged principally in the operation, development, franchising and licensing of the worldwide Pizza Hut, Taco Bell and KFC concepts. Restaurants also operates other smaller U.S. concepts which are managed by Taco Bell (Hot 'n Now and Chevys) and Pizza Hut (East Side Mario's). PFS, PepsiCo's restaurant distribution operation, provides food, supplies and equipment to company-operated, franchised and licensed units, principally in the U.S. Net sales and the related estimated operating profit of PFS' franchisee and licensee operations have been allocated to each restaurant chain.

Pizza Hut, Taco Bell and KFC operate throughout the U.S. Pizza Hut, KFC and, to a lesser extent Taco Bell, operate in 93 countries outside the U.S. Principal international markets include Australia, Canada, Japan, Korea, Mexico, New Zealand, Spain and the U.K. Restaurants has investments in several JVs outside the U.S., the most significant of which are located in Japan and the U.K. PepsiCo also participates in a JV which operates California Pizza Kitchen (CPK), a U.S. casual dining restaurant chain.

In 1995, PepsiCo changed the presentation of its restaurant segment to provide information by each of PepsiCo's major U.S. concepts, which include the smaller concepts managed by Pizza Hut and Taco Bell, and in total for the international operations, to more closely reflect how we currently manage the business. Prior year amounts have been restated.

Unallocated expenses, net included corporate headquarters expenses, minority interests, primarily in the Gamesa (Mexico) and Wedel (Poland) snack food businesses, foreign exchange translation and transaction gains and losses and other items not allocated to the business segments. Corporate identifiable assets consist principally of cash and cash equivalents and short-term investments, primarily held outside the U.S.

PepsiCo has invested in about 80 joint ventures in which it exercises significant influence but not control. As noted above, the JVs are primarily international and principally within PepsiCo's three industry segments. Equity in net (loss) income of these unconsolidated affiliates was ($3) million, $38 million, and $30 million in 1995, 1994 and 1993, respectively. Excluding the initial charge upon adoption of SFAS 121 (see Accounting Changes below), 1995 equity in net income was $14 million. The $24 million decline in 1995 primarily reflected increased losses in our international beverages affiliates in Mexico, reflecting the devaluation of the Mexican peso, costs related to the formation of the GEMEX JV and an unrealized loss on a put option issued in connection with the formation of the GEMEX JV (see Notes 7 and 17). This decline was partially offset by increased equity in net income from our Pepsi-Lipton Tea partnership and SVE. The increase in 1994 primarily reflected increased profit as SVE. Dividends received from these unconsolidated affiliates totaled $29 million, $33 million and $16 million in 1995, 1994 and 1993, respectively.

PepsiCo's year-end investments in unconsolidated affiliates totaled $1.6 billion in 1995 and $1.3 billion in 1994. The increase in 1995 reflected the acquisition of a 27% interest in GEMEX and the investment in Simba (see Note 17), advances to BAESA and investments in international franchised bottling operations in China, partially offset by dividends received and equity in net loss that are discussed above. Significant investments in unconsolidated affiliates at year-end 1995 included $244 million in General Bottlers, $201 million in GEMEX, $168 million in BAESA, $157 million in a KFC Japan JV, $147 million in CPK and $107 million in SVE.

Industry Segments

		Growth Rate 1990 - 1995	1995	1994	1993	1992	1991
Net Sales							
Beverages:	U.S.	7%	$ 6,977	$ 6,541	$ 5,918	$ 5,485	$ 5,171
	International	19%	3,571	3,146	2,720	2,121	1,744
		10%	10,548	9,687	8,638	7,606	6,915
Snack Foods:	U.S.	10%	5,495	5,011	4,365	3,950	3,738
	International	19%	3,050	3,253	2,662	2,182	1,512
		12%	8,545	8,264	7,027	6,132	5,250
Restaurants:	U.S.	11%	9,202	8,694	8,026	7,115	6,258
	International	25%	2,126	1,827	1,330	1,117	869
		13%	11,328	10,521	9,356	8,232	7,127
Combined Segments							
	U.S.	9%	21,674	20,246	18,309	16,550	15,167
	International	20%	8,747	8,226	6,712	5,420	4,125
		12%	$30,421	$28,472	$25,021	$21,970	$19,292
By U.S. Restaurant Chain							
	Pizza Hut	8%	$ 3,977	$ 3,712	$ 3,595	$ 3,183	$ 2,937
	Taco Bell	15%	3,503	3,340	2,855	2,426	2,017
	KFC	9%	1,722	1,642	1,576	1,506	1,304
		11%	$ 9,202	$ 8,694	$ 8,026	$ 7,115	$ 6,258
Operating Profit							
Beverages:	U.S.	11%	$ 1,145	$ 1,022	$ 937	$ 686	$ 746
	International	19%	164	195	172	113	117
		12%	1,309	1,217	1,109	799	863
Snack Foods:	U.S.	9%	1,132	1,025	901	776	617
	International	14%	300	352	289	209	140
		10%	1,432	1,377	1,190	985	757
Restaurants:	U.S.	10%	451	659	685	598	480
	International	8%	(21)	71	93	120	96
		9%	430	730	778	718	576
Combined Segments							
	U.S.	10%	2,728	2,706	2,523	2,060	1,843
	International	14%	443	618	554	442	353
		10%	3,171	3,324	3,077	2,502	2,196
Equity (Loss) Income			(3)	38	30	40	32
Unallocated Expenses, net			(181)	(161)	(200)	(171)	(116)
Operating Profit		11%	$ 2,987	$ 3,201	$ 2,907	$ 2,371	$ 2,112
By U.S. Restaurant Chain							
	Pizza Hut	9%	$ 308	$ 285	$ 338	$ 300	$ 286
	Taco Bell	12%	105	273	256	214	183
	KFC	7%	38	101	91	84	11
		10%	$ 451	$ 659	$ 685	$ 598	$ 480

Geographic Areas

	Net Sales			Segment Operating Profit (Loss)			Identifiable Assets		
	1995	1994	1993	1995	1994	1993	1995	1994	1993
United States	$21,674	$20,246	$18,309	$2,728	$2,706	$2,523	$14,505	$14,218	$13,590
Europe	2,783	2,177	1,819	(65)	17	47	3,127	3,062	2,666
Mexico	1,228	2,023	1,614	80	261	223	637	995	1,217
Canada	1,299	1,244	1,206	86	82	102	1,344	1,342	1,364
Other	3,437	2,782	2,073	342	258	182	2,629	2,196	1,675
Combined Segments	$30,421	$28,472	$25,021	$3,171	$3,324	$3,077	22,242	21,813	20,512
Investments in Unconsolidated Affiliates							1,635	1,295	1,091
Corporate							1,555	1,684	2,103
							$25,432	$24,792	$23,706

Amortization of Intangible Assets

	Growth Rate 1990 - 1995	1995	1994	1993		Growth Rate 1990 - 1995	1995	1994	1993
Beverages	7%	$ 166	$ 165	$ 157	By U.S. Restaurant Chain				
Snack Foods	2%	41	42	41	Pizza Hut	14%	$ 36	$ 38	$ 35
Restaurants	23%	109	105	106	Taco Bell	24%	23	27	23
					KFC	18%	18	22	23
	10%	$ 316	$ 312	$ 304	Total U.S.	16%	77	87	81
					International	61%	32	18	25
						23%	$ 109	$ 105	$ 106

Depreciation Expense

	Growth Rate 1990 - 1995	1995	1994	1993		Growth Rate 1990 - 1995	1995	1994	1993
Beverages	15%	$ 445	$ 385	$ 359	By U.S. Restaurant Chain				
Snack Foods	9%	304	297	279	Pizza Hut	13%	$ 189	$ 178	$ 159
Restaurants	17%	579	539	457	Taco Bell	21%	179	153	122
Corporate		7	7	7	KFC	11%	101	107	101
	14%	$ 1,335	$ 1,228	$ 1,102	Total U.S.	15%	469	438	382
					International	27%	110	101	75
						17%	$ 579	$ 539	$ 457

Identifiable Assets

	Growth Rate 1990 - 1995	1995	1994	1993		Growth Rate 1990 - 1995	1995	1994	1993
Beverages	9%	$10,032	$ 9,566	$ 9,105	By U.S. Restaurant Chain				
Snack Foods	7%	5,451	5,044	4,995	Pizza Hut	8%	$1,700	$1,832	$1,733
Restaurants	14%	6,759	7,203	6,412	Taco Bell	19%	2,276	2,327	2,060
Investments in Unconsolidated Affiliates	9%	1,635	1,295	1,091	KFC	7%	1,111	1,253	1,265
Corporate		1,555	1,684	2,103	Total U.S.	12%	5,087	5,412	5,058
	8%	$25,432	$24,792	$23,706	International	27%	1,672	1,791	1,354
						14%	$6,759	$7,203	$6,412

Capital Spending

	Growth Rate 1990 - 1995	1995	1994	1993		Growth Rate 1990 - 1995	1995	1994	1993
Beverages	11%	$ 566	$ 677	$ 491	By U.S. Restaurant Chain				
Snack Foods	15%	769	532	491	Pizza Hut	1%	$ 168	$ 225	$ 209
Restaurants	10%	750	1,072	1,005	Taco Bell	17%	305	442	442
Corporate		34	7	21	KFC	–	93	69	106
	12%	$ 2,119	$ 2,288	$ 2,008	Total U.S.	8%	566	736	757
U.S.	12%	$ 1,496	$ 1,492	$ 1,388	International	20%	184	336	248
International	13%	623	796	620		10%	$ 750	$1,072	$1,005
	12%	$ 2,119	$ 2,288	$ 2,008					

Acquisitions and Investments in Unconsolidated Affiliates

	1995	1994	1993		1995	1994	1993
Beverages	$ 323	$ 195	$ 711	By U.S. Restaurant Chain			
Snack Foods	82	12	76	Pizza Hut	$ 3	$ 52	$ 219
Restaurants	70	148	589	Taco Bell	34	32	187
	$ 475	$ 355	$ 1,376	KFC	–	–	30
U.S.	$ 73	$ 88	$ 757	Total U.S.	37	84	436
International	402	267	619	International	33	64	153
	$ 475	$ 355	$ 1,376		$ 70	$ 148	$ 589

Five- or Ten-Year Summary

Usually presented in close proximity to the audited financial statements is a five- or ten-year summary of selected financial data. From such a summary, one can determine trends and growth patterns over a fairly long period of time. PepsiCo presented the following summary that includes operating data, financial position data, and seletected statistics and ratios:

Selected Financial Data

(in millions except per share and employee amounts, unaudited) PepsiCo, Inc. and Subsidiaries	Compounded 10-Year 1985-95	Compounded 5-Year 1990-95	Annual 1-Year 1994-95	1995	1994
Summary of Operations					
Net sales	15%	12%	7%	$30,421	28,472
Operating profit	14%	8%	(7)%	$ 2,987	3,201
Gain on stock offering by an unconsolidated affiliate				–	18
Interest expense, net.				(555)	(555)
Income from continuing operations before income taxes and cumulative effect of accounting changes.	14%	8%	(9)%	$ 2,432	2,664
Income from continuing operations before cumulative effect of accounting changes	14%	8%	(10)%	$ 1,606	1,784
Cumulative effect of accounting changes				$ –	(32)
Net income	11%	8%	(8)%	$ 1,606	1,752
Cash Flow Data					
Provided by operating activities	16%	12%	1%	$3,742	3,716
Capital spending	11%	12%	(7)%	2,104	2,253
Operating free cash flow.	43%	12%	12%	$1,638	1,463
Dividends paid	14%	15%	11%	$ 599	540
Purchases of treasury stock				$ 541	549
Acquisitions and investments in unconsolidated affiliates				$ 466	316
Per Share Data and Other Share Information					
Income from continuing operations before cumulative effect of accounting changes	15%	8%	(10)%	$ 2.00	2.22
Cumulative effect of accounting changes				$ –	(0.04)
Net income	12%	8%	(8)%	$ 2.00	2.18
Cash dividends declared	15%	15%	11%	$ 0.780	0.700
Book value per share at year-end	15%	8%	7%	$ 9.28	8.68
Market price per share at year-end	22%	17%	54%	$ 55⅞	36¼
Number of shares repurchased				12.3	15.0
Shares outstanding at year-end				788	790
Average shares outstanding used to calculate income (charge) per share				804	804
Balance Sheet					
Total assets	16%	8%	1%	$25,432	24,792
Long-term debt	22%	8%	(4)%	$ 8,509	8,841
Total debt.	20%	4%	(3)%	$ 9,215	9,519
Shareholders' equity				$ 7,313	6,856
Statistics					
Return on average shareholders' equity				23%	27
Market net debt ratio				18%	26
Historical cost net debt ratio				46%	49
Employees.	12%	9%	2%	480,000	471,000

PepsiCo, Inc.

1993	1992	1991	1990	1989	1988	1987	1986	1985
25,021	21,970	19,292	17,516	15,049	12,381	11,018	9,017	7,585
2,907	2,371	2,112	2,042	1,773	1,342	1,128	829	782
–	–	–	118	–	–	–	–	–
(484)	(472)	(452)	(506)	(433)	(222)	(182)	(139)	(99)
2,423	1,899	1,660	1,654	1,340	1,120	946	690	683
1,588	1,302	1,080	1,091	901	762	605	464	427
–	(928)	–	–	–	–	–	–	–
1,588	374	1,080	1077	901	762	595	458	544
3,134	2,712	2,430	2,110	1,886	1,895	1,335	1,212	817
1,982	1,550	1,458	1,180	944	726	771	859	770
1,152	1,162	972	930	942	1,169	564	353	47
462	396	343	294	242	199	172	160	161
463	32	195	148	–	72	19	158	458
1,011	1,210	641	631	3,297	1,416	372	1,680	160
1.96	1.61	1.35	1.37	1.13	0.97	0.77	0.59	0.51
–	(1.15)	–	–	–	–	–	–	–
1.96	0.46	1.35	1.35	1.13	0.97	0.76	0.58	0.65
0.610	0.510	0.460	0.383	0.320	0.267	0.223	0.209	0.195
7.93	6.70	7.03	6.22	4.92	4.01	3.21	2.64	2.33
41 7/8	42 1/4	33 3/4	25 3/4	21 3/8	13 1/8	11 1/4	8 3/4	7 7/8
12.4	1.0	6.4	6.3	0	6.2	1.9	20.2	66.0
799	799	789	788	791	788	781	781	789
810	807	803	799	796	790	789	787	842
23,706	20,951	18,775	17,143	15,127	11,135	9,023	8,027	5,889
7,443	7,965	7,806	5,900	6,077	2,656	2,579	2,633	1,162
9,634	8,672	8,034	7,526	6,943	4,107	3,225	2,865	1,506
6,339	5,356	5,545	4,904	3,891	3,161	2,509	2,059	1,838
27	24	21	25	26	27	27	24	23
22	19	21	24	26	24	22	28	15
50	49	51	51	54	43	41	46	30
423,000	372,000	338,000	308,000	266,000	235,000	225,000	241,000	150,000

Quarterly Financial Data and Capital Stock Information

Nearly all publicly held companies and many nonpublic companies issue financial information on a quarterly basis to stockholders, regulatory agencies, and others. These quarterly reports are referred to as interim financial reports, for which there are prescribed accounting standards. Quarterly financial data along with capital stock information are frequently summarized in the Annual Report. PepsiCo summarizes its quarterly data and capital stock information as shown below.

Selected Quarterly Financial Data

($ in millions except per share amounts, unaudited)
PepsiCo, Inc. and subsidiaries

	First Quarter (12 Weeks)		Second Quarter (12 Weeks)		Third Quarter (12 Weeks)		Fourth Quarter (16/17 Weeks)		Full Year (52/53 Weeks)	
	1995	1994	**1995**	1994	**1995**	1994	**1995**	1994	**1995**	1994
Net sales	**$6,191**	5,729	**7,286**	6,557	**7,693**	7,064	**9,251**	9,122	**30,421**	28,472
Gross profit	**$3,169**	2,944	**3,735**	3,420	**3,942**	3,684	**4,689**	4,709	**15,535**	14,757
Operating profit	**$ 629**	550	**869**	785	**1,031**	962	**458**	904	**2,987**	3,201
Income before income taxes and cumulative effect of accounting changes	**$ 496**	438	**735**	672	**901**	830	**300**	724	**2,432**	2,664
Provision for income taxes	**$ 175**	155	**248**	225	**284**	289	**119**	211	**826**	880
Income before cumulative effect of accounting changes	**$ 321**	283	**487**	447	**617**	541	**181**	513	**1,606**	1,784
Cumulative effect of accounting changes	**$ –**	(32)	**–**	–	**–**	–	**–**	–	**–**	(32)
Net income	**$ 321**	251	**487**	447	**617**	541	**181**	513	**1,606**	1,752
Income (charge) per share										
Income before cumulative effect of accounting changes	**$ 0.40**	0.35	**0.61**	0.55	**0.77**	0.68	**0.22**	0.64	**2.00**	2.22
Cumulative effect of accounting changes	**$ –**	(0.04)	**–**	–	**–**	–	**–**	–	**–**	(0.04)
Net income per share	**$ 0.40**	0.31	**0.61**	0.55	**0.77**	0.68	**0.22**	0.64	**2.00**	2.18
Cash dividends declared per share	**$ 0.18**	0.16	**0.20**	0.18	**0.20**	0.18	**0.20**	0.18	**0.78**	0.70
Stock price per share										
High	**$ 41**	42½	**49**	37¾	**47⅞**	34⅝	**58¾**	37⅜	**58¾**	42½
Low	**$ 33⅞**	35¾	**37⅞**	29⅞	**43¼**	29¼	**45⅝**	32¼	**33⅞**	29¼
Close	**$ 40¼**	37⅝	**46⅝**	31⅛	**45¾**	33¾	**55⅞**	36¼	**55⅞**	36¼

Capital Stock Information

Cash Dividends Declared Per Share
(In Cents)

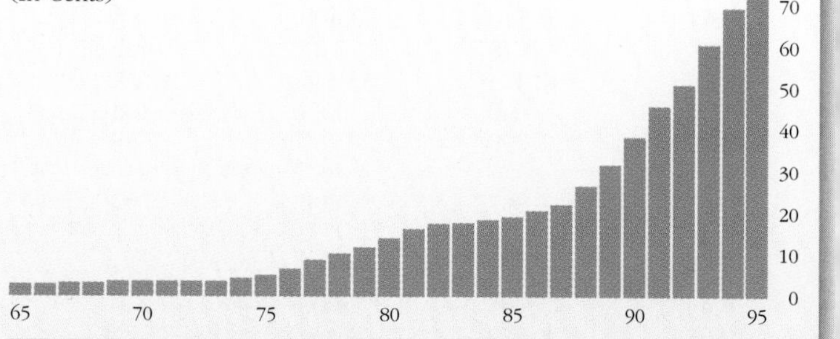

Stock Trading Symbol

PEP

Stock Exchange Listings

The New York Stock Exchange is the principal market for PepsiCo capital stock, which is also listed on the Amsterdam, Chicago, Swiss and Tokyo Stock Exchanges.

Shareholders

At year-end 1995, there were approximately 167,000 shareholders of record.

Dividend Policy

Quarterly cash dividends are usually declared in November, February, May and July and paid at the beginning of January and the end of March, June and September. The dividend record dates for 1996 are expected to be March 8, June 7, September 6 and December 6.

Quarterly cash dividends have been paid since PepsiCo was formed in 1965, and dividends paid per share have increased for 23 consecutive years.

TIME VALUE OF MONEY

▶ STUDY OBJECTIVES ◀

After studying this appendix, you should be able to:

1. *Distinguish between simple and compound interest.*
2. *Solve for future value of a single amount.*
3. *Solve for future value of an annuity.*
4. *Identify the variables fundamental to solving present value problems.*
5. *Solve for present value of a single amount.*
6. *Solve for present value of an annuity.*
7. *Compute the present value of notes and bonds.*

Would you rather receive $1,000 today or a year from now? You should prefer to receive the $1,000 today because you can invest the $1,000 and earn interest on it. As a result, you will have more than $1,000 a year from now. What this example illustrates is the concept of the **time value of money**. Everyone prefers to receive money today rather than in the future because of the interest factor.

Nature of Interest

Interest is payment for the use of another person's money. It is the difference between the amount borrowed or invested (called the principal) and the amount repaid or collected. The amount of interest to be paid or collected is usually stated as a rate over a specific period of time. The rate of interest is generally stated as an annual rate.

The amount of interest involved in any financing transaction is based on three elements:

1. **Principal (p)**: The original amount borrowed or invested.
2. **Interest Rate (i)**: An annual percentage of the principal.
3. **Time (n)**: The number of years that the principal is borrowed or invested.

Simple Interest

Simple interest is computed on the principal amount only. It is the return on the principal for one period. Simple interest is usually expressed as:

Illustration B-1

Interest computation

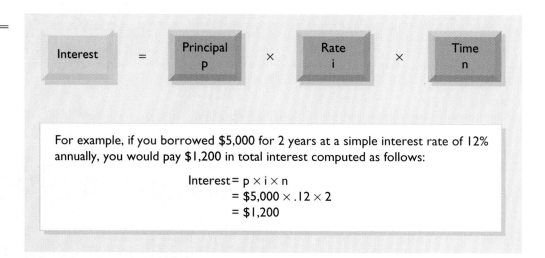

For example, if you borrowed $5,000 for 2 years at a simple interest rate of 12% annually, you would pay $1,200 in total interest computed as follows:

$$\text{Interest} = p \times i \times n$$
$$= \$5,000 \times .12 \times 2$$
$$= \$1,200$$

Compound Interest

Compound interest is computed on principal **and** on any interest earned that has not been paid or withdrawn. It is the return on (or growth of) the principal for two or more time periods. Compounding computes interest not only on the principal but also on the interest earned to date on that principal, assuming the interest is left on deposit.

To illustrate the difference between simple and compound interest, assume that you deposit $1,000 in Bank One, where it will earn simple interest of 9% per year, and you deposit another $1,000 in CityCorp, where it will earn compound interest of 9% per year compounded annually. Also assume that in both cases you will not withdraw any interest until 3 years from the date of deposit. The computation of interest to be received and the accumulated year-end balances are indicated in Illustration B-2.

Illustration B-2

Simple vs. Compound Interest

Bank One				**CityCorp.**		
Simple Interest Calculation	Simple Interest	Accumulated Year-end Balance		Compound Interest Calculation	Compound Interest	Accumulated Year-end Balance
Year 1 $1,000.00 × 9%	$ 90.00	$1,090.00		Year 1 $1,000.00 × 9%	$ 90.00	$1,090.00
Year 2 $1,000.00 × 9%	90.00	$1,180.00		Year 2 $1,090.00 × 9%	98.10	$1,188.10
Year 3 $1,000.00 × 9%	90.00	$1,270.00		Year 3 $1,188.10 × 9%	106.93	$1,295.03
	$ 270.00		$25.03 Difference		$ 295.03	

Note in the illustration above that simple interest uses the initial principal of $1,000 to compute the interest in all 3 years. Compound interest uses the accumulated balance (principal plus interest to date) at each year-end to compute interest in the succeeding year—which explains why your compound interest account is larger.

Obviously if you had a choice between investing your money at simple interest or at compound interest, you would choose compound interest, all other things—especially risk—being equal. In the example, compounding provides $25.03 of additional interest income. For practical purposes compounding assumes that unpaid interest earned becomes a part of the principal, and the accumulated balance at the end of each year becomes the new principal on which interest is earned during the next year.

As can be seen in Illustration B-2, you should invest your money at CityCorp which compounds interest annually. Compound interest is used in most business situations. Simple interest is generally applicable only to short-term situations of one year or less.

▼ SECTION *1* ► *Future Value Concepts*

▼*F*uture Value of a Single Amount

The future value of a single amount is the value at a future date of a given amount invested assuming compound interest. For example, in Illustration B-2, $1,295.03 is the future value of the $1,000 at the end of 3 years. The $1,295.03 could be determined more easily by using the following formula:

$$FV = p \times (1 + i)^n$$

STUDY OBJECTIVE
••••••••••**2**••••••••••
Solve for future value of a single amount.

Where:

$$FV = \text{future value of a single amount}$$
$$p = \text{principal (or present value)}$$
$$i = \text{interest rate for one period}$$
$$n = \text{number of periods}$$

The $1,295.03 is computed as follows:

$$FV = p \times (1 + i)^n$$
$$= \$1,000 \times (1 + i)^3$$
$$= \$1,000 \times 1.29503$$
$$= \$1,295.03$$

Illustration B-3

Time diagram

The 1.29503 is computed by multiplying (1.09 × 1.09 × 1.09). The amounts in this example can be depicted in the following time diagram:

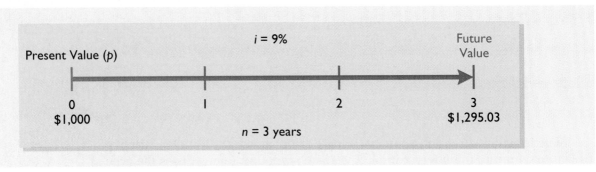

Another method that may be used to compute the future value of a single amount involves the use of a compound interest table. This table shows the future value of 1 for n periods. Such a table is shown below.

TABLE I
FUTURE VALUE OF I

(n) Periods	4%	5%	6%	8%	9%	10%	11%	12%	15%
1	1.04000	1.05000	1.06000	1.08000	1.09000	1.10000	1.11000	1.12000	1.15000
2	1.08160	1.10250	1.12360	1.16640	1.18810	1.21000	1.23210	1.25440	1.32250
3	1.12486	1.15763	1.19102	1.25971	1.29503	1.33100	1.36763	1.40493	1.52088
4	1.16986	1.21551	1.26248	1.36049	1.41158	1.46410	1.51807	1.57352	1.74901
5	1.21665	1.27628	1.33823	1.46933	1.53862	1.61051	1.68506	1.76234	2.01136
6	1.26532	1.34010	1.41852	1.58687	1.67710	1.77156	1.87041	1.97382	2.31306
7	1.31593	1.40710	1.50363	1.71382	1.82804	1.94872	2.07616	2.21068	2.66002
8	1.36857	1.47746	1.59385	1.85093	1.99256	2.14359	2.30454	2.47596	3.05902
9	1.42331	1.55133	1.68948	1.99900	2.17189	2.35795	2.55803	2.77308	3.51788
10	1.48024	1.62889	1.79085	2.15892	2.36736	2.59374	2.83942	3.10585	4.04556
11	1.53945	1.71034	1.89830	2.33164	2.58043	2.85312	3.15176	3.47855	4.65239
12	1.60103	1.79586	2.01220	2.51817	2.81267	3.13843	3.49845	3.89598	5.35025
13	1.66507	1.88565	2.13293	2.71962	3.06581	3.45227	3.88328	4.36349	6.15279
14	1.73168	1.97993	2.26090	2.93719	3.34173	3.79750	4.31044	4.88711	7.07571
15	1.80094	2.07893	2.39656	3.17217	3.64248	4.17725	4.78459	5.47357	8.13706
16	1.87298	2.18287	2.54035	3.42594	3.97031	4.59497	5.31089	6.13039	9.35762
17	1.94790	2.29202	2.69277	3.70002	4.32763	5.05447	5.89509	6.86604	10.76126
18	2.02582	2.40662	2.85434	3.99602	4.71712	5.55992	6.54355	7.68997	12.37545
19	2.10685	2.52695	3.02560	4.31570	5.14166	6.11591	7.26334	8.61276	14.23177
20	2.19112	2.65330	3.20714	4.66096	5.60441	6.72750	8.06231	9.64629	16.36654

In Table 1, n is the number of compounding periods, the percentages are the periodic interest rates, and the 5-digit decimal numbers in the respective columns are the future value of 1 factors. In using Table 1, the principal amount is multiplied by the future value factor for the specified number of periods and interest rate. For example, the future value factor for 2 periods at 9% is 1.18810. Multiplying this factor by $1,000 equals $1,188.10, which is the accumulated balance at the end of year 2 in the CityCorp example in Illustration B-2. The $1,295.03 accumulated balance at the end of the third year can be calculated from Table 1 by multiplying the future value factor for 3 periods (1.29503) by the $1,000.

The following demonstration problem illustrates how to use Table 1.

Illustration B-4

Demonstration Problem using Table 1 for FV of 1

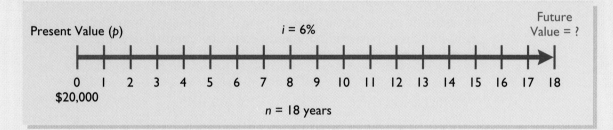

John and Mary Rich invested $20,000 in a savings account paying 6% interest at the time their son, Mike, was born. The money is to be used by Mike for his college education. On his 18th birthday, Mike withdraws the money from his savings account. How much did Mike withdraw from his account?

Present Value (*p*)　　　　　　　　　　*i* = 6%　　　　　　　　　　Future Value = ?

0　1　2　3　4　5　6　7　8　9　10　11　12　13　14　15　16　17　18
$20,000

n = 18 years

Answer: The future value factor from Table 1 is 2.85434 (18 periods at 6%). The future value of $20,000 earning 6% per year for 18 years is **$57,086.80** ($20,000 × 2.85434).

*F*uture Value of an Annuity

The preceding discussion involved the accumulation of only a single principal sum. Individuals and businesses frequently encounter situations in which a series of equal dollar amounts are to be paid or received periodically, such as loans or lease (rental) contracts. Such payments or receipts of equal dollar amounts are referred to as annuities. The future value of an annuity is the sum of all the payments (receipts) plus the accumulated compound interest on them. In computing the future value of an annuity, it is necessary to know the (1) interest rate, (2) the number of compounding periods, and (3) the amount of the periodic payments or receipts.

To illustrate the computation of the future value of an annuity, assume that you invest $2,000 at the end of each year for 3 years at 5% interest compounded annually. This situation is depicted in the following time diagram:

STUDY OBJECTIVE
··········**3**··········

Solve for future value of an annuity.

Illustration B-5

Time diagram for a 3-Year annuity

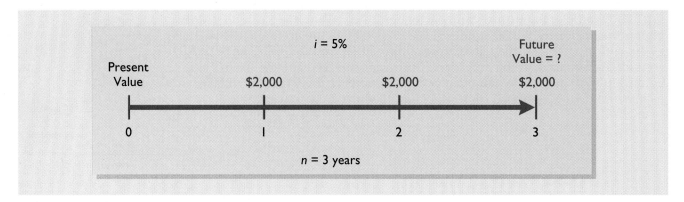

As can be seen from the preceding diagram, the $2,000 invested at the end of year 1 will earn interest for 2 years (year 2 & 3) and the $2,000 invested at the end of year 2 will earn interest for 1 year (year 3). However, the last $2,000 investment (made at the end of year 3) will not earn any interest. The future value of these periodic payments could be computed using the future value factors from Table 1 as shown below:

Illustration B-6

Future value of periodic payment computation

Year Invested	Amount Invested	×	Future Value of 1 Factor at 5%	=	Future Value
1	$2,000	×	1.10250		$2,205
2	$2,000	×	1.05000		2,100
3	$2,000	×	1.00000		2,000
			3.15250		$6,305

The first $2,000 investment is multiplied by the future value factor for 2 periods (1.1025) because 2 years' interest will accumulate on it (in years 2 & 3). The second $2,000 investment will earn only 1 year's interest (in year 3) and therefore is multiplied by the future value factor for 1 year (1.0500). The final $2,000 investment is made at the end of the third year and will not earn any interest. Consequently, the future value of the last $2,000 invested is only $2,000 since it does not accumulate any interest.

This method of calculation is required when the periodic payments or receipts are not equal in each period. However, when the periodic payments (receipts) are the same in each period, the future value can be computed by using a future value of an annuity of 1 table. Such a table is shown below.

(n) Periods	4%	5%	6%	8%	9%	10%	11%	12%	15%
				TABLE 2 **FUTURE VALUE OF AN ANNUITY OF 1**					
1	1.00000	1.00000	1.00000	1.00000	1.00000	1.00000	1.00000	1.00000	1.00000
2	2.04000	2.05000	2.06000	2.08000	2.09000	2.10000	2.11000	2.12000	2.15000
3	3.12160	3.15250	3.18360	3.24640	3.27810	3.31000	3.34210	3.37440	3.47250
4	4.24646	4.31013	4.37462	4.50611	4.57313	4.64100	4.70973	4.77933	4.99338
5	5.41632	5.52563	5.63709	5.86660	5.98471	6.10510	6.22780	6.35285	6.74238
6	6.63298	6.80191	6.97532	7.33592	7.52334	7.71561	7.91286	8.11519	8.75374
7	7.89829	8.14201	8.39384	8.92280	9.20044	9.48717	9.78327	10.08901	11.06680
8	9.21423	9.54911	9.89747	10.63663	11.02847	11.43589	11.85943	12.29969	13.72682
9	10.58280	11.02656	11.49132	12.48756	13.02104	13.57948	14.16397	14.77566	16.78584
10	12.00611	12.57789	13.18079	14.48656	15.19293	15.93743	16.72201	17.54874	20.30372
11	13.48635	14.20679	14.97164	16.64549	17.56029	18.53117	19.56143	20.65458	24.34928
12	15.02581	15.91713	16.86994	18.97713	20.14072	21.38428	22.71319	24.13313	29.00167
13	16.62684	17.71298	18.88214	21.49530	22.95339	24.52271	26.21164	28.02911	34.35192
14	18.29191	19.59863	21.01507	24.21492	26.01919	27.97498	30.09492	32.39260	40.50471
15	20.02359	21.57856	23.27597	27.15211	29.36092	31.77248	34.40536	37.27972	47.58041
16	21.82453	23.65749	25.67253	30.32428	33.00340	35.94973	39.18995	42.75328	55.71747
17	23.69751	25.84037	28.21288	33.75023	36.97351	40.54470	44.50084	48.88367	65.07509
18	25.64541	28.13238	30.90565	37.45024	41.30134	45.59917	50.39593	55.74972	75.83636
19	27.67123	30.53900	33.75999	41.44626	46.01846	51.15909	56.93949	63.43968	88.21181
20	29.77808	33.06595	36.78559	45.76196	51.16012	57.27500	64.20283	72.05244	102.44358

Table 2 shows the future value of 1 to be received periodically for a given number of periods. From Table 2 it can be seen that the future value of an annuity of 1 factor for 3 periods at 5% is 3.15250. The future value factor is the total of the three individual future value factors as shown in Illustration B-6. Multiplying this amount by the annual investment of $2,000 produces a future value of $6,305.

The following demonstration problem illustrates how to use Table 2.

Illustration B-7

Demonstration Problem using Table 2 for FV of an annuity of 1

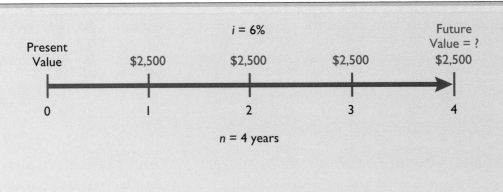

John and Char Lewis' daughter, Debra, has just started high school. They decide to start a college fund for her and will invest $2,500 in a savings account at the end of each year she is in high school (4 payments total). The account will earn 6% interest compounded annually. How much will be in the college fund at the time Debra graduates from high school?

Answer: The future value factor from Table 2 is 4.37462 (4 periods at 6%). The future value of $2,500 invested each year for 4 years at 6% interest is **$10,936.55** ($2,500 × 4.37462).

SECTION 2 ▸ Present Value Concepts

Present Value Variables

STUDY OBJECTIVE
.... 4 ....
Identify the variables fundamental to solving present value problems.

The present value, like the future value, is based on three variables: (1) the dollar amount to be received (future amount), (2) the length of time until the amount is received (number of periods), and (3) the interest rate (the discount rate). The process of determining the present value is referred to as discounting the future amount.

In this textbook, present value computations are used in measuring several items. For example, in Chapter 11, to determine the market price of a bond, the present value of the principal and interest payments is computed. In addition, the determination of the amount to be reported for notes payable and lease liability (Appendix E) involves present value computations.

Present Value of a Single Amount

To illustrate present value concepts, assume that you are willing to invest a sum of money that will yield $1,000 at the end of one year. In other words, what amount would you need to invest today to have $1,000 one year from now? If you want a 10% rate of return, the investment or present value is $909.09 ($1,000 ÷ 1.10). The computation of this amount is shown in Illustration B-8.

STUDY OBJECTIVE
•••••••••• **5** ••••••••••
Solve for present value of a single amount.

$$Present\ Value = Future\ Value \div (1 + i)^1$$
$$PV = FV \div (1 + 10\%)^1$$
$$PV = \$1,000 \div 1.10$$
$$PV = \$909.09$$

Illustration B-8

Present value computation— $1,000 discounted at 10% for 1 year

The future amount ($1,000), the discount rate (10%), and the number of periods (1) are known. The variables in this situation can be depicted in the following time diagram:

Illustration B-9

Finding present value if discounted for one period

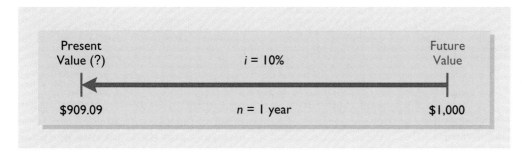

If the single amount of $1,000 is to be received **in 2 years** and discounted at 10% [PV = $1,000 ÷ (1 + 10%)²], its present value is $826.45 [($1,000 ÷ 1.10) ÷ 1.10], depicted as follows:

Illustration B-10

Finding present value if discounted for two periods

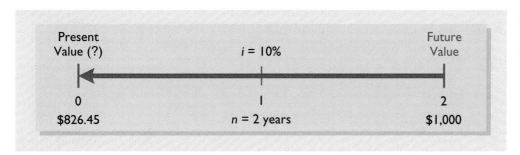

The present value of 1 may also be determined through tables that show the present value of 1 for *n* periods. In Table 3, *n* is the number of discounting periods involved. The percentages are the periodic interest rates or discount rates, and the 5-digit decimal numbers in the respective columns are the present value of 1 factors.

TABLE 3
PRESENT VALUE OF 1

(n) Periods	4%	5%	6%	8%	9%	10%	11%	12%	15%
1	.96154	.95238	.94340	.92593	.91743	.90909	.90090	.89286	.86957
2	.92456	.90703	.89000	.85734	.84168	.82645	.81162	.79719	.75614
3	.88900	.86384	.83962	.79383	.77218	.75132	.73119	.71178	.65752
4	.85480	.82270	.79209	.73503	.70843	.68301	.65873	.63552	.57175
5	.82193	.78353	.74726	.68058	.64993	.62092	.59345	.56743	.49718
6	.79031	.74622	.70496	.63017	.59627	.56447	.53464	.50663	.43233
7	.75992	.71068	.66506	.58349	.54703	.51316	.48166	.45235	.37594
8	.73069	.67684	.62741	.54027	.50187	.46651	.43393	.40388	.32690
9	.70259	.64461	.59190	.50025	.46043	.42410	.39092	.36061	.28426
10	.67556	.61391	.55839	.46319	.42241	.38554	.35218	.32197	.24719
11	.64958	.58468	.52679	.42888	.38753	.35049	.31728	.28748	.21494
12	.62460	.55684	.49697	.39711	.35554	.31863	.28584	.25668	.18691
13	.60057	.53032	.46884	.36770	.32618	.28966	.25751	.22917	.16253
14	.57748	.50507	.44230	.34046	.29925	.26333	.23199	.20462	.14133
15	.55526	.48102	.41727	.31524	.27454	.23939	.20900	.18270	.12289
16	.53391	.45811	.39365	.29189	.25187	.21763	.18829	.16312	.10687
17	.51337	.43630	.37136	.27027	.23107	.19785	.16963	.14564	.09293
18	.49363	.41552	.35034	.25025	.21199	.17986	.15282	.13004	.08081
19	.47464	.39573	.33051	.23171	.19449	.16351	.13768	.11611	.07027
20	.45639	.37689	.31180	.21455	.17843	.14864	.12403	.10367	.06110

When Table 3 is used, the future value is multiplied by the present value factor specified at the intersection of the number of periods and the discount rate. For example, the present value factor for 1 period at a discount rate of 10% is .90909, which equals the $909.09 ($1,000 × .90909) computed in Illustration B-8. For 2 periods at a discount rate of 10%, the present value factor is .82645, which equals the $826.45 ($1,000 × .82645) computed previously.

Note that a higher discount rate produces a smaller present value. For example, using a 15% discount rate, the present value of $1,000 due one year from now is $869.57 versus $909.09 at 10%. It should be also be recognized that the further removed from the present the future value is, the smaller the present value. For example, using the same discount rate of 10%, the present value of $1,000 due in **five** years is $620.92 versus $1,000 due in **one** year is $909.09.

The following two demonstration problems (Illustrations B-11, B-12) illustrate how to use Table 3.

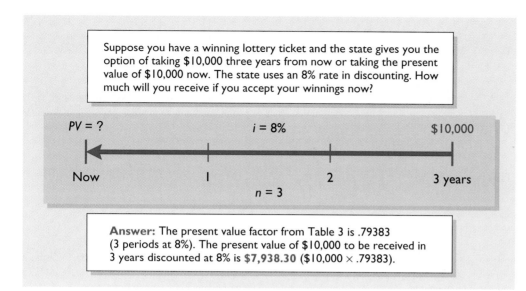

Suppose you have a winning lottery ticket and the state gives you the option of taking $10,000 three years from now or taking the present value of $10,000 now. The state uses an 8% rate in discounting. How much will you receive if you accept your winnings now?

PV = ?   i = 8% $10,000

Now   1   2   3 years
                    n = 3

Answer: The present value factor from Table 3 is .79383 (3 periods at 8%). The present value of $10,000 to be received in 3 years discounted at 8% is **$7,938.30** ($10,000 × .79383).

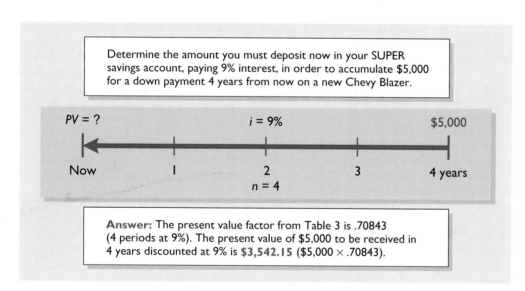

Determine the amount you must deposit now in your SUPER savings account, paying 9% interest, in order to accumulate $5,000 for a down payment 4 years from now on a new Chevy Blazer.

PV = ?   i = 9% $5,000

Now   1   2   3   4 years
                    n = 4

Answer: The present value factor from Table 3 is .70843 (4 periods at 9%). The present value of $5,000 to be received in 4 years discounted at 9% is **$3,542.15** ($5,000 × .70843).

Present Value of an Annuity

The preceding discussion involved the discounting of only a single future amount. Businesses and individuals frequently engage in transactions in which a series of equal dollar amounts are to be received or paid periodically. Examples of a series of periodic receipts or payments are loan agreements, installment sales, mortgage notes, lease (rental) contracts, and pension obligations. These series of periodic receipts or payments are called **annuities**. In computing the present value of an annuity, it is necessary to know the (1) discount rate, (2) the number of discount periods, and (3) the amount of the periodic receipts or payments. To illustrate the computation of the present value of an annuity, assume that you will receive $1,000 cash annually for three years at a time when the discount rate is 10%. This situation is depicted in the following time diagram:

STUDY OBJECTIVE
••••••••••6••••••••••
Solve for present value of an annuity.

Illustration B-13

Time diagram for a 3-year annuity

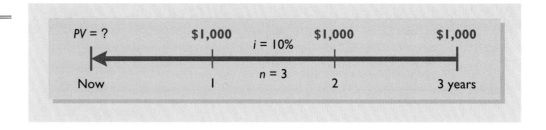

The present value in this situation may be computed as follows:

Illustration B-14

Present value of a series of future amounts computation

Future Amount	×	Present Value of 1 Factor at 10%	=	Present Value
$1,000 (One year away)		.90909		$ 909.09
1,000 (Two years away)		.82645		826.45
1,000 (Three years away)		.75132		751.32
		2.48686		**$2,486.86**

This method of calculation is required when the periodic cash flows are not uniform in each period. However, when the future receipts are the same in each period, there are two other ways to compute present value. First, the annual cash flow can be multiplied by the sum of the three present value factors. In the previous example, $1,000 × 2.48686 equals $2,486.86. Second, annuity tables may be used. As illustrated in Table 4 below, these tables show the present value of 1 to be received periodically for a given number of periods.

TABLE 4
PRESENT VALUE OF AN ANNUITY OF 1

(n) Periods	4%	5%	6%	8%	9%	10%	11 %	12%	15%
1	.96154	.95238	.94340	.92593	.91743	.90909	.90090	.89286	.86957
2	1.88609	1.85941	1.83339	1.78326	1.75911	1.73554	1.71252	1.69005	1.62571
3	2.77509	2.72325	2.67301	2.57710	2.53130	2.48685	2.44371	2.40183	2.28323
4	3.62990	3.54595	3.46511	3.31213	3.23972	3.16986	3.10245	3.03735	2.85498
5	4.45182	4.32948	4.21236	3.99271	3.88965	3.79079	3.69590	3.60478	3.35216
6	5.24214	5.07569	4.91732	4.62288	4.48592	4.35526	4.23054	4.11141	3.78448
7	6.00205	5.78637	5.58238	5.20637	5.03295	4.86842	4.71220	4.56376	4.16042
8	6.73274	6.46321	6.20979	5.74664	5.53482	5.33493	5.14612	4.96764	4.48732
9	7.43533	7.10782	6.80169	6.24689	5.99525	5.75902	5.53705	5.32825	4.77158
10	8.11090	7.72173	7.36009	6.71008	6.41766	6.14457	5.88923	5.65022	5.01877
11	8.76048	8.30641	7.88687	7.13896	6.80519	6.49506	6.20652	5.93770	5.23371
12	9.38507	8.86325	8.38384	7.53608	7.16073	6.81369	6.49236	6.19437	5.42062
13	9.98565	9.39357	8.85268	7.90378	7.48690	7.10336	6.74987	6.42355	5.58315
14	10.56312	9.89864	9.29498	8.24424	7.78615	7.36669	6.98187	6.62817	5.72448
15	11.11839	10.37966	9.71225	8.55948	8.06069	7.60608	7.19087	6.81086	5.84737
16	11.65230	10.83777	10.10590	8.85137	8.31256	7.82371	7.37916	6.97399	5.95424
17	12.16567	11.27407	10.47726	9.12164	8.54363	8.02155	7.54879	7.11963	6.04716
18	12.65930	11.68959	10.82760	9.37189	8.75563	8.20141	7.70162	7.24967	6.12797
19	13.13394	12.08532	11.15812	9.60360	8.95012	8.36492	7.83929	7.36578	6.19823
20	13.59033	12.46221	11.46992	9.81815	9.12855	8.51356	7.96333	7.46944	6.25933

From Table 4 it can be seen that the present value of an annuity of 1 factor for three periods at 10% is 2.48685.[1] This present value factor is the total of the three individual present value factors as shown in Illustration B-14. Applying this amount to the annual cash flow of $1,000 produces a present value of $2,486.85.

The following demonstration problem (Illustration B-15) illustrates how to use Table 4.

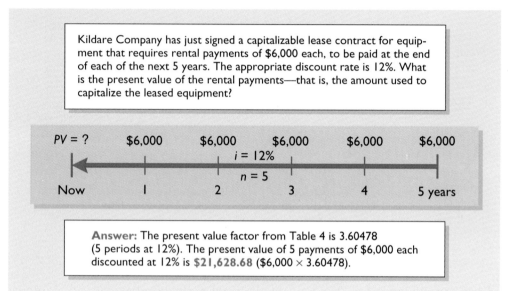

Kildare Company has just signed a capitalizable lease contract for equipment that requires rental payments of $6,000 each, to be paid at the end of each of the next 5 years. The appropriate discount rate is 12%. What is the present value of the rental payments—that is, the amount used to capitalize the leased equipment?

Answer: The present value factor from Table 4 is 3.60478 (5 periods at 12%). The present value of 5 payments of $6,000 each discounted at 12% is **$21,628.68** ($6,000 × 3.60478).

Time Periods and Discounting

In the preceding calculations, the discounting has been done on an annual basis using an annual interest rate. Discounting may also be done over shorter periods of time such as monthly, quarterly, or semiannually. When the time frame is less than one year, it is necessary to convert the annual interest rate to the applicable time frame. Assume, for example, that the investor in Illustration B-14 received $500 **semiannually** for three years instead of $1,000 annually. In this case, the number of periods becomes 6 (3 × 2), the discount rate is 5% (10% ÷ 2), the present value factor from Table 4 is 5.07569, and the present value of the future cash flows is $2,537.85 (5.07569 × $500). This amount is slightly higher than the $2,486.85 computed in Illustration B-14 because interest is computed twice during the same year; therefore interest is earned on the first half year's interest.

Computing the Present Value of a Long-Term Note or Bond

The present value (or market price) of a long-term note or bond is a function of three variables: (1) the payment amounts, (2) the length of time until the amounts are paid, and (3) the discount rate. Our illustration uses a 5-year bond issue.

STUDY OBJECTIVE
••••••••• **7** •••••••••

Compute the present value of notes and bonds.

---

[1]The difference of .00001 between 2.48686 and 2.48685 is due to rounding.

The first variable (dollars to be paid) is made up of two elements: (1) a series of interest payments (an annuity) and (2) the principal amount (a single sum). To compute the present value of the bond, both the interest payments and the principal amount must be discounted—two different computations. The time diagrams for a bond due in 5 years are shown in Illustration B-16.

Illustration B-16

Present value of a bond time diagram

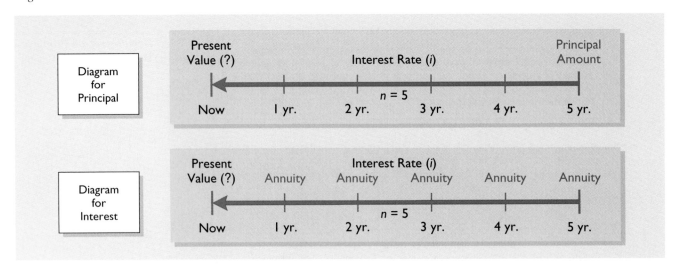

When the investor's discount rate is equal to the bond's contractual interest rate, the present value of the bonds will equal the face value of the bonds. To illustrate, assume a bond issue of 10%, 5-year bonds with a face value of $100,000 with interest payable **semiannually** on January 1 and July 1. If the discount rate is the same as the contractual rate, the bonds will sell at face value. In this case, the investor will receive (1) $100,000 at maturity and (2) a series of ten $5,000 interest payments [($100,000 × 10%) ÷ 2] over the term of the bonds. The length of time is expressed in terms of interest periods, in this case, 10, and the discount rate per interest period, 5%. The following time diagram (Illustration B-17) depicts the variables involved in this discounting situation:

Illustration B-17

Time diagram for present value of a 10%, 5-year bond paying interest semiannually

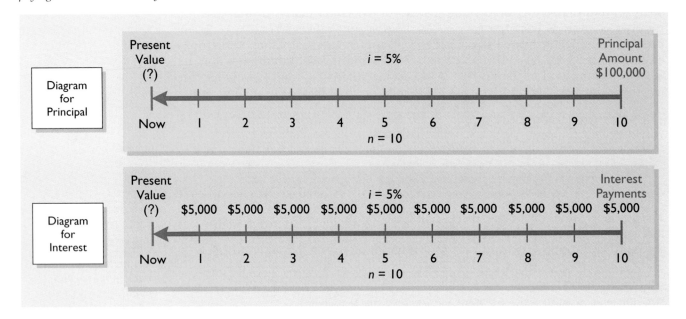

The computation of the present value of these bonds is shown below.

10% Contractual Rate—10% Discount Rate	
Present value of principal to be received at maturity	
$100,000 × PV of 1 due in 10 periods at 5%	
$100,000 × .61391 (Table 3)	$ 61,391
Present value of interest to be received periodically	
over the term of the bonds	
$5,000 × PV of 1 due periodically for 10 periods at 5%	
$5,000 × 7.72173 (Table 4)	38,609*
Present value of bonds	$100,000

*(Rounded).

Now assume that the investor's required rate of return is 12%, not 10%. The future amounts are again $100,000 and $5,000, respectively, but now a discount rate of 6% (12% ÷ 2) must be used. The present value of the bonds is $92,639, as computed below:

10% Contractual Rate—12% Discount Rate	
Present value of principal to be received at maturity	
$100,000 × .55839 (Table 3)	$55,839
Present value of interest to be received periodically	
over the term of the bonds	
$5,000 × 7.36009 (Table 4)	36,800
Present value of bonds	$92,639

Conversely, if the discount rate is 8% and the contractual rate is 10%, the present value of the bonds is $108,111, computed as follows:

10% Contractual Rate—8% Discount Rate	
Present value of principal to be received at maturity	
$100,000 × .67556 (Table 3)	$ 67,556
Present value of interest to be received periodically	
over the term of the bonds	
$5,000 × 8.11090 (Table 4)	40,555
Present value of bonds	$108,111

►Technology in Action

 As discussed in this appendix, the selling price of the bonds can be determined via present value formulas. Many computer spreadsheets and computer programs can perform the discounting functions given the basic information of the situation.

The above discussion relied on present value tables in solving present value problems. Electronic hand-held calculators may also be used to compute present values without the use of these tables. Some calculators, especially the "business" or "MBA" type calculators, have present value (PV) functions that allow you to calculate present values by merely inputing the proper amount, discount rate, periods, and pressing the PV key.

Summary of Study Objectives

1. *Distinguish between simple and compound interest.* Simple interest is computed on the principal only while compound interest is computed on the principal and any interest earned that has not been withdrawn.

2. *Solve for future value of a single amount.* Prepare a time diagram of the problem. Identify the principal amount, the number of compounding periods, and the interest rate. Using the future value of 1 table, multiply the principal amount by the future value factor specified at the intersection of the number of periods and the interest rate.

3. *Solve for future value of an annuity.* Prepare a time diagram of the problem. Identify the amount of the periodic payments, the number of compounding periods, and the interest rate. Using the future value of an annuity of 1 table, multiply the amount of the payments by the future value factor specified at the intersection of the number of periods and interest rate.

4. *Identify the variables fundamental to solving present value problems.* The following three variables are fundamental to solving present value problems: (1) the future amount, (2) the number of periods, and (3) the interest rate (the discount rate).

5. *Solve for present value of a single amount.* Prepare a time diagram of the problem. Identify the future amount,

the number of discounting periods, and the discount (interest) rate. Using the present value of a single amount table, multiply the future amount by the present value factor specified at the intersection of the number of periods and the discount rate.

6. *Solve for present value of an annuity.* Prepare a time diagram of the problem. Identify the future amounts (annuities), the number of discounting periods, and the discount (interest) rate. Using the present value of an annuity of 1 table, multiply the amount of the annuity by the present value factor specified at the intersection of the number of periods and the interest rate.

7. *Compute the present value of notes and bonds.* Determine the present value of the principal amount: Multiply the principal amount (a single future amount) by the present value factor (from the present value of 1 table) intersecting at the number of periods (number of interest payments) and the discount rate. Determine the present value of the series of interest payments: Multiply the amount of the interest payment by the present value factor (from the present value of an annuity of 1 table) intersecting at the number of periods (number of interest payments) and the discount rate. Add the present value of the principal amount to the present value of the interest payments to arrive at the present value of the note or bond.

GLOSSARY

Annuity   A series of equal dollar amounts to be paid or received periodically. (p. B5.)

Compound interest   The interest computed on the principal and any interest earned that has not been paid or received. (p. B2.)

Discounting the future amount(s)   The process of determining present value. (p. B8.)

Future value of a single amount   The value at a future date of a given amount invested assuming compound interest. (p. B3.)

Future value of an annuity   The sum of all the payments or receipts plus the accumulated compound interest on them. (p. B5.)

Interest   Payment for the use of another's money. (p. B2.)

Present value   The value now of a given amount to be invested or received in the future assuming compound interest. (p. B8.)

Present value of an annuity   A series of future receipts or payments discounted to their value now assuming compound interest. (p. B11)

Principal   The amount borrowed or invested. (p. B2.)

Simple interest   The interest computed on the principal only. (p. B2.)

BRIEF EXERCISES (Use Tables To Solve Exercises)

Compute the future value of a single amount.

BEB–1   Don Smith invested $5,000 at 6% annual interest, and left the money invested without withdrawing any of the interest for 10 years. At the end of the 10 years, Don withdrew the accumulated amount of money. (a) What amount did Don withdraw assuming the investment earns simple interest? (b) What amount did Don withdraw assuming the investment earns interest compounded annually?

BEB–2 For each of the following cases, indicate (a) to what interest rate columns and (b) to what number of periods you would refer in looking up the future value factor.

Using future value tables.

1. In Table 1 (future value of 1):

	Annual Rate	Number of Years Invested	Compounded
a.	6%	5	Annually
b.	5%	3	Semiannually

2. In Table 2 (future value of an annuity of 1):

	Annual Rate	Number of Years Invested	Compounded
a.	5%	10	Annually
b.	4%	6	Semiannually

BEB–3 Porter Company signed a lease for an office building for a period of 10 years. Under the lease agreement, a security deposit of $10,000 is made. The deposit will be returned at the expiration of the lease with interest compounded at 5% per year. What amount will Porter receive at the time the lease expires?

Compute the future value of a single amount.

BEB–4 Gordon Company issued $1,000,000, 10-year bonds and agreed to make annual sinking fund deposits of $80,000. The deposits are made at the end of each year into an account paying 5% annual interest. What amount will be in the sinking fund at the end of 10 years?

Compute the future value of an annuity.

BEB–5 David & Kathy Hatcher invested $5,000 in a savings account paying 6% annual interest when their daughter, Sue, was born. They also deposited $1,000 on each of her birthdays until she was 18 (including her 18th birthday). How much will be in the savings account on her 18th birthday (after the last deposit)?

Compute the future value of a single amount and of an annuity.

BEB–6 Ron Watson borrowed $20,000 on July 1, 1996. This amount plus accrued interest at 6% compounded anually is to be repaid on July 1, 2001. How much will Ron have to repay on July 1, 2001?

Compute the future value of a single amount.

BEB–7 For each of the following cases, indicate (a) to what interest rate columns and (b) to what number of periods you would refer in looking up the discount rate.

Using present-value tables.

1. In Table 3 (present value of 1):

	Annual Rate	Number of Years Involved	Discounts Per Year
a.	12%	6	Annually
b.	10%	15	Annually
c.	8%	8	Semiannually

2. In Table 4 (present value of an annuity of 1):

	Annual Rate	Number of Years Involved	Number of Payments Involved	Frequency of Payments
a.	12%	20	20	Annually
b.	10%	5	5	Annually
c.	8%	4	8	Semiannually

BEB–8 (a) What is the present value of $10,000 due 8 periods from now, discounted at 8%? (b) What is the present value of $10,000 to be received at the end of each of 6 periods, discounted at 9%?

Detemining present values.

BEB–9 Smolinski Company is considering an investment which will return a lump sum of $500,000 five years from now. What amount should Smolinski Company pay for this investment to earn a 15% return?

Compute the present value of a single amount investment.

BEB–10 Pizzeria Company earns 11% on an investment that will return $875,000 eight years from now. What is the amount Pizzeria should invest now to earn this rate of return?

Compute the present value of a single amount investment.

BEB–11 Kilarny Company is considering investing in an annuity contract that will return $20,000 annually at the end of each year for 15 years. What amount should Kilarny Company pay for this investment if it earns a 6% return?

Compute the present value of an annuity investment.

Compute the present value of an annuity investment.	**BEB–12** Zarita Enterprises earns 11% on an investment that pays back $110,000 at the end of each of the next four years. What is the amount Zarita Enterprises invested to earn the 11% rate of return?
Compute the present value of bonds.	**BEB–13** Hernandez Railroad Co. is about to issue $100,000 of 10-year bonds paying a 12% interest rate, with interest payable semiannually. The discount rate for such securities is 10%. How much can Hernandez expect to receive for the sale of these bonds?
Compute the present value of bonds.	**BEB–14** Assume the same information as BEJ–9 except that the discount rate was 12% instead of 10%. In this case, how much can Hernandez expect to receive from the sale of these bonds?
Compute the present value of a note.	**BEB–15** Caledonian Taco Company receives a $50,000, 6-year note bearing interest of 11% (paid annually) from a customer at a time when the discount rate is 12%. What is the present value of the note received by Caledonian?
Compute the present value of bonds.	**BEB–16** Galway Bay Enterprises issued 10%, 8-year, $2,000,000 par value bonds that pay interest semiannually on October 1 and April 1. The bonds are dated April 1, 1998, and are issued on that date. The discount rate of interest for such bonds on April 1, 1998, is 12%. What cash proceeds did Galway Bay receive from issuance of the bonds?
Compute the present value of a machine for purposes of making a purchase decision.	**BEB–17** Barney Googal owns a garage and is contemplating purchasing a tire retreading machine for $16,280. After estimating costs and revenues, Barney projects a net cash flow from the retreading machine of $2,790 annually for 8 years. Barney hopes to earn a return of 11 percent on such investments. What is the present value of the retreading operation? Should Barney Googal purchase the retreading machine?
Compute the present value of a note.	**BEB–18** Hung-Chao Yu Company issues a 10%, 6-year mortgage note on January 1, 1998 to obtain financing for new equipment. Land is used as collateral for the note. The terms provide for semiannual installment payments, of $112,825. What were the cash proceeds received from the issuance of the note?
Compute the maximum price to pay for a machine.	**BEB–19** Ramos Company is considering purchasing equipment. The equipment will produce the following cash flows: Year 1, $30,000; Year 2, $40,000; Year 3, $50,000. Ramos requires a minimum rate of return of 15%. What is the maximum price Ramos should pay for this equipment?
Compute the interest rate on a single amount.	**BEB–20** If Kerry Rodriquez invests $1,827 now and she will receive $10,000 at the end of 15 years. What annual rate of interest will Kerry earn on her investment? (Hint: Use Table 3.)
Compute the number of periods of a single amount.	**BEB–21** Maloney Cork has been offered the opportunity of investing $24,719 now. The investment will earn 15% per year and will at the end of that time return Maloney $100,000. How many years must Maloney wait to receive $100,000? (Hint: Use Table 3.)
Compute the interest rate on an annuity.	**BEB–22** Annie Dublin purchased an investment for $11,469.92. From this investment, she will receive $1,000 annually for the next 20 years starting one year from now. What rate of interest will Annie's investment be earning for her? (Hint: Use Table 4.)
Compute the number of periods of an annuity.	**BEB–23** Andy Sanchez invests $8,851.37 now for a series of $1,000 annual returns beginning one year from now. Andy will earn a return of 8% on the initial investment. How many annual payments of $1,000 will Andy receive? (Hint: Use Table 4.)

PAYROLL ACCOUNTING

After studying this appendix, you should be able to:

1. Discuss the objectives of internal control for payroll.
2. Compute and record the payroll for a pay period.
3. Describe and record employer payroll taxes.

Payroll and related fringe benefits often constitute a substantial percentage of current liabilities. In addition, employee compensation is often the most significant expense that a company incurs. For example, General Motors recently reported total employees of 516,000 and labor costs of $31.3 billion. Add to labor costs such fringe benefits as health insurance, life insurance, disability insurance, and so on, and you can see why proper accounting and control of payroll are so important.

It should be emphasized that payroll accounting involves more than paying employees' wages. Companies are required by law to maintain payroll records for each employee, file and pay payroll taxes, and comply with numerous state and federal tax laws applicable to employee compensation. Accounting for payroll has become much more complex as a result of these regulations.

◤Payroll Defined

The term "payroll" pertains to all salaries and wages paid to employees. Managerial, administrative, and sales personnel are generally paid salaries, which are often expressed in terms of a specified amount per month or per year. For example, the faculty and administrative personnel at your college or university are paid salaries. In contrast, store clerks, factory employees, and manual laborers are normally paid wages, which are based on a rate per hour, or on a piecework basis (such as per unit of product). Frequently, the terms "salaries" and "wages" are used interchangeably.

The term "payroll" does not extend to payments made for personal service by professionals such as certified public accountants, attorneys, and architects. Such professionals are independent contractors, and payments to them are called **fees**, rather than salaries and wages. This distinction is important because government regulations relating to the payment and reporting of payroll taxes apply only to employees.

◤Importance of Internal Control to Payroll

Internal control was introduced in Chapter 7. As applied to payrolls, the objectives of internal control are (1) to safeguard company assets against unauthorized payments of payrolls and (2) to assure the accuracy and reliability of the accounting records pertaining to payrolls.

Unfortunately, irregularities often result if internal control is lax. Overstating hours, using unauthorized pay rates, adding fictitious employees to the payroll, continuing terminated employees on the payroll, and distributing duplicate payroll checks are all methods of stealing from a company. Moreover, inaccurate records will result in incorrect paychecks, financial statements, and payroll tax returns.

Payroll activities involve four functions: hiring employees, timekeeping, preparing the payroll, and paying the payroll. For an internal control system to work effectively, these four functions should be assigned to different departments or individuals. To illustrate these functions in more detail, we will examine the case of Academy Company and one of its employees, Michael Jordan.

▶**T**echnology in **A**ction

A Senate hearing revealed that the U.S. Army spent $8 million on unauthorized pay, including payments to 76 deserters and six "ghost" soldiers. The underlying cause was a computer system so lax that it was possible to create new pay records and destroy old ones without leaving an audit trail.

Source: Ann Arbor News, April 13, 1994, p. A4.

Hiring Employees

Posting job openings, screening and interviewing applicants, and hiring employees are responsibilities of the personnel department. From a control standpoint, the personnel department provides significant documentation and authorization. When an employee is hired, the personnel department prepares an authorization form like the one used by Academy Company for Michael Jordan shown in Illustration C-1.

Illustration C-1

Personnel authorization form

ACADEMY COMPANY

Employee Name __Jordan,__ __Michael__ ___ Starting Date __9/01/92__
　　　　　　　　LAST　　　　　FIRST　　　MI

Classification __Skilled-Level 10__　　　Social Security No. __329-36-9547__

Department __Shipping__　　　　　　　　Division __Entertainment__

NEW HIRE	Classification __Clerk__　　Salary Grade __Level 10__ Trans. from Temp. ☐ Rate $__10.00__ per __hour__　　Bonus __N/A__　　Non-exempt ☒ Exempt ☐
RATE CHANGE	New Rate $ __12.00__　　Effective Date __9/1/94__ Present Rate $ __10.00__ Merit ☒ Promotion ☐ Decrease ☐　　Other____ Previous Increase Date __None__　　Amount $____ per ____ Type ____
SEPARATION	Resignation ☐ Discharge ☐ Retirement ☐　Reason ____ ____ Leave of absence ☐　From ____ to ____　Type ____ Last Day Worked ____
APPROVALS	_____BEW_____　__9/1/92__　　_____EMW_____　__9-1-94__ BRANCH OR DEPT. MANAGER　DATE　　DIVISION V.P.　　DATE 　　　　　　　　　　　　　　__James E. Speer__ 　　　　　　　　　　　　　　PERSONNEL DEPARTMENT

Hiring Employees

Personnel

Personnel department documents and authorizes employment.

　　The authorization form is sent to the payroll department, where it is used to place the new employee on the payroll. A chief concern of the personnel department is ensuring the accuracy of this form. The reason is quite simple: one of the most common types of payroll frauds is adding fictitious employees to the payroll.

　　The personnel department is also responsible for authorizing (1) changes in pay rates during employment and (2) terminations of employment. In each instance, the authorization should be in writing, and a copy of the change in status should be sent to the payroll department. Note in Illustration C-1 that Jordan received a pay increase of $2 per hour.

Timekeeping

Timekeeping

Supervisors monitor hours worked through time cards and time reports.

Another area in which internal control is important is timekeeping. Hourly employees are usually required to record time worked by "punching" a time clock. The time of arrival and departure are automatically recorded by the employee when he or she inserts a time card into the clock. The time card for Michael Jordan is shown in Illustration C-2.

In large companies, time clock procedures are often monitored by a supervisor or security guard to make sure an employee punches only one card. At the end of the pay period, the employee's supervisor is required to approve the hours shown by signing the time card. When overtime hours are involved, approval by a supervisor is usually mandatory to guard against unauthorized overtime.

Illustration C-2

Time card

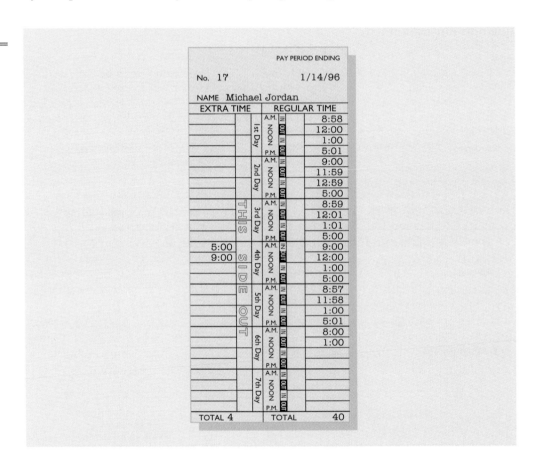

The approved time card is then sent to the payroll department. For salaried employees, a manually prepared weekly or monthly time report kept by a supervisor may be used to record time worked.

Preparing the Payroll

Preparing the Payroll

Two (or more) employees verify payroll amounts; supervisor approves.

The payroll is prepared in the payroll department on the basis of two sources of input: (1) personnel department authorizations and (2) approved time cards. Because of the numerous calculations involved in determining gross wages and payroll deductions, it is customary for a second payroll department employee,

►Accounting in Action ▸ *Business Insight*

The annual pay raise may soon be passé. Large companies such as American Express and Eastman Kodak and some small companies are linking pay more directly to the performance of both the worker and the company. The performance measures include product quality, on-time delivery, and customer satisfaction. If the company and the worker have a good year, a fatter paycheck is the reward. If the reverse is true, down goes the paycheck. Under the plan, a worker's base annual salary remains the same from year to year.

working independently, to verify all amounts, and a payroll department supervisor then approves the payroll. The payroll department is also responsible for preparing (but not signing) payroll checks, maintaining payroll records, and preparing payroll tax returns.

►Accounting in Action ▸ *Business Insight*

Payroll processing is considered by many small business owners to be a tedious and painful chore fraught with legal and tax headaches. As a result, service bureaus that process payrolls for small businesses are becoming increasingly popular. Small businesses appreciate the advantages service bureaus offer: relatively low cost, simplicity, confidentiality, accuracy, and keeping up to date on changes in tax rates and laws.

Paying the Payroll

The payroll is paid by the treasurer's department. **Payment by check minimizes the risk of loss from theft, and the endorsed check provides proof of payment**. For good internal control, payroll checks should be prenumbered, and all checks should be accounted for. All checks must be signed by the treasurer (or a designated agent), and their distribution to employees should be controlled by the treasurer's department. Checks may be distributed by the treasurer or paymaster.

If the payroll is paid in currency, it is customary to have a second person count the cash in each pay envelope and for the paymaster to obtain a signed receipt from the employee upon payment. Thus, if alleged discrepancies arise, adequate safeguards have been established to protect each party involved.

Paying the Payroll

Treasurer signs and distributes checks.

▾Determining the Payroll

Determining the payroll involves computing (1) gross earnings, (2) payroll deductions, and (3) net pay.

Gross Earnings

Gross earnings are the total compensation earned by an employee. There are three major types of gross earnings: wages, salaries, and bonuses.

Total **wages** for an employee are determined by multiplying the hours worked by the hourly rate of pay. In addition to the hourly pay rate, most companies are required by law to pay hourly workers a minimum of one and one-half times the regular hourly rate for overtime work in excess of 8 hours per day

STUDY OBJECTIVE
••••••••▾2•••••••••
Compute and record the payroll for a pay period.

or 40 hours per week. For example, companies involved in interstate commerce are required by the Federal Fair Labor Standards Act to pay one and one-half times the regular wage rate. In addition, many employers pay overtime rates for work done at night, on weekends, and on holidays. The computation of Michael Jordan's gross earnings (total wages) for the 44 hours shown on his time card for the weekly pay period ending January 14 is as follows:

Illustration C-3

Computation of total wages

Type of Pay	Hours	×	Rate	=	Gross Earnings
Regular	40	×	$12.00	=	$480.00
Overtime	4	×	18.00	=	72.00
Total wages					$552.00

This computation assumes that Jordan receives one and one-half times his regular hourly rate ($12.00 × 1.5) for his overtime hours. Union contracts often require that overtime rates be as much as twice the regular rates.

The **salary** for an employee is generally based on a monthly or yearly rate rather than on an hourly basis. These rates are then applied ratably to the payroll periods used by the company. Most executive and administrative positions are salaried. The Federal Fair Labor Standards Act does not require overtime pay for such positions.

▶ *Ethics note*

Bonuses often reward outstanding individual performance; however, a successful corporation also needs considerable teamwork. A challenge is to motivate individuals while preventing an unethical team member from taking another's idea for his or her own advantage.

Many companies have bonus agreements for management personnel and other employees. For example, a recent survey indicated that over 94% of the largest manufacturing companies in the United States provide annual bonuses to their key executives. Bonus arrangements may be based on such factors as increased sales or net income. Bonuses may be paid in cash and/or by granting executives and employees the opportunity to acquire shares of stock in the company at favorable prices (called stock option plans). Bonuses have become very lucrative, as companies attempt to retain the services of key executives—so lucrative, in fact, that they have come under intense public scrutiny.

▲ **A**ccounting in **A**ction ▶ *Business Insight*

In 1995 Amoco Corporation employees received shares of the company's stock equal to 3.5% of their salaries as a result of the company's strong total return to shareholders. Amoco's performance plan awards shares to employees when the return to shareholders meets or exceeds the average of seven major oil companies. Amoco's return of 18.8% was the second highest of the group of competitors.

Source: Denver Post, January 6, 1995.

Payroll Deductions

As anyone who has received a paycheck knows, gross earnings are usually very different from the amount actually received. The difference is attributable to payroll deductions. Payroll deductions do not result in payroll tax expense to the employer. The employer serves only as a collection agency, and it subsequently transfers the deductions to the government and designated recipients. Payroll deductions may be mandatory or voluntary. The former are required by law and consist of FICA taxes and income taxes. The latter are at the option of the employee. Illustration C-4 summarizes the types of payroll deductions.

Illustration C-4

Payroll deductions

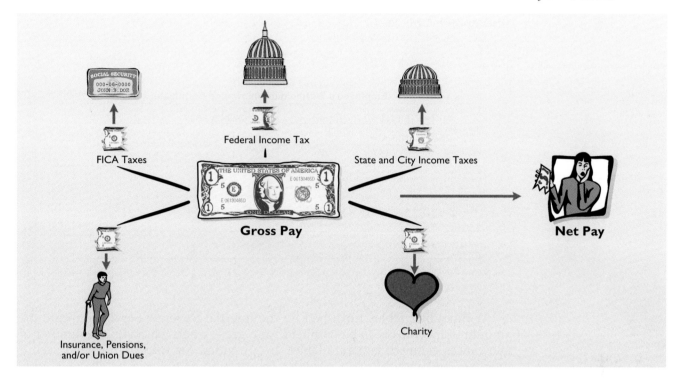

FICA Taxes

In 1937 Congress enacted the Federal Insurance Contribution Act (FICA). **FICA taxes are designed to provide workers with supplemental retirement, employment disability, and medical benefits.** In 1965, benefits were expanded to include Medicare for individuals over 65 years of age. The benefits are financed by a tax levied on employees' earnings. FICA taxes are commonly referred to as **social security taxes**.

   The tax rate and the tax base for FICA taxes are set by Congress, and they are changed intermittently. When FICA taxes were first imposed, the rate was 1% on the first $3,000 of gross earnings, or a maximum of $30 per year. The rate and base have changed dramatically since that time! In 1995, that rate was 7.65% (6.2% Social Security and 1.45% Medicare) on the first $61,200 of gross earnings for each employee, or a maximum of $4,681.80.[1] For purpose of illustration in this chapter, we will assume a rate of 8% on the first $60,000 of gross earnings, or a maximum of $4,800. Using the 8% rate, the FICA withholding for Jordan for the weekly pay period ending January 14 is $44.16 ($552 × 8%).

Income Taxes

Under the United States pay-as-you-go system of federal income taxes, employers are required to withhold income taxes from employees each pay period. The amount to be withheld is determined by three variables: (1) the employee's gross earnings; (2) the number of allowances claimed by the employee for herself or himself, his or her spouse, and other dependents; and (3) the length of the pay

---

[1]The Medicare provision also includes a tax of 1.45% on gross earnings in excess of $61,200. In our end-of-chapter materials, gross earnings will not exceed $61,200.

period. **To indicate to the Internal Revenue Service the number of allowances claimed, the employee must complete an** Employee's Withholding Allowance Certificate (Form W-4). As shown in Illustration C-5, Michael Jordan claims two allowances on his W-4.

Illustration C-5

W-4 form

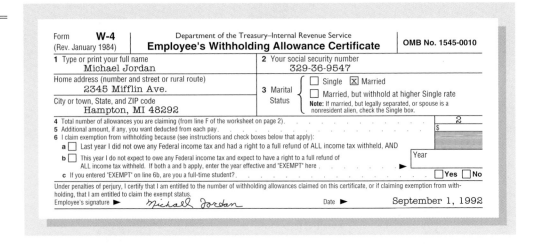

Withholding tables furnished by the Internal Revenue Service indicate the amount of income tax to be withheld from gross wages based on the number of allowances claimed. Separate tables are provided for weekly, biweekly, semi-monthly, and monthly pay periods. The portion of the withholding tax table for Michael Jordan (assuming he earns $552 per week) is shown in Illustration C-6. As indicated in the table, for a weekly salary of $552 with two allowances, the income tax to be withheld is $50.

Illustration C-6

Withholding tax table

MARRIED Persons — **WEEKLY** Payroll Period
(For Wages Paid in 1995)

If the wages are —		And the number of withholding allowances claimed is —										
At least	But less than	0	1	2	3	4	5	6	7	8	9	10
		The amount of income tax to be withheld is —										
490	500	56	49	41	34	27	20	13	5	0	0	0
500	510	57	50	43	36	28	21	14	7	0	0	0
510	520	59	52	44	37	30	23	16	8	1	0	0
520	530	60	53	46	39	31	24	17	10	3	0	0
530	540	62	55	47	40	33	26	19	11	4	0	0
540	550	63	56	49	42	34	27	20	13	6	0	0
550	560	65	58	50	43	36	29	22	14	7	0	0
560	570	66	59	52	45	37	30	23	16	9	1	0
570	580	68	61	53	46	39	32	25	17	10	3	0
580	590	69	62	55	48	40	33	26	19	12	4	0
590	600	71	64	56	49	42	35	28	20	13	6	0
600	610	72	65	58	51	43	36	29	22	15	7	0
610	620	74	67	59	52	45	38	31	23	16	9	2
620	630	75	68	61	54	46	39	32	25	18	10	3
630	640	77	70	62	55	48	41	34	26	19	12	5
640	650	78	71	64	57	49	42	35	28	21	13	6
650	660	80	73	65	58	51	44	37	29	22	15	8
660	670	81	74	67	60	52	45	38	31	24	16	9
670	680	83	76	68	61	54	47	40	32	25	18	11
680	690	84	77	70	63	55	48	41	34	27	19	12

Most states and some cities also require employers to withhold income taxes from the earnings of employees. As a general rule, the amounts to be withheld are determined by applying a percentage specified in the state revenue code to the amount withheld for the federal income tax or to the employee's earnings. For the sake of simplicity, we have assumed that Jordan's wages are subject to state income taxes of 2%, or $11.04 (2% × $552).

There is no limit on the amount of gross earnings subject to income tax withholdings. In fact, the higher the earnings, the higher the amount of taxes withheld.

Voluntary Deductions

Employees may voluntarily authorize withholdings for charitable, retirement, and other purposes. All voluntary deductions from gross earnings should be authorized in writing by the employee. The authorization(s) may be made individually or as part of a group plan. Deductions for charitable organizations, such as the United Fund, or for financial arrangements, such as U.S. savings bonds and repayment of loans from company credit unions are made individually. In contrast, deductions for union dues, health and life insurance, and pension plans are often made on a group basis. For purpose of illustration, we will assume that Jordan has voluntary deductions of $10 for the United Fund and $5 for union dues.

▶ Technology in Action

 With the widespread use of microcomputers, the error-prone task of manually searching tax tables for the proper payroll deductions is becoming extinct even in small businesses. Now computers with entire tax tables stored internally perform this table lookup function without error and accurately calculate all payroll information.

Net Pay

Net pay is determined by subtracting payroll deductions from gross earnings. For Michael Jordan, net pay for the pay period is $431.80, computed as follows:

Gross earnings		$552.00
Payroll deductions:		
FICA taxes	$44.16	
Federal income taxes	50.00	
State income taxes	11.04	
United Fund	10.00	
Union dues	5.00	120.20
Net pay		**$431.80**

Illustration C-7

Computation of net pay

Assuming that Michael Jordan's wages for each week during the year are $552, total wages for the year are $28,704 (52 × $552). Thus, all of Jordan's wages are subject to FICA tax during the year. However, if an employee's wages are $1,200 per week, or $62,400 for the year, only the first $60,000 is subject to FICA taxes. In such case, the maximum FICA withholdings would be $4,800 ($60,000 × 8%).

Recording the Payroll

Recording the payroll involves maintaining payroll department records, recognizing payroll expenses and liabilities, and recording payment of the payroll.

Maintaining Payroll Department Records

To comply with state and federal laws, an employer must keep a cumulative record of each employee's gross earnings, deductions, and net pay during the year. The record that provides this information and other essential data is the employee earnings record. Michael Jordan's employee earnings record is shown in Illustration C-8.

Illustration C-8

Employee earnings record

ACADEMY COMPANY
Employee Earnings Record
For the Year 1996

Name: Michael Jordan   Address: 2345 Mifflin Ave.

Social Security Number: 329-36-9547   Hampton, Michigan 48292

Date of Birth: December 24, 1962   Telephone: 238-9051

Date Employed: September 1, 1992   Date Employment Ended:

Sex: Male   Exemptions: 2

Single: _____   Married: X

1996 Period Ending	Total Hours	Gross Earnings				Deductions						Payment	
		Regular	Overtime	Total	Cumulative	FICA	Fed. Inc. Tax	State Inc. Tax	United Fund	Union Dues	Total	Net Amount	Check No.
1/7	42	480.00	36.00	516.00	516.00	41.28	44.00	10.32	10.00	5.00	110.60	405.40	974
1/14	44	480.00	72.00	552.00	1,068.00	44.16	50.00	11.04	10.00	5.00	120.20	431.80	1028
1/21	43	480.00	54.00	534.00	1,602.00	42.72	47.00	10.68	10.00	5.00	115.40	418.60	1077
1/28	42	480.00	36.00	516.00	2,118.00	41.28	44.00	10.32	10.00	5.00	110.60	405.40	1133
Jan. Total		1,920.00	198.00	2,118.00		169.44	185.00	42.36	40.00	20.00	456.80	1,661.20	

A separate earnings record is kept for each employee, and it is updated after each pay period. The cumulative payroll data on the earnings record are used by the employer in (1) determining when an employee has earned the maximum earnings subject to FICA taxes, (2) filing state and federal payroll tax returns (as explained later in the chapter), and (3) providing each employee with a statement of gross earnings and tax withholdings for the year, as shown in Illustration C-11 on page C15.

In addition to employee earnings records, many companies find it useful to prepare a payroll register to accumulate the gross earnings, deductions, and net pay by employee for each pay period. It provides the documentation for preparing a paycheck for each employee. The payroll register is presented in Illustration C-9, with the data for Michael Jordan shown in the wages section. In this example, Academy Company's total payroll is $17,210, as shown in the gross pay column.

Illustration C-9

Payroll register

ACADEMY COMPANY
Payroll Register
For the Week Ending January 14, 1996

Employee	Total Hours	Earnings			Deductions						Paid		Accounts Debited	
		Regular	Over-time	Gross	FICA	Federal Income Tax	State Income Tax	United Fund	Union Dues	Total	Net Pay	Check No.	Office Salaries Expense	Wages Expense
Office Salaries														
Arnold, Patricia	40	580.00		580.00	46.40	62.00	11.60	15.00		135.00	445.00	998	580.00	
Canton, Matthew	40	590.00		590.00	47.20	64.00	11.80	20.00		143.00	447.00	999	590.00	
Mueller, William	40	530.00		530.00	42.40	55.00	10.60	11.00		119.00	411.00	1000	530.00	
Subtotal		5,200.00		5,200.00	416.00	1,090.00	104.00	120.00		1,730.00	3,470.00		5,200.00	
Wages														
Bennett, Robin	42	480.00	36.00	516.00	41.28	44.00	10.32	18.00	5.00	118.60	397.40	1025		516.00
Jordan, Michael	44	480.00	72.00	552.00	44.16	50.00	11.04	10.00	5.00	120.20	431.80	1028		552.00
Milroy, Lee	43	480.00	54.00	534.00	42.72	47.00	10.68	10.00	5.00	115.40	418.60	1029		534.00
Subtotal		11,000.00	1,010.00	12,010.00	960.80	2,400.00	240.20	301.50	115.00	4,017.50	7,992.50			12,010.00
Total		16,200.00	1,010.00	17,210.00	1,376.80	3,490.00	344.20	421.50	115.00	5,747.50	11,462.50		5,200.00	12,010.00

Note that this record is a listing of each employee's payroll data for the pay period. In some companies, a payroll register is a journal or book of original entry, and postings are made directly to ledger accounts from the register. In other companies, the payroll register is a memorandum record that provides the data for a general journal entry and subsequent posting to the ledger accounts. In the Academy Company situation, the latter procedure is followed. The main payroll report provided by the computer at many companies is the payroll register.

►*T*echnology in *A*ction

In addition to supplying the entry to record the payroll, the output for a computerized payroll system would include (1) payroll checks, (2) a payroll check register sorted by check and department, and (3) updated employee earnings records which become the source for monthly, quarterly, and annual reporting of wages to taxing agencies.

Recognizing Payroll Expenses and Liabilities

From the payroll register in Illustration C-9, a journal entry is made to record the payroll. For the week ending January 14 the entry is:

Jan. 14	Office Salaries Expense	5,200.00	
	Wages Expense	12,010.00	
	FICA Taxes Payable		1,376.80
	Federal Income Taxes Payable		3,490.00
	State Income Taxes Payable		344.20
	United Fund Payable		421.50
	Union Dues Payable		115.00
	Salaries and Wages Payable		11,462.50
	(To record payroll for the week ending January 14)		

Specific liability accounts are credited for the mandatory and voluntary deductions made during the pay period. In the example, debits to Office Salaries and Wages Expense are used for gross earnings because office workers are on a salary and other employees are paid on an hourly rate. In other cases, there may be additional debits such as Store Salaries and Sales Salaries. The amount credited to Salaries and Wages Payable is the sum of the individual checks the employees will receive.

Recording Payment of the Payroll

Payment by check is made either from the employer's regular bank account or a payroll bank account. Each check is usually accompanied by a detachable **statement of earnings** document that shows the employee's gross earnings, payroll deductions, and net pay. The Academy Company uses its regular bank account for payroll checks. The check and statement of earnings for Michael Jordan are shown in Illustration C-10.

Illustration C-10

Check and statement of earnings

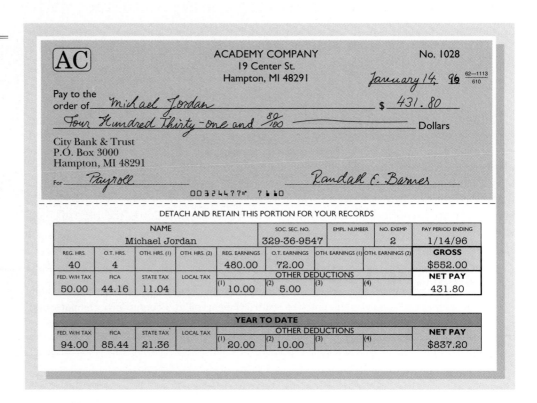

Following payment of the payroll, the check numbers are entered in the payroll register. The entry to record payment of the payroll for Academy Company is as follows:

Jan. 14	Salaries and Wages Payable	11,462.50	
	Cash		11,462.50
	(To record payment of payroll)		

When currency is used in payment, one check is prepared for the net pay. The check is then cashed, and the coins and currency are inserted in individual pay envelopes for disbursement to individual employees.

Before You Go On . . .

► *Review It*

1. Identify two internal control procedures that are applicable to each payroll function.
2. What are the primary sources of gross earnings?
3. What payroll deductions are (a) mandatory and (b) voluntary?
4. What account titles are used in recording a payroll, assuming only mandatory payroll deductions are involved?

► *Do It*

Your cousin Stan is establishing a house-cleaning business and will have a number of employees working for him. From his prior work experience, he is aware that documentation procedures are an important part of internal control. However, he is confused about the difference between an employee earnings record and a payroll register. He asks you to explain the principal differences, because he wants to be sure that he sets up the proper payroll procedures.

Reasoning: You may need to review the material on payroll department records and study Illustrations C-8 and C-9 in order to identify and explain the differences for Stan.

Solution: An employee earnings record is kept for *each* employee. It shows gross earnings, payroll deductions, and net pay for each pay period. It provides cumulative payroll data for that employee. In contrast, a payroll register is a listing of *all* employees' gross earnings, payroll deductions, and net pay for each pay period. It is the documentation for preparing paychecks and for recording the payroll. Of course, Stan will need to keep both documents.

Related exercise material: BEC–1, BEC–2, BEC–3, EC–1, EC–2, EC–3, and EC–4.

▼*E*mployer Payroll Taxes

Payroll tax expense for businesses, both large and small, results from three taxes **levied on employers** by governmental agencies. These taxes are: FICA, federal unemployment tax, and state unemployment tax. Each of these taxes plus such items as paid vacations and pensions are collectively referred to as "fringe benefits." As indicated earlier, the cost of fringe benefits in many companies is substantial.

STUDY OBJECTIVE
••••••••••**3**••••••••••
Describe and record employer payroll taxes.

FICA Taxes

We have seen that each employee must pay FICA taxes. The employer must match each employee's FICA contribution. The matching contribution results in **payroll tax expense** to the employer. The employer's tax is subject to the same rate and maximum earnings applicable to the employee. The account, FICA

►*A*ccounting in *A*ction ► *Business Insight*

Facing a rising tide of disability applications and a backlog of more than 1 million cases, the Social Security Administration plans to shorten the time for processing a claim by two-thirds. One part of the plan is to streamline routing systems in order to reduce by two-thirds the number of people that handle a claim. With 65,000 employees, the Administration collects payroll taxes from 135 million Americans and sends 45 million checks monthly. Only 20% of the checks go to recipients of disability benefits, but the handling of such claims takes slightly more than half of the agency's $4.9 billion budget. Clearly, more efficient systems will be beneficial.

Taxes Payable, is used for both the employee's and the employer's FICA contributions. For the January 14 payroll, Academy Company's FICA tax is $1,376.80 ($17,210.00 × 8%).

Federal Unemployment Taxes

The Federal Unemployment Tax Act (FUTA) is another feature of the federal social security program. Federal unemployment taxes provide benefits for a limited period of time to employees who lose their jobs through no fault of their own. Under provisions of the Act, the employer is required to pay a tax of 6.2% on the first $7,000 of gross wages paid to each employee during a calendar year. The law, however, allows the employer a maximum credit of 5.4% on the federal rate for contributions to state unemployment taxes. Because of this provision, state unemployment tax laws generally provide for a 5.4% rate, and the effective federal unemployment tax rate becomes 0.8% (6.2% − 5.4%). This tax is borne **entirely by the employer**; there is no deduction or withholding from employees. The account Federal Unemployment Taxes Payable is used to recognize this liability. The federal unemployment tax for Academy Company for the January 14 payroll is $137.68 ($17,210.00 × 0.8%).

State Unemployment Taxes

All states have unemployment compensation programs under state unemployment tax acts (SUTA). Like federal unemployment taxes, state unemployment taxes provide benefits to employees who lose their jobs. These taxes are levied on employers.[2] The basic rate is usually 5.4% on the first $7,000 of wages paid to an employee during the year. The basic rate is adjusted according to the employer's experience rating: Companies with a history of unstable employment may pay more than the basic rate. Companies with a history of stable employment may pay less than 5.4%. Regardless of the rate paid, the credit on the federal unemployment tax is still 5.4%. The account State Unemployment Taxes Payable is used for this liability. The state unemployment tax for Academy Company for the January 14 payroll is $929.34 ($17,210.00 × 5.4%).

Recording Employer Payroll Taxes

Employer payroll taxes are usually recorded at the same time the payroll is journalized. The entire amount of gross pay ($17,210.00) shown in the payroll register in Illustration C-9 is subject to each of the three taxes mentioned above. Accordingly, the entry to record the payroll tax expense associated with the January 14 payroll is:

Jan. 14	Payroll Tax Expense	2,443.82	
	FICA Taxes Payable		1,376.80
	Federal Unemployment Taxes Payable		137.68
	State Unemployment Taxes Payable		929.34
	(To record employer's payroll taxes on		
	January 14 payroll)		

Separate liability accounts are used instead of a single credit to Payroll Taxes Payable, because these liabilities are payable to different taxing authorities at

---

[2]In a few states, the employee is also required to make a contribution. In this textbook, including the homework, we will assume that the tax is only on the employer.

different dates. The liability accounts are classified as current liabilities since they will be paid within the next year. Payroll Tax Expense is classified on the income statement as an operating expense.

Filing and Remitting Payroll Taxes

Preparation of payroll tax returns is the responsibility of the payroll department; payment of the taxes is made by the treasurer's department. Much of the information for the returns is obtained from employee earnings records.

For purposes of reporting and remitting, FICA taxes and federal income taxes withheld are combined. **The taxes must be reported quarterly**, no later than one month following the close of each quarter. The remitting requirements depend on the amount of taxes withheld and the length of the pay period. Remittances are made through deposits in either a Federal Reserve Bank or an authorized commercial bank.

Federal unemployment taxes are generally filed and remitted **annually** on or before January 31 of the subsequent year. Earlier payments are required, however, when the tax exceeds a specified amount. State unemployment taxes usually must be filed and paid by the **end of the month following each quarter**. When payroll taxes are paid, payroll liability accounts are debited and cash is credited.

The employer is also required to provide each employee with a Wage and Tax Statement (Form W-2) by January 31 following the end of a calendar year. This statement shows gross earnings, FICA taxes withheld, and income taxes withheld for the year. The required W-2 form for Michael Jordan, using assumed annual data, is shown in Illustration C-11.

The employer must send a copy of each employee's Wage and Tax Statement to the Social Security Administration. This agency subsequently furnishes the Internal Revenue Service with the income data required.

Illustration C-11

W-2 form

Form **W-2 Wage and Tax Statement**

1 Control number	
	OMB No. 1545-0008

2 Employer's name, address and ZIP code	3 Employer's identification number	4 Employer's State number
Academy Company 19 Center St. Hampton, MI 48291	36-2167852	

5 Stat. employee □	Deceased □	Legal rep. □	942 emp. □	Subtotal □	Void □

6 Allocated tips	7 Advance EIC payment

8 Employee's social security number	9 Federal income tax withheld	10 Wages, tips, other compensation	11 Social security tax withheld
329-36-9547	$3240.00	$26,300.00	$2,104.00

12 Employee's name, address, and ZIP code	13 Social security wages	14 Social security tips
	$26,300.00	

16	

Michael Jordan 2345 Mifflin Ave. Hampton, MI 48292	17 State income tax	18 State wages, tips, etc.	19 Name of State
	$526.00		Michigan

20 Local income tax	21 Local wages, tips, etc.	22 Name of locality

▲Accounting in Action ▸ *Business Insight*

The owner of a newly restored Victorian hotel, nestled in a small Massachusetts town, skipped payment of withholding taxes for three quarters because of cash flow problems. Before long, he received a call from the IRS. After months of haggling, the hotel owner was told that unless he paid the $70,000 owed, the IRS would be forced to liquidate the hotel, the land, and dozens of antiques in the inn, which had taken him and his wife years to acquire.

As this story indicates, cash-hungry small businesses are often tempted to skip or delay paying withholding taxes. Increasingly, federal and state agencies are cracking down on such cheaters. Penalties for late or nonpayment can be devastating: Fines are levied at the rate of 5% of taxes owed for each month a payroll tax isn't filed. And in cases where nothing is paid, penalties of 100% can be applied, with interest added, to the unpaid balance. Under the 100% penalty, the government can padlock the doors, seize assets, and hold the officers or certain other employees personally responsible for the penalties.

What happened to the Massachusetts hotel owner? He's now working on a repayment plan, rather than lose his years of hard work.

Before You Go On . . .

▶ *Review It*

1. What payroll taxes are levied on employers?
2. What accounts are involved in accruing employer payroll taxes?

▶ *Do It*

In January, the payroll supervisor determines that gross earnings in Halo Company are $70,000. All earnings are subject to 8% FICA taxes, 5.4% state unemployment taxes, and 0.8% federal unemployment taxes. You are asked to record the employer's payroll taxes.

Reasoning: In recording the taxes, you should remember that (1) the total expense can be debited to one account and (2) separate accounts are required for each of the three liabilities.

Solution: The entry to record the employer's payroll taxes is:

Payroll Tax Expense	9,940	
FICA Taxes Payable ($70,000 × 8%)		5,600
Federal Unemployment Taxes Payable ($70,000 × 0.8%)		560
State Unemployment Taxes Payable ($70,000 × 5.4%)		3,780
(To record employer's payroll taxes on January		
payroll)		

Related exercise material: BEC–4, EC–3, and EC–5.

◢*Summary of Study Objectives*

1. *Discuss the objectives of internal control for payroll.* The objectives of internal control for payroll are (1) to safeguard company assets against unauthorized payments of payrolls, and (2) to assure the accuracy and reliability of the accounting records pertaining to payrolls.

2. *Compute and record the payroll for a pay period.* The computation of the payroll involves gross earnings, payroll deductions, and net pay. In recording the payroll, salaries (or wages) expense is debited for gross earnings, individual tax and other liability accounts are credited for payroll de-

ductions, and salaries (wages) payable is credited for net pay. When the payroll is paid, Salaries and Wages Payable is debited, and Cash is credited.

3. *Describe and record employer payroll taxes.* Employer payroll taxes consist of FICA, federal unemployment taxes, and state unemployment taxes. The taxes are usually accrued at the time the payroll is recorded by debiting Payroll Tax Expense and crediting separate liability accounts for each type of tax.

GLOSSARY

Bonus Compensation to management personnel and other employees, based on factors such as increased sales or the amount of net income. (p. C6)

Employee earnings record A cumulative record of each employee's gross earnings, deductions, and net pay during the year. (p. C10)

Employee's Withholding Allowance Certificate (Form W-4) An Internal Revenue Service form on which the employee indicates the number of allowances claimed for withholding federal income taxes. (p. C8)

Federal unemployment taxes Taxes imposed on the employer that provides benefits for a limited time period to employees who lose their jobs through no fault of their own. (p. C14)

FICA taxes Taxes designed to provide workers with supplemental retirement, employment disability, and medical benefits. (p. C7)

Gross earnings Total compensation earned by an employee. (p. C5)

Net pay Gross earnings less payroll deductions. (p. C9)

Payroll deductions Deductions from gross earnings to determine the amount of a paycheck. (p. C6)

Payroll register A payroll record that accumulates the gross earnings, deductions, and net pay by employee for each pay period. (p. C10)

Salaries Specified amount per month or per year paid to executive and administrative personnel. (p. C2)

Statement of earnings A document attached to a paycheck that indicates the employee's gross earnings, payroll deductions, and net pay. (p. C12)

State unemployment taxes Taxes imposed on the employer that provide benefits to employees who lose their jobs. (p. C14)

Wage and Tax Statement (Form W-2) A form showing gross earnings, FICA taxes withheld, and income taxes withheld which is prepared annually by an employer for each employee. (p. C15)

Wages Amounts paid to employees based on a rate per hour or on a piece-work basis. (p. C2)

DEMONSTRATION PROBLEM

Indiana Jones Company had the following payroll transactions:

Feb. 28   The payroll for the month consists of Sales Salaries $32,000 and Office Salaries $18,000. All wages are subject to 8% FICA taxes. A total of $8,900 federal income taxes are withheld. The salaries are paid on March 1.

   28   Employer payroll taxes include 8% FICA taxes, a 5.4% state unemployment tax, and a .8% federal unemployment tax.

Instructions

(a) Journalize the February payroll transaction.

(b) Journalize the payrolll adjusting entry at February 28.

Solution to Demonstration Problem

(a) Feb. 28	Sales Salaries Expense	32,000	
	Office Salaries Expense	18,000	
	FICA Taxes Payable (8% × $50,000)		4,000
	Federal Income Taxes Payable		8,900
	Salaries Payable		37,100
	(To record February salaries)		
(b) Feb. 28	Payroll Tax Expense	7,100	
	FICA Taxes Payable		4,000
	Federal Unemployment Taxes Payable		400
	(.8% × $50,000)		
	State Unemployment Taxes Payable		2,700
	(5.4% × $50,000)		
	(To record employer's payroll taxes on		
	February payroll)		

Problem-Solving Strategies

1. The formula for determining sales is cash register total divided byy 100% plus the sales tax percentage.

2. All payroll taxes are based on gross earnings.

SELF-STUDY QUESTIONS

Answers are at the end of the appendix.

(SO 1) 1. The department that should pay the payroll is the:
 a. timekeeping department.
 b. personnel department.
 c. treasurer's department.
 d. payroll department.

(SO 2) 2. J. Barr earns $14 per hour for a 40-hour week and $21 per hour for any overtime work. If Barr works 44 hours in a week, gross earnings are:

a. $560.
b. $616.
c. $644.
d. $666.

3. Employer payroll taxes do not include: (SO 3)
 a. federal unemployment taxes.
 b. state unemployment taxes.
 c. FICA taxes.
 d. federal income taxes.

QUESTIONS

1. You are a newly hired accountant with Schindlebeck Company. On your first day, the controller asks you to identify the main internal control objectives related to payroll accounting. How would you respond?

2. What are the four functions associated with payroll activities?

3. What is the difference between gross pay and net pay? Which amount should a company record as wages or salaries expense?

4. Which payroll tax is levied on both employers and employees?

5. Are the federal and state income taxes withheld from employee paychecks a payroll tax expense for the employer? Explain your answer.

6. What do the following acronyms stand for: FICA, FUTA, and SUTA?

7. What information is shown on a W-4 statement? A W-2 statement?

8. Distinguish between the two types of payroll deductions and give examples of each.

9. What are the primary uses of the employees earnings record?

10. (a) Identify the three types of employer payroll taxes. (b) How are tax liability accounts and payroll tax expense classified in the financial statements?

BRIEF EXERCISES

Identify payroll functions.
(SO 1)

BEC–1 Lukas Company has the following payroll procedures:

1. Supervisor approves overtime work.
2. The personnel department prepares hiring authorization forms for new hires.
3. A second payroll department employee verifies payroll calculations.
4. The treasurer's department pays employees.

Identify the payroll function to which each procedure pertains.

Compute gross earnings and net pay.
(SO 2)

BEC–2 Pat Broka's regular hourly wage rate is $14, and she receives an hourly rate of $21 for work in excess of 40 hours. During a January pay period, Pat works 43 hours. Pat's federal income tax withholding is $70, and she has no voluntary deductions. FICA taxes are 8% on the first $60,000 of gross earnings. Compute Pat Broka's gross earnings and net pay for the pay period.

Record a payroll and the payment of wages.
(SO 2)

BEC–3 Data for Pat Broka are presented in BEC–2. Prepare the journal entries to record (a) Pat's pay for the period and (b) the payment of Pat's wages. Use January 15 for the end of the pay period and the payment date.

Record employer payroll taxes.
(SO 3)

BEC–4 In January, gross earnings in the Nigel Company totaled $50,000. All earnings are subject to 8% FICA taxes, 5.4% state unemployment taxes, and 0.8% federal unemployment taxes. Prepare the entry to record January payroll tax expense.

EXERCISES

EC-1 Rose Reed's regular hourly wage rate is $15.00, and she receives a wage of 1½ times the regular hourly rate for work in excess of 40 hours. During a March weekly pay period Rose worked 42 hours. Her gross earnings prior to the current week were $7,000. Rose is married and claims three withholding allowances. Her only voluntary deduction is for group hospitalization insurance at $10.00 per week.

Compute net pay and record pay for one employee.
(SO 2)

Instructions
(a) Compute the following amounts for Rose's wages for the current week.
    1. Gross earnings.
    2. FICA taxes (assume 8% rate on maximum of $60,000).
    3. Federal income taxes withheld (use wage-bracket table in text).
    4. State income taxes withheld (assume 2.0% rate).
    5. Net pay.
(b) Record Rose's pay, assuming she is an office computer operator.

EC-2 Employee earnings records for Kokomo Company reveal the following gross earnings for four employees through the pay period of December 15.

Compute maximum FICA deductions.
(SO 2)

| R. Sunberg | $58,500 | D. Myers | $59,200 |
| C. Carlsen | $59,700 | P. Otto | $60,000 |

For the pay period ending December 31, each employee's gross earnings is $1,000. The FICA tax rate is 8% on gross earnings up to $60,000.

Instructions
Compute the FICA withholdings that should be made for each employee for the December 31 pay period. (Show computations.)

EC-3 Ahmad Company has the following data for the weekly payroll ending January 31.

Prepare payroll register and record payroll and payroll tax expense.
(SO 2, 3)

| | | | Hours | | | | Hourly | Federal Income Tax | Health |
Employee	M	T	W	T	F	S	Rate	Withholding	Insurance
A. Hope	8	8	9	8	10	0	$10	$34	$10
B. Innes	8	8	8	8	8	2	12	37	15
C. Stone	9	10	8	8	9	0	12	58	15

Employees are paid 1½ times the regular hourly rate for all hours worked in excess of 40 hours per week. FICA taxes are 8% on the first $60,000 of gross earnings. Ahmad Company is subject to 5.4% state unemployment taxes and 0.8% federal unemployment taxes on the first $7,000 of gross earnings.

Instructions
(a) Prepare the payroll register for the weekly payroll.
(b) Prepare the journal entry to record the payroll and Ahmad's payroll tax expense.

EC-4 Selected data from a February payroll register for Tia Yue Company are presented below with some amounts intentionally omitted.

Compute missing payroll amounts and record payroll.
(SO 2)

Gross earnings:			
Regular	$8,900	State income taxes	$ (3)
Overtime	(1)	Union dues	100
Total	(2)	Total deductions	(4)
Deductions:		Net pay	7,310
FICA taxes	$ 760	Accounts debited:	
Federal income taxes	1,140	Warehouse wages	(5)
		Store wages	$4,000

FICA taxes are 8% and state income taxes are 2% of gross earnings.

Instructions
(a) Fill in the missing amounts.
(b) Journalize the February payroll and the payment of the payroll.

Determine employer's payroll taxes and record payroll tax expense.
(SO 3)

EC–5 According to a payroll register summary of Modesco Company, the amount of employee's gross pay in December was $700,000, of which $60,000 was not subject to FICA tax and $680,000 was not subject to state and federal unemployment taxes.

Instructions

(a) Determine the employer's payroll tax expense for the month, using the following rates: FICA, 8%; state unemployment, 5.4%; federal unemployment, 0.8%.

(b) Prepare the journal entry to record December payroll tax expense.

PROBLEMS

Identify internal control weaknesses and make recommendations for improvement.
(SO 1)

PC–1 The payroll procedures used by three different companies are described below:

1. In Lindy Company each employee is required to mark the hours worked on a clock card. At the end of each pay period, the employee must have this clock card approved by the department manager. The approved card is then given to the payroll department by the employee. Subsequently, the treasurer's department pays the employee by check.
2. In Selina Company clock cards and time clocks are used. At the end of each pay period, the department manager initials the cards, indicates the rates of pay, and sends them to payroll. A payroll register is prepared from the cards by the payroll department. Cash equal to the total net pay in each department is given to the department manager, who pays the employees in cash.
3. In Winker Company employees are required to record hours worked on clock cards by "punching" a time clock. At the end of each pay period, the clock cards are collected by the department manager. The manager prepares a payroll register in duplicate and forwards the original to payroll. In payroll, the summaries are checked for mathematical accuracy and a payroll supervisor pays each employee by check.

Instructions

(a) ▦▶ Indicate the weakness(es) in internal control in each company.

(b) ▦▶ For each weakness, describe the control procedure(s) that will provide effective internal control. Use the following format for your answer:

(a) Weaknesses	(b) Recommended Procedures

Prepare payroll register and payroll entries.
(SO 2, 3)

PC–2 Banner Drug Store has four employees who are paid on an hourly basis plus time-and-one-half for all hours worked in excess of 40 a week. Payroll data for the week ended February 15, 1996, are presented below:

Employees	Hours Worked	Hourly Rate	Federal Income Tax Withholdings	United Fund
B. Creek	39	$13.00	$?	$ –0–
C. Crowley	42	12.00	?	5.00
E. Irvine	44	13.00	56	7.50
G. Klamath	46	12.00	33	5.00

Creek and Crowley are married. They claim 2 and 4 withholding allowances, respectively. The following tax rates are applicable: FICA 8%, state income taxes 3%, state unemployment taxes 5.4%, and federal unemployment 0.8%. The first three employees are sales clerks (store wages expense), and the other employee performs administrative duties (office wages expense).

Instructions

(a) Prepare a payroll register for the weekly payroll. (Use the wage-bracket withholding table in the text for federal income tax withholdings.)

(b) Journalize the payroll on February 15, 1996, and the accrual of employer payroll taxes.

(c) Journalize the payment of the payroll on February 16, 1996.

(d) Journalize the deposit in a federal reserve bank on February 28, 1996, of the FICA and federal income taxes payable to the government.

PC–3 The following payroll liability accounts are included in the ledger of Carlos Costa Company on January 1, 1996:

Journalize payroll transactions and adjusting entries.
(SO 2, 3)

FICA Taxes Payable	$ 662.20
Federal Income Taxes Payable	954.60
State Income Taxes Payable	102.15
Federal Unemployment Taxes Payable	2,400.00
State Unemployment Taxes Payable	1,954.40
Union Dues Payable	250.00
U.S. Savings Bonds Payable	350.00

In January, the following transactions occurred:

Jan. 10 Sent check for $250.00 to union treasurer for union dues.

12 Deposited check for $1,616.80 in Federal Reserve Bank for FICA taxes and federal income taxes withheld.

15 Purchased U.S. Savings Bonds for employees by writing check for $350.00.

17 Paid state income taxes withheld from employees.

20 Paid federal and state unemployment taxes.

31 Completed monthly payroll register, which shows office salaries $14,600, store wages $27,400, FICA taxes withheld $3,360, federal income taxes payable $1,654, state income taxes payable $360, union dues payable $400, United Fund contributions payable $1,688, and net pay $34,538.

31 Prepared payroll checks for the net pay and distributed checks to employees.

At January 31, the company also makes the following accruals pertaining to employee compensation: FICA taxes (8%), state unemployment taxes (5.4%), and federal unemployment taxes (0.8%).

Instructions

(a) Journalize the January transactions.

(b) Journalize the adjustments pertaining to employee compensation at January 31.

PC–4 For the year ended December 31, 1996, Valley Electric Company reports the following summary payroll data:

Prepare entries for payroll and payroll taxes, and prepare W-2 data.
(SO 2, 3)

Gross earnings:	
Administrative salaries	$180,000
Electricians' wages	370,000
Total	$550,000
Deductions:	
FICA taxes	$ 38,000
Federal income taxes withheld	168,000
State income taxes withheld (2.6%)	14,300
United Fund contributions payable	27,500
Hospital insurance premiums	17,200
Total	$265,000

Valley Company's payroll taxes are: FICA 8%, state unemployment 2.5% (due to a stable employment record), and 0.8% federal unemployment. Gross earnings subject to (1) FICA taxes total $475,000, and (2) unemployment taxes total $400,000.

Instructions
(a) Prepare a summary journal entry at December 31 for the full year's payroll.
(b) Journalize the adjusting entry at December 31 to record the employer's payroll taxes.
(c) The W-2 Wage and Tax Statement requires the following dollar data:

Wages, Tips, Other Compensation	Federal Income Tax Withheld	State Income Tax Withheld	FICA Wages	FICA Tax Withheld

Complete the required data for the following employees:

Employee	Gross Earnings	Federal Income Tax Withheld
A. Osa	$60,000	$27,500
B. Bama	26,000	10,200

ALTERNATE PROBLEMS

Identify internal control weaknesses and make recommendations for improvement.
(SO 1)

PC–1A Selected payroll procedures of Chen Wee Company are described below:

1. Department managers interview applicants and on the basis of the interview either hire or reject the applicants. When an applicant is hired, the applicant fills out a W-4 form (Employer's Withholding Exemption Certificate). One copy of the form is sent to the personnel department and one copy is sent to the payroll department as notice that the individual has been hired. On the copy of the W-4 sent to payroll, the managers manually indicate the hourly pay rate for the new hire.
2. The payroll checks are manually signed by the chief accountant and given to the department managers for distribution to employees in their department. The managers are responsible for seeing that any absent employees receive their checks.
3. There are two clerks in the payroll department. The payroll is divided alphabetically with one clerk having employees A to L and the other employees M to Z. Each clerk computes the gross earnings, deductions, and net pay for employees in the section and posts the data to the employee earning records.

Instructions
(a) Indicate the weaknesses in internal control.
(b) For each weakness, describe the control procedures that will provide effective internal control. Use the following format for your answer:

(a) Weaknesses   (b) Recommended Procedures

Prepare payroll register and payroll entries.
(SO 2, 3)

PC–2A Sure-Value Hardware has four employees who are paid on an hourly basis plus time-and-one-half for all hours worked in excess of 40 a week. Payroll data for the week ended March 15, 1996, are presented below:

Employee	Hours Worked	Hourly Rate	Federal Income Tax Withholdings	United Fund
A. Pima	40	$13.00	$?	$5.00
C. Zuni	42	13.00	?	5.00
E. Hopi	44	13.00	42	8.00
G. Mohav	46	13.00	48	5.00

Pima and Zuni are married. They claim 0 and 4 withholding allowances, respectively. The following tax rates are applicable: FICA 8%, state income taxes 3%, state unemployment taxes 5.4%, and federal unemployment 0.8%. The first three employees are sales clerks (store wages expense) and the other employee performs administrative duties (office wages expense).

Instructions
  (a) Prepare a payroll register for the weekly payroll. (Use the wage-bracket withholding table in the text for federal income tax withholdings.)
  (b) Journalize the payroll on March 15, 1996, and the accrual of employer payroll taxes.
  (c) Journalize the payment of the payroll on March 16, 1996.
  (d) Journalize the deposit in a federal reserve bank on March 31, 1996, of the FICA and federal income taxes payable to the government.

PC–3A The following payroll liability accounts are included in the ledger of Amora Company on January 1, 1996:

Journalize payroll transactions and adjusting entries.
(SO 2, 3)

FICA Taxes Payable	$ 760.00
Federal Income Taxes Payable	954.60
State Income Taxes Payable	108.95
Federal Unemployment Taxes Payable	288.95
State Unemployment Taxes Payable	1,954.40
Union Dues Payable	870.00
U.S. Savings Bonds Payable	360.00

In January, the following transactions occurred:

Jan. 10   Sent check for $870.00 to union treasurer for union dues.
  12   Deposited check for $1,714.60 in Federal Reserve Bank for FICA taxes and federal income taxes withheld.
  15   Purchased U.S. Savings Bonds for employees by writing check for $360.00.
  17   Paid state income taxes withheld from employees.
  20   Paid federal and state unemployment taxes.
  31   Completed monthly payroll register, which shows office salaries $14,600, store wages $28,400, FICA taxes withheld $3,440, federal income taxes payable $1,684, state income taxes payable $360, union dues payable $400, United Fund contributions payable $1,888, and net pay $35,228.
  31   Prepared payroll checks for the net pay and distributed checks to employees.

At January 31, the company also makes the following accrued adjustments pertaining to employee compensation: FICA taxes (8%), federal unemployment taxes (0.8%), and state unemployment taxes (5.4%).

Instructions
  (a) Journalize the January transactions.
  (b) Journalize the adjustments pertaining to employee compensation at January 31.

PC–4A For the year ended December 31, 1996, Wynn Electrical Repair Company reports the following summary payroll data:

Prepare entries for payroll and payroll taxes and prepare W-2 data.
(SO 2, 3)

Gross earnings:	
Administrative salaries	$180,000
Electricians' wages	470,000
Total	$650,000
Deductions:	
FICA taxes	$ 48,000
Federal income taxes withheld	188,000
State income taxes withheld (2.6%)	16,900
United Fund contributions payable	32,500
Hospital insurance premiums	20,300
Total	$305,700

Wynn Company's payroll taxes are: FICA 8%, state unemployment 2.5% (due to a stable employment record), and 0.8% federal unemployment. Gross earnings subject to (1) FICA taxes total $600,000; and (2) unemployment taxes total $450,000.

Instructions

(a) Prepare a summary journal entry at December 31 for the full year's payroll.

(b) Journalize the adjusting entry at December 31 to record the employer's payroll taxes.

(c) The W-2 Wage and Tax Statement requires the following dollar data:

Wages, Tips, Other Compensation	Federal Income Tax Withheld	State Income Tax Withheld	FICA Wages	FICA Tax Withheld

Complete the required data for the following employees:

Employee	Gross Earnings	Federal Income Tax Withheld
A. Ute	$62,000	$28,500
B. Yuma	28,000	10,800

Broadening Your Perspective

DECISION CASE

Quicko Processing Company provides word-processing services for clients and students in a university community. The work for clients is fairly steady throughout the year, but the work for students peaks significantly in December and May as a result of term papers, research project reports, and dissertations.

Two years ago, the company attempted to meet the peak demand by hiring part-time help. However, this led to numerous errors and considerable customer dissatisfaction. A year ago, the company hired four experienced employees on a permanent basis instead of using part-time help. This proved to be much better in terms of productivity and customer satisfaction. However, it has caused an increase in annual payroll costs and a significant decline in annual net income.

Recently, Sue Stone, a sales representative of Hiawatha Services Inc., made a proposal to the company. Under the plan, Hiawatha Services will provide up to four experienced workers at a daily rate of $100 per person for an 8-hour workday. Hiawatha workers are not available on an hourly basis. Quicko Processing would have to pay only the daily rate for the workers used.

The owner of Quicko Processing, Denise Denby, asks you, as the company's accountant, to prepare a report on the expenses that are pertinent to the decision. If the Hiawatha plan is adopted, Denise will terminate the employment of two permanent employees who are each earning an average annual salary of $28,000. The remaining permanent employees each earn an annual income of $28,000. Quicko Processing pays 8% FICA taxes, 0.8% Federal Unemployment Taxes, and 5.4% State Unemployment Taxes. The unemployment taxes apply to only the first $7,000 of gross earnings. In addition, Quicko Processing pays $40 per month for each employee for medical and dental insurance.

Denise indicates that if the Hiawatha Services plan is accepted, her needs for workers will be as follows:

Months	Number	Working Days per Month
January–March	2	20
April–May	3	25
June–October	2	18
November–December	3	23

Instructions

(a) Prepare a report showing the comparative payroll expense of continuing to employ permanent workers compared to adopting the Hiawatha Services Inc. plan.

(b) What other factors should Denise consider before finalizing her decision?

COMMUNICATION ACTIVITY

Prentice Berg, president of the Flying Eagle Company, has recently hired a number of additional employees. He recognizes that additional payroll taxes will be due as a result of this hiring, and that the company will serve as the collection agent for other taxes.

Instructions
In a memorandum to Prentice Berg explain each of the taxes, and identify the taxes that result in payroll tax expense to the employer.

ETHICS CASE

Jack Sprat owns and manages the Spicy-Saucer Restaurant, a 24-hour restaurant near the city's medical complex. Jack employs nine full-time employees and sixteen part-time employees. He pays all of the full-time employees by check, the amounts of which are determined by Jack's public accountant, Clara Hankes. Jack pays all of his part-time employees in currency that he computes and withdraws directly from his cash register. Clara has repeatedly urged Jack to pay all employees by check. But as Jack has told his competitor and friend, Bud Juice, who owns the Tasty Diner, "First of all, my part-time employees prefer the currency over a check, and secondly I don't withhold or pay any taxes or workmen's compensation insurance on those wages because they go totally unrecorded and unnoticed."

Instructions
(a) Who are the stakeholders in this situation?
(b) What are the legal and ethical considerations regarding Jack's handling of his payroll?
(c) Clara Hankes is aware of Jack's payment of the part-time payroll in currency. What are her ethical responsibilities in this case?
(d) What internal control principle is violated in this payroll process?

Answers to Self-Study Questions
1. c   2. c   3. d

APPENDIX · D

SPECIAL JOURNALS AND SUBSIDIARY LEDGERS

▼Section 1 ▸ Expanding the Ledger— Subsidiary Ledgers

▼Subsidiary Ledgers

STUDY OBJECTIVE

··········· **1** ···········

Describe the nature and purpose of a subsidiary ledger.

Imagine a business that has several thousand charge (credit) customers and shows the transactions with these customers in only one account—Accounts Receivable—in the general ledger. It would be virtually impossible to determine the balance owed by an individual customer at any specific time. Similarly, the amount payable to one creditor would be difficult to locate quickly from a single Accounts Payable account in the general ledger.

To provide such information, companies use subsidiary ledgers to keep track of individual balances. A subsidiary ledger is a group of accounts with a common characteristic (for example, all customer accounts—that is, accounts receivable). The subsidiary ledger frees the general ledger from the details of individual balances. A subsidiary ledger is an addition to, and an expansion of, the general ledger.

Two common subsidiary ledgers are:

1. The accounts receivable (or customers') ledger which accumulates transaction data with individual customers.
2. The accounts payable (or creditors') ledger which maintains transaction data with individual creditors.

In each of these subsidiary ledgers, individual accounts are usually arranged in alphabetical order.

The detailed data shown in a subsidiary ledger are summarized in a general ledger account. The accounts for the two ledgers above are Accounts Receivable and Accounts Payable, respectively. The general ledger account that summarizes subsidiary ledger data is called a control account. **Each general ledger control account balance must equal the composite balance of the individual accounts in the related subsidiary ledger at the end of an accounting period.** An overview of the relationship of subsidiary ledgers to the general ledger is shown in Illustration D-1, with the general ledger control accounts in color.

Illustration D-1

Relationship of general ledgers and subsidiary accounts

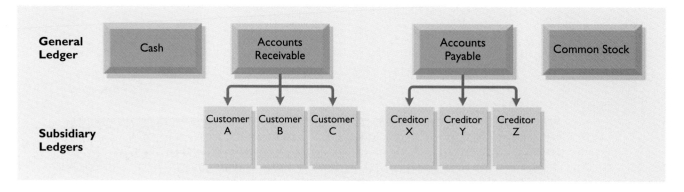

Note that cash and common stock are not control accounts.

Illustration

An example of a control account and subsidiary ledger for Larson Enterprises is provided in Illustration D-3. The explanation column in these accounts is not shown in this and subsequent illustrations due to space considerations.

The example (Illustration D-3) is based on the following transactions:

	Credit Sales				Collections on Account	
Jan. 10	Aaron Co.	$ 6,000		Jan. 19	Aaron Co.	$ 4,000
12	Branden Inc.	3,000		21	Branden Inc.	3,000
20	Caron Co.	3,000		29	Caron Co.	1,000
		$12,000				$ 8,000

Illustration D-2

Sales and collection transactions

The total debits and credits in Accounts Receivable in the general ledger are reconcilable to the detailed debits and credits in the subsidiary accounts. In addition, the balance of $4,000 in the accounts receivable control account agrees with the total of the balances in the individual accounts receivable accounts (Aaron Co. $2,000 + Branden Inc. $0 + Caron Co. $2,000) in the subsidiary ledger.

As shown, postings are made monthly to the control accounts in the general ledger so that monthly financial statements may be prepared. Postings to the individual accounts in the subsidiary ledger are made daily. The rationale for posting daily is to ensure that current account information can be used as a basis for monitoring credit limits, billing customers, and answering inquiries from customers about their account balances.

ACCOUNTS RECEIVABLE SUBSIDIARY LEDGER

Aaron Co.

Date	Ref.	Debit	Credit	Balance
1996				
Jan 10		6,000		6,000
19			4,000	2,000

Branden Inc.

Date	Ref.	Debit	Credit	Balance
1996				
Jan 12		3,000		3,000
21			3,000	------

Caron Co.

Date	Ref.	Debit	Credit	Balance
1996				
Jan 20		3,000		3,000
29			1,000	2,000

GENERAL LEDGER

Accounts Receivable

Date	Ref.	Debit	Credit	Balance
1996				
Jan 31		12,000		12,000
31			8,000	4,000

The subsidiary ledger is separate from the general ledger.	Accounts Receivable is a control account.

Illustration D-3

Relationship between ledgers

▶ Technology in Action

Rather than relying on customer or creditor names in a subsidiary ledger, a computer system expands the account number of the control account in a pre-specified manner. For example, if accounts receivable was numbered 10010, the first account in the accounts receivable subsidiary ledger might be numbered 10010-0001. Most systems allow inquiries about specific accounts in the subsidiary ledger (by account number) or about the control account. With the latter, the system would automatically total all the subsidiary accounts whenever an inquiry to the control account was made.

Advantages of Subsidiary Ledgers

The advantages of using subsidiary ledgers are that they:

1. **Show transactions affecting one customer or one creditor in a single account**, thus providing necessary up-to-date information on specific account balances.
2. **Free the general ledger of excessive details**. As a result, a trial balance of the general ledger does not contain vast numbers of individual account balances.
3. **Help locate errors in individual accounts** by reducing the number of accounts combined in one ledger and by using controlling accounts.
4. **Make possible a division of labor** in posting by having one employee post to the general ledger and a different employee(s) post to the subsidiary ledgers.

Before You Go On . . .

▸ Review It

1. What are the basic principles to be followed in designing and developing an efficient and effective accounting information system?
2. What are the major phases in the development of an accounting information system?
3. What is a subsidiary ledger, and what purpose does it serve?

▸ Do It

Presented below is information related to Sims Company for its first month of operations. Identify the balances that appear in the accounts payable subsidiary ledger and the accounts payable balance that appears in the general ledger at the end of January.

	Credit Purchases			Cash Paid	
Jan 5	Devon Co.	$11,000	Jan 9	Devon Co.	$7,000
Jan 11	Shelby Co.	7,000	Jan 14	Shelby Co.	2,000
Jan 22	Taylor Co.	14,000	Jan 27	Taylor Co.	9,000

Reasoning: Note that only one account appears in the general ledger, but the detail related to this account is shown in the subsidiary ledger.

Solution: Subsidiary ledger balances: Devon Co. $4,000 ($11,000 − $7,000); Shelby Co. $5,000 ($7,000 − $2,000); Taylor Co. $5,000 ($14,000 − $9,000). General ledger Accounts Payable balance $14,000 ($32,000 − $18,000).

Related exercise material: BED–1, BED–2, ED–1, ED–2, ED–3, ED–4, ED–5, and ED–9.

▸SECTION *2* ▸ Expanding the Journal— Special Journals

STUDY OBJECTIVE
•••••••••*2*•••••••••

Explain how special journals are used in journalizing.

So far you have learned to journalize transactions in a two-column general journal and post these entries individually to the general ledger. This procedure is satisfactory in only the very smallest companies. To expedite journalizing and posting transactions, most companies use special journals **in addition to the general journal**.

A special journal is used to record similar types of transactions, such as all sales of merchandise on account, or all cash receipts. The types of special journals used depend largely on the types of transactions that occur frequently in a business enterprise. Most merchandising enterprises use the journals shown in Illustration D-4 to record transactions daily:

Illustration D-4

Use of special journals and the general journal

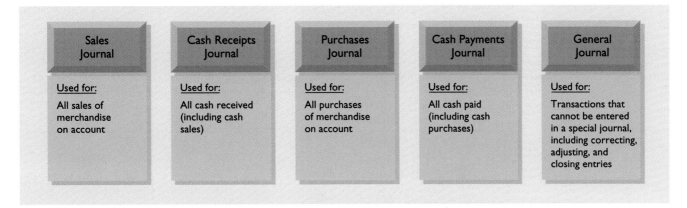

If a transaction cannot be recorded in a special journal, it is recorded in the general journal. For example, if you had special journals only for the four types of transactions listed above, purchase returns and allowances or sales returns and allowances would be recorded in the general journal. Similarly, **correcting, adjusting, and closing entries are recorded in the general journal**. Other types of special journals may be used in some situations. For example, when purchase returns and allowances or sales returns and allowances are frequent, special journals may be used to record these transactions.

Special journals **permit greater division of labor** because several individuals can record entries in different journals at the same time. For example, one employee may be responsible for journalizing all cash receipts, and another for journalizing credit sales. In addition, the use of special journals **reduces the time necessary to complete the posting process**. When special journals are used, monthly postings to some accounts may be substituted for daily postings, as will be illustrated later in the chapter.

Helpful hint Questions: In what journal would you record: (1) the cash purchase of merchandise inventory? (2) the purchase of inventory on credit? (3) a cash sale? (4) the owner's withdrawal of a unit of inventory for personal use? Answers: (1) Cash payments journal; (2) purchases journal; (3) cash receipts journal; (4) general journal.

Sales Journal

The sales journal is used to record sales of merchandise on account. Cash sales of merchandise are entered in the cash receipts journal. Credit sales of assets other than merchandise are entered in the general journal.

Journalizing Credit Sales

All entries in a sales journal are made from sales invoices. Each invoice is prenumbered to ensure that all invoices are journalized. To illustrate, assume that Karns Wholesale Supply has the following credit sales transactions:

Helpful hint Will a special journal or the general journal have fewer daily entries? Answer: The general journal, because in a properly designed system all recurring daily entries should be recorded in a special journal.

Illustration D-5

Credit sales transactions

Date	Customer	Invoice No.	Amount	Date	Customer	Invoice No.	Amount
5/3	Abbot Sisters	101	$10,600	5/21	Abbot Sisters	105	$15,400
5/7	Babson Co.	102	11,350	5/24	Deli Co.	106	21,210
5/14	Carson Bros.	103	7,800	5/27	Babson Co.	107	14,570
5/19	Deli Co.	104	9,300				

Each entry in the sales journal used here results in a debit to Accounts Receivable and a credit to Sales. Since each sale on account involves a debit to Accounts Receivable and a credit of equal amount to Sales, only one line is needed in this sales journal to record each transaction. The sales journal is presented in Illustration D-6.

Illustration D-6

Journalizing the sales journal

	KARNS WHOLESALE SUPPLY				
	Sales Journal				S1
Date	Account Debited	Invoice No.	Ref.	Accts. Receivable Dr. Sales Cr.	
1996					
May 3	Abbot Sisters	101		10,600	
7	Babson Co.	102		11,350	
14	Carson Bros.	103		7,800	
19	Deli Co.	104		9,300	
21	Abbot Sisters	105		15,400	
24	Deli Co.	106		21,210	
27	Babson Co.	107		14,570	
				90,230	

The reference (Ref.) column is not used in journalizing. It is used in posting the sales journal, as explained in the next section. Also, note that, unlike the general journal, an explanation is not required for each entry in a special journal.

If management wishes to record its sales by department, additional columns may be provided in the sales journal. For example, a department store may have columns for home furnishings, sporting goods, shoes, etc. In addition, practically all states and cities require a sales tax be charged on items sold, which the company must remit to the state or city. In this case, it is desirable to add an additional credit column to the sales journal for sales tax payable. Sales tax payable is posted in total at the end of the month, similar to sales.

Posting the Sales Journal

Postings from the sales journal are made **daily to the individual accounts receivable** in the subsidiary ledger and **monthly to the general ledger**, as shown in Illustration D-7.

A check mark (√) is inserted in the reference posting column to indicate that the daily posting to the customer's account has been made. A check mark (√) is used in this illustration because the subsidiary ledger accounts are not numbered. At the end of the month, the column total of the sales journal ($90,230) is posted to the general ledger—as a debit to Accounts Receivable (account No. 4) and a credit to Sales (account No. 60). The insertion of the respective account numbers below the column total indicates that the postings have been made. In both the general ledger and subsidiary ledger accounts, the reference **S1** indicates that the posting came from page 1 of the sales journal.

Proving the Ledgers

To prove the ledgers it is necessary to determine that (1) the total of the general ledger debit balances equals the total of the general ledger credit balances and (2) the sum of the subsidiary ledger balances equals the balance in the control account. The proof of the ledgers is shown in Illustration D-8.

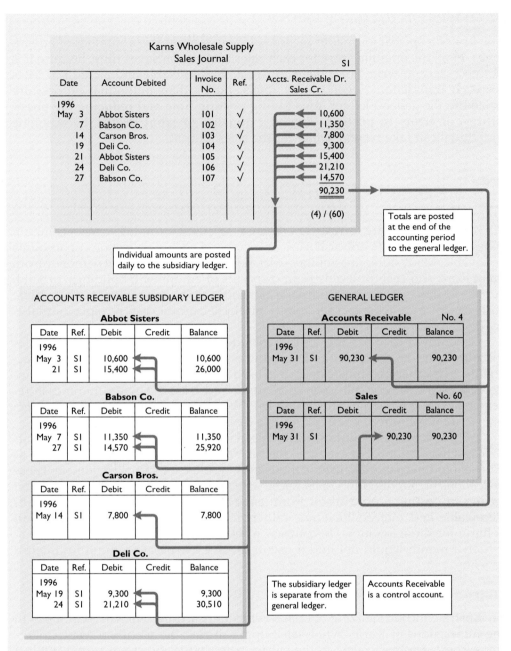

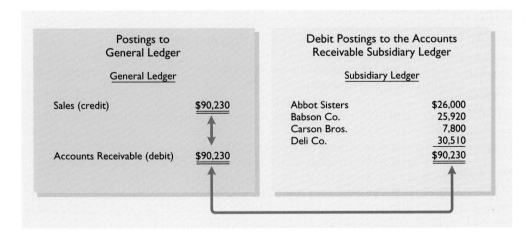

Advantages of the Sales Journal

The use of a special journal to record sales on account has a number of advantages. First, the one-line entry for each sales transaction **saves time**, because it is not necessary to write out a debit to Accounts Receivable and a credit to Sales for each transaction. Second, only totals, rather than individual entries, are posted to the general ledger, thus **saving posting time and reducing the possibilities of errors in posting**. Finally, **a division of labor results**, because one individual can take responsibility for the sales journal.

Cash Receipts Journal

All receipts of cash are recorded in the cash receipts journal. The most common types of cash receipts are cash sales of merchandise and collections of accounts receivable. Many other possibilities exist, however, such as receipt of money from bank loans and cash proceeds from disposals of equipment, buildings, or land. A one-column cash receipts journal is not sufficient to accommodate all possible cash receipt transactions. Therefore, a multiple-column cash receipts journal is used.

Generally, a cash receipts journal includes debit columns for cash and sales discounts and credit columns for accounts receivable, sales, and "other" accounts. The other accounts category is used when the cash receipt does not involve a cash sale or a collection of accounts receivable. A five-column cash receipts journal is shown in Illustration D-9. When a special journal has more than one account column it is referred to as a columnar journal

Additional credit columns may be used if they significantly reduce postings to a specific account. For example, the cash receipts of a loan company, such as Household International, include thousands of collections from customers. These collections are credited to Loans Receivable and Interest Revenue. A significant saving in posting would result from using separate credit columns for Loans Receivable and Interest Revenue, rather than using the other accounts credit column for these amounts. In contrast, a retailer that has only one interest collection a month would not find it useful to have a separate column for interest revenue.

Journalizing Cash Receipts Transactions

To illustrate the journalizing of cash receipts transactions, we will continue with the transactions of Karns Wholesale Supply during the month of May. Collections from customers relate to the entries recorded in the sales journal in Illustration D-6. The entries in the cash receipts journal are based on the following cash receipts transactions:

May 1 Stockholders make an investment of $5,000 in the business.
    7 Cash sales of merchandise total $1,900.
   10 A check for $10,388 is received from Abbot Sisters in payment of invoice No. 101 for $10,600 less a 2% discount.
   12 Cash sales of merchandise total $2,600.
   17 A check for $11,123 is received from Babson Co. in payment of invoice No. 102 for $11,350 less a 2% discount.
   22 Cash is received by signing a note for $6,000.
   23 A check for $7,644 is received from Carson Bros. in full for invoice No. 103 for $7,800 less a 2% discount.
   28 A check for $9,114 is received from Deli Co. in full for invoice No. 104 for $9,300 less a 2% discount.

Karns Wholesale Supply
Cash Receipts Journal

CR1

Date	Accounts Credited	Ref.	Cash Dr.	Sales Discounts Dr.	Accounts Receivable Cr.	Sales Cr.	Other Accounts Cr.
1996 May 1	Common Stock	50	5,000				5,000
7			1,900			1,900	
10	Abbot Sisters	√	10,388	212	10,600		
12			2,600			2,600	
17	Babson Co.	√	11,123	227	11,350		
22	Notes Payable	20	6,000				6,000
23	Carson Bros.	√	7,644	156	7,800		
28	Deli Co.	√	9,114	186	9,300		
			53,769	781	39,050	4,500	11,000
			(1)	(61)	(4)	(60)	(x)

Individual amounts are posted daily to the subsidiary ledger.

Totals are posted at the end of the accounting period to the general ledger.

ACCOUNTS RECEIVABLE SUBSIDIARY LEDGER

Abbot Sisters

Date	Ref.	Debit	Credit	Balance
1996 May 3	S1	10,600		10,600
10	CR1		10,600	--------
21	S1	15,400		15,400

Babson Co.

Date	Ref.	Debit	Credit	Balance
1996 May 7	S1	11,350		11,350
17	CR1		11,350	--------
27	S1	14,570		14,570

Carson Bros.

Date	Ref.	Debit	Credit	Balance
1996 May 14	S1	7,800		7,800
23	CR1		7,800	-------

Deli Co.

Date	Ref.	Debit	Credit	Balance
1996 May 19	S1	9,300		9,300
24	S1	21,210		30,510
28	CR1		9,300	21,210

Accounts Receivable is a control account.

The subsidiary ledger is separate from the general ledger.

GENERAL LEDGER

Cash   No. 1

Date	Ref.	Debit	Credit	Balance
1996 May 31	CR1	53,769		53,769

Accounts Receivable   No. 4

Date	Ref.	Debit	Credit	Balance
1996 May 31	S1	90,230		90,230
31	CR1		39,050	51,180

Notes Payable   No. 20

Date	Ref.	Debit	Credit	Balance
1996 May 22	CR1		6,000	6,000

Common Stock   No. 50

Date	Ref.	Debit	Credit	Balance
1996 May 1	CR1		5,000	5,000

Sales   No. 60

Date	Ref.	Debit	Credit	Balance
1996 May 31	S1		90,230	90,230
31	CR1		4,500	94,730

Sales Discounts   No. 61

Date	Ref.	Debit	Credit	Balance
1996 May 31	CR1	781		781

Further information about the columns in the cash receipts journal (see Illustration D-9) above is as follows:

Debits:

1. **Cash.** The amount of cash actually received in each transaction is entered in this column; the column total indicates the total cash receipts for the month.

2. **Sales Discounts.** The Sales Discounts column is included so that it is not necessary to enter sales discount items in the general journal. As a result, the collection of an account receivable within the discount period is expressed on one line in the appropriate columns of the cash receipts journal.

Credits:

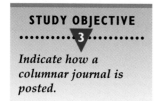

Helpful hint   When is an account title entered in the "Accounts Credited" column of the cash receipts journal? Answer: A *subsidiary ledger* title is entered there whenever the entry involves a collection of accounts receivable. A *general ledger* account title is entered there whenever the entry involves an account that is not the subject of a special column (and an amount must be entered in the "Other Accounts" column). No account title is entered there if neither of the foregoing apply.

3. **Accounts Receivable.** The Accounts Receivable column is used to record cash collections on account. The amount entered in this column is the amount to be credited to the individual customer's account.

4. **Sales.** The Sales column records all cash sales of merchandise. Cash sales of plant assets, for example, are not reported in this column.

5. **Other Accounts.** The Other Accounts column, often referred to as the **sundry accounts column**, is used whenever the credit is other than to Accounts Receivable or Sales. For example, in the first entry, $5,000 is entered as a credit to Common Stock.

In a columnar journal, as in a single-column journal, only one line is needed for each entry. There must be equal debit and credit amounts for each line. When the collection from Abbot Sisters on May 10 is journalized, for example, three amounts are indicated. Note also that the Accounts Credited column is used to identify both general ledger and subsidiary ledger account titles. The former is illustrated in the May 1 entry for the stockholders' investment; the latter is illustrated in the May 10 entry for the collection in full from Abbot Sisters.

When the journalizing of a columnar journal has been completed, the amount columns are totaled, and the totals are balanced to prove the equality of debits and credits. The proof for Karns Wholesale Supply is as follows:

Illustration D-10

Proving the accuracy of the cash receipts journal

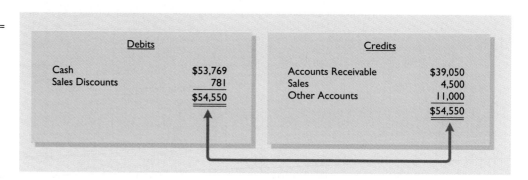

Totaling the columns of a journal and proving the equality of the totals is called **footing** and **cross-footing** a journal.

Posting the Cash Receipts Journal

STUDY OBJECTIVE
·········◢3◣·········
Indicate how a columnar journal is posted.

Posting a columnar journal involves the following procedures.

1. All column totals except the total for the Other Accounts column are posted **once at the end of the month** to the account title specified in the column heading, such as Cash or Accounts Receivable. Account numbers are entered below the column totals to show that they have been posted.

2. The total of the Other Accounts column is not posted. Instead, the **individual amounts comprising the total are posted separately** to the general ledger accounts specified in the Accounts Credited column. See, for example, the credit posting to Common Stock. The symbol (X) is inserted below the total to this column to indicate that the amount ($11,000) has not been posted.

3. The individual amounts in a column, posted in total to a control account (Accounts Receivable, in this case), are posted **daily to the subsidiary ledger** account specified in the Accounts Credited column. See, for example, the credit posting of $10,600 to Abbot Sisters.

Therefore, cash is posted to account No. 1, accounts receivable to account No. 4, sales to account No. 60, and sales discounts to account No. 61. The symbol **CR** is used in the ledgers to identify postings from the cash receipts journal.

Proving the Ledgers

After the posting of the cash receipts journal is completed, it is necessary to prove the ledgers. As shown in Illustration D-11, the general ledger totals are in agreement and the sum of the subsidiary ledger balances equals the control account balance.

Illustration D-11

Proving the ledgers

Accounts Receivable Subsidiary Ledger	
Abbot Sisters	$15,400
Babson Co.	14,570
Deli Co.	21,210
	$51,180

General Ledger Debits	
Cash	$53,769
Accounts Receivable	51,180
Sales Discounts	781
	$105,730

Credits	
Notes Payable	$ 6,000
Common Stock	5,000
Sales	94,730
	$105,730

Purchases Journal

All purchases of merchandise on account are recorded in the purchases journal. Each entry in this journal results in a debit to Purchases and a credit to Accounts Payable. When a one-column purchases journal is used, other types of purchases on account and cash purchases cannot be journalized in it. For example, credit purchases of equipment or supplies must be recorded in the general journal, and all cash purchases are entered in the cash payments journal. As illustrated later, where credit purchases for items other than merchandise are numerous, the purchases journal is often expanded to a multi-column format. The single-column purchases journal for Karns Wholesale Supply is shown in Illustration D-12.

Journalizing Credit Purchases of Merchandise

Entries in the purchases journal are made from purchase invoices. The journalizing procedure is similar to the procedures for a single-column sales journal. In contrast to the sales journal, the purchases journal may not have an invoice number column, because invoices received from different suppliers will not be in numerical sequence. To assure that all purchase invoices are recorded, however, some companies consecutively number each invoice upon receipt and then provide for an internal document number column in the purchases journal.

Illustration D-12

*Journalizing and posting
purchases journal*

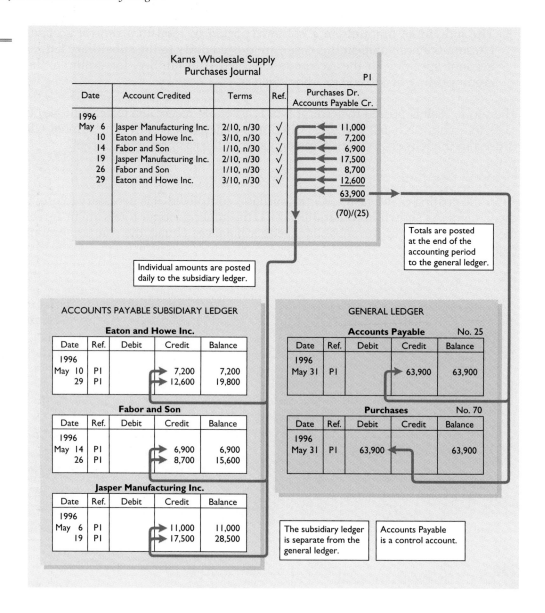

The entries for Karns Wholesale Supply are based on the following assumed transactions:

Illustration D-13

*Credit purchases trans-
actions*

Date	Supplier	Amount	Date	Supplier	Amount
5/6	Jasper Manufacturing Inc.	$11,000	5/19	Jasper Manufacturing Inc.	$17,500
5/10	Eaton and Howe, Inc.	7,200	5/26	Fabor and Son	8,700
5/14	Fabor and Son	6,900	5/29	Eaton and Howe, Inc.	12,600

Posting the Purchases Journal

Helpful hint Postings to
subsidiary ledger accounts are
done daily because it is often
necessary to know a current
balance for the subsidiary
accounts.

The procedures for posting the purchases journal are similar to those for the sales journal. In this case, postings are made **daily** to the **accounts payable ledger** and **monthly** to Purchases and Accounts Payable in the general ledger. In both ledgers, the letter P1 is used in the reference column to show that the postings are from page 1 of the purchases journal.

Proof of the accuracy of the postings to both ledgers in this example is shown by the following tabulation:

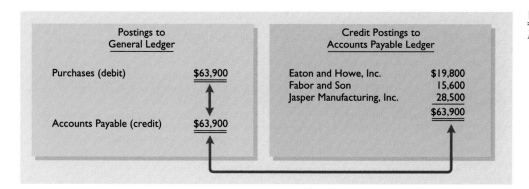

Illustration D-14
Proving the ledgers

Expanding the Purchases Journal

Some companies expand the purchases journal to include all types of purchases on account. Instead of one column for purchases and accounts payable, a multiple-column format is used. The multiple-column format usually includes a credit column for accounts payable and debit columns for purchases of merchandise, purchases of office supplies, purchases of store supplies, and other accounts. Illustration D-15 is an example of a multiple-column purchases journal for Hanover Co. The posting procedures are similar to those used for posting the cash receipts journal illustrated earlier.

Helpful hint A multiple-column purchases journal must be footed and cross-footed to prove the equality of debits and credits.

Illustration D-15
Columnar purchases journal

HANOVER CO.
Purchases Journal — P1

Date	Accounts Credited	Ref.	Accounts Payable Cr.	Purchases Dr.	Office Supplies Dr.	Store Supplies Dr.	Other Accounts Dr. Account	Ref.	Amount
1996									
June 1	Signe Audio	✓	2,000		2,000				
3	Wright Co.	✓	1,500	1,500					
5	Orange Tree Co.	✓	2,600				Equipment	18	2,600
30	Sue's Business Forms	✓	800			800			
			56,600	43,000	7,500	1,200			4,900

Cash Payments Journal

All disbursements of cash are entered in a cash payments journal. Entries in this journal are made from prenumbered checks. Because cash payments may be made for a variety of purposes, the cash payments journal has multiple columns. A four-column journal is shown in Illustration D-16.

Journalizing Cash Payments Transactions

The procedures for journalizing transactions in this journal are similar to those described earlier for journalizing transactions in the cash receipts journal. For example, each transaction is entered on one line, and for each line there must be

Illustration D-16

Journalizing and posting the cash payments journal

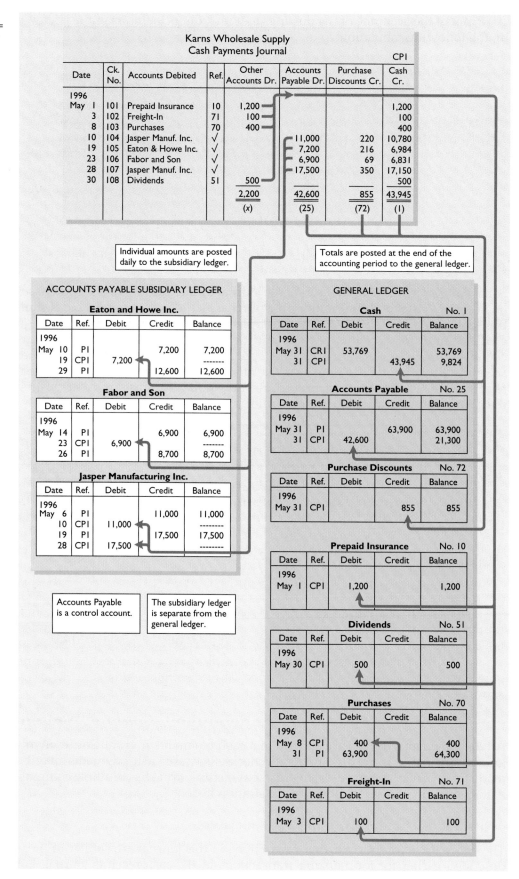

equal debit and credit amounts. The entries in the cash payments journal shown in Illustration D-16 are based on the following transactions for Karns Wholesale Supply:

May 1 Check No. 101 for $1,200 issued for the annual premium on a fire insurance policy.
    3 Check No. 102 for $100 issued in payment of freight when terms were FOB shipping point.
    8 Check No. 103 for $400 issued for the purchase of merchandise.
    10 Check No. 104 for $10,780 sent to Jasper Manufacturing Inc. in payment of May 6 invoice for $11,000 less a 2% discount.
    19 Check No. 105 for $6,984 mailed to Eaton and Howe, Inc. in payment of May 10 invoice for $7,200 less a 3% discount.
    23 Check No. 106 for $6,831 sent to Fabor and Son in payment of May 14 invoice for $6,900 less a 1% discount.
    28 Check No. 107 for $17,150 sent to Jasper Manufacturing Inc. in payment of May 19 invoice for $17,500 less a 2% discount.
    30 Check No. 108 for $500 issued to stockholders as a cash dividend.

Note that whenever an amount is entered in the Other Accounts column, a specific general ledger account must be identified in the Accounts Debited column. The entries for check Nos. 101, 102, and 103 illustrate this situation. Similarly, a subsidiary account must be identified in the Accounts Debited column whenever an amount is entered in the Accounts Payable column, as, for example, the entry for check No. 104.

When the journalizing of the cash payments journal has been completed, the amount columns are totaled. The totals are then balanced to prove the equality of debits and credits.

Posting the Cash Payments Journal

The procedures for posting the cash payments journal are similar to those for posting the cash receipts journal. Specifically, the amounts recorded in the Accounts Payable column are posted individually to the subsidiary ledger and in total to the control account. Purchase Discounts and Cash are posted only in total at the end of the month. When a transaction is recorded in the Other Accounts column, it is posted individually to the appropriate account(s) affected. No totals are posted for this column.

The posting of the cash payments journal is shown in Illustration D-16. Note that the symbol **CP** is used as the posting reference for this journal. After postings are completed, the equality of the debit and credit balances in the general ledger should be determined. In addition, the control account balances should agree with the subsidiary ledger total balance. The agreement of these balances is shown in Illustration D-17.

Illustration D-17

Proving the ledgers

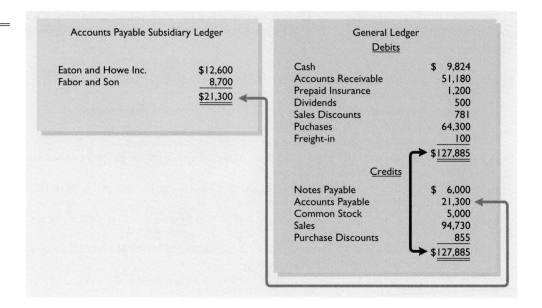

Accounts Payable Subsidiary Ledger	
Eaton and Howe Inc.	$12,600
Fabor and Son	8,700
	$21,300

General Ledger	
Debits	
Cash	$ 9,824
Accounts Receivable	51,180
Prepaid Insurance	1,200
Dividends	500
Sales Discounts	781
Puchases	64,300
Freight-in	100
	$127,885
Credits	
Notes Payable	$ 6,000
Accounts Payable	21,300
Common Stock	5,000
Sales	94,730
Purchase Discounts	855
	$127,885

Effects on General Journal

Special journals for sales, purchases, and cash substantially reduce the number of entries that are made in the general journal. **Only transactions that cannot be entered in a special journal are recorded in the general journal.** For example, the general journal may be used to record such transactions as granting of credit to a customer for a sales return or allowance, receipt of credit from a supplier for purchases returned, acceptance of a note receivable from a customer, and purchase of equipment by issuing a note payable. In addition, correcting, adjusting, and closing entries are made in the general journal.

The general journal has columns for date, account titles and explanation, reference, and debit and credit amounts. When control and subsidiary accounts are not involved, the procedures for journalizing and posting of transactions are identical with those described in earlier chapters. However, when control and subsidiary accounts are involved, two modifications of earlier procedures are required:

1. In **journalizing**, both the control and the subsidiary accounts must be identified.
2. In **posting**, there must be a **dual posting**: once to the control account and once to the subsidiary account.

To illustrate, assume that on May 31, Karns Wholesale Supply returns $500 of merchandise for credit to Fabor and Son because of an error in filling its May 26 order. The entry in the general journal and the posting of the entry are shown in Illustration D-18. Note that if cash is received instead of credit granted on this return, then the transaction is recorded in the cash receipts journal.

Observe in the journal that two accounts are indicated for the debit and two postings are indicated in the reference column. One amount is posted to the control account and the other to the creditor's account in the subsidiary ledger.

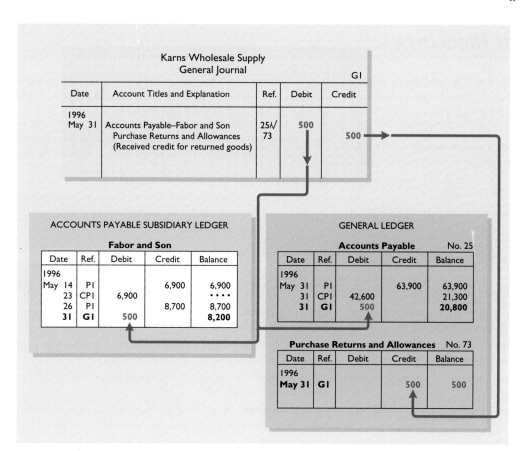

Before You Go On . . .

▶ Review It

1. What type of special journals are usually used to record transactions? Why are special journals used?
2. Explain how transactions recorded in the sales journal and the cash receipts journal are posted.
3. Indicate the types of transactions that are recorded in the general journal when special journals are used.

▶ Do It

The Vilas Company has the following selected transactions: (1) purchase of equipment for cash, (2) cash sale, (3) sales returns and allowances, (4) withdrawal of cash for proprietor's personal use, and (5) sale of merchandise on account. Identify the journals in which each transaction should be entered.

Reasoning: It is necessary to know the content of each special journal and the effect of special journals on the general journal. For example, the sales journal contains only sales on account, and the cash payments journal is used for all cash payments.

Solution: (1) Purchase of equipment for cash—cash payments journal. (2) Cash sale—cash receipts journal. (3) Sales return and allowance—general journal. (4) Withdrawal of cash for proprietor's personal use—cash payments journal. (5) Sale of merchandise on account—sales journal.

Related exercise material: BED–5, BED–6, ED–1, ED–4, ED–5, ED–6, ED–7, and ED–8.

Summary of Study Objectives

1. Describe the nature and purpose of a subsidiary ledger. A subsidiary ledger is a group of accounts with a common characteristic. It facilitates the recording process by freeing the general ledger from details of individual balances.

2. Explain how special journals are used in journalizing. A special journal is used to group similar types of transactions. In a special journal, only one line is used to record a complete transaction.

3. Indicate how a columnar journal is posted. In posting a columnar journal:

(a) all column totals except for the Other Accounts column are posted once at the end of the month to the account title specified in the column heading.

(b) the total of the Other Accounts column is not posted. Instead, the individual amounts comprising the total are posted separately to the general ledger accounts specified in the Accounts column.

(c) the individual amounts in a column posted in total to a control account are posted daily to the subsidiary ledger accounts specified in the Accounts column.

Glossary

Accounts payable (creditors') ledger A subsidiary ledger that contains accounts with individual creditors. (p. D2).

Accounts receivable (customers') ledger A subsidiary ledger that contains individual customer accounts. (p. D2).

Cash payments (disbursements) journal A special journal used to record all cash paid. (p. D13).

Cash receipts journal A special journal used to record all cash received. (p. D8).

Columnar journal A special journal with more than one column. (p. D8).

Control account An account in the general ledger that controls a subsidiary ledger. (p. D2).

Purchases journal A special journal used to record all purchases of merchandise on account. (p. D11).

Sales journal A special journal used to record all sales of merchandise on account. (p. D5).

Special journal A journal that is used to record similar types of transactions such as all credit sales. (p. D4).

Subsidiary ledger A group of accounts with a common characteristic. (p. D2).

Demonstration Problem

Emelia Company uses a five-column cash receipts journal with columns for Cash (Dr.), Sales Discounts (Dr.), Accounts Receivable (Cr.), Sales (Cr.), and Other Accounts (Cr.). Cash receipts transactions for the month of July 1996 are as follows:

July 3   Cash sales total $5,800.

5   A check for $6,370 is received from the Jeltz Company in payment of invoice dated June 26 for $6,500 terms 2/10, n/30.

9   An additional investment of $5,000 in cash is made in the business by a stockholder.

10   Cash sales total $12,519.

12   A check for $7,275 is received from R. Eliot & Co. in payment of a $7,500 invoice dated July 3, terms 3/10, n/30.

15   A customer advance of $700 cash is received for future sales.

20   Cash sales total $15,472.

22   A check for $5,880 is received from Beck Company in payment of $6,000 invoice dated July 13, terms 2/10, n/30.

29   Cash sales total $17,660.

31   Cash of $200 is received on interest earned for July.

Instructions

(a) Journalize the transactions in the cash receipts journal.

(b) Contrast the posting of the Accounts Receivable and Other Accounts columns.

Solution to Demonstration Problem

(a)
EMELIA COMPANY
Cash Receipts Journal
CR1

Date	Accounts Credited	Ref.	Cash Dr.	Sales Discounts Dr.	Accounts Receivable Cr.	Sales Cr.	Other Accounts Cr.
1996							
7/3			5,800			5,800	
5	Jeltz Company		6,370	130	6,500		
9	Common Stock		5,000				5,000
10			12,519			12,519	
12	R. Eliot & Co.		7,275	225	7,500		
15	Unearned Revenues		700				700
20			15,472			15,472	
22	Beck Company		5,880	120	6,000		
29			17,660			17,660	
31	Interest Revenue		200				200
			76,876	475	20,000	51,451	5,900

(b) The Accounts Receivable column is posted as a credit to Accounts Receivable. The individual amounts are credited to the customers' accounts identified in the Accounts Credited column, which are maintained in the accounts receivable subsidiary ledger.

The amounts in the Other Accounts Column are only posted individually. They are credited to the account titles identified in the Accounts Credited column.

Problem-Solving Strategies

1. All cash receipts are recorded in the cash receipts journal.
2. The "accounts credited" indicate items posted individually to the subsidiary ledger or general ledger.
3. Cash sales are recorded in the cash receipts journal—not in the sales journal.
4. The total debits must equal the total credits.

SELF-STUDY QUESTIONS

(SO 1) 1. Which of the following is *incorrect* concerning subsidiary ledgers?
 a. The purchases ledger is a common subsidiary ledger for creditor accounts.
 b. The accounts receivable ledger is a subsidiary ledger.
 c. A subsidiary ledger is a group of accounts with a common characteristic.
 d. An advantage of the subsidiary ledger is that it permits a division of labor in posting.

(SO 2) 2. A sales journal will be used for:

	Credit sales	Cash sales	Sales discounts
a.	no	yes	yes
b.	yes	no	yes
c.	yes	no	no
d.	yes	yes	no

(SO 3) 3. Which of the following statements is correct?
 a. The sales discount column is included in the cash receipts journal.
 b. The purchases journal records all purchases of merchandise whether for cash or on account.
 c. The cash receipts journal records sales on account.
 d. Merchandise returned by the buyer is recorded by the seller in the purchases journal.

(SO 3) 4. Which of the following is *incorrect* concerning the posting of the cash receipts journal?
 a. The total of the Other Accounts column is not posted.
 b. All column totals except the total for the Other Accounts column are posted once at the end of the month to the account title specified in the column heading.
 c. The total of all columns are posted daily to the accounts specified in the column heading.
 d. The individual amounts in a column posted in total to a control account are posted daily to the subsidiary ledger account specified in the Accounts Credited column.

(SO 3)   5. Postings from the purchases journal to the subsidiary ledger are generally made:
   a. yearly.
   b. monthly.
   c. weekly.
   d. daily.

(SO 2)   6. Which statement is *incorrect* regarding the general journal?
   a. Only transactions that cannot be entered in a special journal are recorded in the general journal.
   b. Dual postings are always required in the general journal.
   c. The general journal may be used to record acceptance of a note receivable for an accounts receivable.
   d. Correcting, adjusting, and closing entries are made in the general journal.

QUESTIONS

1. What are the advantages of using subsidiary ledgers?

2. (a) When are postings normally made to (1) the subsidiary accounts and (2) the general ledger control accounts? (b) Describe the relationship between a control account and a subsidiary ledger.

3. Identify and explain the four specific journals discussed in the chapter. List an advantage of using each of these journals rather than using only a general journal.

4. A. Mega Company uses special journals. A sale made on account to K. Hansen for $435 was recorded in a single-column sales journal. A few days later, Hansen returns $70 worth of merchandise for credit. Where should A. Mega Company record the sales return? Why?

5. A $400 purchase of merchandise on account from Julia Company was properly recorded in the purchases journal. When posted, however, the amount recorded in the subsidiary ledger was $40. How might this error be discovered?

6. Why would special journals used in different businesses not be identical in format? Can you think of a business that would maintain a cash receipts journal but not include a column for accounts receivable?

7. The cash and the accounts receivable columns in the cash receipts journal were mistakenly over-added by $4,000 at the end of the month. (a) Will the customers' ledger agree with the Accounts Receivable control account? (b) Assuming no other errors, will the trial balance totals be equal?

8. The column total of a special journal is posted at month end to only two general ledger accounts. One of these two accounts is Accounts Receivable. What is the name of this special journal? What is the other general ledger account to which the month-end total is posted?

9. In what journal would the following transactions be recorded? (Assume that a single-column sales journal and a single-column purchases journal are used.)
   (a) Recording of depreciation expense for the year.
   (b) Gave credit to a customer for merchandise purchased on credit and returned.
   (c) Sales of merchandise for cash.
   (d) Sales of merchandise on account.
   (e) Collection of cash on account from a customer.
   (f) Purchase of office supplies on account.

10. In what journal would the following transactions be recorded? (Assume that a single-column sales journal and a single-column purchases journal are used.)
   (a) Cash received from signing a note payable.
   (b) Investment of cash by a stockholder of the company.
   (c) Closing of the expense accounts at the end of the year.
   (d) Purchase of merchandise on account.
   (e) Received credit for merchandise purchased and returned to supplier.
   (f) Payment of cash on account due a supplier.

11. What transactions might be included in a multiple-column purchases journal that would not be included in a single-column purchases journal?

12. Give an example of a transaction in the general journal that causes an entry to be posted twice (i.e., to two accounts), one in the general ledger, the other in the subsidiary ledger. Does this affect the debit/credit equality of the general ledger?

13. Give some examples of appropriate general journal transactions for an organization using special journals.

BRIEF EXERCISES

BED–1 Presented below is information related to Bradley Company for its first month of operations. Identify the balances that appear in the accounts receivable subsidiary ledger and the accounts receivable balance that appears in the general ledger at the end of January.

Identify subsidiary ledger balances.
(SO 1)

Credit Sales			**Cash Collections**		
Jan. 7	Avon Co.	$9,000	Jan. 17	Avon Co.	$7,000
15	Barto Inc.	$6,000	24	Barto Inc.	$5,000
23	Cecil Co.	$9,000	29	Cecil Co.	$9,000

BED–2 Identify in what ledger (general or subsidiary) each of the following accounts is shown.

Identify subsidiary ledger accounts.
(SO 1)

1. Rent Expense
2. Accounts Receivable—Oliva
3. Notes Payable
4. Accounts Payable—Kerns

BED–3 Identify the journal in which each of the following transactions is recorded.

Identify special journals.
(SO 2)

1. Cash sales
2. Owner withdrawal of cash
3. Cash purchase of land
4. Credit sales
5. Purchase of merchandise on account
6. Receipt of cash for services performed

BED–4 Indicate whether each of the following debits and credits is included in the Cash Receipts journal. (Use "Yes" or "No" to answer this question.)

Identify entries to cash receipts journal.
(SO 2)

1. Debit to Sales
2. Credit to Purchase Discounts
3. Credit to Accounts Receivable
4. Debit to Accounts Payable

BED–5 Sterling Computer Components Inc. uses a columnar Cash Receipts journal. Indicate which column(s) is/are posted only in total, only daily, or both in total and daily.

Indicate postings to cash receipts journal.
(SO 3)

1. Accounts Receivable
2. Sales Discounts
3. Cash
4. Other Accounts

BED–6 Cohen Co. uses special journals and a general journal. Identify the journal in which each of the following transactions is recorded.

Identify transactions for special journals.
(SO 2)

1. Purchased equipment on account.
2. Purchased merchandise on account.
3. Paid utility expense in cash.
4. Sold merchandise on account.

BED–7 Identify the special journal(s) in which the following column headings appear.

Identify transactions for special journals.
(SO 2)

1. Sales Discounts Dr.
2. Accounts Receivable Cr.
3. Cash Dr.
4. Purchase Discount Cr.
5. Purchase Dr.
6. Sales Cr.

EXERCISES

ED–1 Toyama Company uses both special journals and a general journal as described in this chapter. On June 30, after all monthly postings had been completed, the Accounts Receivable controlling account in the general ledger had a debit balance of $320,000 and the Accounts Payable controlling account had a credit balance of $97,000.

Determine control account balances and explain posting of special journals.
(SO 1, 2)

The July transactions recorded in the special journals are summarized below. No entries affecting accounts receivable and accounts payable were recorded in the general journal for July.

Sales journal	Total sales, $161,400
Purchases journal	Total purchases, $54,360
Cash receipts journal	Accounts receivable column total, $135,000
Cash payments journal	Accounts payable column total, $47,500

Instructions

(a) What is the balance of the Accounts Receivable control account after the monthly postings on July 31?

(b) What is the balance of the Accounts Payable control account after the monthly postings on July 31?

(c) To what account(s) is the column total of $161,400 in the sales journal posted?

(d) To what account(s) is the accounts receivable column total of $135,000 in the cash receipts journal posted?

Explain postings to subsidiary ledger.
(SO 1)

ED–2 Presented below is the subsidiary accounts receivable account of Rene Lopaz.

Date	Ref	Debit	Credit	Balance
1996				
Sept. 2	S31	61,000		61,000
9	G4		12,000	49,000
27	CR8		49,000	—

Instructions

▸ Write a memo that explains each transaction.

Post various journals to control and subsidiary accounts.
(SO 1, 3)

ED–3 On September 1 the balance of the Accounts Receivable controlling account in the general ledger of Crampton Company was $10,960. The customers' subsidiary ledger contained account balances as follows: Bannister, $1,440; Crowley, $2,640; Dotson, $2,060; Seaver, $4,820. At the end of September the various journals contained the following information:

Sales Journal: Sales to Seaver, $800; to Bannister, $1,350; to DeLeon, $1,030; to Dotson, $1,100.

Cash receipts journal: Cash received from Dotson, $1,310; from Seaver, $2,300; from DeLeon, $410; from Crowley, $1,800; from Bannister, $1,240.

General journal: An allowance is granted to Seaver, $120.

Instructions

(a) Set up control and subsidiary accounts and enter the beginning balances. Do not construct the journals.

(b) Post the various journals. Post the items as individual items or as totals, whichever would be the appropriate procedure. (No sales discounts given)

(c) Prepare a list of customers and prove the agreement of the controlling account with the subsidiary ledger at September 30, 1996.

Record transactions in sales and purchases journal.
(SO 1, 2)

ED–4 Hariett Company uses special journals and a general journal. The following transaction occurred during September 1996.

Sept. 2 Sold merchandise on account to B. Vell, invoice no. 101, $600, terms n/30.

10 Purchased merchandise on account from C. Cosgrove $700, terms 2/10, n/30.

12 Purchased office equipment on account from J. Wells, $6,500.

21 Sold merchandise on account to L. Scott, invoice no. 102 for $800, terms 2/10, n/30.

25 Purchased merchandise on account from P. Lewis $900, terms n/30.

27 Sold merchandise to R. Cowan for $700 cash.

Instructions

(a) Draw a single-column sales journal (see Illustration D-7) and a single-column purchase journal (see Illustration D-12). (Use page 1 for each journal.)

(b) Record the transaction(s) for September that should be journalized in the sales journal and the purchases journal.

Record transactions in cash receipts and cash payments journal.
(SO 1, 2)

ED–5 Reese Inc. uses special journals and a general journal. The following transactions occurred during May 1996.

May 1 L. Reese invested $72,000 cash in the business in exchange for shares of common stock.

2 Sold merchandise to L. Bean for $6,000 cash.

3 Purchased merchandise for $8,000 from R. L. Sanchez using check no. 101.

14 Paid salary to F. Sparks $700 by issuing check no. 102.

16 Sold merchandise on account to B. Ready for $900, terms n/30.

22 A check of $9,000 is received from C. Moody in full for invoice 101; no discount given.

Instructions

(a) Draw a multiple-column cash receipts journal (see Illustration D-9) and a multiple-column cash payments journal (see Illustration D-16). (Use page 1 for each journal.)

(b) Record the transaction(s) for May that should be journalized in the cash receipts journal and cash payments journal.

ED–6 Alda Company uses the columnar cash journals illustrated in the textbook. In April, the following selected cash transactions occurred:

Explain journalizing in cash journals.
(SO 2)

1. Made a refund to a customer for the return of damaged goods.
2. Received collection from customer within the 3% discount period.
3. Purchased merchandise for cash.
4. Paid a creditor within the 3% discount period.
5. Received collection from customer after the 3% discount period had expired.
6. Paid freight on merchandise purchased.
7. Paid cash for office equipment.
8. Received cash refund from supplier for merchandise returned.
9. Paid cash dividends.
10. Made cash sales.

Instructions

Indicate (a) the journal, and (b) the columns in the journal that should be used in recording each transaction.

ED–7 Vernor Company has the following selected transactions during March:

Journalize transactions in general journal and post.
(SO 1, 2)

Mar. 2 Purchased on account equipment costing $6,000 from Lifetime Company.

5 Received credit memorandum for $300 from Lynch Company for merchandise damaged in shipment to Vernor.

7 Issued a credit memorandum for $400 to Frey Company for merchandise the customer returned.

Vernor Company uses a one-column purchases journal, a sales journal, the columnar cash journals used in the text, and a general journal.

Instructions

(a) Journalize the transactions in the general journal.

(b) ▭▭▭▭▷ In a brief memo to the president of Vernor Company, explain the postings to the control and subsidiary accounts.

ED–8 Below are some typical transactions incurred by Duluth Company.

Indicate journalizing in special journals.
(SO 2)

1. Payment of creditors on account.
2. Return of merchandise sold for credit.
3. Collection on account from customers.
4. Sold land for cash.
5. Sale of merchandise on account.
6. Sale of merchandise for cash.
7. Received credit for merchandise purchased on credit.
8. Sales discount taken on goods sold.
9. Payment of employee wages.
10. Close income summary to retained earnings.
11. Depreciation on building.
12. Purchase of office supplies for cash.
13. Purchase of merchandise on account.

Instructions

For each transaction, indicate whether it would normally be recorded in a cash receipts journal, cash payments journal, single-column sales journal, single-column purchases journal, or general journal.

Explain posting to control account and subsidiary ledger.
(SO 1, 3)

ED–9 The general ledger of the Gonya Company contained the following Accounts Payable control account (in T-account form). Also shown is the related subsidiary ledger.

General Ledger

Accounts Payable

Feb. 15	General Journal	1,200		Feb. 1	Balance	26,025
28	?	?		5	General Journal	265
				11	General Journal	550
				28	Purchases	13,700
				Feb. 28	Balance	9,640

Accounts Payable Ledger

Patee

Feb. 28	Bal.	4,600

Wagner

Feb. 28	Bal.	?

Gruber

Feb. 28	Bal.	3,000

Instructions
(a) Indicate the missing posting reference and amount in the control account and the missing ending balance in the subsidiary ledger.
(b) Indicate the amounts in the control account that were dual-posted (i.e., posted to the control account and the subsidiary accounts).

Prepare purchases and general journals.
(SO 1, 3)

ED–10 Selected accounts from the ledgers of Alps Company at July 31 showed the following:

GENERAL LEDGER

Store Equipment   **No. 153**

Date	Explanation	Ref.	Debit	Credit	Balance
July 1		G1	3,600		3,600

Accounts Payable   **No. 201**

Date	Explanation	Ref.	Debit	Credit	Balance
July 1		G1		3,600	3,600
15		G1		400	4,000
18		G1	100		3,900
25		G1	200		3,700
31		P1		8,600	12,300

Purchases   **No. 510**

Date	Explanation	Ref.	Debit	Credit	Balance
July 31		P1	8,600		8,600

Freight-in   **No. 516**

Date	Explanation	Ref.	Debit	Credit	Balance
July 15		G1	400		400

Purchase Returns and Allowances   **No. 512**

Date	Explanation	Ref.	Debit	Credit	Balance
July 18		G1		100	100
25		G1		200	300

ACCOUNTS PAYABLE LEDGER

Andrew Equipment Co.

Date	Explanation	Ref.	Debit	Credit	Balance
July 1		G1		3,600	3,600

David Co.

Date	Explanation	Ref.	Debit	Credit	Balance
July 14		P1		1,100	1,100
25		G1	200		900

Bradley Co.

Date	Explanation	Ref.	Debit	Credit	Balance
July 3		P1		2,000	2,000
20		P1		700	2,700

Erick Co.

Date	Explanation	Ref.	Debit	Credit	Balance
July 12		P1		500	500
21		P1		600	1,100

Craig Materials

Date	Explanation	Ref.	Debit	Credit	Balance
July 17		P1		1,400	1,400
18		G1	100		1,300
29		P1		2,300	3,600

Gary Transit

Date	Explanation	Ref.	Debit	Credit	Balance
July 15		G1		400	400

Instructions

From the data prepare:

(a) the single-column purchases journal for July.

(b) the general journal entries for July.

ED–11 Olsen Products uses both special journals and a general journal as described in this chapter. Olsen also posts customers' accounts in the accounts receivable subsidiary ledger. The postings for the most recent month are included in the subsidiary T accounts below.

Determine correct posting amount to control account.
(SO 3)

Edmonds		
Bal.	340	250
	180	

Roemer		
Bal.	150	150
	190	

Schulz		
Bal.	–0–	145
	145	

Park		
Bal.	120	120
	190	
	170	

Instructions

Determine the correct amount of the end-of-month posting from the sales journal to the Accounts Receivable controlling account.

PROBLEMS

PD–1 Kimbell Company's chart of accounts includes the following selected accounts:

101 Cash	401 Sales
112 Accounts Receivable	414 Sales Discounts
301 Common Stock	512 Purchase Returns and
	Allowances

Journalize transactions in cash receipts journal and post to control account and subsidiary ledger.
(SO 1, 2, 3)

On June 1 the accounts receivable ledger of the Kimbell Company showed the following balances: Block & Son, $2,500; Field Co., $1,900; Green Bros., $1,600; and Mastin Co., $900. The June transactions involving the receipt of cash were as follows:

June 1 A. J. Kimbell, invested additional cash for common stock, $9,000.

3 Received check in full from Mastin Co. less 2% cash discount.

6 Received check in full from Field Co. less 2% cash discount.

7 Made cash sales of merchandise totaling $6,135.

9 Received check in full from Block & Son less 2% cash discount.

11 Received cash refund from a supplier for damaged merchandise, $200.

15 Made cash sales of merchandise totaling $5,250.

20 Received check in full from Green Bros., $1,600.

Instructions

(a) Journalize the transactions above in a five-column cash receipts journal with columns for Cash, Dr.; Sales Discounts, Dr.; Accounts Receivable, Cr.; Sales, Cr.; and Other Accounts, Cr. Foot and crossfoot the journal.

(b) Insert the beginning balances in the Accounts Receivable control and subsidiary accounts and post the June transactions to these accounts.

(c) Prove the agreement of the control account and subsidiary account balances.

Journalize transactions in cash payments journal and post to the general and subsidiary ledger.

(SO 1, 2, 3)

PD–2 Creek Company's chart of accounts includes the following selected accounts:

101 Cash	306 Dividends
130 Prepaid Insurance	510 Purchases
157 Equipment	514 Purchase Discounts
201 Accounts Payable	

On November 1 the accounts payable ledger of the Creek Company showed the following balances: R. Huff & Co., $3,750; G. Paul, $2,350; R. Snyder, $1,000; and Wicks Bros., $1,900. The November transactions involving the payment of cash were as follows:

Nov. 1 Purchased merchandise, check no. 11, $900.

3 Purchased store equipment, check no. 12, $1,650.

5 Paid Wicks Bros. balance due of $1,900, less 1% discount, check no. 13, $1,881.

11 Purchased merchandise, check no. 14, $2,000.

15 Paid R. Snyder balance due of $1,000, less 3% discount, check no. 15, $970.

16 A dividend is paid in the amount of $500, check no. 16.

19 Paid G. Paul in full for invoice no. 1245, $1,500 less 2% discount, check no. 17, $1,470.

25 Paid premium due on one year insurance policy, check no. 18, $3,000.

30 Paid R. Huff & Co. in full for invoice no. 832, $2,250, check no. 19.

Instructions

(a) Journalize the transctions above in a five-column cash payments journal with columns for Other Accounts, Dr.; Accounts Payable, Dr.; Purchases, Dr.; Purchase Discounts, Cr.; and Cash, Cr. Foot and crossfoot the journal.

(b) Insert the beginning balances in the Accounts Payable control and subsidiary accounts and post the November transactions to these accounts.

(c) Prove the agreement of the control account and the subsidiary account balances.

Journalize transactions in multicolumn purchases journal and post to the general and subsidiary ledgers.

(SO 1, 2, 3)

PD–3 The chart of accounts of Ventura Company includes the following selected accounts:

112 Accounts Receivable	412 Sales Returns and Allowances
126 Supplies	510 Purchases
157 Equipment	512 Purchase Returns and Allowances
201 Accounts Payable	516 Freight-in
401 Sales	610 Advertising Expense

In May the following selected transactions were completed. All purchases and sales were on account except as indicated.

May 2 Purchased merchandise from Vons Company, $8,000.

3 Received freight bill from Acme Freight on Vons purchase, $400.

5 Sales were made to Penner Company, $2,600; Hendrix Bros., $2,700; and Nelles Company, $1,500.

8 Purchased merchandise from Golden Company, $8,000 and Dorn Company, $8,700.

10 Received credit on merchandise returned to Dorn Company, $500.

15 Purchased supplies from Engle Supply, $900.

16 Purchased merchandise from Vons Company, $4,500; and Golden Company, $6,000.

17 Returned supplies to Engle Supply, receiving credit, $100. (Hint: Credit Supplies.)

18 Received freight bills on May 16 purchases from Acme Freight, $500.

20 Returned merchandise to Vons Company receiving credit, $300.

23 Made sales to Hendrix Bros., $2,400; and Nelles Company, $2,200.

25 Received bill for advertising from Ball Advertising, $900.

26 Granted allowance to Nelles Company for merchandise damaged in shipment, $200.

28 Purchased equipment from Engle Supply, $250.

Instructions

(a) Journalize the transactions above in a purchases journal, a one-column sales journal, and a general journal. The purchases journal should have the following column headings: Date, Accounts Credited (Debited), Ref., Other Accounts Dr., Purchases Dr., Freight-in Dr., and Accounts Payable Cr.

(b) Post to both the general and subsidiary ledger accounts. (Assume that all accounts have zero beginning balances.)

(c) Prove the agreement of the control and subsidiary accounts.

PD–4 Selected accounts from the chart of accounts of Susan Company are shown below.

Journalize transactions in special journals.
(SO 1, 2, 3)

101 Cash	401 Sales
112 Accounts Receivable	414 Sales Discounts
126 Supplies	510 Purchases
140 Land	512 Purchase Returns and Allowances
145 Buildings	514 Purchase Discounts
201 Accounts Payable	610 Advertising Expense

During October, Susan Company completed the following transactions:

Oct. 2 Purchased merchandise on account from Mason Company, $16,500.

4 Sold merchandise on account to Parker Co., $8,100. Invoice no. 204; terms 2/10, n/30.

5 Purchased supplies for cash, $80.

7 Made cash sales for the week totaling $9,160.

9 Paid in full the Mason Company on account less a 2% discount.

10 Purchased merchandise on account from Quinn Corp., $4,200.

12 Received payment from Parker Co. for invoice no. 204.

13 Issued a debit memorandum to Quinn Corp. and returned $250 worth of damaged goods.

14 Made cash sales for the week totaling $8,180.

16 Sold a parcel of land for $27,000 cash, the land's book value.

17 Sold merchandise on account to L. Boyton & Co., $5,350, invoice no. 205, terms 2/10, n/30.

18 Purchased merchandise for cash, $2,125.

21 Made cash sales for the week totaling $8,465.

23 Paid in full the Quinn Corp. on account for the goods kept (no discount).

25 Purchased supplies on account from Frey Co., $260.

25 Sold merchandise on account to Green Corp., $5,220, invoice no. 206, terms 2/10, n/30.

25 Received payment from L. Boyton & Co. for invoice no. 205.

26 Purchased for cash a small parcel of land and a building on the land to use as a storage facility. The total cost of $35,000 was allocated $21,000 to the land and $14,000 to the building.

27 Purchased merchandise on account from Schmid Co., $8,500.

28 Made cash sales for the week totaling $8,540.

30 Purchased merchandise on account from Mason Company, $14,000.

30 Paid advertising bill for the month from the Gazette, $400.

30 Sold merchandise on account to L. Boyton & Co., $4,600. Invoice no. 207; terms 2/10, n/30.

Susan Company uses the following journals:

1. Single-column sales journal.

2. Single-column purchases journal.

3. Cash receipts journal with columns for Cash, Dr.; Sales Discounts, Dr.; Accounts Receivable, Cr.; Sales, Cr.; and Other Accounts, Cr.

4. Cash payments journal with columns for Other Accounts, Dr.; Accounts Payable, Dr.; Purchase Discounts, Cr.; and Cash, Cr.
5. General journal.

Instructions
Using the selected accounts provided:

(a) Record, in the appropriate journals, the October transactions.
(b) Foot and crossfoot all special journals.
(c) Show how postings would be made by placing ledger account numbers and check marks as needed in the journals. (Actual posting to ledger accounts is not required.)

Journalize in purchase and cash payments journals, post, prepare a trial balance, prove control to subsidiary, prepare adjusting entries, and prepare an adjusted trial balance.
(SO 1, 2, 3)

PD–5 Presented below are the sales and cash receipts journals for Taco Co. for its first month of operations.

SALES JOURNAL   S1

Date	Account Debited	Ref.	Accounts Receivable Debit Sales Credit
Feb. 3	H. Adams		5,000
9	R. Babcock		6,500
12	B. Chambers		7,000
26	L. Dawson		6,000
			24,500

CASH RECEIPTS JOURNAL   CR1

Date	Accounts Credited	Ref.	Cash Debit	Sales Discounts Debit	Accounts Receivable Credit	Sales Credit	Other Accounts Credit
Feb. 1	Common Stock		30,000				30,000
2			6,500			6,500	
13	H. Adams		4,950	50	5,000		
18	Purchase Returns and Allowances		150				150
26	R. Babcock		6,500		6,500		
			48,100	50	11,500	6,500	30,150

In addition, the following transactions have not been journalized for February 1996.

Feb. 2 Purchased merchandise on account from S. Healy for $2,000, terms 1/10, n/30.
7 Purchased merchandise on account from L. Held for $30,000, terms 1/10, n/30.
9 Paid cash of $1,000 for purchase of supplies.
12 Paid $1,980 to S. Healy in payment for $2,000 invoice, less 1% discount.
15 Purchased equipment for $8,000 cash.
16 Purchased merchandise on account from R. Landly, $2,400, terms 2/10, n/30.
17 Paid $29,700 to L. Held in payment of $30,000 invoice, less 1% discount.
20 Paid a cash dividend of $1,100.
21 Purchased merchandise on account from J. Able for $6,500, terms 1/10, n/30.
28 Paid $2,400 to R. Landly in payment of $2,400 invoice.

Instructions
(a) Open the following accounts in the general ledger.

101 Cash
112 Accounts Receivable
126 Supplies
157 Equipment

158 Accumulated Depreciation—Equipment
201 Accounts Payable
301 Common Stock
306 Dividends

401 Sales
414 Sales Discounts
510 Purchases
512 Purchase Returns and Allowances

514 Purchase Discounts
631 Supplies Expense
711 Depreciation Expense

(b) Journalize the transactions that have not been journalized in a one-column purchases journal, and the cash payments journal (see Illustration D-16).
(c) Post to the accounts receivable and accounts payable subsidiary ledgers. Follow the sequence of transactions as shown in the problem.
(d) Post the individual entries and totals to the general ledger.
(e) Prepare a trial balance at February 28, 1996.
(f) Determine that the subsidiary ledgers agree with the control accounts in the general ledger.
(g) The following adjustments at the end of February are necessary.
1. A count of supplies indicates that $300 is still on hand.
2. Depreciation on equipment for February is $200.
Prepare the adjusting entries and then post the adjusting entries to the general ledger.
(h) Prepare an adjusted trial balance.

PD–6 The post-closing trial balance for Garcia Co. is as follows:

Journalize in special journals, post, and prepare a trial balance.
(SO 1, 2, 3)

GARCIA CO.
Post-Closing Trial Balance
December 31, 1996

	Debit	Credit
Cash	$ 39,500	
Accounts Receivable	15,000	
Notes Receivable	45,000	
Merchandise Inventory	23,000	
Equipment	6,450	
Accumulated Depreciation—Equipment		$ 1,500
Accounts Payable		43,000
Common Stock		84,450
	$128,950	$128,950

The subsidiary ledgers contain the following information: (1) accounts receivable—R. Barton $2,500; B. Cole $7,500; S. Devine $5,000; (2) accounts payable—S. Field $10,000; R. Gilson $18,000; and D. Harms $15,000.

The transactions for January 1997 are as follows:

Jan. 3 Sell merchandise to B. Senton, $2,000, terms 2/10, n/30.
5 Purchase merchandise from S. Warren, $2,200, terms 2/10, n/30.
7 Receive a check from S. Devine, $3,500.
11 Pay freight on merchandise purchased, $300.
12 Pay rent of $1,000 for January.
13 Receive payment in full from B. Senton.
14 Post all entries to the subsidiary ledgers. Issue a credit memo to acknowledge receipt of damaged merchandise of $700 returned by R. Barton.
15 Send D. Harms a check for $14,850 in full payment of account, discount, $150.
17 Purchase merchandise from D. Lapeska, $1,600, terms 2/10, n/30.
18 Pay sales salaries of $2,800 and office salaries, $1,500.
20 Give R. Gilson a 60-day note for $18,000 in full payment of accounts payable.
23 Total cash sales amount to $8,600.
24 Post all entries to the subsidiary ledgers. Sells merchandise on account to B. Cole, $7,700, terms 1/10, n/30.
27 Send S. Warren a check for $950.
29 Receive payment on a note of $40,000 from S. Lava.
30 Return merchandise of $500 to D. Lapeska for credit. Post all journals to the subsidiary ledger.

Instructions

(a) Open general and subsidiary ledger accounts for the following:

101 Cash	412 Sales Returns and Allowances
112 Accounts Receivable	414 Sales Discounts
115 Notes Receivable	510 Purchases
120 Merchandise Inventory	512 Purchase Returns and Allowances
157 Equipment	514 Purchase Discounts
158 Accumulated Depreciation—Equipment	516 Freight-in
200 Notes Payable	726 Sales Salaries Expense
201 Accounts Payable	727 Office Salaries Expense
301 Common Stock	729 Rent Expense
401 Sales	

(b) Record the January transactions in a single-column sales journal, a single-column purchases journal, a cash receipts journal (see Illustration D-9), a cash payments journal (see Illustration D-16), and a general journal.

(c) Post the appropriate amounts to the general ledger.

(d) Prepare a trial balance at January 31, 1997.

(e) Determine whether the subsidiary ledgers agree with controlling accounts in the general ledger.

▶*B*roadening *Your Perspective*

*F*INANCIAL REPORTING PROBLEM—A MINI PRACTICE SET
• •

(The working papers that accompany this textbook are needed in order to work this mini practice set.) This practice set uses a **periodic inventory system**; therefore it should be assigned after coverage of Chapter 9.

Hunt Co. uses both an accounts receivable and an accounts payable subsidiary ledger. Balances related to both the general ledger and the subsidiary ledger for Hunt are indicated in the working papers. Presented below are a series of transactions for Hunt Co. for the month of January. Credit sales terms are 2/10, n/30.

Jan. 3   Sell merchandise on credit to B. Sargent $3,100, invoice No. 510, and to J. Eaton $1,800, invoice No. 511.

5   Purchase merchandise from S. Walden $3,000 and D. Landell $2,200, terms n/30.

7   Receive checks from S. Lowell, $4,000 and B. Jaggar $2,000 after discount period has lapsed.

8   Pay freight on merchandise purchased $180.

9   Send checks to S. Lee for $9,000 less 2% cash discount and D. Nordin for $11,000 less 1% cash discount.

9   Issue credit memo for $300 to J. Eaton for merchandise returned.

10   Summary daily cash sales total $15,500.

11   Sell merchandise on credit to R. Dansig $1,300, invoice No. 512, and to S. Lowell $900, invoice No. 513.

12   Pay rent of $1,000 for January.

13   Receive payment in full from B. Sargent and J. Eaton less cash discounts.

15   Paid cash dividends of $800.

15   Post all entries to the subsidiary ledgers.

16   Purchase merchandise from D. Nordin $15,000, terms 1/10, n/30; S. Lee $14,200, terms 2/10, n/30; and S. Walden $1,500, terms n/30.

17   Pay $400 cash for office supplies.

18   Return $200 of merchandise to S. Lee and receive credit.

20   Summary daily cash sales total $17,500.

21   Issue $15,000 note to R. Mannon in payment of balance due.

21 Receive payment in full from S. Lowell less cash discount.

22 Sell merchandise on credit to B. Sargent $1,700, invoice No. 514 and to R. Dansig $800, invoice No. 515.

22 Post all entries to the subsidiary ledger.

23 Send checks to D. Nordin and S. Lee in full payment less cash discounts.

25 Sell merchandise on credit to B. Jaggar $3,500, invoice No. 516 and to J. Eaton $6,100, invoice No. 517.

27 Purchase merchandise from D. Nordin $14,500, terms 1/10, n/30; D. Landell $1,200, terms n/30; and S. Walden $2,800, terms n/30.

27 Post all entries to the subsidiary ledger.

28 Pay $200 cash for office supplies.

31 Summary daily cash sales total $21,300.

31 Pay sales salaries $4,300 and office salaries $2,600.

Instructions

(a) Record the January transactions in a single-column sales journal, a single-column purchases journal, a cash receipts journal as shown on page D9, a cash payments journal as shown on page D16, and a two-column general journal.

(b) Post the journals to the general ledger.

(c) Prepare a trial balance at January 31, 1997, in the trial balance columns of the work sheet. Complete the work sheet using the following additional information. (**A periodic inventory system is assumed.**)

    (1) Office supplies at January 31 total $500.

    (2) Insurance coverage expires on October 31, 1997.

    (3) Annual depreciation on the equipment is $1,500.

    (4) Interest of $60 has accrued on the note payable.

    (5) Merchandise inventory at January 31 is $16,000.

(d) Prepare a multiple-step income statement and a retained earnings statement for January and a classified balance sheet at the end of January.

(e) Prepare and post adjusting and closing entries.

(f) Prepare a post-closing trial balance and determine whether the subsidiary ledgers agree with the controlling accounts in the general ledger.

DECISION CASE

Smith & Young is a wholesaler of small appliances and parts. Smith & Young is operated by two owners, Paul Smith and Ann Young. In addition, the company has one employee, a repair specialist, who is on a fixed salary. Revenues are earned through the sale of appliances to retailers (approximately 75% of total revenues), appliance parts to do-it-yourselfers (10%), and the repair of appliances brought to the store (15%). Appliance sales are made on both a credit and cash basis. Customers are billed on prenumbered sales invoices. Credit terms are always net/30 days. All parts sales and repair work are cash only.

Merchandise is purchased on account from the manufacturers of both the appliances and the parts. Practically all suppliers offer cash discounts for prompt payments, and it is company policy to take all discounts. Most cash payments are made by check. Checks are most frequently issued to suppliers, to trucking companies for freight on merchandise purchases, and to newspapers, radio, and TV stations for advertising. All advertising bills are paid as received. The company pays dividends monthly to its stockholders. The salaried repairman is paid twice monthly.

Smith & Young currently has a manual accounting system. However, the business is growing and some consideration is being given to an electronic accounting system.

Instructions

(a) Identify the special journals that Smith & Young should have in its manual system. List the column headings appropriate for each of the special journals.

(b) What control and subsidiary accounts should be included in Smith & Young's manual system? Why?

(c) Identify for Paul and Ann the key points they should consider in deciding whether to install an electronic system.

GROUP ACTIVITY

Hard Hat Construction uses a general journal and the following special journals: single-column sales journal, cash receipts journal, single-column purchases journal, and a cash payments journal. Hard Hat also uses control accounts and subsidiary ledgers for accounts receivable and accounts payable.

Instructions

With the class divided into six groups, five groups will choose one journal each and should report to the class on the journalizing and posting of the journal and proving the postings. The sixth group will consider control accounts and subsidiary ledgers. This group should report to the class on the relationship of the accounts, postings to the accounts, and proving the agreement of the accounts.

ETHICS CASE

Triport Products Company operates three divisions, each with its own manufacturing plant and marketing/sales force. The corporate headquarters and central accounting office are in Triport with the plants in Freeport, Rockport, and Bayport, all within 50 miles of Triport. Corporate management treats each division as an independent profit center and encourages competition among them. They each have similar but different product lines. As a competitive incentive, bonuses are awarded each year to the employees of the fastest growing and most profitable division.

Ron Hermann is the manager of Triport's centralized computer accounting operation that keyboards the sales transactions and maintains the accounts receivable for all three divisions. Ron came up in the accounting ranks from the Bayport division where his wife, several relatives, and many friends still work.

As sales documents are keyboarded into the computer, the originating division is identified by code. Most sales documents (95%) are coded, but some (5%) are not coded or are coded incorrectly. As the manager, Ron has instructed the keyboard operators to assign the Bayport code to all uncoded and incorrectly coded sales documents. This is done he says, "in order to expedite processing and to keep the computer files current since they are updated daily." All receivables and cash collections for all three divisions are handled by Triport as one subsidiary accounts receivable ledger.

Instructions

   (a) Who are the stakeholders in this situation?
   (b) What are the ethical issues in this case?
   (c) How might the system be improved to prevent this situation?

CRITICAL THINKING
▸ *A Real-World Focus: Alco Standard Corporation*

ALCO Standard Corporation

Alco Standard Corporation's operations are divided into two business groups: Alco Office Products and Unisource. Alco Office Products sells, leases, and rents various electronic office machines; Unisource markets and distributes papers primarily for office use. The company owns or leases facilities in 49 states and 9 foreign countries.

The President of Alco wrote the following in his letter in a recent annual report:

The creation of Unisource allows us to pursue strategies that are practical only on a unified basis. Our efforts to upgrade information technology, for example, will now be directed to building a common system throughout North America. This unified approach will give us online electronic link suppliers, cutting order entry costs and improving inventory management. As a result, we will be able to improve service to customers with more timely and more accurate order fulfillment, faster inquiry response and enhanced technical support.

Instructions

(a) When a company computerizes customer order entry, what equivalent special journal type must be programmed into such an electronic system?

(b) When a company computerizes inventory management (which involves more timely ordering of new merchandise), what special journal type must be programmed into such an electronic system?

Answers to Self-Study Questions

1. a   2. c   3. a   4. c   5. d   6. b

APPENDIX · E

*O*THER SIGNIFICANT LIABILITIES

▶ STUDY OBJECTIVES ◀

After studying this appendix, you should be able to:

1. *Describe the accounting and disclosure requirements for contingent liabilities.*
2. *Contrast the accounting for operating and capital leases.*
3. *Identify additional fringe benefits associated with employee compensation.*

In addition to the current and long-term liabilities discussed in Chapter 11, several more types of liabilities may exist that could have a significant impact on a company's financial position and future cash flows. These other significant liabilities have been classified in this appendix as (a) contingent liabilities, (b) lease liabilities, and (c) additional liabilities for employee fringe benefits (paid absences and postretirement benefits).

◤Contingent Liabilities

STUDY OBJECTIVE

• • • • • • • • • ▼ • • • • • • • • •

Describe the accounting and disclosure requirements for contingent liabilities.

Helpful hint Another example of a contingency is toxic waste. Corporations have increasingly been held liable for toxic waste cleanup. Some expect that insurance will cover these costs, but insurance companies are arguing that (1) intentional discharges are not covered and (2) general liability policies were never meant to cover this type of situation.

With notes payable, interest payable, accounts payable, and sales taxes payable, we know that an obligation exists to make payment. But suppose that your company is currently involved in a dispute with the Internal Revenue Service (IRS) over the amount of its income tax liability. Do you have to report the disputed amount on the balance sheet as a liability? Or suppose your company is the defendant in a lawsuit in which an adverse decision might result in bankruptcy. How should this major contingency be reported? The answers to these questions are difficult, because these liabilities are dependent—contingent—upon some future event. In other words, a contingent liability is a potential liability that may become an actual liability in the future.

How, then, should contingent liabilities be reported? Guidelines have been adopted that are helpful in resolving these problems. The guidelines require that:

1. If the contingency is **probable**—if it is likely to occur—**and** the amount can be **reasonably estimated**, the liability should be recorded in the accounts.
2. If the contingency is only **reasonably possible**—if it could happen—then it need be disclosed only in the notes accompanying the financial statements.
3. If the contingency is **remote**—if it is unlikely to occur—it need not be recorded or disclosed.

Recording a Contingent Liability

Product warranties are a good example of a contingent liability that should be recorded in the accounts. Warranty contracts result in future costs that may be incurred in replacing defective units or repairing malfunctioning units without charge to the customer for a specified period after the product is sold. Generally, a manufacturer, such as Black & Decker, knows that some warranty costs will be incurred. Moreover, on the basis of prior experience with the product (or

▶Accounting in Action ▸ *Business Insight*

Contingent liabilities abound in the real world. Consider the following: Manville Corp. filed bankruptcy when it was hit by billions of dollars in asbestos product liability claims. Companies having multiple toxic waste sites are faced with cleanup costs that average $10 to $30 million and can reach as high as $500 million depending on the type of waste. For life and health insurance companies and their stockholders, the cost of AIDS is like an iceberg—everybody wonders how big it really is and what damage it might do in the future; according to the U.S. Centers for Disease Control treatment costs could be $8 billion to $16 billion. And frequent-flyer programs are so popular that airlines at one time owed participants more than 3 million round-trip domestic tickets. That's enough to fly at least 5.4 billion miles—free for the passengers but at what future cost to the airlines?

similar products), the company usually can make a reasonable estimate of the anticipated cost of servicing (honoring) the contract.

► *International note*

International accounting standards basically use the same criteria in determining how to account for contingencies.

The accounting for warranty costs is based on the matching principle. To comply with this principle, **the estimated cost of honoring product warranty contracts should be recognized as an expense in the period in which the sale occurs.** To illustrate, assume that in 1996 Denson Manufacturing Company sells 10,000 washers and dryers at an average price of $600 each. The selling price includes a one-year warranty on parts. It is expected that 500 units (5%) will be defective and that warranty repair costs will average $80 per unit. In the year of sale, warranty contracts are honored on 300 units at a total cost of $24,000.

At December 31, it is necessary to accrue the estimated warranty costs on the 1996 sales. The computation is as follows:

Illustration E-1

Computation of estimated product warranty liability

Number of units sold	10,000
Estimated rate of defective units	× 5%
Total estimated defective units	500
Average warranty repair cost	× $80
Estimated product warranty liability	$40,000

The adjusting entry, therefore, is:

Dec. 31	Warranty Expense	40,000	
	Estimated Warranty Liability		40,000
	(To accrue estimated warranty costs)		

Helpful hint The effects of the warranty adjusting entry are an increase in expenses and an increase in liabilities; the effects of the entry to record the honoring of the warranty are a decrease in one liability and either a decrease in assets or an increase in another liability.

The entry to record repair costs incurred in 1996 to honor warranty contracts on 1996 sales is shown in summary form below:

Jan. 1–	Estimated Warranty Liability	24,000	
Dec. 31	Repair Parts/Wages Payable		24,000
	(To record honoring of 300 warranty		
	contracts on 1996 sales)		

Warranty expense of $40,000 is reported under selling expenses in the income statement, and estimated warranty liability of $16,000 ($40,000 − $24,000) is classified as a current liability on the balance sheet.

In the following year, all expenses incurred in honoring warranty contracts on 1996 sales should be debited to Estimated Warranty Liability. To illustrate, assume that 20 defective units are replaced in January 1997, at an average cost of $80 in parts and labor. The summary entry for the month of January is:

Helpful hint The balance in Warranty Expense is always the estimated expense. In terms of matching, the effects are the same as using the percentage-of-sales method to estimate uncollectible accounts receivable.

Jan. 31	Estimated Warranty Liability	1,600	
	Repair Parts/Wages Payable		1,600
	(To record honoring of 20 warranty		
	contracts on 1996 sales)		

Disclosure of Contingent Liabilities

When a contingent liability meets one but not both conditions for recording the contingency described above, or when the contingent liability is only reasonably possible, only disclosure of the contingency is required. Examples of contingencies that may require disclosure are pending or threatened lawsuits and assessment of additional income taxes pending an IRS audit of the tax return.

Helpful hint Why should a contingency be disclosed if it is not probable that it will occur? Answer: If it is reasonably possible, disclosure seems warranted. Such a contingency if it occurs may materially affect the financial statements.

The disclosure should identify the nature of the item, and if known, the amount of the contingency and the expected outcome of the future event. Disclosure is usually accomplished through a note to the financial statements, as illustrated by the following:

Illustration E-2

Disclosure of contingent liability

USAir
Legal Proceedings
The Company and various subsidiaries have been named as defendants in various suits and proceedings which involve, among other things, environmental concerns about noise and air pollution and employment matters. These suits and proceedings are in various stages of litigation, and the status of the law with respect to several of the issues involved is unsettled. For these reasons the outcome of these suits and proceedings is difficult to predict. In the Company's opinion, however, the disposition of these matters is not likely to have a material adverse effect on its financial condition.

Lease Liabilities

STUDY OBJECTIVE
••••••••••**2**••••••••••

Contrast the accounting for operating and capital leases.

A lease is a contractual arrangement between the lessor (owner of the property) and a lessee (renter of the property) that grants the right to use specific property for a period of time in return for cash payments. Leasing is big business. For example, an estimated $125 billion of capital equipment was leased in a recent year. This represents approximately one-third of equipment financed that year. The two most common types of leases are operating leases and capital leases.

▶Accounting in Action ▶ *Business Insight*

As an excellent example of the magnitude of leasing, leased planes account for nearly 40% of the U.S. fleet of commercial airlines. The reasons for leasing include favorable tax treatment, increased flexibility, and low airline income. As passenger volume is expected to double in the next 20 years, some industry analysts estimate that approximately $400 billion in airplanes will be needed, and it is anticipated that much of the financing will be done through leasing. Leasing is particularly attractive to lessors because airplanes have relatively long lives, a ready secondhand market, and a significant resale value. Or take the commercial truck fleet—over one third of heavy-duty trucks are presently leased.

Operating Leases

The renting of an apartment and the rental of a car at an airport are examples of operating leases. **In an operating lease the intent is temporary use of the property by the lessee with continued ownership of the property by the lessor.** The lease (or rental) payments are recorded as an expense by the lessee and as revenue by the lessor. For example, assuming that a sales representative for Western Inc. leases a car from Hertz Car Rental at the Los Angeles airport and that Hertz charges a total of $275, the entry by the lessee, Western Inc., is:

Car Rental Expense	275	
Cash		275
(To record payment of lease rental charge)		

In addition, the lessee may incur other costs during the lease period. For example, in the case above, the lessee may be required to pay for gas and oil. These costs are also reported as an expense.

Capital Leases

In most lease contracts, a periodic payment is made by the lessee and is recorded as rent expense in the income statement. However, in some cases, the lease contract transfers substantially all the benefits and risks of ownership to the lessee, so that the lease is in effect a purchase of the property. This type of lease is called a capital lease because the present value of the cash payments for the lease are capitalized and recorded as an asset.

The lessee must record the lease **as an asset**—that is, as a capital lease—if any **one** of the following conditions exists:

1. **The lease transfers ownership of the property to the lessee.** *Rationale:* If during the lease term, the lessee receives ownership of the asset, the leased asset should be reported as an asset on the lessee's books.
2. **The lease contains a bargain purchase option.** *Rationale:* If during the term of the lease, the lessee can purchase the asset at a price substantially below its fair market value, the lessee will obviously exercise this option. Thus, the lease should be reported as a leased asset on the lessee's books.
3. **The lease term is equal to 75% or more of the economic life of the leased property.** *Rationale:* If the lease term is for much of the asset's useful life, the asset should be recorded by the lessee.
4. **The present value of the lease payments equals or exceeds 90% of the fair market value of the leased property.** *Rationale:* If the present value of the lease payments is equal to or almost equal to the fair market value of the asset, the lessee has essentially purchased the asset. As a result, the leased asset should be recorded on the books of the lessee.

> **Helpful hint** A capital lease situation is one in which although it is legally a rental case, it is *in substance* an installment purchase by the lessee. Accounting standards require that substance over form be used in such a situation.

To illustrate, assume that Gonzalez Company decides to lease new equipment. The lease period is 4 years; the economic life of the leased equipment is estimated to be 5 years. The present value of the lease payments is $190,000 which is equal to the fair market value of the equipment. There is no transfer of ownership during the lease term nor is there any bargain purchase option.

In this example, Gonzalez has essentially purchased the equipment. Conditions 3 and 4 have been met: First, the lease term is 75% or more of the economic life of the asset, and second, the present value of cash payments is equal to the equipment's fair market value. The entry to record the transaction is as follows:

> **Helpful hint** What are the effects on the lessee's balance sheet if a lease meets the criteria to be classified as a capital lease but is incorrectly accounted for as an operating lease? Answer: Assets and liabilities are understated.

Leased Asset—Equipment	190,000	
Lease Liability		190,000
(To record leased asset and lease liability)		

The leased asset is reported on the balance sheet under plant assets. The lease liability is reported as a liability on the balance sheet. **The portion of the lease liability expected to be paid in the next year is reported as a current liability. The remainder is classified as a long-term liability.**

Most lessees do not like to report leases on their balance sheets. The reason is that the lease liability increases the company's total liabilities. This, in turn, may make it more difficult for the company to obtain needed funds from lenders. As a result, companies attempt to keep leased assets and lease liabilities off the balance sheet by not meeting any one of the four conditions mentioned above.

> **Helpful hint** Off-balance sheet financing is a major reporting problem. Some other off-balance sheet items are guarantees, pensions, and long-term commitments.

This procedure of keeping liabilities off the balance sheet is often referred to as **off-balance sheet financing**.

Additional Liabilities for Employee Fringe Benefits

STUDY OBJECTIVE

3

Identify additional liabilities for fringe benefits associated with employee compensation.

In addition to the liabilities for payroll taxes, employers incur other substantial employee fringe benefit costs. Two of the most important additional liabilities are associated with paid absences and postretirement benefits.

Paid Absences

Employees often have rights to receive compensation for future absences when certain conditions of employment are met. The compensation may pertain to paid vacations, sick pay benefits, and paid holidays. When the payment of such compensation is **probable** and the amount can be **reasonably estimated**, a liability should be accrued for paid future absences. When the amount cannot be reasonably estimated, the potential liability should be disclosed. Ordinarily, vacation pay is the only paid absence that is accrued; the other types of paid absences are only disclosed.[1]

To illustrate, assume that Academy Company employees are entitled to one day's vacation for each month worked. If thirty employees earn an average of $110 per day in a given month, the accrual for vacation benefits in one month is $3,300. The liability is recognized at the end of the month by the following adjusting entry:

Jan. 31	Vacation Benefits Expense	3,300	
	Vacation Benefits Payable		3,300
	(To accrue vacation benefits expense)		

This accrual is required by the matching principle. Vacation Benefits Expense is reported as an operating expense in the income statement, and Vacation Benefits Payable is reported as a current liability in the balance sheet. When vacation benefits are paid, Vacation Benefits Payable is debited and Cash is credited. For example if the above benefits for ten employees are paid in July, the entry is:

July 31	Vacation Benefits Payable	1,100	
	Cash		1,100
	(To record payment of vacation benefits)		

The magnitude of unpaid absences has gained employers' attention. Consider the case of an assistant superintendent of schools who worked for around 20 years and rarely took a vacation or sick day. A month or so before she retired, the school district discovered that she was due nearly $30,000 in accrued benefits. Yet the liability was never accrued.

Postretirement Benefits

Helpful hint These costs should be expensed during the working years of the employee because the company benefits during this period.

Postretirement benefits consist of payments by employers to retired employees for (1) health care and life insurance and (2) pensions. For many years the accounting for postretirement benefits was on a cash basis. However, both types of postretirement benefits are now accounted for on the accrual basis.

---

[1]The typical U.S. company provides an average 12 days of paid vacations for its employees at an average cost of 5% of gross earnings.

Postretirement Health Care and Life Insurance Benefits

Providing medical and related health care benefits for retirees—at one time an inexpensive and highly effective way of generating employee goodwill—has turned into one of corporate America's most worrisome financial problems. Runaway medical costs, early retirement, and increased longevity are sending the liability for retiree health plans through the roof for many companies.

Helpful hint Recognizing the impact of retiree health costs on net income, companies are increasingly changing their health plans to shift costs and reduce benefits.

Many companies began offering retiree health care coverage in the form of Medicare supplements in the 1960s. Almost all plans operated on a pay-as-you-go basis—the companies simply paid for the bills as they came in, rather than setting aside funds to meet the cost of future benefits. These plans were accounted for on the cash basis rather than the accrual basis. However, the FASB concluded that shareholders and creditors should know the amount of the employer's obligations. As a result, employers must now use the **accrual basis** in accounting for postretirement health care and life insurance benefits.

►Accounting in Action ► Business Insight

The battle over fringe benefits has grabbed a starring role in the corporate drama of the 1990s, as benefits continue to outpace wages and salaries. Growing far faster than pay, benefits equaled 38% of wages and salaries in a recent year. While vacations and other forms of paid leave still take the biggest bite of the benefits pie, medical costs are the fastest-growing item.

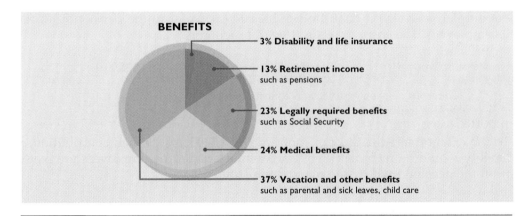

BENEFITS

- 3% Disability and life insurance
- 13% Retirement income such as pensions
- 23% Legally required benefits such as Social Security
- 24% Medical benefits
- 37% Vacation and other benefits such as parental and sick leaves, child care

Pension Plans

A pension plan is an agreement whereby an employer provides benefits (payments) to employees after they retire. Over 50 million workers currently participate in pension plans in the United States. The need for proper administration of and good accounting for pension plans becomes apparent when one appreciates the size of existing pension funds. Most pension plans are subject to the provisions of ERISA (Employee Retirement Income Security Act), a law enacted to curb abuses in the administration and funding of such plans.

Three parties are generally involved in a pension plan. The **employer** (company) sponsors the pension plan. The **plan administrator** receives the contributions from the employer, invests the pension assets, and makes the benefit payments to the **pension recipients** (retired employees). Illustration E-3 shows the three distinct parties involved in a pension plan and indicates the flow of cash among them.

Illustration E-3

Parties in a pension plan

The two most common types of pension arrangements for providing benefits to employees after they retire are defined contribution plans and defined benefit plans.

Defined Contribution Plan.   In a defined contribution plan, the employer's contribution to the plan is defined by the terms of the plan. That is, the employer agrees to contribute a certain sum each period based on a formula.

The accounting for a defined contribution plan is straightforward: The employer simply makes a contribution each year based on the formula established in the plan. As a result, the employer's obligation is easily determined. It follows that **the amount of the contribution required each period is reported as pension expense. A liability is reported by the employer only if the contribution has not been made in full**.

To illustrate, assume that Alba Office Interiors Corp. has a defined contribution plan in which it contributes $200,000 each year to the pension fund for its employees. The entry to record this transaction is:

Pension Expense	200,000	
Cash		200,000
(To record pension expense and contribution to		
pension fund)		

To the extent that Alba did not contribute the $200,000 defined contribution, a liability would be recorded. Pension payments to retired employees are made from the pension fund by the plan administrator.

Defined Benefit Plan.   In a defined benefit plan, the benefits that the employee will receive at the time of retirement are defined by the terms of the plan. Benefits are typically calculated using a formula that considers an employee's compensation level when he or she nears retirement and the employee's years of service. Because the benefits in this plan are defined in terms of uncertain future variables, an appropriate funding pattern is established to assure that enough funds are available at retirement to meet the benefits promised. This funding level depends on a number of factors such as employee turnover, length of service, mortality, compensation levels, and investment earnings. **The proper accounting for these plans is complex and is considered in more advanced accounting courses.**

Postretirement Benefits as Long-term Liabilities

While part of the liability associated with (1) postretirement health care and life insurance benefits and (2) pension plans is generally a current liability, the greater portion of these liabilities extends many years into the future. Therefore, many companies are required to report significant amounts as long-term liabilities for postretirement benefits.

Before You Go On . . .

► *Review It*

1. What is a contingent liability?
2. How are contingent liabilities reported in financial statements.
3. What accounts are involved in accruing and paying vacation benefits?
4. What basis should be used in accounting for postretirement benefits?

Summary of Study Objectives

1. *Describe the accounting and disclosure requirements for contingent liabilities.* If it is probable that (likely to occur) the contingency will happen and the amount is reasonably estimable, the liability should be recorded in the accounts. However, if it is only reasonably possible (it could occur), then it need be disclosed only in the notes to the financial statements. If the possibility that the contingency will happen is remote (unlikely to occur), it need not be recorded or disclosed.

2. *Contrast the accounting for operating and capital leases.* For an operating lease, lease (or rental) payments are re-corded as an expense by the lessee (renter). For a capital lease, the lessee records the asset and related obligation at the present value of the future lease payments.

3. *Identify additional fringe benefits associated with employee compensation.* Additional fringe benefits associated with wages are paid absences (paid vacations, sick pay benefits, and paid holidays), postretirement health care and life insurance, and pensions. The two most common types of pension arrangements are a defined contribution plan and a defined benefit plan.

GLOSSARY

Capital lease   A contractual arrangement that transfers substantially all the benefits and risks of ownership to the lessee so that the lease is in effect a purchase of the property. (p. E5).

Contingent liability   A potential liability that may become an actual liability in the future. (p. E2).

Defined benefit plan   A pension plan in which the benefits that the employee will receive at retirement are defined by the terms of the plan. (p. E8).

Defined contribution plan   A pension plan in which the employer's contribution to the plan is defined by the terms of the plan. (p. E8).

Operating lease   A contractual arrangement giving the lessee temporary use of the property with continued ownership of the property by the lessor. (p. E4).

Pension plan   An agreement whereby an employer provides benefits to employees after they retire. (p. E7).

Postretirement benefits   Payments by employers to retired employees for health care, life insurance, and pensions. (p. E6).

SELF-STUDY QUESTIONS

Answers are at the end of the chapter.

(SO 1)   1. A contingency should be recorded in the accounts when:
   a. It is probable the contingency will happen but the amount cannot be reasonably estimated.
   b. It is reasonably possible the contingency will happen and the amount can be reasonably estimated.
   c. It is reasonably possible the contingency will happen but the amount cannot be reasonably estimated.
   d. It is probable the contingency will happen and the amount can be reasonably estimated.

2. At December 31, Hanes Company prepares an adjusting entry for a product warranty contract. Which of the following accounts are included in the entry?   (SO 1)
   a. Warranty Expense.
   b. Estimated Warranty Liability.
   c. Repair Parts/Wages Payable.
   d. Both (a) and (b).

(SO 2)   3. Lease A does not contain a bargain purchase option, but the lease term is equal to 90 percent of the estimated economic life of the leased property. Lease B does not transfer ownership of the property to the lessee by the end of the lease term, but the lease term is equal to 75 percent of the estimated economic life of the leased property. How should the lessee classify these leases?

Lease A	Lease B
a. Operating lease	Capital lease
b. Operating lease	Operating lease
c. Capital lease	Capital lease
d. Capital lease	Operating lease

4. Which of the following is *not* an additional fringe   (SO 3)
benefit?
   a. Salaries.
   b. Paid absences.
   c. Paid vacations.
   d. Postretirement pensions.

QUESTIONS

1. What is a contingent liability? Give an example of a contingent liability that is usually recorded in the accounts.

2. Under what circumstances is a contingent liability disclosed only in the notes to the financial statements? Under what circumstances is a contingent liability not recorded in the accounts nor disclosed in the notes to the financial statements?

3. (a) What is a lease agreement? (b) What are the two most common types of leases? (c) Distinguish between the two types of leases.

4. Mitchell Company rents a warehouse on a month-to-month basis for the storage of its excess inventory. The company periodically must rent space when its production greatly exceeds actual sales. What is the nature of this type of lease agreement, and what accounting treatment should be accorded it?

5. Rodriguez Company entered into an agreement to lease 12 computers from Rochester Electronics Inc. The present value of the lease payments is $186,300. Assuming that this is a capital lease, what entry would Rodriguez Company make on the date of the lease agreement?

6. Identify three additional types of fringe benefits associated with employees' compensation.

7. Often during job interviews, the candidate asks the potential employer about the firm's paid absences policy. What are paid absences? How are they accounted for?

8. What are the two types of postretirement benefits? During what years does the FASB advocate expensing the employer's costs of these postretirement benefits?

9. What basis of accounting for the employer's cost of postretirement health care and life insurance benefits has been used by most companies and what basis does the FASB advocate in the future? Explain the basic difference between these methods in recognizing postretirement benefit costs.

10. Identify the three parties in a pension plan. What role does each party have in the plan?

11. Tom Broka and Bryant Gumbs are reviewing pension plans. They ask your help in distinguishing between a defined contribution plan and a defined benefit plan. Explain the principal differences to Tom and Bryant.

BRIEF EXERCISES

Prepare adjusting entry for warranty costs.
(SO 1)

BEE–1 On December 1, Filgas Company introduces a new product that includes a one-year warranty on parts. In December 1,000 units are sold. Management believes that 3% of the units will be defective and that the average warranty costs will be $60 per unit. Prepare the adjusting entry at December 31 to accrue the estimated warranty cost.

Contrast accounting for operating and capital lease.
(SO 2)

BEE–2 Prepare the journal entries that the lessee should make to record the following transactions:

1. The lessee makes a lease payment of $100,000 to the lessor in an operating lease transaction.
2. Goldberg Company leases a new building from Brace Construction, Inc. The present value of the lease payments is $600,000. The lease qualifies as a capital lease.

BEE-3 In the Reid Company, employees are entitled to one day's vacation for each month worked. In January, 50 employees worked the full month. Record the vacation pay liability for January assuming the average daily pay for each employee is $100.

Record estimated vacation benefits.
(SO 3)

EXERCISES

EE-1 Red Cliff Company sells automatic can openers under a 75-day warranty for defective merchandise. Based on past experience, Red Cliff Company estimates that 3% of the units sold will become defective during the warranty period. Management estimates that the average cost of replacing or repairing a defective unit is $10. The units sold and units defective that occurred during the last two months of 1996 are as follows:

Record estimated liability and expense for warranties.
(SO 1)

Month	Units Sold	Units Defective Prior to December 31
November	30,000	600
December	32,000	400

Instructions
(a) Determine the estimated warranty liability at December 31 for the units sold in November and December.
(b) Prepare the journal entries to record the estimated liability for warranties and the costs (assume actual costs of $10,000) incurred in honoring 1,000 warranty claims.
(c) Give the entry to record the honoring of 350 warranty contracts in January at an average cost of $10.

EE-2 Murphy Company has the following liability accounts after posting adjusting entries: Accounts Payable $62,000, Unearned Ticket Revenue $24,000, Estimated Warranty Liability $18,000, Interest Payable $12,000, Mortgage Payable $120,000, Notes Payable $80,000, and Sales Taxes Payable $12,000.

Prepare the current liability section of the balance sheet.
(SO 1)

Instructions
(a) Prepare the current liability section of the balance sheet, assuming $30,000 of the mortgage is payable next year.
(b) Comment on Murphy Company's liquidity, assuming total current assets are $300,000.

EE-3 Presented below are two independent situations.

Journal entries for operating lease and capital lease.
(SO 2)

1. Plante Car Rental leased a car to Rockefeller Company for one year. Terms of the operating lease agreement call for monthly payments of $600.
2. On January 1, 1996, Wizard Inc. entered into an agreement to lease 20 computers from Kilgust Electronics. The terms of the lease agreement require three annual rental payments of $120,000 (including 10% interest) beginning December 31, 1996. The present value of the three rental payments is $298,422. Wizard considers this a capital lease.

Instructions
(a) Prepare the appropriate journal entry to be made by Rockefeller Company for the first lease payment.
(b) Prepare the journal entry to record the lease agreement on the books of Wizard Inc. on January 1, 1996.

EE-4 Mercer Company has two fringe benefit plans for its employees:

Prepare adjusting entries for fringe benefits.
(SO 3)

1. It grants employees two days' vacation for each month worked. Ten employees worked the entire month of March at an average daily wage of $100 per employee.
2. It has a defined contribution pension plan in which the company contributes 10% of gross earnings. Gross earnings in March were $35,000. The payment to the pension fund has not been made.

Instructions
Prepare the adjusting entries at March 31.

PROBLEMS

Prepare current liability entries, adjusting entries, and current liability section.
(SO 1)

PE–1 On January 1, 1996, the ledger of Carroll Company contains the following liability accounts.

Accounts Payable	$42,500
Sales Taxes Payable	5,600
Unearned Service Revenue	15,000

During January the following selected transactions occurred:

Jan. 1 Borrowed $15,000 in cash from Midland Bank on a four-month, 12%, $15,000 note.

5 Sold merchandise for cash totaling $7,800 which includes 4% sales taxes.

12 Provided services for customers who had made advance payments of $8,000. (Credit Service Revenue.)

14 Paid state treasurer's department for sales taxes collected in December 1995 ($5,600).

20 Sold 500 units of a new product on credit at $52 per unit, plus 4% sales tax. This new product is subject to a 1-year warranty.

25 Sold merchandise for cash totaling $11,440, which includes 4% sales taxes.

Instructions
(a) Journalize the January transactions.
(b) Journalize the adjusting entries at January 31 for (1) the outstanding notes payable, and (2) estimated warranty liability, assuming that the estimated rate of defective units is 10% and the average warranty repair cost is $41.60.
(c) Prepare the current liability section of the balance sheet at January 31, 1996.

Analyze three different lease situations and prepare journal entries.
(SO 2)

PE–2 Presented below are three different lease transactions in which Casper Enterprises engaged in 1996. Assume that all lease transactions start on January 1, 1996. In no case does Casper receive title to the properties leased during or at the end of the lease term.

	Lessor		
	Lornegren Associates	Potter Co.	Haskell Inc.
Type of property	Bulldozer	Truck	Furniture
Bargain purchase option	None	None	None
Lease term	4 years	6 years	3 years
Estimated economic life	8 years	7 years	5 years
Yearly rental	$13,000	$ 6,000	$ 5,000
Fair market value of leased asset	$80,000	$29,000	$27,500
Present value of the lease rental payments	$48,000	$27,000	$12,000

Instructions
(a) Identify the leases above as operating or capital leases. Explain.
(b) How should the lease transaction for Potter Co. be recorded on January 1, 1996?
(c) How should the lease transactions for Haskell Inc. be recorded in 1996?

ALTERNATE PROBLEMS

Prepare current liability entries, adjusting entries, and current liability section.
(SO 1)

PE–1A On January 1, 1996, the ledger of Midler Company contains the following liability accounts:

Accounts Payable	$52,000
Sales Taxes Payable	7,500
Unearned Service Revenue	16,000

During January the following selected transactions occurred:

Jan. 5 Sold merchandise for cash totaling $16,632, which includes 8% sales taxes.

12 Provided services for customers who had made advance payments of $9,000. (Credit Service Revenue)

14 Paid state revenue department for sales taxes collected in December 1995 ($7,500).

20 Sold 500 units of a new product on credit at $50 per unit, plus 8% sales tax. This new product is subject to a 1-year warranty.

21 Borrowed $18,000 from Midland Bank on a three-month, 12%, $18,000 note.

25 Sold merchandise for cash totaling $11,340, which includes 8% sales taxes.

Instructions
(a) Journalize the January transactions.
(b) Journalize the adjusting entries at January 31 for (1) the outstanding notes payable, and (2) estimated warranty liability, assuming that the estimated rate of defective units is 10% and the average warranty repair cost is $40. (Hint: Use one-half of a month for the City Bank note and one-third of a month for the Midland Bank note.)
(c) Prepare the current liability section of the balance sheet at January 31, 1996.

PE–2A Presented below are three different lease transactions that occurred for Brett Inc. in 1996. Assume that all lease contracts start on January 1, 1996. In no case does Brett receive title to the properties leased during or at the end of the lease term.

Analyze three different lease situations and prepare journal entries.
(SO 2)

	Lessor		
	Hung Delivery	Williams Co.	Cecil Auto
Type of property	Computer	Delivery equipment	Automobile
Yearly rental	$ 8,000	$ 4,000	$ 3,700
Lease term	6 years	4 years	2 years
Estimated economic life	7 years	7 years	5 years
Fair market value of lease asset	$44,000	$19,000	$11,000
Present value of the lease rental payments	$43,000	$13,000	$ 6,400
Bargain purchase option	None	None	None

Instructions
(a) Which of the leases above are operating leases and which are capital leases? Explain.
(b) How should the lease transaction for Williams Co. be recorded in 1996?
(c) How should the lease transaction for Hung Delivery be recorded on January 1, 1996?

►*B*roadening Your Perspective

*F*INANCIAL REPORTING PROBLEMS

A. Refer to the financial statements of PepsiCo, Inc. and the Notes to Consolidated Financial Statements in Appendix A to answer the following questions about contingent liabilities and pension costs.
1. Where does PepsiCo report its contingent liabilities?
2. What is management's opinion as to the ultimate effect of the "various claims and legal proceedings" pending against the company?
3. What is the amount that PepsiCo is contingently liable under guarantees at December 30, 1995 and December 31, 1994?
4. What type of employee pension plan does PepsiCo have?
5. What is the amount of postretirement benefit expense (other than pensions) for 1995?

B. Presented below is the lease portion of the notes to the financial statements of CF Industries, Inc.

Leases

The present value of future minimum capital lease payments and the future minimum lease payments under noncancelable operating leases at December 31, 1993 are:

	Capital Lease Payments	Operating Lease Payments
1994	$ 7,733	$3,067
1995	6,791	2,052
1996	6,730	1,056
1997	6,788	918
1998	6,785	86
Thereafter	13,441	6
Future minimum lease payments	48,268	$7,185
Less equivalent interest	11,391	
Present value	36,877	
Less current portion	5,570	
	$31,307	

Rent expense for operating leases was $7.0 million for the year ended December 31, 1993, $5.3 million for 1992 and $5.6 million for 1991.

Instructions

What type of leases does CF Industries, Inc. use? What is the amount of the current portion of the lease obligation?

DECISION CASE

Presented below is the condensed balance sheet for Express, Inc. as of December 31, 1996:

EXPRESS, INC.
Balance Sheet
December 31, 1996

Current assets	$ 800,000	Current liabilities	$1,200,000
Plant assets	1,600,000	Long-term liabilities	700,000
		Common stock	400,000
		Retained earnings	100,000
Total	$2,400,000	Total	$2,400,000

Express has decided that it needs to purchase a new crane for its operations. The new crane costs $900,000 and has a useful life of 15 years. However, Express' bank has refused to provide any help in financing the purchase of the new equipment, even though Express is willing to pay an above market interest rate for the financing.

The chief financial officer for Express, Lisa Colder, has discussed with the manufacturer of the crane the possibility of a lease arrangement. After some negotiation, the manufacturer of the equipment agrees to lease the crane to Express under the following terms: length of the lease, 7 years; payments, $100,000 per year. The present value of the lease payments is $548,732.

The board of directors at Express is delighted with this new lease. They reason they have the use of the crane for the next seven years. In addition, Lisa Colder notes that this type of financing is a good deal because it will keep debt off the balance sheet.

Instructions

    (a) Why do you think the bank decided not to lend money to Express, Inc.?

    (b) How should this lease transaction be reported in the financial statements?

    (c) What did Lisa Colder mean when she said "leasing will keep debt off the balance sheet"?

Answers to Self-study Questions
1. d   2. d   3. c   4. a

PHOTO CREDITS

● ●

COMPANY INDEX

SUBJECT INDEX